Vincent van Gogh (1853–1890) led a life of anguish, loneliness, and self-deprecation, trying to win love but alienating people instead. The Dutch-born youth worked briefly and unsuccessfully for an international art gallery. Later, as an evangelist sent to a Belgium mining community, he avidly imitated the "poverty of the saints," succeeding only in disturbing the miners rather than "saving" them; he was finally dismissed because of his overzealousness.

Van Gogh's subsequent career as an artist lasted less than ten years, during which time his depression and inner torment deepened. He spent two periods in mental institutions, first with a diagnosis of schizophrenia and later with a diagnosis of some type of epilepsy. At the age of thirty-seven he took his own life.

Our cover is taken from van Gogh's "Ravine in the Peyroulets" (shown above), painted a year before his death. Van Gogh said that he conceived of the mountain in the center of this painting as a looming obstacle, preventing passage.

ABNORMAL PSYCHOLOGY AND MODERN LIFE

6TH EDITION

ABNORMAL PSYCHOLOGY AND MODERN LIFE

6TH EDITION

James C. Coleman
University of California at Los Angeles

James N. Butcher
University of Minnesota

Robert C. Carson
Duke University

SCOTT, FORESMAN AND COMPANY

Glenview, Illinois
Dallas, Tex.
Oakland, N.J.
Palo Alto, Cal.
Tucker, Ga.
London, England

Library of Congress Cataloging in Publication Data

Coleman, James Covington.
    Abnormal psychology and modern life.

    Bibliography: p.
    Includes index.
    1. Psychology, Pathological. 2. Psychotherapy.
I. Butcher, James Neal, 1933–   joint author.
II. Carson, Robert Charles, 1930–   joint author.
III. Title.

RC454.C6   1979   616.8′8   79-19571
ISBN 0-673-15213-8

    45678910-WAK-85848382

Preface

Abnormal Psychology and Modern Life has gained through its earlier editions a justified reputation of leadership in the highly competitive marketplace of texts in this field. We approached the task of preparing this Sixth Edition with great anticipation and eagerness, but also with no small measure of anxiety; we wanted it to be at least as good as its predecessors—a goal that frankly intimidated both of us.

Readers familiar with earlier editions will be able to judge for themselves the extent to which that goal has been accomplished. Such readers will also be aware that, in many ways, this is still James Coleman's book. We would not wish it otherwise. Indeed, perhaps the most compelling impression we both retain from our work on the present edition is of the enormous talent and skill of our senior colleague as a scholar and author. In a myriad of instances we found it impossible to improve upon the depth, conciseness, and clarity of the original prose.

We have, however, done more than merely tinker with the previous edition. While the basic structure of the text remains much as it was, we have extensively reorganized many of the chapters internally and to some extent rearranged the sequence and emphases of chapter progression. We have given somewhat greater attention to biological factors in the causation and maintenance of disorders, especially the more severe ones; for example, a discussion of biological treatment approaches is now included as a separate chapter. We have revamped the treatment sections within chapters, broadening the focus to include newer emphases such as cognitive-behavioral therapy. And, of course, we have updated the entire text with respect to the latest research findings and reconceptualizations of the fundamental issues in the field. All of these changes have been made in keeping with our percep-tions of the intensive development and differentiation of the field since the publication of the last edition.

A particular problem for this edition has been that of maintaining currency with the several revisions of the *Diagnostic and Statistical Manual of Mental Disorders,* Third Edition (DSM-III), that occurred during the period of writing; changes in this document during the final stages of our work required several rewrites, including some at the galley stage. We appreciate the cooperation of Doctors Robert Spitzer, Keith Brodie, and Frederick Hine in response to our efforts to make this book accurately reflect the final version of DSM-III.

One of our ambitions was to shorten the book through compression and elimination of less crucial material. However, we found, as with the mythical dragon of antiquity, that removal of a limb at one point would result in two more growing back at another. We learned that the field of abnormal psychology defies adequate abbreviated treatment. Given the character of previous editions of the book, our decision had to be that thoroughness and comprehensiveness were primary considerations. Thus, the Sixth Edition is only modestly shorter than the Fifth.

As with previous editions, we have endeavored to the extent feasible to make chapters largely independent of one another. The course instructor may therefore take considerable liberty in eliminating certain chapters or in rearranging the sequence in which students are introduced to them. In general, the sequence of the Sixth Edition may be summarized as follows:

Part I sets forth a framework for understanding *abnormal,* or *maladaptive,* behavior, including common misconceptions, accepted definitions, and attempts at classification. A brief historical discussion traces the changing views of mental disorders from ancient to modern times, along with the development of contemporary biological, psychosocial, and sociocultural viewpoints. Included here is the recognition of the need for an interdisciplinary approach to understanding and dealing with abnormal behavior. Part I concludes with an overview of the basic principles of human development and adjustment, both normal and abnormal. The crucial roles of both learning and life stressors in the development and maintenance of abnormal behavior are emphasized throughout, as well as the interaction of biological, psychosocial, and sociocultural factors. Within this context, maladaptive behavior can be viewed as involving not only individuals but also the physical, interpersonal, and sociocultural environments in which they live.

Part II details the clinical pictures, causal factors, and treatment and outcomes of maladaptive patterns. Included here are transient reactions to severe stress, neurotic patterns, physical illness related to psychological factors, personality disorders, addictive disorders, affective disorders, the schizophrenias and paranoia, organic mental disorders and mental retardation, and behavior disorders of childhood and adolescence. Also included here are discussions of the special problems of sexual dysfunctions/variants and suicide.

Part III deals with the areas of assessment, therapy, and prevention. The value of assessment as a continuing aid and check on progress is emphasized. The scope of therapeutic intervention on both biological and psychological frontiers is examined, and ongoing efforts and future prospects toward prevention of maladaptive behavior are explored.

New to this edition is an *Appendix*, listing in full the DSM-III classification, as well as the DSM-II classification for comparison purposes. Also included here is the Rutter et al. classification system, which is particularly helpful when dealing with childhood and adolescent disorders. A comprehensive *Glossary* has been carefully revised to make it of maximal use to the reader; and, as has become an expected standard of this text, the *References* provide a rich source of both classic studies and the most recent research in the field. Again, as has been true of earlier editions, the Sixth Edition is sen-

sitively illustrated to convey in visual terms the reality of the many forms of human experience and behavior. A wide variety of case studies and HIGHLIGHT boxes enrich and enhance the reader's understanding of the field. In this edition, the HIGHLIGHTS are clearly set apart from the text proper but are cross-referenced within the text to indicate the opportune time for the reader to refer to them. Finally, the back endsheets provide a quick overview of the maladaptive behaviors discussed in the text.

We owe debts of gratitude to many people— foremost to James C. Coleman whose earlier work set a brilliant standard and provided an essential basis for this Sixth Edition. To James L. Romig and Joanne M. Tinsley of Scott, Foresman's College Division, we owe our thanks for "discovering" us and for the faith and confidence they generously lavished upon us from the outset of the project. We have had superb editorial assistance from Marguerite Clark, later joined by Sybil Sosin and Chris Arden, who taught us gently but insistently how to convert our sometimes turgid prose into something the reader would be better able to understand. We served an apprenticeship in writing during the past two years under this highly skilled editorial staff. They gave us unstinting critical appraisal when we wandered off the mark, as we sometimes did, and offered warm and supportive guidance when we were lost.

The Sixth Edition has also benefited greatly from comments and critiques, both of the previous edition and of our early drafts, provided by numerous specialists and scholars in the field, among them: Irving E. Alexander, Duke University; Paul H. Blaney, University of Miami; Loren J. Chapman, University of Wisconsin, Madison; James C. Coyne, University of California, Berkeley; Andrew B. Crider, Williams College; Robert R. Dies, University of Maryland; Juris G. Draguns, Pennsylvania State University; Norman L. Farberow, Institute for Studies of Destructive Behaviors and the Suicide Prevention Center, Los Angeles; Ronald A. Farrell, State University of New York, Albany; John R. Graham, Kent State University; Malcolm D. Gynther, Auburn University; Daniel R. Hanson, University of Minnesota; Steven D. Hollon, University of

Minnesota; Philip C. Kendall, University of Minnesota; Mary P. Koss, Kent State University; Benjamin B. Lahey, University of Georgia; Robert E. Lehman, University of Idaho; Brendan A. Maher, Harvard University; Philip A. Mann, University of Northern Iowa; Paul A. Mauger, Georgia State University; William R. Miller, University of New Mexico; Duane H. Reeder, Glendale Community College; Robert I. Watson, Jr., Adelphi University; and Irving B. Weiner, Case Western Reserve University.

Additional clinical case material was provided by Alan Roberts, Gloria Leon, Philip Kendall, and Alan Davidson. Mary Koss drafted certain of the HIGHLIGHT material.

Finally, we should comment on the order in which the authors' names appear for the Sixth Edition. James Coleman's appears first simply because, as we have noted, this is still largely his book. The order of the second and third authors' names was determined alphabetically; our contributions in the preparation of the work were as near equal as we could make them.

J.N.B.
R.C.C.

Contents

Chapter Twenty

Action for mental health and a better world

Appendix:

Systems used in the classification of mental disorders

ABNORMAL PSYCHOLOGY AND MODERN LIFE

6TH EDITION

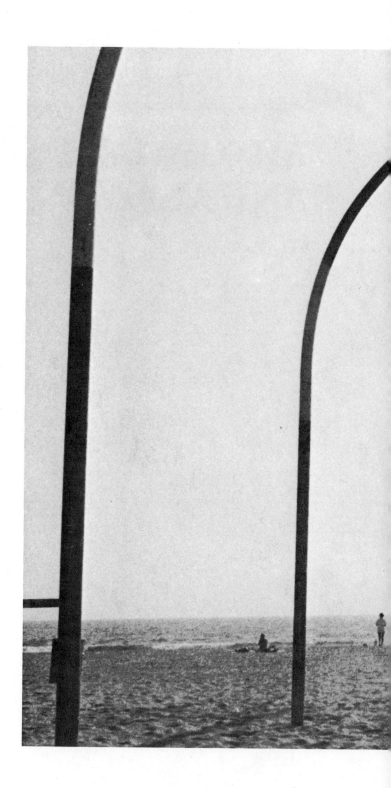

PART 1

Perspectives on abnormal behavior

1

Abnormal behavior in our times

Popular views of abnormal behavior
Abnormal behavior as the scientist sees it
The orientation of this book

The seventeenth century has been called the Age of Enlightenment; the eighteenth, the Age of Reason; the nineteenth, the Age of Progress; and the twentieth, the Age of Anxiety.

Through technology and the advances of science, our understanding of our world has grown and with it a sense of the seemingly limitless opportunity and diversity that our environment makes possible for us. We Westerners have tended to regard this environment as something for us to control and conquer; now we are finding that we are part of it and that what we have done to it is affecting us in many unforeseen ways. Brilliant solutions to problems of production, communication, transportation, and so on have provided us with a host of new problems. Gone is the old faith in the inevitability of progress and continued improvement. Instead, we now seem immersed in worrisome instabilities and uncertainties.

The medical advances that have cut our death rates are making it possible for the world's population to double every thirty-five years or even less—far faster than new food sources can be developed. Economic fluctuations and inflation take their toll in unemployment, dislocation, and poverty for millions of people. Yet grinding poverty and discrimination for some exist side by side with abundance and opportunity for others—leading to social pressures that periodically erupt in violence. Our mobile society, with its constantly disrupted friendships and loss of extended family bonds leaves us with a sense of rootlessness, while constant competition and encounters with bureaucracy in our crowded urban areas tend to be dehumanizing and devaluating.

Meanwhile, the wasteful use of our natural resources, coupled with the pollution of air, water, and soil, threatens the life-support system of all of us. Big and little wars keep breaking out, disrupting both personal and national life and leaving in their wake grief, destruction, and social unrest. And the ever present threat of a global nuclear holocaust further aggravates our anxieties. For the first time in history, life is lived in the shadow of threats and problems on a scale that could end life on this planet—problems largely of human creation but problems we do not yet know how to solve. Some even believe there are no solutions.

As if these larger problems were not enough, we also face new personal dilemmas. The opportunities and diversities that our world offers us also bring frightening complexity and difficult choices in a time when we can no longer simply accept the wisdom and values of our elders. Traditional values and beliefs no longer seem self-evident. Today we are increasingly questioning long-accepted assumptions about religion, education, sex, marriage, the family, and social and political institutions and processes. Yet rejecting the false or the phony is not enough. We also want and need something to believe in and care about, to feel a part of and contribute to.

Small wonder that on every side we see anxious, unhappy, bewildered people who miss the realization of their potentialities because they cannot find satisfactory answers to problems that seem beyond them. The stress of modern life is evident in the incredible amount of tranquilizers, sleeping pills, and alcoholic beverages consumed; in the emergence of heart attacks as the leading cause of death in our society; in the marked increase in suicide among our youth; and in the alarming increase in delinquency and crime, particularly crimes of violence.

Despite the stress of modern life, most people still manage to "muddle through." Some thrive and find fulfillment. But for many people, the stress proves too great. It is startling to note that emotional disturbances incapacitate more people than all other health problems combined. In its 1978 report, the President's Commission on Mental Health wrote that, if present trends continue, new evidence suggests that one person in seven now living in the United States will at some time require professional treatment for emotional disturbances. (See HIGHLIGHT on page 4.)

Mental health has for good reason been designated the country's number-one health concern. Many of us encounter serious difficulties in dealing with life's problems—particularly problems centering around intimate personal relationships and the search for values that will make our lives meaningful. The challenge is to meet these difficulties without being defeated by them—to keep our zest and joy and sense of wonder despite both the big problems and the little annoyances that are part of living.

In studying abnormal psychology, we "beard the lion in its den," as it were. We look squarely

HIGHLIGHT

Estimated incidence of major maladaptive behavior patterns in the United States in 1978

200,000 reported cases of child abuse

200,000 or more individuals attempt suicide* (**26,000** or more individuals die from suicide)

1,000,000 individuals are actively schizophrenic

1,000,000 or more students withdraw from college each year as a result of emotional problems

2,000,000 individuals suffer from profound depression

6,000,000 or more children and teenagers considered emotionally disturbed

7,000,000 individuals are considered mentally retarded

10,000,000 or more juveniles and adults arrested in connection with serious crimes* (**190,000** or more individuals are sent to prison and **500,000** individuals are in prison)

10,000,000 Americans report alcohol-related problems (**1,000,000** individuals are being treated for such)

20,000,000 (at least) individuals suffer from neurotic disturbance

53,500,000 individuals suffer from mild to moderate depression

*The incidence of suicide attempts and serious crimes may be much higher due to the large number that are not reported.

Incidence figures based on Berger (1978), the National Institute of Mental Health (1978), the President's Commission on Mental Health (1978), and Uniform Crime Reports (1978).

at the worst that can happen to the human psyche when individuals with physical and/or psychological deficiencies or inefficiencies meet problems that are just too great. But in seeing what can happen, we also see when and why it happens and what conditions can work in our favor to prevent or undo psychic damage. We find that the events here are lawful: they are understandable and even, within range, predictable and controllable. This knowledge can give us protection and reassurance that we can indeed be "masters of our fate."

Popular views of abnormal behavior

Examples of mental disorders that we have heard or read about are apt to be extreme cases that, isolated and lumped together, give us a "chamber-of-horrors" impression of abnormal behavior rather than the truer picture, in which less spectacular minor maladjustments are far more common. Popular present-day beliefs about abnormal behavior thus tend to be based on atypical and unscientific descriptions. Partly this has been inevitable, because it is only recently that scientific research methods have been turned to an understanding of abnormal behavior.

A brief review of a few cases of mental disorders from history and literature will be of value in giving us a broader perspective, for most of the forms of severe mental disorder that we see today have been observed and reported in other ages too.

Views carried over from history

Some of the earliest historical writings—Chinese, Egyptian, Hebrew, and Greek—provide striking "case histories" of disturbed individuals.[1] Saul, King of Israel in the eleventh century B.C., suffered from recurrent manic-depressive episodes. During an attack of mania (excitement) he stripped off all his clothes in a public place. On another occasion he tried to kill his son Jonathan.

Cambyses, King of Persia in the sixth century B.C., was one of the first alcoholics on record. His alcoholic excesses were apparently associated with periods of uncontrollable rage during which he behaved "as a madman not in possession of his senses" (Whitwell, 1936, p. 38). On one occasion, without making any provision for the feeding of his army, he set out against the Ethiopians, who had greatly enraged him by calling the Persians "dung eaters." He was shortly forced to return to Memphis, where he found the people celebrating the feast of Apis. Furious at what he took to be rejoicing at his failure, he ordered that all the people taking part in the feast be killed. On another occasion he used his friend's son as a target for his arrows to demonstrate that his excessive drinking had not affected his skill. His aim was true and he killed the boy, proving his point, at least to his own satisfaction.

Greek mythology contains many descriptions

The alcoholic excesses of Cambyses often resulted in fits of uncontrollable rage, such as the incident depicted here, for which innocent bystanders paid the price.

of mentally disturbed persons that afford some insight into the nature of the real-life cases from which the descriptions must have been drawn. For example, Hercules seems to have been afflicted with convulsive seizures accompanied by a homicidal fugue-type reaction. His attacks are graphically described by Euripides in the "phrenzy of Hercules": his eyes rolled, his consciousness clouded, he frothed at the mouth, showed violent fury, and attacked persons in his way, then fell, writhed, and finally fell into a deep sleep. Upon awakening, he had complete amnesia for the seizure. During the course of several attacks, Hercules killed two of his own children, two of his brother's children, his best friend, and his teacher. Ajax, too, became mentally disordered and slew a flock of sheep under the impression that he was attacking his enemies. On regaining his senses, he was so overcome with remorse that he committed suicide by throwing himself on his sword.

[1]Sources on which this section is based include the following: Bluemel (1948), Born (1946), Lombroso (1891), Marks (1925), Martindale (1972), Sewell (1943), Whitwell (1936), and Zilboorg & Henry (1941).

Many of the notables of later Greece and Rome, including Socrates, Alexander the Great, and Julius Caesar, apparently suffered from mental disorders of one kind or another, and the ensuing period of the Middle Ages contains innumerable instances of abnormal behavior. The great Oriental conqueror, Tamerlane (1336–1405), for example, was particularly fond of building pyramids of human skulls. One of his architectural achievements is reported to have contained some forty thousand of them.

In more recent times, George III of England (1738–1820)—known as the "mad monarch" —showed a variety of symptoms, including periods of intense excitement and overactivity. During these periods he shifted rapidly from one topic to another, asked precipitate questions without waiting for an answer, ate his food so rapidly that the members of his court had to bolt their food or leave the table hungry, raced up and down stairs, rode his horse to death, and indulged in obscene language.

The French philosopher Jean Jacques Rousseau (1712–1778) developed marked paranoid symptoms during the latter part of his life. He was obsessed with fears of secret enemies and thought that Prussia, England, France, the king, priests, and others were waging a terrible war against him. He believed that these enemies caused him to suffer indigestion, diarrhea, and other internal troubles, but their chief trick was to torture him by overwhelming him with benefits and praise, even going so far as to corrupt vegetable peddlers so that they would sell him better vegetables more cheaply. According to Rousseau, this was undoubtedly designed to prove his baseness and their generosity.

The names of other philosophers, painters, writers, musicians, and celebrities who suffered emotional disturbances would make a long list. Mozart, for example, during the time he was composing the Requiem, thought that he was being poisoned. Beethoven, although miserably poor, was constantly changing his living quarters and sometimes had to pay for lodgings at three or four different places at once. Keats suffered from chronic tension and was subject to spells of uncontrollable laughter and crying.

On one occasion van Gogh cut off his ear and sent it to a prostitute, an action apparently performed in a state of clouded consciousness resulting from his epileptic condition. Schopenhauer, Chopin, and John Stuart Mill suffered from attacks of depression. Rabelais, Samuel Butler, Burns, Byron, and Poe used alcohol excessively. Coleridge acknowledged using opiates before writing "Kubla Khan."

Many rulers and conquerors have been able to indulge seemingly sadistic inclinations. Attila the Hun is remembered mainly for the ruthlessness and barbarity of his conquests. Queen Mary I of England, better known as "Bloody Mary," was responsible for the Marian persecution—the burning of Protestants as heretics during the years 1553 to 1558.

In reviewing these historical instances of abnormal behavior, it should be made clear that we are to some extent evaluating this behavior in the light of present-day concepts of mental disorder. In their own day, some of these people were looked on as perfectly normal, and others as only eccentric or unusual. We may also take note of the fact that, although many individuals with mental disorders have made significant contributions to society and the shaping of history, it has been those men and women of more effective personality adjustment who have carried the major burden in the achievement of social progress.

Ideas carried over from literature and drama

Long before abnormal psychology became an area of scientific study, the masters of fiction and drama developed many brilliant and moving characterizations of abnormal behavior, based on their keen observations of human behavior. Such literary classics, in their descriptions of human abnormality in all of its infinite subtleties of degree and variety, often achieve a lifelike vividness and an emotional force that science cannot achieve. *Othello,* for example, provides an unforgettable insight into the subjective quality of obsessive, violent jealousy.

Of course, literature cannot provide either the theoretical or practical basis for understanding and treating specific cases of abnormal behavior, but it does complement psychol-

Numerous cases in literature depict abnormal behavior that has its roots in extreme jealousy or anger. Shown here, Othello, falsely believing the innocent Desdemona has been unfaithful to him, refuses to listen to her pleas of innocence and later strangles her. And Medea, in a frenzied rage, kills her two children in front of Jason, her unfaithful husband.

ogy in giving a different kind of understanding of such behavior. Literature yields valuable information, for example, about personality dynamics, about mental disorders prevalent during a particular historical period, and about the inner experiences of those who have undergone such disorders.

The writings of the Greek poets and dramatists contain many allusions to abnormal behavior. In his play *Medea*, Euripides (480–406 B.C.) described and analyzed the emotions of jealousy and revenge as displayed by a mother who murders her children. Sophocles (495–406 B.C.) in *Oedipus Rex* and *Electra* has given us the first intimation of incest motives in the shaping of human behavior. And in the *Oresteia* trilogy, Aeschylus clearly described delusional and hallucinatory symptoms arising out of severe feelings of remorse and guilt.

Many of the characters in the plays of William Shakespeare portray the development of abnormal behavior with clinical accuracy. The intense guilt reaction of Lady Macbeth, after planning and participating in the bloody murder of King Duncan, is well brought out in her uneasy sleepwalking and symbolic handwashing:

"It is an accustomed action with her, to seem thus washing her hands: I have known her continue in this a quarter of an hour." (*Macbeth*, Act V, Scene i)

That her compulsive handwashing has failed, however, to "cleanse" her of her feelings of guilt is shown in her admission that

"Here's the smell of the blood still: all the perfumes of Arabia will not sweeten this little hand. Oh, oh, oh!" (Act V, Scene i)

Consider the humor as well as the pathos in the adventures of Don Quixote. Cervantes' hero becomes so overwhelmed by reading the most famous books of chivalry that he believes them to be true. How natural it seems for him

Don Quixote, the noble but deluded idealist, sits in his library surrounded by some of the figures he saw during his various hallucinations.

to accept his "mission" as a knight errant and to sally forth into the world to defend the oppressed and to fight injustice like the heroes of his romances. Even when his excited imagination turns windmills into giants, solitary inns into castles, and galley slaves into oppressed gentlemen, the reader can feel a part of his adventuring. And finally when he is restored to his "right" mind through a severe illness and is made to renounce the follies of knight errantry, most of us probably feel a tinge of disappointment that the hero must give up his dreams and his noble "mission."

De Quincey (1821) revealed something of the "world within" in his description of his opium dreams:

". . . I brought together all creatures, birds, beasts, reptiles, all trees and plants, usages and appearances, that are found in all tropical regions, and assembled them together in China or Indostan. From kindred feelings, I soon brought Egypt and all her gods under the same law. I was stared at, hooted at, grinned at, chattered at, ran into pagodas: and was fixed for centuries at the summit, or in secret rooms; I was the idol; I was the priest; I was worshipped; I was sacrificed. I fled from the wrath of Brama through all the forests of Asia: Vishnu hated me: Seeva laid wait for me. I came suddenly upon Isis and Osiris: I had done a deed, they said, which the ibis and the crocodile trembled at. I was buried for a thousand years in stone coffins; with mummies and sphinxes, in narrow chambers at the heart of external pyramids. I was kissed, with cancerous kisses, by crocodiles: and laid, confounded with all unutterable slimy things, amongst reeds and Nilotic mud." *(Confessions of an English Opium Eater)*

It is interesting to speculate concerning the motivation that prompted other writings. For example, was a sort of vicarious sadism behind the fantasies of Jonathan Edwards when he pictured the brutal torturings in hell of those he considered to be sinners? When he preached on "Sinners in the Hands of an Angry God," his congregation received a terrifying warning:

"The God that holds you over the pit of hell, much as one holds a spider or some loathsome insect over the fire, abhors you, and is dreadfully provoked; His wrath towards you burns like fire; He looks upon you as worthy of nothing else, but to be cast into the fire; He is of purer eyes than to bear to have you in His sight; you are ten times so abominable in His eyes, as the most hateful and venomous serpent is in ours. . . .

"If we knew that there was one person, and but one, in the whole congregation, that was to be the subject of this misery, what an awful thing it would be to think of! . . . But alas! instead of one, how many is it likely will remember this discourse in hell! . . . And it would be no wonder if some persons that now sit here . . . should be there before tomorrow morning. These of you . . . that shall keep out of hell longest, will be there in a little time!" (Edwards, 1809, pp. 489–502)

Many modern writers have attempted to capture, often from their own experience, the pattern of thought processes underlying various types of abnormal behavior. Themes so treated have included schizophrenia, depression, suicide, alcoholism, drug dependence, mental retardation, sexual sadism, and homicide—in fact, almost the entire gamut of behaviors considered to be abnormal.

Some popular misconceptions

Throughout most of history, as we shall see in Chapter 2, beliefs about mental disorders have been generally characterized by superstition, ignorance, and fear. Although successive advances in the scientific understanding of abnormal behavior have dispelled many false ideas, a number of popular misconceptions remain.

The belief that abnormal behavior is always bizarre. The instances of abnormal behavior reported in the mass media, like those recorded in history and literature, are likely to be extreme ones involving murder, sexual assault, airplane hijacking, or other striking deviations from accepted social norms. Patients in mental hospitals and clinics are often pictured as a weird lot who spend their time ranting and raving, posing as Napoleon, or engaging in other bizarre behavior. In fact, most hospitalized patients are quite aware of what is going on around them, and only a small percentage exhibit behavior that might be labeled as bizarre. The behavior of most mental patients, whether in a clinical setting or not, is indistinguishable in many respects from that of "normal" people.

Actually, the term "abnormal" covers a wide range of behaviors. Some types of abnormal behavior are bizarre; but in the great majority of cases, abnormal behavior is so labeled because it is self-defeating and maladaptive. Such self-defeating patterns are a cause of concern, but they are well within the bounds of ordinary human experience. Included here would be the college student who for no apparent reason is so anxious that she can't concentrate on her studies and has to drop out of school, or the youth who creates serious difficulties in his social relationships by telling

In the eighteenth century, an entertaining diversion often involved a visit to the asylum to view the bizarre behavior of the lunatics, as the two "ladies of fashion" are doing here. Unfortunately, the belief that abnormal behavior is always bizarre persists among many to this day.

trivial lies. On a more serious level would be the young husband who mistreats his wife and then attempts suicide when she leaves him, or the adolescent girl who turns to prostitution to pay for her drug habit.

Finally, there are behaviors that are recognized generally as severely abnormal—the adolescent who pours gasoline over an old man and sets him on fire; the indignant youth who insists that his enemies have set up an electronic device that "pours filth into his mind"; the alcoholic who cringes in terror before an imaginary invasion of cockroaches; or the paranoid man who murders several innocent people he believes are plotting against him. Cases like these are unusual, however, and not typical of abnormal behavior in general.

The view that "normal" and "abnormal" behavior are different in kind. A sharp dividing line between "normal" and "abnormal" behavior simply does not exist. There are not "normal" people on the one hand and "abnormal" people on the other—two different and distinct kinds of beings. Rather, adjustment seems to follow what is called a normal distribution, with most people clustering around a central point or average, and the rest spreading out toward the two extremes. Most people are moderately well adjusted, with minor maladaptive patterns; a few at one extreme enter mental hospitals or clinics; and a few at the other extreme lead unusually satisfying and effective lives.

We have probably all known and sympathized with someone who became severely depressed after an unhappy love affair, or someone who began to drink excessively following a serious business failure. These people were showing behavior that differed only in degree from that of patients in mental hospitals or clinics, on the one hand, and from that of "normal, well-adjusted" people on the other.

The lack of a sharp dividing line between normal and abnormal behavior can be seen in a controversial study by Rosenhan (1973) in which eight normal people gained admission to twelve mental hospitals by reporting that they had hallucinations and some anxiety about them. All but one received a diagnosis of schizophrenia, and although they then started acting as "normal" as they could, it was fifty-

two days before the last one gained release. Although the study has been criticized, it demonstrates that serious mental disorder is sometimes inferred, rightly or wrongly, from a few cues.

Not only does the behavior of different individuals range by imperceptible degrees from normal to abnormal, but from time to time most of us shift our position somewhat along the continuum. For example, we may be coping adequately with our problems when some change—perhaps a hurtful divorce, a prolonged illness, a serious financial loss, or several problems at once—may increase the severity of the demands made on us to the point where we can no longer cope with them satisfactorily.

Both normal and abnormal behavior patterns are now seen as attempts to cope with life problems as the individual perceives them. Although people have different adaptive resources, use different methods of coping, and have differing degrees of success, the same general principles apply to understanding both normal and abnormal behavior, however unusual the latter may be.

The view of former mental patients as unstable and dangerous. The common misconception persists that mental disorders are essentially "incurable." As a consequence, persons who have been discharged from mental hospitals or clinics are often viewed with suspicion as being unstable and possibly dangerous. Commonly they are discriminated against in employment or job advancement as well as in the political arena. While it is true that persons with certain forms of mental disorders—such as those associated with severe senile brain damage—will never recover completely, most mental patients respond well to treatment and later meet their responsibilities satisfactorily. Indeed, many achieve a higher level of personality adjustment than before their breakdowns.

Although research on the rate of crime among former mental patients is inconclusive, it appears that their overall arrest record is now somewhat higher than that for the general population (Zitrin et al., 1976). This finding may reflect the recent trend toward earlier release of patients from mental hospitals. It

For centuries the colony of Gheel in Belgium has recognized that the majority of mental patients are not unstable or dangerous. This young man is one of many mental patients who live in private homes and benefit from love, warmth, and interaction with family members.

mental disorder = adaptive failure

suggests that this trend away from long-term hospitalization has not been supplemented by sufficient resources for help in the community. (See HIGHLIGHT on page 12.)

Most persons who recover from even serious mental disorders, however, do *not* later engage in violent or socially disruptive behavior, especially if they had no history of arrests prior to their hospitalization (Rabkin, 1979). Though care should be taken in releasing patients with a history of violence, less than 1 percent of all patients released from mental hospitals or clinics can be regarded as dangerous, and most of them are more likely to be a threat to themselves than to others.

The belief that mental disorder is something to be ashamed of. Many people who do not hesitate to consult a dentist, a lawyer, or other professional person for assistance with various types of problems are reluctant to go to a psychologist or a psychiatrist with their emotional problems. Actually, a mental disorder should be considered no more disgraceful than a physical disorder. Both are adaptive failures.

Nevertheless, there is still a tendency in our society to reject the emotionally disturbed. Whereas most people are sympathetic toward a crippled child or an adult with cancer, they may turn away from the person suffering from an incapacitating mental disorder. Even many psychologists and medical personnel are both uninformed and unsympathetic when they are confronted with persons evidencing mental disorders (Langer & Abelson, 1974; Rabkin, 1972). Yet the great majority of persons suffering mental disorders are doing the best they know how and desperately need understanding and help.

Fortunately, treatment of mental disorders is becoming an integral part of total social and community health programs. But the stigma that has traditionally been attached to mental disorders still lingers in the minds of many people in our society.

The belief that mental disorder is something magical or awe-inspiring.

In some societies people who had hallucinations or showed strange behavior were thought to be possessed by supernatural powers and were regarded with awe. This view lessened with the rise of scientific views but has never been completely abandoned in popular thought and periodically gains new popularity. The idea that people with severe psychological problems should be admired or rewarded has been seen recently in novels like Vonnegut's *Breakfast of Champions* and Kesey's *One Flew Over the Cuckoo's Nest*. Today, in fact, there is a "pop psychology" view in which those labeled "sick" are seen as actually having more accurate and insightful views than the "righteous" people who commit them to institutions. The following excerpt reprinted in *Madness Network News Reader* reflects this view—as does the existence of such a publication.

We are the aged
forbidden to pass among the young
we are the deceivers
caged in by the righteous
we are the insane
walled off by the sane

You, You are the young
    the righteous
    the sane,
If by some quirk
you must enter our colony
we will accept you

For we are the aged
we are the deceivers
we are the insane
and know full well
who we are

(Poem by Patrick George Harrison, *Visions of a Madman*, in Hirsh et al., 1974)

Such writings are critical of the traditional ways of treating disturbed persons and sometimes imply that there is really no such thing as abnormal behavior. They ignore the reality that many people who show "odd behavior" are not simply expressing their individuality but

Patients in state and county mental hospitals from 1880 to 1975

decline

(Approximate figures)

The year 1975 represented the twentieth consecutive year in which the resident population of state and county mental hospitals showed a decline, and this trend is continuing into the 1980s. This decline is considered to be due to a number of factors, including (a) introduction of major tranquilizing and antidepressant drugs; (b) increased availability of alternate care facilities for the aged (for example, nursing homes); (c) reduction in length of stay of first admissions; (d) more effective aftercare facilities; and (e) introduction of outpatient clinics, day hospitals, and related community health facilities.

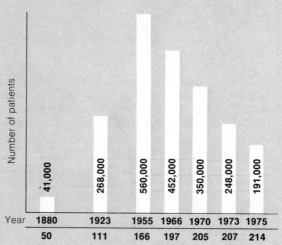

Year	1880	1923	1955	1966	1970	1973	1975
Number of patients	41,000	268,000	560,000	452,000	350,000	248,000	191,000
Population of the U.S. in millions	50	111	166	197	205	207	214

Population of the U.S. in millions
(NIMH, 1978)

are unhappy and confused and incapacitated by their behavior. By idealizing psychological problems, such critics detract from the efforts of professionals to understand and help the people who experience them.

An exaggerated fear of one's own susceptibility to mental disorders. Fears of possible mental disorder are quite common and cause much needless unhappiness. "Other people seem so self-assured and capable. They cannot possibly have the irrational impulses and fantasies I do, or feel the hostility or anxiety or despair that plagues me." Most people feel anxious and discouraged during difficult periods in their lives. Many notice with alarm that they are unreasonably irritable, have difficulty in concentrating or remembering, or even feel that they are "going to pieces." In one study, a representative sample of Americans were asked if they had ever felt they were going to have a "nervous breakdown." Almost one out of five people interviewed replied "yes" (U.S. Department of Health, Education, and Welfare, 1971).

In this connection, it should be mentioned that medical students, in reading about various physical disorders, are likely to imagine that they have many of the symptoms described; the same reaction is likely among those reading about mental disorders and is reflected in the number of students from abnormal psychology classes who seek counseling.

The following letter, illustrating what might be called "students' neurosis," was received by one of the authors:

Dear _____,
I began to suffer from the very symptoms I read about, concerning hysteria, while reading Freud. . . . I verified my guess as to what the problem was by looking at a diagnosis made by a physician.

Since then, I have tried various client-centered therapists and I have not had any success in overcoming the various symptoms of hysteria.

In an effort to save myself, I am scheduled to visit the clinic at _____ University and request adverse counterconditioning in an effort to try to overcome hysteria.

I would like to know if you might suggest an additional form of therapy I might take advantage of in an effort to secure some sense of normality.

Please note, that from what little I have read concerning behavior modification, there may be substitute symptoms unless the unconscious problem is resolved, and client-centered therapy has not been especially helpful.

I would like to thank you for any consideration that you may give this correspondence and any consideration that you may give concerning an additional form of therapy I might take advantage of.

Sincerely,

Feelings of anxiety, crises of self-confidence, and concern about one's own irrational fantasies and actions are common experiences that we all have. In most cases they do not become pervasive or disabling: they are not "symptoms of disorder" but normal reactions. Their universality in human experience can help us see seriously disturbed individuals as less "strange" but need not be cause for personal alarm. A realization that our difficulties are not unique and that other people have these same worries and self-doubts can help reduce the feelings of isolation and of being "different" that often play a part in personal fears of mental disorder.

Abnormal behavior as the scientist sees it

In order to assess, treat, and eventually prevent abnormal behavior, the scientist must work out clear definitions of "normal" and "abnormal," and develop criteria for distinguishing one from the other in actual clinical cases. Unfortunately, this has not proven an easy task.

What do we mean by "abnormal behavior"?

Since the word _abnormal_ literally means "away from the normal," it implies deviation from some clearly defined norm. But what should be our norm? What is normal? In the case of physical illness, the norm is the structural and functional integrity of the body; here the boundary lines between normality and pathology are usually clear. On a psychological level, however, we have no "ideal model" or even "normal model" of human functioning to use as a base of comparison. Thus we suffer considerable confusion and disagreement as to just what is or is not *normal,* a confusion aggravated by our changing values.

In part, too, our difficulty stems from clinicians' preoccupation with abnormal behavior and consequent neglect of the concept of the normal. The philosopher Kaplan (1967) formulated a principle called the "Law of the Instrument," which he finds operative throughout the behavioral sciences. He illustrated it this way: "If you give a small boy a hammer, it will turn out that everything he runs into needs pounding" (p. 325). It follows that clinical psychologists and other "helping personnel," because of the job they are doing, tend to focus on personality difficulties rather than on normal functioning.

From a diversity of approaches used in distinguishing between normal and abnormal behavior, there emerge two basic and conflicting views. One maintains that the concepts of "normal" and "abnormal" are meaningful only with reference to a given culture: abnormal behavior is behavior that deviates from society's norms. The other view maintains that behavior is abnormal if it interferes with the well-being of the individual and/or the group. Let us examine each of these perspectives.

Abnormal as deviation from social norms. The concept of "abnormal" as deviation from societal norms has been well formulated by Ullmann and Krasner (1975), who maintain that *abnormal* is simply a label given to behavior that is deviant from social expectations. Conversely, they maintain that behavior cannot be considered abnormal so long as society accepts it. As *cultural relativists*, they reject the concept of a "sick society" in which the social norms themselves might be viewed as pathological.

"A critical example is whether an obedient Nazi concentration-camp commander would be considered normal or abnormal. To the extent that he was responding accurately and successfully to his environment and not breaking its rules, much less coming to the professional attention of psychiatrists, he would not be labeled abnormal. Repulsive as his behavior is to mid-twentieth century Americans, such repulsion is based on a particular set of values. Although such a person may be held responsible for his acts—as Nazi war criminals were—the concept of abnormality as a special entity does not seem necessary or justified. If it is, the problem arises as to who selects the values, and this, in turn, implies that one group may select values that are applied to others. This situation of one group's values being dominant over others is the fascistic background from which the Nazi camp commander sprang." (Ullmann & Krasner, 1975, p. 16)

The acceptance of complete cultural relativism obviously simplifies the task of defining abnormality: behavior is abnormal if—and only if—the society labels it as such. But serious questions may be raised about the validity of this definition. It rests on the questionable assumption that it is social acceptance that makes behavior normal—that one set of values is as good as another for human beings to adopt. It then follows that the task of the psychotherapist is to ensure that patients conform to the norms their society views as appropriate, regardless of the values on which these norms are based.

This viewpoint was dealt a heavy blow following World War II when a number of Nazi leaders were convicted of genocide and other "crimes against humanity." The Nuremberg trials were based on the assumption that a whole society can develop maladaptive patterns and that there are standards which groups as well as individuals must follow for human survival and well-being.

Abnormal as maladaptive. Some degree of social conformity is clearly essential to group life, and some kinds of deviance are clearly harmful not only to society but to the individual. *However, the present text maintains that the best criterion for determining the normality of behavior is not whether society accepts it but rather whether it fosters the well-being of the individual and, ultimately, of the group.* By *well-being* is meant not simply maintenance or survival but also growth and fulfillment—the actualization of potentialities. According to this criterion, even conforming behavior is abnormal if it is *maladap-*

tive, that is, if it interferes with optimal functioning and growth.

So defined, abnormal behavior includes the more traditional categories of mental disorders—alcoholism, neuroses, and psychoses, for example—as well as prejudice and discrimination against persons because of race or sex, wasteful use of our natural resources, pollution of our air and water, irrational violence, and political corruption—regardless of whether such patterns are condemned or condoned by a given society. All represent maladaptive behavior that impairs individual and/or group well-being. Typically they lead to personal distress, and often they bring destructive group conflict.

Increasingly, the definition of "abnormal behavior" as behavior that is maladaptive has solid scientific support. For in much the same way that the biological sciences are identifying conditions that promote or detract from physical health, the social sciences are delineating conditions that foster or impede psychological and social well-being. For example, research has made it clear that parental neglect, rejection, and lack of love are likely to have serious detrimental effects on a child's early development and later competence.

In defining abnormal behavior as *maladaptive* and in basing our evaluation of given behaviors on available scientific evidence, we are making two value assumptions: (a) that survival and actualization are worth striving for on both individual and group levels; and (b) that human behavior can be evaluated in terms of its consequences for these objectives. As with the assumption of "cultural relativism," such value assumptions are open to criticism on the grounds that they are arbitrary. But unless we value the survival and actualization of the human race, there seems little point in trying to identify abnormal behavior or do anything about it.

In assessing, treating, and preventing abnormal behavior, mental health personnel are concerned not only with the individual but also with the family, community, and general societal setting. Increasingly, the goal of therapy is defined not solely in terms of helping individuals adjust to their personal situations—no matter how frustrating or abnormal—but also in terms of alleviating group and societal conditions that may have brought

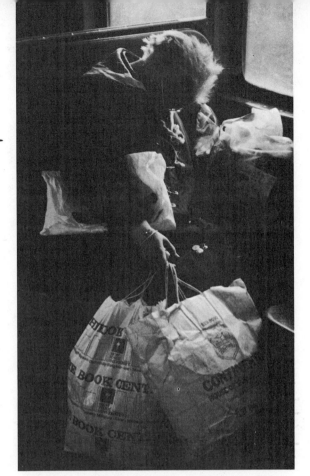

In some societies a nomadic existence is the norm, and individuals have few personal possessions beyond what they can easily carry with them. In our own society, the norm is the opposite. What, then, of individuals, such as the woman shown here, who prefer to own no more than they can carry and who have no permanent homes, living instead on subways and in the streets? Some people might consider her behavior abnormal. Would you?

about the maladaptive behavior or may be maintaining it.

The term *maladaptive* itself has an advantage over the term *abnormal* in shifting the focus to the behavior rather than the person, and implying more possibility for change. It thus becomes the behavior rather than the person that is being judged. A person once seen as "abnormal" may forever thereafter be seen that way, whereas maladaptive behavior today can usually be changed to more adaptive behavior tomorrow. Thus for a variety of reasons the term *abnormal* is less used than formerly. (See HIGHLIGHT on page 17.)

The traditional term *patient,* too, is less often used than formerly, especially in cases of less severe disorder. Many clinicians feel that the term *client* is preferable because it implies more responsibility on the part of the individual for bringing about his or her own recovery; it also carries an implication of therapy as a relearning process rather than as the curing of a disease.

The problem of classification

Classification of phenomena is important in any science—whether we are studying plants, planets, or people. In abnormal psychology, classification involves the delineation of various types, or categories, of maladaptive behavior. Classification is a necessary first step toward introducing some order into our discussion of the nature, causes, and treatment of such behavior—and in communicating about such behavior in agreed-upon and meaningful ways.

None of the various classification schemes developed so far, however, has been completely satisfactory. In 1952 the American Psychiatric Association (APA) adopted a classification of mental disorders, the *Diagnostic and Statistical Manual—Mental Disorders* (DSM), that was based largely on a scheme worked out by the United States Army during World War II. In 1968 the APA adopted a modified classification, DSM-II, worked out in conjunction with the World Health Organization. This international classification permitted mental health workers to compare incidence, types of disorders, treatment procedures, and other relevant data concerning mental disorders throughout the world. However, serious limitations in the DSM-II prompted a further revision of the system.

Current classification of mental disorders. In 1979 a new classification scheme, DSM-III, was released after extensive field trials. Besides specifying more precisely what observable behaviors must be present for a problem to be considered indicative of a particular category, this new scheme has provisions for evaluating an individual on five dimensions, or *axes.*

The first three axes are assessments of the individual's present condition:

I. The particular maladaptive symptoms, or clinical psychiatric syndromes, such as schizophrenia;
II. Any long-standing personality problems (adults) or specific developmental problems (children and adolescents);
III. Any medical, or physical, disorder that may also be present.

The two new dimensions are optional to DSM classification. They provide a framework for assessing the individual's life situation (Axis IV) and recent degree of success in coping with it (Axis V). Axis IV (see HIGHLIGHT on page 18) is a 7-point scale for rating the severity of psychosocial factors that may have been placing the individual under stress, providing both adult and child examples for each. Levels range from "None" at one end of the scale to "Catastrophic" at the other. Axis V (see HIGHLIGHT on page 19) has a 6-point scale for rating the individual's highest level of functioning during the preceding year, again with adult and child examples. Here the levels range from "Superior" to "Grossly impaired." Both these scales can help assure that when different clinicians talk about either severity of stress or "good" adjustment, for example, they are all talking about the same kind of behavior.

Axes IV and V are significant additions. Knowing what demands the individual has been trying to meet is important for an understanding of the problem behavior that has developed. Knowing the individual's general level of success in meeting adjustive demands in the recent past can help in making an appropriate and realistic treatment plan and knowing what to expect.

The latest revision was guided by the broad goal of developing a diagnostic system that is comprehensive and at the same time provides a refinement in the diagnostic categories. Some conditions previously included, such as neurosis, have been redefined into more specific categories, whereas several conditions not previously considered "psychiatric syndromes" have been included, such as tobacco-use disorder, occupational problem, academic underachievement disorder, and caffeine intoxication. Some clinicians, however, are question-

Terms used in referring to abnormal behavior

The comprehensive terms *abnormal behavior, maladaptive behavior, mental disorder,* and *psychopathology* will be used more or less interchangeably in this book. There are, however, some important distinctions to be noted concerning the use of these terms. The following descriptions not only indicate how they and other key terms are used in the present text, but also allude to differences in usage within the field.

Abnormal behavior	Used in a variety of ways to refer to a person's inner personality makeup or outer behavior or both; to refer to specific behavior like phobias or more pervasive patterns like schizophrenia; to mean chronic, long-lasting problems or those—such as drug intoxication—in which symptoms are acute and temporary. Roughly synonymous with *mental disorder* as so defined; however, in a broader context is synonymous with *maladaptive behavior.*
Maladaptive behavior	As used in this book, a term that widens the conceptual framework of *abnormal behavior* to include any behavior that has undesirable consequences for the individual and/or the group—e.g., includes not only disorders like psychoses and neuroses but also such individual or group patterns as unethical business practices, racial prejudice, alienation, and apathy.
Mental disorder	As indicated above, applies to abnormal behavior patterns, covering the whole range from mild to crippling. Although criticized by some on the grounds that it seems to imply not only a mind-body dualism but also a severe disturbance of normal functioning, *mental disorder* nevertheless is a well-established term and is integral to the APA classification system.
Psychopathology	Refers to the study of *abnormal behavior* or *mental disorder;* also used as synonymous with those terms.
Emotional disturbance	Refers to inadequate personality integration and personal distress. Commonly used in referring to maladaptive behavior of children.
Behavior disorder	Used especially in referring to disorders that stem from faulty learning—either the failure to learn needed competencies or the learning of maladaptive coping patterns. May be used more broadly as roughly synonymous with *abnormal behavior.*
Mental illness	Once used as synonymous with *mental disorder* but now ordinarily restricted to disorders involving brain pathology or severe personality disorganization. The label *illness,* although it seems justified when referring to disorders that are severely incapacitating, is hardly appropriate in cases which apparently stem largely from faulty learning.
Mental disease	Formerly used to refer to disorders associated with brain pathology, but rarely used today.
Insanity	Legal term, indicating mental incompetence for managing one's affairs or foreseeing the consequences of one's actions. Denotes serious mental disorder.

In the course of this text, we shall try to clarify these distinctions further. As is the case with most attempts at labeling, none of these terms is completely satisfactory, and professional usage varies a great deal both from person to person and from one school of thought to another.

Axis IV scale for rating severity of psychosocial stressors

Code	Term	Adult examples	Child or adolescent examples
1	None	No apparent psychosocial stressor	No apparent psychosocial stressor
2	Minimal	Minor violation of the law, small bank loan	Vacation with family
3	Mild	Argument with neighbor, change in work hours	Change in school teacher, new school year
4	Moderate	New job, death of close friend, pregnancy	Parental fighting, change to new school, illness of close relative, birth of sibling
5	Severe	Major illness in self or family, bankruptcy, marital separation, birth of child	Death of peer, divorce of parents, arrest
6	Extreme	Death of close relative, divorce, jail term	Death of parent or sibling
7	Catastrophic	Concentration camp experience, devastating natural disaster	Multiple family deaths
0	Unspecified	No information or not applicable	No information or not applicable

From DSM-III (APA, 1979).

ing the appropriateness of including many of these problems under the rubric of "mental disorders."

A complete outline of DSM-III classification, Axes I and II, appears in the Appendix of this book. (An outline of DSM-II also appears for comparison purposes.) These categories may be regarded for purposes of clarity as fitting into several broader groupings:

a) *Organic mental disorders,* including disorders involving brain injuries, senile dementia, and a wide range of other conditions based on brain pathology;

b) *Substance use disorders,* including problems related to drug and alcohol abuse;

c) *Disorders of psychological or sociocultural origin,* in which no known brain pathology is involved as a primary causal factor, such as anxiety disorders, psychosomatic disorders, psychosexual disorders, personality disorders, severe depression, schizophrenia, and other "functional" psychoses;

d) *Disorders arising during childhood or adolescence,* including mental retardation (involving subnormal intellectual and adaptive functioning that originates during early development as a result of biological and/or psychosocial factors) and special problems, such as autism, that may occur in children and warrant separate categorization.

In referring to mental disorders, several qualifying terms are commonly used. *Acute* is a term used for disorders of relatively short duration, while *chronic* refers to long-standing and usually permanent disorders. *Mild, moderate,* and *severe* are used, as might be expected, in referring to the severity of the disorder. *Episodic* is used for disorders that recur, such as some depressive patterns.

Axis V scale for rating level of functioning

Levels	Adult examples	Child or adolescent examples
1 *SUPERIOR* Unusually effective functioning in social relations, occupational functioning and use of leisure time.	Housewife takes excellent care of children and home, has warm relations with family and many close friends and is effectively involved in several community activities.	12-year-old girl is getting superior grades in school, is extremely popular among her peers and excels in many sports.
2 *VERY GOOD* Better than average functioning in social relations, occupational functioning and use of leisure time.	A 65-year-old retired widower does some volunteer work, often sees old friends and pursues many life-long hobbies.	An adolescent boy is getting average grades, works parttime, has several close friends and plays banjo in jazz band.
3 *GOOD* No more than slight impairment in either social or occupational functioning.	A man functions extremely well at a difficult job, but has only one or two good friends.	An 8-year-old boy is doing well in school, has several friends but bullies younger children.
4 *FAIR* Moderate impairment in either social relations or occupational functioning, OR some impairment in both.	A female lawyer has trouble carrying through assignments, has several acquaintances but hardly any close friends.	A 10-year-old girl is doing poorly in school but has adequate peer and family relations.
5 *POOR* Marked impairment in either social relations or occupational functioning OR moderate impairment in both.	A man with one or two friends has trouble keeping a job for more than a few weeks.	A 14-year-old boy is almost failing in school and has trouble getting along with his peers.
6 *GROSSLY IMPAIRED* Marked impairment in both social relations and occupational functioning.	A woman is unable to do any of her housework, and has violent outbursts towards family and neighbors.	A 6-year-old girl needs special help in all subjects and has virtually no peer relationships.
0 *UNSPECIFIED*	No information.	No information.

From the DSM-III (APA, 1979).

Limits of classification. As was the case with earlier editions, DSM-III classification still has some serious limitations, some of which might characterize any scheme. First, the categories are descriptions, not explanations. One must guard against the tendency to think something has been explained when in fact it has only been named.

A second limitation is that only individual behavior is covered. Disturbed families, delinquent subcultures, and violence-prone societies show maladaptive behavior that does not fit into a scheme for classifying individuals. Yet classifying only individual behavior as abnormal implies that when individuals do not fit smoothly into their social milieu, it is the individuals who are at fault and must change. This attitude casts the mental health profession in the role of a force for preserving the status quo.

We shall deal further with this point in the course of the text; in our own discussion, however, we shall consider not only individuals but also pathogenic families and maladaptive group behavior. In addition, we will attempt to show the interaction and the vicious circles that may result from such behaviors.

In defense of the present APA classification, it should be noted that it does provide an idea of the range of behaviors considered to be abnormal in major societies throughout the world. Familiarity with it helps teachers, researchers, clinicians, and students to be sure they are talking about the same thing when they are communicating about abnormal behavior patterns. Nevertheless, it should be emphasized that classification is a human activity that is influenced by time, place, and culture—and therefore subject to change.

The man shown here is a tragic example of the dangerous effects of labeling. Born in a mental hospital to parents with mental problems, Jack Smith was assumed to be mentally retarded and received no formal schooling after age 12, in spite of the fact that he showed interest in learning. His early years were spent in a state orphanage, followed by 38 years in a mental hospital. In 1976, a Michigan judge declared that Mr. Smith was not mentally ill or dangerous, based on findings of a psychiatric evaluation. By that time, however, the 54-year-old man was considered "so impaired that it would be unwise to put him out on the streets" (The New York Times, March 11, 1979, p. 26). Mr. Smith now lives in a nursing home.

The problem of labeling.   Although categories and labels are useful for those working in the field, assigning labels to people may have several harmful effects. Labels imply that there are sharp dividing lines between "normal" and "abnormal" and between different disorders, whereas reality does not exist in such neat categories. People suffering from the same disorder will differ from each other in many ways. But once a label has been assigned to an individual, it may close off further inquiry. It becomes all too easy for those involved to accept the label uncritically as an accurate and complete description of the individual. It is then hard to look at the person's behavior objectively, without preconceptions about how he or she will act. Expectations, in turn, affect interactions with the person, including what kinds of treatment may or may not be tried.

These expectations are also communicated to the patient, who may accept the new identity implied by the label and develop the expected role and outlook. Unnecessary and crippling self-devaluation and hopelessness may result.

Most insidious, perhaps, is the tendency on the part of both patients and clinical workers to see the label as naming the person rather than simply the current behavior. For all these reasons, the present trend is away from rigid classification and labeling. (See HIGHLIGHT on page 21.)

Assessing and treating maladaptive behavior

While keeping in mind the possible drawbacks of labeling, the fact remains that before maladaptive behavior patterns can be treated, they must first be identified. Sometimes assessment and treatment are undertaken at the individual's own request—for example, because of serious feelings of anxiety or depression. In other cases, mental health personnel may make an assessment at the request of courts or other public agencies. In the case of children, parents or teachers may take the initiative in seeking help. Fortunately, more resources for such help are available than ever before.

Getting a broad picture of the problem.
An important early consideration in the assessment process is to determine whether there are physical causes underlying the disorder. Then, assuming that no relevant organic pathology is found, the clinician or clinical team usually collects a great deal of clinical and social information in an attempt to get an overall picture of the individual's problem.

Is the person depressed? Is there a thought disorder? Is there extreme reliance on neurotic defenses or a long history of legal or social difficulties? How well is the person meeting day-to-day demands and fulfilling social responsibilities? Although the trend is away from using assessment data to label behavior, the individual's behavior may be noted at this time as falling into one of the recognized categories, such as schizophrenic disorders.

Medical and psychological findings are integrated into an overall picture that describes the patient's problems, the behavioral context, and the conditions causing special stress, along with hypotheses about possible causal factors in the disorder. It is also important for the clinician to obtain an accurate evaluation of the patient's motivation for change and potential for it, and to identify any environmental factors that might be used to induce change.

A fuller description of the many techniques drawn on for assessment will be given in Chapter 17. It becomes apparent that those charged with deciding when a person's behavior is abnormal—and how abnormal it is—have an awesome responsibility to the individual and to the society.

Helping fields and personnel. At the present time, there are several distinct but closely related professional fields concerned with the study of abnormal behavior and with mental health. The distinction among them is often hard to draw precisely, for even though each has its own functions and areas of work, the contributions in one field are constantly influencing and contributing to the thinking and work in others.

Abnormal psychology has long been referred to as that part of the field of psychology concerned with the understanding, treatment, and prevention of abnormal behavior. However, the term is now relegated largely to titles of courses in colleges and universities that cover the subject matter of abnormal behavior. In other contexts it has generally been replaced by the term *clinical psychology,* the professional field broadly concerned with the study, assessment, treatment, and prevention of abnormal behavior. *Psychiatry* is the corresponding field of medicine, and is thus closely related to clinical psychology. *Social work,* an offshoot of sociology, is concerned with the analysis of social environments and with providing services which assist the adjustment of the patient in both family and community settings. (See HIGHLIGHT on page 22.)

In any given therapy program, a wide range of medical, psychological, and sociological procedures may be used. Such procedures range from the use of drugs through individual or group psychotherapy and encounter groups to sociotherapy aimed at modifying adverse conditions in the client's life situation. Often the latter—as in helping an employer become more understanding and supportive of the client's needs—is as important as treatment directed toward modifying the client's personality makeup and/or behavior.

Of growing importance in helping the maladjusted is the *team approach* to assessment and treatment. This approach involves the coordinated efforts of medical, psychological, social work, and other mental health personnel working together as the needs of each case warrant. Also of key importance is the trend toward providing treatment facilities in the community. Instead of considering maladjustment as a private misery of the individual, which in the past often required one's confinement in a distant mental hospital, this approach integrates family and community resources in the treatment.

In the chapters that follow we shall note many examples of specific therapeutic procedures used with particular disorders. In Chapters 18 and 19 we shall deal in some detail with the goals, procedures, and outcomes—as well as the problems and limitations—of contemporary approaches to biological and psychological therapy; and in Chapter 20 we shall examine community intervention approaches and strategies concerned with the prevention of mental disorders.

HIGHLIGHT

Mental illness as a myth

Psychiatrist Thomas Szasz (1920–   ) has been an outspoken critic of current practices and labels within the field of abnormal psychology (Szasz, 1961, 1970). In his writings, Szasz contends that mental illness is a myth and that traditional treatment can be more harmful than helpful.

According to Szasz, most of the disorders treated by psychiatrists and other mental health practitioners are not illnesses. Instead, he claims, they are simply individual traits or behaviors that deviate from what our society considers morally or socially normal. They are caused by "problems in living"—by unmet needs and by stressful relationships, for example.

Szasz believes that traditional psychiatric treatment harms such people by labeling them as ill. Not only does this labeling encourage them to fulfill society's expectations and act in irresponsible ways; it also implies that they must become patients and accept treatment in order to change. In Szasz's view, this means that they are being encouraged to think and behave in ways considered normal by psychiatrists rather than to attack the social causes of their problems.

The orientation of this book

Throughout this book we shall be attempting to acquire a perspective on abnormal behavior and its place in contemporary society. Although we shall deal with all the major categories of mental disorders, we shall not attempt an encyclopedic coverage, but rather shall focus on those patterns that seem most relevant to an understanding of abnormal behavior. And while we shall not hesitate to include the unusual or bizarre, our emphasis will be on the unity of human behavior, ranging from the normal to the abnormal ends of the continuum.

This text is predicated on the assumption that a sound and comprehensive study of abnormal behavior should be based on the following concepts:

1. *A scientific approach to abnormal behavior.* Any comprehensive view of human behavior must draw upon concepts and research findings from a variety of scientific fields. Of particular relevance are genetics, neurophysiology, sociology, and anthropology, as well as psychology. Such common scientific concepts as causal processes, control groups, dependent variables, placebos, and theories will figure prominently in our discussion. Special emphasis will be placed on the application of learning principles to the understanding and treatment of mental disorders.

In this general context, students are encouraged to take a critical and evaluative attitude toward research findings presented in this text and in other available sources. Scientific research, when properly conducted, does provide us with information having a high probability of being accurate, but many research findings are subject to bias and open to serious question.

2. *An awareness of our existential problems.* There are many experiences and problems common to human existence about which science as yet has had little to say. Included are such vital experiences as hope, faith, courage, love, grief, despair, death, and the quest for values and meaning. Authentic insights into

Personnel in psychotherapy

PROFESSIONAL

Clinical psychologist
Ph.D. in psychology with both research and clinical skill specialization. One-year internship in a psychiatric hospital or mental health center. *Or,* Psy.D. in psychology (a professional degree with more clinical than research specialization) plus one-year internship in a psychiatric hospital or mental health center.

Counseling psychologist
Ph.D. in psychology plus internship in a marital or student counseling setting; normally, the counseling psychologist deals with adjustment problems not involving mental disorder.

Psychiatrist
M.D. degree with internship plus residency training (usually three years) in a psychiatric hospital or mental health facility.

Psychoanalyst
M.D. or Ph.D. degree plus intensive training in theory and practice of psychoanalysis.

Psychiatric social worker
B.A., M.S.W., or Ph.D. degree with specialized clinical training in mental health settings.

Psychiatric nurse
R.N. in nursing plus specialized training in care and treatment of psychiatric patients. M.A. and Ph.D. in psychiatric nursing is possible.

Occupational therapist
B.S. in occupational therapy plus internship training with physically or psychologically handicapped, helping them make the most of their resources.

PARAPROFESSIONAL

Community mental health worker
Capable person with limited professional training who works under professional direction (especially crisis intervention).

Alcohol or drug-abuse counselor
Limited professional training but trained in the evaluation and management of alcohol- and drug-addicted persons.

Pastoral counselor
Ministerial background plus training in psychology. Intership in mental health facility as a chaplain.

In both mental health clinics and hospitals, personnel from several fields may function as an interdisciplinary team in therapy—for example, a psychiatrist, a clinical psychologist, a social worker, a psychiatric nurse, and an occupational therapist may work together.

such experiences can often be gained from literature, drama, and autobiographical accounts that strike a common chord and relate directly to an understanding of human behavior. Material from such fields as art, history, and religion can also provide useful insights into certain aspects of abnormal behavior. However, information from the preceding sources will be distinguished from that obtained through scientific observation.

3. *Respect for the dignity, integrity, and growth potential of the individual.* A basic orientation of this book is well described in the opening statement of the *Ethical Standards of Psychologists,* formulated by the American Psychological Association:

"The psychologist believes in the dignity and worth of the individual human being." (1972, p. 1)

Implicit in this statement is a view of individuals not merely as products of their past conditioning and present situation but as potentially active agents as well—persons who can develop and use their capacities for building the kind of life they choose and a better future world for humankind.

In attempting throughout this volume to provide a perspective for viewing abnormal behavior, we shall focus not only on how maladaptive patterns such as schizophrenia are perceived by clinical psychologists and other mental health personnel, but also on how such disorders feel and are perceived by the individuals experiencing them. In dealing with the major patterns of abnormal behavior, we shall focus on four significant aspects of each: clinical picture, causal factors, treatment, and outcome. And in each case we shall examine the evidence for biological, psychological and interpersonal, and sociocultural factors.

Most of this volume will be devoted to a presentation of well-established patterns of abnormal behavior and to special problem behaviors of our time that are more controversial but directly relevant to any discussion of maladaptive behavior. Initially, however, we shall trace the development of our contemporary views of abnormal behavior from early beliefs and practices, sketch several attempts to explain what makes human beings "tick,"

and review briefly the basic principles of adjustive behavior and the general causes of abnormal behavior.

Finally, after our discussion of the various problem behaviors, we shall devote four chapters to modern methods of assessment and treatment, including the potentialities of modern psychology and allied sciences for preventing mental disorders and for helping humankind achieve a more sane and harmonious world.

At the close of his journeys, Tennyson's Ulysses says, "I am part of all that I have met." It is the authors' hope that readers of this book, at the end of their journey through it, will have a better understanding of human experience and behavior—and that they will consider what they have learned as a meaningful part of their own life experience.

In this introduction we have briefly reviewed the nature and scope of abnormal behavior; we have surveyed some examples of mental disorders from history, literature, and drama; we have noted some popular misconceptions of mental disorders; we have dealt with the scientific problem of what we mean by "abnormal"; we presented a brief summary of the current APA listing of mental disorders; and we have briefly touched on the procedures used in assessment and treatment.

In the course of our discussion, we have emphasized that (a) *abnormal behavior* may be defined as behavior that is *maladaptive;* (b) human behavior falls along a continuum extending from highly adaptive behavior at one extreme to highly maladaptive behavior at the other; (c) a person's position on this continuum of adjustment may shift over time; and (d) the same principles that are used to conceptualize and understand normal behavior are also applicable to abnormal or maladaptive behavior.

Having presented this brief orientation to the study of abnormal behavior, let us now trace the progress that has been made in understanding psychopathology from ancient times to the present.

2

From demonology to the biological viewpoint

Abnormal behavior in ancient times
Demonology in the Middle Ages
Emergence of humanitarian approaches
Development of the biological viewpoint

The mysteries of the human mind and brain have rightly been called the last frontier in our scientific understanding of ourselves and our relationship to the rest of nature. While much progress has been made in our approach to this frontier, we must acknowledge that fundamental problems continue to perplex us and to elude our best efforts to resolve them. The psychology of the abnormal is in this sense no farther advanced than is that of its normal counterpart. The story of our attempts to gain a foothold on understanding abnormality is a fascinating one. Its beginnings are the subject of this chapter.

Many popular misconceptions about mental disorders have roots in the dim historical past, but many of our modern scientific concepts and methods of treatment also had their beginnings long ago. For example, modern brain surgery, as we shall shortly see, had its early precursor many thousands of years ago, and electroshock treatment for severe depression and other serious disorders is antedated by flogging, immersing a person in cold water, and other crude "shock" treatments. Even the method of "free association"—a cornerstone of psychoanalytic therapy, designed to allow repressed conflicts and emotions to enter conscious awareness—is described by the Greek playwright Aristophanes in his play *The Clouds*. Interestingly enough, the scene in which Socrates tries to calm and bring self-knowledge to Strepsiades is complete with a couch.

It is only comparatively recently, however, that mental disorders have been generally recognized as having natural causes. In this chapter we shall trace the evolution of views on psychopathology from ancient times to the turn of the present century, from the superstitious and often cruel treatment given those who suffered from mental disorders to a recognition of the importance of brain pathology in some mental disorders. Then, in Chapter 3 we shall look at further advances and points of view that have developed in this century.

The great advances that have come about in the understanding and treatment of abnormal behavior become all the more remarkable when viewed against the long background of ignorance, superstition, and fear. Yet, as we shall see, we are not yet free of all culturally conditioned constraints that inhibit truly rational approaches to many of our remaining problems.

Abnormal behavior in ancient times

Although human life presumably appeared on earth some three million or more years ago, written records extend back only a few thousand years. Thus our knowledge of "primitive humans" is very limited and often based on extrapolation from so-called primitive peoples who remained isolated and relatively static into modern times. Beginning with the Egyptian and other ancient civilizations, historical information becomes more reliable, although far from complete.

Demonology among the ancients

The earliest treatment of mental disorders of which we have any knowledge was that practiced by Stone Age cave dwellers some half million years ago. For certain forms of mental disorders, probably those in which the individual complained of severe headaches and developed convulsive attacks, the early shaman, or medicine man, treated the disorder by means of an operation now called *trephining*. This operation was performed with crude stone instruments and consisted of chipping away one area of the skull in the form of a circle until the skull was cut through. This opening, called a *trephine*, presumably permitted the evil spirit that supposedly was causing all the trouble to escape—and incidentally may have relieved a certain amount of pressure on the brain. In some cases trephined skulls of primitive people show healing around the opening, indicating that the patient survived the operation and lived for many years afterward (Selling, 1943).

References to mental disorders in the early writings of the Chinese, Egyptians, Hebrews, and Greeks show that they generally attributed such disorders to demons that had taken possession of the individual. This is not surprising when we remember that "good" and "bad" spirits were widely used to explain lightning, thunder, earthquakes, storms, fires, sickness, and many other events that otherwise seemed incomprehensible. It was probably a very simple and logical step to extend this theory to peculiar and incomprehensible behavior in their fellows.

The decision as to whether the "possession" involved good spirits or evil spirits usually depended on the individual's symptoms. If speech or behavior appeared to have a religious or mystical significance, it was usually thought that the person was possessed by a good spirit or god. Such individuals were often treated with considerable awe and respect, for it was thought that they had supernatural powers. In the Bible story, David took advantage of this popular belief when he simulated "madness" in order to escape from Achish, the king of Gath (1 Samuel 21:12–14).

Most possessions, however, were considered to be the work of evil spirits, particularly when the individual became excited and overactive and engaged in behavior contrary to religious teachings. Among the ancient Hebrews, such possessions were thought to represent the wrath and punishment of God. Moses is quoted in the Bible as saying, "The Lord shall smite thee with madness. . . ." Apparently this was thought to involve primarily the withdrawal of God's protection, and the abandonment of the individual to the forces of evil. For example, Saul presumably disobeyed God, so that the spirit of the Lord left him and an evil spirit was thereby permitted to enter. In such cases every effort was made to rid the person of the evil spirit. Jesus reportedly cured a man with an "unclean spirit" by transferring the devils that plagued him to a herd of swine who, in turn, became possessed and "ran violently down a steep place into the sea" (Mark 5:1–13).

The primary type of treatment for demoniacal possession was exorcism, which included various techniques for casting the evil spirit out of the body of the afflicted one. These varied considerably but typically included prayer, incantation, noisemaking, and the use of various horrible-tasting concoctions, such as purgatives made from sheep's dung and wine. In extreme cases more severe measures were often used in an attempt to make the body of the possessed person such an unpleasant place that the evil spirit would be driven out.

Such treatment was originally in the hands of shamans, but was eventually taken over in

This 15th-century German engraving emphasizes the belief held by early Christians that God could protect them from possession by demons.

Greece and Egypt by the priests, who were apparently a curious mixture of priest, physician, psychologist, and magician. Although these priests in the main accepted the beliefs in demonology and used established exorcistic practices, they did make a beginning in the more humane treatment of mental disturbances. For example, as early as 860 B.C. in the temples of Asclepius in Greece, the priests had patients sleep in the temple; supposedly the dreams they had there would reveal what they needed to do to get better. The priests also supplemented the usual prayer and incantation with kindness, suggestion, and recreational measures, such as theatricals, riding, walking, and harmonious music. However, starving, flogging, and chains were still advocated for recalcitrant patients. The popularity of recent motion pictures and books on possession and exorcism suggests that these primitive ideas still have appeal today.

Early philosophical and medical concepts

During the Golden Age of Greece considerable progress was made in the understanding and treatment of mental disorders. Originally, membership in the medical priesthood of the Greek temples of healing was hereditary, but gradually outsiders were admitted and various "schools" began to form. It was in one of these groups that Hippocrates received his early training.

Hippocrates. The great Greek physician Hippocrates (460–377 B.C.) has been called the "father of modern medicine." He denied the intervention of deities and demons in the development of disease, and insisted that mental disorders had natural causes and required treatment like other diseases. His position was unequivocal: "For my own part, I do not believe that the human body is ever befouled by a God" (in Lewis, 1941, p. 37). Hippocrates emphasized the view, earlier set forth by Pythagoras, that the brain was the central organ of intellectual activity and that mental disorders were due to brain pathology. Hippocrates also emphasized the importance of heredity and predisposition and pointed out that injuries to the head could cause sensory and motor disorders.

Hippocrates classified all the varieties of mental disorder into three general categories—mania, melancholia, and phrenitis—and gave detailed clinical descriptions of the specific disorders included in each category, such as alcoholic delirium and epilepsy. Hippocrates relied heavily on clinical observation, and his descriptions, which were based on the daily clinical records of his patients, were surprisingly thorough. It is interesting to note that Hippocrates realized the clinical importance of dreams for understanding the personality of the patient. On this point he anticipated one of the concepts basic to several forms of contemporary psychotherapy.

The methods of treatment advocated by Hip-

pocrates were far in advance of the exorcistic practices then prevalent. For the treatment of melancholia, for example, he prescribed a regular and tranquil life, sobriety and abstinence from all excesses, a vegetable diet, celibacy, exercise short of fatigue, and bleeding if indicated. But for hysteria,[1] which was thought to be restricted to women and caused by the wandering of the uterus to various parts of the body because of its pining for children, Hippocrates recommended marriage as the best remedy. He also believed in the importance of environment, and not infrequently removed his patients from their families.

Hippocrates' emphasis on natural causes, clinical observations, and brain pathology in relation to mental disorders was truly revolutionary. Like his contemporaries, however, Hippocrates had very little knowledge of physiology. (Greek physicians were poor physiologists and anatomists because they deified the human body and dared not dissect it.) Thus in his concept of the "four humors"—blood, black bile, yellow bile, and phlegm—Hippocrates apparently conceived the notion of a balance of physiological processes as essential to normal brain functioning and mental health. In his work *On Sacred Disease,* he stated that when the humors were adversely mixed or otherwise disturbed, physical or mental disease resulted: "depravement of the brain arises from phlegm and bile; those mad from phlegm are quiet, depressed and oblivious; those from bile excited, noisy and mischievous." Although this concept went far beyond demonology, it was too crude physiologically to be of any great value. Yet medical treatment based on such inadequate anatomical and physiological knowledge was to continue for many centuries, often proving both humorous and tragic.

Plato and Aristotle. The problem of dealing with mentally disturbed individuals who committed criminal acts was studied by the great philosopher Plato (429–347 B.C.). He wrote that such persons were in some "obvious" sense not responsible for their acts and should not receive punishment in the same way as normal persons: ". . . someone may

---

[1]The appearance of symptoms of physical illness in the absence of organic pathology.

commit an act when mad or afflicted with disease . . . [if so,] let him pay simply for the damage; and let him be exempt from other punishment." Plato also made provision for mental cases to be cared for in the community as follows: "If anyone is insane, let him not be seen openly in the city, but let the relatives of such a person watch over him in the best manner they know of; and if they are negligent, let them pay a fine . . ." (Plato, n.d., p. 56). In making these humane suggestions, Plato was addressing issues that are still with us today—the issue of "insanity" as a legal defense when a crime has been committed and the proper treatment of persons whose public behavior is considered offensive or dangerous to the social order.

In addition to this emphasis on the more humane treatment of the mentally disturbed, Plato contributed to a better understanding of human behavior by pointing out that all forms of life, human included, were motivated by physiologic needs, or "natural appetites." Perhaps his most significant contribution was that he saw psychological phenomena as responses of the whole organism, reflecting its internal state. He also seems to have anticipated Freud's insight into the functions of fantasies and dreams as substitutive satisfactions, concluding that in dreams, desire tended to satisfy itself in imagery when the higher faculties no longer inhibited the "passions." In his *Republic*, Plato emphasized the importance of individual differences in intellectual and other abilities, pointing also to the role of sociocultural influences in shaping thinking and behavior. Despite these modern ideas, however, Plato shared the belief of his time that mental disorders were partly organic, partly moral, and partly divine.

The celebrated systematist Aristotle (384–322 B.C.), who was a pupil but not a follower of Plato, wrote extensively on mental disorders. Among his most lasting contributions to psychology are his descriptions of the content of consciousness. He, too, anticipated Freud in his view of "thinking" as directed striving toward elimination of pain and attainment of pleasure. On the question of whether mental disorders could be caused by psychological factors like frustration and conflict, Aristotle discussed the possibility and rejected it, and his influence was widespread. Aristotle generally

followed the Hippocratic theory of disturbances in the bile. For example, he believed that very hot bile generated amorous desires and loquacity, and was also responsible for suicidal impulses.

Later Greek and Roman thought.   Work along the lines that had been established by Hippocrates was continued by some of the later Greek and Roman physicians. Particularly in Alexandria, Egypt (which after its founding in 332 B.C. by Alexander the Great became the center of Greek culture), medical practices developed to a high level, and the temples dedicated to Saturn were first-rate sanatoriums. Pleasant surroundings were considered of great therapeutic value for the mental patients, who were provided with constant activities including parties, dances, walks in the temple gardens, rowing along the Nile, and musical concerts. The later Greek and Roman physicians also employed a wide range of other kinds of therapeutic measures, including dieting, massage, hydrotherapy, gymnastics, hynotism, and education, as well as certain less desirable measures, such as bleeding, purging, and mechanical restraints.

Among the Greeks and Romans who continued in the Hippocratic tradition were Asclepiades, Cicero, Aretaeus, and Galen. Asclepiades (born *c.* 124 B.C.) was the first to note the difference between acute and chronic mental disorders, and to distinguish between illusions, delusions, and hallucinations. In addition, he invented various ingenious devices designed to make patients more comfortable. One of these was a suspended hammock-like bed whose swaying was considered very beneficial for disturbed patients. Asclepiades' progressive approach to mental disorders was also evidenced by his opposition to bleeding, mechanical restraints, and dungeons.

Cicero (106–43 B.C.) was perhaps the first to go on record as stating boldly that body ailments could be the result of emotional factors. A century later, Aretaeus saw certain mental disorders as merely an extension of normal psychological processes. He thought that people who were irritable, violent, and easily given to joy and pleasurable pursuits were prone to the development of manic excitement, while those who tended to be serious were more apt to develop melancholia. Aretaeus was the first to describe the various phases of mania and melancholia, and to consider these two pathological states as expressions of the same illness. His insight into the importance of emotional factors and of the pre-psychotic personality of the patient was an extraordinary achievement for his day.

Galen (A.D. 130–200), a devoted elaborator of Hippocratic tradition, did not contribute much that was new to the treatment or clinical descriptions of mental disorders, although he did make many original contributions concerning the anatomy of the nervous system. He also maintained a scientific approach to the field, performing a major service in compiling and integrating the existing material (Guthrie, 1946). In the latter connection, he divided the causes of mental disorders into physical and mental. Among the causes he named were injuries to the head, alcoholic excess, shock, fear, adolescence, menstrual changes, economic reverses, and disappointment in love.

Roman medicine reflected the characteristic pragmatism of the Roman people. Roman physicians wanted to make their patients comfortable and used pleasant physical therapies, such as warm baths and massage. They also followed the principle of "contraris contrarius"—for example, having their patients drink chilled wine while immersed in a warm tub.

Although historians consider the fall of Rome to the barbarians toward the end of the fifth century to be the dividing line between ancient and medieval times, the Dark Ages in the history of abnormal psychology began with Galen's death in A.D. 200. The contributions of Hippocrates and the later Greek and Roman physicians were shortly lost in the welter of popular superstition, and most of the physicians of later Rome returned to some sort of demonology. One notable exception to this trend, however, was Alexander Trallianus (A.D. 525–605), who followed the works of Galen rather closely but placed a great deal of emphasis on constitutional factors—stating, for example, that people with dark hair and a slim build were more likely to be affected by melancholia than persons with light hair and a heavy build. Worthy of note also are some of the clinical cases he recorded (Whitwell, 1936), such as that of a woman who had the delusion that her middle finger was fixed in such a way that it

held the whole world within its power. This caused her great distress for fear she should bend her finger, thus overthrowing the world and destroying everything. Another interesting case was that of a man who was greatly depressed because he was convinced that his head had been amputated. Trallianus reported that he cured this case by suddenly placing a close-fitting leaden cap on the patient's head so that he was able to feel the weight and thought his head had been replaced. In this respect, Trallianus anticipated certain of the more direct "behavioral" therapies in use today in treating psychological disorders.

Survival of Greek thought in Arabia.
During medieval times it was only in Arabia that the more scientific aspects of Greek medicine survived. The first mental hospital was established in Baghdad in A.D. 792; it was soon followed by others in Damascus and Aleppo (Polvan, 1969). In these hospitals the mentally disturbed received more humane treatment than they did in Christian lands, one of many curious discrepancies between Christian concept and practice, of which more will be said.

The outstanding figure in Arabian medicine was Avicenna (c. A.D. 980–1037), called the "prince of physicians" (Campbell, 1926). In his writings Avicenna frequently referred to hysteria, epilepsy, manic reactions, and melancholia. The following case shows his unique approach to the treatment of a young prince suffering from a mental disorder:

"A certain prince . . . was afflicted with melancholia, and suffered from the delusion that he was a cow . . . he would low like a cow, causing annoyance to everyone, . . . crying 'Kill me so that a good stew may be made of my flesh,' finally . . . he would eat nothing. . . . Avicenna was persuaded to take the case. . . . First of all he sent a message to the patient bidding him be of good cheer because the butcher was coming to slaughter him, whereat . . . the sick man rejoiced. Some time afterwards Avicenna, holding a knife in his hand, entered the sickroom saying, 'Where is this cow that I may kill it?' The patient lowed like a cow to indicate where he was. By Avicenna's orders he was laid on the ground, bound hand and foot. Avicenna then felt him all over and said, 'He is too lean, and not ready to be killed; he must be fattened.' Then they offered him suitable food of which he now partook eagerly, and gradually he gained strength, got rid of his delusion, and was completely cured." (Browne, 1921, pp. 88–89)

Unfortunately, most Western medical men of Avicenna's time were dealing with mental patients in a very different way. For a look at what was happening in China, see HIGHLIGHT on page 32.

Demonology in the Middle Ages

During the Middle Ages (about A.D. 500–1500) there was a tremendous revival of the most ancient superstition and demonology, with only a slight modification to conform to current theological demands. Human beings now became the battleground of demons and spirits who waged eternal war for the possession of their souls. Mental disorders were apparently quite frequent throughout the Middle Ages, and their incidence seems to have increased toward the end of the period, when medieval institutions began to collapse. As Rosen (1967) has described it:

"The medieval world began to come apart in the 14th century, and the process of disintegration continued inexorably through the succeeding centuries. Fundamental changes took place in its institutions, its social structure, its beliefs and outlook. It was a period of peasant revolts and urban uprisings, of wars and plagues, and thus an age in which many felt acutely insecure and discontented. An emotional malaise was abroad." (p. 775)

"Mass madness" *hysteria*

The last half of the Middle Ages saw a peculiar trend in abnormal behavior, involving the widespread occurrence of group mental disorders that were apparently mainly cases of hysteria. Whole groups of people were affected simultaneously.

Dance manias, taking the form of epidemics of raving, jumping, dancing, and convulsions, were reported as early as the tenth century. One such episode, occurring in Italy early in the thirteenth century, was recorded by physicians of the time whose records have been reviewed by the medical historian H. E. Sigerist. He has written:

"The disease occurred at the height of the summer heat. . . . People, asleep or awake, would suddenly jump up, feeling an acute pain like the sting of a bee. Some saw the spider, others did not, but they knew that it must be the tarantula. They ran out of the

Madness has been a favorite subject for artists throughout history. Here (opposite page), *a 15th-century drawing by Pieter Brueghel shows peasant women overcome by St. Vitus's dance. And William Blake's 18th-century depiction of Nebuchadnezzar* (left), *king of Babylon who suffered from lycanthropy, is a powerful work based on a biblical description: ". . . he was driven from men, and did eat grass as oxen, and his body was wet with the dew of heaven, til his hairs were grown like eagles' feathers, and his nails like birds' claws" (Daniel 4:33).*

house into the street, to the market place, dancing in great excitement. Soon they were joined by others who like them had been bitten, or by people who had been stung in previous years. . . .

"Thus groups of patients would gather, dancing wildly in the queerest attire. . . . Others would tear their clothes and show their nakedness, losing all sense of modesty. . . . Some called for swords and acted like fencers, others for whips and beat each other. . . . Some of them had still stranger fancies, liked to be tossed in the air, dug holes in the ground, and rolled themselves into the dirt like swine. They all drank wine plentifully and sang and talked like drunken people. . . ." (1943, pp. 103, 106–107)

Actually, the behavior was very similar to the ancient orgiastic rites by which people had worshiped the Greek gods. These had been banned with the advent of Christianity, but were deeply embedded in the culture and were apparently kept alive by secret gatherings. Probably considerable guilt and conflict were engendered; then, with time, the meaning of the dances changed, and the old rites appeared as symptoms of disease. The participants were no longer sinners but the poor victims of the tarantula (Gloyne, 1950).

Known as *tarantism* in Italy, the dancing mania later spread to Germany and the rest of Europe, where it was known as *St. Vitus's dance*. Other peculiar manifestations also ap-

peared. In the fifteenth century, a member of a German convent was overcome with a desire to bite her fellow nuns. The practice was taken up by her companions, and the mania spread to other convents in Germany, Holland, and Italy (A. D. White, 1896).

Isolated rural areas were also afflicted with outbreaks of *lycanthropy*—a mental disorder in which individuals imagined themselves wolves and imitated their behavior. In 1541 a case was reported in which the lycanthrope told his captors, in confidence, that he was really a wolf but that his skin was smooth on the surface because all the hairs were on the inside (Stone, 1937). To cure him of his delusions, his extremities were amputated, following which he died, still unconvinced.

These epidemics continued into the seventeenth century, but apparently reached their peak during the fifteenth and sixteenth centuries—a period noted for oppression, famine, and pestilence. Prior to this period, Europe was ravaged by an epidemic known as the "Black Death," which spread across the continent, destroying millions of human lives and severely disrupting social organization. Undoubtedly many of the peculiar manifestations during this period, including the Children's Crusade, in which thousands of children left their homes to liberate the Holy Sepulcher,

Early views of mental disorders in China

Tseng (1973) traced the development of concepts of mental disorders in China by reviewing the descriptions of the disorders and their recommended treatment in Chinese medical documents. For example, the following is taken from an ancient Chinese medical text supposedly written by Huang Ti (c. 2674 B.C.), the third legendary emperor, but now considered by historians to have been written at a later date, possibly during the seventh century B.C.:

"The person suffering from excited insanity initially feels sad, eating and sleeping less; he then becomes grandiose, feeling that he is very smart and noble, talking and scolding day and night, singing, behaving strangely, seeing strange things, hearing strange voices, believing that he can see the devil or gods. . . ." (p. 570)

Even at this early date, Chinese medicine was based on natural rather than supernatural causes. For example, in the concept of Ying and Yang the human body, like the cosmos, is divided into a positive and a negative force which are both complementary and contradictory to each other. If the two forces are balanced, the result is physical and mental health; if they are not, illness will result. Consequently:

"As treatment for such an excited condition withholding food was suggested, since food was considered to be the source of positive force and the patient was thought to be in need of a decrease in such force." (p. 570)

Chinese medicine apparently reached a relatively sophisticated level during the second century, and Chung Ching, who has been called the Hippocrates of China, wrote two well-known medical works around A.D. 200. Like Hippocrates, he based his views of both physical and mental disorders on clinical observations and implicated organ pathology as the primary cause. However, he also believed that stressful psychological conditions could cause the organ pathology, and his treatment, like that of Hip-

pocrates, utilized both drugs and the regaining of emotional balance through appropriate activities. During this period, for example, the following treatment for excited insanity was recommended:

"If a patient wants to go, let him go; if he wants to stay, let him stay; do not deny him what he wants and do not suppress him. If we comply to his wishes and let him satisfy his needs, then all of his excessive positive force will be appropriately discharged and he will consequently get well." (p 571)

Here it may be noted that the excessive positive force—again involving the concept of Ying and Yang—was based on the idea that some vital organ had lost its essential stability, thus interrupting the normal rhythm of life. And while seemingly a rather passive method of treatment, it was both humane and socially oriented.

As in the West, however, Chinese views of mental disorders were to regress to the belief in supernatural forces as causal agents. From the later part of the second century through the early part of the ninth century, ghosts and devils were implicated in "Ghost-evil" insanity, which presumably resulted from bewitchment by evil spirits. However, the "Dark Ages" in China were not so severe—in terms of the treatment of mental patients—nor did they last so long as in the West. And a return to somatic views as well as the emphasis on psychosocial factors were to occur in the centuries which followed.

In this context, it is interesting to note the conclusion of Tseng that ". . . concepts of how mental illness is perceived and pathology explained have gone through the sequence of supernatural, natural, somatic, and psychological stages in both the East and the West" (p. 573). And in both East and West, there were setbacks—"Dark Ages"—involving a return to prehistoric views of evil spirits and related supernatural causal forces.

were related to the depression, fear, and wild mysticism engendered by the terrible events of the time. People did not dream that such frightening catastrophes were attributable to natural causes and thus would some day be within our power to control, prevent, or even create.

Interestingly, it was during the sixteenth century that Teresa of Avila, a Spanish nun who was later to be canonized, accomplished the beginnings of an extraordinary conceptual leap that influences our thinking to the present day. Teresa, in charge of a group of cloistered nuns who had become hysterical and were therefore in mortal danger from the Spanish Inquisition, argued convincingly that her nuns were not bewitched, but rather were "as if sick" (comas enfermas). Apparently, she did not mean they were sick of body. Rather, with the expression "as if," we have what is perhaps the first suggestion that a mind can be sick just as can a body. It was a momentous suggestion that apparently began as a kind of metaphor but was, with time, reified (viewed as real): mental illness came to be seen as an entity, the "as if" having long since dropped out of use (Sarbin & Juhasz, 1967). As we shall see, the confusion engendered by this reification of a metaphor is still with us.

Mass disorder is not unknown in the present day. Reports of so-called "mass hysteria" occur from time to time in the contemporary press; the affliction is usually one that mimics some type of physical disorder, such as fainting spells or convulsive movements.

Exorcism in medieval times

In the Middle Ages treatment of the mentally disturbed was left largely to the clergy. Monasteries served as refuges and places of confinement. During the early part of the medieval period, the mentally disturbed for the most part were treated with considerable kindliness. Much store was set by prayer, holy water, sanctified ointments, the breath or spittle of the priests, the touching of relics, visits to holy places, and mild forms of exorcism. In some monasteries and shrines exorcism was performed by the gentle "laying on of hands." Such methods were often intermixed with vague ideas of medical treatment derived mainly from Galen, which gave rise to such prescriptions as the following: "For a fiend-sick man: When a devil possesses a man, or controls him from within with disease, a spewdrink of lupin, bishopswort, henbane, garlic. Pound these together, add ale and holy water" (Cockayne, 1864–1866).

As exorcistic techniques became more fully developed, emphasis was placed on Satan's pride, which was believed to have led to his original downfall. Hence, in treating persons possessed by a devil, the first thing to do was to strike a fatal blow at the devil's pride—to insult him. This involved calling the devil some of the most obscene epithets that imagination could devise, and the insults were usually supplemented by long litanies of cursing:

". . . May all the devils that are thy foes rush forth upon thee, and drag thee down to hell! . . . May God set a nail to your skull, and pound it in with a hammer, as Jael did unto Sisera! . . . May . . . Sother break thy head and cut off thy hands, as was done to the cursed Dagon! . . . May God hang thee in a hellish yoke, as seven men were hanged by the sons of Saul!" (From Thesaurus Exorcismorum)

This procedure was considered highly successful in the treatment of possessed persons. A certain bishop of Beauvais claimed to have rid a person of five devils, all of whom signed an agreement stating that they and their subordinate imps would no longer persecute the possessed individual (A. D. White, 1896).

As theological beliefs concerning abnormal behavior became more fully developed and were endorsed by the secular world, treatment of the mentally disturbed became more harsh. It was generally believed that cruelty to people afflicted with "madness" was punishment of the devil residing within them, and when "scourging" proved ineffective, the authorities felt justified in driving out the demons by more unpleasant methods. Flogging, starving, chains, immersion in hot water, and other torturous methods were devised in order to make the body such an unpleasant place of residence that no self-respecting devil would remain in it. Undoubtedly many men and women who might have been restored to health by more gentle and humane measures were driven into hopeless derangement by such brutal treatment.

Witchcraft

During the latter part of the fifteenth century, it became the accepted theological belief that demoniacal possessions were of two general types: (a) possessions in which the victim was unwillingly seized by the devil as a punishment by God for past sins, and (b) possessions in which the individual was actually in league with the devil. The latter persons were supposed to have made a pact with the devil, consummated by signing in blood a book presented to them by Satan, which gave them certain supernatural powers. They could cause pestilence, storms, floods, sexual impotence, injuries to their enemies, and ruination of crops, and could rise through the air, cause milk to sour, and turn themselves into animals. In short, they were witches.

These beliefs were not confined to simple serfs but were held and elaborated upon by most of the important clergymen of this period. No less a man than Martin Luther (1483–1546) came to the following conclusions:

"The greatest punishment God can inflict on the wicked . . . is to deliver them over to Satan, who with God's permission, kills them or makes them to undergo great calamities. Many devils are in woods, water, wildernesses, etc., ready to hurt and prejudice people. When these things happen, then the philosophers and physicians say it is natural, ascribing it to the planets.

"In cases of melancholy . . . I conclude it is merely the work of the devil. Men are possessed by the devil in two ways; corporally or spiritually. Those whom he possesses corporally, as mad people, he has permission from God to vex and agitate, but he has no power over their souls." (*Colloquia Mensalia*)

Those who were judged to have been unwillingly seized by the devil as punishment by God were treated initially in accordance with the established exorcistic practices of the time. As time went on, however, the distinction between the two types of possessions became somewhat obscured, and by the close of the fifteenth century, the mentally ill were generally considered heretics and witches.

More and more concern was expressed in official quarters over the number of witches roaming around and the great damage they were doing by pestilences, storms, sexual depravity, and other heinous crimes. Con-sequently, on December 7, 1484, Pope Innocent VIII sent forth his papal brief, *Summis Desiderantes Affectibus*, in which he exhorted the clergy of Europe, especially Germany, to leave no means untried in the detection of witches. This papal brief was theologically based on the scriptural command "Thou shalt not suffer a witch to live" (Exodus 22:18).

To assist in this great work, a manual, *Malleus maleficarum (The Witches' Hammer)*, was prepared by two Dominican monks, Johann Sprenger and Heinrich Kraemer, both Inquisitors appointed by the pope to act in northern Germany and territories along the Rhine. This manual, revered for centuries in both Catholic and Protestant countries as being almost divinely inspired, was complete in every detail concerning witchcraft and was of great value in witch-hunting. It was divided into three parts. The first confirmed the existence of witches and pointed out that those who did not believe in them were either in honest error or polluted with heresy. The second part contained a description of the clinical symptoms by which witches could be detected, such as red spots or areas of anesthesia on the skin, which were thought to resemble the claw of the devil ("devil's claw") and were presumably left by the devil to denote the sealing of the pact with him. The third part dealt with the legal forms of examining and sentencing a witch.

In accordance with the precepts laid down in the *Malleus*, the accepted way to gain sure proof of witchcraft was to torture the person until a confession was obtained. This method was eminently effective. The victims of these inhuman tortures—writhing in agony and viewed with horror by those they loved—confessed to anything and everything. Frequently they were forced to give the names of alleged accomplices in their evildoing, and these unfortunate persons were in turn tortured until they, too, confessed.

Confessions were often weird, but this seldom deterred the learned judges. For example, James I of England proved, through the skillful use of unlimited torture, that witches were to blame for the tempests that beset his bride on her voyage from Denmark. A Dr. Fian, whose legs were being crushed in the "boots" and who had wedges driven under his fingernails, con-

*Regardless of the supposed cause of an
individual's possession, there's no doubt that
early methods to treat many disorders which were
poorly understood were drastic and often fatal.
The elaborateness of a 16th-century exorcism "en
masse" (bottom left) contrasts sharply with a
physician's attempts to cure fantasy and folly
(bottom right), and even more so with
witch-burning (right), where the "cure" was,
without doubt, a final one.*

fessed that more than a hundred witches had put to sea in a sieve to produce the storms (A. D. White, 1896).

Some writers have suggested that the persecution of witches was partly a means for curbing the eroticism of priests and monks, which centuries of celibacy had not stamped out. Women stirred men's passions; therefore, they must be carriers of the devil. The fact that almost all those persecuted were women and that they were often subjected to sexual indignities suggests that the motivation may not have been purely religious (Alexander & Selesnick, 1966).

Further impetus to these persecutions was undoubtedly given by many of the suspects themselves, who, although mentally disordered by present standards, participated so actively in the beliefs of the time that they often freely "confessed" their transactions with the devil, almost gleefully pointed out the "marks" he had left on their bodies, and claimed great powers as a result of their evildoing. Others, suffering from severe depressions, elaborated on their terrible sins and admitted themselves to be beyond redemption. (Even today many psychotic individuals are convinced of their hopeless guilt and damnation.) This sort of basis for the iron-bound logic of the Inquisitors is well illustrated in the following case of a woman who was probably suffering from psychotic depression.

"A certain woman was taken and finally burned, who for six years had an incubus devil even when she was lying in bed at the side of her husband . . . the homage she has given to the devil was of such a sort that she was bound to dedicate herself body and soul to him forever, after seven years. But God provided mercifully for she was taken in the sixth year and condemned to the fire, and having truly and completely confessed is believed to have obtained pardon from God. For she went most willingly to her death, saying that she would gladly suffer an even more terrible death if only she would be set free and escape the power of the devil." (Stone, 1937, p. 146)

To be convicted of witchcraft was a most serious matter. The penalty usually followed one of three general forms. There were those who were beheaded or strangled before being burned, those who were burned alive, and those who were mutilated before being burned. The treatment accorded a mentally disordered man caught in the wrong period of history is illustrated in the following case:

"In Königsberg in 1636 a man thought he was God the Father; he claimed that all the angels and the devil and the Son of God recognized his power. He was convicted. His tongue was cut out, his head cut off, and his body burned." (Zilboorg & Henry, 1941, p. 259)

There seems to have been little distinction between the Roman and the Reformed churches in their attitudes toward witchcraft, and large numbers of people were put to death in this period.

"A French judge boasted that he had burned 800 women in sixteen years on the bench; 600 were burned during the administration of a bishop in Bamberg. The Inquisition, originally started by the Church of Rome, was carried along by protestant churches in Great Britain and Germany. In protestant Geneva 500 persons were burned in the year 1515. In Trèves some 7000 people were reported burned during a period of several years." (Bromberg, 1937, p. 61)

The full horror of the witch mania and its enthusiastic adoption by other countries, including some American colonies, took place during the sixteenth and seventeenth centuries. And though religious and scientific thought began to change gradually, the idea of mental disorder as representing punishment by God or deliberate association with the devil continued to dominate popular thought until well into the nineteenth century.

Emergence of humanitarian approaches

Any criticism or questioning of the theological doctrine of demonology during the Middle Ages was made at the risk of life itself. Yet even during the latter part of the fifteenth century we

This French engraving of "moonstruck" women dancing in the town square illustrates the commonly held belief that the moon could affect behavior.

find the beginnings again of more scientific intellectual activity. The concepts of demonology and witchcraft, which had long acted to retard the understanding and therapeutic treatment of mental disorders, began to be challenged and attacked by people greater than their time—individuals from the fields of medicine, philosophy, physics, and even as we have seen in the case of Teresa, religion.

Reappearance of scientific questioning in Europe

The first physician known to have spoken out against the code of the witch burners was Agrippa (1486–1535) who is best known as the teacher of Johann Weyer, discussed below. A short time later, Paracelsus (1490–1541) insisted that the "dancing mania" was not a possession but a form of disease, and that it should be treated as such (Zilboorg & Henry, 1941). He also postulated a conflict between the instinctual and spiritual nature of human beings, formulated the idea of psychic causes for mental illness, and advocated treatment by "bodily magnetism," later called *hypnosis* (Mora, 1967).

Although Paracelsus thus rejected demonology, his view of abnormal behavior was colored by belief in astral influences (*lunatic* is derived from the Latin word "luna" or moon): he was convinced that the moon exercised a supernatural influence over the brain—an idea, incidentally, that persists among some people today, including probably some who work as staff

Malleus Maleficarum - Krammer & Spreger

attendants in mental hospitals. Paracelsus defied both the medical and the theological traditions of his time; it did not help matters that his manner in doing so was quite arrogant, and he was hounded and persecuted until his death.

Johann Weyer (1515–1588), a physician and man of letters who wrote under the Latin name of Joannus Wierus, was so deeply impressed by the scenes of imprisonment, torture, and burning of persons accused of witchcraft that he made a careful study of the entire problem of witchcraft and about 1563 published a book, *The Deception of Demons*, which contains a step-by-step rebuttal of the *Malleus maleficarum*. In it he argued that a considerable number, if not all, of those imprisoned, tortured, and burned for witchcraft were really sick in mind or body, and consequently that great wrongs were being committed against innocent people. Weyer's work received the approval of a few outstanding physicians and theologians of his time. In the main, however, it met with vehement protest and condemnation. Father Spina, the author of a polemical book against Weyer, stated: "Recently Satan went to a Sabbath[2] attired as a great prince, and told the assembled witches that they need not worry since, thanks to Weyer and his followers, the affairs of the Devil were brilliantly progressing" (in Castiglioni, 1946, p. 253).

Weyer was one of the first physicians to specialize in mental disorders, and his wide experience and progressive views justify his being regarded as the true founder of modern psychopathology. Unfortunately, however, he was too far ahead of his time. He was scorned by his peers, many of whom called him "Weirus Heriticus" and "Weirus Insanus." His works were banned by the Church and remained so until the twentieth century.

Perhaps there is no better illustration of the spirit of scientific skepticism that was developing in the sixteenth century than the works of the Oxford-educated Reginald Scot (1538–1599), who devoted his life to exposing the fallacies of witchcraft and demonology. In his book *Discovery of Witchcraft*, published in 1584, he convincingly and daringly denied the

THE
Diſcovery of Witchcraft:
PROVING,
That the Compacts and Contracts of WITCHES
with *Devils* and all *Infernal Spirits* or *Familiars*, are but
Erroneous Novelties and Imaginary Conceptions.

Alſo diſcovering, How far their Power extendeth in Killing,
Tormenting, Conſuming, or Curing the bodies of Men, Women, Children,
or Animals, by Charms, Philtres, Periapts, Pentacles, Curſes, and Conjurations.

WHEREIN LIKE WISE
The Unchriſtian Practices and Inhumane
Dealings of *Searchers* and *Witch-tryers* upon *Aged, Melancholly,*
and *Superſtitious* people, in extorting Confeſſions by Terrors and
Tortures, and in deviſing falſe Marks and Symptoms, are notably Detected.

And the Knavery of *Juglers, Conjurers, Charmers, Soothſayers,*
Figure-Caſters, Dreamers, Alchymiſts and *Philterers*; with
many other things that have long lain hidden, fully Opened and Deciphered.

ALL WHICH
Are very neceſſary to be known for the undeceiving of *Judges,*
Juſtices, and *Jurors,* before they paſs Sentence upon Poor, Miſerable and
Ignorant People; who are frequently Arraigned, Condemned, and Executed
for *Witches* and *Wizzards.*

IN SIXTEEN BOOKS.

By REGINALD SCOT *Eſquire.*

Title page of Reginald Scot's Discovery of Witchcraft (1584), *which denied the common belief that demons caused mental disorders.*

existence of demons, devils, and evil spirits as the cause of mental disorders.

"These women are but diseased wretches suffering from melancholy, and their words, actions, reasoning, and gestures show that sickness has affected their brains and impaired their powers of judgment. You must know that the effects of sickness on men, and still more on women, are almost unbelievable. Some of these persons imagine, confess, and maintain that they are witches and are capable of performing extraordinary miracles through the arts of witchcraft; others, due to the same mental disorder, imagine strange and impossible things which they claim to have witnessed." (in Castiglioni, 1946, p. 253)

King James I of England, however, came to the rescue of demonology, personally refuted Scot's thesis, and ordered his book seized and burned. But churchmen also were beginning to question the practices of the time. For example, St. Vincent de Paul (1576–1660), surrounded by every opposing influence and at

---

[2]The word *Sabbath* has no relation to the Biblical Sabbath, but refers to witches' gatherings in which orders were supposedly received from Satan.

the risk of his life, declared: "Mental disease is no different to bodily disease and Christianity demands of the humane and powerful to protect, and the skilful to relieve the one as well as the other."

In the face of such attacks, which continued through the next two centuries, demonology was forced to give ground, and the way was gradually paved for the triumph of observation and reason, culminating in the development of modern experimental and clinical approaches.

Establishment of early asylums and shrines

From the sixteenth century on, monasteries and prisons gradually relinquished the care of persons suffering from mental disorders to special institutions that were being established in increasing numbers. The care received by patients, however, left much to be desired.

Early asylums. In 1547 the monastery of St. Mary of Bethlehem at London was officially made into a mental hospital by Henry VIII. Its name soon became contracted to "Bedlam," and it became widely known for the deplorable conditions and practices that prevailed. The more violent patients were exhibited to the public for one penny a look, and the more harmless inmates were forced to seek charity on the streets of London in the manner described by Shakespeare:

". . . Bedlam beggars, who, with roaring voices . . .
Sometime with lunatic bans, sometime with prayers
Enforce their charity." (*King Lear*, Act II, Scene iii)

Such hospitals, or "asylums" as they were called, were gradually established in other countries (Lewis, 1941). The San Hipolito, established in Mexico in 1566 by the philanthropist Bernardino Alvares, was the first hospital for the care and study of mental disorders to be established in the Americas. The first mental hospital in France, La Maison de Charenton, was founded in 1641 in a suburb of Paris. A mental hospital was established in Moscow in 1764, and the notorious Lunatics' Tower in Vienna was constructed in 1784. This was a showplace in Old Vienna, and the description of the structure and its practices

makes interesting reading. It was an ornately decorated round tower within which were square rooms. The doctors and "keepers" lived in the square rooms, while the patients were confined in the spaces between the walls of the square rooms and the outside of the tower. The patients were put on exhibit to the public for a small fee, and were, in general, treated like animals and criminals.

The Pennsylvania Hospital at Philadelphia, completed under the guidance of Benjamin Franklin in 1756, provided some cells or wards for the mental patients, but the first hospital in the United States devoted exclusively to mental patients was constructed in Williamsburg, Virginia, in 1773.

These early asylums, or hospitals, were primarily modifications of penal institutions, and the inmates were treated more like beasts than like human beings. Selling gives a striking account of the treatment of the chronic insane in La Bicêtre Hospital in Paris. This treatment was typical of the asylums of this period and continued through most of the eighteenth century.

The patients were ordinarily shackled to the walls of their dark, unlighted cells by iron collars which held them flat against the wall and permitted little movement. Ofttimes there were also iron hoops around the waists of the patients and both their hands and feet were chained. Although these chains usually permitted enough movement that the patients could feed themselves out of bowls, they often kept them from being able to lie down at night. Since little was known about dietetics, and the patients were presumed to be animals anyway, little attention was paid to whether they were adequately fed or to whether the food was good or bad. The cells were furnished only with straw and were never swept or cleaned; the patient was permitted to remain in the midst of all the accumulated ordure. No one visited the cells except at feeding time, no provision was made for warmth, and even the most elementary gestures of humanity were lacking. (Modified from Selling, 1943, pp. 54–55)

Treatment of mental patients in the United States was little, if any, better. The following is a vivid description of their plight in this country during colonial times:

"The mentally ill were hanged, imprisoned, tortured, and otherwise persecuted as agents of Satan. Regarded as sub-human beings, they were chained in

*Eighteenth-century views of "Bedlam," exterior
and interior. It was customary to allow the public
to see the lunatics, as the "lady" in the center of
the engraving (bottom left) is doing. One of the
common sights was patients chained to the walls
(bottom right).*

specially devised kennels and cages like wild beasts, and thrown into prisons, bridewells and jails like criminals. They were incarcerated in workhouse dungeons or made to slave as able-bodied paupers, unclassified from the rest. They were left to wander about stark naked, driven from place to place like mad dogs, subjected to whippings as vagrants and rogues. Even the well-to-do were not spared confinement in strong rooms and cellar dungeons, while legislation usually concerned itself more with their property than their persons." (Deutsch, 1946, p. 53)

Some insight into the prevalent forms of treatment in the early American hospitals may be gained from a thesis on "Chronic Mania," written by a medical student in 1796 at the New York Hospital, in which cells or wards were provided in the cellar for the mentally ill patients. He considered that restraint should be avoided as long as possible, "lest the strait jackets, and chains and cells should induce a depression of spirits seldom surmounted." He also doubted the propriety of "unexpected plunging into cold water," of "two to six hours in spring water or still colder," of the "refrigerant plan," of bleeding, purging, vomiting, streams of cold water on the head, blisters, and similar procedures (Russell, 1941, p. 230).

Even as late as 1830, new patients had their heads shaved, were dressed in straitjackets, put on a low diet, compelled to swallow some active purgative, and placed in a dark cell. If these measures did not serve to quiet unruly or excited patients, more severe measures, such as starvation, solitary confinement, cold baths, and other torturelike methods, were used (Bennett, 1947).

The Gheel shrine.   There were a few bright spots in this otherwise tragic situation. Out of the more humane Christian tradition of prayer, the laying on of hands, or holy touch, and visits to shrines for cure of illness, there arose several great shrines where treatment by kindness and love stood out in marked contrast to generally prevailing conditions. The one at Gheel in Belgium, visited since the thirteenth century, is probably most famous—and the story of its founding is an interesting one.

"Somewhere in the dim past there lived a king in Ireland who was married to a most beautiful woman and who sired an equally beautiful daughter. The

good queen developed a fatal illness, and at her death bed the daughter dedicated herself to a life of purity and service to the poor and the mentally bereft. The widowed king was beside himself with grief and announced to his subjects that he must at once be assuaged of sorrow by marrying the woman in his kingdom who most resembled the dead queen. No such paragon was found. But the devil came and whispered to the king that there was such a woman—his own daughter. The devil spurred the king to propose marriage to the girl, but she was appropriately outraged by this incestuous overture and fled across the English Channel to Belgium. There the king overtook her and with Satan at his elbow, slew the girl and her faithful attendants. In the night the angels came, recapitated the body and concealed it in the forest near the village of Gheel. Years later five lunatics chained together spent the night with their keepers at a small wayside shrine near this Belgian village. Overnight all the victims recovered. Here indeed must be the place where the dead girl, reincarnated as St. Dymphna, was buried, and here was the sacred spot where her cures of the insane are effected. In the 15th century pilgrimages to Gheel from every part of the civilized world were organized for the mentally sick. Many of the pilgrims remained in Gheel to live with the inhabitants of the locality, and in the passing years it became the natural thing to accept them into the homes and thus the first 'colony' was formed and for that matter the only one which has been consistently successful." (Karnosh & Zucker, 1945, p. 15)

The colony of Gheel has continued its work into modern times (Aring, 1974, 1975; Belgian Consulate, 1975). In the mid-1970s more than two thousand certified mental patients lived in private homes, worked with the inhabitants, and suffered few restrictions other than not using alcohol. Many types of mental disorders are represented, including schizophrenia, manic and depressive psychoses, psychopathic personality, and mental retardation. Ordinarily patients remain in Gheel until they are considered recovered by a supervising therapist. It is unfortunate that the great humanitarian work of this colony—and the opportunity Gheel affords to study the treatment of mental patients in a family and community setting—has received so little recognition.

Humanitarian reform

Although scientific skepticism had undermined the belief that mental disturbance was

In this collage, Philippe Pinel is shown discovering the deplorable conditions under which mental patients lived at La Bicêtre, urging the townspeople to accept his proposals for reform, and finally releasing the shackles from the inmates.

the devil's work, most early asylums were no better than concentration camps. The unfortunate inmates lived and died amid conditions of incredible filth and cruelty. Humanitarian reform of mental hospitals received its first great impetus from the work of Philippe Pinel (1745–1826) in France.

Pinel's experiment.   In 1792, shortly after the first phase of the French Revolution came to a close, Pinel was placed in charge of La Bicêtre (the hospital for the insane in Paris to which we have previously referred). In this capacity he received the grudging permission of the Revolutionary Commune to remove the chains from some of the inmates as an experiment to test his views that mental patients should be treated with kindness and consideration—as sick people and not as vicious beasts or criminals. Had his experiment proved a failure, Pinel might well have lost his head, but,

fortunately for all, it proved to be a great success. Chains were removed, sunny rooms were provided instead of dungeons, patients were permitted to exercise on the hospital grounds, and kindliness was extended to these poor creatures, some of whom had been chained in dungeons for thirty years or more. The effect was almost miraculous. The previous noise, filth, and abuse were replaced by order and peace. As Pinel said: "The whole discipline was marked with regularity and kindness which had the most favorable effect on the insane themselves, rendering even the most furious more tractable" (Selling, 1943, p. 65).

The reactions of these patients when all their chains were removed for the first time is a pathetic story. One patient, an English officer who had years before killed a guard in an attack of fury, tottered outside on legs weak from lack of use, and for the first time in some forty years saw the sun and sky. With tears in his eyes he exclaimed, "Oh, how beautiful!" (Zilboorg & Henry, 1941, p. 323). Finally, when night came, he voluntarily returned to his cell, which had been cleaned during his absence, to fall peacefully asleep on his new bed. After two years of orderly behavior, including helping to handle other patients, he was pronounced recovered and permitted to leave the hospital.

Pinel was later given charge of the Salpêtrière Hospital, where the same reorganization in treatment was instituted with similarly gratifying results. The Bicêtre and Salpêtrière hospitals thus became the first modern hospitals for the care of the insane. Pinel's successor, Jean Esquirol (1772–1840), continued his good work at the Salpêtrière and, in addition, helped in the establishment of some ten new mental hospitals, which helped put France in the forefront of humane treatment for the mentally disturbed.

It is a curious and satisfying fact of history that Pinel was saved from the hands of a mob who suspected him of antirevolutionary activities by a soldier whom he had freed from asylum chains.

Tuke's work in England.   At about the same time that Pinel was reforming the Bicêtre Hospital, an English Quaker named William Tuke established the "York Retreat," a pleasant country house where mental patients lived, worked, and rested in a kindly religious atmosphere. This represented the culmination of a noble battle against the brutality, ignorance, and indifference of his time. Some insight into the difficulties and discouragements he encountered in the establishment of the York Retreat may be gleaned from a simple statement he made in a letter regarding his early efforts: "All men seem to desert me." This is not surprising when we remember that demonology was still widespread, and that as late as 1768 we find the Protestant John Wesley's famous declaration that "The giving up of witchcraft is in effect the giving up of the Bible." The belief in demonology was too strong to be conquered overnight.

As word of the amazing results obtained by Pinel spread to England, Tuke's small force of Quakers gradually gained support from John Connolly, Samuel Hitch, and other great English medical psychologists. In 1841 Hitch introduced trained women nurses into the wards at the Gloucester Asylum and put trained supervisors at the head of the nursing staffs. These innovations, regarded as quite revolutionary at the time, were of great importance not only in improving the care of mental patients but also in changing public attitudes toward the mentally disturbed. As mental disorders came to be put more on the same footing

Pinel, like the founders of the Gheel colony, sought humane treatment for the mentally disturbed. It is no small wonder, then, that this drawing (top) of a portion of Salpètrière hospital after Pinel's reforms is strikingly similar to the sense of warmth and community in the present-day photo (bottom) of the Gheel colony.

as physical illness, the mystery, ignorance, and fear that had always surrounded them began gradually to give way.

Rush and moral therapy in America.

The success of Pinel's and Tuke's experiments in more humanitarian methods revolutionized the treatment of mental patients throughout the civilized world. In the United States, this was reflected in the work of Benjamin Rush (1745–1813), the founder of American psychiatry. Becoming associated with the Pennsylvania Hospital in 1783, Rush encouraged more humane treatment of the mentally ill, wrote the first systematic treatise on psychiatry in America, *Medical Inquiries and Observations upon the Diseases of the Mind* (1812), and was the first American to organize a course in psychiatry. But even he did not escape entirely from the established beliefs of his time. His medical theory was tainted with astrology, and his principal remedies were bloodletting and purgatives. In addition, he invented and used a torturous device called "the tranquillizer." Despite these limitations, however, we may consider Rush an important transitional figure between the old era and the new.

During the early part of this period of humanitarian reform, the use of "moral therapy" in mental hospitals was relatively widespread. This approach stemmed largely from the work of Pinel and Tuke. As Rees (1957) has described it:

"The insane came to be regarded as normal people who had lost their reason as a result of having been exposed to severe psychological and social stresses. These stresses were called the moral causes of insanity, and moral treatment aimed at relieving the patient by friendly association, discussion of his difficulties, and the daily pursuit of purposeful activity; in other words, social therapy, individual therapy, and occupational therapy." (pp. 306–7)

Moral therapy achieved an almost incredible level of effectiveness—all the more amazing because it was done without the benefit of the antipsychotic drugs so prevalent today, and because, we must surmise, many of the patients so treated were suffering from the then-incurable neurological disease of central-nervous-system syphilis. In the twenty year period between 1833 and 1853, Worcester State Hospital's discharge rate for patients who had

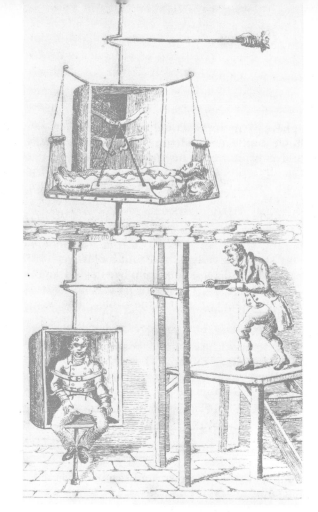

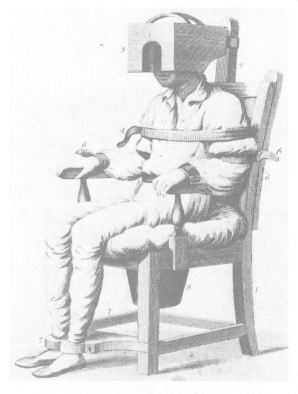

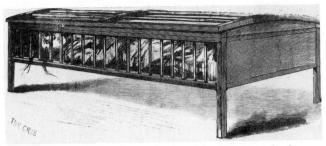

Even after reform of mental institutions had begun, various devices were used to control unmanageable patients: the crib (above), used as late as 1882 to restrain violent patients; the "tranquilizing chair" of Benjamin Rush (opposite page, bottom); and the circulating swing, used in the early 19th century to bring the mentally disordered back to sound reasoning (opposite page, top). It was said that "no well-regulated institution should be without one."

been ill less than one year prior to admission was 71 percent; even for patients with a longer pre-admission disorder it was 59 percent (Bock-hoven, 1972).

Despite its effectiveness, however, moral therapy declined and was nearly abandoned by the latter part of the nineteenth century. The reasons were many and varied. Among the more obvious ones were ethnic and racial prejudice, with the rising immigrant population, and consequent distancing and impersonality between staff and patients, a failure of the leadership to train their own replacements, and the overextension of hospital facilities, reflecting the misguided belief that bigger hospitals would differ from smaller ones only in size.

Two other, less obvious, reasons for the demise of moral therapy are truly ironic. One was the rise of the mental hygiene movement, which focused almost exclusively on the *physical* well-being of mental patients in hospitals, thus condemning them in a subtle way to helplessness and dependency, however much their creature comforts might have improved. The other was the brilliant advances that had been made in biomedical science, fostering the notion that psychosocial influences were irrelevant since all mental disorder would sooner or later yield to a biological explanation and appropriate biologically based treatment.

Needless to say, the anticipated biological cure-all did not arrive, and by the late 1940s or early 1950s, discharge rates were down to about 30 percent. We do better today, with discharge rates above 90 percent, but this is a very recent development.

Notwithstanding their negative effects on the use of moral therapy, both the mental hygiene movement and the biological viewpoint have, of course, many positive accomplishments to their credit. Some of these are reviewed in what follows.

Dix and the beginning of the mental hygiene movement.

Dorothea Dix (1802–1887) was an energetic New England schoolteacher forced into early retirement because of recurring attacks of tuberculosis. In 1841 she began to teach in a women's prison. Through this contact she soon became acquainted with the deplorable conditions prevalent in jails, almshouses, and asylums. In a "Memorial" submitted to the Congress of the United States in 1848, she stated that she had seen "more than 9000 idiots, epileptics and insane in the United States, destitute of appropriate care and protection . . . bound with galling chains, bowed beneath fetters and heavy iron balls attached to drag-chains, lacerated with ropes, scourged with rods and terrified beneath storms of execration and cruel blows; now subject to jibes and scorn and torturing tricks; now abandoned to the most outrageous violations" (Zilboorg & Henry, 1941, pp. 583–84).

As a result of her findings, Dix carried on a zealous campaign between 1841 and 1881 that aroused the people and the legislatures to an awareness of the inhuman treatment accorded the mentally ill. Through her efforts many millions of dollars were raised to build suitable hospitals, and some twenty states responded directly to her appeals. Not only was she instrumental in improving conditions in the United States, but she directed the opening of two large institutions in Canada, and completely reformed the asylum system in Scotland and several other countries. She is credited with the establishment of some thirty-two mental hospitals, an astonishing record considering the ignorance and superstition that still prevailed in the field of mental health. She rounded out her career by organizing the nursing forces of the Northern armies during the

Some of the individuals who have contributed to our contemporary views of psychopathology are shown here.

Teresa of Avila (1515–1582) argued that her hysterical nuns were "as if sick," paving the way for the view that the mind can be just as sick as the body.

Johann Weyer (1515–1588) wrote against the prevalent beliefs in witchcraft and decried the persecution of the mentally ill.

Civil War. A resolution presented by the United States Congress in 1901 characterized her as "among the noblest examples of humanity in all history" (Karnosh & Zucker, 1945, p. 18).

In the last half of the nineteenth century the mental hospital or asylum—"the big house on the hill"—with its high turrets and fortresslike appearance, became a familiar landmark in America. In it mental patients lived under semiadequate conditions of comfort and freedom from abuse. To the general public, however, the asylum was an eerie place, and its occupants a strange and frightening lot.

Little was done by the resident psychiatrists[3] to educate the public along lines that would reduce the general fear and horror of insanity. One principal reason for this, of course, was that the early psychiatrist had very little actual information to impart. Even as late as 1840 no widely used classification of mental disorders had been worked out, and a German teacher, Dr. Heinroth, was still advancing the theory that sin produced insanity and repentance a cure, and that piety was conducive to mental health (Lewis, 1941).

Gradually, however, important strides were made toward changing the attitude of the general public toward mental patients. In America, the pioneering work of Dix in educating the public about mental disorders was followed up by that of Clifford Beers, whose now-famous book, *A Mind That Found Itself*, was published in 1908. Beers, a Yale graduate, described his own mental collapse and told of the bad treatment he received in three typical institutions of the day, and of his eventual recovery in the home of a friendly attendant. Although chains and other torture devices had long since been given up, the straitjacket was still widely used as a means of "quieting" excited patients. Beers experienced this treatment and supplied a vivid description of what such painful immobilization of the arms means to an overwrought mental patient in terms of intensification of inner excitement. He began a campaign to make people realize that this was no way to handle the sick, winning the interest and support of many public-spirited individuals, including the eminent psychologist William James, and the "dean of American psychiatry," Adolf Meyer.

Thus through the combined efforts of many dedicated people, our contemporary mental health movement had its start. As time went on, it contributed greatly to better public understanding of mental disorders, to the development of community mental health programs and facilities, and to the concept of comprehensive health.

Development of the biological viewpoint

With the emergence of modern experimental science in the early part of the eighteenth century, knowledge of anatomy, physiology, neurology, chemistry, and general medicine increased rapidly. These advances led to the

---

[3]It is of interest to note that psychiatrists were formerly called *alienists*—and in some places still are—referring to persons who treat the "alienated" or insane.

Benjamin Rush (1745–1813) was the first American to write a systematic treatise on psychiatry and to organize a course on the subject.

Dorothea Dix (1802–1887) was one of the most important forces worldwide for improving conditions in institutions and asylums during the last half of the 19th century.

Emil Kraepelin (1856–1926), by integrating clinical data, worked out the first systematic classification of mental disorder.

gradual identification of the biological, or organic, pathology underlying many physical ailments. That is, scientists focused on body organs as being diseased and thereby causing physical ailments. It was only another step for these workers to rediscover the idea of mental disorder as an illness based on *pathology of an organ*—in this case the *brain*.

As early as 1757, Albrecht von Haller (1708–1777) in his *Elements of Physiology* emphasized the importance of the brain in psychic functions and advocated studying the brains of the insane by postmortem dissection. The first systematic presentation of this viewpoint, however, was made by the German psychiatrist William Griesinger (1817–1868). In his textbook *The Pathology and Therapy of Psychic Disorders*, published in 1845, Griesinger insisted that psychiatry should proceed on a physiological and clinical basis and emphasized his belief that all mental disorders could be explained in terms of brain pathology. This concept of mental disorders is called the *biological viewpoint*. Although it was perhaps too broadly adopted before limitations of its applicability were recognized, it represents the first great advance of modern science toward the understanding and treatment of mental disorders.

Systematic classification of mental disorders

Although the work of Griesinger received considerable attention, it was his follower, Emil Kraepelin (1856–1926) who played the dominant role in the early development of the biological viewpoint. Kraepelin, whose textbook *Lehrbuch der Psychiatrie* was published in

1883, not only emphasized the importance of brain pathology in mental disorders but also made several related contributions that helped establish this viewpoint. The most important of these was his system of classification. Kraepelin noted that certain symptom patterns occurred with sufficient regularity to be regarded as specific types of mental disease. He then proceeded to describe and clarify these types of mental disorders, working out the scheme of classification that is the basis of our present categories. The integration of the clinical material underlying this classification was a herculean task and represented a major contribution to the field of psychopathology.

Kraepelin looked upon each type of mental disorder as separate and distinct from the others, and thought that the course of each was as predetermined and predictable as the course of measles. Such conclusions led to widespread interest in the accurate description and classification of mental disorders, for by this means the outcome of a given type of disorder could presumably be predicted even if it could not yet be controlled. The subsequent period in psychopathology, during which description and classification were so heavily emphasized, has been referred to as the "descriptive era."

Establishment of brain pathology as a causal factor

During this "descriptive" period, tremendous strides were being made in the study of the nervous system by such scientists as Golgi, Ramón y Cajal, Broca, Jackson, and Head, and the brain pathology underlying many mental

Events leading to the discovery of organic factors in general paresis

1. Differentiation of general paresis as a specific type of mental disorder by the French physician A. L. J. Bayle in 1825. Bayle gave a very complete and accurate description of the symptom pattern of paresis and convincingly presented his reasons for believing paresis to be a distinct disorder.

2. Report by Esmarch and Jessen in 1857 of paretic patients known to have had syphilis and their conclusion that the syphilis caused the paresis.

3. Description by the Scot Argyll-Robertson in 1869 of the failure of the pupillary reflex to light (failure of the pupil of the eye to narrow under bright light) as diagnostic of the involvement of the central nervous system in syphilis.

4. Experiment by Viennese psychiatrist Krafft-Ebing in 1897, involving the inoculation of paretic patients with matter from syphilitic sores. None developed secondary symptoms of syphilis, which led to the conclusion that they must previously have been infected. This crucial experiment definitely established the relationship of general paresis to syphilis.

5. Discovery of the *Spirochaeta pallida* by Schaudinn in 1905 as the cause of syphilis.

6. Development by von Wassermann in 1906 of a blood test for syphilis. Now it became possible to check for the presence of the deadly spirochetes in the bloodstream of individuals before the more serious consequences of infection appeared.

7. Application by Plant in 1908 of the Wasermann test to the cerebrospinal fluid, to indicate whether or not the spirochete had invaded the patient's central nervous system.

8. Development by Paul Ehrlich in 1909, after 605 failures, of the arsenical compound arsphenamine (which he thereupon called "606") for the treatment of syphilis. Although "606" proved effective in killing the syphilitic spirochetes in the bloodstream, it was not effective against the spirochetes that had penetrated the central nervous system.

9. Verification by Noguchi and Moore in 1913 of the syphilitic spirochete as the brain-damaging agent in general paresis. They discovered these spirochetes in the postmortem study of the brains of patients who had suffered from paresis.

10. Introduction in 1917 by Wagner-Jauregg, chief of the psychiatric clinic of the University of Vienna, of the malarial fever treatment of syphilis and paresis. He inoculated nine paretic patients with the blood of a soldier who was ill with malaria and found marked improvement in three patients and apparent recovery in three of the others.

disorders was gradually being uncovered. For example, the syphilitic basis of *general paresis* (syphilis of the brain) was finally established as the result of the brilliant contributions of a number of medical scientists. Similarly, the brain pathology in cerebral arteriosclerosis and in the senile psychoses was established by Alzheimer and other investigators. One success was followed by another, and eventually the organic pathology underlying the toxic psychoses, certain types of mental retardation, and other "organically" caused mental disorders was discovered.

These discoveries were not made overnight but resulted from the combined efforts of many scientists. It is important to remember here that discoveries in science do not usually proceed sequentially from point *a* to *z*. They are more often the result of a very uncoordinated process in which many scientists pursue hypotheses that are later seen as dead ends, go off on tangents, refuse to accept "evidence," experience crises in their thinking, and so on.

Recapping events that have led to scientific discoveries can often belie the excitement, intrigue, and frustration that went into getting there.

With this caution in mind, at least ten different events can be traced in the discovery of the organic pathology underlying general paresis—one of the most serious of all mental illnesses, which produced paralysis and insanity and typically brought about the death of the afflicted subject in from two to five years. These ten events in this long search illustrate the way in which scientists working independently can use research by others in the field in advancing knowledge bit by bit (see HIGHLIGHT).

True, the complete understanding of paresis—why one patient becomes euphoric and another depressed with the same general organic brain pathology—involves an understanding of certain psychological concepts yet to be discussed. Also, of course, progress in treatment has continued, and penicillin has become the preferred method of treatment, avoiding the complications of malaria. But the events noted in the HIGHLIGHT show the way in which, *for the first time in all history, a clear-cut conquest of a mental disorder was made by medical science.*

Advances achieved as a result of early biological views

Let us take a moment here to examine the important advances made in psychopathology up to the turn of the twentieth century, which represented the end of the period during which the biological viewpoint almost completely dominated psychopathology.

1. The early concepts of demonology had finally been destroyed, and the biological viewpoint of mental disorder as based on brain pathology was well established.

2. For general paresis and certain other mental disorders, definite underlying brain pathology had been discovered and appropriate methods of treatment developed.

3. A workable, though not yet completely satisfactory, scheme of classification had been set up.

4. Mental disorders had finally been put on an equal footing with physical illness, at least in medical circles, and for the first time mental patients were receiving treatment based on scientific findings.

5. A great deal of research was under way in anatomy, physiology, biochemistry, and other allied medical sciences, in an attempt to ascertain the brain pathology (or other organic pathology that might be affecting the brain) in other types of mental disorders and to clarify the role of organic processes in all behavior.

These were truly remarkable achievements, yet their effects have not been uniformly positive. The early successes of the biological viewpoint led to false expectations of finding gross physical pathology in all disorders and, as we have seen, to an underestimation of the importance of psychological influences in treatment. Recent research suggests that certain very subtle abnormalities of neural transmission, perhaps due in part to genetic defects, may well be involved in many mental disorders, but this is a far cry from the gross types of damage produced by the action of the syphilitic spirochete.

The successes in demonstrating biological causes for some mental disorders have also had another effect. Even where psychological factors, such as unconscious conflicts, have been blamed for the development of mental disorders, medical language has been used. The popular term *mental illness* implies a mental *disease* in which an *underlying cause,* such as buried conflict, produces the *symptoms* we see in disordered behavior. This view of mental disorders as due to underlying causes that produce symptoms (whether biological or psychological) is known as the *medical model.* It prevailed for many years but is being challenged today by those who assert that the disordered behavior is itself the problem to be tackled—that it is not the symptom of something else but a case of faulty learning, correctable by new learning. This point of view and others emphasizing the importance of psychosocial and sociocultural factors in the causation of both normal and abnormal behavior will be examined in the next chapter.

In this chapter we have traced the development of views of psychopathology from ancient times to the beginning of the twentieth century. We noted the belief in demonology and exorcism, followed by the emergence of early medical concepts during the Golden Age of Greece and the elaboration of many of these concepts by Roman physicians. With the fall of Rome toward the end of the fifth century and the beginning of the Dark Ages, there was a return to the most primitive concepts of demonology, which continued to dominate views of mental disorders for over a thousand years. However, by the beginning of the sixteenth century, there was a reappearance of scientific questioning in Europe followed by more humanitarian approaches and the eventual recognition of the importance of physical pathology in some mental disorders, giving rise to a biological perspective on mental disorders in general.

Understanding this developmental sequence, with its forward steps and reverses, helps us understand the emergence of modern psychopathology and provides us with a perspective for understanding the advances that have come since and are still to come.

3

Psychosocial and sociocultural viewpoints

Development of the psychosocial viewpoint
Emergence of the sociocultural viewpoint
Toward an interdisciplinary approach

Despite the great advances in the understanding and treatment of mental disorders by the turn of the century, many puzzling and important questions remained unanswered.

For one thing, repeated clinical examinations and research studies failed to reveal any biological pathology in most patients with mental disorders. True, a given patient might show some minor deviation in bodily chemistry, but then, so did a great many normal people; furthermore, many patients with the same symptoms did not show the same organic deviation.

To some scientists these discrepancies were a challenge to intensify research, for they felt certain that organic pathology must be there, and that the refinement of their laboratory techniques would make it clear. But there was also a new school of thought emerging that questioned the dominant belief that brain pathology was the sole cause of mental disorders. This was the "revolutionary" view that certain types of mental disorders might be caused by *psychological* rather than biological factors.

Although one might assume that the role of psychological factors in causing mental disorders would have been uniformly recognized long before 1900, such was not the case. Psychology as a science was still in its infancy in 1900, its inception dating back only twenty-one years to Wilhelm Wundt's establishment of the first experimental psychology laboratory at the University of Leipzig in 1879. In addition, early psychology consisted primarily of experimental studies of sense perception. Of course, in 1890 William James had published his monumental work, *Principles of Psychology,* in which he attempted to explain emotion, memory, reasoning, habits, consciousness of self, hysteria, and other aspects of human behavior. However, he was handicapped because little experimental work had been done in these areas, and his brief allusions to abnormal behavior were mainly descriptive and speculative.

This is not to disparage the contributions of the early investigators who helped psychology through its infant period or to minimize the importance of physiological studies as a foundation for what came next. The fact remains, however, that psychology was still in its early stages, and there was little systematic knowledge regarding the role of psychological factors in maladaptive behavior.

Development of the psychosocial viewpoint

In reviewing the development of contemporary psychological thought, we shall examine five explanations of human nature and behavior—psychoanalytic, behavioristic, humanistic, existential, and interpersonal. Although these perspectives represent distinct and sometimes conflicting orientations, they are also, as we shall see, in many ways complementary. All of them take some cognizance of social influences as well as of psychological processes within the individual—hence the term *psychosocial* as a general descriptive label.

The psychoanalytic perspective

The first systematic steps toward understanding psychological factors in mental disorders came about through the astounding contributions of one man—Sigmund Freud (1856–1939). Freud developed his psychoanalytic perspective over a period of five decades of observing and writing. His major principles were based on the clinical study of individual patients who consulted him for treatment of their problems.

In reviewing the psychoanalytic approach, it is useful to divide our discussion into an examination of (a) the roots of psychoanalysis, (b) Freud and the beginnings of psychoanalysis, (c) the basic principles of psychoanalysis, and (d) the impact of psychoanalysis on our views of human nature and human behavior.

Roots of psychoanalytic thought. We find the early roots of psychoanalysis in a somewhat unexpected place—in the study of hypnosis, especially in its relation to hysteria.

1. *Mesmerism.* Our story starts with one of the most notorious figures in psychiatry, Anton

A contemporary engraving of a mesmeric baquet. *The protruding rods, supposedly charged with "animal magnetism," were applied to the affected part of the body to cure it, as in the case of the man on the right of the tub.*

Mesmer (1734–1815), who further developed Paracelsus' notion of the influence of the planets on the human body (see Chapter 2). Their influence was believed to be caused by a universal magnetic fluid, and it was presumably the distribution of this fluid in the body that determined health or disease. In attempting to find a cure for mental disorders, Mesmer came to the conclusion that all persons possess magnetic forces that can be used to influence the distribution of the magnetic fluid in other persons, thus effecting cures.

Mesmer attempted to put his views into practice in Vienna and in various other towns, but it was not until he came to Paris in 1778 that he obtained a following. Here he opened a clinic in which he treated all kinds of diseases by "animal magnetism." The patients were seated around a tub (a *baquet*) containing various chemicals, from which protruded iron rods that were applied to the affected portions of the body; the room was darkened, appropriate music was played, and Mesmer appeared in a lilac robe, passing from one patient to another and touching each one with his hands or his

wand. By this means Mesmer was apparently able to remove hysterical anesthesias and paralyses and to demonstrate most of the phenomena discovered later by the use of hypnosis.

Eventually branded as a charlatan by his medical colleagues, Mesmer was forced to leave Paris, and he shortly faded into obscurity. However, his methods and results were the center of controversy in scientific circles for many years—in fact, mesmerism in the early part of the nineteenth century was as much a source of heated discussion as psychoanalysis was to be in the early part of the twentieth century. This discussion eventually led to a revival of interest in the hypnotic phenomenon as itself an explanation of the "cures" that took place.

2. *The "Nancy school."* One of the physicians who used hypnosis successfully in his practice was the Frenchman Liébeault (1823–1904), who practiced at Nancy. Also in Nancy at this time was a professor of medicine, Bernheim (1840–1919), who became interested in the relationship between hysteria and hypnosis, primarily as a result of Liébeault's success in curing by hypnosis a patient whom Bernheim had been treating unsuccessfully by more conventional methods for some four years (Selling, 1943). Bernheim and Liébeault worked together on the problem and developed the hypothesis that hypnotism and hysteria were related and that both were due to suggestion (Brown & Menninger, 1940). Their hypothesis was based on two lines of evidence: (a) phenomena observed in hysteria, such as paralysis of an arm, inability to hear, or anesthetic areas in which the individual could be stuck with a pin without feeling pain—all of which occurred when there was apparently nothing organically wrong—could be produced in normal subjects by means of hypnosis; and (b) symptoms such as these could be removed by means of hypnosis so that the patient could use the formerly paralyzed arm, or hear, or feel in the previously anesthetized areas. Thus it seemed likely that hysteria was a sort of self-hypnosis. The physicians who accepted this view were known as the "Nancy school."

Meanwhile, Jean Charcot (1825–1893), who was head of the Salpétrière Hospital in Paris and the leading neurologist of his time, had been experimentally investigating some of the phenomena described by the old mesmerists. As a result of his research, Charcot disagreed

It took some time before Charcot (1825–1893), the leading neurologist of his time, believed that there might be a causal relationship between self-hypnosis and hysteria. Once convinced, however, he did much through lectures about hypnosis, such as the one shown here, and research to promote interest in the role psychological factors may play in mental disorders.

with the findings of Bernheim and Liébeault and insisted that there were degenerative brain changes in hysteria. In this Charcot was eventually proved wrong, but work on the problem by so outstanding a scientist did a great deal to awaken medical and scientific interest in hysteria.

In one of the major medical debates of history, in which many harsh words were spoken on both sides, the adherents of the Nancy school finally triumphed. The recognition of one psychologically caused mental disorder (hysteria) spurred research, and it soon became apparent that psychological factors were involved in anxiety states, phobias, and other psychopathology. Eventually Charcot himself, a man of great scientific honesty, was won over to the new point of view and did much to promote an interest in the study of psychological factors in various mental disorders.

Toward the end of the nineteenth century, then, it was clear to many that there were mental disorders with a psychological basis as well as those with a biological basis. But one major question remained to be answered: How do the psychologically caused mental disorders actually come about?

Freud and the beginnings of psychoanalysis. The first systematic attempt to answer this question was made by Sigmund Freud. Freud was a brilliant young Viennese physician who at first specialized in neurology and received an appointment as lecturer on nervous diseases at the University of Vienna. On one occasion, however, he introduced to his audience a neurotic patient suffering from a persistent headache, and mistakenly diagnosed the case as chronic localized meningitis. As a result of this error in diagnosis, he lost his job—although, as he pointed out in his autobiography, greater authorities than he were in the habit of diagnosing similar cases as cerebral tumor. Freud went to Paris in 1885 to study under Charcot and later became acquainted with the work of Liébeault and Bernheim at Nancy. He was impressed by their use of hypnosis with hysterical patients and came away convinced that powerful mental processes may remain hidden from consciousness.

On his return to Vienna, Freud worked in collaboration with an older physician, Joseph Breuer, who had introduced an interesting innovation in the use of hypnosis with his neurotic patients, chiefly women. Unlike hypnotists before him, he directed the patient under hypnosis to talk freely about her problems and about what bothered her. Under these circumstances the patient usually displayed considerable emotion, and on awakening from the hypnotic state felt considerably relieved. Because of the emotional release involved, this method was called the "cathartic method." This simple innovation in the use of hypnosis proved to be of great significance, for not only did it help the patient discharge her emotional tensions by discussion of her problems, but it revealed the nature of the difficulties that had brought about her neurotic symptoms. The patient saw no relationship between her problems and her hysterical symptoms, but the therapist could usually see it quite readily.

Thus was made the discovery of the "unconscious"—the realization of the important role played by unconscious processes in the determination of behavior. In 1893 Freud and Breuer published their joint paper, *On the Psychical Mechanisms of Hysterical Phenomena*, which constituted one of the great milestones of psychodynamics.[1]

Freud soon discovered, moreover, that he could dispense with the hypnotic state entirely. By encouraging the patient to say freely whatever came into her mind without regard to logic or decency, Freud found that she would eventually overcome inner obstacles to remembering and would discuss her problem freely. The new method was called *free association*, and the term *psychoanalysis* was given to the principles involved in analyzing and interpreting what the patient said and did, and in helping her gain insight and achieve a more adequate adjustment.

Freud devoted the remainder of his long and energetic life to the development and elaboration of psychoanalytic principles. His views were formally introduced to American scientists in 1909, when he delivered a famous series of lectures at Clark University at the invitation of G. Stanley Hall, the eminent American psychologist who was then president of the university. These *Introductory Lectures on Psychoanalysis* led to a great deal of controversy that helped publicize the concepts of psychoanalysis to both scientists and the general public.

Basic principles of the psychoanalytic perspective. The psychoanalytic perspec-

tive is both highly systematized and complex, and we shall not attempt to deal with it in detail. Its general principles, however, may be sketched as follows:

1. *Id, ego, and superego.* Basically the individual's behavior is assumed to result from the interaction of three key subsystems within the personality: the id, ego, and superego.

The *id* is the source of instinctual drives, which are considered to be of two types: (a) constructive drives, primarily of a sexual nature, which constitute the *libido,* or basic energy of life, and (b) destructive drives which tend toward aggression, destruction, and eventual death. Thus *life*, or constructive, instincts are opposed by *death*, or destructive, instincts. Here it may be noted that Freud used the term *sex* in a broad sense to refer to almost anything pleasurable, from eating to creating a painting. The id is completely selfish, concerned only with the immediate gratification of instinctual needs without reference to reality or moral considerations. Hence it is said to operate in terms of the *pleasure principle*. While the id can generate mental images and wish-fulfilling fantasies, referred to as the *primary process,* it cannot undertake the realistic action needed to meet instinctual demands.

Consequently a second key subsystem develops—the *ego*—which mediates between the demands of the id and the realities of the external world. The basic purpose of the ego is to meet id demands, but in such a way as to ensure the well-being and survival of the individual. This requires the use of reason and other intellectual resources in dealing with the external world, as well as the exercise of control over id demands. Such adaptive measures of the ego are referred to as the *secondary process,* and the ego is said to operate in terms of the *reality principle.* Freud viewed id demands, especially sexual and aggressive strivings, as inherently in conflict with rules and prohibitions imposed by society.

Since the id-ego relationship is merely one of expediency, Freud introduced a third key subsystem—the *superego*—which is the outgrowth of learning the taboos and moral values of society. The superego is essentially what we refer to as *conscience* and is concerned with right and wrong. As the superego develops, it becomes an additional inner control system that copes with the uninhibited desires of the

---

[1]Psychoanalysis is sometimes referred to as a *psychodynamic* theory because it focuses on the "inner dynamics" of "psychic processes," such as drives and motives, to explain behavior.

id. However, the superego also operates through the ego system and strives to compel the ego to inhibit desires that are considered wrong or immoral. (See HIGHLIGHT on this page.)

Freud viewed the interplay among these intrapsychic subsystems of id, ego, and superego as of crucial significance in determining behavior. Often inner conflicts arise because the three subsystems are striving for somewhat different goals. Mental disorders result when the individual is unable to resolve these conflicts.

2. *Anxiety, defense mechanisms, and the unconscious.* The concept of anxiety is prominent in the psychoanalytic perspective. Freud distinguished among three types of anxiety, or "psychic pain," that people can suffer: (a) *reality* anxiety, arising from dangers or threats in the external world; (b) *neurotic* anxiety, caused by the id's impulses threatening to break through ego controls into behavior that will be punished in some way; and (c) *moral* anxiety, arising from a real or contemplated action in conflict with the individual's superego and arousing feelings of guilt.

Anxiety is a warning of impending danger as well as a painful experience, so it forces the individual to undertake corrective action. Often the ego can cope with the anxiety by rational measures; if these do not suffice, however, the ego resorts to irrational protective measures, such as rationalization, which are referred to as *ego-defense mechanisms.*

These defense mechanisms alleviate the painful anxiety, but they do so by distorting reality instead of by dealing directly with the problem. This creates an undesirable schism between actual reality and the individual's perception of it.

Another important concept in the psychoanalytic perspective is that of the *unconscious.* Freud thought that the conscious part of the mind represents a relatively small area while the unconscious part, like the submerged part of an iceberg, is the much larger portion. In the depths of the unconscious are the hurtful memories, forbidden desires, and other experiences that have been *repressed*— that is, pushed out of the conscious. Although the individual is unaware of such unconscious material, it continues to seek expression and may be reflected in fantasies and dreams when ego controls are temporarily lowered. Until

Relation of id, ego, and superego

This diagram illustrates Freud's concept of the ego as the central integrating core of the personality, mediating between inner demands from the id and the superego and outer demands from the environment.

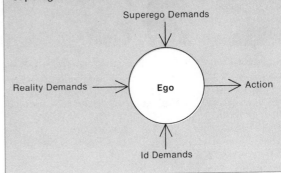

such unconscious material is brought to awareness and integrated into the ego structure—for example, via psychoanalysis— it presumably leads to irrational and maladaptive behavior.

3. *Psychosexual development.* Freud viewed personality development as a succession of stages, each characterized by a dominant mode of achieving libidinal (sexual) pleasure. The five stages he outlined follow:

a) *Oral stage.* During the first two years of life, the mouth is the principal erogenous zone; the infant's greatest source of gratification is assumed to be sucking.

b) *Anal stage.* From age 2 to age 3, the membranes of the anal region presumably provide the major source of pleasurable stimulation.

c) *Phallic stage.* From age 3 to age 5 or 6, self-manipulation of the genitals is assumed to provide the major source of pleasurable sensation.

d) *Latency stage.* In the years from 6 to 12, sexual motivations presumably recede in importance as the child becomes preoccupied with developing skills and other activities.

e) *Genital stage.* After puberty the deepest feelings of pleasure presumably come from heterosexual relations.

Freud believed that appropriate gratification

Sigmund Freud, *1856–1939, the founder of psychoanalysis, emphasized the role of "unconscious" processes and psychosexual stages in the determination of behavior.*

C. G. Jung, *1875–1961, felt that Freud placed undue emphasis on sex, and he focused instead on the "collective unconscious" and "inner self-experience."*

Both **Alfred Adler**, *1870–1937, and* **Karen Horney**, *1885–1952, are known for expanding the focus of psychoanalytic thought to include social-environmental factors in the development of personality.*

during each stage is important if the individual is not to be *fixated* at that level. For example, he held that an individual who does not receive adequate oral gratification during infancy may be prone to excessive eating or drinking in adult life.

In general, each stage of development places demands on the individual and arouses conflicts that must be resolved. One of the most important conflicts occurs during the phallic stage, when the pleasures of self-stimulation and accompanying fantasies pave the way for the Oedipus complex. Oedipus, according to Greek mythology, unknowingly killed his father and married his mother. Each young boy, Freud thought, symbolically relives the Oedipus drama. He has incestuous cravings for his mother and views his father as a hated rival; however, he also dreads the wrath of his dominant male parent and fears especially that his father may harm him by removing his penis. This *castration anxiety* forces the boy to repress his sexual desires for his mother as well as his hostility toward his father. Eventually, if all goes well, the boy identifies with his father and comes to have only harmless tender affection for his mother.

The Electra complex is the female counterpart of the Oedipus complex. It is based essentially on the view that the girl wants to possess her father and replace her mother. For either

sex, resolution of the conflict is considered essential if the young adult is to develop satisfactory heterosexual relationships.

In short, the psychoanalytic perspective holds that about the best we can hope for is a compromise among our warring inclinations, from which we will realize as much instinctual gratification as possible with minimal punishment and guilt. It thus presents a pessimistic and deterministic view of human behavior that minimizes rationality and freedom for self-determination. On a group level, it interprets violence, war, and related phenomena as the inevitable product of the aggressive and destructive instincts present in human nature.

Impact on our views of psychopathology. In historical perspective, psychoanalysis can be seen as the first systematic approach to show how human psychological processes may result in mental disorders. Much as the biological perspective replaced demons and witches with organic pathology as the cause of mental disorders, the psychoanalytic perspective replaced brain pathology with exaggerated ego defenses against anxiety as the cause of at least some mental disorders.

Freud greatly advanced our understanding of both normal and abnormal behavior, and many of the concepts formulated by Freud and his followers have become fundamental to our

Karl Menninger, *b. 1893, has, in essence, remained a proponent of Freud's original principles and has gathered data in support of them.*

Anna Freud, *b. 1895, elaborated the ego-defense mechanisms and pioneered the psychoanalytic treatment of children.*

Erik Erickson, *b. 1902, broadened Freud's psychosexual stages by describing eight psychosocial stages, each offering the child an opportunity to work out a conflict in a healthy or unhealthy way.*

thinking about human nature and behavior. Two of Freud's contributions stand out as particularly noteworthy:

1. He developed techniques such as free association and dream analysis for becoming acquainted with both the conscious and unconscious aspects of mental life. The data thus obtained led Freud to emphasize (a) the dynamic role of unconscious motives and ego-defense processes, (b) the importance of early childhood experiences in later personality adjustment and maladjustment, and (c) the importance of sexual factors in human behavior and mental disorders. Although, as we have said, Freud used the term *sex* in a much broader sense than it is ordinarily used, the idea caught the popular fancy, and the role of sexual factors in human behavior was finally brought out into the open as an appropriate topic for scientific investigation.

2. He demonstrated that certain abnormal mental phenomena occur as a result of attempts to cope with difficult problems and are simply exaggerations of normal ego-defense mechanisms. With the realization that the same psychological principles apply to both normal and abnormal behavior, much of the mystery and fear surrounding mental disorders was dispelled and mental patients were helped to regain their dignity as human beings.

The psychoanalytic perspective has come under attack from many directions, however —from other perspectives as well as from those within the psychoanalytic tradition. It has been criticized for overemphasis on the sex drive; for undue pessimism about basic human nature; for exaggeration of the role of unconscious processes; for failure to consider motives toward personal growth and fulfillment; for neglect of cultural differences in shaping behavior; and for a lack of scientific evidence to support many of its assumptions or to evaluate the success of psychoanalytic therapy. Finally, since therapy frequently takes months, and even years, it has been criticized because it is very expensive.

Variants of the psychoanalytic approach have appeared, due in part, no doubt, to criticisms of the approach. Two of Freud's early students, C. G. Jung and Alfred Adler, soon found themselves in disagreement with various aspects of Freud's approach, particularly what they felt was the undue emphasis placed on sex as a determinant of behavior. Jung, founder of the *analytic* school of psychology, advanced the valuable concepts of "collective unconscious" and "inner self-experience." According to Jung, each individual has a personal unconscious, as well as a collective unconscious consisting of memories established throughout human history and inherited in the brain structure as "primal images" or "archetypes." The individual achieves true "wholeness" only as fantasies, images, and dreams from the personal and collective unconscious become accessible to the conscious self.

Adler differed from Freud and Jung in his emphasis on social rather than inherited determinants of behavior. He viewed people as inherently social beings whose most basic motivation is to belong to and participate in the group. Adler emphasized an active, creative, conscious "self" that plays a central role in the individual's attempt to organize experiences, take responsibility, and achieve fulfillment as a human being.

Karl Menninger has remained more within the general theoretical framework developed by Freud and has been a leading figure in the elaboration and dissemination of psychoanalytic thought in America. He has gathered data from his own clinic—the famed Menninger Clinic in Topeka, Kansas—in support of Freud's principles and has written extensively about them.

Erik Erikson elaborated and broadened Freud's psychosexual stages by describing conflicts that come into focus at eight stages, each of which can be resolved in a healthy or unhealthy way. For example, during the oral stage the child may learn either basic *trust* or basic *mistrust*. Although these conflicts are never fully resolved once and for all, failure to develop toward the appropriate pole of each conflict handicaps an individual for meeting the tasks of the later stages. For example, trust is needed for later competence in many areas of life; a clear sense of identity is a necessary prerequisite for satisfying intimacy with another person; such intimacy, in turn, is an important precondition for becoming a nurturant parent.

Many of Freud's early ideas have thus been revised or discarded. Yet the basic psychoanalytic view is still widely held. There are many practicing psychoanalysts and a number of analytic societies where professionals receive psychoanalytic training in the United States. Although there has been a shift in treatment focus away from the psychoanalytic approach in recent years, a great many books and articles on the method are still published each year.

The behavioristic perspective

While psychoanalysis largely dominated psychological thought about abnormal behavior in the early part of this century, another school—behaviorism—was emerging to challenge its supremacy. Behavioristic psychologists believed that the study of subjective experience —via the techniques of free association and dream analysis—did not provide acceptable scientific data, since such observations were not open to verification by other investigators. In their view, only the study of directly observable behavior and the stimuli and reinforcing conditions that "control" it could serve as a basis for formulating scientific principles of human behavior.

The behavioristic perspective is organized around one central theme: the role of learning in human behavior. Although this perspective was initially developed through research in the laboratory rather than through clinical practice with disturbed individuals, its implications for explaining and treating maladaptive behavior soon became evident.

Roots of the behavioristic perspective. The origins of the behavioristic approach can be traced to the work of the Russian physiologist Ivan Pavlov (1849–1936), but credit for its elaboration belongs largely to three distinguished American psychologists: J. B. Watson (1878–1958), E. L. Thorndike (1874–1949), and B. F. Skinner (b. 1904). We shall examine the contributions of each of these men in turn.

1. *Pavlov and the conditioned reflex.* While performing a series of studies on the salivary response in dogs, Pavlov discovered the phenomenon of the conditioned reflex. He found that stimuli that had been regularly present just before food was presented came to elicit salivation even in the absence of food. For example, even seeing the person who ordinarily brought the food, or hearing his or her footsteps, eventually produced salivation on the part of the dogs. This simple method of learning came to be called *conditioning*. It was destined to become a key building block in the systematic study of learning.

In 1914, while pursuing the study of conditioned reflexes in dogs, one of Pavlov's stu-

Ivan Pavlov (1849–1936), *a pioneer in showing the part conditioning plays in behavior, is shown here with his staff and some of the apparatus used to condition reflexes in dogs.*

dents reported an unusual and dramatic incident. He had conditioned a dog to distinguish between a circle and an ellipse, as demonstrated by the fact that the dog salivated to the ellipse but not to the circle. The ellipse was then gradually altered in shape so that it became more and more like the circle, until the dog could no longer distinguish accurately between the two. During three weeks of subsequent experimentation, the dog's ability to discriminate between the two similar figures not only failed to improve, but became considerably worse, and finally disappeared altogether.

At the same time, the behavior of the dog underwent an abrupt change. The previously quiet and cooperative animal squealed and squirmed in its stand and tore off the experimental apparatus with its teeth. In addition, when taken into the experimental room, the dog now barked violently, instead of going quietly as it had before. Pavlov considered this change in the dog's behavior to be equivalent to an "experimental neurosis."

Thus unusual incidents in the laboratory routine, which might have been overlooked as merely trivial and annoying by an observer less astute than Pavlov, led to a whole new method in the study of abnormal behavior.

On the basis of subsequent experimental findings, Pavlov went on, after the age of eighty, to attempt a rather comprehensive formulation of human psychopathology (Pavlov, 1928). This formulation was based on the speculative assumption that the different reaction patterns shown by dogs in response to the conditioned-reflex techniques would also be reflected on the human level in reactions to life stressors.

While Pavlov's formulations on the functioning of the human brain have not proven definitive, his conditioning techniques and production of "experimental neuroses" paved the way for a vast amount of research in psychopathology.

2. *Watson and "behaviorism."* Pavlov's discovery of conditioning was seized upon by the American psychologist J. B. Watson as a procedure for studying human behavior more objectively. If psychology were ever to become a science, Watson concluded, it must limit itself to the study of events that could be objectively observed.

Starting with this fundamental assumption,

Watson changed the focus of psychology from the study of inner sensations to the study of outer behavior, an approach he called *behaviorism*. His book *Psychology from the Standpoint of a Behaviorist* was published in 1919. As we might expect, this approach placed heavy emphasis on the role of the social environment in "conditioning" personality development and behavior.

In their now-famous experiment with little Albert, an eleven-month-old boy who was fond of animals, Watson and Rayner (1920) dramatically demonstrated how an irrational fear, or phobia, could be readily learned through conditioning. The procedure was simple: the experimenter stood behind the boy and struck a steel bar with a hammer when Albert reached for a white rat. The loud noise elicited a fear response on the boy's part and made him cry. After several repetitions of this experience, Albert became greatly disturbed at the sight of the animal even without the loud noise, and his fear generalized to include other furry animals and objects as well. This demonstration of the development and generalization of an irrational fear suggested that other types of abnormal behavior might also be the result of learning.

Later, Mary Cover Jones (1924) succeeded in eliminating such fears by presenting a white rabbit at a distance when a child, Peter, who was very afraid of white rabbits, was reacting positively to food, an anxiety inhibitor. By bringing the animal gradually closer, always avoiding overbalancing the negative fear tendency by the strength of the positive tendency, the experimenter finally eliminated the boy's fear and replaced it with pleasant feelings toward the white rabbit; these feelings, in turn, generalized to other furry animals.

3. *The contributions of Thorndike and Skinner.* The work of Pavlov and Watson convinced many investigators that all learning is based on conditioned reflexes, and that studying the lawful properties of such conditioned reflexes could explain human behavior—normal and abnormal.

However, the work of E. L. Thorndike was to provide the basis for the development of a second fundamental concept of the behavioristic perspective. In his formulation of the "law of effect," Thorndike (1913) made the observation that responses that have rewarding con-

sequences are strengthened or learned, whereas responses that have negative or aversive consequences are weakened or extinguished. Thus he emphasized the control of human behavior by reward and punishment.

Following this early lead, Skinner (1953) concluded that the most important, understandable, and manipulable determinants of behavior lie outside the organism in environmental events or stimuli; he further concluded that these stimuli can be manipulated to control the learning and behavior of the organism. As Skinner expressed it,

"The practice of looking inside the organism for an explanation of behavior has tended to obscure the variables which are immediately available for a scientific analysis. These variables lie outside the organism, in its immediate environment and in its environmental history." (1953, p. 31)

Skinner's influence on current psychology has been enormous. His concepts of operant conditioning and control of behavior by reinforcement (to be discussed in the next section) have become cornerstones in behavioristic research and have affected the thinking of educators, therapists, correctional personnel, and even physiologists, as we shall see.

Basic principles of the behavioristic viewpoint. As we have noted, *learning* provides the central theme of the behavioristic approach. Since most human behavior *is* learned, the behaviorists have addressed themselves to the question of how learning comes about.[2] In trying to answer this question, they have focused on the effects of environmental conditions (stimuli) on the acquisition, modification, and elimination of response patterns—both adaptive and maladaptive ones.

1. *Respondent (classical) and operant conditioning.* Even prior to learning, a specific stimulus may elicit a specific response. For example, food elicits salivation. Food is thus referred to as an *unconditioned* stimulus, and

---

[2]Distinguished American psychologists who contributed to the development and extension of behavioristic theory include E. C. Tolman, E. R. Guthrie, Clark Hull, R. R. Sears, J. Dollard, N. E. Miller, O. H. Mowrer, K. W. Spence, W. K. Estes, and A. Bandura.

Should this woman find that her response provides the desired stimulus—gum—the principles of operant conditioning would suggest that she may use the same tactic in future, similar situations.

the salivation is called an *unconditioned* response. Through conditioning, the same response may come to be elicited by a wide range of other stimuli in the manner demonstrated by Pavlov. This form of conditioning is called *classical* or *respondent conditioning;* its hallmark is that the response is elicited by the stimulus.

As previously noted, the classic demonstration of respondent conditioning is the experiment cited previously in which little Albert was conditioned to fear a white rat, a fear that generalized to other furry objects. Much of our learning—particularly during infancy and childhood—is based on this kind of conditioning. It can be adaptive, as when we learn to fear and avoid hurtful stimuli, or it can be maladaptive, as when we learn irrational fears or phobias.

In *operant conditioning,* the individual makes a response in an attempt to achieve a desired goal. The individual "operates" on or modifies the environment; hence the term *operant.* The goal in question may be to obtain something that is rewarding or to avoid something that is aversive. Here the response typically precedes the stimulus, as when an individual kicks a coffee machine that has failed to function, causing it to produce coffee. The next time the coffee machine does not work, the

person will probably kick it again. As we grow up, operant learning becomes an important mechanism for discriminating between the desirable and the undesirable—between what will prove rewarding and what will prove unrewarding or aversive—and for acquiring the competencies essential for achieving our goals and coping with our world.

Unfortunately, however, there is no guarantee that what we learn will be accurate or useful. Thus we may learn to value things that will hurt us; we may fail to learn needed competencies for coping, or we may learn coping patterns such as helplessness, bullying, or other irresponsible behavior that is maladaptive rather than adaptive.

2. *Reinforcement.* Essential to both respondent and operant conditioning is *reinforcement*—the strengthening of a new response by its repeated association with some unconditioned stimulus. Such a stimulus is called a *reinforcer* and may be either positive (pleasant) or negative (aversive). In the experiment with little Albert, the reinforcer was the loud noise; successive repetitions of the noise in association with the presentation of the rat strengthened—reinforced—Albert's conditioned fear.

In operant learning, the response may be strengthened because it is repeatedly as-

E. L. Thorndike, *1874–1949, formulated the* law of effect—*a seemingly simple observation that rewarded responses are strengthened and unrewarded responses are weakened—but one which laid the foundations of understanding learning and suggested means for the control of human behavior.*

J. B. Watson, *1878–1958, changed the focus of psychology from the study of inner sensations to the study of outer behavior, an approach he called* behaviorism.

B. F. Skinner, *b. 1904, formulated the concept of operant conditioning as a kind of conditioning in which reinforcers could be used to make a response more or less probable and frequent.*

Albert Bandura, *b. 1925, pioneered the study of* modeling. *He clarified and integrated learning principles in the causation and treatment of maladaptive behavior in his important book,* Principles of Behavior Modification, *as well as in later publications.*

Donald H. Meichenbaum, *b. 1940, has made important recent contributions to the cognitive-behavioral approach to changing maladaptive behavior through the modification of people's self-statements.*

sociated with a reward or with avoiding some aversive condition. For example, a child may learn a response either to receive a reward, such as candy, or to avoid a punishment, such as a spanking. In both "positive" and "negative" reinforcement, the learner is rewarded for making an appropriate response.

Initially a high rate of reinforcement may be necessary to establish a response, but lesser rates are usually sufficient to maintain it. In fact, a learned response appears to be especially persistent when reinforcement is intermittent—when the reinforcing stimulus does *not* invariably follow the response—as demonstrated in gambling when occasional wins seem to keep the response going. However, when reinforcement is consistently withheld over time, the conditioned response—whether classical or operant—eventually *extinguishes.* The subject stops making the response.

There is a special problem in extinguishing a response learned through *avoidance learning,* in which the subject has been conditioned to anticipate an aversive event and to respond in such a way as to avoid it. For example, a boy who has been bitten by a vicious dog may develop a conditioned avoidance response in which he consistently turns away from and avoids all dogs. When he sees a dog, he feels anxious; avoiding contact lessens his anxiety and is thus reinforcing. As a result, his avoidance response is highly resistant to extinction. It also prevents him from having experiences with friendly dogs that could bring about reconditioning. We shall examine the significance of such conditioned avoidance responses in our later discussions of patterns of abnormal behavior.

3. *Generalization and discrimination.* We noted in the experiment conducted by Watson and Rayner that little Albert's fear generalized from white rats to other furry animals. This tendency for a response that has been conditioned to one stimulus to become associated with similar stimuli is referred to as *generalization.* The greater the similarity of stimuli, the greater the likelihood of generalization.

A process complementary to generalization is *discrimination,* which occurs when the individual learns to distinguish between similar stimuli and to respond differently to them. The

ability to discriminate may be brought about through selective reinforcement. For example, since red strawberries taste good and green ones do not, a conditioned discrimination will occur if the individual has experience with both. According to the behavioristic perspective, complex processes like attending, perceiving, forming concepts, and solving problems are all based on an elaboration of this basic discriminative process.

The concepts of generalization and discrimination have many implications for the development of maladaptive behavior. While generalization enables us to use past experience in sizing up new situations, there is always the possibility of making inappropriate generalizations—as when a delinquent youth fails to develop discriminations between "responsible" and "irresponsible" behavior, or a child of wealthy parents learns to regard only rich people as worthy of respect. In some instances, a discrimination that is needed may be beyond the individual's capability—as we noted in the case of Pavlov's production of experimental neuroses in dogs—and may lead to psychological disorganization and inefficient coping behavior.

4. *Modeling, shaping, and learned drives.* Other basic concepts of the behaviorist approach are modeling, shaping, and primary and secondary drives.

Modeling involves precisely what the term implies—demonstration of desired response patterns by parents or others. If the individual is capable of imitating the act modeled and is rewarded for doing so or sees the model being rewarded for such behavior, new performances can be acquired very rapidly. Often, of course, a child spontaneously imitates parental behavior; hence parents are viewed as important models in a child's early development. Unfortunately, a child may imitate maladaptive as well as adaptive behavior.

Often an appropriate response is not available in a person's behavior repertoire, a matter that presents problems for therapy based on the behaviorist approach, since a response cannot be reinforced until it occurs. In such cases it is often possible to *shape* the response by reinforcing successive approximations of the desired behavior. Here behavior that is in the right direction—even though it does not represent the final performance to be achieved—is reinforced, while other responses are not reinforced and hence extinguish. For example, in getting a mute, chronic schizophrenic individual to speak, slight movement of the lips may be reinforced first; later, when the individual starts to make sounds, they are reinforced instead. Thus behavior is gradually shaped until the final goal of coherent speech is achieved.

Behaviorists view motivation as being based on a limited number of primary biological drives, such as hunger and thirst, that are directly related to meeting bodily needs. The many different motives in everyday life are seen as learned extensions of these primary drives. For example, an infant soon learns that parental approval leads to the gratification of bodily needs and thus learns to seek parental approval. With time this seeking may generalize or come to be associated with academic achievement and other behavior valued by the parents. Thus motives for approval, achievement, and so on, are seen as merely extensions of our more basic biological drives and are called *secondary drives*. And as with other learned behavior, motives that lead to maladaptive as well as adaptive behavior may be learned and reinforced.

5. *Cognitive mediation.* According to the stimulus-response framework of original behaviorism, all that is needed to change behavior is to change stimuli in the environment. But because different individuals may assess and respond to an event in different ways, many learning-oriented clinicians are recognizing the need to take account of verbal or cognitive processes in the individual that occur between the stimulus and the response and help to determine what the response is. These are the individual's *mediating processes.* The clinician can modify these processes by modifying the "self-statements" made by the individual—verbalizations of what he or she is experiencing—which are, in essence, verbalizations of the mediating processes.

For example, suppose that two women with essentially the same speaking skills but differing in their levels of speech anxiety are asked to give speeches, and suppose that in both cases several members of the audience walk out in the middle of the speech. The woman with high speech-anxiety is likely to say to

herself: "I must be boring. How much longer must I speak? I knew I could never give a speech," and so forth. These self-statements engender more anxiety and become self-fulfilling prophecies. On the other hand, the woman with low speech-anxiety is more likely to view the audience's departure as a sign of rudeness or to attribute their leaving to external considerations. She is more likely to tell herself something like: "They must have a class to catch. Too bad they have to leave; they will miss a good talk" (Meichenbaum, 1977, p. 1).

Since the first woman's assessment of the situation—that is, her cognitive behavior—has been an important determinant of her increased anxiety, a cognitively oriented behavioral therapist would have her practice and experience reward for more positive self-statements, which in time would be expected to change her self-concept. In later chapters we shall see examples of such cognitive-behavioral therapy.

Impact on our views of psychopathology. By means of a relatively few basic concepts, behaviorism attempts to explain the acquisition, modification, and extinction of all types of behavior. Maladaptive behavior is viewed as essentially the result of (a) a failure to learn necessary adaptive behaviors or competencies, such as how to establish satisfying personal relationships; or (b) the learning of ineffective or maladaptive responses, as in the case of little Albert. Maladaptive behavior is thus seen as resulting from faulty learning and is defined in terms of specific, observable undesirable responses.

For the behaviorist, the focus of therapy is accordingly on changing specific behaviors—eliminating undesirable reactions and bringing about the learning of desirable ones. A number of *behavior-modification* techniques have been developed, based on the systematic application of learning principles. (See HIGHLIGHT on page 65.) Many examples of the application of these techniques will be given in later chapters.

The behavioristic approach has been heralded for its preciseness and objectivity, for the wealth of research it has generated, and for its demonstrated effectiveness in changing specific behaviors. The behavior therapist

Some behavior-modification techniques based on learning principles

Learning principle	Technique	Example in Treatment
Behavior patterns are developed and established through repeated association with positive reinforcers.	Use of positive reinforcement to establish desired behavior.	Wahler (1968) successfully modified extreme oppositional and negativistic behavior on the part of children by having parents reward cooperative behavior with approval and with tokens exchangeable for prized toys. Tokens were gradually eliminated, but dramatic improvement in cooperative behavior remained stable.
The repeated association of an established behavior pattern with negative reinforcers results in avoidance behavior.	Use of negative reinforcement to eliminate undesirable behavior (aversive conditioning).	Wolpe (1965) successfully treated drug addiction in a physician by having him use a portable apparatus to give himself an electric shock whenever he had a craving for the drug.
When an established behavior pattern is no longer reinforced, it tends to be extinguished.	Withdrawal of reinforcement for undesirable behavior.	Lovaas et al. (1965) found that self-injurious behavior of emotionally disturbed children could be reduced by cutting off social reinforcers—e.g., by having parents and others show less attention and concern when such behavior occurred.
Avoidance behavior will be inhibited or reduced if the conditions that provoke it are repeatedly paired with positive stimuli.	Desensitization to conditions that elicit unreasonable fear or anxiety.	In a classic experiment by Mary Cover Jones (1924), a boy's phobia for white rabbits and other furry animals was inhibited by feeding the boy his favorite food while the rabbit was in the background; the rabbit was gradually brought closer during feeding until the boy's fear of the animal was eliminated.
A specified behavior can gradually be established if successive approximations of the behavior are reinforced.	Shaping of desired behavior.	Rekers, Lovaas, and Low (1975) successfully used social reinforcement to develop masculine sex-typed behavior in an 8-year-old boy whose behavior was considered to be inappropriately feminine. They reinforced masculine or neutral behavior with expressions of interest and gave no attention to behavior that was considered feminine. Their treatment was begun in the home, then extended to the school setting in order to maximize generalizability of the treatment. "Masculine" social skills and sports were also taught over a period of several months. A follow-up evaluation when the boy was 12 years old showed that the new behaviors were being maintained.
Reinforcement can operate to modify covert behavior (cognitions) as well as overt behavior.	Cognitive restructuring.	Goldfried, Lineham, and Smith (1978) told highly anxious subjects to imagine being in an anxiety-arousing test situation and then presented them with instructions for reducing their anxiety. Subjects not only learned to react to test situations with less anxiety but responded in other social circumstances with more adaptive attitudes.

specifies what behavior is to be changed and in just what ways. Later, the effectiveness of the therapy can be evaluated objectively by the degree to which the stated goals have been achieved. On the other hand, the behavioristic perspective has been criticized on a number of grounds, including the following:

a) it is concerned only with symptoms and not with underlying problems;

b) it is too mechanistic and ignores the human being, focusing more on the method and the technical aspects than on the person seeking help;

c) it generally fails to include the data of subjective experience—such as self-awareness—which are highly meaningful to the client and help determine the client's reaction to the situation;

d) it fails, in general, to come to grips with the problem of values and meaning in human existence and the question of how human beings *should* relate to each other; and

e) it fails to deal adequately with the problem of self-direction. According to the behavioristic perspective, human beings are completely at the mercy of previous learning and present environmental conditions; these may shape behavior in ways that are good or evil, rational or irrational, adaptive or maladaptive. "Freedom of choice" and "self-determination" are viewed as illusions.[3]

Regarding the first of these criticisms, behaviorists would say that the symptom *is* the problem: get rid of the disturbing behavior and the person's problem disappears or is greatly lessened. The second and third criticisms have become less valid. Individual factors have been given more emphasis (Lazarus, 1971); more attention has been given to the characteristics of the relationship between the client and the therapist (Goldfried & Davison, 1976; Wilson & Evans, 1977); and the importance of cognitive processes, including imagery, has been recognized in current behavior therapy (Cautela, 1973; Meichenbaum, 1977).

The other criticisms are more general and more difficult to deal with empirically.

Paradoxically, however, the most ardent behaviorists, like Watson and Skinner, have repeatedly emphasized the potential use of modern science and technology for planning a better future world. In his famous novel, *Walden Two* (1948), and its nonfiction version, *Beyond Freedom and Dignity* (1971), Skinner has depicted the utopian world he thinks would result from the systematic application of learning principles and behavior-modification procedures to our present world problems. In fact, Skinner (1974) has stated the matter very succinctly: "In the behavioristic view, man can now control his own destiny because he knows what must be done and how to do it" (p. 258). He does not explain how people who have no choice could choose to exert such control.

Whatever its limitations and paradoxes, the behavioristic perspective has had and continues to have a tremendous impact on our contemporary views of human nature and behavior in general and on psychopathology in particular.

The humanistic perspective

The humanistic perspective has been influenced by both the psychoanalytic and the behavioristic perspectives, but it is in significant disagreement with both. The behavioristic perspective, with its focus on the stimulus situation and observable behavior, is seen as an oversimplification that underrates the importance of the individual's psychological makeup, inner experience, and potential for self-direction. At the same time, humanistic psychologists disagree with the negative and pessimistic picture of human nature portrayed by psychoanalytic theory and its stress on the overwhelming power of irrational, unconscious impulses. Rather, the humanistic perspective views our basic nature as "good," emphasizes present conscious processes as well as unconscious processes and past events, and places strong emphasis on our inherent capacity for responsible self-direction.

Some objection has been raised to the use of the term *humanistic* to describe only the more experientially oriented therapies because it seems to imply that other approaches demean the individual or view humans as simply objects with which to tinker. All approaches, of

---

[3]Skinner (1974) has listed twenty criticisms of the behavioristic approach, all of which he considers to be largely or totally unjustified. Bandura (1974), however, has suggested that the behavioristic perspective be broadened to deal with such critical views. For example, he has stated that human beings do have "a capacity for self-direction" and that recognition of this capacity "represents a substantial departure from exclusive reliance upon environmental control" (pp. 861, 863).

course, aim ultimately at more effective, happier human beings and are "humanistic" in that sense, just as all are interested in changing behavior and thus recognize the importance of learning. Their labels indicate their special focus but do not imply that they exclude all other factors.

Roots of the humanistic approach. The humanistic perspective has been heavily influenced by such outstanding psychologists as William James, Gordon Allport, Abraham Maslow, Gardner Murphy, Carl Rogers, and Fritz Perls. Although some of its roots extend deep into the history of psychology—as well as philosophy, literature, and education—others are of relatively recent origin. It appears to have emerged as a major perspective in psychology in the 1950s and 1960s when many middle-class Americans realized their simultaneous material affluence and spiritual emptiness.

As an important new "third force" in contemporary psychology, the humanistic approach recognizes the importance of learning and other psychological processes that have traditionally been the focus of research; but it is also concerned with processes about which we have as yet little scientific information—such as love, hope, creativity, values, meaning, personal growth, and self-fulfillment. In essence, humanistic psychologists feel that modern psychology has failed to address itself to many of the problems that are of crucial significance in the lives of all of us.

Basic principles of the humanistic perspective. The humanistic approach is characterized as much or more by its general orientation toward human beings and their potentialities as by any coherent set of principles of personality development and functioning. It is as much a statement of values as it is a theory of human behavior. There are, however, certain underlying themes and principles that humanistic psychologists hold in common.

1. *Self as a unifying theme.* As we noted at the beginning of this chapter, William James included consciousness of self in his early text written before the turn of the century, but this concept was later dropped by the behaviorists because the self could not be observed by an outsider. Eventually, however, the need for some kind of unifying principle of personality and some way of accounting for an individual's subjective experiences led to the reintroduction of the self-concept in the humanistic perspective.

Here it may be noted that the concept of the self is somewhat analogous to the psychoanalytic concept of the ego in that both represent inferred subsystems concerned with evaluating, problem solving, decision making, and coping. The humanistic viewpoint, however, extends the self-concept to include the individual's sense of identity and relation to the world as well as tendencies toward self-evaluation and self-fulfillment.

Among contemporary humanistic psychologists, Carl Rogers has developed the most systematic formulation of the self-concept, based largely on his pioneering research into the nature of the psychotherapeutic process. Rogers (1951) has stated his views in a series of propositions that may be summarized as follows:

a) Each individual exists in a private world of experience of which the I, me, or myself is the center.

b) The most basic striving of the individual is toward the maintenance, enhancement, and actualization of the self.

c) The individual reacts to situations in terms of the way he or she perceives them, in ways consistent with his or her self-concept and view of the world.

d) Perceived threat to the self is followed by defense—including the narrowing and rigidification of perception and behavior and the introduction of self-defense mechanisms.

e) The individual's inner tendencies are toward health and wholeness; under normal conditions we behave in rational and constructive ways and choose pathways toward personal growth and self-actualization.

In using the concept of self as a unifying theme, humanistic psychologists emphasize the importance of individuality. Because of our great potential for evaluation and learning and the great diversity in our genetic endowments and backgrounds of experience, each one of us is unique. In studying "human nature," psychologists are thus faced with the dual task of describing the uniqueness of each individual and identifying the characteristics that all members of the human race have in common.

Before the turn of the twentieth century, **William James,** *1842–1910, set the stage for the humanistic perspective in a chapter on the concept of the self in his book* Principles of Psychology.
A. H. Maslow, *1908–1970, devoted more than two decades to showing the potentialities of human beings for higher self-development and functioning.*
Carl R. Rogers, *b. 1902, has contributed significantly to the humanistic perspective with his theoretical formulations and his systematic studies on the therapeutic process and its outcomes.*
Thomas S. Szasz, *b. 1920, a psychiatrist, has argued that illness is an inappropriate term for most maladaptive behavior, which he sees as resulting from problems in living rather than from organic causes.*
Fritz Perls, *1893–1970, was influential in the development of therapeutic procedures for enhancing human experiencing and functioning, particularly in the context of confrontation groups.*

2. *Focus on values and personal growth.* Humanistic psychologists place strong emphasis on values and the process of value choices in guiding our behavior and achieving a meaningful and fulfilling way of life. They consider it crucial that each one of us develop values based on our own experience and evaluations rather than blindly accepting values held by people around us; otherwise we deny our own experiences of value and lose touch with our own real feelings.

To evaluate and choose for ourselves requires a clear sense of our own self-identity—the discovery of who we are, of what sort of person we want to become, and why. Only in this way can we actualize our potentialities and achieve responsible self-direction.

The humanistic perspective stresses the problem of values and fulfillment, not only for the individual but for society as well. As Maslow (1969) pointed out, it is essential that we develop a "good society" as well as a "good person," because the actualization of human potentialities on a mass basis is possible only under favorable social conditions.

3. *Positive view of human nature and potential.* In contrast to the psychoanalytic and behavioristic perspectives, the humanistic approach takes a much more positive view of human nature and potential. Despite the myriad instances of violence, war, and cruelty that have occurred from ancient times, humanistically oriented psychologists conclude that under favorable circumstances, human propensities are in the direction of friendly, cooperative, and constructive behavior. They regard selfishness, aggression, and cruelty as pathological behavior resulting from the denial, frustration, or distortion of our basic nature. Similarly, they suggest that although we can be misled by inaccurate information, handicapped by social and economic deprivation, and overwhelmed by the number and complexity of issues we are expected to act upon, we still tend to be rational creatures. We try to find sense and meaning in our experience, to act and think in consistent ways, and to follow standards and principles we believe are good. According to this view, we are not passive automatons but active participants in life with some measure of freedom for shaping both our personal destiny and that of our social group.

Humanistic psychologists believe that as science discovers more about our inherent nature and effective functioning, it will become increasingly possible to make judgments about what is good or bad for humankind, both for individuals and for societies. And as our techniques for modifying personality and behavior become increasingly powerful, psychologists—as well as other scientists—can no longer avoid concern with values or the ethical dilemmas that arise when value choices are made.

Impact on our views of psychopathology. According to the humanistic view, psychopathology is essentially the blocking or distortion of personal growth and natural tendencies toward physical and mental health. Such blocking or distortion is generally the result of one or more of these causal factors: (a) the exaggerated use of ego-defense mechanisms so that the individual becomes increasingly out of touch with reality; (b) unfavorable social conditions and faulty learning; and (c) excessive stress.

Thus humanistic approaches to therapy usually focus on helping individuals drop their defenses, acknowledge what they are actually experiencing, perceive themselves as they really are, achieve needed competencies, and find satisfying values—in essence, to increase their capabilities for personal choice, growth, and fulfillment. As might be expected, humanistic psychologists are keenly interested in encounter groups, awareness training, and other experiential techniques for fostering personal growth, building more satisfying relationships with others, and finding more effective methods of coping.

It is too early to assess the ultimate impact of the humanistic perspective, but it has clearly introduced a new dimension to our thinking about abnormal behavior in its view of psychopathology as a blocking or distortion of the individual's natural tendencies toward health and personal growth rather than as abnormality or deviance per se. In fact, Maslow (1962, 1969) has even expressed concern about the "psychopathology of the normal"—that is, the disappointing and wasteful failure of so many "normal" people to realize their potentialities as human beings.

The humanistic perspective has been

criticized for its diffuseness, for a lack of scientific rigor in its conceptualizations, and for expecting too much from psychology. But while some psychologists would view its goals as "grandiose," others would view them as a useful description of the challenging long-range task that confronts psychology today.

The existential perspective

The existential perspective emphasizes our uniqueness, as individuals, in our quest for values and meaning, and in our freedom for self-direction and self-fulfillment. In these ways it is highly similar to the humanistic perspective, and, in fact, many existential psychologists are also referred to as humanists. However, the existential perspective represents a somewhat less optimistic view of human beings and places more emphasis on the irrational tendencies in human nature and the difficulties inherent in self-fulfillment—particularly in our bureaucratic and dehumanizing mass society. In short, the matter of living seems much more a "confrontation" for the existentialists. And the existentialists place considerably less faith in modern science and more in the inner experience of the individual in his or her attempts to understand and deal with the deepest human problems.

Central themes and concepts of the existential perspective. The existential perspective, like the humanistic approach, is not a highly systematized school of thought, but it is unified around a central concern with the ultimate challenge of human existence—to find sound values, to grow as a person, and to build a meaningful and socially constructive life. Its basic concepts stem mainly from the writings of such European philosophers as Heidegger, Jaspers, Kierkegaard, and Sartre. Especially influential in the development of existential thought in the United States have been the theologian Paul Tillich and the psychologist Rollo May.

1. *Existence and essence.* A basic theme of existentialism is that our existence is given, but what we make of it—our essence—is up to us. The adolescent boy who defiantly blurts out, "Well, I didn't ask to be born" is stating a profound truth; but in existential terms, it is completely irrelevant. For whether he asked to be born or not, here he is in the world and answerable for himself—for one human life. What he makes of his essence is up to him. It is his responsibility to shape the kind of person he is to become and to live a meaningful and constructive life.

However, this is not an easy task in an age of profound social change in which many traditional values and beliefs are being questioned. For this is an age that tends to engender inner confusion and deep emotional and spiritual strain concerning the kind of people we should be and become, and the way of life we should try to build for ourselves.

Essentially, we can resolve this dilemma in one of two ways: (a) by giving up the quest and finding some satisfaction in blind conformity and submergence in the group; or (b) by striving for increased self-definition in the reality of our own existence. Only through the second choice can we find self-fulfillment.

2. *Choice, freedom, and courage.* Our essence is created by our *choices,* for our choices reflect the values on which we base and order our lives. As Sartre put it: "I am my choices."

In choosing what sort of person to become, we are seen as having absolute *freedom;* even refusing to choose represents a choice. Thus the locus of valuing is within each individual. We are inescapably the architects of our own lives. Morris (1966) has stated the situation in the form of three propositions:

"1. I am a *choosing* agent, unable to avoid choosing my way through life.
2. I am a *free* agent, absolutely free to set the goals of my own life.
3. I am a *responsible* agent, personally accountable for my free choices as they are revealed in how I live my life." (p. 135)

The problems of choice and responsibility often become an agonizing burden, for finding satisfying values is a lonely and difficult matter. It requires the *courage* to break away from old patterns if need be and to stand on one's own. In a very real sense, the freedom to shape one's essence is "both our agony and our glory."

Some people lack "the courage to be"—to seek and follow· new paths that offer greater possibilities for self-fulfillment. Often they do not want their essence to be left up to them;

Jean-Paul Sartre, b. 1905, is one of the most influential modern existential thinkers, known for his novels and dramas as well as for his other works of existential philosophy.

Psychologist **Rollo May**, b. 1909, is one of the leading exponents of the existential perspective in America.

The interpersonal model is based largely on the work of **Harry Stack Sullivan**, 1892–1949, who thought it was pointless to speak of the individual personality, since he believed personality existed only in interaction with others.

rather they seek some outside authority such as religion or their social group to advise them on what to believe and how to act. But if blind conformity cuts the individual off from new possibilities for *being* and leads to a wasted life, the individual cannot blame anyone else or evade the consequences. For to flee from one's freedom and responsibility to life is to be *unauthentic,* to *show bad faith,* and to *live in despair.*

3. *Meaning, value, and obligation.* A central theme in the existential perspective is the will-to-meaning. This is considered a basic human characteristic and is primarily a matter of finding satisfying values and guiding one's life by them. As we have noted, this is a difficult and highly individual matter, for the values that give one life meaning may be quite different from those that provide meaning for another. Each of us must find his or her own pattern of values.

This emphasis on individual value patterns, however, is not to be construed as moral nihilism. For there is a basic unity in humankind, and all people are faced with the task of learning to live constructively with themselves and others. Hence, there will be an underlying continuity in the value patterns chosen by different individuals who are trying to live authentically.

Existentialism also places strong emphasis on our *obligations* to each other. The most important consideration is not what we can get out of life but what we can contribute to it. Our lives can be fulfilling only if they involve socially constructive values and choices.

4. *Existential anxiety and the encounter with nothingness.* A final existential theme that adds an urgent and painful note to the human situation is that of *nonbeing* or *nothingness.* In ultimate form it is death, which is the inescapable fate of all human beings.

This encounter with nothingness is unique to human beings: we are the only creatures who live with the constant awareness of the possibility of nonbeing. At each moment, we make our way along the sharp edge of possible annihilation; we can never escape the fact that death will come sometime, somewhere. This awareness is essential for a full grasp of what it means to *be;* it adds a crucial dimension to our existence and immediate experiencing. It is this awareness of our inevitable death and its implications for our living that can lead to *existential anxiety*—to deep concern over whether we are living a meaningful and fulfilling life.

We can overcome our existential anxiety and deny victory to nothingness by living a life that counts for something, that should not be lost. If we are perishable, we can at least perish resisting—living in such a way that nothingness will be an unjust fate.

Impact on our views of psychopathology. Existentialists are very much concerned with the social predicament of modern human beings. They emphasize the weakening of traditional values and the crisis of faith; the depersonalization of the individual in our bureaucratic mass society; and the loss of meaning for many of us. They see us as alienated and estranged—strangers to God, to other human beings, and to ourselves; they view the social context of contemporary life as pushing us toward an awareness of our empty existence, to existential anxiety, and to psychopathology.

Thus the primary focus of the existential therapist is to help the individual clarify his or her values and work out a meaningful way of "being-in-the-world." In this therapy, the individual is assumed to be capable of rational, responsible choice.

From a broad perspective, the major impact of both humanistic and existential perspectives on our views of psychopathology has been their emphasis on our capacity for full functioning as human beings. "Abnormality" is seen as a failure to develop sufficiently our tremendous potentials as human beings, and therapy is not just to move the individual from maladjustment to adjustment but to foster personal growth toward a socially constructive and personally fulfilling way of life.

The existential approach has been severely criticized for its lack of scientific grounding and its reliance on the unique experience of the individual in attempting to understand and deal with maladaptive behavior. It is, of course, flatly in contradiction to the view of the behaviorists that our behavior is determined and choice an illusion. Nevertheless, many of the concepts of the existential perspective—such as freedom, choice, courage, values, meaning, obligation, authenticity, nonbeing, and existential anxiety—have had a profound impact on contemporary thought.

The interpersonal perspective

We are social beings, and many of our problems grow out of our relationships with other people.

As yet, however, there is no systematic view of human nature and behavior based entirely on interpersonal relationships or the social context in which human beings function. Perhaps the closest approximation is the interpersonal viewpoint developed by the psychiatrist Harry Stack Sullivan (1953) and elaborated on by many later psychiatrists, psychologists, and sociologists.[4]

Basic principles of the interpersonal perspective. While the interpersonal perspective is not highly systematized, there are certain principles and concepts that are heavily emphasized. Among the most important of these are the following:

1. *Interpersonal relationships and personality development.* According to Sullivan, one's personality development proceeds through various stages involving different patterns of interpersonal relationships. At first, for example, interactions are mainly with parents, who begin the socialization of the child. Later, with a gradual emancipation from parents, peer relationships become increasingly important; and in young adulthood, intimate relationships are established, culminating typically in marriage. Failure to progress satisfactorily through the various stages of development paves the way for later maladaptive behavior.

In this developmental context, Sullivan was intensely concerned with the anxiety-arousing aspects of interpersonal relationships during early development. Since the infant is completely dependent on "significant others" (e.g., parents and siblings) for meeting all physical and psychological needs, lack of love and care lead to an insecure and anxious human being. Sullivan emphasized the role of early childhood relationships in shaping the self-concept, which he saw as constructed largely out of the reflected appraisals of significant others. For example, if a little girl perceives others as rejecting her or treating her as being of little or no worth, she is likely to view herself in a similar light and to develop a negative self-image

---

[4]It may be noted that G. H. Mead—whose *Mind, Self, and Society* was published in 1934—was an early pioneer in focusing attention on such concepts as communication, social roles, and interpersonal relationships in human behavior.

According to the interpersonal perspective, individuals have certain obligations, rights, duties, and so forth associated with the social roles they play. Often these role expectations are reciprocal, as in the case of a child's right to be comforted when hurt and a mother's obligation to provide comfort and affection.

that almost inevitably leads to maladjustment.

The pressures of the socialization process and the continual appraisal by others lead a child to label some personal tendencies as the "good-me" and others as the "bad-me." It is the "bad-me" that is associated with anxiety. With time, the individual develops a *self-system* that serves to protect him or her from such anxiety through the use of ego-defense mechanisms. Often, if an anxiety-arousing tendency is too severe, the individual perceives it as the "not-me," totally screening it out of consciousness or even attributing it to someone else. However, such actions lead to an incongruity between the individual's perceptions and the world as it really is, and may therefore result in maladaptive behavior. Here we can readily see a similarity between Sullivan's views and those of both Freud and Rogers.

2. *Social exchange, roles, and games.* Three ways of viewing our relationships with other people are helpful in understanding both satisfying and hurtful interactions.

The *social-exchange* view, developed largely by Thibaut and Kelley (1959) and Homans (1961), is based on the premise that we form relationships with each other for the purpose of satisfying our needs. Each person in the relationship wants something from the other, and the exchange that results is essentially a trading or bargaining one. When we feel that we have entered into a bad bargain—that the rewards are not worth the costs—we may attempt to work out some compromise or simply terminate the relationship.

A second way of viewing interpersonal relationships is in terms of social *roles*. Society prescribes role behavior for teachers, generals, and others occupying given positions designed to facilitate the functioning of the group. While each individual lends a personal interpretation to the role, there are usually limits to the "script," beyond which a person in a given role is not expected to go. Similarly, in intimate personal relationships, each person holds certain role expectations—in terms of obligations, rights, duties, and so on—that the other person in the relationship is expected to meet. If one spouse fails to live up to the other's role expectations or finds them uncomfortable, or if husband and wife have different conceptions of what a "wife" or "husband" should be or do, serious complications in the relationship are likely to occur.

Another view of interpersonal relationships focuses on the "games people play." Eric Berne (1964, 1972) has pointed out that such games are not consciously planned but rather involve a sort of role playing of which the persons are either entirely or partially unaware. For example, a woman who lacks self-confidence may marry a man who is very domineering and then complain that she could do all sorts of outstanding things "if it weren't for you."

Such games presumably serve two useful functions: (a) as substitutes for or defenses against true intimacy in daily life, intimacy for which many people are unprepared; and (b) as stabilizers to help maintain a relationship. But they are likely to prove a poor substitute for a more honest relationship. Though called "games" in the sense of being ploys, they are often deadly serious.

3. *Causal attribution in interpersonal relations.* A comparatively recent development in the interpersonal approach is that of *attribution theory*. All we actually see is a series of events, but we often interpret one event as having been "caused" by some earlier event. Sometimes we attribute these "causes" to something in the environment, such as rewards or punishments, and sometimes we assume traits or "dispositions" in other people or in ourselves to account for the behavior that takes place. These dispositions and other causes are not seen but are just assumed to exist, as underlying realities. Assuming them helps us explain consistency in people's behavior and makes it possible to predict what we and others are likely to do in the future.

For example, if a person does something mean, we may assume that he or she has a quality of "meanness" and expect it to cause mean behavior in the future. Or if we do something stupid, we may attribute stupidity to ourselves as a trait in our personality. On the other hand, if we see ourselves as simply conforming to some stupid regulation that has to be followed to get credit for a course, we would view our behavior as caused by the environment and not indicating anything about our own qualities. Theories about this tendency to attribute causes to behavior, including unseen qualities in ourselves or others, are called *attribution theories* (Bem, 1972; Brehm, 1976; Heider, 1958; Jones & Davis, 1965).

According to attribution theorists, the attributions we make are important in our relationships with others because they form the basis for continuing *evaluations* and *expectations*. However inaccurate they may be, they become important parts of our picture of the world and tend to become self-fulfilling prophecies. Also, they tend to make us see other people and ourselves as unchanging and unchangeable, leading us to fall into unnecessary "ruts" in our relationships with one another.

4. *Communication and interpersonal accommodation.* Interpersonal accommodation is the process whereby two persons evolve patterns of communication and interaction that enable them to attain common goals, meet mutual needs, and build a satisfying relationship.

People communicate in many verbal and nonverbal ways, and the individuals in a relationship use many cues in their attempts to interpret what is really being said to them. Sullivan believed that faulty communication is far more common than most people realize, especially in family interactions on an emotional level.

If individuals in a close relationship have a tangle of unresolved misunderstandings and conflicts, they will probably have trouble communicating clearly and openly with each other. In fact, the final phase of a failing marriage is often marked by almost complete inability of the partners to communicate.

In addition to establishing and maintaining effective communication, interpersonal accommodation involves meeting a number of other adjustive demands, such as establishing mutually satisfying role relationships, resolving disagreements constructively, and dealing adequately with external demands that can markedly affect the relationship. Sullivan thought that interpersonal accommodation is facilitated when the motives of the persons in the relationship are complementary, as when both persons are strongly motivated to give and receive affection. When interpersonal accommodation fails and the relationship does not meet the needs of one or both partners, it is likely to be characterized by conflict and dissension, and eventually to be ended.

In Chapter 5, we shall examine some disordered interpersonal relationships and pathogenic family patterns and observe the detrimental effects on the individuals involved. In fact, it has been shown that certain social contexts can literally drive an individual "crazy," while others can be "disorder reducing" or therapeutic in their effects.

Impact on our views of psychopathology. The interpersonal perspective places strong emphasis on unsatisfactory interpersonal relationships as the primary causal factor in many forms of maladaptive behavior. Such relationships may extend back to childhood, as when a boy's self-concept was distorted by parents who evaluated him as worthless or by rigid socialization measures that made it difficult to accept and integrate the "bad-me" into his self-concept. Poor interpersonal relationships may also result from self-defeating "games" that individuals learn to play, or from uncomfortable roles they are given, or from faulty assumptions about the causes of their own or others' behavior. In any case, it is the individual's current interpersonal relationships and their effects on behavior that are of primary concern in the interpersonal perspective.

The focus of interpersonal therapy is on the alleviation of current pathogenic, or problem-causing, relationships and on helping the individual achieve more satisfactory relationships. Such therapy is concerned with verbal and nonverbal communication, social roles, processes of accommodation, the client's causal attributions, especially self-attributions, and the general interpersonal context of behavior. And, as might be expected, emphasis is placed on the use of the therapy situation itself as a vehicle for new learning of interpersonal skills.

In common with the several other approaches described, the interpersonal approach is handicapped by incomplete information concerning most aspects of interpersonal relationships. As a result, many of Sullivan's concepts and those of later investigators lack adequate scientific grounding. Despite such limitations, however, the interpersonal perspective has served to focus attention on the quality of the individual's close personal relationships as a key factor in determining whether behavior will be effective or maladaptive.

In reviewing these psychosocial perspectives regarding human behavior—psychoanalytic, behavioristic, humanistic, existential, and interpersonal—we have seen that each contributes to our understanding of psychopathology, but that none alone seems to account for all the complex types of maladaptive behavior exhibited by human beings. Each has a substantial amount of research evidence to support it, yet each one also depends on generalizations from limited kinds of events and observations. In attempting to explain a complex disorder such as schizophrenia, for example, the behavioristic perspective focuses on faulty learning and on environmental conditions that may exacerbate or maintain such maladaptive behavior, while the humanistic perspective focuses on problems the individual has had relating to values, meaning, and personal growth.

Thus it becomes apparent that adopting one perspective or another has important consequences: it influences our perception of maladaptive behavior as well as the types of evidence we look for and how we are likely to interpret the data. In later chapters we shall utilize concepts from all these viewpoints when they seem relevant, and in many instances we shall find it useful to contrast different ways of explaining and treating the same behavior.

Emergence of the sociocultural viewpoint

By the beginning of the twentieth century, sociology and anthropology had emerged as independent scientific disciplines and were making rapid strides toward understanding the role of sociocultural factors in human development and behavior.[5] Soon it became apparent that

---

[5]Prominent early contributors to this field were Ruth Benedict, Ralph Linton, Abram Kardiner, Margaret Mead, and Franz Boas.

human beings are almost infinitely malleable and that personality development reflects the larger society—its institutions, norms, values, ideas, and technology—as well as the immediate family and other interpersonal relationships to which individuals are exposed. Eventually, too, it became clear that a relationship exists between sociocultural conditions and mental disorders—for example, between the particular stressors in a society and the frequency and types of mental disorders that occur in it. And it was also observed that the patterns of both physical and mental disorders in a given society may change over time as sociocultural conditions change. These sociocultural discoveries have added another dimension to modern thinking concerning abnormal behavior.

Changing interpretations of anthropological findings

The relationships between sociocultural factors such as poverty, discrimination, or illiteracy and maladaptive behavior during childhood or adulthood are complex. It is one thing to observe that some individuals who fall victim to psychological disorders have come from harsh environmental circumstances. However, it is quite difficult to show empirically and unequivocally that these circumstances were both *necessary* and *sufficient* conditions for producing the later disorder.

Evidence that sociocultural factors influence personality adaptation or result in particular abnormal disorders is suggestive at best. It is virtually impossible to conduct controlled experiments. Both economic and ethical restraints prevent investigators from rearing children with similar genetic or biological endowments in diverse social or economic environments in order to find out which variables, if any, played a part in the individuals' later adjustment.

However, natural occurrences in human history have provided a laboratory for the researcher. Groups of human beings have in fact been exposed to very different environments, from the Arctic to the tropics to the deserts. Human societies have developed different means for economic subsistence and different types of family structures for propagating and

maintaining the species under different and often adverse conditions. Human groups have evolved highly diverse social and political systems. It seems that nature has indeed done the social scientists a great favor by providing such a wide array of human groups for study.

Yet the investigator who attempts to conduct cross-cultural research is plagued by numerous technological and methodological problems, such as (a) different language and thought systems; (b) political and cultural climates that prevent objective inquiry; (c) difficulties in finding appropriately trained local scientists to collaborate in the research and prevent the ethnocentric attitudes or values of "outsiders" from distorting the findings; and (d) high costs of large-scale cross-cultural research.

In the earliest cross-cultural studies, Western-trained anthropologists made observations of the behavior of "natives" and considered those behaviors in the context of Western scientific thought. One of the earliest attempts at applying Western-based concepts in other cultures is the classic study of Malinowski (1927), *Sex and Repression in Savage Society*. In this work he attempted to explain the behavior of "savages" using the then dominant psychoanalytic perspective. But Malinowski found little evidence among the Trobriand Islanders of any Oedipal conflict, as described by Freud. He concluded that the sexually based behavior of psychoanalytic theory was not universal but was rather a product of the patriarchal family in Western society.

Shortly thereafter, Ruth Benedict (1934) pointed out that even the Western definition of "abnormality" might not be applicable to behavior in other cultures. Citing various ethnographic reports, she indicated that what is considered abnormal in one society is sometimes considered normal in another. For example, she noted that cataleptic and trancelike states were often valued by "simpler" peoples. Thus she concluded that "normality" is simply a culturally defined concept.

Early research also yielded evidence that some types of abnormal behavior occurred only in certain cultures. (See HIGHLIGHT on page 77.) These and other early anthropological findings led many investigators to take a position of *cultural relativism* concerning abnormal behavior. According to this view, as we saw in Chatper 1, there are no universal standards of

Unusual patterns of behavior considered to be culture-bound disorders

Name of disorder	Culture	Description
Amok	Malaya (also observed in Java, Philippines, Africa, and Tierra del Fuego)	A disorder characterized by sudden, wild outbursts of homicidal aggression in which the afflicted person may kill or injure others. The rage disorder is usually found in males who are rather withdrawn, quiet, and inoffensive prior to the onset of the disorder. Stress, sleep deprivation, extreme heat, and alcohol are among the conditions thought to precipitate the disorder. Several stages have been observed: typically in the first stage the person becomes more withdrawn; then a period of brooding follows in which a loss of reality contact is evident. Ideas of persecution and anger predominate. Finally, a phase of automatism or *Amok* occurs, in which the person jumps up, yells, grabs a knife, and stabs people or objects within reach. Exhaustion and depression usually follow, with complete amnesia for the rage.
Latah	Malay	A fear reaction often occurring in middle-aged women of low intelligence who are subservient and self-effacing. The disorder is precipitated by the word *snake* or by tickling. It is characterized by *echolalia* (repetition of the words and sentences of others) and *echopraxia* (repetition of the acts of others). The disturbed individual may also react with negativism and the compulsive use of obscene language.
Koro	Southeast Asia (particularly Malay Archipelago)	A fear reaction or anxiety state in which the person fears that his penis will withdraw into his abdomen and he will die. This reaction may appear after sexual overindulgence or excessive masturbation. The anxiety is typically very intense and of sudden onset. The condition is "treated" by having the penis held firmly by the patient or by family members or friends. Often the penis is clamped to a wooden box.
Windigo	Algonquin Indian hunters	A fear reaction in which a hunter becomes anxious and agitated, convinced that he is bewitched. Fears center around his being turned into a cannibal by the power of a monster with an insatiable craving for human flesh.
Kitsunetsuki	Japan	A disorder in which victims believe that they are possessed by foxes and are said to change their facial expressions to resemble foxes. Entire families are often possessed and banned by the broader community. This reaction occurs in certain rural areas of Japan where people are superstitious and relatively uneducated.

Based on Kiev (1972), Lehmann (1967), Lebra (1976), and Yap (1951).

Margaret Mead, *1901–1978, the world-famous anthropologist, spent years studying other societies and amassing cross-cultural data. She contributed greatly to our understanding of variations in individual and group behavior patterns—both normal and abnormal. Here she is pictured meeting with schoolchildren in New Guinea.*

"normality" or "abnormality" that can be applied to all societies. In fact, there was for a time a tendency to accept the "anthropologist's veto": any general principle could be rejected if a contrary instance somewhere in the world could be demonstrated. For example, schizophrenia would no longer be viewed as abnormal if its symptoms were somewhere accepted as a normal behavior pattern.

The relativistic view of abnormal behavior is no longer widely held (Strauss, 1979). Instead, it is generally recognized that the more severe types of mental disorder delineated in Western society are, in fact, found and considered maladaptive among peoples throughout the world. Recent research in transcultural psychiatry supports the view that many psychological disturbances are "universal," appearing in most cultures studied (Cooper et al., 1972; Murphy, 1976; World Health Organization, 1973).

For example, although the relative incidence and specific symptoms vary, schizophrenia can probably be found among all peoples, from the most primitive to the most technologically advanced. When individuals become so mentally disordered that they can no longer control their behavior, perform their expected role in the group, or even survive without the special care of others, their behavior is considered abnormal in any society.

However, cultural influences cannot be disregarded. While there appear to be "universals," there is also great reason to believe that cultural factors are very influential in what disorder develops, in the form that it takes, and in its course. How the disordered individual is received and treated and what is expected can influence whether the individual recovers or develops a chronic disorder (Murphy & Hall, 1972).

The importance of cultural influences on the way psychological disorders are expressed has been illustrated in a comparison of psychiatric patients from Italy, Switzerland, and the United States carried out by Butcher and Pancheri (1976). Patients grouped according to diagnostic category produced very similar general personality patterns on the Minnesota Multiphasic Personality Inventory (MMPI, see Chapter 17), but the Italian patients also showed an exaggerated pattern of physical complaints that differentiated them from both the Swiss and American patients, regardless of clinical diagnosis.

This finding was consistent with earlier work by Opler and Singer (1959) and Zola (1966). For example, Zola examined symptom expression in two samples of second-generation American patients (Italian and Irish) at an ear-nose-throat clinic in Boston. When patients were matched on the basis of actual physical disorder, Zola found that the Italian patients made more physical complaints than the Irish. He attributed this difference to a defense mechanism which he called *dramatization*, in which the Italian patients, once identified as ill, tended to exaggerate or dramatize their physical problems to a greater extent than the other patients.

These findings illustrate an important point—the need for greater study of cultural influences on psychopathology. This neglected area of research may yet answer many questions about the origin and course of behavior problems (Draguns, 1979; Marsella, 1979). In a shrinking world, with instant communication and easy transportation, it is of utmost importance for our science and our professional crafts to reflect a world view.

Sociocultural influences in our own society

As we narrow our focus to our own society, we find a number of early studies dealing with the relation of social class and other subgroup factors to the nature and incidence of mental disorders. For example, in a pioneering 1939 study, Faris and Dunham found that a disproportionate number of the schizophrenics ad-

mitted to mental hospitals came from the lower socioeconomic areas of a large city. The rate of admission decreased with distance of residence from these disorganized and deteriorating sections of the city. Studies since then have consistently found a relationship between social class and psychopathology (Dohrenwend & Dohrenwend, 1974).

Early studies concerning social class were gradually augmented by studies dealing with urban-rural, ethnic, religious, occupational, and other subgroups in relation to mental disorders. In one of these—an extensive study of mental disorders in Texas—Jaco (1960) found the incidence of psychoses to be three times higher in urban than in rural areas, and higher among the divorced and separated than among the married or widowed. And in a more recent study by Levy and Rowitz (1974), the highest rates of mental disorders were found in the areas of large cities that were undergoing rapid and drastic social change.

The study of the incidence and distribution of physical and mental disorders in a population, as in the research just cited, is referred to as *epidemiology*. The epidemiological approach serves to indicate both the social conditions that are correlated with a high incidence of given disorders and the "high-risk" areas and groups—those for whom the risk of pathology is especially high. In our later discussion we shall point out high-risk groups with respect to heart attacks, suicide, drug dependence, and other maladaptive patterns of behavior in our society.

This information provides a basis for formulating prevention and treatment programs; in turn, the effectiveness of these programs can be evaluated by means of further epidemiological studies.

Social pathology and community mental health

With the gradual recognition of sociocultural influences, the heretofore almost exclusive concern with the individual patient broadened to include a concern with societal, communal, familial, and other group settings as contributors to mental disorders. It had become apparent that an individual's maladaptive behavior might be caused not by faulty internal processes but by abnormal conditions in the surrounding social environment. As Lennard and Bernstein (1969) put it, "Therapeutic or damaging potentials often inhere in social contexts rather than in individuals . . ." (p. 205).

This concept has led to the community mental health movement, which calls for an assessment of the sociocultural environment as well as of the individual for an understanding of the causation, best treatment, and possible prevention of mental disorders. Smith (1968) has referred to the community mental health movement as "the third mental health revolution."

"The first mental-health revolution unshackled the insane. By calling them sick, it managed to treat them as human. Its monuments and symbols are the great, usually isolated, state mental hospitals. The second revolution came from the spread of dynamic psychiatry (mainly Freud's) and was characterized by individual, one-to-one psychotherapy. Now the third revolution throws off the constraints of the doctor-patient medical model—the idea that mental disorder is a private misery—and relates the trouble, and the cure, to the entire web of social and personal relationships in which the individual is caught." (p. 19)

The sociocultural viewpoint has led to the introduction of programs designed to alleviate social conditions that foster maladaptive behavior and to the provision of community facilities for the early detection, treatment, and long-range prevention of mental disorders. We shall deal with the clinic facilities and other programs—both governmental and private—that have been established as a result of the community mental health movement in later chapters.

Toward an interdisciplinary approach

As the research engendered by the biological, psychosocial, and sociocultural perspectives gradually led to a better understanding of the role of all these factors in mental disorders, it became increasingly apparent that explanation based on only one of the three levels was likely to be incomplete. Usually, interaction of several causal factors produces the disorders that we see. For example, an individual may have a biological predisposition to severe mood swings but may be getting along satisfactorily until some severe crisis brings on a depressive state.

Even in the mental disorder *paresis* (see Chapter 2), it was observed that some patients became depressed and others expansive and happy with approximately the same brain pathology. Similarly, in psychoses associated with senile and arteriosclerotic brain damage, researchers found that some patients became severely disordered mentally with only a small amount of brain damage, whereas others showed only mild symptoms despite relatively extensive brain damage.

Gradually investigators came to realize that even where brain damage was present, the patient's psychological reaction to it and to the resulting change in his or her life situation were of vital importance in determining the overall clinical picture. It also became apparent that the emotional support of family members—as well as the kind of situation to which the patient would be returning after discharge from the hospital—were significant factors in determining the *prognosis*, that is, the likelihood that the patient would improve. On the other hand, in certain functional psychoses in which the patient's disorder was apparently the result of psychological rather than organic factors, it was nevertheless found that the use of organic therapies—such as antidepressant drugs or electroconvulsive shock—produced dramatic results. And finally, the symptoms, prognosis, and reaction to a given treatment might all vary somewhat for individuals from different cultural backgrounds.

Such considerations have led to the emergence of the *interdisciplinary* approach, which calls for the integration of biological, psychosocial, and sociocultural factors into a comprehensive clinical picture. In dealing with a particular case, of course, we may be concerned primarily with one set of determinants or another. For example, one case of

Nahenba tribesman, Zaire

Is "abnormality" in the eye of the beholder?

Throughout history, most people's knowledge of human behavior has been limited to the behavior of their own cultural group—past or present—or that of near neighbors. We live in the first age in which people in all parts of the world have access to knowledge about each other. It was only about a hundred years ago that Western anthropologists began to bring home pictures and stories of the dress and customs of far-away peoples, and the first reaction of Westerners was to see these people as colorful, outlandish, backward, and often incomprehensible.

It is all too easy to regard one's own ways as "normal"—also moral, rational, and superior—and to see different values and customs as inferior and "abnormal." But what seems strange is in large part a matter of what you happen to be used to. Our ways can seem as strange to others as their ways do to us.

Participant in Democratic Convention, 1976, USA

Veiled women, Morocco

Cheerleader clinic, USA

Arab men greeting each other, France

Awareness of the striking differences in values and customs in different parts of the world led many people to see all values as relative—an accident of time and place—and no value as possessing any universal validity. A deeper look, however, reveals that behind the diversity of detail, many universal values and strivings are expressed, such as the need for meaning and predictability, the search for beauty and self-enhancement, the prizing of love and belonging, the enjoyment of chances to demonstrate skill and competence, and the effort to prepare the young for responsible participation in the society. These needs are met in different ways in different cultures, but if they are not met, individual and social disorientation result.

Members of all groups strive for beauty—however different their ideas of what is beautiful.

Body painting, Brazil

Man, Bali

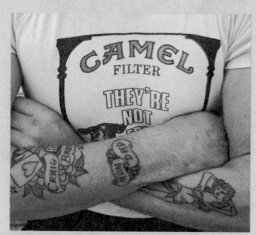

Tattooing, Australia

Woman at cosmetics counter, USA

Woman, India

Asaro mudmen, New Guinea

All groups tend to develop ritual behaviors with meaning for the group—however different the behaviors and the meanings they express.

Bagpipers, Canada

Tribal dance, Bali

Members of all groups enjoy contests of strength and skill according to a set of rules—however different the form of the contest and the rules agreed on.

Rugby game, Korea

Boxing, Thailand

Frog-jumping contest, USA

One result of our new knowledge of each others' ways has been an intermingling of values and customs—a borrowing from each other. Often the interpenetration of cultures creates strains and insecurities as people find old certainties challenged and have unfamiliar demands made on them. Some try to hold onto old ways that have proved sound; others welcome the new just because it is new, regardless of whether it will enrich their lives. In our own society, more open than most to competing ideas, many inconsistent ideas vie for public acceptance.

Amish farm family, USA

Western young people, Eastern meditation, USA

Surveying, Nigeria

Mother and child at Ku Klux Klan event, USA

homicidal behavior may be closely associated with drug intoxication, another with pent-up frustration and hostility, and still another with the learning of criminal values in a faulty environment. Thus the problem becomes one of assessing and dealing with the particular interaction of these three sets of determinants—biological, psychosocial, and sociocultural—in each particular case.

The interdisciplinary approach has led to the integration of research findings from such varied disciplines as genetics, biochemistry, neurophysiology, psychology, sociology, anthropology, and ecology in efforts to understand and cope with abnormal behavior. On a practical level, it has led to the meaningful coordination of medical, psychological, and other mental health personnel in the work to assess, treat, and prevent mental disorders. It has become increasingly apparent to workers in these fields that maladaptive behavior can be fully understood and effectively dealt with only in this comprehensive way.

In this chapter we have reviewed the development of (a) the psychosocial perspectives—psychoanalytic, behavioristic, humanistic, existential, and interpersonal viewpoints; (b) the sociocultural approach, including cross-cultural studies, epidemiological studies, and a recognition of the significance of social pathology and community mental health; and (c) the interdisciplinary approach, integrating the biological, psychosocial, and sociocultural viewpoints into a more comprehensive view of human behavior.

In our review we have seen that no one viewpoint seems to account for the myriad types of maladaptive behaviors exhibited by human beings. In dealing with particular types of disorders or specific cases, we may find one or another approach most useful. In general, however, we need to assess and deal with the interaction of biological, psychosocial, and sociocultural factors involved in the total clinical picture.

4

Personality development and adjustment: An overview

The determinants of development
The patterning of development
Motivation: Human needs and strivings
Adjustive demands and stress
Reactions to life stress

Why are some people alcoholics and others teetotalers, some criminals and others law-abiding citizens, some schizophrenics and others happy and productive individuals? Why are some children autistic and others open and loving, some runaways and others adjusted to their home situations? The task of trying to explain such variations in behavior necessarily begins with a consideration of the broad principles underlying human development and functioning.[1]

Our initial focus in this chapter will be on the developmental process itself. We shall consider not only the basic determinants of development—the individual's genetic endowment, environment, and emerging self-structure—but also the general patterning of development. Here we shall note the orderly sequencing and cumulative nature of the growth process, and the interplay of maturation and learning in producing both likenesses and differences among individuals.

Turning next to adjustment and human behavior, we shall consider the key role of motivation in directing the individual's actions toward the satisfaction of basic needs and strivings; the kinds of adjustive demands that commonly interfere with efforts to achieve need satisfaction; and the behavior patterns that may be brought into play as the individual attempts to cope with such demands.

We shall see that the biological and psychological characteristics that become part of each individual during the process of development are basic resources for coping with each new adjustive demand. We shall also see that the social environment—the groups and subgroups each individual belongs to—as well as the physical environment, influence the way these resources are used. With both normal and abnormal behavior, we are dealing with an interaction of inner and outer determinants and of biological, psychological, and sociocultural factors.

---

[1]This chapter is intended as an overview of the basic principles of personality development and adjustment based on well-established research findings. Although we have represented research from investigators adhering to each of the perspectives of human behavior discussed in Chapter 3, a sizeable portion of the research findings stem from scientists who owe allegiance to no particular perspective but take an eclectic view—as we have done in this text.

The determinants of development

The basic sources of personality development are heredity and environment. However, as a person's genetic inheritance interacts with and is shaped by environmental factors, a self-structure emerges that becomes an important influence in shaping further development and behavior.

Heredity

Although there are millions of different kinds of plants and animals on our planet, each kind breeds true. Oak trees have acorns that grow into more oak trees and never into elms; deer give birth to fawns and never to lambs. It thus becomes apparent that each type of living thing transmits specific hereditary information from one generation to the next. With the breaking of the genetic code, we have learned a great deal about this genetic information: how it is transmitted and how it operates in guiding our development. Nevertheless, many mysteries remain.

At conception—when the egg cell of the female is fertilized by the sperm cell of the male—each new human being receives a *genetic inheritance* that provides potentialities for development and behavior throughout a lifetime. This inheritance influences the development of some traits more than others. Its influence is perhaps most noticeable in physical features, such as eye color and physique, but it also appears to play an influential role in "primary reaction tendencies," such as activity level, sensitivity to stimuli, and adaptability.

Even very young babies differ in their reactions to particular kinds of stimuli. Some are startled at even slight sounds, or cry if sunlight hits their faces; others are seemingly insensitive to such stimulation. Thus, conditions that one baby can tolerate may be quite upsetting to another. Longitudinal (long-term) studies have shown that these reaction tendencies are rela-

The family of composer Johann Sebastian Bach, which produced several famous musicians and composers, would seem to support the role heredity plays in development. However, it might also be significant that Bach's children were exposed to music daily and trained in music from an early age.

tively enduring from infancy to young adulthood.

These primary reaction tendencies are regarded as constitutional rather than genetic characteristics, since prenatal environmental factors may also play a role in their development. The term *constitutional* is used to describe any characteristic that is either innate or acquired so early and in such strength that it is functionally similar to a genetically determined characteristic.

Genetic and constitutional differences help explain why individuals exposed to similar environments may react and develop in highly diverse ways. More directly pertinent to abnormal behavior, either genetic or constitutional influences may create specific vulnerabilities, or *predispositions,* to certain types of stress, significantly increasing the likelihood that a child will experience some particular form of behavior disorder later in life.

While characteristics determined by heredity may influence how we respond to our environment, they may also help *create* the environmental conditions to which we are exposed. For example, being declared either a boy or a girl can have profound effects on a child. Such a decision (not always a clear-cut one or even genetically accurate as we shall see in Chapter 15) unleashes an enormously complex array of forces in interpersonal contacts with parents and others that usually creates an environment

designed to ensure that the child will develop an "appropriate" gender identity. Another example is the attractiveness or unattractiveness of one's features, also largely determined by heredity, and also giving rise to widespread and important variations in the environments that different infants encounter.

Probably the most unique aspect of our human inheritance is a superior brain. It has been described as the most highly organized apparatus in the universe, consisting of some ten billion nerve cells, or neurons, with countless interconnecting pathways as well as myriad connections with other parts of the body. The human brain provides a fantastic communication and computing network with tremendous capabilities for learning and "storing" experience; for reasoning, imagining, and problem solving; and for integrating the overall functioning of the organism. It is the brain that makes possible the enormous adaptability of the human species to varied and changing conditions of existence, but it often does so at a price—a price being paid by those unfortunate persons who are the subject matter of abnormal psychology. The nervous systems of lower organisms are not nearly so flexibly adaptive, but by the same token they are much less likely to go awry or lead to behavior that is ultimately self-injurious.

It would appear that the essential characteristics of human inheritance are basically the same for persons of all racial and ethnic groups. However, the specific features of this endowment vary widely: except for identical twins, no two human beings have ever begun life with the same genetic endowment. Thus heredity not only provides the potentialities for development and behavior typical of the species but also is an important source of individual differences.

Environment

In much the same sense that we receive a genetic inheritance that is the end product of millions of years of biological evolution, we also receive a sociocultural inheritance that is the end product of many thousands of years of social evolution—the significance of which was well pointed up by Huxley (1965):

"The native or genetic capacities of today's bright city child are no better than the native capacities of a bright child born into a family of Upper Paleolithic cave-dwellers. But whereas the contemporary bright baby may grow up to become almost anything—a Presbyterian engineer, for example, a piano-playing Marxist, a professor of biochemistry who is a mystical agnostic and likes to paint in water colours—the paleolithic baby could not possibly have grown into anything except a hunter or food-gatherer, using the crudest of stone tools and thinking about his narrow world of trees and swamps in terms of some hazy system of magic. Ancient and modern, the two babies are indistinguishable. . . . But the adults into whom the babies will grow are profoundly dissimilar; and they are dissimilar because in one of them very few, and in the other a good many, of the baby's inborn potentialities have been actualized." (p. 69)

Because each group fosters its own cultural patterns by systematically teaching its offspring, all its members tend to be somewhat alike—to conform to certain "basic personality types." Individuals reared among headhunters become headhunters; individuals reared in societies that do not sanction violence learn to settle their differences in nonviolent ways. In New Guinea, for example, Mead (1949) found two tribes—of similar racial origin and living in the same general geographical area—whose members developed diametrically opposed characteristics. The Arapesh were a kindly, peaceful, cooperative people, while the Mundugumor were warlike, suspicious, competi-

tive, and vengeful. Such differences appear to be social in origin.

The more uniform and thorough the education of the younger members of a group, the more alike they will become. Thus in a society characterized by a limited and consistent point of view, there are not the wide individual differences typical of a society like ours, where children have contact with many diverse, often conflicting, beliefs. Even in our society, however, there are certain core values that we attempt to perpetuate as essential to our way of life.

Subgroups within a general sociocultural environment—such as family, sex, age, social class, occupational, and religious groups—also foster beliefs and norms of their own, largely by means of *social roles* that their members learn to adopt. Expected role behaviors exist for the student, the teacher, the army officer, the priest, the nurse, and persons occupying other specific positions. The extent to which role expectations can influence development is well illustrated by the assignment of sex roles among the Tchambuli, another New Guinea tribe studied by Mead (1949). In this tribe, women earn the living, handle business transactions, take the initiative in courtship, and head the family in general—while men are expected to be coquettish, prone to gossip, interested in dancing and theatricals, and good at housekeeping. Obviously the sex roles among the Tchambuli, while very unusual on a worldwide scale, tend to channel personality development along lines quite different from those encouraged in our society.

The individual, being a member of various subgroups, is subject to various role demands. And, of course, social roles change as group memberships—or position in a given group—change. In fact, the life of the individual can be viewed as consisting of a succession of roles—child, student, worker, husband or wife, parent, and senior citizen. The various groups may allow the individual considerable leeway in role behavior, but there are limits. Conformity to role demands is induced by the use of positive and negative reinforcers—money, prestige, status, punishment, or loss of membership in the group—as well as through instruction. When social roles are conflicting, unclear, or uncomfortable, or when an individual is unable to achieve a satisfactory role in the group, personality development and adjustment may be impaired.

Each individual interacts with various other persons, typically beginning with family members and gradually extending to peer group members and other significant persons in his or her world. Much of an individual's personality development reflects experiences with these key people. For example, the child who is rejected and mistreated is likely to develop quite differently from one who is accepted and encouraged. Similarly, relationships in a Boy Scout troop will likely have effects on development quite different from relationships in a delinquent gang. The behavior patterns children learn depend heavily on what models they observe, whose expectations they are trying to meet, and what rewards are forthcoming for what behavior.

Since each of us belongs to different subgroups and experiences different interpersonal relationships, we each participate in the sociocultural environment in a unique way. As a consequence of such "differential participation," no two of us grow up in quite the same world. Thus the sociocultural environment, too, is a source of differences as well as commonalities in human development.

In discussing environment and its effects in shaping development, it is important to note the effects of the physical as well as the sociocultural environment. Each physical setting is unique in the particular pattern of favorable and unfavorable conditions it provides and in the special demands it makes on the organisms living within it. As a result, different physical environments may foster somewhat different personality characteristics.

In summary so far, we may say that our genetic endowment provides our potentialities for both biological and psychological development, but the shaping of these potentialities—how we come to perceive, think, feel, and act—depends heavily on our physical and sociocultural environment.

Self as a third determinant

As the infant grows and learns to distinguish between self and nonself, a part of the total

This child's growing sense of and delight with herself will become an important determinant in her further development.

perceptual field is gradually delineated as the "me," "I," or "self." As this self-structure develops, it becomes the integrating core of the personality—the reference point around which the individual's experiences and coping patterns are organized. Problems that arise are perceived, thought about, and acted upon in relation to the self;[2] that is, the individual comes to perceive the self as an active agent in determining his or her own behavior—as indicated by such statements as "I know," "I want," and "I will." In essence, the experience of self-direction involves the self as knower, desirer, and doer; these are the *three key functions* of the self-structure as a centralized decider subsystem.[3]

Fundamental to the functioning of the self-structure are the assumptions that we make about ourselves and our world. These assumptions are based on learning and are of three kinds:

(a) *reality assumptions*—assumptions about how things really are and what kind of person we are;

(b) *possibility assumptions*—assumptions about how things could be, about possibilities for change, opportunities for personal growth and social progress;

(c) *value assumptions*—assumptions about the way things ought to be, about right and wrong, good and bad, desirable and undesirable.

These three sets of assumptions provide us with a *frame of reference*, or *cognitive map*—a consistent view of self in relation to the environment.

These assumptions are not necessarily conscious, however. Although our daily decisions and behavior are in large part shaped by our frame of reference, we may be quite unaware of the assumptions on which it is based—or even of having made assumptions at all. We think we are simply "seeing things the way they are." It is unthinkable that other pictures of the world might be possible or that other rules for "right" might exist. Thus many of our thoughts, actions, and feelings are based on internalized rules and ways of seeing things that we would be hard pressed to articulate or define.

Particular assumptions may be valid or invalid; they may be held with varying degrees of conviction; and, as already indicated, they may be more or less explicit and conscious. Established through learning, they are subject to modification, although our new learning tends to be consistent with our existing assumptions. That is, new experience tends to be *assimilated* into our existing cognitive framework, even if the new information has to be reinterpreted or distorted to make it fit. We tend to cling to existing assumptions and reject or distort new information that is contradictory to them. *Accommodation*—changing our existing framework to make it possible to incorporate such discrepant information—is more difficult and threatening, especially where very important assumptions are challenged.

Because the self is experienced as the very core of our existence, we tend to develop a system of ego-defense mechanisms to maintain the picture of our adequacy and worth and defend ourselves from self-devaluation. Rationalizing our mistakes, blaming others or "bad breaks" for feelings we think we should not have, and avoiding activities in which we think we might not do well are familiar ways in which we protect our self-esteem and avoid anxiety. We shall examine the operation of ego-defense mechanisms in the final section of this chapter.

Several aspects of our frame of reference merit further mention. For one thing, our assumptions about reality, possibility, and value afford us a sense of *self-identity*—a realization of who and what we are—and also a *self-ideal*—a picture of what we could and should be. An unclear self-identity or a marked discrepancy between "real" and "ideal" selves can lead to serious inner conflict. Second, our pattern of assumptions contributes to consistency in perceiving, thinking, feeling, and acting—to the evolution of a characteristic *life-style*. Third, our assumptions serve not only as guides to behavior but also as *inner controls*. For example, value assumptions may prevent us from stealing or behaving in other ways that we consider unethical. Such value assumptions are often referred to as the *superego*, or *conscience*.

When our inner controls are strong enough to direct our behavior in accordance with the expectations and norms of our society, we are said to be *socialized*. In some cases, for reasons we shall examine later, these inner controls do not develop to an adequate degree;

---

[2]The self-structure, like gravity, cannot be observed directly, but is inferred from the finding that psychological functions operate in an integrated manner as part of a unified organism. As Hebb (1960) has pointed out, "The self is neither mythical nor mystical, but a complex mental process" (p. 743). It has a developmental course, is influenced by learning in both structure and degree of differentiation, and can be studied by various experimental procedures. In the present context we shall use the concepts of *ego* and *self* as roughly synonymous.

[3]J. G. Miller (1965) has inferred a "centralized decider subsystem" in all living organisms. The self appears to function as such a decider subsystem in human beings.

Book 3 determinants of personality ① Heredity
② Environment
③ SELF!

88   Chapter Four/Personality development and adjustment

and under certain conditions—such as alcoholic or drug intoxication—they may give way. However, society does its best to see that such restraints are well developed and maintained, for without them, organized social life would be impossible.

As each of us develops a sense of selfhood, we become an increasingly important force in directing our own behavior. While much of our behavior is shaped by external demands and influences, each of us nevertheless typically perceives ourself as an active force in initiating our plans and actions. It is the *I* who is seen as wanting or needing some things while trying to avoid others, and it is the *I* who perceives and responds to new situations in light of our own motives, assumptions, and feelings. In the process, each of us achieves an increasing sense of identity and of *self-direction.*[4] Thus if we view each person as a striving, evaluating, adapting individual—not simply as the passive result of heredity and environment—we may consider the "self" as the third and final determinant of personality.

When we consider the unique pattern of interacting determinants—genetic, environmental, and self—that shape a given individual, we can readily see that the potentialities for individual differences are beyond calculation. Yet as we have seen, these determinants produce commonalities as well as differences in development. On a *universal level,* we share an inheritance that distinguishes human beings from all other living things, and we are born into a sociocultural environment unlike that of any other species. On a *communal level,* members of a given society inherit the genetic legacy of their particular group, which tends to produce similar physical characteristics, and a particular sociocultural environment that tends to produce similarities among them and differentiate them from other cultural groups. On an *individual level,* each of us has a unique genetic inheritance (except for identical twins), and a pattern of learning and experience different from anyone else's. Every person in some respects is *like all other human beings, like some other human beings, and like no other human being.* An understanding of both the uniqueness of each individual and the commonalities among all human beings is essential for an understanding of development and adjustment.

The patterning of development

In contrast to animals lower on the phylogenetic scale, who have "built-in" patterns of behavior and who mature rapidly, the human infant begins life with few built-in patterns and a far greater capacity to learn from experience. But the price of such a high degree of modifiability is initial helplessness and a long period of immaturity, with the necessity of mastering the "know-how" and "know-why" of living. In our society, such learning is coming to require most of the life cycle.

The direction of development

In reviewing the patterning or sequencing of development, we shall focus on the formative period of the life cycle to see how growth is patterned under the combined influence of inner and outer determinants. Within limits, human development follows a predictable sequence and proceeds in a characteristic direction toward increasing differentiation, integration, and complexity. However, the maintenance of the pattern depends on a favorable environment and on the individual's learning essential information and competencies along the way.

Although children's growth is shaped in different ways in different sociocultural settings, there are certain characteristic trends in development that are seen in any society. These trends lead individuals toward responsible self-direction and toward ability to participate in and contribute to society. Here we may briefly note six of these specific but interrelated trends toward personal maturity:

1. *Dependence to self-direction.* One of the most obvious progressions toward maturity is from the dependency of fetus, infant, and

---

[4]Bandura (1978) has presented a systematic analysis of the guiding functions of the self from the perspective of social learning theory.

child to the independence of adulthood. Bound up with this growth toward independence and self-direction is the development of a clear sense of personal identity and the acquisition of information, competencies, and values. In our society this includes sufficient emancipation from family and other social groups to be a person in one's own right.

2. *Pleasure to reality (self-control).* As we have seen, Freud postulated the *pleasure principle*—the tendency to seek pleasure and to avoid pain and discomfort—as fundamental in governing early behavior. However, he thought this principle was in time subordinated to the *reality principle*—the individual's realization of the need to perceive and face reality. This means distinguishing between fantasy and reality, controlling impulse and desire, delaying immediate gratification in the interest of long-range goals, and learning to cope with the inevitable hurts, disappointments, and frustrations of living.

3. *Ignorance to knowledge.* Human infants are born in a state that might be called total ignorance, but they rapidly begin to acquire information about themselves and the world. With time, this information is organized into a coherent pattern of assumptions concerning reality, possibility, and value that provides a stable frame of reference for guiding behavior. If this frame of reference is to prove adequate, it needs to be realistic, to be relevant to the kinds of problems that must be dealt with, and to be one in which the individual has faith. Also, it needs to be flexible enough to be modified by new experience.

4. *Incompetence to competence.* The entire preadult period from infancy through adolescence is directed toward the mastery of intellectual, emotional, social, and other competencies essential for adulthood. Individuals acquire skills in problem solving and decision making, learn to control their emotions and to use them for the enrichment of living, and learn to deal with others and to establish satisfying relationships. Included here, too, is preparation for sexual, marital, occupational, parental, and other roles and relationships associated with adult life.

5. *Diffuse to articulated self-identity.* The emergence of a core self or identity is a gradual process. Its first manifestations involve the infant's differentiation of self from the surrounding environment. And, very early, the sex-typing responses of parents and others produce an awareness of oneself as a boy or a girl. Similarly, various other reactions or feedback from the environment begin to provide the child with a sense of his or her own characteristics over a broad range of traits, both "good" and "bad." The early origins of self-identity are thus acquired largely from external sources of information; the pieces are not necessarily consistent or systematically related, and the child often suffers confusion. The achievement of a self-defined identity, one that is internally consistent and more or less in keeping with the person's "real" characteristics, is by no means an easy task, nor is success assured. Guideposts along the way include the establishment of a confident gender identity and a reasonable plan for one's future life. Many people struggle with "getting it all together" until well into the early adult years, and some never stop struggling. As a rule, however, the person will have achieved a sense of coherent selfhood and future direction by the end of the adolescent years.

In their early quest for knowledge, infants seldom show evidence of a sense of "right" and "wrong." Given time and input from their parents, this, too, will come.

6. *Amoral to moral.* Newborn infants are amoral in the sense that they have no concept of "right" and "wrong." Very early, however, children learn that certain forms of behavior are approved, or "good," while other forms are disapproved, or "bad." Gradually they learn a pattern of value assumptions that operate as inner guides and controls of behavior, which we have referred to as the conscience or superego. Initially they accept these value assumptions blindly, but with increasing maturity they learn to appraise them, and to work out a value orientation that bears their own stamp. Included within any such developing moral orientation is a growing recognition and appreciation of the rights of others and of their sometimes differing views on the nature of reality and of decency.

There are widespread differences in the rate and success with which different persons move toward maturity. But modest progress in each of them is important in the realization of one's growth potential and development into a productive, effective member of society.

Developmental stages and tasks

Intensive studies of infants and children by Gesell (1953), Piaget (1970), and other investigators have shown that human development tends to follow a definite sequence, not only in physical and motor development but also in intellectual, emotional, and social development. Crawling and sitting up come before walking; early diffuse emotional reactions become differentiated into love, humor, grief, and other specific patterns; and language behavior progresses from random vocalizations to the words that eventually become vehicles for thinking.

In the present context, it is not necessary to review the stages of human development—prenatal, infancy, childhood, adolescence, adulthood, and old age—or to delineate the details of development in intellectual or other specific areas. But it is important for our purposes to know that at each stage of development, certain tasks or competencies must be mastered if the individual is to maintain a normal schedule of development. For example, learning to walk and talk are major tasks of in-

fancy; establishing a sense of identity and acquiring the intellectual, emotional, and interpersonal competencies needed for adulthood are key tasks of adolescence.

If developmental tasks are not mastered at the appropriate stage, the individual suffers from immaturities and incompetencies and is placed at a serious disadvantage in adjusting at later developmental levels. A young child who had not learned to walk or talk would be at a serious disadvantage in entering nursery school or kindergarten; the adolescent who does not have friends misses a major opportunity for acquiring the experience and skill in interacting with others that will be helpful later for establishing satisfactory relationships. The demands of a given developmental period may be relatively easy or difficult to meet, depending on how well the tasks at prior developmental levels have been mastered.

Some developmental tasks are set by the individual's own needs, some by the physical and social environment. Members of different socioeconomic and sociocultural groups face somewhat different developmental tasks, and social and technological changes may create new developmental tasks for all of us.

The crucial roles of maturation and learning

Built-in maturational processes[5] provide the potentials for the orderly progression of development, but these potentials can be realized only under favorable environmental conditions.

Critical periods and stimulation. During early development, *critical periods* occur during which certain types of stimulation and learning are essential for normal development. For example, Hunt (1961) showed that if chicks were kept in darkness for up to five days after hatching, they showed no apparent defects in their pecking response; but if the perceptual restriction lasted eight or more days, they were unable to learn to peck. Similarly, Harlow and Harlow (1966) found that if infant

---

[5]*Maturation* refers to growth following birth that is determined primarily by genetic factors and occurs more or less independently of learning.

monkeys were reared in isolation during the first six months after birth, they evidenced serious inadequacies in social and sexual behavior as adolescents and adults.

We know less about critical periods in human development, but some infants appear to be more severely affected than others by early deprivation. However, mental retardation, inability to form warm interpersonal relationships, and antisocial behavior have all been shown to be associated with extreme emotional, social, and intellectual deprivation in infancy. In this context, it is interesting to note the findings of Skeels (1966) on the adult intellectual status of two groups of individuals who had been placed in an orphanage as infants.

One group of thirteen children, ranging from seven months to three years of age, had been transferred from the orphanage to another institution where the adult inmates, though mentally retarded, provided more stimulation and personal contact for the children. A follow-up study twenty-one years later showed an average gain of 31.6 IQ points for this group, as compared with an average loss of 20.6 IQ points for a matched (control) group who had stayed in the original orphanage.

The effects of parental deprivation and of aversive stimulation on children's intellectual, emotional, and social development will be examined in Chapter 5. Here we may simply reemphasize that if needed stimulation and learning are lacking during early critical periods, the functions expected to develop at these times (a) may not appear; (b) may be slower in making their appearance; or (c) may be only partially adequate. And once the critical period has passed, it may be difficult or impossible to correct the physiological and/or psychological deficiencies that have occurred.

Early and later learning. Simple conditioning, as described in Chapter 3, is common in infancy and early childhood, and provides many new response patterns—often without the child's awareness of such learning. However, as their perceptual and cognitive capabilities develop, children become increasingly active agents in pursuing their own interests and shaping their own learning. In fact, by the age of four most children have a fairly clear picture of themselves and their world, and their ability to discriminate, interpret, and evaluate experience makes them less susceptible to simple conditioning.

But while children show similarities in learned abilities, they also show differences. Mischel (1973) has identified five learning-based differences that become apparent early in childhood: (a) Children have acquired different levels of competency in different areas; (b)

Early learning and experiences help lay a foundation for how a child will respond to and assimilate future experiences. For example, this young boy will probably continue to find gardening enjoyable, due in some measure to his early, pleasant experiences with his father.

they have learned different concepts and different strategies for coding and categorizing their experience and thus "process" new information differently in accordance with these strategies and structures; (c) although they have all learned that certain things follow from certain others, what they have learned to expect is quite different, depending on their unique experiences; (d) they have learned to find different situations attractive or disagreeable and thus to seek very different things; and (e) they have learned different ways of coping with impulses and regulating their behavior; they have long since developed a characteristic "style" of dealing with the exigencies of life. Differences in these general areas will continue through childhood and into the adult years.

Such learned variations make some children far better prepared than others for further learning and personal growth. The ability to make effective use of new experience depends very much on what is already there—on the adequacy with which past learning has prepared the child for assimilating new learning in ways that will be facilitative and productive. Partly for this reason, most theories of personality development emphasize the importance of early experience in shaping the main directions that an individual's coping style will take.

So far we have been looking at the factors contributing to personal development and change, and the patterning characteristic of development, especially during the early years. Now we are ready to examine the inner and outer determinants of behavior—strivings from within and adjustive demands that arise out of the person-environment interaction.

Motivation: Human needs and strivings

Human behaviors occur not only in response to external stimulation but also in response to certain energizing conditions within the organism. We call these conditions *motives, needs,* or *strivings* to refer to both their energizing and their goal-directed characteristics. In our brief review of motivation, we shall em-

phasize its key role in determining both the *direction* and the *activation* of human behavior—the goals we pursue and the effort we expend in trying to attain them.

Our motives and needs vary a great deal in their insistence and intensity and in the degree to which their "satisfaction" may be delayed, postponed, or even entirely foregone. Some are an inevitable product of requirements of the living organism, requirements that are continuous or keep recurring; satisfaction of these may not be long delayed if the biological organism is to remain viable. Included here are needs for oxygen, food, fluids, elimination, the maintenance of temperature within a certain range, and so forth. Such needs are, of course, innate and universal in the species. Other needs, such as the need to escape from sources of frustration, may have partly hereditary and partly learned origins. However, even strivings that have an innate base, such as strivings for food or sex, may come to differ greatly in their manner of expression.

The majority of the many human needs and motives are almost wholly a product of the particular experiences that the particular person (with his or her own reaction tendencies) undergoes in the course of learning how to cope with a complicated world. The number of motives that may be learned—and their manner of expression—is virtually limitless. Even within the same society, different individuals can be expected to express different and sometimes contradictory motives.

For present purposes, we shall focus on the basic core of human strivings that we all share in common. These can be considered to fall into two categories, maintenance and actualization strivings, and include attempts to meet both biological and psychological needs, as well as the demands of society.

Strivings toward maintenance and actualization

The motivation of all living organisms is based on their fundamental strivings toward *maintenance* or survival and toward the *actualization* of their potentialities. The individual organism resists disintegration or decay[6] and tends to develop and behave in accordance with its genetic possibilities. Among human beings we see these strivings operating on both biological and psychological levels.

Although we do not fully understand the processes involved, it is apparent that digestive, circulatory, and other body functions operate in such a way as to maintain the body's physiological equilibrium and integration. In the mechanisms for ensuring normal blood chemistry, for maintaining constant body temperature, and for combating invading microorganisms, we see this continuous endeavor of the body to preserve *steady states*—to maintain physiological variables within a range essential to survival—an endeavor generally referred to as *homeostasis*. The tendency toward actualization on the biological level can be seen in physical growth, as well as sexual and parental behavior that perpetuates the species.

If we do not fully understand the forces underlying biological maintenance and actualization, we understand still less the forces related to psychological strivings. They appear, however, to be an extension of the strivings that operate on the biological plane. On the psychological level our maintenance strivings become an attempt to protect the self, and our actualization strivings, an attempt to enhance the self. Damage to the self—as through severe feelings of inadequacy and worthlessness—can disable a person just as surely as can failure of physiological homeostatic mechanisms. Thus we strive to maintain the functional integration of the self-structure.

Living organisms strive to maintain steady states not only internally but also in relation to their environment so as to prevent environmental variations from disrupting their functioning or perhaps even destroying them. This is true with regard to both the physical environment and the social one. Human beings generally attempt to maintain steady states with respect to safety, work, love, marriage, and other conditions they consider important to

---

[6]The tendency of living matter to preserve itself is dramatically illustrated in Wilson's (1925) classic experiment with a sponge. He reduced the sponge to a pulp, squeezed and rolled it flat, and centrifuged it so that no trace of its original form remained. He then allowed the remains to stand overnight. Slowly and in orderly fashion, the material reconstituted itself into the organized sponge it had been before its mistreatment. Similarly, later experiments have shown that completely scrambled cells taken from the liver or kidneys of chick embryos can reconstruct the same organ (Weiss & Taylor, 1960).

Though individuals generally try to maintain steady states, often some find it exhilarating to do just the opposite, as in mountain climbing.

their well-being. On the other hand, well-functioning individuals often feel a need to upset present balances—to impose themselves on a relatively unyielding environment, to generate novel experiences, and to create effects in the world (Berlyne, 1960; White, 1959), quite without respect to the satisfaction of other pressing needs. Motives such as these have often been considered manifestations of basic self-actualizing strivings.

Biological strivings

The biological strivings that appear most relevant to human behavior include strivings to meet our visceral needs and our needs for stimulation and activity, for safety and avoidance of pain, and for sexual gratification.

Visceral strivings. The most basic of all human requirements are those for food, water, sleep, the elimination of wastes, and for other

conditions and substances necessary for life. In order to survive and meet adjustive demands, the organism must constantly renew itself through rest and through taking in nutrients to replace materials used up in the process of living. Prolonged interference with such renewal weakens the organism's resources for coping with even normal adjustive demands and makes it vulnerable to special stresses. Prisoners have sometimes been "broken" by nothing more persuasive than the systematic prevention of sleep or deprivation of food over a period of several days.

Experimental studies of volunteers who have gone without sleep for periods of 72 to 98 hours show increasing psychological disorganization as the sleep loss progresses—including disorientation for time and place and feelings of depersonalization. As Berger (1970) has summarized it, "One thing is sure . . . we must sleep in order to stay sane" (p. 70).

Studies of dietary deficiencies have pointed to marked changes in psychological functioning, the exact change depending largely on the type and extent of the deficiency. Some of these effects were demonstrated in a pioneering study of semistarvation carried out by Keys (1950) and his associates during World War II.

Thirty-two conscientious objectors served as volunteer subjects. The men were first placed on an adequate diet for three months, then placed on a very low calorie diet characteristic of European famine areas for a period of six months, and then provided with a three-month period of nutritional rehabilitation.

During the six-month period of semistarvation, subjects had an average weight loss of 24 percent. At the same time, subjects also showed dramatic personality and behavioral changes. They became irritable, unsociable, and increasingly unable to concentrate on anything but food. In some instances they resorted to stealing food from one another and lying in attempts to obtain additional food rations. Among other psychological changes were apathy, loss of pride in personal appearance, and feelings of inadequacy. By the close of the experiment, there was a marked reduction or disappearance of their interest in sex, and the predominant mood was one of gloom and depression. Food dominated the men's thoughts, conversation, and even daydreams. They even pinned up pictures of chocolate cake instead of pretty women. In some cases, they went so far as to replan their lives in the light of their newly acquired respect for food. The investigators concluded that by the end of the twenty-fifth week, hunger had become the dominant influence in the behavior of their subjects.

In ordinary life, chronic deprivation may result in lowered resistance to stress. Insufficient rest, inadequate diet, or attempts to carry a full work load under the handicap of a severe cold, fatigue, or emotional strain may deplete a person's adjustive resources and result in increased predisposition to personality disorganization.

Stimulation and activity. Research studies, as well as personal accounts of explorers, have shown that psychological integration depends on adequate contact with the outside world.

"People confined to dark, quiet chambers—the traditional 'solitary confinement' of the prisoner or the soundproof room used for training astronauts—often display bizarre stress and anxiety symptoms including hallucinations, delusions, apathy, and fear of losing sanity. Their performance deteriorates." (Haythorn & Altman, 1967, p. 19)

In addition, such individuals become more receptive to information that is "fed-in"—a tendency that suggests why brainwashing may be effective after a long period of solitary confinement.

An unusual and dramatic account of the need for stimulation comes from the experience of Dr. Alain Bombard, who sailed alone across the Atlantic Ocean for sixty-five days on a life raft to prove that shipwrecked people could survive an indefinite length of time. He subsisted solely on the food he could get from the sea. During this period of isolation, Bombard stated, he "wanted terribly to have someone . . . who would confirm my impressions, or better still, argue about them. . . . I began to feel that I would be incapable of discerning between the false and the true" (Bombard, 1954, pp. 106–7).

On the other hand, too much input may lead to "overloading" and to lowered psychological integration and impaired performance. J. G. Miller (1965) found that when messages—in the form of information that had to be acted on—came in too fast, subjects could not handle even the usual number effectively; when such excessive input continued, psychological functioning became disorganized. Similarly, Gottschalk, Haer, and Bates (1972) exposed subjects to overwhelming sensory input in the form of high-intensity sound color movies; they found that such overloading resulted in serious personality disorganization similar to that found in organic brain disturbances. And, as we shall discuss in more detail later, individuals whose current adaptation is disrupted repeatedly by excessive life changes become more vulnerable to illness and even death (Rahe & Arthur, 1978).

In general, there appears to be for each individual an optimal level of stimulation and activity; it varies over time, but stimulation must be maintained within these limits for normal psychological functioning. Under some conditions—such as boredom—we may strive to increase the level of stimulation by doing something different or engaging in an "exciting" activity. On the other hand, under excessive pressure, or "overload," we may strive to reduce the level of input and activity.

Safety and avoidance of pain. From early infancy on we tend to withdraw from painful stimuli and try to avoid objects that have brought us pain or discomfort in the past. The threat or experience of pain is acutely unpleasant and highly motivating.

Severe hunger, thirst, and fatigue can be extremely painful, as can most forms of intense stimulation such as heat, cold, and pressure. Certain emotions—particularly anxiety—are also painful and highly motivating. In fact, anxiety has been referred to as "psychic pain." In this sense, just as pain serves as a warning or indicator to protect us from bodily harm, it can serve also as a safeguard against psychological damage.

The precise influence of physical pain on behavior has never been fully delineated, although experience and observation indicate that it can be very great. Through the centuries, torture and pain have been used to elicit confessions as well as for punishment. When pain is severe and long-continued—as it is in certain types of disease—it may gradually wear down the sufferer's adjustive resources and lead to overwhelming feelings of hopelessness and despair.

Sex. Although the meaning and importance of sexual strivings vary greatly from one person to another, sexual tensions, fantasies, and experiences, as well as problems centering around sexual gratification, usually are important facets of a person's life. Depending on our attitude toward sex and the part it plays in our own life plan, sex can be an important source of satisfaction and self-realization or a source of anxiety and self-devaluation. In any case, sexual motivation is probably second only to the hunger motive in its far-reaching implications for both personal and social living.

Although the sex drive has a hormonal basis and sexual stimulation is innately pleasurable, the strength of an individual's interest in sex depends heavily on past learning. A person indoctrinated with the view that sex is dirty and evil may develop little sexual motivation, and may even find sexual intercourse unpleasant or repugnant. Because of differences in age, cultural viewpoints, and individual life experiences, widespread differences exist in sexual motivation and in the perceived significance of sexual behavior. Approved patterns of sexual gratification also vary considerably from one society to another and within particular societies over a period of time. In our own society sexual codes are being liberalized, but certain sexual patterns—such as incest—are still considered abnormal. We shall deal with these and other aspects of sexual behavior in Chapter 15.

Psychological strivings

The psychological requirements for healthy human development and functioning are influenced by learning and social requirements to a greater degree than are biological requirements, and the goals relating to their gratification are capable of greater variation. A position of leadership, for example, highly valued in our society as a means of meeting needs for adequacy and worth, was found by Mead (1949) to be a nuisance and burden to the Arapesh, who avoided leadership roles whenever possible.

Despite wide individual and group differences in human motives, however, there does appear to be a common core of psychological strivings related to maintenance and actualization. Although psychological requirements are less readily identified than requirements for food, water, sleep, and the like, the following basic core of psychological strivings characterize all of us as human beings.

Understanding, order, and predictability. Human beings strive to understand and achieve a meaningful picture of their world. Otherwise we would have no basis for evaluating new situations and choosing adjustive actions. Unless we can see order and predictability in our environment, we cannot work out an intelligent response to it. Social customs, rules, and laws are in part a reflection of this need for order and predictability.

People do not like ambiguity, lack of structuring, chaos, or events that seem beyond their understanding and control. Even the most "primitive" people develop explanations for lightning, thunder, death, and other frightening phenomena. Accurate or not, such explanations tend to impose order and meaning on seemingly random events, thereby giving a sense of potential prediction and control. Mod-

Parents can do a great deal to meet the young child's need for security as new experiences are met.

ern science is simply a more sophisticated attempt in the same direction.

Our striving for understanding, order, and predictability is evidenced in our tendency to maintain the consistency and stability of our frame of reference. When new information contradicts existing assumptions, we experience *cognitive dissonance*—an unpleasant state of tension—and are uncomfortable until the discrepancy can be reconciled. Such reconciliation, as we have seen, involves assimilation of the new information by either distorting its meaning or, more rarely, accommodating the current belief system to the new input. In fact, Aronson (1973) concluded that cognitive dissonance may result in such acute discomfort that an individual may risk his or her life in an effort to resolve it.

Adequacy, competence, and security.

Each of us needs to feel capable of dealing with life's problems. Seeing oneself as incapable of coping with a stressful situation is conducive to confusion and disorganization.

Feelings of adequacy are heavily dependent on the development of intellectual, social, and other competencies for dealing with adjustive demands. Several investigators have pointed out that even the early playful and investiga-

tory behavior of children involves a process of "reality testing" that fosters the development of learning, reasoning, and other coping abilities.

The need for security develops with and is closely related to the need for adequacy. We soon learn that failure to meet biological or psychological needs leads to unpleasant results. Consequently we strive to maintain whatever conditions can be counted on to assure present and future need gratification. The need for security is reflected in the preference for jobs with tenure, in social security legislation, in insurance against disability and other contingencies, and in society's emphasis on law and order. Feelings of insecurity may have widely differing effects on behavior; but pervasive and chronic feelings of insecurity typically lead to fearfulness, apprehension, and failure to participate fully in one's world. The more adequate we feel and the greater our level of competence, the less aware we are of our need for security and the more we may value the exploration of unfamiliar paths and freedom for self-direction.

In this general context, it is interesting to note that one of the key functions of psychotherapy is to help patients achieve a sense of adequacy, competency, and mastery over their lives. Indeed, Bandura (1977) has argued forcefully that this is the function basic to *all* the varied forms of psychological treatment.

Love, belonging, and approval.   To love and to be loved are crucial to healthy personality development and adjustment. In their extensive study of patterns in child rearing, Sears, Maccoby, and Levin (1957) concluded that the most crucial and pervasive of all the influences toward healthy development of children were the love and warmth imparted by the parents. For the child who feels loved and accepted, many conditions that might otherwise impair development—such as a physical handicap, poverty, or harsh discipline—may be largely neutralized. On the other hand, if a child feels unloved, no lavishing of material benefits on him or her will make up for it: the hurt will distort personal development and perhaps lead to attempts to retaliate, as we shall see in Chapter 14.

Evidence of our needs for love, belonging, and approval is provided in the HIGHLIGHT on this page, which describes the nature and effects of the "silent treatment." The need for close ties to other people continues throughout life and becomes especially important in times of severe stress or crisis. In a study of terminal cancer patients, Bard (1966) concluded that the need for affiliation and human contact is never greater than it is as death approaches. Kubler-Ross (1975) confirms this need in dying patients, but she also notes the tendency of others to withdraw at this critical juncture.

Self-esteem, worth, and identity.   Closely related to the needs for adequacy and social approval is the need to feel good about oneself and worthy of the respect of others.

Self-esteem has its early foundation in parental affirmation of worth and in mastery of early developmental tasks; it receives continual nourishment from the development of new competencies and from achievement in areas deemed important; and eventually it comes to depend heavily on the values and standards of significant others. If we can measure up to those standards—for example, in terms of physical appearance, achievement, or economic status—we can approve of ourselves and feel worthwhile.

Intermeshed with feelings of self-esteem and

HIGHLIGHT

The "silent treatment"

Eloquent testimony to our needs for love, belonging, and approval is provided by the experience of small groups of scientists, officers, and enlisted personnel who voluntarily subjected themselves to isolated antarctic living for the better part of a year. During this period troublesome individuals were occasionally given the "silent treatment" in which a man would be ignored by the group as if he did not exist.

This "isolation" procedure resulted in a syndrome called the "long eye," characterized by varying combinations of sleeplessness, outbursts of crying, hallucinations, a deterioration in habits of personal hygiene, and a tendency for the man to move aimlessly about or to lie on his bunk staring into space. These symptoms cleared up when he was again accepted by and permitted to interact with others in the group.

Based primarily on Rohrer (1961) and on Popkin, Stillner, Osborn, Pierce, and Shurley (1974).

worth is one's sense of self-identity. This, too, is heavily influenced by significant others and by one's status and role in the group. Here it is interesting to note that despite changes in physical appearance, in status, and in social roles, people tend to maintain continuity in their basic feelings of self-identity. That is, we think of ourself as the same *I* or *me* today that we were yesterday and will be tomorrow.

Probably most of us would like to change in certain ways, and many of us work hard at becoming the finer or more capable or more attractive self we would like to be. A few people, as we shall see in Chapter 15, even come to the point of undergoing sex-change surgery to achieve a body consistent with what they feel is their *real* identity. But though we may wish to make some changes in our present self-identity, it is doubtful, in most instances, that we would willingly give it up. When a person's sense of self-identity and continuity becomes disorganized—as happens sometimes in psychotic disorders—the experience is usually acutely painful.

Sargent (1973) has reported on the loss of self-identity often experienced by convicted prisoners and its consequences in terms of self-esteem, worth, and adequacy.

"The prisoners increasingly depend on authority, become susceptible to suggestion, tend toward magical thinking, and become more anxious and impulsive. In some cases the symptoms reach psychotic proportions." (p. 390)

Values, meaning, and hope.

Surprisingly, there has been little research on the human need for values, meaning, and hope. But we can infer such needs from observations of the typical results when people are unable to find satisfying value patterns, are "planless," or lack hope. Values, meaning, and hope appear to act as catalysts: in their presence energy is mobilized, competencies are developed and used, and satisfactions are achieved. Without them, life seems futile and the individual is bored and enervated.

In extreme cases, hopelessness may lead to apathy and even death. For example, reports from prisoner-of-war camps have told of cases in which prisoners who had lost hope simply pulled their blankets over their heads and waited for death to come (Nardini, 1952; *U.S. News and World Report*, 1973).

The universality of the search for meaning and hope has been described by Cantril (1967):

"In the midst of the probabilities and uncertainties that surround them, people want some anchoring points, some certainties, some faith that will serve either as a beacon light to guide them or as a balm to assuage them during the inevitable frustrations and anxieties that living engenders." (p. 17)

Closely related to our needs for values and meaning are our goals and plans, for we live in the future as well as in the past and present. Our goals and plans serve as a focus for both our strivings and our hopes. When we feel uncertain and anxious about the future, personal adjustment and effectiveness are likely to be impaired.

Personal growth and fulfillment.

As already indicated, we strive not only to maintain ourselves and survive but also to express ourselves, to improve, to grow—*to actualize our potentialities*. Huxley (1953) made this point very eloquently:

"Human life is a struggle—against frustration, ignorance, suffering, evil, the maddening inertia of things in general; but it is also a struggle *for* some-

For the isolated child, the opportunities for developing self-esteem, worth, and identity are significantly less than for his peers who have greater access to new experiences and interpersonal relationships.

thing. . . . And fulfillment seems to describe better than any other single word the positive side of human development and human evolution—the realization of inherent capacities by the individual and of new possibilities by the race; the satisfaction of needs, spiritual as well as material; the emergence of new qualities of experience to be enjoyed; the building of personalities." (pp. 162–63)

The strivings for fulfillment take different forms with different people, depending on their abilities, values, and life situations. In general, however, we appear to share certain strivings as human beings: (a) toward developing and using our potentials in constructive and creative ways, as in art, music, writing, science, athletics, and other pursuits that foster creative self-expression; (b) toward the enrichment of living—toward enriching the range and quality of our experiences and satisfactions, as, for example, in travel; (c) toward increasing our relatedness to the world—forming warm

Our needs for loving relationships know no age limits.

and meaningful relationships with others and becoming involved in the "human enterprise"; and (d) toward "becoming a person"—answering the question "Who am I?" and becoming the "self" that we feel we should be. Here it may be noted that the various psychological strivings discussed above may all be considered routes to self-actualization. Many of our deepest satisfactions come through improving our understanding and competence, forming loving relationships with others, and acquiring values that contribute to a meaningful and fulfilling life.

The strivings discussed above appear to represent the basic core of psychological requirements that emerge through normal interaction with the world and that contribute significantly to the direction of behavior. The strength of a given psychological striving and the behaviors for meeting it may vary considerably, of course, from one person to another, and from one social group to the next. It is apparent, too, that biological and psychological strivings are closely interrelated and that failure to meet a particular one may adversely influence our entire motivational structure as well as physical and psychological well-being.

It is in relation to maintenance and actualization strivings that we use the terms *adjustment* and *maladjustment*, which refer to outcomes of these strivings. The term *therapy,* too, becomes meaningful only in this context: the goal of therapy—whatever its particular orientation—is to help individuals meet their needs in a socially constructive way.

Motivation and behavior

The preceding discussion has dealt with the nature of our basic needs and strivings. But they do not operate apart from other psychological processes. In this section we shall consider (a) their role in the mobilization of energy; (b) their influence on other psychological processes; (c) their conscious and unconscious aspects; (d) the priorities among them; and (e) their relation to one's life-style.

Then we shall conclude our review of motivation with a brief look at the needs of groups and the role of social forces in inhibiting and facilitating the development and expression of given motives.

Levels of activation. Motivation accounts for not only the direction but also the activation of behavior—the energy mobilized in pursuit of our goals.

Activation can vary in degree from very low to very high, from deep sleep to intense excitement. At any moment a person's level of activation is influenced by a wide range of individual and situational factors. It is affected by the way one perceives the situation and evaluates its potential satisfaction and frustrations; it is affected by many inner conditions, including biological drives, emotions, and drugs; it is affected by sudden loud noises and strange or novel stimuli; and it is affected by fatigue, disease, and pain.

Usually, efficient task performance requires a moderate level of activation. With too low a level, the person may fail to expend the energy and effort essential for task achievement, while very high levels tend to result in poorly coordinated functioning and impaired performance.

Although there are individual differences in personal tempo and sensitivity or excitability, most people learn to respond to familiar situations with appropriate levels of activation. However, an individual is likely to react with an overly high level of activation in the face of an unfamiliar challenge or under stressful conditions to which he or she is particularly vulnerable. Similarly, conditions such as severe fatigue, intense inner conflict, or faulty assumptions and loss of hope may lead to extreme and inappropriate fluctuations in activation, as well as to slow recovery from the effects of prior activation and energy output.

Motivation, attending, and perceiving.

Needs and motives influence perceiving, reasoning, learning, and other psychological processes. For example, people are most likely to perceive those aspects of the environment that are related to the gratification of immediate or long-term needs. A person lost in the desert and suffering from intense thirst would likely ignore the vivid colors of the sunset and keep scanning the surroundings for some indication of water. This tendency of the organism to single out particular elements considered to be especially relevant to its purposes is called *selective vigilance*.

While motivation may sensitize the individual to particular stimuli, we have already seen that it may also have the opposite effect. People tend to screen out or distort information that is incompatible with their expectations, assumptions, and wishes. Proud parents may selectively perceive the desirable traits and behaviors of their children while tending not to perceive undesirable ones; people often do the same thing in evaluating themselves. This tendency to avoid perceiving unpleasant stimuli or undesired information is sometimes referred to as *perceptual defense*.[7]

Motivation also influences what we learn, as well as how rapidly and how much. And despite our attempts to be logical, our motivation may influence our beliefs and subvert our thought processes in helping us justify our assumptions and behavior. This is why we cannot usually be objective judges in disputes in which we have a vested interest on one side of the issue.

Conscious and unconscious aspects of motivation.

We noted that the concept of unconscious motivation is basic to the psychoanalytic perspective. Over three decades ago W. A. White (1947) concluded that the failure to take unconscious motivation into consideration was "probably the cause of more inadequacies in the understanding of human behavior than any other one thing." Although considerable controversy still exists among psychologists concerning the nature and importance of unconscious processes in human behavior, there is abundant evidence that we are often unaware of what our needs and goals really are. Yet to view consciousness and unconsciousness as separate or unrelated can also lead to erroneous and misleading conclusions. There are probably many more motives of which we are "more or less" aware than there are of which we are either wholly conscious *or* wholly unconscious.

Many of our biological needs operate on an unconscious level, and we may become aware of others—for example, via feelings of hunger and thirst—only when they become pressing. Psychological needs, such as those for security, adequacy, social approval, and self-esteem, may also operate on relatively unconscious

---

[7]An informative discussion of perceptual defense and vigilance may be found in Erdelyi (1974).

levels. Thus we may criticize our associates, join exclusive clubs, and even get married for reasons of which we are unaware. Of course, we may think of good reasons to justify our behavior, but they may not be the real reasons at all.

The degree to which individuals are aware of their motives varies considerably from one person to another. Usually individuals who are seriously maladjusted lack insight into many key facets of their motivational patterns. The following now-classic illustration demonstrates the action of unconscious motivation. It is especially revealing, because in this instance we do know the individual's exact motivational pattern, which is not generally the case.

"During profound hypnosis the subject was instructed to feel that smoking was a bad habit, that he both loved and hated it, that he wanted to get over the habit but he felt it was too strong a habit to break, that he would be very reluctant to smoke and would give anything not to smoke, but that he would find himself compelled to smoke; and that after he was awakened he would experience all of these feelings.

"After he was awakened the subject was drawn into a casual conversation with the hypnotist who, lighting one himself, offered him a cigarette. The subject waved it aside with the explanation that he had his own and that he preferred Camels, and promptly began to reach for his own pack. Instead of looking in his customary pocket, however, he seemed to forget where he carried his cigarettes and searched fruitlessly through all of his other pockets with a gradually increasing concern. Finally, after having sought them repeatedly in all other pockets, he located his cigarettes in their usual place. He took them out, engaged in a brief conversation as he dallied with the pack, and then began to search for matches, which he failed to find. During his search for matches he replaced the cigarettes in his pocket and began using both hands, finally locating the matches too in their usual pocket. Having done this, he now began using both hands to search for his cigarettes. He finally located them but then found that he had once more misplaced his matches. This time however he kept his cigarettes in hand while attempting to locate the matches. He then placed a cigarette in his mouth and struck a match. As he struck it, however, he began a conversation which so engrossed him that he forgot the match and allowed it to burn his finger tips whereupon, with a grimace of pain, he tossed it in the ash tray. . . .

Hierarchy of needs

According to Maslow, needs on the "lower" levels are prepotent as long as they are unsatisfied. When they are adequately satisfied, however, the "higher" needs occupy the individual's attention and effort.

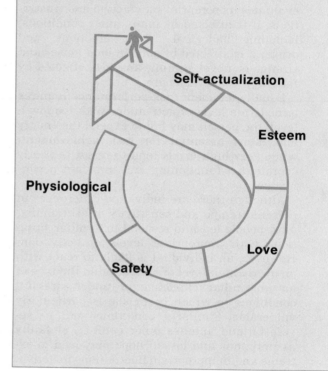

"This behavior continued with numerous variations. He tried lighting a cigarette with a split match, burned his fingers, got both ends of one cigarette wet, demonstrated how he could roll a cigarette, kept stopping to converse or tell a joke, and so on. Several cigarettes were ruined and discarded. When he finally got one going successfully, he took only a few good puffs with long pauses in between and discarded it before it was used up." (Erickson, 1939, pp. 342–45)

Hierarchy of needs. Maslow (1970, 1971) has suggested that human needs form a hierarchy from the most basic biological requirements to the needs for self-actualization (see HIGHLIGHT on page 102). According to this formulation, the level that commands the individual's attention and effort is ordinarily the lowest one on which there is an unmet need. For example, unless needs for food and safety are reasonably well met, behavior will be dominated by these needs. With their gratification, however, the individual is free to devote time and energy to meeting needs on higher levels.

Maslow used the term *deficiency motivation* to refer to motives aimed at meeting the needs on lower levels, since these motives are activated by deficiencies and force the individual to take action to restore equilibrium. He used the term *growth motivation* to refer to motives aimed at meeting the higher-level needs for self-actualization. Although meeting lower-level needs is clearly necessary for maintenance of the organism, Maslow considered a long-term preoccupation with *only* the maintenance needs to be unhealthy because of the resulting failure to develop the individual's uniquely human potentialities.

Maslow's hierarchy concept tends to be borne out by observations of behavior under extreme conditions. Friedman (1949) reported that: "In all survivors of the Nazi concentration camps, one might say the self-preservation instinct became so dominant that it blotted out all other instincts." Similarly, in the Japanese prisoner-of-war camps in World War II, it was a common pattern for those inmates who had been subjected to prolonged deprivation and torture to obtain food at the expense of their fellow prisoners and in other ways surrender the loyalties and values they had held under more normal conditions (Nardini, 1952, 1962).

Under conditions of extreme deprivation, most people do appear likely to sacrifice their higher-level actualization needs to meet more basic needs for survival. As Maslow acknowledged, however, there are many exceptions, as shown by the countless number of people who have remained faithful to ethical, social, or religious values despite severe deprivation, torture, and even certain death.

Motive patterns and life-style.   Each individual tends to develop a relatively consistent life-style, an essential element of which is a continuing *motive pattern* centered around

The goals we strive for in large part reflect the strength of our motivations.

particular strivings and goals. Some persons are concerned primarily with love and relatedness, others with material possessions and power, and still others with personal growth and self-actualization. An individual's motive pattern is in part a product of past rewards and punishments; in part an out-growth of reality, possibility, and value assumptions; and in part a reflection of the demands, limitations, and opportunities of the environment.

Some goals are more appropriate than others in relation to the individual's resources and opportunities, and some are superior to others in the satisfactions they can afford. The pursuit of unrealistically high goals leads to failure and frustration; the pursuit of goals that are too low leads to wasted opportunities and lost satisfactions; the pursuit of "false" goals leads to disillusionment and discouragement. Well-adjusted people tend to have a reasonably accurate view of themselves in relation to their world and hence to have a fairly realistic *level of aspiration.* Maladjusted people, on the other hand, tend to be unrealistic—to set their goals too high or too low or to pursue unrewarding goals. In many cases, maladjusted people seem unable to formulate meaningful life plans and goals and drift through life with little or no sense of direction. Usually such persons experience feelings of dissatisfaction, aimlessness, and being "lost."

Many of our more important motives involve other people. Examples are needs to dominate, to submit, to love, or to aggress against an oppressor. The possibilities that such needs will be satisfied depends very much on the behaviors and motives of the other people in our lives. For example, it is difficult to fulfill a need to dominate in the absence of someone who will "submit." We often find, therefore, that seriously maladaptive expressions of needs occur in situations in which two or more persons are in regular interaction with each other.

Although each of us tends to show a relatively consistent pattern of motives, this pattern undergoes change over time. The key motives of the child are not those of the adolescent, nor are the motives of the adolescent those of the adult or older person. Similarly, changes in one's life situation may lead to the modification of motive patterns. For example, a football player with a serious injury may find it necessary to make changes in his established motive pattern. Broadly speaking, one may develop important new motives, show shifts in the priorities of existing motives, or discard motives that have formerly been of significance. Some of these changes emerge as the products of experience and learning; others seem to result from new requirements at different life stages; and still others are influenced by changed environmental conditions.

Changes in motive patterns are closely related to changes in self-structure, each both causing and resulting from changes in the other. As new demands require new behaviors, we strive to maintain consistency between our sense of self and our picture of what we are doing and need to do in our situation.

Social forces in motivation

Thus far we have viewed motivation primarily in terms of the needs and strivings of the individual. However, environmental factors are of great importance in facilitating or inhibiting given strivings, in making some goals more feasible than others, and in determining the extent to which one's needs are met.

Social inhibition and facilitation of motives. By its system of values and by the manipulation of rewards and punishments, society encourages the gratification of certain needs while it attempts to inhibit or limit that of others. In most societies, for example, patterns of sexual gratification are strictly regulated by society; in general, unusual or unapproved expressions of such desires are punished. Conversely, the pursuit of other needs, such as the need for social approval, may be strongly encouraged.

The rewards and punishments supplied by the group also influence the goals its members seek and the means they learn to use in working toward these goals. In our society, for example, there are strong incentives to strive toward such goals as academic excellence, creative accomplishment, financial success, and leadership. And although a wide range of means for achieving these goals is approved, there nevertheless are limitations: if we use socially disapproved means, we may be punished.

Needs of groups and of society. Social groups have basic needs in much the same sense that individuals do. Their survival depends, for example, on the maintenance of orderly social relationships—which in turn requires the development of various "homeostatic" mechanisms, such as customs and laws and the means for enforcing them.

When normal group functioning or organizational structure is disrupted, groups strive to reestablish a state of equilibrium. This applies to small groups as well as larger ones. If a general is killed in battle, another officer moves up to fill the position; if one member of a family dies, changes in relationships and responsibilities take place as other family members attempt to establish a new pattern of effective functioning.

Whether or not this young boy later joins a neighborhood gang, he will feel the force of its influence as he grows up.

The needs of groups and of society are important determinants of the behavior of individual members. Usually meeting the needs of one's family and other groups, as well as those of the larger society, tends to promote one's own welfare too. However, the needs of the group or the society may conflict with or eclipse the needs of the individual, as when a young mother must work long hours at a monotonous job to support her family or when soldiers are forced to risk their lives in combat.

In concluding our review of human motivation, it may be reemphasized that motives and goals focus our energy and effort, help determine what competencies we need, and provide a basis for deciding between alternative courses of action. And while specific motives and goals may change during the course of our lives, the basic core of biological and psychological needs required for maintenance and actualization—needs that we share in common as human beings—remains essentially the same throughout our lives. In the words of Sullivan (1953), "We are all much more simply human than otherwise" (p. 16).

Adjustive demands and stress

Life would be simple indeed if one's biological and psychological needs were automatically gratified. But as we know, there are many obstacles, both environmental and personal, that may interfere. Such obstacles place adjustive demands on the individual that sometimes lead to severe stress.

The term *stress* has historically been used to refer both to adjustive demands placed on an organism and to the organism's internal responses to such demands. To avoid confusion, we shall refer to adjustive demands as *stressors* and to the frequently maladaptive effects they create within the organism as *stress*.

In the present section, we shall be concerned with three aspects of stressors and stress: (a) types of stressors; (b) factors influencing the severity of stress; and (c) the unique and changing stressor patterns that characterize each person's life.

Types of stressors: frustration, conflict, and pressure

Adjustive demands, or stressors, stem from a number of sources, including biological conditions (e.g., viruses), psychological conditions (e.g., emotional deprivation), and sociocultural conditions (e.g., poverty). Our focus here will be on three psychological stressors, which may be classified as frustration, conflict, and pressure. While we shall consider these types of adjustive demands separately, it will be apparent that they are all closely interrelated.

Frustration. Frustration occurs when one's strivings are thwarted, either by obstacles that block progress toward a desired goal or by absence of an appropriate goal.

A wide range of obstacles, both environmental and internal, can lead to frustration. The frustrations we face depend heavily on such factors as age and other personal characteristics, our life situation, and the society in which we live. Inflation, group prejudice and discrimination, and the death of loved ones are common frustrations stemming from the environment; physical handicaps, lack of needed competencies, and inadequate self-control are sources of frustration that can result from our own personal limitations. Often frustrations arise out of psychological barriers in the form of ethical or moral restraints. Some college students refrain from premarital sexual intercourse, for example, because their moral values make such behavior unacceptable. And, of course, faulty value assumptions, such as the belief that the world owes us a living, may lead to unnecessary frustrations.

Conflict. In many instances stress results from the simultaneous occurrence of two or more incompatible needs or motives: the requirements of one preclude satisfaction of the other(s). On the simplest level, for example, an early marriage may mean foregoing or shortening one's college education; choosing one job may mean turning down another that seems equally desirable. Although we are dealing with frustration and conflict as if they were distinct sources of stress, this differentiation is largely for convenience, since the key element in conflict is often the frustration that will result from either choice. In addition, however, the necessity of making a choice commonly involves cognitive and emotional strain: it is often difficult "to make up one's mind," especially when each alternative offers values that the other does not, and the choice is an important one.

Conflicts with which everyone has to cope may be conveniently classified as approach-avoidance, double-approach, and double-avoidance types.

1. *Approach-avoidance conflicts* involve strong tendencies both to approach and to avoid the same goal. Perhaps an individual wants to join a high-status group but can do so only by endorsing views contrary to personal values; or a former smoker may want to smoke during a party but realize that doing so may jeopardize his or her desire to quit.

Approach-avoidance conflicts are sometimes referred to as "mixed-blessing" dilemmas, because some negative and some positive features must be accepted regardless of which course of action is chosen.

2. *Double-approach conflicts* involve choosing between two or more desirable goals, such as which of two movies to see on the only free night of the week. To a large extent, such simple "plus-plus" conflicts result from the inevitable limitations in one's time, space, energy, and personal and financial resources; and they are usually handled in stride. In more complex cases, however, as when an individual is torn between two good career opportunities, or between present satisfactions and future ones, decision making may be very difficult and stressful.

3. *Double-avoidance conflicts* are those in which the choice is between more or less equally *undesirable* alternatives, such as going to a party when you'd rather stay home or being considered impolite if you cancel out at the last moment. Neither choice will bring satisfaction, so the task is to decide which course of action will be least disagreeable.

It can be seen that this classification of conflicts is somewhat arbitrary, and that various combinations among the different types are perhaps the rule rather than the exception. Thus a "plus-plus" conflict between alternative careers may also have its "plus-minus" aspects growing out of the responsibilities that either imposes. But regardless of how we categorize conflicts, they represent a major source of stress that can become overwhelming in intensity.

Pressure as a type of stressor.   Stress may stem not only from frustrations and conflicts, but also from pressure to achieve specific goals or to behave in particular ways. Such pressures may originate from external or internal sources. A college student may feel under severe pressure to make good grades because her parents demand it, or she may submit herself to such pressure because she wants to gain admission to graduate school.

In general, pressures force a person to speed up, intensify, or change the direction of goal-oriented behavior. All of us encounter many different pressures in the course of everyday living, and often we handle them without undue difficulty. In some instances, however, pressures seriously tax our adjustive resources, and if they become excessive, they may lead to a breakdown of organized behavior.

It is apparent that a given situation may involve elements of all three types of stressors—frustration, conflict, and pressure. For example, a serious financial loss may not only lead to lower living standards but also confront the person with evidence of poor judgment. If such evidence is contrary to the person's self-image as too shrewd to make a poor investment, the resulting cognitive dissonance may add to the complexity of the stressful situation. And although a particular stressor may predominate in any situation, we rarely deal with an isolated demand but usually with a continuously changing complex of interrelated and sometimes contradictory demands.

Factors influencing the severity of stress

The severity of stress is gauged by the degree of disruption in functioning that is entailed. For example, an individual will experience serious disruption of both physiological and psychological functioning if deprived of food for a sustained period.

The actual degree of disruption that occurs or is threatened depends partly on the characteristics of the adjustive demand, partly on the individual, and partly on the cultural and situational context. On a biological level, for example, the severity of stress created by invading viruses depends partly on the strength and number of the invaders, partly on the organism's ability to resist and destroy them, and partly on available medical resources for helping the body's defenses. On a psychological level, the severity of stress depends not only on the nature of the stressor and the individual's resources—both personal and situational—but also on how the stressor is perceived and evaluated. For example, a divorce may be highly stressful for one partner but not for the other.

In any case, the severity of stress depends on the relationship between the size of the demand and the individual's resources for dealing with it. However great the demand, it creates little stress if the individual can easily handle it. Some of the factors that influence severity of stress are importance, duration, and multiplicity of demand; preparedness of the individual; perception of threat; stress tolerance of the individual; and external resources and supports.

Importance, duration, and multiplicity of demands.   Certain stressors—such as the death of a loved one, a divorce, or serious personal illness—tend to be highly stressful for most people (Cochrane & Robertson, 1973; Holmes & Rahe, 1967; Rahe & Arthur, 1978). And ordinarily, the longer a stressor operates, the more severe its effects. Prolonged exhaustion imposes a more intense stress than does temporary fatigue. Often, too, stressors appear to have a cumulative effect. A married couple may maintain amicable relations through a long series of minor irritations or frustrations only to "explode" and dissolve the relationship in the face of the "last straw."

Encountering a number of stressors at the same time makes a difference too. If a man has a heart attack, loses his job, and receives news that his son or daughter has been arrested for drug abuse—all at the same time—the resulting stress will be more severe than if these events occurred separately.

Imminence of the stressor. In most difficult situations, including those involving conflict, the severity of stress increases as the need to deal with the demand approaches. For example, Mechanic (1962), from observations of graduate students, found that although the students thought about their examinations from time to time and experienced some anxiety during the prior three months, anxiety did not become intense until the examinations were nearly upon them. Similar experiences have been reported by sports parachutists as the hour of their next jump approaches (Epstein & Fenz, 1962, 1965). Persons anticipating other stress situations—such as major surgery—have found that the severity of stress increased as the time for the ordeal approached (Janis & Leventhal, 1965).

Perception of threat. It has been amply demonstrated that what is one person's stressor is another person's "piece of cake." If the situation is seen as presenting a serious threat, it is highly stressful, especially if resources for dealing with it are believed to be inadequate—whether they really are or not. And if we are generally unsure of our adequacy and worth, we are much more likely to experience threat than if we feel generally confident and secure.

Often new adjustive demands that have not been anticipated and for which no ready-made coping patterns are available will place an individual under severe stress. That is why the training of emergency workers such as police and firefighters normally involves repeated exposure to controlled or contrived stressors until coping patterns have become "second nature." In the same vein, the course of recovery from the stress created by major surgery can be markedly facilitated when adequate attention is given to providing the patient with realistic expectations beforehand (Janis & Leventhal, 1965). The same sense of adequacy and control can be achieved when the stress has been chosen voluntarily, rather than having been imposed by others or having come unexpectedly (Averill, 1973). Understanding the nature of a stressful situation, preparing for it, and knowing how long it will last, all lessen the severity of the stress when it does come.

Stress tolerance of the individual. The severity of stress in the face of a given stressor depends, too, on the individual's actual resources for withstanding stress in general and on the kind of stressor it is in particular. If a person is marginally adjusted, the slightest frustration or pressure may be highly stressful. The term *stress tolerance* or *frustration tolerance* refers to one's ability to withstand stress without having integrated functioning seriously impaired.

Both biologically and psychologically, people vary greatly in overall vulnerability to stressors as well as in the types of stressors to which they are most vulnerable. Emergencies, disappointments, and other problems that one person can take in stride may prove incapacitating to another. Sometimes early traumatic experiences have left the individual especially vulnerable to certain kinds of stressors.

External resources and supports. Lack of external supports—either personal or material—makes a given stressor more potent and weakens an individual's capacity to cope with it. A divorce or the death of one's mate evokes more stress if one is left feeling alone and unloved than if one is still surrounded by people one cares about and feels close to.

Pressures to violate one's principles or beliefs are less stressful and more easily withstood when one has an ally than when one is alone. It is hardly surprising that studies have found a tendency for individuals exposed to highly stressful situations to turn to others for support and reassurance.

Environmental supports are a complex matter, however, and behavior by one's family or friends that is intended to provide support may actually increase the stress. In his study of graduate students facing crucial examinations, Mechanic (1962) compared the effects of different types of behavior on the part of the spouses:

"In general, spouses do not provide blind support. They perceive the kinds of support the student wants and they provide it. The [spouse] who becomes worried about examinations also may provide more support than the spouse who says, 'I'm not worried, you will surely pass.' Indeed, since there is a chance that the student will not pass, the person who is supportive in a meaningful sense will not give blind assurance. . . . Often a statement to the effect, 'Do the best you can' is more supportive than, 'I'm sure you are going to do well.' The latter statement adds to the student's burden, for not only must he fear the disappointment of not passing, but also the loss of respect in the eyes of his spouse." (p. 158)

Often the culture provides for specific rituals or other courses of action that give support as the individual attempts to deal with certain types of stress. For example, most religions provide rituals that help the bereaved through their ordeal, and in some faiths, confession and atonement help people deal with stresses related to guilt and self-recrimination.

Stressor patterns are unique and changing

Each individual faces a unique pattern of adjustive demands. This is true partly because of differences in the way people perceive and interpret similar situations. But objectively, too, no people are faced with exactly the same pattern of stressors. Each individual's age, sex, occupation, economic status, personality makeup, competencies, and family situation help determine the demands he or she will face. The stressor pattern a child faces will differ in many ways from that of an older person, and the pattern faced by a carpenter will differ from that of a business executive.

Continuing stressors in a person's life.
Sometimes there are key stressors in a person's life that center around a continuing difficult life situation. A person may be stuck in a boring and unrewarding job from which there is seemingly no escape, suffer for years in an unhappy and conflictful marriage, or be severely frustrated by a physical handicap or a chronic health problem.

In other instances, the continuing stress derives from traumatic experiences from which the person has never fully recovered—as in the case of some prisoners of war who endured years of imprisonment, deprivation, and torture before being released. It has recently been suggested that some survivors of World War II

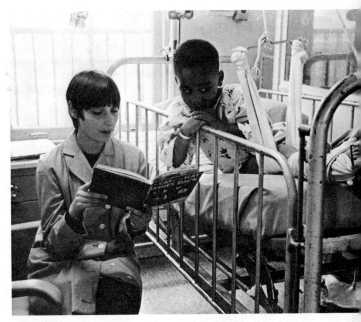

Hospitalization can be a severe stressor for anyone, but especially so for children. Warmth and attention should help to ease this youngster's anxiety.

concentration camps may suffer from disabling effects, such as impoverishment of personality, more than thirty years later (Dor-Shav, 1978). Similarly, the unexpected or violent death of a loved one—particularly a spouse or child—may have a lasting effect on a person's life and attitudes.

Sources of change in stressor patterns.
Stressor patterns do change with time, however—both predictably, as when we enter different life periods, and unpredictably, as when an accident, a death in the family, or a drastic social change makes new demands. Some of these changes bring only minor stress, while others place us under severe or excessive stress. But regardless of severity, the stressor pattern we face today is somewhat different from what it was a week ago; and it will be different in the future from what it is now. The total pattern at any time determines the part any one stressor will play and how much difficulty we are likely to have coping with it. And it is the way that we cope with stressors

over time that shapes the course of our lives.

From time to time, most of us experience periods of especially acute stress. The term *crisis* is used to refer to "a limited period in which an individual or group is exposed to threats or demands which are at or near the limits of their resources" (Lazarus, 1966, p. 407). Crises are often especially stressful because the coping techniques we are accustomed to depending on do not work (Butcher & Koss, 1978; Langsley, 1972).

A crisis may center around a traumatic divorce, or an episode of depression in which the person seriously considers suicide, or the aftermath of a serious injury or disease that forces difficult readjustments in one's self-concept and way of life. The incidence of such crises in the life of the average person is unknown—estimates range from about once every ten years to about once every two years. In view of the complex and rapidly changing society in which we live, the latter estimate may be the more realistic one.

The outcome of such crises has profound significance for the person's subsequent adjustment. An effective new method of coping developed during a period of crisis may be added to the person's previous repertoire of coping behaviors; or inability to deal adequately with the crisis may impair one's ability to cope effectively with similar stressors in the future because of expectation of failure. For this reason "crisis intervention"—providing psychological help in times of severe and special stress—has become an important element in contemporary approaches to treatment and prevention of abnormal behavior. We shall discuss such intervention in more detail in Chapter 20.

It is important to remember that any life change, even a favorable one, places new demands on us and thus is somewhat stressful. The faster such changes come upon us, the greater the stress. Research efforts to determine the relationship between stress and possible physical and mental disorder have been many, and one continuing effort is summarized in the HIGHLIGHT on this page. In addition, the recent DSM-III provides in Axis IV (see page 19) a more formal framework by which the diagnostician can take into account the severity of psychosocial stressors that may be contributing to an individual's maladaptive behavior.

HIGHLIGHT

Measuring life stress

Holmes and his colleagues (Holmes & Rahe, 1967; Holmes & Holmes, 1970; Rahe & Arthur, 1978) have developed the Social Readjustment Rating Scale (SRRS), an objective method for measuring the cumulative stress to which an individual has been exposed over a period of time. This scale measures life stress in terms of "life change units" (LCU) involving the following events.

Events	Scale of Impact
Death of spouse	100
Divorce	73
Marital separation	65
Jail term	63
Death of close family member	63
Personal injury or illness	53
Marriage	50
Fired at work	47
Marital reconciliation	45
Retirement	45
Change in health of family member	44
Pregnancy	40
Sex difficulties	39
Gain of new family member	39
Business readjustment	39
Change in financial state	38
Death of close friend	37
Change to different line of work	36
Change in number of arguments with spouse	35
High mortgage	31
Foreclosure of mortgage or loan	30
Change in responsibilities at work	29
Son or daughter leaving home	29
Trouble with in-laws	29
Outstanding personal achievement	28
Wife begins or stops work	26
Begin or end school	26
Change in living conditions	25
Revision of personal habits	24
Trouble with boss	23
Change in work hours or conditions	20
Change in residence	20
Change in schools	20
Change in recreation	19
Change in church activities	19
Change in social activities	18
Small mortgage or loan	17
Change in sleeping habits	16
Change in number of family get-togethers	15
Change in eating habits	15
Vacation	13
Christmas	12
Minor violations of the law	11

For persons who had been exposed in recent months to stressful events that added up to an LCU score of 300 or above, these investigators found the risk of developing a major illness within the next two years to be very high, approximating 80 percent.

Reactions to life stress

Since stress—beyond a minimal level—threatens the well-being of the organism, it engenders automatic, persistent attempts at its resolution; it forces a person to do something about it. What is done depends on many factors, including one's frame of reference, motives, competencies, stress tolerance, environmental limitations and supports, prior mental set, and social demands and expectations. Recent evidence even suggests that some particularly hardy individuals may be relatively immune to stressors that would impair the functioning of most of us (Kobasa, 1979). Sometimes inner factors play the dominant role in determining one's stress reactions; at other times environmental conditions are of primary importance. Any stress reaction, of course, reflects the interplay of a combination of *inner* and *outer determinants*—some more influential than others, but all working together to make the individual react in a certain way.

In this section we shall begin by considering some general principles of adjustive behavior; then we shall examine the particular characteristics of both task-oriented and defense-oriented coping patterns; and finally we shall conclude this chapter with a brief review of the types and stages of decompensation under excessive stress.

General principles of adjustive behavior

In reviewing certain general principles that underlie reactions to adjustive demands, we shall again find it convenient to utilize the concept of three interactional levels. Thus, on a biological level there are immunological defenses against disease and damage-repair mechanisms; on a psychological and interpersonal level there are learned coping patterns and self-defenses; and on a sociocultural

How we react to stress often depends on the resources available to us.

level there are group resources, such as labor unions, religious organizations, and law-enforcement agencies.

The failure of coping efforts on any of these levels may seriously impair an individual's adjustment on other levels. For example, a breakdown of immunological defenses against disease may impair not only bodily functioning but psychological functioning as well; chronic malfunctioning of psychological coping patterns may lead to peptic ulcers or other "diseases of adaptation"; and the failure of a group on which one depends may seriously interfere with one's own ability to satisfy basic needs.

Reactions are holistic.

We have seen that living organisms tend to maintain their integrity or "wholeness." Basic to this integration of behavior are the neural processes of *excitation* and *inhibition*.

Since all of an individual's adjustive behavior must use the same bodily equipment—sense organs, nervous system, glands, muscles, and so on—the overall adjustive demands of the moment will determine how it is used. If there are several competing demands, the one that is most important, or is perceived as most important, will commandeer the organism's adjustive resources, and some functions or actions will be inhibited while others are facilitated.

This coordination is well illustrated by emergency emotional reactions—for example, in the moment just prior to a traffic accident. Here, digestive and other bodily processes not immediately essential for survival are slowed down or stopped (inhibited) while the driver's resources for increased activity and effort are mobilized (excited)—with a heightening of muscle tonus, the release of stored sugar into the bloodstream, and the secretion of *adrenaline,* a key agent in helping the body react with vigor to immediate, urgent stressor conditions.

In general, the processes of excitation and inhibition provide the organism with the flexibility it needs for dealing with stressors. Only under unusual or pathological conditions does the organism function "segmentally" rather than as an integrated unit. Such segmental action may occur as a consequence of interference with the integrating functions of the higher brain centers by alcohol, drugs, or brain damage; or it may occur as a consequence of excessive psychological stress.

Reactions are economical.

Not only does an organism react to a stressor as an integrated unit, but it responds in a way that entails a minimum expenditure of resources. This, of course, is what we might expect in view of the organism's tendencies toward self-maintenance. One's needs and goals are many, but one's resources, while impressive, are limited.

Selye (1976) has pointed out that organisms that survive—whether they are low or high on the evolutionary scale—tend to employ first those defenses that are least expensive; if these are ineffective, then additional and more expensive resources are brought into operation. If a continuously increasing amount of acid is injected into a dog's veins, for example, the first defense mechanism that appears is over-breathing. If this does not prove effective, more drastic protective mechanisms, such as biochemical changes in the blood, are employed. Similarly, if the head of a social services agency finds the workers unable to handle the caseload, she may find it necessary to add to the staff.

The principle of economy is also relevant in a slightly different context. We tend to maintain our existing patterns of thought and action not only because they provide a basic source of security in dealing with the world but also because it takes less effort to follow established patterns than to modify them or adopt new ones. This tendency to resist change in established ways of perceiving and acting has been referred to as *inertia* on the individual level and as *cultural lag* on the social level. These concepts help explain the tendency of maladaptive behavior patterns to persist long after new, more effective patterns have become available.

Reactions may be automatic or planned.

Reactions to stressful situations may be undertaken with conscious planning, with only partial awareness, or with no conscious involvement at all. In general, an individual's potentials for conscious and automatic functioning represent complementary resources for meeting adjustive demands.

On a biological level, the repair of damaged tissue, immunological defenses against dis-

People often feel anger when they are frustrated —whether it be over trying to appropriate a certain park bench or to have the last word in a spirited argument.

ease, and other corrective and defensive processes take place automatically. Some psychological tension-reducing and repair mechanisms such as crying and repetitive talking also take place automatically. Even if the individual is aware of what he or she is doing, such responses are not usually planned or consciously thought out. Seeing what one wants to see, screening out or distorting threatening information, and repressing painful experiences are other examples of automatic and mainly unconscious processes. Automatic functioning on a psychological level also commonly takes the form of habits, in which responses that were once conscious and planned no longer require the individual's attention.

Automatic functioning can be a boon in processing routine stressors, since it frees one's attention for problems that require careful thought. It is apparent, however, that automatic behavior can also impair effective adjustment. A person who unthinkingly employs habitual patterns of response in coping with a marital problem, for instance, is clearly reducing the chances that the problem will ever be satisfactorily resolved. In all but routine situations, the ability to adapt effectively depends on conscious effort and the flexibility to choose an appropriate response.

Reactions have emotional components.
The particular emotional states accompanying reactions to stressors may vary greatly. Three emotional patterns are of special significance here: anger, fear, and anxiety.

1. *Frustration tends to elicit anger.* Frustrating conditions often elicit anger, accompanied by a tendency to attack and remove the obstacle to one's goals. Where frustration continues, anger may blend into a more enduring attitude of hostility, characterized by feelings of wanting to hurt or destroy the person viewed as the source of frustration. Anger and aggressive feelings may or may not be carried out in aggressive action depending on past learning, the probable consequences, and other factors. Where anger is intense, however, and the individual's inner controls are poorly developed or temporarily lowered by alcohol or other conditions, the result may be impulsive behavior of a destructive nature, such as assault or homicide.[8]

2. *Danger tends to elicit fear.* The perception of danger tends to arouse fear and to impel the individual toward withdrawal or flight.

[8]The role of anger and aggression in human behavior has been ably presented by Berkowitz (1974) and Lefkowitz, Eron, Walder, & Huesmann (1977).

However, the nature of the stress situation and the degree of fear elicited have much to do with the direction and quality of resulting behavior. In the face of extreme danger, the individual may panic or "freeze" and become unable to function in an organized manner. Such behavior is commonly observed in fires and other disasters.

3. *Threat tends to elicit anxiety.* Although closely related to fear, anxiety is a feeling of impending threat in which the specific nature of the danger is often not clearly perceived. Many situations—such as the possibility that one's marriage will end in divorce—may give rise to both fear and anxiety. Stressor situations which induce anxiety are often difficult to cope with since the precise nature of the threat is usually unclear to the individual, yet the anxiety or "psychic pain" demands some sort of protective action. As we shall see, the defenses mustered to cope with anxiety may run the entire gamut of abnormal behavior.

Anger, fear, and anxiety may be aroused singly or in various combinations. Where fear is aroused, anger often follows, for the things we fear are usually actual or potential sources of frustration. These so-called negative emotions may be intermeshed with more positive ones such as love, as when a person has *ambivalent* feelings toward a parent or mate. The specific emotions that occur are heavily influenced by past learning and by the perceived significance of the stress situation to the individual.

Reactions may be task-oriented or defense-oriented. In coping with stress, a person is confronted with two problems: (a) to meet the requirements of the adjustive demand, and (b) to protect the self from psychological damage and disorganization. A person who feels competent to handle a stress situation tends to act in a *task-oriented* way—that is, to direct behavior primarily at dealing with the requirements of the adjustive demand. But when one's feelings of adequacy are seriously threatened by the adjustive demand, reactions will tend to be *defense-oriented*—aimed primarily at protecting the self from hurt and disorganization.

The distinction between task-oriented and defense-oriented reactions is of crucial significance in understanding abnormal behavior. To a very large extent, the person behaving maladaptively may be thought of as someone who has forsaken effective goal-oriented action in favor of preemptive concerns for maintaining the integrity of the self, however ill-advised and self-defeating the effort may prove to be in the long run.

Task-oriented reaction patterns

Since task-oriented reactions are aimed at meeting the demands of the stressor, they tend to be based on an objective appraisal of the situation, to be rational and constructive, and to be consciously directed. The typical steps in such reactions—whether the reaction turns out to be effective or ineffective—are generally flexible enough to enable the individual to change course.

Task-oriented reactions may involve making changes in one's self or one's surroundings or both, depending on the situation. The action may be overt—as in showing one's spouse more affection; or it may be covert—as in lowering one's level of aspiration. And the action may involve retreating from the problem, attacking it directly, or trying to find a workable compromise. Retreat and attack—flight and fight—are fundamental forms of coping with stressors found in all organisms. They appear to be part of the organism's heritage.

Retreat. Simple retreat is a primary type of task-oriented reaction to stress. Many animals seem capable of fairly well-coordinated retreat or flight reactions shortly after birth, but the human infant lacks such built-in patterns. On the other hand, the infant is able to withdraw a hand or foot from a painful stimulus, such as a hot object, and when subjected to sudden, unexpected stimuli may tend to curl up into a ball, apparently manifesting an innate withdrawal reaction. However, although retreat may be an effective task-oriented reaction, the fear that may accompany it can lead to maladaptive behavior.

In addition to retreating from danger physically, the individual may withdraw in various psychological ways—for example, by admitting defeat, avoiding certain types of adjustive demands, or reducing emotional involvement in a situation. Engel (1962) has postulated an innately determined conservation-withdrawal mechanism characteristic of all higher animals wherein, under severe and prolonged frustration, the organism withdraws and conserves energy until such time as a change in conditions might make vigorous emotion and activity once again adaptive. In these ways it is possible to exercise considerable control over the effects of stressors to which one is exposed and thus keep pressures and other problems from becoming excessive. On the other hand, such reactions often bring on additional problems, such as depression, which we shall discuss at length in Chapter 11.

Attack. Where retreat serves to remove the organism from dangerous situations it cannot overcome, attack helps to overcome obstacles and attain goals necessary to its survival. The possible ways of attacking a problem are many; they range from obvious actions, such as physical assault or learning new skills, to subtle means, such as patience or passive resistance. The type of stressor may influence the particular form that an attack reaction takes.

1. *Direct action to end frustration.* In the face of frustration, attack responses are apparently based on tendencies of living organisms toward increased activity and variation in mode of response when obstacles are encountered. For example, someone failing on a job may exert greater effort and go about systematically trying to learn new skills.

2. *Choice to resolve conflict.* In conflict situations, attack may involve analyzing the advantages and disadvantages of various options and making an objective, informed decision. Sometimes, however, when there are many unknowns, the best solution may come through keeping one's options open. The student who is not sure what major to choose may do well to put off a choice as long as possible.

3. *Resistance to pressure.* Usually the individual resists pressure, especially when the pressure is seen as arbitrary and unwarranted. Children, for example, often develop highly effective techniques for coping with perfectionistic parents or teachers. Defiance and rebellion are active forms of resistance, but there are passive forms too, such as inattention, dawdling, helplessness, and deliberate under-

achievement. Resistance to pressure is an attempt by the organism to maintain its own integrity and to be in control of its own actions.

When appropriate to the situation and the resources of the individual, an attack approach usually offers the best channel for using and coordinating resources in constructive action. However, attack behavior may be destructive as well as constructive. With anger and hostility, there is a tendency to destroy as well as attack—a tendency that may lead to socially disapproved and self-defeating behavior.

Compromise. Since most stress situations cannot be dealt with successfully by either retreat or direct attack, it usually becomes necessary to work out some sort of compromise solution. This approach may entail changing one's method of operation, accepting substitute goals, or working out some sort of accommodation in which one settles for part of what was initially wanted.

Individuals faced with starvation may compromise with their consciences and steal "just this one time"; or they may ignore their squeamishness and eat worms, bugs, spiders, or even human flesh. A related form of compromise is the acceptance of substitute goals under conditions of severe frustration. Thus a prisoner may gain some sexual satisfaction from pinup pictures or from wish-fulfilling daydreams. In fact, Masserman (1961) has shown that under sustained frustration, individuals usually become increasingly willing to accept substitute goals—both symbolic and nonsymbolic ones.

When compromise reactions succeed in meeting the essential requirements of the stressor situation, the problem is resolved and the person can go on to other activities. From time to time, however, each of us is likely to make compromises that we cannot fully accept and live with because important needs continue to go unmet. In such instances, additional adjustive action is required.

Task-oriented reactions of all three types—retreat, attack, and compromise—involve the same basic steps: (a) defining the problem, (b) working out alternative solutions and deciding on an appropriate course of action, and (c) taking action and evaluating the feedback. Perhaps the most difficult step in this sequence is that of decision making, or choice.

While a task-oriented approach usually offers the best chance of resolving the stressor situation, it is by no means infallible. Inaccurate information, faulty values, and poor judgment can lead to unsuitable and maladaptive reactions. And even if we choose well and act with skill, factors beyond our control may tip the balance against us. As the poet Burns put it so succinctly,

"The best-laid schemes o' mice an' men,
  Gang aft agley,
An' lea'e us nought but grief an' pain
  For promis'd joy!"

Even if the individual suffers a setback in dealing with severe stress or a crisis situation, the results may not be entirely negative if feedback is utilized in a task-oriented way. For example, the person who is going through a traumatic divorce may gain better self-understanding and improve his or her competencies for future relationships.

Defense-oriented reaction patterns

Defense-oriented reactions to stress, as we have noted, are aimed chiefly at protecting the self from hurt and disorganization.

Two types of defense-oriented reactions are commonly differentiated. The first consists of responses such as crying, repetitive talking, and mourning that seem to function as psychological damage-repair mechanisms. The second type consists of the so-called ego- or self-defense mechanisms, such as denial and rationalization, that function to relieve tension and anxiety and to protect the self from hurt and devaluation.

Of these two types of defensive reaction, an understanding of the second is clearly more important in coming to grips with behavior that is maladaptive. These defense reactions protect the individual from both external threats, such as devaluating failures, and internal threats, such as guilt-arousing desires or actions. They appear to protect the self in one or more of the following ways: (a) by denying, distorting, or restricting the individual's experience; (b) by reducing emotional or self-involvement; and (c) by counteracting threat

or damage. Often, of course, a given defense mechanism may offer more than one kind of protection.

These defense mechanisms are ordinarily used in combination rather than singly, and often they are combined with task-oriented behavior. We all use them to some extent for coping with the problems of living. In fact, Gleser and Sacks (1973) have concluded that we tend to be fairly consistent in the particular mechanisms we use.

Ego-defense mechanisms. Since there are numerous ego-defense mechanisms, we shall review only those that seem immediately relevant to an understanding of abnormal behavior.

1. *Denial of reality.* Probably the simplest and most primitive of all self-defense mechanisms is denial of reality, in which an attempt is made to "screen out" disagreeable realities by ignoring or refusing to acknowledge them. The tendency toward perceptual defense is part of this inclination to deny or avoid reality. One may turn away from unpleasant sights, refuse to discuss unpleasant topics, faint when confronted with a traumatic situation, deny criticism, or become so preoccupied with work that there is no time to deal with marital, child-rearing, or other personal problems. Under extreme conditions, such as imprisonment, an individual may experience the feeling that "This isn't really happening to me." Here the defensive reaction appears, at least temporarily, to provide insulation from the full impact of the traumatic situation. Similarly, Kubler-Ross (1975) has noted that persons having terminal illnesses almost uniformly go through a stage of denial before being able to come to grips effectively with their situation.

2. *Fantasy.* By means of this mechanism, frustration is overcome by the imaginary achievement of goals and meeting of needs. Two common varieties of wish-fulfilling fantasy are the *conquering hero* and *suffering hero* patterns. In the first, one may picture oneself as a great world leader, a courageous astronaut, a celebrated athlete, a famous movie or television star, or other renowned figure who performs incredible feats and wins the admiration of all—the idea being that the individual is capable, powerful, and respected. Frequently hostility is dissipated safely through conquering-hero fantasies in which all who stand in one's way are destroyed or punished. Such fantasies act as safety valves and provide some measure of compensatory gratification for the individual.

In the *suffering hero* pattern, no admission of personal inferiority is necessary, since one is suffering from some dread disease, debilitating handicap, or visitation from unjust fate. When others find out about such difficulties and realize the bravery and courage it took to carry on under such conditions, they will be sympathetic and admiring. Thus, inferior performance or failures are explained away without any threat to one's feelings of adequacy and worth.

3. *Repression.* This is a defense mechanism by means of which threatening or painful thoughts and desires are excluded from consciousness.[9] Although it has often been referred to as "selective forgetting," it is more in the nature of selective remembering. For although the material that is repressed is denied admission to conscious awareness, it is not really forgotten. The soldier who has seen his best friend's head blown off by shrapnel may find the experience so terribly painful that he excludes it from consciousness and becomes "amnesic" with regard to the battle experience. When brought to an aid station, he may be nervous and trembling, unable to recall his name or what has happened to him, and manifesting other signs of his ordeal. But the intolerable battle experience, screened from consciousness, may be brought into awareness by means of hypnosis or sodium pentothal interviews.

Repression is an extremely important self-defense mechanism in that it affords protection from sudden, traumatic experiences until time has somewhat desensitized the individual to the shock. Repression may also help the individual control dangerous and unacceptable desires—and at the same time alleviate the anxiety associated with such desires. The reality of repression in freeing the individual from anxiety has been demonstrated in an interest-ing study by Sommerschield and Reyher (1973). They induced posthypnotic conflicts in their subjects and found that various symptoms, including gastric distress, tension, and anxiety, appeared as the hypnotically induced repression weakened and the conflict threatened to enter consciousness.

Repression, in varying degrees, enters into other defense mechanisms. There is some evidence that it is only when repression fails that stronger, more maladaptive defenses are tried.

4. *Rationalization.* Rationalization is justifying maladaptive behavior by faulty logic or ascribing it to noble motives that did not in fact inspire it. Rationalization has two major defensive values: (a) it helps justify specific behaviors; and (b) it aids in softening the disappointment connected with unattainable goals.

Typically, rationalization involves thinking up logical, socially approved reasons for past, present, or proposed behaviors. With a little effort persons using rationalization may be able to justify to themselves diverting funds needed for essentials to lavish entertainment, neglecting work for cultural pursuits, or marrying someone whom they do not love. Even callous brutality can be rationalized as necessary or even praiseworthy. Adolf Hitler saw the extermination of the Jews as his patriotic duty.

Curiously enough, as Erich Fromm (1955) has pointed out,

"However unreasonable or immoral an action may be, man has an insuperable urge to rationalize it—that is, to prove to himself and to others that his action is determined by reason, common sense, or at least conventional morality." (p. 65)

Rationalization is also used to soften the disappointment of thwarted desires. A common example of such rationalization is the "sour grapes" reaction. Students may justify their mediocre college performance on the grounds that they are refusing to get involved in the "competitive rat race" of modern society. One way of reducing the discrepancy embodied in failure to take action toward a desired goal is to decide that the goal is really not anything worth having anyway.

Frequently, of course, it is difficult to tell where an objective consideration of realities leaves off and rationalization begins. Behaviors that commonly indicate rationalization

[9]Repression may be distinguished from suppression in that it occurs without the awareness of conscious intent of the individual. In suppression, the individual *consciously* decides not to express a feeling or even think about a disturbing event. A critical review of the concept of repression may be found in Holmes (1974).

Rationalization

Psychotic

are (a) hunting for reasons to justify one's behavior or beliefs; (b) being unable to recognize inconsistencies or contradictory evidence; and (c) becoming upset when one's "reasons" are questioned.

5. *Projection.* Projection is a defensive reaction by means of which (a) others are seen as responsible for one's own shortcomings, mistakes, and misdeeds; and (b) others are seen as harboring one's own unacceptable impulses, thoughts, and desires.

Projection is perhaps most commonly evidenced by the first tendency, sometimes called "transfer of blame." The student who fails an examination may feel that the teacher was unfair; the delinquent teenager may blame her problems on a rejecting and nonunderstanding parent; and even the small boy being punished for fighting may protest, "It wasn't my fault—he hit me first." Fate and bad luck are particularly overworked objects of projection. Even inanimate objects are not exempt from blame. The three-year-old who falls off a hobby horse may attack it with blows and kicks; the baseball player who strikes out may carefully examine his bat. In extreme cases, an individual may become convinced that other persons or forces are systematically working against him or her. Such ideas may develop into delusions of persecution involving the supposed plots and conspiracies of "the enemy."

In other projective reactions, individuals may attribute their own unacceptable desires and thoughts to others. This tendency appears to be particularly common among those with rigid moral values and strict conscience development. For example, a man who is sexually attracted to children may insist that a child is behaving seductively toward him. Consequently, the child becomes the offender, while the man remains conveniently "pure," unaware of his own unacceptable inclinations.

6. *Reaction formation.* Sometimes individuals protect themselves from dangerous desires by not only repressing them, but actually developing conscious attitudes and behavior patterns that are just the opposite. Thus they may conceal hate with a façade of love, cruelty with kindness, or desires for sexual promiscuity with moralistic sexual attitudes and behavior. In this way individuals erect obstacles or barriers that reinforce their repression and keep their real desires and feelings from con-

scious awareness and from being carried out overtly.

On a simple level, reaction formation is illustrated by the old story about the spinster who looks hopefully under her bed each night for fear that a man may be lurking there. On a more complex level, reaction formation may be manifested by people who crusade against loose morals, alcohol, "pornography," gambling, or even smoking cigarettes. Often such people have a background of earlier difficulties with these problems themselves, and their zealous crusading appears to be a means of safeguarding themselves against recurrence of their difficulties. This is known as the "reformed sinner syndrome."

Reaction formation, like repression, may have adjustive value in helping the individual maintain socially approved behavior and avoid awareness of threatening and self-devaluating desires. But because this mechanism, too, is self-deceptive and not subject to conscious control, it often results in exaggerated and rigid fears or beliefs that may complicate an individual's adjustive reactions and lead to excessive harshness or severity in dealing with the lapses of others.

7. *Displacement.* In displacement there is a shift of emotion or symbolic meaning away from the person or object toward which it was originally directed to another person or object. Often displacement involves difficult emotions, such as hostility and anxiety. A common subject for cartoons about displacement is the meek office clerk who has been refused a raise by a domineering boss. Instead of expressing hostility toward the employer—which would be dangerous—the clerk goes home and is unreasonably irritable with family members.

In some instances the individual whose hostility has been aroused by an outside person or event may turn the hostility inward, engaging in exaggerated self-accusations and recriminations, and feel severe guilt and self-devaluation. Such intropunitive reactions do protect the individual from expressing dangerous hostility toward others, but may lead to depression and even to attempted or actual suicide.

Through a process of symbolic association, displacement may become extremely complex and deviant. Some phobias, for example, where the person develops a specific fear of some harmless aspect of the environment, appear to be, in reality, symbolically mediated displacements of anxiety relating to personally unacceptable impulses.

8. *Emotional insulation.* Here the individual reduces emotional involvement in situations that are viewed as disappointing and hurtful. Such "emotional anaesthesia" is commonly seen as one phase of a grief reaction following significant loss, as we shall see in Chapter 11.

In more extreme cases of long-continued frustration, as in chronic unemployment or prison confinement, many persons lose hope, become resigned and apathetic, and adapt themselves to a restricted way of life. Such "broken" individuals thus protect themselves from the bitter hurt of sustained frustration by becoming passive recipients of whatever life brings them. Similarly, in extreme forms of alienation the individual may become non-involved and apathetic, feeling isolated, bewildered, and without hope. In certain mental disorders, too, such as chronic schizophrenia, there is often an extreme use of insulation that apparently protects the individual from emotional involvement in a life situation and world that have proved unbearably hurtful.

Up to a point, emotional insulation is an important means of defense against unnecessary disappointment and hurt. But life involves calculated risks, and most people are willing to take a chance on active participation. Emotional insulation provides a protective shell that prevents a repetition of previous pain, but it reduces the individual's healthy, vigorous participation in life.

9. *Intellectualization (isolation).* This defense mechanism is related to both emotional insulation and rationalization. Here the emotional reaction that would normally accompany a painful event is avoided by a rational explanation that divests the event of personal significance and painful feeling. The hurt over a parent's death is reduced by saying that he or she lived a full life or died mercifully without pain. Failures and disappointments are softened by pointing out that "it could have been worse." Cynicism may become a convenient means of reducing guilt feelings over not living up to one's ideals. Even the verbalization of good intentions, as in a glib admission that "I should work harder" or that "I should be less selfish and more interested in the welfare of

others," seems to cut down on guilt and relieve one of the necessity of positive action.

Intellectualization may be employed under extremely stressful conditions as well as in dealing with the milder stressors of everyday life. Bluestone and McGahee have found that this defense mechanism was often used by prisoners awaiting execution. They have described the pattern as follows: " 'So they'll kill me; and that's that'—this said with a shrug of the shoulders suggests that the affect appropriate to the thought has somehow been isolated" (1962, p. 395).

10. *Undoing (atonement).* Undoing is designed to negate or annul some disapproved thought, impulse, or act. Apologizing for wrongs, repentance, doing penance, and undergoing punishment are all forms of undoing.

Undoing apparently develops out of early training in which children learn that once they apologize, make some restitution, or are punished for disapproved behavior, their misdeed is negated and they can start over with a clean slate and with renewed parental approval. As a consequence of such early learning, people commonly develop methods of atoning for or undoing their misdeeds—methods to avoid or ameliorate the punishment and self-devaluation that would otherwise result. The neglectful parent may bring home presents; the unethical executive may give huge sums of money to charity.

The opportunity for confession and the assurance of forgiveness in some religions appear to meet a deep human need to be able to get rid of guilt feelings and make a new beginning. As a defense mechanism, however, undoing operates on an unconscious level. The individual assuages feelings of guilt by making some kind of reparation, but without conscious awareness of the intent of the action.

11. *Regression.* Regression is a defense mechanism in which one returns to the use of reaction patterns long since outgrown. When a new addition to the family has seemingly undermined his status, a little boy may revert to bed-wetting and other infantile behavior that once brought him parental attention. An even more severe example of regression is presented in the HIGHLIGHT on page 120.

We might expect something akin to regression to occur merely on the basis of the frequent failure of newly learned reactions to

An example of extreme regression

This young woman looked like an average 17-year-old girl (left) until she found the photograph of herself taken at the age of 5 (center). Thereafter, she tried to look as much as she could like the pictured child (right).

From her childhood, the girl had been the victim of an extremely contentious and unstable environment. She first showed neurotic symptoms about the age of 4, when her parents began to quarrel violently. When the girl was 7, the mother refused further sexual relations with the father, but the girl slept with the father until she was 13. The mother, suspecting incestuous seduction, obtained legal custody of the girl at this time and removed her to another home.

Resenting the separation from her father, the girl quarreled with her mother, became a disciplinary problem at school, and acquired a police record for delinquency. On the girl's insistence the mother and she visited the father after 3 years, and found him "living with a girl in questionable circumstances." A violent scene ensued, and again the mother took her daughter home, against her wishes.

After this the girl would not attend school, and she became sullen and withdrawn. In her mother's absence she would go on destructive forays of the house, and in one of these forays discovered the early picture of herself. In her subsequent behavior she "appeared to have regressed to a relatively desirable period in life antedating disruptive jealousies and other conflict; moreover, she acted out this regression in unconsciously determined but strikingly symbolic patterns of eliminating the mother as a rival and regaining the father she had lost in her childhood" (adapted from Masserman, 1961, pp. 70–71, case of Dr. John Romano).

 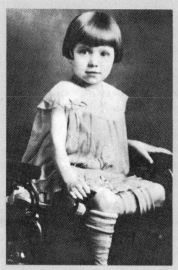 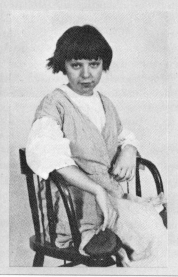

bring satisfaction. In looking for other, more successful modes of adjustment, it would be only natural to try out discarded patterns that previously had brought satisfaction.

However, regression is a more generalized reaction than merely trying out older modes of response when new ones have failed. For in regression the individual retreats from reality to a less demanding personal status—one that involves lowered aspirations and more readily accomplished satisfactions. This point is well illustrated by Bettelheim's reference to a general "regression to infantile behavior" seen in nearly all the prisoners at the Nazi concentration camps of Dachau and Buchenwald.

"The prisoners lived, like children, only in the immediate present: . . . they became unable to plan for the future or to give up immediate pleasure satisfactions to gain greater ones in the near future. . . . They were boastful, telling tales about what they had accomplished in their former lives, or how they succeeded in cheating foremen or guards, and how they sabotaged the work. Like children, they felt not at all set back or ashamed when it became known that they had lied about their prowess." (1943, p. 443)

In our discussion of the psychoses, we shall describe patients whose regression is so extreme that they are no longer able to dress, feed, or otherwise take care of themselves.

12. *Identification.* Identification often takes place in imitative learning, as when a boy identifies with his father and uses him as a model. Identification may also operate as a defense mechanism in enhancing feelings of worth and protecting the individual against self-devaluation.

Growing children soon learn that the way in which they are evaluated by others depends heavily on their family and other group memberships. During adolescence and adulthood, the mechanism of identification is expanded to include a wide range of persons and groups. Not only does society evaluate individuals in the light of their group memberships, but also individuals come to evaluate themselves in the light of their own group memberships. Students may identify with the college they attend and its athletic teams, and many employees identify with the power and prestige of the company for which they work. By doing so, they take as their own some of the desirable attributes of the groups to which they belong. Particularly for persons who feel basically insecure, such identifications may have important supportive and defensive value.

When feelings of adequacy and worth are based too heavily on identification with others, however, the individual becomes highly vulnerable to stress situations in which such identifications prove devaluating—for example, when the values and behavior of the group prove disillusioning, when the group suffers humiliation, or when the group is relegated to low social status. In such cases, the individual's identifications lead to self-devaluation rather than to self-enhancement. This is one reason why the athletic coach whose team loses consistently often winds up out of a job as well.

13. *Introjection.* Introjection is closely related to identification. As a defense reaction it involves the acceptance of others' values and norms as one's own even when they are contrary to one's previous assumptions. After revolutions leading to dictatorial forms of government, for example, many people introject the new values and beliefs as a protection for themselves. By internalizing the socially prescribed values and norms, they can then trust themselves to avoid behavior that would bring social retaliation and punishment.

In describing the use of introjection under extreme conditions, it is again useful to refer to the experiences of Bettelheim at the Nazi concentration camps of Dachau and Buchenwald. Under the cruel and insidious camp experiences, previous values and identifications were broken down and new norms were introjected —Nazi norms.

"A prisoner had reached the final stage of adjustment to the camp situation when he had changed his personality so as to accept as his own the values of the Gestapo. . . . old prisoners were sometimes instrumental in getting rid of the unfit, in this way making a feature of Gestapo ideology a feature of their own behavior." (1943, pp. 447–49)

One aspect of introjection has been referred to as "identification with the aggressor" and is a defensive reaction that seems to follow the principle, "If you can't beat 'em, join 'em." However, it is evident that introjection may lead to seriously distorted and maladaptive behavior.

14. *Compensation.* Compensatory reactions are defenses against feelings of inferiority and inadequacy growing out of real or imagined personal defects or weaknesses, as well as out of the individual's inevitable failures and setbacks. Such reactions may take many forms and may represent constructive, deliberate, task-oriented behavior, as in the case of an individual who attempts to overcome a physical handicap through increased effort and persistence. Demosthenes, the great orator, had to overcome early stuttering, and Wilma Rudolph, crippled and unable to walk until she was eight years old, became an Olympic track winner. Compensatory reactions of this type may be a deciding factor in success, as biographers are quick to point out.

More commonly, compensatory reactions are indirect; there is an attempt to substitute for the defect in some way or to draw attention away from it. The physically unattractive child may develop an exceptionally pleasing personality, the uncoordinated child may turn from athletics to scholarship, and the mediocre nobody may become the Grand Imperial Potentate of some secret order. Much of the cosmetics industry has developed around minimizing undesirable facial features and emphasizing desirable ones.

Unfortunately, not all compensatory reactions are desirable. The child who feels insecure may show off to try to get more attention; the person who feels unloved and frustrated may eat too much. Some people brag about their illustrious ancestors and exaggerate their own accomplishments, while others resort to criticism or innuendoes in attempts to cut others down to their own size. In extreme cases, an individual may engage in antisocial behavior or develop eccentricities in an unconscious attempt to get some attention and evidence of interest and concern from others.

Evaluation of ego-defense mechanisms.

Although defense mechanisms may serve useful protective functions, they usually involve some measure of self-deception and reality distortion and may seriously interfere with the effective resolution of the actual problem. For these reasons, ego-defense mechanisms are considered maladaptive when they become the predominant means of coping with stressors.

Both the "positive" and "negative" functions of such defenses have been well illustrated in an investigation of the ego defenses used by thirty hospitalized women who were awaiting the outcome of breast tumor biopsy (Katz et al., 1970). These researchers found the defense mechanisms of denial and rationalization to be highly effective in coping with anxiety, particularly when used in combination. They also found, however, that many of the women who allayed their anxieties with these defenses did not seek early enough medical help.

In summary, it may be emphasized that these defense mechanisms are, in the main, learned; they are designed to deal with inner hurt, anxiety, and self-devaluation; they operate on relatively automatic and habitual levels; and they typically involve some measure of

Summary chart of ego-defense mechanisms

Denial of reality. Protecting self from unpleasant reality by refusal to perceive or face it

Fantasy. Gratifying frustrated desires by imaginary achievements

Repression. Preventing painful or dangerous thoughts from entering consciousness

Rationalization. Attempting to prove that one's behavior is "rational" and justifiable and thus worthy of self- and social approval

Projection. Placing blame for difficulties upon others or attributing one's own unethical desires to others

Reaction formation. Preventing dangerous desires from being expressed by adopting exaggerated opposed attitudes and types of behavior and using them as "barriers"

Displacement. Discharging pent-up feelings, usually of hostility, on objects less dangerous than those which initially aroused the emotions

Emotional insulation. Reducing ego involvement and withdrawing into passivity to protect self from hurt

Intellectualization (isolation). Cutting off affective charge from hurtful situations or separating incompatible attitudes by logic-tight compartments

Undoing. Atoning for and thus counteracting immoral desires or acts

Regression. Retreating to earlier developmental level involving less mature responses and usually a lower level of aspiration

Identification. Increasing feelings of worth by identifying self with person or institution of illustrious standing

Introjection. Incorporating external values and standards into ego structure so individual is not at their mercy as external threats

Compensation. Covering up weakness by emphasizing desirable trait or making up for frustration in one area by overgratification in another

Based on Anna Freud (1946)

self-deception and reality distortion. A summary chart of the ego-defense mechanisms we have discussed is presented in the HIGHLIGHT on page 122.

Decompensation under excessive stress

As we have seen, stressor conditions create a challenge to the organism's adaptive resources, bringing into play various defensive reactions. Most of the time, these varied defensive reactions are successful in containing the threat. When stressors are sustained or severe, however, the adaptive capabilities of the organism may be overwhelmed, in which case there is a lowering of integrated functioning and eventually a possible breakdown of the organism. This lowering of integration is referred to as *decompensation*. Whether stress becomes "excessive" depends, as we have seen, not only on the nature of the adjustive demand but also on the individual's available resources for coping with it. In this section, we shall deal first with some of the generalized effects of excessive stress. Then we shall move on to specific forms of decompensation on biological, psychological, and sociocultural levels.

Effects of severe stress.   Stress is a fact of life, and our reactions to stress can give us competencies we need and would not develop without being challenged to do so. Stress can be damaging, however, if demands are too severe for our coping resources or if we believe and act as if they were. Severe stress can exact a high cost in terms of lowered efficiency, depletion of adaptive resources, wear and tear on the system, and, in extreme cases, disintegration and death.

1. *Lowering of adaptive efficiency.* On a physiological level, severe stress may result in alterations that impair the body's ability to fight off invading bacteria and viruses. On a psychological level, perception of threat brings a narrowing of the perceptual field and increased rigidity of cognitive processes so that it becomes difficult or impossible for the individual to see the situation objectively or to perceive the range of alternatives actually available. This process often appears to be operative in suicidal behavior.

Our adaptive efficiency may also be impaired by the intense emotions that commonly accompany severe stress. Acute stage fright may disrupt our performance of a public speech; "examination jitters" may lead us to "blow it" despite adequate preparation. In fact, high levels of fear, anger, or anxiety may lead not only to impaired performance but to disorganization of behavior.

2. *Lowering of resistance to other stressors.* In using its resources to meet one severe stressor, the organism may suffer a lowering of tolerance for other stressors. The Canadian physiologist Hans Selye (1976) has repeatedly demonstrated the lethal effects of a succession of noxious stimuli on animals. Similarly, soldiers who develop tolerance for the rigors of combat may show a lowering of resistance to other stressors, such as viral infections or bad news from home.

It appears that the coping resources of the system are limited: if they are already mobilized against one stressor, they are not available for coping with others. This helps explain how sustained psychological stress can lower biological resistance to disease, and how sustained bodily disease can lower resistance to psychological stressors. Interestingly, prolonged stress may lead to either pathological over-responsiveness to stressors—as illustrated by the "last straw" response—or to pathological insensitivity to stressors, as in loss of hope and extreme apathy.

In general, it would appear that severe and sustained stress on any level leads to a serious reduction in the overall adaptive capacity of the organism.

3. *Wear and tear on the organism.* Probably most of us believe that even after a very stressful experience, rest can completely restore us. In his pioneering studies of stress, however, Selye has found evidence to the contrary: "AGING"

"Experiments on animals have clearly shown that each exposure leaves an indelible scar, in that it uses up reserves of adaptability which cannot be replaced. It is true that immediately after some harassing experience, rest can restore us almost to the original level of fitness by eliminating acute fatigue. But the emphasis is on the word *almost*. Since we constantly go through periods of stress and rest during life, even a minute deficit of adaptation energy every day adds up—it adds up to what we call *aging*." (1976, p. 429)

Other independent studies have strongly supported Selye's findings and also indicate that, in general, symptom intensity is directly related to the severity of the adjustive demand placed on the organism (Coleman, 1973; Rahe & Arthur, 1978; Uhlenhuth & Paykel, 1973).

When pressure is severe and long continued, physiological mobilization may become chronic and in time lead to irreversible pathology in bodily organs—ranging from peptic ulcers and high blood pressure to heart attacks or strokes. In some individuals sustained or very severe stress appears to lead to chemical changes that interfere with brain functioning and seriously impair the individual's ability to think, feel, and act in an integrated manner.

Biological decompensation.   A model that helps explain the course of biological decompensation under excessive stress has been advanced by Selye (1976) in his formulation of the *general adaptation syndrome.* Selye found that the body's reaction to sustained and excessive stress typically occurs in three major phases: (a) *alarm and mobilization*—representing a general "call to arms" of the body's defensive forces; (b) *stage of resistance*—in which biological adaptation is at the maximum level of operation in terms of bodily resources used; and (c) *exhaustion and disintegration*—in which bodily resources are depleted and the organism loses its ability to resist so that further exposure to the stress can lead to disintegration and death.

Where decompensation does not run its entire course and result in the death of the organism, maintenance mechanisms attempt to repair damage and reorganize normal function. If the stress has resulted in extensive damage, this restorative process is often a matter of reorganizing "remaining parts and resources," but there is a permanent lowering of the previous level of integration and functioning.

Psychological decompensation.   Personality decompensation under excessive stress appears to follow a course resembling that of biological decompensation.

1. *Alarm and mobilization.* At first there is an alerting of the organism and a mobilizing of resources for coping with the stressor. Typically involved at this stage are emotional arousal and increased tension, heightened sensitivity and alertness (vigilance), and determined efforts at self-control. At the same time, the individual undertakes various coping measures—which may be task-oriented or defense-oriented or a combination of the two—in attempts to meet the emergency. During this stage, symptoms of maladjustment may appear, such as continuous anxiety and tension, gastrointestinal upset or other bodily manifestations, and lowered efficiency—indications that the mobilization of adaptive resources is not proving adequate.

2. *Stage of resistance.* If the stress continues, the individual is often able to find some means for dealing with it and thus to resist psychological disintegration. Resistance may be achieved temporarily by concerted task-oriented coping measures; the use of self-defense mechanisms may also be intensified during this period. Even in the stage of resistance, however, there may be indications of strain, including psychosomatic symptoms and mild reality distortions. During the late phases of this stage the individual tends to become rigid and to cling to previously developed defenses rather than trying to reevaluate the stressor situation and work out more adaptive coping patterns.

3. *Stage of exhaustion.* In the face of continued excessive stress, the individual's adaptive resources are depleted and the coping patterns called forth in the stage of resistance begin to fail. Now, as the stage of exhaustion begins, there is a lowering of integration and an introduction of exaggerated and inappropriate defensive measures. The latter reactions may be characterized by psychological disorganization and a "break with reality," involving delusions and hallucinations. These appear to represent increased disorganization in thought and perception along with a desperate effort to salvage some measure of psychological integration and self-integrity by restructuring reality. Metabolic changes that impair normal brain functioning may also be involved in delusional and hallucinatory behavior. Eventually, if the excessive stress continues, the process of decompensation proceeds to a stage of complete psychological disintegration—perhaps involving continuous uncontrolled violence, apathy, or stupor, and eventually death.

As we shall see, relatively severe psychological decompensation may be precipitated by sudden and extreme stress; but more often the decompensation is a gradual and long-range process. Typically, of course, treatment measures are instituted before decompensation runs its course. Such measures may increase the individual's adaptive capabilities or alleviate the stressor situation so that the process of decompensation is reversed to *recompensation*. We shall illustrate the stress-decompensation sequence with case material in Chapter 6.

Sociocultural decompensation. Although social science is just beginning to make inroads into the understanding of group pathology, it would appear that the concept of decompensation is just as applicable here as on biological and psychological levels. In the face of wars, economic problems, and other internal and external stressors that surpass their adjustive capabilities, societies may undergo varying degrees of decompensation, often resorting to extreme measures in their attempts to maintain their organization and resist disintegration. This process has been depicted by the historian Toynbee and other writers in their descriptions of the decline and fall of Greek and Roman societies.

In completing our immediate discussion of decompensation, it may be emphasized that the outcome in a given situation—on biological and psychological as well as on sociocultural levels—depends on the extent to which any damage can be repaired and remaining resources reorganized. In some instances the functional level may be permanently lowered following excessive stress; in other cases the individual or group may attain a higher level of integration and functioning than before the episode.

Our primary purpose in reviewing personality development and adjustment in this chapter has been to lay the foundation for a better understanding of both normal and abnormal behavior. Toward this end, we have reviewed the primary determinants of human development; we have seen that development normally proceeds in an orderly manner through predictable stages; and we have noted that the quality of development at each stage is limited by what has gone before. We have emphasized the crucial role of learning in shaping personality development and in determining the individual's resources for coping with the problems of living.

In our discussion of personality adjustment, we have dealt with our basic needs and strivings toward both maintenance and actualization; we have examined the nature of both stressors and resulting stress and the factors that determine their severity; and we have reviewed both task-oriented and defense-oriented coping reactions. In the final section of this chapter we noted the course of decompensation under excessive stress—on both individual and group levels.

In the chapter that follows, we shall apply these basic principles of personality development and adjustment to understanding the causes of abnormal behavior.

5

Causes of abnormal behavior

Perspectives on causation
Biological factors
Psychosocial factors
Sociocultural factors

Unraveling the *etiology,* or causal picture, in different forms of abnormal behavior is enormously difficult. Rarely is there a single cause. Typically, biological, psychological, and sociocultural factors all play some role. Yet the same circumstance often affects different individuals differently. Thus, even with a wealth of background information, it is all but impossible to know with certainty the role a given condition has played in a particular case.

We are still a long way from having complete answers about causation; yet we have enough information to piece together hypotheses concerning the probable origins of most of the major types of disordered behavior. It is characteristic of the state of the art, however, that we may associate some of the same factors with high achievement in one individual and personal disaster in another. The student will be well advised to keep this caveat in mind as we proceed.

Perspectives on causation

In attempting to analyze the causal factors in abnormal behavior, we shall find it helpful to review briefly (a) differing current theoretical viewpoints of causation, (b) the distinction between primary, predisposing, precipitating, and reinforcing causes, and (c) the problem of feedback and circularity in abnormal behavior.

Differing viewpoints of causation

In Chapters 2 and 3 we noted the different concepts of psychopathology inherent in the biological, psychosocial, and sociocultural viewpoints. Here we shall review briefly the special emphasis of each of these viewpoints in relation to the etiology of abnormal behavior.

The biological viewpoint emphasizes various *organic conditions* that can impair brain functioning and lead to psychopathology. Included here are a wide variety of conditions, ranging from syphilitic infection to drug intoxication

and nutritional deficiencies. We also noted the possibility that some persons may be predisposed to specific metabolic or biochemical alterations under severe stress, and that these changes may in turn impair bodily functioning, including that of the brain. The latter type of process seems increasingly to be implicated, as we shall see, in certain of the major psychoses, where the transmission of neural impulses from one cell to another may be affected adversely by biochemical derangements.

The psychoanalytic perspective is concerned primarily with *stressful situations* that involve a threat to the individual and therefore elicit *anxiety,* which in turn functions as both a warning of danger and an acutely unpleasant condition demanding alleviation. If the individual copes effectively with the stressor, anxiety is eliminated; however, if the stressor and ensuing anxiety continue, the individual typically resorts to various ego-defense mechanisms, such as denial and rationalization. This process of self-defense leads to an incongruence between reality and the individual's experience; if it becomes extreme, it may result in maladaptive behavior and perhaps lowered personality integration.

Faulty learning is seen as the key cause of psychopathology in the behavioristic perspective but is also recognized as an important causal factor by all the major psychosocial viewpoints. Behaviorists today assume that maladaptive behavior is the result of either (a) the failure to learn necessary adaptive behaviors or competencies, or (b) the learning of maladaptive behaviors. Delinquent behavior based on a failure to learn necessary social values and norms would be an example of the former; the fear response to the white rat learned by little Albert (see page 60) would be an example of the latter. As we have seen, behaviorists also place strong emphasis on conditions that reinforce and hence maintain maladaptive behavior once it begins.

According to the humanistic and existential perspectives, *blocked or distorted personal growth* is a primary cause of psychopathology. Presumably, human nature tends toward cooperation and constructive behavior; if we show aggression, cruelty, or other maladaptive behavior, it is because of distortion of our natural tendencies by an unfavorable environment. Important here is the concept of maintenance versus growth motivation and of the necessity to be and shape ourselves. If we are denied or fail to use opportunities for personal growth and self-fulfillment, the inevitable consequences are anxiety, futility, and despair. This may, in part, explain the low morale among people who are in the midst of a long, hard winter and experience what is sometimes popularly referred to as "cabin fever": most resources must be devoted to simple survival, with no room for personal growth.

The interpersonal perspective places *unsatisfactory interpersonal relationships* at the root of maladaptive behavior. Perhaps the child's self-concept was distorted in early childhood by overcritical parents or by rigid socialization measures that made it difficult to accept and integrate the "bad me" into a comfortable self-concept. And for many adults, unsatisfactory intimate relationships may lead to or maintain maladaptive behaviors on the part of one or both partners. In fact, a relationship in which one feels constantly devaluated, disconfirmed, and thrown off balance can literally "drive one crazy."

The sociocultural perspective emphasizes the role of *pathological social conditions* such as poverty, racial prejudice and discrimination, and destructive violence in the development of abnormal behavior. The stressors to which an individual is exposed and the maladaptive behaviors that may develop are determined in no small part by the social context in which the individual lives.

Not only do immediate social conditions affect the nature and incidence of mental disorders in a given society, but the pattern of mental disorders changes over time as technological innovations and other conditions lead to profound alterations in society. In fact, the patterning of both physical and mental disorders changes with major changes in civilization.

Implicit in most viewpoints is the process of psychological decompensation under excessive stress, which we discussed in the latter part of Chapter 4. Such decompensation usually occurs gradually but may occur suddenly in the face of sudden or acute stressors that are beyond the range of the individual's adjustive resources.

These differing concepts of causation developed in different research traditions, and at one time each tended to claim exclusive truth. Contemporary workers in the field, however, often use concepts from several of them in trying to understand the development of a particular maladaptive pattern.

Thus from the broad framework of personality development and adjustment discussed in Chapter 4, we can regard the causes of abnormal behavior as the outcome of faulty development or severe stress or a combination of the two. In some instances, as in the case of a child who learns criminal values and becomes a hired killer, it is faulty development that appears primarily responsible for the abnormal behavior; in other instances, as in combat fatigue, it is the overwhelming stress that ordinarily plays the dominant role. The type of adjustment we are achieving at any time is always a function of both the level of stress we are experiencing and the personality resources we have for dealing with it. The better our resources, the more stress we can withstand; the more severe the stress, the better the resources we need if we are to cope adequately with it.

Primary, predisposing, precipitating, and reinforcing causes

Regardless of one's theoretical orientation, several terms are in common usage regarding causes of abnormal behavior. *Primary* cause is used to designate the condition without which the disorder would not have occurred—syphilis of the brain in the case of general paresis. A *predisposing* cause is a condition that comes before and paves the way for a possible later occurrence of disorder under certain conditions; an example on the psychological level would be parental rejection, which would probably predispose a child toward difficulty in handling close personal relationships later. A *precipitating* cause is a condition that proves too much for the individual and "triggers" the disorder; an example might be a crushing disappointment. A *reinforcing* cause is a condition that tends to maintain maladaptive behavior that is already occurring; an example would be the extra attention, sympathy, and removal from unwanted responsibility that often come when one is "ill" and may contribute to a delay in recovery. Reinforcing causes have received increased emphasis in recent years.

In a given case, the primary cause may be unknown, or two or more factors may share primary responsibility (see HIGHLIGHT on page 130). Likewise, the exact pattern of predisposing, precipitating, and reinforcing causes may be far from clear. And what precipitates today's "symptoms" may become a predisposing factor in tomorrow's maladaptive behavior. For example, the conditions that precipitate a schizophrenic episode today may serve as predisposing causes for a recurrence of such an episode at a later time.

Feedback and circularity ("vicious circles") in abnormal patterns

Traditionally in the sciences, the task of determining cause-and-effect relationships was to isolate the condition X (cause) that could be demonstrated to lead to condition Y (effect). For example, when the alcohol content of the blood reaches a certain level, alcoholic intoxication occurs. Where more than one causal factor is involved, the term *causal pattern* has been used. Here conditions A, B, C, etc., are described as leading to condition Y. In either case, this concept of *cause* follows a simple linear model, in which a given variable or set of variables leads to a result later in time.[1]

With the introduction of the concept of self-regulating systems, however, causation is often viewed as being more complex than a simple cause-and-effect relationship. For now the effects of *feedback* and relationships of mutual, two-way influence must also be taken into account. Consider, for example, the following situation:

A husband and wife are undergoing counseling for difficulties in their marriage. The husband accuses his wife of drinking excessively, while the wife accuses her husband of rejecting her and showing no affection. In explaining her frustrations to the therapist, the wife views the situation as "I drink because my husband rejects me." The husband sees the problem differently: "I reject my wife because she drinks too much."

Over time a vicious circle develops in which the husband has increasingly withdrawn as his wife has increasingly lost control of her drinking. It becomes extremely difficult, if not impossible, to differentiate cause from effect. Rather, the problem has become a vicious circle: each influences and maintains the behavior of the other.

This hypothetical situation helps point out that new concepts of causal relationships must deal with the more complex factors of feedback loops, information exchange or communication, patterns of interaction, and circularity.

In the remainder of this chapter we shall attempt to delineate the role that several kinds of biological, psychosocial, and sociocultural factors have been found to play in causing maladaptive behavior, either by producing faulty development (thus hampering adjustive ability), or by increasing stress, or both. In some instances, the key causal factors can be seen more clearly with an electron microscope; in others, with a chemical analysis; in still others, with a psychological test or a sociological survey. And although we shall often be discussing biological, psychosocial, and sociocultural factors separately, it is important to bear in mind that their *interaction* is critically important.

Biological factors

Biological factors influence all aspects of our behavior, including our intellectual capabilities, basic temperament, primary reaction tendencies, stress tolerance, and adaptive resources. Thus a wide range of biological conditions, such as faulty genes, diseases, endocrine imbalances, malnutrition, injuries, and other conditions that interfere with normal development and functioning are potential causes of abnormal behavior.

---

[1]It is interesting to note that this concept of "causes" and "effects" does not occur in all thought systems. It was a central feature of Newtonian physics, which American psychologists simply accepted without question until quite recently (Tart, 1975).

In the present section we shall focus on five categories of biological factors that seem particularly relevant to an understanding of the development of maladaptive behavior: (a) genetic defects; (b) constitutional liabilities; (c) physical deprivations; (d) disruptive emotional processes; and (e) brain pathology. Each of these categories encompasses a number of conditions that influence the quality and functional intactness of our bodily equipment.

These conditions may function in varying combinations, and they may serve as primary, predisposing, precipitating, or reinforcing causes of maladaptive behavior. Most frequently, however, their influence is predisposing in character.

Genetic defects

Since our behavior is inevitably influenced by our biological inheritance, genetic defects are clearly a potential cause of psychopathology. The two defects of major concern are chromosomal aberration, or *anomaly*, and faulty genes that may produce abnormality directly or make an individual more vulnerable to later stress.

Chromosomal aberrations. Research in the field of genetics has enabled us to detect chromosomal aberrations and to study their implications for development and behavior.

The first major breakthrough in this area was the discovery that most normal human cells have forty-six chromosomes in which are encoded the hereditary plan—the overall strategy or information for guiding development. When fertilization takes place, the normal inheritance of the new individual consists of twenty-three pairs of chromosomes—one of each pair being from the mother and one from the father. Twenty-two of these chromosome pairs are called *autosomes;* they determine general anatomical and physiological characteristics. The remaining pair, the *sex chromosomes,* determine the individual's sex and certain other characteristics. In the female, both of these sex chromosomes—one from each parent—are designated as *X chromosomes.* In the male, the sex chromosome from the mother is an X but that from the father is different and is called a *Y chromosome.*

Death in Guyana

In late November 1978 the news media reported the shocking story of the mass suicide—or murder—of over 900 persons, members of a religious cult, the People's Temple, who had migrated to the Guyanan jungle from the United States only a few years before. The facts of the gruesome event have been fairly well pieced together, but the questions it raised may never be satisfactorily answered.

Following repeated reports that members of the commune were being mistreated and held against their will, Congressman Leo J. Ryan of California and 17 others had gone to Guyana to investigate. They were allowed to talk to members but as their plane prepared to leave, shooting broke out and five of the party, including the congressman, were killed.

Evidently the founder and leader of the People's Temple, the Reverend Jim Jones, had planned the shootings. He called the people together, told them that the Guyanese authorities would arrest and torture them, and said that he could not allow any of his beloved children to suffer such a terrible fate—they must all choose the dignity of "revolutionary suicide" instead. Two huge vats of Kool-Aid laced with cyanide were prepared, and with armed guards ringing the group to prevent escape, the people were exhorted to drink the potion and give it to their children. Nurses helped the reluctant. At some point Jones shot himself or was shot. A handful escaped into the surrounding jungle, but the rest perished.

Who was the Reverend Jim Jones, and how did he achieve such power over his followers?

Jones had founded the People's Temple in the early 1950s in Indianapolis. It was devoted to fundamentalist Christianity and socialism and drew an interracial following. In 1963, convinced that Indianapolis would soon be destroyed in a nuclear holocaust, Jones moved with over 100 of his followers to Ukiah, California, later going to San Francisco, where his following grew rapidly, with the elderly and the underprivileged disproportionately represented.

Jones staged "miracles," such as cancer "cures," and claimed at various times to be a reincarnation of Jesus, Father Divine, Lenin, and even God himself. But behind the scenes, he was delighting in beatings and other public chastenings of his followers, after which they were expected to say "Thank you, father," and he would embrace them, saying "Father loves you. You're a stronger person now. I can trust you."

Meanwhile, he was developing paranoid fears of assassination by the U.S. government and in 1972 began the commune at Jonestown, Guyana, where he went himself in 1977. At Jonestown many members were stripped, paddled, forced to sign false confessions, and humiliated in other ways. Yet when Jones would ask if they would lay down their and their children's lives for him, they would scream, "I will, father!" Would-be defectors were discouraged by armed guards and by assurances that the CIA would kill them if they returned to the United States.

Jones' physician in the United States was quoted as saying that Jones had a serious illness and was "literally burning his brains with drugs" (Moody & Graham, 1978, p. 10). Did he perhaps know he was dying and did he want to take his loved ones with him? We will probably never know.

Even harder to understand is how such a person could have attracted and held such a devoted following. Yet there have been repeated examples of this kind of blind devotion to charismatic cult leaders and repeated examples of followers being induced to commit acts they had never before thought of committing, including burglary and murder. There have always been cults, but they seem to flourish especially in times of violence, social disorganization, and great uncertainty; for the faithful, they offer security and absolute truth. Often the people who join them are alienated and estranged individuals whose identification with and loyalty to a powerful leader give their lives meaning. There is also an element of

idealism: the group stands for noble values. And there is an element of elitism: in this corrupt and evil world, *we* stand for truth and goodness. Once in the group, individuals are subjected to powerful pressures from other group members.

With this grounding, individuals will do whatever they have to do to prove their absolute commitment to the leader. What they must do depends on the values and mental stability of the leader. But the state of mind that followers can reach is shown in these statements (Moody & Graham, 1978, p. 9):

"My husband and I would have been willing to kill for Jones." (Statement by a woman at Ukiah.)

"I was nothing going nowhere. I was bored and unhappy at home. The Joneses made me feel like I was someone. Just the sound of his voice made you feel like you had power." (Statement by a 16-year-old girl who went with the group from Indiana to California.)

So what "caused" the deaths at Guyana? Was it the madness of the leader? The vulnerabilities of the members that had predisposed them to blind followership? The troubled times in which we live? The isolation of Jonestown? All these factors and others would seem to have played a part, highlighting again the need to look for patterns of interacting factors rather than single causes in trying to understand the puzzles of human behavior.

The basic facts of this tragic event are presented in the December 4, 11, and 18, 1978, issues of *Time*.

Research in developmental genetics has shown that abnormalities in the structure or number of the chromosomes are associated with a wide range of malformations and disorders. Genetic aberrations have been found to be a causal factor in color blindness, hemophilia, and a number of other defects. For example, the presence of an extra chromosome is characteristic of *Down's syndrome,* a type of mental retardation in which there is a *trisomy* (three instead of two) of one autosomal pair, chromosome #21 (see HIGHLIGHT on this page). Here the extra chromosome is the *primary* cause of the disorder, but because the probability of this defect rises sharply with the age of the mother, and possibly the father also, older parental age at conception may be regarded as a possible *predisposing* cause (Matsunaga, Tonomura, Hidetsune, & Yatsumoto, 1978).

Somewhat similar aberrations may also occur in the sex chromosomes, producing a variety of complications that may predispose the person to the development of abnormal behavior. For example, Klinefelter's syndrome also involves 47 chromosomes, but in this case the pathogenic element is an extra X chromosome, XXY in the sex chromosomes; these individuals have male body structures (although they are usually infertile) and a predominantly male gender identity. They are far more likely than boys with the usual 46 chromosomes to develop several kinds of psychopathology, such as juvenile delinquency and mental retardation. Such individuals are said to be "at high risk" for these pathological outcomes.

Studies by Sergovich et al. (1969) and Hanerton et al. (1975) indicate that the incidence of gross chromosomal abnormalities in newborns is approximately one-half of 1 percent. The exact causes of chromosomal anomalies are not yet fully understood. Some have evidently been passed on from one or both of the parents; some apparently occur in the combining of egg and sperm or from genetic mutations occurring after conception.

A search for chromosomal irregularities in schizophrenia and other psychoses has not proved fruitful, and none of the chromosomal anomalies thus far observed has appeared to be directly related to such disorders. Even in the case of Down's syndrome, where a trisomy has been identified, it has been estimated that 65

HIGHLIGHT

Down's syndrome and the trisomy of chromosome 21

This picture of chromosomes shows an aberration involving the trisomy of chromosome 21. Cases of Down's syndrome, a type of mental retardation, reveal this pattern.

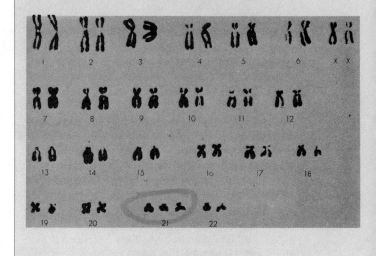

percent of the fetuses spontaneously abort (Creasy & Crolla, 1974). The potential effects of more gross chromosomal irregularities are largely unknown because they ordinarily result in the death of the embryo.

One thing appears certain, however: females are less susceptible to defects from sex-linked genetic disorders because they have two X chromosomes. If one proves faulty, the other member of the pair generally can handle the work of development. Nevertheless, females are sometimes born with a missing or extra sex chromosome (XO, called Turner's syndrome, or XXX), either of which may produce abnormalities. Since males have a single X chromosome paired with a single Y chromosome, a defect in either may mean trouble.

Faulty genes. A major breakthrough in modern genetics has been the development of ultramicroscopic techniques—for example, the combined use of the electron microscope and X-ray diffraction—which makes it possible to study the actual structure of the chromosomes. Each chromosome is made up of a long molecule of DNA (deoxyribonucleic acid) arranged in two strands linked together at regular intervals to form a double spiral, or helix, that looks like a ladder curving round and round. Our genetic instructions are stored in this DNA ladder, or "book."

The "sentences" in this DNA book of instructions are the genes, which follow one another like beads strung together to form a necklace. Genes carry the instructions for specific body traits, such as eye color and blood type, and also the "assembly instruction" for determining organic development. Thus they are the specific units or bearers of an individual's genetic inheritance.

Some genes are called *dominant* genes: their instructions are activated even if the other member of the pair carries contradictory instructions. *Recessive* genes are genes whose instructions are discarded unless the individual has inherited two such genes, one from each parent. In the field of abnormal psychology, however, it is not usual for genetic influences to express themselves in such simple, straightforward ways. This is partly because behavior, unlike physical characteristics such as eye color, is *never* determined exclusively by genetic endowment: it is *always* a product of the interaction of environment with the structural and functional characteristics of the organism. Genes can affect behavior only indirectly, through their influence on the physical and chemical properties of the body, whose development they regulate. An example of one physical effect of genetic endowment can be seen in the HIGHLIGHT on page 134.

The few instances in the field of abnormal psychology in which relatively straightforward predictions can be made on the basis of known laws of inheritance invariably involve gross neurological impairment as a primary feature; here, abnormal behavior arises as a more or less direct consequence of central nervous system malfunction. Examples of such relatively rare disorders include Huntington's chorea (Lynch, Harlan, & Dyhrberg, 1972) and Tay-Sachs disease (Spencer, 1973). Disorders of this type will be described in Chapter 13.

The more interesting (if still largely obscure) genetic influences in abnormal behavior almost certainly do not involve dominant and recessive relationships in one or two pairs of genes. Rather, it is now believed that where pathogenic genetic influences operate, they do so *polygenically*—that is, through the action of many genes together in some sort of additive or interactive fashion. By this schema, the vulnerable individual is the one who has inherited a large number of these genes that, in the aggregate, represent faulty heredity. These faulty genes, in turn, may lead to metabolic difficulties or other faulty functioning that predispose the individual to later difficulty.

Although marked advances have been made in the identification of faulty genes, most of the information we have concerning the role of genetic factors in mental disorders is based not on studies of genes but on family studies. The family history method requires that the investigator observe a large sample of relatives of each *proband* or *index case* (the subject, or carrier of the trait in question, such as schizophrenia) in order to see whether the incidence increases in proportion to the degree of hereditary relationship. In addition, the incidence of the trait in a normal population is compared with its incidence among the relatives of index cases.

Such research is much more difficult and complicated to carry out than may at first appear, and the history of research in this area, particularly with regard to schizophrenic disorders, is littered with many erroneous conclusions and patently biased reports. For example, many studies have been made of the rates at which schizophrenia in one monozygotic (that is, genetically identical) twin is predictive of schizophrenia in the other. Such rates are called *concordance rates*. Reports from such studies have varied between 6 percent and 86 percent.

An *accurate* figure, we now know, would be somewhere around 50 percent, but this figure is hard to interpret because twins almost always share common environments as well as heredity. The main point is that in many instances of this disorder (and very probably in certain other mental disorders) there does seem to be a modest hereditary component—an innate predispositional vulnerability.

The "smallest" wedding

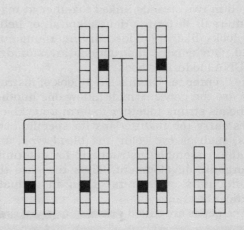

The wedding of "General" Tom Thumb and Miss Lavinia Bump in 1863 united two midgets. The groom was 38 inches tall, the bride 32 inches. Recessive genes probably caused their small stature, as suggested in the schematic drawing of chromosomes (McKusick & Rimoin, 1967). A recessive gene (color) in the paired chromosomes of both parents (top) could be combined in different ways in the paired chromosomes of their offspring (bottom). A combination of two recessive genes (third from left) would give rise to the recessive trait.

Whether an individual with this pathogenic genetic endowment will develop schizophrenia will be determined by many factors that operate after conception. For the most part, we lack definitive knowledge about the nature of these other factors, and how they interact with genetic endowment to produce schizophrenia, perhaps the most serious of the disorders of personality. We shall take up this matter of genetic influences in greater detail in Chapter 12.

It should not be altogether surprising that given a favorable life situation, an individual's inherited vulnerability may never result in abnormal behavior. The weight of evidence suggests, indeed, that *nonoccurrence* of the disorder in a genetically affected person is the *most likely outcome*. The field of physical disease, too, is rife with examples of genetic predispositions that never attain the status of observable disease, including dispositions for diabetes, hypertension, coronary heart disease, and some forms of cancer (Bergsma, 1974; Kaiser Foundation, 1970).

Constitutional liabilities

The term *constitution,* as we have seen, is used to denote the relatively enduring biological makeup of the individual resulting from either genetic or very early environmental influences, often including influences in the prenatal environment. Physique, physical handicaps, basic reaction tendencies, and vulnerability to stress are among the many traits included in this category. Here our focus will be on the role of these constitutional traits in the etiology of maladaptive behavior.

Physique. Perhaps the best known of various scientific attempts to relate physique to personality and psychopathology is the early work of Sheldon and his associates (1954). Sheldon concluded that there are three types of body build, each associated with particular temperamental and other personality characteristics. He believed that physique is not a primary cause of psychopathology but that it does influence the type of disorder the individual is most likely to develop under stress. Although Sheldon's work has received limited support from later investigators—for example, Glueck and Glueck (1968) reported a higher incidence of individuals with muscular physiques among juvenile delinquents and adult criminals—most have been critical of his typology. It seems unlikely that the complexities of human development and behavior can be predicted on the basis of one relatively simple variable, especially a nonpsychological one.

However, a look at everyday situations makes it evident that physique and other aspects of physical appearance do play an important role in both personality development and adjustment. Beauty, for example, is highly valued in our society. One need only attend a social gathering, watch television, or note the billions of dollars spent each year on cosmetics to see the influence of beauty on people's behavior. Snyder, Tanke, and Berscheid (1977) have demonstrated that college males who believed they were talking on the telephone to an attractive female behaved quite differently from those who believed they were talking to an unattractive female. Interestingly, the females *assumed* to be attractive responded to the greater interest shown them and were rated by independent judges listening to recordings of the conversations as in fact *being* attractive. On the other hand, the females assumed to be unattractive responded to their telephone partners' behavior in ways that led the judges to rate them as unattractive. What had been reality only in the minds of the male subjects became "reality" in the behavior of their otherwise unknown female partners. This study suggests that other people's reactions to our (real or imagined) characteristics may determine our own behavior, often in a way that conforms to their expectations.

Perhaps the most significant influence of our physical appearance occurs indirectly—through the view we take of it. A conception of one's body as being too different from the standards valued by one's group can be self-devaluating—as can dissatisfaction over changes in bodily proportions during adolescence and old age.

Physical handicaps. Genetic defects or environmental conditions operating before or after birth may result in physical handicaps. A defect that a child is born with is called a *congenital* defect; in this country an estimated 7 out of every 100 babies are born with mental or physical defects (Solomon, 1973). About a third of these defects are considered to be hereditary; another sixth are due to drugs or disease; the rest—about half in all—result from unknown causes. Some of the aberrations are apparent at birth, while others—such as mental retardation, endocrine disturbances, and heart defects—may not be detected until months or years later. Often such anomalies are minor, but more serious congenital defects constitute one of the five leading causes of death during childhood, accounting for over half a million deaths yearly.

Prenatal conditions that can lead to birth defects and to premature birth include nutritional deficiencies, disease, exposure to radiation, drugs, emotional stress, or excessive use of alcohol or tobacco on the part of the mother.

The most common birth difficulty associated with later mental disorders—including mental retardation, hyperactivity, and emotional disturbances—is low birth weight, which is defined as a birth weight of 5½ pounds or less. This is most often a factor in premature births

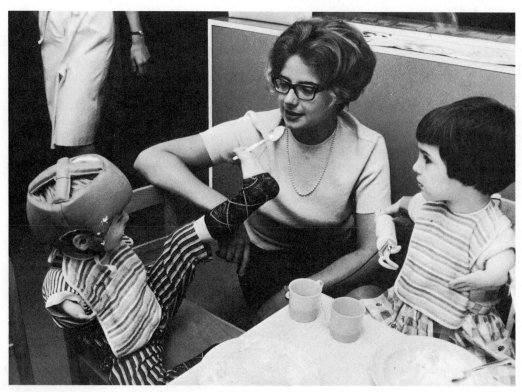

Drugs taken by pregnant women can cause severe physical abnormalities in their infants. During the early 1960s, for example, hundreds of babies were born without arms and/or legs—a tragic side effect of thalidomide, a tranquilizing drug that was widely prescribed in Europe at that time.

but can also occur in full-term births. In any event, it appears that some of the risk factor associated with prematurity may be mitigated by special treatment of the infant, such as systematic stroking and massage, during the first postnatal month (Rice, 1977); unfortunately, the likelihood that such special treatment will occur is, in most families, quite remote.

Mothers who are subjected to severe emotional stress during pregnancy appear to have a much higher incidence of premature deliveries. Even in the case of full-term babies, severe maternal stress appears to be associated with hyperactivity in the fetus during later pregnancy, and after birth to be reflected in feeding difficulties, sleep problems, irritability, and other difficulties in adjustment (Blau et al., 1963; Sontag, Steele, & Lewis, 1969). As might be expected, socioeconomic status has been found to be related to fetal and birth difficulties, the incidence being several times greater among mothers on lower socioeconomic levels (Robinson & Robinson, 1976).

As a consequence of such findings, it would appear that the fetus is not so well protected as many investigators formerly thought—that a variety of biological and psychological conditions affecting the mother during pregnancy can have profound effects on development and adjustment.

Accidents and disease also exact a high toll in our society. Each year accidents alone take the lives of over 100,000 persons and permanently disable approximately a million others.

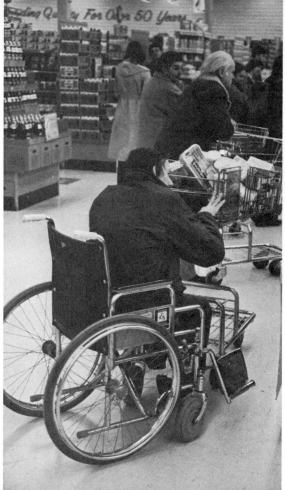

Severe physical disabilities can make dealing with the routine tasks of everyday life just that much more stressful. Many individuals manage to come to terms with their physical limitations and function as independent members of society; others accept the role of a "cripple" or misfit with its ensuing psychological problems.

These figures suggest that accidental injuries are the "neglected disease" of modern civilization, often leaving in their wake physical mutilation, disrupted lives, and severe problems of adjustment.

In addition, over 20 million persons suffer from heart conditions or other serious physical impairments that may be both painful and debilitating; many of these victims are young people. The U.S. Department of Health, Education, and Welfare estimates indicate that approximately one-fifth of this country's under-seventeen age group will, at some time in their lives, suffer from at least one chronic physical condition that adversely affects their adjustment. When such conditions involve severe and long-continued pain, they may gradually

wear down the individual's adjustive resources and lead to discouragement and despair. Chronic disease may also reduce the individual's expected life span.

Except in the case of defects that seriously restrict one's activities, are severely disabling, or are chronically painful, however, the significance of a physical impairment depends primarily on the way the individual evaluates and adjusts to it. Common and undesirable reactions to physical disabilities are feelings of inferiority, self-pity, and hostility. Another obstacle to good adjustment that a disabled person faces is the tendency to accept the role of a "cripple," which society often seems to expect and encourage. This picture is often complicated by family members who either encourage such a sick role or expect performance beyond the individual's capabilities. As a consequence of such obstacles, the individual—whether child, adolescent, or adult—may develop psychological handicaps that are much more disabling than the physical impairment. The effects of severe physical impairments on children are summarized in the HIGHLIGHT on this page.

Primary reaction tendencies.   In discussing the role of heredity and constitution in development, we noted how primary reaction tendencies such as sensitivity, temperament, and activity level affect our interactions with the environment. Primary reaction tendencies also include characteristic ways of reacting to stress. Some infants react to changes in routine or other stress by running a fever; others, by digestive disorders; still others, by sleeping disturbances. Several investigators have attempted to relate such primary reaction tendencies to stress vulnerability and maladaptive behavior.

In a longitudinal study of infant development, Chess, Thomas, and Birch (1965) found that 7 to 10 percent of all babies are "difficult"—they evidence irregular patterns of eating, sleeping, and bowel movement; tend to cry a great deal and to show a predominantly negative mood; and are inclined to be irritable and have difficulty in adjusting to change. These researchers concluded that since the mother does not gain the satisfactions she expected from having her baby, the temperamental difficulty becomes overlaid and complicated by an unsatisfactory mother-infant relationship, with undesirable consequences for both.

In subsequent writing, Thomas, Chess, and Birch (1968) made the point that a poor "fit" between the child's temperamental characteristics and the structure and flexibility of environmental demands, particularly those within the home, can lead to "dissonant stress." Such stress in turn may lead to a behavioral disturbance whose form in part reflects the child's temperamental characteristics. The problem is complicated if the child also exhibits developmental deviations of one sort or another, such as mental retardation. Such deviations increase the likelihood of behavior disorder and thus make a "good fit"

HIGHLIGHT

Forty-one physically handicapped children: How they developed during early school years

Minde, Hackett, Killou, and Silver (1972) studied the psychological development of 41 physically handicapped children—13 female and 28 male—during their early school years in a special school in Montreal, Canada. The following sequence and characteristics of development between the ages of 5 and 9 were highlighted:

1. The cognitive realization, triggered by separation from outside peer group members and exposure to other crippled children, that the "handicap was not going to suddenly disappear" (p. 108).

2. This realization was followed by a period of severe depression in 16 children which varied from 6 weeks to an entire year in duration. During this period, the children talked about the futility of their lives and would not do schoolwork. Some even wished not to have another birthday.

3. The gradual development of emotional readiness to see the physical handicap as part of the self, and a hesitant beginning on the part of the child to incorporate it into his or her self-image and life-style.

During these early school years, the parents of the children appeared to be in a "continuous struggle between their wish to have a fully normal child . . . and their knowledge of the child's handicap" (p. 109). This struggle could not be described in terms of simple "acceptance" or "rejection," but appeared to be considerably more complex. "In facing this conflict of marginality, they chose either normalcy or deviance, but have not yet been able to create an identity for their children that embraces both concepts. They have either made their children into 'sick' people or else spent immense energies to give them a feeling of being 'like everyone else'" (p. 109). Unfortunately, the failure of the parents to resolve this conflict in a constructive way apparently took attention and care away from siblings of the handicapped children who showed a significant increase in behavior disorders during the period of this study.

between temperament and environmental conditions even more crucial if untoward consequences are to be avoided. A number of factors may thus help determine the relationships between constitutionally derived temperamental features and subsequent behavior disorder (Buss & Plomin, 1975; Thomas & Chess, 1977).

Other longitudinal studies have followed children believed to be at high risk by virtue of having abnormal prenatal conditions or having been born to parents with serious problems. Such studies are called *prospective studies*—studies that attempt to "look ahead." They start with subjects who have not yet developed a disorder and try to predict which ones will succumb, or, as in the above case, watch what actually happens and try to identify the conditions that seem to push a child in one direction or the other. These studies are difficult and expensive, however, and can encounter many unforeseen difficulties. As such, most of our evidence still comes from *retrospective studies*—studies that "look back"—in which individuals who have already developed a disorder are studied, and the researcher tries to reconstruct a picture of the probable causes.

Incomplete though our knowledge is, however, one conclusion we can draw is that childhood disturbance is often followed by adult disturbance, though its specific form is a poor predictor of the particular nature of later adult difficulties (Fish, 1975; Hanson, Gottesman, & Meehl, 1977). To at least some extent, early manifestations of vulnerability seem to be diffuse and nonspecific; what later abnormality they are most likely to lead to is hard to predict.

Physical deprivations

Physical deprivation is an important contributor to abnormal development and behavior. Although rarely occurring independently of other contributing factors, malnutrition may be the most serious and widespread of these deprivations. It thereby serves as a good example of the general class of such problems.

Severe malnutrition during infancy not only impairs physical development and lowers resistance to disease, but also stunts brain growth and results in markedly lowered intelligence (Cravioto & DeLicardie, 1975; Dobbing, 1967; Kaplan, 1972). Peterson (1978) has also noted the importance of deficits of thiamine, niacin, and vitamin B_{12} as potential causes of organic brain syndromes, which we shall discuss in more detail in Chapter 13.

In a postmortem study of infants who had died of malnutrition during their first year of life, Winick (1968) found the total brain cell content 60 percent below that of normal infants. Further research on animals showed the same type of effect in the offspring of malnourished mothers (Winick & Rosso, 1973). In the case of babies who suffer severe malnutrition but survive, the stunting of brain growth is considered irreversible, since the period of fastest growth of the brain is from about five months before until ten months after birth. Even in "affluent" America, in a random sample of areas where 75 to 80 percent of the resident families were living either in poverty or close to it, a study by the U.S. Department of Health, Education, and Welfare found that 15 percent of all children studied showed evidence of physical and mental growth retardation associated with malnutrition (Loyd, 1969).

Malnutrition because of faulty diet, resulting in a wide range of physical disorders and generally lowered resistance to stress, is found even in lower middle-income families (Reice, 1974). Among adults, Robinson and Winnik (1973) have reported on the higher incidence of psychoses and other mental disturbances among individuals who follow a "crash diet" to achieve rapid weight loss.

The broader social magnitude of the problem of malnutrition is indicated by estimates that a third of the world's children die of malnutrition before age five and another third lack sufficient protein food for minimum nutritional needs (Brown, 1974; Sanderson, 1975). In fact, it is estimated that over a fourth of the world's people suffer from malnutrition, and the situation is expected to worsen in the years ahead (Brown, 1978).

One of the most sobering aspects of this world picture is the knowledge that the effects of malnutrition continue into later generations. Not only do malnourished children suffer lowered mental and physical capacity, but the children of malnourished mothers also show serious deficits.

Disruptive emotional processes

Emotional processes like fear and anger represent the mobilization of bodily resources to meet emergency situations. Such a mobilization of resources enables a threatened organism either to fight or to flee more effectively. In modern civilization, however, we are rarely confronted with situations that can be met adequately by simple physical attack or flight. Yet we have not experienced a comparable reduction in our emotional excitability: we still become mobilized for physical flight or attack when we feel endangered, and if we feel chronically anxious, our emergency physiological mobilization may become a chronic state.

Mild emotions may be constructive in their overall effect by energizing our actions toward worthwhile goals. But as we get into the intermediate range of intensity, emotions are typically detrimental to problem solving and task performance, and, as the level of emotional tension increases, it becomes increasingly disruptive to organized behavior.

Thus it would appear that severe emotional upheavals actually defeat their emergency function, and that prolonged emotional mobilization produces physiological changes that are not only useless but actually harmful to the organism (Selye, 1976). In Chapter 8 we shall discuss psychosomatic disorders—peptic ulcers, hypertension, and coronary heart disease, for example—in which chronic emotional mobilization typically plays a major role.

Brain pathology

Another set of biological factors, whose role in psychopathology has been better delineated, are the more typical organic disturbances that directly affect the central nervous system. About one-fifth of the patients in mental hospitals, many of them elderly, are suffering from mental disorders associated with organic brain pathology—that is, conditions that result in the destruction of brain tissue or otherwise interfere with normal functioning of the brain. Brain pathology may be temporary, as in the delirium of fever or drug intoxication, or it may be permanent, as in the case of syphilitic infection of the brain. The essential difference here is whether or not the affected brain cells are lethally damaged or are merely prevented temporarily from fulfilling their functions by virtue of various surrounding conditions in the brain. Severe injury to the brain from whatever source, therefore, usually involves long-standing behavioral deficits, although other parts of the brain may be able to compensate for such deficits through special retraining programs.

Another neurophysiological factor receiving intensive study is the way in which defects in the body's defenses against disease and other stresses may contribute to brain pathology. Normally the body produces antibodies to defend itself against invading viruses and other microorganisms; as we shall see in Chapter 8, faulty functioning of the antibody-producing system leaves the body vulnerable to a wide variety of diseases—possibly including degenerative diseases of the central nervous system. Similarly, stress may disrupt the delicate biochemistry of the brain, with adverse consequences for certain predisposed individuals. In fact, a disorganization of thought processes superficially similar to that observed in various severe mental disorders can be induced temporarily in normal people by the injection of certain drugs, such as LSD or mescaline. In Chapter 13 we shall deal with the various mental disorders associated with demonstrable brain pathology.

Psychosocial factors

In comparison with the variables associated with biological causes of maladaptive behavior, those associated with psychosocial causes are more elusive. However, a good deal has been learned about psychological and interpersonal factors that appear to play significant roles in maladaptive behavior. In this section we shall discuss (a) childhood trauma, (b) parental deprivation, (c) pathogenic parent-child relationships, (d) maladaptive family structures, and (e) special frustrations, conflicts, and pressures.

Again we shall see that these factors are by no means independent of each other and that a given condition may function as a primary, predisposing, precipitating, or reinforcing cause. In addition, these psychosocial influences are always interacting with particular genetic and constitutional factors, and the particular setting in which they operate also influences the outcome.

As we have seen, the expression of even genetically based predispositions may be influenced by processes of learning. In the operation of psychosocial influences, learning is of paramount importance. This is true not only of simple learning processes like conditioning but also of more complex varieties of learning in which cognitive elements are central. It is abundantly clear that life experiences leave a more or less permanent record in the individual's nervous system, which both limits and helps channel the individual's reactions to subsequent events. Although learning processes are conceptualized in different ways by the different theorists, there is agreement on their fundamental importance.

Childhood trauma

Most of us have had traumatic experiences that temporarily shattered our feelings of security, adequacy, and worth, and were important in influencing our later evaluations of ourselves and our environment.[2] The following illustrates such an incident.

"I believe the most traumatic experience of my entire life happened one April evening when I was eleven. I was not too sure of how I had become a member of the family, although my parents had thought it wise to tell me that I was adopted. That much I knew, but what the term *adopted* meant was something else entirely. One evening after my step-brother and I had retired, he proceeded to explain it to me—with a vehemence I shall never forget. He made it clear that I wasn't a 'real' member of the family, that my parents didn't 'really' love me, and that I wasn't even wanted around the place. That was one night I vividly recall crying myself to sleep. That experience undoubtedly played a major role in making me feel insecure and inferior."

Such traumas are apt to leave psychological wounds that never completely heal. As a result, later stress that reactivates these early wounds is apt to be particularly difficult for the

This 8-year-old girl has just learned that her parents and three sisters were killed when their car was struck by a train shortly after they had dropped her off at a friend's home. Traumatic experiences of this nature can have a profound effect on later personality development and adjustment.

individual to handle and often explains why one person has difficulty with a problem that is not especially stressful to another. Psychic traumas in infancy or early childhood are especially damaging for the following reasons:

a) Conditioned responses are readily established in situations that evoke strong emotions; such responses are often highly resistant to extinction. Thus one traumatic experience of being unable to swim and almost drowning in a deep lake may be sufficient to establish a fear of water that endures for years or a lifetime.

b) Conditioned emotional responses stemming from traumatic experiences may generalize to other situations. A child who has learned to fear water may also come to be fearful of riding in boats and other situations associated with even the remotest possibility of drowning.

c) Traumatic situations result in emotional conditioning rather than in cognitive learning. Consequently, exposure to similar situations tends to reactivate an emotional response that

---

[2]The terms *psychic trauma* and *traumatic* are used here to mean any aversive experience that inflicts serious psychological damage on the individual.

pre-empts the possibility of a rational appraisal of the situation, which would provide more flexibility of response and be more likely to be adaptive.

The aftereffects of early traumatic experiences depend heavily on the support and reassurance given the child by parents or other significant persons. This appears particularly important when the trauma involves an experience that arouses strong feelings of inadequacy and self-devaluation, such as being ridiculed for stuttering or clumsiness.

Many traumatic experiences in childhood, though highly upsetting at the time, are probably of minor significance in their long-term consequences, and some children are less vulnerable than others and show more resilience and recoverability from hurt that may occur. However, a child exposed to repeated early traumatic experiences is likely to show a disruption in normal personality development. And even though subsequent experiences may have a corrective influence, the detrimental effects of such early traumas may never be completely obliterated.

Although we have emphasized the pathogenic effects of early psychic traumas on personality development and adjustment, acutely hurtful experiences at any age may adversely affect development and adjustment beyond that point. However, in some cases—for example, when a traumatic event is frightening but not overwhelming—the experience may actually tend to immunize the individual to a similar later experience by making it a familiar phenomenon: its limits have been perceived, the individual has seen it in the perspective of other known experiences, and self-defenses have been developed. But in general, early traumas seem to have more far-reaching consequences than later ones, largely because critical evaluation, reflection, and self-defenses are not yet well developed in children. As can be seen in the HIGHLIGHT on page 143, many of the consequences of early trauma can be seen in other species as well.

Parental deprivation

Faulty development has often been observed in infants deprived of emotional stimulation (or "parenting") as a consequence of either (a)

separation from the parent(s) and placement in an institution, or (b) lack of adequate nurturing in the home. Many studies have focused on maternal deprivation, but they are essentially concerned with warmth and stimulation, whether it comes from the mother, the father, or institutional staff members.

Institutionalization. In an institution, as compared with an ordinary home, there is likely to be less warmth and physical contact, less intellectual, emotional, and social stimulation, and a lack of encouragement and help in positive learning.

A study by Provence and Lipton (1962) compared behavior of infants living in institutions with that of infants living with families. At one year of age, the institutionalized infants showed a general impairment in their relationship to people, rarely turning to adults for help, comfort, or pleasure and showing no signs of strong attachment to any person. These investigators also noted a marked retardation of speech and language development, emotional apathy, and impoverished and repetitive play activities. In contrast to the babies living in families, the institutionalized infants failed to show the personality differentiation and learning that "can be thought of both as accomplishments of the first year of life and as the foundation upon which later learning is built" (p. 161). With more severe and pervasive deprivation, development may be even more retarded.

The long-range effects of severe early deprivation of parental love and stimulation are suggested by the early findings of Beres and Obers (1950) in their study of 38 adolescents who had been institutionalized between the ages of about three weeks and three years. At the time of the study, sixteen to eighteen years after discharge from the orphanage, 4 were diagnosed as psychotic, 21 as having a character disorder, 4 as mentally retarded, and 2 as neurotic. Only 7 were judged to have achieved a satisfactory personality adjustment. In general, it would appear that "affectionless psychopathy"—characterized by inability to form close interpersonal relationships and often by antisocial behavior—is a syndrome commonly found among children who have been institutionalized at an early age, particularly before the age of one year; the long-range

Effects of early deprivation and trauma on adult behavior of animals

Early experience	Adult behavior—species
Raised in darkness or with restricted tactual stimulation	Permanent impairment of vision (birds, monkeys, other mammals); retarded use of limbs, abnormal sitting and walking posture (chimps)
Immobilization of movement in early infancy	Inability to fly (buzzards); impaired ability to swim (fish)
Partial starvation in early infancy	Increased hoarding tendency and faster eating rate (rats)
Total social isolation for six months or more after birth	Permanent deficiencies in exploratory, play, sexual, and maternal behaviors, and in grooming (monkeys)
Raised by humans	Preference for human company over own species (chimpanzees, lambs, wild sheep, birds, guinea pigs)
Subjected to aversive stimulation, such as electroshock or loud noise	Modification of emotional reactivity to later stress (rats); greater emotionality and possible timidity in wide range of situations (mice)
Raised in overcrowded environment	Many forms of abnormal behavior in rats, including infant mortality rate as high as 96 percent. Dogs raised in overcrowded conditions neither fought nor mated.
Trained to fight over food	Fighting over food even when not hungry (mice). In comparison, mice trained in noncompetitive or cooperative behavior were far less aggressive.

The material in this chart is based in part on the excellent summary of earlier literature in this field by Beach and Jaynes (1954), and also on Calhoun (1962), Calhoun and Marsden (1973), Davenport, Rogers, and Rumbaugh (1973), Denenberg et al. (1970), Dennis (1941), Harlow (1973), Harlow and Harlow (1966), Harlow and Suomi (1970), Hersher et al. (1962), Lessac and Solomon (1969), and Reisen (1947).

prognosis is considered unfavorable (Rutter, 1972; Tizard & Rees, 1975; Wolkind, 1974).

Although some earlier estimates of the pathological effects of such deprivation were exaggerated, it is now clear that many children deprived of normal parenting in infancy do suffer damage in their personality development. The extent to which early deprivation can be "made up for" by abundant love and attention at a later time is not yet known. It does appear, however, that attachment to some particular adult (typically the mother)—once considered the essential element in healthy development —is not, in fact, the critical factor. Research by Leiderman and Leiderman (1974) comparing "monomatric" with "polymatric" (one mother versus several mothers) households, and by Kagan, Kearsley, and Zelazo (1976) on the effects of early placement in quality day-

care settings, failed to show any substantial deficits in multiple-mothered children. Whether damage that does occur from deprivation is reversible appears to depend on a number of factors, including the duration of prior deprivation and the quality and time of therapeutic enrichment efforts (see HIGHLIGHTS on pages 144 and 145). It does seem clear that restoration becomes increasingly difficult as the child gets older (Freedman, Kaplan, & Sadock, 1976).

Masked deprivation in the home.   By far the greatest number of infants subjected to parental deprivation are not separated from their parents, but rather suffer from inadequate or distorted care at home. Here the parents typically neglect or devote little attention to the child and are generally rejecting.

The effects of such masked deprivation may be devastating. The early work of Ribble (1944, 1945), for example, showed that rejecting, indifferent, or punishing mothers may cause tense, unsatisfied, and negativistic behavior among their infants even at a very early age. Such behavior may even take the form of a refusal to nurse, as a result of which the infant may fall into a semistuporous condition from which arousal is extremely difficult. In fact, Bullard and his associates (1967) have delineated a "failure to thrive" syndrome that "is a serious disorder of growth and development frequently requiring admission to the hospital. In its acute phase it significantly compromises the health and sometimes endangers the life of the child" (p. 689).

In a follow-up study conducted eight months to nine years after hospitalization of such children for treatment, Bullard found that almost two-thirds of the subjects showed evidence "either of continued growth failure, emotional disorder, mental retardation, or some combination of these" (p. 681).

The effects of deprivation vary considerably from infant to infant; in some societies, practices that we would expect to be permanently damaging turn out not to be. For example, Kagan (1973) found that year-old Guatemalan Indian infants who had spent their first year in a psychologically impoverished environment —due to the custom of the culture—were severely retarded in their development, as compared with American-raised infants. However, after the first year, the environment of these infants was enriched, and by the age of eleven, they performed as well or better than American children on problem-solving and related intellectual tasks.

Pathogenic parent-child relationships

A parent-child relationship is always a two-way relationship. As with any continuing relationship, the behavior of each person affects the behavior of the other. Some children are easier to love than others; some parents are more sensitive than others to an infant's needs. Patterns are established for which it is often hard to say which person was originally the most responsible.

HIGHLIGHT

Separation from parents as a traumatic experience

Bowlby (1960, 1973) has summarized the effects on children from 2 to 5 years of age of being separated from their parents during prolonged periods of hospitalization. He cited three stages of their separation experience:

1. Initial protest—characterized by increased crying, screaming, and general activity.

2. Despair—which included dejection, stupor, decreased activity, and general withdrawal from the environment.

3. Detachment—following the children's discharge from the hospital and reunion with their mothers— in which the children appeared indifferent and sometimes even hostile toward their mothers.

The effects of long-term or permanent separation from one or both parents are complex. When the separation occurs as early as 3 months after birth, the infant's emotional upset seems to be primarily a reaction to environmental change and strangeness, and he or she usually adapts readily to a surrogate parent figure. But once attachment behavior has developed, the emotional hurt of separation may be deeper and more sustained, and the child may go through a period of bereavement and have greater difficulty adjusting to the change. It would appear that the age at which the infant is most vulnerable to long-term separation or loss is from about 3 months to 3 years. The long-term consequences of such loss appear to depend not only on the time of its occurrence, but also on the child in question, the previous relationship with the parent, and the quality of subsequent parental care.

The magnitude of the problem of separation from parents is indicated by the statistic that well over 10 million children in the United States have had the experience of losing at least one parent through separation, divorce, or death.

Effects of maternal deprivation on monkeys

In Harlow's (1965, 1973) well-known experiments, monkeys separated from their mothers at birth and raised in isolation with artificial mothers (wire frames covered with terry cloth) treated them like real mothers, spent hours clinging to them, and apparently developed normally (left). At maturity, however, they failed to establish normal sexual relations, and those that bore young were helpless and dangerous mothers.

Another experiment involved raising four motherless monkeys together in one cage (center), permitting them 20 minutes each day in a playroom. Although they appeared normal at one year of age, they spent their early months huddled together.

When the young monkeys were raised under conditions of relatively complete social deprivation, they exhibited various symptoms of maladaptive behavior. The monkey huddling in a corner of a cage (right) has been taken out of isolation and is reacting with a typical response of fear and withdrawal.

In occasional cases we can now identify characteristics in an infant that have been largely responsible for the unsatisfactory relationship that has developed between parent and child. One example is the "difficult baby," described by Chess and her associates (see p. 138), whose irregularities were considered partly responsible for the mutually unsatisfying relationship that developed between mother and child.

Another example is the withdrawn, unresponsive, *autistic* child. It has been observed that the parents of such children often seem cold, emotionally reserved, and "intellectual," and early researchers had blamed this parental coldness and "distance" for the child's autism—thereby adding the burden of guilt to the problems these parents already were fac-

ing. Infantile autism is now recognized as usually related to a congenital neurological deficit in the child; evidently the parents restrict their emotional involvement, often unconsciously, as a way of coping with a profoundly unresponsive child (Schopler, 1978). There is also evidence that some of the disturbance commonly found in the parents of schizophrenic patients is a reaction *to* the child's disturbance rather than the other way around.

Probably more important in shaping the child's personality development, however, is the influence of the parent on the child. Several specific patterns of parental influence appear with great regularity in the background of children who show emotional disturbances and other types of faulty development. Seven of these patterns will be discussed here.

Rejection.   Parental rejection of the child is closely related to "masked deprivation" and may be shown in various ways—by physical neglect, denial of love and affection, lack of interest in the child's activities and achievements, harsh or inconsistent punishment, failure to spend time with the child, and lack of respect for the child's rights and feelings. In a minority of cases, it also involves cruel and abusive treatment. Parental rejection may be partial or complete, passive or active, and subtly or overtly cruel.

In an early study of 379 mothers of five-year-olds, Sears, Maccoby, and Levin (1957) found that cold and rejecting mothers reported a background of feeding problems, persistent bed-wetting, aggressiveness, and slow conscience development in their children. Later, Hurley (1965) found parental rejection to be associated with diminished intelligence during the early school years. He concluded that an unpleasant emotional climate and discouragement have a general inhibiting and suppressing effect on a child's intellectual development and functioning. Pringle (1965) found that many adults who had been rejected in childhood had serious difficulty in giving and receiving affection.

More recent studies have supported and extended these earlier findings. In a ten-year study of 427 children, Lefkowitz et al. (1973) found parental rejection to be a key predictor of aggression in young children; Poznanski (1973) found parental rejection to be a key factor among children suffering from excessive fears; Pemberton and Benady (1973) found an association between parental rejection and lying and stealing on the part of children; and Stierlin (1973) found parental rejection a major reason why adolescents decide to run away from home. In a study of a wide variety of psychological disorders among urban children, Langner et al. (1974) found parental coldness a common factor.

A consideration of why parents reject their children would take us too far afield, but it would appear that a large proportion of such parents have themselves been the victims of parental rejection. In this sense, lack of love has been referred to as a "communicable disease." And, of course, rejection is not a one-way street; the child may also reject the parents. This pattern sometimes occurs when the parents belong to a low-status minority group of which the child is ashamed. Although the results of such rejection have not been studied systematically, it would appear that children who reject their parents deny themselves needed models, loving relationships, and other essentials for healthy development.

Overprotection and restrictiveness.   Parental overprotection involves the "smothering" of the child's growth. Overprotecting parents may watch over their children constantly, protect them from the slightest risk, overly clothe and medicate them, and make up their minds for them at every opportunity. In the case of mother-son relationships, there is often excessive physical contact, in which the mother may sleep with the child for years and be subtly seductive in her relationships with him.

Different parental motivations may lead to overprotection. An early study by Levy (1945) found that in an experimental group of abnormally protective mothers, 75 percent had little in common with their husbands. Such maternal reactions appeared to represent a compensatory type of behavior in which the mother attempted, through her contact with the child, to gain satisfactions that normally should have been obtained in her marriage. It is not uncommon in such cases for the mother to call the child her "lover" and actually to encourage the child in behaviors somewhat typical of courting. A corollary syndrome also occurs between fathers and daughters.

In a study of the family background of children referred to a child guidance clinic, Jenkins (1968) found that those youngsters characterized as "overanxious" were likely to have an infantilizing, overprotective mother. Similarly, in his study of children with excessive fears, Poznanski (1973) found a dependent relationship upon an overprotective mother to be one key reason for the fears. In shielding the child from every danger, this type of mother fails to provide the opportunities needed for reality testing and the development of essential competencies. In addition, her overprotection implies that she regards the child as incapable of coping with everyday problems. It is not surprising that such children often reach adolescence and young adulthood feeling inadequate and threatened by a dangerous world. When the time finally comes for such children to be on their own, they usually find themselves unprepared for the challenge (see HIGHLIGHT on this page).

Closely related to overprotection is restrictiveness. Here the parents rigidly enforce restrictive rules and standards and give the child little autonomy or freedom for growing in his or her own way. Whether justified or not, parental restrictiveness is one of the most commonly heard complaints of adolescents. Restrictiveness may foster well-controlled, socialized behavior, but it also tends to nurture fear, dependency, submission, repressed hostility, and some dulling of intellectual striving (Baumrind, 1971; Becker, 1964). Often, too, extreme behavior on the part of the adolescent is a way of rebelling against severe restrictions. This conflict between rebellion and submission is not infrequently reflected in the sexual behavior of adolescent girls. On a broader scope, the HIGHLIGHT on page 148 suggests some of the effects that overprotection and restrictiveness can have on both individuals and society.

Unrealistic demands.   Some parents place excessive pressures on their children to live up to unrealistically "high" standards. For example, a child may be expected to excel in school and other activities. Where the child has the capacity for exceptionally high-level performance, things may work out; but even here the child may be under such sustained pressure that little room is left for spontaneity or development as an independent person.

Typically, however, the child is never quite able to live up to parental expectations and demands. If a child raises a grade of C to a B, rather than giving praise, the parents may ask why it was not an A. Nothing the child does is good enough. Effort only brings more painful frustration and self-devaluation. Those parents who promote feelings of failure by their excessive demands also tend to discourage further effort on the child's part. Almost invariably such a child eventually comes to feel, "I can't do it, so why try?"

One need only observe a child's eager "Watch me, Mommy," while demonstrating some new achievement, to understand how important the mastery of new competencies and parental recognition for such mastery are to healthy development. And research studies, such as the

One case of overprotection

I was a girl who had almost everything: a beautiful home; money for personal pleasure whenever I asked; nice clothes; and parents who coddled me, picked up after me, and chauffeured me wherever I wanted to go. What didn't I have? Well, I didn't have any knowledge of how to sort out laundry or run a washing machine. I didn't know how to discipline myself to use time properly, to make sure I got enough sleep, to feed myself the right food. I didn't have the basics for coping with life on my own.

My parents—undoubtedly out of love, but with a mixture of guilt added—had, for some reason, overcompensated during my childhood. They had done too much for me. And when the time came for me to be on my own, I struggled for independence from this overprotective nest, stumbled over my newfound physical, moral, and social freedoms, and suffered a crushing fall. But by the time I hit bottom, I had learned one principle that I hope will guide me throughout the rest of my life: I can make it on my own. I learned this the hard way. I only hope that, by sharing my experience, I can help others become independent young adults without the physical and emotional trauma I endured.

Quoted from Traub (1974, p. 41).

investigation of the antecedents of self-respect in children carried out by Coopersmith (1967), have shown that high parental expectations are both common and helpful for the child's development. Yet such expectations need to be realistic, and to take into consideration the capabilities and temperament of each child.

Too often, expectations become a matter of what the parents value rather than what the child may need. A professional football player may have his heart set on his son's following in his footsteps, when actually the son lacks both capability and interest. In some instances unrealistic demands may take the form of parental overdependence on the child. Parents who are unhappy with each other or in other ways are failing to find a meaningful and fulfilling life may focus on the child for meeting their own needs.

Not infrequently, unrealistic parental demands focus around moral standards—particularly with regard to sex, alcohol, and related matters. For example, the parents may instill in the child the view that masturbation or any other sexual activity is terribly sinful and can lead only to moral and physical degeneration. The child who accepts such rigid parental standards is likely to face many guilt-arousing and self-devaluating conflicts.

In still other instances, parental demands are unrealistically low, and the parents do not care what happens as long as the child stays out of trouble. Coopersmith (1967) found that the children of such parents were significantly lower in both achievement and self-esteem than were children whose parents had high but realistic expectations for them. Thus we can see that unrealistic expectations and demands—either too high, too low, or distorted and rigid—can be important causes of faulty development and maladjustment.

Overpermissiveness and indulgence. It happens less commonly than is popularly supposed, but sometimes one or both parents will cater to the child's slightest whims and in so doing fail to teach and reward desirable standards of behavior. In essence, the parent surrenders the running of the home to an uninhibited son or daughter. Pollack (1968), for example, has quoted a permissive father who finally rebelled at the tyranny of his nine-year-old daughter, and in a near tantrum exploded with, "I want one thing clearly understood—I live here, too!" (p. 28).

Overly indulged children are characteristically spoiled, selfish, inconsiderate, and demanding. Sears (1961) found that high permissiveness and low punishment in the home were correlated positively with antisocial, aggressive behavior, particularly during middle and later childhood. Unlike rejected, emotionally deprived children, who often find it difficult to enter into warm interpersonal relationships, indulged children enter readily into such relationships but exploit people for their own purposes in the same way that they have learned to exploit their parents. In dealing with authority, such children are usually rebellious since, for so long, they have had their own way. Overly indulged children also tend to be impatient, to approach problems in an aggressive and demanding manner, and to

Do we effectively develop and utilize the resources of our youth?

"The energy, idealism, and intelligence of youth are the prime resources of each nation; if these resources are to be wisely spent, our youth must be involved in the mainstream of national life." This view, expressed by Eisenberg (1970, p. 1692) has been elaborated on by Bronfenbrenner (1974):

"Our children are not entrusted with any real responsibilities. Little that they do really matters. They are given duties rather than responsibilities; the ends and means have been determined by someone else and their job is to fulfill an assignment involving little judgment, decision making or risk. This practice is intended to protect children from burdens beyond their years, but there is reason to believe it has been carried too far in contemporary American society and has contributed to the alienation of young people and their alleged incapacity to deal constructively with personal and social problems. The evidence indicates that children acquire the capacity to cope with difficult situations when they have an opportunity to take on consequential responsibilities in relation to others and are held accountable for them." (p. 60)

In a similar vein, recent reports by both governmental and private agencies have urged that young people be given the opportunity to participate more fully in our social institutions and to assume more responsibility for themselves and others. Through the guise of protecting our children, we may be losing the valuable new outlooks and solutions they can bring to the problems of our future well-being. That is, we may be conditioning children "to believe in a future which is based on the past and to believe that any changes in this model can only be initiated by chance or by experts" (Nicholson, 1979).

find it difficult to accept present frustrations in the interests of long-range goals (Baumrind, 1971).

The fact that their important and pampered status in the home does not transfer automatically to the outside world may come as a great shock to indulged youngsters; confusion and adjustive difficulties may occur when "reality" forces them to reassess their assumptions about themselves and the world.

Faulty discipline. Parents have been particularly confused during recent years about appropriate forms of discipline. Sometimes a misinterpretation of psychological findings and theories has led to the view that all punishment and frustration should be avoided lest the child be "fixated" at that level of development. In other cases parents have resorted to excessively harsh discipline, convinced that if they "spare the rod" they will spoil the child. And in still other cases parents have seemed to lack general guidelines, punishing children one day and ignoring or even rewarding them the next for doing the same thing.

As we have noted, overpermissiveness and lack of discipline tend to produce a spoiled, inconsiderate aggressive child—and an insecure one as well. On the other hand, overly severe or harsh discipline may have a variety of harmful effects, including fear and hatred of the punishing person, little initiative or spontaneity, and less friendly feelings toward others. When accompanied by rigid moral standards, overly severe discipline is likely to result in a seriously repressed child who lacks spontaneity and warmth and devotes much effort toward controlling impulses that are, in fact, natural but are assumed to be sinful. Such children often subject themselves to severe self-recrimination and self-punishment for real or imagined mistakes and misdeeds. Overly severe discipline, combined with restrictiveness, also may lead to rebellion and socially deviant behavior as children grow older and are subjected increasingly to outside influences that may be incompatible with parental views and practices.

When severe discipline takes the form of physical punishment for broken rules—rather than withdrawal of approval and privileges—the result tends to be increased aggressive behavior on the part of the child (Eron et al., 1974; Lefkowitz et al., 1973, 1977; Steinmetz & Straus, 1973). Apparently physical punishment provides a model of aggressive behavior that the child then tends to emulate.

Similarly, inconsistent discipline makes it difficult for the child to establish stable values for guiding behavior. When the child is punished one time and ignored or rewarded the next for the same behavior, he or she is at a loss to know what behavior is appropriate. Deur and Parke (1970) found that children with a history of inconsistent reward and punishment for aggressive behavior were more resistant to punishment and to the extinction of their aggressive behavior than were children who had experienced more consistent discipline. This study supports earlier findings showing a high correlation between inconsistent discipline and later delinquent and criminal behavior.

In the past, discipline was conceived as a method for both punishing undesirable behavior and preventing such behavior in the future. At the present time discipline is thought of more positively as providing needed structure and guidance for promoting healthy growth on the part of the child. Where coercion or punishment is deemed necessary, it is considered important that the parent make it clear exactly what behavior is considered inappropriate; it is also considered important that the child know what behavior is expected, and that positive and consistent methods of discipline be worked out for dealing with infractions. In general, it would appear that freedom should be commensurate with the child's level of maturity and ability to use it constructively.

Inadequate and irrational communication. Parents can discourage a child from asking questions and in other ways fail to foster the "information exchange" essential for helping the child develop a realistic frame of reference and essential competencies. Such limited and inadequate communication patterns have commonly been attributed to socially disadvantaged families, but these patterns are not restricted to any one socioeconomic level.

Such patterns may take a number of forms. Some parents are too busy with their own concerns to listen to their children and try to understand the conflicts and pressures they are facing. As a consequence, these parents often fail to give needed support and assistance during crisis periods. Other parents may have forgotten that the world often looks different to a child or adolescent and that rapid social change can lead to a very real communication gap between generations.

In other instances faulty communication may take more deviant forms in which the messages become completely garbled because the listener distorts, disconfirms, or blocks out the speaker's intended meaning. A good example of such pathological communication is provided by Haley (1959). The setting is a meeting in the hospital involving a schizophrenic young man, his parents, and his therapist. Some time prior to the meeting, the patient had sent his mother a Mother's Day card containing the inscription, "For Someone Who's Been Like a Mother To Me." We pick up the conversation at the point following a confrontation between mother and son concerning the obliquely hostile inscription:

"*Patient:* Well, I meant to sting you just a tiny bit by that outside phrase.
Mother: You see I'm a little bit of a psychiatrist too, Simon, I happen to be—(laughing). So I felt so—when you talked to (the therapist) I brought along that card—I wanted to know what's behind your head. And I wanted to know—or you made it on purposely to hurt me—Well, if you did, I—I . . .
Patient: (interrupting) Not entirely, not entire . . .
Mother: (interrupting and overlapping) I'll take all—Simon, believe me. I'll take all the hurt in the world if it will help you—you see what I mean?
Therapist: How can you . . .
Mother: (continuing) Because I never meant to hurt you—Huh?
Therapist: How can you hurt anybody who is perfectly willing to be hurt? (short pause)
Father: What's that?
Mother: I uh—a mother sacrifices—if you would be—maybe a mother you would know too. Because a mother is just a martyr, she's sacrificing—like even with Jesus with his mother—she sacrificed too. So that's the way it goes on, a mother takes over anything what she can help . . .
Therapist: (interrupting) What mother?
Mother: (continuing) her children.
Patient: (interrupting and overlapping) Well, uh, I'll tell you Ma—listen, Ma, I didn't mean to—to sting you exactly that outside part there.
Therapist: Well, you said so.
Patient: Oh, all right, but it—it wasn't that exactly. No, I'm not giving ground—uh—it's hard to explain this thing. Uh—uh—what was I going to say? Now I forgot what I was going to say. (short pause) I mean I felt that this—this is what I mean, uh—that I felt that you could have been a better mother to me than you were. See there were things.
Mother: Uh . . .
Father: Well you said . . .
Patient: (interrupting) You could have been better than you were. So that's why—that's that—I felt—it was, uh—uh, was all right to send it that way.
Mother: Well, if you meant it that way that's perf—that's what I wanted to know—and that's all I care you see. But I still say, Simon, that if you would take your father and mother just like they're plain

people—you just came here and you went through life like anybody else went through—and—and don't keep picking on them and picking them to pieces—but just leave them alone—and go along with them the way they are—and don't change them—you'll be able to get along with everybody, I assure you.
Patient: (interrupting) I mean after all a card is a card—why I'd—it seems to me kind of silly (anguish in his voice and near weeping) to bring that thing in here—they have sold them at the canteen, Ma . . .
Therapist: Are you anxious now . . .
Patient: Why . . .
Therapist: Are you anxious now because she said . . .
Patient: I shouldn't be blamed for a thing like that, it's so small . . .
Mother: (overlapping) I'm not blaming you.
Patient: (continuing) I don't even remember exactly what the thing was.
Mother: (overlapping) Well, that's all I wanted to know (laughs).
Patient: (continuing) I didn't want to—to—to—to blame you or nothing." (Haley, 1959, p. 360)

This conversation continued in similar fashion until the patient conceded that what he had meant by the inscription was that his mother had been a *real* mother to him. This produced a considerable reduction in general tension, but it was, of course, at the expense of reality.

Although the preceding illustration is an extreme example of pathological communication, some parents apparently follow similar patterns. One such pattern that conveys contradictory messages has been referred to by Bateson (1960) as the *double bind*. For example, a mother may complain of her son's lack of affection toward her, but freeze up and show strong disapproval when he tries to be demonstrative. Similarly, parents may convey one message by their words and another by their behavior. Thus a father may deplore lying and admonish his daughter "never to tell a lie" while obviously lying a good deal himself.

It is not uncommon for families, particularly those headed by disturbed parents, to communicate various myths that essentially redefine reality, including the reality of the child's own personal characteristics or those of other family members. A special instance of such communication involves implicit rules that some aspect of reality will be treated as though it does not exist, a process known as *masking*. For example, a 28-year-old man treated by one of the authors repeatedly referred to his nocturnal seminal emissions as "bed-wetting." When this curious redefinition of a natural process was pointed out, he claimed not to know "what else it could be," which was in fact a partially accurate claim. His early (and late) family life had been characterized by a systematic and total masking out of all information pertaining to sex and sexual functions.

An even more subtle and damaging communication pattern involves contradicting or undermining the child's statements, conclusions, or even experience in the world, so that he or she is left confused, devalued, and disconfirmed as a person. Lidz, Fleck, and Cornelison (1965) provide a poignant example in describing the attempt of a schizophrenic young woman to communicate with her parents:

"The daughter carefully prepared in advance what she wished to convey, and we tried to prepare the parents to listen carefully and to reply meaningfully. The patient, to the surprise of her psychiatrist, freely poured out her feelings to her parents and in heart-rending fashion told them of her bewilderment and pleaded for their understanding and help. During the height of her daughter's pleas, Mrs. _____ off-handedly turned to one of the psychiatrists, tugged at the waist of her dress and blandly remarked, 'My dress is getting tight. I suppose I should go on a diet. . . .' The next day the patient relapsed into incoherent and silly behavior." (p. 182)

Faulty patterns of communication have been found to be more common in the backgrounds of emotionally disturbed adolescents and young adults than in those of young people more adequately adjusted. Normal families tend to show a much higher incidence of supportive interactions and communications that foster the unity of the family (Alexander, 1973).

Undesirable parental models.   Important in any relationship are the behaviors that one individual shows to the other. This is particularly true in parent-child interactions. Since children tend to observe and imitate the behavior of their parents, parental behavior can have a highly beneficial or detrimental effect on the way a youngster learns to perceive, think, feel, and act (see HIGHLIGHT on page 152). We may consider parents as undesirable models if they have faulty assumptions about real-

ity, possibility, and values, or if they depend excessively on defense mechanisms in coping with their problems—as when they consistently project the blame for their own mistakes onto others, if they lie and cheat, if they refuse to face and deal realistically with problems, or if there is a marked discrepancy between their proclaimed values and the values reflected in their actual behavior.

A parent who is emotionally disturbed, addicted to alcohol or drugs, or otherwise maladjusted may also serve as an undesirable model. In his extensive study of emotional disturbances in children, Jenkins (1966) found that nearly half of a group of children diagnosed as "overanxious-neurotic" had mothers who were described as neurotic because of extreme anxiety, nervousness, and related symptoms. Concurrently, the children characterized by habitual delinquent behavior typically had inadequate father figures as well as backgrounds combining poverty, parental neglect, and a bad neighborhood. Similarly, Anthony (1969) found a much higher incidence of maladaptive behavior among children with psychotic parents than among a control group with nonpsychotic parents.

Several investigators, including Green, Gaines, and Sandgrund (1974), have found that child abusers tend to come from families in which the parents had been rejecting and abusive. In fact, the typical severe child abuser—who may even commit murder—often has been reared in a family having multiple problems (Kaplun & Reich, 1976).

Undesirable parental models are undoubtedly an important reason why mental disorders, delinquency, crime, and other forms of maladaptive behavior tend to run in families. But it should be pointed out that there is nothing inevitable in the effects of parental pathology on the child's development. The pathology of one parent may be compensated for by the wisdom and concern of the other, or an alcoholic parent may perhaps serve as a "negative model," showing the child what *not* to be like. Kadushin (1967) has cited a number of studies in which children coming from homes with undesirable parental models have grown up to be successful and well-adjusted adults. And Bleuler (1974) found that even the extreme stress of being reared by a psychotic parent did not prevent half to three-quarters

Imitative learning of aggression from adult models

The extent to which children may imitate adult models is graphically illustrated in a study by Bandura, Ross, and Ross (1963). In this sequence, an adult model (top) throws, batters, and kicks a large inflated doll.

After viewing an adult model perform such actions, in person or on film, each child in the experimental group underwent mild frustration and was then observed in a playroom supplied with a variety of toys—including crayons, a tea set, a mallet, a dart gun, and an inflated doll—which could be used in aggressive on nonaggressive play. A control group (who saw no aggressive model) underwent the same mild frustration. Children who had seen the adult model were nearly twice as aggressive in their play activities as the control group. Some children, such as those depicted here, imitated the adult model almost exactly.

of the children he studied from remaining normal.

Although the reasons for such favorable outcomes are not clear, it is useful to emphasize that specific pathogenic parent-child patterns always take place in a broader social context. The latter may tend to minimize or exacerbate the influence of a particular condition. A summary of faulty parent-child relationships is presented in the HIGHLIGHT on page 154.

Pathogenic family structures

In the previous sections we considered particular patterns of faulty parent-child relationships; here we will focus on more comprehensive patterns of family pathology. The current research on families as group systems has revealed that maladjustive behavior on the part of the child may be fostered by the general family environment as well as by the child's relationships with one or both parents.

In reviewing the effects of the family system on development, we again encounter the problem of establishing criteria for differentiating between what is "healthy" and what is maladaptive; for, as in the case of the individual, we have no model of the "ideal" family. However, several types of families can be identified that clearly have a detrimental influence on child development in our society. For present purposes, we shall briefly describe four such types of families.

These four types are by no means discrete, and a given family may show a wide range of pathogenic behaviors. These family patterns have been labeled "pathogenic" because of the high frequency with which they are associated with problems in child development and later psychopathology. It may be emphasized, however, that an apparently healthy family may also have children who show seriously maladaptive behavior.

Inadequate families.   This type of family is characterized by inability to cope with the or-

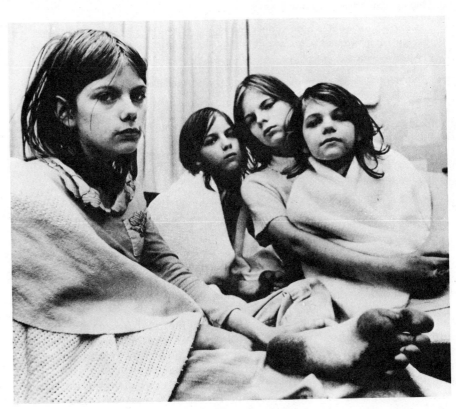

These orphans, turned out of the house by an uncle, were found wandering barefoot in subzero temperatures. Two were suffering from frostbite. A family situation of this type can have lasting impact on a child's psychological, as well as physical, development.

Summary chart of faulty parent-child relationships

Undesirable condition	Typical effect on child's personality development
Rejection	Feelings of anxiety, insecurity, low self-esteem, negativism, hostility, attention-seeking, loneliness, jealousy, and slowness in conscience development
Overprotection—domination	Submissiveness, lack of self-reliance, dependence in relations with others, low self-evaluation, some dulling of intellectual striving
Overpermissiveness—overindulgence	Selfishness, demanding attitude, inability to tolerate frustration, rebelliousness toward authority, excessive need of attention, lack of responsibility, inconsiderateness, exploitativeness in interpersonal relationships
Perfectionism, with unrealistic demands	Lack of spontaneity, rigid conscience development, severe conflicts, tendency toward guilt and self-condemnation if there is failure to live up to parental demands
Faulty discipline:	
Lack of discipline	Inconsiderateness, aggressiveness, and antisocial tendencies
Harsh, overly severe discipline	Fear, hatred of parent, little initiative or spontaneity, lack of friendly feelings toward others
Inconsistent discipline	Difficulty in establishing stable values for guiding behavior; tendency toward highly aggressive behavior
Inadequate and irrational communications	As in case of ''double bind'' communications, the tendency toward confusion, lack of an integrated frame of reference, unclear self-identity, lack of initiative, self-devaluation
Undesirable parental models	The learning of faulty values, formulation of unrealistic goals, development of maladaptive coping patterns

The exact effects of faulty parent-child relationships on later behavior depends on many factors, including the age of the child, the constitutional and personality makeup of the child at the time, the duration and degree of the unhealthy relationship, his or her perception of the relationship, and the total family setting and life context, including the presence or absence of alleviating conditions and whether or not subsequent experiences tend to reinforce or correct early damage. There is no uniform pattern of pathogenic family relationship underlying the development of later psychopathology, but the conditions we have discussed often act as predisposing factors.

dinary problems of family living. It lacks the resources, physical or psychological, for meeting demands with which most families can satisfactorily cope. Consequently, the inadequate family relies heavily on continued outside assistance and support in resolving everyday problems. The incompetencies of such a family may stem from immaturity, lack of education, mental retardation, or other shortcomings of the parents. Sometimes, of course, environmental demands are so severe that they overtax the adjustive resources of families that would normally be more adequate.

A family that is floundering against odds too great for its resources, for whatever reason, cannot give its children the feeling of safety and security they need, or adequately guide them in the development of essential competencies. Nor can financial or other outside assistance be counted on to meet the needs of such families, for families, like individuals, need to feel they are self-directing and in control of their own destinies.

Antisocial families. Here the family espouses values not accepted by the wider community. In some families the parents are overtly or covertly engaged in behavior that violates the standards and interests of society, and they may be chronically in difficulty with the law. Such antisocial values usually handicap marital and other family relationships, as well as providing undesirable models for the child.

Children in such families may be encouraged in dishonesty, deceit, and other undesirable behavior patterns; or they may simply observe and imitate the undesirable behavior and attitudes of their parents. In some cases, children may develop a high degree of courage, self-discipline, and loyalty to the family group at the expense of identification with the society as a whole. More often, the models they see are immature and self-seeking, and the social interactions they observe and take part in are shallow and manipulative—a poor preparation for mature, responsible adulthood. Here it is of interest to note that Langner and Michael (1963), in an extensive study of mental health and mental disorder in a congested urban area, found a higher mental health risk for children who disapproved of their parents' character than for those who experienced a broken home.

Discordant and disturbed families. In a discordant family one or both of the parents is not gaining satisfaction from the relationship and may express feelings of frustration and disillusionment in hostile ways such as nagging, belittling, and doing things purposely to annoy the other person. A common source of conflict and dissatisfaction is value differences, which may lead to serious disagreements about a variety of topics, including sexual behavior and how money is spent. Whatever the reasons for difficulties, seriously discordant relationships are likely to be frustrating, hurtful, and generally pathogenic in their effects on both the adults and the children.

Discordant families are usually characterized by faulty communication patterns such as those described on page 149. Often they involve what have been called *fraudulent*

Children learn the values and prejudices of their parents at an early age.

interpersonal contracts, of which there are several variants. In a common one, A offers a particular kind of relationship (with certain implied "rules" of behavior), which B accepts and proceeds to act on; then A shifts the rules in midstream, blaming B for inappropriate behavior. B is put down for doing what A had seemed to want—a fertile ground for increasing resentment, retaliation, and dissension. As one might expect, children who grow up in discordant families are likely themselves to find it difficult to establish and maintain marital and other intimate relationships.

In a *disturbed* family, one or both of the parents behave in grossly eccentric or abnormal ways and may keep the home in constant emotional turmoil. Such homes differ greatly, but it is common to find (a) parents who are fighting to maintain their own equilibrium and are unable to give the child needed love and guidance; (b) gross irrationality in communication patterns as well as faulty parental models; and (c) almost inevitably, the enmeshment of the child in the emotional conflicts of the parents. Lidz et al. (1965) described two such patterns they found to be especially prominent in the family backgrounds of schizophrenic patients: (a) *Marital schism,* in which both parents are constantly embroiled in deep-seated conflict; and (b) *Marital skew,* wherein the healthier marital partner, in the interest of minimizing open disharmony, essentially accepts and supports the frequently bizarre beliefs and behavior of the spouse. Schism and skew are roughly equivalent, respectively, to discordant and disturbed family patterns. In either instance, the children are caught up in a very unwholesome psychological environment.

Homes in which the parents are discordant or disturbed have been found to be associated with a high incidence of psychological disorders among children and adolescents (Langner et al., 1974; Wolkind & Rutter, 1973). Parental quarreling, conflict, and general tension are unfortunate conditions for the growing children, representing a threat to their "base of operations" and the only security they know. For this reason, it often appears that maladjusted parents who are able to establish a harmonious relationship with each other despite their individual problems are much less damaging to the child than are maladjusted—or possibly even otherwise well-functioning—parents who live in disharmony.

Disrupted families.   Disrupted families are incomplete, whether as a result of death, divorce, separation, or some other circumstance. Owing partly to greater cultural acceptance of divorce, more than a million divorces are now occurring yearly in the United States, with a rate of increase averaging about 8 percent each year. Although certain persons contribute disproportionately to such figures through multiple divorces and remarriages, the statistics nevertheless provide a sobering commentary on the strains and difficulties of extended intimate relationships. It is estimated that, at any one time, over 10 percent of the ever-married adult population is currently separated or divorced (Bloom, Asher, & White, 1978). Estimates predict that, as of 1980, over three million households will be headed by divorced mothers alone.

Stressful as unhappy marriages are, dissolution of a marital relationship can also be enormously stressful and produce much disorder, both mental and physical. The divorced and separated are markedly overrepresented among psychiatric patients, although the direction of the causal relationship is not always clear. In their comprehensive review of the effects of marital disruption, Bloom et al. (1978) concluded that such disruption is a major source of psychopathology, physical illness and death, suicide, and homicide.

Divorce can have traumatic effects on a child. Feelings of insecurity and rejection may be aggravated by conflicting loyalties and, sometimes, by the spoiling the child receives while staying with one or the other parent— maybe not the one he or she would prefer to be with.

It has been commonly assumed that the loss of a father is more traumatic for a son than for a daughter, but some doubt has been raised about this assumption. It is now believed that absence of the father has adverse effects on the formation of a secure gender identity for both girls and boys (Hetherington, Cox, & Cox, 1978). For example, Hetherington (1973) found that "the effects of father absence on daughters appear during adolescence and manifest themselves mainly as an inability to interact appropriately with males" (p. 52). In this context, one is also reminded of the bitterness of the daughter of a naval officer who stated, "I despise my father. He was never there. He was in the Navy 120 years" (*Time,* 1967, p. 30).

The long-range effects of family disruption on the child may vary greatly, even being favorable in many instances as contrasted to remaining in a home torn by marital conflict and dissension (Hetherington et al., 1978). Detrimental effects may be minimized if a substitute model for the missing parent is available, if the remaining family members are able to compensate for the missing parent and reorganize the family into an effective functioning group, or if the home is reconstituted by a successful remarriage that provides an adequate environment for child rearing. And if the remaining parent—usually the mother—is able to cope with her own emotional upset as well as the confusion, anxiety, or depression that may be aroused in the child, she may help ease the transition through this crisis period.

Unquestionably, parental separation or divorce involves very real stresses for children; it is hardly surprising that some succumb to these stresses and develop maladaptive responses. Delinquency and other maladaptive behaviors are much more frequent among children and adolescents from disrupted homes than among those from intact ones. We are beginning to learn, however, that we are not always justified in inferring that the disrupted home has caused the maladaptive behavior. Since both broken homes and delinquency are most common among families in lower socioeconomic circumstances, it seems equally likely that both the broken homes and the childhood deviance are in large part caused by the stressors of poverty and exclusion from the mainstream of society.

Pathogenic interpersonal relationships and interactions are by no means confined to the family, but may also involve the peer group and other individuals outside the family. Particularly during adolescence, when young people are becoming progressively independent of parental controls, their relationships outside the family are likely to be important influences on their further development.

Severe stress

The various causes of abnormal development we have discussed—such as psychic trauma and family disruption—are also sources of severe stress. In addition, certain other stressors in our society appear directly relevant to understanding maladaptive behavior.

Devaluating frustrations. In contemporary life there are a number of frustrations that lead to self-devaluation and hence are particularly difficult to cope with. Among these are failure, losses, personal limitations and lack of resources, guilt, and loneliness.

1. *Failure.* The highly competitive setting in which we live almost inevitably leads to occasional failures. No team is likely to win all the time, nor can all succeed who aspire to become movie or television stars or to achieve high political office. For each person who suc-

ceeds, there is an inevitable crop of failures. Furthermore, some people seem to court failure by setting unrealistically high goals or by undertaking new ventures without adequate preparation.

Some individuals fall into a pattern in which, to avoid the possibility of clear failure, they develop strategies of "incompetence" that keep others' demands for performance to a minimum. It is difficult to fail, after all, when nothing much is expected of one. The difficulty with this strategy, as in the case of many other strategies designed to cut short-term losses, is that over time the individual is driven inexorably into a position of degrading ineptitude from which it becomes increasingly difficult to escape; competence does not flourish in the absence of practice of the pertinent skills.

Some evidence suggests that this pattern of motivated incompetence may have been, in the past at least, especially likely to develop in girls and women as a means of coping with societal sex-role expectations (Horner, 1968, 1970). However, this trend may be undergoing significant change at this time (Bardwick, 1971; Romer, 1975).

Repeated failures or failure in an endeavor in which we are emotionally involved and want very much to succeed, such as marriage, can be especially devaluating and frustrating. Often it is important that failure experiences be "worked through," that we not only accept them but that we learn from them. In this context, it is interesting to note a report by Harmeling (1950) that the Eskimos at Cape Prince of Wales conducted a primitive form of psychodrama in their community igloo during the six-month winter. Accompanied by an orchestra of drums, they staged a pantomime of the failure experiences in their lives and laughed at their own mistakes thus objectively viewed. In our own culture much of the comedy of professional comedians would seem to serve a similar function.

2. *Losses.* Closely related to failure are the many losses that people inevitably experience—losses involving objects or resources they value or individuals with whom they strongly identify.

Among the most distressing material losses are those of money and status. In our society money gives its owner security, self-esteem, and the use of desired goods and services; thus

an appreciable financial loss is apt to lead to severe self-recrimination and discouragement. Similarly, loss of social status—whether it stems from loss of economic position or some other cause—tends to devalue an individual in his or her own eyes as well as in the eyes of others.

Interpersonal losses are probably more stressful than material ones for most people. As we noted in Chapter 4, for example, Holmes and Holmes (1970) found death of spouse, divorce, and marital separation to be the three most stressful events reported by adults in our society. In fact, bereavement appears to be an important cause of illness and death (Klerman &

Izen, 1977). Here it may be noted that the death rate for widowers is double that for married men, and that 75 percent of American women will one day be widowed (Caine, 1974; Harvey & Bahr, 1974).

3. *Limitations beyond one's control.* Being "on the low end of the totem pole" with regard to material advantages and possessions is a powerful source of frustration, one afflicting members of disadvantaged minorities in our society with special severity. Constant exposure to TV commercials and other advertising depicting desirable objects and experiences in our allegedly affluent society—while seeming to be "on the outside looking in"—can be

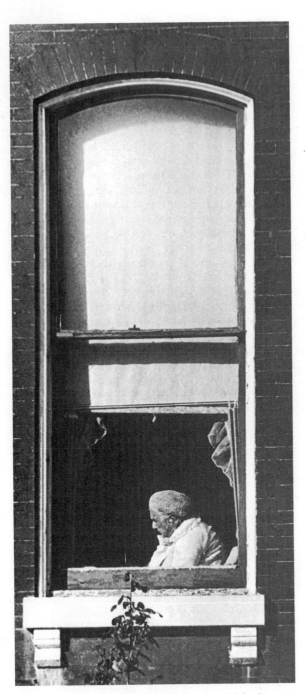

The elderly and handicapped are particularly subject to the agonizing effects of loneliness.

highly frustrating for those whose aspirations and hopes seem to have been bypassed by society. But probably from time to time most of us make envious *status comparisons* in which we see others as more favorably endowed with personal and material resources than we are.

In addition, physical handicaps and other personal limitations that restrict one's activities—and possibly attractiveness to members of the opposite sex—can be highly stressful. Here again, comparison with others who seem more favorably endowed can increase frustration and self-devaluation.

A related problem is the sense of personal helplessness that many of us feel, the sense that important events in our lives occur independently of our own actions or behavior. The coveted promotion goes to a co-worker who does not deserve it, while one's own stellar performance goes unrecognized. Under such circumstances, we feel little control over our destiny. This sense of noncontingency between outcomes and behavior has been formalized in recent years in terms of the concept of *learned helplessness,* believed to be important in the determination of certain types of psychological depression (Seligman, 1975). We shall have more to say about this concept in Chapter 11.

4. *Guilt.* To understand feelings of guilt it is useful to note that (a) we all learn to make certain assumptions about right and wrong; (b) we then apply these value assumptions in appraising our own behavior; and (c) we learn, often by hard experience, that wrongdoing leads to punishment. Thus, behaving in ways that we consider immoral leads to both self-devaluation and apprehension. Because of this orientation, depressed persons commonly search back through past events, locating and exaggerating misdeeds that have presumably led to their present difficulties.

Guilt is heavily infused with self-recrimination and anxiety, and is likely to be particularly stressful if it seems that nothing can be done to rectify one's misdeed. In fact, Gelven (1973) concluded that "Of all the forms of mental suffering, perhaps none is as pervasive or as intense as the ache of guilt" (p. 69).

5. *Loneliness.* Probably most people experience painful feelings of isolation and loneliness at some time in their lives. As the novelist Thomas Wolfe (1929) has expressed it,

"Which one of us has known his brother? Which of us has looked into his father's heart? Which of us has not remained forever prison-pent? Which of us is not forever a stranger and alone?" (p. 3)

Being unloved and lonely has been called "the greatest poverty." Perhaps for more people than we ever realize, the world is a lonely place.

A pervasive source of frustration related to all of the stresses we have mentioned—but particularly pertinent to understanding loneliness—is the inability to find meaning in one's life. Without meaning life is wasted, futile, and empty. There is little reason to try to be concerned, or even to hope. Thus again we see the great need for self-identity, for feelings of relatedness, and for values that give direction to life.

Value conflicts.   As we have seen, our values play a key role in determining the choices we make. If our value assumptions are unclear or contradictory, or if we have little faith in them, we are likely to experience difficulties in making choices and directing our behavior in ways that bring satisfaction. Such difficulties inevitably increase the stress we experience.

Here we shall briefly mention some core conflicts of modern life that frequently lead to such tension and inner turmoil that the individual's adjustive capacities are seriously impaired.

1. *Conformity vs. nonconformity.* Group pressures toward conformity inevitably develop as a group tries to maintain itself and achieve its goals, although the degree of conformity required varies greatly from one situation to another and from one group to another. For example, the conformity needed in a military group is considerably greater than that needed in a classroom. In any group, however, certain ground rules are established and members are under some pressure to conform to them.

Usually people are most likely to conform to the demands of groups in which they value membership and which have the greatest power to meet or to frustrate their needs. Thus it is often easier for teenagers to repudiate adult norms than it is for them to go against peer group pressures. But adults too are likely

to find it difficult to go against the expectations, demands, and pressures of peer groups that are important to them.

We have seen in Chapter 4 that healthy development involves the achievement of an integrated core of self-identity, a sense of who and what one is and what one values. In some ways this may be seen as the key developmental task of the adolescent years. Failure in this task has been described by Erikson (1968) as *identity diffusion.* The person suffering from identity diffusion is confused about what values to accept, sometimes attempting to solve the problem by strong identification with deviant groups. Often such a person pursues a "negative identity": one may not know who or what one *is,* but one can be reasonably certain that one is not "that"—referring to any value that parents and other adults hold dear. Identity diffusion is often found in the histories of persons who later develop more serious forms of personality disorganization.

2. *Caring vs. noninvolvement.* Because of the impersonality and anonymity of modern urban society, many people find it difficult to experience a sense of relatedness to others or of concern for the human enterprise. And since efforts on behalf of others can jeopardize one's own safety, the risks associated with "getting involved" may seem too great a price to pay for helping "strangers." As Seaman (1966) has put it,

"Often it seems painful but realistic to conclude that, in the last analysis, you and your family are alone, and the only ones you can count on for help and support are yourselves. No one else cares." (p. 35)

The conflict between commitment and noninvolvement is by no means confined to interactions with strangers or to participation in broader programs to right social injustices. Even in close interpersonal relationships, an individual may choose to remain somewhat aloof. All caring has hazards, since the one who invests affection is vulnerable to being hurt, and a painless outcome can never be guaranteed. Noninvolvement, on the other hand, exacts a price in lost satisfactions, feelings of estrangement and alienation, and a lack of meaning in one's existence.

3. *Avoiding vs. facing reality.* Perhaps the

first requisite of maturity is the ability to see oneself and the surrounding world objectively and to make the best of realities. But this is no simple task. Reality is often unpleasant and anxiety-arousing, and may undermine efforts to feel good about oneself and one's world. For example, facing the realization that failure in an important venture resulted from one's own inadequacies would be self-devaluating. Hence a person may tend to avoid facing this reality by rationalizing or using other defense mechanisms.

Similarly, a proud father may screen out the fact that his son is drinking too much, or is unduly preoccupied with drugs and neglecting his studies; or he may attempt to minimize the undesirable behavior by saying that young people go through "phases" and that there is really no cause for concern.

Although screening out unpleasant reality—whether it relates to ourselves or the environment—may temporarily help us feel adequate in facing life's problems, it may also keep us from making needed changes in our frame of reference and modes of adjustment.

4. *Fearfulness vs. positive action.* It has been said that anyone who lives in the latter half of the twentieth century and does not experience a certain amount of fear and anxiety is either stupid, insensitive, or atrophied. But many people, instead of taking constructive action to improve conditions, overreact to perceived dangers with disproportionate feelings of fear and inadequacy.

Although most people are familiar with the increased tension and desire to flee that accompany fear, few realize that fatigue, worry, indecision, and oversensitivity may also be disguised manifestations of fear. The pervasive effects of fear are illustrated by the man who is afraid to go out in the dark alone after watching a terrifying murder mystery on television; if he does go out anyway, he is prone to jump at the slightest sound. This increased sensitivity is characteristic of the many frightened, insecure persons who go through life overreacting to the slightest threat. Their fears rob them of courage and cripple their reasoning and other adjustive capacities.

Probably all of us experience some degree of fear in facing the problems of living. The brave person is not the one who experiences no fear, but the one who acts courageously despite fear. Not realizing this, many people expend their efforts trying to deny or conceal their fears, instead of learning to function effectively in spite of them.

5. *Integrity vs. self-advantage.* The term *integrity* refers essentially to being honest with oneself and others. At times it may appear that one's needs would best be served by actions that are strongly in conflict with one's ethical beliefs. An individual may be tempted, for example, to cheat on an examination, to be devious in a business transaction, to lie in order to achieve some end, or simply to fail to stand up for values in which he or she believes. The temptation to engage in such behavior may be especially great when one sees others engage in it with seemingly successful results. In fact, a certain amount of deceit appears both common and acceptable in our society. But most people find it guilt-arousing and self-devaluating to behave in ways that conflict with what they believe to be right. In addition, lack of self-integrity usually leads to a loss of respect from others and makes it virtually impossible to build satisfying interpersonal relationships.

6. *Sexual desires vs. restraints.* As a result of social prohibitions centering around sexual behavior, many people experience intense conflict in this area. Initially, sexual conflicts may be related to masturbation and may persist as a running battle between strong sexual desires and the belief that masturbation is a vile habit engaged in only by those who lack moral fiber and willpower. With the advent of adolescence and young adulthood, sexual conflicts are likely to arise over questions of premarital and extramarital relations.

Adding to young people's difficulty is the confusion and disagreement they see around them concerning what is acceptable and unacceptable in sexual behavior. In recent years our society has become more permissive with respect to norms governing sexual expression; but guidelines are far from clear, and sexual values may differ markedly among different geographic, ethnic, socioeconomic, and religious groups as well as from one person to another. It is not surprising, then, that many young people experience intense conflict as they try to work out an acceptable code of sexual ethics to guide their behavior.

Pressures of modern living. In contemporary American society, most of us in a general way face the pressures of competing with others for finite resources of one kind or another, meeting educational, occupational, and marital demands, and coping with the complexity and rapid pace of modern living. Each of these creates its own special kind of stress.

1. *Competition.* In our highly competitive society, we compete for grades, athletic honors, jobs, marital partners, and almost everything else we want. In this competitive struggle we are encouraged to surpass others, to excel, and to "get to the top." While we may give grudging credit for "a good try," it is success that gains the rewards. The winning team attracts the crowds, the outstanding student gains the opportunity for admission to graduate school and advanced training. Consequently, many people feel compelled to drive themselves mercilessly toward high levels of achievement, subjecting themselves in the process to sustained and severe pressure.

Competitive pressures have been acclaimed as leading to greater productivity, to an increased sense of purpose, and to higher standards of excellence. Yet inappropriate or indiscriminate competition, particularly competition where one person can achieve or succeed only at the expense of others, may be especially harmful for the individual and divisive to the group. If competition leads to sustained "overloading," it may ultimately be harmful to winners and losers alike.

2. *Educational, occupational, and family demands.* Closely related to the pressures of competition are those of sustained effort stemming from educational, occupational, and family demands. The long hours of study, the tension of examinations, and the sustained concentration of effort over many years result in considerable stress for many students. Where a student is handicapped by inefficient study habits, inadequate financial resources, personal problems, or other difficulties, the continuing effort for academic achievement may be highly stressful.

Occupational demands can also be highly stressful, and many jobs make severe demands in terms of responsibility, time, and performance. Buck (1972) has reported a negative relationship between pressure on the job and the mental health of the worker. In addition, if the individual is not really interested in or well suited to the work, occupational demands are likely to be a major source of stress, regardless of the actual demands of the work situation.

Every student can probably identify to an extent with the frustrations of class registration, just one of the stressful demands education can make.

Marriage and family life make demands on both partners. These demands may be especially stressful if either partner is immature and poorly prepared for the responsibilities involved, if there are basic incompatibilities between the partners, or if financial or other problems make the external situation unfavorable. Particularly if a marriage is already making difficult adjustive demands, the arrival of children and problems of parenthood may markedly increase the pressures on both partners.

3. *Complexity and pace of modern living.* The mere complexity and pace of modern living tend to "overload" the human organism; the stress of living under such highly complicated and demanding conditions can play havoc on both biological and psychological levels. The role of severe stress in the incidence of heart attacks and other "psychosomatic" disorders, as well as the general lowering of adaptive efficiency over time has been well documented in numerous studies.

Many other frustrations, conflicts, and pressures could be mentioned in our discussion, including insufficient time to deal with the many adjustive demands that confront us and the necessity of making choices before adequate information is available. And ever lurking in the background are the possibility of thermonuclear war and the other problems of global scope that characterize our contemporary world.

Sociocultural factors

Every era and generation understandably tends to regard its own special problems and frustrations as being uniquely demanding. By and large, such claims are probably unwarranted in any precise, quantitative sense. Life *is* hard; it always has been and it always will be. There is no denying, however, that patterns and sources of stress do vary from time to time and from place to place. Among the conditions especially characteristic of our time and place in history that put adjustive demands on most of us, directly or indirectly, are the problems of

war and violence, deviance-producing social roles, group prejudice and discrimination, economic and employment problems, and rapid technological and social change, including the threat of worldwide shortages of basic resources.

War and violence

A history of the United States—or of the world in general—must of necessity devote a sizable amount of space to a consideration of wars. Although wars have sometimes been accepted as necessary to achieve or maintain freedom and human rights, the conditions of warfare have placed great stress on large numbers of people. Privation, mutilation, death, grief, and social disorganization have been inevitable accompaniments of war.

Today we live in the shadow of the new and incredibly destructive instruments of modern warfare, which are becoming available to an increasing number of nations on our planet. Although most people try not to think about the possibility that humanity may be consumed in a thermonuclear holocaust, it does exist and adds its own distinctive note of fear to our lives. In fact, many young people are cynical about preparing for the future because they do not expect to have a future.

While "small wars" and civil violence continue to smolder on our planet, we have also witnessed an ever increasing rate of violent crime in our own society—an increase that makes many communities unsafe even in the daytime and adds its own grim note to the uncertainties of our times.

Deviance-producing social roles

An organized society sometimes calls on its members to perform roles in which the prescribed behaviors are either deviant in and of themselves or may produce maladaptive reactions in persons asked to perform them. The soldier who is called upon by his society to kill and maim other human beings may subsequently develop very serious feelings of guilt. Military officialdom in Germany during the Nazi holocaust willingly participated in the most heinous and cold-blooded mass murders humankind has ever known. Some of our own street gangs demand extreme cruelty and callousness on the part of their members.

In an experiment that had to be prematurely terminated because of its disturbing effects on the participating subjects (see HIGHLIGHT on this page), Zimbardo and his associates (1975) have demonstrated the power of the roles of "guard" and "prisoner" to produce extremely maladaptive behavior in otherwise normal persons in just a few days. In the meantime, well-organized terrorist groups throughout the world, who feel that world society is ignoring their just claims, train their members for destruction and murder that threaten the security of all of us.

Group prejudice and discrimination

One of the most destructive forms of group prejudice is that of racial discrimination. While it is loudly decried in our society, it seems to be among our most ingrained cultural habits. All of society suffers as a result of this prejudice, but the victims lose most by it.

One index of the toll that such conditions take is Harlem's rate of admissions to mental hospitals—much greater than that of the rest of New York City—and its startlingly high rates for suicide, drug abuse, delinquency, crime, and other maladaptive behaviors. Racial discrimination, poverty, and social disorganization tend to debase and confuse human beings. Children reared in such a setting have the almost impossible task of trying to learn what is predictable and possible, of striving to develop healthy motives and values, and of attempting to achieve educational and other competencies essential for effective participation in our highly technological society. A report of the National Institute of Mental Health (1969) concluded that

". . . a child of parents at the bottom of the socioeconomic scale who comes into the world with the same basic intellect as a child of parents at the top is less likely, for lack of stimulation and opportunity, to develop it. Moreover, poverty often interferes with the development not only of intelligence but also of a healthy personality. There is evidence, too, of an association between poverty on the one hand

The Stanford prison experiment

Social psychologist Philip Zimbardo and his colleagues at Stanford University (Zimbardo et al., 1975) conducted a simulation experiment designed to explore the possible causes of deviant prison behavior. Using a "mock prison" set up in a basement of a university psychology building, they planned a two-week experience for normal, young male subjects who were randomly assigned to the roles of "guards" and "prisoners." Eleven subjects became guards and ten became prisoners. Two investigators served as "superintendent" and "warden."

Investigators went to considerable length to simulate real prison conditions, building an oppressive physical environment and detailing a set of arbitrary and restrictive rules that the guards were to enforce. Subjects were given distinctive uniforms: guards wore khaki uniforms and dark glasses; prisoners wore short, loosely fitting smocks with identification numbers on front and back. Deindividuation and impersonality were encouraged. Guards were expected to harass prisoners, but they were instructed not to become brutal.

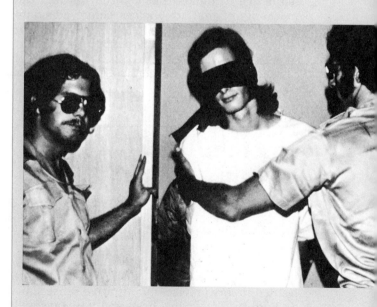

It is evident that the conditions of this experiment were sufficient to unleash subtle forces that may reside in all of us. Guards soon became actively hostile, cruel, and sadistic. Passive hostility in the prisoners, part of their original "script," gave way to demeaning obedience. The situation rapidly became one of surprising psychological and physical brutality.

One of the prisoners went on a hunger strike; others made plans to contact an attorney to seek release. No inmate simply announced he was quitting the experiment. The "prisoners" accepted their roles so well that they could not escape, and some guards developed their roles so well that they began to exceed appropriate limits of behavior. They invented elaborate punishments to inflict upon uncooperative prisoners, forcing them to sleep on the floor, refusing to remove uneaten food from jail cells, not allowing use of toilet facilities, etc. Reactions of the prisoners ranged from acute anxiety to depression. One prisoner developed a severe psychosomatic rash that so alarmed the investigators that they "released"

him for medical attention. Another became hysterical and had to be removed. The situation became so "inhuman" that the experiment was officially terminated just six days after it began—eight full days earlier than had been planned—by which time even the investigators were finding it difficult to maintain their researchers' roles.

Investigators and subjects alike were clearly unprepared for the behaviors that ensued in this supposed simulation. The environment and interpersonal processes gave rise to extraordinarily maladaptive behaviors. Most of the normal young men who served as subjects reported surprise and confusion at their own behaviors. They exhibited behaviors of which they had thought themselves incapable. They had lost their objective self-awareness. In short, though the experiment was not "completed" as originally planned, it clearly demonstrated the enormous power that social situations and social roles can have on human behavior.

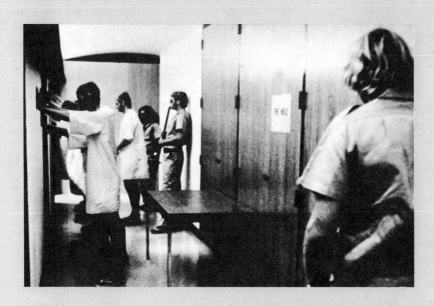

and, on the other, ignorance and distrust of democratic ideals and institutions. Violence, too, breeds in an atmosphere of deprivation and despair." (p. 2)

The more recent report of the President's Commission on Mental Health (1978) essentially echoes many of these same conclusions. Thus we see the beginning of the vicious circle of educational underachievement, menial jobs, broken homes, maladaptive behavior, and the perpetuation of the culture of poverty.

The effects of group prejudice and discrimination are by no means limited to racial minorities in our society. In recent years, for example, we have witnessed the struggle for women's rights in educational, occupational, marital, and other areas where women have not had equal opportunity with men. Similarly, we could point to the discrimination against older people who are forced to adjust to arbitrary retirement, a marked reduction in income, and feelings of no longer being useful or even wanted.

Economic and employment problems

Continuing inflation coupled with high unemployment—and the likelihood that both will continue—are sources of stress for many people in our society. Inflation, for example, has imposed special hardships on people whose finances cannot keep pace with the economic spiral, such as those on fixed retirement incomes. Unemployment has placed a burden on a sizable segment of our population, bringing with it both financial hardships and self-devaluation. In fact, unemployment can be as debilitating psychologically as it is financially (Nelson, 1974).

As an indication of the toll that unemployment exacts, periods of extensive unemployment are typically accompanied by increases in certain types of maladaptive behavior, such as depression, suicide, and crime (Brenner, 1973). Hardest hit by economic and employment problems are those at the bottom of the social ladder who are already handicapped by poorer education, poorer nutrition, more broken or unstable families, overcrowding, inadequate housing, and feelings of helplessness and of rejection by the larger society.

Even for many people who *are* employed, a major source of stress is job dissatisfaction. Job dissatisfaction is related to anxiety, tension, and a wide range of psychosomatic disorders; it has also been related to impaired marital and family relationships.

Whatever the possibilities for job satisfaction in an increasingly computerized and complicated society, the demand for it seems to be increasing (Gartner & Riessman, 1974). People are no longer content with only money as a return for their investment of time and energy; today there appears to be a widespread and growing demand for meaningful employment and for the integration of education, work, and increased leisure into a more fulfilling life pattern.

Accelerating technological and social change

Accelerating change in our contemporary world has played havoc with established norms and values and with many people's assumptions about the meaning of human existence. With the advent of the space age, we are confronted with a new perspective of time and space and the problem of finding the meaning of human existence in a universe in which Earth may be no larger in relation to the whole than an atom is to the earth.

The rate and pervasiveness of change today are different from anything our ancestors ever experienced, and all aspects of our lives are affected—our education, our jobs, our family life, our leisure pursuits, our economic security, and our beliefs and values. Constantly trying to keep up with the new adjustments demanded by these changes is a source of considerable stress. In fact, Toffler (1970) proposed the term "future shock" to describe the profound confusion and emotional upset resulting from social change that has become too rapid.

Simultaneously, we confront an inevitable squeeze as the consumable natural resources of the earth dwindle and as our environment becomes increasingly noxious with pollutants —while environmentalists vie with those who feel their jobs will be threatened by tighter controls. No longer are Americans confident that the future will be better than the past or that technology will solve all our problems. On the contrary, events such as the threatened meltdown of a nuclear electricity generating plant remind us that attempts for solutions frequently create new problems and hazards (*Time*, April 9, 1979). Meanwhile, from the developing countries we hear a crescendo of demands for a more equitable world economic system, and increasingly we are hostage to the instabilities of world markets.

As a result, many people in our society are groping about, bewildered and bitter, unable to find satisfying values to guide their lives. Some seek security in cults or esoteric philosophies, others in authoritarian political movements. Despite their television sets, well-stocked refrigerators, and other signs of material affluence, the meaning of life seems to be escaping them. In essence, they are suffering from *existential anxiety*—from doubt and concern about their ability to find a meaningful and fulfilling way of life.

Rapid change and pervasive anxiety are by no means restricted to the United States. Vast social changes seem to be the order of the day throughout the world; unfortunately, these changes are accompanied by considerable turmoil and stress as competing ideologies vie for adherents, new alignments of power develop, and old patterns and values give way to new ones.

In this chapter we have reviewed different models of causation in maladaptive behavior and our changing views of causal relationships leading to today's broad perspective in which the key factors are seen as faulty personality development or excessive stress, or a combination of the two. We defined the concepts of primary, predisposing, precipitating, and reinforcing causes; and we emphasized the concept of feedback and circularity in establishing the "vicious circles" that often characterize the clinical picture in abnormal behavior. We then reviewed some of the specific biological, psychosocial, and sociocultural factors that are commonly involved in the development of abnormal behavior in our society. Throughout we have emphasized the interaction of these factors in the total causal pattern.

We shall find this general perspective on causation helpful as we turn now to an examination of specific patterns of abnormal behavior.

Patterns of abnormal (maladaptive) behavior

6

Transient reactions to severe stress

Traumatic reactions to combat

Reactions to civilian catastrophes

Reactions to sustained or difficult stressors

Prevention of stress disorders: Emotional "inoculation"

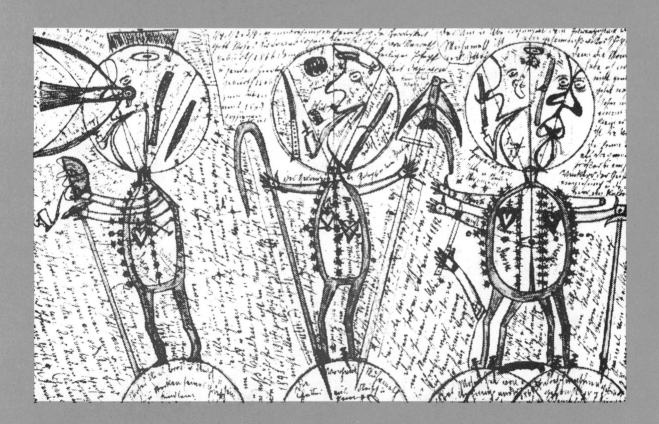

As we noted previously, any one of us may break down if the going gets tough enough. When conditions of overwhelming stress occur—as in terrifying accidents, imprisonment, physical mutilation, military combat, or intensely disrupting interpersonal relationships—temporary, or transient, mental disorders may develop, even in previously stable personalities. The personality decompensation may be sudden, as in the case of an individual who has gone through a severe accident or fire; or it may be gradual, as in the case of a person who has been subjected to conditions in a prisoner-of-war camp or even to a very difficult situation in civilian life. Usually the individual shows good recoverability once the stressful situation is over, although in some cases there is residual damage to the self-structure and an increased vulnerability to certain types of stressors. In the case of individuals who are marginally adjusted to begin with, of course, the situational stressor may precipitate more serious and lasting psychopathology.

Perhaps the special value of starting our discussion of the kinds of abnormal behavior with these transient reactions to severe stress, particularly with reactions to the acute stress of combat, lies in the perspective that they can give us on the development of more typical maladaptive patterns that occur in less extreme situations. Abhorrent as war is, it has provided a research setting that can perhaps never be duplicated in civilian life: a "laboratory" in which the effects of severe environmental stressors on the personality integration of thousands of men could readily be evaluated. Grinker (1969), in referring to efforts to help soldiers who had developed transient reactions to combat during World War II, put it succinctly:

"The entire range of factors from the biological to the sociological were sharply etched in miniature and required only a magnified view for understanding. Likewise time was compressed so that in rapid succession we could view predisposition, precipitation, breakdown, and recovery." (p. 3)

Through these efforts, and those in later wars, marked strides have been made in the understanding and treatment of psychopathology. These forward strides have led, in turn, to a better understanding of mental disorders by the general public. For the first time, millions of people became aware of the potential effects of extreme stress on personality integration. They learned that such stress could seriously impair adaptive behavior or even incapacitate the individual; and they learned that this was not a disgrace—it could happen to anyone.

We shall begin our discussion with the psychological casualties of past wars, particularly those cases involving army personnel subjected to combat; then we shall attempt to show the implication of these findings for the general population. Next we shall examine transient reactions to civilian catastrophes and to other situations of sustained and severe stress. Although we shall see similarities between combat and civilian stress reactions, we shall also see differences. Finally, we shall look at attempts that have been made to prevent the development of stress disorders prior to the onset of stressful situations.

Traumatic reactions to combat

During World War I traumatic reactions to combat conditions were called "shell shock," a term coined by a British pathologist Col. Frederick Mott, who regarded such reactions as organic conditions produced by minute hemorrhages of the brain. It was gradually realized, however, that only a very small percentage of such cases represented physical injury from concussion of exploding shells or bombs. Most of these men were suffering instead from the general combat situation with its physical fatigue, ever present threat of death or mutilation, and severe psychological shocks. During World War II, traumatic reactions to combat passed through a number of classifications, such as "operational fatigue" and "war neuroses," before finally being termed "combat fatigue" or "combat exhaustion" in the Korean War and the Vietnam War.

Even the latter terms were none too aptly chosen, since they implied that physical exhaustion played a more important role than was usually the case. However, they did serve to distinguish such disorders for purposes of treatment from neurotic, psychotic, and other disorders that happened to occur under war conditions but might well have occurred in civilian life—for example, among individuals showing a history of maladaptive behavior that was aggravated by the increased stress of combat service. In the great majority of cases, men who became psychological casualties under combat conditions had adjusted satisfactorily to civilian life and to prior military experiences.

It has been estimated that in World War II 10 percent of the American men in combat developed combat exhaustion; however, the actual incidence is not known, since many received therapy at their battalion aid station and were returned to combat within a few hours. Records were kept mainly on men evacuated from the front lines who were considered the more seriously disturbed cases. Of the slightly over 10 million men accepted for military service during World War II, approximately 1,363,000 were given medical discharges, of which approximately 530,000—39 percent—were for neuropsychiatric reasons (including combat exhaustion, psychosis, neurosis, and other personality weaknesses or disorders that made them unsuitable for military life). In fact, combat exhaustion was the disability causing the single greatest loss of manpower during that war (Bloch, 1969). In the Korean War the incidence of combat exhaustion dropped from an initial high of over 6 percent to 3.7 percent; 27 percent of medical discharges were for psychiatric reasons (Bell, 1958). In the Vietnam War the figure dropped to less than 1.5 percent for combat exhaustion, with a negligible number of discharges for psychiatric disorders (Allerton, 1970; Bourne, 1970).

The marked decrease in combat exhaustion cases in the Vietnam War was apparently due to a number of factors, including (a) improved methods of selection and training; (b) confidence in military leadership; (c) the sporadic nature of the fighting, in which brief intensive encounters were followed by periods of relative calm and safety—as contrasted with weeks and months of prolonged combat that many soldiers went through in World War II and the Korean War; and (d) a policy of rotation after twelve months of service (thirteen months for Marines). Each soldier was given a DEROS (date of expected return from overseas), which indicated a clear time when the exceptional

stress would be over for him. This knowledge of a definite end to the stressful situation appears to have made it more bearable at the time (Kormos, 1978). We shall discuss the possible long-range, or residual, effects of combat later in this chapter.

Clinical picture in combat exhaustion

The specific symptoms in combat exhaustion have varied considerably, depending on the branch of the service, the severity and nature of the traumatic experience, and the personality makeup of the individual. Common symptoms among combat troops have been dejection, weariness, hypersensitivity, sleep disturbances, and tremors. In air-corps personnel, after long combat flying, the more typical symptoms have included anxiety, frequently with accompanying dejection and depression, phobias toward combat missions, irritability, tension, and startle reactions. In addition, where the stress has been cumulative, symptoms have often differed from those brought on by a sudden and particularly intense combat situation.

Despite such variations, however, there was surprising uniformity in the general clinical picture for those soldiers in World War II and later in the Korean War who developed combat exhaustion. The first symptoms were a failure to maintain psychological integration, with increasing irritability, disturbances of sleep, and often recurrent nightmares.

"The irritability is manifested externally by snappishness, overreaction to minor irritations, angry reactions to innocuous questions or incidents, flareups with profanity and even tears at relatively slight frustrations. The degree of these reactions may vary from angry looks or a few sharp words to acts of violence.

"Subjectively, the state of irritation is perceived by the soldier as an unpleasant 'hypersensitiveness' and he is made doubly uncomfortable by a concomitant awareness of his diminishing self-control. One patient put this very vividly by saying—'The first thing that brought home to me the fact that I was slipping was this incident: A fellow next to me took some cellophane off a piece of hard candy and crumpled it up, and that crackling noise sounded like a forest fire. It made me so mad I wanted to hit him. Then I was ashamed of being so jumpy.'

"In association with this 'hypersensitiveness' to minor external stimuli, the 'startle reaction' becomes manifest (increasingly so as time goes on). This is a sudden leaping, jumping, cringing, jerking or other form of involuntary self-protective motor response to sudden, not necessarily very loud noises, and sometimes also to sudden movement or sudden light.

"The disturbances of sleep, which almost always accompany the symptom of increased irritability, consist mainly in the frustrating experience of not being able to fall asleep even upon those occasions when the military situation would permit. Soldiers have to snatch their rest when they can. . . . Opportunities for sleep become very precious and an inability to use them very distressing. Difficulties were experienced also in staying asleep because of sudden involuntary starting or leaping up, or because of terror dreams, battle dreams, and nightmares of other kinds.

"This triad of increased 'sensitivity,' irritable reactions and sleep disturbances represents the incipient state of 'combat exhaustion.' It usually does not lead to referral [for treatment]. It may exist without much change for days, weeks, or even months. Sooner or later, often upon the occasion of some incident of particularly traumatic significance to the soldier, the marginal and very unstable equilibrium is upset and the soldier becomes a casualty." (Bartemeier et al., 1946, pp. 374–75)

When the combat casualties reached the aid station or the clearing station, they presented a somewhat typical pattern of symptoms, differing only in the degree of personality decompensation.

"In the majority of cases they followed a stereotyped pattern: 'I just can't take it any more'; 'I can't stand those shells'; 'I just couldn't control myself.' They varied little from patient to patient. Whether it was the soldier who had experienced his baptism of fire or the older veteran who had lost his comrades, the superficial result was very similar. Typically he appeared as a dejected, dirty, weary man. His facial expression was one of depression, sometimes of tearfulness. Frequently his hands were trembling or jerking. Occasionally he would display varying degrees of confusion, perhaps to the extent of being mute or staring into space. Very occasionally he might present classically hysterical symptoms." (Menninger, 1948, p. 143)

In extreme experiences of unusually traumatic combat, a soldier might repress the episode so that he was amnesic for the entire battle experience.

The following diary covers a period of about six weeks of combat in the South Pacific during World War II and illustrates the cumulative effect of combat stresses on an apparently stable personality.

"Aug. 7, 1942. Convoy arrived at Guadalcanal Bay at approximately 4 A.M. in the morning. Ships gave enemy a heavy shelling. At 9 A.M. we stormed the beach and formed an immediate beachhead, a very successful landing, marched all day in the hot sun, and at night took positions and rested. Enemy planes attacked convoy in bay but lost 39 out of 40 planes.

"Aug. 8, 1942. Continued march in the hot sun and in afternoon arrived at airport. Continued on through the Jap village and made camp for the night. During the night Jap navy attacked convoy in battle that lasted until early morning. Enemy had terrific losses and we lost two ships. This night while on sentry duty I mistook a horse for a Jap and killed it.

"Aug. 19, 1942. Enemy cruiser and destroyer came into bay and shelled the beach for about two hours. The cruiser left and the destroyer hung around for the entire morning. We all kept under shelter for the early afternoon a flying fortress flew over, spotting the ship and bombed it, setting it afire we all jumped and shouted with joy. That night trouble again was feared and we again slept in foxholes.

"Aug. 21, 1942. The long awaited landing by the enemy was made during the night 1500 troops in all and a few prisoners were taken and the rest were killed. Bodies were laying all over the beach. In afternoon planes again bombed the Island. [Here the writing begins to be shaky, and less careful than previously.]

"Aug. 28, 1942. The company left this morning in higgins Boats to the end of the Island, landed and started through thick Jungle and hills. It was hot and we had to cut our way through. In afternoon we contacted the japs. our squad was in the assault squad so we moved up the beach to take positions the enemy trapped us with machine gun and rifle fire for about two hours. The lead was really flying. Two of our men were killed, two were hit by a hand greade and my corporal received a piece of shrampnel in back,—was wounded in arm, out of the squad of eight we have five causitry. We withdrew and were taken back to the Hospital.

"Sept. 12, 1942. Large jap squadron again bombed Island out of 35 planes sent over our air force knocked down 24. During the raid a large bomb was dropped just sevety yards from my fox hole.

"Sept. 13, 1942. At on o'clock three destroyers and one cruiser shelled us contumally all night The ships turned surch lights all up and down the beach, and stopped one my foxhole seveal time I'm feeling pritty nervese and scared, afraid I'll be a nervas reack be for long. slept in fox hole all night not much sleep. This morning at 9:00 we had a nother air raid, the

Still under North Vietnamese fire, a Navy corpsman looks up in anguish from the body of a Marine whose life he tried to save. Combat reactions among men fighting in Southeast Asia were often traced to particular experiences of this nature.

raid consisted of mostly fighter planes. I believe we got several, this afternoon. we had a nother raid, and our planes went out to met them, met them someplace over Tulagi, new came in that the aircraft carrier wasp sent planes out to intersept the bombers. This eving all hell broke lose. Our marines contacted enemy to south of us and keep up constant fire all night through.

"Sept. 14, 1942. This morning firing still going on my company is scaduted to unload ships went half ways up to dock when enemyfire start on docks, were called back to our pososeion allon beach, company called out again to go after japs, hope were lucker than we were last time [part of this illegible]. Went up into hills at 4:00 P.M. found positions, at 7:00 en 8 sea planes fombed and strifed us, 151942 were strifed biy amfibious planes and bombed the concussion of one through me of balance and down a 52 foot hil. I was shaking likd a leaf. Lost my bayanut, and ran out of wathr. I nearves and very jumpy, hop I last out until morning. I hope sevearly machine s guns ore oping up on our left flank there going over our heads

"Sept. 16. this morning we going in to take up new possissons we march all moring and I am very week and nerves, we marched up a hill and ran in to the affaul place y and z company lost so many men I hardly new what I was doing then I'm going nuts.

"Sept. 17. don't remember much of this day.

"Sept. 18. Today I'm on a ship leaving this awful place, called Green Hell. I'm still nearves and shakey." (Stern, 1947, pp. 583–86)

In the Vietnam War, soldiers were seldom exposed to prolonged periods of shelling and bombardment; combat reactions were typically more sudden and acute as a result of some particular overwhelming combat experience. This is well illustrated in the following case.

"A 21-year-old rifleman was flown directly to the hospital from an area of fighting by a helicopter ambulance. No information accompanied him, he had no identifying tags on his uniform, and he was so completely covered with mud that a physical description of his features was not possible. His hands had been tied behind him for the flight, and he had a wild, wide-eyed look as he cowered in a corner of the emergency room, glancing furtively to all sides, cringing and starting at the least noise. He was mute, although once he forced out a whispered 'VC' and tried to mouth other words without success. He seemed terrified. Although people could approach him, he appeared oblivious to their presence. No manner of reassurance or direct order achieved either a verbal response or any other interaction from him.

"His hands were untied, after which he would hold an imaginary rifle in readiness whenever he heard a helicopter overhead or an unexpected noise. The corpsmen led him to the psychiatric ward, took him to a shower, and offered him a meal; he ate very little. He began to move a little more freely but still offered no information.

"He was then given 100 mg. of chlorpromazine

(Thorazine) orally; this dose was repeated hourly until he fell asleep. He was kept asleep in this manner for approximately 40 hours. . . . Although dazed and subdued upon awakening, his response in the ward milieu was dramatic. This was aided by the presence of a friend from his platoon on an adjoining ward, who helped by filling in parts of the story that the patient could not recall. The patient was an infantryman whose symptoms had developed on a day when his platoon had been caught in an ambush and then was overrun by the enemy. He was one of three who survived after being pinned down by enemy fire for 12 hours. His friend told him that toward the end of that time he had developed a crazed expression and had tried to run from his hiding place. He was pulled back to safety and remained there until the helicopter arrived and flew him to the hospital.

"Within 72 hours after his admission the patient was alert, oriented, responsive, and active—still a little tense but ready to return to duty. He was sent back to duty on his third hospital day and never seen again at our facility. It should be noted that he had no history of similar symptoms or emotional disorder." (Bloch, 1969, p. 42)

In the recorded cases of combat exhaustion among soldiers in all of these wars, the common core was usually overwhelming anxiety. In World War II, however, an exception was noted in the case of troops from India to whom admission of fear was unacceptable. They rarely showed anxiety reactions, instead resorting occasionally to self-mutilation and other "honorable" ways of avoiding further combat (Williams, 1950).

It is interesting to note that, in most cases, wounded soldiers have shown less anxiety or other combat exhaustion symptoms—except in cases of permanent mutilation. Apparently the wound, in providing an escape from the stressful combat situation, removes the source of the anxiety. A similar difference was found among Israeli soldiers hospitalized during the Yom Kippur War.[1] Those soldiers hospitalized for physical injuries—even severe ones such as paralysis or loss of limb—showed no appreciable psychological disturbances. However, those hospitalized because of psychiatric

problems—such as severe symptoms of depression, thought disorders, and obsessiveness—were quite disturbed about their physical symptoms, even minor ones—more so than the seriously physically injured (Merbaum & Hefez, 1976).

In fact, it has not been unusual for a soldier to admit that he has prayed to be hit or to have something "honorable" happen to remove him from battle. Upon approaching full recovery and the necessity of returning to combat, an injured soldier may sometimes show prolongation of his symptoms or a delayed traumatic reaction of nervousness, insomnia, and other symptoms that were nonexistent when he was first hospitalized.

Causal factors in combat exhaustion

In a combat situation, with the continual threat of injury or death and repeated narrow escapes, one's ordinary methods of coping are relatively useless. The adequacy and security feelings the individual has known in a relatively safe and dependable civilian world are completely undermined. As one combat medic in Vietnam expressed it,

"I was always afraid. In fact, I can't remember not being afraid. For one thing, a combat medic doesn't know what's happening. Especially at night, everybody screaming or moaning and calling, 'Medic, medic.' I always saw myself dying, my legs blown off, my brains spattered all about, shivering in shock, and talking madly. This is what I *saw* in reality." (Polner, 1968, p. 18)

However, we must not overlook the fact that in all the wars we have been discussing, 90 percent or more of the soldiers subjected to combat have not become psychiatric casualties, although most of them have evidenced severe fear reactions and other symptoms of personality disorganization that were not serious enough to be incapacitating. In addition, many soldiers have tolerated almost unbelievable stress before they broke, while others became casualties under conditions of relatively slight combat stress.

Consequently, it appears that to understand traumatic reactions to combat, we need to look at the wars we have known and examine other

---

[1]The Yom Kippur War began on October 6, 1973, the Jewish Holy Day of Atonement (Yom Kippur), when the Egyptian and Syrian forces attacked Israel in an effort to regain control of the Sinai Peninsula and the Golan Heights. A ceasefire was agreed to on October 23, and on November 11, a peace agreement calling for talks to resolve differences was signed.

factors such as constitutional predisposition, personal maturity, loyalty to one's unit, and confidence in one's officers—as well as stress.

Biological factors.

Do constitutional differences in sensitivity, vigor, and temperament affect one's resistance to the stress of combat? The probabilities are that they do, but there is a dearth of actual evidence.

Factors about which we have more information are the conditions of battle that tax the soldier's physical stamina. Grinker and Spiegel described this vividly in a World War II study:

"Battle conditions are notoriously destructive to health. Frequently men must go for days without adequate sleep or rest. . . . The purely physiological effects of nearby blasts are also a factor. Many men are repeatedly subjected to minimal doses of blast. They are knocked over by the compression wave, or perhaps blown slightly off the ground, if they are lying prone. In some instances they are temporarily numbed or even stunned. . . . Lastly, the continued auditory irritation of constant explosions, bangs, snaps of machine guns, whines of artillery shells, rustle of mortars . . . wears down resistance." (1945, pp. 68–70)

Add other factors that have often occurred in combat situations—such as severe climatic conditions, malnutrition, and disease—to the strain of continual emotional mobilization, and the result is a general lowering of the individual's physical and psychological resistance to all stressors.

Psychosocial factors.

A number of psychological and interpersonal factors may contribute to the overall stress load experienced by soldiers and predispose them to break down under the increased burden of combat. Such factors include a reduction in personal freedom, frustrations of all sorts, and separation from home and loved ones. Letters from home that create worry or hurt add to the soldier's already difficult adjustive burden—particularly since he is far away and helpless to take any action. A soldier who has withstood months of combat may break when he finds that his wife has been unfaithful, or when she stops writing, or when she writes that she is leaving him for someone else.

Most central, of course, are the many stresses arising from the combat situation itself. Several of these combat stressors will be considered here.

1. *Fear and anxiety.* Although not all soldiers experience the same degree of threat and anxiety in combat situations, emergency mobilization of emotional resources continues as long as the crisis exists. With time, increasingly severe feelings of threat and anxiety usually occur as the soldier experiences narrow escapes and sees buddies killed or wounded.

The hypersensitivity shown in the startle reaction follows directly from this continued fear and anxiety. Consequently, the buzz of a fly or the striking of a match may produce marked overreactions. This hypersensitivity is, of course, intensified when the stimulus bears a direct association with some traumatic combat experience. A soldier who has been strafed by attacking planes may be terrified by the sight of approaching aircraft. As continued emotional mobilization and fatigue take their toll of adjustive resources, the common symptom of irritability makes its appearance and adds to the soldier's anxiety by making him aware of his diminishing self-control. In our normal lives, too, prolonged emotional stress and fatigue tend to increase irritability and keep our nerves "on edge."

Difficulties in falling asleep and other sleep disturbances are common accompaniments of fear and sustained emotional arousal, and in combat conditions, soldiers often go for days without adequate sleep. However, the dynamic significance of the recurrent nightmares is not fully understood. How and why does the traumatic material become reactivated during sleep, when the soldier desperately needs quiet and rest? In some cases the repeated dreams are so terrifying that the soldier is even afraid to go to sleep. It may be, however, that the continual reliving of a traumatic battle experience in dreams gradually serves to discharge the anxiety associated with it and to desensitize the individual to the point where he can assimilate the experience.

Stupor or amnesia in severe combat exhaustion cases is thought to result from temporary repression, enabling the individual to avoid consciousness of the traumatic experience until its emotional intensity has cooled down to the point where he can tolerate memory of it. Here the defensive function of repression is clearly demonstrated, since the repressed material can be brought to consciousness in full detail under the influence of hypnosis or various drugs, such as sodium pentothal.

2. *Strangeness, unpredictability, and inability to take action.* Strangeness and unpredictability can be a source of severe threat and stress. When the soldier knows what to expect and what to do, the chances are much better of coming through with a minimum of psychological disorganization (Rachman, 1978). But even the best training cannot fully prepare a soldier for all the conditions of actual battle. The factor of unpredictability also partly explains the effectiveness of new "secret weapons" for which enemy soldiers are not prepared.

Conditions that necessitate immobilization in the face of acute danger also lower the soldier's stress tolerance. The case cited on page 174—the soldier who was pinned down by enemy fire for twelve hours in an enemy ambush—shows the effects of immobilization on a person in extreme danger. Some activity or duty to perform, even though it does not lessen the danger, appears to provide an outlet for tension and thus helps the soldier keep his fear and anxiety within manageable limits.

3. *The necessity of killing.* Having to kill enemy soldiers and sometimes civilians can also be an important factor in combat reactions. Most of us have strong moral convictions against killing or injuring others, and for some soldiers it is psychologically almost impossible to engage in ruthless killing. In extreme cases, such soldiers may even be unable to defend themselves when attacked. In other instances, the soldiers engage in killing but later experience intense feelings of guilt, together with fear of retaliation and punishment.

A good fighter, a machine gunner, one day killed five of the enemy almost simultaneously. "His first reaction was elation—but suddenly he felt that it was wrong to enjoy this and thereupon developed anxiety with some depression, so severe that he was incapacitated." (Saul, 1945, p. 262)

Over time, soldiers may become habituated to killing enemy soldiers and may even take pride in it—perhaps as a job well done, a feeling reinforced by the praise of buddies. In this context, Lifton (1972) has referred to "numbed warfare," in which the enemy is reduced to nonhuman status—to "Huns" or "Gooks"—so

A soldier crouches beside the body of the man he has just shot. Perhaps this is the first time he has realized that he is capable of killing another human being.

the soldier can feel that he is merely getting rid of animals or scum or devils. This attitude was epitomized by the statement of an American officer that the mass slaughter of civilians at My Lai was "no big deal."

On the other hand, the soldier may come to see further combat as the means by which he will inevitably receive dreaded retaliation and punishment for his actions. Thus, anxiety arising out of combat experience may reflect not only a simple fear of death or mutilation but also emotional conflicts and guilt feelings generated by the experience of killing.

4. *Length of combat duty.* The longer a soldier is in combat, the more vulnerable—and more anxious—he is likely to feel. Although, as Tuohy (1967) found, most soldiers on their arrival in Vietnam had the notion of their invulnerability—that anyone but themselves was likely to get killed—they soon found that Vietnam was a dangerous place and that "war really is hell." This time of realization is when many soldiers show their first signs of anxiety. And after a soldier has been in combat and has seen many of his buddies killed and wounded as well as having had narrow escapes himself, he usually loses whatever feeling of invulnerability he may have had. Often the death of a buddy leads to a serious loss of emotional support as well as to feelings of guilt if the soldier cannot help feeling glad that it was his buddy and not himself who was killed. When a soldier has almost completed the number of missions or duration of duty necessary for rotation, he is particularly apt to feel that his "luck has run out" and that the next bullet will "have his name on it."

The effect of prolonged combat in lowering stress tolerance was exemplified in World War II by "the old sergeant syndrome," in which men of established bravery exhibited anxiety, depression, tremulousness, and impairment of self-confidence and judgment after prolonged combat experience—usually 150 to 350 days of combat (Bell, 1958).

5. *Personal characteristics.* Any personality characteristics that lower the individual's resistance to stress or to particular types of stressors may be important in determining his reactions to combat. Personal immaturity—often stemming from parental overprotection—is commonly cited as making the soldier more vulnerable to combat stress.

In their study of personality characteristics

of Israeli soldiers who had broken down in combat in the Yom Kippur War, Merbaum and Hefez (1976) found that over 25 percent reported psychological treatment prior to the war and another 12 percent had had difficulties previously in the six-day Israeli-Arab war of 1967. Thus about 37 percent of these men had clear histories of some instability that may have predisposed them to breakdown under the special stress of war. On the other hand, the others—over 60 percent—had not shown earlier difficulties and would not have been considered to be at risk for such breakdown.

A background of personal maladjustment does not always make an individual a "poor risk" for withstanding the stresses of combat. Some individuals are so accustomed to anxiety that they can cope with it more or less automatically, whereas soldiers who are feeling severe anxiety for the first time may be terrified by the experience, lose their self-confidence, and go to pieces. It has also been observed that sociopaths, though frequently in trouble in the armed services during peacetime for disregarding rules and regulations, have often demonstrated good initiative and effective combat aggression against the enemy. However, the soldiers who function most effectively and are most apt to survive the rigors of combat usually come from backgrounds that fostered self-reliance, ability to function in a group, and ready adjustment to new situations (Bloch, 1969; Borus, 1974; Grinker, 1969; Lifton, 1972).

Sociocultural factors. In the preceding section our focus was on psychosocial factors related to combat stress. Here we are concerned with more general sociocultural factors that may play an important part in determining an individual's adjustment to combat. These include the clarity and acceptability of war goals, the identification of the soldier with his combat unit, *esprit de corps*, and the quality of leadership.

1. *Clarity and acceptability of war goals.* In general, the more concretely and realistically war goals can be integrated into the values of the individual in terms of "his stake" in the war and the worth and importance of what he is doing, the greater their supportive effect will be on him. The individual who is fighting only because he is forced to, or to "get the damned war over with," is not as effective and does not stand stress as well as the soldier who knows what he is fighting for and is convinced of its importance. Time and again men who have felt strongly about the rightness of their cause and its vital importance to themselves and their loved ones have shown incredible endurance, bravery, and personal sacrifice under combat conditions. (See HIGHLIGHT on this page.)

2. *Identification with combat unit.* It has been found particularly important to maintain good group identification in combat troops. The soldier who is unable to identify himself with or take pride in his group lacks the feeling of "we-ness" that is a highly supportive factor in maintaining stress tolerance. Lacking this, he stands alone, psychologically isolated and less able to withstand combat stress. In fact, the stronger the sense of group identification, the less chance that the soldier will crack up in combat.

When a soldier has been removed because of combat exhaustion, he often returns to his unit with feelings of apprehension that his unit will not accept him or have confidence in him in the future (Tuohy, 1968). If the group does accept him, he is likely to make a satisfactory readjustment to further combat; if it does not, he is highly vulnerable to subsequent breakdown.

3. *Esprit de corps.* Closely related to group identification is *esprit de corps*, the morale of the group as a whole. The spirit of the group seems to be contagious. When the group is generally optimistic and confident prior to battle, the individual is also apt to show good morale. If the unit has a reputation for efficiency in battle, the individual soldier is challenged to exhibit his maximum effort and efficiency.

On the other hand, when the unit is demoralized or has a history of defeats and a high loss of personnel, the individual is likely to succumb more easily to anxiety and panic. This is particularly true if there is also a lack of confidence in leaders or in the importance of immediate combat objectives.

4. *Quality of leadership.* Confidence in military leaders is of vital importance. When the soldier in a combat situation respects his leaders, has confidence in their judgment and ability, and can accept them as relatively strong father or brother figures, his morale and resistance to stress are bolstered. On the other hand, lack of confidence or actual dislike of leaders is highly detrimental to morale and to combat stress tolerance.

HIGHLIGHT

Breakdown of combat personnel who had been most resistant to personality decompensation

In studying the eventual breakdown of the World War II army personnel who had been most resistant to personality decompensation, Sobel (1949) found that such individuals seemed to have been protected by five "defensive layers." These were surrendered progressively in the face of too-severe stress and threat. Distant ideals like "democracy" and "the four freedoms" went first. Loyalty to the group was the last to be given up.

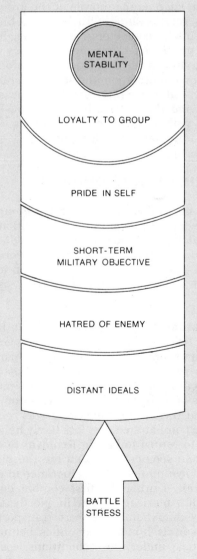

Several other supportive factors merit brief mention. The "buddy system," in which the individual is encouraged to develop a close personal relationship with another member of his unit, often provides needed emotional support. The pursuit of short-range military objectives appears, in general, to cause less stress than the pursuit of long-range ones, where there always seems to be another hill or town to take. Finally, hatred of the enemy apparently tends to raise the combat soldier's stress tolerance.

In summary, it may be emphasized that the terrifying nature of the combat situation is usually only one of the causes of combat exhaustion. A complex of other factors may be involved, such as the morale of the group, the soldier's relationships with buddies, his confidence in the competence of leaders, his degree of physical fatigue, the adequacy of his training, his family situation and problems, and his own motivation and stress tolerance in general. And as we have seen, the duration of combat and the approach of rotation—when the war will become "somebody else's war"—are also important considerations.

Treatment and outcomes

In most cases the decompensation brought on by the acute stress of combat conditions has been quickly reversed when the soldier has been taken out of combat and given brief therapy—usually warm food, sedation to help him get some rest, and supportive psychotherapy.

Importance of treatment near the battle zone.   In World War II, many men were able to return to combat after a night or two of rest. Soldiers whose symptoms proved resistant to such treatment were evacuated to medical facilities behind the lines. It was found, however, that the farther the soldier was removed from the combat area, the less likely he was to be able to return to battle. Removal to an interior zone seemed to encourage the maintenance of symptoms and a reluctance to return to his unit. During the first combat engagements of American forces in North Africa, combat exhaustion cases were transported to base hospitals hundreds of miles behind the battle lines; under these conditions less than

10 percent of the soldiers were able to return to duty (Menninger, 1948). In contrast, approximately 60 percent of those treated immediately within fifteen to twenty miles of the front lines were sent back to combat duty, and apparently the majority readjusted successfully (Ludwig & Ranson, 1947). Such statistics varied, however, ranging from a high of 80 to 90 percent returning to duty where the soldiers were from units with only a month or so of combat, down to 30 to 35 percent for "old" divisions.

Comparable statistics were obtained in the Korean War, with some 65 to 75 percent of the U.S. soldiers treated at the division level or forward being returned to combat duty, and less than 10 percent of those showing up as repeaters (Hausman & Rioch, 1967). Statistics for the Vietnam War are not entirely clear, but the percentage of U.S. soldiers who responded favorably to treatment appears even higher (Allerton, 1970; Bloch, 1969).

The lessons learned in World War II were translated in the Korean and Vietnam Wars into the principles of *immediacy, proximity,* and *expectancy.*

1. *Immediacy* refers to the early detection of signs of combat exhaustion, such as sleeplessness, tremulousness, and crying spells, and the removal of the soldier for immediate treatment.

In the Vietnam War, for example, officers were taught to watch for these symptoms in combat personnel. When a soldier manifested such symptoms he was taken to the nearest outpost, where a specially trained medic administered to him—usually urging him to review the traumatic events, reassuring him, providing him with a hot meal when possible, and recommending medication for ensuring a restful night. The soldier was then returned to duty the next morning.

2. *Proximity* refers to the treatment of the soldier as near as possible to his combat unit and the battle zone. In the Vietnam War, as we have seen, mild cases were taken to the nearest outpost and given brief supportive therapy by specially trained medics. Soldiers who showed more severe combat reactions or whose symptoms did not respond to this brief supportive therapy were often evacuated by helicopter to the division base camp, where a similar but more intensive program of rest and supportive therapy was instituted. Usually after three days of such treatment the soldier felt "like his old self again" and could return to his unit. In exceptionally resistant cases, the soldier was sent to a hospital in the zone of the interior containing a psychiatric ward staffed by medical, psychological, and social work personnel.

3. *Expectancy* refers to (a) a "duty-expectant" attitude—the attitude that anxiety, fear, and tension are not conditions of sufficient severity to require permanent removal from battle and that every soldier, despite anxieties and traumatic experiences, is expected to perform combat duties; and (b) the removal, insofar as possible, of any gain to the soldier from maintaining these symptoms—for example, reassignment to noncombatant duty when not fully justified—such as apparently occurred in World War II.

Such an approach on the part of treatment personnel—who often were themselves in the forward area under enemy fire—reminded the soldier that he was a morally responsible person who could hold up as the going got tougher and perform his combat duties despite his fear and tension.

In essence, personal responsibility and a "doing role" were stressed rather than a "sick role," with a relinquishing of responsibility for one's recovery and behavior. The result was that most soldiers found themselves able to bear much more stress than they would have believed possible and that the number of combat exhaustion cases who were declared unfit for further combat duty was minimized.

Residual effects.   In a minority of cases, the residual effects of combat exhaustion persist for a sustained period of time (see HIGHLIGHT on this page). In other cases, soldiers develop psychological problems for the first time when they leave the armed forces. For example, some soldiers who have stood up exceptionally well under intensive combat experiences have developed what might be called "delayed combat reactions"—or post-combat syndrome[2]—upon their return home, often in response to relatively minor stresses in the home situation that they had previously been capable of

[2]The DSM-III classification lists *post-traumatic stress disorder* as a subcategory of anxiety disorders. These stress disorders can be either *acute* (occurring within 6 months of the traumatic event) or *chronic* (enduring for 6 months or more after the traumatic event).

HIGHLIGHT

Residual effects of combat exhaustion among outpatients at a VA clinic

Twenty years after the end of World War II Archibald and Tuddenham (1965) made a follow-up study of residual effects of combat exhaustion in 62 combat exhaustion cases. This chart compares the incidence of several symptoms in this group and in 20 veterans who had not suffered combat exhaustion during the war. In addition to the symptoms listed here, the more severe combat exhaustion cases revealed various other symptoms, including difficulties in work and family relationships, social isolation, and narrowing of interests. Alcoholism was a problem for about 20 percent of both groups.

In many cases, symptoms had appeared to clear up when the stress was over, only to reappear in chronic form later. It seems evident that intense and sustained stress can lead to lasting symptoms even if the victims receive follow-up care. Although the combat exhaustion veterans were receiving assistance at a Veterans Administration outpatient psychiatric clinic, they were not receiving additional disability compensation as a result of prolonged stress reaction.

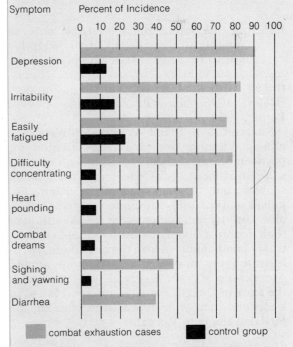

Chart adapted from Archibald and Tuddenham (1965), omitting statistics for noncombat psychiatric military cases.

Feelings of depression, guilt, and anxiety strike some soldiers while they are still in the combat zone. Others experience such reactions after their return to a normal civilian environment.

handling. Evidently these soldiers suffered some long-term damage to their adaptive capabilities, in some cases complicated by memories of killing enemy soldiers or civilians, tinged with feelings of guilt and anxiety (Haley, 1978; Horowitz & Solomon, 1978; Polner, 1968).

Shatan (1978) found six common responses among Vietnam veterans being treated for post-combat syndrome: (a) guilt feelings and self-punishment; (b) feelings of being scapegoated; (c) rage and other violent impulses against indiscriminate targets; (d) loss of sensitivity and compassion; (e) alienation of their feelings about themselves; and (f) mistrust of and doubts of love toward others. He illustrated the post-combat syndrome among American soldiers who served in Vietnam with the story of Dwight Johnson, who was killed in a robbery attempt in Detroit after winning the Medal of Honor in Vietnam:

"Jon Nordheimer's front-page *New York Times* story [1971] sensitively described Sgt. Dwight Johnson's apathy and alienation, his demoralization by unemployment, and his suspicion that he was being exploited by the army, even when he was in the hospital. His government's highest martial honor weighed heavily around his neck each time he was praised for slaughter—and thereby forced to recall that he was the sole survivor of his tank crew, buddies during eleven months of warfare. While the army used him in recruiting drives, empty promise piled upon empty promise and his cynicism grew.

"Johnson had been placed in restraints and narcotized for 24 hours immediately after his final day of combat—the action for which he received the supreme distinction. Yet, 48 hours later, he was back in the U.S. with a non-psychiatric discharge. His emotional difficulties received no official interest until he became a 'hot property.' His treatment began more than a year after his return home, at the Valley Forge Army Hospital. There he was diagnosed as suffering from 'depression caused by post-Vietnam adjustment problems.'

"On several occasions, he asked his psychiatrist how society would react if he were to respond to the black dilemma in Detroit with the same uncontrolled ferocity that had earned him the highest recognition in battle. He found his ultimate answer, not in a distant jungle but on the floor of a hometown grocery. There he lived out his haunting fantasies and nightmares of being killed at point-blank range." (pp. 46–47)

Similarly, in a follow-up study of ninety-two combat veterans of the Vietnam War, Polner (1968) cited a number of cases in which combat experiences continued to disturb the men after their return to civilian life. In most instances the difficulties appeared to center around guilt feelings over killing. For example, one veteran said, "I can't sleep, I'm a murderer." He continued,

"We were outside Bac Lieu, out on an eight-man patrol along with 15 ARVNs [South Vietnamese soldiers]. Our orders were to move ahead and shoot at anything suspicious. My God, how I remember that damned day! It was hot and sticky. The mosquitoes were driving me crazy. And there was this boy, about 8 or 9. He had his hand behind his back, like he was hiding something. 'Grab him,' someone screamed, 'he's got something!' I made a move for him and his hand moved again. 'Shoot!' I fired. Again and again, until my M-2 was empty. When I looked he was there, all over the ground, cut in two with his guts all around. I vomited. I wasn't told. I wasn't trained for that. It was out-and-out murder. . . .

"You know I killed nine people as an adviser." (p. 12)

Many of the other veterans interviewed by Polner, however, felt that they had simply done their duty in a worthwhile cause.

In another study of Vietnam returnees, Strange and Brown (1970) compared combat and noncombat veterans who were experiencing emotional difficulties. The combat group showed a higher incidence of depression and of conflicts in their close interpersonal relationships. They also showed a higher incidence of aggressive and suicidal threats but did not actually carry them out. In a later study of veterans of Vietnam who were making a satisfactory readjustment to civilian life, DeFazio, Rustin, and Diamond (1975) found that the combat veterans still reported certain symptoms twice as often as the noncombat veterans. Based on a questionnaire checklist obtained from 207 veterans separated from the armed forces for over 5 years, DeFazio et al. found the following percentages of combat veterans still reporting symptoms: (a) frequent nightmares—68 percent; (b) considers self a hothead—44 percent; (c) many fears—35 percent; (d) worries about employment—35 percent; (e) difficulties with emotional closeness —35 percent; (f) tires quickly—32 percent. Often the symptoms appeared to be exacerbated by stimuli associated with the soldier's combat experiences. For example, two combat veterans reported that each time the temperature in their apartments rose to about 75 to 80 degrees Fahrenheit, they experienced an increase in terrifying nightmares.

It is not known why some soldiers suffer from post-combat reaction, while others do not. Worthington (1978) found that U.S. soldiers who experienced problems readjusting after their return home from the Vietnam War also tended to have had greater difficulties before and during their military service than soldiers who adjusted readily. The environmental or social context to which a soldier returns can also make a great difference in his ability to readjust after a stressing ordeal (see HIGHLIGHT on page 184).

The importance of an accepting environment for soldiers who break down under stress is highlighted by Merbaum's (1977) one-year follow-up of Israeli psychiatric war casualties from the Yom Kippur War. He retested and reinterviewed the men, comparing these results with his earlier ones. On retesting, the men not only continued to show extreme anxiety, depression, and extensive physical complaints but in many instances appeared to have become more disturbed over time. Merbaum suggested that this worsening of psychiatric status had probably been produced by the attitudes of the community and expectations of the individual. There is a stigma attached to psychological breakdown in combat in a country that is so reliant upon the strength of its army for its very survival. Many of these men were experiencing extreme loneliness and self-recrimination about what they perceived as failure on their part.

Reactions to civilian catastrophes

In civilian life, people exposed to plane crashes, automobile accidents, explosions, fires, earthquakes, tornadoes, sexual assault, or other terrifying experiences frequently show psychological "shock" reactions—transient personality decompensation.

In an early study of reactions to civilian

Failure to readjust after captivity: a tragic ending

When the POWs held in North Vietnam were finally released in 1973, most Americans felt relieved that the Asian war was at last over. The prisoners who returned—some after many years of captivity—were welcomed back into society. But a few of the returning prisoners found the United States to be at least as hostile an environment as a North Vietnamese POW camp.

One such soldier, Jerry L., returned to the United States to find himself facing charges of collaboration with the enemy and the possibility of a military court martial. His alleged behavior during captivity had received adverse publicity, and Jerry's friends and relatives reacted by treating him with coldness and suspicion. Shortly after his return, Jerry died of self-inflicted gunshot wounds.

Two psychologists were asked by the district attorney's office to construct a "psychological autopsy" (see Chapter 16) to clear up the circumstances surrounding the unexpected death. In conducting their investigation, Selkin and Loya (1979) encountered resistance from Jerry's family and from the military. Jerry's wife and other family members believed that the government had mistreated Jerry and that his death was related to the military's lack of support and medical attention plus the extreme anxiety caused by the charges of collaboration. As a result,

the family was at first reluctant to provide information about Jerry's early life, though they later became more cooperative. Meanwhile, military officials initially refused to release Jerry's records—though they, too, finally decided to cooperate.

Selkin and Loya discovered that Jerry had been following what appeared to be a "suicidal life course that had begun long before the war in Vietnam" (p. 89). Jerry had long tended to drink heavily when under stress and had a history of delinquency and other maladjustments. Despite this, the military had provided Jerry with little psychiatric attention after his release. Although he spoke briefly with a "partially trained" psychiatrist, he was not offered psychological help or a psychiatric follow-up after he returned home. It was apparent that "no one in any official capacity made an honest attempt to understand him or take a careful look at his life situation" (p. 90).

This investigation indicates both the relationship of prior psychological problems to adjustment after captivity and the importance of the environment to the successful repatriation of prisoners of war. A few days after the psychological autopsy was reported, the government dropped all charges against other POWs who had been accused of collaborating with the enemy.

catastrophes, it was found that over half of the survivors of the disastrous Cocoanut Grove nightclub fire—which cost the lives of 492 people in Boston in 1942—required treatment for severe psychological shock (Adler, 1943). Similarly, when two commuter trains collided in Chicago in 1972, leaving 44 persons dead and over 300 injured, the tragedy also left scores of persons with feelings of fear, anxiety, and guilt (Uhlenhuth, 1973). More than 80 of them attended a voluntary "talk session" arranged by the psychiatric adult outpatient clinic of the University of Chicago. More recently, psychological evaluation of 8 of the 64 survivors of the collision of two jet planes on Santa Cruz de Tenerife Island in 1977, in which 580 people died, indicated that all the survivors studied suffered from serious emotional problems (Perlberg, 1979).

Clinical picture in civilian "shock" cases

Civilian "shock" cases may show a wide range of symptoms depending on the nature and severity of the terrifying experience, the degree of surprise, and the personality makeup of the individual. A "disaster syndrome" has been delineated that appears to characterize the reactions of many victims of tornadoes, fires, and other civilian catastrophes. This syndrome may be described in terms of both initial reactions to the traumatic experience and possible complications that arise later and are thus called *post-traumatic symptoms*.

Initial "disaster syndrome." The early syndrome typically involves the three following stages:

The first reaction to an unexpected disaster, such as a fire, is usually shock and disorientation. Victims are generally passive and suggestible, depending on others to take charge of the situation.

1. *Shock stage,* in which the victim is stunned, dazed, and apathetic. Frequently unaware of the extent of personal injuries, the victim tends to wander about aimlessly until guided or directed by someone else, and is unable to make more than minimal efforts to help either him or herself or others. In extreme cases the individual may be stuporous, disoriented, and amnesic for the traumatic event.

2. *Suggestible stage,* in which the victim tends to be passive, suggestible, and willing to take directions from rescue workers or others less affected by the disaster. Here the individual often expresses extreme concern over the welfare of others involved in the disaster and attempts to be of assistance; however, his or her behavior tends to be inefficient even in the performance of routine tasks.

3. *Recovery stage,* in which the individual may be tense and apprehensive and show generalized anxiety, but gradually regains psychological equilibrium—often in the process showing a need to repetitively tell about the catastrophic event.

These three stages are well illustrated in the *Andrea Doria* disaster, in which 52 persons died and over 1600 were rescued.

"On July 25, 1956, at 11:05 P.M., the Swedish liner *Stockholm* smashed into the starboard side of the Italian liner *Andrea Doria* a few miles off Nantucket Island, causing one of the worst disasters in maritime history. . . . During the phase of initial shock the survivors acted as if they had been sedated . . . as though nature provided a sedation mechanism which went into operation automatically. [During the phase of suggestibility] the survivors presented themselves for the most part as an amorphous mass of people tending to act passively and compliantly.

They displayed psychomotor retardation, flattening of affect, somnolence, and in some instances, amnesia for data of personal identification. They were nonchalant and easily suggestible. [During the stage of recovery, after the initial shock had worn off and the survivors had received aid,] they showed . . . an apparently compulsive need to tell the story again and again, with identical detail and emphasis." (Friedman & Linn, 1957, p. 426)

In some cases the clinical picture may be complicated by intense feelings of grief and depression (see HIGHLIGHT on this page). Where the individual feels that his or her own personal inadequacy contributed to the loss of loved ones in the disaster, the picture may be further complicated by strong feelings of guilt. This pattern is well brought out in the following case of a husband who failed to save his wife in the jet crash at Tenerife in 1977.

"Martin's story is quite tragic. He lost his beloved wife of 37 years and blames himself for her death, because he sat stunned and motionless for some 25 seconds after the [other plane] hit. He saw nothing but fire and smoke in the aisles, but he roused himself and led his wife to a jagged hole above and behind his seat. Martin climbed out onto the wing and reached down and took hold of his wife's hand, but 'an explosion from within literally blew her out of my hands and pushed me back and down onto the wing.' He reached the runway, turned to go back after her, but the plane blew up seconds later . . . .

"[Five months later] Martin was depressed and bored, had 'wild dreams,' a short temper and became easily confused and irritated. 'What I saw there will terrify me forever,' he says. He told [the psychologist who interviewed him] that he avoided television and movies, because he couldn't know when a frightening scene would appear." (Perlberg, 1979, pp. 49–50)

In some instances "the guilt of the survivors" seems to center around the view that they may have deserved to survive no more or perhaps even less than others. As one stewardess expressed it after the crash of a Miami-bound jet in the Everglades of Florida which took many lives, "I kept thinking, I'm alive. Thank God. But I wondered why I was spared. I felt, it's not fair . . ." (*Time,* Jan. 15, 1973, p. 53).

Post-traumatic "disaster syndrome." As in combat cases, certain civilians who undergo such terrifying experiences reveal a somewhat typical post-traumatic pattern that may endure for weeks, months, or even years (Mod-

HIGHLIGHT

The emotional aftermath of a devastating tornado

"Many saw it coming. At first it looked like a huge, mushroom-shaped black cloud with three narrow stems. Then the stems merged into one devastating funnel, six-tenths of a mile wide. Winds in the funnel reached 318 miles an hour, four times the force of a hurricane. . . . The tornado took only 22 minutes to cut a horrifying 16-mile path from the outskirts of Xenia, directly through the main intersection of town. . . . Almost half of the seven-square-mile town [was] destroyed in a tornado that may have been the largest ever observed on earth. . . .

The power of the storm was incredible. . . . Automobiles were wrapped like untidy Band-Aids around the shattered trees. . . . Of 2,757 homes damaged by the storm, 1,095 were totally destroyed. The three-story high school and both junior high schools were demolished. . . . Twenty-five people died quickly; seven others lingered a day or two in hospitals before they expired. About 2,500 were injured, some very seriously. . . ." (Schanche, 1974, pp. 18–19)

The immediate reactions of "direct victims," who had lived through the full impact of the tornado, tended to follow the stages of the acute "disaster syndrome"—initial feelings of disbelief and numbness, followed by repetitive talking about the disaster experience, and gradual progress toward assimilation of the experience and adjustment to it. Where loved ones were lost, the pattern was, of course, much more complicated.

Prominent among the residual symptoms two months after the disaster were anxiety reactions relating to fear of another tornado and feelings of depression that had not yet fully cleared up. The most significant residual effects were found among the very young, who appeared to develop a "school phobia" characterized by fear of leaving home and refusal to return to school. Often this pattern appeared to be exacerbated by parents who were afraid to let the children leave.

While the "direct survivors" of the disaster were most seriously affected, the "indirect survivors" who had not experienced the major impact of the tornado also evidenced emotional reactions, such as guilt for being spared, difficulty in sleeping, and uncharacteristic conflicts with their husbands or wives. As Schanche expressed it, "Such natural disasters seem invariably to suck an emotional storm in their wake that frequently cuts a wider swath than the disaster itself. In this psychological aftermath, the nonvictims often suffer as much, if not more, than the direct victims of the tragedy" (p. 19).

lin, 1967; Schanche, 1974; Warnes, 1973). It includes the following symptoms: (a) anxiety, varying from mild apprehension to episodes of acute anxiety commonly associated with situations that recall the traumatic experience; (b) chronic tension and irritability, often accompanied by fatigability, insomnia, the inability to tolerate noise, and the complaint that "I just can't seem to relax"; (c) repetitive nightmares reproducing the traumatic incident directly or symbolically; (d) complaints of impaired concentration and memory; and (e) feelings of depression. In some cases the individual may withdraw from social contact and avoid experiences that might increase excitation—commonly manifested in the avoidance of interpersonal involvement, loss of sexual interest, and an attitude of "peace and quiet at any price."

This post-traumatic syndrome may be complicated by a physical mutilation that necessitates changes in one's way of life; it may also be complicated by the psychological effects of disability compensation or damage suits, which tend to prolong post-traumatic symptoms (Keiser, 1968; Okura, 1975).

Causal factors in civilian "shock" cases

The causes behind civilian "shock" reactions seem to be similar to those involved in traumatic reactions to combat. Here, too, the world, which has seemed relatively secure and safe, suddenly becomes a terrifying place.

One survivor of the jet crash in the Everglades remembered reading a book one minute and the next "waking up in a puddle of water with one shoe, my jacket and glasses gone, and an engine lying not far from my head." (*Time*, Jan. 15, 1973, p. 53)

During the initial reaction to the catastrophe, symptoms of being stunned, dazed, and "numbed," appear to stem in part from psychological decompensation associated with the traumatic event; they also appear in part to be defense mechanisms protecting individuals from the full impact of the catastrophe until they are better prepared to assimilate the trauma into their life experience. The stage of suggestibility apparently results from the individual's temporary inability to deal with the situation alone, plus a tendency to regress to a passive-dependent position in which one feels

safer knowing that someone else is in charge.

During the stage of recovery, the recurrent nightmares and the typical need to tell about the disaster again and again with identical detail and emphasis appear to be mechanisms for reducing anxiety and desensitizing the individual to the traumatic experience. The tension, apprehensiveness, and hypersensitivity that often accompany the recovery stage appear to be residual effects of the shock reaction and to reflect the individual's realization that the world can become overwhelmingly dangerous and threatening. As we have seen, feelings of guilt about having failed to protect loved ones who perished may be quite intense, especially in situations where some responsibility can be directly assigned.

Contrary to popular opinion, panic reactions are not common among people in the impact area of a disaster. For example, most victims of floods and hurricanes do not panic. Instead, *panic*, defined as acute fear followed by flight behavior, tends to occur only under fairly specific conditions: (a) when a group of persons is directly threatened, for example, by fire; (b) when the situation is viewed as one in which escape is possible at the moment but maybe only for a few minutes or not for everyone; and (c) when the group is taken by surprise and has no prearranged plan for dealing with such a disaster (McDavid & Harari, 1968).

Under such conditions there may be a complete disorganization or demoralization of the group, with each individual striving for self-preservation; the emotional, panic-stricken behavior of others seems to be contagious, and a person may be overwhelmed by fear. Behavior may be extremely irrational and nonadaptive and can actually result in needless loss of life. For example, in the disastrous Iroquois Theater fire in Chicago in 1903, 500 people were killed in less than eight minutes due to trampling and asphyxiation rather than burns. Similarly, in the catastrophic Cocoanut Grove fire, no lives need have been lost had people exited in an orderly way. Instead, the exits were jammed by a rush of panic-stricken people so that many were trampled and those behind them could not get out.

In broader perspective, however, most civilians function relatively well in catastrophes, and, in fact, many behave with heroism (Rachman, 1978).

Both precipitating and predisposing conditions in civilian life are apt to differ considerably from those in combat situations, for in the former the individual is not typically far from home, extremely fatigued, or exposed to prolonged fear and conflict over physical danger. But here, too, predisposing factors may determine which individuals develop traumatic reactions and which do not, and why some recover much more rapidly than do others (see HIGHLIGHT on this page).

In both acute and long-term chronic reactions, conditioned fear—the fear associated with the traumatic experience—appears to be a key causal factor. Thus prompt psychotherapy following the traumatic experience is considered important in preventing such conditioned fear from "building up" and becoming resistant to change.

Treatment and outcomes

Mild reassuring therapy and proper rest (induced by sedatives if necessary) usually lead to the rapid alleviation of symptoms in civilian "shock" reactions. It would also appear that repetitive talking about the experience and repetitive reliving of the experience in fantasy or nightmares may serve as built-in repair mechanisms in helping the individual adjust to the traumatic experience. As Horowitz has concluded from his own experimental findings and a review of available literature,

"A traumatic perceptual experience remains in some special form of memory storage until it is mastered. Before mastery, vivid sensory images of the experiences tend to intrude into consciousness and may evoke unpleasant emotions. Through such repetitions the images, ideas, and associated affects may be worked through progressively. Thereafter, the images lose their intensity and the tendency toward repetition of the experience loses its motive force." (1969, p. 552)

While the majority of civilian "shock" reactions clear up in a matter of days or weeks, a minority of cases, as we have seen, evidence a post-traumatic syndrome that may persist over a sustained period of time. Here the individual often remains sensitized to certain types of hazardous situations and simply does not regain self-confidence in dealing with them. In a study by Leopold and Dillon (1963) of 34 sea-

Anguishing memories of an air disaster

In September 1978 an airliner collided with a private airplane in the vicinity of the San Diego, California, airport, killing all 137 passengers aboard the two planes and 7 people on the ground. Unlike many other air disasters, the wreckage and remains of the victims were not scattered widely but were instead concentrated in an area smaller than a city block. The force with which the planes struck the ground left few recognizable aircraft parts or human beings intact.

Disaster workers called to the scene to give aid and clear away the debris were generally unprepared for the calamity they witnessed. One police officer reported that "it was like stepping suddenly into hell . . . we were standing in a pile of human tissue mixed with tiny pieces of airplane" (Davidson, 1979a). Several hundred police officers and fire fighters worked five days in temperatures that soared over 100 degrees to clean up the area. Most of the people involved in the cleanup operation—even veterans of many years of police work—were stunned by the horrible circumstances. Apparently, one reason why such experienced people were so adversely affected by the situation was that "it looked very different from what people expected a plane crash to look like—they had no frame of reference for such a calamity and really lost their equilibrium" (Davidson, 1979b). Many developed psychological symptoms—depression, loss of appetite, inability to sleep, and anxiety.

In order to help the disaster workers, a group of psychologists from the San Diego area offered free psychological counseling. Within a few days of the accident, over 30 police officers and fire fighters along with about 50 civilians sought counseling. Interestingly, very few relatives or friends of people who perished in the crash sought help, presumably because many of the victims were not San Diego residents. Several reasons were pointed to for why so many police officers—a group traditionally sceptical of mental health professionals and wary of being viewed by their superiors as "weird"—sought help: (a) a large number of officers experienced unexpected problems as a result of this experience; (b) these officers had no effective outlet for the feelings of anger and frustration they were experiencing; (c) their superior officers indicated that it would be appropriate for them to discuss their feelings with professional psychologists; and (d) the counseling was set up outside of the police department's influence, thus assuring anonymity.

The counseling—crisis intervention therapy (see Chapter 20)—focused on providing support and reassurance and allowing individuals to vent their pent-up or unmanageable emotions. For most of the individuals involved, brief crisis intervention was effective in providing symptom relief. But a few individuals required more extensive long-term psychotherapy. The following description is of a 42-year-old police officer who suffered a severe reaction to the stress of the San Diego air crash.

Don had been a model police officer during his 14 years on the force. He was highly evaluated by his superiors, had a masters degree in social work, and had attained the rank of sergeant. While patrolling in a squad car, he heard that there had been an accident, and he quickly drove to the scene to give aid to any survivors. When he arrived he wandered around "in a daze," looking for someone to help—but there was only destruction. He later remembered the next few days as a bad dream.

He was quite depressed for several days after the cleanup, had no appetite, couldn't sleep, and was impotent. Images and recollections of the accident would come to him "out of nowhere." He reported having a recurring dream in which he would come upon an airplane crash while driving a car or flying a plane. In his dream, he would rush to the wreckage and help some passengers to safety.

Don decided that he needed help and sought counseling. Because of his deteriorating mood and physical condition, he was placed on medical leave from the police force. Eight months after the accident he was still in therapy and had not returned to work. During therapy it became apparent that Don had been experiencing a great deal of personal dissatisfaction and anger prior to the crash. His prolonged psychological disorder was not only a result of his anguish over the air crash but also a vehicle for expressing other problems (Davidson, 1979a).

Based on Davidson, 1979a, 1979b; O'Brien, 1979

men who survived an explosion and fire on board a gasoline tanker, it was found that $3^1/_2$ to $4^1/_2$ years after the disaster, 12 of the survivors—who had succeeded in lowering a lifeboat and getting away from the inferno—had never returned to sea work or had been forced to give it up as a result of post-traumatic symptoms. Of those who continued to work at sea, all showed similar post-traumatic symptoms—tension, fearfulness, and anxiety aboard ship.

In general, the more stable and better integrated the personality and the more favorable the individual's life situation, the more quickly he or she will recover from a civilian "shock" reaction. It would also appear to be important to work through the traumatic experience if post-traumatic symptoms are to be avoided. For example, Leopold and Dillon (1963) concluded that with prompt psychotherapy after the disaster, the post-traumatic syndromes evidenced by the seamen could have been prevented.

Reactions to sustained or difficult stressors

In addition to the decompensation under acute stress seen in combat exhaustion and civilian "shock" reactions, less severe disturbances may also occur when the individual continues for an extended time in a situation where he or she feels threatened, seriously dissatisfied, or inadequate. Such situations occur in both military and civilian life. Regimentation, such as occurs in the army or in a correctional setting, is difficult for most people and intolerable for some. Living in a society from which an individual feels alienated may also lead to emotional disorder.

The symptoms that may develop vary greatly, depending on the individual and the stressful situation. In the military, gambling, drinking, and going to prostitutes are common means of reducing feelings of boredom and frustration. Some soldiers develop a particu-

Drug abuse is sometimes a response to prolonged stress in military as well as civilian life. Here a soldier is receiving emergency treatment for an overdose.

larly embittered attitude and are resistant, irritable, fault-finding, and highly resentful about being "shoved around"; others, particularly those exposed to a highly restricted environment, such as assignment to an isolated outpost, may show a wide range of other symptoms.

Apathy is a fairly common reaction to continued severe, inescapable stress, such as extreme poverty or continued discrimination, perhaps because it partially shields the individual from the hurtful situation. A common defensive reaction in POW camps was to "play it cool"—that is, to put out the minimum essential effort and try not to become emotionally involved.

In the discussion that follows, we shall focus on reactions to two extreme examples of chronic severe stress in wartime settings and three kinds of stress related to difficult life problems that any one of us may face.

Reactions of prisoners of war and concentration-camp survivors

One of the best descriptions of reactions to the difficult situation of being a prisoner of war is that of Commander Nardini, an eyewitness and participant, who described the effects of imprisonment and mistreatment of American soldiers following the fall of Bataan and Corregidor during the early part of World War II.

"Our national group experience accustoms us to protection of individual rights and recourse to justice. The members of this group found themselves suddenly deprived of name, rank, identity, justice, and any claim to being treated as human beings. Although physical disease and the shortages of food, water, and medicine were at their highest during this period, emotional shock and reactive depression . . . undoubtedly contributed much to the massive death rate during the first months of imprisonment.

"Conditions of imprisonment varied from time to time in different places and with different groups. In general there was shortage, wearisome sameness, and deficiency of food; much physical misery and disease; squalid living conditions; fear and despair; horrible monotony . . . inadequate clothing and cleansing facilities; temperature extremes; and physical abuse.

" . . . Hungry men were constantly reminded of

their own nearness to death by observing the steady, relentless march to death of their comrades. . . . Men quibbled over portions of food, were suspicious of those who were in more favored positions than themselves, participated in unethical barter, took advantage of less clever or enterprising fellow prisoners, stole, rummaged in garbage, and even curried the favor of their detested captors. There was a great distortion of previous personality as manifested by increased irritability, unfriendliness, and sullen withdrawal. . . . Hungry, threatened men often found it difficult to expand the horizon of their thinking and feeling beyond the next bowl of rice. . . .

"Disease was abundant . . . fever, chills, malaise, pain, anorexia, abdominal cramps from recurrent malaria (acquired in combat), and dysentery plagued nearly all and killed thousands. . . . most men experienced bouts of apathy or depression. These ranged from slight to prolonged deep depressions where there was a loss of interest in living and lack of willingness or ability to marshal the powers of will necessary to combat disease. An ever present sign of fatal withdrawal occurred 3 to 4 days before death when the man pulled his covers up over his head and lay passive, quiet, and refusing food.

" . . . One of the most distressing features was the highly indefinite period of imprisonment. The future offered only visions of continued hunger, cold, disease, forced labor, and continued subservience in the face of shouting, slappings, and beatings. . . . Strong hostility naturally arose from the extreme frustration. . . . Little could be done with these hostile feelings. . . . It was not possible to demonstrate recognizable signs of hostility to the captors for obvious reasons. Therefore, where there were mixed groups of Allied prisoners, much hostility was turned from group to group and in other instances to individuals within the group. . . . In many cases hostile feelings were obviously turned inward and joined with appropriate feelings of frustration to produce serious waves of depression. . . . Self pity, in which some indulged, was highly dangerous to life. . . ." (Nardini, 1952, pp. 241–44)

Similar reactions were observed among prisoners held by the North Koreans and Chinese Communists during the Korean War (Lifton, 1954; Segal, 1954; Strassman, Thaler, & Schein, 1956). Here, however, the picture was further complicated by "brainwashing" techniques, described in the HIGHLIGHT on page 192.

A common syndrome manifested by POW's during the Korean War was delineated by Farber, Harlow, and West (1956). They referred to this syndrome as "DDD"—debility, dependency, and dread. *Debility* was induced by semistarvation, disease, and fatigue, and led to

Brainwashing of American prisoners during the Korean War

In his novel *1984,* George Orwell (1949) described the process of "brainwashing," in which the environment around a person is controlled so completely that the effects are similar to those of removing the person's brain and literally washing it clean of all thoughts considered socially undesirable by those in control. Orwell's fictional concept became a frightening reality during the Korean conflict, when the Chinese Communists launched a systematic program to indoctrinate prisoners of war with Communist values and to achieve their collaboration.

During the early part of the war, the men captured by the North Koreans were subjected to a variety of cruelties, including forced "death marches," inadequate diet, exposure to freezing weather without adequate clothing or shelter, and vicious beatings for minor or alleged transgressions. Physical treatment improved somewhat after the Chinese Communists took charge of all POWs—but with the improvement came the emotional assault of brainwashing. The approach used by the Communists can be described in terms of three phases, which were in simultaneous and continuous operation: isolation, thought control, and political conditioning.

Phase	How carried out	Results
Isolation	Removal of leaders: officers transferred to a separate camp, and natural leaders, as they emerged, removed silently to "reactionary" camps. Informers rewarded to discourage personal ties and interaction. Home ties cut—pessimistic, complaining letters delivered while other mail withheld. In some instances a prisoner was subjected to complete isolation, increasing his need for companionship and making him more suggestible—"softening him up" for thought control	Creation of a group of "isolates" with low morale and no *esprit de corps.* Social and emotional isolation robbed soldier of usual sources of strength and prevented him from validating his beliefs and values through discussion with others. Led to loss of strength to resist, increased suggestibility, and vulnerability to both threats and bribes.
Thought control	Prisoners forced to choose between "cooperation" and possible starvation, torture, and death. Ethical values, loyalty, religion, and self-identity placed in direct opposition to self-preservation and bodily needs: resistees subjected to threat, punishment, and marginal living conditions; cooperators rewarded with increased food, privileges in camp, and promises of early repatriation. Guilt feelings concerning prior behavior stimulated by mandatory "confessions" and self-criticism. Alternate harshness and friendliness by "inscrutable authority."	Fear, anxiety, guilt, confusion, and conflict about how to behave. "Playing it cool"—being inconspicuous, holding back strong feelings, being minimally communicative and noncommittal on everything, "cooperating" a little when necessary but avoiding major collaboration. Withdrawal of emotional involvement, marked apathy. Listlessness and apparent indifference.

Phase	How carried out	Results
Political conditioning	Daily "instruction" with repetitious teaching of communist catch phrases and principles. Appeals to be "open-minded" and to "just listen to our side of the story." Only anti-American books and newspapers available, stressing inequalities and injustices in U.S. Communists portrayed as "peace seekers," prisoner offered "opportunity to work for peace." Intensive pressure applied to those who seemed most susceptible; those already convinced used to indoctrinate others. Constant use of reward for cooperation and punishment for resistance.	Little actual conversion to communism but considerable confusion and doubt about America's role in war; poor morale and discipline; breakdown of group loyalty. Men turned against each other—"progressives" versus "reactionaries." Difficulty in relating to others even after release. Five percent later won commendation as resisters; 15 percent were judged to have complied unduly; the remaining 80 percent were relatively passive. Twenty-six men actually chose to stay in North Korea after release, but several were later repatriated.

When prisoners were first released, they were apathetic, detached, dazed, without spontaneity, and at the same time tense and suspicious of their new surroundings. Large memory gaps were present, particularly for the period of their capture and for so-called death marches. They were ambivalent in their feelings about the Chinese Communists, showed strong guilt about all phases of their POW experience, and were not anxious to return home to the U.S. This "zombie reaction" wore off after three to five days and was followed by a period of greater spontaneity. However, they still appeared "suspended in time"—confused by their newly acquired status and incapable of making decisions concerning future courses of action. All the men felt alienated from others who had not shared their POW experience and were apprehensive about homecoming; they tended to band together in small, uneasy groups and maintained isolation from nonrepatriates.

On their return home, some got into difficulty over indiscriminate outbursts of misdirected, long-pent-up hostility. Expecting at last to be free of stress, some became disillusioned and discouraged in their efforts to adjust to economic and other changes and to communicate with others. Physical disabilities, chronic fatigue, and a confused self-picture complicated the adjustment problems of many. But although some drank too much or managed other escape measures, the majority of these men eventually made adequate adjustments. In a few cases their weathering of the prison experience seemed to have given them increased inner strength and greater capacity for achievement.

Material for this chart taken from Kinkead (1959); Lifton (1954); Schein, Schneier, and Barker (1961); Segal (1954); Strassman, Thaler, and Schein (1956); and West (1958). For information on the application of similar techniques to civilian populations—for example, in Russia and China—see Hinkle and Wolff (1956); Hunter (1954); Lifton (1961); and Watzlawick, Beavin, and Jackson (1967).

The physical stresses and psychological horrors of life in concentration camps left permanent scars on many of those who survived the ordeal.

a sense of terrible weariness and weakness. *Dependency* was produced by a variety of techniques, including the use of solitary confinement, the removal of leaders and other accustomed sources of support, and occasional and unpredictable respites that reminded the prisoners that they were completely dependent on their captors for what happened to them. *Dread* was described as a stage of chronic fear that their captors attempted to induce—fear of death, of pain, of nonrepatriation, and of permanent deformity or disability due to neglect or inadequate medical treatment. The net effect of these conditions was a well-nigh intolerable state of mental and physical discomfort that rendered the men more amenable to brainwashing.

In the Vietnam War, soldiers were better prepared in terms of what to expect and what to do in the event of capture. Consequently they fared much better, in general, than did the POWs of earlier wars. However, occasional exceptions were noted. For example, Kushner (1973)—a medical doctor and fellow prisoner —reported that two of the twenty-two men in a Viet Cong POW camp in which conditions were particularly bad simply gave up and died.

Descriptions of prisoners in Nazi concentra-tion camps, who were subjected to even more inhuman and sadistic conditions, emphasize similar reactions (Bettelheim, 1943, 1960; Chodoff, 1970; Eitinger, 1961, 1962, 1969; Frankl, 1963; Friedman, 1948; Hafner, 1968). Inmates of concentration camps also showed greater use of the defense mechanisms of denial and isolation of affect. The feeling that "This isn't really happening to me" was widespread. Chodoff (1970) has cited the case of a young prisoner "who would not see the corpses she was stepping over" and the even more poignant picture "of her fellow inmates who refused to believe that the smoke arising from the crematorium chimneys came from the burning corpses of their mothers" who had been selected—because of age—to be killed first. Isolation of affect apparently reached the degree of almost total emotional anesthesia in the case Chodoff cited of a young female prisoner who stated "I had no feelings whatsoever" while being stripped naked and having all her hair shaved off in front of SS troopers (p. 83).

Concentration-camp inmates also tended to form hopes of deliverance via miraculous events, possibly because their situation was even more hopeless than that of the POWs, and any hope would have been unrealistic.

For many former POWs, the bright promise of a happy return to family and home was fulfilled. But others found that joy soon turned to bitterness as they struggled to pick up the threads of their past lives.

The most obvious causal factors in reactions to long-continued stressful situations such as being a prisoner of war or a concentration-camp inmate are, of course, the environmental stressors—the conditions in the environment whose demands, over a period of time, are too great for comfortable accommodation. But the unusual stressors are not the whole story. Here, as in the case of other disorders, the individual's reaction depends on the whole pattern of biological, psychosocial, and sociocultural factors.

Some individuals adjust with a minimum of strain to the same situations that are too much for others. Likewise, a supportive group increases the individual's ability to withstand stress. Rachman (1978) pointed out that having an active and socially responsible task to perform during the repeated terrifying bombing raids in England during World War II helped people learn to cope with the continued threat they were all experiencing.

About half of the American prisoners in Japanese POW camps during World War II died during their imprisonment; an even higher incidence of deaths occurred among inmates of Nazi concentration camps. Among those who survived the ordeal, there was often residual organic as well as psychological damage and a lowering of tolerance to stress of any kind.

The residual damage to survivors of concentration camps was often extensive and commonly included anxiety, insomnia, headaches, irritability, depression, nightmares, impaired sexual potency, and "functional" diarrhea (that is, diarrhea that occurs in any situation of stress, even relatively mild stress). Such symptoms were attributed not only to the psychological stressors of concentration-camp experiences but also to biological stressors, such as head injuries, prolonged malnutrition, and serious infectious diseases (Eitinger, 1964, 1969, 1973; Sigal et al., 1973; Warnes, 1973).

Among returning POWs, psychological problems are often masked by the feelings of relief and jubilation that accompany release from confinement. Even when there is little evidence of residual physical pathology, however, survivors of prisoner-of-war camps commonly evidence impaired resistance to physical illness, low frustration tolerance, frequent dependence on alcohol and drugs, irritability, and other indications of emotional instability (Chambers, 1952; Goldsmith & Cretekos, 1969; Hunter, 1978; Strange & Brown, 1970; Wilbur, 1973).

Another measure of the toll taken by the prolonged stress of being in a POW or concentration camp is the higher death rate after return to civilian life. Among returning POWs from the Pacific area after World War II, Wolff (1960) found that within the first six years, nine times as many died from tuberculosis as would have been expected in civilian life, four times as many from gastrointestinal disorders, over twice as many from cancer, heart disease, and suicide, and three times as many from accidents. Comparable figures have been reported for concentration-camp survivors by Eitinger (1973).

Aware that problems may show up years after release, military psychologists and psychiatrists are following the Vietnam War POWs on a long-term basis with checkups every year. This group differs from previous POW returnees in being almost entirely composed of flight crew personnel—who are officers and somewhat older than the rank and file of combat personnel. In the examination made two years after their return, it was found that the longer the imprisonment had been, the more likely the individual was to be diagnosed as having a psychiatric problem (O'Connell, 1976). Harshness of POW treatment and degree of social isolation were also related to later psychiatric problems (Hunter, 1976). The most frequent problems requiring professional attention were depression and marital difficulties (Hunter, 1978).

Nardini (1962) has suggested the following qualities as being positive factors in both physical and psychological survival of POW experiences: a philosophical, fatalistic, yet non-defeatist attitude; intense application of life energies to the present; ability to retain hope in the face of very great hardships; ability to manage hostility and fight depression; personal maturity and ego strength; a strong sense of self-identity and self-respect; and the intangible but all-inclusive determination to live. Frankl (1963) has emphasized similar characteristics as fostering survival in concentration camps. Of course, in both POW and concentration camps, chance factors often played an important or even crucial role in the survival or death of the prisoner.

Here it may be noted that the "reentry problem" is often a difficult one for both POWs and concentration-camp survivors as they try to ad-

just to the sudden and major change in their world as well as to social changes that have taken place during their imprisonment (see HIGHLIGHT on page 197). While most former prisoners do make a successful readjustment, some will spend the remainder of their lives "rattling the emotional chains" forged by the inhuman conditions of their imprisonment.

Reactions to difficult life problems

The situations we have been describing seem quite remote to most of us. The chances of experiencing firsthand the terrors of war or confinement in a prisoner-of-war camp are quite low. Even natural disasters like floods, fires, tornadoes, and plane crashes, though more common, still never involve most of us. However, situations do not have to be as severe or generally devastating as combat, imprisonment, or natural calamities to precipitate psychological stress reactions (see HIGHLIGHT on page 198). Many people face less dramatic but intensely stressful situations—sometimes over an extended period of time—that require great adjustive effort and can produce long-range psychological problems. Among the situations of this type are unemployment, bereavement, and divorce or separation.

The stress of unemployment. Managing the stress associated with chronic unemployment requires great coping strength, especially for people who have previously earned an adequate living and suddenly find themselves destitute, with no way to better their condition. The following excerpt from Terkel's book *Hard Times* provides a good illustration of the stressors of the Great Depression, the means people used to cope with the harsh circumstances, and the long-range impact of these difficult problems.

"**Ward James**   *He is seventy-three. He teaches at a fashionable private school for boys, out East. He was born in Wisconsin; attended school there.*
" 'BEFORE THE CRASH, I was with a small publishing house in New York. I was in charge of all the production and did most of the copy. It was a good job. The company was growing. It looked like a permanent situation. I was feeling rather secure. . . .
" 'Until 1935, I had my job with this publishing

The permanent POWs

Being in combat or captured by the enemy are not the only stress situations caused by war. One medic's experiences may present a different perspective on being a "prisoner of war."

Pete Rios (1973) was seriously wounded and left for dead in Vietnam. Saved by a buddy who was also seriously wounded, the soldiers, the only survivors of their combat unit, were finally removed from the battle site by helicopter.

"A week later we were flown to Travis AFB, Calif., and psychologically we were in pretty bad shape because we knew we were permanently disabled. . . ."

After one day at Travis, Rios was sent to Walter Reed Army Hospital in Washington, D.C., where he was given intensive physical therapy; at the end of his two-month stay, he could walk with leg braces and crutches. But then he was discharged from the Army and sent to a veteran's hospital, where he was told it was "impossible" for him to walk with such a "young [recent] injury." His actual achievement was discounted.

"I suppose the main thing I object to is always being categorized as 'a patient.' There is a nurse, a patient. There is a doctor, a patient. Never Pete Rios. You are in a wheelchair, so you are 'a spinal-cord injury'—not a person. You are 30 years old, and you've had more than your share of experiences, but you are treated as if you were a child. . . .

"Since you are 'a patient' and expected not to think, you should not ask questions about your own body. You don't need to know why your bowels won't work, why you can't have sexual relations, why you are spastic, why one foot is colder than another, why you have pain. . . .

"I have been disappointed to find that the public seems cognizant only of the fact that many Americans (about 47,000) were killed or missing in Vietnam and that the remaining hundreds of thousands who served there came home. Nobody seems to think of the fact that 153,000 were wounded or that 7,750 came back blind or with missing or useless legs. . . . If you want to see the aftermath of Vietnam, take a stroll through the second-floor spinal injuries section at Hines [Veterans Hospital]. . . .

"People not only don't give a damn today, but some of them are downright antagonistic toward you. . . ."

Rios tells the story of the time he was seated in a special section for wheelchairs at a restaurant— ahead of some patrons who had been waiting longer than he had. An older woman berated him for being disrespectful to his elders, and asked him how he had gotten hurt. When he told her he had been shot in Vietnam, she replied, "you certainly deserved it."

"Where do you suppose are the people and the flags," he wonders. "They were greatly in evidence for the returning prisoners of war. . . .

"Most severely disabled veterans, frankly, are not overly impressed that an American prisoner spent 22 years in China or eight years in Hanoi. We're glad, of course, that they came back.

"But now we are the only POWs.

"Guys who are blind or crippled are going to be POWs as long as they live.

"There is no time limit—not eight years, nor 22—on that kind of imprisonment."

---

house. They insisted I take a month vacation without pay and a few other things, but it wasn't really too distressing. It became tougher and tougher.

" 'I was fired. No reasons given. . . .

" 'I was out of work for six months. I was losing my contacts as well as my energy. I kept going from one publishing house to another. I never got past the telephone operator. It was just wasted time. One of the worst things was occupying your time, sensibly. You'd go to the library. You took a magazine to the room and sat and read. I didn't have a radio. I tried to do some writing and found I couldn't concentrate.

The day was long. There was nothing to do evenings. I was going around in circles, it was terrifying. So I just vegetated.

" 'With some people I knew, there was a coldness, shunning: I'd rather not see you just now. Maybe *I'll* lose my job next week. On the other hand, I made some very close friends, who were merely acquaintances before. If I needed $5 for room rent or something, it was available.

" 'I had a very good friend who cashed in his bonus bonds to pay his rent. I had no bed, so he let me sleep there. (Laughs.) I remember getting down to my last

Violence in the schools— a new challenge for teachers

Most people would not consider a career in public education to be dangerous and physically challenging. But teaching in the public schools, especially some schools in large metropolitan areas, has recently become as potentially dangerous as such professions as urban police work. O'Toole (1978) described a wave of violence in the public schools in which about 3 percent of all teachers were physically assaulted during the 1977–1978 school year—more than 60,900 by students and a few thousand more by outside intruders and angry parents. Teachers have been pushed down stairs, sexually assaulted, and held up at gunpoint. In Texas, one teacher was murdered by a 13-year-old boy. The following example of school violence in Los Angeles is typical:

Recently, a teacher who was grading papers in her classroom was shot four times in the stomach by a young man who attempted to rape her. This was not the first time she had been assaulted in her nine years of teaching. When she first started teaching, she was stabbed with a darning needle by one of the girls in her class; another time, a male student kicked her in the head. She had reported these incidents of violence, but school administrators had taken no action to punish the offenders or to make classrooms more secure. The publicity centering around the shooting incident, however, prompted officials to provide some additional funding for security—but not enough to make the schools safe (*Los Angeles Herald Examiner,* April 4, 1979).

Many teachers fear for their safety and take great precautions to avoid incidents—such as never remaining in the building alone and never going to more isolated areas of the school. But despite such precautions, the danger remains.

Violence and the threat of violence are not the only problems urban teachers face. According to Chicago Teachers' Union official John Kotsakis, "It's the day-to-day stuff that wears you down—the filth, the overcrowded and run-down buildings, the same three kids calling you the same obscenity every day, the snapped antenna on your car" (O'Toole, 1978, p. 90). As a result, teachers are increasingly suffering from anxiety, fatigue, depression, and a variety of other psychological problems, including psychosomatic illness and low self-esteem.

It appears that many individuals who were previously devoted to teaching are rethinking their career choices out of fear for their own health and safety. Some teachers' groups—including the Chicago Teachers' Union and the United Federation of Teachers in New York City—have reacted to these problems by setting up psychological support programs in which teachers can obtain help in coping with assault and other job-related stresses. According to O'Toole, such programs, coupled with "administrative cooperation, better discipline and strict security, have yielded encouraging signs" (p. 90).

---

pair of pants, which looked awful. One of my other friends had just got a job and had an extra pair of pants that fit me, so I inherited them. (Laughs.)

" 'I went to apply for unemployment insurance, which had just been put into effect. I went three weeks in succession. It still hadn't come through. Then I discovered the catch. At that time, anybody who earned more than $3,000 a year was not paid unemployment insurance unless his employer had O.K.'d it. It could be withheld. My employer exercised his option of not O.K.'ing it. . . .

" 'I finally went on relief. It's an experience I don't want anybody to go through. It comes as close to crucifixion as . . . . You sit in an auditorium and are given a number. The interview was utterly ridiculous and mortifying. In the middle of mine, a

more dramatic guy than I dived from the second floor stairway, head first, to demonstrate he was gonna get on relief even if he had to go to the hospital to do it.

" 'There were questions like: Who are your friends? Where have you been living? Where's your family? I had sent my wife and child to her folks in Ohio, where they could live more simply. Why should anybody give you money? Why should anybody give you a place to sleep? What sort of friends? This went on for half an hour. I got angry and said, "Do you happen to know what a friend is?" He changed his attitude very shortly. I did get certified some time later. I think they paid $9 a month.

" 'I came away feeling I didn't have any business living any more. I was imposing on somebody, a

Unemployment remains a major problem for many segments of our population. Regular trips to the unemployment office can be psychologically destructive to those whose future seems to offer only more of the same.

great society or something like that. . . .'

"Do you recall the sentiments of people during the depths of the Depression?

" '. . . Everyone was emotionally affected. We developed a fear of the future which was very difficult to overcome. Even though I eventually went into some fairly good jobs, there was still this constant dread: everything would be cut out from under you and you wouldn't know what to do. It would be even harder, because you were older. . . .

" 'Before the Depression, one felt he could get a job even if something happened to this one. There were always jobs available. And, of course, there were always those, even during the Depression [who said]: If you wanted to work, you could really get it. Nonsense.

" 'I suspect, even now, I'm a little bit nervous about every job I take and wonder how long it's going to last—and what I'm going to do to cause it to disappear.

" 'I feel anything can happen. There's a little fear in me that it might happen again. It does distort your outlook and your feeling. Lost time and lost faith. . . .' " (Terkel, 1970, pp. 421–23)

Ward James started his ordeal with self-confidence and demonstrated competence. Many victims of chronic unemployment, however, have no such resources to help them. For

some population subgroups—especially young minority males—there is now and always has been an economic depression, more pervasive and just as debilitating as the Great Depression was for the white majority. Indeed, for young black men the rates of unemployment today are over twice those for whites during the 1930s.

The impact of chronic unemployment upon the individual's self-concept, sense of worth, and feeling of belongingness is shattering. To be continuously unemployed and poor in an affluent society is a defeating and oppressing circumstance that produces psychological exhaustion as certainly as the other major calamities described earlier. The vulnerability of the lower socioeconomic segment of the population to these difficult conditions helps explain why it contributes a disproportionately higher number of victims to penal institutions and to mental hospitals than do other population classes.

The stress of bereavement. In contemporary Western society, death is an unwelcome intruder. Most people think of death as a remote event that will happen at sometime in the far distant future—when they will have pretty well completed their lives anyway. In spite of the fact that death is a certainty for us all and the loss of friends and relatives is inevitable, many of us deny and ignore it—and remain unprepared. When someone close to us dies, we are psychologically upended. Often the first reaction is disbelief. Then, as we begin to realize the significance of what has happened, our feelings of sadness, grief, and despair (even, perhaps, anger at the departed person) frequently overwhelm us.

Grief over the loss of a loved one is a natural process that seems to allow the survivors to mourn their loss and then free themselves for life without the departed person. The following description of the grief process was provided by Janis et al. (1969):

" . . . Typically, the normal grief pattern following the loss of a loved one begins with a period of numbness and shock. Upon learning of the death, the person reacts with disbelief. For several days his feelings may be blunted and he may be in a semidazed state, punctuated by episodes of irritability and anger. In some instances the protest reactions take the extreme form of outbursts of impotent rage, as when adult brothers and sisters bitterly blame one another for having failed to do something that might have prolonged the life of their elderly parent. This initial phase usually ends by the time of the funeral, which often can release the tears and feelings of despair that had been bottled up in the grief-stricken person. Thereafter, a very intense grief reaction ensues: The mourner weeps copiously, yearns for the lost person, and wishes he had been more helpful and considerate while the loved one was still alive. He may openly express a hopeless form of protest combined with despair, repeating over and over such phrases as 'Oh God, why did this have to happen?' and 'Why couldn't I have prevented it?' These attacks of agitated distress are likely to alternate with periods of more silent despair, during which the sufferer is preoccupied with memories of the dead person.

"For many days and perhaps weeks the mourner remains somewhat depressed and apathetic, expresses a general sense of futility, and becomes socially withdrawn, although he still goes through the motions of carrying out his usual social obligations. During this period of despair, he is likely to suffer from insomnia, psychosomatic intestinal disorders, loss of appetite, restlessness, and general irritability. A tendency to deny the fact of the death may persist for many weeks; the mourner continues to think of the dead person at times as still alive and present in the house. There is also a tendency to idealize the dead person in memory and . . . to seek companion-

ship mainly with persons who are willing to limit their conversation to talking about him.

"The mourner is usually able to return to work and resume other daily activities, such as talking with friends and relatives, after about two or three weeks. But he may continue to withdraw from certain types of social affairs that used to give him pleasure. After a month or two the most acute symptoms begin to subside, but there may still be residual sadness, yearning, and attacks of acute grief during the ensuing months." (pp. 179–80)

Some individuals do not go through the normal process of grieving, perhaps because of their personality makeup or as a consequence of the particular situation: the individual may, for instance, be expected to be stoical about his or her feelings or may have to manage the affairs of the family. Other individuals may develop exaggerated or prolonged depression after the normal grieving process should have run its course. Such pathological reactions to the death of another person are more likely to occur in people who have a history of emotional problems and who harbor a great deal of resentment and hostility against the deceased, thus experiencing intense guilt. They are usually profoundly depressed and often have suicidal preoccupations. The following case illustrates a pathological grief reaction:

Marilyn, a 37-year-old woman, lived with her 63-year-old invalid mother. Marilyn had always lived in her parents' home except for two brief periods when she was hospitalized for depression at ages 18 and 24. She had never married because she felt obligated to care for her mother and to help raise her two younger sisters (now ages 30 and 32, married, and living in distant cities). In her early thirties she had resigned herself to her situation: feeling duty-bound to support her mother, she gave up on the idea of having a family of her own and threw herself into her full-time secretarial work, attending to her rather overbearing mother in the evenings. She had no outside social life and no close friends.

One evening Marilyn came home from work and found her mother dead. She was stunned and became quite confused. Without calling for assistance, she simply tucked her mother in bed and went about business as usual. She went to work for the next two days but acted so unusual that her supervisor sent her home. The next day, her worried supervisor came to her home to check on her. He found the mother dead in bed and Marilyn sitting on the floor in a stuporous condition. She was hospitalized and

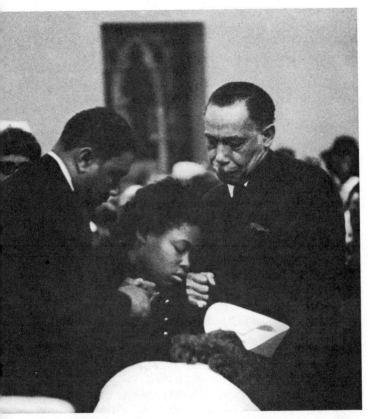

Giving vent to grief is an important part of working through the experience of a significant loss. Support and understanding from those around us can ease the process.

treated with antidepressant medication, electroconvulsive therapy, and limited psychotherapy. After six months she was discharged from the hospital. On the following day she attempted to take her own life with an overdose of sleeping medication. She was discovered in a coma by a neighbor, and was then given emergency treatment. Afterwards, she was returned to the psychiatric hospital for further treatment.

During her second hospital admission Marilyn was given further electroshock and antidepressant treatment along with psychotherapy. After two months, she was discharged and was placed in an aftercare facility, where she was supervised during reentry into her work and social world.

The stress of divorce or separation.   The
deterioration or termination of an intimate re-

lationship is one of the more potent of stressors and one of the more frequent reasons why people seek psychotherapy. Divorce, though more generally accepted today, is still a tragic and usually stressful outcome to a relationship of closeness and trust. We noted in Chapter 5 that marital disruption is a major source of psychopathology, with individuals who are recently divorced or separated markedly overrepresented among people with psychological problems.

Many factors make a divorce or separation unpleasant and stressful for everyone concerned: the acknowledgment of failure in a relationship important to both oneself and the society; the necessity of "explaining" the failure to family and friends; the loss of valuable friendships that frequently accompanies the rupture; the economic uncertainty and hardships that both partners frequently experience; and when children are involved, the problem of custody, living arrangements, and so on.

After the divorce or separation, new problems often emerge. The readjustment to a single life-style, perhaps after many years of marriage, is often a very difficult experience. Since in many cases it seems that friends as well as assets have to be divided, new friendships need to be made. New opposite-sex relationships may require a great deal of personal change. Even where the separation has been relatively agreeable, new adaptation and coping strength will be needed. Thus it is not surprising that many people seek counseling after the breakup of a significant relationship.

The following case illustrates how the stress in a marital breakup can adversely affect a quite capable and generally well-functioning person.

Janice was a petite, attractive 33-year-old manager of an office that employed over fifty people. She had always been very competent and got a great deal of satisfaction out of her career. For several months, however, she had been quite upset and depressed about her marital situation and unable to sleep. She had lost 12 pounds because of her poor appetite and was experiencing painful "burning" feelings in her stomach; she was worried about having ulcers.

Janice's second marriage had begun to show signs of trouble almost from the start. Shortly after the wedding, two years before, her husband's drinking had increased. He often stayed out quite late and on two occasions did not come home at all. Usually he lied about his whereabouts, but for the first few months Janice was tolerant of his transgressions, trying to make this second marriage work. Her husband, whom she regarded as a charming person she "couldn't stay mad at" was always forgiven, and they "had a great time making up." In the most recent incident, however, he had returned late at night with "evident traces of another woman." This was the final straw, and Janice moved out.

The intense stress she was experiencing over the breakup of the marriage appeared to be directly related to her sense of failing in life for a second time. Her first marriage had ended in divorce after, interestingly, her husband of seven years developed a severe drinking problem, stayed away from home a great deal, and frequently abused her physically.

Janice's marital problems did not interfere with her performance at work; but, besides depression and physical problems, she began to experience problems with her teenage daughter. As a result, she entered psychotherapy, hoping that it would help her know herself better and understand why she had married two "losers."

Many other difficult life situations present continuing stressful demands. In Chapter 20 we shall look at "crisis intervention"—a recently developed approach to managing adjustment problems that stem from especially stressful situations. Often it is possible to intervene in such situations before the psychological problems become unmanageable for the individual, giving brief supportive therapy and in some cases lessening the demands of the environment at least temporarily.

Prevention of stress disorders: emotional "inoculation"

If we know that extreme or prolonged stress can produce maladaptive psychological reactions that have a predictable course, is it possible to intervene in the situation early in the process to *prevent* the development of emo-

tional disorder? When it is known that an unusually stressful situation is about to occur, is it possible to "inoculate" the individual by providing information about it ahead of time and suggesting some possible ways of coping with it? If preparation for the stressors of battle can help soldiers avoid breakdown, why not prepare people in civilian life to competently meet anticipated special stressors?

Janis has done just this with patients about to undergo dangerous surgery. His findings have provided a substantial base for preventive efforts aimed at reducing emotional problems of patients following their surgery (Janis, 1958; Janis et al., 1969).

Janis (1958) conducted interviews before and after the surgery to determine the relationship between level of preoperative fear and level of adjustment after the surgery. He found that patients with moderate fear did better than those with either high or low fear. His findings are summarized in the HIGHLIGHT on page 203.

Janis then administered a questionnaire to 150 college students who had recently undergone surgery. Again he classified subjects' level of preoperative fear, but this time he used seven categories for post-operative adjustment, including feelings of anger, complaints about hospital staff, and emotional disturbance in recalling the operation. Again he found that individuals with either a high or a low level of preoperative fear showed worse adjustment after the surgery than did individuals with a moderate degree of pre-operative anxiety.

An important finding in Janis' work is that the individual who is outwardly calm and appears to feel invulnerable to real danger is likely to have more post-crisis problems than individuals who have been "part-time worriers" beforehand.

Janis suggests that the "work of worrying" may involve processes similar to the "work of mourning" following bereavement. In this case, however, it is accomplished before the trauma, helping the individual understand and "work through" the dangerous and aversive situation and be emotionally ready to adjust to it when it comes. Later studies, too, have shown that when patients are prepared for the experience of surgery by being given accurate information about the procedures and a

Level of preoperative fear and adjustment after surgery

Fear level before surgery	Response after surgery
High anticipatory fear—patients greatly worried about suffering pain or being mutilated by the surgery.	Extreme anxiety, emotional outbursts, fearfulness about participating in post-operative treatments. Feeling of deep vulnerability.
Moderate anticipatory fear—patients occasionally worried and tense; felt somewhat vulnerable to the realistic threats of the surgery, asked for information and reassurance.	Least emotional disturbance of the three groups. High morale, cooperative in post-operative treatment.
Low anticipatory fear—patients constantly cheerful and optimistic about surgery, denying feeling worried. Appeared to have unrealistic expectations, felt invulnerable to danger.	Acute preoccupation with their invulnerability, angry and resentful toward staff for being "mistreated." Often uncooperative in post-operative treatment.

Based on Janis (1958)

warning about the pain and discomfort they will experience, they are less likely to experience a severe emotional reaction to surgery (Egbert et al., 1964).

Recent work in cognitive-behavioral therapy has also focused on "stress inoculation" training to prepare individuals for difficult events they will be facing (Meichenbaum & Cameron, 1973; Meichenbaum, Turk, & Burstein, 1975). Here individuals are prepared to tolerate an anticipated threat by changing the things they say to themselves before the crisis.

A three-stage process is employed. The first provides information about the stressful situation and about ways people can deal with such dangers. In the second phase, self-statements that promote effective adaptation—for example, "Don't worry, this little pain is just part of the treatment"—are rehearsed. In the third phase, the individual practices making such self-statements while being exposed to a variety of ego-threatening or pain-threatening stressors, such as unpredictable electric shocks, stress-inducing films, or sudden cold. This last phase allows the person to apply the new coping skills learned earlier. We shall discuss stress-inoculation training and the use of self-statements in greater detail in Chapter 19.

In this chapter we have discussed transient reactions to stress that occur under conditions of unusual and excessive stress, such as military combat and civilian catastrophes. These disorders may involve a variety of symptoms, including intense anxiety, denial, repression, apathy, depression, and the lowering of ethical standards. In most cases the symptoms recede as the stress diminishes, especially if the individual is given brief supportive psychotherapy. However, in extreme cases, such as those involving the survivors of concentration camps, there may be residual damage.

There are many relatively common situations of special stress in contemporary society that require great adjustive efforts. Natural disasters, such as floods, fires, and tornadoes often produce catastrophic results in both material and psychological terms. Less physically threatening life events such as divorce, unemployment, and the death of a loved one are often highly stressful even for emotionally mature and well-adjusted people. The study of transient reactions to intensely stressful situations has enabled psychologists to understand better the development of such problems as anxiety disorders, to which we now turn.

7

The neuroses: Anxiety, somatoform, and dissociative disorders

The basic nature of the neuroses

Anxiety disorders

Somatoform disorders

Dissociative disorders

General causal factors, treatment, and outcomes

In our discussion of transient reactions to severe stress, we dealt primarily with stable personalities who had been subjected to excessive stressor demands. In this chapter we shall look at disorders in which faulty learning, often in early development, has led to persistent feelings of threat and anxiety in facing the everyday problems of living. In these cases, ordinary methods of coping, including the "normal" use of ego-defense mechanisms, have proven inadequate, and the individual has come to rely increasingly on more extreme defensive reactions. While these defenses may help alleviate the acute feelings of threat and anxiety, they exact a high price in self-defeating behavior.

Although neurotic behavior is maladaptive, it does not involve gross distortion of reality or marked personality disorganization, nor is it likely to result in violence to the individual or to others. Rather, we are dealing here with individuals who are typically anxious, ineffective, unhappy, and often guilt-ridden; they do not ordinarily require hospitalization but nevertheless are in need of therapy. The incidence of neuroses is difficult to determine, but it has been estimated that there are at least 20 million individuals in the United States who suffer from neurotic disorders.

The term *neurosis* was coined by the Englishman William Cullen and first used in his *System of Nosology,* published in 1769, to refer to disordered sensations of the nervous system. It reflected the long-held belief that neurological malfunction must be involved in neurotic behavior. This belief endured until the time of Freud, himself a neurologist, who postulated that neurosis stemmed from intrapsychic conflict rather than disordered reactions in the nervous system. This view became widely accepted; significantly, however, it broadened the scope of neurotic behaviors—that is, any nonpsychotic disorder that might have psychological conflict at its base could be considered neurotic. In more recent years, the role of faulty learning to avoid anxiety has also been recognized in the origins of neuroses.

The history of the meaning of the term "neurosis" is important because it reflects a movement away from a very specific definition to a much broader, all-encompassing one. Today, the term has become broadly descriptive, and, coupled with often indiscriminate use of

the term, its effectiveness as a diagnostic category has been limited. To say that an individual is behaving neurotically says, in essence, only that his or her behavior is one of many that stem from the psychological and emotional factors involved in anxiety-avoidance mechanisms.

For this reason, the DSM-III, the latest classification scheme for clinicians, has divided neurotic disorders into more specific categories—the major new ones being anxiety disorders, somatoform disorders, and dissociative disorders—which we shall discuss in this chapter. Also included in the broad category of neurotic disorders are some affective disorders and psychosexual disorders (which we shall cover in Chapters 11 and 15 respectively). It is hoped that these categories will provide the specificity needed in diagnosis. Ingrained patterns of usage will be slow to change, however, and most current research and treatment personnel will likely continue to use the term *neurosis* for some time to come. The important thing to remember here is that the term is a broadly descriptive one.

We shall begin by considering the basic nature of neurotic behavior; then we shall examine several specific neurotic patterns and describe the clinical picture, causal factors, and pertinent aspects of treatment for each one. Finally, we shall deal with more general causal factors, methods of treatment, and outcomes in the neuroses.

The basic nature of the neuroses

While the neuroses embrace a wide range of behaviors, the common core is a maladaptive life-style typified by defense-oriented behavior aimed at avoiding or lessening anxiety. Basic to this neurotic life-style are (a) the *neurotic nucleus*—the faulty evaluation of reality and the tendency to avoid rather than cope with stress; and (b) the *neurotic paradox*—the tendency to maintain this life-style despite its self-defeating and maladaptive nature.

The neurotic nucleus

The neurotic nucleus is a circular process in which the individual feels basically inadequate, evaluates everyday problems as threatening, and attempts to deal with the resulting anxiety by avoidance and defense-oriented reactions. The end result is a self-defeating life-style that blocks personal growth and self-fulfillment. Usually neurotic individuals have trouble establishing and maintaining satisfying interpersonal relationships, feel vaguely guilty for trying to avoid rather than cope with reality, and are dissatisfied and unhappy with their way of life.

Three key facets of the neurotic nucleus merit brief mention:

1. *Feelings of inadequacy and anxiety.* Neurotic individuals feel basically inadequate and insecure in a world they perceive as dangerous and hostile. Consequently, they see many everyday situations as threatening—situations that would not be so evaluated by most people. This "threat vulnerability" leads to a dread of competitive situations and a tendency to overreact to minor setbacks and failures. Even success may contribute to their underlying sense of inadequacy: a job promotion, for example, may raise fears that their "real lack of ability" will inevitably be exposed.

2. *Avoidance instead of coping.* Typically neurotic individuals develop a life-style characterized by defensive and avoidant behavior that enables them to escape somewhat from anxiety-arousing stress. For example, alleged physical ailments may provide an excuse for lack of competitive achievement, or irrational fears enable the person to avoid certain anxiety-arousing situations. However, their defenses are rarely adequate, and a considerable amount of anxiety usually remains. This anxiety may be augmented by the fact that such individuals often realize the irrationality of their own behavior.

3. *Self-defeating behavior and blocked personal growth.* In essence, neurotic individuals are enmeshed in a quagmire of "covering up," defending, escaping, and avoiding—a coping pattern that inevitably leads to rigid, egocentric, and self-defeating behavior. Since they often feel that they are fighting for their very lives in a hostile and threatening world, their main energies are focused on clinging rigidly to the defenses they have been able to

erect; it is not surprising that they have no time or energy for concern for others. This lack of both flexibility and concern for others, in turn, usually plays havoc with their personal relationships, adding to their difficulties. In short, their life-style, together with the complications it creates, is not only self-defeating and maladaptive but tends to block their growth and fulfillment.

Usually neurotic individuals vaguely sense that something is missing, that they are not fulfilling themselves or leading a truly meaningful life. They live with feelings of futility and unhappiness and lack a sense of joy in living.

The neurotic paradox

Human beings tend to be highly pragmatic about doing what works and modifying behavior that is not meeting adjustive demands. Yet neurotic individuals cling to their established coping pattern despite the fact that it is ineffective and self-defeating and brings them continuing dissatisfaction and unhappiness. This puzzling situation is referred to as the *neurotic paradox.*

The neurotic paradox can be understood in terms of two basic patterns: (a) the immediate relief from anxiety that comes momentarily from avoidance of situations perceived as threatening; and (b) the continued and inappropriate perception of certain everyday situations as threatening. The defensive maneuver does bring short-term relief and thus is reinforced. But it prevents the individual from ever discovering whether the situation would in fact be manageable. The net effect of these two patterns is the tendency to maintain the neurotic behavior despite its self-defeating nature.

For example, let us take the case of an insecure young man who is very much in love and engaged to be married. His fiancée, however, abruptly breaks the engagement. He reacts with intense feelings of self-devaluation, anxiety, and depression, coupled with a considerable measure of hostility. Thereafter his behavior follows a new pattern. Whenever a relationship with a woman begins to get serious, he experiences anxiety and breaks it off. He has acquired a conditioned fear of close relationships with members of the opposite sex, and his anxiety and avoidance behavior do not permit him to try out the possibility that he might be more successful this time. Thus the fear and avoidance behavior are maintained because they are reinforced by reduction of anxiety. Moreover, his defensive behavior, based on the expectation of rejection, tends to ensure that he will in fact be rejected.

The basic pattern we are dealing with in the neuroses thus involves conditioned fears that render the individual particularly vulnerable to stressors with which most people can cope effectively. This vulnerability, in turn, leads to a causal chain of *stress —anxiety —avoidance— reinforcement*. Thus paradoxically, the neurotic avoidance is both self-defeating and self-perpetuating.

Keeping these observations in mind, we shall now turn to a discussion of the neurotic categories of anxiety disorders, somatoform disorders, and dissociative disorders.

Anxiety disorders

As we have seen, anxiety and the individual's efforts to control it are viewed as key factors in the development of neurotic problems. In the anxiety disorders, either of these two factors— that is, the anxiety itself or the individual's efforts to resist or defend against it—is the central feature of the clinical picture. Anxiety disorders are fairly common, and it is estimated that about 2 to 4 percent of the general population have at some time been diagnosed as having either a phobic disorder or some other anxiety disturbance.[1] Included in our discussion of anxiety disorders will be generalized anxiety disorder, obsessive-compulsive disorder, and phobic disorder.

Generalized anxiety disorder (anxiety states)

Although anxiety is a central feature of all the neurotic patterns, all but this one include

avoidance mechanisms that succeed to some extent in allaying the feelings of threat. Here, however, such mechanisms have not been perfected, and feelings of threat and anxiety are the central feature.

Generalized anxiety disorder is characterized by chronic (at least six months' duration) diffuse anxiety and apprehensiveness, which may be punctuated by recurring episodes of more acute, disabling anxiety. But since neither the chronic anxiety nor the acute anxiety attacks appear to stem from any particular threat, the pervasive anxiety is said to be "free-floating." While there are no data available on the incidence of generalized anxiety disorders per se, the experience of acute anxiety is one of the most common patterns of the neurotic disorders.

Clinical picture in generalized anxiety disorder. Individuals suffering from generalized anxiety disorder live in a relatively constant state of tension, worry, and diffuse uneasiness. They are oversensitive in interpersonal relationships, and frequently feel inadequate and depressed. Usually they have difficulty concentrating and making decisions, dreading to make a mistake. The high level of tension they experience is often reflected in strained postural movements, overreaction to sudden or unexpected stimuli, and continual nervous movements. Commonly, they complain of muscular tension, especially in the neck and upper shoulder region, chronic mild diarrhea, frequent urination, and sleep disturbances that include insomnia and nightmares. They perspire profusely and their palms are often clammy; they may show cardiovascular changes such as elevated blood pressure and increased pulse rate. They may experience breathlessness and heart palpitations for no apparent reason.

No matter how well things seem to be going, individuals with neurotic anxiety are chronically apprehensive and anxious. Their vague fears and fantasies—combined with their general sensitivity—keep them continually upset, uneasy, and discouraged. Not only do they have difficulty making decisions, but after decisions have been made they worry excessively over possible errors and unforeseen circumstances that may lead to disaster. The lengths to which they go to find things to worry about are remarkable; as fast as one cause for

[1]Incidence statistics relative to the various neurotic patterns are rough estimates based on cases diagnosed in clinics and hospitals. Sources for these estimates include APA (1979), Templer and Lester (1974), and Woodruff, Guze, and Clayton (1972).

208

People suffering from generalized anxiety disorder live in an almost continuous state of tension, worry, and vague uneasiness. Their condition may be manifested in a variety of ways, including moments in which they have difficulty concentrating and making decisions and anxiety attacks—periods of acute panic lasting anywhere from a few seconds to an hour or more in which they suffer severe physiological and psychological distress.

worry is removed, they find another, until relatives and friends lose patience with them (see HIGHLIGHT on page 210).

Even after going to bed, people who suffer from neurotic anxiety are not likely to find relief from their worries. Often they review each mistake, real or imagined, recent or remote. When they are not reviewing and regretting the events of the past, they are anticipating all the difficulties that may arise in the future. Then, after they have crossed and recrossed most of their past and future bridges and managed to fall asleep, they frequently have anxiety dreams—dreams of being choked, being shot, falling from high places, or being chased by

murderers, with the horrible sensation that their legs will move only in slow motion.

The persistent raised level of anxiety may be punctuated from time to time by acute *anxiety attacks*[2]—recurring periods of acute panic that last anywhere from a few seconds to an hour or more. Typically, these attacks come on suddenly, mount to high intensity, and then subside—all in the absence of any obvious cause, such as a life-threatening situation or physical exertion. Symptoms vary from one

[2]In the DSM-III classification, diagnosis of anxiety attack falls into "panic disorder," a subcategory of the anxiety disorders.

person to another, but they can include "palpitations, shortness of breath, profuse sweating, faintness and dizziness, coldness and pallor of the face and extremities, urge to urinate, gastric sensations and an ineffable feeling of imminent death" (Lader & Mathews, 1970, p. 377). The physiological symptoms, together with the sensation of impending death or catastrophe, make an anxiety attack a terrifying experience.

Usually the attack subsides after a few minutes. If it continues, the individual may frantically implore someone to summon a doctor. After medical treatment has been administered, commonly in the form of reassurance and a sedative, the person quiets down. Such attacks vary in frequency from several times a day to once a month or even less often. They may occur during the day, or the person may awaken from a sound sleep with a strong feeling of apprehension that rapidly develops into an attack. Between attacks the individual may appear to be relatively unperturbed, but mild anxiety and tension usually persist.

Many anxiety-neurotic individuals show mild depression as well as chronic anxiety (Prusoff & Klerman, 1974; Downing & Rickels, 1974). This finding is not unexpected in view of their generally gloomy outlook on the world. Nor is it surprising that excessive use of tranquilizing drugs, sleeping pills, and alcohol often complicates the clinical picture in anxiety neuroses.

Causal factors in generalized anxiety disorder. Anxiety reactions are considered normal when the stressful situation is sufficiently severe to justify them. In neurotic reactions the anxiety is considered pathological because it tends to be chronic and is elicited by stressors that the average individual handles without too much difficulty. Four kinds of causal factors appear relevant here.

1. *Modeling.* As we have seen in our discussion of faulty development, a tense and anxious parent can transmit anxiety to even a very young infant. If interactions with such a faulty parental model continue, the child may learn anxiety reactions similar to those of the parent. In his studies of the behavior disorders of children, Jenkins (1966, 1968, 1969) found that overanxious children tend to have neurotic mothers who are themselves anxious. As one

neurotic young adult expressed the problem in the course of psychotherapy, "I guess there is more of my overanxious neurotic mother in me than I had realized."

Jenkins (1968, 1969) also pointed out that anxiety-neurotic individuals often come from families in which parents place high expectations on their child while at the same time they reject his or her actual accomplishments as substandard. Children reared in such a setting often appear to adopt perfectionistic parental standards and to become self-critical and anxious about failure to meet these standards.

After ten years of very successful practice, a 34-year-old dentist noted that his practice had declined slightly during the closing months of the year. Shortly after this he began to experience mild anxiety attacks and complained of continual worry, difficulty in sleeping, and a vague dread that he was "failing." As a result, he increased his hours of practice during the evenings from one to five nights and began driving himself beyond all reason in a desperate effort to "insure the success of his practice." Although his dental practice now increased beyond what it had been previously, he found himself still haunted by the vague fears and apprehensions of failure. These, in turn, became further augmented by frequent heart palpitations and pains that he erroneously diagnosed as a heart ailment, incapacitating if not fatal. At this point his anxiety became so great that he voluntarily came to a clinic for assistance.

In the course of psychological diagnosis and treatment, it was revealed that the patient had had a history of early chronic emotional insecurity. No matter what his accomplishments, his parents rejected and belittled him. When he once proudly told them that the school counselor had informed him he had a very high IQ, the parents demanded to know why he didn't make better grades. He remembered occasionally receiving presents, such as a model airplane set, that were always beyond his age level so that his father would have to help him assemble the kit. Meanwhile a very high level of aspiration led him to keep trying desperately to accomplish something that would gain the parental support he so badly needed. Years later, despite the obvious evidence of success in his practice, his reaction to the slight decline was out of all proportion to the actual degree of threat and eventually led to a rather common form of anxiety reaction.

2. *Inability to handle "dangerous" impulses.* Anxiety-neurotic individuals are likely to experience intense anxiety in situations that elicit "dangerous" feelings—feelings they think they should not have. The handling of

Fantasies of anticipated harm in anxiety neuroses

In a study of 32 anxiety-neurotic individuals, Beck, Laude, and Bohnert (1974) found unrealistic expectations and fantasies of harm associated with these patients' heightened levels of anxiety and with anxiety attacks. The degree of anxiety was related to the severity of, and perceived likelihood of, the anticipated harm.

These expectations and fantasies centered around both physical and psychological dangers—such as being involved in an accident, becoming sick, being violently attacked, failing, and being humiliated or rejected by significant others. In this context, the following examples are instructive.

Patient	Fantasy of anticipated harm	Stimuli triggering anxiety
Physician Male, age 32	Fear of sudden death	Any gastrointestinal symptoms
Teacher Male, age 25	Fear of inability to function as a teacher and of ending up on skid row	Anticipation of giving lecture
Homemaker Female, age 30	Fear of physical catastrophe happening to member of family	Sirens, news of deaths, fires, accidents, etc.
Student Male, age 26	Fear of psychological harm, school failure, rejection by everyone, illness	Schoolwork, confrontation with people, any physical symptom
Laborer Male, age 35	Continuous visual fantasies of accident, fear of imminent death	Any noises that might suggest danger (e.g., traffic noises)
Psychologist Male, age 40	Fear of heart attack, cerebral hemorrhage, fainting in public and subsequent disgrace	Physical sensations in chest or abdomen, back pains, hearing about heart attacks
Artist Female, age 35	Fear of heart attacks	Exertion, anticipation of exertion, reading or hearing about heart attacks
Student Male, age 18	Fear of appearing foolish and subsequent rejection by others	Contact with or anticipated contact with others

Often the fantasies and images reported by a given patient were related to past personal experiences. For example, in the preceding cases, the homemaker had experienced the death of a close friend and the artist's mother had died of a heart attack. These investigators concluded that the expectations and fantasies of anxious patients "not only hold up mirrors to their psychopathology but provide entry points for treating it" (p. 325).

hostility, for example, is usually especially difficult for such an individual, who typically feels forced to take a compliant, subservient, self-suppressing attitude toward others as the price of security, love, and acceptance. This blocking of personal strivings, however, leads inevitably to strong feelings of aggression and hostility, yet it seems that these feelings must be controlled and denied at all costs to avoid possible rejection by others and to maintain the self-image of a worthy person. Repression thus appears to be the main defensive technique used by anxiety-neurotic individuals. But the repression is not complete, as evidenced by the continuing diffuse anxiety. Furthermore, repressed impulses and fears may find indirect means of expression. For example, repressed hostility may reveal itself in fantasies of killing or injuring other people, perhaps even someone the anxiety-neurotic individual loves or feels strongly dependent on for acceptance and security.

An 18-year-old male student developed severe anxiety attacks just before he went out on dates. In therapy it was revealed that he came from a very insecure home in which he was very much attached to an anxious, frustrated, and insecure mother. Intellectually capable and a good student, he had entered college at 16. But during his two years on campus he had difficulty getting dates, especially with college women of his choice. The student he had been dating recently, for example, would not make any arrangements to go out until after 6:00 P.M. of the same day, after her chances for a more preferable date seemed remote. This had increased his already strong feelings of inferiority and insecurity and had led to the development of intense hostility toward the opposite sex, mostly on an unconscious level.

About two months before coming to the college clinic for assistance, he had experienced the anxiety-arousing fantasy of choking the young woman to death when they were alone together. As he put it, "When we are alone in the car, I can't get my mind off her nice white throat and what it would be like to choke her to death." At first he put these thoughts out of his mind, but they returned on subsequent nights with increasing persistence. Then, to complicate the matter, he experienced his first acute anxiety attack. It occurred in his car on the way over to pick up his date and lasted for only a few minutes, but he was panic-stricken and thought that he was going to die. After that he experienced several additional attacks under the same conditions.

The relationship of the repressed hostility to the persistent fantasies and anxiety attacks seemed clear in this case. Yet it was not at all apparent to the young man, who was at a complete loss to explain either his fantasies or the anxiety attacks.

Similarly, repressed sexual desires may threaten to break through existing defenses and elicit intense anxiety. For example, a man may attempt to repress homosexual impulses that he considers immoral and incompatible with his self-concept. For a time the repression protects him, but repression is rarely—if ever—complete, and the individual is likely to experience periodic flare-ups of anxiety even though he may be unaware of the reason for them. In addition, some change in his life situation—perhaps a friendly relationship with a man he considers effeminate—may intensify his homosexual impulses, posing a major threat to his repressive defenses and eliciting intense anxiety.

3. *Anxiety-arousing decisions.* We have noted that individuals suffering from anxiety neurosis tend to have difficulty in making decisions. Under certain conditions—such as conflicts involving moral values or possible loss of security and status—acute anxiety and extreme indecision may occur.

Thomas G., a 44-year-old Protestant minister, upon discovery of his wife's infidelity, began to experience chronic anxiety and conflicts. He was quick to take the blame for the failure of the marriage, sure that his inattentiveness to the needs of his wife and children had driven her away. Yet he was angry at her for creating a public embarrassment for him. He was contemplating a divorce, but such an action would violate his convictions. He was also torn by the feeling that because his marriage had failed he had failed the church, too, and must resign from the ministry. But he loved his work so much that he could not imagine being without it.

During the week before he came for therapy, he had been unable to sleep, lying awake worrying about his problems. He could not eat and complained of a strong burning sensation in his stomach and feelings of being constantly choked up. He was unable to think clearly enough to prepare his sermon for Sunday or to follow through on several commitments he had made previously.

Mr. G.'s present stress only exaggerated problems he had had for many years. He reported that he had always been an insecure and dependent person who found a great deal of emotional support in the church and in his strong, independent wife. She was a "take charge" person who had always handled all their personal matters, including shopping for his clothes. Any thought of an end to either his marriage or his position with the church made him extremely anxious and insecure. But now it seemed that continuing in the marriage and in his current position would be intolerable.

In cases where the neurotically insecure person has achieved some degree of real success and consequently of security, anxiety attacks may develop when the proposed behavior jeopardizes this security.

A successful business executive developed acute anxiety attacks about once every two or three months. His wife was eight years older than he, and he was no longer physically attracted to her. He had found himself increasingly interested in younger women and had begun to think how much more enjoyable it would be to have a younger, more companionable wife. During this period he met a woman with whom he was sure he had fallen in love. It was shortly thereafter that the anxiety attacks began to occur. They were preceded by a period of several days of increased tenseness and anxiety, but the attacks came on suddenly and were intense.

This man, too, was at a complete loss to explain his attacks. But the explanation was not difficult to find. He had had a poverty-stricken and insecure childhood and felt basically inferior, insecure, and threatened by a harsh world. These feelings had been intensified when he had failed college courses in his

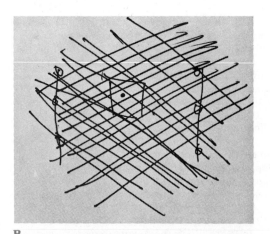

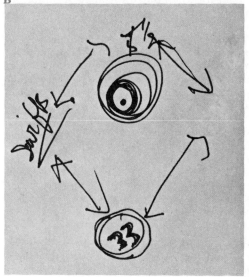

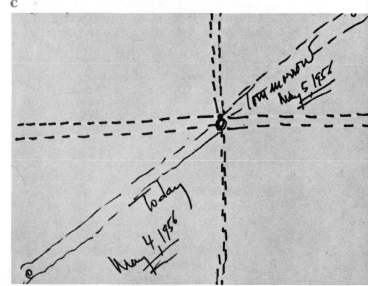

Drawing is often considered a primitive but effective method of communicating one's inner thoughts and feelings. Of course, the therapist must exercise caution to avoid misinterpretation. The four pictures shown here were drawn by a woman assessed as suffering from an acute anxiety disorder. Although she was a successful businesswoman, having risen progressively through jobs of greater and greater responsibility, she felt herself incapable of achieving further advancement—that she had "reached the end of the line." Subsequently, she experienced feelings of frustration, inadequacy, and anxiety.

Sketch A was drawn hurriedly under great tension. The smoking buildings on the left represent New York City, the woman's place of employment, and the buildings on the right, her desired place of employment. Separating the two is the middle structure, which contains the "aggressive, agitated figures of her male competitors in the business world."

In Sketch B, the woman appeared to represent herself in a cage by the boxed-in dot. She then partially blotted out the crude diagram "by rapidly placed crosshatching, as though to deny the admission that she found herself so trapped."

Sketch C appears to represent "the merry-go-round on which she has been moving, from one firm to another, around and around, always seeking advancement, without finding any satisfying fulfillment." Finally, Sketch D indicates her anxiety over her present dilemma—"What road today? What road tomorrow?" (Adapted from Brown, 1957, pp. 171–74)

second year, even though the failure had resulted primarily from excessive outside work. He had been able to achieve some security, however, by marrying a strong, older woman who had instilled considerable self-confidence and initiative in him. The relationship had proved very fruitful financially, and the man was living in a style which, as a youth, "I hadn't dared to imagine in my wildest dreams!" His persistent thoughts about divorcing his wife, on whom he felt dependent for his security and style of life, thus represented a severe threat to the moderately successful adjustment he had been able to achieve. The anxiety attacks followed.

Life often poses problems in which the pursuit of increased satisfactions involves giving up present hard-won security and taking new risks. For the anxiety-neurotic person, this is likely to prove a difficult and anxiety-arousing conflict situation.

4. *Reactivation of prior trauma.* A stressful situation that parallels some earlier trauma may elicit intense anxiety in an individual who is basically insecure. The following reactions are those of a man who sought treatment after being absent from his job for three days as a result of "sickness."

"I've just reached the point where I can't go on. Got no fight left. And not enough guts to end it here. Best damn job I ever had. Almost can see my way out of debt. And it's all going to hell, and I'm getting so I don't care about anything, except not going back to work. I can't kid myself, I just can't take it anymore. And I'll have to confess I have no faith left in anything including your profession. Or faith in myself. Maybe if I can tell someone how I feel, how balled up I am, I can see the light. I can't afford to take time off work. I can't afford to relax a couple of weeks on some warm beach, or forget my troubles with some floozy blonde. Hell, that's for the books on the best seller's lists. I've just got to go about acting like my normal stupid self and something's got to blow. It goes in waves. Sometimes, I'm alright and then I get anxiety feelings, and my heart pounds. I get to shaking all over, and think I'm going to die. God, it's awful!"

Interestingly enough, the primary cause of the intense anxiety reactions in this case was found to be associated with a new and rather critical supervisor at work. In response to criticisms from the supervisor that may have annoyed but did not completely disrupt the behavior of other employees, this man became anxious and depressed. His reaction was traced to his relationship with his father, who had died some five years before. From his

earliest memory, the patient had idolized his father and had practically lived for occasional hard-won compliments from him. Conversely, when his father had criticized him, the patient had been so upset that he would go to his room completely distraught and cry for hours at a time. Now, as an adult, this dependent, insecure individual experienced these same feelings of distress when criticized by an exacting supervisor. Apparently the new supervisor had reactivated an old "weak spot" and thus precipitated the anxiety reaction.

Although we have emphasized the inadequacy, oversensitivity, and low stress tolerance of individuals suffering from anxiety disorders, it may be pointed out that they often put up a good battle in view of their faulty evaluations of themselves and their environment. As Portnoy (1959) has pointed out: "To the picture of an anxious individual apprehensively coping with life in the face of inner and outer dangers must also be added the picture of a human being with courage, able to endure this much anxiety without the more massive defenses and character distortions which characterize the other psychiatric syndromes" (p. 320). And as we have noted in our discussion of combat reactions, some anxiety-prone individuals can function effectively when confronted with an actual danger that both demands and permits definitive action.

Aspects of treatment. Individuals suffering from anxiety disorders often find some relief in mild tranquilizers, although such medication is not likely to modify their basic lifestyle. Psychotherapy is typically directed at helping them discriminate between real and imagined dangers, learn more effective methods of coping, and modify conditions in their life situation that are serving to maintain the maladaptive behavior. They usually respond well to treatment, although it appears that their chronic anxiety is seldom completely removed. But as we shall see in the general section on treatment, newer therapeutic innovations are providing a brighter picture concerning the outcome of treatment.

Obsessive-compulsive disorder

In obsessive-compulsive disorders, individuals feel compelled to think about something that

One of the most famous manifestations of obsessive-compulsive behavior in English literature is the continuous hand-washing of Lady Macbeth.

they do not want to think about or to carry out some action against their will. These individuals usually realize that their behavior is irrational but cannot seem to control it.

The incidence of obsessive-compulsive disorders has been variously estimated to be from about 12 to 20 percent of the anxiety disorders. Age and sex differences have not been systematically studied.

Clinical picture in obsessive-compulsive disorder. As Nemiah (1967) has pointed out, obsessive-compulsive behaviors cover a wide range:

"The phenomena may be manifested psychically or behaviorally; they may be experienced as ideas or as impulses; they may refer to events anticipated in the future or actions already completed; they may express desires and wishes or protective measures against such desires; they may be simple, uncomplicated acts and ideas or elaborate, ritualized patterns of thinking and behavior. . . . " (p. 916)

Most of us have experienced minor obsessional thoughts, such as persistent thoughts about a coming trip or date, or a haunting melody that we cannot seem to get out of our minds. In the case of obsessive reactions, however, the thoughts are much more persistent, appear irrational to the individual, and interfere considerably with everyday behavior.

Neurotic-obsessive thoughts may center around a wide variety of topics, such as concern over bodily functions, committing immoral acts, attempting suicide, or even finding the solution to some seemingly unsolvable problem. Particularly common are obsessive thoughts of committing some immoral act. A wife may be obsessed with the idea of poisoning her husband, a daughter with the thought of pushing her mother down a flight of stairs (see HIGHLIGHT on page 215).

Even though obsessive thoughts are usually not carried out in action, they remain a source of torment to the individual. This pattern is well illustrated in a classic case described by Kraines (1948) of a woman who

"complained of having 'terrible thoughts.' When she thought of her boyfriend she wished he were dead; when her mother went down the stairs, she 'wished she'd fall and break her neck'; when her sister spoke of going to the beach with her infant daughter, the patient 'hoped that they would both drown.' These thoughts 'make me hysterical. I love them; why should I wish such terrible things to happen? It drives me wild, makes me feel I'm crazy and don't belong to society; maybe it's best for me to end it all than to go on thinking such terrible things about those I love.'" (p. 183)

As in the case of obsessive thoughts, most of us show some compulsive behavior—stepping over cracks in sidewalks, walking around ladders instead of under them, or turning away when a black cat crosses our path—but without the degree of compulsiveness of the neurotic individual. Most of us also resort to minor obsessive-compulsive patterns under severe pressure or when trying to achieve goals that

Obsessions of infanticide

Obsessions of infanticide—the murder of a newborn or preadolescent child—were a central clinical feature in 44 of 1317 consecutive patients at the University of Kansas Medical Center. Thirty-eight of these patients were women; 6 were men. Of the patients, 17 were diagnosed as schizophrenic—all of the male patients were so considered—and were characterized by bizarre and paranoid ideation; 11 were diagnosed as depressive even though they evidenced both depressive and obsessional ideation; and 7 were diagnosed as suffering from obsessive-compulsive neurosis.

Interestingly enough, in the latter group "the obsessional thoughts were typically experienced not so much as an impulse to harm the child but as an apprehension that such an impulse might occur and be uncontrollably acted upon" (p. 238). These patients then viewed the child as an object to be avoided if possible, for fear they would harm him. At the same time they expressed feelings of guilt and self-devaluation often reflected in statements such as "I'm not a good mother" (p. 238). Eventually the situation became so anxiety arousing that the patients sought hospitalization.

The following excerpt was written spontaneously by a 32-year-old mother and was considered typical of these obsessive-compulsive patients:

"When I found out I was pregnant I did not want the baby because of all my physical problems and my nervousness. I felt I wasn't equipped to handle another child just then, but I didn't and wouldn't do anything to harm the baby I was carrying. And I seemed in time to become adjusted to my pregnancy. The premature arrival of the baby upset me because I had lost three premature babies. When he had trouble the first few days of life, my fears for him were great. He was in the hospital three weeks. When it was time to go home, I became very tense and fearful of caring well for him. . . . He was home for six weeks and then became (severely) ill with bronchitis. (This) lasted nine days. During this illness my fears, my appetite loss, and the bad dreams all began. I felt I had failed in my care as a mother. Since bringing him home (the second time) I notice that I can't feel tender or relaxed or loving as I want to, and I do everything automatically." (p. 238)

This mother, like the other obsessive-compulsive patients, felt fearful of impending loss of control and the inadvertent acting out of her fantasies of infanticide.

In contrast to the neurotic group, the clinical picture in the psychotic group was dominated by actual impulses to harm the child which might well have been acted on.

Based on Button and Reivich (1972).

we consider of critical importance. Many historical figures have shown an "obsessive-compulsive" adherence to their goals despite discouragement and ridicule: Columbus persisted for 18 years in his efforts to secure financial backing for his expedition to "India," and Darwin assembled evidence for 22 years before he would present his ideas on evolution.

In neurotic-compulsive disorders, people feel compelled to perform some act which seems strange and absurd to them and which they do not want to perform. Such compulsive acts may vary from relatively mild ritual-like behavior, such as making the sign of the cross periodically during the day, to more extreme behavior, such as washing one's hands as often as ten times each hour. The performance of the compulsive act usually brings a feeling of reduced tension and satisfaction (Carr, 1974; Hodgson & Rachman, 1972). On the other hand, anxiety mounts if the person tries to resist the compulsion.

An obsessive-compulsive disorder is considered maladaptive because it represents irrational and exaggerated behavior in the face of stressors that are not unduly upsetting to most people, and because such patterns reduce the flexibility of behavior and the capability for self-direction. In general, such behavior takes place in the context of a personality characterized by feelings of inadequacy and insecurity, rigid conscience development, a tendency toward feelings of guilt, and high vulnerability to threat.

Causal factors in obsessive-compulsive disorder.

Either the obsessive thoughts or the compulsive actions may predominate in a given case, but both are parts of a total reaction pattern, and their causes are essentially the same. Several patterns have been delineated.[3]

1. *Substitutive thoughts and activities.* Sometimes individuals who suffer from an obsessive-compulsive disorder defend themselves from anxiety by persistently thinking of or doing something else each time threatening thoughts or impulses make their appearance. A fearful person walking in a lonely place late at night might have the following continually persisting thought: "There is nothing to be afraid of—I am not afraid." In this way the individual attempts to allay the underlying fear. In essence, "safe" obsessive thoughts are substituted for more unpleasant or dangerous ones.

The same causal pattern may underlie compulsive preoccupation with some activity, such as working on a new invention, writing the "truly great" novel, or developing a system to beat the horses. The task may never be completed, but by working on it so hard the individual is kept too busy to deal with unpleasant problems and is too engrossed to think disturbing thoughts. In many cases the compulsive behavior may, of course, be directed toward a constructive task. It is judged neurotically compulsive if it is used as an escape from marital, sexual, interpersonal, or other problems, and if it interferes with effective living.

In some instances, substitutive thoughts may be more complicated, and may involve the defense mechanism of *reaction formation*. Here the individual may think or act in ways directly contradictory to the dangerous thoughts or impulses. For example, a prisoner may repress dangerous thoughts about killing a hated guard and persistently think about "brotherly love."

[3]Obsessive thoughts and compulsive actions may, of course, occur as part of other clinical syndromes. Masserman (1961) has cited the case of a soldier who in an acute fatigue state kept throwing out his arms in a peculiar gesture. This gesture could not be explained until the patient recalled under narcosis (a drug-induced state of relaxation) that in the heat and excitement of a night battle, he had machine-gunned a friend, and had suffered a remorse so great that he had an overpowering desire to throw away his gun and run blindly from the unbearable horror of the situation. In our later discussion of psychotic disorders, we shall see how obsessive-compulsive disorders may be related to delusional and hallucinatory behavior.

Obsessive fantasies may also help satisfy repressed desires and provide a substitute for overt action.

A farmer developed obsessive thoughts of hitting his three-year-old son over the head with a hammer. The father was completely unable to explain his "horrible thoughts." He stated that he loved his son very much and thought he must be going insane to harbor such thoughts. In the treatment of this case it was revealed that the patient's wife had suffered great pain in childbirth and had since refused sexual relations with him for fear of again becoming pregnant. In addition, she lavished most of her attention on the son, and their previously happy marriage was now torn with quarreling and bickering.

The farmer's obsessive thoughts of violence toward his son had apparently developed out of a combination of repressed hostility toward the boy, who had replaced him in his wife's affection, and wishful thinking in the direction of a return to his previously happy marital state, once the son was out of the way. However, the man vigorously and sincerely denied this explanation when it was suggested to him. Because his fantasies were lacking in affect, they did not seem to him to represent his real feelings at all; at the same time, they permitted expression of his hostility without any attendant feelings of guilt. Of course, not all individuals with obsessive thoughts of violence toward loved ones escape guilt feelings.

2. *Guilt and fear of punishment.* Obsessive-compulsive behavior often seems to stem from feelings of guilt and self-condemnation. Lady Macbeth's symbolic handwashing after her participation in the bloody murder of King Duncan is a well-known literary example of ritualistic behavior aimed at the cleansing of guilt for immoral behavior. In the following case, the development of obsessive-compulsive patterns seems to be associated with a belief that "unforgivable" behavior will inevitably be punished.

A 32-year-old high-school cooking teacher developed marked feelings of guilt and uneasiness, accompanied by obsessive fears of hurting others by touching them or by their handling something she had touched. She dreaded to have anyone eat anything she had prepared, and if students in her cooking class were absent, she was certain they had been poisoned by her cooking. In addition, she developed the obsessive notion that a rash at the base of her scalp was a manifestation of syphilis, which would gnaw at her brain and make a "drooling idiot" of her.

Accompanying the obsessive fears were compulsions consisting primarily of repeated hand-washings and frequent returns to some act already performed to reassure herself that the act had been done right, such as turning off the gas or water.

In treatment the patient was self-centered but highly sensitive and conscientious. She had graduated from college with honors and considered herself highly intelligent. About three years before her present difficulties she had married a noncollege man of whom she had been very much ashamed because of his poor English, table manners, and other characteristics which she thought led to a very poor social showing. As a result, she had rejected him in her thinking and behavior and had treated him in what she now considered a very cruel manner. On one occasion she had also been unfaithful to him, which was directly opposed to her moral training.

Over a period of time, however, she came to realize that he was a very fine person and that other people thought highly of him despite his lack of social polish. In addition, she gradually came to the realization that she was very much in love with him. At this point she began to reproach herself for her cruel treatment of him. She felt that he was a truly wonderful husband, and that she was completely unworthy of him. She was sure her past cruelty and unfaithfulness could never be forgiven. "Heaven knows that every word he says is worth fifty words I say. If I were real honest and truthful I would tell my husband to leave me."

This woman's obsessive fear of contaminating other people and of having syphilis apparently grew out of a feeling that her past "sins" had caught up with her. They also served the function of protecting her from acting upon her occasionally returning desire for sexual relations with other men.

In some instances the individual may attempt to counteract forbidden desires or be cleansed of guilt by means of compulsive rituals. For example, a high-school senior's hostile fantasies toward her domineering mother were so acutely traumatic that she repressed them. However, this repression proved to be a precarious defense, and the dangerous hostility threatened to break through into consciousness. As a result, the patient developed a compulsive defensive ritual: at crucial moments she felt compelled to make the sign of the cross, repeating "God protect my dearly beloved mother." Yet she had not the vaguest idea why she had to perform this action. It seemed sense-

less and silly to her and was interfering with her classwork and social relationships.

3. *Assurance of order and predictability.* A rigid ordering of behavior can be temporarily adaptive in a particularly difficult situation. The autobiographical accounts of Admiral Richard Byrd, who spent 6 solitary months in the antarctic, and of Dr. Alain Bombard, who sailed alone across the Atlantic for 65 days on a life raft (see page 95), show that the two men—dedicated scientists—reacted to their isolation and loneliness in almost identical ways.

"Both explorers found that while their lives were threatened daily by the hazards of their milieu, it was the constancy of their surroundings which seemed like a force which would destroy them. Both men felt that they could control themselves and their environment only by thoroughly organizing their days, assigning themselves to a strict routine of work, and spending no more than one hour at a time doing a task. In this way, each felt he proved to himself that he could control both himself and his environment. . . . Both men used the same mechanisms to fight off depression: controlling their thoughts, dwelling only on pleasant past associations and experiences and refusing to allow themselves to think about the anxiety-producing aspects of their situations." (Solomon et al., 1957)

Similarly, the neurotic-compulsive individual, confronted with a world that seems highly dangerous, may attempt to maintain some semblance of order and control by becoming unduly meticulous and methodical. A rigid pattern of behavior helps prevent anything from going wrong, and hence provides some security and predictability. But if the slightest detail gets out of order, the entire defensive structure is endangered and the individual feels threatened and anxious.

A case that illustrates this pattern is that of a patient who, prior to hospitalization, had had his life ordered in the most minute detail. He arose in the morning precisely at 6:50, took a shower, shaved, and dressed. His wife had breakfast ready precisely at 7:10 and followed a menu that he worked out months in advance. At exactly 7:45 he left for the office where he worked as an accountant. He came home precisely at 5:55, washed, then read the evening paper, and had dinner precisely at 6:30, again as per menu. His schedule was equally well worked out for evenings and weekends, with a movie on Tuesday, reading on Wednesday, rest on Monday and

Thursday, and bridge on Friday. Saturday morning he played golf and Sunday morning and evening he attended church. Saturday evening usually involved having guests or visiting others. He was fastidious in his dress. Each shirt had to be clean and unwrinkled, his suit pressed every two days, and so on. His demands, of course, also included his wife, who was inclined to be easy-going and was upset when he "blew up" at the smallest variation from established routine.

By means of his carefully ordered existence the patient had managed to make a reasonably successful adjustment until he became involved in a business deal with a friend and lost a considerable sum of money. This proved too much for him and precipitated a severe anxiety reaction with considerable agitation and depression, necessitating hospitalization.

In this case the individual's primary means of defense against *external* threats was to try to impose rigid order, thus making the world safer and more predictable. By such a compulsive adherence to a daily routine, particularly a socially desirable and ethical one, an individual may also establish automatic control over dangerous inner desires. Situations that might stimulate such desires or permit their expression are thereby avoided.

In a general sense, this pattern seems similar to the repetitive and rigid rituals long used by people of early or underdeveloped civilizations as a means of warding off evil forces in an unpredictable world. To be effective, such rituals must be faithfully observed and performed in rigidly prescribed ways.

Aspects of treatment. Therapy in obsessive-compulsive disorders tends to follow three basic strategies: (a) helping the individual to discriminate between thought and action, to accept "forbidden" desires as common to most people, and to integrate them into his or her self-structure; (b) helping the individual to discriminate between objective and imagined dangers and to respond selectively to each; and (c) blocking obsessive-compulsive rituals by consistently rewarding departures from such neurotic behavior. All these strategies are aimed at eliminating neurotic defenses and helping the individual realize that catastrophe does not follow their removal.

Although changing a person's basic obsessive-compulsive life-style is not always possible, therapy does ordinarily lead to a marked alleviation of symptoms and paves the way for long-range improvement. The following case represents the nature and outcome of treatment in one rather typical case.

A middle-aged married woman had the compulsion to shake every article of her own clothes and those of her children. The shaking ritual—which occupied over an hour of her time each morning—required that each piece of clothing be shaken three times in each of three different directions and at each of three different levels. In addition, most of the clothes had to be brushed inside and out; whenever anything was washed, it had to be washed three times. The woman also found it difficult to stop washing her hands once she had started and repeatedly felt a compulsion to rub her hands together in each of three different ways.

Interview assessment indicated that much of the woman's compulsive behavior was associated with vague fears of germs and disease. A treatment program was formulated that (a) helped her discriminate between stimuli that were objectively "dirty" and unhygienic and those that were not—thus eliminating unnecessary fears and helping her make realistic decisions about standards of cleanliness; (b) consistently reinforced her behavior when she abandoned her compulsive rituals; and (c) utilized verbal instructions by the therapist to prevent their repetition whenever possible.

Therapy began in February, and by November of the same year the woman's ritualistic behavior had been completely eliminated. She was able to make her own decisions about cleaning and washing and was more confident about her standards of cleanliness. (Adapted from Mather, 1970)

Phobic disorder

A phobia is a persistent fear of some object or situation that presents no actual danger to the person or in which the danger is magnified out of all proportion to its actual seriousness. The following list of the common phobias and their objects will give some hint of the variety of situations and events around which phobias may be centered:

Acrophobia—high places
Agoraphobia—open places
Algophobia—pain
Astraphobia—storms, thunder, and lightning
Claustrophobia—closed places
Hematophobia—blood
Mysophobia—contamination or germs
Monophobia—being alone

Nyctophobia—darkness
Ocholophobia—crowds
Pathophobia—disease
Pyrophobia—fire
Syphilophobia—syphilis
Zoophobia—animals or some particular animal

Some of these phobias involve an exaggerated fear of things that most of us fear to some extent, such as darkness, fires, disease, and snakes. Others, such as phobias of open places or crowds, involve situations that do not elicit fear in most people. In many cases people develop particular phobias that are not part of a neurotic pattern; this is the case with most snake phobias.

Based on a survey of a Vermont community, Agras, Sylvester, and Oliveau (1969) estimated the overall presence of phobic individuals in the general population to be 7.7 percent, though only .2 percent of the population were bothered by severely disabling phobias.

Phobic disorder occurs more commonly among adolescents and young adults than among older people. It is also more frequently diagnosed in females than in males, possibly because strong fears have traditionally been more compatible with female roles than with male roles in our society.

Clinical picture in phobic disorder.
Most of us have minor irrational fears, but in phobic disorders such fears are intense and interfere with everyday activities. For example, phobic individuals may go to great lengths to avoid entering a small room or passageway, even when it is essential for them to do so. People who suffer from phobias usually admit that they have no real cause to be afraid of the object or situation, but say they cannot help themselves. If they attempt to approach rather than avoid the phobic situation they are overcome with anxiety, which may vary from mild feelings of uneasiness and distress to a full-fledged anxiety attack.

Phobic individuals usually show a wide range of other symptoms in addition to their phobias, such as tension headaches, back pains, stomach upsets, dizzy spells, and fear of "cracking up." At times of more acute panic, such individuals often complain of feelings of unreality, of strangeness, and of "not being themselves." Feelings of depression frequently accompany phobias, and many patients report serious interpersonal difficulties that are producing problems for them. In some instances, they also have serious difficulty in making decisions—a condition that Kaufman (1973) somewhat facetiously called *decidophobia*.

The particular phobias that develop are often influenced by cultural factors. For example, a phobia of flying would not likely have become common until we entered the age of commercial air travel. In some cases, phobic reactions may also be obsessive, as when a persistent obsessive fear of contamination dominates the neurotic's consciousness.

Causal factors in phobic disorder.
Phobias may occur in a wide range of personality patterns and abnormal syndromes, reflecting the part that anxiety and avoidance play in many manifestations of abnormal behavior. In general, phobias have been thought of as attempts to cope with specific internal or external dangers by careful avoidance of situations likely to bring about whatever is feared. Recently the focus has shifted from specific phobias to the more general role of phobias in an overall neurotic life-style of defensive and avoidant behaviors.

Three major causal patterns have been emphasized in the development of phobias: conditioning and avoidance learning, defense against threatening impulses, and the displacement of anxiety.

1. *Conditioning and avoidance learning.* As we saw in Watson's case of "little Albert" —who was conditioned to fear a white rat—a phobia may be the learned result of prior trauma in the feared situation. And this fear, as happened in the case of little Albert, may generalize to similar situations.

Phobias of this type are not difficult to understand because most of us probably have mild phobias based on previous learning. A person who has been attacked and bitten by a vicious dog may feel uneasy around dogs, even though some reconditioning experiences have intervened. A pervasive pattern of fear and avoidance behavior can be learned in much the same way. For example, if a little girl's fumbling attempts to master new skills are ridiculed by her parents, or if she is discouraged from becoming independent, she may never develop the confidence she needs to cope with

Common situations that elicit phobias include closed spaces, heights, and crowds.

new situations. In effect, she learns that avoidance is the "appropriate" response to risk or uncertainty.

In addition, a phobia may generalize to a fear of situations only minimally related to the basic trauma.

An 18-year-old woman had been given strict "moral" training concerning the evils of sex, and she associated sexual relations with vivid ideas of sin, guilt, and hell. This basic orientation was reinforced when she was beaten and sexually attacked by a young man on her fifteenth birthday. Nevertheless, when the young man she was dating kissed her and "held her close," it aroused intense sexual desires—which were extremely guilt arousing and which led to a chain of avoidance behaviors. First she stopped seeing him in an effort to get rid of her "immoral" thoughts; then she stopped all dating; then she began to feel uncomfortable with any young man she knew; and finally she became fearful of any social situations where men might be present. At this point her life was largely dominated by her phobias, and she was so "completely miserable" that she requested professional help.

The role of classical conditioning in the development of most phobias remains unclear, since few phobias and obsessions can actually be traced to a specific traumatic event in the person's life. Although similarities can be noted between avoidance learning in animal studies and in the appearance of phobias in humans (Marks, 1977), the processes by which phobias are acquired do not seem to follow a simple S–R model. In many cases, the phobic response appears more powerful or longer lasting than a conditioned stimulus would elicit. Eysenck (1976) suggests abandoning the idea of a single-trial conditioning in favor of a model that includes incubation or enhancement effects.

2. *Defense against threatening impulses.* A phobia may represent a defensive reaction that protects the individual from situations in which repressed aggressive or sexual impulses might become dangerous. Thus a husband may develop a phobia of lakes, swimming pools, and other bodies of water because on previous occasions he had persistent ideas of drowning his wife; similarly, a young mother may develop a phobia of being alone with her unwanted baby because of recurring fantasies about strangling him.

3. *Displacement of anxiety.* A phobia may represent a displacement of anxiety from a threat that originally elicited it to some other object or situation. This concept is strongly emphasized in the psychoanalytic perspective and stems largely from Freud's case history of little Hans, published in 1909.

According to Freudian theory, a small boy desires to possess his mother sexually and is jealous and hostile toward his father. He therefore fears his father—and in particular dreads being castrated. This fear of the avenging father may then be displaced to some external and formerly innocuous object. In the case of 5-year-old Hans, the horse pulling the carriage in which he and his mother were riding fell down and was hurt. Hans had become very frightened, and according to Freud this dramatic situation led to the displacement of his fear of castration by his father to a fear of being bitten by horses. Freud concluded that phobias represent displaced anxiety associated with the Oedipus complex (see p. 56) and thus develop only in people with disturbed psychosexual development.

Later investigators have disagreed with Freud's interpretation of little Hans' phobia, and have pointed out that many kinds of stressful situations may lead to phobic reactions through the mechanism of displacement. For example, a basically insecure person who feels that he may be discharged from his job for inefficiency may develop an elevator phobia. Since he works in an office on the fortieth floor of a large building, this makes it impossible for him to get to work—which in turn protects him from the possible embarrassment and self-devaluation of being fired.

Regardless of how it begins, phobic behavior tends to be reinforced by the reduction in anxiety that occurs each time the individual avoids the feared situation or stressor. In addition, phobias may be maintained in part by secondary gains, such as increased attention, sympathy, and some control over the behavior of others. For example, a phobia of driving may enable a homemaker to escape from responsibilities outside the home, such as shopping or transporting her children to and from school.

Aspects of treatment. Newer methods of behavior therapy have proven highly effective in the treatment of specific phobias as well as more extensive phobic disorders; consequently, it is rarely necessary for the individual to continue to suffer the personal distress occasioned by phobic behaviors. Usually one of two basic strategies is followed in treatment. The first—based on the assumption that phobias are symbolic representations of what was originally feared—focuses on helping the patient understand the phobia and learn more effective techniques for coping with the anxiety and with the feared situation. However, this approach has not proven very effective. As Salzman has pointed out,

"It has been known for some time that understanding, alone, is ineffectual in resolving the phobic state. It is a commonplace that, while the patient may have adequate insight into the origin, symbolism, and function of his phobia, he is still unable to risk the initial venture into the heretofore out-of-bounds area of living." (1968, pp. 464–65)

Consequently, the second major strategy, involving desensitization and other behavior-modification techniques, is being increasingly used to deal directly with the hierarchy of fears and avoidance behaviors. For example, the woman described on page 221, who had become fearful of any situation where men might be present, was first taught to relax while imagining herself in a social situation in which men were present. Next, she was encouraged to attend such a gathering, and found herself able to do so without experiencing the usual fear. Treatment then proceeded through each step of the fear hierarchy until she could behave normally in heterosexual relationships. For a more detailed look at the treatment of an individual with multiple phobias, see the HIGHLIGHT on this page.

Other behavior-modification techniques that can be used in the treatment of phobias will be dealt with later. Here it may be pointed out that the successful treatment of phobias may lead to changes in the patient's entire life-style. This is well brought out in a case cited by Bandura, Blanchard, and Ritter (1969), in which the individual had been successfully treated for a fear of snakes.

"My success in gradually overcoming this fear of snakes has contributed to a greater feeling of confidence generally in my abilities to overcome any other problem which may arise. I have more faith in myself." (p. 197)

HIGHLIGHT

Treatment of a patient with multiple phobias by a desensitization technique using imagery

Frankel (1970) has reported on the treatment of a 26-year-old married woman who suffered from disabling fears of sexual relations, earthquakes, and enclosed places. The background of the case, the treatment procedure, and the outcome are summarized below.

Symptoms

1. The sexual fear. The woman reported that she had been able to have sexual relations with her husband only about 10 times in their 3 years of marriage. Her sexual phobia appeared to have a learned basis. She had been molested by an older male at age 5, had been raped by a gang of juvenile delinquents when she was 15, had been "pawed" by intoxicated male visitors of her divorced mother, and had had sexual relations with 3 men prior to her marriage—each of whom had professed love for her but stopped seeing her after the sexual contact. In an effort to "hold her husband" she had had sexual relations with him a few times, but she always had a "cold feeling, like I'm going to suffocate—like I can't breathe" during sexual relations. In the third month of marriage, the couple conceived a son, after whose birth they had sexual relations only twice.

2. The earthquake fear. The woman stated that several times a day her thoughts were occupied by an uncontrollable fear of being in an earthquake. Her sequence of thoughts was always the same. First she would imagine that the ground was shaking and the house rocking, and that she rushed to pick up the baby. She would next imagine herself standing in a doorway, with the house collapsing around her. At this point the anxiety would become "unbearable." The recurrent thoughts about being in an earthquake were especially prominent when she tried to go to sleep, with the result that she was physically tired, irritable, and anxious during the day. Although a physician had prescribed tranquilizers, she reported that they did not help. On several occasions, she had arisen during the night, picked up her son, and rushed to a doorway. Interestingly enough, she had never been in an earthquake, nor did she personally know anyone who had.

3. Fear of closed places. The woman reported that she had always been fearful of elevators, small rooms, and even being surrounded by people. However, she did not recall ever being locked up in a small enclosure, and did not know anyone who had. She would climb many flights of stairs rather than take an elevator. Just prior to seeking therapy, she had been caught up in a large crowd greeting a visiting dignitary. She reported feeling anxiety, panic, and fear of suffocation. She screamed and pushed people out of the way until she was able to flee.

Treatment

Since the woman's most disabling fear was that of earthquakes, it was decided to treat that fear first, then the fear of sexual relations, and finally the fear of enclosed places. The treatment procedure employed was a variation of implosive therapy, in which the woman was instructed to proceed through sequences of thoughts and images of herself in the fear-producing situation.

"The implosive technique raises the client's anxiety level and maintains it until it passes a peak and begins to decline. This reduction in anxiety is seen as the beginning of extinction of the fear response, but it also may be seen as providing the occasion for reinforcement for the toleration of a high degree of anxiety. That is, the ability to proceed through an imagery sequence which elicits high anxiety is itself reinforced first by success in sustaining anxiety and then by mastery implied by its reduction." (p. 497)

Thus, whenever the woman became "too upset to go on"—a point at which she had previously put the imagery "out of her mind"—she was encouraged to continue with the description of her imagery and her feelings toward it. For example, in the earthquake sequence where she imagined that the house was collapsing around her as she stood in the doorway with her son, she was asked such questions as "What's happening now?" "What's happening next?"

"The content produced by the client involved the house collapsing on her, her son trapped under her as large beams fell on her, the earthquake finally ending, her being pinned under beams and being unable to move, screaming for help for several hours with no one coming to her aid, and finally being able to move a beam, stand up, walk away from the rubble, and breathe a sigh of relief at being alive and unharmed." (p. 498)

The imagery sequences lasted from 15 to 30 minutes, and the remainder of each 50-minute therapy session centered on the discussion of the vividness of the imagery sequences and the feelings they elicited. Since the woman could come in only once a week for therapy, she was instructed to proceed along the entire imagery sequence on her own whenever the fear of earthquakes entered her thoughts. She was instructed not to put the thoughts "out of her mind" under any circumstances. This treatment was continued until the fear of earthquakes no longer troubled her. A similar procedure was used in dealing with her sexual fear and her fear of enclosed places.

Outcome

The entire treatment procedure lasted five months, but the fear of earthquakes was reduced from the highest to the lowest rating (on a 10-point scale) in four sessions. The woman reported that she thought less and less about earthquakes and had no difficulty sleeping. Even though a mild earthquake did occur about six weeks after treatment began, she stated that she was "not bothered in the slightest by its occurrence." Six months after the treatment ended, she showed no recurrence of the fear or evidence of substitution of other fears.

With respect to the sexual phobia, treatment enabled the woman to resume sexual relations with her husband. At first she did not enjoy the sex act; six months after treatment ended she felt increasing pleasure and confidence but was still unable to have an orgasm; and at the end of a year she reported that she was able to gain a great deal of pleasure in sex and to have an orgasm about once in every three or four sexual experiences. Her overall relationship with her husband improved also.

The fear of enclosed places decreased from a fairly high rating to zero after seven sessions. During the fifth session of treatment, the woman remembered that she had accidentally been trapped in an airtight cabinet at about age 6 and would have suffocated if her mother had not found her in time. Memory of the event came after she successfully rode down three floors in an elevator. Thus it would appear that behavior change can be followed by "insight."

Frankel reported that none of the fears reappeared after the conclusion of treatment and that no substitute symptoms appeared. He also emphasized that the treatment was largely self-administered, a marked advantage over more typical therapy approaches.

In essence, discovering that they can safely perform behaviors that they formerly avoided can help phobic individuals gain confidence in themselves and in their ability to cope with stressful situations in general.

Somatoform disorders

"Soma" means *body,* and somatoform disorders involve a neurotic pattern in which the individual complains of bodily symptoms that suggest the presence of a physical problem, but for which no organic basis can be found. Such individuals are typically preoccupied with their state of health and with various presumed disorders or diseases of bodily organs. Though no organic basis exists, these individuals sincerely believe their symptoms are real and serious, and they should not be confused with persons who feign physical illness (malingerers) in order to obtain some special treatment.

In our discussion we shall focus on three distinct somatoform patterns: hypochondriasis, psychogenic pain disorder, and conversion disorder. While all three involve the neurotic development of physical symptoms, the patterns of causation and the most effective treatment approaches may differ somewhat. A fourth pattern involving complaints of bodily symptoms but not included in the current classification is neurasthenic disorders, described in the HIGHLIGHT on page 225.

Hypochondriasis

One of the most frequently seen somatoform patterns is hypochondriasis, which is characterized by the individual's multiplicity of complaints about physical illness—complaints that are usually not restricted to any logical symptom pattern and which express a preoccupation with health matters and unrealistic fears of disease. Although hypochondriacal individuals repeatedly seek medical advice, their fears are not in the least lessened by their doctors' reassurances; in fact, they are disappointed when no physical problem is found.[4]

Clinical picture in hypochondriasis.   Individuals with this disorder may complain of uncomfortable and peculiar sensations in the general area of the stomach, the chest, the head, the genitals, or anywhere else in the body. They usually have trouble giving a precise description of their symptoms. They may begin by mentioning pain in the stomach, which on further questioning is not a pain but a gnawing sensation, or perhaps a feeling of heat. Their general mental orientation keeps them constantly on the alert for new illness manifestations. Hypochondriacal patients are likely to be avid readers of popular magazines on medical topics, and are apt to feel certain they are suffering from every new disease they read or hear about. Tuberculosis, cancer, tumors, and numerous other diseases are readily diagnosed by these individuals. Their morbid preoccupation with bodily processes, coupled with their ignorance of medical pathology, often leads to some interesting diagnoses. One patient diagnosed his condition as "ptosis of the transvex colon," and added, "If I am just half as bad off as I think, I am a dead pigeon."

This attitude appears to be typical: such individuals are sure they are seriously ill and cannot recover. Yet—and this is revealing—despite their exaggerated concern over their health, they do not usually show the fear or anxiety that might be expected of those suffering from such horrible ills. The fact is that they are usually in good physical condition. Nevertheless, they are not malingering; they are sincere in their conviction that their symptoms represent real illness.

A classic illustration of the shifting symptoms and complaints in a very severe case of hypochondriacal disorder is presented in the

---

[4]A related somatoform pattern, which we are not discussing in detail here, is *somatization disorder (Briquet's syndrome),* in which a neurotic reaction is superimposed on actual physical problems and usually starts earlier than hypochondriasis. The physical problems may be undetectable medically (menstrual difficulties are an example) and may have been induced by psychological factors, but they cause the individual real discomfort, and a whole lifelong adjustment pattern is organized around them.

Neurasthenic disorder

In outpatient mental health and medical clinics, a frequent pattern of complaints centers on chronic mental and physical fatigue, various aches and pains, and a general lack of vigor and interest in life. This pattern, referred to as *neurasthenia*, has been considered to be relatively common among young adults, particularly frustrated homemakers. The DSM-III classification no longer includes neurasthenia as a neurotic category. However, the frequency with which this disorder has been diagnosed in the past—it is said to be the most commonly diagnosed disorder in the Soviet Union—warrants our giving it separate consideration.

Clinical picture

The principal complaint in neurasthenic disorder is tiredness. Mental concentration is difficult and fatiguing; such individuals are easily distracted and accomplish little. They lack the vigor required to carry activities through to completion. Even minor tasks seem to require herculean effort. They usually spend a good deal of time sleeping in an attempt to counteract fatigue; yet regardless of the amount of sleep they get, they awaken unrefreshed.

Typically, neurasthenic individuals sleep poorly and feel "just rotten" when they drag themselves out of bed in the morning. On the rare occasions when they feel refreshed, they are completely upset by minor emotional setbacks, such as some criticism of their behavior, and their fatigue and listlessness return. Even when things seem to be going relatively well, the fatigue tends to get worse as the day wears on, although by evening they may feel somewhat better and may go to a movie or a party without experiencing anything like their usual exhaustion. In fact, one of the most significant things about this fatigue is its selective nature. Such individuals often show relatively good energy and endurance in doing anything that really interests them.

It is important here to note two symptoms that distinguish these individuals from those suffering from severe depression. First, neurasthenic individuals do *not* report being depressed; instead, they report feelings of listlessness and frustration. Second, neurasthenic individuals do not show the deep emotional involvement typical of depressed persons; rather, they are somewhat more apathetic and withdrawn.

Causal factors

Historical attempts to explain the causal factors of neurasthenic reactions centered around the concept of "nerve weakness," which is the literal meaning of the older term *neurasthenia*. Beard (1905), an early American psychiatrist who first applied the term to the fatigue syndrome, attributed the condition to prolonged conflict and overwork, which presumably depleted the nerve cells of essential biochemical elements. This conception later gave rise to the Weir Mitchell method of treatment for "nervous exhaustion," which involved a long period of complete rest and relaxation for the patient.

Neurasthenic patients, however, rarely reveal a history of overwork, nor is rest what they most need. Rather, it appears to be prolonged frustration, discouragement, and hopelessness that reduces motivation and leads to the characteristic listlessness and fatigue. In addition, there are likely to be sustained emotional conflicts centering around hostility toward one's mate and guilt over the abandonment of cherished goals.

Much of the psychological benefit derived from these patterns is due to the individual's obvious sincerity—the complaints are made without awareness of their actual function. The neurasthenic individual often gets credit for putting up a noble battle against heavy odds. Thus, as in other neurotic reactions, neurasthenic symptoms may have important secondary gains. They tend to force others to show sympathy and concern, and may be used aggressively to control the behavior of others.

In understanding the causal factors of neurasthenic patterns, it is important to note that feeling fatigued and unable to cope with the world is common in our high-pressure society, but the normal individual carries on and makes a fairly satisfactory adjustment. Neurasthenic individuals, by contrast, are typically people who lack self-confidence, are overdependent on others, and feel completely inadequate in the face of a situation they perceive as frustrating and hopeless. Their symptoms enable them to escape the necessity of dealing with such a threatening world.

Aspects of treatment

Neurasthenic reactions are frequently very resistant to treatment. Tranquilizing drugs may alleviate some of the underlying anxiety but have not proven very helpful. In general, treatment to date has centered around helping patients gain some understanding of their problems, learn more effective coping techniques, and achieve enough self-confidence and courage to stop feeling sorry for themselves and get back into the "battle of life."

following letter that a hospitalized patient wrote to her anxious relatives.

"Dear Mother and Husband:

"I have suffered terrible today with drawing in throat. My nerves are terrible. My head feels queer. But my stomach hasn't cramped quite so hard. I've been on the verge of a nervous chill all day, but I have been fighting it hard. It's night and bedtime, but, Oh, how I hate to go to bed. Nobody knows or realizes how badly I feel because I fight to stay up and outdoors if possible.

"I haven't had my cot up for two days, they don't want me to use it.

"These long afternoons and nights are awful. There are plenty of patients well enough to visit with but I'm in too much pain.

"The nurses ignore any complaining. They just laugh or scold.

"Eating has been awful hard. They expect me to eat like a harvest hand. Every bite of solid food is agony to get down, for my throat aches so and feels so closed up. . . .

"With supper so early, and evening so long, I am so nervous I can't sleep until so late. I haven't slept well since I've been here. My heart pains as much as when I was at home. More so at night. I put hot water bottle on it. I don't know if I should or not. I've been wanting to ask some Dr.

"I had headache so badly in the back of my head last night and put hot water bottle there. My nurse said not to.

"They don't give much medicine here. Mostly Christian Science it seems! Well I must close or I never will get to sleep. My nurse gets off at 8:15 so she makes me go to bed by then.

"My eyes are bothering me more.

"Come up as soon as you can. My nose runs terrible every time I eat.

"The trains and ducks and water pipes are noisy at night.

Annie"
(Menninger, 1945, pp. 139–40)

Individuals suffering from hypochondriasis often show a morbid preoccupation with digestive and excretory functions. Some keep charts of their bowel movements, and most are able to give detailed information concerning diet, constipation, and related matters. Many of them also keep up with "the latest" in medical treatment, by reading newspapers or popular magazines, and are prone to the indiscriminate use of a wide range of self-medications. However, they do not show the losses or distortions of sensory, motor, and visceral functioning that occur in conversion disorder; nor do their complaints have the bizarre delusional quality—such as "insides rotting away" or "lungs drying up"—that is typical of somatic complaints in psychosis.

Causal factors in hypochondriasis.   Most of us are interested in our bodily functioning and state of health. Hypochondriacal patients, however, show a morbid exaggeration of this common interest and concern—an exaggeration that sometimes seems to function like a phobia of illness and dying, but more commonly enables them to avoid certain difficult life stressors and achieve various interpersonal gains.

1. *Overemphasis on bodily functions in early life.* A variety of early experiences may predispose an individual to the later development of hypochondriacal reactions. The child may learn to be oversensitive to and concerned with bodily processes from the model presented by a parent who is inclined to be hypochondriacal. Similarly, when the parent is continually commenting on and worrying about the child's every sneeze, cough, digestive upset, or other possible illness manifestation, the child, in turn, may learn to attach undue significance to such manifestations. A third important predisposing factor is an actual early illness or injury—which focuses everyone's attention on the child's physical condition and may lead to a highly gratifying position in the family, in terms of attention and care.

2. *A disappointing life situation as a precipitating factor.* Predisposed individuals are especially likely to experience hypochondriacal reactions during their forties or fifties, when they are forced to the realization that their life is more than half over and that their life pattern is fairly well determined—for better or worse. When their evaluation of their life situation is unfavorable—that is, when they feel they have failed to achieve their hopes and dreams, and perhaps find their occupational and marital situation far from satisfactory—the stage is set for a hypochondriacal or other maladaptive disorder.

3. *Maintenance of the pattern by reinforcement.* The hypochondriacal pattern enables the individual to avoid the demands and

stresses of an unpleasant life situation while at the same time gaining sympathy and support from significant others, plus some measure of control over other people's behavior. We obviously cannot hold a "sick" person responsible for the same level of achievement we expect of well persons. Thus hypochondriacal patients are protected from feelings of inadequacy or unfavorable judgments by others, and they need no longer strive toward difficult or unattainable achievements or accept other unpleasant responsibilities. In a general way, the anxiety aroused by their stressful life situation—often including their failure to achieve important goals—is displaced to a concern and preoccupation with their body and its functioning.

In addition, the increased attention that these individuals devote to themselves and receive from others may endow them and their bodies with increased significance. Most of us feel fairly important when we have the undivided attention of physicians and the sympathetic interest of our family and friends. And by maneuvering their symptoms with a measure of finesse, hypochondriacal individuals can often control the behavior of those around them. For example, when some activity is planned in which they do not wish to participate, an unexpected intensification of their pain or other symptoms may force the others to give up their plans. In one case a mother very effectively kept either her husband or son at home and attentive to her every need by well-timed complaints, often including statements that she could feel a heart attack coming on. Usually they did not believe her, but if they left her alone, they paid a high price on their return. The recitation of what she had "gone through" in their absence, accompanied by the theme of "Look what you did to me," exacted its toll, preventing her from being ignored very long or often.

Aspects of treatment. These individuals are usually very resistant to treatment, since they must believe in their symptoms if they are to keep their anxiety at a manageable level. Such patients, therefore, are apt to discontinue therapy when told there is nothing organically wrong with them, but as long as a therapist is willing to listen to their long list of complaints,

they are usually willing to continue in "treatment."

Psychogenic pain disorder

Psychogenic pain disorder is characterized by the report of severe and lasting pain. Either no physical basis is apparent, or the reaction is greatly in excess of what would be expected from the physical pathology. Psychogenic pain disorder is believed to be fairly common among psychiatric patients and is more commonly diagnosed among women.

Clinical picture in psychogenic pain disorder. The reported pain may be vaguely located in the area of the heart or other vital organs, or it may center in the lower back or limbs. (Tension headaches and migraines would not be included here, since they involve underlying physiological changes, such as muscle contractions.) People with psychogenic pain disorders flirt with an invalid life-style. They tend to "doctor-shop"—seeking both a physical confirmation of their pain and some desired medication. This behavior continues in spite of the fact that several visits to doctors have failed to indicate any underlying physical problem. Sadly enough, in many cases psychogenic pain patients actually wind up being disabled—either through addiction to pain medication or through the crippling effects of surgery they have been able to obtain as treatment for their condition.

Causal factors in psychogenic pain disorder. Although the diagnosis of psychogenic pain disorder requires that no adequate organic basis to the pain be found, some vaguely related injury or physical problem may be found in the medical history of a pain patient. The past incident may well serve more as perceived "justification" for the patient's physical concern rather than as a predisposing factor to the present pain.

Faulty learning appears to be a likely causal factor in psychogenic pain disorder. As in the other somatoform disorders, parental emphasis on bodily functions and the focus on illness or pain as a means of avoiding unpleasant tasks may play an important role in establishing the patient's invalidism.

Aspects of treatment.
Psychological treatment of patients with psychogenic pain has traditionally been fraught with difficulty, since the patients believe that their pains are physically based; as such, they are not open to psychological interpretation of their pain. Furthermore, histories of pain behavior have usually included medically induced complications, such as addiction to pain-killing medications, that must be dealt with in the total treatment program.

Since there is often no way to distinguish between psychogenic pain and organically based pain, many clinicians treat pain behavior without consideration of its origin (Cox, Chapman, & Black, 1978). In recent years, however, behavior modification has been gaining wide acceptance in the treatment of pain behavior, regardless of origin. Pain treatment programs, pioneered by Fordyce (1979), involve the use of reinforcement to encourage adaptive behavior, as well as extinction procedures to eliminate pain-related behavior and attitudes.

The following case, which includes a 10-year follow-up, can be helpful in providing an overall perspective on severe pain behavior.

Mrs. X., a 50-year-old obese homemaker and mother of four children was admitted to a pain treatment program. At the time of her admission, she complained of pain in her back, legs, neck, and knee. She had been unable to stoop or bend for the past 7 years. She had difficulty in sleeping, walking, or sitting, and had weakness in her legs. She reported that it hurt her to wear clothes, and even to breathe, and that she was depressed and unable to do housework other than prepare light meals and change pillowcases. She reported "funny noises" in the back of her skull, sweating at night, and pain "in all muscle groups of the body." She was taking 16 to 20 pain pills a day, including aspirin, Darvon, Valium, and Librium.

Mrs. X. reported that her childhood health had been relatively normal, except that she had had asthma. Her first complaints of back pain began with her first pregnancy at age 16. Since that time she had had numerous operations (e.g., an appendectomy, a vaginal repair, a urethral hernia repair, a hysterectomy, and surgery for varicose veins). Her first admission to the hospital because of chronic pain was

at age 40. At that time, no organic cause for the pain was found. There followed in the next 10 years multiple admissions to the hospital for back pain, whiplash, acute gastric distress (due to the large number of medications she was taking); in addition, she sought numerous outpatient evaluations by neurology, neurosurgery, arthritis, and physical medicine and rehabilitation clinics. She also received psychological consultations, and on three occasions she was treated with psychotherapy. Additional records revealed innumerable visits to general practitioners and specialists. None of the treatments she received was successful.

At the time of her admission to the pain treatment program, Mrs. X. lived with her husband and youngest daughter. Her husband, a skilled blue-collar worker, had himself had back pain for 17 years. Mr. and Mrs. X. had little in common except their need for constant medical attention—he for his back pain and she for her many medical complaints. Mrs. X. reported that she was fearful of following her own vocational plans (she had previous experience as a librarian and shop clerk) because of her husband's "rigidity." She was quite angry with her husband, and it appeared that she tried to punish him as well as communicate with him through her many pain behaviors.

Mrs. X's therapy involved an 8-week behavior modification program for chronic pain, designed to extinguish all nonverbal and verbal behaviors that communicated to others that she had pain and to reinforce responses, such as exercise and work, incompatible with her pain behavior. Medications were placed in a "pain cocktail," which was a concoction of all of the medications she was taking in a single liquid which disguised the form and taste of the medication. These medications were administered on a time-contingent basis 6 times a day, rather than a pain contingent basis. The medications in the liquid were reduced each week until there were no active ingredients in the "cocktail." Mrs. X. was informed that the reduction in medication was taking place.

During the program, all the staff avoided any reinforcement of Mrs. X.'s pain complaints. About the fourth week, Mrs. X. was assigned a "job," which required increasing work during the remainder of her hospitalization. During the 8-week period, her husband was seen weekly to teach him to stop reinforcing his wife's pain behaviors and to reinforce activity and work.

During the early part of her hospitalization, Mrs. X. was angry, complained, and had spells of crying. She was unable to walk from her bed to the dining room without receiving pain medication. About a month later she began to exhibit exceedingly inappropriate behavior, such as talking to herself in a mirror, lying on the hall floor and kicking, and making sexual advances toward younger female patients. These behaviors were interpreted as substitutes for Mrs. X.'s now-unreinforced pain behaviors, and the staff was instructed to ignore them. With time, Mrs. X.'s work and activity levels increased and her inappropriate behaviors subsided.

At the time of her discharge from the program, Mrs. X. was functioning at a physical and activity level considered normal for her age and sex, and she was using no pain medications. Six months following the program she became somewhat depressed but she required no formal treatment other than the support of her social worker.

In the 10 years since she entered the pain treatment program, Mrs. X. has been leading a normal life and has been employed as a librarian and shop clerk.

Conversion disorder

Conversion disorder, earlier called *hysteria*, involves a neurotic pattern in which symptoms of some physical malfunction or loss of control appear without any underlying organic pathology. It is one of the most intriguing and baffling patterns in psychopathology, and we still have much to learn about it.[5]

The term *hysteria* was derived from the Greek word meaning "uterus." It was thought by Hippocrates and other ancient Greeks that this disorder was restricted to women and that it was caused by sexual difficulties, particularly by the wandering of a frustrated uterus to various parts of the body because of sexual desires and a yearning for children. Thus the uterus might lodge in the throat and cause choking sensations, or in the spleen, resulting in temper tantrums. Hippocrates considered marriage the best remedy for the affliction.

This concept of the relationship between sexual difficulties and unfounded body ailments was later advanced in modified form by Freud. He used the term *conversion hysteria* to indicate that the symptoms were an expression of repressed and deviated sexual energy—that is, the psychosexual conflict was seen as *converted* into a bodily disturbance. For example, a sexual conflict over masturbation might be "solved" by developing a para-

lyzed hand. This was not done consciously, of course, and the person was not aware of the origin or meaning of the physical symptom.

In contemporary psychopathology, reactions of this type are no longer interpreted in Freudian terms as the "conversion" of sexual conflicts or other psychological problems into physical symptoms. Rather, the physical symptoms are now usually seen as serving a defensive function, enabling the individual to escape or avoid a stressful situation.

In World War I conversion disorder, or conversion hysteria, was the most frequent type of psychiatric syndrome. For many soldiers the war involved a highly threatening approach-avoidance conflict, in which military orders and doing one's duty were pitted against the fear of being killed or maimed in the crude bayonet charges that characterized this war. Here, conversion symptoms—such as being paralyzed in the legs or unable to straighten one's back—enabled the soldier to avoid the combat situation without being labeled a coward or being subjected to court-martial. These reactions were also relatively common among combat personnel in World War II. They typically occurred in association with the highly stressful conditions of combat and involved men who ordinarily would be considered stable.

Conversion disorders were once relatively common in both civilian and military life, but today they constitute only 5 percent of all neuroses treated. Interestingly enough, their decreasing incidence seems to be closely related to our growing sophistication about medical and psychological disorders: a conversion disorder apparently loses its defensive function if it can be readily shown to lack an organic basis. In an age that no longer believes in such phenomena as being "struck" blind or suddenly afflicted with an unusual and dramatic paralysis with no organic basis, the cases that occur increasingly simulate more exotic physical diseases that are harder to diagnose, such as mononucleosis or convulsive seizures.

Even highly psychologically sophisticated people have been known to develop conversion symptoms under stress, however.

A 29-year-old physician in the first year of a psychiatric residency was experiencing a great deal of stress

---

[5]In the DSM-II classification, conversion disorder was called *hysterical neurosis, conversion type.*

from problems in both his personal life and his hospital work. His marriage was deteriorating and he was being heavily criticized by the rather authoritarian chief of psychiatry for allegedly mismanaging some treatment cases. Shortly before he was to discuss his work in an important hospital-wide conference being conducted by the chief psychiatrist, he had an "attack" in which he developed difficulty in speaking and severe pains in his chest. He thought his condition was probably related to a viral infection, but physical findings were negative.

Clinical picture in conversion disorder.

The symptoms in conversion disorder are great imitators, and the range of symptoms is practically as diverse as for physically based ailments.

In describing the clinical picture in conversion disorder, it is useful to think in terms of three categories of symptoms: sensory, motor, and visceral.

1. *Sensory symptoms*. Any of the senses may be involved in sensory conversion reactions. The most common forms are as follows:

Anesthesia—loss of sensitivity
Hypesthesia—partial loss of sensitivity
Hyperesthesia—excessive sensitivity
Analgesia—loss of sensitivity to pain
Paresthesia—exceptional sensations, such as tingling

Some idea of the range of sensory symptoms that may occur in conversion disorders can be gleaned from Ironside and Batchelor's (1945) study of hysterical visual symptoms among airmen in World War II. They found blurred vision, photophobia (extreme sensitivity to light), double vision, night blindness, a combination of intermittent visual failure and amnesia, deficient stereopsis (the tendency to look past an object during attempts to focus on it), restriction in the visual field, intermittent loss of vision in one eye, color blindness, jumbling of print during attempts to read, and failing day vision. They also found that the symptoms of each airman were closely related to his performance duties. Night fliers, for example, were more subject to night blindness, while day fliers more often developed failing day vision. Results of a later study of student military aviators who developed conversion disorders are reported in the HIGHLIGHT on page 231.

The other senses may also be subject to a wide range of disorders; the HIGHLIGHT on page 232 presents an interesting case of hysterical deafness. A puzzling and unsolved question in hysterical blindness and deafness is whether the individual actually cannot see or hear, or whether the sensory information is received but screened from consciousness (Theodor & Mandelcorn, 1973). In general, the evidence supports the latter hypothesis, that the sensory input is screened from consciousness.

2. *Motor symptoms*. Motor conversion reactions also cover a wide range of symptoms, but only the most common need be mentioned here.

Paralysis conversion reactions are usually confined to a single limb, such as an arm or a leg, and the loss of function is usually selective. For example, in "writer's cramp" the person cannot write but may be able to use the same muscles in shuffling a deck of cards or playing the piano. Tremors (muscular shaking or trembling) and tics (localized muscular twitches) are common. Occasionally there are contractures that usually involve flexing of the fingers and toes, or there is rigidity of the larger joints, such as the elbows and knees. Paralyses and contractures frequently lead to walking disturbances. A man with a rigid knee joint may be forced to throw his leg out in a sort of arc as he walks. Another walking disturbance worthy of mention is *astasia-abasia*, in which the individual can usually control leg movements when sitting or lying down, but can hardly stand and has a very grotesque, disorganized walk, with both legs wobbling about in every direction.

The most common conversion disturbances of speech are *aphonia*, in which the individual is able to talk only in a whisper, and *mutism*, in which he or she cannot speak at all. Interestingly enough, a person who can talk only in a whisper can usually cough in a normal manner. In true laryngeal paralysis both the cough and the voice are affected. Aphonia is a relatively common conversion reaction and usually occurs after some emotional shock, whereas mutism is relatively rare. Occasionally, symptoms may involve convulsions, similar to those in epilepsy. However, such individuals show few of the usual characteristics of true epilepsy—they rarely, if ever, injure themselves, their pupillary reflex to light remains unaffected, they are still able to control excretory functions, and they do not have attacks when others are not present.

HIGHLIGHT

Conversion reactions in student naval aviators

Mucha and Reinhardt (1970) have reported on a study of 56 student aviators with conversion reactions who were assessed at the U.S. Naval Aerospace Medical Institute in Pensacola, Florida. In the group, representing 16 percent of a total population of 343 patients at the Institute, four types of symptoms were found. These were, in order of frequency: visual symptoms (most common), auditory symptoms, paralysis or paresthesias (prickling sensations) of extremities, and paresthesia of the tongue.

Generally, the 56 students came from middle-class, achievement-oriented families. The fathers of 80 percent of them were either high-school or college graduates and were either professional men or white-collar workers. Interestingly enough, 89 percent of the cases had won letters in one or more sports in high school or college; all were college graduates and presently were flight students, officer candidates, or officers.

Commenting on the relatively high incidence of conversion reactions among the patients at the Institute, Mucha and Reinhardt emphasized three conditions which they considered of etiological significance:

1. Unacceptability of quitting. In the students' previous athletic training, physical illness had been an acceptable means of avoiding difficult situations, whereas quitting was not. Moreover, the present training environment tended to perpetuate this adaptation, since the military is also achievement-oriented, and does not tolerate quitting as a means of coping with stress situations.

2. Parental models and past experience. Seventy percent of the parents of these students had had significant illnesses affecting the organ system utilized in the students' disorders; and a majority of the students had had multiple physical symptoms prior to enlistment—often as a result of athletic injuries.

3. Sensitization to the use of somatic complaints. As a result of their previous experience, the students were sensitized to the use of somatic complaints as a face-saving means of coping with stressful situations.

"When faced with the real stress of the flight training program and with frequent life-or-death incidents, they resorted to this unconscious mechanism to relieve the stress and to avoid admitting failure. To admit failure would be totally unacceptable to the rigid demands of their superegos." (p. 494)

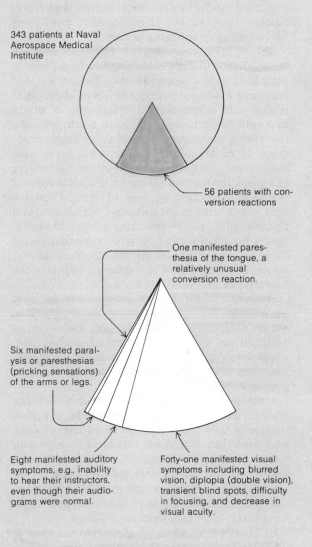

343 patients at Naval Aerospace Medical Institute

56 patients with conversion reactions

One manifested paresthesia of the tongue, a relatively unusual conversion reaction.

Six manifested paralysis or paresthesias (pricking sensations) of the arms or legs.

Eight manifested auditory symptoms, e.g., inability to hear their instructors, even though their audiograms were normal.

Forty-one manifested visual symptoms including blurred vision, diplopia (double vision), transient blind spots, difficulty in focusing, and decrease in visual acuity.

3. *Visceral symptoms*. Visceral conversion reactions also cover a wide range, including headache, "lump in the throat" and choking sensations, coughing spells, difficulty in breathing, cold and clammy extremities, belching, nausea, and so on. Occasionally, persistent hiccoughing or sneezing occurs.

Actual organic symptoms may be simulated to an almost unbelievable degree. In a pseudo-attack of acute appendicitis, the person not only may evidence pain in the lower abdominal region and other typical symptoms of acute appendicitis, but also may have a temperature far above normal. Cases of conversion reactions of malaria and tuberculosis have also been cited in the literature. In the latter, for example, the individual may show all the usual symptoms—coughing, loss of weight, recurrent fever, and night sweats—without actual organic disease. Even cases of pseudo-pregnancy have been cited, in which the menstrual cycle ceases, there is an enlargement of the abdominal area, and the woman experiences morning sickness.

Since the symptoms in conversion disorder can simulate almost every known disease, accurate diagnosis can be a problem. However, in addition to specialized medical techniques, several criteria are commonly used for distinguishing between conversion disorders and organic disturbances:

a) A certain *belle indifference*, in which the patient describes what is wrong in a rather matter-of-fact way, with little of the anxiety and fear that would be expected in a person with a paralyzed arm or loss of sight. Mucha and Reinhardt (1970) reported that all of the 56 student fliers in their study (p. 231) evidenced this pattern, seeming to be unconcerned about long-range effects of their disabilities.

b) The frequent failure of the dysfunction to conform clearly to the symptoms of the particular disease or disorder. For example, no wasting away or atrophy of the "paralyzed" limb occurs in paralyses that are conversion reactions, except in rare and long-standing cases.

c) The selective nature of the dysfunction. For example, in conversion blindness the individual does not usually bump into people or objects; "paralyzed" muscles can be used for some activities but not others; and uncontrolled contractures usually disappear during sleep.

The story of Anne: a case of a deafness conversion reaction

Anne, a young woman of 19, became "deaf," apparently as a result of family tensions. Her relations with her mother had been particularly strained, and the deafness was thought to be a type of avoidant behavior for screening out her mother's nagging voice. Anne showed no overt startle responses to sudden loud noises; however, she revealed covert responses to sound in the first of two trials to measure muscle contractions via an electromyogram (EMG). The first EMG trial revealed muscle contractions in Anne's neck when a loud sound was made, but the second trial 60 seconds later revealed no contractions. Some strong inhibitory neural changes must have come into operation in the brief time between the two trials, because complete inhibition of muscle contractions—covert ones, at least—is seemingly beyond the voluntary control of anyone suddenly exposed to loud noise.

Since Anne could read lips, the therapist combined conditioning with suggestion—telling Anne that she would soon be able to hear. The conditioning involved the removal of a negative reinforcer, which was an electric shock that closely followed the sounding of of a tone for 150 trials. The first time the shock was withheld, the EMG picked up a burst of covert muscle contractions. These promising early results of treatment were given an unexpected boost when a near-accident caused Anne's hearing to be suddenly restored. Crossing a busy street, she was narrowly missed by a driver who honked his horn and shouted at her. The hearing that she instantly regained has subsequently remained intact.

Adapted from Malmo (1970).

d) The interesting fact that under hypnosis or narcosis the symptoms can usually be removed, shifted, or reinduced by the suggestion of the therapist. Similarly, if the individual is suddenly awakened from a sound sleep, he or she may be tricked into using a "paralyzed" limb.

Where conversion symptoms are superimposed on an actual organic disorder, the difficulty in making a diagnosis may be increased. However, it is usually fairly easy to distinguish between a conversion reaction and *malingering*. Malingerers are consciously perpetrating a fraud by faking the symptoms of a disease, and this fact is reflected in their demeanor. Individuals with a conversion reaction are usually dramatic and apparently naive; they are concerned mainly with the symptoms and willingly discuss them. If inconsistencies in their behaviors are pointed out, they are usually unperturbed. To the contrary, malingerers are inclined to be defensive, evasive, and suspicious; they are apt to be reluctant to be examined and slow to talk about their symptoms, lest the pretense be discovered. Should inconsistencies in their behaviors be pointed out, malingerers immediately become more defensive. Thus conversion disorder and malingering are considered distinct patterns, although sometimes they overlap.

The phenomenon of *mass hysteria,* as typified by outbreaks of St. Vitus's dance and biting manias during the Middle Ages (see p. 31) is a form of conversion disorder that has become a rarity in modern times. However, an outbreak of mass hysteria that resulted in the temporary shutting down of a textile mill has been reported by Kerckhoff and Back (1969). It involved a "mysterious illness"—with symptoms of nausea and a body rash—allegedly caused by an insect in a shipment of cloth that had arrived from England. The report quoted one victim:

" 'Some of those women were deathly sick. They were passing out, and they were taking them out of here like flies. I don't know what happened to me.' State and Federal health officials were called into the case; but the victims were reported to be suffering from 'nothing more than extreme anxiety.' " (p. 46)

Episodes of hysteria have frequently been reported in Malaysian schools. Teoh, Soewondo, and Sidharta (1975) reported a number of instances of epidemic hysteria that had a common pattern "beginning with one hysterical girl, followed by a few others, and winding up eventually with one or two dozen girls screaming, shouting and hyperventilating[6] away." The episodes were usually associated with some catastrophe or major event in the schools or hostels—floods, examinations, or sporting events.

[6]*Hyperventilation* refers to excessive breathing, in which too much oxygen is taken in relative to the carbon dioxide exhaled. The result is often buzzing noises in the head or fainting.

"The clinical characteristics of the outbreaks were monotonously similar. The girls would scream, shout, and run aimlessly all over in terror, with severe hyperventilation followed by muscular twitchings and tetanic spasms of the limbs. Some would fall on the floor in a trancelike state, as though in a stupor. Occasionally one or two of the subjects would speak on behalf of the group, voicing their misdemeanors and frustrations. Very often they became abusive. They characteristically took hints and cues from one another. Most of the subjects could not recollect much of what had happened and would swear amnesia. A few complained of . . . moodiness and depression, while others were seized by the attacks without warning. On questioning, the girls would complain of seeing different fearsome objects during the same outbreak. Some would see dark flying objects or an ugly woman eight feet tall. The occupants of one hostel complained that a hungry spirit was always stealing their food and raiding the refrigerator. Others complained of ghosts stealing their underwear and jamming their doors." (p. 260)

Suggestibility clearly plays a major role in the development of mass hysteria, in which a conversion reaction in one individual rapidly spreads to others.

Causal factors in conversion disorder. In the development of a conversion disorder, the following chain of events typically occurs: (a) a desire to escape from some unpleasant situation; (b) a fleeting wish to be sick in order to avoid the situation (this wish, however, is suppressed as unfeasible or unworthy); and (c) under additional or continued stress, the appearance of the symptoms of some physical ailment. The individual sees no relation between the symptoms and the stress situation. The particular symptoms that occur are usually those of a previous illness or are copied from other sources such as illness symptoms observed among relatives or on television or read about in magazines. However, they may also be superimposed on an existing organic ailment, be associated with anticipated secondary gains, or be symbolically related to the conflict situation.

Unfortunately, the neurophysiological processes involved in the simulation of various disease symptoms, such as malarial fever, are not well understood. However, there is increasing research evidence of the remarkable extent to which individuals can control their own bodily functions. For example, recent studies with animals and humans have shown that blood pressure, heart rate, kidney function, and even the distribution of blood flow can be altered by selective reinforcement procedures (Schwartz, 1978). Although we have much to learn about the physiological mechanisms involved, it seems possible for bodily functioning to be markedly altered to meet the psychological needs of the individual.

1. *Personality and role factors.* What can be said about the personality of the individual who attempts to solve serious problems by getting sick? Most of us at some time or other have probably solved some problem or avoided something we did not want to do by pleading sickness. In fact, the common saying "I don't feel like doing it" or "I don't feel up to it" show the prevalence of this type of reaction. Individuals who develop a conversion disorder, however, unconsciously commit themselves to this pattern in the face of everyday life problems that most persons can deal with more effectively.

In relation to persons who respond with other neurotic patterns, these individuals tend to be highly suggestible and dramatic—that is, "histrionic personalities" who are excitable but shallow in emotional responsiveness, particularly capable of ignoring, denying, and repressing undesirable perceptions, prone to exaggeration, and demanding and manipulative in interpersonal relationships (Alarcon, 1973; Chodoff, 1974; O'Neill & Kempler, 1969; Slavney & McHugh, 1974; Verbeek, 1973). Women who have conversion disorders have, in addition, been described as sexually seductive but often unresponsive in actual sexual relations.

The following excerpts from a therapy hour provide an excellent illustration of personality factors often found in patients being treated for conversion disorder.

"The patient, a 30-year-old married woman, sought therapy because of nervousness, depression, headaches, and severe menstrual cramps. She entered the office with a despondent air which contrasted sharply with her colorful, almost flashy, dress. She wore a low-cut blouse and crossed her legs in a seductive manner as she sat down. The following interchange took place.

Pt.: Well, you know what's bothering me. Why don't you talk today.

[The patient's attempt to control the interchange is immediately apparent.]

Th.: Silent

Pt.: I don't know why I come here. I have been coming to see you for six months now (actually four months) and I feel worse than ever. My head hurts so much (patient dramatically touches head) and I wonder more each day if life is worth living. [This communication illustrates the patient's attention-seeking and histrionic behavior; there is also some obvious dishonesty.]

Th.: Silent

Pt.: I keep thinking that life isn't worth living. I'm worrying that I may kill myself.

Th.: I have noticed that when I don't respond to you immediately you begin to complain more and feel sicker.

Pt.: (Suddenly angry) You get me so mad. I come here for help and all you can do is interpret. You and your worship of Freud. I know all about the years you spent studying but I'm not impressed. Somebody like me is miserable and finds every minute of life pure hell and you attribute all kinds of unconscious motives to my suffering. You don't know how much courage it takes for me to just go on from hour to hour.

[The communication again illustrates the patient's controlling and attention-seeking behavior.]

Th.: Somehow I can't feel your misery as that powerful or real. Can't we go beyond it and look at what's so unsatisfying in your life?

Pt.: (Angrily exploding) I only wish you could feel what I'm feeling. (She reaches for an ash tray on the desk and postures as if she is going to throw it on the floor; then she changes her mind and shouts.) Damn you, nobody cares, nobody, nobody, nobody. (Sobs for several minutes while the therapist is silent, then slowly and dramatically) I guess you win, there's no beating you at your own game while I am so sick and helpless. I need you too much. (Suddenly she perks up and smiles coquettishly.) Well, what do you want me to talk about today. [Here she is again controlling, playing as if helplessly dependent, and demonstrating a reluctance to assume responsibility.]" (Halleck, 1967, pp. 751–52)

In describing the "sick role" enactment of the individual showing symptoms of conversion disorder, it is useful to note that (a) the role is useful only in a culture that provides sympathy and support for sick persons and enables them to avoid normal responsibilities; (b) the role is enacted or modeled on the basis of information the individual has concerning the physical ailment he or she is simulating; (c) the role tends to be self-perpetuating, since it has been reinforced by anxiety reduction and other gains—in essence, it has worked. Here it may be emphasized again that these individuals are not consciously aware of playing a sick role, for if they were, the psychological benefit to them would be lost. This need not be considered a mysterious phenomenon, since the literature on learning includes many instances in which behavior is altered by reinforcement without the person's awareness of the relationship between the changed behavior and the reinforcing conditions (Bandura, 1977).

2. *Avoidance of or defense against threat.* Typically conversion disorder makes possible avoidance or defense against a threatening situation. This avoidance pattern seemed clear in the case of a youth who fainted on his way to the altar on two separate occasions, each time planning to wed the same woman. In another instance, a divorcée lost her sense of smell when she noticed a sweet and pungent odor that she suspected to be marijuana in the room of her adolescent son—on whom she was strongly dependent for affection and meaning in her life. In an early report, Halpern (1944) cited 15 cases of hysterical amblyopia—markedly diminished visual acuity—in the armed forces, which developed at a port of embarkation and cleared up when the soldiers were removed from the conflict situation by hospitalization. These reactions have sometimes been called "gangplank fever."

Conversion disorders may also represent a defense against dangerous desires and impulses. Abse (1959) has cited the case of a middle-aged male patient who suffered total paralysis of his legs after his wife left him for another man. During the course of treatment it became apparent that he had a strong wish to pursue his wife and kill her and her lover. Although the wish had been repressed, it was quite intense, and the paralysis apparently represented a massive defense against the possibility that this wish might be carried out.

Sometimes, conversion disorders seem to stem from feelings of guilt and the necessity for self-punishment. In one case, for example, a female patient developed a marked tremor and partial paralysis of the right arm and hand after she had physically attacked her father. During this incident she had clutched at and torn open his shirt with her right hand, and apparently the subsequent paralysis represented a sort of symbolic punishment of the "guilty party," while preventing a recurrence of her hostile and forbidden behavior.

3. *Secondary gains stemming from actual illness or injury.* In some instances symptoms develop following physical illness or an accident in which the individual may or may not have been injured. If pneumonia temporarily enables a patient to avoid unpleasant occupational responsibilities—as well as receive the sympathy and attention of others—the invalidism may unconsciously be prolonged. An injury may lead to the same pattern.

Not uncommonly, these symptoms develop following some accident or injury as a result of which the individual hopes to receive monetary compensation. These reactions usually occur after accidents in which the individual might have been seriously injured but is actually only shaken up or slightly injured. Later, in discussions with family or friends, it may be agreed that the individual would have had a strong legal case if there had been an injury. "Are you sure you are all right? Could you possibly have injured your back? Perhaps there *is* something wrong with it." With the aid of a sympathetic lawyer, the individual may proceed to file suit for compensation for alleged injuries.

Here it is especially hard to distinguish between the malingerer's deliberate simulation of injury and the unconscious deception of an individual suffering from conversion disorder (Lewis, 1974). Apparently in many conversion reaction cases there is a combination of the two, in which conscious acting is superimposed on unconscious acting or role playing. In these cases the patient shows an amazingly rapid recovery once there has been proper compensation for the "injuries."

Whatever specific causative factors may be involved, however, the basic motivational pattern underlying conversion disorder seems to be to avoid or reduce anxiety-arousing stress by getting sick—thus converting an intolerable emotional problem into a face-saving physical one. Once the response is learned, it is maintained because it is repeatedly reinforced—both by anxiety reduction and by the interpersonal gains—in terms of sympathy and support—that result from being sick.

Aspects of treatment. The symptoms in conversion disorder can usually be removed by means of hypnosis or narcosis interviews, thus paving the way for a more extensive therapy program aimed at alleviating the conditions that appear to have influenced the development and maintenance of the reaction. While more extensive treatment may be necessary to modify the individual's basic life-style, the preceding measures are usually effective in helping the person through an immediate crisis and avoiding a chronic pattern of dealing with a given problem by "sickness." This is particularly true where the stressor can be alleviated to some extent.

Dissociative disorders

Like somatoform disorders, dissociative disorders are ways of avoiding stress while gratifying needs—in a manner permitting the person to deny personal responsibility for his or her unacceptable behavior. In the case of dissociative disorders, however, the person avoids the stress by, in essence, escaping—dissociating—from his or her core personality.[7] Dissociative patterns include psychogenic (psychologically induced) amnesia and fugue states, multiple personality, and depersonalization. These patterns are relatively rare, constituting less than 2 percent of all the neuroses.

Psychogenic amnesia and fugue

Amnesia is partial or total inability to recall or identify past experience. It may occur in neuroses, psychoses, or brain pathology, including delirium, brain injury, and diseases of the nervous system. Where the amnesia is caused by brain pathology, it usually involves an actual failure of retention. That is, either the information is not registered and does not enter memory storage, or, if stored, it cannot be retrieved: it is truly lost.

Psychogenic amnesia, on the other hand, is usually limited to a failure to recall. The "forgotten" material is still there beneath the level of consciousness, as becomes apparent under hypnosis or in narcosis interviews and in cases where the amnesia spontaneously clears up. As we have noted, amnesia is fairly common in reactions to intolerably traumatic experiences, such as those occurring under combat conditions and in "shock" conditions in civilian life. In the neurotic pattern known as *psychogenic amnesia*, however, the reaction occurs in the face of stressful life situations with which most people deal more effectively.

Clinical picture in psychogenic amnesia and fugue. In typical psychogenic amnesic reactions, individuals cannot remember their names, do not know how old they are or where they reside, and do not recognize their parents, relatives, or friends. Yet their basic habit patterns—such as their ability to read, talk, and so on—remain intact, and they seem quite normal aside from the amnesia.

In this amnesic state a person may retreat still further from real-life problems by going away in what is called a "fugue state." A fugue reaction is a defense by actual flight—the individual is not only amnesic but also wanders away from home. Days, weeks, or sometimes even years later such individuals may suddenly find themselves in a strange place, not knowing how they got there and with complete amnesia for the period of the fugue. Their activities during the fugue may vary from merely going on a round of motion pictures to traveling across the country, entering a new occupation, and starting a new way of life.

Causal factors in psychogenic amnesia and fugue. The pattern in psychogenic amnesia is essentially the same as in conversion disorder, except that instead of avoiding some unpleasant situation by getting sick the person does it by avoiding thoughts about it. This avoidance of certain thoughts may represent a pattern of avoidance learning without awareness, or it may involve more conscious suppression. In patterns involving suppression, individuals apparently tell themselves that they will not remember some traumatic event or situation; subsequently they try to believe and behave as though they actually were amnesic. For example, in a study of 98 amnesia cases, primarily among military personnel, Kiersch (1962) found 41 to be of this "feigned" type.

In psychogenic amnesia we typically find an egocentric, immature, highly suggestible personality faced with an acutely unpleasant situation from which he or she sees no escape.

---

[7]In the DSM-II classification, dissociative disorder was called *hysterical neurosis, dissociative type.*

There is often a conscious impulse to "forget" and run away from it all, but this solution is too cowardly to be accepted. Eventually, however, the stress becomes so intolerable that large segments of the personality and all memory for the stressful situation are repressed, while more congenial patterns carry on. As O'Neill and Kempler (1969) have pointed out, psychogenic amnesia is highly selective and involves only material that is basically intolerable or threatening to the self.

During such dissociative reactions the individual appears normal and is able to engage in complex activities, that are often of a wish-fulfilling or compensatory nature. This is well illustrated in an interesting case described by Masserman (1961).

"Bernice L., a forty-two-year old housewife, was brought to the Clinics by her family, who stated that the patient had disappeared from her home four years previously, and had recently been identified and returned from R———, a small town over a thousand miles away. On rejoining her parents, husband and child she had at first appeared highly perturbed, anxious, and indecisive. Soon, however, she had begun to insist that she really had never seen them before, that her name was not Bernice L. but Rose P. and that it was all a case of mistaken identity; further, she threatened that if she were not returned to her home in R——— immediately, she would sue the hospital for conspiracy and illegal detainment. Under treatment, however, the patient slowly formed an adequate working rapport with the psychiatrist, consented to various ancillary anamnestic procedures such as amytal interviews and hypnosis, and eventually dissipated her amnesia sufficiently to furnish the following history:

"The patient was raised by fanatically religious parents, who despite their evangelical church work and moralistic pretenses, accused each other of infidelity so frequently that the patient often questioned her own legitimacy. However, instead of divorcing each other, the parents had merely vented their mutual hostility upon the patient in a tyrannically prohibitive upbringing. In the troubled loneliness of her early years the patient became deeply attached to her older sister, and together they found some security and comfort; unfortunately, this sister died when the patient was seventeen and left her depressed and unconsolable for over a year. After this, at her parents' edict, the patient entered the University of A——— and studied assiduously to prepare herself for missionary work. However, during her second semester at the University, she was assigned to room with an attractive, warm-hearted and gifted girl, Rose P., who gradually guided the patient to new in-

terests, introduced her to various friendships, and encouraged her to develop her neglected talent as a pianist. The patient became as devoted to her companion as she had formerly been to her sister, and was for a time relatively happy. In her Junior year, however, Rose P. became engaged to a young dentist, and the couple would frequently take the patient with them on trips when a chaperone was necessary. Unfortunately, the patient, too, fell 'madly in love' with her friend's fiancé, and spent days of doubt and remorse over her incompatible loves and jealousies. The young man, however, paid little attention to his fiancée's shy, awkward, and emotionally intense friend, married Rose P. and took her to live with him in Canada. The patient reacted with a severe depression, the cause of which she refused to explain to her family, but at their insistence, she returned to the University, took her degree, and entered a final preparatory school for foreign missionaries.

"On completion of her work she entered into a loveless marriage with a man designated by her parents and spent six unhappy years in missionary outposts in Burma and China. The couple, with their two children, then returned to the United States and settled in the parsonage of a small midwest town. Her life as a minister's wife, however, gradually became less and less bearable as her husband became increasingly preoccupied with the affairs of his church, and as the many prohibitions of the village (e.g., against movies, recreations, liberal opinions and even against secular music) began to stifle her with greater weight from year to year. During this time the patient became increasingly prone to quiet, hazy reminiscences about the only relatively happy period she had known—her first two years in college with her friend, Rose P.—and these years, in her daydreaming, gradually came to represent all possible contentment. Finally, when the patient was thirty-seven, the culmination of her disappointments came with the sickness and death of her younger and favorite child. The next day the patient disappeared from home without explanation or trace, and her whereabouts, despite frantic search, remained unknown to her family for the next four years.

"Under treatment in the Clinics, the patient recollected that, after a dimly remembered journey by a devious route, she finally reached A———, the college town of her youth. However, she had lost all conscious knowledge of her true identity and previous life, except that she thought her name was Rose P. Under this name she had begun to earn a living playing and teaching the piano, and was so rapidly successful that within two years she was the assistant director of a conservatory of music. Intuitively, she chose friends who would not be curious about her past, which to her remained a mysterious blank, and thereby eventually established a new social identity which soon removed the need for introspections and ruminations. Thus the patient lived for four years as though she were another person until the almost inevitable happened. She was finally identified by a girlhood acquaintance who had known both her and the true Rose P. in their college years. The patient at first sincerely and vigorously denied this identification, resisted her removal to Chicago, where her husband was now assigned, and failed to recognize either him or her family until her treatment in the Clinics penetrated her amnesia. Fortunately, her husband proved unexpectedly understanding and cooperative, and the patient eventually readjusted to a fuller and more acceptable life under happily changed circumstances." (pp. 35–37)

In his analysis of this case, Masserman pointed out that the patient's behavior enabled her to flee from an intolerable mode of living as Mrs. Bernice L., the unhappy wife, and to substitute an intensely desired way of living, personified by Rose P., the loved and successful artist. Her "new personality" was in no sense completely novel, but represented an unconscious selection and integration of certain patterns of the old.

It is interesting to note that a person rarely engages in activities that would have been morally incompatible with his or her pre-fugue personality. Thus, in her identity as Rose P., the patient neither married again nor engaged in any direct sexual activity, since "bigamy or unfaithfulness, conscious or not, would have been untenable."

Multiple personality

Dual and multiple personalities have received a great deal of attention and publicity in fiction, television, and motion pictures. Actually, however, they are rare in clinical practice. Only slightly more than a hundred cases can be found in psychological and psychiatric records.

Clinical picture in multiple personality. Multiple personality is a dissociative reaction, usually due to stress, in which the patient manifests two or more complete systems of personality. Each system has distinct, well-developed emotional and thought processes and represents a unique and relatively stable personality. The individual may change from one personality to another at periods varying from a few minutes to several years, though

the former is the more common time frame. The personalities are usually dramatically different; one may be gay, carefree, and fun-loving, and another quiet, studious, and serious.

Various types of relationships may exist between the different personalities. Usually the individual alternates from one personality to the other, and cannot remember in one what happened in the other. Occasionally, however, while one personality is dominant and functions consciously, the other continues to function subconsciously and is referred to as a *co-conscious* personality. In these cases the co-conscious personality is usually intimately aware of the thoughts of the conscious personality and of things going on in the world, but indicates its awareness through automatic writing (in which the individual writes a message without full awareness or conscious control) or in some other roundabout way. The conscious personality, however, usually knows nothing of the co-conscious personality.

Relationships may become highly complicated when there are more than two personalities, as in the case described in the HIGHLIGHT on pages 240–241. Some of the personalities may be mutually amnesic while others are only one-way amnesic.

Causal factors in multiple personality. In a sense, we are all multiple personalities, in that we have many conflicting and warring tendencies and frequently do things that surprise both ourselves and others. This is illustrated by many common sayings, such as "I don't know why I did it" or "I didn't think he had it in him." It is also illustrated by the changed behavior many persons indulge in at conventions when they are away from their families and associates and "cut loose." In pathological cases, there is evidently such a deep-seated conflict between contradictory impulses and beliefs that a resolution is achieved through separating the conflicting parts from each other and elaborating each into a more-or-less autonomous personality system. In this way the individual is able to carry out incompatible systems of behavior without the stress, conflict, and guilt that would otherwise occur.

The pattern of conflict between personalities is well brought out in Lipton's comprehensive and excellent analysis of the case of Sara and

Maud K., excerpts of which are given below.

" . . . in general demeanor, Maud was quite different from Sara. She walked with a swinging, bouncing gait contrasted to Sara's sedate one. While Sara was depressed, Maud was ebullient and happy.

" . . . in so far as she could Maud dressed differently from Sara. Sara had two pairs of slippers. One was a worn pair of plain gray mules; the other, gaudy, striped, high-heeled, open-toed sandals. Sara always wore the mules. Maud would throw them aside in disgust and don the sandals. Sara used no make-up. Maud used a lot of rouge and lipstick, painted her fingernails and toenails deep red, and put a red ribbon in her hair. She liked red and was quickly attracted by anything of that color. Sara's favorite color was blue.

"Sara was a mature, intelligent individual. Her mental age was 19.2 years, IQ, 128. A psychometric done on Maud showed a mental age of 6.6, IQ, 43. Sara's vocabulary was larger than Maud's, and she took an intelligent interest in words new to her. When Maud heard a new word, she would laugh and mispronounce it, or say, 'That was a twenty-five cent one.' In sharp contrast to Sara, Maud's grammar was atrocious. A typical statement was, 'I didn't do nuttin'.' Sara's handwriting was more mature than Maud's.

"Sara did not smoke and was very awkward when she attempted it. Maud had a compulsion to smoke. At times she insisted she 'had to' and would become agitated and even violent if cigarettes were denied her. She would smoke chain fashion as many cigarettes as were permitted but two would satisfy her for a while. . . .

"Maud had no conscience, no sense of right and wrong. She saw no reason for not always doing as she pleased. She felt no guilt over her incestuous and promiscuous sexual relationships. Sara on the other hand had marked guilt feelings over her previous immoral sexual behavior.

"It seemed that Sara changed to Maud at the point when Sara's feeling of guilt was greatest." (1943, pp. 41–44)

Judging from the previous history of this patient, it would appear that the development of a dissociated personality in the form of Maud had, among other things, enabled Sara to gratify her sexual desires by engaging in promiscuous sexual relations without conscious knowledge and hence without guilt feelings. Apparently Sara reverted to Maud when her guilt feelings over her own previous promiscuous sexual behavior became too intense and self-devaluating.

Further light is cast on Sara's background by the report of two of her previous high-school friends that "she was 'boy crazy' and was always chasing after some boy, often being rude to her girlfriends, that she dyed her hair red, and that she smoked and used Listerine to deceive her mother about smoking. Sara denied all this but Maud readily recalled it" (Lipton, 1943, p. 47). It is interesting to note that this patient later became psychotic, apparently as a result of the failure of the dissociative reaction to solve her inner conflicts satisfactorily.

Because multiple personalities can be induced experimentally, the question has been raised as to whether the cases reported by therapists are in fact artificial creations produced inadvertently by suggestions of the therapist. Regarding this problem, Berman (1975) has pointed out:

"Certainly there are good reasons for doubting the tales of split personalities: The therapists' intense involvement with their patients; their own belief in the reality of splitting; the use of hypnosis and other methods of suggestion. While some cases may be fictitious, and while in others a therapist's expectations may have unconsciously encouraged the birth of the personalities detected, I believe that true cases of multiple personality do occur. One way to detect these genuine cases is to learn if the split appeared before therapy began, or if the reported personalities led separate lives outside the consulting room." (p. 78)

Berman described the case of a woman named Veronica who, at admission to the hospital, reported that "she has felt that there is a second person named Nelly whom she becomes periodically. She is currently afraid that Nelly is getting out of control." A few days after her admission to the hospital a dramatic transition took place. She appeared "not to be herself"—she talked differently, walked differently, and seemed confused by her surroundings. She insisted that she was Nelly and not Veronica. Over a period of weeks Veronica and Nelly alternated personalities, with the shift usually coming after a period of sleep.

Depersonalization disorder

A relatively more frequent dissociative disorder that occurs predominantly in adolescents and young adults is *depersonalization*, in which there is a loss of the sense of self. Such individuals feel that they are, all of a sudden, different—for example, that they are someone else or that their body has become drastically changed and has become, perhaps, quite grotesque. Frequently the altered state is reported as an "out of body experience" in which individuals feel that they are, for a time, floating above their physical bodies and observing what is going on below. Reports of "out of body experiences" have included perceptions that the person has visited other planets or a relative who is in another city. The disorder is often precipitated by acute stress resulting from such factors as toxic illness, an accident, or some other traumatic event. The following case provides a typical example.

Charlotte D., a recently separated 19-year-old woman, was referred to an outpatient mental health service by her physician because she had experienced several "spells" in which her mind left her body and went to a strange place in another state. The first instance had occurred two months earlier, a few days after her husband had left her without explanation. Since then, she had had four episodes of "traveling" that had occurred during her waking state and had lasted for about 15 to 20 minutes. She described her experiences as a dreamy feeling in which her arms and legs were not attached to her body and other people around her were perceived as zombie-like. Typically she felt dizzy and had pains in her stomach for hours after each spell.

Individuals who experience depersonalized states are usually able to function between episodes, at least marginally, but they often experience a great deal of anxiety associated with the episode and with fears of losing control. These characteristics distinguish neurotic depersonalization disorders from the feelings of depersonalization that sometimes occur with the personality deterioration and severe regression of psychosis, as we shall see in Chapter 12.

Aspects of treatment for dissociative disorders.   Treatment for dissociative disorders is essentially the same as for conversion disorder. Usually the immediate amnesia can be readily cleared up by means of hypnosis or narcosis interviews, and in some cases, as we have noted, the individual's amnesia clears up spontaneously. The latter appears especially likely

HIGHLIGHT

The three faces of Evelyn

Most of us are familiar with the classic case of multiple personality reported by Thigpen and Cleckley (1954), which was widely publicized and made into the movie *The Three Faces of Eve*. From psychological studies of the patient undertaken independently and using the Semantic Differential technique, Osgood and Luria (1954) concluded that the three "personalities" indeed had very different affective meaning systems, but they were anxious to analyze another multiple personality in order to further substantiate their findings.

A recent opportunity to conduct a detailed objective study of another case of multiple personality was presented when the late psychiatrist, R. F. Jeans, referred his patient, Gina, a single, 31-year-old woman of Italian descent, to Osgood, Luria, and Smith for independent study using objective psychological uation procedures (Osgood, Luria, Jeans, & Smith, 1976).

Gina was the youngest of nine children of immigrant parents. Her parents were fairly old when Gina was born. Gina considered her mother to be a domineering woman, while she saw her father as a passive and ineffectual man. The mother believed that Gina had a great deal of ability and pushed her to achieve and get ahead in life. Gina had high educational aspirations and had earned a Master's degree. At the time she sought psychological help she was employed as an editor and test developer for a large publishing firm.

Gina was referred to therapy by a group of her friends who were concerned about her somnambulism (sleepwalking), episodic amnesia, and unusual and inefficient behavior. Gina said she often was awakened during the night by the sound of her mother's name, but her roommate reported that it was Gina herself who screamed out the mother's name. Gina was a rather masculine woman in appearance and interests. She had not had much experience with men and seldom dated. When she was 28 years old she had a brief "platonic" affair with a former priest. A short time later she became quite involved with a married man (T.C.) who promised to get a divorce but failed to do so. She reportedly had not dated other men since because she wanted to remain faithful to T.C.

In the beginning of therapy, Gina's sexual identification problems were prominent. She had repressed her feminine identification, although the content of her reported dreams revealed that a feminine identification was still "quite lively and increasingly unwilling to remain shut out of consciousness." At this point, one of Gina's other personalities who called herself "Mary Sunshine" began to emerge. She was quite the opposite of Gina—in sexual identification, attitudes, and mannerisms. Mary Sunshine was a vivacious, bubbling, seductive personality whom Jeans viewed as a warmer, nicer, and more accepting person than Gina.

Interestingly, Gina became aware of Mary Sunshine through several puzzling events. Neither she nor her roommate liked hot chocolate although empty cups that had had chocolate in them kept showing up near Gina's bed. Also, in spite of her high income and her generally frugal existence, Gina found her bank account depleted at the end of each month. She once found herself on the phone ordering a sewing machine even though she knew nothing about sewing. Gina also became surprised at having certain emotions that she had never before experienced. Once, while watching a movie, for example, she began to experience tender emotions which were not in keeping with Gina's usual tough self. The new personality, Mary Sunshine, alternated with Gina for some time.

After a period of therapy a third personality, Evelyn, appeared—an apparent balance of the personalities of Gina and Mary. Therapeutic improvement came rapidly after Evelyn emerged and began to accumulate information about Gina and Mary. Evelyn learned to live without the extreme defenses of either Gina or Mary. She began to date and eventually married. Nine years after the termination of therapy she was reportedly happily married with no recurrence of her previous problems.

Late in therapy, a double form of the Semantic Differential was administered by the therapist and given a blind analysis by Osgood, Luria, and Smith. They were told only that there were three accessible personalities who communicated by "inner conversations"; that the patient was 32 years old, white, childless, single, and worked as an editor; and that the patient had eight older siblings (two brothers). The ten scales used were as follows: Valuable—Worthless; Clean—Dirty; Tasty—Tasteless; Large—Small; Strong—Weak; Deep—Shallow; Fast—Slow; Active—Passive; Hot—Cold; Relaxed—Tense.

The descriptions generated by blind interpretations of the three personalities clearly validated Jeans' clinical descriptions (Osgood, Luria, & Smith, 1976):

Gina was described as a moralistic, straightlaced person. She was seen as tense, inhibited, and quite self-critical, as well as disturbed and full of hatred. She also was considered to derive gratification from her disorder.

Mary was described as an ebullient person, more relaxed and "much more full of love of people." She was also viewed as a rather childish and playful person who placed no value on her job. She seemed to accept fraudulence as a way of life. Mary had a more active interest in males and sex than either Gina or Evelyn.

Evelyn represented a balance between Gina and Mary. She seemed more mature than the "childish" Mary and more relaxed than Gina. She placed more emphasis on reality and a job and task orientation. The blind interpretation suggested that the personality represented by Evelyn was probably the product of the preceding therapy.

in psychogenic fugue disorders in which the individuals find themselves in an even worse situation than the one from which they were trying to escape. Where the conflict and subsequent dissociative disorder stem from some special stress rather than a chronic life situation, and the situation changes or the stress can be alleviated, amelioration of symptoms via hypnosis or other treatment procedures is likely to be followed by a more adequate life adjustment. Also of key importance in treatment is helping the patient learn more effective methods of coping, which make the neurotic avoidant behavior unrewarding and unnecessary.

For a look at an additional pattern that reflects neurotic characteristics, see the HIGHLIGHT on page 243. Whether or not "existential neurosis" occurs as a distinctive form of neurotic disorder, many individuals experience feelings akin to it, and it would seem to merit consideration and treatment by many psychologists and psychiatrists.

General causal factors, treatment, and outcomes

In our preceding discussion we have focused on the basic nature of neurotic behavior, various specific neurotic patterns, and some aspects of treatment. Now let us take a more detailed look at general causal factors, treatment strategies, and outcomes in the neurotic disorders.

Development and maintenance of neuroses

In the development and maintenance of neurotic behavior, as of other psychopathology, it is relevant to consider the role of biological, psychosocial, and sociocultural factors.

Biological factors. The precise role of genetic and constitutional factors in the neuroses has not been delineated. Ample evidence from army records and civilian studies indicates that the incidence of neurotic patterns is much higher in the family histories of neurotic individuals than in the general population, but the extent to which such findings reflect the effect of heredity is not known.

In a study of concordance rates of neuroses in identical and fraternal twins in the military, Pollin et al. (1969) found that among identical twins the rate was only $1\frac{1}{2}$ times as high as it was among fraternal twins. Since the environmental background of identical twins is likely to be more similar than that of fraternal twins, these investigators concluded that heredity plays a minimal role in the development of neuroses. After an evaluation of available evidence, Cohen (1974) came to a similar conclusion: "the concept of a genetically based disease or defect cannot provide a satisfactory explanation for the diversity and variability of most neurotic phenomena" (p. 473).

Sex, age, glandular functioning, and other physiological factors have also been investigated without illuminating the causal picture. It is known, of course, that stress tolerance is lowered by loss of sleep, poor appetite, and increased irritability associated with prolonged emotional tension—but such conditions are by no means exclusive to the neuroses. A more promising possibility centers around constitutional differences in ease of conditioning. For example, extreme sensitivity and autonomic lability (instability) may predispose the individual to a "surplus" of conditioned fears and hence to avoidance behavior. But as yet the evidence is inconclusive; a great deal more research is needed to clarify the role of constitutional and other biological factors in the development of neuroses.

Psychosocial factors. The psychological and interpersonal causal factors in maladaptive behavior that we reviewed in Chapter 5 are especially applicable to the neuroses. Particularly relevant here are early psychic trauma, pathogenic parent-child and family patterns, and disturbed interpersonal relationships.

Also of particular relevance are the several theoretical "viewpoints of causation" that we reviewed. Here it is useful to comment on concepts from four of these viewpoints.

1. *Anxiety-defense.* Traditionally, the neuroses have been explained within the framework of anxiety-defense as set down by Freud and elaborated by later investigators. According to this view, threats stemming from internal or external sources elicit intense anxiety; this anxiety, in turn, leads to the exaggerated use of various ego-defense mechanisms and to maladaptive behavior. Although today other causal factors are also taken into account, anxiety-defense remains a useful concept in many cases, as we have seen.

2. *Faulty learning.* In recent years faulty learning has become the most widely used explanation for both the development and the maintenance of neurotic behaviors. Faulty learning is seen in the acquisition of maladaptive approaches to stressful situations, as well as in the typical failure of neurotic individuals to learn the competencies and attitudes needed for coping with normal life problems. For an individual who feels basically inadequate and insecure in a competitive and hostile world, making the effort to become competent is especially difficult; relying on a defensive and avoidant life-style is less threatening and brings enough short-term alleviation of anxiety to be repeatedly reinforced.

3. *Blocked personal growth.* We have noted the emphasis placed by the humanistic and existential perspectives on values, meaning, personal growth, and self-fulfillment; we have also seen how stressful one's life situation can become when it is devoid of meaning and hope, as depicted by reports of former inmates of concentration and POW camps. In civilian life, lack of meaning and blocked personal growth often appear to stem from a lack of needed competencies and resources or a feeling that duty requires one to remain in a self-stifling role. As a result, the individual's main efforts are devoted to simply trying to meet basic needs, rather than to personal growth. Such a life-style can ultimately bring feelings of anxiety, hostility, and futility—feelings that underlie many neurotic reactions.

4. *Pathogenic interpersonal relationships.* Certain interactions within families and other early relationships can set the stage for children to develop a neurotic life-style in later life. For example, parents who overprotect or indulge their children may prevent them from developing the independent, effective coping techniques required in their adult years. Or insecure parents may instill their own excessive concern with ailments in their children. Much

Is there an existential neurosis?

As we have seen, existentialists point to the breakdown of traditional values, the dehumanization of human beings in a mass society, and the difficulty in finding meaning in modern existence. Shaping one's own identity, finding satisfying values, and living a constructive and meaningful life are essential quests that are proving exceptionally difficult for many people.

Maddi (1967) has suggested the term "existential neurosis" to refer to the individual's inability to succeed in this quest. He has described it basically as follows:

The personal identity out of which this neurosis originates involves a definition of self as simply an embodiment of biological needs and a player of social roles. Such a self-identity is highly vulnerable to various stresses, such as rapid social change and new role expectations, interpersonal relations that victimize a poorly differentiated and confused individual, and acute awareness of the superficiality of one's existence. The resulting symptom pattern is characterized by chronic alienation, aimlessness, and meaninglessness. (Adapted from pp. 311–25)

Not all students of psychopathology would consider the syndrome described by Maddi to be a distinct pattern of neurosis, although most would readily agree that feelings of purposelessness and alienation are severely disturbing to the individual and often play a key role in the development of neurotic behavior.

Many people in our society, after "taking stock," are confronted with the sickening realization that their busy and seemingly important lives have really not proven meaningful or fulfilling. Thus the question of whether there is an existential neurosis seems a meaningful one, and a question likely to be answered in the affirmative by many psychologists and psychiatrists.

of what a person becomes in later life—attitudes, values, and often even particular symptoms—can be traced to interactions within the family during the formative years.

It is apparent that the preceding views of psychosocial causation are interrelated and may apply in varying degrees to a given case. As Bandura (1969) has pointed out, the causal factors attributed to a particular neurotic case usually depend heavily on the orientation of the therapist. Psychoanalysts are likely to unearth anxiety-arousing desires and exaggerated

The induction of "experimental neuroses" in animals

An unusual series of experiments on "neurotic" behavior in animals has been carried out by Dr. Jules Masserman. Although we do not know how far the findings of such studies can be applied on the human level, there clearly are many parallels between human reactions to conflict and those observed in Masserman's animal subjects. Masserman's studies were carried out with both cats and monkeys.

The first step in Dr. Masserman's procedure was to condition the animals to respond to a food signal—a light, a bell, or an odor—by pressing a treadle which was connected to a switch. A proper response opened the plastic lid of a food box in which the animal found the reward (A). When this behavior had been learned, conflict was introduced by associating a noxious stimulus with the feeding situation. Cats were subjected

to a brief electric shock or had a strong puff of air directed at their heads when they tried to obtain the food. Monkeys were commonly exposed to a toy snake, which was presented in the food box or through the wall of the apparatus. These stimuli all produced strong avoidance reactions when initially presented. After a few experiences with the noxious stimulus the basic conflict was well established; the animal faced the choice of resisting fear in order to satisfy hunger or withdrawing and remaining hungry in order to avoid the fear.

Under these conditions many apparently neurotic reactions were observed. Cats displayed typical symptoms of anxiety; they crouched and trembled; their hair stood on end and their pupils dilated; their breathing was rapid, shallow, and irregular; their pulses were

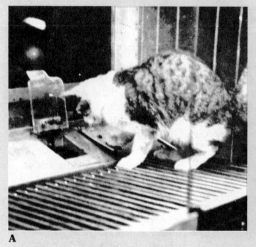

A

B

C

ego-defense mechanisms; behaviorists to point out learned maladaptive patterns and their maintenance through reinforcement; humanistic and existential psychologists to discover blocked personal growth and existential anxiety, and interpersonal theorists to emphasize pathogenic social interactions. Nevertheless, all of these concepts are useful in understanding the development of neurotic behaviors. For an interesting look at how one experimenter induced neurotic behavior in animals, see the HIGHLIGHT above.

Sociocultural factors. Reliable data on the incidence of neurotic disorders in other societies is meager. Kidson and Jones (1968) failed to find classical neurotic patterns among the aborigines of the Australian western desert; but they did note that as these groups were increasingly exposed to contemporary civilization, hypochondriacal concerns and other somatic complaints occurred. In general, however, it would appear that conversion disorder is more common among the people of underdeveloped countries, while anxiety and

rapid; their blood pressure was markedly increased. They showed severe startle reactions and phobic aversions to sudden lights or sounds, to constricted spaces or to restraint, and to any sensory stimulation in the modality associated with the traumatic experience. Some refused to take any food even when it was presented outside the food box on the floor of the cage. Animals that had willingly entered the cage and had resisted removal during the initial learning period became eager to escape after conflict had been established. Often they would crouch near the sliding glass door of the experimental cage, waiting to be removed (B, C.).

Monkeys, in addition to anxiety and phobic reactions like those shown by the cats, displayed even more profound disturbances. Somatic and motor dysfunc-

tions included diarrhea and gastrointestinal disorders resulting in rickets and severe neuromuscular weakness. In contrast to their previous behavior, some monkeys after experimental treatment spent long periods in stereotyped, repetitive activity, such as "pacing" back and forth in the experimental cage (D). Sometimes this behavior alternated with states of tense, apprehensive immobility (E). Some animals would stare fixedly for hours if left undisturbed (F). Often these monkeys would sleep or lie immobile in their home cages until midafternoon. Homosexual and autoerotic activity increased markedly, even in the presence of receptive females. One monkey attempted coitus only once in six months. "Neurotic" animals also lost their former positions of dominance in relation to other animals and were frequently attacked by other members of the colony.

D

E

F

obsessive-compulsive disorders are more common in technologically advanced societies.

In our own society, neurotic disorders are found among all segments of the population. There appear to be significant differences, however, in the incidence and types of patterns manifested by particular subgroups. In general, neurotic individuals from the lower educational and socioeconomic levels appear to show a higher than average incidence not only of conversion disorder but also of aches, pains, and other somatic symptoms. Neurotic indi-

viduals from the middle and upper classes, on the other hand, seem especially prone to anxiety and obsessive-compulsive disorders—with such subjective symptoms as "unhappiness" and general feelings of dissatisfaction with life.

Although there has been little systematic research on the effects of specific sociocultural variables in the development of neurotic disorders, it seems clear that the social environment influences both the individual's likelihood of adopting a neurotic reaction and the particular form that reaction is most likely to take. Thus, as social conditions continue to change in our own society and elsewhere, we can expect that there will be corresponding changes in both the incidence and prevailing types of neurotic behavior.

Treatment and outcomes

The treatment of neuroses may involve a wide range of goals and procedures. Treatment may be aimed at alleviating distressing symptoms, changing the individual's basic defensive and avoidant life-style, or both; it may include drug therapy or psychotherapy, or some combination of these approaches. As we have noted, anxiety, phobic, and conversion disorders usually respond more readily to treatment than do other neurotic patterns, but the outlook for the neuroses is generally favorable.

For present purposes, we shall keep our discussion brief and focused on the aspects of treatment that are particularly relevant to the neuroses.

Drug therapy and other biological approaches.
A large proportion of the patients seen by medical practitioners are neurotic individuals seeking relief from their various aches and pains. Most often minor tranquilizing drugs such as Valium or Librium are prescribed. These drugs are used—and misused—for relief of tension and for relaxation; they may also reduce anxiety and stabilize emotional reactivity. Neurotic individuals frequently attempt to control their anxiety or other symptoms by self-medication.

Available statistics indicate that some 70 percent or more of neurotic patients show some alleviation of symptoms following drug therapy, and most of them are able to function more effectively (Covi et al., 1974; Engelhardt, 1974; Kline, 1967; Prusoff & Klerman, 1974). But these drugs can have undesirable effects—such as drowsiness—and in some cases the patient develops an increasing tolerance for and dependence on the drug. In addition, many persons expect too much of drug medication, and the masking of their symptoms may prevent them from seeking needed psychotherapy.

Another drug treatment approach that has been attempted with neurotic individuals is psychedelic therapy (Cohen, 1976; Natale et al., 1978), which involves the use of d-lysergic acid diethylamide (LSD) along with psychotherapy sessions. In the full-blown psychedelic state, ego functioning is disrupted temporarily and the person becomes "an observer" who is free to experience sensory inputs without critically self-monitoring them. Without the usual pressure of "the critical self" the patients become very suggestible and can be quite open to therapeutic direction. It has been reported that some very rigid individuals have gained new insights about life and death and later become more flexible toward new life approaches through this experience.

Psychedelic therapy, however, is not widely used because its effectiveness has not been sufficiently demonstrated. Translating insights from an altered state of consciousness into practice in the "normal" state of awareness is difficult at best. A more serious deterrent to the therapeutic use of psychedelic drugs, however, is their potential danger. Some individuals may become psychotic when given psychedelic drugs.

Other biological treatment procedures have been used for the neuroses with mixed results. Electrosleep—a relaxed state of sleep induced by means of the application of low-intensity electric current to the brain—has led to both promising and disappointing results with individuals suffering from anxiety disorders (Hearst et al., 1974; Rosenthal & Wulfsohn, 1970). Similarly, biofeedback-induced muscle relaxation has produced mixed findings in the treatment of chronic anxiety (Blanchard & Epstein, 1978; Blanchard & Young, 1974).

An interesting method of treatment that progresses from biological measures to psychotherapy is Morita therapy, which has produced favorable results in the treatment of anxiety disorders, neurasthenic disorders, and obsessional fears (Gibson, 1974; Kora & Ohara, 1973). Initially the patient is subjected to absolute bed rest for a period of four to seven days with no reading, writing, visitors, or other such external stimuli permitted. By the end of this period, the patient usually finds positive reinforcement in responding to external stimuli. Then begins a graded series of tasks, starting with light work and proceeding through heavy manual labor to a focus on interpersonal relationships and finally the establishment of purposive, goal-directed behavior designed to eliminate the neurotic life-style and reorient the individual's life pattern.

Psychological approaches.

Individual psychotherapy, behavior therapy, and group and family therapy have been utilized in the treatment of the neuroses.

1. *Individual psychotherapies.* These therapies are oriented toward helping individuals achieve greater knowledge and understanding of themselves and their problems. The various types of therapy included in this general category differ somewhat in their specific goals and procedures—each reflecting the particular psychosocial perspective on which it is based—but all stress the need for self-understanding, a realistic frame of reference, a satisfying pattern of values, and the development of effective techniques for coping with adjustive demands.

These objectives sound deceptively easy to achieve; actually they share a number of stumbling blocks. First is the problem of creating a therapeutic situation in which neurotic individuals feel safe enough to lower their defenses, explore their innermost feelings, thoughts, and assumptions, and begin to recognize the possibility of other options. Second is the problem of providing opportunities for neurotic individuals to learn new ways of perceiving themselves and their world, and new ways of coping. Third is the problem of helping them transfer what they have learned in the therapy situation to real life; even when they understand the nature and causes of their self-defeating behavior and have learned that more effective coping techniques are available, they may still be "unable to risk the initial venture into the heretofore out-of-bounds area of living" (Salzman, 1968, p. 465). Fourth is the problem of changing conditions in their life situation that may be maintaining the neurotic life-style. For example, a domineering and egocentric husband who will not participate in the therapy program may tend to block his wife's efforts toward self-direction and make it more difficult for her to give up her insecure, neurotic behavior; he may even manage to sabotage the entire treatment program.

2. *Behavior therapy.* As we have seen, behavior therapy focuses on (a) removing specific symptoms or maladaptive behaviors; (b) de-

veloping needed competencies and adaptive behaviors; and (c) modifying environmental conditions that may be reinforcing and maintaining the maladaptive behaviors. In this last context, Bandura (1969) has stated, "A treatment that fails to alter the major controlling conditions of the deviant behavior will most certainly prove ineffective" (p. 50).

The behavior therapy method most commonly used in the treatment of the neuroses is systematic desensitization. Here, as we have seen, clients are placed—symbolically or actually—in situations that are increasingly closer to the situation they find most threatening, and an attempt is made to associate the fear-producing situations with states that are antagonistic to anxiety, such as relaxation.

As we saw in our discussion of specific types of neuroses, some maladaptive behaviors—such as conversion paralyses—may be extinguished by removing reinforcements that have been maintaining the behavior while simultaneously providing reinforcements for more responsible coping patterns. Other maladaptive behaviors—such as obsessive thoughts and compulsions—can often be removed by mild aversive conditioning (Bandura, 1969, 1973; Stern, Lipsedge, & Marks, 1973).

In recent years many behaviorists have been using behavior therapy to change cognitive or covert (unobservable) behavior (Mahoney, 1978; Meichenbaum, 1977). Individuals who are experiencing neurotic problems, such as anxiety attacks, may be viewed as behaving anxiously in response to internal states (cognitions). Here the therapist attempts to change the behavior by changing the individual's inner thoughts and beliefs that may be causing, or reinforcing, the neurotic behavior.

Although behavior therapy is usually directed toward changing specific "target behaviors"—such as removing phobias—it often seems to have more far-reaching positive results (Marks, 1978). A client who overcomes a specific phobia gains confidence in his or her ability to overcome other problems. Ultimately such a patient learns that coping effectively with adjustive demands is more rewarding than trying to avoid them. Thus while cognitive therapies usually focus more on modifying the basic neurotic life-style of the patient and behavior therapy focuses more on the removal of specific target behaviors, the outcomes of

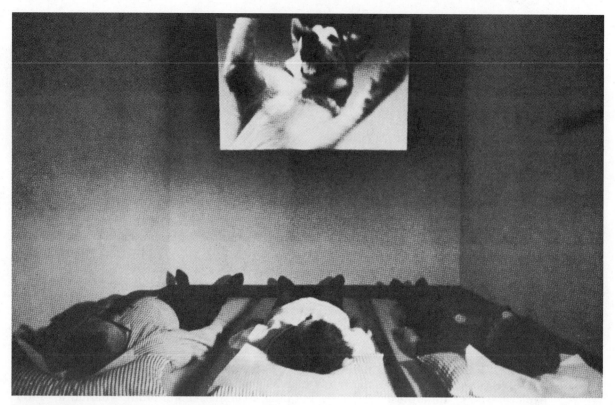

Patients with cynophobia, or fear of dogs, watch a series of slides of dogs, beginning with small, cuddly ones and progressing to lunging, hostile ones, like the snarling German shepherd shown here. Eventually the phobia sufferers should be able to overcome their fear and touch live animals.

these two forms of therapy are often comparable (Sloane et al., 1975).

3. *Family therapy.* Often there are pathogenic family interactions that are keeping the neurotic individual in a continually "sick situation." As Melville (1973) has expressed it, "In a family there is no such thing as one person in trouble" (p. 17). As a consequence of such findings, increasing emphasis has been placed on treating the family system rather than focusing primarily on the individual (Fox, 1976; Gurman & Kniskern, 1978).

Here it may be pointed out that it often requires a great deal of courage and persistence on the part of the neurotic individual to face problems realistically and give up the defensive and avoidant life-style that has helped alleviate feelings of inadequacy and anxiety. For some, this seems too great a task, and they present themselves in such a way as to put the whole responsibility for their well-being and happiness on the therapist.

As Weiss and English so succinctly described it nearly forty years ago,

"There's my story, doctor (after taking plenty of time to tell it in detail). Now you pat me . . . and take my pains away . . . and give me inspiration and happiness and tell me how to be successful, and while you are about it, get my mother-in-law out of the house and I'll pay you when I get a job." (1943, p. 119)

Despite the difficulties involved, however, powerful forces are aligned on the side of psychotherapy. For one thing, those who seek help are usually experiencing considerable inner distress, so that they are motivated to change. When helped to understand their problems and learn more effective and satisfying ways of coping with them, they usually find the courage to "see it through." Although outcomes vary considerably, it appears that from 70 to 90 percent of the people who receive appropriate kinds of help for their neurotic behavior benefit from it (Bergin & Lambert, 1978).

In concluding our discussion of the neuroses, several additional points may be mentioned. Fear of committing suicide is a common neurotic symptom, but the actual incidence of suicide among neurotic individuals does not appear to be higher than for the general population. Nor does the life span of these individuals appear adversely affected by their chronic tension and somatic disturbances, although there are few conclusive statistics on this point. The question has also been raised as to whether neurotic behavior is likely to develop into psychotic behavior; the answer seems to be a definitive *no*. However, in a minority of cases of neurotic behavior—5 percent or less—excessive stress may lead to severe personality decompensation and psychotic patterns.

Finally, the question has been raised as to how a neurosis affects creativity and productiveness. Many authors have declared neurotic individuals to be "pleasantly different" and more likely than the "normal" person to be innovative and productive. In general, however, the evidence indicates that by relying on defensive strategies, neurotic individuals reduce their potential for positive accomplishment as well as their enjoyment of life.

In the beginning of this chapter we focused on the basic nature of the neuroses—characteristics that seem common to various patterns of neurotic behavior. We noted that these characteristics may be described in terms of the *neurotic nucleus* and the *neurotic paradox*. The neurotic nucleus involves (a) pervasive anxiety resulting from basic feelings of inadequacy and the evaluation of everyday problems as threatening; (b) a tendency to avoid such problems by means of various defensive maneuvers rather than to cope with them; (c) self-defeating and maladaptive behavior which blocks personal growth and leads to feelings of futility and unhappiness. Why does the neurotic individual cling to such self-defeating patterns of behavior? This is the neurotic paradox, which can be explained in terms of (a) the immediate short-term relief from anxiety which results from defensive and avoidance maneuvers; and (b) immediate resort to these maneuvers at the first sign of the feared stressor, thus preventing a testing of the situation to see if the fears are realistic. The net result is the tendency to cling rigidly to the defensive and avoidant life-style that characterizes the neuroses.

We then discussed the clinical pictures, causal factors, and treatment and outcomes characteristic of specific neurotic patterns, including anxiety disorders, somatoform disorders, and dissociative disorders. And to round out our discussion, we surveyed the general role of biological, psychosocial, and sociocultural factors in the development of neurotic behavior; we noted that processes emphasized in different theoretical perspectives, such as anxiety-defense, faulty learning, blocked personal growth, and pathogenic interpersonal relations were all relevant to an understanding of the neuroses. Finally, we noted some contemporary approaches to treatment.

8

Psychological factors and physical illness

Psychological factors in health and disease

Classic psychosomatic symptom patterns

General causes of psychosomatic disorders

Treatment and outcomes

Traditionally, the medical profession has concentrated research efforts on understanding and controlling the organic factors in disease. In psychopathology, on the other hand, interest has centered primarily on uncovering psychological factors that may lead to the development of mental disorders. Today we realize that both these approaches are limited: although an illness may be primarily physical or primarily psychological, it is always a disorder of the whole person—not just of the lungs or the psyche. Fatigue or a bad cold may lower tolerance for psychological stress; an emotional upset may lower resistance to physical disease; behavioral dispositions, such as excessive alcohol use, may contribute to the impairment of various organs, like the brain and liver. In short, the individual is a psychobiological unit in continual interaction with the environment. Likewise, the life situation of an individual has much to do with the onset of a disorder, its form and duration, and whether or not recovery occurs. Recovery is apt to be more rapid for the patient eager to get back to work than for the one who will be returning to a frustrating job or an unpleasant home.

The interdisciplinary approach to treatment of all disorders considered to have psychological factors in their causal pattern is often referred to as the *psychosomatic approach,* or increasingly today as *behavioral medicine.* This approach fits contributing biological, psychosocial, and sociocultural factors into the total picture. Its emphasis, however, is essentially on the role psychological factors play in the occurrence and maintenance of physical illness. It is now reflected in medical and psychological thinking, with respect to the treatment not only of physical illnesses brought on primarily by emotional tension, but also of those cases where only physical causes are obvious. We might, for example, ask whether emotional factors may have lowered the resistance of a tuberculosis patient and hence contributed to the onset of the disease. We might also ask how the individual will react to the changes in life situation brought about by the disease. Some patients apparently give up when medically the chances seem good that they will recover. Others with more serious organic pathology recover or survive for long periods of time. In fact, Flanders Dunbar, a pioneer in the field of psychosomatic medicine, concluded that it is often "more important to know what kind of

patient has the disease than what kind of disease the patient has" (1943, p. 23).

Since this is a text about abnormal psychology, we cannot go deeper into primarily physical diseases like tuberculosis, in which the primary cause is the tubercle bacillus, however important psychological and sociological factors may also be involved in the outcome of the disease. We are mainly concerned in this chapter with the *psychosomatic disorders*—physical disorders in which psychological factors play a major causative role.

The psychosomatic disorders were renamed *psychophysiologic disorders* in the 1952 classification of the DSM, with ten subtypes listed according to the body system affected—cardiovascular, genitourinary, and so on. In the present DSM-III classification, the category of psychophysiologic disorder has been dropped. As we have seen, all patients are now rated separately on different axes for psychiatric symptoms, developmental personality factors, and accompanying physical disorders. Thus there is no place on the first two axes for the classic psychosomatic disorders, which are physical illnesses even though psychologically induced. To overcome this problem and permit some sort of psychiatric coding for these disorders, Axis I provides a category called *Psychological factors affecting physical condition,* to be used when a physical disorder, coded on Axis III, involves psychological factors that have either *definitely* or *probably* played a role in the initiation or exacerbation of the disorder.

In the present chapter, after a broader consideration of the role of psychological factors in both health and illness, we shall look at five classic psychosomatic patterns.

Psychological factors in health and disease

Research has repeatedly yielded evidence that mental and emotional processes are implicated in some way both in good health and in the majority of the physical diseases that afflict humankind. But definitive proof of such relationships, and a beginning understanding of what is happening in the body, are relatively recent accomplishments. The boundaries of this field seem virtually limitless. In this section we shall summarize some of the evidence of the close relationship between psychological and physical processes. Then we shall introduce briefly two of the physiological mechanisms that may be involved when physical illness follows stress or chronic negative emotions.

Emotions and health

The sometimes devastating effects of attitudes of hopelessness and helplessness on organic functioning have long been known, partly through anthropological research on "voodoo death" and similar phenomena (see HIGHLIGHT on pages 252–253). Today, many surgeons will not undertake a major operation until they are convinced that the patient is reasonably optimistic about the outcome. In the literature there are numerous reports of "apathy deaths" in situations such as concentration and prisoner-of-war camps; and every year in our cities there are reports of "unexplained" deaths among persons who believed themselves to be in hopeless circumstances— for example, after having ingested dosages of poisonous substances that were actually too small to be lethal.[1] The HIGHLIGHT on page 254 examines cases in which individuals have actually set their own date for death—while they were in good health—and kept the date.

Less dramatically, but in many ways of equal or greater importance, the effects of multiple life changes on a variety of illnesses have been amply documented in the research on significant life changes and subsequent health status, as outlined in Chapter 4. To cite only two examples, Rahe (1974) noted a study on the health status of physicians that demonstrates a marked correspondence between health problems experienced and amount of change-related stress undergone in an immediately preceding period. Similarly, in a study of 192 men between the ages of 30 and 60, Payne (1975) found that long-standing physical *and* psychological health problems were related to larger degrees of life change,

---

[1]Such phenomena have been extensively reviewed by both Seligman (1975) and Jones (1977).

HIGHLIGHT

Voodoo sorcery, psychosomatic disorders, and death

Although attributing death to voodoo spells may appear naive, Cannon (1942)—in what is probably still the most comprehensive study of the scientific literature on the subject—has cited a good deal of evidence to substantiate its occurrence. Included among Cannon's sources were competent scientific observers who had lived among the natives of Africa, Australia, New Zealand, and South America, as well as nearby Haiti. One such observer was Leonard (1906), whom Cannon quoted as follows:

"I have seen more than one hardened old Haussa soldier dying steadily and by inches because he believed himself to be bewitched; no nourishment or medicine that were given to him had the slightest effect either to check the mischief or to improve his condition in any way, and nothing was able to divert him from a fate he considered inevitable." (Leonard, p. 257)

Another statement, from *The Australian Aboriginal* by Basedow (1927), concerns the effect of "bone pointing" on its victim:

"The man who discovers that he is being boned by an enemy is, indeed, a pitiable sight. He stands aghast, with his eyes staring at the treacherous pointer, and with his hands lifted as though to ward off the lethal medium, which he imagines is pouring into his body. His cheeks blanch and his eyes become glassy and the expression of his face becomes horribly distorted. . . . He attempts to shriek but usually the sound chokes in his throat, and all that one might see is froth at his mouth. His body begins to tremble and the muscles twitch involuntarily. He sways backwards and falls to the ground, and after a short time appears to be in a swoon; but soon after he writhes as if in mortal agony, and, covering his face with his hands, begins to moan. After a while he becomes very composed and crawls to his wurley. From this time onwards he sickens and frets, refusing to eat and keeping aloof from the daily affairs of the tribe. Unless help is forthcoming in the shape of a counter-charm administered by the hands of the Nangarri, or medicine-man, his death is only a matter of a comparatively short time." (pp. 178–79)

Cannon's study of such sources led him to answer in the affirmative the question of whether those who

had reported voodoo deaths exercised good critical judgment, and in the negative to that of whether the deaths might have been due to natural causes or poisoning rather than to black magic. He cited the example of Dr. P. S. Clarke, who reported having attended a native in North Queensland to whom an evil spell proved fatal in a few days, even though routine hospital tests preceding death and a postmortem examination disclosed no pathological physical causes. In further support of his conclusions Cannon received a letter from Dr. J. B. Cleland, author of an article on voodoo death in the *Journal of Tropical Medicine and Hygiene* (1928) who "entirely ruled out" the possibility that the deadly effects of bone pointing among Australian natives might be caused by poisoning.

Then how can we account for the effectiveness of voodoo death spells? Cannon emphasized three interrelated factors:

1. Debilitating consequences of intense fear. Studies of humans—and other animals—have shown that intense fear, continued over time, may have serious and even fatal consequences. The deaths of soldiers within 3 to 4 days of suffering severe emotional shock and "malignant anxiety," and the results of postmortem findings in such cases have seemed, according to Cannon, to "fit well with fatal conditions reported from primitive tribes" (p. 180). In many cases, of course, physiological disturbances induced by fear are exacerbated by the victim's refusal of food and liquids.

2. Deep-seated nature of tribal superstitions. The firm belief of primitive peoples in the calamitous effects of voodoo spells explains the very real terror the spells have inspired. Cannon noted that the victim of bone pointing succumbs to dread, as described above, because ". . . death is sure to intervene. This is a belief so firmly held by all members of the tribe that the individual not only has that conviction himself but is obsessed by the knowledge that all his fellows likewise hold it" (p. 176).

3. Abandonment of victim. As Cannon noted, in some groups the member marked for death "becomes a pariah, wholly deprived of the confidence and social support of the tribe" (p. 176). All people

who stand in any kinship to him withdraw their sustaining support; in addition the group appoints a ceremonial leader, a person of very near kin, who conducts the fateful ritual of mourning. Thus effectively cut off from the ordinary world and placed in the world of the dead, the victim—highly suggestible and fearful—responds to group expectations and "assists in committing a kind of suicide" (p. 174).

Although there is a dearth of more recent systematic data on the effects of voodoo sorcery, Watson (1973) has reported findings which strongly support Cannon's data and conclusions. While serving in an African jungle hospital in central Zaire, Watson reported that he witnessed an average of one "death by cursing" every three months. As in the cases described by Cannon, the victims typically became comatose and died, some gradually and others on the same day they were admitted to the hospital. Although it is not known how such death curses work, we saw in Chapter 6 that feelings of hopelessness and despair were considered key factors in the death of prisoners in concentration and prisoner-of-war camps.

Are there target dates for death?

Many cases have been reported of terminally ill patients who managed to stay alive until an important event took place, such as a birthday, a wedding anniversary, or the birth of a grandchild. Of the first four presidents of the U.S. to die, three died on the Fourth of July. Sigmund Freud and Carl Sandburg have been cited as examples of persons where specific dates became "emotionally invested deadlines" for living.

The prospect of life without the companionship of one's mate has caused many happily married older people to say that they want to die when their mates do, and in many instances they do die shortly after the death of their spouses. Similarly, many middle-aged persons, when asked, will state that they want to live until New Year's Day of the year 2000, to see the dawning of the twenty-first century.

A number of cases have also been recorded of persons in good health who actually died on the target dates for death that they set for themselves. Harry Oliver, a two-time Oscar-winning art director in the film industry, died on the Fourth of July at the age of 85—as he predicted he would. One of the most interesting cases with respect to target dates for death is that of Mark Twain (shown at right). He was born on November 30, 1835, when Halley's comet made its spectacular appearance in the sky, and he died—as he had predicted—on April 21, 1910, when Halley's comet returned. Death was attributed to angina pectoris, but the question still remains as to the underlying cause. Was it the excitement surrounding the fiery comet's return, or the conviction that the incontrovertible date for death had arrived?

Based on Fischer and Dlin (1972), Rawitch (1973), and Weisman (1972).

even when the changes had been favorable. Evidently the amount of adjustment required overtaxed the individuals' resources.

Often it appears that any severe stress serves to pave the way for, precipitate, or aggravate a physical disorder in a person already predisposed to it (G. W. Brown, 1972). A person who is allergic to a particular protein may find resistance further lowered by emotional tension; similarly, where an invading virus has already entered the body—as is thought to be the case in multiple sclerosis—emotional stress may interfere with the body's normal defensive forces or immunological system.

In like manner, any stress may tend to aggravate and maintain certain specific disorders, such as rheumatoid arthritis (Robinson et al., 1972). As another pioneer in psychosomatic disorders, Day (1951), once pointed out, "To develop chronic active pulmonary tuberculosis a person needs some bacilli, some moderately inflammable lungs . . . and some internal or external factor which lowers the resistance to the disease." He noted further that unhappiness was among the stressors that could lower resistance. Here we can see the potential role of stress in the development of physical disorders, including those labeled "psychosomatic" as well as many that are not.

The relationship between psychological factors and good health has also been well documented (e.g., Jones, 1977); that is, positive emotions seem often to produce a certain immunity to physical disease or to be associated with speedy and uncomplicated recoveries when disease does strike. In fact, this is so much the case that it complicates efforts to determine the true effectiveness of new treatment techniques, such as new drugs. The patient who *believes* the treatment is going to be effective has a much better chance of showing improvement than does the patient who is neutral or pessimistic—even when the treatment is subsequently shown to have no physiological effects. This has become known as the *placebo effect,* and it accounts in part for the controversies that arise periodically between the scientific community and the general public regarding the efficacy of certain drugs or other treatments—Laetrile in the treatment of cancer being a recent example. It has even been suggested that, had it not been for the placebo effect, the profession of medicine as we know it would not have survived to the present century, because until this century the profession in fact had very little else to offer sufferers of disease. Perhaps its survival and prosperity from ancient times is in part a tribute to the power of "faith" in healing (Shapiro & Morris, 1978).

The fundamental unity of mind and body is perhaps nowhere better documented than in health and illness. The development of psychosomatic disorder, as described later in this chapter, is only one example of this enormous influence of mental factors on bodily functioning.

Autonomic excess and "classic" psychosomatic illness

The classic notion of psychosomatic disorder, proceeding from the early work of Dunbar (1943) and F. Alexander (1950), was predicated on the idea that strong emotions in themselves, whether consciously recognized or not, would over time produce pathologic anatomical and physiological changes in certain organ systems. As is well known, strong emotions are accompanied by various internal bodily changes—such as elevated heart rate, dumping of stored sugar into the bloodstream, and secretion of hormones from the inner core of the adrenal glands—many of which are readily perceived by the aroused person. These often very intrusive bodily changes are a product chiefly of autonomic nervous system arousal. It was but a short step for early researchers to infer that internal stressors, such as personality-based conflicts, could bring about the observed breakdown in certain organ systems through aberrant or excessive autonomic nervous system activity. To a large extent, they appear to have been right, although—as so often happens—their early conceptions were frequently oversimplified.

The psychological processes in the classic psychosomatic disorders, such as peptic ulcer, are seen as similar in many ways to the underlying dynamics of neurosis, described in the preceding chapter. That is, the person typically has acquired unrealistic fears or anxieties that severely limit both effective coping behaviors and the likelihood of need gratification. Instead, defensive and ultimately self-defeating strategies are repeatedly invoked, leading to frustration and continued high arousal. Under these conditions, some persons—for reasons that remain unclear—develop psychosomatic disorders more readily than neurotic disorders, although development of one reaction by no means precludes development of the other.

Selye and the stress-response system

While the classic psychosomatic disorders involve excesses and aberrations of autonomic nervous system activity, this is only one of the pathways by means of which the mental and emotional life of the individual may adversely affect biological functioning. Selye's (1976) general adaptation syndrome, briefly mentioned in Chapter 4, depicts three stages of response to continuing stressors: alarm and mobilization, resistance, and exhaustion. The autonomic nervous system is implicated most significantly in the first of these stages. As severely stressful circumstances continue to impinge upon the organism, the second stage, resistance, comes into play, followed finally, if the stress continues, by the depletion of adaptive resources and significant damage or death to the organism. In the second and third stages, it seems to be the endocrine (hormonal) system that is mainly involved, although interaction with the autonomic nervous system is maintained at many levels.

When severe stress becomes chronic and constant, therefore, we are obliged to shift our attention somewhat away from the autonomic system per se (where the adrenal gland's central core or *medulla* plays a prime role) to certain influences of the adrenal *cortex* (the covering mantle of the adrenal gland). Under the influence of the anterior pituitary—which is in turn influenced by hypothalamic (emotional) stimulation—the adrenal cortex releases into the bloodstream certain hormonal substances that have profound effects on physiological functioning. One group of these substances, the *glucocorticoids* (including hydrocortisone, corticosterone, and cortisone) are involved in sugar metabolism and are especially important in this context.

As part of a stress-response mechanism, the glucocorticoids have paradoxical effects. They promote an increase in available blood sugar for energy mobilization and facilitate blood redistribution, but they also hamper inflammatory processes by which the body controls tissue damage, and they reduce resistance to infection and possibly other pathological processes. Their specific effects include the following: (a) delay of growth of new tissue around a wound, including surgically acquired ones; (b) inhibition of the formation of disease-fighting antibodies and general impairment of the immunological surveillance system; (c) decrease in the number of circulating white blood cells, which are also critical in fighting infections; and (d) depression of thyroid activity with a resulting inhibition of bodily growth and decreased production of the sexual and reproductive hormones.

Small wonder, then, that the endocrine stress-response system has been implicated as a significant factor in diseases and dysfunctions ranging from cancer to infertility (see HIGHLIGHT on page 257). It is also seen as the probable mediating factor in the increased in-

cidence of illness and death following bereavement (Engel, 1961; Klerman & Izen, 1977). And it would be surprising if this system were not responsible, at least in part, for the relationship between illness and recent life changes (Holmes & Masuda, 1974; Rahe, 1974; Rahe & Arthur, 1978).

Classic psychosomatic symptom patterns

The clinical picture in psychosomatic disorders tends to be *phasic:* typically there is an upsurge of symptoms followed by their waning or disappearance. The sequence of their appearance and disappearance appears to be directly related to the amount of stress the individual is experiencing. For example, an assembly-line worker's ulcers may be quiescent during a three-week vacation. However, there are many exceptions to this general trend. It is also of interest to note that there are often marked differences between the sexes in the incidence of specific disorders; some are much more common among men and others more common among women.

Even in the case of the more or less "standard" psychosomatic diseases, however, the same diseases sometimes occur without any significant psychological components. For example, not all ulcers are psychosomatic. And a further caveat is appropriate at the outset. As with disorders manifested exclusively by mental or behavioral phenomena, psychosomatic ailments do not seem to appear from nowhere in an individual who is not in some sense predisposed toward the particular condition in question. Many unwise statements about psychosomatic disorders—not all of them by laypersons—may be traced to a failure to recognize the importance of underlying predispositional factors in virtually any disorder that is alleged to have a psychosomatic component.

The complexities to be taken into account are well illustrated in what is perhaps the foremost

Psychosomatic cancer—a viable concept?

Beginning with the pioneering research of Lawrence LeShan (LeShan & Worthington, 1955), the idea that the development and course of malignant tumors might be influenced by psychological factors has gained increasing attention. Research in this area has gradually focused on the hypothesis that an attitude of passivity and hopelessness in the face of life stressors, including the stressor of being told one has cancer, somehow encourages the proliferation of cancerous cells (Schmale, 1971). Indeed, one version of this hypothesis states that we all produce cancerous cells from time to time but that usually these are promptly detected by our immune surveillance mechanisms and destroyed. According to this view, clinically dangerous forms of cancer develop in individuals who lack the appropriate defensive-immune response. In this chapter we have briefly sketched how such a lack might be produced by psychological causes through the effects of stress on the adrenocortical hormones, which in turn are implicated in the immune response.

These ideas have been put to practical therapeutic use in a systematic program of cancer therapy at the Cancer Counseling and Research Center in Fort Worth, Texas (Simonton, Mathews-Simonton, & Creighton, 1978). Here the usual forms of cancer therapy (surgery, radiation, and chemotherapy) are supplemented with a variety of psychological techniques designed to create the positive emotions and confident sense of control over one's illness that can stimulate the immune system to more normal functioning again. For example, the patients do relaxation exercises, which allay anxiety, and carry out reg-

ular periods of imagery, during which they visualize their white blood cells successfully attacking and removing the cancer cells. Working with only very advanced cases diagnosed as medically incurable, Simonton et al. have reported very encouraging results. In some cases there have been remissions; even where this has not proved possible, the rate of progress of the disease seems often to have been retarded, and there has been a reduction of pain as well as of side effects from chemotherapy or radiation, so that the quality of the patients' lives has been dramatically improved.

Simonton et al. explicitly acknowledge that they are working with the placebo effect. But to acknowledge the reality of the placebo effect is, in effect, to acknowledge the power of the patient's belief system to affect the course of his or her illness. Simonton et al. have taken the next step of trying to develop and use this potential ally. First they help their patients recognize the role that their negative emotions and beliefs have played in the development of their cancers, and then they help their patients give up this illness-causing belief system and develop one that can lead toward health instead.

The work of Simonton et al. raises the exciting possibility that we may be able to gain a greater measure of control over even the dread disease of cancer through learning more adaptive attitudes and emotional responses. This work is in its infancy, however, and their findings will need to be rigorously evaluated and replicated by other investigators before we can be certain of the therapeutic benefits of this approach.

---

of the classic psychosomatic illnesses—peptic ulcer—which we shall discuss next. Then we shall follow with a discussion of other classic psychosomatic disorders, including anorexia nervosa, migraine and tension headaches, hypertension, and heart attacks.

Peptic ulcers

Peptic ulcers first came into prominence in our Western culture during the early part of the nineteenth century. In the beginning they were observed primarily in young women, but in the second half of the nineteenth century there was a shift, and today the incidence of ulcers is some two or three times higher among men than women. Contemporary civilization apparently is conducive to the chronic emotional reactions that lead to peptic ulcers, and it is estimated that about one in every ten Americans now living will at some time develop a peptic ulcer.

The ulcer itself results from an excessive

flow of the stomach's acid-containing digestive juices, which eat away the lining of the stomach or duodenum, leaving a crater-like wound. Although dietary factors, disease, and other organic conditions may also lead to ulcers, it is now recognized that worry, repressed anger, resentment, anxiety, dependency, and other negative emotional states may stimulate the flow of stomach acids beyond what is needed for digestion. The result is that the stomach begins to digest itself, which is the specific precondition for ulcer formation.

It has long been believed that conflicts centering on dependency needs are especially likely to be found in individuals who develop ulcers. In support of this belief we have available something of a landmark study (Weiner, Thaler, Reiser, & Mirsky, 1957).

Relying on prior evidence of a high rate of gastric secretion in ulcer-prone individuals, as indicated in part by a high level of pepsinogen in the blood serum, Weiner and his colleagues tested a population of 2073 army draftees and chose for study those men found to be maximum and minimum gastric secreters. These were groups of men, in other words, who should be at maximum and minimum risk for ulcer formation by virtue of constitutional predisposition. Membership in one or the other group did in fact predict the incidence of ulcer formation during the stress of basic training. Of perhaps even greater importance, however, is the fact that a battery of psychological tests also correctly predicted the group in which pepsinogen-level recruits would fall, and even correctly identified at an above-chance level which high-pepsinogen recruits would develop ulcers. These test results showed evidence of major unresolved dependency (in Freudian terms "oral") conflicts, with resultant frustration and suppressed hostility.

The important point established by this study was that *neither* a high pepsinogen level *nor* dependency conflicts was alone responsible for the development of peptic ulcer. Taken together, however, they constituted a pathogenic predisposition that, on exposure to a special stressor (basic training), could be expected to challenge the equilibrium of a dependent individual, thus producing an abnormally high risk of ulcer formation.

The dependency of the ulcer-prone individual is not always obvious at the behavioral level. In fact, such an individual may seem to be quite independent or autonomous. The dependency,

however, may be revealed by a test of the individual's underlying personality organization.

The relationship between ulcer-related gastric distress and psychic dependency is illustrated in the following case report.

George P., a single, white, 50-year-old male, was admitted to the hospital for the fifth time in six years with complaints of severe stomach pain, "heartburn," and generalized weakness and malaise. He vomited persistently following the ingestion of any solid food. He anticipated that he would be treated with medication and possibly stomach surgery, as he had been in the past, and he resolutely denied any possible connection between his ailment and emotional factors.

George had left his parents' home early in his youth after a dispute with his father. With the nation in the midst of the depression of the 1930s, George had spent most of his time traveling around the country, taking on temporary jobs when he could find them. When he was 21, he had returned home because his father was dying of stomach cancer. After his father's death, George essentially took up the role of his mother's chief friend and confidant, a relationship that lasted for some 20 years until his mother's death. During this period, George engaged in various unprofitable business ventures. He evidenced little, if any, interest in women other than his mother, and his sexual experience was confined to occasional visits to prostitutes. He described this period in his life in idyllic terms.

The 20-year period with his mother was interrupted only by a four-year tour in the navy during World War II. George had apparently adjusted reasonably well to his period of military service, during which he was a cook and was not exposed to combat action. It was shortly after his departure from military service that George had had his first bout with stomach distress and had been admitted to the hospital. His second serious attack occurred some 10 years later, shortly after his mother's death. This second attack was diagnosed as peptic ulcer, and a surgical resection of the stomach wall was performed the following year, followed by three additional hospital admissions for the same complaint in the ensuing four years.

George's behavior on the hospital ward on these visits was significant. He was very demanding of attention from the staff, although diagnostic studies confirmed that he was not in any gross physical danger. He appeared to make himself at home in the hospital, ordering staff members about in an imperious manner. It was plain that he had no interest in an early discharge, notwithstanding the stabilization of his physical condition. Staff members were in agreement that George would be very unlikely to accept formal psychological treatment for his problems. He was referred for outpatient care consisting of medication checks and superficial counseling (Adapted from Goldstein & Palmer, 1975, pp. 177–87).

George P.'s problems with dependency, particularly on his mother, are perhaps fairly obvious. We may also assume a reasonable likelihood that he was biologically predisposed to develop this particular malady. The psychosomatic aspects of peptic ulcer are not always so clear-cut; yet we probably know more about peptic ulcer than we do about any other allegedly psychosomatic illness. The case of peptic ulcer, therefore, provides a good opening to the field. Alas, it may also encourage an unwarranted optimism about the ease of identifying specific causal factors in these disorders.

Anorexia nervosa

Anorexia nervosa is a disorder of food ingestion in which the individual, by refusing food or by vomiting shortly after eating, produces a marked reduction in bodily mass to the point of threatened death by starvation. Once apparently quite rare, the incidence of the disorder has increased alarmingly in recent years, for reasons that remain obscure. Some consider anorexia nervosa to be related to conversion neurosis. However, given its widespread and very serious effects on various organ systems, it seems wiser to include it within the psychosomatic category. In the DSM-III, anorexia nervosa is classified as one of several "eating disorders."

Criteria for the diagnosis of anorexia nervosa have become more or less formalized in recent years (see HIGHLIGHT on page 261). The disorder is much more common in females than in males, on the order of 20 to 1 (Crisp, 1977), a discrepancy that may suggest differing underlying mechanisms in the two sexes. Estimates of the death rate from anorexia nervosa range from a low of 3 or 4 percent to a high of 25 percent (Bemis, 1978). Its occurrence must therefore always be regarded as a clinical emergency requiring prompt and vigorous therapeutic intervention.

Perhaps the strongest evidence for a psychogenic etiology in females with this disorder is the peculiar and virtually universal ces-sation of menstruation, typically occurring well before starvation has set in and often even prior to a perceptible loss in weight. The sensitivity of the menstrual cycle to emotional factors and to stress has been well established in numerous contexts.

Several other psychosocial characteristics have been noted. Patients are usually reported as being from the upper socioeconomic levels. Onset of the disorder is confined largely to the adolescent or young adult years. A history of unusual or bizarre eating habits, including uncontrolled eating binges, is common. A distorted bodily image, particularly an overestimation of one's physical dimensions, is almost universal. In terms of enduring personality characteristics, these patients are usually described as sensitive, dependent, introverted, anxious, perfectionistic, selfish, and unusually stubborn. They almost invariably report a decrement or disappearance of sexual interest and motivation. Typically, they have been extremely conscientious in regard to conventional "duties" such as school work (Bemis, 1978; Bruch, 1978; Palazzoli, 1978).

The mothers of anorexic patients are normally described in very unflattering terms: excessively dominant, intrusive, overbearing, markedly ambivalent; we must register caution here, however, in light of the possibility that mothers respond in these ways to the self-starvation of their children. By contrast, the fathers of anorexic girls are usually described as "emotional absentees."

Anorexia often begins when life changes are requiring new or unfamiliar skills concerning which the person feels inadequate, such as occurs in going off to college, getting married, or even reaching puberty. The characteristic internal conflict activated by such events seems to be, on the one hand, a desire to achieve an autonomous selfhood and, on the other, a pronounced fear of attaining the status of an independent adult (Bruch, 1978; Palazzoli, 1978). Food then becomes the phobic and obsessional context in which this drama is played out.

Not infrequently, the disorder begins as an extension of the ritual of normal dieting, which is common among young women. What distinguishes the normal dieter from the one who converts it into a dangerous flirtation with disaster remains a mystery. In any event, there

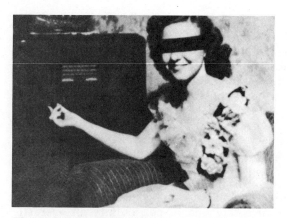

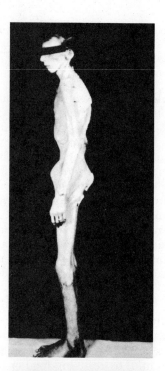

The woman in these pictures was diagnosed as suffering from a severe case of anorexia nervosa. At age 18 (above left), she weighed 120 pounds — within the normal range for her height of 5½ feet. She lost weight over a period of some 19 years, during which time she was married and divorced; at the age of 37, she was admitted to the hospital weighing 47 pounds (above right). During her stay she began a behavior therapy program that involved removal of all normal reinforcements such as mail, television, and magazines; provision of such reinforcements was made contingent on her eating adequate amounts of food and on her gaining weight. She made some progress in both of these areas—gaining 17 pounds in slightly over 3 months–and was discharged from the hospital. She continued her improvement as an outpatient, but at a lessened rate, gaining about 10 pounds in 11 months for a total weight of 74 pounds. At this time it was considered prudent to readmit her to the hospital to hasten her rate of progress. She was put on essentially the same program as previously, and in 5 weeks her weight had risen to 88 pounds (bottom right). She was discharged shortly thereafter (Bachrach, Erwin, & Mohr, 1965).

A follow-up of this woman's progress some 16 years later (Erwin, 1977) illustrates the frequent chronicity of this disorder and the difficulty in maintaining therapeutic gains. Erwin reported that during the 4 months after her second hospital discharge, the patient maintained a "reasonable" weight, increasing at one point to 90 pounds. Thereafter, however, she regularly lost weight, and though therapy brought intermittent weight gains, at the time of the 16-year follow-up, she weighed 55 pounds, only 8 more than she had weighed at the outset of therapy.

seems to be increasing acknowledgment that the syndrome of anorexia may be the extreme end of a continuum. We may thus speak meaningfully of a pre-anorexic state, in which individuals have extreme but not yet self-injurious aversions to food.

The case of Mary S., including her marked activity in the face of dwindling energy resources and her unfailing denial of the growing seriousness of her condition, is in most respects fairly typical of the anorexic syndrome:

"Mary S., aged sixteen and one-half years, grew disgusted with a close friend who began to put on weight by eating candy. The two girls agreed to go on a reducing diet, although Mary weighed only 114 pounds. A year later she graduated from high school and obtained a job as a stenographer. She began to lead a very busy life, working every day and going dancing at night with a young man who paid her attention. As her activities increased, her weight loss became more apparent; and soon her menses disappeared. Up to this time her dieting had been a voluntary control of eating, but now her appetite failed. Some months later one of the patient's sisters lured her boyfriend from her; Mary began to feel tired, and had to force herself to keep active. The onset of dizzy spells caused her to consult a doctor, who suggested a tonsillectomy. After the operation she refused to eat, but continued her active pace, including dancing every night. She now weighed 71 pounds. Two months later she became so dizzy and weak that she could no longer walk, and was finally brought to the hospital weighing 63 pounds. In three days, two and a half years after beginning her diet, Mary S. was dead of bronchopneumonia." (Nemiah, 1961, p. 10)

Anorexia nervosa, then, is a very puzzling and paradoxical psychosomatic entity. Quite literally, its victims, apparently without "intention," engage in a protracted program of self-destruction, refusing others' most urgent efforts to rescue them. It seems likely that the etiology of anorexia nervosa involves a substantial psychological component, although its features and mode of operation remain, to a large extent, a matter of speculation. Then, at some point in the process of withdrawal from eating, biological factors seem to become implicated, taking the behavior beyond conscious control and rendering it increasingly intractable. The best current guess is that such biological alteration is localized in the region of the hypothalamus, a richly interconnected structure in the brain involved in the regulation of motives and emotions (Bemis, 1978).

HIGHLIGHT

Criteria for diagnosis of anorexia nervosa

1. Onset before age 25.
2. Anorexia with accompanying weight loss of at least 25 percent of original body weight.
3. A distorted, implacable attitude toward eating, food, and weight that overrides hunger, admonitions, reassurance, and threats.
4. No known medical illness that could account for the anorexia and weight loss.
5. No other known psychiatric disorder.
6. At least two of the following manifestations:
   —Cessation of menstruation
   —Soft, downy hair over body surface
   —Persistent resting pulse of 60/min or less
   —Periods of overactivity
   —Binges of compulsive eating
   —Vomiting, which may be self-induced.

Based on Feighner et al. (1972).

Migraine and tension headaches

Although headaches can result from a wide range of organic conditions, the vast majority of them—about 9 out of 10—seem to be related to emotional tension. An estimated 50 million or more Americans suffer from recurrent tension and migraine headaches, with the overall incidence apparently being higher among women than men. Research in this area has focused primarily on migraine, an intensely painful headache that recurs periodically. Although typically involving only one side of the head, migraine is sometimes more generalized; it may also shift from side to side. In addition to these "ordinary" types of migraine headache, there is the sharp, stabbing "cluster" type that occurs in multiple episodes, often following a period of REM sleep (the period of sleep characterized by rapid eye movements and dreaming). For unknown reasons, ordinary migraine occurs about four times as often in females as in males, but the opposite is true for the cluster variety, in approximately the same ratio.

Migraine headaches

The side-view drawing of the head at left below shows the location of pain-sensitive cranial arteries, with the dotted lines marking the areas where the headache is felt as various parts of the arteries dilate.

The graph traces the course of a headache induced during a discussion which evoked feelings of hostility in a subject. Both the changes in the amplitude of the artery pulsations and the corresponding increase

and diminution in the intensity of the pain reported are shown. The headache was completely relieved by means of an injection which the subject believed would end the suffering but which actually could have had no physical effect.

Head redrawn from H. G. Wolff's *Headache and other head pain*, revised by Donald J. Dalessio. Copyright © 1948, 1963, 1972 by Oxford University Press, Inc. Reprinted by permission.

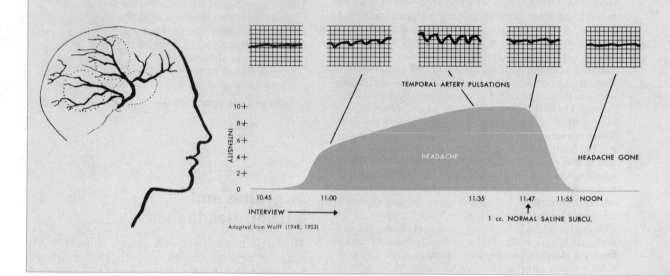

TEMPORAL ARTERY PULSATIONS

HEADACHE

HEADACHE GONE

INTENSITY

10+
8+
6+
4+
2+
0

10:45   11:00   11:35   11:47   11:55 NOON

INTERVIEW ⟶

1 cc. NORMAL SALINE SUBCU.

Adapted from Wolff (1948, 1953)

Migraine was described extensively by Galen and other medical writers of antiquity, but the cause of the pain remained a mystery until recently, when interest was focused on the pain-sensitive arteries of the head. By dilating these arteries with an injection of histamine, researchers found it possible to reproduce the pain of migraine. Turning to actual cases of migraine, they discovered that the onset of the headaches was accompanied by progressive dilation of these cranial arteries. In addition, persons with unilateral headaches showed dilation of the cranial artery only on the side where the pain occurred. As the attack subsided, either spontaneously or following the administration of drugs, the pain diminished and the arteries returned to their normal size.

It has also been shown that a variety of experimentally induced stressors—frustrations, excessive demands for performance, and threatening interviews—cause vascular dilation among migraine sufferers but not among other persons. The HIGHLIGHT on this page traces the course of a headache induced during a discussion that evoked feelings of hostility in the subject—a migraine sufferer.

The vast majority of headaches are so-called "simple" tension headaches. These, too, involve stress and vascular changes, but the changes are different from those in migraine headaches. Here, emotional stress leads to contraction of the muscles surrounding the skull; these contractions, in turn, result in vascular constrictions, which cause headache pain.

Both tension and migraine headaches usually make their appearance during adolescence and reoccur periodically during periods of stress, often being so painful as to be temporarily incapacitating unless they are alleviated or stopped by some form of treatment. Of the two types, however, migraine headaches are usually more painful and difficult to treat than simple tension headaches, in which the pain can often be relieved with simple analgesics, with muscle-relaxant drugs, or with certain relaxation-inducing psychological procedures, including biofeedback.

The presumed psychological underpinnings of psychogenic (psychologically induced) headaches are less clear than in the case of peptic ulcer. However, there seems to be a growing consensus among clinicians that it is important to the typical headache-prone person to be in *control* of events impinging on him or her. Such individuals are usually described as highly organized and perfectionistic in their character makeup (Williams, 1977). In one instance, a highly skilled nurse, who specialized in the demanding field of cardiac emergencies and who was subject to excruciatingly severe migraine attacks, went to a clinic for therapy but was so bent on maintaining control of virtually every aspect of the therapeutic relationship that she managed to sabotage it with a regularity astonishing to both herself and her therapist.

Hypertension

Of the various organ systems, the cardiovascular system is probably the most sensitive to emotional stress. During states of calm, the beat of the heart is regular, pulse is even, blood pressure is relatively low, and the visceral organs are well supplied with blood. With stress, however, the vessels of the visceral organs are constricted, and blood is directed in greater quantity to the muscles of the trunk and limbs—changes that help put the body on an emergency footing for maximum physical exertion. The tightening or restricting of the tiny vessels to visceral organs forces the heart to work harder. As it beats faster and with greater force, the pulse quickens and blood pressure mounts. Usually, when the crisis passes, the body resumes normal functioning and the blood pressure returns to normal. But under continuing emotional strain, high blood pressure may become chronic.

About 12 percent of Americans suffer from chronically high blood pressure, or *hypertension*. It is the primary cause of more than 60,000 deaths each year, and a major underlying factor in another million or more deaths a year from strokes and cardiovascular disease. Hypertension is also a risk factor in kidney failure, blindness, and a number of other physical ailments. For reasons that are not entirely clear but apparently relate in part to diet, the incidence of hypertension is about twice as high among blacks as among whites (Edwards, 1973; Mays, 1974). In fact, for every black person who dies from sickle-cell anemia, an estimated one hundred die from hypertension.

Unlike the other psychosomatic disorders we have dealt with, there are usually no symptoms to signal high blood pressure. The individual experiences no personal distress. In severe cases, some persons complain of headaches, tiredness, insomnia, or occasional dizzy spells—symptoms often easy to ignore—but most persons suffering from hypertension receive no warning symptoms. In fact, Nelson (1973) reported on one survey encompassing three middle-class neighborhoods in Los Angeles which revealed that a third of the adults tested had high blood pressure; only half of them had been aware of it. As Mays (1974) has described the situation,

"In most instances . . . the disease comes as silently as a serpent stalking its prey. Someone with high blood pressure may be unaware of his affliction for many years and then, out of the blue, develop blindness or be stricken by a stroke, cardiac arrest or kidney failure." (p. 7)

Since there is no such thing as "benign hypertension," high blood pressure is considered an insidious and dangerous disorder. Ironically, high blood pressure is both simple and painless to detect by means of a medical examination.

In many cases a physical cause of hypertension can be identified. For example, it may be attributable to certain diseases of the kidney, to a narrowing of the aorta or one of its arteries, to the excessive use of certain drugs, or to dietary factors. But a number of investigators have shown that chronic hypertension may be triggered by emotional stress. For example, a highly stressful job markedly increases the risk of high blood pressure (Edwards, 1973), and the stresses of ghetto life—as well as dietary factors—have been identified as playing a key role in the high incidence of hypertension among black people (Mays, 1974). The normal regulation of blood pressure, however, is so complex that when it goes awry in a particular case, identifying the causal factors is extremely difficult. Kidney dysfunction, for example, may be a cause or an effect of dangerously elevated pressures—or both.

Obvious preexisting organic factors can be ruled out in 90 to 95 percent of hypertension cases (Byassee, 1977); thus the condition is often called *essential* hypertension (*essential* being a term used to denote an absence of known physical causes). Recently, obesity, long suspected as an etiological factor, has emerged as a possible underlying factor in several other known correlates of hypertension, such as poor diet and lack of exercise (Ostfeld & D'Atri, 1977). Obesity, of course, can and frequently does have a marked relationship to the current level of experienced stress.

The classical psychodynamic interpretation of hypertension is that affected persons suffer from suppressed rage, and there is scattered evidence to support this hypothesis. Although there is high incidence of hypertension in the black ghetto population, among whom suppressed rage might be expected to run high (Harburgh et al., 1973), the suppressed-rage hypothesis concerning the etiology of essential hypertension cannot be said to be firmly established in respect to all, or even necessarily a majority, of affected persons.

More recently, a variant of the suppressed-rage hypothesis of essential hypertension has been proposed by McClelland (1979). According to this view, the essential hypertensive individual is driven not so much by rage and the need to suppress it as by power motives and the need to inhibit their expression, unexpressed anger then being a frequent accompaniment. In a well-conceived study designed to test these ideas, McClelland found that personality measures of "need for power" and "activity inhibition" were indeed jointly associated with elevated blood pressures. Moreover, he demonstrated that this inhibited

power motive syndrome in men in their 30s accurately predicted elevated pressure and signs of hypertensive disease in these same men twenty years later.

As the following case illustrates, hypertensive reactions may appear even in young people.

Mark _____, a senior in law school, evidenced episodes of extreme hypertension whenever he was subjected to stress. He became aware of these episodes when he failed to pass his physical examination for induction into the armed forces because of exceptionally high blood pressure. In a later check at a medical clinic, under nonstressful conditions, his blood pressure was normal; however, under simulated stress conditions, his blood pressure showed extreme elevation, and it happened again when he returned for another physical examination at the induction center.

Although most people show temporary alterations in blood pressure under stress, it would appear that under severe and sustained stress, persons like Mark run a high risk of developing chronic hypertension.

Heart attacks

Heart attacks are often referred to as "the twentieth-century epidemic." More people in the United States die from heart attacks than from any other cause, to say nothing of the many additional thousands who survive but suffer crippling effects.[2] For unknown reasons women are rarely victims of heart attacks before menopause; afterward, however, their rate is the same as that for men. Although there are various types and causes of heart attacks, a very frequent antecedent is hypertension—itself a leading psychosomatic disorder.

In a study of sudden cardiac death, Rahe and Lind (1971) gathered life-change data on 39 subjects over the last three years prior to their

---

[2]Although "heart attack" implies a sudden episode rather than a continuing condition, it is a "wastebasket" term that includes a variety of heart disorders, such as cardiac arrest, coronary insufficiency, coronary thrombosis, myocardial infarction, and angina pectoris. The broader terms *cardiac ischemia* and *coronary heart disease* are sometimes used as roughly synonymous with *heart attack*.

sudden cardiac deaths. (Their chart showing the estimated stressfulness of various life-change units is on page 110). Both for those with prior histories of coronary heart disease and for those without, there was a threefold increase in the number and intensity of life-change units during the final six months of their lives as compared to the rest of the three years prior to death.

Similarly, in a study of 50 patients, aged 40 to 60, admitted consecutively to a hospital following their first heart attack—as contrasted with 50 healthy controls—Thiel, Parker, and Bruce (1973) found significant differences between the two groups with respect to the incidence of divorce, loneliness, excessive working hours, sleep disturbances, nervousness, anxiety, and depression. While leaving room for exceptions resulting primarily from biological factors, these investigators, as well as Rahe and Lind, concluded that their findings point to a direct relationship between life stressors and heart attacks.

In a study of 229 men from three countries (Finland, Sweden, and the United States) who had recently survived a myocardial infarction (one type of heart attack), it was found that common background factors included heavy work responsibility, time urgency coupled with hostility when slowed by others, and dissatisfaction with the achievement of life goals (Romo, Siltanen, Theorell & Rahe, 1974). Again it would appear that severe stress and heart attacks tend to be causally related.

Stress is not, of course, exclusively a product of the environment, unrelated to one's personal idiosyncrasies. Some individuals seem to carry their stress around with them, so to speak, and manage to convert the most ordinary of life circumstances into a struggle for dominance, power, and control. This is the all-too-familiar Type A person, originally described by Friedman and Rosenman (1959). The Type A pattern has been described in terms of an eagerness to compete, frequent engagement with self-imposed deadlines, intense desire for recognition, mental and physical alertness and quickness, and strong drives toward self-selected but poorly defined goals.

Type A males in the 39 to 49 age range are said to run a risk of coronary heart disease that is six times greater than that of Type B men —men who are less impatient and exhibit traits that are otherwise opposite to those of Type A (Suinn, 1977). It is patently clear, then, that this notoriously lethal and disabling type of disease is in part caused by personal proclivities that are unrelated to the other risk factors in coronary disease, such as hypertension, obesity, smoking, and diet. The implication is that a change of life-style may be quite as important as, say, a change of diet in preventing coronary disease. Unfortunately, there is no real assurance that the one is any more easy to change than the other.

Other specific reaction patterns

We have now made a fair sampling of some of the major types of specific psychosomatic disorders. In our discussion of peptic ulcers, anorexia nervosa, psychogenic headache, hypertension, and heart attacks, most of the principal dimensions of psychosomatic illness have been introduced, at least in passing.

A large number of other physical diseases have also been considered at various times— and often with less justification—to be predominantly psychosomatic. A good example here is the problem of asthma, a disorder of the breathing apparatus in which air exchange is rendered difficult because of bronchiolar constriction. Not so very long ago, this bronchiolar constriction was assumed to be caused by emotional problems, sometimes even a specific type of emotional conflict. Further research, however, has cast doubt on the concept of asthma as caused entirely by psychological factors (Alexander, 1977). Current thinking emphasizes the importance of predisposing physical factors: in many—perhaps most— cases of asthma there may be some type of innate vulnerability to interference with the autonomic regulation of breathing. Support for this position is provided by the fact that asthma attacks sometimes occur at times when the individual is not under stress; here, apparently, the triggering factors are biological.

On the other hand it is clear that emotional upheaval may trigger an attack in a predisposed person. It is also clear that some asthmatics learn to use their symptoms—or the threat of their emergence—to control the people around them.

A similar situation exists with respect to several other disorders that had often been assumed to be psychologically caused. It is now recognized that *either* biological or psychological factors may play the triggering role in given cases of skin eruptions, allergies, ulcerative colitis, chronic diarrhea, rheumatoid arthritis, varied menstrual disorders, Raynaud's disease (a serious circulatory disorder), chronic disturbances of the sleep cycle, enuresis, insatiable hunger and obesity, excessive sweating, hiccoughs, and varied endocrine disturbances.

General causes of psychosomatic disorders

In this section we shall be concerned both with the general causes of psychosomatic disorders and with the problem of organ specificity—of why, under stress, one individual develops peptic ulcers, another hypertension, and still another migraine headaches.

Much remains to be learned about the interacting roles of biological, psychosocial, and sociocultural variables in predisposing an individual to psychosomatic disorders as well as in precipitating and maintaining them. However, the primary causal factor that underlies all of these disorders is *life stress*. In essence, chronic emotional tension elicited by life situations perceived as threatening can cause profound changes in the physiological functioning of the human body; these changes, in turn, can trigger the development of the various disorders we refer to as psychosomatic.

In general, the development of psychosomatic disorders appears to involve the following sequence of events: (a) the arousal of negative emotions in response to stressful situations—the degree of arousal depending not only on the nature of the stressful situation, but also on the individual's perception of the situation and stress tolerance for it; (b) the failure of these emotions to be dealt with adequately—either through appropriate expression or through a changed frame of reference or improved

competence—with the result that the emotional arousal continues on a chronic basis; and (c) the concentration of organ system response—either the concentration of damaging effects on specific organs or more generalized changes that render the body more vulnerable to varied pathogens. In the discussion that follows, we shall be concerned with the possible significance of particular biological, psychosocial, and sociocultural variables in contributing to this chain of events.

Biological factors

A number of biological factors have been implicated in psychosomatic disorders, directly or indirectly. These include genetic factors, differences in autonomic reactivity, somatic weakness, and alterations in corticovisceral control mechanisms.

Genetic factors. Research by Gregory and Rosen (1965) has demonstrated that the brothers of ulcer patients are about twice as likely to have ulcers as comparable members of the general population. Increased frequencies of hypertension, migraine, and other reactions have also been reported for close relatives of individuals with these disorders.

Although we now know that learning could be a factor in such family resemblances, further research evidence is needed, and genetic factors should not be ruled out. In fact, it would probably be difficult to discover any disease of humankind in which genetic factors could be ruled out entirely.

The implicated *interaction* of genetic and psychological influences is illustrated in the findings of Liljefors and Rahe (1970), who studied the role of life stress in coronary heart disease among twins. The subjects consisted of 32 pairs of identical male twins, between 42 and 67 years of age, in which only one twin in each pair suffered from coronary heart disease. These investigators found that the twins suffering from heart disease were more work oriented, took less leisure time, had more home problems, and, in general, experienced greater dissatisfactions in their lives.

Differences in autonomic reactivity. In our earlier discussion of personality development in Chapter 4, we noted that individuals vary significantly in "primary reaction tendencies." Even very young infants reveal marked differences in their sensitivity to aversive stimuli; some infants react to such stressors by developing a fever, others by digestive upset, and still others by disturbances in sleeping. Such differences in reactivity continue into adult life, and presumably help account for individual differences in susceptibility to psychosomatic disorders, as well as for the disorder that a given individual is most likely to develop.

In connection with the latter point, Wolff (1950) suggested that people can be classified as "stomach reactors," "pulse reactors," "nose reactors," and so on, depending on what kinds of physical changes stress characteristically triggers in them. For example, a person who characteristically reacts to stressful situations with a rise in blood pressure will be particularly vulnerable to hypertension, whereas one who reacts with increased secretion of stomach acids will be more likely to develop peptic ulcers.

Somatic weakness. The organ affected may be one that is especially vulnerable. Factors as diverse as heredity, illness, or prior trauma may produce somatic weakness in a particular organ system, making it more vulnerable to stress than others. The person who has inherited or developed a "weak" stomach presumably will be prone to gastrointestinal upsets during anger or anxiety. The person who has an inherited tendency to respond to stressors with increased cardiac output and vasoconstriction may be at risk for the development of chronic hypertension (Friedman & Iwai, 1976).

Presumably, the weakest link in the chain of visceral organs will be the organ affected. However, caution must be exercised to avoid *ex post facto* reasoning, since it would not be safe to conclude when a particular organ system is affected that it must have been weak to begin with. Also, as we shall see, conditioning may play a key role in determining which organ system is involved.

Inadequate corticovisceral control mechanisms.   Other biological explanations have focused on the role of cortical control

mechanisms in regulating autonomic functioning (see HIGHLIGHT on page 268). According to one hypothesis, corticovisceral control mechanisms may fail in their homeostatic functions, so that the individual's emotional response is exaggerated in intensity and physiological equilibrium is not regained within normal time limits (Halberstam, 1972; Lebedev, 1967). Such faulty control might well be central to deficient hypothalamic regulation of *both* the autonomic nervous system and the adrenocortical hormones. A combination of response stereotypy and faulty visceral control mechanisms appears to predispose the individual to psychosomatic disorders in the face of continued stress.

In assessing the role of biological factors in psychosomatic disorders, most investigators would take into consideration each of the factors we have described. Perhaps the greatest emphasis at present would be placed on the characteristic autonomic activity of given individuals, the vulnerability of affected organ systems, and possible alterations in cortical control mechanisms that normally regulate autonomic and endocrinologic functioning.

Psychosocial factors

The role of psychosocial factors in psychosomatic disorders is still not altogether clear. Factors that have been emphasized include personality characteristics, including failure to learn adequate coping patterns, the kind of stressor, interpersonal relationships, and learning in the autonomic nervous system.

Personality characteristics and inadequate coping patterns.   The work of Dunbar (1943, 1954) and a number of other early investigators raised the hope of identifying specific personality factors associated with particular psychosomatic disorders—for example, rigidity, high sensitivity to threat, and chronic underlying hostility among those who suffer from hypertension. The ability to delineate ulcer types, hypertensive characters, accident-prone personalities, and so on, would, of course, be of great value in understanding, assessing, and treating psychosomatic disorders—and perhaps even in preventing them.

More recent research evidence, however,

suggests that such an approach is oversimplified. For example, although Kidson (1973) found hypertensive patients as a group to be significantly more insecure, anxious, sensitive, and angry than a nonhypertensive control group, a sizable number of the control-group members also showed these characteristics. Similarly, Jenkins (1974), using Friedman and Rosenman's Type A formulation described earlier (p. 265), gave test questionnaires to 2700 men who had not had heart attacks up to that time and then followed them over a four-year period. The men who had scored high on Type A behavior had twice as many heart attacks during this follow-up period as those who had scored low. Nevertheless, the majority of high scorers did not have heart attacks, and some of the low scorers did.

So even though personality makeup seems to play an important role, we still do not know why some individuals with similar personality characteristics do *not* develop psychosomatic disorders; nor can we account adequately for the wide range of personality makeup among the individuals who suffer from psychosomatic disorders. Usually we can at best conclude only that particular personality factors are weakly but significantly correlated with the occurrence of a psychosomatic disorder.

A related approach has focused on the possible relationship between an individual's attitudes toward stressful situations and the coping pattern, both psychological and physiological, that he or she develops. Graham (1962) found the following attitude and coping patterns fairly typical:

Ulcers—feels deprived of what is due, and wants to get what is owed or promised and to get even;
Migraine—feels something has to be achieved, drives self to reach a goal, and then feels let down;
Eczema—feels frustrated but is helpless to do anything about it except take it out on himself or herself;
Hypertension—feels endangered, threatened with harm, has to be ready for anything, to be on guard.

Partial and suggestive support for the hypotheses in relation to eczema (hives) and hypertension was obtained in a quite ingenious way: by hypnotically inducing the pertinent "attitudes" in normal subjects and finding that the predicted changes in their physiology did in fact occur (Graham, Kabler, & Graham, 1962). Subsequently, Gottlieb, Gleser, and Gottschalk (1967) replicated this result and were able also

Biological clocks

The 24-hour rhythmic fluctuations observable in the activity and metabolic processes of plants and animals—indeed, all living creatures on earth—are referred to as *circadian* cycles, from the Latin words meaning "about a day." Thus, normal functioning for each system or individual appears to follow a biological clock; and an upset in this cycle, caused by changes in schedule or other factors, may cause malfunctioning in the form of somatic or psychosomatic complaints.

Thousands of experiments with lower animals have established the relationship between biological clocks and normal functioning. And humans—although found to be somewhat more adaptable to environmental changes than lower animals—have revealed similar cyclic fluctuations in activity and sleep, body temperature, chemical constituents of the blood, and so on. Interestingly enough, these cycles have remained essentially the same even for human subjects who have lived in caves, cut off from all means of knowing whether it was day or night for periods as long as several months.

In studies of disturbances in circadian cycles in humans—e.g., a sudden reversal of sleep schedules from night to daytime—subjects have demonstrated various degrees of adaptability. And in experiments that simulated manned space flights, some subjects reacted well to unusual schedules of work and rest—e.g., working for 4 hours, then resting for 4 hours—while others were unable to adapt to them.

A report prepared for the National Institute of Mental Health by Weitzman and Luce (1970) has noted the potential adverse effects of technological change—including abrupt time changes associated with jet travel—on "the invisible circadian cycle that may govern our susceptibility to disease or shock, our emotions, our performance, our alertness or stupefaction" (p. 279).

to produce a decrease in skin temperature (thought to be associated with the pathology underlying Raynaud's disease, p. 266) by inducing a feeling of mistreatment and desire to strike back. The chief importance of studies of this type is that they circumvent the problem of reactivity—the possibility that a patient's attitude may have been caused by having the disease in question, rather than the other way around. However, this work has proved difficult to replicate (Peters & Stern, 1971) and has not been followed up in a systematic manner.

Many individuals suffering from psychosomatic disorders appear unable to express their emotions adequately by verbal means, nor have they effectively learned to use various ego-defense mechanisms—such as rationalization, fantasy, and intellectualization—to alleviate their emotional tension. As a consequence, they rely primarily on repression, which does screen their feelings from conscious awareness. However, the physiological components of the emotion continue and may finally lead to structural damage.

Normally, when individuals are subjected experimentally to frustrating experiences, blood pressure rises and the heart beats more rapidly. But when they are then given an opportunity to express physical or verbal aggression against the frustrator, there is a rapid return to normal blood pressure and heart rate. If they are permitted only fantasy aggression or no aggression at all, however, there is a much slower return to normal physiological functioning (Hokanson & Burgess, 1962). Thus besides looking at people's ability to cope with the stress of frustration or conflict or whatever, it seems necessary to consider their ability to deal adequately with the accompanying emotional tensions.

In general, it would appear that the possible role of attitudes, coping patterns, and other personality factors merits further exploration. At present, however, it seems likely that these factors are only a part of the total causal pattern rather than being of primary or unique causal significance.

Kind of stressor. Approaching the problem from the standpoint of the environmental stressor rather than the personality of the patient, F. Alexander (1950) hypothesized that each type of psychosomatic disorder could be associated with a particular kind of stressor. He concluded that peptic ulcers, for example, are typically associated with frustration of the needs for love and protection. Presumably, the frustration of these needs gives rise to such emotions as anxiety and anger, and these emotions, in turn, trigger excessive secretions of stomach acid—leading eventually to peptic ulcers. Except in the specific case of ulcers, however, subsequent research has failed to

demonstrate a consistent relationship between particular disorders and particular stressors. Rather it would appear that a wide range of stressful situations can lead to a given type of disorder—and, conversely, that a wide range of disorders can result from a given type of stressor.

While efforts to relate specific stressors to specific psychosomatic disorders have not generally been successful, stress is a key underlying theme in these disorders. Stress may serve as a predisposing, precipitating, or reinforcing factor in the causal pattern, or it may merely aggravate a condition, such as rheumatoid arthritis, which might have occurred anyway. Often stress appears to speed up the onset, increase the severity of the disorder, and/or interfere with the body's immunological defenses and other homeostatic functions.

Interpersonal relationships. In our previous discussions, we have repeatedly noted the destructive effects that stressful interpersonal patterns—including marital unhappiness and divorce—may have on personality adjustment. Such patterns may also influence physiological functioning. In fact, death rates from varied causes, including physical disease, are markedly higher in persons who have recently undergone marital disruption or divorce than in the general population (Bloom, Asher, & White, 1978).

Loss of a spouse through death also puts the survivor at risk. For example, in a study of widowers, Parkes, Benjamin, and Fitzgerald (1969) reported that during the six-month period following the death of their wives, the widowers' death rate was 40 percent above the expected rate. In fact, the incidence of cardiac deaths among them was so high that the investigators referred to "this pattern as "the broken-heart syndrome."

Other studies have focused on the role of pathogenic family patterns. For example, studies of asthmatic patients have found that the mothers of such patients have in many cases felt ambivalent toward their children and tended to reject them, while at the same time being overprotective and unduly restrictive of the children's activities (Lipton, Steinschneider, & Richmond, 1966; Olds, 1970). Since individuals coming out of such family backgrounds tend to be overdependent and insecure, it would hardly be surprising if they should react with chronic emotional mobilization to problems that do not seem threatening to most people. On the other hand, as we have seen, a strictly psychosomatic interpretation of asthma is questionable. Severe asthma is a terrifying and life-threatening disorder. It would not be surprising on this basis alone to discover that asthmatic children are overdependent and insecure, or that their mothers tend to become ambivalent, protective, and restrictive after the asthma appears.

Learning in the autonomic nervous system. Although Pavlov and other investigators have demonstrated that autonomic responses can be conditioned—as in the case of salivation—it was long assumed that an individual could not learn to control such responses voluntarily. We now know that this assumption is not valid. Not only can autonomic reactivity be conditioned involuntarily via the classical Pavlovian model, but operant learning in the autonomic nervous system can apparently also take place.

Thus the hypothesis has developed that psychosomatic disorders may arise through accidental conditioning and reinforcement of such patterns. "A child who is repeatedly allowed to stay home from school when he has an upset stomach may be learning the visceral responses of chronic indigestion" (Lang, 1970, p. 86). Similarly, an adolescent girl may get little or no attention from being "good," but the reactions that follow her starving herself to the point of severe weight loss may make her the center of attention. If this pattern is continued, she might learn to avoid weight gain at all costs and correspondingly learn a profound aversion to food. The increasing alarm of her parents and others would presumably serve as a potent reinforcement for her to continue in her dietetically errant ways.

Although causal factors other than conditioning are now thought to play a role in most cases of psychosomatic disorders, it seems clear that regardless of how a psychosomatic response may have developed, it may be elicited by suggestion and maintained by the reinforcement provided by secondary gains. The role of suggestion was demonstrated by a study in which 19 of 40 volunteer asthmatic subjects developed asthma symptoms after breathing the mist of a salt solution that they were told contained allergens, such as dust or pollen. In fact, 12 of the subjects had full-fledged asthma attacks. When the subjects then took what they thought was a drug to combat asthma (actually the same salt mist), their symptoms disappeared immediately (Bleeker, 1968). Here we see the effect of suggestion on an autonomically mediated response. Why the other 21 subjects remained unaffected is not clear.

In short, it would appear that some psychosomatic disorders may be acquired or maintained or both in much the same way as other behavior patterns. Indeed, this is a basic tenet of the currently resurgent field of behavioral medicine, in which various behavior modification techniques are employed in a systematic manner to alter overt and/or covert organismic reactions related to physical disease processes (Williams & Gentry, 1977).

Sociocultural factors

The incidence of specific disorders, both physical and mental, varies in different societies, in different strata of the same society, and over time, as we have seen. In general, psychosomatic disorders, including ulcers, hypertension, anorexia nervosa, tension headaches, and heart attacks, occur among all major industrialized societies. On the other hand, such disorders appear to be extremely rare among nonindustrialized societies like the aborigines of the Australian Western Desert (Kidson & Jones, 1968) and among the Navajo Indians of Arizona and certain isolated groups in South America (Stein, 1970). As these societies are exposed to social change, however, gastrointestinal, cardiovascular, and other psychosomatic disorders begin to make their appearance. There is evidence of change in the nature and incidence of psychomatic disorders in Japan paralleling the tremendous social changes that have taken place there since World War II (Ikemi et al., 1974). For example, the incidence of hypertension and heart attacks has increased markedly with the post-war westernization of Japanese culture.

In our own society, a number of early studies found a disproportionately high incidence of psychosomatic disorders at the two extremes of the socioeconomic scale (Faris & Dunham, 1939; Pasamanick, 1962; Rennie & Srole, 1956). More recently, however, reports have cast doubts on these early findings. After an extensive review of the literature, Senay and Redlich (1968) found that psychosomatic disorders were no respectors of social class or other major sociocultural variables. Similarly, Kahn (1969) found that only a small number of executives develop peptic ulcers; in fact, blue-collar workers who are dissatisfied with their jobs are more likely to develop ulcers than successful business executives who are moving up on the occupational ladder. And while black people in our society show a higher incidence of hypertension than whites, this finding is confounded by different dietary habits, including the excessive use of salt by many black citizens (Mays, 1974).

This statement is not meant to minimize the importance of ghetto life stressors, but to point out that stress is common in other communities as well. For example, we noted that one survey found a third of the adults in three middle-class neighborhoods in Los Angeles to be suffering from hypertension. Although a higher stress level probably contributes to the higher incidence of hypertension among blacks than among whites, it apparently does not provide the entire explanation.

In general, it would appear that any sociocultural conditions that markedly increase the stressfulness of living tend to play havoc with the human organism and lead to an increase in psychosomatic disorders as well as other physical and mental problems.

Treatment and Outcomes

As we saw earlier in the chapter, the distinction between the classic psychosomatic disorders and other illnesses that have psychogenic components has become blurred; thus the treatment for almost any physical illness may include not only the physical procedures appropriate to the particular illness but also an attempt to lessen the stressfulness of the individual's situation and encouragement of an optimistic attitude. There are, however, more specific forms of intervention in the case of the classic psychosomatic disorders.

Though a particular environmental stressor may have been a key causal factor in the development of a psychosomatic illness, removal of this stressor, even combined with development of more effective coping techniques, may be insufficient for recovery if organic changes have taken place. Furthermore, such changes may have become irreversible.

Treatment, therefore, starts with an assessment of the nature and severity of the organic pathology currently involved as well as the roles of psychosocial and organic factors in the total causal pattern. In hypertension, for example, the role of dietary factors may far outweigh that of current psychosocial conditions in causation. Dietary patterns, however, reflect cultural patterns and attitudes that also may have to be reckoned with. Thus a thorough assessment involving the past and present roles of biological, psychosocial, and sociocultural factors seems to be an essential starting point for formulating an effective treatment program.

Except for psychosomatic disorders involving serious organic pathology, treatment is similar to that for the neuroses; the outcomes of treatment are likewise reasonably favorable. Instead of going into detail concerning the methods of treatment and outcomes for each type of psychosomatic disorder, we shall briefly summarize the general treatment measures that are used.

Biological measures

Aside from immediate and long-range medical measures, such as emergency treatment for bleeding ulcers or long-range treatment for coronary heart disease, biological treatment typically focuses on the use of mild tranquilizers aimed at reducing emotional tension. Such drugs, of course, do not deal with the stressful situation or the coping reactions involved. But by alleviating emotional tension and distressing symptoms, they may provide the individual with a "breathing spell," during which to "regroup" his or her coping resources.

Other drugs, such as those used to control high blood pressure, are prescribed on a more specific basis. Dietary measures may be indicated in certain psychosomatic reactions, including peptic ulcers, migraine headaches, and hypertension. Acupuncture as a method of treatment is still undergoing intensive research; although it does appear useful in alleviating certain types of pain, such as that of tension and migraine headaches, a notable problem here has been that of disentangling acupuncture and placebo effects (Berk, Moore, & Resnick, 1977; Chaves & Barber, 1973; Gaw, Chang, & Shaw, 1975). Electrosleep—cerebral electrotherapy—has produced mixed results in the treatment of psychosomatic disorders as it has in the neuroses. Preliminary findings appear promising in the use of this method for insomnia, but more research is needed (Hearst, Cloninger, Crews, & Cadoret, 1974; Miller, 1974; Rosenthal, 1972).

Morita therapy, which progresses from biological to psychological measures and was described on page 246, has been reported as being effective with a number of psychosomatic as well as neurotic disorders (Murase & Johnson, 1974).

Psychosocial measures

Although family therapy has shown promising results in the treatment of anorexia nervosa and other psychosomatic disorders, cognitive psychotherapies—aimed at helping patients understand their problems and achieve more effective coping techniques—have been relatively ineffective. The most promising psychological measures appear to lie in the direction of behavior therapy and biofeedback.

Behavior therapy. Behavior-modification techniques are based on the assumption that since autonomic responses can be learned, they can also be unlearned via extinction and differential reinforcement. In one case, the patient, June C., was a 17-year-old girl who had been sneezing every few seconds of her waking day for a period of 5 months. Medical experts had been unable to help her, and Kushner, a psychologist, volunteered to attempt treatment by behavior therapy.

"Dr. Kushner used a relatively simple, low power electric-shock device, activated by sound—the sound of June's sneezes. Electrodes were attached to her forearm for 30 minutes, and every time she sneezed she got a mild electric shock. After a ten-minute break, the electrodes were put on the other arm. In little more than four hours, June's sneezes, which

had been reverberating every 40 seconds, stopped. Since then, she has had only a few ordinary sneezes, none of the dry, racking kind that had been draining her strength for so long. 'We hope the absence of sneezes will last,' said Dr. Kushner cautiously. 'So do I,' snapped June. 'I never want to see that machine again.' " (*Time*, 1966, p. 72)

In a follow-up report, Kushner (1968) stated that a program of maintenance therapy had been instituted, and at the end of 16 months the intractable sneezing had not recurred.

Wolpe (1969) has reported a strategy involving deconditioning of the anxiety reaction to particular stresses. Using this technique, he has reported success with peptic ulcers, migraine, neurodermatitis (an eruption of the skin, usually involving severe itching, believed to be psychogenically caused), and many other psychosomatic disorders.

Since Wolpe's early work, a large number of studies have been done on the effects of various behavioral relaxation techniques in selected psychosomatic disorders. Results claimed have been highly variable and sometimes quite disappointing. For example, simple tension headaches have proven quite amenable to general relaxation treatment procedures (Cox, Freundlich, & Meyer, 1975; Tasto & Hinkle, 1973), whereas the same kinds of procedures have so far been somewhat disappointing when used in the treatment of essential hypertension (Schwartz, 1978; Surwit, Shapiro, & Good, 1978).

The limits of behavior therapy alone in treating psychosomatic disorders remain to be established, and a great deal of work is continuing in this area. Taking a broad view, it may turn out that the greatest contribution of behavioral approaches to health maintenance will be in the area of altering self-injurious "habits," such as smoking and excessive alcohol use, in systematic programs that teach "self-control" (Ainslie, 1975; Goldfried & Merbaum, 1973; Rimm & Masters, 1974). Behavioral approaches to the control of pain also appear promising (Weisenberg, 1977).

Biofeedback. In bowling or serving a tennis ball, we receive immediate feedback and can correct our behavior accordingly, but such feedback is usually not available with respect to autonomic functions, such as heart rate and brain waves. The new biofeedback devices are designed to provide such feedback: they monitor these functions and convert the information into signals like lights or sounds that the individual can readily perceive.

In an early study involving the control of heart rate, for example, Lang, Stroufe, and Hastings (1967) provided subjects with equipment that measured heart rate. The subjects received visual feedback on the dial and were instructed to maintain their heart rates within prescribed limits. Although the subjects could not explain how they did it, they gradually became able to do so: somehow, mental set and exposure to feedback information enabled them to achieve the desired result.

More recent studies have dealt with control of a wide range of psychosomatic and other disorders, including hypertension, headache, backache, muscular spasms, teeth grinding, epilepsy, sexual impotency, and irregular heartbeat. However, the actual magnitude and duration of results is a matter of some controversy. For example, Davis, Saunders, Creer, and Chai (1973) used relaxation training facilitated by biofeedback training in the treatment of bronchial asthma in children. Asthma symptoms were reduced in nonsevere cases but not in cases considered as severe. Similarly, as in the case of general relaxation training for hypertension, biofeedback treatment of this condition has yielded somewhat equivocal results (Surwit et al., 1978).

On the other hand, Murata (1973), Blanchard and Young (1974), and Budzynski (1974) have pointed to the success of biofeedback in treating migraine and tension headaches. In fact, Budzynski reported that 81 percent of his patients with migraine headaches were helped to a significant extent by biofeedback training. Comparable results have been reported by Friar and Beatty (1976).

As in the case of behavior therapy for psychosomatic disorders, biofeedback training, which may be seen as a special application of behavioral techniques, is currently undergoing enormous expansion and development into virtually all areas of psychosomatic medicine (Fuller, 1978); in fact, to some investigators (e.g., Katkin & Obrist, 1978) it seems that the field is developing faster than is warranted by sound research data. (See Chapter 19 for more information on behavioral techniques).

Sociocultural measures

Treatment measures here are concerned with modifying conditions in the community and broader society that place large numbers of people under severe and sustained stress. They are also concerned with changing cultural patterns that make people more vulnerable to certain types of psychosomatic disorders.

As we learn more about the role of biological, psychosocial, and sociocultural factors in the etiology of psychosomatic disorders, it becomes increasingly possible to delineate "high-risk" individuals and groups—such as the heart attack-prone Type A personalities and groups living in a precarious and rapidly changing life situation. This, in turn, enables treatment efforts to focus on early intervention and even prevention. In this context, counseling programs—aimed at fostering changes in maladaptive life-styles of individuals and families and remedying pathological social conditions—seem eminently worthwhile.

In this chapter we have noted the increased understanding of the role of psychological factors in physical health and disease. Psychological factors have specific effects that seem to be mediated primarily by the autonomic nervous system and by the stress-response system, as conceptualized in Selye's general adaptation syndrome. Prolonged reactions to stress seem to be a common denominator.

We have also surveyed the field of classic psychosomatic disorders, pointing out that with the general psychological approach to all medical problems, these are no longer seen as distinct from other illnesses. Five of the classic psychosomatic symptom patterns—peptic ulcer, anorexia nervosa, migraine and tension headaches, hypertension, and heart attacks—were described in some detail, and it was pointed out that simplified hypotheses as to causation are rarely feasible. However, inasmuch as many of these reactions seem in part to be learned (although it may require a biologically vulnerable individual to learn them), it should be possible in principle to unlearn them. This idea is the foundation for many of the newer and more promising forms of treatment.

9

Personality disorders and crime

Personality disorders
Antisocial (psychopathic) personality
Criminal behavior

In this chapter we shall be dealing with disorders that typically do not stem from defenses against anxiety, as in the neuroses; or from emotional tension, as in the psychosomatic disorders; or from personality decompensation, such as we shall see in the psychoses. Rather, they stem from immature and distorted personality development, resulting in individuals with persistent maladaptive ways of perceiving, thinking, and relating to the world around them that usually cause significant impairment of functioning and in some cases cause subjective distress.[1] Essentially they are "acting out" patterns rather than intrapsychic disturbances. Often these patterns of personality and behavior are recognizable by adolescence, and they continue into adult life. Traditionally, the terms *personality disorders* and *character disorders* have been used interchangeably to describe these problems.

The category of personality disorders is a broad one, with behavior problems that differ greatly in form and severity. On the mildest end of the spectrum we find individuals who generally function adequately but would be described by their relatives or associates as troublesome or eccentric. They have characteristic ways of approaching situations and other people that make them difficult to get along with, yet they are often quite capable or even gifted in the work world. At the other end of the spectrum are individuals whose more extreme and in many cases unethical "acting out" against society makes them less able to function in a normal setting; many are incarcerated in prisons or maximum security hospitals, although their ability to manipulate others may keep them from getting caught.

The prevalence of personality disorders is unknown, since many of these individuals never come in contact with mental health or legal agencies. Many such individuals, however, do become identified through the correctional system. Others eventually show up in the statistics of alcohol treatment programs or through court-ordered evaluations. Although we have no accurate estimates as to what percentage of incarcerated individuals would be classified as having personality disorders, it is believed that the figure would be quite high.

In this chapter we shall first consider the several types of disordered personality that have been identified, then examine one of them—antisocial personality—in greater detail, and finally look at criminal behavior, in which these disorders often—but not always—play a role. Personality disorders are also often a factor in several disorders that will be considered in other chapters, such as alcoholism and pathological gambling (Chapter 10), sexual deviations (Chapter 15), and delinquency (Chapter 14). Although "juvenile delinquency" does in fact sometimes represent the early stages of a lifelong process of personality disorder, it often does not: much of the acting-out behavior of adolescence, including much delinquency, is limited to the adolescent years. This is why delinquency will be discussed with the other special disorders of childhood and adolescence.

Personality disorders

Individuals with personality problems that disrupt social relations and cause other people great difficulty can be found in almost everyone's daily life. In his autobiography, Benjamin Franklin (1771) wrote about being "taken" by such an individual. As a young man he was put to great inconvenience by a politician who kept promising to help him secure a loan to buy a printing press in England:

"The governor, seeming to like my company, had me frequently to his house, and his setting me up was always mention'd as a fixed thing. I was to take with me letters recommendatory to a number of his friends, besides the letter of credit to furnish me with the necessary money for purchasing the press and types, paper, etc. For these letters I was appointed to call at different times, when they were to be ready, but a future time was still named. Thus he went on till the ship, whose departure too had been several times postponed, was on the point of sailing. Then, when I call'd to take my leave and receive the letters, his secretary, Dr. Bard, came out to me and said the governor was extremely busy in writing, but would be down at Newcastle before the ship, and there the letters would be delivered to me." (p. 39)

---

[1]Sometimes behavior patterns similar to those in the personality disorders are determined primarily by the residual effects of head injuries or other brain pathology. Such cases will be considered in our discussion of brain disorders (Chapter 13).

When Franklin arrived in England there were no letters. He located a friend who related to Franklin that in all probability the man had not even written the letters and that anyone who knew him would not depend on him. He was also reputed to be involved in schemes with an attorney who was "a very knave." Franklin summarized the governor's character problems:

But what shall we think of a governor's playing such pitiful tricks, and imposing so grossly on a poor ignorant boy! It was a habit he had acquired. He wish'd to please everybody; and having little to give, he gave expectations. He was otherwise an ingenious, sensible man, a pretty good writer, and a good governor for the people, tho' not for his constituents, the proprietaries, whose instructions he sometimes disregarded. (p. 41)

Apparently, although the governor's "habits" placed many people in difficult situations and resulted in a severe lack of trust among his constituents, he also seemed adept at winning some positive acclaim. Like many individuals with personality disorders, the irresponsibility and disregard for others seemed to be offset by charm and ability.

Clinical picture in personality disorders

Although people like the governor have been around for some time—probably since the beginning of human interaction—their behavior patterns are rather new to clinical texts and diagnostic manuals: they were not clearly described until the publication of the American Psychiatric Association's first *Diagnostic and Statistical Manual* (DSM-I) in 1952. Before that, they were regarded as "disorders of character" found in people who were otherwise essentially normal—problems "without psychosis" (Murray, 1938).

Although several types of personality disorders have been delineated, according to the particular distorted trait pattern that is prominent, individuals with personality disorders have several features in common:

a) Perhaps most characteristic in all of them is the pattern of disrupted personal relationships. Whether they are narcissistic or dependent or passive-aggressive, they usually leave a trail of interpersonal problems marked by the difficulties they have caused others.

b) Another characteristic of these individuals is their perception that any difficulties they are experiencing have come about through bad fortune or through the action of others. Thus they have usually no feeling that they are at fault or need to change. Instead, they typically perceive the world as wrong, and they often show an angry, demanding quality in their manner.

c) Since they are blameless and others are causing all the difficulties, these individuals feel no responsibility toward other people. They are frequently manipulative, self-seeking, without guilt for unethical behavior, and without remorse for hurting others. They appear to have a callous disregard for the welfare of others and an overriding concern for taking care of themselves.

d) Whatever the particular trait pattern they have developed (obstinacy, covert hostility, or suspiciousness, for example), it colors each new situation they meet and leads to a repetition of the same maladaptive patterns of behavior. For example, the dependent person "wears out" a relationship with someone, such as a spouse, by incessant and extraordinary demands; then when the spouse tires of the situation and leaves, the person immediately goes into another dependent relationship and repeats the behavior. Thus personality disorders are marked by considerable consistency over time, with no apparent learning from previous troubles.

e) The lack of responsibility these individuals show for others is accompanied by an avoidance of responsibility for the problems they create. Rather than assume blame, they project it onto others. An example is the man who believes he is doing society a service by stealing products made by a large corporation because "the corporation is too big and rich."

f) It follows from the preceding that these disorders are in a sense disorders of reputation: they are marked by the imprint the behavior has on others rather than by the pain felt by the individual. Typically these individuals are known not by what they have reported to the clinician but by the report of others. They rarely take the initiative in seeking therapy and when referred for therapy by others have little or no motivation to profit from it. Instead, they are likely to disrupt or sabotage it—or to leave it if possible.

All these characteristics lead to the fractured and deteriorated relationships that are the hallmark of the personality disorders.

Types of personality disorder

The several special types of personality disorder are classified according to the particular characteristic (dependence, avoidance, etc.) that is most prominent, although in given cases the dividing lines are often unclear. This characteristic, in turn, is predictive of what kind of disordered relationships can be expected.

Often, of course, an individual will show some characteristics of more than one type, making diagnosis difficult. And in many cases personality disorders are part of a larger pattern of pathology. For example, an individual who is addicted to drugs might also be characterized as having a dependent personality. In this case, the long-continuing personality disorder might well have been a causal factor in the development of the addiction. As we saw in Chapter 1, the DSM-III classification has separate axes for recording psychiatric symptom disorders and long-term personality features. Here the drug problem would be recorded on Axis I and the dependent personality disorder on Axis II.

A special caution is in order regarding the use of labels for personality disorders. Perhaps more misuse of labels occurs here than in other categories. There are three special problems. One is the comparative paucity of research on these disorders; they are not as sharply defined as other categories, nor do we have as clear a set of criteria for them. For example, although Small and Small (1971) found a number of common characteristics in a group of individuals classified as passive-aggressive personalities, these were hospitalized cases and may not have been representative of all passive-aggressive personalities.

A second problem is that the personality characteristics that are features of the personality disorders can also be found, on a smaller scale and less intensely expressed, in many normal individuals. For example, liking one's

Many of the traits associated with character disorders are seen in less extreme form in the general population. A social psychologist's experiment on vandalism highlights the pervasiveness of these characteristics and the difficulties in setting the point at which they should be considered abnormal. An automobile was "abandoned" on a New York City street and photographers hidden to record the action. In the first picture, a white middle-class family strips the car of its most valuable components; in the second, a man takes the best tires. Finally, after the car had been completely stripped, wanton destruction began; passersby broke windows and bashed in the metal until only a useless hulk remained. Should the behavior of these individuals be considered pathological? (Based on Zimbardo, 1973.)

work and being conscientious about the details of one's job does not make one a "compulsive personality" nor does being economically dependent automatically make a spouse a dependent personality. Applying diagnostic labels to people who are functioning well enough to be outside a hospital setting is always risky; it is especially so where diagnosis involves judgment about characteristics that are also typical of normal individuals.

A third problem is that personality disorders are defined by inferred traits rather than by clearly observed behaviors. There are objective behavioral criteria for drug intoxication or somatization disorder but not for dependent or compulsive personality patterns. Traits are inferred from consistencies in behavior but can never be seen directly. For this reason, some researchers have questioned the whole concept of traits (e.g., Mischel, 1968), urging instead that predictions always be based on observable behavior.

Some day a more objective scheme for the personality disorders may be devised. In the meantime, however, the trait-based categories will continue to be used, with the recognition that they are more dependent on the observer's judgment than one might wish.

With these cautions, we shall look at three clusters of personality disorders that have been identified.

Paranoid, schizoid, and schizotypal personality disorders.

Individuals with these disorders all often seem odd or eccentric, although their eccentricities take three quite different forms.

Paranoid personality is characterized by suspiciousness, hypersensitivity, rigidity, envy, excessive self-importance, and argumentativeness, plus a tendency to blame others for one's own mistakes and failures and to ascribe evil motives to others. Such individuals are constantly expecting trickery and looking for clues to validate their expectations, while disregarding all evidence to the contrary. They are keenly aware of power and rank, envious of those in high places, and disdainful of those who seem weak or soft.

Schizoid personality is characterized by an inability to form social relationships and a lack of interest in doing so. Such individuals seem unable to express their feelings and are seen by others as cold and distant; they often lack social skills and can be classified as "loners," with solitary interests and occupations.

The following case of a schizoid personality illustrates a fairly severe personality problem in a man who was functioning adequately as judged both by occupational criteria and by his own standards of "happiness." When he sought help, it was at the encouragement of his supervisor and his physician.

Bill D., a highly intelligent but quite introverted and withdrawn 33-year-old computer analyst, was referred for psychological evaluation by his physician, who was concerned that Bill might be depressed and unhappy. At the suggestion of his supervisor, Bill had recently gone to the physician for rather vague physical complaints and because of his gloomy outlook on life. Bill had virtually no contact with other people. He lived alone in his apartment, worked in a small office by himself, and usually saw no one at work except for the occasional visit of his supervisor to give him new work and pick up completed projects. He ate lunch by himself and about once a week, on nice days, went to the zoo for his lunch break.

Bill was a life-long loner: as a child he had very few friends and always preferred solitary activities over family outings (he was the oldest of five children). In high school he had never dated and in college had gone out with a woman only once—and that was with a group of students after a game. He had been active in sports, however, and had played varsity football in both high school and college. In college he had spent a lot of time with one relatively close friend—mostly drinking. However, this man, also a rather introverted person, now lived in another city.

Bill reported that he has a hard time making friends; he never knows what to say in a conversation. On a number of occasions he has thought of becoming friends with other people but simply can't think of the right words, so "the conversation just dies." He reported that he has given some thought lately to changing his life in an attempt to be more "positive," but it never seems worth the trouble. It is easier for him not to make the effort because he becomes very anxious and embarrassed when someone tries to talk with him. He is happiest when he is alone.

Schizotypal personality is characterized by seclusiveness, oversensitivity, avoidance, and eccentricities of communication and behavior. Such individuals are egocentric and frequently tend to see chance events as related to themselves. Autistic and superstitious thinking are common, though reality contact is usually maintained. Their oddities in thinking, talking, and other behavior are similar to those often seen in more severe form in schizophrenic patients; in fact, they might previously have been diagnosed as exhibiting borderline or latent schizophrenia.

Histrionic, narcissistic, antisocial, and borderline personality disorders.

Individuals with these personality disorders have in common a tendency to be dramatic, emotional, and erratic. Their acting-out behavior is more colorful, more forceful, and more likely to get them into contact with mental health or legal authorities than is true of disorders in the first cluster.

Histrionic personality is characterized by immaturity, excitability, emotional instability, a craving for excitement, and self-dramatization (an attention-seeking device that is often seductive in nature). Sexual adjustment is usually poor and interpersonal relationships are stormy. These individuals often show dependence and helplessness and are quite gullible. Usually they are self-centered, vain, and overconcerned about approval from others, who see them as overly reactive, shallow, and insincere.

Narcissistic personality is characterized by an exaggerated sense of self-importance and a preoccupation with receiving attention. These persons are grandiose and constantly expect and demand special treatment from others. Yet the fragility of their self-esteem is revealed by their preoccupation with how others are regarding them. They are interpersonally exploitative in serving their own goals, disregarding the rights and feelings of others.

Antisocial personality is characterized by continuing violation of the rights of others through aggressive, antisocial behavior, without remorse or loyalty to anyone. Some antisocial personalities have enough intelligence and social charm to devise and carry out elaborate schemes for conning large numbers of people. Imposters fit in this category. Because this pattern has been studied more fully than the others, it will be examined in some detail later in this chapter.

Borderline personality is characterized by instability, reflected in drastic mood shifts and behavior problems. Often these persons display

intense anger outbursts with little provocation, and they may show a disturbance in basic identity which preoccupies them and produces a basically negative outlook. Such individuals are frequently described as impulsive and unpredictable, angry, empty, and periodically unstable. They may have short episodes that appear psychotic. A low frustration tolerance is common.

Avoidant, dependent, compulsive, and passive-aggressive personality disorders.

In this cluster of disorders, unlike the others, there is often anxiety and fearfulness, making it difficult in some cases to distinguish them from the neuroses. Because of this anxiety, individuals suffering from these disorders are more likely than the others to seek help.

Avoidant personality is characterized by hypersensitivity to rejection and apprehensive alertness to any sign of social derogation; such individuals readily see ridicule or disparagement where none was intended. There is a lifelong pattern of limited social relationships and reluctance to enter into social interaction. These individuals are too fearful of criticism and rebuff to seek out other people, yet they desire affection and are often lonely and bored. Unlike the schizoid personality, they do not enjoy their aloneness: their inability to relate comfortably to other people is a source of acute distress and low self-esteem.

Dependent personality is characterized by extreme dependence on other people and acute discomfort—even panic—at having to be alone. These individuals usually build their lives around other persons and subordinate their own needs to keep the other person involved with them. They lack self-confidence and feel helpless even when they have actually developed good work skills or other competencies. They function well as long as they are not required to be on their own. The following case is one in which a woman with a dependent personality experienced such distress following desertion by her husband that she sought help.

Sarah D., a 32-year-old mother of two and a part-time tax accountant, came to a crisis center late one evening after Michael, her husband of a year and a half, abused her physically and then left home. Although he never physically harmed the children, he frequently threatened to do so when he was drunk. Sarah appeared acutely anxious and worried about

Individuals with certain types of personality disorders are frequently "loners," appearing cold and distant and avoiding social interaction. Some, like schizoid personalities, find their solitariness a sanctuary—to others it is a prison of which their own fears are the lock.

the future and "needed to be told what to do." She wanted her husband to come back and seemed rather unconcerned about his regular pattern of physical abuse. At the time, Michael was an unemployed resident in a day treatment program at a halfway house for paroled drug abusers that taught abstinence from all addictive substances through harassment and group cohesiveness. He was almost always in a surly mood and "ready to explode."

Although Sarah had a well-paying job, she voiced great concern about being able to make it on her own. She realized that it was foolish to be "dependent" upon her husband, whom she referred to as a "real loser." (She had had a similar relationship with her first husband, who had left her and her oldest child when she was 18.) Several times in the past few months Sarah had made up her mind to get out of the marriage but couldn't bring herself to break away. She would threaten to leave, but when the time came to do so, she would "freeze in the door" with a numbness in her body and a sinking feeling in her stomach at the thought of "not being with Michael."

Compulsive personality is characterized by excessive concern with rules, order, efficiency, and work, coupled with an insistence that everyone do things their way and an inability to express warm feelings. Such individuals tend to be overinhibited, overconscientious, overdutiful, and rigid, and to have difficulty relaxing or doing anything just for fun. There is usually a preoccupation with trivial details and poor allocation of time.

The symptoms of this disorder are somewhat similar to those of neurotic compulsive disorders. In obsessive-compulsive neurosis, however, the individual suffers from the persistent intrusion of particular undesired thoughts (obsessions) or actions (compulsions) that are a source of extreme anxiety because the individual recognizes that they are irrational but cannot seem to control them. Obsessive personalities, on the other hand, have a whole life-style characterized by obstinacy and compulsive orderliness. Although they may be anxious about getting all their work done in keeping with their exacting standards, they are not anxious about their compulsiveness itself (Pollak, 1979).

Passive-aggressive personality is characterized by hostility expressed in indirect and nonviolent ways as, for example, by procrastination, obstructionism, pouting, stubbornness, intentional inefficiency, or "forgetting." These individuals resent and manage not to comply with demands others make on them; the behavior is most apparent in their work situations but also occurs in their social relationships. Resentment against authority figures, coupled with a lack of assertiveness, is typical.

Causal factors in personality disorders

Establishing the causal factors in personality disorders has not progressed as far as with many other disorders, partly because such disorders were not even included in the official classifications before 1952 and partly because they are less amenable to thorough study. Many individuals with these disorders are never seen by clinical personnel, as we have seen. Those who do come to the attention of clinicians or legal authorities have already developed the "full-blown disorder" so that only *retrospective* study is possible—that is, going back through what records may exist in an effort to reconstruct the chain of events that may have led to the disorder. As we saw in Chapter 5, researchers have more confidence in *prospective* studies, in which groups of individuals are observed before a disorder appears and followed over a period of time to see which individuals develop problems and what causal factors have in fact been present.

Research on causal factors in disordered personality is also made more difficult by the fact that it is general traits of personality rather than specific behavior patterns that are being studied, and it is hard to identify the point at which "inability to express anger directly," for example, ceases to be within the normal range and becomes pathological.

Heredity and constitution. Early theorists saw body type as a predisposing factor in mental disorder. They hypothesized links between physique and emotional temperament that would predict what kind of disorder would be most likely *if* the individual should develop a disorder but not whether one would in fact develop (Kretschmer, 1921; Sheldon, 1954). Research has failed to support their predictions, however. Where physique is a factor in the development of a disorder—or of personality traits generally—it seems to be indirect. For example, an unattractive physique may lead others to see and treat an individual in a deprecating way; the individual may then develop an unhealthy self-concept, leading to greater susceptibility to maladjustment.

It has also been suggested that the constitutional reaction tendencies that infants display (high or low vitality, special sensitivity, and so on) may predispose the individual to the development of particular personality disorders. So far, this remains a hypothesis: there is no evidence linking particular constitutional reaction tendencies to the development of personality disorders, with the possible exception of the antisocial personality, to be discussed later.

Psychosocial factors. In Chapter 3 we discussed several general theories of personality development; in Chapter 4 we looked at the general role of biological, psychosocial, and sociocultural factors in both development and adjustment; and in Chapter 5 we looked at factors associated with the development of abnormal behavior, including several pathogenic family patterns that are conducive to the development of particular faulty personality patterns in children. Much of the discussion there seems relevant to an understanding of the probable antecedents of the various personality disorders. Precise causal patterns remain in the sphere of speculation and inference, however. Except to some extent for antisocial personality, research has not yet established particular antecedents for these disorders.

Sociocultural factors. We are even less able to point to specific sociocultural causes of personality disorder. We do know, however, that incidence and form of psychopathology in general vary somewhat with time and place, and some clinicians believe that personality disorders have increased in this society in recent years (Smith, 1978). If this is true, we can expect to find the increase related to changes in the assumptions. priorities, and activities in our culture generally. Is our present high value on impulse gratification, instant solutions, and pain-free benefits leading more people to develop the self-centered, manipulative, and irresponsible life-style that we see in more extreme form in the personality disorders? Only further research can clarify this picture.

Treatment and outcomes

People with personality disorders are usually considered to be especially resistant to therapy. For example, speaking of antisocial personalities, Ellis (1977) pointed out that

"[they] are exceptionally difficult to treat with psychotherapy. They only rarely come for treatment on a voluntary basis; and when they are treated involuntarily, they tend to be resistant, surly, and in search of a "cure" that will involve no real effort on their part. Even when they come for private treatment, they are usually looking for magical, effortless "cures," and they tend to stay in treatment only for a short period of time and to make relatively little improvement." (p. 259)

In many cases people with personality disorders who are seen clinically are there as part of another person's treatment—as, for example, in couple counseling, where the partner identified as the "patient" has a spouse with a personality disorder. Or a child referred to a child guidance center may have a parent with a personality disorder. In these cases, of course, the problems of the so-called patient may be due in no small measure to the great strain that the family member with severe personality disorder is causing to other family members. The narcissistic father, who is so self-centered and demanding of attention from others that family relationships are constantly strained, leaves little room for small children to grow into self-respecting adults. Likewise, a mother whose typical manner of responding to others is through passive-aggressive maneuvers such as procrastination, obstruction, and pouting may create an unhealthy family atmosphere that frustrates the child's development.

A child subjected to such extreme, inescapable, and often quite irrational behavior on the part of one or both parents may become the "weak link" that breaks, bringing the family into therapy. Many a child or family therapist has quickly concluded after seeing a child in the family context that psychological attention, if it is to be effective at all, must be focused upon the parental relationships. The following case clearly illustrates the problem:

Mrs. A. brought her 7-year-old son, Christopher, to a mental health center for treatment because he was fearful of going out and recently had been having bad nightmares. Mrs. A. sought help at the recommendation of the school social worker after Chris refused to return to school. She voiced a great deal of concern for Chris and agreed to cooperate in the treatment by attending parent effectiveness training sessions. However, she seemed quite reluctant to talk about getting her husband involved in the treatment. After much encouragement, she agreed to try to bring him to the next session. He adamantly refused to participate, however. Mrs. A. described him as a "very proud and strong-willed man" who was quite suspicious of other people. She felt that he might be afraid people would blame him for Chris's problems. She reported that he had been having a lot of problems lately—he had seemed quite bitter and resentful over some local political issues and tended to blame others (particularly minority group people) for his problems. He refused to come to the clinic because he "doesn't like social workers."

After several sessions of therapy, Mrs. A. confessed to her therapist that her husband's rigid and suspicious behavior was disrupting the family. He would often come home from work and accuse her of, for example, "talking with Jewish men." He was a very domineering person who set strict house rules and enforced them with loud threats and intimidation. Both Mrs. A. and Chris were fearful of his tyrannical demands, but his suspicious nature made it difficult for them to explain anything to him. Mrs. A. also felt a great deal of sympathy for her husband because she felt that deep down inside he was very frightened; she reported that he kept numerous guns around the house and several locks on the doors for protection against outsiders, whom he feared.

Because they usually enter treatment only at someone else's insistence and do not believe that there is any need for them to change, individuals with personality disorders typically put the responsibility for treatment on others and are adept at avoiding the focus of therapy themselves. In addition, the difficulty they have in forming and maintaining good relationships generally tends to make the therapeutic relationship a stormy one at best. The pattern of acting out, typical in their other relationships, is carried into the therapy situation, and instead of dealing with their problem at the verbal level, they may become angry at the therapist and loudly disrupt the sessions. Or they may behave in socially inappropriate ways outside the session to show the therapist that the therapy is not working.

When questioned about such behavior, these individuals often drop out of treatment or become even more entrenched in their defensiveness. In some cases, however, confrontation can be quite effective. For individuals who become identified with a therapy group, or who are sufficiently "hooked" into couple therapy not to flee the session when their behavior comes under scrutiny, the intense feedback from peers or spouse often is more acceptable than confrontation by a therapist in individual treatment (Gurman & Kniskern, 1978; Lubin, 1976).

In some situations, therapeutic techniques must be modified. For example, Leeman and Mulvey (1973), recognizing that traditional individual psychotherapy tended to encourage dependency in already too dependent personalities, developed a treatment strategy in individual outpatient therapy for altering the individual's basic life-style of dependency instead of fostering it. First, they informed the patient at the outset that the therapy would be brief. Next, they made it clear that they "would not assume responsibility for managing the patient's life" (p. 36) and that they expected strength on the part of the patient "both to tolerate feelings and to behave in more adaptive and self-satisfying ways" (p. 36). Therapy sessions were then kept focused on relationships outside of therapy rather than on the treatment relationship, and demands were made on the patient to *change* his or her behavior—not just to understand it. Several highly dependent patients, including one "veteran" of ten years of individual psychotherapy, responded favorably to this treatment, and most reported that they were doing much better two and a half years later.

In general, therapy for individuals with personality disorders is much more likely to be effective in situations like prisons, where acting-out behavior can be constrained and the individual cannot leave the situation (Vaillant, 1975). Outpatient treatment is not promising in most cases. The tenacity of these disorders and the failure of the individuals either to profit from ordinary therapy or to learn from their life experiences is shown in the following case of an individual diagnosed as a passive-aggressive personality:

Charles, age 29, was, on first encounter, a highly successful salesman in a large retail shoe store. He was a handsome, friendly, and outgoing person who quickly impressed customers and gained ready admirers. His relationships with co-workers and employers, however, was an entirely different matter. He was a very disorganized person who couldn't keep the bookkeeping and stock in order. He was a procrastinator who promised everything but delivered nothing. He responded to criticism by his employers with smiles and promises but was never able to get organized. He never expressed anger toward his supervisor or disgruntled customers but seldom fulfilled their demands.

One evening, after he had been criticized for his sloppiness, he was directed to straighten out his "mess" and lock up the store after everyone else had left. He failed to comply and actually left the store open with the lights on. This was the last straw for his employer, and Charles was fired.

Over the years, his stubborn and passive-aggressive actions lost him several other jobs. In each situation he was able to secure a sales position quite readily but in short order his behavior angered his employers and the ensuing criticisms made him even more intractable.

He entered therapy at his wife's insistence because of marital problems they were experiencing. His behavior toward his wife was similar to his behavior in other personal relationships: he was obstinate and unyielding even though he always smiled and never lost his temper. After only two weeks in therapy he began to miss sessions until after a month he stopped coming altogether because "he had to look for work."

Antisocial (psychopathic) personality

Antisocial personality, as we have seen, is a personality disorder in which the outstanding characteristics are a marked lack of ethical or moral development and an apparent inability to follow approved models of behavior. Basically, these individuals are unsocialized and seemingly incapable of significant loyalty to other persons, groups, or social values. These characteristics often bring them into repeated conflict with society. The terms *psychopathic personality* and *sociopathic personality* are also commonly used in referring to this disorder.

The category called *antisocial personality* includes a mixed group of individuals: unprincipled business people, shyster lawyers, quack doctors, high-pressure evangelists, crooked politicians, imposters, drug pushers, a sizeable number of prostitutes, and assorted delinquents and criminals. Few of these individuals find their way into community clinics or mental hospitals. A much larger number are confined in penal institutions, but a history of repeated legal or social offenses is not sufficient justification for assuming that an individual is psychopathic. In point of fact, the great majority of psychopaths manage to stay out of corrective institutions, although they tend to be in constant conflict with authority (see HIGHLIGHT on this page).

The worldwide incidence of psychopathic personality is not known. In the United States, however, incidence is estimated to be about 3 percent of American males and about 1 percent of American females (APA, 1979). Onset is in early childhood for males but typically not until the onset of puberty for females.

Clinical picture in antisocial personality

Typically intelligent, spontaneous, and very likeable on first acquaintance, antisocial personalities are deceitful and manipulative, callously using others to achieve their own ends. Often they seem to live in a series of present moments, without consideration for the past or future. The following example is illustrative.

Two 18-year-old youths went to visit a teenager at her home. Finding no one there, they broke into the house, damaged a number of valuable paintings and other furnishings, and stole a quantity of liquor and a television set. They sold the TV to a mutual friend for a small sum of money. Upon their apprehension by the police, they at first denied the entire venture and then later insisted that it was all a "practical joke." They did not consider their behavior particularly inappropriate, nor did they think any sort of restitution for damage was called for.

In other cases antisocial individuals are capable of assuming responsibility and pursuing long-range goals, but they do so in unethical ways with a complete lack of consideration for the rights and well-being of others. In describing the "Case of Dan," a wealthy actor and disc jockey, McNeil (1967) pointed to Dan's lifestyle of abusing other people for his own amusement and profit. Dan had

"an unbelievable set of deceptive ways to deal with the opposition. Character assassination, rumor mon-

HIGHLIGHT

Wanted: Everyday psychopaths

Most antisocial individuals who have been studied have been cases who were institutionalized, leaving us in ignorance about the far larger number who never get caught. Widom (1977) tried an ingenious approach for reaching this larger group. She ran advertisements in the local newspapers which read:

"Are you adventurous? Psychologist studying adventurous, carefree people who've led exciting, impulsive lives. If you're the kind of person who'd do almost anything for a dare and want to participate in a paid experiment, send name, address, phone, and short biography proving how interesting you are to. . . ." (p. 675)

Widom had hoped to attract psychopathic individuals and apparently did just that. When given a battery of tests, those who responded turned out to be similar in personality makeup to institutionalized psychopathic individuals. Although she did not go further than this in studying these individuals, her method suggests a way of making contact with samples of uninstitutionalized psychopathic personalities.

gering, modest blackmail, seduction, and barefaced lying were the least of his talents. He was a jackal in the entertainment jungle, a jackal who feasted on the bodies of those he had slaughtered professionally." (p. 86)

Also included in the general category of antisocial personality are "hostile psychopaths," who are prone to acting out the impulses in remorseless and often senseless violence.

Only individuals 18 or over are diagnosed as antisocial personalities. According to the current DSM-III classification, this diagnosis is made if the following criteria are met: (a) if there were at least two instances of deviant behavior such as theft, vandalism, or unusually aggressive behavior before age 15; (b) if there have been at least three behavior problems such as financial irresponsibility, illegal occupation, and poor work history since age 15 and no period longer than five years without such a problem; (c) if the antisocial behavior is not a symptom of another mental disorder.

To fill in the clinical picture, let us begin by summarizing characteristics that antisocial personalities tend to share; then we shall describe three quite different cases which illustrate the wide range of behavior patterns that may be involved.

Common characteristics. While all the following characteristics are not usually found in a particular case, they are typical of antisocial personalities in general.

1. *Inadequate conscience development and lack of anxiety and guilt.* Antisocial personalities are unable to understand and accept ethical values except on a verbal level. They make glib verbalizations and claims of adherence to high standards of morality that have no apparent connection with their behavior. Because of the marked discrepancy between their level of intelligence and their level of conscience development, they have been referred to as "moral morons."

Antisocial personalities tend to "act out" tensions and problems rather than worry them out. Their apparent lack of anxiety and guilt, combined with the appearance of sincerity and candor, may enable them to avoid suspicion and detection for stealing and other illegal activities. They often show contempt for those they are able to take advantage of—the "marks."

2. *Irresponsible and impulsive behavior; low frustration tolerance.* Antisocial individuals generally have a callous disregard for the rights, needs, and well-being of others. They are typically chronic liars, and have learned to take rather than earn what they want. Prone to thrill-seeking and deviant and unconventional behavior, they often break the law impulsively and without regard for the consequences. They seldom forego immediate pleasure for future gains and long-range goals. They live in the present, without realistically considering either past or future. External reality is used for immediate personal gratification. Unable to endure routine or to shoulder responsibility, they frequently change jobs.

3. *Ability to put up "a good front" to impress and exploit others, projecting blame onto others for their own socially disapproved behavior.* Often antisocial individuals are charming and likeable, with a disarming manner that easily wins friends. Typically, they have a good sense of humor and an optimistic outlook. If detected in lies they will often seem sincerely sorry and promise to make amends— but not do so. They seem to have good insight into other people's needs and weaknesses and are very adept at exploiting them. For example, many psychopaths engage in unethical sales schemes in which they use their charm and the confidence they inspire in others to make "easy money." They readily find excuses and rationalizations for their antisocial conduct, typically projecting the blame onto someone else. Thus they are often able to convince other people—as well as themselves—that they are free of fault.

4. *Rejection of authority and inability to profit from experience.* Antisocial individuals behave as if social regulations do not apply to them: they do not play by the rules of the game. Frequently they have a history of difficulties with educational and law-enforcement authorities. Yet, although they often drift into criminal activities, they are not typically calculating professional criminals. Despite the difficulties they get into and the punishment they may receive, they go on behaving as if they will be immune from the consequences of their actions.

5. *Inability to maintain good interpersonal relationships.* Although initially able to win the liking and friendship of other people, antisocial personalities are seldom able to keep close friends. Irresponsible and egocentric, they are usually cynical, unsympathetic, ungrateful, and remorseless in their dealings. They seemingly cannot understand love in others or give it in return. As Horton, Louy, and Coppolillo (1974) have expressed it, the psychopathic personality "continues to move through the world wrapped in his separateness as though in an insulator, touched rarely and never moved by his fellow man" (p. 622).

Antisocial personalities pose a menace not only to chance acquaintances but also to family and friends. Manipulative and exploitive in sexual relationships, they are irresponsible and unfaithful mates. Although they often promise to change, they rarely do so for any length of time.

Many of the preceding characteristics may be found in varying degrees in neurotic individuals, in those dependent on drugs, and in those showing other maladaptive behavior patterns. In the case of the antisocial personality, however, these characteristics are extremely pronounced and occur apart from other "symptoms" of psychopathology. Whereas most neurotic individuals, for example, are beset by worry and anxiety and have a tendency to avoid difficult situations, antisocial personalities act on their impulses fearlessly, with little or no thought for the difficulties they may be incurring.

Patterns of behavior.

The following cases are useful in illustrating the range and variability of behavior that may be found among individuals labeled as psychopathic personalities.

"Donald S., 30 years old, has just completed a three-year prison term for fraud, bigamy, false pretenses, and escaping lawful custody. The circumstances leading up to these offenses are interesting and consistent with his past behavior. With less than a month left to serve on an earlier 18-month term for fraud, he faked illness and escaped from the prison hospital. During the ten months of freedom that followed he engaged in a variety of illegal enterprises; the activity that resulted in his recapture was typical of his method of operation. By passing himself off as the "field executive" of an international philanthropic foundation, he was able to enlist the aid of several religious organizations in a fund-raising campaign. The campaign moved slowly at first, and in an attempt to speed things up, he arranged an interview with the local TV station. His performance during the interview was so impressive that funds started to pour in. However, unfortunately for Donald, the interview was also carried on a national news network. He was recognized and quickly arrested. During the ensuing trial it became evident that he experienced no sense of wrongdoing for his activities. He maintained, for example, that his passionate plea for funds "primed the pump"—that is, induced people to give to other charities as well as to the one he professed to represent. At the same time, he stated that most donations to charity are made by those who feel guilty about something and who therefore deserve to be bilked. This ability to rationalize his behavior and his lack of self-criticism were also evident in his attempts to solicit aid from the very people he had misled. Perhaps it is a tribute to his persuasiveness that a number of individuals actually did come to his support. During his three-year prison term, Donald spent much time searching for legal loopholes and writing to outside authorities, including local lawyers, the Prime Minister of Canada, and a Canadian representative to the United Nations. In each case he verbally attacked them for representing the authority and injustice responsible for his predicament. At the same time he requested them to intercede on his behalf and in the name of the justice they professed to represent. . . .

"By all accounts Donald was considered a willful

and difficult child. When his desire for candy or toys was frustrated he would begin with a show of affection and if this failed he would throw a temper tantrum; the latter was seldom necessary because his angelic appearance and artful ways usually got him what he wanted. Similar tactics were used to avoid punishment for his numerous misdeeds. At first he would attempt to cover up with an elaborate façade of lies, often shifting the blame to his brothers. If this did not work, he would give a convincing display of remorse and contrition. When punishment was unavoidable he would become sullenly defiant, regarding it as an unjustifiable tax on his pleasures.

"Although he was obviously very intelligent, his school years were academically undistinguished. He was restless, easily bored, and frequently truant. His behavior in the presence of the teacher or some other authority was usually quite good, but when he was on his own he generally got himself or others into trouble. Although he was often suspected of being the culprit, he was adept at talking his way out of difficulty. . . .

"His sexual experiences were frequent, casual, and callous. When he was 22 he married a 41-year-old woman whom he had met in a bar. Several other marriages followed, all bigamous. In each case the pattern was the same: he would marry someone on impulse, let her support him for several months, and then leave. One marriage was particularly interesting. After being charged with fraud Donald was sent to a psychiatric institution for a period of observation. While there he came to the attention of a female member of the professional staff. His charm, physical attractiveness, and convincing promises to reform led her to intervene on his behalf. He was given a suspended sentence and they were married a week later. At first things went reasonably well, but when she refused to pay some of his gambling debts he forged her name to a check and left. He was soon caught and given an 18-month prison term. As mentioned earlier, he escaped with less than a month left to serve.

"It is interesting to note that Donald sees nothing particularly wrong with his behavior, nor does he express remorse or guilt for using others and causing them grief. Although his behavior is self-defeating in the long run, he considers it to be practical and possessed of good sense. Periodic punishments do nothing to decrease his egotism and confidence in his own abilities, nor do they offset the often considerable short-term gains of which he is capable." (Hare, 1970, pp. 1–4)

The most dangerous psychopathic personalities from the standpoint of society as a whole are those who are not only intelligent and completely unscrupulous but also show sufficient self-control and purposefulness of behavior to achieve high political office. This point is well illustrated by the case of Nazi Field Marshal Goering.

"Goering had a better family background than most of his Nazi associates. His father had been Governor of German Southwest Africa and Resident Minister at Haiti. Hermann attended several boarding schools but he was bored and restless till he got to the Military Academy, where he settled down to his studies. He entered the army as an infantryman but he took flying lessons surreptitiously and got himself transferred to the Air Force against the wishes of his superior officers. He was a courageous and impetuous flyer and after the death of Richthofen he took charge of The Flying Circus.

"At the close of the First World War Goering went to Sweden where he worked as a mechanic and as a civil aviator. He married a wealthy woman and was able to return to Germany and enroll at the University of Munich. In Munich he met Hitler and joined the Nazi movement. . . .

"Goering's manner of living is described as 'Byzantine splendor' and as 'piratical splendor.' He built a pretentious country home near Berlin and furnished it magnificently with tapestries and paintings and antiques. He had a private zoo. He required his servants to address his wife as Hohe Frau, thus giving her the distinction of nobility. He felt that the Germans liked his display of luxury—that it gave food for their imagination and gave the people something to think about. Goering was given to exhibitionism and he had a passion for uniforms, gold braid, medals, and decorations. . . . Goering would strut and swagger in private and public. In political rallies he made himself a flamboyant master of pomp and pageantry. He was an exhibitionist in the psychopathic pattern.

"Goering was coarse and gross. He was a Gargantuan eater and drinker. He was ribald in jest. He laughed uproariously when his pet lion urinated on a lady's dress. He once horrified his men and women guests at his country estate by having a bull and a cow mate before them. Personally he enjoyed the spectacle and declared that it was an old Teutonic custom.

"'Our Hermann' was popular with the masses and they smiled goodnaturedly at his antics and self-display. He demanded that they make sacrifices in order to win victory and exhorted them to choose guns instead of butter. He patted his fat belly and said that he had lost forty pounds in the service of his country. The Germans appreciated his sense of humor. . . .

"Goering was unscrupulous in his exercise of authority. He was said to be courageous, hard, challenging and authoritative in the Prussian manner. He was described as an affable, hearty butcher. . . .

When he was made Chief of the Prussian Police he told his men to shoot first and inquire afterward. 'If you make a mistake, don't talk about it.' 'The faults which my officials commit are my faults; the bullets they fire are my bullets.' Goering regarded his bullets as an effective form of propaganda. He introduced the concentration camp and declared that it was not his duty to exercise justice, but to annihilate and exterminate. He reintroduced decapitation as an honest old German punishment. Goering is given credit for plotting the Reichstag Fire and for the planning and direction of the Blood Purge. Goering admitted that he had no conscience; his conscience was Adolf Hitler.

"Like many a psychopath Goering had a tender side. He was fond of animals, including his lion cubs. He declared that 'He who torments an animal hurts the feelings of the whole German people.' . . .

"Goering was often considered the most normal and the most conservative of the Nazi leaders. Like most psychopaths he would appear normal in his social relationships and he might seem genial and kindly with his humor and laughter. His pattern of behavior, however, identifies him as a constitutional psychopath and he presents a fair example of this personality disorder." (Bluemel, 1948, pp. 78–82)

Found guilty as a war criminal at the Nuremberg trials following World War II, Goering was sentenced to death on the gallows. However, he managed to evade his punishment by obtaining a capsule of cyanide—an extremely fast-acting poison—and taking his own life.

One of the most interesting types of persons found in the category of antisocial personality is the impostor, whose abilities are often outstanding and might seemingly have been channeled in socially approved ways. This is well brought out in the following unusual case.

One of the boldest impostors of recent times was Ferdinand Waldo Demara, Jr. As an adolescent, he ran away from a rather tragic family situation and after unsuccessful attempts first to become a Trappist monk and then to teach school, he joined the army. Soon thereafter he went AWOL, joined the navy, and was assigned to duty on a destroyer during World War II. Here, by a ruse, he got hold of some navy stationery with which he managed to obtain the transcript of college grades of an officer who was on leave. He then "doctored" this transcript by substituting his own name and adding some courses; when photostated, it looked so impressive that he used it to apply for a commission. While waiting for his commission to come through, he amused himself by obtaining other records, including the full credentials of a Dr. French, who had received a Ph.D. degree in psychology from Harvard. Informed during a visit to Norfolk that he could expect his commission as soon as a routine security check was completed, he realized that such a check would surely expose him. Under cover of darkness, he left his navy clothes on the end of a pier with a note that "this was the only way out."

Now that Demara was "dead"—drowned in the oily waters off Norfolk—he became Dr. French. He obtained an appointment as Dean of Philosophy in a small Canadian college and taught courses in general, industrial, and abnormal psychology. Eventually, however, he had a disagreement with his superior and reluctantly left.

During this period he had become friends with a physician by the name of Joseph Cyr and had learned a considerable amount about the practice of medicine from him during the cold winter months when neither man had much to occupy his time. Interested in the possibility of getting a license to practice in the States, the trusting doctor had given Demara a complete packet including his baptism and confirmation certificates, school records, and his license to practice medicine in Canada.

Using these credentials, without Dr. Cyr's knowledge, Demara now obtained a commission for himself as lieutenant in the Royal Canadian Navy. His first assignment was to take sick call each morning at the base. To help solve his problem of lack of knowledge in the field, he went to his superior officer and stated that he had been asked to work up a rule-of-thumb guide for people in lumber camps, most of whom did not have physicians readily available. His senior officer, delighted with the project, prepared a manual covering the most serious medical situations, which served as a basic guide for amateur diagnosticians. Demara then used this manual faithfully as his own. He also studied medical books and evidently picked up considerable additional knowledge.

Assigned to duty on the aircraft carrier HMCS *Magnificent,* Demara was criticized by his senior medical officer for his lack of training in medicine and surgery, especially for his deficiency in diagnosing medical problems. Learning of the report, Demara took characteristic bold action. He commandeered several seamen's compartments in the lower area of the ship, posted them with quarantine signs, and sent there for observation the patients whom he was having trouble diagnosing—in the meantime giving them penicillin. The chief medical officer knew nothing of this plan—Demara had confided only in a bosun's mate—and the reports of Demara's performance, based only on cases that Demara reviewed with his superior officer, became more favorable.

Perhaps the climax of Demara's incredible career

came during the Korean War when—still as Lieutenant Cyr—he was assigned as the ship's doctor to the Canadian destroyer *Cayuga.* As the *Cayuga* proceeded to the combat zone, Demara studied medical books and hoped that his skill would never be put to the test. But fate decreed otherwise. One afternoon the destroyer spotted a small Korean junk littered with wounded men who had been caught in an ambush. "Dr. Cyr" was summoned and knew that there was no escape for him.

"Nineteen suffering men were lifted tenderly from the junk. Three were so gravely wounded that only emergency surgery could save them. Demara had read books on surgery, but had never seen an operation performed.

"The self-taught 'M.D.' cleaned and sutured the 16 less seriously wounded men, while gathering his courage for the great ordeal. Then he commandeered the captain's cabin as an emergency operating room. Working hour after hour with slow, unskilled hands, but drawing on all the resources of his great memory and natural genius, Demara performed miracles, while the ship's officers and dozens of enlisted men helped and watched.

"From one wounded man he removed a bullet that had lodged near the heart; from the second, a piece of shrapnel in the groin. For the third man, Demara collapsed a lung which had been perforated by a bullet.

"The operations began at midnight. When the pseudo surgeon looked up after the last operation the light of dawn was shining through the portholes. Drenched in his own sweat, with the cheers of officers and crew ringing in his ears, he took a long drink of the ship's rum, went to his cabin, and collapsed in a stupor of sleep."

When his ship was sent to Japan for refitting, an eager young press officer seized on "Dr. Cyr's" exploits and wrote them up in full. His story was released to the civilian press, and the "miracle doctor" became world famous. This publicity proved to be Demara's temporary undoing, for it led to queries from the real Dr. Joseph Cyr as to whether the physician mentioned in the press releases was a relative, and when Dr. Cyr saw the newspaper picture, he was shocked to find it was that of an old friend.

Dropped from the Canadian navy without fanfare—largely because he had managed to get a license to practice medicine in England and was now a licensed physician—Demara went through a difficult period. Wherever he went, he was soon recognized, and he lost job after job. He managed to work for a year at a state school for retarded children and did so well that he received a promotional transfer to a state hospital for the criminally insane. Here he found that the patients seemed to like him and that he was able to communicate with them. The experience began to bother him and he started to drink heavily and eventually resigned.

One morning after a prolonged drinking bout, he woke up in a southern city and realized his drinking was getting out of hand. He joined the local chapter of Alcoholics Anonymous as Ben W. Jones, whose credentials he had acquired along the way. With the help of sympathetic friends in Alcoholics Anonymous and a few fraudulent references obtained by ingenious methods, he was hired as a guard in a state penitentiary. Here he did a remarkable job, instituting a number of badly needed reforms in the maximum security block. Again he found himself able to communicate with the men, and he was promoted to assistant warden of maximum security. Ironically, one of his reform measures was to ask the townspeople to contribute old magazines, and before long one of the prisoners read the issue of *Life* that contained his picture and case history and recognized the new assistant warden.

Trying to get away lest he wind up as a prisoner in the same penitentiary, Demara was jailed in a nearby state and given considerable publicity but eventually released. Some time later he telephoned Dr. Crichton, from whose report most of this material has been adapted, to say "I'm on the biggest caper of them all. Oh, I wish I could tell you." (Summarized from Crichton, 1959; quoted passages from Smith, 1968.)

By way of a postscript, it may be mentioned that in early 1970 there was a newspaper report of Demara functioning successfully as a minister in a small northwestern community, this time with the congregation's full knowledge of his past. As we shall see, many persons labeled as "antisocial personalities" do eventually settle down to responsible positions in the community.

Causal factors in antisocial personality

Although the causal factors in antisocial personality are still not fully understood, it would appear that these factors differ from case to case as well as from one socioeconomic level to another. Contemporary research in this area has variously stressed constitutional deficiencies, the early learning of antisocial behavior as a coping style, and the influence of particular family and community patterns.

Constitutional factors. Because the antisocial individual's impulsiveness, acting out, and intolerance of discipline tend to appear early in life, several investigators have focused

And he turned blue in the face from preaching laboriously to the heathens!

During the 1960's Ferdinand Waldo Demara, the "great impostor," turned to the religious life and took up residence in an interfaith monastery in central Missouri.

on the role of constitutional deficiencies as causative factors in antisocial personality disturbances.

1. *Malfunction of inhibitory mechanisms in the central nervous system.* In a review and interpretation of studies indicating a relatively high incidence of EEG abnormalities among psychopathic personalities, particularly involving slow-wave activity in the temporal lobe of the brain, Hare (1970) concluded that such abnormalities reflect the malfunction of inhibitory mechanisms in the central nervous system, and that "this malfunction makes it difficult to learn to inhibit behavior that is likely to lead to punishment" (pp. 33–34).

It may be emphasized, however, that most psychopathic personalities do not show abnormal EEGs, and when they do, there is no conclusive evidence that the EEG patterns are directly related to the development of their behavior. In addition, many individuals who show similar EEG patterns are not psychopathic. So when brain anomalies do occur in psychopathic individuals, they are probably interactive factors rather than primary determinants of the maladaptive behavior.

2. *Deficient emotional arousal.* A good deal of research evidence indicates that psychopathic individuals are deficient in emotional arousal; this presumably renders them less prone to fear and anxiety in stressful situations and less prone to normal conscience development and socialization.

In an early study, for example, Lykken (1957) concluded that psychopathic individuals have fewer inhibitions about committing antisocial acts because they suffer little anxiety. Similarly, Eysenck (1960) concluded that psychopathic individuals are less sensitive to noxious stimuli and have a slower rate of conditioning than normal individuals. As a result, psychopathic individuals presumably fail to acquire many of the conditioned reactions essential to normal avoidance behavior, conscience development, and socialization. Support for this viewpoint is found in the more recent findings of Chesno and Kilmann (1975) who concluded that sociopathic individuals, as contrasted with normal persons, "were relatively unsuccessful in acquiring active avoidance responses" (p. 150).

Hare (1970) and other later investigators have reported comparable findings with respect to the psychopathic individual's lack of normal fear and anxiety reactions and failure to learn readily from punishment. However, the latter point merits qualification. Schmauk (1970) confirmed earlier observations that such individuals were less adept than nonpsychopathic individuals in learning to avoid physical and social punishments, but found them to be more adept than normal persons in learning to avoid the loss of money—a type of punishment that was apparently *meaningful* to them. These findings are more understandable when it is added that the individuals observed in this experiment were inmates of a penal institution where physical and social punishments were relatively mild for most forms of misbehavior, whereas money was both hard to come by and very valuable for obtaining niceties beyond the grim prison fare.

In addition, it may be noted that while the lack of normal emotional arousal may be based on constitutional deficiencies, it may also be based partially on learning. Often in the past psychopathic individuals have managed to avoid the full consequences of their antisocial behavior by such devices as lies and plausible excuses, dramatic shows of remorse, and empty but convincing promises of "good" behavior in the future. In fact, the absence of anxiety attributed to these individuals has been questioned by Vaillant (1975), who believes that they have simply learned to handle their anxiety differently. In Vaillant's view, rather than succumb to anxiety like neurotic individuals, they conceal it and in most cases find ways to escape from it. When they cannot flee, they may experience the anxiety, but they hide their feelings. Vaillant believes that this concealment of anxiety was learned because anxiety was intolerable to the parents. He points out that escaping from anxiety-arousing situations is an immature defense like those found in adolescence.

3. *Stimulation seeking.* In his study of criminally psychopathic individuals, Hare (1968) reported that these individuals operate at a low level of arousal and are deficient in autonomic variability. He considered these characteristics—together with their lack of normal conditioning to noxious and painful stimuli—indicative of a "relative immunity" to stimulation that would likely cause them to seek stimulation and thrills as ends in themselves. In a study comparing psychopathic and normal individuals, Fenz (1971) also found that the former seemed to have an insatiable need for stimulation.

Such findings support the earlier view of Quay (1965), who concluded that psychopathic behavior is, in essence, an extreme form of stimulation-seeking behavior:

"The psychopath is almost universally characterized as highly impulsive, relatively refractory to the effects of experience in modifying his socially troublesome behavior, and lacking in the ability to delay gratification. His penchant for creating excitement for the moment without regard for later consequences seems almost unlimited. He is unable to tolerate routine and boredom. While he may engage in antisocial, even vicious, behavior, his outbursts frequently appear to be motivated by little more than a need for thrills and excitement. . . . It is the impulsivity and the lack of even minimal tolerance for sameness which appear to be the primary and distinctive features of the disorder." (p. 180)

Thrill seeking is one hallmark of the antisocial personality.

What such extreme stimulation-seeking might mean in the total context of a personality also characterized as impulsive, lacking in judgment, deficient in inner reality and moral controls, and seemingly unable to learn from punishment and experience can only be surmised. Though further investigation is needed, it seems plausible that stimulation-seeking "unchecked by conditioned fear response is a two-edged sword for antisocial behavior" (Borkovec, 1970, p. 222).

Family relationships. Perhaps the most popular generalization about the development of the antisocial personality is the assumption of some form of early disturbance in family relationships.

1. *Early parental loss and emotional deprivation.* A number of earlier studies reported that an unusually high number of antisocial individuals had experienced the trauma of losing a parent at an early age—usually through the separation or divorce of their parents. For example, Greer (1964) found that 60 percent of one group he studied had lost a parent during childhood, as contrasted with 28 percent for a control group of neurotic individuals and 27 percent for a control group of normal subjects.

Since many normal people have experienced the loss of a parent at an early age, it would seem to require considerably more than parental loss to produce a psychopathic personality. In reviewing the available evidence, Hare (1970) suggested that the factor of key significance was not the parental loss per se, but rather the emotional disturbances in the family relationships created before the departure of a parent.

This point is supported by the findings of Wolkind (1974) who found a high incidence of "affectionless psychopathy" in a group of 92 institutionalized children. In many of these cases the antisocial disorder seemed to have been caused by pathogenic family situations prior to the children's being placed in an institution.

2. *Parental rejection and inconsistency.* A number of studies have attempted to relate parental rejection and inconsistent discipline to inadequate socialization and antisocial personality. After an extensive review of the available literature, McCord and McCord (1964) concluded that severe parental rejection and lack of parental affection were the primary causes of psychopathic personality.

Another aspect of this picture has been pointed out by Buss (1966), who concluded that two types of parental behavior foster psychopathy. In the first, parents are cold and distant toward the child and allow no warm or close relationship to develop. A child who imitates this parental model will become cold and distant in later relationships; although the child learns the formal attributes and amenities of social situations, he or she does not develop empathy for others or become emotionally involved with them.

The second type of parental behavior involves inconsistency, in which parents are capricious in supplying affection, rewards, and punishments. Usually they are inconsistent in their own role enactments as well, so that the child lacks stable models to imitate and fails to develop a clear-cut sense of self-identity. Often the parents reward not only "superficial conformity" but "underhanded nonconformity"— that is, nonconformity that goes undetected by outsiders. Thus, they reinforce behaviors that lead to psychopathic behavior. Similarly, when the parents are both arbitrary and inconsistent in punishing the child, avoiding punishment becomes more important than receiving rewards. Instead of learning to see behavior in terms of right and wrong, the child learns how to avoid blame and punishment by lying or other manipulative means.

In Chapter 5 we noted that among the damaging effects of parental rejection and inconsistent discipline are slow conscience development and aggression on the part of the child. We also noted that children subjected to inconsistent reward and punishment for aggressive behavior were more resistant to the extinction of such behavior than were children who experienced more consistent discipline. However, it seems desirable to exercise caution in using parental rejection and inconsistency as basic explanations of psychopathic personalities. In the first place, these same conditions have been implicated in a wide range of later maladaptive behaviors. In addition, many children coming from such family backgrounds do not become antisocial personalities or evidence other serious psychopathology. Thus further explanation is needed.

3. *Faulty parental models and family interactions.* In an early study of 40 male antisocial personalities, Heaver (1943) emphasized the influence exerted by faulty parental models—typically a mother who overindulged her son and a father who was highly successful, driving, critical, and distant.

Greenacre (1945) added a number of details that have been supported by later studies of antisocial individuals from middle-class families. The father is a successful and respected member of the community and is distant and fear-inspiring to his children. The mother, on the other hand, is indulgent, pleasure-loving, frivolous, and often tacitly contemptuous of her husband's importance. When such families are heavily dependent on the approval and admiration of their communities—as in the case of some clergy and politicians—it is crucial that they maintain the illusion of a happy family by concealing and denying any evidence of bickering or scandal. Thus the children learn that appearances are more important than reality, and they, too, become part of the show-window display, where a premium is put on charm and impressing others rather than on competence and integrity. This need to please and to win social approval for their parents' sake seems to bring out a precocious but superficial charm in some of these children, together with great adroitness in handling people for purely selfish ends.

The son in such a family cannot hope to emulate his successful and awe-inspiring father, but, aware of the extension to himself of the high evaluation that is placed on his father, he develops a feeling of importance and of being exempt from the consequences of his actions. Frequently the prominence of the father does, in fact, protect the child from the ordinary consequences of antisocial behavior. If we add one additional factor—the contradictory influence of a father who tells his son of the necessity for responsibility, honesty, and respect for others, but who himself is deceitful and manipulative —we appear to have a family background capable of producing a middle-class psychopathic personality.

Supporting this explanation is Hare's (1970) finding of a high incidence of psychopathic personalities—particularly fathers—in the families of children who later manifest such behavior themselves. In this context, Hare concluded that "at least part of a psychopath's behavior results from modeling another individual's psychopathic behavior" (p. 107).

The intermittent reinforcement of short-term gains and success in avoiding punishment also make the psychopathic life-style especially resistant to change. With relative freedom from anxiety, guilt, and remorse, there is little motivation to learn different patterns.

Sociocultural factors.   Antisocial personality is thought to be more common in lower socioeconomic groups. Although we have emphasized the part played by constitutional and family factors in the formation of psychopathic personalities, it would appear that social conditions such as those found in our urban ghettos also produce their share of antisocial individuals. An environment characterized by the breakdown of social norms and regulations, disorganization, undesirable peer models, and pervasive alienation from and hostility toward the broader society appears to produce inadequate conscience development, lack of concern for others, and destructive, antisocial behavior. On a family level, the picture is often aggravated by broken homes, parental rejection, and inconsistent discipline, leading to distrust, a confused sense of personal identity, self-devaluation, and feelings of hurt and hostility. The end result may be overt aggressive behavior, directed especially at the representatives of "conventional" society.

In one high school in a disadvantaged area, two youths held a teacher while a third poured gasoline over him and set him on fire. Fortunately, another teacher came to the rescue and was able to extinguish the flames before the teacher was seriously burned. The youths were apprehended and detained in a juvenile facility, since they were under 18 years of age. Interviewed by a social worker, they showed no remorse for their act, did not consider it wrong, and were disappointed that they had not succeeded in killing the teacher. The youths were not in any of his classes, nor did they know him personally. The apparent leader of the group stated that "Next time we'll do it right, so there won't be nobody left around to identify us."

Melges and Bowlby (1969) have pointed out that such individuals believe other people cannot be counted on and see their own future as out of their control. In essence, they feel helpless and hopeless—as well as resentful and hostile—in relation to their aversive life situations. Seeing no possible way they can "make it," they lash out to make others suffer too.

Another possible explanation for the development of an antisocial personality has been suggested by Smith (1978), who sees such an orientation as encouraged and rewarded by the materialistic, competitive, marketplace values of our capitalistic society. Psychopathic individuals, he feels, simply carry these prevalent tendencies to extremes. While this view offers a plausible explanation for some typically psychopathic behaviors, such as manipulativeness, superficial charm, and concern only

for outward appearances, it does not seem sufficent to explain the extreme lawlessness and senseless destructive behaviors that also accompany this disorder.

Although some cultural groups appear to have a relatively high rate of psychopathy in their group members, others have relatively low rates. Among the Hutterites, a relatively socially isolated religious sect who live on large communal farms, there is a negligible incidence of antisocial personality disorders. Perhaps the close-knit social structure with its strong emphasis on traditional values punishes or fails to reinforce the expression of antisocial behaviors. In addition, the adults to which the children are exposed during their early development provide nonpsychopathic role models. The low rate of psychopathic disorders among the Hutterites may also result from a natural selection process in which individuals who have deviant social characteristics leave the group so that neither they nor their offspring contribute to the statistics.

In summary, antisocial personalities are a mixed group of individuals who nevertheless have certain characteristics in common. Although the causal factors are not clear and may differ from case to case, varying combinations of constitutional, psychosocial, and sociocultural factors appear to be involved.

Treatment and outcomes

Since most individuals with antisocial personalities do not exhibit obvious psychopathology and can function effectively in most respects, they seldom come to the attention of mental hospitals or clinics. Those who run afoul of the law may participate in rehabilitation programs in penal institutions, but usually are not changed by them. Even if more and better therapeutic facilities were available, effective treatment would still be a challenging task.

Some early case reports pointed to favorable results with intensive psychotherapy, but, in general, traditional psychotherapeutic approaches have not proven effective. Nor have various biological measures, including electroconvulsive shock therapy, the use of drugs, and psychosurgery, fared any better.

More recently, behavior therapists have dealt

successfully with specific antisocial behaviors, and modern behavior therapy techniques appear to offer promise of more effective treatment (Sutker, Archer, & Kilpatrick, 1979). However, behavior therapy is also somewhat at a disadvantage since we are dealing with a total life-style rather than with a specific maladaptive behavior, like a phobia, that can be targeted for treatment. And, as we have noted, intermittent reinforcement by short-term gains and successful avoidance of punishment, combined with a lack of anxiety and guilt, leave the antisocial individual with little motivation to change.

On the basis of an extensive review of research findings, Bandura (1969) has suggested three steps that can be used to modify antisocial behavior through the application of learning principles: (a) the withdrawal of meaningful reinforcements for disapproved antisocial behavior, and, where appropriate, the use of punishment for such behavior; (b) the modeling of desired behavior by "change agents"— the therapist and/or other behavioral models who are admired—and the use of a graded system of rewards or reinforcers for imitating such behavior; and (c) the reduction of material incentives and rewards as the individual's behavior is increasingly brought under the control of self-administered, symbolic rewards. Essentially, the objective is to effect the gradual transfer of evaluative and reinforcement functions from the environment to the antisocial individual by helping him or her develop inner controls that minimize the need for external ones.

An important facet of this approach is providing situations in which one individual's improved behavior becomes a model for others in treatment. Patients can thus function as "change agents" for each other while furthering the long-range modification of their own behavior. Such a program requires a controlled situation in which the therapist can administer or withhold reinforcement and the individual cannot run away.

Vaillant (1975), too, believes that antisocial individuals can be effectively treated only in settings where behavioral control is possible—in other words, where psychotherapy is on an outpatient basis, it is doomed to failure. He has found control necessary, also, to prevent self-destructive behavior and to overcome the individual's fears of intimacy. Like other investigators, he has concluded that punishment is ineffective for controlling sociopathic behavior and that such individuals (i.e., sociopaths) "should work for liberty, not pay for past mistakes."

Vaillant also pointed out that one-to-one therapeutic relationships (even meeting several times a week) were rarely adequate to change sociopathic behavior. What seemed to work best was an acceptable group membership that provided both an opportunity to learn to care for others and a place to be accepted by peers.

"Only acceptance by peers can circumvent the sociopath's profound fear that he may be pitied. Only acceptance by 'recovered' peers can restore his defective self-esteem. Finally, the psychopath needs to absorb more of other people than one person, no matter how loving, can ever provide. Sociopaths need to find groups to which they can belong with pride." (p. 183)

Fortunately, many antisocial personalities improve after the age of forty even without treatment, possibly because of weaker biological drives, better insight into their self-defeating behavior, and the cumulative effect of social conditioning. Such individuals are often referred to as "burned-out psychopaths." However, these individuals can create a great deal of havoc before they reach 40—as well as afterward if they do not change. In view of the distress and unhappiness they inflict on others and the social damage they cause, it seems desirable—and more economical in the long run—to put increased effort into the development of effective treatment programs.

Criminal behavior

Serious crime is an extreme form of acting out against other individuals or the society as a whole. Thus it is more closely related to personality disorder than to other forms of maladaptive behavior, and many—though by no means all—criminals would be classified as having personality disorders. "Crime" is a legal category rather than a psychological one, however: a crime is a violation of a law. Thus what is defined as a crime depends on the society.

In our own society, two types of crimes have been defined: *felonies* and *misdemeanors.* Felonies are serious crimes such as murder and robbery for which there are severe legal penalties, including later restriction of citizen rights to vote and hold office. Misdemeanors, as the name implies, are minor offenses such as disorderly conduct and vagrancy. Whether a particular behavior is classified as a felony or a misdemeanor varies considerably from state to state—illustrating once again the importance of social definitions in the labeling of behavior as "abnormal."

Incidence

Official figures compiled by the Federal Bureau of Investigation indicate that the crime rate is higher in the United States than in most other countries, and that the rate for many crimes is continuing to rise. For 1977 the FBI reported the commission of over 10 million serious crimes, including homicide, forcible rape, robbery, aggravated assault, burglary, larceny, and auto theft. Rapes were up 11 percent from the year before. There were 19,120 murders that year, and although the overall rate for robberies was down slightly, some types of robberies had increased. For example, there were fewer street robberies but more gas station robberies, and in the preceding 4-year period, the rate for bank robberies had jumped 93 percent.[2] In actual fact, the problem of crime in the U.S. is even more serious since it has been estimated that from one-third to one-half of all serious crimes are not reported to the police (Uniform Crime Reports, 1978).

Some investigators have pointed out that the figure for serious crime is not as ominous as it seems, since over a million of the cases are auto thefts, which many people feel should not be included in this classification. But there would appear to be little room for complacency when it is realized that *violent* crimes—the first four types listed above—increased 11 times faster than population size during the 1960s, and that during the first half of the

---

[2]Based on reports of some 11,000 state and local law enforcement agencies to the FBI.

HIGHLIGHT

Crime clock

In an average 24-hour period in 1977 in the United States, the following crimes took place:

Violent crimes

     53 murders—one every 27 minutes
   180 forcible rapes—one every 8 minutes
1,108 robberies—one every 78 seconds
1,440 aggravated assaults—one every minute

Property crimes

  2,618 motor vehicle thefts—one every 33 seconds
  8,640 burglaries—one every 10 seconds
17,280 larceny thefts—one every 5 seconds

Actually, of course, crimes do not occur at such regular intervals, but these figures show the relative frequency of the crimes in the various categories.

Based on Uniform Crime Reports, 1978.

1970s they rose even faster—over 15 times as fast as population size (see HIGHLIGHT on this page).

Among lower-income groups, blacks are almost twice as likely as whites to be victims of crimes of violence and slightly more likely than whites to be victims of crimes against property. Middle- and upper-income groups, whether black or white, are about equally exposed to crime, but much more often to crimes against property than to crimes against the person. By and large, whites tend to victimize whites and blacks to victimize blacks. Contrary to popular belief, criminals most often strike in the vicinity in which they live, and often they know their victims personally.

Crime rates vary considerably from one region of the country to another, from city to city, and from metropolitan to suburban and rural areas. They are much higher in the West than in the Northwest or South, higher in New York City and Los Angeles than in Philadelphia, and much higher in metropolitan centers than in smaller cities and rural areas. However, the crime rate is increasing more rapidly in the latter than in metropolitan centers.

More than 10 million Americans are arrested each year for having committed, or for suspicion of having committed, a serious crime

(Megargee, 1979). Among these, the lowest class in the general population is overrepresented (Gunn, Robertson, Dell, & Way, 1978). Approximately 80 percent of both juvenile and adult offenders are male; the great majority of violent crimes are committed by males. However, American females are committing an increasing number of murders, armed robberies, assaults, and other serious crimes, and their rate is increasing faster than that for males. In 1977, 10 percent of all murders were committed by persons under 18 years of age, and 43 percent by persons under 25. As a consequence of apprehension and conviction for such crimes, over 500,000 individuals, including over 80,000 women, are in federal, state, and local prisons. In addition, more than a million others, both male and female, are on probation.

The cost of crime in the United States each year is estimated at over $85 billion, an incredible and wasteful financial toll; and this says nothing of the toll in human resources and human suffering (see HIGHLIGHTS on pages 297 and 298).

Causal factors in criminal behavior

In our discussion of the personality disorders, we noted the importance of pervasive personal pathology, pathogenic family and peer patterns, general sociocultural factors that foster antisocial behavior, and severe stress. These same factors have also been examined in relation to adult criminal behavior, as have some additional factors, including chromosomal aberrations, crime as a profession, and organized crime.

Heredity and constitutional factors. A number of early investigators attributed criminal behavior to heredity. Prominent among these investigators were Lombroso and his followers, who became known as the "Italian School of Criminology" (Lombroso-Ferrero, 1911). According to Lombroso, the criminal was a "born type" with "stigmatizing" features—such as a low forehead, an unusually shaped head and jaw, eyebrows growing together above the bridge of the nose, and protruding ears. Supposedly such features clearly distinguished the criminal from normal people.

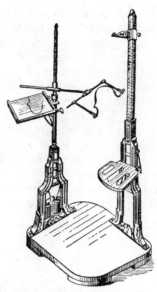

Italian criminologist Cesare Lombroso believed that criminals could be identified by specific physical characteristics, including the shape of the head. By measuring the skulls of known criminals with devices like this "craniograph," he compiled a classification of "criminal types."

These stigmata were considered to be a throwback to the "savage" and thus to signal an individual predisposed to criminal behavior.

Although Lombroso's view has long since been discarded, a number of recent investigators have dealt with the possibility that an extra Y chromosome—a genetic anomaly that may occur in males—is associated with much criminal behavior. Although there are many exceptions, men of the XYY chromosomal type are characterized by unusual height, borderline intelligence, and a tendency to show episodes of extremely aggressive behavior.

The earliest study in this area was that of Jacobs and her colleagues (1965) who published their findings on 197 mentally abnormal inmates of a special security institution in Scotland. All were considered to have violent and dangerous criminal tendencies. Seven—3.5 percent—were of the XYY chromosomal type.

In an intensive review of later research findings, Jarvik, Klodin, and Matsuyama (1973) reported that the total frequency of XYY males in the criminal population approximated 2 percent. This frequency is about 15 times

Facts about homicide

Homicides are classified, in terms of intent, into: (1) first degree murder, characterized by premeditation and planning, or committed during a felony, such as rape or robbery; (2) second degree murder, in which there is no premeditation or planning, e.g., as when the homicide is committed "in the heat of passion"; and (3) manslaughter, committed without malice or intention, as when a driver accidentally kills a pedestrian in a crosswalk. Relevant to these three categories are the following data concerning homicide in the United States.

Incidence

For reasons that are unclear, the homicide rate started to rise sharply in 1963 and has continued to rise since, increasing 240 percent from 1963 to 1975. In 1977, 19,120 homicides were committed in the United States. For each actual murder, many more attempts are unsuccessful and the victim lives (80 percent of gunshot victims and 90 percent of stab victims). Thus, homicidal acts are far more common in our society than the statistics on homicide would indicate.

Who kills whom?

Ten percent of all homicides are committed by youths under 18 years of age, and 43 percent by persons under 25. Males outnumber females as victims at a ratio of 4 to 1, and as offenders in a ratio of 5 to 1. More murder victims are individuals in the 20- to 29-year age bracket than in any other 10-year age span. In the great majority of murders, the victims are of the same race. Blacks are disproportionately represented as both victims and offenders. Apprehending the offender is often relatively easy, since in about 40 percent of the cases offender and victim are relatives, friends, or close acquaintances. About half of family killings involve spouse killing spouse. Another 7 percent or so involve "lover's quarrels." In 1977 about 7 percent of murders resulted from drunken arguments. Homicides associated with felonies—usually armed robbery involving strangers—make up about 30 percent of all homicide cases.

Methods or weapons used

By far the greatest number of homicides result from shooting (63 percent), followed by cutting or stabbing (19 percent), use of other impersonal weapons such as clubs or poisons (7 percent), and use of personal weapons, such as hands (9 percent). The high incidence of murders committed by firearms is not surprising in view of the widespread possession of guns by civilians in the U.S.

Motives

As we have noted in listing the three categories of homicide, motives may be diverse, or the homicide may even be accidental. However, aside from murders committed for calculated monetary gains by individuals associated with organized crime, homicide is typically considered a "crime of passion." It often results from quarrels combined with a lowering of inner reality and ethical restraints; for example, intoxicants complicate the motivational picture in about half of all homicide cases. In some instances the victim—for whatever reason—seems to invite being killed, as by striking the first blow; and, as we shall see, homicide may be associated with such mental disorders as schizophrenia and paranoia.

Psychosocial factors

Although diverse personality types may commit homicide, offenders tend to come from homes or neighborhoods in which violence is an aspect of daily life. Often they have a history of violent tendencies and behavior. In ghetto slums, homicide rates are disproportionately high. Homicide rates also show marked cross-cultural differences—with Iceland and Colombia, South America, representing extremes in rates of incidence among the major countries. Iceland's rate is zero, while that for Colombia is 5 times that of the United States.

In general, it would appear that an increase in homicidal acts tends to accompany technological and social change.

Statistics are approximate, based on available 1977 data (Uniform Crime Reports, 1978).

Facts about rape

Rape is defined in the Uniform Crime Reports (1978), somewhat broadly, as "carnal knowledge of a female forcibly and against her will." It is the fastest-growing violent crime in our society and is the source of considerable apprehension among women. There are also a number of misconceptions about rape among both men and women. What are the facts?

Incidence

During 1977 there were 63,020 rapes reported to the FBI—double the number reported ten years before. Furthermore, the incidence was undoubtedly higher than these figures would indicate, for rape is an "underreported" crime. In fact, it is estimated that for each rape that is reported, there are anywhere from 3 to 10 others that are not reported.

Who rapes whom?

Of those arrested for rape in 1977, 56 percent were under 25. Most of their victims were also young, with half under 21. Contrary to expectations, rape occurred most frequently not in a "dark alley" but in the woman's home. In approximately 60 percent of the cases, the man and woman were strangers; in the remainder, the offender was an acquaintance or relative of the victim. Almost always offender and victim were of the same race. A high proportion of the reported rapes involved multiple offenders—group rapes.

What happens to rapists?

Even for reported rapes, the chance of a conviction is small: rape has the lowest conviction rate of any major crime. In one study, 635 rape complaints led to identification of only 167 suspects, of whom 45 were charged and 10 were subsequently convicted—a conviction rate of less than 2 percent (Hotchkiss, 1978). Thus most men who have raped are free in the community. Abel et al. (1978) report that the rapists they studied (who were currently free in the community) had raped anywhere from 5 to 100 times. Rapists convicted for the first time are usually paroled after serving about four years in prison, although the recidivism rate for convicted rapists is 70 percent.

Why do men rape?

There are two hypotheses about why men rape:

1. *The psychopathology hypothesis.* This hypothesis attributes rape to personal pathology on the part of the rapist, centering around defects in perception, judgment, and/or impulse control. Tests have shown that imprisoned rapists are more disturbed than other violent prisoners but are similar to them in general personality makeup. The personality profile of the men who rape and do not get caught may be very different; so far we do not know.

2. *The social control hypothesis.* This hypothesis holds that rapists differ from other men not in the type of attitudes they hold but in the degree to which they hold certain attitudes that are prevalent in our culture having to do with sex, men, women, and violence. For example, there is a myth, *not* upheld by research evidence (Kirkpatrick & Kanin, 1957), that women really enjoy being roughed up during sex. Other examples of beliefs in our culture that can be viewed as supportive of rape are the belief that women have an unconscious wish to be raped—a belief held by 71 percent of a group of Minnesota residents; nearly as many also believed that rape victims were mostly women of ill repute (Hotchkiss, 1978). Such beliefs would encourage false perceptions of a rape situation on the part of both men and women.

So far, research to test this hypothesis has led to conflicting results. One study found no difference between rapists, normal men, and police officers in degree of acceptance of rape-supportive beliefs (Feild, 1978). Another study found rapists extremely aroused by tape recordings of erotic situations involving force, whereas non-rapist men were only slightly aroused by these situations but much more aroused by erotic situations not involving force (Abel et al., 1978). More research on why men rape is urgently needed if effective preventive programs are to be developed.

that found for the male population in general.

Presumably the extra Y chromosome stimulates excessive production of testosterone, the male hormone that has been linked by some investigators to aggression. However, this hypothesis is not as simple as it first seems. For one thing, not all XYY males are aggressive. In addition, their crimes are more often against property than persons. To resolve this seeming paradox, Ginsburg (1974) has advanced evidence to show that the aggressiveness of an XYY male depends on whether the extra chromosome is inherited from an aggressive father or a mild one; he has also suggested that when aggression does occur it may reflect defects in brain structure and functioning stemming from this genetic anomaly rather than from excessive testosterone.

More recently, Witkin et al. (1976) have even questioned the hypothesis that the extra Y chromosome predisposes the individual to violence. At the present time there is simply no convincing evidence that the XYY male has a genetic predisposition to criminal behavior.

Other biological factors.
Tendencies toward violent behavior have been related to several other biological variables, including brain damage, mental retardation, psychomotor epilepsy, and degenerative brain changes associated with old age. An estimated 10 to 20 million Americans have some form of minor brain damage, and a number of investigators are exploring the possibility of a link between such conditions and criminal behavior, particularly in conjunction with other factors such as severe stress or the use of alcohol or other drugs (Kiester, 1974).

Although a disproportionately high incidence of abnormal EEGs has been reported for both male and female prisoners, there is no conclusive evidence of the relation of brain lesions to serious crime except in a distinct minority of cases (Climent et al., 1973; Small, 1966). Interestingly enough, Small, while studying prisoners convicted of felonies, found that those with abnormal EEGs were less likely to have engaged in "skilled" criminal behavior but were usually guilty of repeated theft; those with no demonstrable evidence of central nervous system lesions accounted for the most serious crimes, such as assault, murder, and forcible rape.

Personal and family pathology.
As we have pointed out, although crime is a legal term and not a psychiatric one, Gunn et al. (1978) have found that about a third of sentenced prisoners could be regarded, on the basis of psychiatric examination, to be psychiatric cases. Even among criminals who show no biological pathology related to their criminal behavior, personal pathology is common. In an early study, Arief and Bowie (1947) found that a group of shoplifters fell into 18 psychiatric categories. In a study of 300 bad-check writers, MacDonald (1959) found not only a high incidence of psychopathic personalities and chronic alcoholics but also a lesser number of schizophrenic, manic, senile, and mentally retarded individuals. The most common forms of psychopathology associated with serious crimes appear to be antisocial personality, alcoholism, and drug dependence; however, there is also a disproportionately high number of borderline and actual psychotic individuals (Guze, Goodwin, & Crane, 1969; Sutker & Moan, 1973). Severe life stress, particularly in conjunction with personal pathology, also appears to be an important factor in triggering impulsive acts of violence and other antisocial behavior.

Many criminals who show pervasive personal pathology come from homes torn by conflict and dissension, often resulting in parental separation or divorce; also frequently found in their family backgrounds are parental rejection and inconsistent and severe punishment. These characteristics appear to be particularly common in—but not exclusive to—prison inmates who have committed crimes of violence (Climent et al., 1973; Sutker & Moan, 1973). Again, however, it is risky to draw causal inferences, since many persons who come from backgrounds similar to those just described do not evidence personal pathology and do not engage in criminal behavior. The life history of one young killer is outlined in the HIGHLIGHT on page 301.

Sociocultural influences.
Often personal pathology appears to stem primarily from social pathology, as evidenced by the unusually high incidence of both juvenile and adult offenses in the slums of our large cities. These areas are characterized by severe social disorganization that leads to a very different form of

socialization. The values of the larger society are often held in low repute or rejected altogether, and widespread feelings of helplessness and hopelessness combined with hostility toward established authority are characteristic. Under such conditions, aggressive and illegal behavior may become the norm for an entire subgroup.

1. *Crime as a profession.* The concept of *differential association,* first developed by Sutherland in the late 1930s, has provided a framework for understanding the importance of subcultural influences in the "training" of professional criminals—people such as hired killers, burglars, and forgers. As Sutherland and Cressey (1966) noted, the basic process of socialization is much the same for everyone: the individual comes to accept the values and behavioral standards emphasized by those with whom he or she associates on a repeated and intimate basis—most notably, parents and peers.

In the case of a young person growing up in a subculture where criminal behavior is the norm, the values and standards internalized—and the skills learned—are likely to be quite different from those emphasized in conventional society. Thus, individuals who become professional criminals usually acquire their training in much the same way that legitimate professionals do: by responding to the learning opportunities, values, and reinforcements that their environment has provided. Unlike the antisocial personality, they are "socialized"—but in a deviant way.

Typically, professional criminals specialize in a particular type of crime, such as forgery or burglary, and develop a particular style of operation. Their goal is to make money in the quickest and safest way possible. In general, they attempt to avoid violence, since it would greatly increase the risk of detection and imprisonment. Often they are highly skilled. Their crimes are usually well planned and may even be rehearsed. Possible arrest and imprisonment are hazards of their profession for which they are prepared; if they are imprisoned, they try to adapt to prison life and do "easy time."

The term *dyssocial personality* has been used to describe these individuals. By and large, they do not appear to show significant psychopathology aside from their adherence to the values and codes of their own group. Stojanovich (1969) has sounded a note of caution, however. While many professional criminals he studied did manifest so-called dyssocial characteristics—such as predatoriness, good control of inner impulses, and ability to profit from experience—others showed characteristics more typically associated with the antisocial personality.

2. *Organized crime.* It is difficult to assess or discuss the nature and incidence of organized crime, since it has not been defined legally in the same sense as individual criminal *acts* like forcible rape and homicide. In addition, organized crime actively maintains a low level of social visibility. In general, however, the "organized criminal" is an individual who commits criminal acts while occupying a position in an organization specifically set up for perpetrating specific criminal activities.

The largest criminal organization in the United States, by all accounts, is La Cosa Nostra, also known as "the mafia," "the syndicate," and "the mob." About 70 percent of the mob's illegal income is estimated to be derived from gambling, and most of the remainder from narcotics, hijacked goods, and interest from loan sharking.

As our society changes, the patterns of organized crime also change; and activities that the syndicate once found economically rewarding—such as prostitution—may now be deemphasized in favor of more lucrative pursuits, such as gambling or drug traffic. In recent years, Cosa Nostra money has also been invested in various legitimate businesses, thus supplementing its income. In his authoritative book *Theft of a Nation,* Cressey (1969) estimated Cosa Nostra's minimum contribution to our political campaigns at about 15 percent of their total cost. Operating in most, if not all, of the big cities and many smaller ones, the syndicate represents a powerful and pervasive force.

To fight against organized crime, law-enforcement agencies must obtain evidence and seek convictions; however, since violence and intimidation are such an integral part of organized crime, evidence is extremely difficult to obtain. Sometimes witnesses are promised protection and even relocated to a different part of the country with changed identities, but even these precautions have not al-

The "kid nobody wanted"

Exploding into the headlines in the early 1950s was the story of Billy Cook, "hard-luck" killer from Joplin, Missouri, whose days were ended in the gas chamber at San Quentin. He was captured by a Mexican posse in Lower California after a murderous rampage which extended across several states from Missouri to California. Cook's life motto was "Hard Luck," which he had tattooed on the knuckles of his left hand.

"Hard luck" was an appropriate motto for the youth: his mother died when he was 5 years old, and his father thereupon abandoned him, with his brothers and sisters, in a mine cave. In addition, he was handicapped with a deformed right eyelid. Nobody wanted Billy when he was offered for adoption, resentful and squint-eyed, and it was only a matter of time until his tantrums became too much for the county-appointed guardians to control. Billy quit school at the age of 12, and when brought before the court he was sent to the reformatory at his own request. From then on, almost all of his life was spent behind bars, first in the reformatory and then in the state penitentiary, to which he was "graduated" at 18.

Released from prison, Cook looked up his father and announced his intention to "live by the gun and roam." He got a job washing dishes, bought a gun, and was on his way—stealing his first car from a Texas mechanic with whom he hitched a ride. Robbed and locked in the trunk, the mechanic escaped to freedom by prying open the lid, but the next kidnap victims—an Illinois farmer, his wife, and three small children who picked Cook up near Oklahoma City when the first stolen car broke down—were not so lucky. Not daring to set them free, Cook forced them to drive back and forth through four states while he decided what to do with them. It was a three-day nightmare which included a foiled escape attempt; it finally ended in Joplin where Cook shot them and threw their bodies down a mine shaft.

A horrible pattern of kidnapping and murder had been set in motion, and as the hunted Cook desperately attempted to elude the law, he hitched three more rides and took the cars' occupants as captives. He spared the life of one kidnap victim, a Blythe, California, deputy officer whom he left tied up in the desert; but he shot and killed a Seattle businessman—the crime for which he eventually received the death penalty. The big interstate manhunt that was on for Cook spread into Mexico when he was reported seen there with two companions—California prospectors who picked him up below the border and were his prisoners for eight days. When Cook

was apprehended, less than a month had gone by since he had a hitched the ride with the Texas mechanic. But though the time was brief, the toll was high: 9 people kidnapped, 6 killed.

As if in explanation of his deeds, Billy Cook said when arrested, "I hate everybody's guts, and everybody hates mine."

Both before and after the Billy Cook case, a number of gruesome homicide cases have been reported. Among these are the cases of Jack the Ripper, the Boston Strangler, Richard Speck, the Manson family, and the finding of the bodies of over 30 teen-age boys interred beneath the home of a "model citizen" in a Chicago suburb. In the case of Billy Cook, however, there seems to be an almost classic portrayal of the extent to which extreme parental and societal rejection, undesirable peer group models, and a life spent mainly as an inmate of penal institutions combined to produce a psychopathic killer.

Based on *Life* (1951) and *Time* (1951, 1952).

ways been adequate. Since organized crime is a major threat to any society based on justice, law, and order, we need to find more effective methods of dealing with it.

3. *Changes in criminal types.* During the early 1960s a number of investigators noted the growing prevalence of individuals who committed criminal acts primarily for ego-satisfaction and "kicks." A thrill is derived from performing some taboo act—usually a senseless act of violence—which serves to intensify the present moment, clearly differentiating it from the routine of daily life. Whereas professional criminals carefully calculate their acts, usually with an eye on material gain with minimum risk, this new criminal type commits violent acts on impulse, simply because it "makes me feel good." As one youth told Yablonsky (1962) after a gang killing,

"If I would of got the knife, I would have stabbed him. That would of gave me more of a build-up. People would have respected me for what I've done and things like that. They would say, 'There goes a cold killer.' "

Typically, the illegal acts of such criminals are spontaneous and unpremeditated; in most cases there is no evidence that they have even had prior contact with their victims. Even when they participate in planned criminal acts, they are still interested primarily in kicks. Unlike most other criminals, they seek no gain other than the pleasure to be derived from the criminal act itself.

More recently still, another new group of criminals has emerged, who now constitute a large segment of today's prison population. As Alexander (1974) has described them,

"They are mostly losers, mostly poor and black. Their chief crime, in Huey Newton's memorable phrase, is being 'illegitimate capitalists,' unemployables whose only hope of enjoying the good things of life is in ripping off the system." (p. 35)

The poor, the powerless, and the undereducated are much more likely to be caught, prosecuted, punished, or even held in jails for months before being tried. And if found guilty, their sentence is likely to be more severe.

While the affluent have probably always fared somewhat better, there is evidence of a widening "class gap" in the organization and administration of our legal system. As Doleschal and Klapmuts (1974) have pointed out, the rich, powerful, and intelligent members of our society are rarely caught, prosecuted, or punished. This gap increases the resentment of those at the bottom and heightens their feelings of not being part of the broader society, thus also increasing their feelings of justification in simply taking what they want (see HIGHLIGHT on page 303).

Admittedly the causes of violence and other forms of crime in the United States are both complex and varied. But as a former United States Attorney General pointed out,

"Much crime develops from poverty and deprivation. Most victims of crime are the poor themselves. There will be no marked crime reduction until we understand that—but more importantly, until we act upon it." (Saxbe, 1974, p. 12)

Approaches to dealing with criminals

We have yet to find what might be considered the ideal method for dealing with individuals convicted of crime. Early forms of punishment seemed to center on revenge or retribution, such as execution and physical torture. Early in the nineteenth century, imprisonment gained popularity; and in the twentieth century efforts to rehabilitate and resocialize the criminal have grown as we have sought to "understand" and "correct" patterns of criminal behavior.

The trends in dealing with criminal behavior have in many ways paralleled those used for psychopathology in general—that is, a movement from incarceration to correction. It is obvious that many of the same procedures will be needed for successful treatment, such as early detection and correction of unhealthy personality trends, correction of undesirable social conditions, and provision of adequate treatment personnel and facilities. But since crime represents a vast range of individuals and behaviors, it is also apparent that no simple formula or single generalization can either explain it or suggest an easy solution to it. Because its complex social, economic, and psychological bases are not fully understood, its eradication must be considered a long-range, rather than an immediately achievable, goal.

Blackout crime

The blackout that struck New York City in July 1977 lasted 25 hours and brought with it a wave of vandalism and plundering that left hundreds of stores and entire city blocks devastated. As *Time* (July 25, 1977) described it,

"Roving bands of determined men, women and even little children wrenched steel shutters and grilles from storefronts with crowbars, shattered plate-glass windows, scooped up everything they could carry, and destroyed what they could not. First they went for clothing, TV sets, jewelry, liquor; when that was cleaned out, they picked up food, furniture and drugs. Said Frank Ross, a black police officer in Bedford-Stuyvesant: "It's like a fever struck them. They were out there with trucks, vans, trailers, everything that could roll. . . ." (p. 12)

Why do people who are normally law abiding sometimes go on a rampage of theft and lawlessness when civil catastrophes strike? Many explanations have been given for "blackout crime," including the following: (a) oppressive heat results in frustration, which leads to aggression (in a previous blackout in New York in winter, the orgy of looting had not occurred); (b) there is a "crowd effect" in which individual responsibility diminishes and people commit crimes for which they do not consider themselves accountable; (c) a high rate of unemployment and other conditions of ghetto life produce a high level of frustration and resentment that can lead to looting in the confusion of a disaster as a way of "getting even" for a time.

Were the looters members of a starving underclass in this case? Not according to a survey of 2706 adults arrested for looting. Over 45 percent of them were employed (a rate higher than that found among other arrested groups) and many had strong community ties. They also had cleaner criminal records than other arrested groups.

Prison inmates march with drill-like precision. In the prison environment convicts lose their individuality; each one becomes a number. Subject to rigid regimentation, deprived of their civil rights, and exposed to highly undesirable models, it is not surprising that many return to the community unrehabilitated—traumatized by prison experiences and bearing the additional burden of the label "ex-con." Because of the high rate of recidivism, many jails and prisons have been referred to by investigating committees as "crime hatcheries," or breeding grounds of bitter social outcasts.

For present purposes let us briefly examine three aspects of the treatment of criminal offenders: (a) the traditional reliance on punishment, (b) attempts at rehabilitation, and (c) some correctional trends and prospects.

Traditional reliance on punishment.

In 1843, Jeremy Bentham concluded that if punishment were certain, swift, and severe, many a person would avoid criminal behavior. The view is still widely held that punishment is the most effective way of making offenders realize the error of their ways and curing them of their criminal tendencies. Such punishment has actually been thought to serve three purposes: (a) revenge by society—"giving the criminal his or her due"; (b) protection of soci-

ety; and (c) deterrence from future crimes—both for the offenders who are punished and for others, through example.

1. *Revenge.* The familiar term "bringing a criminal to justice" implies a revenge orientation: the criminal is seen as having a debt to pay. As Henley (1971) has noted, "Many crime victims carry unseen and long-lasting psychological scars" (p. 39). He might have added that many also carry physical injuries that impair their health and earning ability. And in the tens of thousands of cases where victims are killed, great suffering and hardship may result for their loved ones. Emphasis on revenge and retaliation against criminals is based on the premise that the guilty, who have brought distress to others, ought to suffer.

Another basis for this approach is the view that if society does not establish legal procedures for punishing criminal offenders, individual citizens or groups will take the law into their own hands. Even with established laws, our early history reveals numerous incidents of lynchings and illegal hangings.

2. *Protection of society.* Imprisonment was developed in large part as a way to protect the rest of society. But imprisonment is usually only for a limited time, and unfortunately it may simply serve to expose the offender to prison codes of behavior, to reinforce criminal values, to permit learning of new criminal skills or refining of old ones, and to augment the individual's degradation and feeling of separateness from society. In fact, prisons have been called "universities of crime."

There are also repeated reports of young offenders who are subjected to sexual assault by tougher convicts and sent back to society filled with confusion, shame, and hatred. In other cases, prisoners are the victims of stabbings and other forms of physical assault. The net effect of imprisonment may thus be that the offender returns to society more hardened and alienated than before imprisonment—and a greater threat to society than ever.

Menninger (1968) has referred to imprisonment as the "crime of punishment." And Alexander (1974) points out that "the most hardened wardens agree that 90 percent of prisoners could be released without constituting any menace to society" (p. 35). The problem is that not even the most experienced criminologists can positively identify the 10 percent who will again commit crimes of violence.

3. *Deterrence.* Punishment and detention for criminal acts are usually based partly on the premise that such an experience will deter the offender in the future and keep others from committing similar acts. The failure of our present system to do this is shown by the rapidly rising crime rates and by the fact that the rate of recidivism (re-arrest for new crimes following release from prison) is over 66 percent nationwide and as high as 90 percent in some areas of the country, including New York City (Goldfarb, 1974; Murphy, 1970).

Several factors limit the deterrent effect of punishment. One is the uncertainty and delay that often surround the punishment. Many offenders are never caught; of those arrested, many are never convicted. In addition, the long delay that commonly separates sentencing from the offense lessens the impact of punishment as a deterrent force. Spiraling caseloads have strained our judicial system to the point where there are often delays of several months or longer between arrest and trial.

Another factor limiting the deterrent effect of punishment is the lack of guilt feelings among many of those who are punished. Many prisoners, for example, see themselves as victims of society rather than as perpetrators of crimes. Similarly, many imprisoned offenders see their problem as one of having gotten caught—as "bad luck" rather than "bad character."

Logically, it might seem that the more severe the punishment allotted, the greater its deterrent effect would be, but for certain crimes at least—including homicide and rape—this has not been the case (Melville, 1973; Schwartz, 1968). For example, states that have used the death penalty have had homicide rates as high or higher than those that have not. For other types of crimes, the deterrent effect of increasingly severe and certain punishment may be different, but no conclusive evidence is presently available. In addition, severe penalties may lead to the takeover of some criminal activities—such as drug peddling—by organized crime if the profits are considered worth the risk. In any event, punishment does nothing to change the personal or social reasons why individuals commit crimes; thus it is hardly surprising that using punishment to deter crime has not been notably successful.

Rehabilitation. Less than 4 percent of the persons working in penal institutions are treatment staff—the rest are guards, administrators, and other personnel. Less than 13 percent of state and local correctional personnel handle all the probations and parolees, although the latter constitute more than two-thirds of the nation's criminal offender population. In view of these figures, both treatment facilities in penal institutions and supervision facilities for parolees appear to be sadly inadequate, which helps explain the high recidivism rate. Imprisonment of some offenders may be necessary, and imprisonment can have positive value providing it includes meaningful opportunities for rehabilitation—for reeduca-

Some rehabilitation programs attempt to prepare offenders to "make it" successfully on the outside by teaching them vocational skills. Others, like the creative writing and potting classes shown above, encourage self-expression and creativity.

tion and resocialization, including the development of a sense of purpose and responsibility to society and vocational and social skills. But imprisonment without such redeeming characteristics is neither a major deterrent to criminal behavior nor a helpful form of treatment.

Concern for rehabilitation rather than punishment of criminal offenders led, some years ago, to a greater use of indeterminate sentences and parole to shorten the time in prison, as well as to a variety of innovative attempts at behavior change during imprisonment (see HIGHLIGHT on page 308).

1. *Indeterminate sentences and paroles.* In view of the deplorable conditions existing in penal institutions, the courts became increasingly reluctant to send offenders to prison unless it was considered absolutely necessary; thus the indeterminate sentence came into wide use. It was intended to (a) enable qualified rehabilitation personnel to determine—within broad limits—when an offender should be released; (b) introduce flexibility into the widely disparate ideas of different judges about the appropriate sentences for convicted offenders; and (c) facilitate return to the community of prisoners who could meet qualifications for parole.

Unfortunately, the indeterminate sentence also makes the fate of prisoners more subject to the whim of those in power, particularly when it is capriciously applied. Prisoners may be kept longer instead of released earlier. And putting in time is no longer enough. Prisoners must conform in ways that may seem alien or impossible or even wrong to them. Many inmates would prefer a clear penalty to an indeterminate sentence in which they have to please the authorities in order to get out. In addition, this whole structure is based on the questionable assumption that law-enforcement personnel can predict the behavior of paroled offenders.

As a consequence of such considerations, the indeterminate sentence has been subjected to severe criticism and is being used less than it formerly was.

2. *Innovative approaches to treatment.* A number of other innovative approaches to dealing with criminal offenders have also been suggested, and some have been tried out on a limited basis. Among these have been study and work furloughs and restitution programs,

in which the individual is given a job and works to pay the victim for property damaged or stolen instead of serving time in prison. Twenty-one states now have such restitution programs; they are most often used for juveniles.

There has also been a limited attempt at sexual integration of prisons, conjugal visits, and integration of family and institutional treatment programs. Although imprisonment means different things to different people, it tends in general to be degrading, as well as to create serious sexual problems that may lead to homosexual behavior—particularly since about half of the prisoners are under 25 years of age. And where the prisoner is married and has a family, imprisonment places a tremendous burden on the spouse and children. To help counteract this problem, prisons in Mexico, Sweden, India, and a number of other countries allow conjugal visits. In the United States the first prison to allow conjugal visits was the Mississippi State Penitentiary. This practice, including overnight visits by friends of unmarried prisoners, seems to be gaining support in the United States.

Other innovative approaches to rehabilitation range from transcendental meditation through behavior therapy techniques to the use of drugs and other medical measures for prisoners who have brain abnormalities that apparently make them prone to anger and impulsive violence. However, the involuntary "treatment" of offenders by medical and psychological procedures has become a matter of considerable controversy centered around the issue of the offender's rights (see HIGHLIGHT on page 309).

In England an entire prison was organized as a therapeutic environment. Enhanced personal adjustment for the individuals was possible in this setting, as indicated, for example, by fewer fights among inmates than is typical in traditional prison settings. However, long-term success was disappointing, as measured by the number of prisoners staying out of prison following release: about the same percent as usual (70 percent) had been reconvicted after two years (Gunn et al., 1978).

While some people feel that rehabilitation has not been given a fair chance, the high rate of recidivism has led to general disillusionment with this approach. As Schwartz (1975) has

Is a therapeutic prison possible?

A unique correctional institution named The Patuxent Institution was established in Jessup, Md., in 1955 to demonstrate decades of progress in correctional psychology and to serve as a model facility for treatment of criminal offenders. Designed for some 400 to 500 serious offenders, it was staffed by a large number of mental health personnel and aimed specifically at treatment and rehabilitation, but it was also run as a maximum security institution with the usual complement of guards and related personnel. Prisoners sent there had to be legally sane but to have shown persistent, aggravated antisocial behavior.

Despite the well-intentioned plans, Patuxent had become a focus of controversy by 1975. Criticisms centered around several features:

1. Since all commitments to Patuxent were for an indeterminate period of time, prisoners could in effect be kept there for life, and in fact only 135 had been considered sufficiently "cured" to be released during the first 18 years of the institution's existence. (Another 337 had been released against staff advice.)

2. Although the treatment was based on behavior modification principles, with a prisoner earning more privileges as he worked his way up through four levels, there were accusations of guard brutality and overuse of negative reinforcers, such as solitary confinement.

3. There was resentment at the notion of enforced treatment, which some felt violated an individual's rights and encouraged shamming—a false front on the part of the prisoners to obtain approval and release. Although participation in treatment was theoretically voluntary, those who refused treatment felt they were discriminated against by the staff; in any case, without taking part in the treatment, there was no possible way that they could ever get out of prison. There seemed to be a basic inconsistency in expecting to make a therapeutic milieu out of a situation that allowed inmates no real choice.

The controversy led in 1977 to a change in Maryland law ending indeterminate sentencing, and the resulting changes have been instructive. Those who come now must have at least three years of their sentence left to serve but come to Patuxent by their own choice. Workers at the institution say that the whole environment of the institution has changed and is much healthier.

The program is essentially the same, with a "graded tier" system of four levels of increasing privileges, those in the fourth level are essentially self-governing and may seek parole. In addition, every inmate has a job to perform at the institution and takes part in educational and vocational programs, which have recently been expanded.

The Patuxent Institution is currently the only correctional institution in the United States defined specifically as a treatment and rehabilitation institution. Currently there are 475 inmates, all under treatment, with 150 more waiting to come. The inmates are divided into four units of about 120 each; for each unit there is one psychiatrist, two psychologists, and three social workers. Each inmate's progress is reviewed every six months by staff and once a year by a Board of Review. Patuxent operates independently of Maryland's Division of Corrections and determines and supervises its own paroles. It also has its own halfway house for released inmates (Gluckstern, 1979).

We know from many studies that personal choice of an activity is more likely to lead to active and responsible participation in it than is involuntary recruitment. Has the new element of voluntary entry into the Patuxent program produced more serious participation in its rehabilitative program, and will these individuals, after release, be more able to cope responsibly in the community and more likely to do so? It is too early to tell, but careful records are being kept of what happens to those who are released. If their recidivism rate is lowered, and there are other signs of effective rehabilitation, the institution will indeed become the model it originally hoped to be.

expressed it, " 'Rehabilitation' in prison is at best a myth and at worst a fraud" (p. 5). In any event, there is a strong trend at the present time away from the goal of rehabilitation and back toward punishment.

Some correctional trends and prospects.

While serious efforts are being made to improve law-enforcement and correctional procedures, there is a good deal of disagreement among governmental agencies, law-enforcement officials, criminologists, and other social scientists concerning the most effective measures to take. There appears, however, to be increasing agreement on the following points:[3]

a) At the present time, no methods of rehabilitation have been found that are both predictably effective and socially acceptable. Therefore, some people must be imprisoned to protect society.

b) Such criminal offenders should be given a flat maximum sentence to "fit the crime," but with provision for time off for good behavior—for example, for each day the individual abides by prison rules.

c) Rehabilitation programs should be available in prison for those who want them, but participation in such programs should not be made a condition of parole, at least until they have been proven effective.

d) Giant human warehouses such as Attica and San Quentin should be phased out and replaced by smaller, more flexible, and less dehumanizing prisons. Prison facilities such as libraries should be improved.

e) Treatment of prisoners should not vary with respect to sex, race, or social class. Standards for correctional personnel should be established and maintained, and adequate facilities for helping paroled prisoners make the transition to society should be available (see HIGHLIGHT on page 310).

Implicit in the above measures is the realization that prison is not presently a good place to send people for rehabilitation—especially those who have not committed violent or serious crimes. As Guthrie (1975) quoted one former state prison official as saying, "If you had a friend who was having some adjustment

---

[3]Based in part on Holden (1975) and Schwartz (1975):

Prisoners' rights vs. "treatment" for offenders

During the eighteenth and nineteenth centuries the criminal offender was viewed as having "free will" and being "morally depraved." Because the criminal was viewed as a serious menace to society, the primary method of crime control centered around detection and long periods of imprisonment. During the latter part of the nineteenth century and the first half of the twentieth, the preceding view changed to one emphasizing "treatment" and "rehabilitation" of the offender, based largely on the assumption that his behavior was the result of underlying maladjustment. The individual was "sick" and needed treatment.

In the latter half of this century, a new view of criminology has emerged which views our society, rather than the criminal offender, as "sick." In essence, the offender is the end product of the failures of the "establishment." From this viewpoint, more drastic methods of "treatment"—such as long prison sentences and the use of powerful behavior modification techniques—are considered both misdirected and a violation of the offender's rights as a person, for the emphasis is on forcing the offender to adjust to a sick society, rather than on changing pathological social conditions which presumably resulted in the criminal behavior.

In the light of available evidence, it would seem more realistic to adopt an interactional view which focuses on needed changes both in society and in criminal offenders. Until the former can be achieved, however, the immediate problem of what to do with offenders who commit violent criminal acts such as homicide, assault, robbery, and rape is a difficult one to resolve.

Milestones in dealing with criminal behavior in the United States

1817   Inauguration in New York State of the first parole system in the U.S.

1841   Adoption by the city of Boston, Massachusetts, of probation procedures—the first in the U.S.

1855   Opening of an institution for the criminally insane—the first in the U.S.— adjacent to Auburn State Prison, New York

1915   Formal report by Paul E. Bowers, psychiatrist at Indiana State Prison, of comprehensive studies on the relationship between crime and mental illness

1930   Congressional passage of law reorganizing federal prisons and providing for medical services to prisoners

1940   First publication of the *Journal of Criminal Psychopathology*

1948   Utilization in the New Jersey prison system of group therapy techniques

1952   Inauguration by the State of Wisconsin of the first program in the U.S. for adequate treatment of sex offenders

1956   The rendering, by the U.S. Court of Appeals for the District of Columbia, of the Durham decision, in which the provision is made that a defendant is not criminally responsible if the criminal act was the product of mental disease or mental defect

1958   Congressional passage of Public Law 752, providing for psychiatric examination of convicted federal offenders before imposition of sentence

1965   Congressional passage of the Prisoner Rehabilitation Act, authorizing the daytime release of selected inmates for education or work in nearby communities

1965   The rendering, by the U.S. Supreme Court, of the Miranda decision, which requires that persons accused of a crime be informed of their right to counsel before being questioned

1970   Congressional passage of "preventive detention" and other anticrime legislation

1972   Supreme Court decision holding that the death penalty as imposed under some state laws violates the Eighth Amendment of the Constitution, which bans "cruel and unusual punishment." However, the precise meaning of the decision remains unclear, and further action is expected.

1976   Federal judge in Alabama, holding that the prisons are fraught with "massive constitutional infirmities," set minimum standards the state must provide its prisoners to meet guarantees of the United States Constitution. The order required that mental health services be offered to prisoners.

In addition to the events listed, there has been a trend during the 1970s toward the use of clinical psychologists and psychiatrists as "expert witnesses" in selected criminal cases. Such testimony is directed toward providing a jury with information concerning a defendant's mental status and assisting the jury in drawing inferences from certain types of psychological data. For a discussion of the role of psychologists and psychiatrists as expert witnesses, the reader is referred to the Group for the Advancement of Psychiatry (1974), Silber (1974), Silverman (1969), and Monahan (1976).

problems unrelated to crime, you wouldn't think of sending him to San Quentin for a couple of months to get rehabilitated" (p. 5). Probation or early parole for such offenders and a concentrated effort to integrate institutional, family, and community facilities into a broadly based correctional program would be expected to have better results.

Ultimately, of course, any effective approach to crime must elicit citizen and community involvement. Only with such involvement will it be possible to incorporate ex-offenders into the community in responsible ways and deal adequately with both the causes of crime and the injustices in our legal system.

We began this chapter with a description of personality disorders, a cluster of disorders in which there are persistent maladaptive patterns of perceiving, thinking, and relating to the environment that result in either significant problems in social relationships or subjective distress or both. Such individuals have a common core of immaturity, self-centeredness, lack of feeling for others, manipulativeness, and a tendency to "act out" and project blame for their problems onto others. Many of the traits characteristic of personality disorders also occur in other individuals in mild enough form not to interfere with their successful functioning. For most of the personality disorders, little research has been conducted on causal patterns.

In the case of antisocial, or psychopathic, personality, in which the individual is callous and unethical, without loyalty or close relationships but often with superficial charm and intelligence, both constitutional and learning factors seem to be important. Anxiety and other factors associated with excessive stress do not seem to be prominent features. These disorders begin and are often recognized in childhood or adolescence but only individuals 18 or over are given a diagnosis of antisocial personality. Treatment is fraught with difficulties, because these individuals rarely see any need for it and blame others for their problems. Traditional psychotherapy is ineffective, but where control is possible, as in an institution, newer methods incorporating meaningful reinforcement have had some success.

In the latter part of this chapter, we dealt with crime, noting the increasing incidence and social dangers, as well as the complex causal patterns that may be involved. Unlike the offenders whose behavior stems from poverty or social disorganization, professional criminals and those involved in organized crime often show a high level of emotional stability and are well socialized—except that they have adopted the values of a subgroup of society. With the social changes of the 1960s and 1970s, two "new" kinds of criminals have become common—the one who commits crimes for "kicks" and the alienated, hostile ghetto-dweller who sees no other way to participate in the benefits of the society. Finally, we looked at some of the past and present approaches to dealing with criminals.

10

Addictive disorders: Substance abuse, obesity, and pathological gambling

Alcohol abuse and alcohol dependence

Drug abuse and drug dependence

Other addictive disorders: Extreme obesity and pathological gambling

The misuse of drugs may take the form of dependence or abuse. In traditional usage, *dependence* signified psychological reliance on a particular drug, while *addiction* was reserved for physiological dependence, as indicated by withdrawal symptoms if the drug were discontinued. Recently, however, *drug dependence* has been commonly used to denote either psychological or physiological dependence. The term *drug abuse* is used to indicate excessive use of a drug, regardless of whether an individual has reached the point of true dependence on it. We shall follow this terminology although, as will be indicated later, there is some disagreement within the field on the most suitable nomenclature, and the new DSM-III classification has retained the traditional definitions.

Another useful distinction is between *substance use* disorders and *substance-induced* disorders. Substance use disorders are patterns of maladaptive behavior that center around taking the substance, while substance-induced disorders are states that result from the drug itself. For example, alcohol dependence would be considered an alcohol use disorder, whereas delirium tremens would be considered an alcohol-induced disorder. Sometimes alcohol-induced states are useful in diagnosing the substance use disorder of alcohol dependence.

The most commonly used problem drugs are the *psychoactive*—mind-altering—drugs: alcohol, barbiturates, minor tranquilizers, amphetamines, heroin, and marijuana. Some of these drugs, such as alcohol, can be purchased legally by adults; others, such as the barbiturates, can be used legally under medical supervision; still others, such as heroin, are illegal. Currently, drug legislation—particularly in relation to marijuana—is a controversial matter.

The increasing problem of drug abuse and dependence in our society has caused both public and scientific attention to be focused on it. In the past, abuse and dependence—particularly in relation to alcohol and heroin—were considered to be manifestations of "moral weakness." But exhortation and other treatment approaches based on this concept—such as imprisonment—proved singularly ineffective. Thus, until recently, little progress was made toward the identification of causal factors or the development of effective methods of treatment. Although our present knowledge concerning drug abuse and dependence is far from complete, investigating them as maladaptive patterns of adjustment to life's demands rather than as moral deficiencies is leading to rapid progress in both understanding and treatment. Such an approach, of course, does not necessarily abandon the idea that the individual has some personal responsibility for the development and maintenance of the problem; the prevalent concept of drug dependence and abuse as "disease" has in our judgment clouded the issue in an unfortunate way.

In addition to the abuse and dependence disorders that involve a particular substance, there are disorders that have all the features of an addictive condition but do not involve substances with chemically addicting properties. Two of these disorders, pathological gambling and the gross overeating involved in extreme obesity, are included in this chapter because the maladaptive behavior involved and the treatment approaches effective with them suggest that they have a great deal in common with the drug abuse disorders.

Alcohol abuse and alcohol dependence

As we noted in Chapter 1, Cambyses, King of Persia in the sixth century B.C., had the dubious distinction of being one of the first alcoholics on record. People of many other early cultures, including the Egyptian, Greek, and Roman, made extensive and often excessive use of alcohol. Beer was first made in Egypt around 3000 B.C. The oldest surviving winemaking formulas were recorded by Marcus Cato in Italy almost a century and a half before the birth of Christ. About 800 A.D. the process of distillation was developed by an Arabian alchemist, thus making possible an increase in both the range and the potency of alcoholic beverages.

Incidence and effects of problem drinking

The terms *alcoholic* and *alcoholism* have been the subject of some controversy recently and are used somewhat differently by different groups. Some, such as the World Health Organization, use the term *alcoholic* for any person with life problems related to alcohol, while others, like the National Council on Alcoholism, use a more restrictive definition: other diagnostic signs must be present for an individual to be classified as an alcoholic. Some behaviorists are recommending a still more restrictive definition: they prefer to use the term *problem drinkers* for most alcohol abusers, conceptualizing "problem drinking" as a continuum, with "alcoholics" a smaller subgroup at the extreme end (Miller, in press; Miller & Caddy, 1977). In this chapter we will use the term *alcoholic* in the more prevalent sense to refer to individuals with serious drinking problems, whose drinking impairs their life adjustment in terms of health, personal relationships, and/or occupational functioning (President's Commission on Mental Health, 1978).

However defined, alcoholism is on the rise in the United States. An estimated 10 million adult Americans experience episodes of abusive use of alcohol. These episodes range from infrequent to frequent and may be manifestations of early, intermediate, or later phases of alcoholism. Yet only 1 million of these individuals are currently receiving treatment for their drinking problem.

The potentially detrimental effects of excessive alcohol—for the individual, his or her loved ones, and society—are legion. Bengelsdorf (1970a) has pointed out that

" . . . its abuse has killed more people, sent more victims to hospitals, generated more police arrests, broken up more marriages and homes, and cost industry more money than has the abuse of heroin, amphetamines, barbiturates, and marijuana combined." (p. 7)

In addition to the serious problems they create for themselves, excessive drinkers pose serious difficulties for, on the average, some 4 to 6 other persons, including mates, children, friends, employers, and even total strangers, as in cases where they are involved in automobile accidents while under the influence of alcohol. The National Institute on Alcohol Abuse and Alcoholism and other national agencies agree that alcohol abuse is by far the most devastating drug problem in the United States today.

Alcohol has been associated with over half the deaths and major injuries suffered in automobile accidents each year, and with about 50 percent of all murders, 40 percent of all assaults, 35 percent or more of all rapes, and 30 percent of all suicides. About one out of every three arrests in the United States results from the abuse of alcohol. The financial drain imposed on the economy by alcoholism is estimated to be over $25 billion a year, in large part comprised of losses to industry from absenteeism, lowered work efficiency, and accidents, as well as the costs involved in the treatment of alcoholics. The life span of the average alcoholic is about 12 years shorter than that of the average nonalcoholic, and alcohol now ranks as the third major cause of death in the United States, behind coronary heart disease and cancer.[1]

Alcoholism in the United States cuts across all age, educational, occupational, and socioeconomic boundaries. It is considered a serious problem in industry, in the professions, and in the military; it is found among such seemingly unlikely candidates as airline pilots, surgeons, law-enforcement officers, and teenagers. The once popular image of the alcoholic as an unkempt resident of Skid Row is inaccurate. In fact, the latter group constitutes less than 5 percent of all alcoholics; it is even estimated that half or more of the people on Skid Row—such as the Bowery in New York—are either moderate drinkers or nondrinkers. (For information on other myths about alcoholism, see HIGHLIGHT on page 316).

Problem drinking may develop during any life period from early childhood through old age. However, the great majority of extreme problem drinkers are men and women who are married and living with their families, still hold jobs—often important ones—and are accepted members of their communities. And al-

---

[1]The statistics in this section are based on Celentano and McQueen (1978); DeLint and Schmidt (1976); National Institute on Alcohol Abuse and Alcoholism (1978); President's Commission on Mental Health (1978); Schmidt (1977); U.S. Dept. of Health, Education, and Welfare (1974); and *U.S. News & World Report* (April 14, 1975).

Alcoholism in the United States cuts across all age, educational, occupational, and socioeconomic boundaries. The public image of the alcoholic as an unkempt resident of Skid Row is fallacious; less than 5 percent of the country's alcoholics are in that category.

though alcoholism has traditionally been considered to be more prevalent among males than females, this distinction seems to be disappearing in our society. Since many women do not work outside the home, it is often easier for them to conceal their alcoholism.

The commonly used incidence figure of 5 males to 1 female is considered a conservative estimate (Efron, Keller, & Gurioli, 1974). A recent survey by Celentano and McQueen (1978) showed that 81 percent of the men drank alcohol, with 26 percent considering themselves heavy drinkers, while 68 percent of the women were drinkers but only 8 percent considered themselves heavy drinkers.

Our present discussion will center on the problem of severe alcohol abuse and dependence in the United States. This problem, however, is by no means limited to any particular country or racial or ethnic group but is found all over the world. In fact, there has been a recent upsurge of alcoholism in a number of industrialized nations (Foulks & Katz, 1973; Kamien, 1975).

Clinical picture of alcohol abuse and dependence

The Roman poet Horace, in the first century B.C., wrote lyrically about the effects of wine:

"It discloses secrets; ratifies and confirms our hopes; thrusts the coward forth to battle; eases the anxious mind of its burthen; instructs in arts. Whom has not a cheerful glass made eloquent! Whom not quite free and easy from pinching poverty!"

Unfortunately, the effects of alcohol are not always so benign or beneficial. According to the Japanese proverb, "First the man takes a drink, then the drink takes a drink, and then the drink takes the man."

General effects of alcoholic intoxication. Alcohol is a depressant which attacks and numbs the higher brain centers, impairing judgment and other rational processes and lowering self-control. As behavioral restraints decline, more primitive emotional responses appear, and the drinker may indulge in the satisfaction of impulses ordinarily held in check. In fact, alcohol has been called a "catalyst" for violence, including homicide, assault, and rape.

Some degree of motor incoordination soon becomes apparent, and the drinker's sense of discrimination and perception of cold, pain, and other discomforts are dulled. Typically the drinker experiences a sense of warmth, expansiveness, and well-being. In such a mood, unpleasant realities are screened out and the drinker's feelings of self-esteem and adequacy rise. Casual acquaintances become the best and most understanding of friends, and the drinker enters a generally pleasant world of unreality in which worries are temporarily left behind.

When the alcohol content of the bloodstream reaches 0.1 percent, the individual is considered to be intoxicated (see HIGHLIGHT on page 318). Muscular coordination, speech, and vision are impaired, and thought processes are confused. Even before this level of intoxication is reached, however, judgment becomes impaired to such an extent that the person misjudges his or her condition. For example, drinkers are certain of their ability to drive safely long after their driving has in fact become quite unsafe.

When the blood alcohol reaches approximately 0.5 percent, the entire neural balance is upset and the individual "passes out." Here unconsciousness apparently acts as a safety device, since concentrations above 0.55 percent are usually lethal.

In general, it is the amount of alcohol actually concentrated in the bodily fluids, not the amount consumed, that determines intoxication. However, the effects of alcohol vary for different drinkers, depending on personality,

Some common misconceptions about alcohol and alcoholism

1. Alcohol is a stimulant.

2. Alcohol is essential to the treatment of certain diseases.

3. You can always detect alcohol on the breath of a person who has been drinking.

4. One ounce of 86 proof liquor contains more alcohol than a 12-ounce can of beer.

5. Body size has little or nothing to do with how much liquor a person can hold.

6. Drinking several cups of coffee can counteract the effects of alcohol and enable the drinker to "sober up."

7. Alcohol can help a person sleep more soundly.

8. Impaired judgment does not occur before there are obvious signs of intoxication.

9. The individual will get more intoxicated by "mixing" liquors than by taking comparable amounts of one kind—e.g., bourbon, Scotch, or vodka.

10. Exercise or a cold shower helps speed up the metabolism of alcohol.

11. People with "strong wills" need not be concerned about becoming alcoholics.

12. Alcohol cannot produce a true addiction in the same sense that heroin does.

13. One cannot become an alcoholic by drinking just beer.

14. Alcohol is far less dangerous than marijuana.

15. In a heavy drinker, damage to the liver shows up long before brain damage appears.

16. The physiological withdrawal reaction from heroin is more dangerous than is withdrawal from alcohol.

17. Most alcoholics who have successfully completed treatment can safely resume social drinking.

physical condition, amount of food in the stomach, and duration of the drinking. In addition, the user of alcohol may gradually build up a tolerance for the drug so that ever increasing amounts may be needed to produce the desired effects. The attitude of the drinker is important, too: although actual motor and intellectual abilities decline in direct ratio to the blood concentration of alcohol, many persons who consciously try to do so can maintain apparent control over their behavior, showing few outward signs of being intoxicated even after drinking relatively large amounts of alcohol.

Exactly how alcohol works on the brain is not yet fully understood, but several physiological effects are common. One is a tendency toward increased sexual stimulation but, simultaneously, lowered sexual performance. As Shakespeare wrote in *Macbeth*, alcohol "provokes the desire, but it takes away the performance."

An appreciable number of problem drinkers also experience "blackouts"—lapses of memory. At first these occur at high blood alcohol levels, and the individual may carry on a rational conversation and engage in other relatively complex activities but have no trace of recall the next day. For heavy drinkers even moderate drinking can elicit a memory lapse.

A third curious phenomenon associated with alcoholic intoxication is the "hangover," which many drinkers experience at one time or another. Some observers consider the hangover to be a mild form of withdrawal. As yet, no one has come up with a satisfactory explanation or remedy for the symptoms of headache, nausea, and fatigue characteristic of hangovers.

Alcohol dependence and deterioration. Although many investigators have maintained that alcohol is a dangerous systemic poison even in very small amounts, newer studies indicate that in moderate amounts—up to about three shots of whiskey, half a bottle of wine, or four glasses of beer per day—alcohol is not harmful to most people and may actually be beneficial to reduce the tension of everyday life stress (U.S. Dept. of Health, Education, and Welfare, 1974). For pregnant women, however, these amounts are believed to be dangerous; in fact, no safe level

has been established (see HIGHLIGHT on page 319).

For individuals who drink immoderately, the picture is highly unfavorable. For one thing, the alcohol that is taken in must be assimilated by the body, except for about 5 to 10 percent which is eliminated through breath, urine, and perspiration. The work of assimilation is done by the liver, but when large amounts of alcohol are ingested, the liver may be seriously overworked and eventually suffer irreversible damage. In fact, over time the excessive drinker has a 1-in-10 chance of developing cirrhosis of the liver, a pathological condition in which liver cells are irreparably damaged and replaced by fibrous scar tissue.

For another thing, alcohol is a high-calorie drug. A pint of whiskey—enough to make about 8 to 10 ordinary cocktails—provides about 1200 calories, which is approximately half the ordinary, caloric requirement for a day. Thus, consumption of alcohol reduces the drinker's appetite for other food. Since alcohol has no nutritional value, the excessive drinker often suffers from malnutrition. Furthermore, heavy drinking impairs the body's ability to utilize nutrients, so the nutritional deficiency cannot be made up by popping vitamins. The excessive intake of alcohol also impairs the activity of the white blood cells in fighting disease and is associated with a greatly increased risk of cancer (U.S. Dept. of Health, Education, and Welfare, 1974). And in addition to the other problems, the excessive drinker usually suffers from chronic fatigue, oversensitivity, and depression.

Initially alcohol may seem to provide a useful crutch for dealing with the stresses of life, especially during periods of acute stress, by helping screen out intolerable reality and enhancing the drinker's feelings of adequacy and worth. Eventually, however, the excessive use of alcohol becomes counterproductive, resulting in lowered feelings of adequacy and worth, impaired reasoning and judgment, and gradual personality deterioration. Behavior typically becomes coarse and inappropriate, and the drinker assumes increasingly less responsibility, loses pride in personal appearance, neglects spouse and family, and becomes generally touchy, irritable, and unwilling to discuss the problem. As judgment becomes impaired, the excessive drinker may be unable to hold a

Alcohol levels in the blood after drinks taken on an empty stomach by a 150-pound male drinking for one hour*

Effects	Time for all alcohol to leave the body– Hours	Alcohol concentration in blood– Percent	Amount of beverage
Gross intoxication	10	0.15	5 highballs (1¹/₂ oz. whiskey each) or 5 cocktails (1¹/₂ oz. whiskey ea.) or 27¹/₂ oz. ordinary wine or ¹/₂ pint whiskey
Clumsiness–unsteadiness in standing or walking	8	0.12	4 highballs or 4 cocktails or 22 oz. ordinary wine or 6 bottles beer (12 oz. ea.)
Exaggerated emotion and behavior–talkative, noisy, or morose	6	0.09	3 highballs or 3 cocktails or 16¹/₂ oz. ordinary wine or 4 bottles beer
Feeling of warmth, mental relaxation	4	0.06	2 highballs or 2 cocktails or 11 oz. ordinary wine or 2 bottles beer
Slight changes in feeling	2	0.03	1 highball or 1 cocktail or 5¹/₂ oz. ordinary wine or 1 bottle beer
	0		

Calories

5¹/₂ oz. wine	115
12 oz. beer	170
1¹/₂ oz. whiskey	120

*Blood alcohol level following given intake differs according to the person's weight, the length of the drinking time, and the sex of the drinker.
(*Time*, 1974)

job and generally becomes unqualified to cope with new demands that arise. By this time, the drinker's general health is likely to have deteriorated, and brain and liver damage may have occurred. General personal disorganization and deterioration may be reflected in loss of employment and/or marital breakup.

Stages in alcohol dependence. Excessive drinking can progress insidiously from early- to middle- to late-stage alcoholism. (The HIGHLIGHT on page 320 presents some of the common "early warning signs" of excessive drinking.) In an extensive study of over 2000 drinkers who had progressed to late-stage physiological and psychological dependence, Jellinek (1952, 1971) found that the following stages had been common in the development of their dependence.

1. *The prealcoholic symptomatic phase.* Drinkers who later lost control had started out drinking in conventional social situations but soon had experienced a rewarding relief from tension—a feeling that was strongly marked in their case, either because their tensions were greater than others' or because they had not learned to handle them effectively. Initially, they tended to seek this relief of tension only occasionally. Gradually, however, their tolerance for tension decreased to such an extent that they resorted to alcohol almost daily. This transition from occasional to frequent drinking took from several months to as long as two years.

2. *The prodromal phase.* The second phase was marked by sudden onset of blackouts: the drinker might show few, if any, signs of intoxication and might be able to carry on a reasonable conversation or go through quite elaborate activities but with no memory of these events the next day. Occasionally, average drinkers experience such amnesic episodes when they drink excessively during a state of emotional or physical exhaustion, but this is very rare. Accordingly, Jellinek considered this amnesia without loss of consciousness and sometimes even without intake of extremely large amounts of alcohol to be an indication of a heightened susceptibility to alcohol in the subjects he was studying.

Certain correlated behaviors now made their appearance, among which were (a) surreptitious drinking, in which the drinker sought oc-

Is there a "fetal alcohol syndrome"?

A great deal of recent research indicates that heavy drinking by an expectant mother can affect the health of the unborn baby. Studies of newborn infants whose mothers drank heavily during pregnancy have found frequent physical and behavioral abnormalities. Such infants are lighter and smaller than average and sometimes show facial and limb irregularities (Jones & Smith, 1975; NIMH, 1978; Smith, Jones, & Hanson, 1976; Streissguth, 1976; and Ulleland, 1972). In fact, *The Third Report on Alcohol and Health* (HEW, 1978) reports that alcohol abuse in pregnant women is the third leading cause of birth defects (the first two being *Down's syndrome,* or mongolism, and *spina bifida,* or incomplete formation and fusion of the spinal canal).

The exact mechanisms by which alcoholism produces fetal damage have not been identified. Some investigators believe that the damage is caused by ethanol crossing the placental barrier and reaching the fetus (Smith et al., 1976; Streissguth, 1976). Other investigators, however, raise questions about the whole concept of a "fetal alcohol syndrome" (Johnson, 1974). For example, they point out that it is not clear to what extent the alcohol is responsible and to what extent the damage may be resulting from other factors usually associated with heavy drinking, such as nutritional deficit. But no one disputes the damage that occurs.

How much drinking endangers the newborn's health? The HEW report warns against drinking more than one ounce of alcohol per day or the equivalent (2 12-ounce cans of beer or 2 5-ounce glasses of wine, for example). However, the actual amount of alcohol that can safely be ingested during pregnancy is not known.

casions for having a few drinks, unknown to others, for fear of being misjudged; (b) preoccupation with alcohol, which often took the form of worrying about whether there would be enough to drink at an upcoming social gathering—and perhaps having several drinks ahead of time in anticipation of a possible shortage; (c) avid drinking, in which the drinker gulped the first one or two drinks; (d) guilt feelings about this drinking behavior, with a dawning recognition that it was out of the ordinary; and (e) avoidance of references to alcohol in conversation.

3. *The crucial phase.* The third stage was characterized by the loss of control over drinking: any consumption of alcohol now seemed to trigger a chain reaction that continued until the drinker was either too intoxicated or too sick to drink any more. Celentano and McQueen (1978) have reported that 26.4 percent of a representative group of male drinkers and 13.5 percent of the female drinkers reported having experienced this loss of control while drinking.

Although they had lost the ability to regulate their drinking once they began, Jellinek's subjects could still control whether they would drink on any given occasion. This was evidenced by periods of abstinence or "going on the wagon" following recovery from severe intoxication.

As control was lost, these individuals began to rationalize their drinking behavior, producing the familiar alcoholic alibis. They convinced themselves that they had not really lost control on a particular occasion—or that they had had good reason for getting intoxicated. These justifications also served to counter the social pressures that arose as their behavior became more conspicuous.

In spite of their rationalizations, however, there had been a marked lowering of self-esteem, and some drinkers now attempted to compensate for this trend with extravagant expenditures and other grandiose behaviors as well as by projecting the blame for their difficulties onto others. But these defenses did not work well and they remained remorseful, which further increased their tension and provided added reason for drinking. This remorse, however, together with social pressures, sometimes also led to periods of total abstinence. As tensions persisted, some decided that their troubles arose not from drinking per se, but rather from the type of beverage they were drinking. So now they attempted to control their problem by changing their pattern— consuming different beverages, setting up rules about drinking only after a certain hour of the day, and so on.

During this phase they usually began drinking in the afternoon and were intoxicated during the evening. The aftereffects of the evening's drunkenness caused some loss of work

HIGHLIGHT

Early warning signs of drinking problems

1. Frequent desire—increase in desire, often evidenced by eager anticipation of drinking after work and careful attention to maintaining supply.

2. Increased consumption—an increase that seems gradual but is marked from month to month. The individual may begin to worry about it at this point and lie about the amount consumed.

3. Extreme behavior—the commission of various acts that leave the individual feeling guilty and embarrassed the next day.

4. "Pulling blanks"—inability to remember what happened during an alcoholic bout.

5. Morning drinking—either as a means of reducing a hangover or as a "bracer" to help start the day.

A person who exhibits this pattern of behavior is well on the road to loss of control. The progression is likely to be facilitated if there is environmental support for heavy or excessive drinking from the spouse or the individual's job situation or sociocultural setting.

time, but they still struggled to maintain their employment and social standing, even though they now had begun a pattern of progressive withdrawal from their environment.

The entire struggle subjected them to severe stress. They began to drop friends and quit jobs. In some cases, of course, they were abandoned by associates and dismissed by employers, but usually they took the initiative as an anticipatory defense. This process led to increased isolation and to further centering of their behavior around alcohol. They now became concerned with how their activities might interfere with their drinking rather than the other way around.

About this time, too, they began to take steps to protect their supply by laying in a large stock of alcoholic beverages which they hid in the most unlikely places. Similarly, their neglect of proper nutrition began to aggravate the effects of heavy drinking, and the first hospitalization for some alcoholic complaint occurred in some cases. Improper nutrition and other complications also induced a marked decrease in sexual drive, a factor which tended to increase their hostility toward their spouses and give rise to the well-known "alcoholic jealousy syndrome," in which they blamed their loss of sexual drive on their mates' alleged extramarital affairs.

By now, they had begun to feel unable to start the day without a drink to steady themselves. This was the beginning of "morning drinking" and foreshadowed the start of the chronic phase.

4. *The chronic phase.* As alcohol became increasingly dominant in their lives, they found themselves intoxicated during the daytime on a weekday and might continue in this state for several days until they were entirely incapacitated. These drawn-out drinking bouts were usually associated with a marked impairment of thinking and with ethical deterioration—processes which, however, were still reversible. They were no longer selective about their drinking companions, and if their normal sources of liquor were not available, they drank almost anything, even hair tonic or rubbing alcohol. At this time alcoholic psychoses might occur.

Also commonly noted at this time was a loss of tolerance for alcohol, now believed to result from liver damage. Half the amount previously required might now be sufficient to produce an alcoholic stupor. Indefinable fears and tremors became persistent and were especially pronounced as soon as the alcohol disappeared from the drinker's system. Consequently the symptoms were "controlled" by continuous drinking.

In this chronic phase, rationalizations began to fail as they were mercilessly tested against reality. And in many of the group—approximately 60 percent—vague religious desires began to develop. As the rationalization system finally gave way, some of them admitted defeat and became amenable to treatment. Those who did not seek and receive outside help continued to drink compulsively. They were unable to help themselves.

Here it should be emphasized that although the stages outlined by Jellinek appear to characterize the course followed by many drinkers who become alcoholics, others do not fit this pattern. For example, there are so-called "spree" drinkers who remain sober and handle responsible positions for long periods of time, but then in the face of some stressful situation will lose control completely—usually winding up in a hospital or jail. It has also been shown that blackouts may not be experienced or may occur in later stages of alcoholism. And in some instances, individuals appear to skip even the social drinker phase, becoming what has been referred to as "instant alcoholics." Finally a new trend has become apparent in our society, involving "multiple addictions," in which dependence on alcohol is complicated by the concurrent use of barbiturates, amphetamines, tranquilizers, and/or other psychoactive drugs. This is apparently particularly common among young alcoholics and, of course, may markedly change the nature and course of the clinical picture.

Psychoses associated with alcoholism. Several acute psychotic reactions fit the DSM-III classification of substance-induced disorders. These reactions may develop in individuals who have been drinking excessively over long periods of time or who have a reduced tolerance for alcohol for other reasons—for example, because of brain lesions. Such acute reactions usually last only a short time and generally consist of confusion, excitement, and delirium. They are often called *alcoholic psychoses* because they are marked by a temporary loss of contact with reality. There are four commonly recognized subtypes of such disorders.

1. *Pathological intoxication* is an acute reaction that occurs in persons whose tolerance to alcohol is chronically very low (such as epileptics or those of an unstable personality makeup) or in normal persons whose tolerance to alcohol is temporarily lessened by exhaustion, emotional stress, or other conditions. Following the consumption of even moderate amounts of alcohol, these individuals may suddenly become disoriented and may evidence a homicidal rage—sometimes committing violent crimes. This confused, disoriented state is usually followed by a period of deep sleep, with complete amnesia afterward. The following case history illustrates this pattern.

The patient was hospitalized following an altercation in a bar in which he attacked and injured a woman and her escort. On admission to the hospital he seemed very friendly and cooperative—in fact, almost servile in his desire to please those in authority. His personal history revealed that he had been involved in five such incidents during the previous two years. His family background was torn with bickering and dissension. Both parents were stern disciplinarians and severely punished him for the most minor disapproved behavior. He was taught to feel that sex was very evil.

In his previous altercations he had been arrested twice for disturbing the peace. In each case these incidents took place in bars where, after a few drinks, he would become aggressive, loud, and abusive, daring any and all to do anything about it. His latest escapade and arrest involved an attack on a woman; this had apparently been provoked by her kissing her escort and making what the patient interpreted as sexual overtures in public. He approached the woman in a threatening manner, slapped her, knocked her escort out when he attempted to intervene, and then hit her several times with his fists before he was forcibly restrained by other customers. He was amnesic for the entire episode, apparently "coming to" on his way to the hospital.

It was felt in this case that the woman's behavior aroused unacceptable and therefore threatening sexual desires in the patient, against which he defended himself by becoming hostile and attacking her. The alcohol apparently served to lower his normal behavioral restraints, permitting his hostility to be expressed in overt antisocial behavior.

2. *Delirium tremens* is probably the best known of the various alcoholic psychotic reactions. A fairly common occurrence among those who drink excessively for a long time, this reaction may follow a prolonged alcoholic debauch, appear during a period of abstinence, be associated with a head injury or infection, or occur upon the withdrawal of alcohol after prolonged drinking.

The delirium usually is preceded by a period of restlessness and insomnia during which the person may feel generally uneasy and apprehensive. Slight noises or sudden moving objects may cause considerable excitement and agitation. The full-blown symptoms include (a) disorientation for time and place in which, for example, a person may mistake the hospital for a church or jail, friends are no longer recognized, and hospital attendants may be identified as old acquaintances; (b) vivid hallucinations, particularly of small, fast-moving animals like snakes, rats, and roaches, which are clearly localized in space; (c) acute fear, in which these animals may change in form, size, or color in terrifying ways; (d) extreme suggestibility, in which a person can be made to see almost any form of animal if its presence is merely suggested; (e) marked coarse tremors of the hands, tongue, and lips—as implied by the name of this disorder; and (f) other symptoms, including perspiration, fever, a rapid and weak heartbeat, a coated tongue, and a foul breath.

The delirium typically lasts from three to six days and is generally followed by a deep sleep. When the person awakens, there are few symptoms—aside from possible slight remorse—but frequently the individual will have been rather badly scared, and may not resume drinking for several weeks or months. Usually, however, there is eventual resumption, followed by a return to the hospital with a new attack. The death rate from delirium tremens as a result of convulsions, heart failure, and other complications once approximated 10 percent (Tavel, 1962). With such newer drugs as chlordiazepoxide, however, the current death rate during delirium tremens and acute alcoholic withdrawal has been markedly reduced.

The following is a brief description of a 43-year-old male delirium tremens patient.

The subject was brought forcibly to the psychiatric ward of a general hospital when he fired his shotgun at 3:30 A.M. while "trying to repel an invasion of cockroaches." On admission he was confused and disoriented and had terrifying hallucinations involving "millions and millions" of invading cockroaches. He leaped from his bed and cowered in terror against the wall, screaming for help and kicking and hitting frantically at his imaginary assailants. When an attendant came to his aid, he screamed for him to get back out of danger or he would be killed too. Before the attendant could reach him he dived headlong on his head, apparently trying to kill himself.

The subject's delirium lasted for 3½ days, after which he returned to a state of apparent normality, apologized profusely for the trouble he had caused everyone, stated he would never touch another drop, and was discharged. However, on his way home he stopped at a bar, had too much to drink, and on emerging from the bar collapsed on the street. This time he sobered up in jail, again apologized for the trouble he had caused, was extremely remorseful, and was released with a small fine. His subsequent career is unknown.

3. In *acute alcoholic hallucinosis*, the main symptoms are auditory hallucinations. At first the individual usually hears a voice making certain simple statements. With time, however, the hallucinations usually extend to the voices of several people, all of them critical and reproachful. The individual's innermost private weaknesses, particularly sexual ones, are itemized and discussed, and various horrible punishments are then proposed. The clanking of chains, the sharpening of knives, the sound of pistol shots, or footsteps approaching in a threatening manner may be heard. Terror-stricken, the individual may scream for help or attempt suicide.

This condition may continue for several days or even weeks, during which time the person is depressed but fairly well oriented and coherent, apart from the hallucinations. After recovery, he or she usually shows considerable remorse as well as some insight into what has happened.

Investigators are less inclined than formerly to attribute this psychotic reaction solely to the effects of alcohol. Generally, it seems to be related to a broad pattern of maladaptive behavior, as in the following case.

The subject was hospitalized after a suicide attempt in which he slashed his wrists. He had been hospitalized once before after a similar incident in which he tried to hang himself with a bath towel. He was unmarried and lived alone.

The patient had been drinking excessively for a three-year period. He was not in the least particular about what he drank as long as it contained alcohol. For several days prior to his last suicide attempt he had heard voices that accused him of all manner of "filthy sex acts." He was particularly outraged when they accused him of having committed homosexual acts with his mouth and of having had relations with animals. He complained of a terrible taste in his mouth and imagined that his food had been poisoned as a means of punishing him for his sins. He was generally fearful and apprehensive and slept poorly

After a stay of two weeks in the hospital, the patient made a good recovery and was discharged. At this time he seemed to have some insight into his difficulties, stating that he felt that his sexual problems had something to do with his suicide attempt.

The psychotic symptoms of this individual were apparently triggered by alcohol, but it seems probable that they could have been similarly brought on by other drugs, illness, exhaustion, or other types of stress.

4. *Korsakoff's psychosis* was first described by the Russian psychiatrist Korsakoff in 1887.

The outstanding symptom is a memory defect (particularly with regard to recent events) which is concealed by falsification. Individuals may not recognize pictures, faces, rooms, and other objects that they have just seen, although they may feel that these people or objects are familiar. Such persons increasingly tend to fill in gaps with reminiscences and fanciful tales that lead to unconnected and distorted associations. These individuals may appear to be delirious, hallucinated, and disoriented for time and place, but ordinarily their confusion and disordered conduct are closely related to their attempts to fill in memory gaps. The memory disturbance itself seems related to an inability to form new associations in a manner that renders them readily retrievable. Such a reaction usually occurs in older alcoholics, after many years of excessive drinking.

The symptoms of this disorder are now considered to be due to vitamin B deficiency and other dietary inadequacies. A diet rich in vitamins and minerals generally restores the patient to more normal physical and mental health. However, some personality deterioration usually remains in the form of memory impairment, blunting of intellectual capacity, and lowering of moral and ethical standards.

Causes of alcohol abuse and dependence

In trying to identify the causes of problem drinking, some researchers have stressed the role of genetic and biochemical factors; others have viewed it as a maladaptive pattern of adjustment to the stress of life; still others have emphasized sociocultural factors, such as the availability of alcohol and social approval of excessive drinking. As with most other forms of maladaptive behavior, it would appear that there may be several types of alcohol dependence in which there are somewhat different patterns of biological, psychosocial, and sociocultural causal factors.

Biological factors. In the alcohol-dependent person, cell metabolism has adapted itself to the presence of alcohol in the bloodstream and now demands it for stability. When the alcohol in the bloodstream falls below a certain level, there are withdrawal symptoms. These

324

may be relatively mild, involving a craving for alcohol, tremors, perspiration, and weakness, or more severe, with nausea, vomiting, fever, tachycardia, convulsions, and hallucinations. The shortcut to ending them is to take another drink.

In terms of learning principles, each drink now serves to reinforce alcohol-seeking behavior because it reduces the unpleasantness. As Bandura (1969) has expressed it, "After the person thus becomes physically dependent on alcohol, he is compelled to consume large quantities of liquor both to alleviate distressing physical reactions and to avoid their recurrence" (p. 533). In essence, a recurrent cycle of alcohol-induced need-arousal and need-reduction is established.

A question that has been raised is whether certain individuals start out with a physiological predisposition to alcoholism—perhaps leading to an unusual craving for alcohol once it has been experienced, and hence a greater-than-average tendency toward loss of control. Presumably such a craving could result from some genetic vulnerability.

Research studies over the past three decades have shown that alcohol dependence does tend to run in families (Goodwin, 1976, 1979). In a study of 259 hospitalized alcoholics, for example, Winokur et al. (1970) found that slightly over 40 percent had had an alcoholic parent—usually the father. Whether this familial incidence results from shared genes or a shared alcoholic environment is a matter of some controversy. In an early study, Roe, Burks, and Mittelmann (1945) followed the case histories of 36 children who had been taken from severely alcoholic parents and placed in foster homes. The likelihood of their becoming alcoholic turned out to be no greater than that of a control group of 25 children of nonalcoholic parents. Some years later, in a review of a number of available studies, Rose and Burks (1968) reported comparable results, thus casting doubt on the genetic hypothesis.

More recent studies, however, have strongly supported the genetic viewpoint. For example, Goodwin et al. (1973) found that children of alcoholic parents who had been adopted by non-alcoholic foster parents still had nearly twice the number of alcohol problems by their late twenties as did a control group of adopted children whose real parents did not have a history of alcoholism. In another study, Goodwin and

Research studies over the past 30 years have shown that alcohol dependence tends to run in families. However, the great majority of children who have alcoholic parents do not themselves become alcoholics. Thus the role genetic factors play in the development of alcoholism remains unclear.

his colleagues (1974) compared the sons of alcoholic parents who were adopted in infancy by nonalcoholic parents with those raised by their alcoholic parents. Both adopted and non-adopted sons later evidenced high rates of alcoholism—25 percent and 17 percent respectively. These investigators concluded that it was being born to an alcoholic parent rather than being raised by one that increased the risk of the son's becoming an alcoholic.

On the other hand, the great majority of children who have alcoholic parents do not themselves become alcoholics—whether or not they are raised by their real parents. Thus we do not know the precise role of genetic factors in the etiology of alcoholism though available evidence suggests that they might be important as predisposing causes. Of course, constitutional predisposition to alcoholism could be acquired as well as inherited. But it is not known whether there are acquired conditions, such as endocrine or enzyme imbalances, that increase an individual's vulnerability to alcoholism.

Some research has suggested that certain

ethnic groups, particularly orientals and native Americans, have abnormal physiological reactions to alcohol. Fenna et al. (1971) and Wolff (1972) found that oriental and Eskimo subjects showed a hypersensitive reaction, including flushing of the skin, a drop in blood pressure, and nausea following the ingestion of alcohol. The relatively lower rates of alcoholism among oriental groups are tentatively considered to be related to a faster metabolism rate. Schaefer (1977), however, has questioned these and other metabolism studies as a basis for interpreting cultural differences in alcoholism rates and, using more explicit criteria of metabolism rate, found no differences in alcohol metabolism between a group of Reddis Indians and Northern European subjects (Schaefer, 1978). He concluded that further research into metabolism rate differences and sensitivity to alcohol needs to be integrated with studies focusing upon relative stress in various cultures.

Psychosocial factors.   Not only do alcoholics become physiologically dependent on alcohol; they develop a powerful psychological dependency as well. Since excessive drinking is so destructive of an individual's total life adjustment, the question arises as to why psychological dependence is learned. A number of psychosocial factors have been advanced as possible answers.

   1. *Psychological vulnerability.* The query as to why some individuals lose control over their drinking is often posed in terms of psychological vulnerability. In other words, is there an "alcoholic personality"—a type of character organization that predisposes a given individual to the use of alcohol rather than to some other defensive pattern of coping with stress?

   In efforts to answer this question, investigators have reported that alcoholics, in terms of pre-alcoholic personality, tend to be emotionally immature, to expect a great deal of the world, to require an inordinate amount of praise and appreciation, to react to failure with marked feelings of hurt and inferiority, to have low frustration tolerance, and to feel inadequate and unsure of their ability to play expected male or female roles. With respect to the last characteristic, for example, Winokur et al. (1970), Pratt (1972), and McClelland et al. (1972) have viewed heavy drinking by some young men as an attempt to prove their masculinity and achieve feelings of adequacy and competency. Similarly, Wilsnack (1973a, 1973b) concluded that the potential female alcoholic places strong value on the traditional female role, while at the same time her sense of adequacy as a female is highly fragile.

"She may manage to cope with her fragile sense of feminine adequacy for a number of years, but when some new threat severely exacerbates her self-doubts she turns to alcohol in an attempt to gain artificial feelings of womanliness. Her excessive drinking may then begin a vicious circle that culminates in the alcoholic's characteristic loss of control over her drinking." (1973 a, p. 96)

   Beckman (1978) found that female alcoholics have lower self-esteem than either male alcoholics or women who have no history of alcohol abuse. Antisocial personality and depression are two clinical syndromes that have also been commonly associated with later excessive drinking (Jones, 1968, 1971; Seixas & Cadoret, 1974; Weissman et al., 1977; Woodruff et al., 1973).

   While such findings provide promising leads, it is difficult to assess the role of specific personality characteristics in the development of alcoholism. Certainly there are many persons with similar personality characteristics who do not become alcoholics, and others with dissimilar ones who do. The only characteristic that appears common to the backgrounds of most problem drinkers is personal maladjustment, yet most maladjusted people do not become alcoholics. But the personality of alcoholics may be a result rather than a cause of their dependence on alcohol—for example, a depressed person may turn to the excessive use of alcohol, or the excessive use of alcohol may lead to depression, or both.

   It is apparent that longitudinal studies are needed to determine whether or not there are personality characteristics that predispose one to the loss of control. One prospective analysis has in fact found evidence of such factors. Loper et al. (1973) compared the performance of male alcoholics on psychological tests taken several years before, while they were in college, with that of a sample of their classmates who did not later develop problems with alcohol. The alcoholics had differed from their nonalcoholic classmates in being more immature, impulsive, and antisocial.

Although the significance of pre-alcoholic personality factors remains unclear, alcoholics do tend to show a distinct cluster of personality traits once their drinking pattern has been established. Included here are low stress tolerance, a negative self-image, and feelings of inadequacy, isolation, and depression. By the time the alcoholic comes to the attention of a clinic or hospital, he or she also tends to manifest a lack of responsibility, impaired impulse control, and a decided tendency toward deceitfulness, characteristics that have apparently resulted from environmental stressors such as marital breakup or unemployment, and the exaggerated use of ego-defense mechanisms—particularly denial, rationalization, and projection. In this context, Wikler (1973) has pointed out that during the later stages of alcoholism, there tends to be a "curious twist in the alcoholic's thinking" (p. 10). For example, instead of blaming herself for drinking excessively and letting the dinner burn, a wife may excuse herself and project the blame onto her husband, who is now perceived as a "nag." And as the alcoholic's life situation continues to deteriorate and stress increases, there is a tendency to rely increasingly on such ego-defense mechanisms.

2. *Stress, tension reduction, and reinforcement.* A number of investigators have pointed out that the typical alcoholic is discontented with his or her life situation and is unable or unwilling to tolerate tension and stress (AMA Committee on Alcoholism and Drug Dependency, 1969). In fact, Schaefer (1971) has concluded that alcoholism is a conditioned response to anxiety. The individual presumably finds in alcohol a means of relieving anxiety, resentment, depression, or other unpleasant feelings. Each drink relieves tension at the moment; thus the behavior is reinforced. Eventually, drinking becomes the habitual pattern for coping with stress.

Some investigators hold that anyone who finds alcohol to be tension-reducing is in danger of becoming an alcoholic, even without an especially stressful life situation. However, if this were true, we would expect alcoholism to be far more common than it is, since alcohol tends to reduce tensions for most persons who use it. In addition, this model does not explain why some excessive drinkers are able to maintain control over their drinking and continue to function in society, while others are not.

At the opposite end of the spectrum are investigators who reject the view that alcoholism is a learned maladaptive response, reinforced and maintained by tension reduction. They point out that the long-range consequences of excessive drinking are too devastating, far outweighing its temporary relief value. However, as Bandura (1969) has pointed out,

"This argument overlooks the fact that behavior is more powerfully controlled by its immediate, rather than delayed, consequences, and it is precisely for this reason that persons may persistently engage in immediately reinforcing, but potentially self-destructive behavior. . . ." (p. 530)

It seems that alcoholics drink to feel better at the moment, even though they know they will feel worse later.

3. *Marital and other intimate relationships.* As we have noted, alcoholism tends to run in families. But while genetic factors may be an influence, it is clear that an alcoholic parent also constitutes a highly undesirable model for the child. Thus children of alcoholics may have special problems in learning who they are, what is expected of them, and what to esteem in others. Further, their range of coping techniques is likely to be more limited than that of the average child.

Of course, in some cases they may learn to perceive the parent as a negative model—as someone *not* to emulate or model their behavior after. Here it would appear that an alcoholic parent creates so many problems for the family that the child comes to see the alcoholic behavior as highly aversive. This learning process is well illustrated in the case of a 26-year-old Miami divorcée.

"After attending a Dade County alcohol rehabilitation center for the past three months, Barbara is sober and plans to remain that way. She fears, however, that her drinking may have permanently hurt her children. 'They remember my wine-drinking days when I'd throw up in their wastebasket. Now if they see me drinking a Coke, my older girl will come over and taste it and then reassure the younger one: "It's O.K." ' " (*Time*, April 22, 1974, p. 81)

Excessive drinking often begins during crisis periods in marital or other intimate personal relationships, particularly crises which lead to hurt and self-devaluation. For example, in a study of 100 middle- and upper-class women who were receiving help at an alcoholism treatment center, Curlee (1969) found that the trauma which appeared to trigger the alcoholism was related to a change or challenge in the subject's role as wife or mother, such as divorce, menopause, or children leaving home (the so-called empty-nest syndrome). Many women appear to begin their immoderate drinking during their late thirties and early forties when such life situation changes are common.

After a review of available literature, Siegler, Osmond, and Newell (1968) described a more extreme pattern of family interaction in alcoholism:

"Alcoholism, like drug addiction and schizophrenia, is best seen as a form of family interaction in which one person is assigned the role of the 'alcoholic' while others play the complementary roles, such as the martyred wife, the neglected children, the disgraced parents, and so forth. As this deadly game is played by mutual consent, any attempt to remove the key actor, the alcoholic, is bound to create difficulties for the other family members, who will attempt to restore their former game. As the game is of far greater interest to the family than to the therapist, the family is almost bound to win. The family may succeed in including the therapist as another role in the game." (p. 579)

Since in this conceptualization alcoholism represents a long drawn-out family game which is circular and self-reinforcing, it appears relatively useless to ask how it all began.[2]

A husband who lives with an alcoholic wife is often unaware of the fact that, gradually and inevitably, many of the decisions he makes every day are based on the expectation that his wife will be drinking. In a case such as this, the husband is becoming "drinking-wife-oriented." These expectations, in turn, may make the drinking behavior more likely. Eventually the entire marriage may center around the drinking of the alcoholic spouse. And in some in-

stances, the husband or wife may also begin to drink excessively, possibly through the reinforcement of such behavior by the drinking mate, or to blank out the disillusionment, frustration, and resentment that are often elicited by an alcoholic spouse. Of course, such relationships are not restricted to marital partners but may also occur in those involved in love affairs or close friendships (Al-Anon, 1971).

Excessive use of alcohol is the third most frequent cause of divorce in the United States (and often a hidden factor in the two most common causes—financial and sexual problems). Persons who abuse alcohol are about 7 times more likely to be divorced or separated than nonabusers (Levitt, 1974). The deterioration in their intimate interpersonal relationships, of course, further augments the stress and disorganization in their life situations.

General sociocultural factors. In a general sense, our culture has become dependent on alcohol as a social lubricant and a means of reducing tension. Thus numerous investigators have pointed to the role of sociocultural as well as physiological and psychological factors in the high rate of alcohol abuse and alcohol dependence among Americans.

Here it is of interest to note the conclusions of Pliner and Cappell (1974) concerning the reinforcing effects of social drinking in our society, in which liquor has come to play an almost ritualistic role in promoting gaiety and pleasant social interaction.

"According to the present results, if it is the case that much of the early drinking experience of . . . individuals takes place in such convivial social settings, drinking will be likely to become associated with positive affective experiences. This reinforcing consequence may in turn make drinking more probable in the future. Thus, to the extent that a social context can enhance the attraction of alcohol, for some individuals it may play a crucial role in the etiology of pathological patterns of alcohol consumption." (p. 425)

Bales (1946) outlined three cultural factors that appear to play a part in determining the incidence of alcoholism in a given society: (a) the degree of stress and inner tension produced by the culture; (b) the attitudes toward drinking fostered by the culture; and (c) the degree

---

[2]An informative discussion of the games alcoholics play may be found in Steiner (1977).

to which the culture provides substitute means of satisfaction and other ways of coping with tension and anxiety. This has been borne out by cross-cultural studies.

The importance of the level of stress in a given culture is shown in studies of preliterate societies. In a pioneering study of 56 preliterate societies, Horton (1943) found that the greater the insecurity level of the culture, the greater the amount of alcohol consumption—due allowance having been made for the availability and acceptability of alcohol. And in a study of 57 tribal societies, Schaefer (1974) reported that people tended to drink to excess in societies in which the spirits of dead ancestors were believed to be unpredictable, malicious, and capricious. On the other hand, people in societies in which the families were dominated by father-son interaction tended to abstain from excessive drinking.

Rapid social change and social disintegration also seem to foster excessive drinking. For example, the U.S. Public Health Service's Alaska Native Medical Center has reported excessive drinking to be a major problem among Eskimos in many places in rural Alaska (*Time*, April 22, 1974). This problem is attributed primarily to rapid change in traditional values and way of life, in some cases approaching social disintegration. It is perhaps also relevant to note that alcoholism is a major problem in the world's two superpowers—the United States and the Soviet Union.

The effect of cultural attitudes toward drinking is well illustrated by Muslims and Mormons, whose religious values prohibit the use of alcohol, and by Orthodox Jews, who have traditionally limited their use largely to religious rituals. The incidence of alcoholism among these groups is minimal. On the other hand, the incidence of alcoholism is proportionately higher among the French and Irish, where cultural approbation is greater—in fact, the French appear to have the highest rate of alcoholism in the world, approximating 10 to 12 percent of the population. Thus it appears that religious sanctions and social custom can determine whether alcohol is one of the modes of coping commonly used in a given group or society.

But while there are many reasons why people drink—as well as many conditions that can predispose them to do so and reinforce drinking behavior—the combination of factors that result in a person's becoming an alcoholic are still unknown.

Treatment and outcomes

A multidisciplinary approach to treatment of drinking problems appears to be most effective because the problems are often complex, thus requiring flexibility and individualization of treatment procedures. Also, the needs of the alcoholic change as treatment progresses.

Formerly it was considered essential that treatment of a problem drinker take place in an institutional setting, which removes the individual from an aversive life situation and makes more control possible over his or her behavior. However, an increasing number of problem drinkers are now being treated in community clinics, especially those who do not require hospitalization for withdrawal treatment. Halfway houses are also being used increasingly to bridge the gap between institutionalization and return to the community and to add to the flexibility of treatment programs.

The objective of a traditional treatment program is recovery of the alcoholic: physical rehabilitation, control over the craving for liquor, abstinence from drinking, and realization on the part of the individual that he or she can cope with the problems of living and lead a much more rewarding life without alcohol.

Biological measures.   Included here are a variety of treatment measures ranging from detoxification procedures to brain surgery.

1. *Medical measures in detoxification.* In acute intoxication, the initial focus is on detoxification, or elimination of alcoholic substances from the individual's body; on treatment of withdrawal symptoms; and on a medical regimen for physical rehabilitation. These can best be handled in a hospital or clinic, where drugs, such as chlordiazepoxide, have largely revolutionized the treatment of withdrawal symptoms. Such drugs function to overcome motor excitement, nausea, and vomiting, prevent delirium tremens and convulsions, and help alleviate the tension and anxiety associated with withdrawal. There is a

These paintings were done by W——, a 40-year-old male with a history of alcoholism, repeated loss of employment, and hospitalization for treatment. His interest in painting, which gradually became the key aspect of his treatment program at an alcoholism treatment center, also led to a new way of life following his discharge. In the first painting (top), W—— depicted alcoholism as a magnet-like vise that drew and crushed his consciousness. He symbolized his feelings in sober periods between drinking sprees as the chained tree, and the nebulous higher power to which he looked for help as a descending dove. The egg and the eye, a motif W—— used in earlier work to depict his unrealistic view of alcohol, are merged into a straining muscular arm reaching back to the more placid past and unattainable dream castles, that is, futile quests with which W—— associated his past abuses of alcohol. In the second painting, the overriding concept is of constructive action. Three portals are depicted, (left) one leading to a world "blown to hell"; another (right) with two entrances, one leading downward to an abyss, the other to barrenness; and finally a third portal (middle) in the shape of a cross, symbolic of hope, that leads upward to a pleasant landscape, representing goal or purpose.

growing concern, however, that the use of tranquilizers at this stage does not promote long-term recovery. Accordingly, some detoxification clinics are exploring alternative approaches, including a gradual weaning from the alcohol instead of a sudden cutoff.

Detoxification is optimally followed by psychosocial measures, including family counseling and the use of community resources relating to employment and other aspects of the individual's social readjustment. Maintenance doses of mild tranquilizers are also used at times to reduce anxiety and help the individual sleep. Such use of tranquilizers may be less effective than no treatment at all, however. Usually patients must learn to abstain from tranquilizers as well as from alcohol, since they tend to misuse the one as well as the other. And under the influence of tranquilizers, they may even return to the use of alcohol.

Disulfiram (Antabuse), a drug that creates extremely uncomfortable effects when followed by alcohol, may be administered to prevent an immediate return to drinking. However, such deterrent therapy is seldom advocated as the sole approach, since pharmacological methods alone have not proven effective in treating alcoholism. For example, an alcoholic may simply discontinue the use of Antabuse when he or she is released from the hospital or clinic and begin to drink again (see HIGHLIGHT on this page). In fact, the primary value of drugs of this type appears to lie in their interruption of the alcoholic cycle for a period of time, during which therapy may be undertaken.

2. *Psychedelic therapy.* The chronic, severe type of alcoholic has been a nemesis for alcohol treatment and rehabilitation programs. The attitudes and beliefs of extreme alcoholics, along with their low motivation and hopelessness, make them generally inaccessible to outside help. Yet, many of these "lost souls" have come back to become contributing members of society after having had an unusual event, such as a religious experience, that has altered their conception of themselves. One treatment approach based on this fact is psychedelic therapy, which attempts to provide alcoholics with a "transcendental" experience that may serve as a basis for new insights. Cohen (1976) pointed out:

"It is the selected, severe, problem alcoholic who has been a prime target for *psychedelic psychotherapy.* He is often alienated from society as a 'lost' person without sustaining faiths or beliefs. It is said that most problem drinkers must 'hit bottom' before they can rehabilitate themselves. This 'hitting bottom' seems to consist of a number of factors. It consists of the long-delayed acknowledgment that one is a drunk, that one's drinking is out of control, that help is needed, and that the situation is catastrophic. An LSD experience may provide some of these insights. The alcoholic's self-esteem tends to be low and his destructive life is obvious. Furthermore, his subsequent behavior can be an easy measure of success or failure." (p. 190)

Although some highly successful results have been obtained (Hoffer & Osmond, 1967), psychedelic therapy has not become widely used because (a) the "insights" often do not translate into behavior change; (b) behavior changes, when they do occur, are often quite transitory and the alcoholic soon resumes drinking; and (c) the potential dangers of inducing other problems, such as a psychotic break, are great.

HIGHLIGHT

A young teacher's continuing battle with alcoholism

Mary _____ is an intelligent, attractive, elementary-school teacher who is married to a writer some 10 years her senior. At age 29 she had been teaching for 7 years, and as a result of her high degree of competence had been given increasingly difficult classes. Mary stated that after a difficult day at school she had many unresolved problems that she needed to discuss with someone but seldom could do so with her husband, who was under sustained pressure himself and away on assignments a good deal of the time.

Thus, with her husband either away or too busy to talk, Mary turned to alcohol:

"I started having two or three cocktails every evening to 'settle my nerves.' And as the pressure seemed to build up about 3 years ago, I found myself drinking heavily every night to blot out the events of the day. I seemed to have this insatiable craving for alcohol, and I could hardly wait to get home after school to get a drink. And on weekends, I was drunk from Friday evening through Sunday. On Monday mornings, my hangovers were something awful, and I started calling in sick. I knew my drinking was interfering with my work, but I couldn't seem to cope with either. Frankly, I became just plain desperate."

The principal of Mary's school became aware of the problem and suggested that she take a sick leave and obtain medical assistance. Examination revealed serious liver damage, and the physician informed Mary that if she continued to drink she would kill herself. He prescribed Antabuse to help her stop drinking. Although she had the prescription filled, Mary did not take the drug right away: "I was so terrified by what the doctor told me that I just had to have a drink to calm me down. Then I was going to try the Antabuse, I really was." That drink led to 3 days of intoxication and finally to convulsions. Mary was hospitalized.

When she improved sufficiently to leave the hospital, Mary volunteered to join a local chapter of Alcoholics Anonymous and to continue seeing a therapist. Her crucial battle with alcoholism was just beginning.

3. *Brain surgery.* In a report from Göttingen University in Germany, Fritz Roeder and his associates (1974) stated that

"Our research has revealed that dependence on drugs or alcohol assumes the proportions of a natural urge after a certain period and, like the sexual drive or the urge to eat, is controlled by a certain brain center. Neutralizing this center, which is no more than 50 cubic millimeters in volume, will cure the patient for all time." (p. 106)

No undesirable side effects were reported by these investigators after 22 operations, but such a drastic procedure as brain surgery in the treatment of alcoholism is a highly controversial matter. At this time it would appear to be a treatment of last resort, justified only in the case of patients in the most advanced stages of alcoholism where all other treatment measures have been proven ineffective.

In general, biological measures alone have not proven adequate in the treatment of alcoholism, although medical measures focusing on detoxification and general health problems are often of crucial importance in the total treatment program.

Psychosocial measures. Although individual psychotherapy is sometimes effective, the focus of psychosocial measures in the treatment of alcoholism more often involves group therapy, environmental intervention, behavior therapy, and the approach of Alcoholics Anonymous.

1. *Group therapy.* In the rugged give-and-take of group therapy, alcoholics are usually forced to face their problem and recognize its possible disastrous consequences, but also to begin to see new possibilities for coping with it. Often, but by no means always, this double recognition paves the way for learning more effective methods of coping and other positive steps toward dealing with their drinking problem.

In some instances the spouses of alcoholics and even their children may be invited to join in group therapy meetings. In other situations, family treatment is itself the central focus of therapeutic effort. In the latter case, the alcoholic individual is seen as a member of a disturbed family in which all the members have a responsibility for cooperating in treatment.

Since family members are frequently the persons most victimized by the alcoholic's addiction, they often tend to be judgmental and punitive, and the alcoholic, who has already passed harsh judgment on himself or herself, tolerates this further source of devaluation very poorly. In other instances, members of a family may unwittingly encourage an alcoholic to remain addicted, as, for example, when a wife with a need to dominate her husband finds that a continually drunken and remorseful spouse best meets her need.

2. *Environmental intervention.* As with other serious maladaptive behaviors, the total treatment program in alcoholism usually requires measures to alleviate the patient's aversive life situation. As a result of their drinking, alcoholics often become estranged from family and friends, and their jobs are lost or jeopardized. Typically the reaction of those around them is not as understanding or supportive as it would have been if they had a physical illness of comparable magnitude. Simply helping them learn more effective coping techniques may not be enough if the social environment remains hostile and threatening. For alcoholics who have been hospitalized, halfway houses—designed to assist them in their return to family and community—are often an important adjunct to the total treatment program.

Relapses and continued deterioration are generally associated with a lack of close relationships with family or friends, or with living in a high-risk environment. In a study of black male alcoholics, for example, King et al. (1969) have pointed to the ghetto cycle of broken homes, delinquency, underemployment, alcoholism, and, once again, broken homes. In general, it would appear unlikely that an alcoholic will remain abstinent after treatment unless the negative psychosocial factors that operated in the past are dealt with.

As a consequence, the concept of a "community reinforcement approach" has been developed. This approach focuses on helping problem drinkers achieve more satisfactory adjustments in key areas of their lives, such as marriage, work, and social relations. Unfortunately, it is not always possible to make these needed changes. But this approach seems to offer a promising conceptual basis for the direction of future treatment programs.

3. *Behavior therapy.* One of the most

rapidly developing treatment modalities for alcohol abuse disorders is behavior therapy, of which several types exist. One is aversive conditioning procedures, involving a wide range of noxious stimuli. The Romans used this technique by placing a live eel in a cup of wine; forced to drink this unsavory cocktail, the alcoholic presumably would feel disgusted and from then on be repelled by wine.

Today there are a variety of pharmacological and other deterrent measures that can be employed after detoxification has been accomplished. One approach utilizes the intramuscular injection of emetine hydrochloride, an emetic. Prior to the nausea that results from the injection, the patient is given alcohol, so that the sight, smell, and taste of the beverage become associated with severe retching and vomiting. With repetition, this classical conditioning procedure acts as a strong deterrent to further drinking—probably in part because it adds an immediate and unpleasant physiological consequence to the more general socially aversive consequences of excessive drinking.

Among other aversive methods has been the use of mild electrical stimulation which presumably enables the therapist to maintain more exact control of the aversive stimulus, reduces possible negative side effects and medical complications, and can even be administered by means of a portable apparatus that can be used by the patient for self-reinforcement. Utilizing a procedure which paired electrical stimulation with stimuli associated with drinking, Claeson and Malm (1973) reported successful results—no relapses after 12 months—in 24 percent of a patient group that consisted mostly of advanced-stage alcoholics.

Another approach, called *covert sensitization,* involves extinguishing the drinking behavior by associating it with noxious mental images rather than chemical or electrical stimuli (Cautela, 1967). Positive results have been reported, with reduction of drinking for a time. However, the long-term effects of covert sensitization generally have not been impressive. To expect such stimuli as images (which are under the control of the individual) to change a deeply ingrained life pattern is perhaps unrealistic. Covert sensitization procedures might be effectively used as an early

step, with other treatment procedures then employed while the person is abstinent. The most important effect of any type of aversion therapy with alcoholics seems to be this temporary extinction of drinking behavior, making it possible for other psychosocial methods to be used effectively (Davidson, 1974).

Other behavioral techniques have also been receiving a great deal of attention, partly because they are based on the hypothesis that some problem drinkers need not give up drinking altogether but can learn to drink moderately (Miller, 1978; Nathan, 1977; Sobell & Sobell, 1978). Sobell and Sobell (1973) have described the range of procedures utilized in what they term "individualized behavior therapy" for alcoholics. This treatment used both individual and group procedures but attempted to tailor the treatment to meet the needs of each particular patient.

"Procedures included subjects being videotaped while intoxicated under experimental conditions, providing subjects when sober with videotape self-confrontation of their own drunken behaviors, shaping of appropriate controlled drinking or non-drinking behaviors respective to treatment goal, the availability of alcoholic beverages throughout treatment, and behavior change training sessions. 'Behavior change training sessions' is a summary phrase to describe sessions which concentrated upon determining setting events for each subject's drinking, training the subject to generate a series of possible alternative responses to those situations, to evaluate each of the delineated alternatives for potential short- and long-term consequences, and then to exercise the response which could be expected to incur the fewest self-destructive long-term consequences. Behavior change training sessions consisted of discussion, role playing, assertiveness training, role reversal or other appropriate behavioral techniques, respective to the topics under consideration during a given session." (p. 601)

Other investigators (Lovibond & Caddy, 1970) have conducted blood alcohol discrimination training sessions, which are aimed at getting the alcoholic to control drinking by becoming aware of intoxicating levels of alcohol in the blood. Miller and Muñoz (1976) and Miller (1978) used behavioral self-control training to teach alcoholics to monitor and reduce their alcohol intake. Patients kept records of their drinking behavior and the therapy sessions focused upon determining blood alcohol concentration based upon their intake. Strategies for increasing future intake control were discussed along with identifying alternatives to alcohol consumption.

Self-control training techniques, in which the goal of therapy is to get the alcoholic to reduce alcohol intake without necessarily abstaining altogether, has a great deal of appeal for drinkers. It is difficult, of course, for individuals who are extremely dependent upon the effects of alcohol to abstain totally from drinking. Thus, many alcoholics fail to complete traditional treatment programs. The idea that they might be able to learn to control their alcohol intake while at the same time enjoying the continued use of alcohol might serve as a motivating element.

Several approaches to learning controlled drinking have been attempted (Lloyd & Salzberg, 1975), and some recent work has suggested that some alcoholics can learn to control their alcohol intake (Miller, 1978; Miller & Caddy, 1977). Whether the alcoholic who has learned to recognize intoxicating levels of alcohol and to limit intake to lower levels will maintain these skills over long periods of time has not been sufficiently demonstrated.

Most workers in the field still assume that total abstinence should be the goal for all problem drinkers. Some groups, such as Alcoholics Anonymous, are rather adamant in their opposition to programs aimed at controlled drinking for alcohol-dependent individuals. This controversy is not likely to be resolved in the near future since the controlled drinking research has not produced unequivocal results, nor has it been persuasive enough to win a large number of followers.

4. *Alcoholics Anonymous.* A practical approach to the problem of alcoholism which has met with considerable success is that of Alcoholics Anonymous (AA). This organization was started in 1935 by two individuals, Dr. Bob and Bill W. in Akron, Ohio. Bill W. recovered from alcoholism through a "fundamental spiritual change," and immediately sought out Dr. Bob, who, with Bill's assistance, achieved recovery. Both in turn began to help other alcoholics. Since that time AA has grown to over 10,000 groups with over a million members. In addition, AA groups have been established in many other countries of the world.

Alcoholics Anonymous operates primarily as a nonprofessional counseling program in which both person-to-person and group relationships are emphasized. AA accepts both teenagers and adults with drinking problems, has no dues or fees, does not keep records or case histories, does not participate in political causes, and is not affiliated with any religious sect, although spiritual development is a key aspect of its treatment approach. To ensure the anonymity of the alcoholic, only first names are used. Meetings are devoted partly to social activities, but consist mainly of discussions of the participants' problems with alcohol, often with testimonials from those who have recovered from alcoholism. Here, recovered members usually contrast their lives before they broke their alcohol dependence with the lives they now live without alcohol.[3]

An important strength of AA is that it lifts the burden of personal responsibility by helping alcoholics realize that alcoholism, like many other problems, is bigger than they are. Henceforth, they can see themselves not as weak-willed or lacking in moral strength, but rather simply as having an affliction—they cannot drink—just as other people may not be able to tolerate certain types of medication. By mutual help and reassurance through participation in a group composed of others who have shared similar experiences, many an alcoholic acquires insight into his or her problems, a new sense of purpose, greater ego strength, and more effective coping techniques. And, of course, continued participation in the group helps prevent the crisis of a relapse.

An affiliated movement, Al-Anon Family Groups, has been established for the relatives of alcoholics. By meeting together and sharing their common problems and experiences, the wives or husbands of alcoholics are helped to better understand the nature of alcoholism, the effects of the spouses' drinking upon them personally, and the best techniques for helping their alcoholic mates, as well as themselves. They learn to understand, for example, the necessity of their alcoholic spouses' attendance at AA meetings several nights a week on a sustained basis if relapses are to be prevented.

---

[3]The term *alcoholic* is used by AA and its affiliates to refer either to individuals who currently are drinking excessively or to persons who have recovered from such a problem but must continue to abstain from alcohol consumption in the future.

They are also helped to see their mates in a less "drinking-wife-" or "drinking-husband-oriented" perspective, and they are provided with suggestions for reasonable courses of action. Finally, they are relieved from guilt feelings over being the causes of their spouses' drinking, for they come to realize that many factors may contribute but that the initial choice of using alcohol as a coping mechanism lies with the individual.

An outgrowth of the Al-Anon movement has been the Ala-teen movement, designed to help teenagers understand the drinking problems of their parents and find support in a group setting.

Results of treatment. Statistics on the long-range outcome of treatment for alcoholism vary considerably, depending both on the population studied and the treatment facilities and procedures employed. They range from a very low rate of success for hardcore alcoholics to recoveries of 70 to 90 percent where modern treatment and aftercare procedures are utilized. The outcome is most likely to be favorable when the drinking problem is discovered early, when the individual realizes that he or she needs help, and when adequate treatment facilities are available. Fontana and Dowds (1975) have reported a "honeymoon effect" following treatment of severe alcohol abuse, however. They found a frequent pattern to be a decrease in alcohol consumption following treatment but a return to initial drinking levels at a six-month follow-up.

Over the past few years, great progress has been made in the treatment of alcoholism by the introduction of employee programs in both government and industry. Such programs have proven highly effective in detecting drinking problems early, in referring drinkers for treatment, and in ensuring the effectiveness of aftercare procedures. When it is realized that an estimated 5 percent of the nation's work force are alcoholics and an additional 5 percent are considered alcohol abusers, it is apparent that such programs can make a major impact in coping with the alcohol problem in our society (Alander & Campbell, 1975).

Unfortunately, many alcoholics refuse to admit they have an alcohol problem or seek assistance before they "hit bottom"—which in many cases is the grave. Nor is there a miracle "cure" for those who do seek treatment. Nevertheless, it would appear that for the great majority of alcoholics there is a treatment program that can be tailored to their needs and provide a good chance for recovery.

Drug abuse and drug dependence

Aside from alcohol, the psychoactive drugs most commonly associated with abuse and dependence in our society appear to be (a) narcotics, such as opium and its derivatives; (b) sedatives, such as barbiturates; (c) stimulants, such as cocaine and amphetamines; (d) anti-anxiety drugs, such as meprobamates; and (e) hallucinogens, such as LSD and PCP (see HIGHLIGHT on page 336). Caffeine and nicotine are also drugs of dependence, and disorders associated with tobacco withdrawal and caffeine intoxication are included for the first time in the present APA classification, but we shall not deal with them in our present discussion.

Drug abuse and dependence may occur at any age but seem to be most common during adolescence and young adulthood. Clinical pictures vary markedly, depending on the type, amount, and duration of drug usage, the physiological and psychological makeup of the individual, and, in some instances, the social setting in which the drug experience occurs. Thus it appears most useful to deal separately with some of the drugs more commonly associated with abuse and dependence in contemporary society.[4]

---

[4]It may be noted that the most common action of all drugs—even those which are medically prescribed—is their alteration of cell metabolism. Typically, this change in cellular action is a temporary one designed to help combat the patient's problem. Nevertheless, the changes that drugs bring about in "target cells" are in a direction *away from normal functioning*. Thus, medication does not result in cells performing "better than ever." Of course, some drugs—such as hormones—do replace or supplement substances which are normally present in the body, and in this sense, they may improve the normal functioning of various organs and cells; but in general, drugs tend to block some important functions of cells. Hence, the general rule of thumb is the fewer drugs the better.

Opium and
its derivatives (narcotics)

People have used opium and its derivatives for over 5000 years. Galen (A.D. 130–201) considered theriaca, whose principal ingredient was opium, to be a veritable panacea:

"It resists poison and venomous bites, cures inveterate headache, vertigo, deafness, epilepsy, apoplexy, dimness of sight, loss of voice, asthma, coughs of all kinds, spitting of blood, tightness of breath, colic, the iliac poisons, jaundice, hardness of the spleen, stone, urinary complaints, fevers, dropsies, leprosies, the trouble to which women are subject, melancholy and all pestilences."

Even today, opium derivatives are still used for some of the conditions Galen mentioned.

Opium is a mixture of about eighteen nitrogen-containing agents known as *alkaloids*. In 1805 it was found that the alkaloid present in the largest amount (10 to 15 percent) was a bitter-tasting powder that proved to be a powerful sedative and pain reliever; it was thus named *morphine* (after Morpheus, god of sleep in Greek mythology). After introduction of the hypodermic needle in America about 1856, morphine was widely administered to soldiers during the Civil War, not only to those wounded in battle but also to those suffering from dysentery. As a consequence, large numbers of Civil War veterans returned to civilian life addicted to the drug, a condition euphemistically referred to as "Soldier's Illness."

Scientists concerned with the addictive properties of morphine hypothesized that one part of the morphine molecule might be responsible for its analgesic properties[5] and another for its addictiveness. Thus, at about the turn of the century it was discovered that if morphine were treated by an inexpensive and readily available chemical called *acetic anhydride*, it could be converted into another powerful analgesic called *heroin*. Heroin was hailed with enthusiasm by its discoverer, Heinrich Dreser (Boehm, 1968). Leading scientists of his time agreed with Dreser on the merits of heroin, and the drug came to be widely prescribed in place of morphine for pain relief and related medicinal purposes. However, heroin

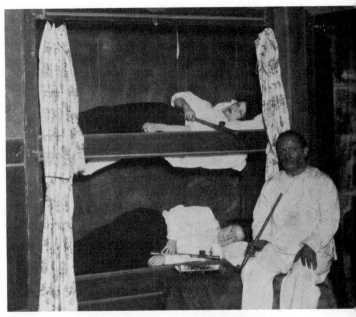

Holding long opium pipes, two women and a man escape into altered states of consciousness in an opium den that flourished in New York City at the turn of the century.

turned out to be a cruel disappointment, for it proved to be an even more dangerous drug than morphine, acting more rapidly and more intensely and being equally if not more addictive. Eventually heroin was removed from use in medical practice.

As it became apparent that opium and its derivatives—including codeine, which is used in some cough syrups—were perilously addictive, the United States Congress enacted the Harrison Act in 1914. Under this and later acts, the unauthorized sale and dispensation of certain drugs became a federal offense; physicians and pharmacists were held accountable for each dose they dispensed. Thus, overnight, the role of a narcotic user changed from that of addict—which was considered a vice, but tolerated—to that of criminal. And now, unable to obtain drugs through legal sources, many turned to illegal ones, and eventually to other criminal acts as a means of maintaining their suddenly expensive drug supply. The number of addicts declined, however, and remained at about 40,000 for several decades.

During the 1960s there was a rapid increase in the use of heroin—the peak year being 1969

---

[5]An analgesic is a drug that alleviates pain without inducing unconsciousness.

HIGHLIGHT

Psychoactive drugs commonly involved in drug abuse

Classification	Drugs	Usage	Medical Usage	Tolerance	Physiological Dependence	Psychological Dependence
Sedatives	Alcohol (ethanol)	Reduce tension Facilitate social interaction "Blot out"	No	Yes (reverse tolerance later)	Yes	Yes
	Barbiturates Nembutal (pentobarbital) Seconal (secobarbital) Veronal (barbital) Tuinal (secobarbital and amobarbital)	Reduce tension Induce relaxation and sleep	Yes	Yes	Yes	Yes
Stimulants	Amphetamines Benzedrine (amphetamine) Dexedrine (dextroamphetamine) Methedrine (methamphetamine)	Increase feelings of alertness and confidence Decrease feelings of fatigue Stay awake for long periods	Yes	Yes	No	Yes
	Cocaine (coca)	Decrease feelings of fatigue Increase endurance Stimulate sex drive	No	No (minimal)	No	Yes
Narcotics	Opium and its derivatives Opium Morphine Codeine Heroin	Alleviate physical pain Induce relaxation and pleasant reverie Alleviate anxiety and tension	Yes, except heroin	Yes	Yes	Yes
	Methadone (synthetic narcotic)	Treatment of heroin dependence	Yes	Yes	Yes	Yes

Classification	Drugs	Usage	Medical Usage	Tolerance	Physiological Dependence	Psychological Dependence

Psychedelics and hallucinogens	Cannabis
	  Marijuana
	  Hashish
	Mescaline (peyote)
	Psilocybin (psychoto-
	  genic mush-
	  rooms)
	LSD (lysergic acid
	  diethylamide-25)
		Induce changes
		  in mood,
		  thought, and
		  behavior
		"Mind
		  expansion"
			No, ex-
			cept in
			research
				No—
				possible
				reverse
				tolerance
				(mari-
				juana)
					No	Yes

	PCP (phencyclidine)	Induce stupor	No	No	No	Yes

Antianxiety drugs (minor tranquilizers)	Librium
	  (chlordiazepoxide)
	Miltown (meprobam-
	  ate)
	Valium (diazepam)
	Others, e.g.,
	  Compōz (scopol-
	  amine)
		Alleviate ten-
		  sion and
		  anxiety
		Induce relaxa-
		  tion and
		  sleep
			Yes	Yes	Yes	Yes

In reviewing this list, it is important to note that it is by no means complete; for example, it does not include new drugs, such as Ritalin, which are designed to produce multiple effects; it does not include the less commonly used volatile hydrocarbons, such as glue, paint thinner, gasoline, cleaning fluid, and nail-polish remover, which are highly dangerous when sniffed for their psychoactive effects; and it does not include the antipsychotic and antidepressant drugs, which are abused, but relatively rarely. We shall deal with these as well as the antianxiety drugs in our discussion of therapy with drugs in Chapter 18. It also should be emphasized that abuse can occur with both prescriptive and nonprescriptive drugs, and with both legal and illegal drugs.

when there were an estimated 150,000 or more addicts in New York City alone, and some 300,000 in the country as a whole—and public attention was focused on the "heroin epidemic" (Bazell, 1973; Greene & Dupont, 1974). Largely as a result of strict control by federal and local authorities, programs of public education, and more effective methods of detection and treatment, heroin addiction markedly decreased during the 1970s.

Effects of morphine and heroin. Morphine and heroin are commonly introduced into the body by smoking, "snorting" (inhaling the bitter powder), eating, "skin popping," and "mainlining," the last two being methods of introducing the drug via hypodermic injection. *Skin popping* refers to injecting the liquefied drug just beneath the skin, and *mainlining* to injecting the drug into the bloodstream. In the United States, the young addict usually progresses from snorting to mainlining.

Among the immediate effects of heroin is a euphoric spasm of 60 seconds or so, which many addicts compare to a sexual orgasm. This is followed by a "high," during which the addict typically is in a lethargic, withdrawn state in which bodily needs, including those for food and sex, are markedly diminished; pleasant feelings of relaxation, euphoria, and reverie tend to dominate. These effects last from 4 to 6 hours and are followed—in addicts—by a negative phase which produces a desire for more of the drug.

The use of opium derivatives over a period of time usually results in a physiological craving for the drug. The time required to establish the drug habit varies, but it has been estimated that continual usage over a period of 30 days or longer is sufficient. Users will then find that they have become physiologically dependent upon the drug, in the sense that they will feel physically ill when they do not take it. In addition, users of opium derivatives gradually build up a tolerance to the drug so that ever larger amount are needed for the desired effects (see HIGHLIGHT on this page).

When persons addicted to opiates do not get a dose of the drug within approximately 8 hours, they start to experience *withdrawal symptoms*. The character and severity of the reaction depends on many factors, including the amount of the narcotic habitually used, the

HIGHLIGHT

Tolerance in drug usage

Tolerance to a drug develops in an individual when the same dosage produces decreased effects after repeated use. Drugs that produce tolerance include alcohol, heroin, and barbiturates. As an individual's tolerance to a drug increases, he or she tends to increase the dose taken. The degree of tolerance and the rate at which it is acquired depend on the specific drug, the person using it, and the frequency and magnitude of its use.

The mechanisms by which physiological tolerance is acquired are not fully understood. There is some evidence that the central nervous system develops some degree of tolerance for various drugs; but, in addition, learning may play an important role in changing an individual's attitude toward a drug and response to it after repeated use. Thus with some drugs, such as marijuana, the individual may learn to control some effects and maintain relatively normal functioning.

Two aspects of drug tolerance that merit brief mention are "cross-tolerance" and "reverse tolerance." "Cross-tolerance" may occur when the individual who develops tolerance to one drug also shows tolerance to drugs whose effects are similar. A heavy drinker, for example, may show tolerance not only to alcohol but also to barbiturates, tranquilizers, and anesthetics. "Reverse tolerance" may occur in the use of some drugs, such as the hallucinogens; here, with experience, the desired effects may be achieved through the use of smaller doses. Both physiological and psychological (learning) factors appear to play a significant part in this process.

Based on Commission of Inquiry into the Non-Medical Use of Drugs (1970).

intervals between doses, the duration of the addiction, and especially the addict's health and personality.

Contrary to popular opinion, withdrawal from heroin is not always dangerous or even very painful. Many addicted persons are able to withdraw without assistance. However, in some instances withdrawal is both an agonizing and a perilous experience.

Initial symptoms usually include a running nose, tearing eyes, perspiration, restlessness, increased respiration rate, and an intensified desire for the drug. As time passes, the symptoms become more severe, usually reaching a peak in about 40 hours. Typically there is chilliness alternating with vasomotor disturbances of flushing and excessive sweating, vomiting, diarrhea, abdominal cramps, pains in the back and extremities, severe headache, marked tremors, and insomnia in varying degrees. Beset by these discomforts, the individual refuses food and water, and this, coupled with the vomiting, sweating, and diarrhea, results in dehydration and weight losses of as much as 5 to 15 pounds in a day. Occasionally there may be delirium, hallucinations, and manic activity. Cardiovascular collapse may also occur, and may result in death. If morphine is administered at any point along the way, the subjective distress of the addict ends, and physiological equanimity is restored in about 5 to 30 minutes.

Usually the withdrawal symptoms will be on the decline by the third or fourth day, and by the seventh or eighth day will have disappeared. As the symptoms subside, the individual resumes normal eating and drinking, and rapidly regains lost weight. An additional hazard now exists in that after withdrawal symptoms have ceased, the individual's former tolerance for the drug also will have disappeared, and death may now result from taking the former large dosage of the drug.

In rare cases individuals have enough self-control to use opiates without allowing them to interfere with their work and ruin their lives, but the danger in the use of such drugs—especially heroin—is very great. Tolerance may be built up so rapidly that larger and more expensive amounts of the drug are soon required, and withdrawal treatments are likely to do little to end the problem. Most addicted individuals—even after withdrawal—find it extremely difficult to break their dependency. Biochemical alterations appear to be at least partly responsible for the individual's continued craving for the narcotic drug even after completion of the withdrawal treatment.

Typically, the life of a narcotic addict becomes increasingly centered around obtaining and using drugs, so the addiction usually leads to socially maladaptive behavior as the individual is eventually forced to lie, steal, and associate with undesirable companions in order to maintain a supply of the drug. Contrary to the common picture of a "dope fiend," how-

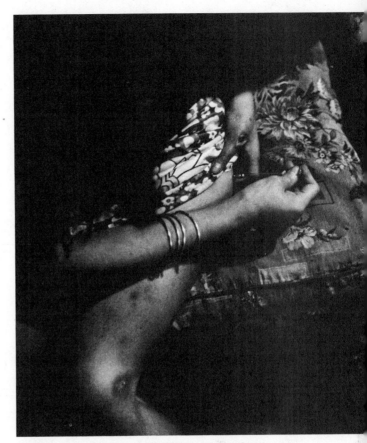

Unable to find any more functioning surface veins into which she can inject heroin, a 26-year-old addict shoots the drug directly into skin tissue. The abscesses on her hand and leg were caused by impure drugs and dirty needles. This young woman later died of an overdose.

ever, most narcotic addicts are not major criminals. Those who have police records usually confine themselves to petty offenses, and very few commit crimes of violence. Female addicts, for example, commonly turn to prostitution as a means of financing their addiction.

Along with the lowering of ethical and moral restraints, addiction has adverse physical effects on the well-being of the individual. Lack of an adequate diet may lead to ill health and increased susceptibility to a variety of physical ailments. The use of unsterile equipment may also lead to a variety of ailments, including liver damage from hepatitis. In addition, the use of such a potent drug as heroin without medical supervision and government controls to assure its strength and purity can result in fatal overdosage. Injection of too much heroin can cause coma and death. Between May 1976 and April 1977 there were more than 1200 deaths associated with heroin usage in the United States, 92 of which were teenagers who died from overdoses or heroin-related infections (Project DAWN, 1977).

Usually, however, addiction to opiates leads to a more gradual deterioration of well-being. The ill health and general personality deterioration often found in opium addiction do not result directly from the pharmacological effects of the drug, but are generally the product of the sacrifice of money, proper diet, social position, and self-respect, as the addict becomes more desperate in an effort to procure the required daily dosage. On the other hand, narcotic addicts with financial means to maintain both a balanced diet and an adequate supply of the drug without resorting to criminal behavior may maintain their drug dependence over many years without any appreciable symptoms of either physical or mental disorder.

The following case history gives a brief view of a teenage addict arrested by the Los Angeles police.

"The boy was seventeen years of age. He had a pleasant way of talking, punctuating his remarks with an occasional smile. His excellent grammar and quiet manners indicated a good home and background. . . .

"Is this a 'dope fiend'? This is an inaccurate . . . term, but by all common standards and definitions the answer would be yes. Gene R_____, the boy in custody, is a confirmed heroin addict, a 'mainliner' injecting heroin directly into the main blood vessels of his arm. His body requires five 'pops' every day, costing him from $20 to $25 every twenty-four hours. He has managed to earn this amount by 'introducing' other teen-agers into the mysteries of . . . heroin. The police report five separate cases where Gene R_____ has inflicted the dope habit upon 'girl friends,' all minors. Investigation indicates that four of these girls now pay for his, and their own, drug supply by means of prostitution." (Los Angeles Police Department, 1952, pp. 3–4)

This case, although reported in the early fifties, is of particular interest, since it would still appear typical of the narcotic scene among middle-class teenagers who become addicted to heroin today—except that the daily cost of maintaining the habit has greatly increased.

Causal factors in addiction to narcotics.
There is no single causal pattern that fits all addiction to narcotic drugs. In addition to the physiological and psychological dependence that itself becomes a driving factor, life stress, personal maladjustment, and sociocultural conditions enter into the total causal picture. Although the following categorization of causal factors is somewhat artificial, it does provide a convenient means of ordering our discussion.

1. *Neural bases for physiological addiction.* Research teams have isolated and studied receptor sites for narcotic drugs in the brain (Goldstein, et al., 1974; Pert & Snyder, 1973). Such receptor sites are specific nerve cells into which given psychoactive drugs fit like keys into the proper lock. This interaction of drug and brain cell apparently results in the action of the drug, and in the case of narcotic drugs leads to addiction. Preliminary findings indicate that there are two or more receptor sites mediating the effects of these drugs; apparently one site mediates the pleasurable euphoria, while another mediates the painkilling action.

Recently it has been learned that the human body produces its own opium-like substances, called *endorphins,* in the brain and pituitary gland. These substances are produced in response to stimulation and are believed to play a role in the organism's reaction to pain (Akil, Watson, Sullivan, & Barchas, 1978). Some investigators suspect that the endorphins may play a role in drug addiction, speculating that chronic underproduction of the endorphins may lead to a craving for narcotic drugs. Hollt et al. (1975) experimented on animals to determine whether drugs like heroin or methadone produce actual changes in the receptor sites; they found only transient changes and no modification of the underlying receptor mechanisms.

Research on humans has not been extensive at this point. However, some indication that the endorphins may be a factor in addiction was suggested in a study by Su et al. (1978). These researchers attempted to block methadone withdrawal by administering endorphins and found that endorphins were moderately effective in reducing withdrawal symptoms.

Research on the role of endorphins in drug addiction has generally been inconclusive and disappointing. According to Watson and Akil (1979), before the anatomical and physiological bases of addiction and drug tolerance can be understood, many complex problems of measurement must be resolved.

2. *Addiction associated with the relief of pain.* Many patients are given narcotic drugs, such as morphine, to relieve pain during illness or following surgery or serious injury. The vast majority of such patients never develop an addiction, and when their medication is discontinued, they do not again resort to the use of morphine. Those narcotic addicts who blame their addiction on the fact that they used drugs during an illness usually show personality deficiencies which predisposed them to the use of drugs—such as immaturity, low frustration tolerance, and the ability to distort and evade reality by way of a flight into drug-induced fantasy.

3. *Addiction associated with psychopathology.* During the 1960s, studies placed strong emphasis on the high incidence of psychopathic personalities among heroin addicts. In a comparison between a group of 45 young institutionalized male addicts and a control group of nonaddicts, Gilbert and Lombardi (1967) found that distinguishing features were "the addict's psychopathic traits, his depression, tension, insecurity, and feelings of inadequacy, and his difficulty in forming warm and lasting interpersonal relationships" (p. 536). Similarly, in a study of 112 drug abusers admitted to Bellevue Psychiatric Hospital in New York, Hekimian and Gershon (1968) found that heroin users usually showed psychopathic personality characteristics.

Although very little research has been done on female narcotics users, Chinlund (1969) reported a psychopathic personality pattern as being characteristic of female addicts studied over a period of seven years in New York City. He concluded that a female addict has three key goals: (a) a conscious wish to lose control of her drug usage so that she can blame her failures on the drug; (b) a desire to obliterate all sense of time—to blot out what is happening in her frustrating life situation; and (c) a need to deny cause-and-effect relationships in her life—for example, the relationship between her sexual activity and pregnancy.

While the thrill-seeking and uninhibited behavior characteristic of psychopathic personalities appears to render them particularly vulnerable to drug dependence, including heroin addiction, the picture of the typical addict

seems to have changed during the 1970s. In an extensive study, Berzins et al. (1974) assessed the personality makeup of 1500 hospitalized opiate addicts, 750 males and 750 females. They found that the majority of addicts—60 percent—showed a variety of emotional disturbances and related characteristics that did not fit any consistent personality profile. The remaining 40 percent of the subjects, however, could be classified into two groups:

"Type I subjects were characterized by high levels of subjective distress, nonconformity, and confused thinking; they attributed a wide range of psychopathology to themselves and also deprecated themselves *as addicts.* In contrast . . . Type II subjects appeared self-satisfied both as persons and as addicts." (p. 72)

In fact, it was concluded that had Type II subjects not been hospitalized for opiate addiction, they might have been regarded as above average in personal-social competence.

On the basis of their findings, Berzins and his associates speculated that "Type I subjects may employ drugs to control or attenuate feelings of anxiety, depression, distress, and so on, while Type II subjects may use them to enhance hedonistic pursuits or, possibly, to reduce feelings of hostility and resentment" (p. 72). Type I subjects constituted 33 percent of the total addict population and were considered more amenable to treatment than Type II subjects, who constituted only 7 percent of the total addict population. Although Type II subjects were not labeled as psychopathic, they did evidence many characteristics of this personality disorder.

In general, it would appear that narcotic dependence tends to develop in association with psychopathic personality and other psychopathology (Sutker & Archer, 1979). As in the case of alcoholism, however, it seems essential to exercise caution in distinguishing between personality traits before and after addiction, for the high incidence of psychopathology among narcotic addicts may in part result from the long-term effects of addiction rather than precede it.

4. *Addiction associated with sociocultural factors.* The influence of sociocultural factors in drug dependence, including alcohol and opium addiction, is well depicted in the experience of the Meo, a tribal people who inhabit the mountains of several countries in Southeast Asia (Westermeyer, 1971). Although alcohol is used, it is employed with rigid restraints, and alcoholism does not occur. On the other hand, opium is a major cash crop and is widely used among the Meo, and opium addiction does occur. Westermeyer (1974) also reported the widespread use of opium in Laos. He noted that "Most Western observers have depicted the Oriental opium den as an unsavory place that leads only to ruin" (p. 237), but found that in Laos the opium den tended to play about the same role as the neighborhood tavern in Western countries.

In our own society there are so-called narcotic subcultures, in which addicts can obtain drugs and protect themselves against the sanctions of society. Apparently the majority of narcotic addicts do participate in the drug culture. The decision to join this culture has important implications for the future life of addicts, for from that point on they will center their activities around their role of drug user. In short, their addiction becomes their way of life.

With time, most young addicts who join the drug culture become increasingly withdrawn, indifferent to their friends (except those in the drug group), and apathetic about sexual activity. They are likely to abandon scholastic and athletic endeavors, and to show a marked reduction in competitive and achievement strivings. Most of these addicts appear to lack good sex-role identification, and to experience feelings of inadequacy when confronted with the demands of adulthood. While feeling progressively isolated from the broader culture, they experience a bolstering of their feelings of group belongingness by continued association with the addict milieu; at the same time, they come to view drugs both as a means of revolt against constituted authority and conventional values and as a device for alleviating personal anxieties and tensions.

Treatment and outcomes.   Treatment for heroin addiction is initially similar to that for alcoholism, in that it involves building up the addict both physically and psychologically and providing help through the withdrawal period. Addicts often dread the discomfort of withdrawal, but in a hospital setting it is not abrupt and usually involves the administration of a synthetic drug that eases the distress.

After withdrawal has been completed,

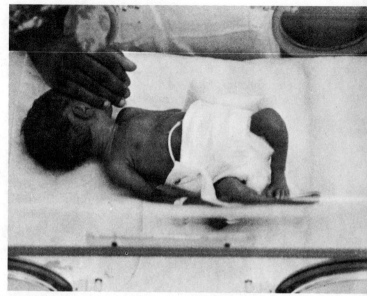

Infants such as this one, whose mothers are dependent on opium, morphine, heroin, or methadone, may be born addicted and may show serious withdrawal symptoms from birth to about 4 days. If the problem is not detected and treated, the infant may die of a convulsion or of dehydration. There have been no follow-up studies to determine how prenatal exposure to narcotics may influence later development and behavior.

treatment focuses on helping the former addict make an adequate adjustment to his or her community and abstain from the further use of narcotics. Traditionally, however, the prognosis has been unfavorable. Despite the use of counseling, group therapy, and other measures, only about 13 percent of persons discharged from government rehabilitation programs in England did not become readdicted (Stephens & Cottrell, 1972). These and comparable findings from studies in the United States led to the hypothesis that withdrawal does not remove the craving for heroin and that a key target in treatment must be the alleviation of this craving.

An approach to dealing with the problem of physiological craving for heroin was pioneered by a research team at the Rockefeller University in New York. Their approach involved the use of methadone in conjunction with a rehabilitation program (counseling, group therapy, and other procedures) directed toward the "total resocialization" of the addict (Dole &

Nyswander, 1967; Dole, Nyswander, & Warner, 1968). Methadone hydrochloride is a synthetic narcotic which is related to heroin and is equally addictive physiologically. Its usefulness in treatment lies in the fact that it satisfies the addict's craving for heroin without producing serious psychological impairment. For example, of 863 volunteer addicts—all of whom were between the ages of 20 and 50, had injected heroin for at least four years, and had failed in other treatment programs—750 stopped using heroin. Although they were now methadone addicts, they were nonetheless productive and responsible members of their communities. The results of a four-year trial showed that nine out of ten former heroin addicts had abstained from the further use of heroin—a figure that contrasts sharply with the poor record of success achieved by most earlier treatment programs.

In evaluating the preceding study, it may be pointed out that the average age of addicts in the program was older than that of the addict population in general, and participants were perhaps more strongly motivated to undertake treatment than are most younger heroin addicts. In a second study of criminal addicts, Dole and Robinson (1969) randomly selected 12 who were prison inmates to receive the methadone treatment, as well as a control group of 16 convict-addicts. All had been addicts for at least five years, had had five or more jail sentences, and had volunteered for treatment. The results were impressive: none of the 12 addicts who were treated with methadone became readdicted to heroin, and 9 had no criminal convictions during a 50-week follow-up period. Of the 16 controls, by contrast, all but one became readdicted after release from jail, and 15 were also convicted of crimes committed during the same follow-up period. These investigators concluded that at least 50 percent of all criminal addicts could be rehabilitated permanently by the methadone program of treatment. Similarly, in a five-year study of a methadone maintenance program involving over 2000 narcotic addicts, Gearing (1970) reported that previous antisocial behavior, as measured by arrests and related criteria, was eliminated or markedly reduced, and that there was a corresponding increase in employment and social adjustment.

As a result of such impressive preliminary

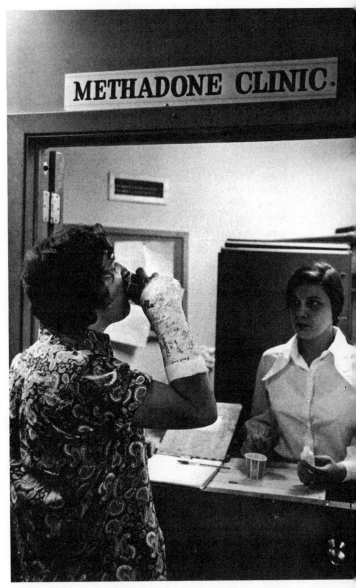

At the Methadone Clinic of Long Beach Memorial Hospital in New York, a patient drinks his methadone medication under the supervision of a nurse. Each patient enrolled at the clinic has an individual methadone bottle with his or her name on it. After patients have had their dosage, the bottles are refilled by the nurse and stored in a safe until the next visit. Methadone medication is only part of a complete drug therapy program available at the clinic.

findings, the federal government in 1972 agreed to a licensing program for physicians and clinics utilizing methadone in the treatment of narcotic addicts. But as methadone treatment became more widely employed, it became apparent that methadone alone is not sufficient to rehabilitate narcotic addicts. Although some former addicts do make good adjustments with little ancillary treatment, most require vocational training and other supportive measures if the overall treatment program is to prove effective. It would also appear essential that methadone treatment be monitored very carefully, since there are a limited but rising number of reports of liver damage and other undesirable side effects following the long-term use of methadone (Thornton & Thornton, 1974). In addition, it is important to prevent the illicit use of methadone, since there are serious dangers—including overdosage—when it is not used in a well-organized heroin treatment program (Greene, Brown, & Dupont, 1975).

There is also the ethical problem of weaning the addict from heroin only to addict him or her to another narcotic drug that may be required for life. A response might be that addicts on methadone can function normally and hold jobs—not possible for most heroin addicts. In addition, methadone is available legally, and its quality is controlled by government standards. Nor is it necessary to increase the dosage over time. In fact some patients can eventually be taken off methadone without danger of relapse to heroin addiction. Many heroin addicts can also be treated without undergoing initial hospitalization, and during treatment are able to hold jobs and function in their family and community settings (Newman & Cates, 1977).

The barbiturates (sedatives)

In the 1850s, new chemical compounds known as *bromides* were introduced. They immediately became popular as sedatives and were taken by millions of people. But with use came abuse; and the excessive consumption of bromides resulted in toxic psychoses—involving delusions, hallucinations, and a variety of neurological disturbances—which for a time

became a leading cause of admissions to mental hospitals (Jarvik, 1967).

In the 1930s powerful sedatives called *barbiturates* were introduced. While the barbiturates have their legitimate medical uses, they are extremely dangerous drugs commonly associated with both physiological and psychological dependence as well as with lethal overdoses. Yet the result of an 18-month survey by a subcommittee of the United States Senate, released in 1972, indicated that as many as a million Americans, most of them between 30 and 50 years old, were addicted to barbiturate drugs (Bayh, 1972). And it would appear that the number of addicted persons has not appreciably decreased since that time. Literally billions of barbiturate pills, including pills with fixed combinations of barbiturates and amphetamines, are manufactured each year in the United States. Between May 1976 and April 1977, 18 percent of drug-related deaths involved barbiturate usage (Project DAWN, 1977).

Effects of barbiturates. The barbiturates are widely used by physicians to calm patients and/or induce sleep. They act as depressants—somewhat like alcohol—to slow down the action of the central nervous system. Shortly after taking the drug, the individual experiences a feeling of relaxation in which tensions seem to disappear, followed by a physical and intellectual lassitude and a tendency toward drowsiness and sleep—the intensity of such feelings depending on the type and amount of the barbiturate taken. Strong doses produce sleep almost immediately; excessive doses are lethal because they result in paralysis of the respiratory centers of the brain.

Excessive use of barbiturates leads to increased tolerance as well as to physiological and psychological dependence. The barbiturates most often involved in such abuse are the short-acting ones such as Seconal ("red devils") and tuinal ("rainbows"): long-acting barbiturates, such as phenobarbital, are not so subject to abuse because of their failure to produce quick results.

In addition, excessive use of barbiturates leads to a variety of undesirable side effects, including sluggishness, slow speech, impaired comprehension and memory, lability of affect, motor incoordination, and depression. Problem solving and decision making require great effort, and the individual usually is aware that his or her thinking is "fuzzy." Prolonged excessive use of this class of drugs leads to brain damage and personality deterioration. And, whereas with opiates tolerance increases the amount needed to cause death, this is not true for the barbiturates, which means that users can easily ingest a fatal overdose, either intentionally or accidentally. Indeed, barbiturates are associated with more suicides than any other drug.

Causal factors in barbiturate abuse and dependence.

Though many young people experiment with barbiturates, or "downers," most do not become dependent. In fact, the individuals who do become dependent on barbiturates tend to be middle-aged and older persons who often rely on them as "sleeping pills" and who do not commonly rely on other classes of drugs except, possibly, alcohol and the minor tranquilizers (see HIGHLIGHT on this page). Often these persons are referred to as "silent abusers" since they take the drugs in the privacy of their homes and ordinarily do not become public nuisances. As with alcoholism, barbiturate dependence seems to occur in the emotionally maladjusted person who seeks relief from feelings of anxiety, tension, inadequacy, and the stresses of life.

An exception to the above picture has occurred in recent years with the introduction of "new, improved" diet pills. Previous diet pills had usually been amphetamines alone, but the new pills are fixed-ratio combinations of amphetamines and barbiturates—the latter being added to reduce the "jitteriness" often caused by the amphetamines. Unfortunately, both of these drugs are highly addictive, either separately or in combination, and since the addition of barbiturates may make the amphetamines more tolerable, "addiction prone" persons may rapidly increase their pill intake, thus increasing the possibility of addiction to both drugs (Kunnes, 1973).

In addition to being used with amphetamines, barbiturates are also commonly used with alcohol. Some teenagers claim they can achieve a "far out" effect—a kind of controlled hypersensitivity—by combining bar-

The use and abuse of minor tranquilizers

Antianxiety drugs, such as Librium, Miltown, and Valium, are widely used in our society for reducing anxiety and tension, particularly in relation to specific life stressors, However, these minor tranquilizers are potentially dangerous because of possible side effects, because of ill-advised practices associated with their use, and because physiological and psychological dependence may result from their continued use.*

Drowsiness and motor impairment are common side effects of the minor tranquilizers. Thus it is illegal in many states to drive while under the influence of tranquilizers; such drugs can also be dangerous to people in occupations that require continual alertness and a high level of motor coordination. In fact, it would appear that far more accidents, both on and off the job, are associated with the misuse of legal drugs than with the use of illegal ones. There is also evidence that meprobamates like Miltown have been involved in an increasing number of suicide attempts. And, of course, mixing mild tranquilizers with other psychoactive drugs may have potentiating or other undesirable effects; e.g., a medically prescribed barbiturate for sleeping may be much more potent than intended when taken with alcohol and a tranquilizer.

The practice of mixing prescription drugs appears to be relatively common, and many people take two or more types of minor tranquilizers each day. Another practice common among many husbands and wives, is to use each other's tranquilizers, thus negating intended medical supervision.

Even when used as prescribed, it should be recognized that the continual use of minor tranquilizers in heavy dosage can build up tolerance and dependence; abrupt cessation of usage may then lead to serious withdrawal symptoms.

*Here we are dealing with prescription drugs, but over-the-counter (OTC) preparations, such as Compōz, Cope, and Nervine are also subject to these dangers.

biturates, amphetamines, and alcohol. However, one possible "far out" effect of combining barbiturates and alcohol is death, since each drug *potentiates* (increases the action of) the other (see HIGHLIGHT on page 347).

Treatment and outcomes.

As with many other drugs, it is often essential in treatment to distinguish between barbiturate intoxication, which results from the toxic effects of overdosage, and the symptoms associated with withdrawal of the drug from addicted users. We are concerned primarily with the latter. Here the symptoms are more dangerous, severe, and long-lasting than in opiate withdrawal. The patient becomes anxious and apprehensive and manifests coarse tremors of the hands and face; additional symptoms commonly include insomnia, weakness, nausea, vomiting, abdominal cramps, rapid heart rate, elevated blood pressure, and loss of weight. Between the sixteenth hour and the fifth day convulsions may occur. An acute delirious psychosis often develops, which may include symptoms similar to those in delirium tremens.

For individuals used to taking large dosages, the withdrawal symptoms may last for as long as a month, but usually they tend to abate by the end of the first week. Fortunately, the withdrawal symptoms in barbiturate addiction can be minimized by the administration of increasingly smaller doses of the barbiturate itself, or by another drug producing pharmacologically similar effects. The withdrawal program is still a dangerous one, however, especially if barbiturate addiction is complicated by alcoholism or dependence on other drugs.

Although the elimination of psychological dependence on barbiturates may also require psychotherapy or other treatment, readdiction is not so severe a problem as in the case of opiate addiction, where the individual is believed to have an overpowering craving for the drug even after the physical dependence has been broken.

The amphetamines and cocaine (stimulants)

In contrast to the barbiturates, which depress or slow down the action of the central nervous system, the amphetamines and cocaine have chemical effects that stimulate or speed it up.

The amphetamines.

The earliest amphetamine to be introduced—Benzedrine, or amphetamine sulfate—was first synthesized in 1927 and became available in drugstores in the early 1930s as an inhalant to relieve stuffy noses. However, the manufacturers soon learned that some customers were chewing the wicks in the inhalers for "kicks." Thus, the stimulating effects of amphetamine sulfate were discovered by the public before the drug was formally prescribed as a stimulant by physicians. In the late 1930s two newer amphetamines were introduced—Dexedrine (dextroamphetamine) and Methedrine (methamphetamine hydrochloride). The latter preparation is a far more potent stimulant of the central nervous system than either Benzedrine or Dexedrine, and hence is considered more dangerous. In fact, its abuse is lethal in an appreciable number of cases.

Initially these preparations were considered to be "wonder pills" that helped people stay alert and awake and function temporarily at a level beyond normal. During World War II military interest was aroused in the stimulating effects of these drugs, and they were used by both allied and German soldiers to ward off fatigue (Jarvik, 1967). Similarly, among civilians, amphetamines came to be widely used by night workers, long-distance truck drivers, students cramming for exams, and athletes striving to improve their performances. It was also discovered that the amphetamines tend to suppress appetite, and they became popular among persons trying to lose weight. In addition, they were often used to counteract the effects of barbiturates or other sleeping pills that had been taken the night before. As a result of their many uses, the amphetamines were widely prescribed by doctors.

Since the passage of the Controlled Substance Act of 1970 (DEA, 1979), the amphetamines have been classified as "schedule II" substances—that is, drugs with high abuse potential that require a prescription for each purchase. As a result, medical use of the amphetamines has declined in recent years, and they are more difficult to obtain legally. Nevertheless, it is apparently easy to find illegal "street" sources of the amphetamines, which thus remain among the most widely abused drugs.

Today the amphetamines, or "pep pills," are used medically for curbing the appetite when weight reduction is desirable; treating individuals suffering from narcolepsy—a disorder in which people cannot prevent themselves from continually falling asleep during the day; and treating hyperactive children. Curiously enough, the amphetamines have a calming rather than a stimulating effect on many of these youngsters. Amphetamines are still also sometimes prescribed for alleviating mild feelings of depression and relieving fatigue and maintaining alertness for sustained periods of time.

1. *Causes and effects of amphetamine abuse.* Despite their legitimate medical uses, amphetamines are not a magical source of extra mental or physical energy, but rather serve to push users toward a greater expenditure of their own resources—often to a point of hazardous fatigue. In fact, athletes have damaged their careers by using "speed" to try to improve their stamina and performance (Furlong, 1971). It has also been suggested that amphetamines are much too freely prescribed for weight reduction, in view of their short-term effectiveness and possible dangers.

As with other drugs, the effects of amphetamines vary with the type, the dosage, the length of time they are taken, and the physical and psychological state of the individual user. Although amphetamines are not considered to be physiologically addictive, the body does build up tolerance to them very rapidly. Thus, habituated users may consume pills by the mouthful several times a day whereas such amounts would be lethal to nonusers. In some instances, users inject the drug to get faster and more intense results. To get "high" on amphetamines, persons may give themselves from 6 to 200 times the daily medical dosage usually prescribed for dieters. If lesser amphetamines do not provide a sufficient reaction, they may use Methedrine, or "speed," to produce the desired high. In some instances, amphetamine abusers go on "sprees" lasting several days.

For the person who exceeds prescribed dosages, consumption of amphetamines results in heightened blood pressure, enlarged pupils, unclear or rapid speech, profuse sweating,

One girl who gambled with barbiturates and lost

Judi A. was a young attractive girl from a middle-class family who apparently was seeking something that eluded her. She died of an overdose of barbiturates. The newspaper account of her death began with a statement from the autopsy report:

"The unembalmed body for examination is that of a well-developed, well-nourished Caucasian female measuring 173 cm. (68 inches), weighing 100–110 pounds, with dark blonde hair, blue eyes, and consistent in appearance with the stated age of. . . .

"Judi A. had lived only 17 years, 5 months and 27 days before her nude body was found on a grimy bed which had been made up on the floor of a run-down apartment in Newport Beach [California].

"The inside of her mouth and her tongue were a bright red. The fingers of both hands were stained with the same color . . . A small pill was found on the bed near the body, another was discovered on the floor.

"Judi's death was classified as an accident because there was no evidence that she intended to take her own life. Actually it was about as accidental as if she'd killed herself while playing Russian roulette.

"Judi didn't intentionally take too many reds. She was familiar with them, had taken them before, knew what to expect. She'd even had an earlier scare from a nonfatal overdose.

"But her mind, clouded by the first few pills, lost count and she ingested a lethal number. She was dying before she swallowed the last pill. . . ." (Hazlett, 1971, p. 1)

A complete investigation was ordered, in which it came to light that Judi took drugs when she was unhappy at home, apparently often feeling unloved and unwanted. Following the breakup of her parents' marriage, she lived with her grandparents—who seemed to have been unaware of her drug problem and hence had not attempted to help her with it.

Judi escalated the odds against herself by combining barbiturates with alcohol. Her friends said she was not particularly different from the other girls they knew, most of whom also took pills in combination with beer or wine. In Judi's case, however, the combination was lethal. She never found the something that eluded her, but she did find death.

tremors, excitability, loss of appetite, confusion, and sleeplessness. In some instances, the jolt to body physiology from "shooting" Methedrine can raise blood pressure enough to cause immediate death. In addition, the chronic abuse of amphetamines can result in brain damage as well as a wide range of psychopathology, including a disorder known as *amphetamine psychosis,* which investigators consider to be very similar to paranoid schizophrenia.

Suicide, homicide, assault, and various other acts of violence are associated with amphetamine abuse. In the United States, Ellinwood (1971) studied 13 persons who committed homicide under amphetamine intoxication and found that, in most cases, "the events leading to the homicidal act were directly related to amphetamine-induced paranoid thinking, panic, emotional lability, or lowered impulse control" (p. 90). And a study of 100 hospital admissions for amphetamine intoxication revealed that 25 of the subjects had attempted suicide while under the influence of the drug (Nelson, 1969).

2. *Treatment and outcomes.* Withdrawal from the amphetamines is usually painless physically, since physiological addiction is absent or minimal. In some instances, however, withdrawal on a "cold turkey" basis from the chronic excessive use of amphetamines can result in cramping, nausea, diarrhea, and even convulsions (AMA, 1968a; Kunnes, 1973).

But psychological dependence is another matter, and abrupt abstinence commonly results in feelings of weariness and depression. The depression usually reaches its peak in 48 to 72 hours, often remains intense for a day or two, and then tends to lessen gradually over a period of several days. However, mild feelings of depression and lassitude may persist for weeks or even months after the last dose. Where brain damage has occurred, residual effects may also include impaired ability to concentrate, learn, and remember, with resulting social, economic, and personality deterioration.

Cocaine. Like opium, cocaine is a plant product discovered and used in ancient times. It was widely used in the pre-Columbian world of Mexico and Peru (Guerra, 1971). And it has been endorsed by such diverse figures as Sig-

HIGHLIGHT

The cocaine episode in the life of Sigmund Freud

In a lecture to a psychiatric society in 1885, Freud described the effects of ingesting from 50 to 100 mg. of cocaine hydrochloride: he felt a profound sense of elation, greater physical endurance, and increased mental agility. Post reported Freud as having stated:

" 'I take very small doses of it regularly against depression . . . with the most brilliant success. [The effects were] exhilarating and lasting euphoria, which in no way differs from the normal euphoria of a healthy person. . . . You perceive an increase in self-control and possess more vitality and capacity for work. . . .' " (pp. 225–26)

Freud reported that he had no craving for the further use of the drug, even after repeated dosage, nor did he experience unpleasant after effects such as those that follow "exhilaration brought about by alcohol."

mund Freud (see HIGHLIGHT on this page) and the legendary Sherlock Holmes. Its use appears to have increased in the United States.

Like opium, cocaine may be ingested by sniffing, swallowing, or injecting. And like the opiates, it precipitates a euphoric state of four to six hours' duration, during which the user experiences feelings of peace and contentment. However, this blissful state may be preceded by headache, dizziness, and restlessness. When cocaine is chronically abused, acute toxic psychotic symptoms may occur which are similar to those in acute schizophrenia and encompass frightening visual, auditory, and tactual hallucinations, such as the "cocaine bug" (Post, 1975). In rare cases it is fatal (Wetli & Wright, 1979).

Because of its anesthetic qualities, cocaine is sometimes used as a substitute for morphine. Unlike the opiates, however, cocaine is a cortical stimulant, inducing sleeplessness and excitement, as well as stimulating and accentuating sexual processes. Consequently, individuals with deviant sexual patterns have been known to administer it as an impetus to seduction. Dependence on cocaine also differs from that on opiates, in that tolerance is not increased appreciably with its use, nor is there any physiological dependence.

However, psychological dependence on cocaine, like addiction to opiates, often leads to a centering of behavior around its procurement, concurrent with a loss of social approval and self-respect. The following case illustrates this pattern:

The subject was a strikingly pretty, intelligent woman of 19 who had divorced her husband two years previously. She had married at the age of 16 and stated that she was terribly in love with her husband but that he turned out to be cruel and brutal.

The woman was too ashamed of her marital failure (her parents had violently opposed the marriage and she had left home against their will) to return to her home. She moved away from her husband and got a job as a cocktail waitress in the same bar where her husband had been accustomed to taking her. She was severely depressed, and several of his friends insisted on buying her drinks to cheer her up. This process continued for almost a year, during which she drank excessively but managed to hold her job.

Following this, she met a man in the bar where she worked who introduced her to cocaine, assuring her that it would cheer her up and get rid of her blues. She states that it both "hopped me up and gave me a feeling of peace and contentment." For a period of several months she purchased her supplies of cocaine from this same man until she became ill with appendicitis and was unable to pay the stiff price he asked. Following an appendectomy, she was induced to share his apartment as a means of defraying her expenses and ensuring the supply of cocaine which she had now become heavily dependent on psychologically. She stated that she felt she could not work without it. During this period she had sexual relations with the man although she considered it immoral and had severe guilt feelings about it.

This pattern continued for several months until her "roommate" upped his prices on the cocaine, on the excuse that it was getting more difficult to obtain, and suggested that she might be able to earn enough money to pay for it if she were not so prudish about whom she slept with. At this time the full significance of where her behavior was leading seems to have dawned on her and she came voluntarily to a community clinic for assistance.

Treatment for psychological dependence on cocaine does not differ appreciably from that for other drugs which involve no physiological dependence. Aversion therapy, group techniques, and related procedures may all be utilized. However, as in the case with other such drugs, feelings of tension and depression may have to be dealt with during the immediate withdrawal period.

LSD and related drugs (hallucinogens)

The hallucinogens are drugs whose properties are thought to induce hallucinations. In fact, however, these preparations do not so often "create" sensory images as distort them, so that the individual sees or hears things in different and unusual ways.

The major drugs in this category are LSD (lysergic acid diethylamide), mescaline, and psilocybin. PCP, or "angel dust," has recently become popular as well (see HIGHLIGHT on page 350). Our present discussion will be restricted largely to LSD because of its unusual hallucinogenic properties and its potentialities for research into brain functioning.

LSD. The most potent of the hallucinogens, the odorless, colorless, and tasteless drug LSD can produce intoxication with an amount smaller than a grain of salt. It is a chemically synthesized substance first discovered by the Swiss chemist Hoffman in 1938.

1. *Effects of LSD.* Hoffman was not aware of the potent hallucinatory qualities of LSD until some five years after his discovery, when he swallowed a small amount. This is his report of the experience:

"Last Friday, April 16, 1943, I was forced to stop my work in the laboratory in the middle of the afternoon and to go home, as I was seized by a peculiar restlessness associated with a sensation of mild dizziness. On arriving home, I lay down and sank into a kind of drunkenness which was not unpleasant and which was characterized by extreme activity of imagination. As I lay in a dazed condition with my eyes closed (I experienced daylight as disagreeably bright) there surged upon me an uninterrupted stream of fantastic images of extraordinary plasticity and vividness and accompanied by an intense kaleidoscope-like play of colours. This condition gradually passed off after about two hours." (Hoffman, 1971, p. 23)

Hoffman followed up this experience with a series of planned self-observations with LSD, some of which he described as "harrowing." Researchers thought LSD might be useful for the induction and study of hallucinogenic states or "model psychoses," which were thought to be related to schizophrenia. About 1950, LSD was introduced into the United

States for purposes of such research as well as to ascertain whether it might have medical or therapeutic uses. Despite considerable research, however, LSD has not proven therapeutically useful.

After taking LSD, a person typically goes through about eight hours of changes in sensory perception, lability of emotional experiences, and feelings of depersonalization and detachment. The peak of both physiological and psychological effects usually occurs between the second and fourth hours. Physiological effects include increased heart rate, elevation in blood pressure, augmented muscle tone, and faster and more variable breathing.

As LSD takes effect, the most important psychic manifestation is a tremendous intensification of sensory perception. Objects seem to become clearer, sharper, brighter, and endowed with dimensions not perceived before. One young woman lost herself in contemplation of a flower, seeing in it colors she had never seen before, hearing the movements of its petals, and feeling that at last she understood its essential nature. Another phenomenon associated with the drug has been called "humanity identification"—a sensation in which one feels oneself to be in emphatic concert with all humankind in the experiencing of such universal emotions as love, loneliness, or grief.

In addition to the intensity of the basic perceptual and affective reactions that occur in the early stages of the LSD experience, Katz, Waskow, and Olsson (1968) have pointed to certain contradictory aspects of that experience. These include the following:

"1. Very strong but opposing emotions occurring approximately at the same time, emotions which may not have a cognitive counterpart;
2. A feeling of being out of control of one's emotions and thoughts;
3. A feeling of detachment from the real world;
4. A feeling of perceptual sharpness, but at the same time perceptions of the outer world as having an unreal quality;
5. The perception of the world and others as 'friendly' but 'suspicious.' " (p. 13)

The LSD "trip" is not always pleasant. It can be extremely harrowing and traumatic, and the distorted objects and sounds, the illusory colors, and the new thoughts can be menacing

A violent drug with an angelic name—"angel dust"

Phencyclidine or PCP, known on the streets as "angel dust," was developed as a tranquilizer in the 1950s. Because of its unpredictable and at times violent effects, it was not made commercially available for human consumption.

More recently, illegally manufactured PCP has been showing up on the streets—with disastrous results. In July–August 1975 in New York, 32 percent of drug-related emergencies involved PCP, an increase from 13 percent from 1973 (*Behavior Today,* 1977).

If taken in moderate doses, the drug produces a stuporous condition or coma, which lasts for hours or days. Prolonged comas or psychoses that resemble paranoid schizophrenia are common. Several violent murders have been committed by PCP users, and there have been extreme cases of self-mutilation such as attempts to tear out one's eyes.

PCP was implicated in an April 1979 gun battle at a San Antonio, Texas, parade in which 2 spectators were killed and at least 50 more injured. The gunman, Ira Attebery, took his own life; at the autopsy, traces of PCP were found in his blood.

According to relatives and acquaintances, Attebery suffered from delusions that the police were always watching and following him and that people stole things from him (*Chicago Sun Times,* April 29, 1979, p. 11). His relatives attributed Attebery's paranoid delusions to trauma over a 1971 accident in which his truck collided with an automobile, killing two people. But the medical examiner in San Antonio stated that PCP, rather than the earlier accident, explains the incident, claiming: "While there may have been some previous mental trauma, the influence of PCP is more spectacular, and I would ascribe his behavior to the drug" (*Chicago Sun Times,* May 6, 1979, p. 42).

and terrifying. For example, Rorvik (1970) has cited the case of a young British law student who tried to "continue time" by using a dental drill to bore a hole in his head while under the influence of LSD. In other instances, persons undergoing "bad trips" have set themselves aflame, jumped from high places, and taken other drugs which proved a lethal combination. Of 114 subjects admitted to the Bellevue Hospital in New York City with acute psychoses induced by LSD, 13 percent showed over-whelming fear and another 12 percent experienced uncontrollably violent urges; suicide or homicide had been attempted by approximately 9 percent (Rorvik, 1970). In a study of chronic users of LSD, Blacker and his associates (1968) found that the "bum trip" usually began in a context of ire. For example, one of their subjects reported that he had taken LSD when he was angry with his mother. Initially his trip had been beautiful; then it exploded. He suddenly became very fearful, thought he could hear monsters coming up the stairs, and was convinced that they would come through the door to his room and eat him.

The setting in which LSD is taken appears to be influential in determining its effect, but a favorable milieu alone is no guarantee against adverse reactions. Even a single dose can trigger serious psychological complications. For example, in a study of 52 persons admitted to a New York hospital with LSD-induced psychoses, it was found that 26 had taken the drug only one time, and only 12 of the subjects had shown evidence of serious maladjustment prior to their LSD psychosis (AMA, 1968b). On the other hand, the same individual may be affected differently by the drug at different times. In fact, the preceding investigators cited cases of persons who had used LSD 100 or more times without apparent difficulty and then suddenly had developed severe, adverse reactions.

An interesting and unusual phenomenon that may occur following the use of LSD is the *flashback:* an involuntary recurrence of perceptual distortions or hallucinations weeks or even months after taking the drug. These experiences appear to be relatively rare among individuals who have taken LSD only once—although they do sometimes occur. On the other hand, it has been conservatively estimated that about 1 in 20 consistent users experiences such flashbacks (Horowitz, 1969). Some persons react with fear to these recurrent images, which "seem to have a will of their own"; extreme anxiety and even psychotic reactions may result. It has been estimated that about 3 percent of persons who use LSD under illegal conditions experience such psychotic reactions.

Some studies have indicated that LSD may cause chromosomal damage and a lowering of

Fear shows in the eyes of this young woman, who is undergoing a terrifying drug "trip."

immunological defenses to disease, but others have challenged these reports. In any event, users of LSD do not develop physiological dependence, nor do they build up tolerance requiring increasingly large doses of the drug. However, some chronic users have developed psychological dependence, in the sense that they focus their life around this type of drug experience.

While even the research use of LSD is definitely contraindicated for persons who are maladjusted or under severe emotional stress, the dangers appear to be low for persons who take it under careful supervision in research settings. After a review of available evidence, McWilliams and Tuttle (1973) concluded: "The danger of long-lasting psychological damage is low when the drug is used by emotionally stable individuals in secure, controlled settings . . . indicating the drug's relative safety for continued research" (p. 341).

2. *Use of LSD for self-improvement.* Despite the possibility of adverse reactions, the remarkable effects of LSD were widely publicized during the 1960s, and a number of relatively well-known people experimented with the drug and gave glowing accounts of their "trips." In fact, during this period an "LSD Movement" was under way, based on the conviction that the drug could "expand the mind" and enable one to use talents and realize potentials previously undetected. As a result, a considerable number of people attempted to use LSD as a vehicle for achieving greater personal insight, increased sensitivity, mystic experiences, and better understanding of their place in the universe. This category included a sizable number of painters, writers, and composers, who attempted to use the drug not only for personal growth but also as a means of creating more original and meaningful works of art.

There is no evidence that LSD enhances creative activity, however: no recognized works of art have apparently been produced under the influence of the drug or as a consequence of a psychedelic experience. And although several artists have claimed improved creativity stemming from their LSD experiences, objective observers recognize few, if any, refinements (AMA, 1968b). In fact, under the direct influence of LSD, the drawings of one well-known American painter showed

progressive deterioration; later, when asked if he felt his LSD experience had improved his creativity, he replied in the negative (Rinkel, 1966).

3. *Treatment and outcomes.* For acute psychoses induced by LSD intoxication, treatment requires hospitalization and is primarily a medical matter. Often the outcome in such cases depends heavily on the personal stability of the individual prior to taking the drug; in some cases prolonged hospitalization may be required.

Fortunately, brief psychotherapy is usually effective in treating psychological dependence on LSD as well as in preventing the recurrence of flashbacks which may still haunt the individual as a result of a "bad trip." As in the case of trauma experienced in combat or civilian disasters, therapy is aimed at helping the individual work through the painful experience and integrate it into his or her self-structure.

Mescaline and psilocybin. Two other well-known hallucinogens are mescaline and psilocybin. Mescaline is derived from the small, disclike growths ("mescal buttons") at the top of the peyote cactus; psilocybin is a drug obtained from a variety of "sacred" Mexican mushrooms known as *psilocybe mexicana.*

These drugs have been used for centuries in the ceremonial rites of Indian peoples living in Mexico, the American Southwest, and Central and South America. In fact, they were used by the Aztecs for such purposes long before the Spanish invasion. Both drugs have mind-altering and hallucinogenic properties, but their principal effect appears to be enabling the individual to see, hear, and otherwise experience events in unaccustomed ways—transporting him into a realm of "nonordinary reality."

As with LSD, there is no definite evidence that mescaline and psilocybin actually "expand consciousness" or create new ideas; rather, they seem primarily to alter or distort experience.

Marijuana

Although marijuana may be classified as a mild hallucinogen, there are significant differences in the nature, intensity, and duration of its effects as compared with those induced by LSD, mescaline, and other major hallucinogens.

Marijuana comes from the leaves and flowering tops of the hemp plant, *cannabis sativa*. The plant grows in mild climates throughout the world including parts of India, Africa, Mexico, and the United States. In its prepared state, marijuana consists chiefly of the dried green leaves—hence the colloquial name "grass." It is ordinarily smoked in the form of cigarettes ("reefers" or "joints") or in pipes, but it can also be baked into cookies and other foods. In some cultures the leaves are steeped in hot water and the liquid is drunk, much as one might drink tea. Marijuana is related to the stronger drug, hashish, which is derived from the resin exuded by the cannabis plant and made into a gummy powder. Hashish, like marijuana, may be smoked, chewed, or drunk.

Both marijuana and hashish can be traced far back into the history of drug usage. Cannabis was apparently known in ancient China (Blum, 1969; Culliton, 1970), and was listed in the herbal compendiums of the Chinese emperor Shen Nung, written about 2737 B.C.

Until the late 1960s marijuana use in the United States was confined largely to members of lower socioeconomic minority groups and to people in entertainment and related fields. In the late 1960s, however, there was a dramatic increase in its use among youth in our society, and during the early 1970s it was estimated that over half the teenagers and young adults had experimented with marijuana in social situations, with about 10 percent presumably going from occasional to habitual use. In 1978 an estimated 43 million people in the United States had used marijuana and over 16 million were current users (NIDA, 1978).

Effects of marijuana.   The specific effects of marijuana vary greatly, depending on the quality and dosage of the drug, the personality and mood of the user, the user's past experience with the drug, the social setting, and the user's expectations. However, there is considerable consensus among regular users that when marijuana is smoked and inhaled, the individual gets "high." This state is one of mild euphoria distinguished by increased feelings of well-being, heightened perceptual acuity, and

pleasant relaxation, often accompanied by a sensation of drifting or floating away. Sensory inputs are enhanced: music sounds fuller, colors look brighter, smells seem richer, and food tastes better. Somehow the world seems to become more meaningful, and even minor events may take on extraordinary profundity. Often there is a stretching out or distortion of the individual's sense of time, so that an event lasting but a few seconds may seem to cover a much longer span. Short-term memory may also be affected, as when one notices a bite taken out of a sandwich but does not remember having taken it. For most users, pleasurable experiences, including sexual intercourse, seem to be greatly enhanced. When smoked, marijuana is rapidly absorbed and its effects appear within seconds to minutes, but seldom last more than 2 to 3 hours. The effects of THC (a synthetically produced drug that appears to be the active ingredient in cannabis) are slower in making their appearance, requiring 30 minutes to over 2 hours following oral ingestion.

Marijuana may lead to unpleasant as well as pleasant experiences. For example, if an individual takes the drug while in an unhappy, angry, suspicious, or frightened mood, unsavory events may be magnified. And with high dosages, as well as with certain unstable or susceptible individuals, marijuana can produce extreme euphoria, hilarity, and overtalkativeness; it can also produce intense anxiety and depression as well as delusions, hallucinations, and other psychotic like behavior.

It is of interest to note, however, that in a study reported by Nelson (1969), only 3 hospital admissions for marijuana abuse or intoxication were reported out of 90,733 consecutive admissions, while thousands of admissions and hundreds of deaths were associated with the abuse of alcohol, barbiturates, and amphetamines. The U.S. Drug Enforcement Agency's report on drug-related deaths between May 1976 and April 1977 found that only one death out of 3,809 was induced by marijuana (Project DAWN, 1977).

The short-range physiological effects of marijuana include a moderate increase in heart rate, a slowing of reaction time, a slight contraction of pupil size, bloodshot and itchy eyes, a dry mouth, and an increased appetite. Continued use of high dosages over time tends to produce lethargy and passivity. Here marijuana appears to have a depressant as well as a hallucinogenic effect. However, the effects of long-term and habitual use of the drug are still under investigation, although a number of possible adverse side effects have been related to the prolonged heavy use of marijuana or less frequent use of the more potent hashish (Maugh, 1974).

Marijuana has often been compared to heroin, but the two drugs have little in common with respect either to tolerance or to physiological dependence. Although studies conducted in Eastern countries have found evidence of tolerance to marijuana at high dosage levels over long periods of time, studies in the U.S.—which have involved lower dosages for shorter time periods—have failed to find evidence of tolerance (HEW, 1971). In fact, habitual users often show "reverse tolerance." This may be due in part to the users' having learned the proper method of smoking and to the suggestive influence of anticipated effects. In any event, habitual users rarely feel it necessary to increase their doses to maintain desired effects. In addition, many habitual users of marijuana claim the ability to "turn off" its effects or "come down" from a marijuana "high" if conditions in the situation require it, and a limited amount of research evidence tends to support their claim (Cappell & Pliner, 1973). Nor does marijuana lead to physiological dependence, as heroin does, so discontinuance of the drug is not accompanied by withdrawal symptoms. Marijuana can, however, lead to psychological dependence, in which the individual experiences a strong need for it whenever he or she feels anxious and tense.

Some key questions concerning marijuana. Aside from alcohol, no drug has triggered so much debate and confusion in our society as marijuana. Many persons, including members of the drug subculture, see no dangers in its use and even consider it a boon to humanity; other persons see serious dangers in its use and feel that the possession or use of marijuana should be subject to severe legal sanctions.

What are the facts about marijuana? Unfortunately, despite an increasing amount of research, we still do not have adequate answers to a number of pertinent questions.

1. *What are the reasons for using marijuana?* In the late 1960s and 1970s, the reasons for using marijuana appeared to run the gamut: (a) curiosity, thrill-seeking, and easy euphoria; (b) peer pressure for doing the "in thing" with a given group; (c) desire for self-improvement through gaining new insights and help in realizing one's potential; and (d) urge to diminish stressful conflicts, insecurities, and anxieties. The last reason was often associated with the discouragement of slum life as well as with the disillusionment of many youth during the 1960s, including teenage runaways, who "dropped out" of the mainstream of society and joined drug subcultures.

Feeney (1976) has proposed a hypothesis to explain what takes place in the recreational use of marijuana that involves neurological, behavioral, and subjective processes. He suggests that marijuana may induce variability in the information-processing mechanisms of the higher brain centers which, in turn, could produce variability in the individual's experience and responses, even to familiar events. Thus the drug-induced neurological variability could retard habituation of classical reinforcers and lead to "novel experience from commonplace events." He refers to this experience as the "marijuana window" and suggests that it may also help individuals overcome fear of the unfamiliar.

2. *Is there a specific personality pattern associated with marijuana use?* A number of psychological studies have been directed toward this question but results are far from conclusive. Several studies (Graham & Cross, 1975; Hogan, Mankin, Conway, & Fox, 1970) have found important personality differences between chronic users and nonusers. Users showed more spontaneity, adventuresomeness, and novelty seeking, while nonusers appeared well socialized, conforming, and respectful of authority; they strove for traditional values and rarely acted on impulse. However, most of the published research has examined personality differences only after the marijuana use has begun.

One recent study reported observations of three groups of college students: (a) nonusers of marijuana, (b) continuous users of marijuana, and (c) students who switched to marijuana during the period of the study. Kay et al.

(1978) had tested a large group of college students on several occasions with the California Psychological Inventory (CPI), the Adjective Check List (ACL), and a drug questionnaire. Replicating Hogan et al. (1970), they found personality differences between users and nonusers; they also found that marijuana users of the 1970s were similar to those of the 1960s in personality correlates.

The nonusers who later switched to marijuana use provide an interesting comparison. Most of them had switched to marijuana use within their first year at college. In terms of their measured personality characteristics they appeared to fall between the users and nonusers, showing some characteristics of both other groups. Their original CPI scores also suggested more flexibility than the nonuser group. Over time, they came to resemble the user group in their self-descriptions on the Adjective Check List. The authors concluded that individuals with certain personality characteristics such as flexibility are more likely to use marijuana than conforming, conservative individuals.

3. *Does the use of marijuana have harmful effects?* In the fourth of a series of reports on the use of marijuana, the National Institute of Drug Abuse (NIDA, 1976) summarized findings from research projects that had been funded by this agency. The essential thrust of the report was that marijuana poses serious threats to highway safety in ways similar to alcohol intoxication.

With regard to the harmfulness of marijuana to the physical health of habitual or heavy users, the findings were inconclusive—though suggestive. For example, there was some evidence of (a) adverse effects on cardiac functioning, (b) irritation of the lungs resulting from deep inhalation, (c) weakening of the body's immune mechanisms, (d) a decrease of male sex hormones, and (e) brain damage. Until more definitive research findings become available, it seems probable that the controversy concerning the possible hazards of marijuana use is likely to continue.

Marijuana has been found to be beneficial in some medical treatment, particularly in relieving the pain of glaucoma and the painful side effects of chemotherapy for cancer. Specifically, marijuana suppresses the vomiting reaction produced by chemotherapy. In New Mexico, a court has ruled in favor of permitting a patient to use marijuana to relieve pain, but has provided no legal means by which the patient could obtain the drug.

4. *Does the use of marijuana enhance creativity?* Most investigators have given a definite "no" to this question (Braden et al., 1974; Yolles, 1969). Although marijuana may induce fantasies that seem creative, at least to the person experiencing them, what actually is produced in terms of writing, painting, or other creative pursuits is usually evaluated as no better—and often worse—than usual. As with the use of LSD and other hallucinogens, individuals may think they have found "the key to the universe"; when they "come down," however, it is not there.

Conceivably, enhanced feelings, perceptions, and thoughts experienced while under the influence of hallucinogenic drugs can be translated into creative productivity, including new insights about the self, and even self-enhancement. As yet, however, this remains to be proved.

5. *Should marijuana be legalized?* Defenders of marijuana have long argued that the drug is no more dangerous than alcohol—and possibly less so, since it is not appreciably related to violence or crime in the United States. They have pointed out that legalization would provide freer access to a source of pleasure and tension reduction; would ensure a safer product since the federal government could supervise its production, distribution, and sale; and would provide another source of revenue through taxation. In addition, they consider it illogical to sanction the use of drugs that are known to be dangerous, such as alcohol and nicotine-containing tobacco, while making the use of marijuana illegal.

Penalties for the possession of small amounts of marijuana—but not for "pushing"—have been reduced by the federal government and most states from a felony to a misdemeanor, thus making penalties much less severe. In 1973, Oregon became the first of several states to completely remove the criminal penalties for the private possession and use of marijuana; the new law provides that persons found in possession of up to 1 ounce of marijuana (enough for about 20 cigarettes) can be charged only with the violation of an ordinance and fined, in effect making the use of marijuana no more criminal than parking a car in an illegal place.

The opponents of legalization have taken a variety of stands against it, one being that the use of marijuana leads to the use of "hard" drugs. But even though a high proportion of heroin addicts have also used marijuana, this is not proof of a causal relationship between the two; in fact, an even larger proportion of heroin users have probably used alcohol and other drugs. And the vast majority of marijuana users never become involved with heroin. A second argument has been that the removal of governmental restrictions would inevitably lead to a marked increase in marijuana use, a result that has apparently not occurred so far. Perhaps of key importance is the point that the legalization of any drug before we have definitive evidence concerning its long-range effects is taking a major and unnecessary risk.

Until we know more about the long-term effects of marijuana use, it would appear that legalization of this drug does present a certain element of risk. But it seems likely to many observers that if present trends continue, the federal government and most states may follow the pattern set by Oregon, or even possibly legalize marijuana subject to restrictions similar to those for alcohol. A major step in this direction was taken by Alaska, which in 1975 became the first state to legalize the use of marijuana at home; however, continued prohibitions were maintained against its sale or public use.

Other addictive disorders: Extreme obesity and pathological gambling

Not all addictive disorders involve the use of substances with chemical properties that induce dependency. People can develop "addic-

tions" to certain activities that can be just as life-threatening as severe alcoholism and just as damaging, psychologically and socially, as drug abuse. We are including two such disorders in this chapter. They are similar to other addictions in their behavioral manifestations and their etiologies as well as in their resistance to change.

Extreme obesity

To see the widespread problem of obesity, just look around at almost any social event or public place and count the number of individuals who are seriously overweight. Jeffrey and Katz (1977) estimate that from 40 to 80 million Americans fall in this category. Obesity is one of the most serious health problems in the United States today.

In this discussion we are concerned with *hyperobesity*—extreme obesity in which the individual is 100 pounds or more above ideal body weight. Such obesity is not simply an unattractive characteristic. It can be a dangerous, life-threatening disorder, resulting in such conditions as diabetes, musculoskeletal problems, high blood pressure, and other cardiovascular diseases that can place the individual at high risk for heart attacks. Although some cases of extreme obesity result from metabolic or hormonal disorders, most individuals who are obese become so simply through taking in more calories than they burn off.

Obesity, as a disorder, may be placed in several diagnostic categories, depending on which characteristics are being emphasized. If we focus on the physical changes, for example, we may view obesity as a psychosomatic disturbance, since psychological factors lead to the physical changes. Many clinicians, however, view the central problem not as the excessive weight itself but as the long-standing habit pattern of overeating. Thus obesity resulting from gross, habitual overeating is considered to be more like those problems found in the personality disorders—especially those involving loss of control of an appetitive nature (Kurland, 1967; Leon, Eckert, Teed, & Buchwald, 1978).

Causes of persistent overeating. What prompts people to overeat persistently to the point of obesity, even though they are aware of the detrimental effects on their health and are quite conscious of society's expressed adoration of the "body beautiful"? Several potential causal factors have been explored; and although results are not conclusive, biological and learning factors seem to be the most important.

1. *Biological factors.* It is clear that constitutional-biological factors are important. Some people seem to be able to eat high-calorie foods without significant weight gain, while others become overweight easily and have a constant struggle *not* to gain weight. There is a tendency for most people to gain weight with advancing age, but this could be related to reduced activity as well as to the fact that older people need fewer calories but are likely to continue their earlier eating habits. As already indicated, some individuals have metabolic or endocrine anomalies that can produce obesity at any age, though these cases seem to be relatively rare.

Obesity in adulthood is related to the number and size of the *adipose* cells (fat cells) in the body (Hirsch, 1972). Individuals who are obese have markedly more adipose cells than people of normal weight. When weight is lost, the size of the cells is reduced but not their number. There is some evidence that the total number of adipose cells stays the same from childhood onward (Crisp, Douglas, Ross, & Stonehill, 1970). It is possible that overfeeding infants and young children may cause them to develop more adipose cells and may thus predispose them to overweight or obesity in adulthood.

2. *Psychosocial factors.* In many cases the key determinants of excessive eating and obesity appear to be family behavior patterns. In some families the customary diet or overemphasis on food consumption may produce obesity in many or all family members. Here the fat baby may be seen as the healthy baby and there may be great pressure on infants and children to eat more than they want. In other families eating (or overeating) becomes a habitual means of alleviating emotional distress.

There are currently three quite different psychological views concerning the causes of gross habitual overeating.

a) According to the *psychodynamic* view, obese individuals are fixated at the oral stage of psychosexual development (Bychowski, 1950). They are believed to eat to excess and orient their lives around oral gratification because their libidinal energies and psychological growth have not advanced to a more mature level.

This view has been elaborated recently by Bruch (1973), who distinguishes between *developmental* obesity and *reactive* obesity. She sees developmental obesity as developing in childhood as a response to parental rejection or other severe disturbance in the parent-child relationship. Supposedly, the parents overcompensate for their rejection by overfeeding and overprotecting the child. Such children never learn to distinguish different internal signals because the mother responds to all signs of distress by giving them food. Bruch sees this pattern as leading to a distorted perception of internal states—that is, a lack of awareness of satiation when enough food has been ingested. She also views obesity as a symptom of underlying depression and postulates that weight loss would make an obese person more depressed. In a study by Silverston and Lascelles (1966), however, obese persons who lost a great deal of weight became less depressed.

Reactive obesity is defined by Bruch as obesity that occurs in adults as a reaction to trauma or stress. Here individuals are thought to use the defense mechanism of overfeeding themselves to lessen their feelings of distress. Research has not demonstrated that obesity occurs as a reaction to trauma or that it serves as a substitute for depression.

b) According to the *externality* hypothesis, eating is under the control of external cues instead of the individual's internal state. Whereas hunger and its satisfaction dictate the eating patterns of persons of normal weight, obese persons are seen as being at the mercy of environmental inducements. Regardless of how recently or amply they have eaten, they may be prompted to eat again simply by the sight or smell of food.

This reliance upon external cues is pointedly illustrated in the complaint of an obese 29-year-old patient:

I crave food . . . everywhere I go, whatever I do, I am reminded of food. Today after breakfast, I rode to work on the bus. The advertisements made me so hungry that I had to stop at the coffee shop for rolls

We do not know why people become obese. One theory suggests that obese people are more sensitive to external cues, that is, environmental inducements to eat, rather than to their own internal state. Regardless of how recently or amply they have eaten, they may be prompted to eat again simply by the sight or smell of food.

before I went into the office. When I watch TV I find myself constantly eating—I want everything. I can't stop. My big downfall is "munchies"—peanuts, potato chips, brownies. Going to the grocery store, I lose control and before you know it I have to get another grocery cart—and the first one is just full of junk. I can sit down in the evening to write a letter and before I know it the jar of peanuts is completely gone!

Other investigators, however, reject the externality hypothesis (Leon & Roth, 1977). Rodin (1974) found obese persons no more sensitive to external cues than persons of normal weight. Leon and Roth (1977), too, in a review of research on this hypothesis, found the evidence highly equivocal.

c) The simplest explanation—and therefore the easiest to accept—seems to be found in the *behavioral* view. Both the weight gain and the tendency to maintain overweight can be explained most simply in terms of learning principles (Jordan & Levitz, 1975; Leon & Chamberlain, 1973; Stuart, 1971).

For all of us, eating behavior becomes conditioned to a wide range of environmental stimuli. For example, people are encouraged to eat at parties and movies, while watching TV, and even at work. Eating is reinforced in all these situations, and it is difficult to avoid the many inducements to eat. Thus there is a wide assortment of seemingly unavoidable reinforcers and conditioned stimuli in the lives of most Americans.

Obese persons, however, have been shown to be conditioned to more cues—both internal and external—than persons of normal weight. Anxiety, anger, boredom, and social inducements all may lead to eating behavior. Eating in response to such cues is then reinforced because the taste of good food is pleasurable and the individual's emotional tension is reduced. All this increases the probability that overeating will continue at an even higher level.

But with such frequent overfeeding, obese persons may then learn not to be responsive to satiety cues, no longer feeling full when they have had enough. Meanwhile, physical activity, because its short-term effects are often aversive rather than pleasant, tends *not* to be reinforced, especially as pounds accumulate. Thus the obese individual becomes less and less active.

3. *Sociocultural factors.* Different cultures have very different concepts of beauty as regards the human form. Some value slimness, others, a more rounded contour. In some cultures, obesity is even valued as a sign of social influence and power.

Within our own society, obesity seems to be related to social class, occurring six times as often in lower-class adults and nine times more often in lower-class youngsters (Stunkard et al., 1972). Here, however, obesity may be related to a high carbohydrate diet in lower-class families.

Treatment of extreme obesity. Losing weight is a preoccupation of many Americans and the sale of dietary aids and weight-loss programs is a big business. Jeffrey and Katz (1977) estimated that over $16,000 is spent every minute—a total of $8 billion a year—on diet pills, diet aids, diet books, diet programs, and so on. Diet plans abound, with new programs emerging as often as clothing fads. Each one promises instant weight loss with minimum effort and no discomfort. In actuality, the success rate of most dietary devices and programs is quite low. In fact, the average outcome from diets has been reported to be a regaining of 105 percent of the weight lost (Stuart, 1967).

Cyclic loss and regaining is dangerous, however, because it may do serious damage to the cardiovascular system, further compounding the problem. Thus a person is better off maintaining obesity than using "the rhythm method of girth control."

Treatment of extreme obesity has included a variety of approaches including dietary programs, group self-help programs, medical measures ranging from appetite-suppressing drugs to intestinal bypass surgery, and behavioral management techniques.

Dietary programs alone are relatively unsuccessful. Most obese patients who seek professional help have failed on many diets in the past. Some of the most successful dietary programs are the self-control behavioral management programs, conducted in groups and including the use of follow-up booster sessions (Kingsley & Wilson, 1977).

There are also a number of weight-loss group programs conducted by commercial organizations like TOPS (Take Off Pounds Sensibly) and Weight Watchers (Bumbalo & Young, 1973). These programs provide strong group pressures to reduce weight by public praise of weight loss and public disapproval and "punishments" for failures. Thus they provide both community support and encouragement to maintain better eating habits. Individuals who remain with these group programs lose about 14 pounds on the average (Garb & Stunkard, 1974); however, less than a third of those who begin the programs stay for 24 months.

Fasting or starvation diets under medically controlled conditions generally produce weight loss in hyperobese patients—with some studies reporting losses of over 100 pounds (Leon, 1976). However, this method of rapid weight loss may involve several dangerous potential complications such as hypertension, gout, renal failure, and a breakdown in electrolyte homeostasis (Munro & Duncan, 1972; Runcie & Thompson, 1970).

Psychological distress may also accompany such starvation, with severe personality deterioration and psychosis occurring in some cases (Swanson & Dinello, 1970). And maintaining the lower weight level remains a problem: patients tend to regain the lost weight rapidly. After reviewing the research on therapeutic fasting, Leon (1976) concluded that "the equivocal weight maintenance results and the number of serious physical complications associated with prolonged starvation suggests that this technique should be used only in extreme situations" (p. 572).

Another questionable medical treatment of the hyperobese patient has centered on the use of *anorexigenic drugs* to reduce the patient's appetite. Diet pills, such as the amphetamines, suppress the desire for food and, as a result, have been extensively used. However, maintenance of weight loss once the diet pills are gone often becomes a problem.

Moreover, diet pills often present a problem in their own right. As we have seen, the amphetamines are addicting substances and are particularly dangerous when used in combination with other substances such as alcohol. The general ineffectiveness of amphetamines for long-term weight control and their high abuse potential has made these drugs of doubtful value in weight-reduction programs.

Another experimental medical treatment for

extreme obesity has been the *jejunoileal bypass operation*. This surgical procedure involves disconnecting and bypassing a large portion of the small intestine. The operation results in a reduction of the food-absorptive capacity of the intestine, thus producing a drastic weight loss—typically over a hundred pounds in less than a year (Payne, Dewind, & Commons, 1963). However, severe postoperative side effects have been reported, including diarrhea, hair loss, electrolyte imbalance, and death in as high as 6 percent of the cases. The dangers and the undesirable side effects of this surgical procedure make it a last ditch effort in cases of extreme obesity.

The most effective psychological treatment procedures for the extremely obese patient are behavioral management methods, which teach the individual to take off weight gradually through reduced food intake and exercise (Jeffery, Wing, & Stunkard, 1978). A number of methods using positive reinforcement, self-monitoring, and self-reward can produce moderate weight loss over time. In general, these procedures, based upon positive reinforcement, are more effective than classical conditioning procedures such as aversive conditioning in which shock or unpleasant thoughts may be paired with eating behavior (Leon, 1976).

The treatment of extremely obese patients is often a difficult and frustrating task for all concerned. Even with the most effective treatment procedures—behavioral management training—treatment failures abound. The following case underscores the importance of individual motivation in treatment and shows the similarity of the disorder to the other addictive disorders discussed in this chapter.

Beth was referred at age 15 by her adoptive parents for treatment for her obesity. She had always been a chubby child, and her weight now had reached 208½ pounds. Throughout her grade-school years other children called her names like "moose" or "fatty," which she learned to ignore. Her adoptive parents were both overweight, as were her natural parents. Beth's 12-year-old brother was not overweight.

Beth was receiving average grades in 10th grade, but she seldom participated in the extra-school activities and did not date. At the first treatment session she stated that she wanted to lose weight. She was started on a token system in which she received monetary rewards for eating balanced meals with smaller portions, having no between-meal snacks, and taking regular exercise.

Although she reportedly complied with the point system and earned rewards for the first three weeks she nevertheless lost little weight. She reported that she had cut down on high-calorie snacks but was still eating large portions at mealtimes. The treatment sessions focused upon problems occurring in her school and with her family that were related to her eating problem. Ways of maintaining her diet were also explored, as were issues concerning the decision to eat and her commitment to change. The primary emphasis was on self-control and self-management techniques. She was also taught a system of self-monitoring of her food intake.

During the next five weeks, there was a gradual increase in her weight—until she weighed more than before beginning treatment. The attention-getting value of her weight was explored with her parents in several sessions. A contingency contract was set up whereby the therapist canceled sessions when Beth arrived without having kept her weight records—something she was now inclined to do.

After sixteen sessions of individual treatment and counseling with the parents over a period of five months, Beth's weight was down to 207¼ pounds. The therapist confronted her with her lack of commitment toward actual behavioral change and pointed out the difference between wanting to lose weight and wanting to change her eating style.

Two weeks later, Beth came to the final session having decided that her independence in eating what she wanted was more important to her at this point in her life than changing her eating patterns. She had decided that she really did not want to stop overeating. Everyone was expecting too much of her at school (she complained that her brother got all the attention in the family because of his good academic performance). She felt that she could lose weight if she wanted to but admitted that she never had really tried during the past months.

The poor outcome in this example illustrates the tenacity of the problem of extreme obesity. As in Beth's case, many patients lose interest in the remote goal and choose to remain obese rather than make the difficult and persistent effort required to lose weight and keep from regaining it.

Pathological gambling

Although the behavior pattern known as *pathological* or *compulsive gambling* does not

Gambling in our society takes many forms, from casino gambling in Las Vegas to informal numbers games on the street.

involve a chemically addictive substance, it can be considered an addictive disorder because of the personality attributes that tend to characterize the individuals and the similar treatment problems involved. It also involves behavior maintained by short-term gains despite long-term disruption of the individual's life.

Gambling is usually defined as wagering on games or events in which chance largely determines the outcome. In modern societies money is typically the item of exchange; in other societies, seashell currency, beads, jewelry, and food are often used. The ancient Chinese frequently wagered hairs of their head—and sometimes even fingers, toes, and limbs—on games of chance (Cohen & Hansel, 1956). Occasionally the Mojave Indians wagered their wives (Devereaux, 1950). But regardless of the item of exchange, gambling seems to be an enduring human proclivity. Judging from written history and the studies of anthropologists, gambling has occurred and continues to occur almost universally and among all social strata.

Clinical picture in pathological gambling. Gambling in our society takes many forms, from casino gambling in Las Vegas, to betting on horse races (legally or otherwise), to numbers games, lotteries, dice, bingo, and cards. The exact sums that change hands in legal and illegal gambling are unknown, but it has been estimated that habitual gamblers in the United States lose more than 20 billion dollars each year.[6]

If one were to define gambling in its broadest sense, even playing the stock market might be considered a game of chance. Sherrod (1968) has humorously pointed to the need for a clearer definition of terms:

"If you bet on a horse, that's gambling. If you bet you can make three spades, that's entertainment. If you bet cotton will go up three points, that's business. See the difference?" (p. 619)

In any event, gambling appears to be one of our major national pastimes, with some 50

---

[6]Statistics in this section are based on Solomon (1972), Strine (1971), and Livingston (1974).

percent of the population gambling at one time or other on anything from Saturday-night poker games to the outcome of sporting events such as the World Series and the Super Bowl. Usually, such gambling is a harmless form of social entertainment; the individual places a bet and waits for the result. Win or lose, that is that. But while most people can take it or leave it, an estimated 6 to 10 million Americans get "hooked" on gambling.

These pathological gamblers[7] are habitual losers who are practically always out of luck, usually in debt, and sometimes in jail. Despite their difficulties, however, they tend to be of average intelligence or above, and many have completed one or more years of college. They are usually married and often have responsible managerial or professional positions that provide a reasonably good income (see HIGHLIGHT on page 363). It is generally assumed that far more men than women are pathological gamblers, but there are no reliable data concerning the actual sex ratio.

Causal factors in pathological gambling.
One of the first attempts to explain the role of psychological factors in pathological gambling was made by Sigmund Freud. Using the compulsive gambling of Dostoevsky as an example, Freud concluded that such gamblers were guilt-ridden masochists who wanted to be punished. Freud emphasized Dostoevsky's hatred of his father and subsequent guilt feelings after his father was murdered when Dostoevsky was eighteen years old.

Although a few psychologists and psychiatrists have dealt with the topic of pathological gambling, very little systematic research has been done and the causal factors are not yet well understood. It seems to be a learned pattern that is highly resistant to extinction. Often the person who becomes a pathological gambler has won a substantial sum of money the first time he or she gambled; chance alone

would dictate that a certain percentage of individuals would have such "beginner's luck." Bolen and Boyd (1968) consider it likely that the reinforcement an individual receives during this introductory phase is a significant factor in later pathological gambling. And since anyone is likely to win from time to time, the principles of intermittent reinforcement could explain the addict's continued gambling despite excessive losses. Bolen and Boyd were struck particularly by the similarity between slot-machine players and Skinner's laboratory pigeons; the latter, placed on a variable reinforcement schedule, "repetitively and incessantly pecked to the point of exhaustion and eventual demise while waiting the uncertain appearance of their jackpot of bird seed" (1968, p. 629).

Despite their awareness that the odds are against them, and despite the fact that they rarely or never repeat their early success, compulsive gamblers continue to gamble avidly. To "stake" their gambling they often dissipate their savings, neglect their families, default on bills, and borrow money from friends and loan companies. Eventually they may resort to writing bad checks, embezzlement, or other illegal means of obtaining money, feeling sure that their luck will change and that they will be able to repay what they have taken. Whereas others view their gambling as unethical and disruptive, they are likely to see themselves as taking "calculated risks" to build a lucrative business. Often they feel alone and resentful that others do not understand their activities.

In a pioneering and well-controlled study of former pathological gamblers, Rosten (1961) found that as a group they tended to be rebellious, unconventional individuals who did not seem to fully understand the ethical norms of society. Half of the group described themselves as "hating regulations." Of 30 men studied, 12 had served time in jail for embezzlement and other crimes directly connected with their gambling.

Rosten also found that these men were unrealistic in their thinking and prone to seek highly stimulating situations. In the subjects' own words they "loved excitement" and "needed action." Although the men admitted that they had known objectively the all-but-impossible odds they faced while gambling,

---

[7]Although these individuals have traditionally been called *compulsive gamblers,* they more closely resemble psychopathic personalities or addictive individuals than obsessive-compulsive personalities (Bolen, Caldwell, & Boyd, 1975; Moran, 1970). In DSM-III pathological gamblers are classified under a separate heading: "Disorders of impulse control not elsewhere classified."

A case of pathological gambling

John_____was a 40-year-old rather handsome man with slightly greying hair who managed an automobile dealership for his father. For the previous two years, he had increasingly neglected his job and was deep in debt as a result of his gambling activities. He had gambled heavily since he was about 27 years old. His gambling had occasioned frequent quarrels in his first marriage and finally a divorce. He married his second wife without telling her of his problem, but it eventually came to light and created such difficulty that she took their two children and returned to her parents' home in another state.

John joined an encounter group in the stated hope that he might receive some assistance with his problems. In the course of the early group sessions, he proved to be an intelligent, well-educated man who seemed to have a good understanding of his gambling problem and its self-defeating nature. He stated that he had started gambling after winning some money at the horse races. This experience convinced him that he could supplement his income by gambling judiciously. However, his subsequent gambling—which frequently involved all-night poker games, trips to Las Vegas, and betting on the races—almost always resulted in heavy losses.

In the group, John talked about his gambling freely and coherently—candidly admitting that he enjoyed the stimulation and excitement of gambling more

than sexual relations with his wife. He was actually rather glad his family had left since it relieved him of certain responsibilities toward them as well as feelings of guilt for neglecting them. He readily acknowledged that his feelings and behavior were inappropriate and self-defeating, but stated that he was "sick" and that he desperately needed help.

It soon became apparent that while John was willing to talk about his problem, he was not prepared to take constructive steps in dealing with it. He wanted the group to accept him in the "sick role" of being a "pathological gambler" who could not be expected to "cure" himself. At the group's suggestion he did attend a couple of meetings of Gamblers Anonymous but found them "irrelevant." It was also suggested that he try aversive therapy, but he felt this would not help him.

While attending the group sessions, John apparently continued his gambling activities and continued to lose. After the eighth encounter group session, he did not return. Through inquiry by one of the members, it was learned that he had been arrested for embezzling funds from his father's business, but that his father had somehow managed to have the charges dropped. John reportedly then left for another state and his subsequent history is unknown.

they had felt that these odds did not apply to them. Often they had the unshakable feeling that "tonight is my night"; typically they had also followed the so-called Monte Carlo fallacy—that after so many losses, their turn was coming up and they would hit it big. Many of the men discussed the extent to which they had "fooled" themselves by elaborate rationalizations. For example, one gambler described his previous rationalizations as covering all contingencies: "When I was ahead, I could gamble because I was playing with others' money. When I was behind, I had to get even. When I was even, I hadn't lost any money" (Rosten, 1961, p. 67).

It is of interest to note that within a few months after the study, 13 of Rosten's 30 subjects either had returned to heavy gambling, had started to drink excessively, or had not been heard from and were presumed to be gambling again.

Later studies strongly support the earlier findings of Rosten. They describe pathological gamblers as typically immature, rebellious, thrill-seeking, superstitious, and basically psychopathic (Bolen & Boyd, 1968; Bolen, Caldwell, & Boyd, 1975; Custer, 1976; and Graham, 1978).

The most comprehensive study is that of Livingston (1974), who observed, interviewed, and tested 55 mostly working-class men who had joined Gamblers Anonymous to try to stop gambling. Livingston found that these men often referred to their "past immaturity" in explaining their habitual gambling. They also described themselves as having a "big ego" and acknowledged a strong need for recognition and adulation from others.

Although these men had usually been able to cover their losses early in their gambling careers, the course was downhill, leading to financial, marital, job, and often legal problems. Eventually things got so bad that it seemed the only way out of their difficulties was the way they got in—by gambling.

A more recent study by Graham (1978) compared the psychological test performance of pathological gamblers with that of alcoholics and heroin addicts. The three groups of addicts showed many similar characteristics. The individuals in each group were self-centered, narcissistic, tense, nervous, and anxious; they overreacted to stress and were pessimistic

and brooding. They were characterized by acting-out, impulsive behavior; they had periodic outbursts of anger, were frustrated with their own lack of achievement, were reluctant to open up emotionally for fear of being hurt, often showed superficial remorse, and were passive-dependent and manipulative. They stated a desire to "turn over a new leaf" but showed a poor prognosis for behavior change in traditional therapy. These similarities suggest that similar personality characteristics may be involved as predisposing factors in the three disorders.

Treatment and outcomes. Treatment of pathological gamblers is still a relatively unexplored area. However, Boyd and Bolen (1970) have reported on a study in which eight pathological gamblers and their spouses were treated together through group psychotherapy—an approach based on the finding that the pathological gambler's marital relationship is generally chaotic and turbulent, with the spouse frequently showing seriously maladaptive behavior patterns also. There was a complete cessation of gambling in three of these cases and a near cessation in the other five. The extent to which changes in the gamblers' marital relationships influenced the outcome of treatment can only be surmised— six of the eight couples showed a significant improvement. Other treatment approaches, including aversion therapy and covert sensitization (Cotler, 1971) and cognitive behavioral therapy (Bannister, 1975) have been tried with individual cases, but further studies are needed before we can evaluate the potential effectiveness of psychotherapy in the treatment of this disorder.

Some pathological gamblers who want to change find help through membership in Gamblers Anonymous. This organization was founded in 1957 in Los Angeles by two pathological gamblers who found that they could help each other control their gambling by talking about their experiences. Since then, groups have been formed in most of the major cities in the United States. The groups are modeled after Alcoholics Anonymous, and the only requirement for membership is an expressed desire to stop gambling. In group discussions, members share experiences and try to gain insight into the irrationality of their gambling and to realize its inevitable consequences. As with Alcoholics Anonymous, members try to help each other maintain control and prevent relapses. Gamblers Anonymous has no policy for influencing legislation to control gambling but emphasizes the view that those who gamble are personally responsible for their own actions.

Unfortunately, only a small fraction of pathological gamblers find their way into Gamblers Anonymous. Of those who do, only about 1 in 10 manages to overcome the addiction to gambling (Strine, 1971).

In this chapter we have reviewed the nature and effects of the major drugs that are associated with abuse and dependence. We also have examined some of the causal factors involved in such abuse and dependence—the characteristics of the drugs themselves, the physical and psychological makeup of the individual, and the social setting in which the drugs are used.

Many psychoactive drugs, especially alcohol and tranquilizers, have constructive personal and social uses. However, most of these mind-altering drugs also have potentially harmful effects, particularly if they are abused. Consequently, society feels it necessary to exercise some control over their use; most drugs considered potentially dangerous if abused are legally available only by prescription. However, in the case of certain controversial drugs it is often difficult to exercise effective controls. This is particularly true if large segments of the population simply ignore such controls, as has been the case with marijuana.

We have also examined two patterns of behavior—extreme obesity and pathological gambling—that do not involve dependence on a particular substance but appear to have many features of addictive disorders. The "compulsive" appetite with which some individuals approach food or gambling resembles very closely that of the severe alcoholic or drug addict, and the self-destructive behavior, maintained by short-term and intermittent reinforcement, is very difficult to change.

11

Affective disorders

Milder forms of affective disturbance

Varieties of affective disorder

Causes of affective disorder

Treatment and outcomes

The term *affect* is roughly equivalent to *emotion* or, especially in the present context, to *mood*. The affective disorders are mood disorders, in which extreme and inappropriate levels of mood—extreme elation or deep depression—dominate the clinical picture. By contrast, the schizophrenic and paranoid disorders to be discussed in the next chapter are predominantly disturbances of *thought*, although often they have some distortion of affect, too. A disorder of the thought processes is not usually a notable feature in affective disorders, however, except perhaps where the disorder reaches extreme intensity; even here, the disturbed thinking often seems in some sense "appropriate" to the extremes of emotion that the person is experiencing. For example, the delusional idea that one's internal organs have totally deteriorated—an idea not uncommonly held by severely depressed persons—ties in with the person's whole mood of despondency.

Affective psychoses are not new in the history of humankind. Descriptions of affective disorders are found among the early writings of the Egyptians, Greeks, Hebrews, and Chinese; similar descriptions are found in the literary works of Shakespeare, Dostoevsky, Poe, and Hemingway. As we noted in Chapter 1, Saul, King of Israel in the eleventh century B.C., suffered from manic and depressive episodes, and King George III of England was subject to periods of manic overactivity, although it is now believed that George's maniacal behavior was secondary to a serious physical disease known as *porphyria*. The list of historical figures who suffered from recurrent depression is a long and celebrated one, including Moses, Rousseau, Dostoevsky, Queen Victoria, Lincoln, Tchaikovsky, and Freud. Here it is apparent that we are again dealing with mental disorders that appear to be common to the human race, both cross-culturally and historically.

Fortunate indeed is the adult person who has never experienced at least mild depression from time to time. As we shall see, there is reason to conceive of such mild affective disturbance as being *on the same continuum* as the more severe disorders on which we shall be concentrating; the difference seems chiefly to be one of degree, not of kind. At some point along this continuum, however, as we encounter the more extreme psychotic phenomena, subtle biological factors very likely become implicated, rendering the person less amenable to psychological treatment approaches.

Our discussion will start with the mild disturbances regarded as essentially normal, then go on to the disorders observed on the neurotic level, and finally focus on the disorders identified as psychotic. We shall have more to say about depression and depressive phenomena, especially in the earlier sections of this chapter; they are much more common than their manic counterparts. Later sections will consider the causes, treatment, and outcomes of affective disorders.

Milder forms of affective disturbance

Sadness, discouragement, pessimism, and a sense of hopelessness about being able to improve matters are familiar themes to most people, as is the tendency of such feelings to cluster together in a state of feeling known colloquially as "the blues." Most of us are prone to repeated cycles in and out of this state throughout our lives. Depression is unpleasant, even noxious, when we are in it, but it usually does not last very long; sometimes, it seems almost to be self-limiting. As we come out of it, we often experience it as having been in some sense useful: we were "stuck," and now we can move on; the former situation was easier to get out of than we thought it could be, and our newer perspective encompasses all sorts of possibilities.

This familiar scenario contains certain hints that may be significant to depression generally, including its more severe forms. The more important of these are that (a) depression, in its mild form, may actually be adaptive; (b) depression seems to be involved chiefly with psychic repair following some stress, particularly one involving significant loss; and (c) depression may, at least under some circumstances, be self-limiting. We shall have occasion to return to these points in what follows.

"Normal" depression

While the distinction between "normal" and "abnormal" is especially fuzzy here, any reasonable estimate would suggest that normal depressions far surpass abnormal ones in terms of the numbers of persons affected at a given time. Most people suffering from normal depression will not seek or need the specialized services of a mental health professional—although, in doubtful cases, it is certainly better to err on the conservative side and seek such assistance.

Normal depressions are almost always the result of more or less obvious recent stress. We shall consider some of these kinds of depression below.

Grief and the grieving process.

We usually think of grief as the psychological process one goes through following the death of a loved one. While this may be the most common and intense form of grieving, many other types of loss will give rise to a similar state in the affected person. Loss of a favored status or position (including one occasioned by "promotion" out of it), separation or divorce, financial loss, the breakup of a romantic affair, retirement from a valued occupation, separation from an important friend, absence from home for the first time, or even the disappearance or death of a cherished pet may all give rise to the symptoms of acute grief.

Whatever the source, the condition has certain characteristic qualities. The grieving person will normally "turn off" on events that would normally provoke a strong response; figuratively, he or she seems to roll up in a ball, fending off any and all possibilities of additional involvement and hurt by the simple expedient of losing interest in nearly all external happenings. At the same time, the griever often becomes very actively involved in fantasies that poignantly depict the now unavailable former situation of satisfaction and gratification. Initially very painful, these fantasies, if only by sheer repetition, gradually lose their capacity to evoke pain—a process of erasure (Sullivan, 1956).

In the typical instance, the capability for response to the external world is gradually regained, sadness abates, zest returns, and the person moves out again into a more productive engagement with the fluctuations of life. This is the normal pattern; some people, however, become stuck somewhere in the middle of the sequence, in which case they enter into a more serious psychological status to be described in a later section.

Ignoring for the moment such potential complications, it is easy to see grief as having an adaptive function. In fact, the lack of grief under conditions in which it would seem warranted would generally be of concern to a mental health professional. On the other hand, as we have seen in Chapter 8, a prolonged sense of hopelessness may endanger physical health.

Other normal mood variations.

Many situations in life other than obvious loss can provoke depressive feelings, and some people seem especially prone to develop a depressive response. It is a commonplace observation, for example, that doctoral candidates in various fields, including those in clinical psychology, frequently undergo pronounced depressive reactions promptly following completion of their final oral exams. A seemingly similar phenomenon is the so-called postpartum depressive reaction of some new mothers (and sometimes fathers) on the birth of a child. Possibly it reflects a feeling of "let down" after sustained effort and anticipation, or perhaps the reality never quite matches the expectation, leading to feelings of depression.

A large number of college students experience greater or lesser bouts with depression during their college years of supposed freedom and personal growth. Normal depressions among college students were studied by Blatt, D'Afflitti, and Quinlan (1976) in an effort to determine the basic dimensions of the experience. In brief, they found that the depression was similar for males and females, and that it involved chiefly three main psychological variables: (a) dependency, the sense that one is in need of help and support from others; (b) self-criticism, the tendency to exaggerate one's faults and engage in self-devaluation; and (c) inefficacy, the sense that events in the world are independent of—not contingent upon—one's own actions or efforts. As we shall see, themes of this sort also dominate the thinking of more severely depressed persons, giving credence to the notion of a continuum from normal to abnormal depression.

The birth of a child is sometimes followed by a period of depression, usually short lived. In some cases, however, such depression can be sufficiently extreme to lead to rejection of the infant.

The conservation-withdrawal hypothesis

As we noted in Chapter 4, in a seemingly hopeless situation or following prolonged frustration, many animals eventually suspend their emergency coping activity, appear to "shut down" physically in an energy-conserving manner, and for all practical purposes detach themselves from ongoing activity in the environment. After a time, should danger not materialize, they become aroused again and are able to reassess the situation, which has perhaps changed in the interim.

Noting the seeming adaptiveness of this behavior pattern, Engel (1962) hypothesized that it is an innately programmed product of the selective forces of evolution, one that is, in fact, shared by human beings. While Engel's hypothesis is not easily tested, the resemblance to human depression is impressively strong on a number of points. According to this view, more severe human depression would represent a case in which the adaptive mechanism has gone awry.

Varieties of affective disorder

The point on the severity continuum at which affective *disturbance* becomes affective *disorder* is, in the final analysis, a matter of clinical judgment. Unfortunately, while criteria exist for exercising this judgment, they are not precise enough to guarantee consensus among different clinicians. Although the more severe forms of affective disorder are obviously abnormal to even the casual observer, there is a gray area where distinction between normal and abnormal is difficult.

It is customary to differentiate the affective disorders on three principal dimensions: (a) *severity*—that is, neurotic or psychotic; (b) *type*—whether depressive, manic, or mixed symptoms predominate; and (c) *duration*—whether the disorder is acute, chronic, or intermittent, with periods of relatively normal functioning between the episodes of disorder. The following discussion is organized around these distinctions.

Neurotic affective disorder

Neurotic affective disorders are disorders of mood in which the person is seriously incapacitated, but not to the extent that contact with reality is impaired. We shall deal first with the long-recognized condition of *neurotic depression,* and then address the question of whether or not we should entertain the possibility of a classification that, for want of a better term, might be called *neurotic mania.*

Neurotic depression.

In neurotic depressive reactions the individual reacts to some distressing situation with more than the usual amount of sadness and dejection and often fails to return to normal after a reasonable period of time.[1] Although such reactions may last for weeks or even months, they do eventually clear up. In some cases a mildly depressed mood remains after more severe symptoms have abated. The incidence of neurotic depression appears to be higher in females than males.

The general appearance of the individual is one of dejection, discouragement, and sadness. Typically there is a high level of anxiety and apprehensiveness, together with diminished activity, lowered self-confidence, constricted interests, and a general loss of initiative. The person usually complains of difficulty in concentrating, although actual thought processes are not slowed up. He or she often has difficulty in going to sleep and, during the night, may awaken and be unable to go back to sleep. In many cases the individual has somatic complaints and experiences feelings of tension, restlessness, and hostility. Most persons suffering from neurotic depression can describe the traumatic situation that led to their depression, although they may not be able to explain their overreaction to it.

The following is typical of a conversation with a neurotically depressed individual and illustrates the characteristic feeling tone.

Pt.: Well, you see, doctor, I just don't concentrate good, I mean, I can't play cards or even care to talk

on the phone, I just feel so upset and miserable, it's just sorta as if I don't care any more about anything.

Dr.: You feel that your condition is primarily due to your divorce proceedings?

Pt.: Well, doctor, the thing that upset me so, we had accumulated a little bit through my efforts—bonds and money—and he (sigh) wanted one half of it. He said he was going to San Francisco and get a job and send me enough money for my support. So (sigh) I gave him a bond, and he went and turned around and went to an attorney and sued me for a divorce. Well, somehow, I had withstood all the humiliation of his drinking and not coming home at night and not knowing where he was, but *he* turned and divorced me and this is something that I just can't take. I mean, he has broken my health and broken everything, and I've been nothing but good to him. I just can't take it, doctor. There are just certain things that people—I don't know—just can't accept. I just can't accept that he would turn on me that way.

In severe cases the person may be unable to work and may sit alone hopelessly staring into space, able to see only the dark side of life. In such cases hospitalization may be needed for treatment as well as to safeguard against possible suicide.

In addition, the neurotically depressed individual usually reveals low stress tolerance, together with rigid conscience development and a proneness to guilt feelings. Typically the stress situation seems to center around the individual's "Achilles' heel"—that is, some stress situation that reactivates earlier conflict or trauma. For example, the death of one's husband may reactivate insecurities and conflicts associated with the death of one's father many years before. Thus it is not surprising that feelings of anxiety often complicate the clinical picture in neurotic depressive reactions (Downing & Rickels, 1974; Prusoff & Klerman, 1974). A sizable number of such persons manifest "pathological mourning" not only immediately after the death of a loved one but also on anniversaries of the death (Volkan, 1973).

Often in neurotic depression the picture is complicated by hostility the individual has felt toward the loved one. This hostility has typically been repressed because of its dangerous and unethical implications, but it may have manifested itself in hostile, guilt-arousing fantasies. When the loved one dies, the person's

---

[1]The current DSM-III classification has two major categories for affective disorders: (a) *major affective disorders* and (b) *other specific affective disorders,* which includes the less severe varieties. While it might seem that a neurotic depression would always be represented under *dysthymic disorder (depressive neurosis),* one of the subcategories in this second group, it might sometimes be represented in the first group, since major affective disorders are not always of psychotic severity during all episodes. In addition, DSM-III deals with the apparently widespread occurrence of "minor" depression by providing a category called *adjustment disorder with depressed mood,* entirely separate from the two affective disorder categories. Since this may engender confusion for students, we have departed from strict adherence to DSM-III here and have simply organized our presentation around "neurotic affective disorder" and "the affective psychoses."

The symptoms of neurotic depression generally include dejection, lethargy, and discouragement. In most cases, the reaction can be traced to some specific situation or event, perhaps the breakup of a relationship or the loss of a job.

grief is augmented by this intense guilt, as if the hostile fantasies had somehow brought about the tragedy. Where the individual was indeed partially responsible for the loved one's death, as in an automobile accident, these feelings of guilt and self-condemnation may be extremely severe.

Like other neurotic individuals, those suffering from neurotic depression sometimes use their symptoms to force support and sympathy from others. In one case a woman telephoned her therapist to say that she was going to commit suicide. Special precautions were taken—such as alerting family members to be "on guard"—but the woman made no serious suicide attempt. In a later therapeutic session the therapist asked her why she had called him and threatened suicide. The woman explained that she thought the therapist was not taking her symptoms and hopeless situation seriously enough and was not showing proper sympathy and appreciation for her desperate plight. By her threat of suicide she hoped to make him realize that he "just had to do something for her immediately."

Virtually all therapists undergo multiple experiences of this type with their depressed clients and even with some who are not obviously depressed. It cannot be stressed too strongly, however, that the assessment of suicide risk is a professional judgment, and one not to be taken lightly. *All* suicide threats should be carefully evaluated, including those that come from neurotically depressed persons. We shall have more to say about suicide and preventive intervention in Chapter 16.

As has been implied, depressions of neurotic severity usually are preceded by definite and readily identified stressors. Some investigators believe that in certain instances they may also occur "endogenously"—that is, in the absence of prior precipitating stressors. It must be noted, however, that the probability of discovering precipitating stressors is known to be proportional to the care of the diagnostician in taking an adequate history (Leff, Roatch, & Bunney, 1970).

Is there a neurotic mania?   Most clinicians are familiar with a type of person who is chronically overactive, dominating, counterdependent, deficient in self-criticism, and perhaps excessively optimistic concerning the outcome of various plans and schemes; such persons are by no means a rare breed. It would be unfortunate, however, to confuse this person's behavior with that of the classical manic syndrome. Such persons are almost invariably found to have underlying anxiety which they are defending against by overactivity in the standard fashion of neurotic conflict, and their problems are perhaps best considered as a subgroup of mild neurotic disorders.

Incidentally, these individuals are unlikely to present themselves for treatment at a psychological or psychiatric clinic. The more common pattern is for them to show up initially in medical clinics with beginning psychosomatic disease—perhaps as Type A patients with coronary problems (see Chapter 8).

In any case, although it is clear that depressive episodes of less than psychotic level occur, it is not so clear that there is a neurotic level of mania. The DSM-III provides for classifying a manic episode as being of less than psychotic severity, but it may be a category for which no cases occur.

The affective psychoses

As has already been suggested, there is no clear discontinuity in behavior as we move, say, from normal through neurotic to psychotic depression: progressively more of the individual's personality is involved, and the connection between the "real world" and the individual's experience and behavior gradually widens. Thus, at the psychotic end of the continuum there are two key characteristics: (a) the patient's total personality is involved in the manifestations of the disorder, and (b) there is a pervasive loss of contact with reality. Other typical differences between neurotic and psychotic behaviors are summarized in the HIGHLIGHT on page 373.

The affective psychoses fall in the DSM-III classification under the general rubric of *major affective disorders*. Two subtypes of major affective disorder are recognized. Depending on whether the individual becomes only depressed or has also exhibited symptoms of mania at some time in his or her life, the diagnosis is *major depressive disorder or bipolar disor-*

der.[2] In either case, the disorder may be recorded as mild, moderate, severe, or psychotic.

Major depressive disorder.   A major depressive disorder is a severe affective disorder in which only depression occurs.[3] It may occur in a single episode or may be recurrent. The diagnosis of major depressive disorder shares with its bipolar counterpart the difficulty that it necessarily involves some uncertainty about whether the individual may develop an attack of mania at some time in the future, in which case the correct diagnosis will have been bipolar affective disorder.

Of the two types, major depressive disorder occurs much more frequently and has increased in recent years, while bipolar disorder has decreased. In fact, it has been estimated that some 8 to 10 persons in 100—about 25 million Americans—will evidence a severe depressive episode at some time in their lives (Brown, 1974). Over 2 million of these will suffer profound depressions (President's Commission on Mental Health, 1978). The great majority of cases occur between the ages of 25 and 65, although such reactions may occur anytime from early childhood to old age. Poznanski and Zrull (1970) have described depressive reactions among children ranging from 3 to 12 years of age, and cases have been observed even after age 85. The incidence is higher among females than males, with a ratio of about 3 to 2.

In our discussion, we shall focus on three degrees of increasingly psychotic depression that have traditionally been distinguished for major depressive disorders.

1. *Subacute major depressive disorder.* The outstanding symptoms in subacute major depressive disorder are a loss of enthusiasm and a general slowing of mental and physical activity. The individual feels dejected and discouraged. Work and other activities require

---

[2]The essential distinction here is based on the idea that psychotic depressions may occur either alone (sometimes called unipolar depressive disorder) or as part of a bipolar disorder in which manic episodes also occur. In listing manic reactions only under bipolar disorders, the present classification assumes that manic disorder does not occur independently of depressive disorder. Hence all cases of psychotic mania would be diagnosed as bipolar disorder even though no depressive episode has yet occurred.

[3]The category of major depressive disorder includes the two formerly used categories of *psychotic depressive reaction* and *involutional melancholia*.

HIGHLIGHT

Comparison of neurotic and psychotic behavior

	Neurotic behavior	Psychotic behavior
General behavior	Maladaptive avoidance behavior, with mild impairment of personal and social functioning.	Severe personality decompensation; marked impairment of contact with reality; severe impairment of personal and social functioning.
Nature of symptoms	Wide range of psychological and somatic symptoms, but no hallucinations or other extreme deviations in thought, affect, or action.	Wide range of symptoms, with extreme deviations in thought, affect, and action —e.g., delusions, hallucinations, emotional blunting, bizarre behavior.
Orientation to the environment	Slight, if any, impairment of orientation to environment with respect to time, place, and person.	Frequent loss of orientation to environment with respect to time, place, and person.
Insight (self-understanding)	Frequently, some understanding of own maladaptive behavior, but with a seeming inability to change it.	Markedly impaired understanding of current symptoms and behavior.
Physically destructive behavior	Behavior rarely dangerous or physically injurious to anyone.	In some cases behavior may be dangerous to self or others.
Etiology	Emphasis on failure to acquire needed competencies, and/or on learned maladaptive behaviors.	Emphasis on maladaptive learning, decompensation under excessive stress, and possible biochemical irregularities.

tremendous effort and somehow do not seem worth bothering with anyway. Feelings of unworthiness, failure, sinfulness, and guilt dominate the individual's sluggish thought processes; loss of interest extends to eating and is usually reflected in loss of weight and digestive difficulties, such as constipation. Conversation is carried on in a monotone, and questions are answered with a meager supply of words. In general, the individual prefers just to sit alone, contemplating past sins and seeing no hope for the future. As we have noted, suicidal preoccupation is common and actual suicide attempts may be made.

Despite the mental and motor retardation, however, the person shows no real clouding of consciousness or actual disorientation. Memory remains unimpaired, and the person is able to answer questions fairly satisfactorily if allowed sufficient time. Many of these individuals have some insight into their condition and understand that they need treatment, although

they may not admit that they are depressed but rather emphasize various bodily ailments such as headaches, fatigue, loss of appetite, constipation, and poor sleep. The following is an excerpt from a conversation between a therapist and a 25-year-old woman who had been classified as a subacute depressive.

Th.: Good morning, how are you today?
Pt.: (Pause) Well, okay I guess, doctor. . . . I don't know, I just feel sort of discouraged.
Th.: Is there anything in particular that worries you?
Pt.: I don't know, doctor . . . everything seems to be futile . . . nothing seems worth while any more. It seems as if all that was beautiful has lost its beauty. I guess I expected more than life has given. It just doesn't seem worth while going on. I can't seem to make up my mind about anything. I guess I have what you would call the "blues."
Th.: Can you tell me more about your feelings?
Pt.: Well . . . my family expected great things of me. I am supposed to be the outstanding member of

the family . . . they think because I went through college everything should begin to pop and there's nothing to pop. I . . . really don't expect anything from anyone. Those whom I have trusted proved themselves less than friends should be.

Th.: Oh?

Pt.: Yes, I once had a very good girlfriend with whom I spent a good deal of time. She was very important to me . . . I thought she was my friend but now she treats me like a casual acquaintance (tears).

Th.: Can you think of any reason for this?

Pt.: Yes, it's all my fault. I can't blame them—anybody that is . . . I am not worthy of them. I have sinned against nature. I am worthless . . . nobody can love me. I don't deserve friends or success. . . .

Th.: You sinned against nature?

Pt.: Well . . . I am just no good. I am a failure. I was envious of other people. I didn't want them to have more than I had and when something bad happened to them I was glad. Now I am being repaid for my sins. All my flaws stand out and I am repugnant to everyone. (Sighs) I am a miserable failure. . . . There is no hope for me.

2. *Acute major depressive disorder.* In acute major depressive disorders the mental and physical slowing down is increased. These individuals become increasingly inactive, tend to isolate themselves from others, do not speak of their own accord, and are extremely slow to respond. Alternatively, they may be agitated, with much pacing, hand-wringing, and the like. Feelings of guilt and worthlessness become more pronounced and these patients become increasingly self-accusatory. They may hold themselves responsible for plagues, floods, or economic depressions, and may insist that they have committed all sorts of horrible sins that will bring disaster on everyone. Delusions may take a hypochondriacal turn, and in keeping with their morbid mood, they may believe that their brains are being eaten away, that their "insides are slowly petrifying," or that their bowels are completely stopped up. One hospitalized patient maintained that he had not had a bowel movement for over a month. Another would refuse to eat because he had no stomach and was only a "living shell." He usually blamed these ailments on early sex practices or other sins that had undermined his health and for which he was now being punished.

The individual experiencing acute depression sees absolutely no hope that things will

ever improve. Feelings of unreality and mild hallucinations occasionally occur, particularly in connection with ideas of sin, guilt, and disease. There is a considerable danger of suicide, since death generally seems the only way out. The reactions of this 47-year-old patient are fairly typical:

Th.: Good morning, Mr. H., how are you today?

Pt.: (Long pause—looks up and then head drops back down and stares at floor.)

Th.: I said good morning, Mr. H. Wouldn't you like to tell me how you feel today?

Pt.: (Pause—looks up again) . . . I feel . . . terrible . . . simply terrible.

Th.: What seems to be your trouble?

Pt.: . . . There's just no way out of it . . . nothing but blind alleys . . . I have no appetite . . . nothing matters anymore . . . it's hopeless . . . everything is hopeless.

Th.: Can you tell me how your trouble started?

Pt.: I don't know . . . it seems like I have a lead weight in my stomach . . . I feel different . . . I am not like other people . . . my health is ruined . . . I wish I were dead.

Th.: Your health is ruined?

Pt.: . . . Yes, my brain is being eaten away. I shouldn't have done it . . . If I had any willpower I would kill myself . . . I don't deserve to live . . . I have ruined everything . . . and it's all my fault.

Th.: It's all your fault?

Pt.: Yes . . . I have been unfaithful to my wife and now I am being punished . . . my health is ruined . . . there's no use going on . . . (sigh) . . . I have ruined everything . . . my family . . . and now myself . . . I bring misfortune to everyone . . . I am a moral leper . . . a serpent in the Garden of Eden . . . why don't I die . . . why don't you give me a pill and end it all before I bring catastrophe on everyone. . . . No one can help me. . . . It's hopeless . . . I know that . . . it's hopeless.

3. *Depressive stupor.* In the most severe degree of psychomotor retardation and depression, individuals become almost completely unresponsive and inactive. They are usually bedridden and utterly indifferent to all that goes on around them. They refuse to speak or eat and have to be tube-fed and have their eliminative processes taken care of. Confusion concerning time, place, and person is marked and there are vivid hallucinations and delusions, often involving grotesque fantasies about sin, death, and rebirth. The following

The isolation and inactivity shown by this hospitalized patient are typical of individuals suffering from acute depression.

brief description illustrates this severe depressive reaction.

The patient lay in bed, immobile, with a dull, depressed expression on his face. His eyes were sunken and downcast. Even when spoken to, he would not raise his eyes to look at the speaker. Usually he did not respond at all to questions, but sometimes, after apparently great effort, he would mumble something about the "Scourge of God." He appeared somewhat emaciated, his breath was foul, and he had to be given enemas to maintain elimination. Occasionally, with great effort, he made the sign of the cross with his right hand. The overall picture was one of extreme vegetativelike immobility and depression.

With the newer treatment methods today, most depressive reactions can be rapidly ameliorated, and few hospitalized patients remain severely depressed for an extended period of time.

Bipolar affective disorder. As has already been implied, manic and depressive affective disorders sometimes seem to be related, at least at the psychotic level and at least in some patients. The sixth-century physician Alexander Trallianus was probably the first to recognize recurrent cycles of mania and melancholia in the same person, thus anticipating by several hundred years Bonet's (1684) "folie maniaco-mélancolique" and Falret's (1854) "folie circulaire." It remained for Kraepelin, however, in 1899, to introduce the term *manic-depressive psychosis* and to clarify the clinical picture. Kraepelin described the disorder as a series of attacks of elation and depression, with periods of relative normality in between and a generally favorable prognosis.

Bipolar affective disorder is distinguished by at least one episode of mania. Bipolar disorders are classified as depressive, manic, or mixed,[4]

---

[4]Within the DSM-III there is a subcategory under *other specific affective disorders* for individuals who show persistent mood swings of mild or moderate—but not psychotic—severity, alternating between euphoria and depression. This subcategory is called *cyclothymic disorder.* Formerly, persons experiencing this pattern were considered to have a "personality disorder" rather than a neurotic reaction. The danger implicit in this revised classification is the subtle one of suggesting a continuity between long-term cyclothymic tendencies and major bipolar affective disorder, in which the individual has both manic and depressive episodes. There is no convincing evidence for any such continuity.

according to their predominant pattern. Even though a patient is exhibiting only manic features, it is assumed that there is in fact a bipolar disorder. Substantial manic or mixed patterns are much less common than the depressive pattern.

The clinical features of the depressive form of bipolar affective disorder are very similar to those of major depressive disorder, as already described, and there are the same variations in severity. The essential difference is that these depressive episodes alternate with manic ones, either closely or separated by an interval of relatively normal functioning.

In the manic form of bipolar affective disorder, the individual becomes elated or euphoric to an extraordinary degree, and there is a marked acceleration of mental and behavioral processes. The relative frequency of 20 symptoms in manic disorders is shown in the HIGHLIGHT on this page.

Here, too, three degrees of increasingly psychotic severity are roughly discriminable.

1. *Subacute mania.* The mildest form of psychotic manic disorder is characterized by moderate elation, flightiness, and overactivity. Individuals with subacute mania feel "simply great," have unbounded confidence in their ability and knowledge, and will unhesitatingly express their opinion on any and all subjects. Their thinking is speeded up and they may become particularly witty and entertaining. They seem tireless and get practically no sleep, stating that they feel so well that they do not need any. During the day they engage in ceaseless activity, talking, visiting, keeping luncheon and other engagements, telephoning, writing, and working on various sure-fire schemes. Numerous appointments are made, postponed, and canceled. The mail frequently seems too slow to these persons, and they are fond of sending telegrams and special delivery letters and making long-distance telephone calls.

The overall picture frequently appears at first to be one of aggressive, brilliant, sociable individuals who have many commendable enthusiasms and wonderful plans for the future. Initially they may seem exciting persons to be with, but they soon reveal their self-centeredness, become domineering, monopolize the conversation, and show difficulty in sticking to the subject. They are intolerant of criticism and may unsparingly denounce as a stupid fool

---

HIGHLIGHT

Frequency of various symptoms shown by 52 manic patients

Taylor and Abrams (1973) reported the following symptoms in 23 male and 29 female manic patients. These investigators noted that while these patients evidenced the classical symptoms of mania, they also evidenced many symptoms characteristic of schizophrenia. As a consequence, they concluded that this may help explain the confusion in diagnosis which often occurs between these two disorders, particularly between manic reactions and acute schizophrenic episodes.

Symptom	Percent patients affected
Mood disorder	100
Irritable	80.8
Expansive	65.5
Euphoric	30.8
Labile, with depression	28.8
Hyperactivity	100
Rapid/pressured speech	100
Flight-of-ideas	76.9
Grandiose delusions	59.6
Assaultive/threatening behavior	48.1
Incomplete auditory hallucinations	48.1
Persecutory delusions	42.3
Confusion	32.7
Singing/dancing	32.7
Head decoration	32.7
Autochthonous ideas	26.9
Visual hallucinations	26.9
Nudity/sexual exposure	23.1
Fecal incontinence/smearing	19.2
Olfactory hallucinations	15.4
Catatonia (posturing, catalepsy, mannerisms, stereotypes, automatic cooperation)	13.5

---

anyone who dares to disagree with them or interfere with their plans. The details of these plans are seldom worked out; very few of them are ever put into action, and these few are not completed. However, these individuals easily rationalize such failures to follow through and concede no mistakes. Money is spent recklessly, and in a short period of time entire savings may be dissipated. Moral restraint gives way, and these individuals may engage in numerous promiscuous sexual acts and in alcoholic excesses.

Although these persons rarely show marked delusions or hallucinations, they show very poor judgment and usually lack insight into their condition. Any suggestion that they seek professional assistance is met with angry abuse. They are ready with a rebuttal to all charges made against them and may threaten legal action against anyone who dares to interfere with them.

The following conversation with a subacutely manic patient reveals the elated mood and pressure toward activity typical of this reaction pattern. The patient was a woman of 46.

Dr.: Hello, how are you today?

Pt.: Fine, fine, and how are you, Doc? You're looking pretty good. I never felt better in my life. Could I go for a schnapps now? Say, you're new around here, I never saw you before—and not bad! How's about you and me stepping out tonight if I can get that sour old battleship of a nurse to give me back my dress. It's low cut and it'll wow 'em. Even in this old rag, all the doctors give me the eye. You know I'm a model. Yep, I was No. 1—used to dazzle them in New York, London and Paris. Hollywood has been angling with me for a contract.

Dr.: Is that what you did before you came here?

Pt.: I was a society queen . . . entertainer of kings and presidents. I've got five grown sons and I wore out three husbands getting them . . . about ready for a couple of more now. There's no woman like me, smart, brainy, beautiful and sexy. You can see I don't believe in playing myself down. If you are good and know you're good you have to speak out, and I know what I've got.

Dr.: Why are you in this hospital?

Pt.: That's just the trouble. My husbands never could understand me. I was too far above them. I need someone like me with savoir faire you know, somebody that can get around, intelligent, lots on the ball. Say, where can I get a schnapps around here—always like one before dinner. Someday I'll cook you a meal. I've got special recipes like you never ate before . . . sauces, wines, desserts. Boy, it's making me hungry. Say, have you got anything for me to do around here? I've been showing these slowpokes how to make up beds but I want something more in line with my talents.

Dr.: What would you like to do?

Pt.: Well, I'm thinking of organizing a show, singing, dancing, jokes. I can do it all myself but I want to know what you think about it. I'll bet there's some schnapps in the kitchen. I'll look around later. You know what we need here . . . a dance at night. I could play the piano, and teach them the latest steps. Wherever I go I'm the life of the party.

2. *Acute mania.* The symptoms in acute mania are similar to those in subacute mania but are more pronounced. This condition may develop out of a subacute reaction or may develop suddenly with little or no warning except for a short period of insomnia, irritability, and restlessness. Elation and pressure of activity become more pronounced, and the individual may laugh boisterously and talk in a raucous voice.

Individuals suffering from acute mania become increasingly boastful, dictatorial, and overbearing, and may order everyone around as if they were their superdictators. Irritability is easily provoked, and their mood may change rapidly from gaiety to anger. Both before and during hospitalization, violent behavior is common, and such individuals may break up furniture, deface the walls, and assault nurses and other patients. They are continually on the go, walking back and forth, gesturing to themselves, singing, and banging on the walls and door, demanding release. Even persons who have had the most rigid moral backgrounds will show a complete abandonment of moral restraint and may be obscene in their talk, expose themselves, and make sexual advances to those around them.

There is a wild flight of ideas, frequently leading to incoherent speech. The alternation in ideas may be so rapid that at one moment the person engages in erotic activities and the next delivers a profound religious dissertation. There may be some confusion and disorientation for time, place, and person, with a tendency to misidentify other people.

Transient delusions and hallucinations may occur, in which the person may have grandiose ideas of wealth and ability or may hear voices and carry on conversations with imaginary persons. Occasionally there may be short periods of relative calmness in which such individuals show some insight into their noisy behavior and may even apologize for it. In general, however, insight and judgment are severely impaired, and periods of insight are shortly followed by a resumption of manic activity.

The following brief description of an acute manic patient, though made a number of years ago and involving a relatively extreme case, still serves to illustrate various typical symptoms of acute mania.

"On admission she slapped the nurse, addressed the house physician as God, made the sign of the cross, and laughed loudly when she was asked to don the hospital garb. This she promptly tore into shreds. She remained nude for several hours before she was restrained in bed. She sang at the top of her voice, screamed through the window, and leered at the patients promenading in the recreation yard. She was very untidy and incontinent, smearing her excreta about the floor and walls. Frequently she would utter the words, 'God, Thou Holy One,' cross herself, laugh, and then give vent to vile expletives while she carried out suggestive movements of the body. She yelled for water, and, when this was proffered, she threw the tin cup across the room." (Karnosh & Zucker, 1945, p. 78)

3. *Delirious mania.* In the most severe type of manic reaction the individual is confused, wildly excited, and violent. The condition may develop out of subacute or acute mania but often appears suddenly with few warning signs. The individual becomes incoherent and disoriented and may experience vivid auditory and visual hallucinations. It is impossible to converse with such a patient. There is extreme psychomotor overactivity, and the individual is violent and destructive and spends days and nights in restless pacing, singing, screaming, gesticulating, and incoherent shouting.

During these episodes the eyes may show a peculiar glare and the features may be contorted beyond recognition. Such individuals may refuse food one moment and devour everything they can get hold of the next. Their behavior is obscene and entirely shameless, and personal habits completely deteriorate. They may smear their excreta on themselves or on the walls. They are dangerous to those about them and may seriously injure themselves. In short, they fulfill the popular notion of a "raving maniac."

This condition places a tremendous burden on all bodily functions, and the patient loses weight rapidly and may become utterly exhausted. As might be expected, vulnerability to heart attacks and strokes is increased and resistance to disease is lowered, particularly among older patients.

The following scene, which took place in the courtyard of a state mental hospital before the advent of newer treatment procedures, illustrates the extreme excitement that may occur during a severe manic reaction.

A manic patient had climbed upon the small platform in the middle of the yard and was delivering an impassioned lecture to a number of patients sitting on benches surrounding the platform. Most of the audience were depressed patients who were hallucinating and muttering to themselves and not paying a bit of attention to the speaker. However, the speaker had an "assistant" in the form of a subacutely manic patient who would move rapidly around the circle of benches shaking the occupants and exhorting them to pay attention. If anyone started to leave, the assistant would plump him back in his seat in no uncertain terms. In the background were a number of apparently schizophrenic patients who were pacing a given number of steps back and forth, and beyond was a high wire fencing surrounding the yard.

The speaker herself was in a state of delirious mania. She had torn her clothing to shreds and was singing and shouting at the top of her voice. So rapidly did her thoughts move from one topic to another that her "speech" was almost a complete word hash, although occasional sentences such as "You goddam bitches" and "God loves everybody, do you hear?" could be made out. These points were illustrated by wild gestures, screaming, and outbursts of song. In the delivery of her talk, she moved restlessly back and forth on the platform, occasionally falling off the platform in her wild excitement. Her ankles and legs were bleeding from rubbing the edge of the platform during these falls, but she was completely oblivious of her injuries.

Fortunately, the degree of excitement in manic reactions can now be markedly reduced by means of various drugs, and scenes such as this need no longer occur. The typical stages in a manic reaction are summarized in the HIGHLIGHT on page 379.

As has already been suggested, there is a strong belief among clinicians and researchers that major manic disorder does not exist as a disease entity apart from depressive disorder, giving rise in former times to the practice of labeling all instances of manic disorder as representing manifestations of "manic-depressive psychosis." The listing of mania as a subcategory of major bipolar disorder in the current DSM-III classification is essentially a continuation of this idea.

Strictly speaking, we do not really know whether there is such an entity as unipolar manic disorder. In a recent review of the literature, Depue and Monroe (1978) pointed out that response to treatment with lithium salts seems significantly greater in established bipolar cases than in those involving only

HIGHLIGHT

Stages of a manic episode based on daily behavior ratings of a hospitalized patient

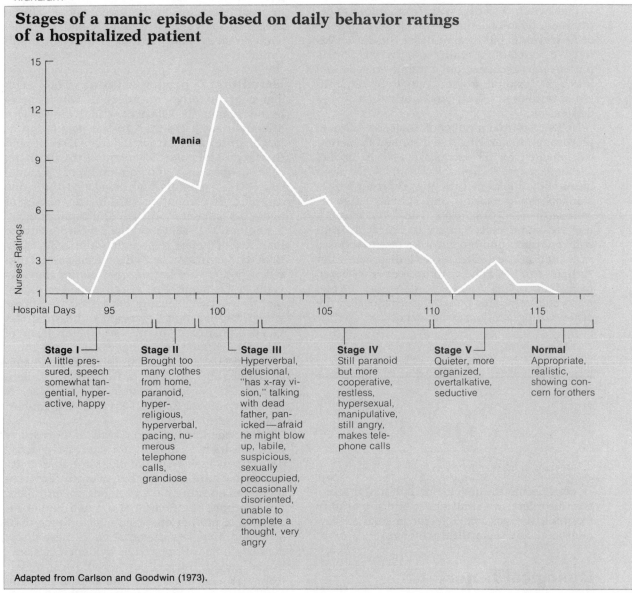

Stage I
A little pressured, speech somewhat tangential, hyperactive, happy

Stage II
Brought too many clothes from home, paranoid, hyperreligious, hyperverbal, pacing, numerous telephone calls, grandiose

Stage III
Hyperverbal, delusional, "has x-ray vision," talking with dead father, panicked—afraid he might blow up, labile, suspicious, sexually preoccupied, occasionally disoriented, unable to complete a thought, very angry

Stage IV
Still paranoid but more cooperative, restless, hypersexual, manipulative, still angry, makes telephone calls

Stage V
Quieter, more organized, overtalkative, seductive

Normal
Appropriate, realistic, showing concern for others

Adapted from Carlson and Goodwin (1973).

depression, suggesting different underlying mechanisms in the two types of reaction. Thus they concluded that the distinction has some validity. At the same time, they also cautioned that cases manifesting (so far) only manic or only depressive symptoms sometimes respond very positively to this type of intervention, perhaps indicating an underlying unity in at least some instances.

Jenner et al. (1967) cited an unusual case of a bipolar patient whose manic phase lasted 24 hours and was then followed by a depressive phase of equal length. This cycle had persisted for 11 years. Similarly, Bunney, Murphy, Goodwin, and Borge (1972) referred to the case of a patient who switched between mania and depression every 48 hours over a period of two years. Such cases are atypical, however. There is likely to be a 1- to 10-day period of relative normality between the end of depression and the start of mania. A day-to-day account of one patient's switch from depression to mania is chronicled in the HIGHLIGHT on page 381.

The switch the other way, from mania to depression, usually happens suddenly, with little or no warning, but in some cases there is an extensive period of normality in between. Thus a patient may recover from a manic episode and leave the hospital or clinic only to be readmitted several months or years later with a severe depression.

In a substantial number of cases, the clinical picture in bipolar affective disorders is further complicated by the excessive use of alcohol (Reich, Davies, & Himmelhoch, 1974). In other cases the clinical picture may show a distinct schizophrenic coloring and is referred to as *schizoaffective psychosis*. The latter pattern has led some investigators to speculate that schizophrenia and bipolar affective psychoses may not be separate mental disorders, but rather extremes of a continuum characterized by a shattering of thought processes at one end and relatively pure mood disturbances at the other, with gradations in between.

Causes of affective disorder

In considering the development of major affective disorders, we shall again find it useful to examine the possible roles of biological, psychosocial, and sociocultural factors.[5]

Biological factors

A biological basis for severe manic and depressive reactions is suggested by the fact that once the reaction is underway, it becomes relatively "autonomous" until it runs its course or is interrupted by drugs or other intervention. Attempts to establish a biological basis for these disorders have run the familiar gamut from

---

[5]An overview of research on depression and the delineation of causal models may be found in Akiskal and McKinney (1975), Becker (1977), and Blaney (1977).

genetic and constitutional factors through neurophysiological and biochemical alterations; even various related considerations, such as sleep disturbances, have been implicated.

Hereditary predisposition. The incidence of affective disorders is considerably higher among the relatives of individuals with affective psychosis than in the population at large. In an early study, Slater (1944) found that approximately 15 percent of the brothers, sisters, parents, and children of "manic-depressive" patients had developed the same disorder, as compared with an expectancy of about 0.5 percent for the general population.

Kallmann (1958) found the concordance rate for these disorders to be much higher for identical than for fraternal twins; he also noted that when both twins became psychotic, they developed the same type of reaction. For example, if one twin became depressed, the other would also become depressed rather than develop a distinctly manic or bipolar form of disorder. Other studies have supported these earlier findings in terms of incidence and concordance rates (Abrams & Taylor, 1974; Allen, Cohen, Pollin, & Greenspan, 1974; Helzer & Winokur, 1974; Reich, Clayton, & Winokur, 1969; Rosenthal, 1968).

The evidence for some kind of hereditary predisposition to manic and depressive disorders is persuasive but not clear-cut as to magnitude because the factors of early environment and learning have been left uncontrolled. For example, the finding of a much higher incidence of mother-offspring concordance than of father-offspring concordance in these disorders could be interpreted as evidence of a sex-linked genetic factor, but it could also result from early environment and learning if the child is more influenced by the mother than the father during the early years. In short, the precise role of heredity is far from clear, although it seems realistic to consider it an important interactional factor in the total picture.

Neurophysiological factors. Following the early lead of Pavlov, a great deal of interest has been expressed in the possibility that imbalances in excitatory and inhibitory processes may predispose some people toward extreme mood swings. It is suggested that manic disor-

HIGHLIGHT

The "switch" from depression to mania

Clinical study of patients in a metabolic research ward at the National Institute of Mental Health, Bethesda, Maryland, led a team of investigators to suspect that a biological switch mechanism may be a factor in sudden cyclic shifts from depression to mania. As an example of how the switch occurs, they described the case of a female patient. Twelve days prior to the onset of a manic episode, the woman was deeply depressed. For the next seven days she stayed in bed in her room, avoiding contact with the nurses and staff. She appeared sad and deep in thought. Then the "countdown" to switch day proceeded as follows:

'Switch day' minus 5   Patient remains alone, depressed but beginning to come out of it. She says to a nurse: 'I guess I'm in one of my low periods.'

'Switch day' minus 4   Patient still appears depressed and still secludes herself in her room, but there are times when she actually seems pleasant and not brooding.

'Switch day' minus 3   In the morning, the nurses find that the patient 'appears to be functioning on a good level' and not depressed. Her behavior is rated as normal. She says how good it would be to go home on a pass the next day and expresses concern about a new female patient.

'Switch day' minus 2   Patient is normal and spends the day out on a pass with her mother.

'Switch day' minus 1   Patient is still normal and returns from pass 'in excellent spirits.' She recounts many of the events at home: 'I washed my windows, gave my dog a bath, took care of other odds and ends and got my hair cut and styled.'

'Switch day'   Patient was up entire night. Sudden onset of mania was noted around midnight. After midnight she became loud, threatening, and seductive, and provoked fights. She was very angry, sarcastic, euphoric at times, talking continuously. By afternoon, she was shouting, had dressed gaudily and had put on bizarre makeup.

"For the next 25 days she continued to be manic, very loud, threatening, shouting continuously, bizarre in dress, obnoxious, provocative, and extremely angry, with moods frequently vacillating from tears to forced laughter. By 'switch day' plus 26, she began to come down slowly. The cycle was starting again." (Bunney, Paul, & Cramer, 1971, pp. 1–2)

On the assumption that "Something must be happening in the body as well as the mind" of such patients, these NIMH investigators studied biochemical changes in 6 manic-depressive patients, who, with one exception, were not on medication. It was found that there was a brief but marked elevation in a biogenic amine (adenosine 3', 5'-monophosphate) in the urine of the depressed patients on the day of the switch. Patients with the most rapid onset of mania also showed the most marked elevation in this biogenic amine on the switch day. Although these investigators considered the biological alteration as a possible switch mechanism, it was their impression that identifiable environmental stressors also played a part. However, they were unable to identify such stressors in the change out of mania. This impression was supported in an additional study of patients switching from mania into depression as well as from depression to mania (Bunney, Murphy, Goodwin, & Borge, 1972).

ders may result from excessive excitation and weakened inhibition, and depressive disorders from excessive inhibition.

To support this viewpoint, several investigators have pointed out that in monkeys— highly excitable and unequilibrated animals— the processes of excitation do in fact predominate over the processes of inhibition. In many other species, including humans, there is a greater equilibrium of excitatory and inhibitory processes, but within any species there are wide individual differences, probably stemming from both genetic and environmental influences. Presumably such neurophysiological differences could predispose some individuals to affective disorders under stress.

In considering the possible role of neurophysiological factors in manic and depressive reactions, it is relevant to note Engel's (1962) conclusion that the central nervous system is apparently "organized to mediate two opposite patterns of response to a mounting need." The first is an active, goal-oriented pattern directed toward achieving the gratification of needs from external sources; the second, in contrast, is a defensive pattern aimed at reducing activity, heightening the barrier against stimulation, and conserving the energy and resources of the organism. The latter, as we have seen, is known as the conservation-withdrawal reaction. Manic reactions appear to be an exaggerated form of the first response pattern, while depression appears to be an extreme form of the second.

But though the psychomotor retardation of the depressive and the psychomotor overactivity of the manic do suggest polar opposites in neural functioning, as well as behavior, this view appears to be oversimplified as an explanation of manic and depressive disorders. It does not explain, for example, how the two types of extreme affect can sometimes be observed to exist simultaneously in the same patient. In any event, a great deal more research is needed before we can arrive at definitive conclusions concerning the role of neurophysiological factors in the severe affective disorders.

Biochemical factors. Kraepelin considered manic-depressive psychoses to be toxic, and a good deal of research effort has been directed toward finding possible metabolic alterations and brain pathology in individuals with these disorders. Increasingly prominent since the 1960s has been the "catecholamine hypothesis," in which both mania and depression are viewed as being related to the level of catecholamines (various biogenic amines) in the brain.

Biogenic amines serve as neural transmitters or modulators that regulate the extent to which nerve impulses are conveyed across the synapse from one neuron to the next. A growing body of evidence suggests that various biological therapies often used to treat severe affective disorders—such as electroconvulsive therapy, potent antidepressant drugs, and lithium carbonate—may affect the normal functioning of certain biogenic amines in the brain. This, in turn, would affect the transmission of nerve impulses within the brain. One of the catecholamines, *norepinephrine,* has been implicated as playing an especially important role in the biochemistry of severe affective disorders. For a time it was hypothesized that mania and depression were due simply to functional excess and deficiency, respectively, of norepinephrine, but evidently the situation is more complex.

Although we have not yet pinpointed the underlying biochemical mechanisms involved, the evidence that such mechanisms play a causal role, especially in the maintenance of these disorders, is becoming quite compelling.[6] This case rests essentially on three facts that are beyond reasonable dispute: (1) a predisposition to this type of disorder may be genetically transmitted; (2) the behavioral symptoms of the disorder often abate promptly with certain biological interventions; and (3) certain profound alterations of bodily function, such as changes in the sleep cycle, not uncommonly accompany the affective symptoms.

Psychosocial factors

Growing awareness of a biological factor in the etiology of affective disorder does not, of

---

[6]Evidence bearing on the biochemistry of the major psychoses has recently been reviewed by both Barchas et al. (1978) and Berger (1978), the latter from the standpoint of the presumed site of action and pharmacology of drugs known to have a substantial effect on the course of these disorders.

course, imply that psychosocial factors are irrelevant. In Chapters 4 and 5 we outlined various ways in which biological influences may interact with life experience to produce an observed behavior. In the present case, evidence for an important psychological element in most of these types of disorder is at least as strong as evidence for biological factors. Most likely, then, we are dealing with a complex interaction between the two.

Stress as a precipitating factor. In Chapter 8, on psychosomatic disorders, we learned something of the ways in which psychosocial stressors may lead to altered body functioning. We are now in a position to suggest that such stressors may also affect the delicately balanced biochemistry of the brain, at least in predisposed persons. Consider, for example, the following statement:

"In addition to immediate changes in the formation, concentration, and pathway of metabolism of the [biogenic amines], long-term changes in biochemical mechanisms can result from behavioral states. Certain [stressors], such as exposure to aversive stimuli, seem to alter the reuptake mechanisms for norepinephrine, a finding which suggests that there are changes in the way in which a neuroregulator functions at synapse, with potential alterations in its effects on [the receptor neuron]. . . . Thus, a behaviorally induced change in reuptake mechanisms could lead to subsequent long-term behavioral changes due to receptor alterations no longer responsive to immediate behavioral states. Whether such mechanisms are relevant to the processes of depression, a disorder most effectively treated by drugs which alter reuptake, remains to be determined." (Barchas et al., 1978, p. 967)

What this summary of recent research suggests, in other words, is that psychosocial stressors may cause long-term changes in the extent to which impulses are transmitted from one brain neuron to another, and that these changes may be implicated in the onset and maintenance of affective disorders.

Evidence of interactions between biological and psychosocial factors of the kind described here represent a breathrough of enormous importance in our understanding of the major affective disorders. At the same time, this evidence should not be allowed to blind us to the probability that in some affective distur-

bances—certainly the milder normal and neurotic depressions—the contribution of an abnormal biological factor will turn out to be minimal or nonexistent. We have already seen that the milder depressions almost always have clear stressor antecedents; the occurrence of depressive affect following "losses," for instance, would seem understandable on psychological grounds alone—not requiring the postulation of extraordinary biochemical changes.

In the case of psychotic affective disorders, too, most investigators have been impressed with the high incidence of aversive life events that apparently have served as precipitating factors. Beck (1967) has provided a broad classification of the most frequently encountered precipitating circumstances: (a) situations that tend to lower self-esteem; (b) thwarting of important goals or the posing of an insoluble dilemma; (c) physical disease or abnormality that activates ideas of deterioration or death; (d) single stressors of overwhelming magnitude; (e) several stressors occurring in a series; and (f) insidious stressors unrecognized as such by the affected person. Later studies are in general agreement with Beck's observations (Briscoe et al., 1973; Brown, 1972; Paykel, 1973). The HIGHLIGHT on page 384 summarizes the stressors that had most often preceded severe depression in one study.

An interesting example of the apparent role of aversive life events as precipitating causes of psychotic affective disorders is that described by Hartmann (1968) of a patient who, between the ages of 44 and 59, had six severe manic episodes, all of which required hospitalization, and a number of depressive episodes, two of which required hospitalization. Typically this patient tended to be overactive in his general functioning, but during the early autumn he usually either ran for a political office himself or took an active role in someone else's campaign. In the process, he would become increasingly manic; when the ventures led to defeat—which they almost invariably did—he would become depressed in November or December.

Other descriptions of major affective disorders somewhat subtly convey the notion that these disorders often occur *de novo*—out of the blue, so to speak—in the absence of either notable personal distress or significant psychosocial antecedents. This implies that such episodes must be *endogenous*—caused from within—rather than precipitated by life events. Since the issue is an important one, we shall take a closer look at the evidence.

Estimates of the proportion of affective disorders preceded by precipitating stressors vary from almost none (Winokur & Pitts, 1964) to almost all (Leff et al., 1970; Paykel, 1973; Travis, 1933). In general, studies that adhere most closely to precise research methodology tend to produce the highest estimates of antecedent stress. Partly as a result of such data, there is currently considerable doubt as to the validity of sharply distinguishing an endogenous subset of affective disorders (Prange, 1973; Stainbrook, 1977; Thompson & Hendrie, 1972; White, Davis, & Cantrell, 1977). The "spontaneous" occurrence of affective disorders seems to be at best an infrequent phenomenon, and even where that seems to be the case we may have overlooked a stressor that was not obvious.

If we take the position—and the data seem to justify doing so—that some people *are* more prone than others to develop affective disorders, then it would seem reasonable to suppose that these high-risk individuals would react more intensely to subtle, easily overlooked stressors than would individuals less at risk for this type of disorder. And if there is a threshold above which biological factors that increase symptom intensity play an important role with progressive mood deviation, then these high-risk, low-stress cases would exhibit relatively severe symptoms. Unfortunately, the available evidence does not permit us to evaluate this hypothesis directly.

Predisposing personality characteristics.

Beck (1967) argues convincingly that psychosocial stressors provoke severe depressive psychoses only in persons who already have a negative cognitive set, consisting of negative views of the self, negative views of the world, and negative views of the future. According to this hypothesis, the stressor merely serves to activate negative cognitions that have heretofore been dormant. The result is an abnormally extreme negative affect. Obviously, Beck's "negative cognitive set" is in the nature of a *psychological* predisposing variable.

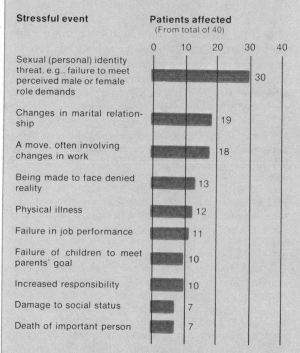

HIGHLIGHT

Stressors preceding severe depression

In an intensive study of 40 depressed patients, Leff, Roatch, and Bunney (1970) found that each patient had been subjected to multiple stressful events prior to early symptoms and to a clustering of such events during the month preceding the actual breakdown in functioning. The chart shows the ten types of stressors most frequently involved.

Stressful event	Patients affected (From total of 40)
Sexual (personal) identity threat, e.g., failure to meet perceived male or female role demands	30
Changes in marital relationship	19
A move, often involving changes in work	18
Being made to face denied reality	13
Physical illness	12
Failure in job performance	11
Failure of children to meet parents' goal	10
Increased responsibility	10
Damage to social status	7
Death of important person	7

Strikingly similar to the findings of Leff and her associates are those of Paykel (1973). In that study, which involved 185 depressed patients, it was found that comparable stressful events preceded the onset of the depressive breakdown. In order of significance, these events were categorized as (a) marital difficulties, (b) work moves or changes in work conditions, (c) serious personal illness, and (d) death or serious illness of an immediate family member. More recent reports have supported these findings (Brown, 1972; Brown, 1974; Schanche, 1974).

It might also be expected that exaggerated mood swings in the child would be fostered by observations of similar emotional patterns in the parents, and would then persist as learned maladaptive response patterns. The high incidence of affective disorders in the families of manic and depressive patients would have provided greater than average opportunity for such learning. In their study of 14 depressed children, for example, Poznanski and Zrull (1970) reported that 5 of the parents were depressed at the time of the child's referral; one father had committed suicide, apparently during an episode of depression. These investigators concluded:

". . . in those cases where parental depression was known, one source of the child's depression could be based on identification with the parent, particularly the parent's affective reaction to stress and difficulties within his own life." (p. 14)

Attempts to delineate a typical personality pattern for adults who later suffer serious affective episodes have met with limited success. In general, however, manic patients—whatever their childhood backgrounds may have been—are described as ambitious, outgoing, energetic, sociable, and often highly successful, both prior to their psychotic breakdown and after remission. As contrasted with controls, they tend to place a higher conscious value on achievement, are very conventional in their beliefs, and are deeply concerned about what others think of them. Depressive patients share these characteristics, but they appear to be more obsessive, anxious, and self-deprecatory. They also tend to show an unusually rigid conscience development, which prevents the overt expression of hostile feelings and makes them particularly prone to feelings of guilt and self-blame when things go wrong.[7] On the other hand, patients in both groups differ greatly in personality makeup, and there are many persons who show these typical personality traits but do not suffer psychotic episodes.

[7]The description of characteristics that are commonly ascribed to the personality makeup of manic and depressive patients is based on the following references: APA (1979), Akiskal and McKinney (1975), Bagley (1973), Beck (1971), Becker (1977), Becker and Altrocchi (1968), Chodoff (1972), Ferster (1973), Lewinsohn and Graf (1973), Libet and Lewinsohn (1973), and Peto (1972).

Feelings of helplessness and loss of hope. Feelings of helplessness and hopelessness have been emphasized as basic to depressive reactions by investigators of differing theoretical orientations. Bibring (1953), a psychoanalyst, held that the basic mechanism of depression is "the ego's shocking awareness of its helplessness in regard to its aspirations . . . such that the depressed person . . . has lost his incentives and gives up, not the goals, but pursuing them, since this proves to be useless" (p. 39). In later studies, other investigators have referred to "learned helplessness" in severe depression; presumably the individual, perceiving no way of coping with the stress, eventually stops fighting and gives up (Hiroto & Seligman, 1975; Seligman, 1973, 1975; Weiss, 1974).

Laboratory experiments have identified conditions that can lead to "learned helplessness," but attempts to relate such conditions directly to clinical depression have not fared very well. Nevertheless, the hypothesis remains somewhat attractive, and it may eventually prove more robust in those recently proposed revisions that emphasize the kinds of cognitive mediations to which the conditions of helplessness give rise. According to this idea, depression will occur only to the extent that helplessness inspires a negative cognitive set.[8] The relation between cognition and affect in the affective disorders is clearly a complex one (see HIGHLIGHT on page 387).

Feelings of helplessness and hopelessness and their behavioral consequences have been dealt with from a behavioristic viewpoint by several investigators. Lazarus (1968) has concluded that "depression may be regarded as a function of inadequate or insufficient reinforcers . . . some significant reinforcer has been withdrawn" (pp. 84–85). Similarly, Lewinsohn (1974) has concluded that feelings of depression—along with other symptoms of this clinical picture—can be elicited when the individual's behavior no longer results in accustomed reinforcement or gratification. The failure to receive positive reinforcement, in turn, leads to a reduction in effort and activity, thus resulting in even less chance of coping with

[8]Evaluation of the learned helplessness hypothesis on depression was recently the subject of an entire issue of the *Journal of Abnormal Psychology* (February 1978).

aversive conditions and achieving need gratification. In essence, the individual is caught in a vicious circle of learned helplessness and hopelessness.[9]

While the behavioristic perspective seems helpful in understanding depressive reactions, it would seem at first glance less applicable to manic reactions. However, one might speculate that the latter represent an attempt to obtain needed reinforcers via an indiscriminate increase in activity level. As in the case of depressive reactions, however, such reinforcers are not forthcoming. Here the conclusion of Ferster (1973) seems directly applicable: "It seems likely . . . that any factor which causes a temporary or long-term reduction in positively reinforced ways of acting . . . will also produce bizarre or irrational behavior as a by-product" (p. 859). Not adequately accounted for in this explanation, however, are the feelings of euphoria that characterize manic reactions.

Extreme defenses against stress.   Manic and depressive psychoses may be viewed as two different but related defense-oriented strategies for dealing with severe stress.

In the case of mania, individuals try to escape their difficulties by a "flight into reality." In less severe form, this type of reaction to stress is shown by the person who goes on a round of parties to try to forget a broken love affair, or tries to escape from a threatening life situation by restless activity, occupying every moment with work, athletics, sexual affairs, and countless other crowded activities—all performed with professed gusto but with little true enjoyment.

In mania this pattern is exaggerated. With a tremendous expenditure of energy, the manic individual tries to deny feelings of helplessness and hopelessness and to play a role of competence. Once this mode of coping with difficulties is adopted, it is maintained until it has spent itself in emotional exhaustion, for the only other alternative is an admission of defeat and inevitable depression. This is well brought out in the following case of a subacutely manic patient.

Some theorists hypothesize that feelings of helplessness underlie the development of depressive reactions. The individual who continually finds—for whatever reason—that "nothing I do makes a difference" eventually loses hope and stops doing anything.

"He neglected his meals and rest hours, and was highly irregular, impulsive, and distractible in his adaptations to ward routine. Without apparent intent to be annoying or disturbing he sang, whistled, told pointless off-color stories, visited indiscriminately, and flirted crudely with the nurses and female patients. Superficially he appeared to be in high spirits, and yet one day when he was being gently chided over some particular irresponsible act he suddenly slumped in a chair, covered his face with his hands, began sobbing, and cried, 'For Pete's sake, doc, let me be. Can't you see that I've just got to act happy?' " (Masserman, 1961, pp. 66–67)

---

[9]Several variations of this behavioristic hypothesis are described by Eastman (1976). And Blaney (1977) has recently provided a detailed comparison between behavioristic and cognitively oriented formulations of the depressive state.

Unfortunately, as manic disorders proceed, any defensive value they may have had is negated, for thought processes are speeded up to a point where the individual can no longer "process" incoming information with any degree of efficiency. In a manner of speaking, "the programmer loses control of the computer," resulting in severe personality decompensation.

In the case of depression, the person apparently gains some relief from the intolerable stress situation by admitting defeat and withdrawing psychologically from the fight. Also, the slowing down of thought processes may serve to decrease suffering by reducing the sheer quantity of painful thoughts. However, these feelings of relief are gained at the expense of a sense of adequacy and self-esteem, and thus are accompanied by marked guilt and self-accusation. Like the soldier who panics and flees from combat, the individual may feel relieved to be out of an intolerable situation but also feel guilty and devaluated.

Since depressive patients tend to blame themselves for their difficulties, they often go over the past with a microscope, picking out any possible sins of omission or commission and exaggerating their importance in relation to the present difficulties. They may even accuse themselves of selfishness, unfaithfulness, or hostile acts that did not occur. These self-accusations seem to be attempts to explain and find some meaning in their predicament and at the same time achieve some measure of expiation and atonement.

The traditional Freudian view of depression as a defense against stress has emphasized guilt related to bereavement. Apparently normal grief and depression may be intensified to a pathological degree if the individual feels guilty about having had strong feelings of hostility toward the deceased and/or some responsibility for the loved one's death. Here the turning inward of hostility, coupled with self-recrimination, apparently helps the individual work through the severe guilt and depression. This pattern is illustrated in the following case.

The patient, a 24-year-old woman, had eloped two years previously with a young man of whom her parents disapproved. Following the elopement the parents disowned her and refused to have anything to do with her. The patient and her husband then

HIGHLIGHT

The relation between cognition and affect in manic and depressive disorders

In attempting to understand manic and depressive reactions, it is helpful to remember that we all experience moods. We may feel particularly elated and self-confident at one time and vaguely anxious and depressed at another. In a pioneering study of euphoric and depressed moods in normal subjects, Johnson (1937) found striking differences in people's whole manner and approach to problems, depending on whether they were in a euphoric mood or a depressed one. In euphoric moods, subjects made more spontaneous and unnecessary conversation and reached decisions much more easily. In addition, they made more expansive movements in such psychomotor functions as writing. Depression, on the other hand, resulted in a very definite regression to childhood events in thought and memory, increased difficulty in making decisions, more cramped and smaller script and figures, and a judgment of distances as being greater than they actually were.

Although there is as yet little direct research evidence on the relationship between cognition and affect in patients suffering affective disorders, the development of new experimental techniques involving induction of (temporary) mood states in normal subjects may be expected to provide promising leads. For example, in one such study, subjects demonstrated markedly greater expansiveness or constriction in graphic expression and greater sociability or inactivity following the induction of a happy or depressed mood (Strickland, Hale, & Anderson, 1975). Potts (1977) demonstrated a similar effect in regard to preferences for varied activities.

Findings like these in normal subjects help us understand the effects of the more exaggerated mood swings in the affective disorders. Whereas our cognitive processes ordinarily maintain adequate control over our perceptions and reactions to stress situations, it appears that in affective disorders, the affective processes take over and largely determine an individual's appraisal of events and experiences. It is possible, of course, that changes in cognition—as when one begins to perceive one's life situation as hopeless—may precede and pave the way for the affective reaction, or the relationship between cognition and affect may involve a vicious circle, in which each augments the other.

traveled to California, where he obtained employment as a shipping clerk in a wholesale company.

The daughter and her parents did not correspond, although the daughter had severe guilt feelings about letting her parents down—they had had great ambitions for her in college and had looked forward to her future marriage to a wealthy youth whose parents were old friends. During her first year in California she became pregnant and just before the baby was to arrive wired her parents of the forthcoming event. Unfortunately, the baby died during birth and the handsome presents her parents sent for the baby only served to intensify her disappointment. However, the event served to reestablish relations, and the parents made immediate arrangements to drive to California to visit the patient and her husband. But on the way they were involved in a tragic automobile accident. The father was killed outright and the mother died on the way to the hospital.

Upon the receipt of this news, the patient became extremely depressed and attempted suicide by taking an overdose of sleeping tablets. Emergency medical attention saved her life but she remained depressed and was extremely anxious and tense, unable to sit still or concentrate on any topic except her parents' death. She blamed herself for it and paced the floor in great agitation, muttering to herself and bewailing her guilt. During this period the following conversation took place.

Dr.: You feel that you are to blame for your parents' death?

Pt.: Yes, oh why didn't I obey them. Now they are dead . . . I have killed them. They were wonderful to me and I have repaid them by disobedience and murder. I deserve to die too. Oh God! I have killed my baby and now my parents! I don't deserve to live. . . . I am no good, evil. I will be punished too . . . Oh God what have I done!

It was thought in this case that the patient had felt considerable hostility toward her parents following their rejection of her, as well as guilt for disobeying them. She had never been able to express this hostility even to her husband. Apparently it added considerably to her guilt feelings and played an important part in the severe self-recrimination and depression which followed their death. With antidepressant medication and brief psychotherapy, she showed a rapid and apparently full recovery.

It may be that the remission of depressive disorders even without treatment occurs because the effort at expiation and atonement has been successful. In such cases, there may be a gradual working through of feelings of unworthiness and guilt, in which the individual pays the price for past failures by self-punishment and is thereby cleansed and ready for another go at life.

In bipolar reactions, the shift from mania to depression may tend to occur when the defensive function of the manic reaction breaks down. Similarly, the shift from depression to mania may tend to occur when the individual, devaluated and guilt-ridden by inactivity and inability to cope, finally feels compelled to attempt some countermeasure, however desperate.

While the view of manic and depressive psychoses as extreme defenses seems plausible up to a certain level of severity of disorder, it is becoming very difficult, as we have seen, to account satisfactorily for the more extreme versions of these states without appealing to contributory biological causation. It seems as though certain biological mechanisms become involved at some point and thereafter tend to maintain the disorder. The effectiveness of biological treatment in terminating severe episodes lends support to this hypothesis.

Establishment of a reinforced social role. Curiously enough, the manic patient tends to play a social role well suited to eliciting rejection from others, while the depressive patient seems to elicit either rejection or sympathy and support but rarely neutrality. In their discussion of "playing the manic game," Janowsky, Leff, and Epstein (1970) have observed:

"The acutely manic patient is often able to alienate himself from family, friends, and therapists alike. This knack is based on the facile use of maneuvers which place individuals relating to the manic in positions of embarrassment, decreased self-esteem, and anxious self-doubt. Those dealing with the manic frequently find themselves on the defensive, attempting to justify their actions and motivations. Commonly, they feel 'outsmarted' and 'outmaneuvered.' " (p. 253)

The manic individual apparently feels that wishing to rely on others or to be taken care of is threatening and unacceptable. Instead, such an individual maintains self-esteem and feelings of adequacy and strength by establishing a social role in which control of other people is possible (Janowsky, El-Yousef, & Davis, 1974). The HIGHLIGHT on page 390 describes several

The frantic and seemingly senseless activity of the manic individual may be a screen to ward off the bitter and painful thoughts that eventually trigger yet another depressive episode.

techniques by which such control may be achieved.

On the other hand, the depressed individual tends to adopt a role that places others in the position of providing support and care—and thus reinforcement (Ferster, 1973; Janowsky et al., 1970). Positive reinforcement does not necessarily follow, however. Depressive behavior can, and frequently does, elicit negative feelings and rejection in other persons, especially perhaps in mixed-sex interactions (Hammen & Peters, 1977, 1978). Coyne (1976) has suggested that the presence or absence of support may depend on whether the depressed individual is skillful enough to circumvent and turn to advantage the negative affect he or she tends to create in the other person. Especially if the other person is prone to guilt feelings—the skillful depressive patient may be able to extract considerable sympathy and support, at least over the short term.

Depressive behavior as an attempt to communicate. Other investigators have seen depressive reactions as an attempt to communicate a particular message. As Hill (1968) has expressed it,

"Symptoms, then, whether they be verbal expressions, deviant behavior, or simple motor postures or movements, are forms of communication. They are postures in the sense that they communicate the internal need state of the patient, his distress, his fear and anger, his remorse, his humble view of himself, his demands, and his dependency." (p. 456)

Particularly in interpersonal relations with significant others, depressive reactions can often be seen as attempts of the individual to communicate feelings of discouragement and despair—to say, in effect, "I have needs that you are failing to meet." Too often, however, this communication goes unheeded. Thus in failing marriages, which are commonly associated with depressive reactions, we may see one partner trying to communicate his or her unmet expectations, distress, and dependency —and then becoming increasingly depressed and disturbed when the other partner fails to make the hoped-for response.

General sociocultural factors

The incidence of psychotic affective disorders seems to vary considerably among different societies: in some, manic episodes are more frequent, while in others, depressive episodes are more common.

In early studies, Carothers (1947, 1951, 1959) found manic disorders fairly common among the East Africans he studied, but depressive disorders relatively rare—the exact opposite of their incidence in the United States. He attributed the low incidence of depressive disorders to the fact that in traditional African cultures the individual has not usually been held personally responsible for failures and misfortunes. The culture of the Kenya Africans Carothers observed may be taken as fairly typical in this respect:

Their behavior in all its major aspects is group-determined. Even religion is a matter of offerings and invocations in a group; it is not practiced individually and does not demand any particular attitude on the part of the individual. Similarly, grief over the death of a loved one is not borne in isolation, but appropriate rites are performed amid great public grieving. In these rites, widowed persons express their grief dramatically in ways prescribed by custom, and then resume the tenor of their life as if no bereavement had occurred.

Psychologically speaking, Kenyans receive security because they are part of a larger organism and are not confronted with the problems of individual self-sufficiency, choice, and responsibility that play such a large part in our culture. They do not set themselves unrealistic goals, and they have no need to repress or feel guilty about "dangerous" desires. Their culture actively discourages individual achievement of success, does not consider sexual behavior as evil, and is tolerant of occasional outbursts of aggressive hostility.

In addition, Kenyans feel a great humbleness toward their natural environment, which is often harsh in the extreme. They always expect the worst, and hence can accept misfortunes with equanimity. Here too, responsibility and blame are automatically placed on forces outside themselves. Although they attempt to counteract misfortune and assure success in their ventures by performing appropriate rituals, the outcome is in the hands of the gods. They are not personally responsible and hence do not ordinarily experience self-devaluation or the need for ego-defensive measures. When excessive stress and decompensation do occur, there tends to be a complete

disorganization of personality—as in the hebephrenic type of schizophrenia, which is the most common type of psychotic reaction. (Adapted from Carothers, 1947, 1951, 1953)

Needless to say, much has changed in Africa since Carothers made these observations, and more recent data suggest a quite different picture. In general, it appears that as societies develop toward the more "advanced" forms of Western European and American culture, their members become more prone to the development of what might be called Western-style affective disorders (Marsella, 1979).

Even in nonindustrialized countries where depressive disorders are relatively common, they seem less closely associated with feelings

Playing the manic game

Janowsky and his associates (1970, 1974), noting the extent to which manic patients intentionally induce discomfort in other people, pointed to the following techniques that are used in "playing the manic game."

1. Manipulating the self-esteem of others—either lowering or raising it—as a means of exerting leverage over them.

2. Discovering areas of sensitivity and vulnerability in others for purposes of exploitation.

3. Projecting responsibility in such a way that other people become responsible for the manic's own actions.

4. Progressively testing limits—avoiding limits that have been imposed by challenging them or finding loopholes in them.

5. Creating interpersonal distance between themselves and others by deliberately evoking the anger of and alienating staff members.

Although the reasons for the use of these techniques are not clear, these investigators suggest that the manic's feeling of being threatened by and unable to rely on others may be a contributing factor. In any event, these interpersonal maneuvers appeared typical of the clinical picture in mania and disappeared when the manic episode remitted.

of guilt and self-recrimination than in the developed countries (Kidson & Jones, 1968; Lorr & Klett, 1968; Zung, 1969). In fact, among several groups of Australian aborigines, Kidson and Jones (1968) found not only an absence of guilt and self-recrimination in depressive reactions but also no incidence of attempted or actual suicide. In connection with the latter finding, they stated:

"The absence of suicide can perhaps be explained as a consequence of strong fears of death and also because of the tendency to act out and project hostile impulses." (p. 415)

These conclusions are generally supported in Marsella's (1979) comprehensive review of the cross-cultural literature concerning depression. While various methodological problems make it inadvisable at this time to assert with certainty that depression occurs less frequently in cultures other than our own, there is little doubt that it generally takes a different form from that customarily seen here. For example, in some non-Western cultures, symptoms of depression tend to lack substantial psychological components, being limited to the so-called vegetative manifestations, such as sleep disturbance, anorexia, weight loss, and loss of sexual interest. Interestingly, in some such cultures there is not even a *concept* of depression that would be reasonably comparable to our own.

In our own society, the role of sociocultural factors in affective disorders remains unclear, but it would appear that conditions that increase life stress lead to a higher incidence of these as well as other disorders. For example, Jaco (1960) found that while psychotic affective disorders were distributed more evenly in the population than schizophrenia, the incidence was significantly higher among the divorced than among the married and about 3 times higher in urban than in rural areas. Bloom, Asher, and White (1978) have confirmed that divorce is a frequent precipitant of serious depression. There is also some evidence that the incidence of psychotic depression is higher in the upper socioeconomic classes (Bagley, 1973). However, there is no way of knowing the extent to which diagnostic biases and artifacts may have influenced these observations.

Treatment and outcomes

Antidepressant, tranquilizing, and antianxiety drugs are all used with the more severely disturbed manic and depressive patients. The role of medication in the milder forms of affective disturbance remains somewhat equivocal at this time, and most such patients are likely to do as well with only psychological forms of therapy (Segal, Yager, & Sullivan, 1976).

Lithium, a simple mineral salt, was first tried for the treatment of affective disorders in the 1940s by Cade of Australia but was found to have adverse side effects. Thanks to a series of refinements since then, however, lithium therapy has become highly effective in the treatment of manic psychoses and, more recently, in the treatment of some depressive psychoses as well (Davis, 1976; Depue & Monroe, 1978; Segal, Yager, & Sullivan, 1976). It is widely believed that lithium is effective in depression only where the underlying disorder is bipolar in nature. Lithium therapy is often effective in preventing the cycling between manic and depressive episodes.

For most psychotic depressive patients, the drug treatment of choice will be one of the antidepressants such as imipramine or amitriptyline. These drugs are often effective in prevention as well as treatment for patients subject to recurrent episodes (Davis, 1976; Hollon & Beck, 1978; Prien, Klett, & Caffey, 1973; Raskin, 1974).

Since an estimated 60 percent or more of depressed patients are also anxious, tranquilizing and antianxiety drugs are commonly used in combination with antidepressants (Cole, 1974; Raskin, 1974). Here it is useful to note the reminder of Lehmann (1968) that

"Depression and anxiety are two symptoms which very often co-exist in the same patient. They are nevertheless different symptoms and they may vary independently in their intensity. Of the two symptoms, anxiety is by far the more conspicuous and depression the more dangerous." (p. 18)

Unfortunately, antidepressant drugs usually require a few days before their effects are manifested. Thus electroconvulsive therapy (ECT) is often used with patients who present an immediate and serious suicidal risk (Brown, 1974; Hurwitz, 1974). There is a complete remission of symptoms in depressive patients after about 4 to 6 convulsive treatments in over 90 percent of the cases. Maintenance dosages of antidepressant and antianxiety drugs ordinarily are then used to maintain the treatment gains achieved until the depression has run its course. If necessitated as a last resort, electroconvulsive therapy should be used very sparingly, however, because of its distressing side effects, including temporary memory loss and disorientation, and because there is some evidence that it may produce permanent brain damage (Fink, 1979).

Treatment is not ordinarily confined to drugs or drugs plus electroconvulsive therapy, but usually is combined with individual and/or group psychotherapy directed at helping the patient develop a more stable long-range adjustment. The need for such therapy is indicated by the findings of Hauri (1974) and Hauri, Chernik, Hawkins, and Mendels (1974), who studied the sleeping patterns of former depressed patients. While these patients were overtly recovered, they tended to evidence a "depressive life-style" in their dreams; they also showed significantly more sleep disturbances than a matched "normal" control group, including delayed onset of sleep, more REM (rapid eye movement) sleep, and greater night-by-night variability in sleep patterns.

A number of techniques of psychotherapy have been developed particularly for the treatment of depression. The following case of a 37-year-old homemaker who had been depressed since the recent death of her mother will serve as an example. The treatment program was directed toward reinforcing behavior incompatible with depression and relieving feelings of helplessness and hopelessness. The therapist began the program by observing the patient in her home.

"The therapist recorded each instance of 'depressive-like' behavior, such as crying, complaining about somatic symptoms, pacing, and withdrawal. He also noted the consequences of these behaviors. Initially, she had a high rate of depressive

behaviors and it was noted that members of her family frequently responded to them with sympathy, concern, and helpfulness. During this time, her rate of adaptive actions as a housewife and mother were very low, but she did make occasional efforts to cook, clean house, and attend to the children's needs. . . .

"The therapist, in family sessions, instructed her husband and children to pay instant and frequent attention to her coping behavior and to gradually ignore her depressed behavior. They were taught to acknowledge her positive actions with interest, encouragement, and approval. Overall, they were not to decrease the amount of attention focused on the patient but rather switch the contingencies of their attention from 'sick woman' to 'housewife and mother.' Within one week, her depressed behavior decreased sharply and her 'healthy' behavior increased.

"A clinical experiment was then performed to prove the causal link between her behavior and the responses generated in her family. After the 14th day, the therapist instructed the family members to return to providing the patient with attention and solicitude for her complaints. Within three days, she was once again showing a high level of depressive behavior, albeit not as high as initially. When the focus of the family's attentiveness was finally moved back to her coping skills and away from her miserableness, she quickly improved. One year after termination, she was continuing to function well without depressive symptoms." (Liberman & Raskin, 1971, p. 521)

A promising therapeutic innovation has been developed by Beck and his colleagues, whose cognitively oriented views on depression were discussed earlier in the chapter. Their approach involves a highly structured systematic effort at correcting the aberrant cognitions that are presumed to underlie the depressed state. Preliminary work comparing the outcomes of this type of therapy with those of antidepressant medication suggests that specific cognitive therapy may be at least as effective as drugs in alleviating depression (Rush, Beck, Kovacs, & Hollon, 1977). Other cognitive and cognitive behavioral therapies for depressive disorders have been developed at a high rate in recent years and are showing considerable promise (Hollon, 1979). In the overall treatment program, it is important to deal also with unusual stressors in the patient's life, since an unfavorable life situation may lead to a recurrence of the depression as well as necessitating longer treatment.

Proper nursing care is important during the more severe manifestations of depression because depressed patients are frequently very ingenious in their efforts to put an end to their suffering. Despite patients' seemingly earnest assurance that they will do nothing to harm themselves, they may cut their wrists with a small fragment of glass or set fire to their clothing with a cleverly concealed match. Because of the likelihood of suicide attempts, it is considered hazardous for family members to try to care for severely depressed patients at home.

Even without formal therapy, as we have noted, the great majority of manic and depressive patients recover within less than a year. And with modern methods of treatment, the general outlook has become increasingly favorable—so much so that most hospitalized patients can now be discharged within 60 days. While relapses may occur in some instances, these can usually be prevented by maintenance therapy.

The mortality rate for depressive patients appears to be about twice as high as that for the general population, however, because of the higher incidence of suicide (Leonard, 1974; Zung & Green, 1974). Thus while the development of effective drugs and other new approaches to therapy have brought greatly improved outcomes for patients with affective disorders, the need clearly remains for still more effective treatment methods, both immediate and long term. Also, there appears to be a strong need for additional studies of factors that put people at high risk for depressive disorders, and the application of relevant findings to early intervention and prevention.

In this chapter we have dealt with disturbances and disorders of mood. We examined the milder forms of depression, neurotic-level depression, and finally the major affective psychoses, in which mania or depression or both may be involved. We pointed out that when mania is part of the picture, the disorder is considered to be of the bipolar type. These disorders tend to recur, usually with periods of normal behavior in between. While emphasizing the importance of life stress and predisposing personality characteristics, we also noted the growing body of research indicating that neurophysiological and biochemical factors are often significantly involved in the etiology of the more severe forms of affective disorders. With or without treatment, these disorders tend to run their course, but drugs and psychotherapy can usually shorten their duration, and maintenance medication can often prevent their recurrence.

12

The schizophrenias and paranoia

The schizophrenias

Paranoia

As we saw in Chapter 11, the psychotic affective disorders involve chiefly a disturbance of mood; to the extent that disruptions of perceptual, cognitive, and information-processing mechanisms occur in the psychotic affective disorders, they seem secondary to the more primary mood dysfunction. By and large, the opposite is true in schizophrenic and paranoid disorders.

With the schizophrenias and the related paranoid syndromes, we move into a realm of behavioral disorder that represents in many ways the ultimate in psychological breakdown. The symptoms of these disorders include the most extreme to be found in human behavior, and they include virtually all of the pathological processes encountered thus far in our survey plus something more. What that "something more" may be, as we shall see, is not readily grasped or defined, but it is clearly within the psychotic range defined in Chapter 11: the schizophrenic individual's personality is pervasively involved, and there is a more or less gross break with reality as most of us conceive it.

In addition to a temporary worsening of their schizophrenic symptoms under stress, many schizophrenic persons also display other symptomatology from time to time. Frequently they engage in neurotic defense reactions; often they are bothered with psychosomatic ailments of one sort or another, particularly in the early or acute phases of the disorder; often they show pronounced personality or character deviations prior to breakdown; finally, they are capable of extremes in mood that are easily the equal of anything seen in the psychotic affective disorders. As in the case of other disorders, too, strong predispositional elements can often be detected in the backgrounds of these persons, and precipitating stressors of one kind or another can usually be identified. In short, the schizophrenic disorders may truly be said to be the arena in which all the major problems of the mental health disciplines come together.

The schizophrenias

The schizophrenias are a group of psychotic disorders characterized by gross distortions of reality, withdrawal from social interaction, and disorganization and fragmentation of perception, thought, and emotion. While the clinical picture may differ in schizophrenic reactions, the disorganization of experience that typifies acute schizophrenic episodes is well illustrated in the following description:

"Suspicious and frightened, the victim fears he can trust neither his own senses, nor the motives of other people . . . his skin prickles, his head seems to hum, and 'voices' annoy him. Unpleasant odors choke him, his food may have no taste. Bright and colorful visions ranging from brilliant butterflies to dismembered bodies pass before his eyes. Ice clinking in a nearby pitcher seems to be a diabolic device bent on his destruction.

"When someone talks to him, he hears only disconnected words. These words may touch off an old memory or a strange dream. His attention wanders from his inner thoughts to the grotesque way the speaker's mouth moves, or the loud scrape his chair makes against the floor. He cannot understand what the person is trying to tell him, nor why.

"When he tries to speak, his own words sound foreign to him. Broken phrases tumble out over and over again, and somewhat fail to express how frightened and worried he is." (Yolles, 1967, p. 42)

Schizophrenic disorders were at one time attributed to a type of "mental deterioration" beginning early in life. In 1860 the Belgian psychiatrist Morel described the case of a 13-year-old boy who had formerly been the most brilliant pupil in his school but who, over a period of time, lost interest in his studies, became increasingly withdrawn, seclusive, and taciturn, and appeared to have forgotten everything he had learned. He talked frequently of killing his father, and evidenced a kind of inactivity that bordered on stupidity. Morel thought the boy's intellectual, moral, and physical functions had deteriorated as a result of hereditary causes and hence were irrecoverable. He used the term *démence précoce* (mental deterioration at an early age) to describe the condition and to distinguish it from disorders of old age.

The Latin form of this term—*dementia praecox*—was subsequently adopted by the German psychiatrist Kraepelin to refer to a group of rather dissimilar conditions that all seemed to have the feature of mental deterioration beginning early in life. Actually, however, the term was rather misleading, since the dis-

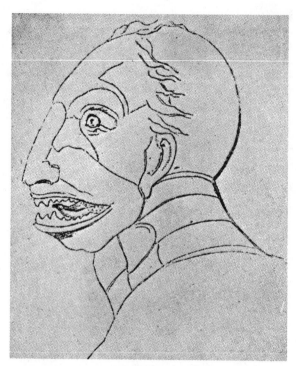

"Ghost of a Flea," a drawing of one of his own hallucinations by William Blake (1757–1827), the English poet and painter. According to Blake, the flea was in his room and told him that fleas contained the damned souls of bloodthirsty men. In both his poetry and his visual art, Blake gave many evidences of schizophrenic ideation (Born, 1946).

order usually becomes apparent not during childhood but during adulthood, and there is no conclusive evidence of permanent mental deterioration.

It remained for a Swiss psychiatrist, Bleuler, to introduce in 1911 a more acceptable descriptive term for this disorder. He used *schizophrenia* (split mind) because he thought the disorder was characterized primarily by disorganization of thought processes, a lack of coherence between thought and emotion, and an inward orientation away from reality. The "splitting" thus does not imply multiple personalities but a splitting within the intellect and between the intellect and emotion.

It is by no means clear that schizophrenia is a unitary process, however. The existence of a single diagnostic label—in this case, *schizophrenia*—does not by itself establish similarity of underlying organization in each

case of schizophrenia, any more than does a medical diagnosis of high blood pressure, which can be due to many different underlying conditions. Thus many clinicians today believe that there may be several schizophrenias, with different causal patterns and dynamics.

Schizophrenic disorders occur in all societies, from the aborigines of the Australian western desert and the remote interior jungles of Malaysia to the most technologically advanced societies. Apparently mental disorders are not simply the result of the jungle being made of concrete.

In the United States the estimated incidence of schizophrenia is about 1 percent of the population, a figure that has been quite stable over time. There are approximately one million *actively* schizophrenic persons in the United States at the present time (Berger, 1978), but only about 600,000 are treated in a typical year. About one-fourth of the patients admitted each year to mental hospitals and clinics are diagnosed as being schizophrenic, and since schizophrenic individuals often require prolonged or repeated hospitalization, they usually constitute about half the patient population for all available mental hospital beds (President's Commission on Mental Health, 1978).

Although schizophrenic disorders sometimes occur during childhood or old age, about three-fourths of all first admissions are between the ages of 15 and 45, with a median age of just over 30. The incidence rate is about the same for males and females. Because of their complexity, their high rate of incidence, especially during the most productive years of life, and their tendency to recur and/or become chronic, the schizophrenias are considered the most serious of all psychotic disorders, as well as among the most baffling.

A case study

We depart somewhat from our usual format in discussing the clinical syndromes in order to capitalize on the pedagogic potential of a unique and uniquely well-documented case study involving the schizophrenic syndrome. It involves a family of six persons—two biological parents and their four, monozygotic, quadruplet daughters—where all four daughters became schizophrenic prior to age 25. Some appreciation of just how remarkable this circumstance is can be derived from the combined improbability of viable quadruplicate births, identical heredity, and perfect concordance for schizophrenia: a fairly liberal estimate is that it would occur once in every one and one-half *billion* births! We are indebted for the thorough knowledge we have of this family to David Rosenthal (1963) and his colleagues, working under the auspices of the National Institute of Mental Health. For obvious reasons, certain specific data, such as names and dates, have been omitted or falsified in the final report, and we shall honor that consideration in our own synopsis. Should the reader be prepared at this point to jump to the conclusion that these are obviously cases of genetically determined disorder, we counsel a more judicious approach until more information is in hand.

Background and early years. Some time in the early 1930s, quadruplet girls were born to Mr. and Mrs. Henry Genain, the product of a marriage occasioned by Mr. Genain's threatening to kill the reluctant Mrs. Genain unless she consented to it. Except for their low birth weights, ranging from Nora's 4 lb., 8 oz., to Hester's 3 lb., the girls appeared to be reasonably normal babies, albeit premature. Hester had to be fitted with a truss (an abdominal compression device) because of a bilateral hernia, but was nevertheless discharged from the hospital with her sisters as basically healthy some six weeks after the birth. These were the only children the Genains ever had, partly because of pronounced difficulties in their sexual relationship.

The most pervasive, if not necessarily the most formative, feature of the girls' early life was their fame. From birth they received a great deal of attention from the media and the public. Early on, in fact, their parents started charging admission (25 cents) to members of the public to visit the home and view the babies, a scheme that terminated when the parents became concerned about the possibility of kidnaping or the transmission of some disease to the children. In subsequent years the children were encouraged in dancing and singing as a team, and they performed often at various functions and at school assemblies. Their fame as performers was apparently limited by a decided lack of talent, although there was once a

suggestion that a Hollywood motion-picture firm might be interested in them; nothing came of this. Partly as a result of their "celebrity" status, the girls tended to stick very closely together for mutual protection; they rebuffed intrusions even from children their own age, with the result that they became social isolates. They were markedly encouraged in this social isolation by their parents, who shared certain peculiar but very strong anxieties about the dangers of "the outside world." Possibly because of irritation from her truss, Hester began to masturbate regularly by the age of three, a habit she continued for many years to the considerable consternation of her parents.

Notwithstanding their genetic identity and physical similarity, the girls were sharply differentiated by their parents virtually from birth. In fact, they were treated as though they were two sets of twins—a superior and talented set consisting of Nora and Myra, and an inferior, problematic set consisting of Iris and Hester—the latter, the "runt of the litter," so to speak, and the one regarded from an early age as being "oversexed." Complying with these parental attributions, the girls did in fact form themselves into two pairs for purposes of mutual support and intimacy-exchange; when threatened from the outside, however, they became a true foursome.

Mr. Genain's derived fame resulted in his being elected (and reelected for more than 20 years) to a minor political office, having been pushed into running by his ambitious wife. His job was not very demanding, and he spent most of his time drinking and hounding the members of his family concerning his various fears and obsessions. Prominent among these were that there would be break-ins at the home unless he patrolled the premises constantly with a loaded gun, and, especially as the girls developed into adolescence, that unless he watched over them with total dedication they would get into sexual trouble or be raped.

In fact, he imposed almost unbelievable restrictions and surveillance on the girls until the point of their breakdowns. By contrast, he was himself sexually promiscuous and is reported to have sexually molested at least two of his daughters; quite possibly Myra, who distanced herself from him with singular persistence, was the only one of the girls to escape his attentions in this respect. Beginning at an early age, and persisting through early adult-hood, Mr. Genain insisted on being present when his daughters dressed and undressed. He also insisted on watching them change their sanitary pads during menstruation. In general, this weak, ineffectual, alcoholic man imposed his will on the remainder of the family through the institution of terror, aided and abetted by his fairly constant drunkenness.

Mr. Genain's preoccupation with sexuality, while extreme and almost preemptive of any-thing else, was at least matched by that of his wife. Mrs. Genain managed to see sexuality and sexual threats in the most innocuous of circumstances, and yet was curiously impervi-ous to certain real sexual phenomena occurring before her eyes, so to speak. When the girls complained to her about Mr. Genain's sexual attentions, she dismissed these happenings with the rationale that Mr. Genain was merely testing their virtue; if they objected to his ad-vances, then clearly all was well! Not that she saw Mr. Genain as a paragon of virtue; on the contrary, she recited his many faults of breed-ing and grossness to anyone who would listen. Nevertheless, she stuck by him to the end (a typically alcoholic end), and by and large confirmed and supported his bizarre construc-tions of reality. Hester, the chronic mastur-bator, was a particular thorn in her side—all the more so when she discovered that, at about age 12, Hester had apparently seduced Iris into the practice of mutual masturbation, which Iris professed to like very much. Apparently unable to think of any more appropriate re-sponse to this dilemma, the parents—on the advice of an obviously unqualified physician—forced the two girls to submit to clitoral cir-cumcisions, a measure whose drastic quality was exceeded only by its lack of success in alter-ing the offending behavior. In general, how-ever, Mrs. Genain enjoyed the status accorded her as the mother of quadruplets, and she re-mained unfailingly involved in the girls' lives in a sort of overwhelming and intrusive way. Most of her affection, such as it was, was re-served for the "good" quads, Nora and Myra.

Adolescence, young adulthood, and breakdown.
Except for their extreme social isolation, the girls had a relatively uneventful junior high school experience. They were re-garded by their teachers as conforming, hard-

working and "nice," except for some competi-tion among them in respect to grades and adult approval. Hester clearly lagged behind the others, and Iris could not quite keep up with the remaining two in academic performance. Essentially the same pattern continued into high school. In the summer preceding the girls' senior year, Hester, whose behavior had be-come somewhat peculiar and who was appar-ently suffering from some type of psychoso-matic gastrointestinal distress, finally became disturbed to the point that her parents could hardly manage her. She was very tempera-mental, often did not seem to know what she was doing, was destructive of household fur-nishings, would tear both her own and her sis-ters' clothing, and on one occasion struck Nora with such force as to render her unconscious. Hester had just turned 18; she never thereafter regained a full measure of effective mental functioning.

The other three girls completed their senior year of high school, engaging in a kind of con-spiracy of silence regarding the missing Hes-ter, who remained at home. Outwardly, they appeared to be normal adolescents, although they were not permitted to have boyfriends, and they continued to have various physical difficulties, including menstrual irregularities and persistent enuresis (bed-wetting). Follow-ing their graduations, they obtained modest employment as office workers. However, they continued to be constantly hounded and spied upon by their suspicious father, lest they be-come involved in sexual liaisons. They were not permitted to date. Of the three, Myra main-tained the most independence, essentially defy-ing her father's edict that she not go out at night to meetings and the like.

None of the three young women was com-fortable in the world of work, feeling in-adequate to the responsibilities heaped upon them by allegedly insensitive bosses. Nora was the first to evidence unusual "nervousness," and in her twentieth year began to have a series of vague physical complaints. She even-tually quit her job and took to her bed at home, gradually becoming more disturbed. She would stand on her knees and elbows until they be-came irritated and bled, began to walk and talk in her sleep, and moaned and groaned a great deal, especially at mealtime. Her behavior con-tinued to deteriorate until, at age 22, she underwent her first of several hospital admissions with the diagnosis of schizophrenia.

In the meantime, Iris had likewise become increasingly disturbed, also resigning from her job. She was troubled by "spastic colon," vomiting, insomnia, and the belief that people were paying her undue attention. In fact, Mr. Genain was at the time paying her a great deal of attention, which disturbed her greatly. Within several months after Nora's first admission, Iris "just went to pieces." She screamed, was markedly agitated, complained of hearing voices and of people fighting, and drooled at meals, being unable to swallow anything but liquids. She, too, was hospitalized for the first of many admissions toward the end of her twenty-second year. The diagnosis was schizophrenia.

Myra did not break down until her twenty-fourth year. Onset was similar to that of her sisters: vomiting, panic, insomnia, and waking up at night screaming. Myra resisted hospitalization at this time, and in fact was not hospitalized until the entire family was shortly thereafter moved to the Clinical Center of the National Institute of Mental Health (NIMH), where, as a unit, they underwent the lengthy and detailed study of which this history is one product. On arrival at the Center, Myra was found to be autistic, disordered in thought, and markedly impaired in judgment and reality testing. She was diagnosed as schizophrenic.

It may be significant that in each of the cases of Nora, Iris, and Myra, deterioration began shortly following an incident in which a man had made rather insistent "improper advances." In paradoxical but characteristic fashion, both parents had minimized the significance of these incidents when the girls complained.

Course and outcome.   By the time of their arrival at the Clinical Center at age 24, Nora had undergone three separate hospital admissions and Iris five. Hester had somehow escaped this fate, although she was often bizarre and frankly psychotic at home. With all four of the daughters simultaneously disturbed in varying degrees, the home atmosphere had become truly chaotic.

Once at the NIMH, the sisters were offered varied forms of high-grade treatment and care, including the new antipsychotic medications

that had recently become available. They remained at NIMH for three years, Myra being the only one capable of attaining a sustainable discharge. The other three sisters had to be transferred to a state hospital at the end of their NIMH stay. Mr. Genain died of liver disease in the interim.

It is important to note that, while the earliest symptoms of the quads were similar in certain respects, the courses and outcomes of their disorders differed markedly and to some extent in ways that could have been predicted. The most serious and "regressed" of the types of schizophrenia is *hebephrenic*. In the various diagnoses accorded to them in the course of their hospitalizations, Nora and Myra were never so diagnosed, although Nora was sometimes regarded as having "hebephrenic features." By contrast, Iris and Hester moved through the "milder" catatonic and undifferentiated phases of disorganization into full hebephrenic disorganization. The quads' outcomes show a corresponding pattern. At last report, Myra was working steadily, married, and doing well. Nora was making a marginal adjustment outside of the hospital. Iris was still fluctuating between periods of severe disturbance and periods of relative lucidity in which she could manage brief stays outside of the hospital. Hester remained continuously hospitalized in a condition of severe hebephrenic psychosis and was considered essentially a "hopeless case." Thus, the quads manifested the full range of possible outcomes associated with a schizophrenic breakdown.

Interpretive comment.   We have here, then, four genetically identical young women, all of whom experienced schizophrenic disorders. The disorders, however, were very different in severity, chronicity, and eventual outcome. Quite obviously, these differences must be ascribed to differences in the environments the twins experienced, including their intrauterine environments, which presumably contributed to their modest variations detectable at birth. Clearly Hester, in relative parental disfavor from the beginning, faced the harshest environmental conditions, followed closely by her "twin," Iris. The outcome for these young women was one of unmitigated disaster. Myra was perhaps the most favored youngster and clearly the one who experienced the least noxious parental input. Nora was a close second in this respect but had the misfortune of being her deranged father's "favorite." Nora, and especially Myra, despite heredity identical to that of Hester and Iris, escaped the terrible fate of their less fortunate sisters. We see here the enormous power of environmental forces in determining destiny.

But let us look again. The fact is that we have four genetically identical individuals, all of whom became schizophrenic within a period of six years—three of them within a period of some two years. Is this not a compelling case for genetic determination? It is, and indeed there is ample evidence, in the family background of at least *Mr.* Genain, that he harbored some very pathogenic genes that were probably passed on to his daughters. On the other hand, we must raise the question as to what would have happened to these girls even if *no* pathogenic genes were involved. As Rosenthal (1963) points out, these parents failed spectacularly in the most elementary tasks of parenthood. Can we imagine that the Genain sisters would have been reasonably well-adjusted had they possessed no defective genes? That seems very unlikely.

In the final analysis, it makes sense to conclude that *both* heredity and environment, operating in some complex interaction, contributed to the Genain sisters' problems. In this instance, unfortunately, it is difficult to make even an estimate of the relative magnitude of the two types of influence. In some other instances of schizophrenic disorder, one can make a shrewd guess—based on genetic history, developmental experience, and the like—about the relative contribution from each of these two broad sources of behavioral variation. As we have seen, however, and as we shall see again in this chapter, the central fact always is the interaction between the two.

We shall have occasion to refer to the Genains from time to time in the pages that follow.

Clinical picture in schizophrenia

Sometimes schizophrenic disorders develop slowly and insidiously. Here the early clinical picture may be dominated by seclusiveness, gradual lack of interest in the surrounding world, excessive daydreaming, blunting of affect, and mildly inappropriate responses. This pattern is referred to as *process schizophrenia,* and the outcome is considered generally unfavorable—partly because the need for treatment is usually not recognized until the behavior pattern has become firmly entrenched. In many cases, however, schizophrenia has a sudden onset, typically marked by intense emotional turmoil and a nightmarish sense of confusion. This pattern, which usually appears to be related to specific precipitating stresses, is referred to as *reactive schizophrenia.* Here the symptoms usually clear up in a matter of weeks, though in some cases an acute episode is the prelude to a more chronic pattern.

This process-reactive distinction, however, should be viewed not as a dichotomy, but rather as a continuum. In fact, it would not be wholly inaccurate to view the continuum as normally distributed in the familiar bell-shaped curve, with relatively few patients falling at either the process or reactive extremes and most falling somewhere in the middle. Of the Genain quadruplets, Hester—who never seemed quite as well off mentally as her sisters and who seemed to move in imperceptible steps toward increasing deterioration—would be considered a relatively pure *process* type. By contrast, Myra, the least disturbed before her breakdown, the last to succumb, and the only one to regain effective control of her life, would be considered a relatively more *reactive* case.

In both process and reactive schizophrenia, specific syptoms are many and vary greatly from one individual to another, as well as with time. The basic experience in schizophrenia, however, seems to be one of disorganization in perception, thought, and emotion.

The DSM-III classification summarizes a number of criteria characteristic of schizophrenic disorders, including the following:

Disorganization of a previous level of functioning. This is perhaps the cardinal sign of schizophrenic breakdown; it distinguishes the schizophrenias from various developmental anomalies, such as infantile autism, in which the person has never attained a suitable degree of integrated behavioral functioning. The impairment always occurs in areas of routine daily functioning, such as work, social relations, and self-care, such that observers note that the person is not him- or herself any more. (See HIGHLIGHT on this page.)

Disturbance of language and communication.

Often referred to as "formal thought disorder," this, too, is conventionally considered a prime indicator of the presence of a schizophrenic disorder. Basically, there is a failure to conform to the semantic and syntactic rules governing verbal communication in the individual's known language—*not* attributable to low intelligence, poor education, or cultural deprivation. Meehl (1962) aptly referred to the process as one of "cognitive slippage"; others have referred to it as "derailment of associations." However labeled, the phenomenon is readily recognized by experienced clinicians: the patient seems to be employing words in common usage and in combinations that sound communicative, but in the final analysis the listener becomes aware of understanding little or nothing of what has been said. Meehl cited as an example the statement, "I'm growing my father's hair." (See HIGHLIGHT on page 402.)

Content of thought.

Disturbances in the content of thought usually involve certain rather standard types of delusion. Prominent among these are the false beliefs that one's thoughts, feelings, or actions are being controlled by external agents, that one's private thoughts are being broadcast indiscriminately to others, that thoughts are being inserted involuntarily by alien forces, or that some mysterious agency has robbed one of one's thoughts. Other absurd delusions of varied content are also commonly observed, including delusions of grotesque bodily changes.

Perception.

Major perceptual disruption often accompanies the manifestations already indicated. A breakdown in perceptual filtering is frequently observed, wherein the patient seems unable to sort out and properly dispose of the great mass of sensory information to which all of us are exposed in most waking moments. As a result, everything "gets through," overwhelming the meager resources the person has for appropriate information-processing. This

HIGHLIGHT

Regression to "primary" thought processes in schizophrenia

Some investigators, particularly those adhering to the psychoanalytic perspective, have emphasized regression to more primitive levels of thinking as a primary feature of schizophrenia. In essence, more highly differentiated and reality oriented "secondary" thought processes, which follow the rules of logic and take external reality into consideration, are replaced by "primary" thought processes, which involve illogical ideas, fantasy, and magical thinking. Presumably, such primary thought processes characterize the thinking of children. They live in a world that is partly fantasy and partly real, and develop all manner of fantastic notions about things and events around them. They talk to imaginary playmates, personify inanimate objects, and attribute various powers to these figments of their imagination. Not uncommonly, they feel that they are the center of the world and develop ideas of omnipotence.

The regressed schizophrenic individual does not, however, perceive, think, and feel in ways precisely like those of a child. For example, children, unlike schizophrenic individuals, can usually distinguish between their fantasies and the world of reality, and most children, despite their fantasies, imperfect logic, and lack of perspective, are clearly not schizophrenic. Thus it would appear that regression in schizophrenia does not represent a return to childhood, but rather a defensive pattern that enables the individual to assume a position of dependency and hence avoid problems and responsibilities that he or she perceives as overwhelming.

point is well illustrated in the following excerpts from statements of schizophrenic persons:

"I feel like I'm too alert . . . everything seems to come pouring in at once . . . I can't seem to keep anything out . . . ."

"My nerves seem supersensitive . . . objects seem brighter . . . noises are louder . . . my feelings are so intense. . . . things seem so vivid and they come at me like a flood from a broken dam."

"It seems like nothing ever stops. Thoughts just keep coming in and racing round in my head . . .

Schizophrenic writings

The personality decompensation in psychotic reactions is frequently manifested in the content and form of patients' letters and other spontaneous writings. These examples clearly reveal the "loosening" and deviations of thought, the distortion of affect, and the lowered contact with reality so common among schizophrenic individuals. The postcard is a reproduction of a card sent by a paranoid schizophrenic man.

> To: The football department and its members present and future
>   The University of New Mexico, Albuquerque, N. M.
>
> I depend on correct, honest supplementation of this card by telepathy as a thing which will make clear the meaning of this card. There exists a Playing of The Great Things, the correct, the constructive, world or universe politics, out-in-the-open telepathy, etc. According to the Great Things this playing is the most feasible thing of all; but it is held from newspaper advertising and correct, honest public world recognition, its next step, by telepathic forces (it seems), physical dangers, and lack of money. Over 10,000 cards and letters on this subject have been sent to prominent groups and persons all over the world. Correct, honest contact with the honest, out-in-the-open world. This line of thought, talk, etc. rule. The plain and frank. Strangers. The Great Things and opposites idea. References: In the telepathic world the correct playings. Please save this card for a history record since it is rare and important for history.

The handwritten excerpts are from a letter written by an 18-year-old woman, also diagnosed as paranoid schizophrenic. As is apparent from the first and last parts of the letter, shown here, the handwriting is of two quite different types, suggestive of the writer's emotional conflict and personality disorganization. Lewinson (1940) included this letter in her study of handwriting characteristics of different types of psychotic patients. Among such patients generally, she found that handwriting typically showed abnormal rhythmic disturbances, with rigidity or extreme irregularity in height, breadth, or depth.

and getting broken up . . . sort of into pieces of thoughts and images . . . like tearing up a picture. And everything is out of control . . . I can't seem to stop it."

It is estimated that approximately 50 percent of patients diagnosed as schizophrenic experience this breakdown of perceptual selectivity during the onset of their disorders (Freedman & Chapman, 1973). Other even more dramatic perceptual phenomena include hallucinations—perceptions for which there are no discernible external stimuli. Hallucinations in the schizophrenias are normally in the auditory mode, although they can also be visual and even olfactory. The typical hallucination is one in which a voice or voices keep up a running commentary on the individual's behaviors or thoughts. Often the voices are accusatory.

Affect.   The schizophrenic syndromes often include an element of clearly inappropriate emotion, or *affect*. In the more severe or chronic cases, the picture is one of emotional shallowness or "blunting": on casual observation, the person appears virtually not to have emotions in his or her behavioral repertoire, such that even the most compelling and dramatic events produce at most an intellectual recognition of what is happening. In other instances, particularly in the acute phases, the patient may show very strong affect, but the type of emotion is discordant with the situation or with the content of his or her thoughts. For example, such a patient may laugh uproariously upon receipt of the news of a parent's death.

Sense of self.   The schizophrenic person often is perplexed about his or her identity, including gender identity, and, in addition, frequently is confused about the boundaries separating the self from the rest of the world. The latter confusion is often associated with frightening "cosmic" or "oceanic" feelings of being somehow intimately tied up with universal powers, and appears to be related to ideas of external control and similar delusions.

Volition.   Almost universally, disruption of goal-directed activity initiated by the individual occurs, whether in apparent motivation or inability to carry through a course of action.

For example, the person may be quite unable to marshal sufficient resources to maintain minimum standards of personal hygiene.

Relationship to the external world.   Ties to the external world of reality are almost invariably loosened in the schizophrenic disorders, and in extreme instances the withdrawal may be nearly complete. This detachment is usually accompanied by the elaboration of an inner world in which the person develops illogical and fantastic ideational constructions having little or no relationship to reality as perceived by others. Since the days of Bleuler, this process has generally been referred to as *autism*.

Motor behavior.   Various peculiarities of movement are sometimes observed in the schizophrenias; indeed, this is the chief and defining characteristic of the catatonic subtype of schizophrenia, of which more will be said later in the chapter. These motor disturbances range from an excited sort of hyperactivity to a marked decrease in all movement or an apparent motor clumsiness. Also included here are various forms of rigid posturing, ritualistic mannerisms, and bizarre grimacing.

Associated features.   Finally, the DSM-III classification notes that "almost any psychiatric symptom" may be present in a schizophrenic disorder; likewise, many of the same symptoms described above are present in other disorders. It may be surmised that such a circumstance will often lead to problems in differential diagnosis; this is, in fact, a very common problem when patients present a mixed symptom picture.

Various other primary features have also been ascribed to schizophrenic disorders by different clinicians. Among these is *anhedonia,* defined by Meehl (1962) as "a marked, widespread, and refractory defect in pleasure capacity which, once you learn how to examine for it, is one of the most consistent and dramatic behavioral signs of the disease" (p. 206). Another primary sign of schizophrenia, according to both Meehl (1962) and Bleuler (1950) is that of profound ambivalence, with conflicting motives, thoughts, and feelings. Most of us experience some mixed feelings toward our loved ones from time to time, but the positive and

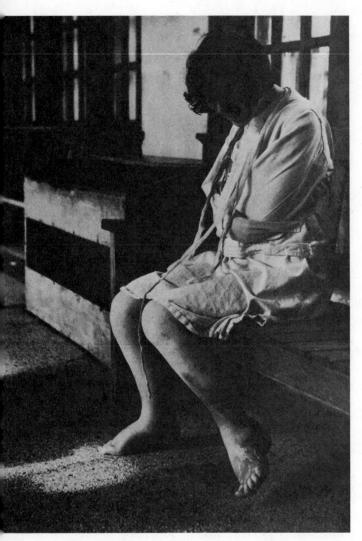

In some schizophrenic episodes a person may experience extreme excitement and engage in impulsive destructive acts directed toward self or others. At one time such people were routinely placed in straitjackets, but improved methods of treatment have now made such crude procedures unnecessary.

negative typically succeed each other and do not occur at the same time, at least not consciously.

In any case, it will be clear that the clinical picture in schizophrenia often includes bizarre elements that may be unintelligible to either the individual or observers. A patient may show peculiarities of movement, gesture, and expression; act out inappropriate sexual and other fantasies; or simply sit apathetically star-ing into space. We shall elaborate on these and other behavior anomalies in describing the various types of schizophrenia.

On the other hand, not all the symptoms occur in every case. There is, in fact, no constant, single, universally accepted "sign" of the presence of a schizophrenic process. Thus the symptom picture may differ markedly from one schizophrenic patient to another. Also, the symptom picture may change greatly over time, sometimes even as a result of the individual's being labeled as a schizophrenic and given a "sick" role to which he or she then conforms. Most schizophrenic patients "fade in and out of reality" as a function of their own inner state and the environmental situation. A patient may be in "good contact" one day and evidence delusions and hallucinations the next. Likewise, an acute shizophrenic reaction may clear up fairly rapidly or may progress to a chronic condition.

One consequence of the fact that "almost any psychiatric symptom" may be evidenced in a schizophrenic reaction is that virtually anyone could deliberately perform in such a way as to be diagnosed as schizophrenic. This was one of the truly unassailable points made in Rosenhan's (1973) controversial study mentioned in Chapter 1, in which he and several students got themselves hospitalized as schizophrenic by reporting hallucinations. We suspect that few people would be inclined to take advantage of this opportunity voluntarily, but we will note in a later section that some, in fact, do.

Types of schizophrenia

The American Psychiatric Association's DSM-III classification lists five formal subtypes of schizophrenia, which are summarized in the HIGHLIGHT on page 405. We shall focus on four of these in our present discussion: undifferentiated, paranoid. catatonic, and disorganized (hebephrenic). Of these, the undifferentiated and paranoid types are the most common.

Undifferentiated type. As the term implies, this is something of a "wastebasket" category. The individual so diagnosed meets the usual criteria for being schizophrenic—including (in varying combinations) delusions, hallucinations, thought disorder, and gross

HIGHLIGHT

Types of schizophrenia

Undifferentiated type	A pattern of symptoms in which there is a rapidly changing mixture of all or most of the primary indicators of schizophrenia. Commonly observed are indications of perplexity, confusion, emotional turmoil, delusions of reference, excitement, dreamlike autism, depression, and fear. Most often, this picture is seen in patients who are in the process of breaking down and becoming schizophrenic. However, it is also seen when major changes are occurring in the adjustive demands impinging on a person with an already-established schizophrenic psychosis. In such cases it frequently foreshadows an impending change to another primary schizophrenic subtype.
Paranoid type	A symptom picture dominated by absurd, illogical, and changeable delusions, frequently accompanied by vivid hallucinations, with a resulting impairment of critical judgment and erratic, unpredictable, and occasionally dangerous behavior. In chronic cases, there is usually less disorganization of behavior than in other types of schizophrenia, and less extreme withdrawal from social interaction.
Catatonic type	Often characterized by alternating periods of extreme withdrawal and extreme excitement, although in some cases one or the other reaction predominates. In the withdrawal reaction there is a sudden loss of all animation and a tendency to remain motionless for hours or even days, in a stereotyped position. The clinical picture may undergo an abrupt change, with excitement coming on suddenly, wherein the individual may talk or shout incoherently, pace rapidly, and engage in uninhibited, impulsive, and frenzied behavior. In this state, the individual may be dangerous.
Disorganized (hebephrenic) type	Usually occurs at an earlier age than most other types of schizophrenia, and represents a more severe disintegration of the personality. Emotional distortion and blunting typically are manifested in inappropriate laughter and silliness, peculiar mannerisms, and bizarre, often obscene, behavior.
Residual type	Mild indications of schizophrenia shown by individuals in remission following a schizophrenic episode.

bizarreness—but does not clearly fit into one of the other subtypes because of a mixed symptom picture. Persons in the acute, early phases of a schizophrenic breakdown frequently exhibit undifferentiated symptoms, as do those who are in transitional phases from one to another of the standard subtypes, which in fact happens rather often. Each of the Genain sisters was given an undifferentiated diagnosis at least once, and all but Myra received such a diagnosis on several different occasions.

The case of David F. illustrates the onset of an undifferentiated schizophrenic episode (Bowers, 1965). David felt great apprehension about his future as he approached the end of his undergraduate days. He also felt inadequate in his relationship with his girlfriend, Laura—a relationship characterized by emotionally charged separations and reconciliations, as well as by sexual experimentation, in which David frequently doubted his sexual adequacy. When Laura dated another boy and refused to tell David the details, David thought the date had involved intercourse, and he wrote a vindictive poem in which he called Laura a whore. After mailing the poem he felt guilty, and he was quite disturbed to find that his best friend sided with Laura. David began to stay in his room more, attending only a few classes.

These excerpts from David's diary were written shortly before his hospitalization.

". . . and there's old Hawthorne's bosom serpent for you eating away hissing all night I lie there and I lie there and think and think and think all the time trying not to think I think anyway or reminisce rather (delightful pastime) until pow I feel like the top of my head blows off and I smash my fist into something and begin all over again like a one cycle engine." (p. 348)

"Tuesday, March 10, 10 P.M. I can't cope, I can't come to grips . . . it's Hawthorne's disease blazing away, red guilt or little stringy black warts (they're growing with a virulence I swear I never noticed before) . . . music helps a bit and I've conducted the Eroica all over the room three times already today, waving my arms and occasionally hitting things . . . all very dramatic . . . to think I worried myself about sleeping too much last fall! I've given the jargon a once over; it stems from incest drives, castration fears, masturbation complexes, homosexual doubts, oedipal fixations bullshit bullshit it was around before the jargon and its got me . . . already at table I've been making curious unconscious slips as if the synapses suddenly rot away and I come disconnected its all right its all right I'm going to be a lawyer and make lots of money and grow up to be as weak as my father as torn as my mother look ahead !!" (p. 349)

"Midnight Tuesday. . . . Boy, that Nathan and Laura business really pulled the cork I'm bad or mad or just dull? Down on my knees before the crescent moon I got my pants dirty. This is undoubtedly one of the most prolix records of a scarringover process (I'm sealing like one of those puncture proof tires, but in slow motion) I should be back to my habitual state of callousness in a couple of days with no apparent damage, maybe I can even go on staving off like this ('a poem is a momentary stay against confusion" Frost . . . this is quite a poem) till I die." (p. 351)

"Thursday, March 12, 11 A.M. I'm out! I'm through . . . boomed out of the tunnel sometime last night and it's raining stars. . . . whooey . . . its nice out there's time for everything. . . . I can do it I did it and if it happens again I'll do it again twice as hard I got a dexamyl high going and I'm not on dexamyl and I've been up for forty eight or more hours and I'm giddygiddygiddy and I took a test this morning and it was on Voltaire and I kicked him a couple of good ones for being down on Pascal that poor bastard with his shrivelled body and bottomless abysess they're not bottomless!! You get down far enough and it gets thick enough and black enough and then you claw claw claw your way out and pretty soon you're on top

again. And I licked it by myself, all alone. No pandering psychiatrists or priests or friends by myself. Now, I must admit I'm a little leery; I dashed back to the typewriter to give it form to write it down and sew it in my vest like Pascal so if the Thing hits me again I'll have this in my vest and I'll kick it in the teeth again but Pascal saw God and yet still it hit him again . . . will it hit me again? Who cares . . . I just sat in on one of those weddings of the soul and I tooted tooted . . . I don't care I can use it I can run on it it will be my psychic gasoline now I don't have to sleep sleep all the time to get away with it . . . but if I lose my typewriter?" (p. 351)

"Saturday, March 14, 11 A.M. . . . Falling asleep last night a thousand million thoughts bubbled then the number the age 18 what happened when I was 18? (my stomach hurts . . . it really physically does . . . that blue bear has all kinds of tricks . . . I'm going out for coffee) Well I DO have to go out to get some money but I MUST be merciless with the blue bear. He has no quarter for me. . . . and not scare myself with eery consequences . . . the newspaper odds are AGAINST automobile deaths, that was the resistance mechanism trying to stop me again I'm hot on your tail blue bear that doesn't mean anything what does that mean it means that I'm feeling the denied homosexual instincts, feeling the woman in me and getting over her that's it that's what Faulkner's bear was a woman I have the quotes up on my wall I wrote them down a week ago. . . . woman is a bear you must kill the bear to be a man no that isn't what I've got on my wall the quotes go 'Anyone could be upset by his first lion." (p. 356)

David was hospitalized four days after writing this. His experiences illustrate well the massive breakdown of filtering, the panic at loss of control, and the desperate attempts to understand what is going on that are typical in early undifferentiated schizophrenia.

Fortunately, like David, most patients recover from such acute undifferentiated episodes within a period of weeks or months. However, recurrent episodes are not uncommon in this type of disorder, especially in the absence of vigorous follow-up treatment. Myra Genain's breakdown was similar to David's, but she required several years of psychotherapy to ensure a lasting recovery. In some few instances, treatment efforts prove of little or no avail, and the early undifferentiated disorder slides inexorably into a more chronic phase, typically developing into more specific subtype symptoms.

Paranoid type.   Formerly about one-half of all schizophrenic first admissions to mental hospitals and clinics were of the paranoid type. In recent years, however, the incidence of the paranoid type has shown a substantial decrease, while the undifferentiated type has shown a marked increase.

Frequently paranoid-type patients show a history of growing suspiciousness and of severe difficulties in interpersonal relationships. The eventual symptom picture is dominated by absurd, illogical, and changeable delusions. Persecutory delusions are the most frequent and may involve a wide range of ideas and all sorts of plots. The individual may become highly suspicious of relatives or associates and may complain of being watched, followed, poisoned, talked about, or influenced by electrical devices rigged up by "enemies."

All the attention patients receive may lead them to believe that they must possess remarkable qualities or be some great person. Why else would their enemies persecute them so? Consequently, they may develop delusions of grandeur and believe that they are the world's greatest economist or philosopher, or some prominent person of the past, such as Napoleon, the Virgin Mary, or even Christ. These delusions are frequently accompanied by vivid auditory, visual, and other hallucinations. Patients may hear singing, or God speaking, or the voices of their enemies, or they may see angels or feel electric rays piercing their bodies at various points.

The individual's behavior becomes centered around these delusions and hallucinations, resulting in loss of critical judgment and in erratic, unpredictable behavior. In response to a command from a "voice," such an individual may break furniture or commit other violent acts. Occasionally paranoid schizophrenic patients can be dangerous, as when they attack people they are convinced have been persecuting them. In general, they show less extreme withdrawal from the outside world than individuals with most other types of schizophrenia.

The following conversation between a doctor and a patient diagnosed as chronic paranoid schizophrenic illustrates well the illogical, delusional picture, together with continued attention to external data that are misinterpreted, which these individuals experience.

Dr.: What's your name?
Pt.: Who are you?
Dr.: I'm a doctor. Who are you?
Pt.: I can't tell you who I am.
Dr.: Why can't you tell me?
Pt.: You wouldn't believe me.
Dr.: What are you doing here?
Pt.: Well, I've been sent here to thwart the Russians. I'm the only one in the world who knows how to deal with them. They got their spies all around here though to get me, but I'm smarter than any of them.
Dr.: What are you going to do to thwart the Russians?
Pt.: I'm organizing.
Dr.: Whom are you going to organize?
Pt.: Everybody. I'm the only man in the world who can do that, but they're trying to get me. But I'm going to use my atomic bomb media to blow them up.
Dr.: You must be a terribly important person then.
Pt.: Well, of course.
Dr.: What do you call yourself?
Pt.: You used to know me as Franklin D. Roosevelt.
Dr.: Isn't he dead?
Pt.: Sure he's dead, but I'm alive.
Dr.: But you're Franklin D. Roosevelt?
Pt.: His spirit. He, God, and I figured this out. And now I'm going to make a race of healthy people. My agents are lining them up. Say, who are you?
Dr.: I'm a doctor here.
Pt.: You don't look like a doctor. You look like a Russian to me.
Dr.: How can you tell a Russian from one of your agents?
Pt.: I read eyes. I get all my signs from eyes. I look into your eyes and get all my signs from them.
Dr.: Do you sometimes hear voices telling you someone is a Russian?
Pt.: No, I just look into eyes. I got a mirror here to look into my own eyes. I know everything that's going on. I can tell by the color, by the way it's shaped.
Dr.: Did you have any trouble with people before you came here?
Pt.: Well, only the Russians. They were trying to surround me in my neighborhood. One day they tried to drop a bomb on me from the fire escape.
Dr.: How could you tell it was a bomb?
Pt.: I just knew.

Although there is considerable disorganization in paranoid schizophrenia, it is not so extreme as to cause the person to give up attempts to understand and deal with life problems. Interestingly, it is often the case that the person developing a paranoid reaction has exhibited unusual intelligence before the breakdown. A case cited by Enders and Flinn (1962)—which represents a typical paranoid schizophrenic reaction—will help fill in the symptom picture for this reaction type. It is a particularly interesting case, since it involves an officer in the Air Force, whose rigorous selection and training procedures screen out individuals with conspicuous emotional difficulties. In addition, the patient had had an excellent service record as a pilot and had tolerated severe combat stress.

"The case to be reported occurred in a 41-year-old command pilot with 7,500 hours, who had flown 135 combat missions . . . . At the time of his illness, he was a chief pilot in a command headquarters. He was an excellent pilot . . . and had consistently received superior ratings because of his conscientious and dependable performance. The overt onset of his illness was related to a period of TDY [temporary tour of duty] at a conference where flight procedures on a new type aircraft were being drafted. However, in retrospect, it was learned that for several weeks he had been preoccupied and upset, had sensed that he could read other people's minds by radio waves, and suspected those with whom he worked of being 'queer.'

"While at the conference, he developed ideas of reference, believing that certain comments which his companions made, or which he heard over the radio, had hidden meanings and were directed toward him. For example, when the conferees spoke of 'take-off,' he did not know whether they were referring to an airplane or a woman, and suspected they were suggesting he should have an illicit sexual relationship. He developed the delusional idea that his associates were trying to 'teach' him something, and puzzled them several times when he confronted them with a demand that they tell him openly whatever they wanted him to learn. They became further concerned when he became increasingly upset, tearful and incoherent, and when he did not improve after several days of 'rest' at his brother's home, he was admitted to the hospital.

"On admission, he was suspicious of those about him, wondering whether they were dope-peddlers or communists, and he refused to talk to people who could not assure him they were cleared for top secret. He believed that he was accused of taking dope, that there were concealed microphones about the ward, and he had hallucinations consisting of voices which accused him of being 'queer.' He was often apprehensive and tearful, but this alternated with periods when he was inappropriately jovial. He was oriented in all spheres, and physical and neurological exams were entirely normal.

"A review of the patient's past history revealed no other evidence of emotional disturbance. He was the second of four children of a strict, moralistic, financially successful farm family. He did well in school and one year of college, but always felt inadequate in comparison with his peers. . . . He had been married for 18 years and had five children. He used alcohol only rarely, and there was no evidence that toxic or exogenous factors could have been implicated in his psychosis.

"The patient received psychotherapy and began to improve within a few days after admission. For this reason, no drug or other somatic treatment was instituted. He continued to improve over the course of the next several weeks and seemed greatly relieved after telling of an isolated extramarital adventure during the TDY. He gradually gained insight into the unreality of his experiences and was discharged from the hospital after one month."

[Following his discharge from the hospital, the officer was assigned to duties associated with supply and ground training, which he handled without difficulty. Despite his apparent recovery, however, some residuals of his previous thought disturbance remained in the background.]

". . . He wondered at times whether he had not been partly right about the events on TDY, and whether his fellow conferees had not been playing a practical joke on him. He had recently considered going to his Wing Commanding Officer to ask whether the experiences had been part of some kind of 'test' of his mental stability, but had decided against this because it might create an unfavorable impression if he were being tested. He had decided that whatever had happened, it was best forgotten, and through the use of this suppressive mechanism had continued to function effectively. Because of his clear-cut history of a psychotic disorder without an underlying organic basis, as well as the evidence of a continuing minimal thinking disorder, return to flying status was not considered to be consistent with flying safety." (pp. 730–31)

In commenting on this case, Enders and Flinn emphasized the patient's lifelong rigid, moralistic code, which made him unable to tolerate an impulse toward promiscuous behavior. As a result, he projected this unethical impulse to outside agencies; he now misconstrued comments heard on the radio or made by his companions as suggesting illicit activities.

The typical paranoid schizophrenic patient is in some basic sense different from his or her more deteriorated cohorts, although no more able to "make it" successfully in normal social interactions. While paranoid schizophrenia may become chronic, the patient so affected rarely undergoes the pronounced regression and deterioration found in other forms of chronic schizophrenia. It is as though the paranoid resolution protects the patient from more gross forms of disorganization of thought. Paranoid forms of thought, of course, are by no means limited to schizophrenic or even psychotic persons and do have the adaptive merit of providing a transfer-of-blame mechanism whereby personal failings are attributed to external forces or conditions with the result that the individual's self-esteem can remain high (see HIGHLIGHT on page 410).

Interestingly, the diagnosis of paranoid schizophrenia never occurred in the 43 separate diagnostic appraisals accorded the Genain sisters during the course of their contact with mental health professionals up to the point of Rosenthal's (1963) report. Perhaps a negative identification with their very paranoid parents forestalled such a development.

Catatonic type. Catatonic reactions often make their appearance with dramatic suddenness, but usually the patient has shown a background of eccentric behavior, often accompanied by some degree of withdrawal from reality. Though at one time very common in Europe and North America, catatonic reactions have seemingly become less frequent in recent years.

The central feature of catatonia is the pronounced motor symptoms, either of an excited or a stuporous type, which sometimes make for difficulty in differentiating this condition from a psychotic affective disorder. As in the case of the Genains, all of whom had early diagnoses of catatonia, the clinical picture is often an early manifestation of a disorder that will become chronic and intractable unless the underlying process is somehow arrested.

Violence is not uncommon in the excited catatonic patient. Some catatonic patients alternate between periods of extreme withdrawal and extreme excitement, but in most cases one reaction or the other is predominant. In a study of 250 patients diagnosed as suffering from catatonic schizophrenia, Morrison (1973) found that 110 were predominantly withdrawn, 67 were predominantly excited, and 73 were considered "mixed." No significant differences were found between these groups with

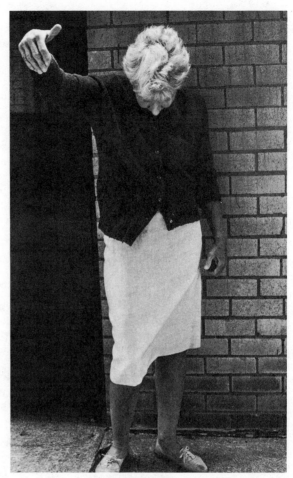

With her arm raised in a rigid, uncomfortable pose, a woman diagnosed as catatonic schizophrenic stands silent and motionless, apparently oblivious to her surroundings. Catatonic schizophrenic patients may alternate between periods of extreme withdrawal and extreme excitement, but in most cases one reaction or the other predominates.

regard to age, sex, or education.

In the withdrawal reaction there is a loss of all animation and a tendency to remain motionless in a rigid, stereotyped position—mute and staring into space. The same position may be maintained for hours or even days, and the hands and feet may become blue and swollen because of the immobility. One patient felt that he had to hold his hand out flat because the forces of "good" and "evil" were waging a "war of the worlds" on his hand, and if he moved it, he might tilt the precarious balance in favor of

An assassin diagnosed as chronic paranoid schizophrenic

Sirhan B. Sirhan, the convicted assassin of Senator Robert F. Kennedy, was diagnosed as chronic paranoid schizophrenic by expert witnesses—psychologists and psychiatrists—appointed by the court.

Although proud of his deed and believing himself to have been a great patriot who acted on behalf of the Arab people (Kennedy had proposed a short time previously that the United States send 50 military aircraft to Israel), Sirhan seemed to have no recollection of the actual assassination. Diamond (1969), who examined Sirhan, suspected that the amnesia covered a psychotic break. He hypnotized Sirhan and was able to observe an entirely different individual, one who vividly remembered killing Kennedy and who was intensely emotional when asked any question about the Arab-Israeli conflict. For example, when asked about a terrifying experience of his boyhood, the bombing of Jerusalem by the Israelis in 1948, Sirhan "suddenly crumpled in agony like a child, sobbing and shivering in terror. The tears poured down his face" (p. 54).

According to Diamond, Sirhan planned the killing under self-hypnosis and lacked conscious awareness of it (see facing page). An example of a "truly split" personality, whose arrogance and "cool front" provided a "simulation of sanity," Sirhan apparently preferred to think of himself as a sane patriot and be convicted of the assassination—rather than face his psychotic behavior and the possibility of being declared criminally insane.

Pages from Sirhan's "trance" notebooks were introduced in evidence at his trial for Robert F. Kennedy's murder. Commenting on them, Diamond (1969) said: "Sirhan's trances obviously took his mind into a voodoo world. He thought he saw Kennedy's face come before him in the mirror, blotting out his own image, and he began to write kill-Kennedy orders to himself . . . 'RFK must die,' he wrote, 'Robert F. Kennedy must be assassinated before June 5, 1968.' . . . Actually his self-hypnosis worked better than he knew. Without real knowledge or awareness of what was happening in the trances, he rigorously programmed himself for the assassination exactly the way a computer is programmed by magnetic tape. In his unconscious mind there existed a plan for the fulfillment of his sick, paranoid hatred of Kennedy and all who might want to help the Jews. In his conscious mind there was no awareness of such a plan or that he, Sirhan, was to be the instrument of assassination" (p. 50). While interesting and persuasive, it may be pointed out that other clinical psychologists or psychiatrists might place a different interpretation on these comments from Sirhan's notebook.

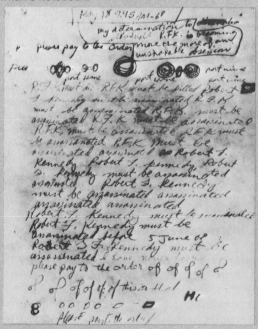

the forces of evil. Surprisingly, despite their apparent lack of attention to their surroundings while in this condition, such patients may later relate in detail events that were going on around them.

Some of these patients are highly suggestible and will automatically obey commands or imitate the actions of others *(echopraxia)* or repeat phrases in a stereotyped way *(echolalia)*. If the patient's arm is raised to an awkward and uncomfortable position, he or she may maintain it in this attitude for minutes or even hours. Ordinarily, however, patients in a catatonic stupor are extremely negativistic. They are apt to resist stubbornly any effort to change their position and may become mute, resist all attempts at feeding, and refuse to comply with even the slightest request. They pay no attention to bowel or bladder control, and saliva may drool from their mouths. Their facial expression typically becomes vacant, and their skin appears waxy. Threats and painful stimuli have no effect, and they have to be dressed and washed and have their eliminative processes taken care of.

Suddenly and without warning, the catatonic patient may pass from a state of extreme withdrawal to one of great excitement, during which he or she seems to be under great "pressure of activity." The patient may talk or shout excitedly and incoherently, pace rapidly back and forth, openly indulge in sexual activities such as masturbation, attempt self-mutilation or even suicide, or impulsively attack and try to kill other persons. The suddenness and the extreme frenzy of these attacks make such patients very dangerous to both themselves and others. The excitement may last a few hours, days, or even weeks.

The following case illustrates some of the symptoms typical of catatonic reactions.

On admission, the patient, a 35-year-old male, appeared apathetic and withdrawn. He would answer questions only after they had been repeated several times and then his speech was so indistinct that it was difficult to understand what he said. After a period of 3 weeks on the ward, his behavior underwent a rather dramatic shift and he became mildly excited, heard the voice of God talking to him, and spent a good deal of time on his knees praying aloud. He occasionally turned to other patients and beseeched them to "get religion" before the devil got them. During this period the following conversation occurred with the ward physician:

Dr.: How are you today, Mr.———?
Pt.: I am fighting, doctor—fighting sin and evil.
Dr.: Sin and evil?
Pt.: Yes, sin and evil. You know what sin and evil are, and you should be down here praying with me for your salvation. . . . God knows the answers. He has imparted some of his knowledge to Churchill. He knows but others are confused. He is the true hero of the British Empire. The Bible states that "By a man's actions ye shall judge him," and he is a man of action.
Dr.: Do you feel that you have found any answers?
Pt.: I am fighting, doctor. The devil tries to confuse you, but I am fighting. Why do people die, doctor? Why did my mother have to die? That's the crucial point, how can you beat sin and evil, how can you keep from moral and physical decay? God has all the answers!

On one occasion the patient impulsively attacked another patient on the ward who had asked him if he was trying to polish the ward floor with his knees. Afterwards, he stated that it was the devil who directed the attack.

Although the matter is far from settled, some clinicians interpret the catatonic patient's immobility as a way of coping with the reduced filtering ability and increased vulnerability to stimulation: it seems to provide a feeling of some control over external sources of stimulation though not necessarily over inner ones. Freeman has cited the explanation advanced by one patient: "I did not want to move, because if I did everything changed around me and upset me horribly so I remained still to hold onto a sense of permanence" (1960, p. 932).

Disorganized (hebephrenic) type. Disorganized or hebephrenic disorders usually occur at an earlier age and represent a more severe disintegration of the personality than in the other types of schizophrenia. Fortunately, they are considerably less common than the other forms.

Typically the individual has a history of oddness, overscrupulousness about trivial things, and preoccupation with religious and philosophical issues. Frequently, he or she is brooding over the dire results of masturbation or minor infractions of social conventions. While schoolmates are enjoying normal play and social activities, this person is gradually becoming more seclusive and more preoccupied with fantasies.

As the disorder progresses, the individual becomes emotionally indifferent and infantile. A silly smile and inappropriate, shallow laughter after little or no provocation are common symptoms. If asked the reason for their laughter, patients may state that they do not know or may volunteer some wholly irrelevant and unsatisfactory explanation. Speech becomes incoherent and may include considerable baby talk, childish giggling, a repetitive use of similar sounding words, and a derailing of thought along the lines of associated meanings that may give a punlike quality to speech. In some instances speech becomes completely incoherent.

Hallucinations, particularly auditory ones, are common. The voices heard by hebephrenic patients may accuse them of immoral practices, "pour filth" into their minds, and call them vile names. Delusions are usually of a sexual, religious, hypochondriacal, or persecutory nature and are changeable and fantastic. For example, one patient insisted not only that she was being followed by enemies but that she had already been killed a number of times.

In occasional cases, patients become hostile and aggressive. They may exhibit peculiar mannerisms and other bizarre forms of behavior. These may take the form of word salad (meaningless, stereotyped repetition of words or sentences), facial grimaces, talking and gesturing to themselves, sudden inexplicable laughter and weeping, and in some cases an abnormal interest in urine and feces, which patients may smear on walls and even on themselves. Obscene behavior and absence of any modesty or sense of shame are characteristic. Although outbursts of anger and temper tantrums may occur in connection with fantasies, these patients are indifferent to real-life situations, no matter how horrifying or gruesome they may be.

The clinical picture in hebephrenic schizophrenia is well illustrated in the following interview:

The patient was a divorcée, 32 years of age, who had come to the hospital with bizarre delusions, hallucinations, and severe personality disintegration and with a record of alcoholism, promiscuity, and possible incestuous relations with a brother. The following conversation shows typical hebephrenic responses to questioning.

Dr.: How do you feel today?
Pt.: Fine.

This drawing depicts a "tree man" holding a bleeding human head. The young woman who drew it, diagnosed as disorganized or hebephrenic schizophrenic, described her creation as a "comical print." Preoccupation with bizarre fantasies is considered characteristic of hebephrenic schizophrenic patients.

Dr.: When did you come here?
Pt.: 1416, you remember, doctor (silly giggle).
Dr.: Do you know why you are here?
Pt.: Well, in 1951 I changed into two men. President Truman was judge at my trial. I was convicted and hung (silly giggle). My brother and I were given back our normal bodies 5 years ago. I am a policewoman. I keep a dictaphone concealed on my person.
Dr.: Can you tell me the name of this place?
Pt.: I have not been a drinker for 16 years. I am taking a mental rest after a "carter" assignment or "quill." You know, a "penwrap." I had contracts with Warner Brothers Studios and Eugene broke phonograph records but Mike protested. I have been with the police department for 35 years. I am made of flesh and blood—see, doctor (pulling up her dress).
Dr.: Are you married?
Pt.: No. I am not attracted to men (silly giggle). I have a companionship arrangement with my brother. I am a "looner" . . . a bachelor.

The prognosis is poor if a schizophrenic patient becomes hebephrenic. As we have seen,

Iris and Hester, the two Genain sisters who seemed unable to manage outside of the hospital, were also the only two of the sisters to exhibit out-and-out hebephrenic behavior. To at least some extent, the disorganized, hebephrenic variety of schizophrenia may be regarded as the "last stop" on a downward-coursing path of "process" schizophrenic psychosis. At this point, no form of treatment intervention yet discovered has marked likelihood of effecting more than a very modest "recovery."

Other schizophrenic patterns. The remaining subcategories of schizophrenia contained in the DSM-III classification deserve brief mention, though we shall not discuss them in detail. The *residual* type is a category used for persons regarded as having recovered from schizophrenia but as still manifesting some subclinical signs of their past disorder.

Schizoaffective disorder (manic or depressive or mixed) is applied to individuals who show features of both schizophrenia and severe affective disorder. In the DSM-III classification, this disorder is not listed as a formal category of schizophrenic disorder but rather under "Psychotic disorders not elsewhere classified." This, no doubt, reflects the fact that schizoaffective disorder presents something of a taxonomic problem, and current controversy prevails over whether these persons should be considered basically schizophrenic or basically affectively disordered, or a group unto themselves. Probably most clinicians lean in the direction of the first choice, although the course of the disorder (rapid onset and often rapid resolution) more nearly approximates that usually seen in the affective psychoses. As recently pointed out by T. Carson and Adams (1980), it may also be possible that the individual has two disorders at once—as happens on the physical level when an individual suffers from both influenza and high blood pressure at the same time.

Also included in the category of "Psychotic disorders not elsewhere classified" is *schizophreniform disorder*, a category reserved for schizophrenic psychoses of less than six months' duration. It may include any of the symptoms described above, but is probably most often seen in an undifferentiated form. At the present time, all new cases of schizophre-

nia would likely receive a diagnosis of schizophreniform disorder. Prognosis for this disorder is better than for established forms of schizophrenia, and it would appear likely that by keeping it out of the formal category of schizophrenic disorder, the potentially harmful effects of labeling may be minimized.[1]

Biological factors in schizophrenia

Despite extensive research on schizophrenia, the etiology of this disorder is still unclear. Primary responsibility for its development has been attributed variously to (a) biological factors, including heredity and various biochemical and neurophysiological processes; (b) psychosocial factors, including faulty learning, pathogenic interpersonal and family patterns, and decompensation under excessive stress; and (c) sociocultural factors, especially as influences on the types and incidence of schizophrenic reactions. These three sets of factors are not mutually exclusive, of course, and it seems likely that all are involved.

Heredity. In view of the disproportionate incidence of schizophrenia in the family backgrounds of schizophrenic patients, a number of investigators have concluded that genetic factors must play an important causal role. While the evidence seems persuasive, it remains circumstantial, based on demonstrations of high concordance rates among close relatives of schizophrenics.

1. *Twin studies*. Twin studies, as we noted in Chapter 5, are designed to find out whether the concordance rate is greater for *identical* (monozygotic) twins, who develop from a single fertilized egg and share the same genetic inheritance, than it is for *fraternal* twins, whose genetic inheritance is comparable to that of other siblings.

While the incidence of schizophrenia among twins is no greater than for the general popula-

---

[1]There is currently considerable controversy over whether two of the personality types, *borderline personality disorder and schizotypal personality disorder* (see pages 278–279) may in fact be related generically and perhaps genetically to schizophrenia. A whole issue of the authoritative government publication *Schizophrenia Bulletin* (1979, Vol. 5) was devoted to papers taking different positions on this controversy.

tion, early studies—which tended to be methodologically naive by modern standards—found very high rates for schizophrenia among monozygotic, or identical, twins relative to fraternal twins or ordinary siblings. More recent studies using refinements in methodology have reported substantially lower concordance rates for both kinds of twins.

In a major study in Norway, Kringlen (1967) found a 38 percent concordance rate for identical twins, as contrasted with 10 percent for fraternal twins; Cohen, Allen, Pollin, and Hruber (1972), studying a large sample of twin pairs who were veterans of the American armed forces, found a concordance rate of 23.5 percent for identical and 5.3 percent for fraternal twins.[2] Similarly, Gottesman and Shields (1972) found a concordance rate of 42 percent for identical and 9 percent for fraternal twins. They also found that the concordance was much higher for identical twins with severe schizophrenic disorders than for those with mild schizophrenic symptoms. In severe cases, when one identical twin became schizophrenic, it was usually just a question of time before the other did also. The lowest concordance rate thus far reported is 6 percent, but this was obtained in a study in which no "age-correction" factor was employed and in which a very narrow definition of concordance was applied (Tienari, 1968). In other words, no adjustment, or correction, was made in the 6 percent figure for the nonschizophrenic co-twins who were not yet beyond the age of risk for schizophrenia (about age 45) and who might later become schizophrenic, and "concordance" was accepted only when the co-twin showed a definite schizophrenic psychosis rather than some other form of severe disorder. This study illustrates the extent to which the concordance rate that is found can depend on the definitions and methods of the researcher.

If schizophrenia were exclusively a genetic disorder, the concordance rate for identical twins would, of course, be 100 percent. In fact, however, there appear to be more *discordant* than *concordant* pairs, notwithstanding the remarkable example of the Genain sisters. On the other hand, there is clearly *some* concordance. What this means is that a twin may have a *predisposition* for schizophrenia if he or she has an identical twin who is schizophrenic. But the fact is that somewhat over half of the identical twins of schizophrenic patients do not develop schizophrenia. It would appear that the environment determines whether the predisposition is actualized or not. Thus, even with a predisposition for schizophrenia, the chances are good for a lifetime of adequate mental health.

2. *Children reared apart from their schizophrenic parents.* Several studies have attempted to eliminate the possible influence of being raised by schizophrenic parents as a causal factor of schizophrenia. In a follow-up study of 47 persons who had been born to schizophrenic mothers in a state mental hospital and placed with relatives or in foster homes shortly after birth, Heston (1966) found that 16.6 percent of these subjects were later diagnosed as schizophrenic. In contrast, none of the 50 control subjects selected from among residents of the same foster homes—whose mothers were not schizophrenic—later became schizophrenic. In addition to the greater probability of being labeled schizophrenic, Heston found that the offspring of schizophrenic mothers were more likely to be diagnosed as mentally retarded, neurotic, and psychopathic. They also had been involved more frequently in criminal activities, and had spent more time in penal institutions. Thus Heston concluded that children born to schizophrenic mothers, even when reared without contact with them, were more likely not only to become schizophrenic but also to suffer a wide spectrum of other disorders. Heston's findings have been confirmed by other investigators.

These findings could mean that the genes involved in schizophrenia are very diffuse in their effects, but other quite tenable hypotheses present themselves. For example, some researchers (e.g., Mednick, 1978) have noted a pronounced tendency for schizophrenic women to mate with psychopathic and criminally disposed men, who may therefore also have made an abnormal genetic contribution to these offspring of schizophrenic mothers.

Other studies of children having schizophrenic mothers and/or fathers but adopted at an early age and reared by presumably normal

---

[2]The lower concordance rates in the Cohen et al. (1972) study may be partially explained by the fact that the veteran sample was not representative of the general twin population, since it consisted entirely of men who had been considered fit for military service.

parents have found from 20 to 31.6 percent developing disorders in the "schizophrenic spectrum" (Rosenthal, 1970; Rosenthal et al., 1971; Wender, 1972; Wender et al., 1974). In general, these "adoption studies" have provided the strongest evidence yet obtained for the genetic transmission of a vulnerability to schizophrenia, and evidence from this type of study continues to build in a most impressive manner (Kety et al., 1978; Kinney & Jacobsen, 1978). Thus, for example, the biological relatives of adopted children who become schizophrenic are invariably found to have a greater incidence of schizophrenia and "schizophrenic spectrum" disorders than the biological relatives of otherwise matched adoptees who do *not* become schizophrenic (Kety et al., 1978).

3. *Family studies.* Another line of research has studied the incidence of schizophrenia among children reared by their schizophrenic parents. Rieder (1973) found a wide spectrum of psychopathology reported among the adult offspring of schizophrenic parents, ranging from schizophrenia to psychopathic personality disorders. The offspring of schizophrenic parents also showed a high incidence of psychological maladjustment as children—estimated at 20 percent—with two types being prominent, a withdrawn schizoid type and a hyperactive, antisocial, delinquent type. Thus Rieder concluded that the offspring of schizophrenic parents differ from the offspring of nonschizophrenic parents.

In the same vein, Kringlen (1978) has shown that 28 percent of the children born to parents who had both become schizophrenic at some point in their adult lives were classifiable as psychotic or borderline psychotic; 20 percent of these children of schizophrenic parents had developed clinical schizophrenia. But—and this observation deserves special note—28 percent of the children of such unions were diagnosed as entirely normal. That is, nearly one-third of these children escaped any form of psychopathology despite what must have been very heavy genetic risk *and* the environmental hazards of association with two psychotic parents! Evidently having two schizophrenic parents increases the risks of poor mental health—but it need not always have ill effects.

4. *Studies of high-risk children.* The research strategy of monitoring over time children known to be at high risk for schizophrenia by virtue of having been born to a schizophrenic parent is basically one intended to identify the environmental factors that cause breakdown (or resistance to it) in predisposed persons. As we have seen in Chapter 5, this strategy, pioneered by Mednick and Schulsinger (1968), and followed up by numerous additional research projects (e.g., Garmezy, 1978a, 1978b), has thus far not paid off very well in terms of isolating specific environmental factors. What it *has* done is show abundantly once again that having a schizophrenic parent is a very good predictor of psychological disorder, including schizophrenia. It seems extremely likely that much of this predictability is mediated by the genetic transmission of vulnerability; *how* much, again, we do not yet know (see HIGHLIGHT on page 416).

Biochemical factors. Research into the possibility of biochemical abnormalities in schizophrenic patients was given impetus in the 1950s when a connection was made between schizophrenic symptoms and the long-established fact that the presence of some chemical agents in the bloodstream, even in minute amounts, can produce profound mental changes (Huxley, 1954). Lysergic acid (LSD) and mescaline, for example, can lead to a temporary disorganization of thought processes and a variety of psychotic-like symptoms that have been referred to as "model psychoses." Such findings encouraged investigators to look for an *endogenous hallucinogen*—a chemical synthesized within the body under stressful conditions that might account for the hallucinations and disorganization of thought and affect in schizophrenia and other psychotic disorders.

The idea of autointoxication by errant chemicals manufactured within the patient's own body is not new, however. In fact, national news magazines have been reporting new "discoveries" in this area on approximately a yearly basis for at least the last quarter-century. Typically, the outcome is that when the pertinent research is repeated in another laboratory, the miraculous "breakthrough" suddenly disappears. For example, one such "discovery" was eventually traced to elements in the diets offered hospitalized mental patients and had nothing to do with the disorder.

A perspective on genetics and psychiatric disorder

Many people would like to be able to conclude, once and for all, that schizophrenia (or some other psychiatric disorder) is *either* genetically *or* environmentally caused. The fallacy of this type of thinking is well illustrated in an example provided by Gottesman (1978). Galactosemia is a serious blood disease affecting children who have a certain pair of recessive genes. Virtually all children with the recessive genes get the disease—yet we cannot say that the disease is "caused" by the genetic defect because the disease occurs only when these children ingest milk, which is, of course, a quite universal "environmental" input. Most people, nevertheless, would conclude that galactosemia is a genetic disease. The genetic defect is seen as the primary and predisposing cause, with milk ingestion as the precipitating cause.

The important point is that for any disorder of humankind there seems always to be an interaction of genetic and environmental causes. When the genetic predisposition for a disorder is relatively rare but the relevant environmental factor is very common, as in the case of galactosemia, the disease or disorder is considered "genetic." When the opposite conditions hold, which seems to be the case, for example, with Legionnaire's disease, the disorder is considered to be environmentally caused. In point of fact, it seems likely that both genetic and environmental factors must be operative to produce the disorder in both of the aforementioned cases—and in virtually any other disorder. In terms of this kind of cause-specificity and weighting of genetic and environmental influences, schizophrenia seems to fall midway between galactosemia and Legionnaire's disease.

In sum, available research studies indicate that genetic factors play an important role in the etiology of schizophrenia. However, an inherited predisposition

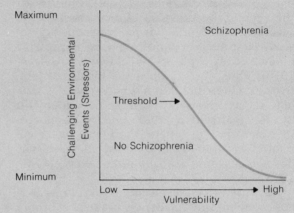

(Chart adapted from Zubin & Spring, 1977)

to schizophrenia would appear to be not an "all-or-nothing" factor but rather one of degree. Thus a mild degree of predisposition would presumably lead to schizophrenia only in persons subjected to severe stressors. On the other hand, a high degree of predisposition would increase the probability of becoming schizophrenic, since a lower level of stress could trigger it. Further research in this area is needed, however, especially on the specific environmental factors that may contribute to breakdown.

This is not intended to minimize the importance of genetic factors in schizophrenia, but merely to emphasize that their specific role is, at present, unknown. It is conceivable—however unlikely—that the shared genetic endowment of the Genain sisters was only a minimal factor in the development of their disorders. The relationship between biological vulnerability and environmental factors in the causation of schizophrenia is illustrated in the chart above.

It seems exceedingly unlikely that the riddle of schizophrenia will be solved so simply.

If schizophrenia turns out to be in part biochemically caused—a hypothesis entirely consistent with the genetic evidence—it seems more likely that it will turn out to be due to some form of deficit in the *regulation* of chemicals that occur naturally in the nervous systems of all of us. At present, as in the case of

the psychotic affective disorders, the best hypothesis is that there is aberrant biochemistry relating to the biogenic amines that control transmission of nervous impulses across synapses in the brain. Among the more attractive of the current ideas in this area is the so-called "dopamine hypothesis" of schizophrenia (Davis, 1978; Sachar et al., 1978; Snyder, 1978). Dopamine is a catecholamine like nor-

Art by emotionally disturbed individuals

Richard Saholt (1924–   ) was a shy, fearful child with a belittling, abusive father. Naturally left-handed, he was forced to change handedness, back and forth, several times and developed a severe speech impediment. While serving in World War II, he survived many weeks of fighting at subzero temperatures in the Italian Alps, where he patrolled behind enemy lines and witnessed explosions that mutilated or killed many of his buddies. Ninety percent of his outfit died.

Home from the war, he had nervous twitches, was jumpy and scared, and suffered from depression, stomach trouble, and blackouts. In five years he started and quit 15 schools and lost 30 jobs. Each year for 29 years he sought compensation for service-connected disability but was turned down. Twice he attempted suicide.

Unable to express his torment verbally, he began to collect words and pictures to create dozens of montages such as those shown here—montages of war, insanity, terror, and violence. It was these montages that helped him gain a total disability pension in 1974, with a diagnosis of chronic undifferentiated schizophrenia.

But the montages have brought him recognition and appreciation as an artist, and ironically the validation of his claim by the Veterans Administration has given him feelings of exoneration and—at last—sanity. He says, "For myself, I can accept that my cries and tries went unheeded for so long. What I don't accept is that other people have to still endure such pain. I hope, by these works, to increase the awareness of the physical, mental, and social ills of today."

These paintings, all in different media and all almost exactly the same size, were done by a neurotic patient with obsessive-compulsive tendencies. These tendencies are manifested in the paintings by the rigidity and sameness of the brush strokes, the seeming need to cover the entire canvas, and the obvious attempt at symmetry.

In an effort to break the patient from his rigid mold, the therapist gave him a piece of paper twice as large as the ones on which the previous paintings had been done. The patient, however, folded the paper to the same size as the previous paintings and did the same kind of painting (below).

These three paintings are part of a series of approximately 20 paintings done over a six-month period by a patient diagnosed as anxiety neurotic. The first painting (above) indicates great hostility toward women, evidenced by the beetle on the forehead, pointed ears, and bald head. At this stage also the patient, while showing some obvious art ability, had difficulty fininshing the painting, especially the background and edges.

The second painting (top right) was done after about three months in therapy. The fragmentation of the image was interpreted as indicating the patient's feelings of ambivalence and confusion at this stage.

The same woman is shown in the third painting (bottom right) but she now has hair, the scarab is gone from her forehead, the pointed ears are modified, and her facial expression is less hostile. The patient, while not completely relieved of his hostility and paranoia toward women, was considered to have reached a point where he could express his feelings in a socially acceptable manner.

Louis Wain (1860–1939) was a well-known and popular artist who painted pictures of cats in human situations, such as wearing glasses and having teaparties. In the mid-1920s he suffered a schizophrenic breakdown and thereafter was confined to mental institutions, where he continued to paint. These paintings show his transition from realistic and recognizable portraits to representations that became increasingly stylized and ornamental—and in the end unrecognizable. Wain's paintings are remarkable for the clues they provide to his mental state and the distortions of perception that are characteristic of schizophrenia.

Louis Wain.

These paintings were made by a male patient diagnosed as suffering from undifferentiated schizophrenia. Over a period of about nine years, he did hundreds of paintings in which the tops of the heads of males were always missing, though the females were complete. He was unable to communicate verbally, and when asked about his life would often draw a "comic strip" that told a story, such as the one shown here.

In an attempt to maneuver the patient into a position to complete a man's head, the therapist made the outline of a suit of clothes on a canvas, low enough so that a head would logically fit in the picture, and urged the patient to finish the drawing. The patient, however, painted only a suit.

A

B

A patient diagnosed as schizophrenic, paranoid type, was unable to respond at all when asked by the therapist to make an original drawing. Therefore, with the therapist's help, a picture (A) was selected from a magazine for the patient to copy. One of his first attempts was picture B, a pencil drawing on manila paper showing great visual distortion, as well as an inability to use colors and difficulty in using letters of the alphabet.

The evident visual distortion was a diagnostic aid for the therapist, who was able to learn from it that the patient, who was extremely fearful, saw things in this distorted way, aggravating his fear. In picture C the patient has shown obvious improvement, although it was not until a year after therapy began that he was able to execute a painting with the realism of picture D.

C

D

epinephrine, of which it is in fact a chemical forerunner. Dopamine is the transmitter substance involved in certain important brain pathways.

According to the simplest form of the dopamine hypothesis, schizophrenia is the product of a functional excess of dopamine at pertinent synaptic sites. A variant of this view is that the schizophrenic person has a superabundance of dopamine receptor sites within the brain. The most important—albeit indirect—evidence for the general hypothesis is that the clinical effectiveness of the various antipsychotic drugs is highly correlated with the extent to which they block dopamine action at the synaptic receptor. Correlation does not, of course, establish a causal relationship, and many questions remain to be answered before the dopamine theory is substantiated. The most basic question has been voiced by Matthysse (1978): "Granted that [antipsychotic] drugs are dopamine blockers, why is dopamine blockade good for schizophrenia?" (p. 148).

Although a satisfactory answer to this question may not be soon forthcoming, the dramatic advances in this general field in very recent years give us reason to be very optimistic about achieving an eventual understanding of the biochemistry of schizophrenic disorders. As in the case of the affective disorders, a complete understanding will likely entail an appreciation of the manner in which psychological factors interact with biochemical balances in the brain.

Neurophysiological factors. A good deal of research has focused on the role of neurophysiological disturbances in schizophrenia. These disturbances are thought to include an imbalance in excitatory and inhibitory processes and inappropriate arousal. Such processes would be expected to disrupt the normal attentional and information-processing capabilities of the organism, and there seems to be a growing consensus that such disturbances underlie and are basic to the cognitive and perceptual distortions characteristic of individuals diagnosed as schizophrenic (Wynne, Cromwell, & Matthysse, 1978).

In addition, difficulties in maintaining attention and deficiencies in autonomic arousal sometimes occur prior to schizophrenic breakdown; that is, they are often present in individuals who are merely "at risk" for schizophrenia (Buchsbaum et al., 1978; Mednick, 1978; Spring & Zubin, 1978; Erlenmeyer-Kimling & Cornblatt, 1978). As yet, however, the role of these neurophysiological divergences in the development of schizophrenia is not clear.

Findings of abnormal neurophysiological processes in schizophrenia do not necessarily imply that such abnormalities are genetic in origin. Many could be the product of faulty early conditioning or of biological deviations caused by other factors. For example, problems of this sort could as likely arise from mechanical difficulties in the birth process as from genetic predestination. In fact, the frequency of obstetrical complications in the histories of persons who later become schizophrenic is markedly above that of the general population (McNeil & Kaij, 1978).

Any complete theory of the origins of schizophrenic breakdown will, of necessity, have to take into account the kinds of observations reviewed in this section. In the meantime, it is reasonable to take the view that *anything* that reduces the adaptive capacity of the organism, including varied biological factors, may result in an increased probability of schizophrenic breakdown at some point in the life cycle.

Psychosocial factors in schizophrenia

Laing (1967) has speculated:

"The experience and behavior that are labelled schizophrenic are a special sort of strategy that a person invents in order to live in an unlivable world. He cannot make a move . . . without being beset by contradictory pressures both internally, from himself, and externally, from those around him. He is in a position of checkmate." (p. 56)

This viewpoint contrasts sharply with that in which schizophrenia is held to be caused by biological factors. Here schizophrenic individuals are seen as persons who escape from an unbearable world and seemingly unsolvable conflicts by altering their inner representations of reality. Although biological factors may complicate the clinical picture, the origins of the disorder are held to be primarily psychosocial.

In this section we shall deal with the psychosocial patterns that appear particularly relevant to the development of schizophrenia: (a) early psychic trauma and increased vulnerability; (b) pathogenic parent-child and family interactions; (c) faulty learning and coping; (d) social role problems; and (e) excessive stress and decompensation.

Early psychic trauma and increased vulnerability.   A number of investigators have placed strong emphasis on the early traumatic experiences of children who later become schizophrenic.

In a pioneering study of the psychoses of children and adolescents, Yerbury and Newell emphasized the total lack of security in human relationships, the severely disturbed home life, and the brutal treatment that many of these children had experienced. Of 56 psychotic cases,

"Ten of them had been shocked by the deaths of parents. . . . Four were so disoriented upon learning of their adoption that they could not reconcile themselves to the true situation. Four children had lived with mentally ill mothers who were finally hospitalized. Sex traumas were reported in 14 cases of children who were overwhelmed with guilt and fear. . . . Three children were horrified by incest in the home, and three girls had become pregnant. . . . Six children had been tormented, beaten, tied, and confined by their companions so that they were terrified in the company of children, and felt safe only with adults." (1943, p. 605)

Similarly, Bettelheim (1955) cited the poignant case of a boy who was rejected by his mother and placed in an orphanage. Here he never learned the names of any of the other boys but referred to them as "big guys" and "little guys"; he lived in a terrifying world of shadowy figures who had the power to beat him up and hurt him without reason.

Karl Menninger has provided a vivid picture of the defenses—and special vulnerabilities—of adolescents and young adults who have suffered deep hurts and have come to view the world as a dangerous and hostile place:

"Children injured in this way are apt to develop certain defenses. They cover up, as the slang expression puts it. They deny the injury which they have experienced or the pain which they are suffering. They erect a façade or front, 'All's well with me,' they seem to say. 'I am one of the fellows; I am just like everybody else. I am a normal person.' And indeed they act like normal persons, as much as they can. . . . Often they are noticeable only for a certain reticence, shyness, perhaps slight eccentricity. Just as often, they are not conspicuous at all. . . .

"What is underneath that front? . . . There is intense conflict and tension and anxiety and strong feelings of bitterness, resentment and hate toward those very people with whom the external relationships may be so perfectly normal. 'I hate them! They don't treat me right. They will never love me and I will never love them. I hate them and I could kill them all! But I must not let them know all this. I must cover it up, because they might read my thoughts and then they wouldn't like me and wouldn't be nice to me.'

"All this is covered up as long as possible. . . . For the chief problem in the person who is going to develop what we call schizophrenia is, 'How can I control the bitterness and hatred I feel because of the unendurable sorrow and disappointment that life has brought to me?' . . .

". . . the regimen under which they live has much to do with their successful adaptation. Given certain new stresses, the façade may break down and the underlying bitterness and conflict may break through. . . ." (1948, pp. 101–4)

Instead of withdrawing, children who have been traumatized may try to relate aggressively to other people. Such children are highly vulnerable to hurt, however, and their existence is usually an anxious one. Often their lives are a series of crises, precipitated by minor setbacks and hurts that they magnify out of all proportion (Arieti, 1974). In other instances, the individual manifests a pattern of somewhat disorganized paranoid ideation often coupled with rebellious behavior involving pathological lying, episodes of unbridled aggression, and various types of delinquent behavior.

Although most children who undergo early psychic trauma show residual effects in later life, most do not become schizophrenic. Conversely, not all schizophrenic patients have undergone such traumatic childhood experiences. Thus early psychic trauma appears to be only one among many interactional factors that may contribute to schizophrenia. Anthony (1978) has even suggested that early traumatic experiences may be less important than the

A group of young men stand outside their ward at a residential mental hospital. A number of researchers have emphasized the early traumatic experience of children and adolescents who become schizophrenic—the total lack of security in human relationships, the severely disturbed home life, and the brutal treatment that many of these young people may have experienced.

overall continuing context in which they occur:

"The 'headline' experiences—the attacks, the paranoid accusations, the incestuous approaches, the brutalities—seem easier for the child to endure than the constant confusions, mystifications, inconsistencies, and other seemingly minor problems of everyday living. It is not abnormality itself that proves so disturbing but the oscillations between normality and abnormality, and the wider these are, the more difficult it is for the child to sustain." (p. 481)

We turn now to some of these less dramatic influences.

Pathogenic parent-child and family interactions. Studies of interactions in schizophrenic families have focused on such factors as (a) "schizophrenogenic" parents; (b) destructive marital interactions; (c) pseudomutuality and role inflexibility; (d) faulty communication; and (e) the undermining of personal authenticity. Here it may be noted that the focus of research has shifted from parent-child to total family interactions.[3]

1. *"Schizophrenogenic" mothers and fathers.* Many studies have been made of the parents of individuals who have developed schizophrenia—particularly the mothers of male patients. Typically, these mothers have

been characterized as rejecting, dominating, cold, overprotective, and impervious to the feelings and needs of others. While verbally such a mother may seem accepting, basically she rejects the child. At the same time, she depends on the child rather than the father for her emotional satisfactions and feelings of completeness as a woman. Perhaps for this reason she tends to dominate, possessively overprotect, and smother the child—encouraging dependence on her. Often combined with this behavior, observers note rigid, moralistic attitudes toward sex that make her react with horror to any evidence of sexual impulses on the child's part. In many instances the mother is overtly seductive in physical contacts with her son, thus augmenting his sexual conflicts. In general, the mother-son relationship in schizophrenia appears to foster immaturity and anxiety in the youth—depriving him of a clear-cut sense of his own identity, distorting his views of himself and his world, and causing him to suffer from pervasive feelings of inadequacy and helplessness.

Nor are the daughters of such mothers likely to fare very well either. In this connection, we refer the reader's attention to the description of Mrs. Genain given at the beginning of this chapter.

Although the "schizophrenogenic" mother has long been a favorite target of investigators, the fathers have not come through unscathed—especially in regard to schizophrenic daugh-

[3]A comprehensive review of family interaction in disturbed and normal families may be found in Jacob (1975).

ters. Available studies have typically described a somewhat inadequate, indifferent, or passive father who appears detached and humorless—a father who rivals the mother in his insensitivity to others' feelings and needs. Often, too, he appears to be rejecting toward his son and seductive toward his daughter. At the same time, he is often highly contemptuous and derogatory toward his wife, thus making it clear that his daughter is more important to him. This treatment of the wife tends to force her into competition with her daughter, and it devaluates her as a model for her daughter's development as a woman. In fact, the daughter may come to despise herself for any resemblance to her mother. Against this background, the daughter often moves into adolescence feeling an incestuous attachment to her father, which creates severe inner conflict and may eventually prove terrifying to her. The problems of the Genain sisters in attempting to cope with their seriously disturbed father are relevant here.

As might be expected, studies have shown a high incidence of emotional disturbance on the part of both mothers and fathers of schizophrenics. Kaufman et al. (1960) reported that both the mothers and fathers of 80 schizophrenic children and adolescents studied were emotionally disturbed: the mothers almost uniformly used psychotic-like defense patterns, and the fathers used seriously maladaptive coping patterns. Later studies, such as that of Tsuang, Fowler, Cadoret, and Monnelly (1974), have generally supported earlier findings.

As was indicated in Chapter 5, however, we cannot reasonably assume that disturbance always passes from parent to offspring: it can work in the other direction as well. And quite aside from the original source of psychopathology, it would appear that once it begins, the members of a family may stimulate each other to increased displays of pathological behavior. For example, studies by Mishler and Waxler (1968) and Liem (1974) both contain quite unequivocal evidence that parents' attempts to deal with the disturbed behavior of schizophrenic sons and daughters had pathological effects on their own behavior and communication patterns.

2. *Destructive marital interactions.* Of particular interest here is the work of Lidz and his associates, which continued over some two

decades. In an initial study of 14 families with schizophrenic offspring (mentioned briefly in Chapter 5), Lidz et al. (1965) failed to find a single family that was reasonably well integrated. Eight of the 14 couples lived in a state of severe chronic discord in which continuation of the marriage was constantly threatened—a condition the investigators called *marital schism.* A particularly malignant feature was the chronic undermining of the worth of one marital partner by the other, which made it clear to the children that the parents did not respect or value each other. Each parent expressed fear that the child would resemble the other parent; a child's resemblance to one parent was a source of concern and rejection by the other parent.

The other 6 couples in this study had achieved a state of equilibrium in which the continuation of the marriage was not constantly threatened but in which the relationship was maintained at the expense of a basic distortion in family relationships; in these cases, family members entered into a "collusion" in which the maladaptive behavior of one or more family members was accepted as normal. This pattern was referred to as *marital skew.* The Genain family, for example, would be considered severely skewed since it was organized chiefly around the bizarre actions and ideas of Mr. Genain. Lidz (1978) believes that a major effect of such severe family disturbance is the encouragement of "egocentric cognitive regression" in youngsters subjected to it, giving rise eventually to the distinctive cognitive derangements characteristic of the schizophrenic state. In these and other cases regarding parental influences, of course, both biological and psychological influences are likely to be involved.

3. *Pseudo-mutuality and role inflexibility.* Wynne et al. (1958) found that schizophrenic family relationships often had the appearance of being mutual, understanding, and open, but in fact were not—a condition they termed *pseudo-mutuality.* These investigators also found considerable rigidity in the family role structure, which tended to depersonalize the children and block their growth toward maturity and self-direction.

Similarly, Bowen (1959, 1960), studying the backgrounds of 12 schizophrenic patients, found "striking emotional distance" between the parents typical. He referred to the emotional barrier as having the characteristics of an "emotional divorce." Although the parents in such families often maintained a façade of love—for example, making a big drama out of giving each other presents at Christmas—there was an underlying withdrawal accompanied by severe disappointment and often hostility. The patient's function had often been that of an unsuccessful mediator between the parents. In the case of the male patients, however, the most common pattern was an intense association between mother and son that excluded the father. Bowen also noted that, as the years passed, the son was threatened by signs of the mother's aging or by other characteristics that might prevent her from being the strong person upon whom he was dependent, while the mother was threatened by any signs of personality growth that might prevent the son from remaining "her baby."

Pseudo-mutuality seems related to a variety of role distortions in schizophrenic families. Stabenau et al. (1965) found that such families were characterized by the assignment of inflexible and simplified roles to each member. Brodey has expressed this as an analogy, using a model based on the theater:

"The family drama is unlike the modern theatre. It is more like the morality play of medieval times. Actors take allegorical role positions that are stereotyped and confined—one is Good; another, Evil; a third, Temptation." (1959, p. 382)

In general, it would appear that the rigid and inflexible roles played by the family members permit a façade of continuing relatedness with each other and with the world, and make the business of living seemingly understandable and controllable. But basically the role provided for the child is destructive to personal growth.

4. *Faulty communication.* Bateson (1959, 1960) was one of the first investigators to emphasize the conflicting and confusing nature of communications among members of schizophrenic families. As we noted in Chapter 5, he used the term *double-bind* to describe the effect of one such pattern. Here the parent presents to the child ideas, feelings, and demands that are mutually incompatible. For example, the mother may be verbally loving and accept-

ing but emotionally anxious and rejecting; or she may complain about her son's lack of affection but freeze up or punish him when he approaches her affectionately. The mother subtly but effectively prohibits comment on such paradoxes, and the father is too weak and ineffectual to intervene. In essence, such a son is continually placed in situations where he cannot win. He becomes increasingly anxious; presumably, such disorganized and contradictory communications in the family come to be reflected in his own thinking.

Singer and Wynne (1963, 1965a, 1965b) have linked the thought disorders in schizophrenia to two styles of thinking and communication in the family—*amorphous* and *fragmented*. The amorphous pattern is characterized by failure in differentiation; here, attention toward feelings, objects, or persons is loosely organized, vague, and drifting. Fragmented thinking involves greater differentiation but lowered integration, with erratic and disruptive shifts in communication. Feinsilver (1970) found supporting evidence for such amorphous and fragmented thinking in the impaired ability of members of schizophrenic families to describe essential attributes of common household objects to each other. And Bannister (1971) has found that schizophrenic thinking tends to be even more "loose" and disordered when the individual is dealing with persons and interpersonal relationships than when dealing with objects.

In their recent work, Singer and Wynne continue to be impressed with the fundamental communicational difficulties of schizophrenic families. They also acknowledge that parent-child influences in this respect tend to be two-way, that is, the behavior of either parent or child may affect the behavior of the other (Singer, Wynne, & Toohey, 1978).

5. *Undermining personal authenticity.* The philosopher Martin Buber (1957) pointed out that a confirmation of each person's authenticity is essential to normal interpersonal relationships.

"In human society at all its levels, persons confirm one another in a practical way, to some extent or other, in their personal qualities and capacities, and a society may be termed human in the measure to which its members confirm one another. . . ." (p. 101)

Such confirmation apparently is often denied the person who later becomes schizophrenic. Several investigators have noted that the members of schizophrenic families consistently disqualify one or more members' statements and actions. In one family, for example, the father strongly approved of whatever the younger son did while he was equally disapproving of the behavior of the older son. Thus the brothers might make similar statements about some matter, and the father would agree with one and find some basis for disqualifying or discrediting the statement of the other. Similarly, at Christmas time, the younger son's present to his father was praised and appreciated, while that of the older son was criticized and found disappointing by the father. The mother and younger sister went along with this differential treatment. Later, at the age of 27, the older son was hospitalized and diagnosed as a paranoid schizophrenic.

Such contradictory and disconfirming communications subtly and persistently mutilate the self-concepts of one or more of the family members, usually that of a particular child, as in the preceding example. The ultimate of this mutilation process occurs when

". . . no matter how [a person] feels or how he acts, no matter what meaning he gives his situation, his feelings are denuded of validity, his acts are stripped of their motives, intentions, and consequences, the situation is robbed of its meaning for him, so that he is totally mystified and alienated." (Laing & Esterson, 1964, pp. 135–36)

In the general context of faulty parent-child and family interactions, we may note that Lidz (1968, 1973) has characterized the parents of schizophrenics as "deficient tutors": they create a family milieu inappropriate for training a child in the cognitive abilities essential for categorizing experience, thinking coherently, and communicating meaningfully. Coupled with feelings of inadequacy and other damage to the child's emerging self-concept, this may help explain the later cognitive distortions, communication failures, difficulties in interpersonal relationships, and identity confusion that commonly occur in schizophrenia.

Yet most of the children from families with pathogenic characteristics do not become schizophrenic. Thus pathogenic family interactions cannot be the sole cause in those that do.

It should be noted that, by and large, controlled laboratory tests of the clinical observations reported above concerning schizophrenic families have failed to confirm the alleged differences between families that have produced schizophrenic offspring and families that have not. Three possible reasons appear for this failure to confirm in the laboratory the observations that seem so compelling to clinicians who work with these families. First, the differences may not exist, and clinicians' expectations may be influencing what they see, especially when adequate control groups are not observed. Second, normal families also often have peculiarities of communication and systematic denials of personal identity; there may be differences, but perhaps they are not large enough to show up within the constraints of the procedures employed. Third, the constraints imposed by experiment and systematic measurement may themselves have reduced the differences between normal and pathological families to undetectable levels. At this point, not all the evidence is in.

Faulty learning and coping. It appears that faulty learning typically plays a key role in schizophrenia, as it does in most other forms of maladaptive behavior. From early traumatic experiences—both within the family setting and in the outer world—the child may learn conditioned fears and vulnerabilities that lead to perception of the world as a dangerous and hostile place. Perhaps of even greater importance is faulty learning on a cognitive level, resulting from irrationalities in social interaction, attempts to meet inappropriate or impossible expectations and demands, and observation of pathological models.

1. *Deficient self-structure.* Such faulty learning is typically reflected in (a) grossly inaccurate assumptions concerning reality, possibility, and value; (b) a confused sense of self-identity coupled with basic feelings of inadequacy, insecurity, and self-devaluation; (c) personal immaturity, often reflected in overdependence on others and overemphasis on being a "good boy" or a "good girl"; and (d) a lack of needed competencies coupled with ineffective coping patterns. These characteristics appear capable of paving the way for schizophrenic and other seriously maladaptive behaviors. If we consider the developmental problems of the Genain sisters in this light, we can see how very difficult it must have been for them, as members of a tightly knit and socially isolated foursome, to gain the understandings and skills they needed.

The results of such faulty learning are often seen in such individuals' attempts to deal with inner impulses and establish satisfying interpersonal relationships. In the sexual sphere, schizophrenic individuals' problems are often complicated by rigidly moralistic attitudes toward sexual behavior. At the same time, they usually have had few, if any, meaningful sexual relationships. As a consequence, their sexual fantasies—like those of the early adolescent—may be somewhat chaotic and encompass a wide range of sexual objects and behaviors. Such fantasies often lead to severe inner conflicts and to self-devaluation. Similarly, the hostility they may feel toward people important to them is apt to be particularly difficult for such "good" individuals to handle: they tend to view such hostility as both immoral and dangerous and do not know how to express it in socially acceptable ways. At the same time, they may be completely upset at being the object of hostility from those on whom they feel dependent.

Lack of competencies in dealing with sexual and hostile fantasies and impulses, combined with a general deficiency in social skills, usually leads to disappointment, hurt, and devaluation in intimate interpersonal relationships. As we shall see, the stresses which commonly precipitate schizophrenic episodes typically center around the difficulties in such relationships. The inability of such individuals to establish and maintain satisfying interpersonal relationships does not void their needs for acceptance, approval, and love; it only reduces their chances for meeting these needs.

2. *Exaggerated use of ego-defense mechanisms.* Feeling inadequate and devaluated and lacking an adequate frame of reference and needed competencies, such individuals, not surprisingly, learn to rely excessively on ego-defense mechanisms rather than on task-oriented coping patterns. These defense mechanisms often include psychosomatic elements that have substantial secondary gain by "excusing" the person's withdrawal and nonperformance, particularly in early stages of the disorder. This was apparently the case with the Genain sisters, though somatic symptoms conceivably may also express an underlying biological defect. In any case, the development of a schizophrenic process does not preclude the use of neurotic forms of coping.

The exaggerated use of many ego-defense mechanisms is common. Emotional insulation protects these individuals from the hurt of disappointment and frustration. Regression enables them to lower their level of aspiration and accept a position of dependence. Projection helps them maintain feelings of adequacy and worth by placing the blame for their failures on others and attributing their own unacceptable desires to someone else. Wish-fulfilling fantasies give them some measure of compensation for feelings of frustration and self-devaluation.

The exaggerated use of such defense mechanisms as projection and fantasy appears particularly likely to predispose an individual to delusions and hallucinations, which not only represent the breakdown of organized perception and thought processes, but also—as part of schizophrenic reorganization of reality—may have marked defensive value. Delusions of grandeur and persecution enable these individuals to project the blame for their own inadmissible thoughts and behaviors; hallucinations—such as voices that "pour filth into their minds" or keep them informed of what their "enemies" are up to—may serve a comparable defensive purpose. Delusions of grandeur and omnipotence may grow out of simple wishful thinking and enable them to counteract feelings of inferiority and inadequacy. Hallucinations, such as conversations in which they hear the voice of God confer great power upon them and assign them the mission of saving the world, may likewise have comparable defensive value.

In acute schizophrenic episodes the initial picture is somewhat different, as we have seen, and is dominated by massive disorganization of thought, with panic at the loss of control over thoughts and feelings and desperate attempts to understand the terrifying experience. As yet the individual has not developed defenses to cope with the situation, but no one can continue indefinitely in this state of panic and confusion. Either the acute schizophrenic episode clears up eventually, or various extreme defenses, such as the ones mentioned above, are likely to develop.

Although extreme ego-defense mechanisms

are commonly observed in schizophrenic patients, it is often unclear to what extent they were a causal factor, as opposed to a reaction to the frightening experience of disorganization. Here it may be emphasized that a schizophrenic breakdown often appears to represent a total defensive strategy. In essence, the individual seems to withdraw from the real world and evolve a defensive strategy that makes it possible to distort and "reshape" aversive experiences so that they can be assimilated without further self-devaluation. Even though this defensive system may be illogical and far from satisfactory, it relieves much of the inner tension and anxiety and protects the individual from complete psychological disintegration.

Social role problems.   Social role behavior has been tied into the development and course of schizophrenic reactions in several different ways. A factor emphasized by Cameron and Margaret (1949, 1951) in their intensive studies of schizophrenic patients was the failure of such individuals to learn appropriate role-taking behavior. Inflexible in their own role behavior and uncomprehending of the role behavior of others, they do not know how to interact appropriately with other people.

Laing (1967, 1969, 1971) has carried this view of role behavior a step further, to the schizophrenic's creation of his or her own social role as protection from destructive social expectations and demands. Describing the so-called normal world as a place where all of us are "bemused and crazed creatures, strangers to our true selves, to one another, and to the spiritual and material world" (1967, p. 56), Laing maintains that a split arises between the false outer self and the true inner self. When the split reaches a point where it can no longer be tolerated, the result is a psychotic breakdown which usually takes the form of schizophrenia. In this view the "madness" labeled schizophrenia represents the individual's attempts to recover a sense of wholeness as a human being.

In essence, according to Laing, the individual dons the "mask of insanity" as a social role and a barricade. Behind this "false self" and often turbulent façade, however, the real person—the "true inner self"—remains. In this hidden inner world, despite the outward role of madness, the schizophrenic individual's hopes and aspirations may remain very much

intact. Accordingly, Laing thinks treatment should focus less on removing "symptoms" than on finding a path to this remote and often inaccessible sanctuary and assisting the individual to regain wholeness as a person.

Laing thus suggests that at least some schizophrenic phenomena may represent partially voluntary enactments on the part of the patient. On reflection, it is not wholly incredible—given the miserable possibilities available to many persons for basic need gratification—that some should opt for the schizophrenic way of life. Though it may entail a certain amount of self-stigmatization and renunciation of personal liberties, these might be mild penalties to pay for escape from constant failure, contempt, rejection, and often brutality. For many, life in a modern mental hospital is distinctly more pleasant on many dimensions than would be life "outside"—in, let us say, an urban ghetto. Given our society's commitment to care for those who appear to be unable to care for themselves, and given the frequency of personal situations of hopelessness and despair, it may be that we should expect this form of "dropping out"—that an *absence* of it would be the occasion for surprise (R. Carson, 1971).

In any event, we do know that the occurrence of schizophrenic symptoms depends to a remarkable extent on the context in which the individual is being observed (Levy, 1976; Ritchie, 1975; Shimkunas, 1972). Such symptoms may come and go or be otherwise modified, depending on what demands are currently being placed on the patient. For example, a demand for intimate exchange appears to exacerbate schizophrenic symptoms. We also know that a certain subset of mental patients diagnosed as schizophrenic are quite skillful in controlling both the diagnoses they receive and the likelihood of their discharge from the hospital (Braginsky, Braginsky, & Ring, 1969; Drake & Wallach, 1979). In some ways, these are deeply disconcerting findings that mock much of the research reported. They will require careful consideration by future investigators—if only to weed out from studies those who are feigning their symptoms.

Excessive stress and decompensation.   Brown (1972) found a marked increase in the severity of life stress during the 10-week period prior to an actual schizophrenic breakdown. Problems typically centered around difficulties in intimate personal relationships. Forgus and DeWolfe (1974) found that schizophrenic patients seemed to have been defeated by their whole life situation as well as by difficulties in close personal relationships.

As we noted, the course of decompensation in reactive schizophrenia tends to be sudden, while that in process schizophrenia tends to be gradual. The actual degree of decompensation may vary markedly, depending on the severity of stress and the makeup of the individual. And the course of recovery or recompensation may also be relatively rapid or slow. Similarly, the degree of recovery may be complete, leading to a better integrated person than before; it may be partial but sufficient for adequate adjustment; or the individual's defenses may be stabilized on a psychotic level, eventuating in chronic schizophrenia.

General sociocultural factors in schizophrenia

While disorders of thought and emotion are common to schizophrenia the world over, cultural factors may influence the type, the symptom content, and even the incidence of schizophrenic disorders in different societies. For example, one of the more puzzling findings is that first admission rates for schizophrenia are very high in the Republic of Ireland (Southern Ireland), but not among Irish Catholics residing elsewhere, including Northern Ireland (Murphy, 1978). One possibility is that different diagnostic criteria are employed in the Irish Republic. Even though criteria have been agreed on internationally, there is still variation in the strictness or looseness with which diagnoses are made in different parts of the world (Gurland & Kuriansky, 1978).

Systematic differences in the content and form of a schizophrenic disorder between cultures and even subcultures were documented by Carothers (1953, 1959) in his studies of different African groups. Carothers found the hebephrenic type of schizophrenia to be most common among African tribal groups in remote areas. He attributed this finding to a lack of well-developed ego-defense mechanisms among the members of these groups, thus making a complete disorganization of personality more likely when schizophrenia did occur.

Similarly, Field (1960) described the initial schizophrenic breakdown among natives in rural Ghana as typically involving a state of panic. Here it was observed that when individuals were brought quickly to a shrine for treatment, they usually calmed down and in a few days appeared recovered. But when there was considerable delay before reaching the shrine, the individual often developed a classic hebephrenic disorder.

In a more recent study of schizophrenia among the aborigines of West Malaysia, Kinzie and Bolton (1973) found the acute type to be by far the most common subtype; they also noted that symptom content often "had an obvious cultural overlay, for example, seeing a 'river ghost' or 'men-like spirits' or talking to one's 'soul' " (p. 773). However, the clinical picture seems to be changing as rural Africans and other people from developing nations are increasingly exposed to modern technology and social change (Copeland, 1968; Kinzie & Bolton, 1973; Torrey, 1973).

An important consideration in cross-cultural studies is that opinions concerning what is "normal" by professionals from another culture may not always correspond with the opinions held by members of the community in question. For example, in describing the schizophrenic disorders of members of the Hawaii-Japanese community, professional observers emphasized seclusiveness and shallow, blunted emotionality. Community members, on the other hand, were impressed by evidence of uncontrolled emotionality and distrust, behaviors that are strongly counter to the values of that community (Katz et al., 1978).

Focusing on sociocultural factors within our own society, Murphy (1968) summarized the picture as follows:

"There is a truly remarkable volume of research literature demonstrating an especially high rate of schizophrenia . . . in the lowest social class or classes . . . of moderately large to large cities throughout much of the Western world. It is not altogether clear what is the direction of causality in this relationship—whether the conditions of life of the lowest social classes are conducive to the development of schizophrenia, or schizophrenia leads to a decline in social class position—but present evidence would make it seem probable that some substantial part of the phenomenon results from lower class conditions of life being conducive to schizophrenia." (p. 152)

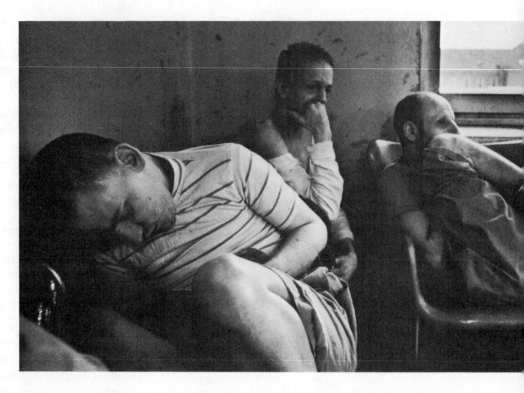

In the past schizophrenic patients generally received custodial treatment, particularly in large, overcrowded state mental institutions. Under such conditions, the rate of discharge for patients was only about 30 percent.

Levy and Rowitz (1972) also found both a higher incidence of schizophrenia and a greater likelihood of relapse on lower socioeconomic levels, especially in areas of large cities that are undergoing rapid and drastic social change. Apparently the social disorganization, insecurity, poverty, and harshness characteristic of urban slums intensify personal problems and tend to increase the likelihood of schizophrenic and other psychopathology.

In a sophisticated review of the impressive evidence relating social class and the incidence of schizophrenia, Kohn (1973) suggested that the conditions of lower-class existence impair the individual's ability to deal in a resourceful manner with varied life stressors. The correlation is decidedly imperfect, however, for we know that some lower-class persons emerge from their backgrounds with superabundant resourcefulness. Here it may also be emphasized that alleged ethnic differences in the incidence and clinical pictures of schizophrenia—for example, between blacks, Chicanos, and Anglo-Americans—disappear when social class, education, and related socioeconomic conditions are equated.

In concluding our review of causal factors in schizophrenia, it may be pointed out that research on the causation of human behavior is, as Shakow (1969) expressed it, "fiendishly complex," even with normal subjects.

"Research with disturbed human beings is even more so, particularly with those with whom it is difficult to communicate, among them schizophrenics. The marked range of schizophrenia, the marked variance within the range and within the individual, the variety of shapes that the psychosis takes, and both the excessive and compensatory behaviors that characterize it, all reflect this special complexity. Recent years have seen the complication further enhanced by the use of a great variety of therapeutic devices, such as drugs, that alter both the physiological and psychological nature of the organism. Research with schizophrenics, therefore, calls for awareness not only of the factors creating variance in normal human beings, but also of the many additional sources of variance this form of psychosis introduces." (Shakow, 1969, p. 618)

Or as Bannister (1971) has pointed out, "We will eventually have to develop a theory of what makes all people march before we can say very much about why some people march to a different drummer" (p. 84).

In general, however, it appears that there is no one clinical entity or causal sequence in schizophrenia. Rather we seem to be dealing with several types of maladaptive behavior resulting from an interaction of biological, psychosocial, and sociocultural factors; the role of these factors undoubtedly varies according to the given case and clinical picture. Often the interaction appears to involve a vicious spiral, in which life stress triggers metabolic changes that impair brain functioning, the latter, in turn, intensifying anxiety and panic as the individual realizes he or she is losing control. And so the spiral continues until more permanent defensive patterns are established, treatment is undertaken, or the disorder "has run its course." In severe instances, the "course" may be as long as 40 years. It is important to note that although full recovery is rare after such a lengthy period of disorder, it does sometimes occur (M. Bleuler, 1978).

Treatment and outcomes

Until recent times, the prognosis for schizophrenia was generally unfavorable. Under the routine custodial treatment in large mental hospital settings, the rate of discharge approximated only 30 percent.

For most schizophrenic individuals, the outlook today is not nearly so dark. Improvement in this situation came with dramatic suddenness when the phenothiazines—major tranquilizing drugs—were introduced in the 1950s. Chemotherapy, together with other modern treatment methods, permits the majority of cases to be treated in outpatient clinics; a schizophrenic individual who enters a mental hospital or clinic as an inpatient for the first time has an 80- to 90-percent chance of being discharged within a matter of weeks or, at most, months. However, the rate of readmission is still extremely high, with 45 percent of all discharged patients being readmitted during the first year after release. Overall, about one-third of schizophrenic patients recover, which means technically that they remain symptom-free for five years; another third show partial recovery; and a final third remain

Conditions associated with favorable outcomes in the treatment of schizophrenia

1. Reactive rather than process schizophrenia, in which the time from onset of full-blown symptoms is 6 months or less.
2. Clear-cut precipitating stressors.
3. Adequate heterosexual adjustment prior to schizophrenic episode.
4. Good social and work adjustment prior to schizophrenic episode.
5. Minimal incidence of schizophrenia and other pathological conditions in family background.
6. Involvement of depression or other schizoaffective pattern.
7. Favorable life situation to return to and adequate aftercare in the community.

In general, the opposite of the preceding conditions —including poor premorbid adjustment, slow onset, and relatives with schizophrenia—are indicative of an unfavorable prognosis.

Here it may be noted that in a 5-year follow-up study of 61 schizophrenic individuals in the U.S., Hawk, Carpenter, and Strauss (1975) failed to find any differences in long-range outcomes between acute and other subtypes of schizophrenia. (Data could be obtained on only 61 out of the original sample of 131 cases.) While this sample is too small to be definitive, this study is part of an International Pilot Study of Schizophrenia (IPSS) designed to include transcultural data on over 1200 patients in 9 countries— Colombia, Czechoslovakia, Denmark, India, Nigeria, Taiwan, U.S.S.R., the United Kingdom, and the United States.

Based on Caffey, Galbrecht, and Klett (1971), Fenz and Velner (1970), Hawk, Carpenter, and Strauss (1975), Morrison (1974), Roff (1974), Stephens, Astrup, and Mangrum (1966), Turner, Dopkeen, and Labreche (1970), and Yarden (1974).

largely or totally disabled. The ratio appears less favorable for children and adolescents than for adults (Bender, 1973; Gross & Huber, 1973; Morrison, 1974; Roff, 1974). For an overview of conditions that would suggest a favorable prognosis in schizophrenia, see the HIGHLIGHT on this page.

As we have done with respect to other disorders, we shall postpone until later chapters a detailed discussion of the various kinds of

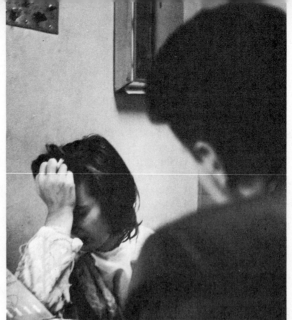

The prognosis for schizophrenia has brightened in recent years. These three photographs show the very noticeable improvement this schizophrenic woman made after only a few days of treatment.

When first admitted to the hospital, she had been agitated and crying, then became withdrawn, convinced that everyone around her was hostile. In her first interview with her therapist, she answered a few questions, but then hid her face with her hand and only shrugged her shoulders in answer to further questions. But after three days of hospitalization she was able to talk more openly to her therapist.

Her treatment involved an intensive program of specially prescribed therapies, including drugs (chlorpromazine) and psychotherapy. This woman was released after only seven weeks. Follow-up treatment included periodic visits to a community health clinic, continuing medication, and the understanding of her husband and family. (Based on Wilson, 1964.) All photos: Alfred Eisenstaedt. Time-Life Books.

treatment employed for schizophrenia. Here we note merely that contrary to widespread belief, such treatment is by no means limited to biological forms of intervention. Indeed, a breakthrough in the fashioning of a demonstrably powerful form of psychosocial intervention in schizophrenia is the most hopeful development to appear in the past quarter century (Paul & Lentz, 1977). Briefly, this treatment involves the use of a token economy program for hospitalized schizophrenic patients; we shall say more of this remarkable advance in Chapters 19 and 20.

It seems fitting to end our consideration of the schizophrenic syndromes with some conclusions from a major international conference on schizophrenia, recently held at the University of Rochester. The following points were cited by Joseph Zubin (1978), a leading researcher in the area:

"1. First, schizophrenia today is much less disabling than in the first half of this century.

2. The course of the disorder, even when little or no therapeutic or custodial intervention takes place, is rather varied.

3. The assumption that psychosocial therapeutic approaches are of limited value is no longer tenable.

4. Close relationships with family or important others in itself is not disabling to the schizophrenic, but close involvement with hostile environments is.

5. Social impoverishment leads to clinical impoverishment, whereas social enrichment leads to clinical improvement.

6. The vulnerability concept is regarded as useful by all participants." (p. 641)

And so, that is where we are today in respect to this most crippling of psychological disorders. One cannot help but wonder what would have been the fate of the Genain sisters—especially that of the beleaguered and tragic Hester—had they been born twenty years later.

Paranoia

The term *paranoia* has been in use a long time. The ancient Greeks and Romans used it to refer more or less indiscriminately to any mental disorder. Our present, more limited use of the term stems from the work of Kraepelin, who reserved it for cases showing delusions and impaired contact with reality but without the severe personality disorganization characteristic of schizophrenia.[4]

Currently two main types of psychoses are included under the general heading of paranoid disorders. (A third type is described briefly in the HIGHLIGHT on page 430.)

a) *Paranoia,* with a delusional system that develops slowly, becomes intricate, logical, and systemized and centers around delusions of persecution and/or grandeur. Aside from the delusions, the patient's personality remains relatively intact, with no evidence of serious disorganization and no hallucinations (unlike paranoid schizophrenia, discussed on pp. 407–409).

b) *Acute paranoid disorder,* with transient and changeable paranoid delusions, lacking either the logical and systematic features of paranoia or the bizarre fragmentation and deterioration often found in paranoid schizophrenia. Usually the condition is related to some evident stress and is a transient phenomenon. Paranoid states often color the clinical picture in other types of psychopathological reactions.[5]

Our primary focus in this section is on paranoia. Paranoia is rare in clinic and mental hospital populations, but this provides a somewhat misleading picture of its actual occurrence.

Many exploited inventors; persecuted teachers, business executives, or other professionals; fanatical reformers; morbidly jealous spouses; and self-styled prophets fall in this category. Unless they become a serious nuisance, these individuals are usually able to maintain themselves in the community and do not recognize their paranoid condition nor seek help to alleviate it.

In some instances, however, they are potentially dangerous, and in virtually all instances they are inveterate "injustice-detectors," very inclined to institute legal actions of one sort or another.

---

[4]There is a marked dearth of recent research on paranoia, and in this section we have been forced to draw on a number of earlier but seemingly definitive studies.

[5]Comprehensive reviews of early studies of paranoid states may be found in Tanna (1974) and in Meissner (1978).

Clinical picture in paranoia

In paranoia the individual feels singled out and taken advantage of, mistreated, plotted against, stolen from, spied upon, ignored, or otherwise mistreated by "enemies." The delusional system usually centers around one major theme, such as financial matters, a job, an invention, an unfaithful spouse, or other life affairs.[6] For example, a woman who is failing on the job may insist that her fellow workers and superiors have it in for her because they are jealous of her great ability and efficiency. As a result, she may quit her job and go to work elsewhere, only to find friction developing again and her new job in jeopardy. Now she may become convinced that the first company has written to her present employer and has turned everyone here against her so that she has not been given a fair chance. With time, more and more of the environment is integrated into her delusional system as each additional experience is misconstrued and interpreted in the light of her delusional ideas. (See HIGHLIGHT on page 431.)

Although the evidence that paranoid persons advance to justify their claims may be extremely tenuous and inconclusive, they are unwilling to accept any other possible explanation and are impervious to reason. A husband may be convinced of his spouse's unfaithfulness because on two separate occasions when he answered the phone the party at the other end hung up. Argument and logic are futile. In fact, any questioning of his delusions only convinces him that his interrogator has sold out to his enemies.

Milner cited the case of a paranoid man, aged 33, who murdered his wife by battering her head with a hammer. Prior to the murder, he had become convinced that his wife was suffering from some strange disease and that she had purposely infected him because she wished him to die. He believed that this disease was due to a "cancer-consumption" germ. He attributed his conclusion in part to his wife's alleged sexual perversion and also gave the following reasons for his belief:

---

[6]At one time it was customary to distinguish several types of paranoid disorders in accordance with the delusional ideas manifested—whether persecutory, grandiose, erotic, jealous, or litigious. But a classification in terms of delusional content has been found not to be very helpful.

HIGHLIGHT

Folie à deux

A relatively neglected phenomenon in the functional psychoses is that of *folie à deux*—a form of psychological "contagion" in which one person copies and incorporates into his own personality structure the delusions and other psychotic patterns of another person. Familial relationships between individuals in 103 cases studied by Gralnick (1942) fell within one of the following four categories:

sister ⇌ sister	40 cases
husband ⇌ wife	28 cases
mother ⇌ child	24 cases
brother ⇌ brother	11 cases

Among the explanatory factors—all environmental—emphasized by Gralnick were the following: (a) length of association, (b) dominance-submission, (c) type of familial relationship, and (d) pre-psychotic personality. The high incidence in the husband-wife category is particularly striking, since common heredity would play no part as an etiological factor in these cases.

In a more recent study, Soni and Rockley (1974) have reported on 8 cases of *folie à deux* seen at a European hospital. Their findings support those of Gralnick and emphasize the role of pathological pre-psychotic characteristics, such as increased suggestibility and submissive roles, as well as the type of relationship, in explaining why these patients acquired the delusions of their partners.

"1. His wife had insured him for a small sum immediately after marriage.

"2. A young man who had been friendly with his wife before their marriage died suddenly.

"3. A child who had lived in the same house as his wife's parents suffered from fits. (He also believed that his wife's parents were suffering from the same disease.)

"4. For several months before the crime his food had had a queer taste, and for a few weeks before the crime he had suffered from a pain in the chest and an unpleasant taste in the mouth." (1949, p. 130)

Although ideas of persecution predominate, many paranoid individuals develop delusions of grandeur in which they endow themselves with superior or unique ability. Such "exalted" ideas usually center around Messianic missions, political or social reforms, or remarkable inventions. Paranoid persons who are religious may consider themselves appointed by God to save the world and may spend most of their time "preaching" and "crusading." Threats of fire and brimstone, burning in hell, and similar persuasive devices are liberally employed. Many paranoid persons become attached to extremist political movements and are tireless and fanatical crusaders, although they often do their cause more harm than good by their self-righteousness and their condemnation of others.

Some paranoid individuals develop remarkable inventions that they have endless trouble in patenting or selling. Gradually they become convinced that there is a plot afoot to steal their invention, or that enemies of the United States are working against them to prevent the country from receiving the benefits of their remarkable talents. Hoffman cited the case of an individual who went to Washington to get presidential assistance in obtaining a patent for a flamethrower that, he claimed, could destroy all the enemies of the United States. He would patiently explain who he was. "There's God who is Number 1, and Jesus Christ who is Number 2, and me, I am Number 3" (1943, p. 574).

Aside from the delusional system, such an individual may appear perfectly normal in conversation, emotionality, and conduct. Hallucinations and the other obvious signs of psychopathology are rarely found. This normal appearance, together with the logical and coherent way in which the delusional ideas are presented, may make the individual most convincing.

In one case an engineer developed detailed plans for eliminating the fog in San Francisco and other large cities by means of a system of reflectors which would heat the air by solar radiation and cause the fog to lift. The company for whom he worked examined the plans and found them unsound. This upset him greatly and he resigned his position, stating that the other engineers in the company were not qualified to pass judgment on any really complex and advanced engineering projects like his. Instead of attempting to obtain other employment, he then devoted full time trying to find some other engineering firm that would have the vision and technical proficiency to see the great potentialities of his idea. He would present his plans convincingly but become highly suspicious and hostile when questions concerning their

HIGHLIGHT

Sequence of events in paranoid mode of thinking

A number of investigators have concluded that the most useful perspective from which to view paranoia is in terms of a *mode of thinking*. The sequence of events which appears to characterize this mode of thinking may be summarized as follows:

1. Suspiciousness—the individual mistrusts the motives of others, fears he or she will be taken advantage of, is constantly on the alert.

2. Protective thinking—selectively perceives the actions of others to confirm suspicions, now blames others for own failures.

3. Hostility—responds to alleged injustices and mistreatment with anger and hostility, becomes increasingly suspicious.

4. Paranoid illumination—the moment when everything "falls into place"; the individual finally understands the strange feelings and events being experienced.

5. Delusions—of influence and persecution that may be based on "some grain of truth," presented in a very logical and convincing way; often later development of delusions of grandeur.

Over time, the paranoid individual may incorporate additional life areas, people, and events into the delusional system, creating a "pseudo community" whose purpose is to carry out some action against him or her. Paranoid individuals who respond in this manner may come to feel that all the attention they are receiving from others is indicative of their unique abilities and importance, thus paving the way for delusions of grandeur.

Based in part on Swanson, Bohnert, and Smith (1970).

feasibility were raised. Eventually, he became convinced that there was a conspiracy among a large number of engineering firms to steal his plans and use them for their own profit. He reported his suspicions to the police, threatening to do something about the situation himself unless they took action. As a consequence of his threats, he was hospitalized for psychiatric observation and diagnosed as suffering from paranoia.

The delusional system is apt to be particularly convincing if one accepts the basic premise or premises upon which it is based. For example, where the delusional system develops around some actual injustice, it may be difficult to distinguish between fact and fancy. As a result, the individual's family and friends, as well as well-meaning public officials, may be convinced of the truth of the claims. However, the individual's inability to see the facts in any other light, typical lack of evidence for far-reaching conclusions, and hostile, suspicious, and uncommunicative attitude when the delusional ideas are questioned usually provide clues that something is wrong.

The following case history is a rather classical description of a mild paranoia; it reveals the development of a logically patterned delusional system and the pertinent selection of environmental evidence that involves more and more individuals in the supposed conspiracy. Despite this woman's delusional system, however, she was not severely out of touch with reality; there are many nonhospitalized cases in the community who reveal similar symptomatology to a more serious degree.

The patient was a 31-year-old nurse who was commissioned a second lieutenant in the Army Nurse Corps shortly after the beginning of World War II. From the start she found it difficult to adjust to fellow nurses and to enlisted men under her supervision, the difficulty apparently arising from her overzealousness in carrying out ward regulations in the minutest detail. In any event, "No one could get along with her." After some 2 years of service, she was transferred to [a new assignment].

". . . Initially she made an excellent impression, but soon showed herself to be a perfectionist, a hypercritical and domineering personality who insisted on the immediate, precise, exact and detailed execution of orders. Within a 14-week period she was transferred on three separate occasions from post to post, and at each new post her manner and her attitude, despite her precise and meticulous efficiency, constituted a virtual demand that nurses, wardmen, patients, and medical officers conform to her exceedingly rigid ideas about the management of ward and even departmental routines. . . .

"During the course of her last assignment, she received every possible help. She requested additional responsibility and was, therefore, assigned, as charge nurse, to the Eye, Ear, Nose, and Throat Clinic. Within a week she lodged a complaint with the commanding officer of the hospital, accusing the enlisted men of conspiring against her, the nurses of lying about her, and the officer in charge of lack of

co-operation. She was, therefore, transferred to one of the wards, where she expected wardmen, nurses and patients to execute her orders on the instant, in minute and exact detail, and where she violently berated them because of their inability to do so. A week later, the responsible medical officer requested that she be relieved from duty there. Instead, she discussed the problem with the chief nurse and promised to correct her attitude. Within four days, the patients as a group requested her removal. Two weeks later, the ward officer repeated his request. She was, therefore, given a five-day leave, and during her absence all ward personnel were contacted in an attempt to help her adjust when she returned to duty.

"During this period she became convinced that she was being persecuted. She grew tense and despondent, kept rigidly to herself, was unable to sleep in a room with a ticking clock, and frequently burst into tears. As she herself said, 'Some of the nurses deliberately went out of their way to annoy and criticize me. They wanted to make me trouble. That's why I was so upset.' On three separate occasions, she requested the appointment of a Board of Officers to investigate these alleged discriminatory acts. Finally she demanded that a Board of Officers be convened to determine her efficiency as a nurse. Instead, she was ordered to report to our hospital for psychiatric observation.

"On admission, few details of her military history were known. She seemed alert and co-operative, was well oriented in all three spheres [time, place, person], and was thought to be in complete contact. Extreme care, however, was necessary when addressing her. Even fellow patients would warn newcomers to the ward. 'Be careful what you say when she's around. She won't mean it, but she'll twist your statements without changing your words, and give them some meaning you never intended.' In addition, she was bitter about the unfair treatment she had received in the Army, wished to reform the Medical Department and the Army Nursing Corps, and indignantly repudiated the existence of any condition that could justify placing her under NP [neuropsychiatric] observation. . . .

"The diagnosis of 'paranoia, true type' was made, and she was returned to the United States, one month after admission to the hospital, a rigid and overzealous individual whose inelasticity had antagonized her associates and aroused severe emotional strain within herself, firmly convinced that she was being persecuted because of the necessary and badly needed work which she had much too efficiently performed. . . . she was received in the States as a patient in the very hospital to whose psychiatric section she had previously, for so brief a period of time, been assigned as ward nurse." (Rosen & Kiene, 1946, pp. 330–33)

Paranoid individuals are not always as dangerous as we have been led to believe by popular fiction and drama, but there is always the chance that they will decide to take matters into their own hands and deal with their enemies in the only way that seems effective. In one instance, a paranoid school principal became convinced that the school board was discriminating against him and shot and killed most of the members of the board. In another case a paranoid man shot and killed a group of 7 persons he thought had been following him. The number of husbands and wives who have been killed or injured by suspicious paranoid mates is undoubtedly large. As Swanson, Bohnert, and Smith (1970) have pointed out, such murderous violence is commonly associated with jealousy and the loss of self-esteem; the spouse feels that he or she has been deceived, taken advantage of, and humiliated. Paranoid persons may also get involved in violent and destructive subversive activities as well as in political assassinations.

Causal factors in paranoia

Most of us on various occasions may wonder if we are not "jinxed," when it seems as if everything we do goes wrong and the cards seem to be "stacked against us." If we are generally somewhat suspicious and disposed to blame others for our difficulties, we may feel that most people are selfish and ruthless and that honest people, no matter what their ability, do not have a fair chance. As a result, we may feel abused and become somewhat bitter and cynical. Many people go through life feeling underrated and frustrated and brooding over fancied and real injustices. Meissner (1978) regards such attitudes as a normal and essential phase of personality development, a necessary component in the achievement of personal identity and autonomy. Most people, according to this view, are able to grow beyond this phase in development, where a central feature is the "need for an enemy." Some few are not, however, in which case they entertain paranoid explanations of their problems on a chronic basis.

Meissner doubts very much that it is possible to make a sharp distinction between paranoid ideation and schizophrenia, and thus between paranoid schizophrenia and other types of paranoid syndromes. We have already noted that individuals with paranoid schizophrenia tend not to show the extensive cognitive disorganization seen in other forms of schizophrenia. It should also be noted that biological factors have rarely been implicated in the paranoid disorders, as they have been in schizophrenia—although it must be acknowledged that very little work has been done in this area. It has seemed to most observers that psychosocial factors are sufficient to account for the development of paranoid forms of thought. In any event, if Meissner's assertion concerning a continuity between the schizophrenias and the paranoid syndrome proves correct, a major implication is that all the etiological factors identified as being important in schizophrenia (perhaps especially those pertaining to paranoid schizophrenia) might also be implicated in paranoia.

It may also be noted that the maintenance of a severely paranoid "fix" on the world does indeed require drastic derangements of the organism's basic cognitive and perceptual equipment, although it does not require that such equipment be subject to virtual functional annihilation. If it did, it would render paranoia impossible as an effective coping strategy.

Faulty learning and development. Most individuals who later become paranoid seem as children to have been aloof, suspicious, seclusive, stubborn, and resentful of punishment. When crossed, they became sullen and morose. Rarely did they show a history of normal play with other children or good socialization in terms of warm, affectionate relationships (Sarvis, 1962; Schwartz, 1963; Swanson, Bohnert, & Smith, 1970).

Often the family background appears to have been authoritarian and excessively dominating, suppressive, and critical; frequently, some family members have practiced "mind reading" the thoughts of other family members. Such a family has often been permeated with an air of superiority that was a cover-up for an underlying lack of self-acceptance and feelings of inferiority, creating for the child, in turn, the

In paranoia a person feels singled out and taken advantage of, mistreated, plotted against, stolen from, spied upon, ignored, or otherwise mistreated by "enemies."

necessity of proving superiority. Inevitably the family background of such individuals colors their feelings about people in general and their way of reacting to others. Inadequate socialization is likely to keep them from understanding the motives and point of view of others and lead them to suspicious misinterpretation of unintentional slights. Also they tend to enter into social relationships with a hostile, dominating attitude that drives others away. Their inevitable social failures then further undermine their self-esteem and lead to deeper social isolation and mistrust of others.

In later personality development these early trends merge into a picture of self-important, rigid, arrogant individuals who long to dominate others and readily maintain their unrealistic self-picture by projecting the blame for difficulties onto others and seeing in others

the weaknesses they cannot acknowledge in themselves. They are highly suspicious of the motives of other people and quick to sense insult or mistreatment. Such individuals lack a sense of humor—which is not surprising, since they view life as a deadly serious struggle—and are incapable of seeing things from any viewpoint but their own. Typically, they categorize people and ideas into "good" and "bad" and have difficulty in conceiving of something as having both good and bad qualities or shades of gray. Their goals and expectations are unrealistically high, and they refuse to make concessions in meeting life's problems by accepting more moderate goals. They expect to be praised and appreciated for even minor achievements, and when such praise is not forthcoming, they sulk and withdraw from normal contacts.

Although such individuals may have broad interests and appear normal in general behavior, they are usually unable to relate closely to other persons; they appear inaccessible, are overly aggressive, and maintain a somewhat superior air. Meissner (1978) views these personality traits as in large measure manifestations of a desperate attempt to maintain autonomy and a related inordinate fear of submission to the will of others, as though such submission would constitute nothing less than total personality disintegration.

Failure and inferiority. The lives of paranoid individuals are replete with failures in critical life situations—social, occupational, and marital—stemming from their rigidity, their unrealistic goals, and their inability to get along with other people. Such failures jeopardize their view of themselves as being adequate, significant, and important and expose their easily wounded pride to what they interpret as the rejection, scorn, and ridicule of others.

Their failures are made more difficult to cope with by their utter inability to understand the causes. Why should their efforts to improve the efficiency of the company—which people approve in principle—lead to such negative reactions from others? Why should people dislike them when they are striving so hard to do the best possible job down to the very last detail? Unable to see themselves or the situation objectively, they simply cannot understand how they tend to alienate others and why they are rebuffed and rejected.

Although their feelings of inferiority are masked behind their air of superiority and self-importance, many aspects of their behavior give them away. Clues in profusion are found in their continual craving for praise and recognition, their hypersensitivity to criticism, their exact and formal adherence to socially approved behavior, and their conscientious and overzealous performance of the most minute occupational tasks.

In essence, then, the paranoid individual is confronted with experiences of failure that in effect say, "People don't like you," "Something is wrong with you," "You are inferior." But he or she is incapable of dealing with the problem in a task-oriented way, instead tending to intensify the existing defenses, becoming more rigid, opinionated, and prone to blame others. This defensive pattern is a protection against having to face unbearable feelings of inferiority and worthlessness. In this connection, Meissner (1978) reports the case of a young man who was sexually seduced by his drunken mother. He lived in terror that his "sin" would be discovered, and in the process developed an elaborate paranoid system of thought.

Elaboration of defenses and the "pseudocommunity." A rigid, self-important, humorless, and suspicious individual such as we have described becomes understandably unpopular with other people—in effect, an aversive stimulus. Thus, as Lemert (1962) has noted, the paranoid person frequently becomes in fact a target of actual discrimination and mistreatment. Ever alert to injustices, both imagined and real, such an individual easily finds "proof" of persecution.

In this context, Grunebaum and Perlman (1973) have pointed to the naivete of the preparanoid person in assessing the interpersonal world—in terms of who can be trusted and who cannot—as a fertile source of hurtful interactions. As they express it, "The ability to trust others realistically requires that the individual be able to tolerate minor and major violations of trust that are part of normal human relationships" (p. 32). But the preparanoid individual is unprepared for the "facts of life," tending to both trust and mistrust inappropriately and to overreact when others are perceived, accurately or not, as betraying the trust.

Some persons do not go beyond this stage, simply continuing as paranoid personalities, continually expecting—and inducing—rejection and rebuff.

Where paranoia develops, it usually does so gradually, as mounting failures and seeming betrayals force these individuals to an elaboration of their defensive structures. To avoid self-devaluation, they search for "logical" reasons for their lack of success. Why were they denied a much-deserved promotion? Why was it given to someone less experienced and obviously far less qualified? They become more vigilant, begin to scrutinize the environment, search for hidden meanings, and ask leading questions. They ponder like a detective over the "clues" they pick up, trying to fit them into some sort of meaningful picture.

Gradually the picture begins to crystallize—a process commonly referred to as "paranoid illumination." It becomes apparent that they are being singled out for some obscure reason, that other people are working against them, that they are being interfered with. In essence, they protect themselves against the intolerable assumption "There is something wrong with me" with the projective defense "They are doing something to me." Now they have failed not because of any inferiority or lack on their part but because others are working against them. They are on the side of good and the progress of humankind while their enemies are allied with the forces of evil. With this as their fundamental defensive premise, they proceed to distort and falsify the facts to fit it and gradually develop a logic-tight, fixed, delusional system.

Cameron (1959) has referred to this process as the building up of a paranoid "pseudo-community" in which the individual organizes surrounding people (both real and imaginary) into a structured group whose purpose is to carry out some action against him or her. Now the most trivial events may take on an ominous meaning. If a new employee is hired, the person was obviously planted as a spy. If a subordinate makes a mistake, it is done to discredit his or her competence as a supervisor. Even the most casual conversation of others may have a hidden and sinister meaning. This pseudo-community is not all-inclusive, however, but remains limited in scope to those stressor areas—such as occupational failure—that present the greatest threat to the individual's feelings of adequacy and worth. In other life areas not directly involved with the paranoid system, the individual may be quite rational and may function adequately. Over a period of time, of course, additional life areas and experiences may be incorporated into the delusional system.

In many cases the attention these individuals think they are receiving leads them to believe that they are persons of great importance, for why else would their enemies go to all this trouble? In one case, it was pointed out to a hospitalized patient that if his enemies were persecuting him in the way he insisted they were, it would be costing them about $10,000 per day, which was obviously a ridiculous figure. The patient drew himself up proudly and replied, "Why shouldn't they? After all, I am the world's greatest atomic scientist." As might be expected, the particular content of the grandiose ideas that develop is closely related to the individual's education, vocation, and special interests. A man with strong religious convictions may develop the notion that he is a great religious savior, whereas a man interested in science is more likely to envision himself as a great inventor.

The role of perceptual selectivity in the development of these delusional systems should be emphasized. Once these individuals begin to suspect that others are working against them, they start carefully noting the slightest signs pointing in the direction of their suspicions and ignore all evidence to the contrary. As Swanson, Bohnert, and Smith (1970) have pointed out,

"Suspicious thinking is remarkably rigid thinking. The suspicious person has something on his mind constantly. He looks at the world with a definite expectation. Suspiciousness requires intense attention. The paranoid reads more between the lines than he sees in the lines themselves, thus overlooking the obvious." (p. 14)

With this frame of reference, it is quite easy, in our highly competitive, somewhat ruthless world, to find ample evidence that others are working against us. The attitude itself of paranoid individuals leads to a vicious circle, for their suspiciousness, distrust, and criticism of others drive their friends and well-wishers away and keep them in continual friction with other people, generating new incidents for them to grasp hold of and magnify. Often people do in fact have to conspire behind their backs in order to keep peace and cope with their eccentricities.

One additional factor often mentioned in connection with the development of paranoia is that of sexual maladjustment. Like schizophrenic patients, most paranoid individuals reveal sexual difficulties, not infrequently centering around homosexual conflicts. The factor of homosexuality was, in fact, strongly emphasized by Freud, who concluded that paranoia represents the individual's attempt to deal with homosexual tendencies that the ego is not prepared to acknowledge. Most contemporary investigators, however, believe that the critical factors in paranoia are the individual's serious difficulties in interpersonal relationships generally, compounded by overwhelming feelings of inadequacy and inferiority. While underlying sexual conflicts, both heterosexual and homosexual, may be involved in the clinical picture, they do not appear to be of primary significance.

Many early schizophrenic and paranoid patients make allusions to being "queer" or "gay," or to the thought that other people think they are. On investigation, it turns out that they typically have never engaged in homosexual behavior and show no indication of wishing to do so. Here it may be that they have finally hit upon an "explanation" for the feeling of being so different from others, and for the slights and contempt they believe are emanating from others. An explanation of this sort may be better than no explanation at all as far as the troubled person is concerned.

Treatment and outcomes

In the early stages of paranoia, treatment with individual and/or group psychotherapy may prove effective, particularly if an individual voluntarily seeks professional assistance. Here, behavior therapy appears to show particular promise; for example, the paranoid ideation may be altered by a combination of aversive conditioning, removal of factors in the person's life situation that are reinforcing the maladaptive behavior, and development of more effective coping patterns.

Once the delusional system is well established, however, treatment is extremely difficult. It is usually impossible to communicate with such individuals in a rational way concerning their problems. In addition, they are not prone to seek treatment, but are more likely to be seeking justice for all the wrong done to them. Nor is hospitalization likely to help, for they are likely to see it as a form of punishment. They are apt to regard themselves as superior to other patients and will often complain that their families and the hospital staff have had them "put away" for no valid reason; seeing nothing wrong with themselves, they refuse to cooperate or participate in treatment.

Eventually, however, they may realize that their failure to curb their actions and ideas will result in prolonged hospitalization. As a result,

they may make a pretext of renouncing their delusions, admitting that they did hold such ideas but claiming that they now realize the ideas are absurd and have given them up. After their release, they are often more reserved in expressing their ideas and in annoying other people, but they are far from recovered. Thus the prognosis for paranoia has traditionally been unfavorable.

In our consideration of psychoses involving schizophrenia and paranoia, we have dealt with clinical manifestations considerably different from those found in the neuroses, the psychosomatic illnesses, or even the psychotic disorders of affect. In schizophrenia we noted severely impaired contact with reality and marked personality disorganization—involving disturbances in thought, affect, and behavior. We examined the major types of schizophrenia—undifferentiated, paranoid, catatonic, and hebephrenic and attempted to identify the differences among them. We then dealt with various causal factors, noting that we still do not fully understand the development of schizophrenia. However, we examined evidence pointing to the significant role of genetic factors in schizophrenia; we also noted the possible role of neurophysiological and biochemical alterations in the impairment of normal brain functioning in schizophrenia, including the breakdown of coherent thought patterns. The precise nature of these alterations remains to be ascertained, as well as whether they precede or result from the mental disorder. We also considered the significance of various psychosocial factors, regarded by many investigators to be of primary importance in the etiology of schizophrenia. Finally, we noted that innovations in chemotherapy, psychosocial therapy, and programs in outpatient clinics have resulted in an increasingly favorable outlook for the schizophrenic patient.

In the latter part of the chapter we examined paranoia, characterized by the development of a highly systematized delusional system. Here, the evidence indicates that psychosocial factors are of primary importance. Paranoid disorders involve less personality disorganization than most other types of psychosis, but they are resistant to current methods of treatment.

13

Organic mental disorders and mental retardation

Organic mental disorders

Mental retardation

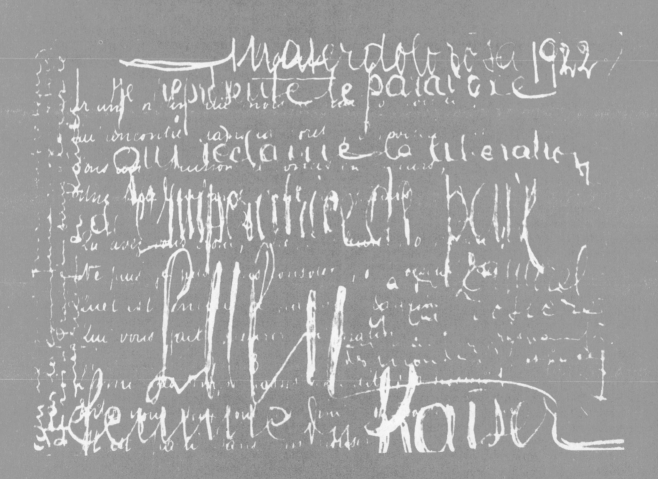

In contrast to most kinds of abnormal behavior, there are certain problems that arise partly as a consequence of gross structural defects in the brain tissue. Such defects impair the normal physiological functioning of those parts of the brain affected—thus, in turn, producing deficits in the mediation of effective thought, feeling, and action.

When such gross structural defects in the brain occur before birth or at a very early age, the typical result is mental retardation, the severity depending on the defect. In mental retardation, the individual fails to develop an optimal level of the various skills that underlie adequate and independent coping with environmental demands. Most mentally retarded persons do not suffer from gross brain damage, but virtually all those individuals who are *severely* retarded have demonstrable organic pathology.

Sometimes the intact brain sustains damage after it has completed all or most of its biological development. A wide variety of injuries, diseases, and toxic chemicals may result in the functional impairment or death of neural cells and, in turn, lead to inadequate psychological functioning and perhaps psychotic behavior.

The person who sustains serious brain damage after he or she has mastered the basic tasks of life is in a very different situation from the person who starts life with a deficit. When brain injury occurs in an older child or adult, there is a *loss* in established functioning. In contrast, the person who began life with severe mental retardation never had these functions to begin with. The difference is an extremely important one psychologically.

In this chapter we will discuss both situations. The first and largest part of the chapter will be devoted to the *organic mental disorders*—mental disorders that occur when there has been damage to the normal brain. Then, in the latter part of the chapter, we shall look at *mental retardation*, in which the individual fails to develop a normal level of intellectual functioning. In both cases, we shall see that the physical deficit in the brain is only one cause of the individual's behavior. In fact, in the case of individuals with mild retardation, as we shall see, there may be no physical deficit at all.

Organic mental disorders

Disorders that have resulted from interference with the functioning of a normal brain may involve only limited behavioral deficits or a wide range of psychopathology, depending on (a) the location and extent of neural damage, (b) the premorbid (pre-disorder) personality of the individual, and (c) the nature of the individual's life situation. There are many cases involving severe brain damage in which mental change is astonishingly slight, whereas in other cases mild brain damage leads to a psychotic reaction. These variations are explained by the fact that the individual is a functional unit and reacts as such to all stressors, whether they are organic or psychological. A well-integrated person can withstand brain damage or any other stress better than a rigid, immature, or otherwise psychologically handicapped person. Similarly, the individual who has a favorable life situation is likely to have a better prognosis than one who does not. Since the nervous system is the center for integration of behavior, however, there are limits to the amount of brain damage an individual can tolerate or compensate for without exhibiting impaired functioning (see HIGHLIGHT on page 440).

The regenerative capacities of the central nervous system are limited too. Cell bodies and neural pathways in the brain do not have the power of regeneration, which means that their destruction is permanent. However, the central nervous system abounds in back-up apparatus. If a given circuit is knocked out, others may take over, and functions lost as a result of brain damage may often be relearned. The degree of recovery from disabilities following an irreversible brain lesion may be relatively complete or limited, and recovery may proceed rapidly or slowly. Since there are limits to both the plasticity and the relearning ability of the brain, however, extensive brain damage may lead to a permanent loss of function and result in a wide range of physical and psychological symptoms. In general, especially with

Implications of brain damage

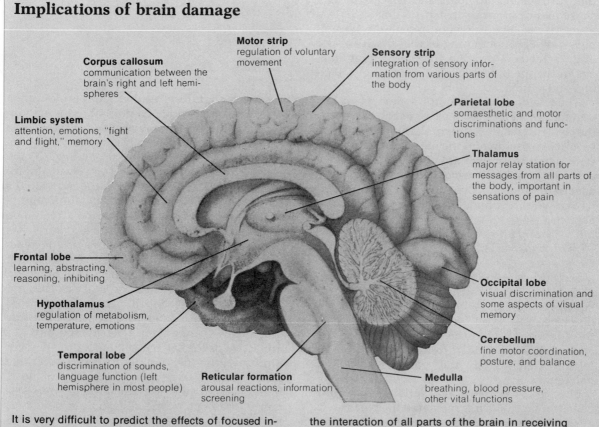

Motor strip
regulation of voluntary movement

Sensory strip
integration of sensory information from various parts of the body

Corpus callosum
communication between the brain's right and left hemispheres

Parietal lobe
somaesthetic and motor discriminations and functions

Limbic system
attention, emotions, "fight and flight," memory

Thalamus
major relay station for messages from all parts of the body, important in sensations of pain

Frontal lobe
learning, abstracting, reasoning, inhibiting

Occipital lobe
visual discrimination and some aspects of visual memory

Hypothalamus
regulation of metabolism, temperature, emotions

Cerebellum
fine motor coordination, posture, and balance

Temporal lobe
discrimination of sounds, language function (left hemisphere in most people)

Reticular formation
arousal reactions, information screening

Medulla
breathing, blood pressure, other vital functions

It is very difficult to predict the effects of focused injuries to the brain. Although there is some localization of function (as indicated in this drawing of the right cerebral hemisphere) and damage to a particular area may cause severe impairment of function, the brain's great back-up resources may be able in time to make up for the deficiency. The sheer number of neurons, or nerve cells, in the brain—10 to 12 billion—provide a redundancy of capability within each given area, to offset some cell loss. Also, the interaction of all parts of the brain in receiving and transmitting information will often permit an area to share related information to compensate for loss of function elsewhere. In addition, the brain has some capability for the repair of damage. The limits of these resources, however, can be reached; and while damage in some areas may lead only to a temporary loss of function, destruction in other areas—as well as extensive damage to any brain area—may result in complete and permanent loss.

severe damage, the greater the amount of tissue damage, the greater the impairment of function.

Brain disorders may be *acute* or *chronic*, the primary consideration being whether the brain pathology is reversible. An acute disorder is likely to be temporary and reversible, whereas a chronic disorder is usually irreversible because of permanent damage to the nervous system. This classification is not a hard and fast one, because an acute condition may leave some residual damage after the major symptoms have cleared up, while a chronic condition may show some alleviation of symptoms over time. However, a general picture can be given of the two types.

1. *Acute brain disorders* are caused by diffuse impairment of brain function. Such impairment may result from a variety of conditions, including high fevers, nutritional deficiencies, and drug intoxication. Symptoms range from mild mood changes to acute delirium. The latter may be complicated by hallucinations, delusions, and other personality disturbances.

The prognosis in acute brain disorders is good; such conditions usually clear up over a short period of time. In some cases, however, the lowering of cortical controls may precipitate a latent psychosis that persists after the immediate brain pathology has cleared up.

2. *Chronic brain disorders* result from injuries, disease, drugs, and a variety of other conditions. The permanent destruction of brain tissue is reflected in some degree of impairment of higher integrative functions. Where the damage is severe, such symptoms typically include the following:

a) Impairment of orientation—especially for time but often also for place and person;

b) Impairment of memory—notably for recent events and less for events of the remote past, with a tendency to confabulate, that is, to "invent" memories to fill in gaps;

c) Impairment of learning, comprehension, and judgment—with ideation tending to be concrete and impoverished—and with inability to think on higher conceptual levels and to plan;

d) Emotional impairment—with emotional overreactivity and easy arousal to laughter or tears, or with a blunting of affect;

e) Impairment of inner reality and ethical controls—with lowering of behavioral standards and carelessness in personal hygiene and appearance.

These symptoms may also occur in acute brain disorders; however, in such cases delirium and hallucinations or stupor are more likely to dominate the clinical picture. Depending on the severity of symptoms—in either acute or chronic disorders—the clinical picture may be referred to as *mild, moderate,* or *severe.*

Traditionally the organic mental disorders have been classified by disease entity or recognizable disorder, such as Huntington's chorea, general paresis, and so on. But these are basically physical disorders with various kinds of related psychopathology. In the DSM-III, physical disorders are coded on Axis III, and psychiatric categories are derived from Axes I and II (psychiatric or personality conditions). Thus, with the exception of the senile and presenile dementias, the traditional organic men-

tal disorders no longer appear as psychiatric categories. Instead, only particular clusters of symptoms based on brain damage and often seen in the various organically based psychoses are listed on Axis I. In our discussion, we will first describe these clusters of symptoms and then go on to describe the clinical picture, causal factors, and treatment approaches for five of the most common mental disorders associated with brain damage.

Organic symptom syndromes

"Syndromes" are groups of symptoms that tend to cluster together. The organic symptom syndromes include many symptoms similar to those that occur in the schizophrenias and the affective psychoses but that in this case reflect underlying brain pathology. The specific brain pathology may vary from some type of brain disease to the results of withdrawal of a chemical substance on which the patient has become physiologically dependent. For our purposes we shall group these symptom syndromes into four categories: (a) delirium and dementia, (b) amnestic syndrome and hallucinosis, (c) organic delusional syndrome and organic affective syndrome, and (d) organic personality syndrome.

It should be noted that more than one syndrome may be present in a given patient at the same time, and that syndromes and patterns of syndromes may change over the course of development of a particular disorder. At the behavioral level they often mimic the types of disorders we have been discussing in previous chapters, sometimes causing serious diagnostic errors to be made (Geschwind, 1975; Malamud, 1975).

Delirium and dementia. *Delirium* is characterized by a relatively rapid onset of widespread disorganization of the higher mental processes; it is caused by a generalized disturbance in brain metabolism. Information-processing capacities are more or less severely impaired, affecting such basic processes as attention, perception, memory, and thinking. Frequently, there is abnormal psychomotor activity and disturbance of the sleep cycle. In terms of the functional integrity of the brain, delirium is only one step above coma and, in fact, may lead to coma. The delirious person is essentially unable to carry out purposeful mental activity of any kind; current experience appears to make no contact with the individual's previously acquired store of knowledge.

Delirious states rarely last more than a week, terminating in recovery or, less often, in death. They tend, therefore, to be associated with acute rather than chronic brain disturbances. They may result from head injury, toxic or metabolic disturbances, oxygen deprivation, insufficient delivery of blood to brain tissues, or alcohol or other drugs in an addicted person.

Dementia has as its essential feature a noteworthy decrement or deterioration in intellectual functioning occurring after the completion of brain maturation (after, that is, about 15 years of age), in which the individual is otherwise alert and attuned to events in the environment. Memory functioning is invariably affected, and there is usually also marked indication of deficit in abstract thinking, acquisition of new knowledge or skill, problem solving, and judgment.

Normally, dementia is also accompanied by an impairment in emotional control and in moral and ethical sensibilities. It may be progressive or static; occasionally it is even reversible. Its course depends to a large extent on the nature of the etiology.

Etiologic factors in dementia are many and varied. They include degenerative processes that affect some individuals—usually older people but not always. Repeated cerebrovascular accidents (strokes), certain infectious diseases such as syphilis and meningitis, intracranial tumors and abscesses, certain dietary deficiencies, head injury, anoxia, and the ingestion or inhalation of toxic substances have all been implicated in the production of dementias.

Amnestic syndrome and hallucinosis.

The essential feature of the *amnestic syndrome* is a striking deficit in the ability to remember ongoing events more than a few minutes after they have taken place. Immediate memory and memory for events that occurred before the development of the disorder are largely unimpaired, as is memory for words and concepts. An amnestic individual, then, is constrained to live for the most part only in the present or the remote past; the recent past is for most practical purposes unavailable.[1]

In contrast to the dementia syndrome, overall cognitive functioning in the amnestic syndrome remains more or less intact. Theoretically, the disorder simply affects the relationships between the short-term and long-term memory systems, such that the contents of the former are not stored in the latter in a way that permits ready accessibility or retrieval.

A common reaction in the amnestic syndrome is for the individual to resist acknowledging the difficulty and to "fill in the gaps" with fanciful materials, a process known as *confabulation*. In the most common forms of amnestic syndrome, those due to alcohol or barbiturate addiction, the disorder is normally irreversible.

A wide range of other pathogenic factors may produce the amnestic syndrome. In these cases, depending on the nature and extent of damage to the affected neural structures and on the treatment undertaken, the syndrome may in time abate wholly, in part, or not at all.

The syndrome of *hallucinosis* has as its essential feature the persistent occurrence of hallucinations in the presence of known or suspected brain involvement; the term is not used where hallucinations are part of a more pervasive mental disorder like schizophrenia. These "false perceptions" arise in a state of full wakefulness, when the patient is alert and otherwise well oriented. The hallucinations most often involve the sense of hearing but may affect any sense; for example, visual hallucinations typically accompany psychedelic drug intoxication.

The course of the syndrome varies with the underlying pathology, but rarely exceeds one month, assuming discontinuance of the causative agent. As in the case of the amnestic syndrome, the most common etiologic factor is severe or long-standing alcohol dependency.

Organic delusional syndrome and organic affective syndrome.   The *organic*

---

[1]Whether the recent past is unavailable in some absolute sense is a question subject to differing interpretations. There is some evidence that these patients may recognize or even recollect events of the recent past if given sufficient cues, which suggests that the information *has* been stored. Thus the difficulty may be in the *retrieval* mechanism (Warrington & Weiskrantz, 1973).

delusional syndrome is one in which false beliefs or belief systems arise in a setting of known or suspected brain damage and are the chief clinical manifestation. These delusions vary in content depending to some extent on the particular organic etiology. For example, a distinctly paranoid delusional system is commonly seen with long-standing abuse of amphetamine drugs, whereas grandiose and expansive delusions are more characteristic of the patient with advanced syphilis (general paresis). In addition to infectious processes and the abuse of certain drugs, etiological factors in the organic delusional syndrome include head injury and intracranial tumors.

The *organic affective syndrome,* as the term implies, refers to manic or depressive states that are secondary to impairment of cerebral function. While the organic delusional syndrome may clinically mimic some forms of schizophrenic disorder, the organic affective syndrome closely resembles the symptoms seen in either depressive or manic affective disorders. The reaction may be minimal or severe, and the course of the disorder varies widely depending on the nature of the organic pathology. Etiological factors include head injury, withdrawal of certain drugs, intracranial tumors or tumors of the hormone-secreting organs, and excessive use of steroids (adrenocortical hormones) or certain other medications.

Organic personality syndrome. The essential feature of the *organic personality syndrome* is a change in the individual's general personality style or traits following brain damage. Normally the change is in a distinctly negative direction; it may include impaired social judgment, lessened control of emotions and impulses, diminished concern about the consequences of one's behavior, and inability to sustain goal-directed activity.

There are multiple etiologies associated with the organic personality syndrome, and the course of the disorder depends on its etiology. Occasionally, as when it is induced by medication, it may be transitory. Very often, however, it is the first sign of an impending deterioration, as when a kindly and gentle old man undertakes sexual advances toward a child or when a conservative businessman suddenly begins to engage in unwise financial dealings. Some evidence indicates that a common feature in the organic personality syndrome may be damage to the frontal lobes (Blumer & Benson, 1975; Hecaen & Albert, 1975; Sherwin & Geschwind, 1978).

These symptom syndromes may appear singly or in combination in the various types of mental disorder associated with brain pathology. In general, disorders involving the syndromes of delirium, dementia, amnesis, hallucinosis, or delusional thinking may be regarded as roughly equivalent to a psychotic level of functioning. Delirium is nearly always acute and short-lived, whereas disorders that have prominent elements of dementia, amnestic syndrome, or organic personality syndrome usually prove to have a chronic course—that is, they normally involve irreversible changes in the brain tissue.

The DSM-III classification lists about 50 different forms of mental disorder in which organic disturbance is present; many of these are related to drug usage and involve only temporary physiological disruption (see Chapter 10). The disorders we will be discussing in the rest of this section are longer-term disorders in which there is major, often permanent, brain pathology but in which the individual's emotional, motivational, and behavioral reactions to his or her awareness of the lost function also play an important role. Indeed, it is often impossible to distinguish between maladaptive behavior directly caused by neurological dysfunction and that which is basically part of the individual's psychological defensive or compensatory reaction to the deficits and disabilities experienced (Geschwind, 1975).

The five organic mental disorders we will be discussing in the next sections are general paresis, disorders involving brain tumors, disorders involving head injury, and the two "old-age psychoses"—senile and presenile dementias, and disorders associated with cerebral arteriosclerosis.

General paresis

General paresis is one of several forms of invasion of the central nervous system by the organism responsible for syphilitic infection, the spirochete *treponema pallidum.* As we saw in Chapter 2, it occupies a very important place in the history of the mental health disciplines.

Despite the availability of medical resources for cure in the early stages, syphilis is still a significant medical problem (see HIGHLIGHT on page 445). Unless properly treated, it eventually disables and then kills its victims.

The general paretic form of advanced syphilis typically begins with an organic personality syndrome. From there it advances to stages involving the amnestic syndrome and usually the organic affective and delusional syndromes. The final stage is that of profound dementia, deteriorating into delirium and death.

The syphilitic infection itself advances in definable stages; only in the fourth or last stage do we find the full-blown general paretic disorder. The first obvious symptom of syphilis is a sore or *chancre* appearing at the site where the spirochetes have gained entrance to the body, typically the mucous membranes of the genitals. Even if untreated, the sore disappears within four to six weeks, to be followed in another three to six weeks by the appearance of a more or less generalized skin rash, which was once called the *Great Pox*. Disappearance of the rash and other associated symptoms initiates the third stage of syphilis, in which the disease appears to become latent. In fact, the spirochetes continue to multiply and are carried by the bloodstream to various bodily organs, where they proceed to destroy tissue; they seem to have a particular affinity for nervous tissue. The fourth stage is one in which the accumulated damage produced during the supposed latent period manifests itself in a wide range of disabilities, including general paresis in some cases.

Clinical picture in general paresis.

General paresis has also been variously called *general paralysis of the insane, dementia paralytica,* and *paresis*. Approximately 5 percent of untreated syphilitics eventually develop general paresis. The first symptoms usually appear about 10 to 15 years after the primary infection, although the incubation period may be as short as 2 years or as long as 40. Unless the person receives treatment, the outcome is always fatal, death usually occurring within 2 to 3 years after the initial symptoms.

General paresis is associated with a wide range of behavioral and psychological symp-

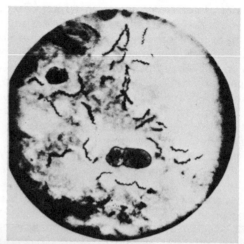

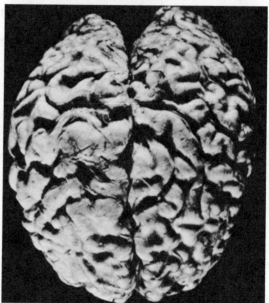

General paresis results when the spirochetes invade the cerebral cortex (top). A postmortem examination typically reveals thickening of the meninges surrounding the brain and atrophy of the convolutions, especially in the frontal and temporal lobes (bottom).

toms. During the early phase of this disorder, the individual typically becomes careless and inattentive and makes mistakes at work. At first the person may notice these mistakes but will attribute them to fatigue; later, they go unnoticed. Personal habits may show some deterioration, and the once-neat person may

Some dimensions of the problem of sexually transmitted disorders

Sexually transmitted diseases (STDs) have been increasing throughout the world. There are about 20 types of sexually transmitted diseases, of which gonorrhea, syphilis, and genital herpes have shown the greatest worldwide increase in recent years. The most common STD—gonorrhea—is out of control in many countries; in some countries, the annual incidence of gonorrhea appears to vary between 5 and 10 percent for the age group 15 to 30. In general, the incidence of STD is twice as high among teenagers as for the general population.

In the United States there are an estimated half-million or more Americans with untreated syphilis, with about 100,000 new cases occurring each year. There are also over two and one-half million new cases of gonorrhea each year, although only about 800,000 are officially reported. In the mid-1970s new cases of syphilis and gonorrhea were occurring at the rate of over 7,000 a day in the U.S.—about 5 new cases per second—with half the victims between 15 and 24 years of age. It has been estimated that in large cities, more than 1 out of 3 high-school students will contract a sexually transmitted disease before graduation; if present trends continue, the incidence rate is expected to reach 1 out of 2.

STDs are almost never acquired by any means other than personal physical contact. The recent marked increase in cases is apparently related to an increased casualness in sexual behavior as well as to the declining use of prophylactic devices—notably the condom—since the advent of birth-control pills.

Much more prevalent than syphilis, gonorrhea is commonly considered a relatively mild disease, but it can cause sterility and may affect the joints, heart, and other organs. Because gonorrheal infection can cause blindness, the law requires that silver nitrate drops or penicillin be placed in the eyes of all new-born infants. Typical early symptoms of gonorrhea include acute inflammation of the genital and urinary tract, with a discharge of pus. In many cases, however, especially in women, the symptoms are not pronounced and the victim is unaware of having contracted the disease. Antibiotics are usually highly effective in the treatment of both gonorrhea and syphilis, but there are far more untreated than treated cases. Also, it appears that certain strains of the gonococcus have developed resistance to the more commonly used antibiotics, rendering effective treatment less certain than a decade ago.

Another serious STD is genital herpes, which causes recurrent episodes of fever and extremely painful genital lesions. Up to 50 percent of the babies born to women with genital herpes are stillborn or have birth defects unless they are born by cesarean section. It is believed that the incidence of genital herpes has increased dramatically; but since physicians are not required to report cases of this disease, actual incidence rates are unknown. It has also been speculated that this presumed increase is due to an especially virulent form of this disease brought to the United States by Vietnam veterans. There is no known cure for genital herpes.

Based on Benenson (1975), Kaiser Permanente Medical Care Program (1973), and Porter and Kane (1975).

become slovenly. Comprehension and judgment suffer, and the individual may show a tendency to evade important problems or may react to them with smug indifference. Accompanying these symptoms is a blunting of affect, so that the individual ceases to share in the joys, sorrows, or anxieties of loved ones. Such individuals seem unable to realize the seriousness of their behavior and may become irritable or resort to ready rationalizations if their behavior is questioned. Overly sentimental behavior is typical, and this phase may involve promiscuous sexual patterns.

As the disorder progresses, a number of well-delineated physical symptoms make their appearance. The pupils are irregular in size and the pupillary reflex to light is either sluggish or entirely absent. Typically, speech functions become badly disturbed, with considerable stuttering and slurring of words. A phrase that routinely gives trouble and is of diagnostic significance is "Methodist Episcopal." This may be mispronounced in a number of ways, such as "Meodist Epispal" or "Methdist Pispal." Writing is similarly disturbed, with tremulous lines and the omission or transposition of syllables. Frequently, the individual has a rather vacant, dissipated look, with a silly grin.

Where the spirochetes have also damaged neural pathways within the spinal cord, there may be difficulty in motor coordination. Such individuals typically have a shuffling, unsteady walk, referred to as *locomotor ataxia*. In addition, there may be tremors of the face, lips, and fingers and an absence of tendon reflexes, such as the knee jerk. During this period convulsive seizures may also appear.

Paralleling these physical symptoms is a progressive personality deterioration. Paretic individuals tend to be unmannerly, tactless, unconcerned with their appearance, and unethical in their behavior. Memory defects, which may be noticeable in the early phases of the illness, become more obvious. These individuals may be unable to remember what they did just a short time before—for example, they may ask when dinner will be served only a few minutes after they have finished eating it. This memory impairment extends to less immediate events, and memory losses are made up for by various fabrications. As their intellectual processes are increasingly impaired, paretic individuals become unable to comprehend the simplest problems and may optimistically squander their money on harebrained schemes or become involved in a variety of antisocial acts.

This entire picture of personality deterioration is usually colored by emotional reactions in the form of either marked euphoria, depression, or apathy. Thus, three categories are commonly used to distinguish clinical types of paretic individuals—*expansive, depressed,* and *demented*—although these types are by no means always distinct, and depressed individuals frequently change categories by becoming euphoric. As the disease enters the terminal period, the extensive brain damage leads to a similar picture for all three types, in which the individual leads a vegetative life, expresses little interest in anything, becomes inarticulate in speech, and can no longer manage personal care. Convulsive seizures usually become common. Finally, a terminal infection or breakdown of body functioning leads to death.

The following[2] is a classic example of the expansive type of paresis and well illustrates the euphoria, poorly systematized delusions of grandeur, and ludicrous nature of the plans these individuals make.

"C. W. flew planes from the United States to North Africa. His route began in Florida, passed through Natal, Ascension Island, and terminated in Dakar. His earlier health record was excellent, save for some 'difficulty' in his early twenties. Now, at 38, he was strong, well liked, and an expert pilot in the ferry command. He had completed a dozen or more trips.

"As he flew his plane eastward on his last journey, C. W. was unusually gay. 'It's a great world,' he sang. 'My rich aunt in Oklahoma is going to leave me $30,000,000.'

"During the periods of relief by his co-pilot, he talked loudly and became chummy with other members of the crew. As a matter of fact, he offered to loan the navigator $50,000. Landing safely in Dakar, his high spirits continued. Then his friends found him buying several 'diamonds' from an Arab street merchant, spending most of his cash for this purpose.

" 'Boy,' he exclaimed, 'I got a swell bargain! Six diamonds for $100 cash now and $100 more on my next trip! I sure fooled that Arab; he's never going to collect the rest from me.'

" 'How do you know the diamonds are genuine?' he was asked.

" 'I tested them,' he boasted, 'I struck one with a hammer and it proved hard; diamonds are hard.'

"Upon the return journey, C. W. continued the story of his expected wealth and the sum grew with the distance of travel.

" 'It's $40,000,000 I am getting and I expect to share some of it with you guys,' he announced. When his co-pilot received this astounding information with doubt and anxiety, C. W. could not understand it. When the co-pilot asked him to rest, he assured him that his body was perfect, that he didn't need rest. Then he added that he could fly the plane without gas, which he tried to prove by doing some fancy maneuvers in the sky.

" 'Funny,' he said later, 'no one seemed to believe me. Even when I offered them a million each they weren't happy, but looked at each other in such a puzzled way. It made me laugh, how they begged me to rest and how worried they looked when I refused. I was the boss and I showed them.'

"When the plane landed in Brazil by a miracle, C. W. was examined by a physician, forced into another plane and brought to Florida. Upon examina-

---

[2]From Fetterman, J. L., *Practical Lessons in Psychiatry,* 1949. Courtesy of Charles C Thomas, Publisher, Springfield, Illinois.

tion he was talkative, eyes gleaming, exuberant with statements of wealth and power. 'I am now one of the richest men in the world.' he said. 'I'll give you $5,000,000 to start a hospital. My eyes are jewels, diamonds, emeralds,' . . ." (Fetterman, 1949, pp. 267–68)

Frequently, the early signs of general paresis are not recognized by family and friends until an acute episode of some sort occurs. The family of one patient noticed nothing particularly wrong until one day he went to a bar instead of to his office and there became noisy and expansive. Actually, for several months there had been less obvious symptoms, including forgetfulness of business appointments and peculiar color combinations in dress, but no one had noticed anything seriously amiss.

Although much is now known about general paresis, a number of questions still puzzle investigators. Why do only some 5 to 10 percent of untreated syphilitics develop general paresis? Why do a higher percentage of whites than blacks develop general paresis after syphilitic infection? Why do far more male than female syphilitics develop general paresis? Some investigators hold that the syphilitic spirochetes attack the most vulnerable organs of the individual's body and that general paresis develops in persons whose brain tissue has an especially low resistance to syphilis. Other investigators have suggested that different strains of spirochetes may account for many of these differences. But the final answers to these questions are not yet available.

Treatment and outcomes. After penicillin had been developed and found effective in the treatment of syphilis, there was a spectacular drop in the number of cases. Thus during the late 1950s the problem of syphilis was considered solved.

During the period from 1960 to 1970, however, the number of cases of reported syphilis doubled. The increase continued into the 1970s with well over 100,000 new cases being reported each year, and probably an equal or greater number of unreported cases. It is estimated that there may be as many as a half million cases of undetected and untreated syphilis in the U.S. as a whole (Krugman & Ward, 1973).

According to statistics gathered from 102 cities in 1969, the sources of infection in syphilis were, in order of frequency, (a) friend of the opposite sex, 47 percent; (b) stranger of the opposite sex, including prostitutes and casual pickups, 20 percent; (c) homosexual contact, 17 percent; and (d) marital partner, 16 percent (Strage, 1971). Contrary to a widely held popular misconception, it is currently estimated that 5 percent or less of syphilis is spread by prostitutes.

The specific outcomes in cases of paresis receiving medical treatment depend to a large extent on the amount of cerebral damage that has taken place before treatment is started. If the damage is not extensive, the adaptive capacities of the individual—both neurological and psychological—may leave only a small impairment of brain function. Unfortunately, in many cases treatment is not undertaken until the disease has produced extensive and irreparable brain damage. Here about all that can be hoped for is to prevent further inroads of the deadly spirochete. In such cases, the intellectual picture may show considerable improvement, but the patient's previous level of ability is never regained. For treated paretics as a group, the following rough estimates of outcome may be made:

a) Some 20 to 30 percent show good recovery and can resume their former occupation and activities.

b) Another 30 to 40 percent show some improvement, but usually require a transfer to less complex occupational duties as a consequence of residual intellectual or personality impairment.

c) 15 to 25 percent show no improvement.

d) 10 percent die during the course of treatment (or within a 10-year period following the instigation of treatment).

As with other mental disorders, psychotherapy may be an essential aspect of the total treatment program.

The only fully adequate approach to cerebral syphilis is the prevention of syphilitic infection, or early detection and treatment where infection has taken place. In the United States, facilities are provided for the free diagnosis and treatment of syphilis; most states require examinations before marriage; and public education has been vigorously supported by governmental, educational, and religious agencies. It is also mandatory in all states for physicians to report cases of syphilis to local health authorities, though it is probable that some doctors succumb to pressures not to report cases they treat. Unfortunately, many people do not seek diagnosis and treatment due to inadequate information or to the stigma attached to sexually transmitted diseases.

In efforts directed toward finding and treating all infected cases, it has become common practice for patients with infectious syphilis to be interviewed for sex contacts. Every effort is then made to locate these individuals and screen them for possible syphilitic infection. For example, a successful search was conducted in a case involving a Sacramento, California prostitute, named as a contact by an infected male; she, in turn produced a list of 310 male contacts. Although they were chiefly interstate truck drivers scattered over 34 states, Canada, and Mexico, authorities were able to locate them and ask for blood tests (*Los Angeles Times,* 1970). In another case, cited by Strage (1971), an infected homosexual male was able to produce a file of nearly 1000 male contacts together with the details of their sexual acts and preferences.

To improve the efficiency of case-finding, investigators have extended interviews to include not only sex contacts of patients but also friends and acquaintances, whose sexual behavior is assumed to be similar to that of the patient; this is called *cluster testing.*

Although we now have the medical means to eradicate syphilis, it remains a major health problem in our society because its roots are social as well as medical. However, with the cooperation of international and national agencies, better education, and more adequate facilities for diagnosis and treatment, there is every reason to believe that syphilis can eventually be controlled or even eliminated as a public health problem.

Disorders involving brain tumors

In the writings of Felix Plater (1536–1614), we find the following rather remarkable account of "A Case of Stupor due to a Tumour in the Brain, Circular like a Gland":

"Caspar Bone Curtius, a noble knight, began to show signs of 'mental alienation' which continued through a period of two years until at last he became quite stupefied, did not act rationally, did not take food unless forced to do so, nor did he go to bed unless compelled, at table he just lay on his arms and went to sleep, he did not speak when questioned even when admonished, and if he did it was useless. Pituita dropped from his nose copiously and frequently: this condition continued for about six months, and finally he died. . . . At the post mortem when the skull was opened and the lobes of the brain separated, a remarkable globular tumor was found on the upper surface of the Corpus Callosum, resembling a gland fleshly, hard and funguslike, about the size of a medium sized apple, invested with its own membranes and having its own veins, lying free and without any connection with the brain itself. . . . This tumour, by its mass, produced pressure on the brain and its vessels, which caused stupor, torpor, and finally death. Some doctors who had seen this case earlier attributed it to sorcery, others just to the humors, but by opening the skull we made clear the abstruse and hidden cause." (1664)

A tumor is a new growth involving an abnormal enlargement of body tissue. Such growths are most apt to occur in the breast, the uterus, the prostate, the lungs, or the intestinal tract, although they are sometimes found in the central nervous system. In adults, brain tumors occur with the greatest frequency between the ages of 40 and 60.

Some brain tumors are malignant, in that they destroy the brain tissue in which they arise; others are benign in that they are not destructive except by reason of the pressure they exert. Since the skull is a bony, unyielding con-

Brain tumors can cause a variety of personality alterations. Below is a picture of a meningioma— a tumor of one of the meninges, or coverings of the brain.

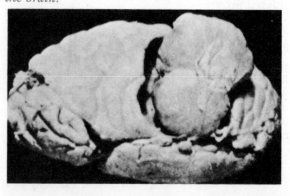

tainer, a relatively small tumor in the brain may cause marked pressure and thus may interfere seriously with normal brain functioning. Unlike their benign counterparts, malignant brain tumors usually originate in malignancies in other organs, typically the lungs; the cancer cells are transported to the brain by a process known as *metastasis*.

Clinical picture in disorders involving brain tumors.

The clinical picture that develops in cases of brain tumor is extremely varied and is determined largely by (a) the location, size, and rapidity of growth of the tumor, and (b) the personality and stress tolerance of the individual. Brain tumors may lead to any or all of the recognized organic symptom syndromes discussed earlier.

The brain tumor itself may result in both localized and general symptoms. Damage to a particular part of the brain may result in localized disturbances of sensory or motor functions. General symptoms appear when the tumor becomes large enough to result in greatly increased intracranial pressure. Common early symptoms are persistent headache, vomiting, memory impairment, listlessness, depression, and "choked disc"—a retinal anomaly due to swelling of the optic nerve when cerebrospinal fluid is forced into it by intracranial pressure.

As the tumor progresses and the intracranial pressure increases, there may be clouding of consciousness, disorientation for time and place, carelessness in personal habits, irritability, convulsive seizures, vomiting, sensorimotor losses, hallucinations, apathy, and a general impairment of intellectual functions. Terminal stages are usually similar to other types of severe brain damage, in which the patient is reduced to a vegetative stupor and eventual death.

Some idea of the relative frequency of symptoms that may occur in brain tumor cases may be gleaned from an early study by Levin (1949), who intensively analyzed 22 cases admitted to the Boston Psychopathic Hospital. These patients ranged in age from 22 to 65 years, the majority falling between the ages of 40 and 60 years. There were 11 males and 11 females. Prior to hospitalization the range of symptoms shown by these patients included the following:

Symptoms prior to hospitalization	Number of cases
Memory impairment or confusion	13
Depression	9
Seizures	8
Headaches	8
Complaints of visual impairment	6
Drowsiness	6
Irritability	6
Indifference	5
Restlessness	4
Complaint of generalized weakness	4
Loss of sense of responsibility	3
Paranoid ideas	2
Tendency to be combative	2
Euphoria	2
Aphasia	2

The interval between the onset of the symptoms and hospitalization varied from 1 week to 6 years, with an average interval of 17 months. In most cases, symptoms were evident 6 months or more prior to admission to the hospital. In this connection, however, it has been pointed out that minor personality changes and depression often serve to mask the more definitive symptoms of a brain tumor—with the result that accurate diagnosis and appropriate treatment are often delayed (Schwab, 1970).

Patients' emotional reactions to the organic damage and to the resulting intellectual impairment vary. Initially, they may be overly irritable, drowsy, and mildly depressed. As the disorder progresses, however, they may have some insight into the seriousness of their condition and become severely depressed, anxious, and apprehensive. Patients who have less insight into their condition usually react to the brain damage and their failing functions by becoming expansive and euphoric. Such patients seem unconcerned about their illness and may joke and laugh in a most unrestrained and hilarious manner. Such reactions are apparently compensatory and are especially frequent in advanced stages when there is considerable brain damage or pressure.

Serious tumors, especially those with psychological complications, are most common in the frontal, temporal, and parietal lobes. Frontal-lobe tumors often produce subtle peculiarities such as inability to concentrate, personal carelessness, a loss of inhibitions, and absentmindedness that later becomes a memory defect. Often, too, the individual becomes silly and prone to punning and general jocularity. In an analysis of 90 patients with frontal-lobe tumors, Dobrokhotova (1968) found three common forms of emotional disorder: (a) the absence of spontaneity; (b) disinhibition and lability of affect—often with euphoria; and (c) forced emotions, which were abruptly expressed and terminated.

Tumors involving the special sensory areas in the brain may result in hallucinations of sight, hearing, taste, and smell. It has been estimated that about half of the patients with brain tumors evidence hallucinations sometime during the course of their illness. Visual hallucinations predominate and may involve dazzling, vividly colored flashes of light, as well as various kinds and sizes of animals and other objects. In temporal-lobe tumors, "Lilliputian hallucinations" are sometimes found, in which patients see small figures that they usually know are not real. Such hallucinations apparently result from irritation of the visual pathways passing through the temporal lobe. Similarly, irritation of the olfactory pathways may result in the perception of peculiar odors, such as rubber burning. Auditory hallucinations may include buzzing, ringing, roaring, and occasionally voices and conversations.

Although personality change is so common in brain-tumor cases that is has in the past been attributed directly to the tumor, we now realize that these symptoms are neither inevitable nor solely the result of the tumor. As we have noted, adjustive reactions are typically a function of both the stress situation (including biological, psychosocial, and sociocultural stressors) and the personal maturity, stability, and level of stress tolerance of the individual.

A most dramatic example of the importance of the patient's pre-illness personality in determining the psychological effects of brain pathology is provided in John Gunther's (1949) moving account of his son Johnny's struggle against a malignant brain tumor. Johnny was 16 and in his junior year at preparatory school when the tumor was discovered. During the 14 months that preceded his death, he was subjected to two major operations and a variety of other treatment procedures.

Throughout his ordeal, Johnny never lost his courage, his ambition, his sense of humor, or his mental alertness. Although his strength and general physical condition deteriorated steadily and he suffered increasing visual impairment, he fought to carry on a normal pattern of activity and to keep up with his studies by being tutored at home. Through tireless and determined effort, he managed to take and pass college entrance examinations—a 6-hour ordeal that followed an hour of standing in line—and to graduate with his class. By this time his physical impairment had become so great that it was a struggle simply to tie his shoelaces or even fasten his belt. At graduation late in May, he could only walk very slowly down the long aisle and grasp his diploma with his weak left hand. Less than a month later, Johnny died.

Treatment and outcomes. Treatment of brain-tumor cases is primarily a medical matter and thus is outside the scope of our present discussion. However, it may be noted that the degree of recovery of the patient in such cases depends both on the size and location of the growth and on the amount of brain tissue that may have to be removed with the tumor. In some cases there seems to be full recovery, while in others there may be a residue of symptoms, such as partial paralysis and a reduction in intellectual level. Where tumors are well advanced and require extensive surgery, the mortality rate is high.

The following case, summarized from a report by Brickner, reveals a postoperative reduction in general intellectual capacity and the overcompensatory reaction of the patient to his changed life situation.

The patient was a man of 40 who had been a successful broker on the New York Stock Exchange. During the operation to remove his tumor, large portions of the frontal lobes of the brain were removed on both sides. As a result, the patient's general adjustive capacities—including comprehension, judgment, restraint, memory, and learning capacity—were markedly lowered.

The following is an excerpt from Brickner's extensive case record on this man.

"**B.:** One thing your illness lost you is the knowledge that you're not perfect.

A.: It's a damned good thing to lose.

B.: Do you really believe in your heart that you are perfect?

A.: Yes. Of course we all have faults. I have faults like everyone else.

B.: Name some of your faults.

A.: I don't think I have any.

B.: You just said you had.

A.: Well, they wouldn't *predominate* on the Exchange.

B.: I mean personal faults.

A.: Yes, I have personal faults. I never give a man an opportunity to do what he wants to do on the Exchange, if I know it.

B.: Is that a fault?

A.: That's being a good broker.

B.: Can you name a personal fault? Do you really believe you're perfect?

A.: You bet I do—pretty near perfect—they don't come much more perfect than I am." (1936, pp. 47–48)

About twenty years ago, German (1959) found that about 40 percent of all brain tumors were potentially curable; about 20 percent were capable of being arrested for periods of 5 years or more; and the remainder were fatal within a short period of time. Since then, newer methods of detecting and pinpointing brain tumors and improved treatment procedures have resulted in a marked improvement in outcomes (Peterson, 1978). We shall discuss neuropsychological assessment in Chapter 17. The success of treatment, most of which involves surgery, depends on the nature of the tumor, its location, the amount of brain tissue that has been displaced, and the amount of surgery required for the complete removal of the tumor (Freedman, Kaplan, & Sadock, 1976).

Disorders involving head injury

Since ancient times, brain injuries have provided a rich source of material for speculation about mental functions. Hippocrates pointed out that injuries to the head could cause sensory and motor disorders, and Galen included head injuries among the major causes of mental disorders.

Head injuries occur frequently, particularly as a result of falls, blows, and accidents. It has been estimated that well over a million persons suffer head injuries each year in automobile and industrial accidents; and a sizable number of cases are the result of bullets or other objects actually penetrating the cranium. Yet relatively few persons with head injuries find their way into mental hospitals, since many head in-

juries do not involve appreciable damage to the brain. Even when a head injury results in a temporary loss of consciousness, the damage to the brain is usually minor.

Most of us have received a blow on the head at one time or other, and in giving the case history of a mental patient, relatives often remember some such incident to which they attribute the observed difficulties. Patients, too, are apt to search their own childhood for evidence of having fallen on their heads or having been hit on the head. Apparently, blaming a head injury is a convenient method of escaping the "disgrace" of a functional mental disorder and at the same time avoiding any hereditary stigma to the family. Consequently, it should be emphasized that only with severe brain injury is there apt to be any residual handicap.

Clinical picture in disorders with head injuries. Head injuries usually give rise to immediate acute reactions, the severity of which depends on the degree and type of injury. These acute reactions may then clear up entirely or develop into chronic disorders.

Perhaps the most famous historical case is the celebrated American crowbar case reported by Dr. J. M. Harlow in 1868. Since it is of both historical and descriptive significance, it merits a few details:

"The accident occurred in Cavendish, Vt., on the line of the Rutland and Burlington Railroad, at that time being built, on the 13th of September, 1848, and was occasioned by the premature explosion of a blast, when this iron, known to blasters as a tamping iron, and which I now show you, was shot through the face and head.

"The subject of it was Phineas P. Gage, a perfectly healthy, strong and active young man, twenty-five years of age . . . Gage was foreman of a gang of men employed in excavating rock, for the road way. . . .

"The missile entered by its pointed end, the left side of the face, immediately anterior to the angle of the lower jaw, and passing obliquely upwards, and obliquely backwards, emerged in the median line, at the back part of the frontal bone, near the coronal suture. . . . The iron which thus traversed the head, is round and rendered comparatively smooth by use, and is three feet seven inches in length, one and one fourth inches in its largest diameter, and weighs thirteen and one fourth pounds. . . .

"The patient was thrown upon his back by the explosion, and gave a few convulsive motions of the extremities, but spoke in a few minutes. His men (with whom he was a great favorite) took him in their arms and carried him to the road, only a few rods distant, and put him into an ox cart, in which he rode, supported in a sitting posture, fully three quarters of a mile to his hotel. He got out of the cart himself, with a little assistance from his men, and an hour afterwards (with what I could aid him by taking hold of his left arm) walked up a long flight of stairs, and got upon the bed in the room where he was dressed. He seemed perfectly conscious, but was becoming exhausted from the hemorrhage, which by this time, was quite profuse, the blood pouring from the lacerated sinus in the top of his head, and also finding its way into the stomach, which ejected it as often as every fifteen or twenty minutes. He bore his sufferings with firmness, and directed my attention to the hole in his cheek, saying, 'the iron entered there and passed through my head.' " (1868, pp. 330–32)

Sometime later Dr. Harlow made the following report.

"His physical health is good, and I am inclined to say that he has recovered. Has no pain in head, but says it has a queer feeling which he is not able to describe. Applied for his situation as foreman, but is undecided whether to work or travel. His contractors, who regarded him as the most efficient and capable foreman in their employ previous to his injury considered the change in his mind so marked that they could not give him his place again. The equilibrium or balance, so to speak, between his intellectual faculties and animal propensities, seems to have been destroyed. He is fitful, irreverent, indulging at times in the grossest profanity (which was not previously his custom), manifesting but little deference for his fellows, impatient of restraint or advice when it conflicts with his desires, at times pertinaciously obstinate, yet capricious and vacillating, devising many plans of future operations, which are no sooner arranged than they are abandoned in turn for others . . . his mind is radically changed, so decidedly that his friends and acquaintances said he was 'no longer Gage.' " (1868, pp. 339–40)

It is evident from the above account that Gage acquired an organic personality syndrome from his encounter with the errant crowbar. This relatively dramatic syndrome, however, is not common as a sequel to head injury.

Fortunately, the brain is an extraordinarily well-protected organ, but even so, a hard blow on the head may result in a skull fracture in which portions of bone press upon or are driven into the brain tissue. Even without a fracture, the force of the blow may result in small, pin-

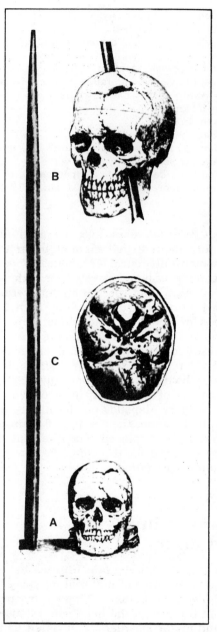

Harlow illustrated his famous crowbar case by these drawings, showing (A) the comparative sizes of the tamping iron and the cranium through which it passed; (B) a view of the cranium showing just where the iron passed through, and also a large section of the skull which was entirely torn away and later replaced; and (C) an upward view from inside the skull, giving the position and relative size of the hole that was made and showing a deposit of new bone partially closing it over.

point hemorrhages throughout the brain or in the rupturing of larger blood vessels in the brain.

The person rendered unconscious by a head injury usually passes through stages of stupor and confusion on the way to recovering clear consciousness. This recovery of consciousness may be complete in the course of minutes, or it may take hours or days. In rare cases an individual may live for extended periods of time without regaining consciousness.

The specific symptoms, of course, depend largely on the nature of the injury. Normally, if a head injury is sufficiently severe to result in unconsciousness, the person experiences *retrograde amnesia,* or inability to recall events immediately preceding the injury. Apparently, such trauma interferes with the brain's capacity to consolidate into long-term storage the events that were being mentally processed at the time of the trauma.

During the coma that follows severe cerebral injury, pulse, temperature, and blood pressure are all affected and survival may be uncertain. The duration of the coma is determined primarily by the extent of the injury. If the patient survives, the coma is usually followed by delirium, in which acute excitement may be manifested, with disorientation, hallucinations, and generally anxious, restless, and noisy activity. Often there is incessant talking in a disconnected fashion, with no insight into the disturbed condition. Gradually the confusion clears up and the individual regains contact with reality. Again, the severity and duration of residual symptoms will depend primarily on the nature and extent of the cerebral damage, the premorbid personality of the patient, and the life situation to which he or she will return.

Some degree of bleeding, or *intracerebral hemorrhage,* occurs in most cases of head injury. In severe head injuries there is usually gross bleeding or hemorrhaging at the site of the damage. When the hemorrhaging involves small spots of bleeding—often microscopic sleeves of red cells encircling tiny blood vessels—the condition is referred to as *petechial hemorrhages.* There is some evidence of petechial hemorrhages in most brain injuries, but in fatal cases they are usually multiple or generalized throughout the brain.

Professional boxers are likely to suffer such petechial hemorrhaging from repeated blows to the head; they may develop a form of encephalopathy (area or areas of permanently damaged brain tissue) from the accumulated damage of such injuries. Consequently, some former boxers suffer from impaired memory, inability to concentrate, involuntary movements, and other symptoms—a condition popularly referred to as being "punch-drunk." Johnson (1969) found abnormal EEG's in 10 of 17 retired boxers; and Earl (1966) noted that two former welterweight champions suffered so much brain damage in their professional fights that confinement in mental institutions ended their careers before they reached the age of 30.

With one-time injuries, however, syndromes produced by head injury are usually limited to delirium and perhaps some features of the dementia, amnestic, and hallucinosis syndromes —all on a temporary basis. Where the trauma results in the permanent loss of neural tissue, however, all these syndromes may occur in their full-blown and irreversible forms; the person may also experience personality disturbance, affective and delusional syndromes, and a variety of physical impairments and disabilities.

Treatment and outcomes. Immediate treatment for brain damage due to head injury is primarily a medical matter and need not concern us here except for the notation that prompt treatment may prevent further injury or damage—for example, when blood clots must be removed from the brain. In severe cases immediate medical treatment may have to be supplemented by a long-range program of reeducation and rehabilitation.

Although many patients make a remarkably good recovery, even after severe brain injury, others show various residual symptoms. Common aftereffects of moderate brain injury are chronic headaches, anxiety, irritability, dizziness, easy fatigability, and impaired memory and concentration. Where the brain damage is extensive, the patient's general intellectual level may be markedly reduced, especially where there have been severe frontal-lobe lesions. In addition, various specific neurological and psychological defects may follow localized brain damage: occipital-lobe lesions may impair vision, parietal-lobe lesions may result in sensory aphasia (see HIGHLIGHT on this page), and so on. Some 2 to 4 percent of head-injury cases develop posttraumatic epilepsy, usually within 2 years of the head injury but sometimes much later. In general, the longer the period between the injury and the first convulsive seizure, the more likely seizures are to persist. (See HIGHLIGHT on page 456.)

In a minority of brain-injury cases—some 2 to 3 percent—there are personality changes, such as those described in the historic case of Phineas Gage. Among older people and individuals who have suffered extensive damage to the frontal lobes, the symptom picture may be complicated by markedly impaired memory for recent events and by confabulation.

The great majority of patients suffering from mild concussion recover within a short time. In moderate brain injuries, a sizable number of patients recover promptly, a somewhat larger number suffer from headaches and other symptoms for prolonged periods, and a few patients develop chronic incapacitating symptoms. In general, an estimated 50 percent of patients with moderate brain injuries show symptoms after 6 months, and about 40 percent after 18 months.

In severe brain-injury cases, the prognosis is less favorable (Jennett et al., 1976). Some patients have to adjust to lower levels of occupational and social functioning, while others are so impaired intellectually that they can never adjust to conditions outside an institution. Often, however—even in cases where considerable amounts of brain tissue have been destroyed—patients with previously stable, well-integrated personalities are able to make a satisfactory adjustment. And in many cases there is improvement with time, due largely to reeducation and to the taking over of new functions by intact brain areas.

In general, the following factors indicate a favorable prognosis in cases of head injury: (a) a short period of unconsciousness or posttraumatic amnesia, (b) nonstrategic location of the brain lesion, (c) a well-integrated premorbid personality, (d) motivation to recover or make the most of residual capacities, (e) a favorable life situation to which to return, and (f) an appropriate program of retraining (Brooks, 1974).

Various other factors may also have a direct bearing on the outcome of brain injuries. As we mentioned earlier, the results of brain damage

HIGHLIGHT

Impairment of language and related sensorimotor functions resulting from brain damage

In many cases, brain damage results in fairly specific language and related sensorimotor functions. Among the more common of these are:

Auditory aphasia—Loss of ability to understand spoken words

Expressive aphasia—Loss of ability to speak required words

Nominal aphasia—Loss of ability to recall names of objects

Formulation aphasia—Loss of ability to formulate sentences

Paraphasia—Garbled speech, marked by inappropriate word use, transposed sounds, and ungrammatical sentences

Alexia (dyslexia)—Loss of ability to read (less severe in dyslexia)

Agraphia—Loss of ability to express thoughts in writing

Acalculia—Loss of ability to do simple arithmetic

Apraxia—Loss of ability to perform simple voluntary acts

With reeducation, impaired or lost language and related sensorimotor functions can often be recovered —either partially or totally.

in infancy differ from those in adolescence and adulthood, although in both instances the results may range from death to any number of neurological disorders, including epilepsy and mental retardation. Moreover, individuals who are also victims of alcoholism, drug dependence, arteriosclerosis, or other organic conditions may have an unfavorable outlook. Alcoholics, in particular, are prone to head injuries and other accidents, and do not have good recovery records. Severe emotional conflicts sometimes appear to predispose an individual to accidents and also may delay recovery. Although malingering is thought to be rare in brain-injury cases, the hope of receiving monetary compensation—for example, from an insurance settlement—may influence individuals to exaggerate and maintain symptoms.

Senile and presenile dementias

It is a banal and commonplace observation that the organs of the body deteriorate with aging, a process, biologists tell us, that begins virtually at birth. The cause or causes of such deterioration, however, remain largely obscure: science has not yet solved the riddle of aging. Of course, the brain—truly the master organ—is not spared in the generalized aging process. As time goes on, it too "wears out," or degenerates. Mental disorders that sometimes accompany this brain degeneration and occur in old age are called *senile dementias*. Unfortunately, there are a number of rare conditions that result in degenerative changes in brain tissue earlier in life. Disorders associated with such earlier degeneration of the brain are known as *presenile dementias*.

Not only is the age of onset different in the presenile dementias; they are also distinguished from the senile dementias by their different behavioral manifestations and tissue alterations (see HIGHLIGHT on this page). One exception to this is Alzheimer's disease, a rare presenile dementia in which, for unknown reasons, the same kind of deterioration seen in senile dementia typically starts in the 40s or 50s and proceeds rapidly. It is so similar in clinical picture and in the associated brain changes to the later-appearing senile degeneration that we will discuss them together as *seniliform dementias*.

The onset of seniliform dementia in older patients is usually gradual, involving slow physical and mental letdown. In some cases a physical ailment or some other stressful event is a dividing point, but usually the individual passes into a psychotic state almost imperceptibly, so that it is impossible to date the onset of the disorder precisely. The clinical picture may vary markedly from one person to another, depending on the nature and extent of brain degeneration, the premorbid personality of the individual, and the particular stressors that have been in operation.

Symptoms often begin with the individual's gradual withdrawal from active engagement with life. There is a narrowing of social and

Presenile dementias

In addition to Alzheimer's disease, two other forms of presenile dementia occur with sufficient frequency to deserve mention: Pick's disease and Huntington's chorea.

Pick's disease
Even rarer than Alzheimer's disease, Pick's disease (first described by Arnold Pick of Prague in papers published in 1892) is a degenerative disorder of the nervous system of unknown cause, usually having its onset in persons between 45 and 50. Women are apparently more subject to Pick's disease than men, at a ratio of about 3 to 2. Onset is slow and insidious, involving difficulty in thinking, slight memory defects, easy fatigability, and, often, character changes with a lowering of ethical inhibitions. At first there is a rather circumscribed atrophy of the frontal and temporal lobes; as the atrophy becomes more severe, the mental deterioration becomes progressively greater and includes apathy and disorientation as well as impairment of judgment and other intellectual functions. The disease usually runs a fatal course within 2 to 7 years.

Huntington's chorea
Huntington's chorea is a genetically determined degenerative disorder of the central nervous system. It was first described by the American neurologist George Huntington in 1872. With an incidence rate of about 5 cases per 100,000 persons, the disease usually occurs in individuals between 30 and 50. Behavior deterioration often becomes apparent several years before there are any detectable neurological manifestations (Lyle & Gottesman, 1977). The disease itself is characterized by a chronic, progressive chorea (involuntary, irregular, twitching, jerking movements) with mental deterioration leading to dementia and death within 10 to 20 years. Although Huntington's chorea cannot be cured or even arrested at the present time, it can be prevented, at least in theory, by genetic counseling, since its occurrence is a function of known genetic laws.

other interests, a lessening of mental alertness and adaptability, and a lowering of tolerance to new ideas and changes in routine. Often there is a self-centering of thoughts and activities and a preoccupation with the bodily functions of eating, digestion, and excretion. As these various changes—typical in lesser degree of many older people—become more severe, additional symptoms, such as impairment of memory for recent events, untidiness, impaired judgment, agitation, and periods of confusion, make their appearance. Specific symptoms may vary considerably from day to day; thus the clinical picture is by no means uniform until the terminal stages, when the patient is reduced to a vegetative level. There is also, of course, individual variation in the rapidity of progression of the disorder, and in rare instances there may be a reversal of psychotic symptomatology and a partial recovery.

Seniliform dementias may take any of the following five forms. It may be emphasized, however, that there is generally a considerable overlapping of symptoms from one form to another.

1. *Simple deterioration.* This is, as the name suggests, a relatively uncomplicated exaggeration of the "normal" changes characteristic of old age. The patient gradually loses contact with the environment and develops the typical symptoms of poor memory, tendency to reminisce, intolerance of change, disorientation, restlessness, insomnia, and failure of judgment. This is the most common of the seniliform psychotic reactions, constituting about 50 percent of the entire group.

The following case—involving an engineer who had retired some 7 years prior to his hospitalization—is typical of simple seniliform deterioration.

During the past five years, he had shown a progressive loss of interest in his surroundings and during the last year had become increasingly "childish." His wife and eldest son had brought him to the hospital because they felt they could not longer care for him in their home, particularly because of the grandchildren. They stated that he had become careless in his eating and other personal habits, was restless and prone to wandering about at night, and could not seem to remember anything that had happened during the day but was garrulous concerning events of his childhood and middle years.

After admission to the hospital, the patient seemed to deteriorate rapidly. He could rarely remember

HIGHLIGHT

Key types of epilepsy and possible relationship to maladaptive behavior

Accounts of epileptic seizures are found throughout the recorded history of human beings. They are caused by brain lesions or other pathology which result in a disturbance of the rhythm of electrical discharges of brain cells. Epilepsy affects about 1 person in 100 in the United States—between 2 and 3 million people—and may be increasing in frequency. Cases occur among all age groups, but more commonly in children and adolescents than in adults. In over half the known cases, the age of onset is under 15 years.

Epileptic seizures are infinitely varied in form, but for practical purposes they may be classified into the three main types described below. Typical EEG patterns for these three types are contrasted at right with recordings of normal brain waves.

1. Grand mal: "great illness." The most prevalent and spectacular form of epileptic seizure, grand mal, occurs in some 60 percent of the cases. Typically, just before the seizure, the individual experiences a warning, such as an unpleasant odor. During an attack the individual loses consciousness and breathing is suspended. Muscles become rigid, jaws clenched, arms extended, and legs outstretched, and the individual pitches forward or slumps to the ground. With the return of air to the lungs, movements, instead of being rigid (tonic), become jerking (clonic). Muscular spasms begin, the head strikes the ground, the arms repeatedly thrust outward, the legs jerk up and down, the jaws open and close, and the mouth foams. Usually in about a minute the convulsive movements slow, the muscles relax, and the individual gradually returns to normality—in some cases after a deep sleep lasting from a few minutes to several hours. Another, less common, form of convulsive seizure, much like a modified grand-mal attack, is known as *Jacksonian epilepsy;* here, motor disturbances occurring in one region spread over the side in which they originate, and sometimes over the entire body.

2. Petit mal: "small illness." In petit-mal seizures there is usually a diminution, rather than a complete loss, of consciousness. The individual stops whatever he or she is doing, stares vacantly ahead or toward the floor, and then in a few seconds resumes previous activity. In some cases, these seizures may

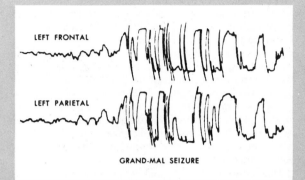

GRAND-MAL SEIZURE

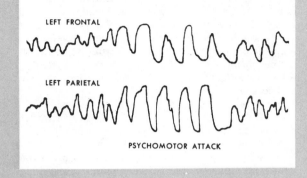

PSYCHOMOTOR ATTACK

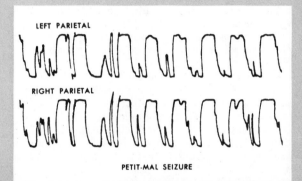

PETIT-MAL SEIZURE

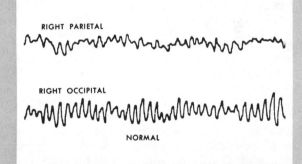

NORMAL

occur several times a day; unlike grand-mal seizures, they rarely have an advance warning or aura. With onset usually occurring in childhood or adolescence, petit-mal attacks are rare after the age of 20.

3. Psychomotor epilepsy. Psychomotor attacks occur in about 10 percent of child, and 30 percent of adult, epileptics. Attacks usually last from a few seconds to minutes, but in some rare cases they may last considerably longer. Their principal feature is a psychic disturbance, which varies greatly from one individual to another. Despite a lapse or clouding of consciousness, activity continues and these individuals appear to be conscious; during the attack they may perform routine tasks or some unusual or antisocial act. A very small percentage of cases may even involve self-mutilation or homicidal assault. The Flemish painter Van Gogh was subject to psychomotor attacks, for which he was later amnesic. On one occasion he cut off one of his ears, wrapped it in a sack, and presented it to a prostitute. In a more serious case, a brain-injured soldier subject to psychomotor epilepsy reported a dream in which he found himself trying to ward off attackers. Actually, he had beaten his 3-year-old daughter to death, but was completely amnesic for the tragic episode.

Fortunately, drug medication and other treatment measures make it possible to prevent seizures in 80 percent or more of epileptics. Often treatment procedures also focus on helping the individual cope with personal problems such as feelings of inferiority associated with the affliction. Educational efforts by professional and lay organizations have succeeded in dispelling many misconceptions concerning epilepsy and in helping epileptics live normal lives. For example, epileptics are no longer branded as poor employment risks—on the contrary, they show a relatively low incidence of on-the-job accidents. Also, legal restrictions on the operation of motor vehicles have been changed, so that epileptics are permitted to drive when it is established that they have been free of seizures (with or without medication) for 2 to 3 years. In general, most epileptics make adequate educational, marital, and occupational adjustments.

Based on Batchelor and Campbell (1969), Flor-Henry (1969), Holvey and Talbott (1972), Jasper (1969), Pryse-Phillips (1969), Rodin (1973, 1978), Stearman (1973), and Sutherland and Trait (1969).

what had happened a few minutes before, although his memory for remote events of his childhood remained good. When he was visited by his wife and children, he mistook them for old friends, nor could he recall anything about the visit a few minutes after they had departed. The following brief conversation with the patient, which took place after he had been in the hospital for 9 months, and about 3 months prior to his death, shows his disorientation for time and person:

Dr.: How are you today, Mr. ___?

Pt.: Oh . . . hello . . . (looks at doctor in rather puzzled way as if trying to make out who he is).

Dr.: Do you know where you are now?

Pt.: Why yes . . . I am at home. I must paint the house this summer. It has needed painting for a long time but it seems like I just keep putting it off.

Dr.: Can you tell me the day today?

Pt.: Isn't today Sunday . . . why, yes, the children are coming over for dinner today. We always have dinner for the whole family on Sunday. My wife was here just a minute ago but I guess she has gone back into the kitchen.

2. *The paranoid type.* In this type of seniliform disorder, the memory loss and other manifestations of degeneration are usually not so pronounced as in other types of seniliform reactions. Confusion and other disturbances of consciousness are not common, and often the individual remains oriented for time, place, and person. In other words, the dementia and amnestic syndromes are not prominent features of this reaction type, at least not in its early phases. Rather, the person develops a pronounced delusional syndrome chiefly involving ideas of persecution. Common among such delusions is the stubbornly held idea, in the absence of any evidence, that the spouse has become sexually unfaithful. Or, alternatively, such individuals may develop the notion that relatives have turned against them and are trying to rob and kill them. Their suspicions are confirmed by the noxious gases they smell in their room, or by the poison they taste in their food. Fortunately, such delusions are poorly systematized and rarely lead to overt physical attacks on alleged persecutors. Approximately 30 percent of psychoses associated with seniliform brain deterioration take a paranoid form.

The following case is fairly typical of this reaction type, except for the prominent amnestic features.

A woman of 74 had been referred to a hospital after the death of her husband because she became uncooperative and was convinced that her relatives were trying to steal the insurance money her husband had left her. In the hospital she complained that the other patients had joined together against her and were trying to steal her belongings. She frequently refused to eat, on the grounds that the food tasted funny and had probably been poisoned. She grew increasingly irritable and disoriented for time and person. She avidly scanned magazines in the ward reading room but could not remember anything she had looked at. The following conversation reveals some of her symptoms:

Dr.: Do you find that magazine interesting?

Pt.: Why do you care? Can't you see I'm busy?

Dr.: Would you mind telling me something about what you are reading?

Pt.: It's none of your business . . . I am reading about my relatives. They want me to die so that they can steal my money.

Dr.: Do you have any evidence of this?

Pt.: Yes, plenty. They poison my food and they have turned the other women against me. They are all out to get my money. They even stole my sweater.

Dr.: Can you tell me what you had for breakfast?

Pt.: . . . (Pause) I didn't eat breakfast . . . it was poisoned and I refused to eat it. They are all against me.

Paranoid seniliform disorders tend to develop in individuals who have been sensitive and suspicious. Existing personality tendencies are apparently intensified by degenerative brain changes and the stress accompanying advancing age.

3. *The presbyophrenic type.* This seniliform psychosis is characterized by fabrication, a jovial, amiable mood, and marked amnesia. Such persons may appear superficially alert and may talk volubly in a rambling, confused manner, filling gaps in present memory with events that occurred 20 or 30 years before. They usually show a peculiar restlessness or excitability and engage in continual aimless activity; for example, an individual may fold and unfold pieces of cloth as if ironing, or may collect various discarded objects with a great show of importance. This type of disorder appears to occur most frequently in individuals who have been lively, assertive, and extroverted in their younger days; it accounts for less than 10 percent of all seniliform psychoses.

4. *Depressed and agitated types.* Here the

individual is severely depressed and agitated and usually suffers from hypochondriacal and nihilistic delusions, often expressing morbid ideas about cancer, syphilis, and other diseases. Delusions of poverty are also common, and such individuals may feel that they are headed for the poorhouse, that nobody wants them, and that they are a senseless burden on their children and just generally "in the way." In some cases, the person becomes self-accusatory and develops delusions of great sin. In many respects the symptoms resemble those in psychotic depressions, for which the early phases of the disorder are very often mistaken, and the possibility of suicide must be guarded against. This type constitutes less than 10 percent of seniliform reactions.

5. *Delirious and confused types.* In these cases there is severe mental clouding in which patients become extremely restless, combative, resistive, and incoherent. They recognize no one and are completely disoriented for time and place. Such delirious states are often precipitated by acute illness or by traumas, such as a broken leg or hip. Although transient delirious episodes often occur in seniliform dementia, chronic confusion and delirium are uncommon except in terminal states; they account for less than 10 percent of seniliform reactions.

With appropriate treatment, many persons with seniliform dementia show some alleviation of symptoms. In general, however, deterioration continues its downward course over a period of months or years. Eventually patients become oblivious of their surroundings, bedridden, and reduced to a vegetative existence. Resistance to disease is lowered, and death usually results from pneumonia or some other infection.

On the other hand, important as is the brain degeneration in the seniliform dementias, the causal picture in the behavior that we see is much broader. Since the same additional causal factors are often found in the disorders associated with brain deterioration due to cerebral arteriosclerosis, and since similar treatment methods are often effective, we will first present the clinical picture of this other old-age psychotic disorder and then take up the causal factors and treatment approaches for both.

Disorders involving cerebral arteriosclerosis

Disorders with cerebral arteriosclerosis are similar to seniliform dementias, but there are certain differences in both anatomical and behavioral symptoms.[3] The typical vascular pathology in cerebral arteriosclerosis involves a "hardening" of the arteries of the brain. Large patches of fatty and calcified material known as *senile plaques* accumulate at particular points on the inside lining of the blood vessels and gradually clog the arterial channel. Circulation becomes sluggish and may eventually be blocked altogether.

This blocking, in turn, may result in *cerebrovascular insufficiency* due to impaired circulation in the brain areas supplied by the vessel, or in *intracerebral hemorrhage,* involving a rupture of the vessel with intracranial bleeding. Of course, damage to a large vessel will do more harm than damage to a small one. When the narrowing or eventual blockage is gradual and involves small blood vessels, cerebral nutrition is impaired and there are areas of softening as the brain tissue degenerates. Such areas of softening are found in some 90 percent of patients suffering from arteriosclerotic brain disease. The HIGHLIGHT on page 460 shows the damage to the brain caused by cerebral arteriosclerosis.

A sudden blocking or rupture in a small vessel is referred to as a *small stroke* and may result in a variety of transient psychological and physical symptoms, ranging from mental confusion and emotional lability to acute indigestion, changes in handwriting, and unsteadiness in gait. Frequently, individuals suffer a succession of small strokes resulting in cumulative brain damage and the gradual personality change described earlier as organic personality syndrome.

When the blockage or rupture involves a large vessel, the individual suffers a major stroke (*cerebrovascular accident*—CVA). Here there is both focal and generalized impairment of brain function, resulting in coma

[3]The term *arteriosclerosis* includes a number of diseases of the blood vessels of which atherosclerosis is by far the most common and important. Atherosclerosis involves an arterial lesion characterized by a thickening of the arterial wall and a reduction in blood flow.

Three cases of cerebrovascular pathology

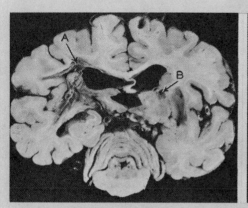 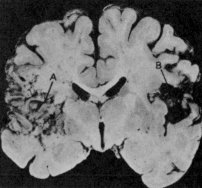 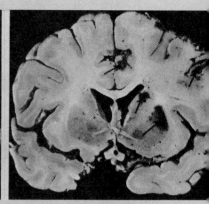

These pictures show cross sections of the brains of persons who suffered from cerebral arteriosclerosis. At the left is a section from the brain of a man who died at 43 after suffering from hypertension and two strokes that had resulted in some paralysis on both sides, emotional lability, and convulsions. The arrows indicate the areas where the cerebrovascular accidents and the specific brain damage occurred.

The center picture is of a section through the frontal lobes of a man who likewise suffered from two strokes; his strokes, however, were separated by an interval of 17 years. The arrow A points to a softening correlated with a recent stroke, which was associated with two months of paralysis on one side; the arrow B points to a cavity resulting from the earlier stroke, which had been associated with aphasia.

Arrows in the picture at right point to scattered emboli in another patient's brain, resulting in many tiny hemorrhages and widespread local damage.

or an acute confusional state. If the individual survives, the acute symptoms may largely clear up, but typically there will be some degree of residual brain damage.

Cerebrovascular accidents kill more than 200,000 Americans each year; about 3 million persons in the United States are handicapped or incapacitated by cerebral arteriosclerosis. The incidence and severity of psychopathology in the latter cases is not known, but it would appear from recent research that the relationship between disturbed behavior and the occurence of cerebral arteriosclerosis in the elderly is much weaker than was formerly believed. Some disturbed oldsters show little sign of arteriosclerotic disease, and many with the disease do not develop disturbed behavior (Ernst et al., 1977; Goldfarb, 1974).

Although cerebral arteriosclerosis may occur in young adulthood or middle age, it usually has its onset after age 55 with the sex ratio being about equal (Holvey & Talbott, 1972). This disorder appears to be most common among persons on lower socioeconomic levels, but it occurs in all economic groups. The average age of first admission for persons manifesting psychoses associated with cerebral arteriosclerosis is between 70 and 75.

Clinical picture in disorders with cerebral arteriosclerosis. In about half the cases of disorders with cerebral arteriosclerosis, symptoms appear suddenly. Here individuals are usually admitted to a medical facility in an acute confusional state resulting from a cerebrovascular accident. Such persons show marked clouding of consciousness, disorientation for time, place, and person, incoherence, and often hemiplegia (paralysis of one side of the body). Convulsive seizures are also relatively common and may precede the acute attack, occur at the same time, or appear at a later point in the illness. In severe cases the patient may die without a clearing of the confusional state.

Acute delirious or demented states may last for days, weeks, or even months, with an eventual remission of the acute symptoms. In these cases, there may be varying degrees of residual brain damage and impairment in physical and mental functions. Often the individual is able to compensate for the brain damage, particularly with the help of special rehabilitative measures designed to alleviate physical handicaps and clear up possible aphasic conditions. Sometimes, however, there is a progressive loss of mental efficiency, accompanied by other psychological symptoms such as emotional lability, irritability, and hypochondriacal concern over bodily functions. In many cases, there appears to be an accentuation of earlier maladaptive traits following severe cerebrovascular accidents.

When the onset of the disorder is gradual, early symptoms may include complaints of weakness, fatigue, dizziness, headache, depression, memory defect, periods of confusion, and lowered efficiency in work. Often there is a slowing up of activity and a loss of zest in living. There may be a considerable delay between the appearance of such symptoms and the hospitalization of the individual.

By the time of hospitalization, the clinical picture is usually similar to that in senile dementia. The memory defect has now increased, although it may be somewhat uneven—for example, it may be more severe when the patient is tired or under emotional stress. Emotional lability becomes pronounced, and the individual may be easily moved to tears or highly irritable, with a tendency to "flare up" at the slightest provocation. Usually the flare-up is brief and ends with tears and repentance. Increased irritability may be accompanied by suspiciousness and poorly organized delusions of persecution.

By this time, there is also a more pronounced impairment of concentration and general intellectual functioning. Interest in the outside world and in others is markedly reduced, as are the individual's initiative and work capacity. Judgment is impaired and in some instances there is a lowering of moral controls. Frequently there are feelings of depression associated with some insight into failing physical and mental powers. As in cases with an acute onset, there may be marked fluctuations in the clinical picture, but the usual course of the disease is in the direction of increasing deterioration and death.

Comparison with the clinical picture in seniliform dementia. The clinical aspects of seniliform dementia and psychosis with cerebral arteriosclerosis are so much alike that a differential diagnosis is frequently very difficult to make. In some cases, there is a mixture of the two disorders—a senile reaction may be superimposed on an arteriosclerotic condition or vice versa. However, mixed reactions are not nearly so common as might be expected, and usually one condition or the other predominates.

Among the clinically distinguishing features of these two disorders are the following: (a) seniliform dementia is usually gradual and progressive and lasts longer, while psychosis with cerebral arteriosclerosis is more apt to be brought on by a cerebrovascular accident and to run a brief and stormy course ending in death; (b) in seniliform dementia there is usually more pronounced intellectual impairment, and paranoid patterns are more common; (c) symptoms common in the arteriosclerotic group but less often seen in seniliform dementia are headaches, dizziness, convulsive seizures, depression, and strong emotional outbursts; and finally (d) the symptoms in cerebral arteriosclerotic disorders typically show more pronounced fluctuations. But although these differences are observable in early and intermediate states, all patients who suffer advanced brain destruction become very much alike.

Causal factors in the psychoses of old age

Early investigators seized on brain damage as the only important factor in the causation of both seniliform dementia and disorders with cerebral arteriosclerosis. But in recent years, with the increased interest and attention devoted to mental disorders of old age, those early beliefs have undergone considerable revision.

Although cerebral damage alone, when

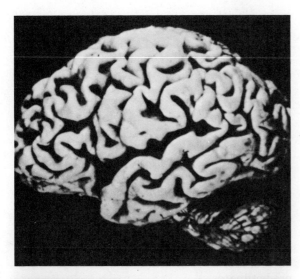

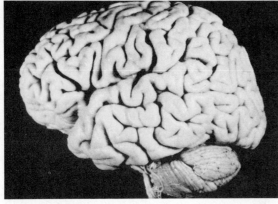

This is the brain (top) of a 79-year-old man who had been hospitalized with a diagnosis of senile dementia; his symptoms included marked confusion, memory defects, especially for recent events, slight aphasia, paranoid ideation, and agitated depression. The cortex shows extensive, diffuse atrophy with a narrowing of the convolutions and a widening of the fissures throughout. Below it, for comparison, is a normal brain.

sufficiently extensive, may produce marked mental symptoms, it has become evident that with most patients the organic changes are only one set of interactive factors. In the total clinical picture, the prior personality organization of the individual and the stressfulness of the life situation are also of key importance. And since specific brain pathology, personality makeup, and stress factors vary from person to person, we find a somewhat different causal pattern in each case.

Biological factors. A number of early studies showed a high incidence of senile and arteriosclerotic brain disease in the family backgrounds of elderly psychotics (Mayer-Gross, 1944; Post, 1944). However, more recent findings, including observations of aging in twins (Kallman, 1961), indicate that it is unrealistic to consider genetic or constitutional factors as *primary* causal agents in these mental disorders. This view, of course, does not exclude a role for such factors in the rapidity of physiological aging.

In recent years the effects of senile and arteriosclerotic changes in brain metabolism have been somewhat less strongly emphasized in the causal pattern of old-age psychoses. In cases involving major strokes, gross disturbances in circulatory and metabolic processes are apparent, and we have noted the confusional states and other symptoms that may result. However, only a small minority of persons who suffer a severe stroke develop persistent psychotic disorders.

In mental disorders having a gradual onset, the role of metabolic factors is even less clear. A diminished flow of blood and lower oxygen consumption accompany senile psychoses, but they are no longer considered of primary etiologic significance (Terry & Wisniewski, 1974). And while prolonged malnutrition, endocrine malfunction, and other metabolic factors are implicated in some cases, they are not ordinarily considered of primary causal significance.

Nor does the extent of brain pathology ordinarily account for the psychotic disorders of old age, a point dramatically demonstrated by Gal (1959), who did a postmortem study of 104 patients ranging in age from 65 to 94 and found a lack of correlation between brain damage and behavior. Extensive cerebral damage was found in some patients who had manifested only mild mental symptoms, while minimal cerebral damage was found in others who had shown severe psychopathology.

With progressive cerebral impairment, of course, the degree of residual brain capacity shapes the response in greater measure. This point was well brought out by Ullmann and Gruen in summarizing their findings with 84 patients who had suffered strokes and had shown mild, moderate, or severe degrees of cerebral deficit.

Retirement brings radical changes in an individual's life style— many of them unwelcome. Days that used to be filled with productive tasks stretch out before one—empty not only of meaningful occupation but of the companionship of former colleagues. It is not surprising that some individuals begin to undergo marked changes in mental and physical health at this period in their lives.

"Patients who have experienced mild strokes with little or no residual mental impairment react to the stress in their own idiosyncratic fashion. Some will integrate the experience successfully; others will become enmeshed in psychopathological maneuvers of varying severity. In patients with moderate or severe brain damage, the situation is quite different. Here the unique features of the stroke are highlighted, the chief of these being that the very organ governing the adaptation to stress is itself impaired. The resulting clinical picture has to be evaluated now, not only in terms of what the experience means to the patient, but also in terms of the capacity the patient has for evaluating the situation." (1961, p. 1009)

Psychosocial factors. It has been said that next to dying, the recognition that we are aging may be the most profound shock we experience in our lifetime. How older individuals react to their changed status and to the difficult stressors of this age period depends heavily on their personality makeup as well as on the challenges, rewards, and frustrations of their life situation. As important as actual brain changes are, the majority of old-age psychoses depend heavily—and often primarily—on psychosocial and sociocultural factors.

1. *The role of the pre-psychotic personality.* A number of studies have shown that individuals who are handicapped psychologically by undesirable personality traits are especially vulnerable to psychoses and other mental disorders in old age. Obsessive-compulsive trends,

rigidity, suspiciousness, seclusiveness, social inadequacy, and poor adaptability to change are some of the traits that have been emphasized in the background of such individuals. Even negative attitudes toward growing old, which lead to self-devaluation and a negative self-image, can be serious adjustment handicaps during this period of life.

2. *Stressors characteristic in old age.* An older person faces numerous real problems and insecurities that are not characteristic of earlier life periods. In fact, the unfavorable environmental circumstances of older people are often more hazardous to mental health than are organic brain changes. Even well-integrated personalities may break down under the combined assault of cerebral changes and a stressful life situation.

a) *Retirement and reduced income.* Retirement is often the brand that marks a person as a member of the "old age" group. It can be quite demoralizing if it is forced upon the individual. Repeated studies have shown that most older persons are productive workers and that many would prefer to keep on working when they reach retirement age (Offir, 1974).

Many people depend greatly on their work for status, for self-identity, for satisfying interpersonal relationships, and for meaning in their lives. Retirement often does not meet these needs, and there is a tendency to react with the feeling that one's usefulness and worth are at an end—a reaction conducive to rapid physical and mental deterioration.

Retirement usually leads also to a severe reduction in income, which further augments the older person's adjustive burden. Most older Americans depend on social security benefits, pensions, and/or savings; for many this means trying to get along on less money than when they were working. The rampant inflation of the last decade has made financial adjustment even more difficult. Today many millions of older Americans are living in or near poverty.

b) *Fear of invalidism and death.* The gradual physical deterioration of one's body and the increased possibility of falling prey to some chronic and debilitating disease tend to make one more preoccupied with bodily functions and with the possibility of failing health, symptoms common among older people. Such concern is aggravated when the individual has a history of medical difficulties that are likely to be aggravated by the aging process. Whereas a young person usually expects to make a complete recovery from sickness, many illnesses among older people become chronic and the individual has to adjust to living with them. When chronic illness and failing health lead to pain, invalidism, and dependence on others, the individual faces a difficult life situation.

With aging and physical deterioration, such individuals are also confronted with the inescapable fact of their own impending death. Some older people react with equanimity, often stemming from deep religious faith in the meaningfulness of human existence and in the certainty of a life hereafter. Others die as they have lived, with little concern for life or human existence. In fact, they may welcome death as a solution to unsolvable problems and a meaningless life. This is sometimes true also of older people who have lost their friends and loved ones and who feel that they have "outlived their time." However, for many older people the realization that life is drawing to a close is a highly stressful experience.

c) *Isolation and loneliness.* As the individual grows older, he or she is faced with the inevitable loss of loved ones, friends, and contemporaries. The death of the mate with whom one may have shared many years of close companionship often poses a particularly difficult adjustment problem. This is especially true for women, who in the U.S. outlive their spouses by an average of some 7 years.

Other factors, too, may contribute to social isolation. Children grow up, marry, and move away; impairment of vision or hearing and various chronic ailments may make social interaction difficult; an attitude of self-pity or an inward centering of interest may alienate family and friends alike. In many instances, the older person also becomes increasingly rigid and intolerant and is unable to make effective use of the opportunities for meaningful social interaction that still remain.

Of course, retirement, lowered income, impaired health, and loneliness are not just matters of inability to maintain a particular lifestyle or to interact with loved ones. In a larger view, they involve the inability to contribute productively and to feel oneself a vital and needed part of the human enterprise. In essence, they progressively destroy the older person's links with the world and feelings of living a meaningful existence.

General sociocultural conditions. The sociocultural context provides the "climate" in which aging takes place.[4] The importance of this context is suggested by the fact that in the United States, the urban rate of first admissions to mental hospitals and related facilities for both senile dementia and psychosis with cerebral arteriosclerosis is approximately twice as high as the rural rate. But we do not know how much this indicates that urban living, with its faster pace, noise, crowds, and other stressors is more conducive to the development of these disorders and how much it indicates that more persons with old-age psychoses are cared for at home in rural areas. The picture is also complicated by the fact that in rural areas the older person enjoys higher social status and is generally able to work productively for a longer period.

In our urban industrial society, the problems of old age have caught us largely unprepared. We have not provided ample conditions for utilizing the experience and wisdom of older people; nor have we provided conditions essential for them to live in reasonable comfort and dignity. In fact, the term "role obsolescence" has been used to refer to society's attitude to-

---

[4]A useful source of information concerning the problems of aging in our own and other societies may be found in the *Annals of the American Academy of Political and Social Science* (Sept. 1974).

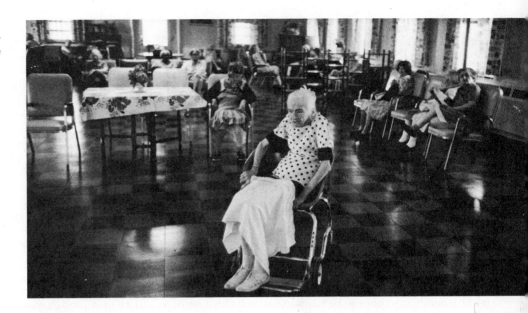

Nursing homes too often become "storehouses" for the elderly—particularly if the onset of senility or cerebral impairment has made them difficult to care for at home. Unfortunately, the emotionally barren environment of such institutions can be a major factor in further deterioration.

ward older persons as having outlived their usefulness. In our youth-oriented culture, many older people come to perceive themselves as obsolete and worthless—and tend to behave accordingly.

Not infrequently, children assume a patronizing and protective attitude toward their aging parents, and in other ways tend to deprive them of dignity, responsibility, and a feeling of importance. Many parents are treated as unwanted burdens, and their children may secretly wish that they would die to relieve them of financial and other responsibilities. In a study of older people in France, De Beauvoir (1970) has pointed out that when the French go away for vacations, they sometimes deposit their aged parents in rest homes. Then, on their return home, they "forget" to pick them up, abandoning them like dogs in a kennel. In the United States, too, many older people are "deposited" in rest or nursing homes to die, even though they may be in relatively good health. The effects of being cast aside simply for "being old" are likely to be devastating, and, in documented instances, even lethal.

Treatment and outcomes for the old-age psychoses

Whether or not to hospitalize the aged person who is mentally disordered (or indeed the younger one) is often a problem. Individuals manifesting such symptoms as confusion, violent and noisy behavior, depression, antisocial behavior, and disorientation for time, place, and person, usually require institutionalization. However, many investigators regard hospitalization as a last resort, feeling that the sudden change in environment and manner of living is especially stressful for the older person and may lead to a feeling of complete hopelessness. In any event, effective treatment of the mental disorders of later life requires a comprehensive use of medical, psychological, and sociological procedures, as indicated by the needs of the individual.

Medical treatment includes both accurate diagnosis and a wide range of procedures, including surgery, drugs, and dietary changes, designed to ameliorate specific physical disorders and to improve the overall health and well-being of the patient. Antipsychotic and antianxiety drugs have proven very valuable in controlling psychotic symptoms and alleviating anxiety and tension, but they are generally not effective in reversing the mental deterioration found in advanced cases of seniliform and arteriosclerotic brain disorders.

There have been favorable reports on the use of group psychotherapy in treating mental disorders associated with old age, but additional research is needed for delineating the most effective psychological treatment procedures. In many hospital settings, "token economies" have proven helpful: desired behavior is rewarded by tokens that the patients can exchange for things they want. A key aspect of the best of such reinforcement procedures is that they parallel the organization of outside society and help counteract tendencies toward progressive institutional dependence and chronicity.

Therapy with older patients is also directed toward creating an environment in which the person can function successfully. In a hospital setting or nursing home this includes the provision of comfortable surroundings, together with stimulating activities that encourage the use of whatever capacities remain. Such therapy also includes working with family members in an attempt to help them understand the nature of the patient's disorder and to encourage them to be supportive and show that they care. Where the patient is convalescing at home, follow-up visits by the social worker may be of great value in helping both the patient and the family to adjust.

Even seemingly minor innovations in treatment have shown promising results. In one interesting study, for example, Volpe and Kastenbaum (1967) worked with a group of older men who were so physically and psychologically incapacitated that they required around-the-clock nursing care. These men could perform no services for themselves, were agitated and incontinent, and had a record of striking at each other and tearing off their clothes. Some simple amenities were provided on the ward— games, cards, a record player, and a decorated bulletin board; the men were dressed in white shirts and ties; and at 2 P.M. each day they were served beer in 12-ounce bottles with crackers and cheese. Within a month there was a noticeable change in the group's behavior. The amount of medication they needed dropped sharply, incontinent and agitated behavior decreased significantly, and social responsiveness—as indicated by requests for and participation in parties and dances—markedly increased. The improvement of these men was attributed to their being treated with dignity as responsible individuals, and to the consequent *"expectancies of mutual gratification on the part of patients and staff members."* In essence, the expectations and demand characteristics of the ward had been changed to

those of a social situation instead of a medical one, and the men were cared for in much the same way as in the era of moral treatment, as described in Chapter 2.

The extent to which meaningful social roles and expectations may help older people cope with the emotional problems of this life period is illustrated by the following rather unusual case. It involves a professional man who was admitted to a mental hospital for treatment as a result of severe anxiety, indecision, and depression.

The patient's disorder was apparently precipitated by his retirement from the firm for which he had worked for over 40 years. In the course of his hospitalization, the patient evidenced little improvement until the hospital received a letter from his firm inquiring about his condition. They were experiencing difficulty without him and needed his help. Upon receipt of the news the patient showed marked improvement. He was given a leave of absence and returned to his old job. A follow-up study a year later revealed that he was handling his responsibilities with unimpaired judgment, appeared younger, showed good stamina, and reported regularly to work. At this time, he was 80 years old.

It seems clear that the expectation and reinforcement of "normal" social behaviors can often bring about marked behavioral changes in a relatively short time. Kahana and Kahana (1970) found that even such a simple measure as moving young and old people into the same ward appeared to be beneficial for both. The younger ones often tried to help the elderly, which provided them with a sense of purpose; their active interest, in turn, increased the elderly individuals' sense of importance.

Thus, the psychological prognosis in the psychoses of old age is far from hopeless. Even without complete recovery, many patients can return to their homes, and many others can remain in their homes while being treated in community clinics.[5]

Although the outcome in cases of seniliform and arteriosclerotic brain disorders has traditionally been considered unfavorable because

---

[5]A summary of recent developments in the rehabilitation and treatment of organically impaired older persons through community resources may be found in Skigen and Solomon (1978).

of the irreversibility of the brain damage, recent evidence indicates that behavioral recovery or improvement is possible in about half of the cases when appropriate treatment is provided. Blau (1970) has pointed out that at the Boston State Hospital, which has an active treatment program for elderly patients and fosters aftercare in the community, almost half of the patients over 60 years of age are discharged within 6 months of their admission.

Interestingly, both the greatest number of deaths and the greatest number of improvements among hospitalized elderly psychotic patients occur during the first year after admission. For patients who require continued care in the hospital, about 75 percent die within the first 5 years. In general, the following are considered favorable indicators with respect to outcome: (a) a well-integrated prepsychotic personality; (b) mild, rather than severe, cerebral pathology; (c) absence of such conditions as severe overweight, hypertension, and alcoholism; (d) average or above-average intelligence, education, and technical competence; and (e) a favorable life situation to which to return.

Increasingly aware of the problems confronting senior citizens, federal, state, and local groups are focusing on all aspects of growing old. Scientists in many areas of the biological and social sciences are investigating the pathological and normal aspects of aging and are exploring—in their respective fields—ways to minimize the hazards of the aging process. Senior citizen centers and other community centers and clinics for assisting older people with retirement and other problems are increasing. Specifically designed housing developments also are being built for the elderly; and a number of older people are experimenting with "communal living."

Elderly people are also trying to help one another avoid the special stressors that increase their vulnerability to mental disorders. An encouraging trend here is the growth of such organizations as the National Association of Retired Persons, which numbers over 5 million members. It provides an impressive array of services for its members and fosters legislation to protect the rights and the welfare of older people in our society (Offir, 1974). It does seem important, however, as Neugarten (1974) has pointed out, that senior citizens not form too strong an age-group identification, which only strengthens the attitudes toward age that tend to divide our society into age-conscious groups. The broader perspective she advocates is a focus of the Gray Panthers, which was started by elderly citizens but now includes all age groups and works toward better health services and greater social justice in the society as a whole.

At the same time we all need to prepare ourselves for the problems typical of this life period, in the hope that so doing will help us avoid the mental and behavioral deterioration often associated with it. We need to plan ahead for an active and useful life that will take full advantage of the opportunities that are open to us. Of course, many of the adjustments of old age are highly specific to the situation of the given individual and hence cannot be fully anticipated, but at any age it is important to maintain mental alertness, flexibility, and adaptability while continuing to grow and fulfill one's potential. In short, old age does pose special problems, but it is by no means incompatible with a meaningful and fulfilling life, nor is it necessarily accompanied by gross mental deterioration.

Mental retardation

The American Association on Mental Deficiency (AAMD) has defined *mental retardation* as "significantly subaverage general intellectual functioning existing concurrently with deficits in adaptive behavior, and manifested during the developmental period" (AAMD, 1973, p. 11). Mental retardation is thus defined in terms of *level of behavioral performance;* the definition says nothing about causal factors—which may be primarily biological, psychosocial, or sociocultural, or a combination of these.

The American Psychiatric Association has adopted the same definitional approach for its latest classification, DSM-III, listing mental retardation as a disorder beginning before the age of 18. By definition, any functional equivalent of mental retardation that has its onset after age 17 must be considered a dementia rather than mental retardation. The distinction is an important one because, as has been pointed out, the psychological situation of the individual who acquires a pronounced impairment of intellectual functioning after attaining maturity is vastly different from that of the individual whose intellectual resources were subnormal throughout all or most of his or her early development. Some of the more important differences will become apparent in what follows.

Mental retardation is considered to be a specific disorder, but it may occur in combination with other disorders. In fact, the prevalence of other psychiatric disorders among retarded individuals is markedly in excess of that of the general population.

Mental retardation occurs among children throughout the world; in its most severe forms it is a source of great hardship to parents as well as an economic and social burden on the community. The incidence of mental retardation in the United States is estimated to be about 6.8 million persons (see HIGHLIGHT on this page). This figure is based on a cutoff point of about IQ 70, which is the cutoff point used by the AAMD. Most states have laws providing that individuals with IQs below 70 who evidence socially incompetent or disapproved behavior can be classified as mentally retarded and committed to an institution.

The incidence of mental retardation seems to increase markedly at ages 5 to 6, to peak at age 15, and to drop off sharply after that. For the most part, these changes in incidence reflect changes in life demands. During early childhood, individuals with only a mild degree of intellectual impairment, who constitute the vast majority of the mentally retarded, often appear to be relatively normal. Their subaverage intellectual functioning becomes apparent only when difficulties with schoolwork lead to a diagnostic evaluation. When adequate facilities are available for their education, children in this group can usually master essential school skills and achieve a satisfactory level of socially adaptive behavior (see HIGHLIGHT on page 469). Following the school years, they usually make an acceptable adjustment in the

HIGHLIGHT

Incidence of mental retardation in the United States

Level of retardation	Approximate incidence
Mild (IQ 50–70)	6,332,100
Moderate and severe (IQ 20–49)	420,000
Profound (IQ 0–19)	105,000

Adapted from Robinson and Robinson (1976), p. 37.

community and thus lose the identity of mentally retarded.

Levels of mental retardation

It is important to remind ourselves once again that any classification system in the behavioral field will have strong features of both arbitrariness and pragmatism. In mental retardation, attempts to define varying levels of impairment have tended to rely increasingly on measurement—largely measurement by means of IQ tests (Robinson & Robinson, 1976). In the above-quoted AAMD definition, for example, the phrase "significantly subnormal general intellectual functioning" translates directly and officially into an IQ test score that is more than two standard deviations below the population mean—i.e., a cutoff representing about the 3rd percentile, which is a point below which only some 3 percent of the population score. This means an IQ of close to 70, depending on the particular test used.

It is not improper to define mental retardation this way, provided we keep in mind the implications of the definition. The original IQ tests were devised for the explicit purpose of predicting academic achievement among schoolchildren. Other IQ tests developed later were validated largely on the basis of how well they could predict scores on the original ones. Generally, then, what IQ tests measure is an individual's likely level of success in dealing

Difficulties of mentally retarded people in learning basic academic skills

The basic learning processes of most mentally retarded children—aside from a minority with serious neurological defects—are not essentially different from those of normal children. However, retarded children learn at a slower rate than normal children and are less capable of mastering abstractions and complex concepts. These limitations are especially apparent in learning language and other symbolic skills requiring a high level of abstract ability.

Problems that retarded children typically encounter in learning basic academic skills may be summarized as follows:

1. Difficulty in focusing attention. Studies have shown that such children's poor learning is often due to the fact that their attention is focused on irrelevant aspects of learning situations. Once they know what stimulus dimensions are important—for example, attending to form when the shape of the letters is important in learning the alphabet—they may quickly master appropriate discrimination skills and show marked improvement in performance and learning.

2. Deficiency in past learning. Most formal learning requires prior learning. For example, a child who has not learned basic verbal, conceptual, and problem-solving skills will fall farther behind when he or she begins schooling. Thus a number of programs have been established to help disadvantaged children of preschool age develop basic skills requisite for learning in school.

3. Expectancy of failure—a self-fulfilling prophecy. Because of having experienced more failure in learning attempts than other children, the mentally retarded child tends to begin tasks with a greater expectancy of failure and to engage in avoidance behavior as well. Often such children feel that forces beyond their control determine the outcome of their actions. Thus, if they succeed in a task, they may not perceive their success as due to their own efforts or ability. They become passive, lose their initiative, and begin to rely too much on others. To counteract this tendency, learning experiences must be programmed into manageable components that can yield continuing experiences of success.

Special education classes should thus be directed at helping the mentally retarded discriminate relevant from irrelevant stimuli in learning and problem-solving situations; they should associate new learning with the children's present information, needs, and life situations; and they should structure learning tasks in a sequence of steps that can be readily mastered by the retarded and so provide experiences of success. Such measures, of course, are useful in all educational settings, but are particularly important in training mentally retarded children.

Based on Bijou (1966), Hagen and Huntsman (1971), Hyatt and Rolnick (1974), Karnes et al. (1970), MacMillan and Keogh (1971), Tarver and Hallahan (1974), and Robinson and Robinson (1976).

with conventional academic materials, and in fact they do this very well when properly utilized.[6] Thus when we speak of varying *levels of mental retardation,* we are to a large extent speaking of levels of capacity to succeed in schoolwork.

Of course, this reliance on IQ scores is tempered somewhat by the other main part of the definition—the presence of concurrent "deficits in adaptive behavior." That is, the diagnosis of mental retardation is reserved for individuals who achieve low IQ test scores *and* demonstrate adaptational deficiencies, particularly in the areas of personal independence and social responsibility. The same dual criteria are involved in the officially recognized "levels" of retardation, although the IQ score often tends in practice to be the dominant consideration. This is appropriate at the lower end

---

[6]In the view of the present authors, it is most unfortunate that "general intelligence" has come to be thought of almost exclusively as a matter of IQ and therefore as facility in handling school tasks. There is surely more to the popular notion of "intelligence" than the talent for getting good grades in school. We would hold, too, that academic talent, which is mostly what IQ tests measure, is but a limited aspect of intellectual fitness. In this context, it is worth noting that the frequent charge of cultural bias on the part of IQ tests is unavoidably accurate: the educational system is the main depository of the dominant culture's products, and facility to deal with it will inevitably come easier to those trained from infancy in its concepts and values.

of the scale, since an individual with an IQ of 50 or below will inevitably exhibit gross deficiencies in adaptive behavior as well. At the higher ranges of "retarded" IQ scores, however, behavioral adaptiveness and IQ score seem to be at least partially independent of each other.

Both the American Association on Mental Deficiency and the American Psychiatric Association classifications recognize four levels of retarded mental development, as follows:

a) *Mild mental retardation (IQ 52–67).* As shown in the Highlight on page 468, this group constitutes by far the largest number of those labeled mentally retarded. Persons in this group are considered "educable," and their intellectual levels as adults are comparable to those of average 8- to 11-year-old children. Their social adjustment often approximates that of the adolescent, although they tend to lack the normal adolescent's imagination, inventiveness, and judgment. Ordinarily they do not show signs of brain pathology or other physical anomalies, but often they require some measure of supervision due to limited ability to foresee the consequences of their actions. With early diagnosis, parental assistance, and special educational programs, the great majority can adjust socially, master simple academic and occupational skills, and become self-supporting citizens.

b) *Moderate mental retardation (IQ 36–51).* Individuals in this group are likely to fall in the educational category of "trainable." In adult life, individuals classified as moderately retarded attain intellectual levels similar to those of average 4- to 7-year-old children. While some of the brighter ones can be taught to read and write a little, and some manage to achieve a fair command of spoken language, their rate of learning is relatively slow, and the level of conceptualizing extremely limited. Physically, they usually appear clumsy and ungainly, and they suffer from bodily deformities and poor motor coordination. A distinct minority of these children are hostile and aggressive; more typically they present an affable and somewhat vacuous personality picture.

In general, with early diagnosis, parental help, and adequate opportunities for training, most of the moderately retarded can achieve partial independence in daily self-care, acceptable behavior, and economic usefulness in a family or other sheltered environment. Whether or not they require institutionalization usually depends on their general level of adaptive behavior and the nature of their home situation.

c) *Severe mental retardation (IQ 20–35).* Individuals in this group are sometimes referred to as "dependent retarded." Among these individuals, motor and speech development are severely retarded, and sensory defects and motor handicaps are common. They can develop limited levels of personal hygiene and self-help skills, which somewhat lessen their dependence, but they are always dependent on others for care. However, many profit to some extent from training and can perform simple occupational tasks under supervision.

d) *Profound mental retardation (IQ under 20).* The term "life support retarded" is sometimes used in referring to individuals in this category. Most of these persons are severely deficient in adaptive behavior and unable to master any but the simplest tasks. Useful speech, if it develops at all, is rudimentary. Severe physical deformities, central nervous system pathology, and retarded growth are typical; convulsive seizures, mutism, deafness, and other physical anomalies are also common. These individuals must remain in custodial care all their lives. However, they tend to have poor health and low resistance to disease and thus a short life expectancy.

Severe and profound cases of mental retardation can usually be quite readily diagnosed in infancy because of the presence of physical malformations, grossly delayed habit training, and other obvious symptoms of abnormality. But although these individuals show a marked impairment of overall intellectual functioning, they may have considerably more ability in some areas than in others. Indeed, in very occasional cases, seriously retarded persons may show a high level of skill in some specific aspect of behavior that does not depend on abstract reasoning. Thus one seriously retarded individual was able to remember the serial number on every dollar bill he was shown or had ever seen; another was able to tell the day of the week of a given date in any year, without resorting to paper and pencil or even to making other numerical calculations. In other exceptional cases, a retarded person may show considerable talent in art or music. Viscott (1970) provided a detailed case study of a "musical idiot savant"; Hill (1975) cited the case of a mildly retarded individual with a diagnosed IQ of 54 who could play 11 different musical instruments by ear and possessed outstanding skill in calculating dates. Similarly, Morishima (1975) cited the case of a famous Japanese painter whose assessed IQ was 47. However, such unusual abilities among the retarded are rare.

Contrary to common understanding, the distribution of IQ scores in the U.S. does not precisely fit "normal curve" expectations, especially at the lower IQ ranges where there tends to be a frequency bulge, with nearly 200,000 more cases than would be expected (Robinson & Robinson, 1976). This finding suggests the operation of an intruding factor that tends to inflate the numbers of cases at lower IQ ranges—probably the presence of major genetic abnormalities and/or brain injury that are not characteristic of mild retardation.

Mental retardation and organic brain dysfunction

Some instances of mental retardation—something on the order of 25 percent of the cases—occur with known organic pathology. In these cases retardation is severe or profound and the clinical picture does not differ in essential respects from the dementia type of symptom syndrome described earlier.

In the present section we shall consider five biological conditions that may lead to mental retardation, noting some of the possible interrelations between them. Then we shall review some of the major clinical types of mental retardation associated with these organic causes.

1. *Genetic-chromosomal factors.* Mental retardation tends to run in families. This is particularly true of mild retardation. However, poverty and sociocultural deprivation also tend to run in families, and with early and continued exposure to such conditions, even the inheritance of average intellectual potential may not prevent subaverage intellectual functioning.

As we noted in Chapter 5, genetic and chromosomal factors play a much clearer role in the etiology of relatively rare types of mental retardation such as Down's syndrome. Here, specific chromosomal defects are responsible for metabolic alterations that adversely affect development of the brain. Genetic defects leading to metabolic alterations may, of course, involve many other developmental anomalies besides mental retardation. In general, the mental retardation most often associated with known genetic-chromosomal defects is moderate to severe in degree.

2. *Infections and toxic agents.* Mental retardation may be associated with a wide range of conditions due to infection. If a pregnant woman has syphilis or gets German measles, her child may suffer brain damage. Brain damage may also result from infections occurring after birth, such as viral encephalitis.

A number of toxic agents, such as carbon monoxide and lead, may cause brain damage during fetal development or after birth. In some instances, immunological agents, such as antitetanus serum or typhoid vaccine, may lead to brain damage. Similarly, certain drugs taken by the mother during pregnancy may lead to congenital malformations; an overdose of drugs administered to the infant may result in toxicity and brain damage. In rare cases, brain damage results from incompatibility in blood types between mother and fetus—conditions known as Rh, or ABO, system incompatibility. Fortunately, early diagnosis and blood transfusions can now minimize the effects of such incompatibility.

3. *Prematurity and trauma (physical injury).* Follow-up studies of children born prematurely and weighing less than about 5 pounds at birth have revealed a high incidence of neurological disorders and often mental retardation. In fact, very small premature babies are many times more likely to be mentally retarded than normal infants (MacDonald, 1964; Rothschild, 1967).

Physical injury at birth can also result in retardation. Isaacson (1970) has estimated that in 1 birth out of 1000 there is brain damage that will prevent the child from reaching the intelligence level of a 12-year-old. Although normally the fetus is well protected by its fluid-filled bag during gestation, and its skull appears designed to resist delivery stressors, accidents do happen during delivery as well as after birth. Difficulties in labor due to malposition of the fetus or other complications may irreparably damage the infant's brain. Bleeding within the brain is probably the most common result of such birth trauma. *Anoxia*—lack of sufficient oxygen to the brain stemming from delayed breathing or other causes—is another type of birth trauma that may damage the brain. Anoxia may also occur after birth as a result of cardiac arrest associated with operations, heart attacks, near drownings, or severe electrical shocks.

4. *Ionizing radiation.* In recent years a good deal of scientific attention has been focused on the damaging effects of ionizing radiation on sex cells and other bodily cells and tissues. Radiation may act directly on the fertilized ovum or may produce gene mutations in the sex cells of either or both parents, which, in turn, may lead to defective offspring.

Sources of harmful radiation were once limited primarily to high-energy X rays used for diagnosis and therapy, but the list has grown to include leakages at nuclear power plants and nuclear weapons testing, among others.

5. *Malnutrition and other biological factors.* As we noted in Chapter 5, deficiencies in protein and other essential nutrients during early development can result in irreversible physical and mental damage. Protein deficiencies in the mother's diet during pregnancy, as well as in the baby's diet after birth, have been pinpointed as particularly potent causes of lowered intelligence.

A limited number of cases of mental retardation are also associated with other biological agents, such as brain tumors that either damage the brain tissue directly or lead to increased cranial pressure and concomitant brain damage. In some instances of mental retardation—particularly of the severe and profound types—the causes are uncertain or unknown, although extensive brain pathology is evident.

Mental retardation stemming primarily from biological causes can be classified into several recognizable clinical types, of which four will be discussed here. The HIGHLIGHT on page 473 presents information on other well-known forms.

Down's syndrome (mongolism). Down's syndrome, first described by Langdon Down in 1886, is the most common of the clinical conditions associated with moderate and severe mental retardation. The term *mongolism* has often been used in referring to this syndrome because persons so afflicted frequently have almond-shaped eyes. About 1 in every 600 babies born in the United States is diagnosed as having Down's syndrome, a condition that "has lifelong implications for physical appearance, intellectual achievement and general functioning" (Golden & Davis, 1974, p. 7).

A number of physical features are often found among children with Down's syndrome, but very few of these children have all of the characteristics commonly thought of as typifying this group. In addition to almond-shaped eyes, the skin of the eyelids tends to be abnormally thick; the face and nose are often flat and broad, as is the back of the head; and the tongue, which seems too large for the mouth, may show deep fissures. The iris of the eye is frequently speckled. The neck is often short and broad, as are the hands, which tend to have creases across the palms. The fingers are stubby and the little finger is often more noticeably curved than the other fingers.

Well over 50 percent of these persons have cataracts, which are not congenital but tend to make their appearance when the child is about 7 or 8 (Falls, 1970). These cataracts aid in diagnosis, but fortunately they rarely become serious enough to warrant surgery. Interestingly enough, there appears to be little, if any, correlation between the number of physical symptoms of Down's syndrome and the degree of mental retardation.

Death rates for children with Down's syndrome have decreased dramatically in the past half century. In 1929 the life expectancy at birth for such children was about 9 years, with most of the deaths being due to gross physical anomalies and a large proportion occurring in the first year. Today, thanks to antibiotics, surgical correction of lethal anatomical defects, and better general medical care, many more of these children are living to adulthood (Smith & Berg, 1976). In fact, overall, the mortality rate for this group is only 6 percent higher than that for the general population, though it is still higher than that in the early years and for those who live beyond 40 (Forssman & Akesson, 1965). At present, the average life expectancy for live-born Down's syndrome children at birth is about 16 years; by age 1, it increases to about 22 years (Smith & Berg, 1976).

The term *mongolian idiot* was widely used

Other disorders associated with mental retardation

Clinical type	Symptoms	Causes
No. 18 trisomy syndrome	Peculiar pattern of multiple congenital anomalies, the most common being low-set malformed ears, flexion of fingers, small jaw, and heart defects	Autosomal anomaly of chromosome 18
Tay-Sach's disease	Hypertonicity, listlessness, blindness, progressive spastic paralysis, and convulsions (death by the third year)	Disorder of lipoid metabolism, carried by a single recessive gene
Turner's syndrome	In females only; webbing of the neck, increased carrying angle of forearm, and sexual infantilism	Sex chromosome anomaly (XO)
Klinefelter's syndrome	In males only; features vary from case to case, the only constant finding being the presence of small testes after puberty	Sex chromosome anomaly (XXY)
Niemann-Pick's disease	Onset usually in infancy, with loss of weight, dehydration, and progressive paralysis	Disorder of lipoid metabolism
Bilirubin encephalopathy	Abnormal levels of bilirubin (a toxic substance released by red cell destruction) in the blood; motor incoordination frequent	Often, Rh (ABO) blood group incompatibility between mother and fetus
Rubella, congenital	Visual difficulties most common, with cataracts and retinal problems often occurring together and with deafness and anomalies in the valves and septa of the heart	The mother's contraction of rubella (German measles) during the first few months of her pregnancy

Based on American Psychiatric Association (1968, 1972), Christodorescu et al. (1970), Donoghue, Abbas, and Gal (1970), Holvey and Talbott (1972), Johnson et al. (1970), Nielsen et al. (1970), Robinson and Robinson (1976).

in the past, but it was misleading, inasmuch as most of these children show only moderate mental retardation. Despite their limitations, they are usually able to learn self-help skills, acceptable social behavior, and routine manual skills that enable them to be of assistance in a family or institutional setting. The social adjustment of children with Down's syndrome is often helped by their tendency to be affectionate and relatively docile, although these traits are by no means universal.

Traditionally, the cause of mongolism was assumed to be faulty heredity. A number of early studies demonstrated, however, that more than one case of mongolism in a family was very infrequent, occurring in less than one family in 100. As a consequence of this finding, investigators turned to the study of metabolic factors and concluded that mongolism was probably due to some sort of glandular imbalance. Then, in 1959, the French scientists Lejeune, Turpin, and Gauthier found 47 chromosomes in several mongoloid cases. A trisomy of chromosome 21 has now been identified as a characteristic of mongoloid children (see the photograph on p. 132).

A child with Down's syndrome today has a much greater life expectancy than did his counterparts half a century ago.

Researchers have long believed that the "extra" chromosome in Down's syndrome is in some way contributed by the mother. But in 1973 it was learned that in certain instances it is in fact contributed by the father (Sasaki & Hara, 1973; Uchida, 1973). The reason for the trisomy of chromosome 21 is not clear, but the anomaly seems definitely related to parental age at conception.

It has been known for many years that the incidence of Down's syndrome increases in regular fashion with the age of the mother. A woman in her 20s has about 1 chance in 2000 of having a Down's syndrome baby, whereas the risk for a woman in her 40s is 1 in 50 (Holvey & Talbot, 1972).[7] Evidence of this type led naturally to the speculation that the capacity of the older woman to produce a chromosomally normal fetus was somehow impaired by the aging process.

Quite recent research, however, strongly suggests that age of fathers at conception is also implicated, particularly at the higher ranges of paternal age (Stene et al., 1977). In one study involving 1,279 cases of Down's syndrome in Japan, Matsunaga and associates (1978) demonstrated an overall increase in incidence of the syndrome with advancing paternal age when maternal age was controlled. The risk for fathers aged 55 years and over was more than twice that for fathers in their early 20s. Curiously, these investigators noted that, in their sample, fathers in their early 40s had a lower risk factor than somewhat younger or older men.

Thus, it seems that advancing age in either parent increases the risk of the trisomy 21 anomaly. As yet we do not understand how aging produces this effect. A reasonable guess is that aging is related to cumulative exposure to varied environmental hazards, such as radiation, that might have adverse effects on the processes involved in zygote formation or development.

But whatever the cause of the chromosomal anomaly, the end result is the distortion in the growth process characteristic of this clinical syndrome. There is no known effective treatment. When parents have had a child with Down's syndrome, they are usually quite concerned about having further children. In such cases genetic counseling may provide some indication of the risk—which may be quite small—of abnormality in additional children. In recent years, the technique known as *amniocentesis* has made it possible to diagnose most cases of Down's syndrome *in utero*, thus permitting parents to make a rational choice concerning termination of the pregnancy if the fetus is abnormal.

---

[7]It should be noted that, as in the case of all birth defects, the risk of having a Down's syndrome baby is very high for teenage mothers.

Phenylketonuria (PKU). Phenylketonuria is a rare metabolic disorder, occurring in about 1 in 20,000 births; retarded individuals in institutions who suffer from PKU number about 1 in 100 (Holmes et al., 1972; Schild, 1972).

In PKU the baby appears normal at birth but lacks an enzyme needed to break down phenylalanine, an amino acid found in many foods. The genetic error manifests itself in pathology only when phenylalanine is ingested, something that is virtually certain to occur if the child's condition remains undiagnosed. It is in this respect analogous to the problem of galactosemia mentioned in the previous chapter. In any event, if the condition is undetected, the amount of phenylalanine in the blood increases and eventually produces brain damage.

The disorder usually becomes apparent between 6 and 12 months after birth, although such symptoms as vomiting, a peculiar odor, infantile eczema, and seizures may occur during the early weeks of life. Often the first symptoms noticed are signs of mental retardation, which may be moderate to severe depending on the degree to which the disease has progressed. Motor incoordination and other neurological manifestations relating to the severity of brain damage are also common, and often the eyes, skin, and hair of untreated PKU patients are very pale.

PKU was identified in 1934 when a Norwegian mother sought to learn the reason for her child's mental retardation and peculiar musty odor. She consulted with many physicians to no avail until Dr. Asbjorn Folling found phenylpyruvic acid in the urine and concluded that the child had a disorder of phenylalanine metabolism (Centerwall & Centerwall, 1961).

Most older PKU patients show severe to profound mental retardation, with the median IQ of untreated adult phenylketonurics being about 20. Curiously, however, a number of PKU individuals have PKU relatives with less severely affected intelligence. And Perry (1970) has reported the cases of two untreated PKU patients with superior intelligence. These findings have made PKU something of an enigma. It results from a liver enzyme deficiency involving one or more recessive genes, and 1 person in 70 is thought to be a carrier. However, there may be varying degrees of

Both of these sisters were afflicted with PKU, but the younger one, at the left, was immediately placed on a special diet and the course of the disease was arrested.

PKU, or possibly another genetic factor may lessen the destructive potential of the enzyme defect (Burns, 1972).

Methods for the early detection of PKU have been developed, and dietary and related treatment procedures are now utilized. With early detection and treatment—preferably before an infant is 6 months old—the deterioration process can usually be arrested so that levels of intellectual functioning may range from borderline to normal. However, a few children suffer mental retardation despite restricted phenylalanine intake and other treatment measures.

For a baby to inherit PKU, it appears that both parents must carry the recessive genes. Thus when one child in a family is discovered to have PKU, it is important that other children in such families be screened as well.

Cretinism (thyroid deficiency). Cretinism provides a dramatic illustration of mental retardation resulting from endocrine imbalance. In this condition, the thyroid either has failed to develop properly or has undergone degeneration or injury; in either case, the infant suffers from a deficiency in thyroid secretion. Brain damage resulting from this insufficiency is most marked when the deficiency occurs during the prenatal and early postnatal periods of rapid growth.

In the valleys of central Switzerland and other geographical areas where iodine is deficient in the soil, and therefore in food grown in it, cretinism was once a common affliction. In such areas infants often were born with defective thyroid glands that remained undeveloped or atrophied later. Because cretinism was observed to run in families in such areas, it was thought to be invariably a hereditary disorder. In 1891, however, Dr. George Murray published his discovery that the injection of thyroid gland extract was beneficial in cases of *myxedema* — a disorder resulting from thyroid deficiency in adult life and characterized by mental dullness. This discovery, in turn, led to the treatment of cretinism with thyroid gland extract and to the realization that this condition, too, was the result of thyroid deficiency.

Although most cases of cretinism result from lack of iodine in the diet, thyroid deficiency may also occur as a result of birth injuries (involving bleeding into the thyroid) or of infectious diseases such as measles, whooping cough, or diphtheria. Less frequently, it may be a result of a genetically determined enzyme defect. The resulting clinical picture will depend on the age at which the thyroid deficiency occurs, as well as on the degree and duration of the deficiency.

Typical descriptions of individuals with cretinism involve cases in which there has been severe thyroid deficiency from an early age, often even before birth. Such an individual has a dwarflike, thick-set body and short, stubby extremities. Height is usually just a little over 3 feet, the shortness accentuated by slightly bent legs and a curvature of the spine. The individual walks with a shuffling gait that is easily recognizable and has a large head with abundant black, wiry hair; thick eyelids give the person a sleepy appearance; the skin is dry and thickened and cold to the touch. Other pronounced physical symptoms include a broad, flat nose, large and flappy ears, a protruding

abdomen, and failure to mature sexually. The sufferer reveals a bland personality and sluggish thought processes. Most individuals with cretinism fall within the moderate and severe categories of mental retardation, depending on the extent of brain damage. In cases with less pronounced physical signs of cretinism, the degree of mental retardation is usually less severe.

Early treatment of cretinism with thyroid gland extract is considered essential; infants not treated until after the first year of life may have permanently impaired intelligence. In long-standing cases, thyroid treatment may have some ameliorating effects, but the damage to the individual's nervous system and general physical development is beyond repair.

As a result of public health measures on both national and international levels with respect to the use of iodized salt and the early detection and correction of thyroid deficiency, severe cases of cretinism have become practically nonexistent in the United States and most, but not all, other countries.

Cranial anomalies. Mental retardation is associated with a number of conditions in which there are relatively gross alterations in head size and shape, and for which the causal factors have not been definitely established (Wortis, 1973). In *macrocephaly* ("large-headedness"), for example, there is an increase in the size and weight of the brain, an enlargement of the skull, and visual impairment, convulsions, and other neurological symptoms resulting from the abnormal growth of glia cells that form the supporting structure for brain tissue. Other cranial anomalies include *microcephaly* and *hydrocephalus,* which we shall discuss in more detail.

1. *Microcephaly.* The term *microcephaly* means "small-headedness." It refers to a type of mental retardation resulting from impaired development of the brain and a consequent failure of the cranium to attain normal size. In an early study of postmortem examinations of brains of microcephalic individuals, Greenfield and Wolfson (1935) reported that practically all cases examined showed development to have been arrested at the fourth or fifth month of fetal life. Fortunately, this condition is extremely rare.

Early diagnosis and treatment of hydrocephalus can keep brain damage and intellectual impairment to a minimum.

The most obvious characteristic of microcephaly is the small head, the circumference of which rarely exceeds 17 inches, as compared with the normal size of approximately 22 inches. Penrose (1963) also described microcephalic youngsters as being invariably short in stature but having relatively normal musculature and sex organs. Beyond these characteristics, they differ considerably from one another in appearance, although there is a tendency for the skull to be cone-shaped, with a receding chin and forehead. Microcephalic children fall within the moderate, severe, and profound categories of mental retardation, but the majority show little language development and are extremely limited in mental capacity.

Microcephaly may result from a wide range of factors that impair brain development, including intrauterine infections and pelvic irradiation of the mother during the early months of pregnancy (Koch, 1967). Miller (1970) noted a number of cases of microcephaly in Hiroshima and Nagasaki that apparently resulted from the atomic bomb explosions

during World War II. The role of genetic factors is not as yet clear. Treatment is ineffective once faulty development has occurred, and, at present, preventive measures focus on the avoidance of infection and radiation during pregnancy.

2. *Hydrocephalus.* Hydrocephalus is a relatively rare condition in which the accumulation of an abnormal amount of cerebrospinal fluid within the cranium causes damage to the brain tissues and enlargement of the cranium.

In congenital cases of hydrocephalus, the head is either already enlarged at birth or begins to enlarge soon thereafter, presumably as a result of a disturbance in the formation, absorption, or circulation of the cerebrospinal fluid (Wortis, 1973). The disorder can also develop in infancy or early childhood following the development of a brain tumor, subdural hematoma, meningitis, or other such conditions. Here the condition appears to result from a blockage of the cerebrospinal pathways and an accumulation of fluid in certain brain areas.

The clinical picture in hydrocephalus depends on the extent of neural damage, which, in turn, depends on the age at onset and the duration and severity of the disorder. In chronic cases the chief symptom is the gradual enlargement of the upper part of the head out of all proportion to the face and the rest of the body. While the expansion of the skull helps minimize destructive pressure on the brain, serious brain damage occurs nonetheless, leading to intellectual impairment and such other effects as convulsions and impairment or loss of sight and hearing. The degree of intellectual impairment varies, being severe or profound in advanced cases.

A good deal of attention has been directed to the surgical treatment of hydrocephalus, and with early diagnosis and treatment this condition can usually be arrested before severe brain damage has occurred (Geisz & Steinhausen, 1974).

Mental retardation and sociocultural deprivation

It was formerly believed that all mental retardation was the result of faulty genes or of other causes of brain pathology. In recent years, however, it has become apparent that adverse sociocultural conditions, particularly those involving a deprivation of normal stimulation, may play a primary role in the etiology of mental retardation.[8]

Two subtypes of mental retardation fall in this general category: (a) mental retardation associated with extreme sensory and social deprivation, such as prolonged isolation during the developmental years, as may have happened in the case of the wild boy of Aveyron discussed in the HIGHLIGHT on page 479; and (b) cultural-familial retardation, in which the child is not subjected to extreme isolation but rather suffers from an inferior quality of interaction with the cultural environment and with other people. Since such sociocultural impoverishment may be associated with genetic deficiency in some cases, the child born to a family in such circumstances may be doubly jeopardized. In any event, it has proven all but impossible to assess adequately the differential influences of nature and nurture in these cases. The field is rife with controversy and, regrettably, has involved one publicized case in which a researcher allegedly manipulated his statistics to prove that mental retardation is hereditary (Dorfman, 1978).

Since the great majority of all retarded individuals are of the cultural-familial type, our discussion will focus on this form of retardation.

Cultural-familial mental retardation. Children who fall in this category are usually mildly retarded; they make up the majority of persons labeled as mentally retarded. These children show no identifiable brain pathology and are usually not diagnosed as mentally retarded until they enter school and have serious difficulties in their studies. As a number of investigators have pointed out, however, most of these children come from poverty-stricken, unstable, and often disrupted family backgrounds characterized by a lack of intellectual stimulation, an inferior quality of interaction with others, and general environmental

---

[8]American behavioral scientists have used the terms *psychosocial deprivation, psychosocial disadvantage, cultural-familial retardation,* and *sociocultural deprivation* somewhat interchangeably. We shall use the latter term as a more general category in ordering our present discussion.

deprivation (Birns & Bridger, 1977; Braginsky & Braginsky, 1974; Feuerstein, 1977; Heber, 1970).

"They are raised in homes with absent fathers and with physically or emotionally unavailable mothers. During infancy they are not exposed to the same quality and quantity of tactile and kinesthetic stimulations as other children. Often they are left unattended in a crib or on the floor of the dwelling. Although there are noises, odors, and colors in the environment, the stimuli are not as organized as those found in middle-class and upper-class environments. For example, the number of words they hear is limited, with sentences brief and most commands carrying a negative connotation." (Tarjan & Eisenberg, 1972, p. 16)

In fact, three-fourths of the nation's mentally retarded come from homes that are socially, economically, and culturally disadvantaged.

Since a child's current level of intellectual functioning is based largely on previous learning—and since schoolwork requires complex skills such as being able to control one's attention, follow instructions, and recognize the meaning of a considerable range of words—these children are at a disadvantage from the beginning because they have not had an opportunity to learn requisite background skills or be motivated toward learning. Thus with each succeeding year, unless remedial measures are undertaken, they tend to fall farther behind in school performance. They also fall farther behind in relative ratings on intelligence tests, which, as we have seen, are measures of ability for schoolwork.

A report by the American Psychological Association (1970) noted the following:

"Mental retardation is primarily a psychosocial and psychoeducational problem—a deficit in adaptation to the demands and expectations of society evidenced by the individual's relative difficulty in learning, problem solving, adapting to new situations, and abstract thinking." (p. 267)

This statement was not intended to minimize the possible role of adverse biological factors, including genetic deficiencies, in the total causal pattern. Certainly many of these children reveal histories of prematurity, inadequate diets, and little or no medical care. But in the great majority of cases of cultural-familial mental retardation, no neurological or

HIGHLIGHT

The "wild boy of Aveyron"

In 1800, long before the development of psycho-therapy, Jean-Marc Itard attempted to inculcate normal human abilities in a "wild boy" who had been captured by peasants in the forests of Aveyron, France. The boy, who appeared to be between 10 and 12 years old, had been exhibited in a cage for about a year by his captors when Itard rescued him. From an examination of the scars on the boy's body, as well as observation of his personal habits, Itard concluded that he had been abandoned at the age of about 2 or 3.

At first Victor (as Itard named the boy) seemed more animal than human. He was oblivious to other human beings, could not talk, and howled and ate off the ground on all fours like an animal. He evidenced unusual sensory reactions; for example, he did not react if a pistol was fired next to his ear, but he could hear the crack of a nut or the crackling of underbrush at a great distance. No adverse reaction seemed to result from his going unclothed even in freezing weather. In fact, Victor had a fine velvety skin, despite his years of exposure.

Victor exhibited animal-like behavior in many ways. He had an obstinate habit of smelling any object that was given to him—even objects we consider void of smell. He knew nothing of love and perceived other human beings only as obstacles—in other words, like the wild animals he had known in the forest. He was typically indifferent and uncomplaining but, very occasionally, he showed a kind of frantic rage and became dangerous to those around him. If he had any sense of self-identity, it was apparently more that of an animal than a human.

Philippe Pinel, Itard's teacher, diagnosed Victor's condition as congenital idiocy—concluding that the boy was incapable of profiting from training. But Itard, although only 25 years old and inexperienced in comparison with Pinel, disagreed; in his view, Victor's savage behavior was the result of early and lengthy isolation from other humans. He believed that human contact and intensive training would enable the boy to become a normal person, and, ignoring Pinel's advice, he began his attempt to civilize "the wild boy of Aveyron."

No procedures had yet been formulated that Itard could use in treating Victor; thus he developed a program based on principles which included the following: (a) without human contact a human infant—unlike a lower animal—cannot develop normally; (b) the instinct to imitate is the learning force by which our senses are educated, and this instinct is strongest in early childhood and decreases with age; and (c) in all human beings, from the most isolated savage to the most educated individual, a constant relationship exists between needs and ideas—the greater the needs, the greater the development of mental capacities to meet them.

In attempting to train Victor, Itard developed methods that have had considerable impact on the subsequent treatment of children with serious learning disabilities. Instructional materials were provided to broaden Victor's discrimination skills in touch, smell, and other sensory modalities, appropriate to his environment; language training was begun through the association of words with the objects Victor wanted; and modeling and imitation were used to reinforce Victor's learning of desired social behaviors.

Initial results were indeed promising. Victor learned to speak a number of words and could write in chalk to express his wants. He also developed affectionate feelings toward his governess.

In June 1801, Itard reported to the Academy of Science in Paris on the rapid progress in the first 9 months of training. But in November 1806, he could only report that despite significant advances in several areas, Victor had not been made "normal" in the sense of becoming a self-directing and socially adjusted person. Being brought into the proximity of girls, for example, only upset the boy, leaving him restless and depressed, and Itard had to abandon his hope for a normal sexual response as a means of fostering Victor's motivation and socialization.

After devoting 5 1/2 years to the task, Itard gave up the attempt to train "the wild boy of Aveyron." As for Victor, he lived to be 40, but never progressed appreciably beyond the achievements of that first year.

The story of Victor is of absorbing interest to both laymen and scientists. A motion picture that portrays Itard's work with Victor—*The Wild Child*—was produced by François Truffaut. In scientific circles, the lack of conclusive answers will keep psychologists and others puzzling over the question of whether Victor was a congenital mental retardate, a brain-damaged child, a psychotic, or simply a child who had been so deprived of human contact during early critical periods of development that the damage he had sustained could never be completely remedied.

Based on Itard (1799; tr. Humphrey & Humphrey, 1932) and Silberstein and Irwin (1962).

physical dysfunction has been demonstrated. Thus efforts to understand mild mental retardation have focused increasingly on the role of environmental factors in impeding intellectual growth.

The problem of assessment. Since mental retardation is defined in terms of both intellectual (academic) and social competence, it is essential to assess both of these characteristics before labeling a person as mentally retarded.

Unfortunately, neither of the preceding tasks is an easy one. Errors in the assessment of IQ can stem from a variety of sources, including (a) errors in administering tests; (b) personal characteristics of the child, such as a language problem or lack of motivation to do well on tests; and (c) limitations in the tests themselves. The latter point had been succinctly stated by Wortis (1972):

"An IQ score, at best, can indicate where an individual stands in intellectual performance compared to others. What others? His nation? His social class? His ethnic group? No intelligence test that has ever been devised can surmount all of these complicating considerations and claim universal validity." (p. 22)

The HIGHLIGHT on this page presents a parable that dramatizes Wortis's conclusion.

While the assessment of social competence may seem less complicated, especially if it is based on clinical observations and ratings, it is subject to many of the same errors as the measurement of intelligence. Of particular importance are the criteria used by the person or persons doing the assessing. For example, if children are well adapted socially to life in an urban ghetto but not to the demands of a formal school setting, should they be evaluated as evidencing a high, intermediate, or low level of social competence? Competence for what? Again the conclusions of Wortis concerning the assessment of intelligence would appear to apply.[9]

To label a child as mentally retarded—as significantly subaverage in intellectual and adaptive capability—is an act likely to have profound effects on both the child's self-

---

[9]Comprehensive discussions of the problems in assessing and labeling the mentally retarded may be found in Mittler (1977) and Robinson and Robinson (1976).

The animal school

"The animals got together in the forest one day and decided to start a school. There was a rabbit, a bird, a squirrel, a fish and an eel, and they formed a Board of Education. The rabbit insisted that running be in the curriculum. The bird insisted that flying be in the curriculum. The fish insisted that swimming be in the curriculum, and the squirrel insisted that perpendicular tree climbing be in the curriculum. They put all of these things together and wrote a curriculum guide. Then they insisted that ALL the animals take ALL the subjects.

"Although the rabbit was getting an A in running, perpendicular tree climbing was a real problem for him; he kept falling over backwards. Pretty soon he couldn't run anymore. He found that instead of making an A in running he was making a C and, of course, he always made an F in perpendicular tree climbing. The bird was really beautiful at flying, but when it came to burrowing in the ground, he couldn't do so well. He kept breaking his beak and wings. Pretty soon he was making a C in flying as well as an F in burrowing, and he had a hard time with perpendicular tree climbing.

"The Moral of the story is . . ." (Anonymous, 1977)

---

concept and the reactions of others—and thus on his or her entire future life. Most immediately, it may lead to institutionalization. And over the long term, it may be a self-fulfilling prophecy fueled by the tendency to behave in ways consistent with one's self-concept as well as with others' expectations. Obviously it is a label that has profound ethical and social implications.

Treatment, outcomes, and prevention

A number of recent programs have demonstrated that significant changes in adaptive capacity are possible through special education and other rehabilitative measures. The degree of change that can be expected is related, of course, to the individual's situation and level of mental retardation.

Treatment facilities and methods. One problem that often inflicts great anxiety on parents of a mentally retarded child is whether or not to put their child in an institution. In general, the children who are institutionalized fall into two groups: (a) those who, in infancy and childhood, manifest severe mental retardation and associated physical impairment, and who enter the institution at an early age, and (b) those who have no physical impairments but show mild mental retardation and failure to adjust socially in adolescence, eventually being institutionalized chiefly because of delinquency or other problem behavior. Here social incompetence is the main factor in the decision. The families of those in the first group come from all socioeconomic levels, whereas a significantly higher percentage of the families of those in the second group come from lower educational and occupational strata.

Studies suggest that, in general, mentally retarded children are likely to show better emotional and mental development in a reasonably favorable home situation than in an institution (Golden & Davis, 1974). Thus institutionalization is not recommended where the child makes a satisfactory adjustment at home and in school.

The effect of being institutionalized in adolescence depends heavily, of course, on the institution's facilities as well as on the individual. For the many retarded teenagers who do not have families in a position to take care of them, community-oriented residential care seems particularly promising (Seidl, 1974; Thacher, 1978).

Fortunately, as we have seen, most retarded individuals do not need to be institutionalized. For those who do, however, state institutions for the mentally retarded are often desperately overcrowded, and in many instances woefully inadequate in terms of the quality of treatment programs offered (Robinson & Robinson, 1976; Tarjan et al., 1973). In 1970, the President's Committee on Mental Retardation reported that in many instances such facilities were no better than prisoner-of-war camps. Since then, some facilities have been greatly improved, but most lack the necessary funds and personnel to provide high-quality rehabilitative programs. Moreover, most private facilities—which are often but not always superior to public ones—are beyond the means of the average family.

For the mentally retarded who do not require institutionalization, educational and training facilities have also been inadequate. In 1970 an estimated 2 million mentally retarded persons who could use job training and become self-supporting members of their communities were not getting this training (President's Committee on Mental Retardation, 1970). Although conditions may have improved somewhat, it would still appear that the majority of mentally retarded persons in the United States are never reached by services appropriate to their specific needs.

This neglect is especially tragic in view of what we now know about helping these individuals. For example, classes for the mildly retarded, which usually emphasize reading and other basic school subjects, budgeting and money matters, and the development of occupational skills, have succeeded in helping many people become independent, productive members of the community.

Classes for the moderately and severely retarded usually have more limited objectives, but they emphasize development of self-care and other skills that will enable individuals to function adequately and to be of assistance in either a family or institutional setting. Just mastering toilet training and learning to feed and dress themselves may mean the difference between remaining at home and having to be placed elsewhere.

In many more cases than had formerly been thought possible, institutionalized individuals have been found able to get along in the community with adequate preparation and help. For example, Clark, Kivitz, and Rosen (1969) reported on a special project undertaken at the Elwyn Institute in Pennsylvania.

The goal of this program was the successful discharge to independent living in the community of the institutionalized mentally retarded. The entire staff was oriented toward rehabilitation; emphasis was placed on the development of practical vocational skills; special programs provided remedial teaching and the learning of socialization skills; and counseling and assessment assured the individualization of training to meet each person's needs. As a result of this program, many mentally retarded persons who had been institutionalized for from 2 to 49 years were discharged and obtained skilled or semiskilled jobs in the community while coping successfuly with everyday problems. Some married and had families; none had to be readmitted to the institution. (p. 82)

The teacher in the first photo uses a puppet to hold the attention of her retarded pupils as she teaches them basic skills. In the art therapy group, the therapist encourages cooperative planning and decision making as the youngsters work together on a mural.

Today about 70 percent of the approximately 150,000 individuals still in institutions for the retarded are severely or profoundly retarded, and even many individuals with this level of handicap are being helped to be partly self-supporting in community programs (Brown, 1977; Robinson & Robinson, 1976; Rodman & Collins, 1974; Sullivan & Batareh, 1973; Thacher, 1978; Zucker & Altman, 1973). These developments reflect both the new optimism that has come to prevail, and also, in many instances, judicial decisions favorable to the "rights" of retarded individuals and their families.

During the 1970s, there was a rapid proliferation of alternate forms of care for the mentally retarded. These include, but are not limited to, the use of decentralized regional facilities for short-term evaluation and training, small private hospitals specializing in rehabilitative techniques, group homes or "halfway houses" integrated into the local community, nursing homes for the elderly retarded, placement of severely retarded children in more "enriched" foster-home environments, and varied forms of support to the family for own-home care (see HIGHLIGHT on page 483).

These varied programs are still too new to permit comprehensive evaluation of their effectiveness in dealing with different groups of retardates and differing levels of retardation. At the least, however, it is clear that they provide a much expanded flexibility in considering the needs of any given retarded individual at any particular point in his or her development and rehabilitation (Robinson & Robinson, 1976).

Although much remains to be learned about the most effective educational and training procedures to use with the mentally retarded —particularly the moderate and severe types— new techniques, materials, and specially trained teachers have produced encouraging results. For example, computer-assisted in-

Two innovative deinstitutionalization approaches

Motivated in part by the discovery in the late 1960s by University of Illinois psychologist Marc Gold that even a severely retarded person could be taught, with patience, to assemble a 15-part bicycle brake, professionals and parents of retarded youngsters in many communities began a serious reassessment of long-term biases about the supposed limits of rehabilitation for the retarded. The major result was a proliferation of programs intended to be alternatives to the typical, forbidding public institution. Two such programs were those developed by the Macomb-Oakland Regional Center (MORC) near Detroit and the Eastern Nebraska Community Office of Mental Retardation (ENCOR) in Omaha. These two programs have essentially the same goals—rehabilitation of the retarded toward the achievement of self-esteem, limited competencies, and economic independence—but they differ substantially in their mode of approach.

The MORC program emphasizes placement of children in "community training homes," of which there are over a hundred in operation. These are the private homes of foster parents who have been specially trained in techniques such as behavior modification, speech therapy, and so on. In addition to their foster homes, MORC runs 12 duplexes called "developmental training homes" for children and adults with special, restricting problems. The duplexes are patterned after standard suburban housing developments. Less-disabled retarded adults live in groups of seven or eight in residences distributed throughout the community; they learn self-care and social skills in these residences, and, during the day, attend sheltered workshops and other vocational training programs.

One measure of the success of MORC's approach is that a group of seriously disabled adult charges was recently awarded a subcontract by a private manufacturing firm to cut and drill aluminum components for solar-heating panels, work that would have been completely beyond their capacity a short time before. In fact, individuals with their level of retardation usually would not have even been allowed to work with such tools.

The basic approach of ENCOR, on the other hand, is to rent houses or apartments in the community to be shared by two or three retarded persons; thereafter, the residents are closely supervised by professional staffers to ensure the maintenance of an adequate living arrangement and continued progress toward economic independence. Roommates are selected on the basis of possession of complementary skills, insofar as possible. For example, a non-reader who can cook might be placed with someone who can read but is helpless in the kitchen. Over time, it is hoped, the skills that each possesses separately will become shared ones. A number of the living units sponsored by ENCOR have become almost entirely self-sufficient—again a development that could not possibly have occurred had these patients remained under the old institutional regimen (Thacher, 1978).

struction has been introduced in Canadian programs for the retarded and has been found to be more efficient as well as less expensive than traditional tutor-guided instruction (Brebner et al., 1977; Hallworth, 1977). Operant conditioning methods are being used increasingly to teach a wide variety of skills (see HIGHLIGHT on page 484).

Typically, educational and training procedures involve mapping out target areas of improvement, such as personal grooming, social behavior, basic academic skills, and simple occupational skills. Within each area, specific skills are divided into simple components that can be learned and reinforced before more complex behaviors are required. Target areas are not selected arbitrarily, of course, but realistically reflect the requirements of the individual's life situation. Training that builds on step-by-step progression and is guided by such realistic considerations can bring these individuals repeated experiences of success and lead to substantial progress even by those previously regarded as uneducable.

For more mildly retarded youngsters, the question of what schooling is best is likely to be a vexing one for both parents and school officials. For many years, organized parents' groups have fought an uphill battle to ensure the availability of special education classes for retarded children in the public schools, having learned that isolation from age-peers tends to

Therapeutic pyramids and the "double-change" phenomenon

A boy, Randy, and his therapist, Dawn, shared an exciting experience which is the subject of the following unusual case study by Whalen and Henker.

"Randy is an 11-year-old boy who lives in a state hospital. He is severely retarded; his estimated IQ is 32. Although there are 70 children on his ward, he spends most of his time alone, staring into space or passively watching what is going on around him. He often stands with his arms extended, oscillating his fingers and moving his head from side to side while making bizarre grimaces and clicking sounds with his tongue or teeth. He doesn't speak. He doesn't play. He has neither friends nor enemies among the other children.

"About 11 o'clock each morning Randy can be found stationed by the front door to his ward, eagerly scanning the faces of all who enter. He is waiting for his therapist, Dawn. To those who know and observe Randy, it is remarkable that he seems to know when it is time for his therapy session. He correctly anticipates this event, even though he cannot ask questions or understand explanations, and he certainly has never learned the significance of a clock.

"When Dawn arrives, Randy becomes visibly excited. His mannerisms stop and his smile broadens as his young therapist greets him and escorts him to a special room in another building. She pretends to carry on a conversation with Randy by taking two roles, asking him questions and then answering them for him. Randy's facial expressions and gestures seem to indicate that he is participating, although on a nonverbal level. More importantly, he receives more verbal stimulation in this short period than during the remainder of the day on his overcrowded, understaffed hospital ward.

"While delivering a monologue about the day's events, Dawn prepares for the session. Simple toddlers' toys are pulled out of a cupboard—a 'busy box,' a few blocks, a pounding board, and a hammer. A box of sugared cereal and a carton of chocolate yogurt are opened, and Randy is given a taste of each. Then Dawn announces, loudly, that it is time to go to work. The first item on today's agenda is a review of what Randy learned in the past week. Dawn says, 'Look at me, Randy.' When his attention is secured, she quickly claps her hands and says, 'You do it.' As Randy imitates the simple response, Dawn exclaims, 'Good boy!' and gives Randy a spoonful of yogurt, which is for him a special treat. Dawn then goes through some other activities that, by this time in therapy, are relatively simple for Randy—raise

your hand, dial the phone, throw the ball, pound the pegboard. For each task she uses the same sequence of procedures: secure attention, present the training stimulus (a nonverbal demonstration or a verbal direction), elicit the response, and then administer the rewards—praise, physical affection, and food.

"After this warm-up phase, Dawn tries a much harder task, a verbal direction which involves two discriminations. She places a block and a hammer on the table in front of Randy and asks him to hand her the hammer. Randy must choose both the correct object and the correct act. He first picks up the hammer and begins to pound the table. Although he has learned to respond to the direction 'Hand me . . .' and the label, 'Hammer,' he can't yet link the two together. He performs the only response he has ever learned involving a hammer—he pounds the table. Dawn says, 'No,' replaces the hammer, and repeats her verbal request. This time she includes a nonverbal prompt—she holds out her hand. Randy seems to understand the desired act but not the correct object as he places the block in her hand. Again Dawn says 'No' and shakes her head. Next time, she gives Randy more help. She places the hammer on top of the block and holds out her hand as she says, 'Give me the hammer.' With these cues, Randy makes the correct response and Dawn is delighted. Enthusiastic praise and a big hug accompany his food treat.

"Now Dawn settles into the difficult and often tedious job of 'fading the prompts' and teaching Randy to respond to the verbal direction alone, with no gestures or other artificial cues. To achieve this goal she must demand slightly more from Randy on each trial; she must help him less and less. If she prompts too completely or too frequently, he will show no improvement. But if her demands are too great, he may stop responding entirely. She must allow him enough time to practice his new response, but she must change the training task before he becomes too bored or frustrated. In short, multiple therapeutic decisions must be made at each stage of the learning sequence."

The remedial approach described in this situation is widely used in behavior therapy with mental retardates; what is unusual and dramatic about it is that Dawn, the therapist, is also mentally retarded. Both she and Randy resided in the same state institution for mental retardates.

Dawn dressed appropriately and seemed normal in appearance and movement. However, her vocabulary was very limited and her speech poorly articulated —at times being almost unintelligible. Her case history was replete with special-incident reports: she had thrown chairs through windows, run away, and destroyed property. She also had frequently engaged in physical and verbal assaults on companions as well as on hospital personnel, and her diagnosis of congenital cerebral defect was accompanied by the label "passive aggressive character with psychotic episodes." Though only mildly retarded (her IQ was 60), she was kept from family care placement by her unsuitable social behavior. She had been institutionalized for 11 of her 24 years.

Dawn's therapy sessions with Randy were part of a systematic research study of the "therapeutic pyramid concept"—in which professional therapists prepare moderately retarded adolescents and young adults to teach severely retarded children in simple social behaviors. Behavior therapy techniques are used in the training of "assistants," who use analogous methods with their younger "trainees." The key goal is to facilitate improvement in both assistants and trainees—in other words, to bring about a "double change."

And indeed this double-change phenomenon did occur in the case of Randy and Dawn. Randy learned to imitate gestures, respond to simple verbal requests and relate to another person. And Dawn, for her part, acquired both occupational and social skills. As an assistant, she learned to arrive at work regularly and on time, assume responsibility, take pride and find satisfaction in her work, earn a salary, and manage her money. She also learned to relate to members of the research staff. In addition, she became uncomfortable about her poor articulation and tendency to "mouth off," and asked for help in improving her behavior. The ultimate consequence of her participation in the pyramid project came in her release from the hospital. She since has been reported adjusting well to her foster home.

As might be expected, research with therapeutic pyramids has shown that the greatest gains are achieved by assistants like Dawn, even though the results have been favorable for trainees as well. Among the assistants, gains have commonly been observed in improving speech skills, developing interpersonal competencies, developing a sense of personal responsibility, and building self-esteem. The success of the initial pyramid project has led to the initiation of similar programs in outpatient clinics, foster-care homes, and special schools.

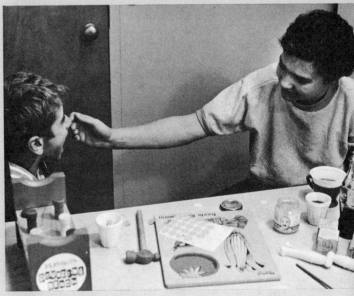

Based on previously unpublished material by Carol K. Whalen, University of California at Irvine, and Barbara Henker, University of California at Los Angeles. Sources also include Guerney (1969) and Whalen and Henker (1971).

compound the problems of these children. Too often, however, success in getting a retarded child into a public school has meant that the child is treated as very special indeed, and—along with other retarded students—becomes isolated *within* the school.

We have begun to learn that this type of "special" education may have very serious limitations in terms of the social and educational development of the child, and that many such children fare better by attending regular classes for at least much of the day. Of course, programs of this type—called "mainstreaming"—do require careful planning and a high level of teacher skill (Birns & Bridger, 1977; Budoff, 1977).

New frontiers in prevention.   The problem of preventing mental retardation involves the question of genetic factors as well as the need to control a wide range of biochemical, neurophysiological, and sociocultural conditions. Inevitably, it is a problem concerned with human development in general.

Until rather recently the most hopeful approach to the prevention of mental retardation has been through routine health measures for pregnant women and the use of diagnostic measures to ensure the early detection and, if possible, correction of pathology. In recent years, however, two new frontiers have opened up in the field of prevention. The first involves work in genetics which has revealed the role of certain genetic defects in faulty development—as in Tay-Sachs disease—and tests that have been devised to identify parents who have these faulty genes, thus making it possible to provide them with genetic counseling. There are now over 200 clinics in the United States where such counseling is available.

The second frontier in prevention involves the alleviation of sociocultural conditions that deprive children of the necessary stimulation, motivation, and opportunity for normal learning and development. In this connection, Keniston (1977) has said, "It is time to match the strong American tradition of healing individual parents and children with equal efforts to change the factors that make those parents and children need healing. To put it another way, it is time for Americans to start holding the social and economic institutions of our society just as accountable for their influence on family life as we traditionally have held par-

ents" (p. 6). And Birns and Bridger (1977) have emphasized that social reforms will need to include a revamping of the educational system to serve better the varying needs of all children. This "new horizon" was well delineated by the late President John F. Kennedy:

"Studies have demonstrated that large numbers of children in urban and rural slums, including preschool children, lack the stimulus necessary for proper development in their intelligence. Even when there is no organic impairment, prolonged neglect and a lack of stimulus and opportunity for learning can result in the failure of young minds to develop. Other studies have shown that, if proper opportunities for learning are provided early enough, many of these deprived children can and will learn and achieve as much as children from more favored neighborhoods. The self-perpetuating intellectual blight should not be allowed to continue." (1963, p. 286)

President Kennedy's report directed the attention of the nation to the tragic and costly problem of mental retardation. It was not until 1970, however, when the President's Committee on Mental Retardation, the American Psychological Association, and other concerned organizations stressed the necessity for a "broad spectrum" approach that real impetus was given to implementing essential measures for the prevention of mental retardation. This broad spectrum approach focused on three ways of providing a more supportive sociocultural setting or preventing children from being harmed by adverse environmental conditions:

1. *Application of existing knowledge.* The first phase of this approach involved the provision of more adequate medical and general health care for mother and baby—prior to and during pregnancy, and after birth of the baby—particularly for the socially disadvantaged and other high-risk groups.

2. *Community services.* Next, the approach focused on the provision of community-centered facilities that would provide a coordinated range of diagnostic, health, education, employment, rehabilitation, and related services. This phase of the program included the training of needed personnel.

A particularly important development in this area has involved efforts to reach high-risk children early with the intensive cognitive stimulation believed to underlie sound development of mental ability. Project Head Start is a well-known example operating at the local community level. And at the national level a similar intention is manifested in specialized television programming for children, such as *Sesame Street* and *The Electric Company*. Rigorous assessment of the effectiveness of such efforts is not yet complete, but they do appear to have positive effects on many children. Somewhat ironically, children least in need of them—the children of relatively affluent families in which education is strongly valued and in which the parents are likely to encourage their children's exposure to such enriching experiences—seem to benefit the most.

The Milwaukee Project (Heber et al., 1972) provides an example of a rigorously controlled experiment demonstrating the benefits of an early intervention program for children considered to be at high risk for retardation. Fifty high-risk newborn subjects were randomly assigned to the treatment and control groups. Beginning in the fourth week of life, the children assigned to the treatment group received a structured program involving sensory stimulation and opportunities for development of language, problem solving, and interpersonal relating. The mothers of these subjects also received special training in homemaking and child care. No special program was given to the control group children or their mothers. When the children reached age 5½, the mean IQ of those in the treatment group was 125 while that of the control group children was 92.

3. *Research.* Finally, emphasis was placed on the facilitation and acceleration of research on all phases of the problem: causality, educational procedures, social effects on the family, psychological effects on the individual, and the changing role and functions of state and community agencies.

It is unfortunate that the initiatives begun by the Kennedy administration have eroded in recent years with increased demands on the federal budget for programs seen as having greater national importance, and as the funds committed for helping the retarded have increasingly suffered devaluation through inflation. Beginning with the Nixon administration, there were serious cutbacks in training and research in all of the mental health disciplines—a trend only now beginning to level off. As a result, we have not been able to capitalize fully on our increased understanding of how to reverse or prevent the deficits experienced by mentally retarded youngsters.

In this chapter we first examined the principal symptom syndromes associated with neurological organic brain dysfunction occurring in the adult years; then we saw how they manifest themselves in five organic mental disorders: those involving general paresis, head injuries, brain tumors, seniliform brain degeneration, and cerebral arteriosclerosis. These disorders may be acute or chronic and may involve mild, moderate, or severe impairment of psychological functioning. Typically they involve such symptoms as impairment of orientation for time, place, and person; emotional shallowness and lability; and impairment of learning, comprehension, and judgment. There are significant differences in the clinical picture from one type of disorder to another, however, and also from one individual to another.

Three interrelated factors are of key importance in determining both the severity of symptoms and the likelihood of successful treatment in disorders associated with brain damage: (a) the nature and extent of the organic pathology; (b) the personality and stress tolerance of the individual; and (c) his or her life situation—including the situation to which he or she will return following hospitalization. As we have observed, the second and third factors are often as important as the first, except in cases of very severe brain damage.

In the last section of the chapter, we dealt with the major problem of mental retardation in our society. We noted the intellectual and social criteria used in assessing mental retardation, the levels of retardation—from mild to profound—and the fact that the great majority of mental retardates fall in the mild range and have no apparent brain pathology. We then examined the role of organic factors in the development of several clinical types of mental retardation, and dealt at some length with the role of adverse sociocultural conditions in the majority of cases of mild mental retardation.

We then considered approaches to the education and training of the mentally retarded and emphasized the current view that the great majority can become not only self-respecting but self-supporting members of the community. Finally, we identified genetic counseling and improvement of sociocultural conditions as frontiers in the prevention of mental retardation—new areas of hope that have yet to be fully implemented.

14

Behavior disorders of childhood and adolescence

Maladaptive behavior in different life periods

Disorders of childhood and adolescence

Delinquent behavior

Planning better programs to help children and youth

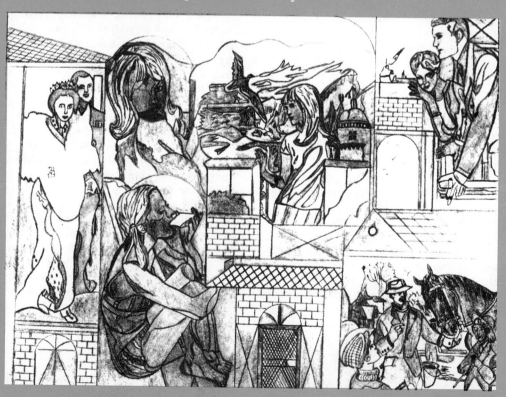

"We love our own children and take as good care of them as we can, but as a society we tolerate a great deal of unnecessary damage and pain among children. Do Americans love children? Yes, when the children are their own; not nearly as well, when the children are other people's.

"People who think about children's policy know the results of that split view all too well. Of all age groups in America, children are the most likely to be poor. Overall, the [Carnegie] Council estimates that fully a quarter to a third of all American children are born into families with financial strains so great that their children will suffer basic deprivations. In this rich, powerful, and productive land, we prefer not to notice the children who risk freezing to death for lack of heat in tarpaper shacks without plumbing in rural Maine. We discount the slum children who have never slept in a bed of their own or seen a doctor." (Keniston, 1977, p. 274)

Only in this century have childhood behavior disorders become the focus of special study. During the nineteenth century, little account was taken of the special characteristics of psychopathology in children, and maladaptive patterns relatively specific to childhood, such as autism and hyperactivity, received virtually no attention at all.

An important step forward came in 1896 with Witmer's founding of the first psychological clinic at the University of Pennsylvania, which provided services for children as well as adolescents and adults. It is of interest to note that of the first two children treated at the clinic, one had a "speech disorder" and the other was a "chronic bad speller." In 1906 Witmer founded a journal, *The Psychological Clinic*, in which he and his students published case reports on a wide range of behavior problems of children. The goal was not to apply a diagnostic label to the child, but to study and understand the child's behavior so that appropriate educational procedures or treatment could be undertaken.

A closely related development was that of the child guidance movement. In 1909 the Juvenile Psychopathic Institute was founded in Chicago under the direction of William Healy, a psychiatrist. This institute fostered the view that the antisocial behavior of children could be modified by psychological methods. As a result of the pioneering work of Healy and Witmer, child guidance clinics were established throughout the United States, and by 1940 such clinics had become an accepted feature of the mental health field.

Since then, marked strides have been made in understanding, assessing, and treating the maladaptive behavior patterns of children and youth. But our facilities are woefully inadequate in relation to the magnitude of the task. In the final section of this chapter, we shall give detailed consideration to some of the special factors involved in both treatment and prevention of children's problems. First, however, we shall note some general characteristics of maladaptive behavior in children, as compared with disorders in adults, and then examine some of the disorders that are relatively specific to the period of childhood and adolescence and the special problem of juvenile delinquency.

Maladaptive behavior in different life periods

Since personality differentiation, developmental tasks, and typical stressors differ for childhood, adolescence, and adulthood, we would expect to find some differences in maladaptive behavior patterns in these different life periods. Three special characteristics of childhood disorders have been noted:

1. *Differences in clinical picture.* The clinical picture in childhood disorders is somewhat different from that at other ages both because some disorders, such as autism, are primarily problems of childhood, and because even the disorders that occur at all life periods reflect the developmental level of the individual experiencing them. For example, the suicidal impulses commonly found in adolescent and adult depression are fairly rare in childhood depression (Kovacks & Beck, 1977). And in childhood schizophrenia, although there is the characteristic schizophrenic withdrawal and inability to relate to others, delusions and hallucinations are less common; when they do occur, they are more transient and less well systematized (Elkind & Weiner, 1978). In fact, most of the emotional disturbances of childhood tend to be relatively short-lived, undifferentiated, and changeable, as compared to those of later life periods.

2. *Special vulnerability from limited perspective and dependency on adults.* Since personality differentiation in childhood is not as advanced as in adolescence or adulthood, children do not have as clear-cut a view of themselves and their world as they will have at a later age. They have less self-understanding and have not yet developed a stable sense of identity and an adequate frame of reference regarding reality, possibility, and value. The threats of the immediate moment are less tempered by considerations of the past or future and thus tend to be seen as disproportionately important. As a result, children often have more difficulty in coping with stressful events than they will have when they are older.

Likewise, children are more dependent on other people than are adults. Though in some ways this dependency serves as a buffer against outer dangers, it also makes them highly vulnerable to experiences of rejection, disappointment, and failure. On the other hand, although their inexperience and lack of self-sufficiency make them more easily upset by problems that seem minor to the average adult, children typically recover more quickly from their hurts.

Children's limited perspective, as might be expected, leads them to use childlike concepts to explain what is happening. For example, in the comparatively rare case of child suicide, the child may be trying to rejoin a dead parent or sibling or pet. For the very young, suicide— or violence against another person—may be undertaken without any real understanding that death is final.

3. *Frequent masking of underlying problems.* Often childhood depressive reactions and other emotional problems are not expressed directly. Among young children, for example, depression and discouragement may be masked by irritability, temper tantrums, low frustration tolerance, hyperactivity, or sleep disturbances; among older children, an underlying depression may be masked by "acting out"—through disobedience, running away, or delinquent behavior (Cytryn & McKnew, 1974; Kovacs & Beck, 1977; Ossofsky, 1974; Poznanski & Zrull, 1970).

Of course, such masking of emotional problems is by no means restricted to children. Depression in adulthood may be similarly masked by inability to sleep, gastrointestinal upsets, or chronic fatigue. But the masking in childhood may mean that no clear, identifiable pattern of psychopathology emerges even in a child whose behavior is chronically maladaptive. (See HIGHLIGHT on page 491.)

Despite these somewhat distinctive characteristics of disturbances in childhood, there is no sharp line of demarcation between the maladaptive behavior patterns of childhood and those of adolescence, nor between those of adolescence and those of adulthood. Thus although our focus in this chapter will be on the behavior disorders of children and adolescents, we shall find some inevitable overlapping with those of later life periods. In this context, it is useful to emphasize the basic continuity of an individual's behavior over the years as he or she attempts to cope with the problems of living.

Disorders of childhood and adolescence

In this section we shall discuss the following disorders of childhood and adolescence: (a) hyperactive (kinetic) syndrome, (b) unsocialized disturbance of conduct (unsocialized aggressive reaction), (c) disturbances of emotion, (d) autism, (e) stuttering, and (f) other symptom disorders. With the exception of autism, these disorders are less stable than most of the abnormal behavior patterns we have discussed in earlier chapters, and also more amenable to treatment. Often they are referred to simply as *emotional disturbances,* to indicate that they are not so much *disorders* as problems with which the child needs help. If such assistance is not received, however, the developmental problems of childhood sometimes merge almost imperceptibly into more serious and chronic disorders when the child passes into adulthood.

Classification of childhood and adolescent disorders

Diagnosis of the psychological disorders of childhood has traditionally been a rather confused practice. Often the same classification system used for adult disorders has been applied to children without allowing for the special considerations that enter into childhood disturbances, such as the often mixed clinical picture, the special influence of environmental factors, and the confounding effects of developmental processes. The use of adult-based diagnostic categories for problems of childhood and adolescence often results in a misfitted classification and meaningless prognostic evaluation.

It was the intention of the American Psychiatric Association in its latest revision of the Diagnostic and Statistical Manual (DSM-III) to provide for a more extensive accounting of the problems of childhood and adolescence and to bring the U.S. classification scheme into line with the classification system used internationally—the ninth edition of the World Health Organization's International Classification of Diseases (ICD-9). The DSM-III, however, includes problems that have not traditionally been considered mental disorders, such as "reading disorder" and "arithmetic disorder." Its labeling of these behaviors as mental disorders has been criticized as neither accurate nor "good for children" (Garmezy, 1978).

At present, the most adequate diagnostic system for disorders of childhood and adolescence is a scheme proposed by Rutter, Shaffer, and Sturge (n.d.). This system, based on the mental-disorders section of the ICD-9, uses a multiaxial framework. Disorders are coded on four axes; a fifth axis is added to code abnormal social situations to which a child may be subject.

Axis One is for psychiatric syndromes, both psychotic and nonpsychotic. It includes several familiar categories like schizophrenic psychoses and affective psychoses but also includes a number of categories that are specific to childhood and adolescence, such as disturbances of conduct, hyperkinetic syndrome of childhood, and disturbances of emotions specific to childhood and adolescence.

Axis Two is for specific delays in development and includes delays in academic learning and delays in speech, language, or motor development. Calling these problems *delays* rather than *disorders* seems more constructive and far less stigmatizing. Axis Three is for indicating level of intellectual functioning, from normal intelligence to profound retardation. Axis Four is for indicating medical problems that may be present.

Axis Five lists several kinds of abnormal psychosocial situations, and the clinician is to indicate as many as apply in the given case. Examples of the situations listed are mental disturbances in other family members, inadequate or inconsistent parental control, and inadequate social, linguistic, or perceptual stimulation.

The clinician is asked to make a coding for each axis whether or not there is abnormality on each one. For any axis where no problem is present, the code is 0; thus anyone using the diagnosis can be sure that all the information thought to be relevant was included. In this chapter we will be depending most heavily on this Rutter et al. classification. (A more complete summary of this classification is in the Appendix.)

Hyperactive (hyperkinetic) syndrome

Hyperactivity is a common presenting symptom[1] among children seen at child guidance clinics and related facilities. It occurs with the greatest frequency before the age of 8 and tends to become less frequent and of shorter duration thereafter. Typically it disappears or shows marked alleviation by the middle teens unless brain damage is involved. An estimated 5 percent of elementary school children in the United States are diagnosed as hyperactive (Pelham, 1978). The hyperactive syndrome is much more frequent among boys than among girls.

Clinical picture in hyperactive syndrome. As the term implies, hyperactive children typically show excessive or exagger-

---

[1]*Presenting symptoms* refer to the clinical picture at the time the client is first seen by professional personnel. *Presenting complaint* and *referral problem* are synonymous terms.

Hyperactive children tend to be overactive, restless, and easily distractible. They do not typically show deficits in intelligence, but tend to talk incessantly and to be socially uninhibited and immature. Usually they do poorly in school, commonly showing specific learning disabilities, such as a difficulty in learning to read or in mastering other basic school subjects.

ated muscular activity—for example, aimless or haphazard running or fidgeting. Difficulty in sustaining attention is another central feature of the disorder; in fact, the DSM-III classification calls this disturbance "Attention deficit disorder with hyperactivity." Such children are highly distractible and do not follow instructions or respond to demands placed on them. Impulsive behavior and a low frustration tolerance are also characteristic.

Hyperactive children do not typically show deficits in intelligence, but tend to talk incessantly and to be socially uninhibited and immature. They do not appear to be anxious, although their overactivity, restlessness, and distractibility are often interpreted as indications of anxiety. Usually they do poorly in school, commonly showing specific learning disabilities, such as difficulty in learning to read or in learning other basic school subjects. Hyperactive children pose the majority of behavior problems in the elementary grades.

The following case, involving an 8-year-old girl, reveals a somewhat typical clinical picture:

The subject was referred to a community clinic because of overactive, inattentive, and disruptive behavior. She was a problem to her teacher and to other students because of her hyperactivity and uninhibited behavior. She would impulsively hit other children, knock things off their desks, erase material on the blackboard, and damage books and other school property. She seemed to be in perpetual motion—talking, moving about, and darting from one area of the classroom to another. She demanded an inordinate amount of attention from her parents and her teacher, and she was intensely jealous of other children, including her own brother and sister.

Despite her hyperactive behavior, inferior school performance, and other problems, she was considerably above average in intelligence. Nevertheless, she felt "stupid" and had a seriously devaluated self-image. Neurological tests revealed nothing significant.

Causal factors in hyperactive syndrome. There are no known genetic or chromosomal defects associated with hyperactivity. However, there is a higher-than-average number of premature births among hyperactive children, a substantial number of whom show so-called soft neurological signs such as perceptual-motor coordination deficits. Satterfield et al. (1974) found a higher-than-average incidence of abnormal EEGs among hyperactive children, as did Grunewald-Zuberbier et al. (1975). Rosenthal and Allen (1978) interpret these findings as possibly indicating lower overall cortical arousal among such children. They also cite other evidence of "cortical immaturity," such as attentional deficit, and conclude that hyperkinesis may be explained by a dysfunction of inhibition processes in the forebrain area. However, they also point out that better definitions of "hyperactivity" and more rigorous studies are needed before the hyperkinetic syndrome can definitely be related to brain dysfunction.

Typically hyperactivity is manifested very early in life. Where it develops in later childhood, special stressors leading to anxiety and emotional upset are likely to be key factors. Actually, hyperactivity is a relatively nonspecific pattern in children, and it may occur in anxious, depressed, schizophrenic, or autistic children, as well as in those who clearly evidence brain damage or some kind of brain dysfunction. The controversy surrounding the concept of minimal brain damage as an explanation for hyperactivity is discussed in the HIGHLIGHT on page 494.

Currently, the hyperactive syndrome is considered to have multiple causes and multiple effects. Thus labeling a child as "hyperactive" may not indicate much in the way of etiology or appropriate treatment procedures; in addition, such a label may devalue the child in the eyes of the parents and play havoc with the child's self-image if he or she is told about it (Arnold, 1973; Loney, 1974). In general, it would appear that a thorough assessment, including neurological and psychosocial testing, is essential for understanding the causes in any particular case.

Treatment and outcomes. Although the hyperactive syndrome was first described more than a hundred years ago, there is some disagreement over the most effective methods of treatment, especially regarding the use of drugs to calm the hyperactive child. Here, as with other problem behaviors, variations in treatment procedures may be required to meet the needs of individual children.

Interestingly enough, cerebral stimulants such as the amphetamines often have a quieting effect on hyperactive children—just the opposite of what we would expect from their effect on adults (see Chapter 10).[2] Such medication decreases the children's overactivity and distractibility and at the same time increases their attention and ability to concentrate. As a result, they are often able to function much better both at home and at school. In fact, many hyperactive children who have not been acceptable in regular classes are enabled to function and progress in a relatively normal manner. The medication does not appear to affect their intelligence, but rather seems to help them use their basic capacities more effectively (NIMH, 1971). Although such drugs do not "cure" the hyperactivity, they have been found beneficial in about half to two-thirds of the cases in which medication appears warranted.

Some concern has been expressed, however, about the effects of such drugs, particularly when used in heavy dosage over time. Safer and Allen (1973) concluded from a longitudinal study of 63 hyperactive children—49 of whom were on medication and 14 of whom were used as controls—that Dexedrine and Ritalin, two of the most commonly used drugs, can have a suppressing effect on normal growth in height and weight. However, in a carefully controlled study, Beck, Langford, Mackay, and Sum (1975) failed to find such effects. Nevertheless, the use of such drugs should be carefully monitored in order to avoid harmful side effects and addiction. Some of the questions that have been raised concerning the use of these drugs are discussed in the HIGHLIGHT on page 495. The use of drug therapy with children will be taken up again in Chapter 18 (see pages 626–627).

Caffeine, another cortical stimulant, may also be useful in reducing hyperactivity among many of these children, two cups of coffee per day apparently being sufficient (Schnackenberg, 1973). But further research is essential

---

[2]It has also been demonstrated that amphetamines have the same quieting effect on children who are not hyperactive (Rapoport et al., 1978).

Minimal brain dysfunction (MBD)

In a three-part study sponsored by the U.S. Dept. of Health, Education, and Welfare (Chalfant & Scheffelin, 1969; Clements, 1966; Paine, 1969), children with minimal brain dysfunction (MBD) have been described as

"... of near average, average, or above average general intelligence with certain learning and/or behavioral disabilities ranging from mild to severe, which are associated with deviations of function of the central nervous system. These deviations may manifest themselves by various combinations of impairment in perception, conceptualization, language, memory, and control of attention, impulse, or motor function. These aberrations may arise from genetic variations, biochemical irregularities, perinatal brain insults or other illnesses or injuries sustained during the years which are critical for the development and maturation of the central nervous system, or from other unknown organic causes." (Paine, 1969, p. 53)

The ten outstanding characteristics of children with MBD are considered, in order of frequency, to be: (1) hyperactivity, (2) perceptual-motor impairments, (3) emotional lability, (4) general coordination deficits, (5) disorders of attention (short attention span, distractibility, perseveration), (6) impulsivity, (7) disorders of memory and thinking, (8) disorders of speech and hearing, (9) specific learning disabilities (reading, writing, spelling, and arithmetic), and (10) neurological signs, including EEG irregularities.

Although the concept of MBD is widely used, it remains controversial. Criticism has been directed especially at the practice of inferring that children have MBD simply because they display "typical symptoms" (e.g., poor perceptual-motor coordination, difficulty in learning to read, attention problems, and hyperactivity) without conducting tests to determine if they actually have a neurological defect. It has also been pointed out that the intellectual,

emotional, and behavioral manifestations of minimal brain dysfunction may vary greatly from child to child. For example, children with MBD do not necessarily have reading difficulties, nor are they necessarily hyperactive; in fact, they sometimes evidence a low level of motor activity. In their study on the relationship between MBD and school performance, Edwards, Alley, and Snider (1971) found "no evidence that a diagnosis of MBD, based on a pediatric neurological evaluation . . . is a useful predictor of academic achievement" (p. 134).

On the other hand, the specific "symptoms" of young children with serious learning problems are often so remarkably similar that the concept of a neurological learning disability syndrome can hardly be ruled out. In effect, the "computers" of some children seem to function atypically in the processing of auditory and visual information; and it seems likely in such cases that neurological evaluation would reveal brain dysfunction—or even actual brain damage.

Even a clear diagnosis of brain dysfunction or damage may not be particularly useful, of course, unless the precise nature of the disorder can be determined, as well as its significance for behavior, treatment, and outcome. Thus, while the concept of minimal brain dysfunction may be a useful one, there is a strong trend away from using such a vague label (Mayer & Scheffelin, 1975; McGlannan, 1975; Trotter, 1975). Labeling a child as suffering from "minimal brain dysfunction" often provides little specific information, is devaluating to the child, and, in general, "hurts more than it helps."

Based on Bryan (1974), Chalfant and Scheffelin (1969), Clements (1966), Edwards, Alley, and Snider (1971), Lievens (1974), Mayer and Scheffelin (1975), McGlannan (1975), Paine (1969), Trotter (1975), and Tymchuk, Knights, and Hinton (1970).

before the value of "coffee breaks for hyperactive children" can be adequately assessed.

Another effective approach to treating hyperactive children involves behavior therapy techniques featuring positive reinforcement and the programming of learning materials and tasks in such a way as to minimize error and maximize immediate feedback and success (Pelham, 1978). The focus of behavioral treatment strategies is to help hyperactive children learn to shift their attention less fre-

quently and to behave reflectively rather than impulsively. (See HIGHLIGHT on page 496.) This approach is particularly effective when combined with the use of medication and with the cooperation of parents as change agents in a total treatment program (Feighner & Feighner, 1974; Hewett & Forness, 1974; Johnson & Katz, 1973; O'Dell, 1974).

Several investigators have reported that impulsive behavior in children can be successfully modified by the use of cognitive-

Drug therapy with children

A number of important questions have been raised concerning the increasing use of drugs in the treatment of certain behavior disorders of children. The principal questions include:

1. Who is being selected for treatment? Few investigators would question the usefulness of amphetamines or related drugs for treating many cases of hyperactivity, but many question the adequacy of assessment procedures used in identifying children who actually need medication. For example, a clear-cut distinction is not always made between the child who appears to need chemotherapy because of minimal brain dysfunction (MBD) and the child whose inattention and restlessness may be the result of hunger, crowded classrooms, irrelevant curriculum content, or anxiety and depression stemming from a pathogenic home situation.

2. Are drugs sometimes being used simply to "keep peace in the classroom"? Those who raise this question point to the possibility that children who manifest bewilderment, anger, restlessness, or lethargy at school may only be showing a normal reaction to educational procedures which fail to spark their interest or meet their needs. To label such children as "sick"—e.g., as evidencing hyperactivity or some other behavior disorder—and to treat them through medication, these investigators maintain, is to sidestep the difficult and expensive alternative of providing better educational programs. Possibly such an approach also reinforces the notion—all too prevalent in our culture—that if things are not going well, all the individual has to do is take some type of drug.

3. Do the drugs have harmful side effects? Even in the small dosages usually prescribed for children,

drugs sometimes have undesirable side effects. Such symptoms as decreased appetite, dizziness, headache, and insomnia have been reported in some cases with stimulants, such as methylphenidate-hydrochloride (Ritalin), and recently these drugs have been implicated in suspected growth retardation. Minor tranquilizers also may have adverse side effects, including lethargy. And even with drugs that seem to produce minimal side effects, the possibility of adverse long-range effects resulting from sustained usage during early growth and development is still being assessed.

The consensus among investigators seems to be that drug therapy for children should be used with extreme caution, and only with those children for whom other alternatives simply do not work, such as the hyperactive child who shows definite indications of MBD and cannot control his or her behavior without drug therapy. It is also considered important that drug therapy be undertaken only with the informed consent of the parent, as well as the child if he or she is old enough, and that the child not be given the sole responsibility for taking the medication—a procedure that can lead to drug abuse. At the same time, there is a need to avoid exaggerated public attitudes against the use of drug therapy for children who genuinely need it. Finally, children who do benefit from drug therapy may also need other therapeutic measures for dealing with coexisting problems, such as learning deficiencies and psychological, interpersonal, and family difficulties.

Based on Beck, Langford, Mackay, and Sum (1975), Cole (1975), Eisenberg (1971), Hayes, Panitch, and Barker (1975), Martin and Zaug (1975), Whalen and Henker (1976), and Winsberg et al. (1975).

behavioral techniques in which behavioral contingencies for desired behavior are combined with training in learning to use verbal self-instructions (Kendall & Finch, 1978; Kendall & Finch, 1979; Meichenbaum, 1977; Meichenbaum & Goodman, 1971).

In a case reported by Kendall and Finch (1976), a 9-year-old boy was referred to a psychiatric facility for children· because of problems at school. The teacher had described him as hyperactive, impulsive, and oversensitive to criticism. After only a

month in 4th grade, he had been demoted to 3rd grade because of his inability to adjust.

During the initial interview, the child was constantly moving about. He climbed into and out of chairs, talked rapidly about many topics, and changed the direction and purpose of his behavior without apparent reason. Test data also suggested overactivity/impulsivity to be the central problem.

Therapy sessions started with the therapist working on a maze and talking aloud as he thought through each step he was performing—defining the problem, indicating the focus of his attention and the approach he was using, and including coping statements such as (after an error made intentionally), "I should have gone slower and thought and been more careful." After the therapist finished the maze, the boy worked it, instructing himself aloud in the same way.

After going through several other mazes in this way, except that the self-instructions were whispered, the use of self-instructions for target behaviors was rehearsed. For example, to learn not to switch topics during a conversation, the boy practiced the following self-instruction: "What should I remember? I'm to finish talking about what I start to talk about. O.K. I should think before I talk and remember not to switch. If I complete what I'm talking about before I start another topic, I get to keep my dimes. I can look at this card (cue) to remind me" (p. 854).

The boy was given several coins, one of which was subject to forfeit each time he switched to some other topic in the middle of what he was saying. Whatever he had left at the end of the session he could keep. It was hoped that this verbal rehearsal and reinforcement for success would help the boy develop control over his own behavior.

The child's in-therapy behavior became less hyperactive, his test performance improved, and the teacher noted improvements in the classroom. Apparently one of the ways to deal with the problems associated with hyperactivity is to teach children to "stop and think" before undertaking a behavior so that they can then guide their own performance by deliberate self-instructions.

Even without treatment, hyperactive disturbances tend to clear up in the middle teens. The reason for this change is not clear. However, many hyperactive children who show signs of minimum brain dysfunction have a poor prognosis if left untreated. Even though the excessive and exaggerated activity may diminish over time, these individuals may continue to have many serious problems into their teens and even adult years (Pelham, 1978; Weiss et al., 1975). This group has been found to have a higher-than-average incidence of delinquency and other maladaptive behavior during adolescence and beyond (Solomon, 1972).

Unsocialized disturbance of conduct

This disturbance is also sometimes referred to as *unsocialized aggressive reaction*. In an extensive study of the behavior problems of 1500 disturbed children, Jenkins (1968) found that

HIGHLIGHT

Token reinforcement programs in the classroom

During the last two decades there has been a systematic attempt to use token reinforcement programs in the classroom as a form of therapy—for example, in modifying the behaviors of hyperactive children that are interfering with their own learning and that of other children.

The basic essentials of such a token reinforcement program typically involve (a) instructions to the class concerning behaviors that will be reinforced; (b) a method of making a potentially reinforcing stimulus—e.g., a token—contingent upon given behavior; and (c) rules governing the exchange of tokens for back-up reinforcers, such as low-calorie candy or the privilege of listening to music through earphones. These essentials must be adapted, of course, to the particular classroom setting, the children, the teacher, and the parents.

Usually there is a "fading" later on in the actual use of tokens and tangible back-up reinforcers; for when more positive and constructive behaviors have been established, they may usually be maintained by praise and related intangible reinforcement that would not have been effective initially.

In general, such token reinforcement programs have been found to be generally effective in achieving such stated objectives as (a) reducing hyperactive and disruptive behaviors; (b) increasing attention, study behavior, and academic achievement; and (c) improving interpersonal and other competencies. Often such programs also yield secondary gains in the form of increased attendance as well as more positive self-concepts on the part of the children.

nearly a third fell in this category. In many ways similar to the psychopathic personality pattern we have described for adults (see Chapter 9), this reaction is much more common among boys than among girls.

Clinical picture in unsocialized disturbance of conduct. The following case is typical of the unsocialized conduct disturbance and illustrates many of the symptoms commonly found.

Craig, an eight-year-old boy, had already established himself as a social outcast by the time he entered first grade. He had been expelled from kindergarten two times in two years for being unmanageable. His mother brought him to a mental health center at the insistence of the school when she attempted to enroll him in the first grade. Within the first week of school, Craig's quarrelsome and defiant behavior had tried the special education teacher, who was reputedly "excellent" with problem children like him, to the point that she recommended his suspension from school. His classmates likewise were completely unsympathetic to Craig, whom they viewed as a bully. At even the slightest sign or movement on his part the other children would tell the teacher that Craig was "being bad again."

At home, Craig was uncontrollable. His mother and six other children lived with his domineering grandmother. Craig's mother was ineffective at disciplining or managing her children. She worked long hours as a domestic maid and "did not feel like hassling with those kids" when she got home. Her present husband, the father of the three youngest children (including Craig), had deserted the family.

In general, unsocialized aggressive children manifest such characteristics as overt or covert hostility, disobedience, physical and verbal aggressiveness, quarrelsomeness, vengefulness, and destructiveness. Lying, solitary stealing, and temper tantrums are common. Such children tend to be sexually uninhibited and inclined toward sexual aggressiveness. Some may engage in fire-setting, vandalism, and even homicidal acts.

Causal factors in unsocialized disturbance of conduct.

There appears to be general agreement among investigators that the family setting of the unsocialized aggressive child is typically characterized by rejection, harsh and inconsistent discipline, and general frustration. Frequently the parents have an unstable marital relationship, are emotionally disturbed or sociopathic, and do not provide the child with consistent guidance, acceptance, or affection. In a disproportionate number of cases the child lives in a home broken by divorce or separation, and may have a stepparent or a series of stepparents. But whether the home is broken or not, the child is overtly rejected—he or she is unwanted and knows it.

Wolkind (1974) found that the unsocialized aggressive reaction was common among children who had been institutionalized at an early age. This was true even in relatively good insti-

tutional settings. He used the term *affectionless psychopathy* to refer to such children and concluded that their antisocial behavior had been heavily influenced by their early family life prior to entering the institution. Evidently the trauma of institutionalization had further exacerbated antisocial trends that had started very early in an inadequate home.

Treatment and outcomes.

Therapy for the unsocialized aggressive child is likely to be ineffective unless some means can be found for modifying the child's environment. This is difficult where the parents are maladjusted and in conflict between themselves. And often an overburdened parent who is separated or divorced and working simply does not have the time or inclination to learn and practice a more adequate parental role. In some cases the circumstances may call for removal of the child from the home and placement in a foster home or institution, with the expectation of later return to the home if intervening therapy with the parents appears to justify it. Unfortunately, children often interpret this as further rejection—not only by their parents but by society as well. And unless the changed environment offers a warm, kindly, acceptant—and yet consistent and firm—setting, they are likely to make little progress.

By and large, society tends to take a punitive, rather than rehabilitative, attitude toward the antisocial aggressive youth. Thus, the emphasis is on punishment and on "teaching the child a lesson." Such "treatment," however, appears to intensify rather than correct the behavior. Where treatment is unsuccessful, the end product is likely to be a psychopathic personality with a long future of antisocial aggressive behavior. In a longitudinal study of antisocial aggressive behavior in childhood, Robins (1970) found that such behavior is highly predictive of sociopathic behavior in later adolescence and adulthood; similar findings have been reported by Wolkind (1974).

The advent of behavior therapy techniques has, however, made the outlook much brighter for children who manifest unsocialized aggressive reactions. Particularly important is training of the parents in control techniques, so that they function as therapists in reinforcing desirable behavior and modifying the environmental conditions that have been reinforc-

These photographs depict children, diagnosed as "emotionally disturbed" or "behaviorally disordered," interacting with their teachers or counselors at the Loyola University Guidance Center or Day School in Chicago.

The Guidance Center serves children who have significant difficulty in everyday living in their community but who can continue to attend a regular school and live at home. After an intensive individual diagnostic evaluation, a treatment program is developed that includes both the child and the parents. This program includes a variety of treatment methods such as individual play therapy, group therapy for children or adults, and family therapy.

The Day School serves very emotionally disturbed children who cannot attend regular public school. Each child is studied as an individual and treated accordingly, but the treatment is based on the theory that the child has not received or has not been able to accept an optimal amount of love and affection.

Children in the Day School spend a great deal of their time relating to adults, learning to receive and give affection and, at the same time, slowly learning to control their behavior.

ing the maladaptive behavior. The changes brought about when they consistently accept and reward the child's positive behavior and stop focusing attention on the negative behavior may finally change their perception of and feelings toward the child, leading to the basic acceptance that the child has so badly needed.

Though effective techniques for behavioral management can be taught to parents (Patterson & Reid, 1973), often they have difficulty carrying out treatment plans. If this is the case, other techniques may have to be employed to ensure that the parent or person responsible for the child's discipline is sufficiently assertive to follow through on the program. Shoemaker and Paulson (1976) described a program of assertiveness training for mothers, in which women who had children with aggressive behavior problems were taught more effective skills in self-expression and verbal discipline. Ratings of the children's behavior showed improvement following the assertiveness training.

Disturbances of emotion: anxiety and withdrawal disturbances

Anxiety and withdrawal disturbances have so much in common that we shall deal with them together under the general heading of *disturbances of emotion*. Jenkins (1968) classified 287 of the 1500 disturbed children he studied—about a fifth—as suffering from reactions of these two types. Both are much more common among boys than among girls. (Another possible disturbance of emotion—childhood depression—is discussed in the HIGH-LIGHT on this page.

Clinical picture in anxiety and withdrawal disturbances.
Children with anxiety and withdrawal disturbances appear to share the following characteristics: (a) oversensitivity, (b) unrealistic fears, (c) shyness and timidity, (d) pervasive feelings of inadequacy, (e) sleep disturbances, and (f) fear of school. However, the children diagnosed as suffering from an anxiety disturbance typically attempt to cope with their fears by becoming overdependent on others for support and help,

Does childhood depression exist as a clinical syndrome?

Clinicians working in child psychiatry and child psychology have long recognized a pattern of symptoms that seemed indicative of depression. Spitz (1946) first described the problem, which he called *anaclitic depression,* as a pattern similar to adult depression that occurred in children experiencing prolonged separation from the mother. This syndrome included developmental retardation and such symptomatic behavior as weepiness, sadness, immobility, and apathy. More recent research (Rutter, 1971) has shown that while separation from the mother is often associated with short-term distress, long-term disorder does not result from such loss or separation if there is a substitute parental person.

Childhood depression is recognized as a diagnostic entity in the International Classification of Diseases (ICD-9); it is called *adjustment reaction* and includes behaviors such as withdrawal, crying, avoidance of eye contact, physical complaints, poor appetite, and even aggressive behavior. The "reality" of childhood depression is accepted so strongly that some investigators (Ossofsky, 1974) even believe that it can be diagnosed in infancy and successfully treated with imipramine, an antidepressant medication.

However, many other investigators doubt the existence of such a syndrome (Lefkowitz & Burton, 1978; Schulterbrandt & Raskin, 1977). For one thing the symptoms listed are common in many normal children (MacFarlane, Allen & Honzik, 1954; Werry & Quay, 1971). For another, cross-cultural studies of depression do not support the idea of a childhood depression syndrome (Marsella, 1979). One investigator, Makita (1973), noted that out of 3,000 cases of disturbed children in Japan, not one was diagnosed as childhood depression.

whereas those who manifest a withdrawal reaction apparently attempt to minimize their anxiety by turning away from the frightening outer world and withdrawing into themselves.

1. *Anxiety disturbance.* Anxiety disturbance is characterized by unrealistic fears, oversensitivity, self-consciousness, nightmares, and chronic anxiety. The child lacks self-confidence, is apprehensive in new situations, and tends to be immature for his or her age. Such children often are described by their parents as prone to be shy, sensitive, nervous,

Children with anxiety and withdrawal disturbances tend to be oversensitive, shy, timid, and fearful.

submissive, easily discouraged, worried, and frequently moved to tears. Typically they are overdependent, particularly on their parents. The following case involving "school phobia" illustrates the clinical picture in this disturbance.

Johnny was a highly sensitive 6-year-old boy who suffered from numerous fears, nightmares, and chronic anxiety. He was terrified of being separated from his mother, even for a brief period. When his mother tried to enroll him in kindergarten, he became so upset when she left the room that the principal arranged for her to remain in the classroom. But after two weeks this had to be discontinued, and Johnny had to be withdrawn from kindergarten since his mother could not leave him even for a few minutes.

Later when his mother attempted to enroll him in the first grade, Johnny manifested the same intense anxiety and unwillingness to be separated from her. At the suggestion of the school counselor, Johnny's mother brought him to a community clinic for assistance with the problem. The therapist who initially saw Johnny and his mother was wearing a white clinic jacket, and this led to a severe panic reaction on Johnny's part. His mother had to hold him to keep him from running away, and he did not settle down

until the therapist removed his jacket. Johnny's mother explained that "He is terrified of doctors, and it is almost impossible to get him to a physician even when he is sick."

2. *Withdrawal disturbance.* In the withdrawal disturbance, as already indicated, children apparently attempt to minimize their anxiety by turning inward—in effect detaching themselves from a seemingly dangerous world. The results of this defensive strategy have been described by Jenkins (1969):

"In turning away from objective reality, these children turn away from the normal practice of constantly checking their expectations against experience. With such turning away, their capacity to distinguish fact from fancy tends to deteriorate. They function inefficiently and fail to develop effective patterns of behavior." (p. 70)

Children manifesting the withdrawal disturbance tend to be seclusive, timid, and unable to form close interpersonal relationships. Often they appear listless and apathetic and are prone to daydreaming and unrealistic fantasies. The following case is fairly typical:

Tommy was a small, slender, 7-year-old boy from a middle-class family. He was enrolled in the second grade at school but failed to function adequately in the classroom. In referring him to the school counselor, the teacher described him as withdrawn, shy, oversensitive, and unable to make friends or to participate in classroom activities. During recess he preferred to remain in the classroom and appeared preoccupied with his thoughts and fantasies. He was seriously retarded in reading achievement and other basic school subjects. Psychological assessment showed that he was superior in intelligence but suffered from extreme feelings of inadequacy and a pervasive attitude of "I can't do it."

Causal factors in anxiety and withdrawal disturbances. A number of causal factors have been emphasized in the overanxious and the withdrawal reactions. The more important of these appear to be the following:

a) Unusual constitutional sensitivity, easy conditionability by aversive stimuli, and the building up and generalization of "surplus fear reactions."

b) Undermining of feelings of adequacy and security by early illnesses, accidents, or losses that involved pain and discomfort. The traumatic effect of such experiences is often due partly to such children's finding themselves in unfamiliar situations, as during hospitalization.

c) The "modeling" effect of an overanxious and protective parent who sensitizes the child to the dangers and threats of the outside world. Often the parent's overprotectiveness communicates a lack of confidence in the child's ability to cope, thus reinforcing the child's feelings of inadequacy.

d) The failure of an indifferent or detached parent to provide adequate guidance for the child's development. Although the child is not necessarily rejected, neither is he or she adequately supported in mastering essential competencies and in gaining a positive self-concept. Repeated experiences of failure, stemming from poor learning skills, may lead to subsequent patterns of anxiety or withdrawal in the face of "threatening" situations.

Sometimes children are made to feel that they must earn their parents' love and respect through outstanding achievement, especially in school. Such children tend to be overcritical of themselves and to feel intensely anxious and devaluated when they perceive themselves as failing. These children are perfectionists who may actually do well but are left with a feeling of failure because they are sure they should have done better.

e) Inadequate interpersonal patterns, which typically extend beyond the family. The withdrawal reaction, in particular, "occurs in children who have found human contact more frustrating than rewarding" (Jenkins, 1970, p. 141). For the overanxious child, interpersonal relationships may be somewhat less aversive than for the withdrawn child; nevertheless, they are probably not actually satisfactory.

The various causal factors that we have been discussing in relation to the anxiety and withdrawal disturbances of childhood can obviously occur in differing degrees and combinations. All of them, however, are consistent with the view that these disorders essentially result from maladaptive learning.

Treatment and outcomes. The anxiety and withdrawal disturbances of childhood may continue into adolescence and young adulthood—the first leading to neurotic avoidance behavior and the latter to increasingly idiosyncratic thinking and behavior. Typically, however, this is not the case. As such children grow and have wider interactions in school and peer-group activities, they are likely to benefit from such corrective experiences as making friends and succeeding at given tasks. Teachers, who have become more and more aware of the needs of both overanxious and shy, withdrawn children—and of ways of helping them—often are able to ensure success experiences for such children and to foster constructive interpersonal relationships. Behavior therapy procedures, employed in structured group experiences within educational settings, can often help speed up and ensure favorable outcomes. Such procedures include assertiveness training, help with mastering essential competencies, and desensitization.

This last procedure may be limited in its application to young children, however, for a number of reasons, including the inability of younger children to relax while imagining emotionally charged stimuli (Hatzenbuehler & Schroeder, 1978). With children, desensitization procedures must be explicitly tailored to the particular problem, and *in vivo* methods (using graded real-life situations) may be more effective than use of imagined situations. For example, Montenegro (1968) described the successful treatment of a 6-year-old boy, Romeo, who showed pathological anxiety when he was separated from his mother. The treatment included the following procedures.

(a) Exposure of the child to a graded series of situations involving the actual fear-arousing stimulus—that is, separation from the mother for increasingly longer intervals.

(b) Use of food during these separations as an anxiety inhibitor—which might involve taking the child to the hospital cafeteria for something to eat.

(c) Instruction of the parents on how to reduce the child's excessive dependence on the mother—for example, through letting him learn to do things for himself.

After ten consecutive sessions, Romeo's separation anxiety was reduced to the point that he could stay home with a competent baby-sitter for an hour, and then for increasingly longer periods. During the summer he was enrolled in a vacation church school, which he enjoyed; and when the new semester began at public school, he entered the first grade and made an adequate adjustment. It may be emphasized that the cooperation of the parents —particularly the mother—was a key factor in the treatment program.

Autism

The boy is 5 years old. When spoken to, he turns his head away. Sometimes he mumbles unintelligibly. He is neither toilet trained nor able to feed himself. He actively resists being touched. He dislikes sounds. He cannot relate to others, and avoids looking anyone in the eye. He often engages in routine manipulative activities, such as dropping an object, picking it up, and dropping it again. While seated, he often rocks back and forth in a rhythmic motion for hours. Any change in routine is highly upsetting to him. He is in a school for severely psychotic children at UCLA. His diagnosis is childhood autism.

Autism in infancy and childhood was first described by Kanner (1943). It afflicts some 80,000 American children—about 1 child in 2500—and occurs about 4 or 5 times more frequently among boys than girls (Schreibman & Koegel, 1975; Treffert, 1970). It is usually iden-

tified before the child is 30 months of age (Rutter, 1978); often it is apparent in the early weeks of life. Autistic children come from all socioeconomic levels, ethnic backgrounds, and family patterns.

Clinical picture in autism.   In autism, the child seems apart or aloof from the earliest stages of life; consequently, this disorder is often referred to as "early infantile autism." Mothers remember such babies as never being "cuddly," never reaching out when being picked up, never smiling or looking at them while being fed, and never appearing to notice the comings and goings of other persons. In fact, autistic children do not evidence any need for affection or contact with anyone, usually not even seeming to know or care who their parents are.

Absence or severely restricted use of speech is characteristic of autistic children. If speech is present, it is almost never used to communicate except in the most rudimentary fashion, as by saying "yes" when asked if they want something to eat, or by the echolalic ("parrot-like") repetition of a few words. Often autistic children show an active aversion to auditory stimuli, crying even at the sound of a parent's voice. However, the pattern is not always consistent: autistic children "may at one moment be severely agitated or panicked by a very soft sound and at another time be totally oblivious to loud noise" (Ritvo & Ornitz, 1970, p. 6).

Self-stimulation is characteristic of these children, usually taking the form of such repetitive movements as head banging, spinning, and/or rocking, which may continue by the hour. Other bizarre as well as repetitive behavior is typical. This is well described by Gajzago and Prior (1974) in the case of a young autistic boy:

"A was described as a screaming, severely disturbed child who ran around in circles making highpitched sounds for hours. He also liked to sit in boxes, under mats, and [under] blankets. He habitually piled up all furniture and bedding in the center of the room. At times he was thought deaf though he also showed extreme fear of loud noises. He refused all food except in a bottle, refused to wear clothes, chewed stones and paper, whirled himself, and spun objects. . . . He played repetitively with the same toys for months, lining things in rows, collected objects such as bottle tops, and insisted on having two of everything, one in each hand. He became extremely upset if interrupted and if the order or arrangement of things were altered." (p. 264)

In contrast to the behavior just described, some autistic children are often skilled at fitting objects together. Thus, their performance on puzzles or form boards may be average or above. However, even in the manipulation of objects, difficulty with meaning is apparent. For example, when pictures are to be arranged in an order that tells a story, the autistic child shows a marked deficiency in performance.[3]

Many autistic children become preoccupied with and form strong attachments to unusual objects such as rocks, light switches, film negatives, or keys. In some instances, the object is so large or bizarre that merely carrying it around interferes with other activities. When their preoccupation with the object is disturbed—for example, by its removal or by attempts to substitute something in its place—or when anything familiar in their environment is altered even slightly, they may have a violent temper tantrum or a crying spell that continues until the familiar situation is restored. Thus autistic children are often said to be "obsessed with the maintenance of sameness."

Finally, and of key importance, autistic children seem to have a blurred and undifferentiated concept of self. Apparently they do not perceive themselves as the center of their world and lack a central reference point for "anchoring" or integrating perceptions. Bettelheim (1967, 1974) has referred to this condition as "the absence of I" or "the empty fortress."

In summary, autistic children typically show difficulties in relationships to other people, in perceptual-cognitive functioning, in their lan-

Childhood schizophrenia

Schizophrenia in childhood is found less frequently than autism. The symptomatic behavior in childhood schizophrenia is similar to that in autism, but the onset is gradual and occurs later—usually after the age of 10 or in adolescence. Typically, schizophrenic children have undergone a period of seemingly normal development before beginning to show withdrawal, thought disturbances, and inappropriate emotional behavior.

The long-range prognosis in childhood schizophrenia appears only slightly more favorable than for autism (Bender, 1973; Roff, 1974). The major tranquilizing drugs so helpful in the treatment of adult schizophrenic patients have not proved effective with either autistic or schizophrenic children, although they do have a calming effect.*

*More detailed comparison of autism and childhood psychoses may be found in Rutter and Schopler (1978), Rutter (1977), and L. K. Wing (1976).

guage development, and in their development of a sense of identity (L. K. Wing, 1976). They also engage in bizarre and repetitive activities and demonstrate a fascination with unusual objects and an obsessive need to maintain the sameness of the environment. This is indeed a heavy set of handicaps.

Because the clinical picture in autism tends to blend almost imperceptibly with that of childhood schizophrenia, a differential diagnosis is often difficult to make. The chief distinguishing feature appears to be the age of onset, with autism becoming evident very early and schizophrenia appearing more gradually and much later, after several years of apparently normal development (see HIGHLIGHT on this page). As Bettelheim (1969) has put it, "While the schizophrenic child withdraws from the world, the autistic child fails to ever enter it" (p. 21).

Causal factors in autism. No brain pathology has been delineated in infant or childhood autism, and since it does not run in families, it cannot be attributed directly to a hereditary defect. In their review of genetic factors in autism and childhood schizophrenia, Hanson and Gottesman (1976) found no evi-

[3]Although some have regarded autistic children as potentially of normal intelligence, this view has been challenged by a number of investigators who consider many if not most of these children to be mentally retarded (Goodman, 1972). Some autistic children, however, show markedly discrepant abilities. In this context, Goodman described the case of an "autistic-savant" who showed unusual ability at an early age in calendar calculating (rapidly determining the day of any calendar date in history) as well as in other areas, such as naming the capitals of most states and countries. Yet his language development was severely retarded, and he showed the indifference to others and related symptoms characteristic of autistic children.

dence for a genetic basis of autism. The possibility remains, however, that defective genes or damage from radiation or other conditions during prenatal development may play a key role in the etiological pattern. Thus, while Judd and Mandell (1968) failed to find significant chromosomal abnormalities in a carefully selected group of 11 autistic children, subtler constitutional defects cannot be ruled out. In fact, most investigators believe that autism begins with some type of inborn defect that impairs the infant's perceptual-cognitive functioning—the ability to process incoming stimulation and to relate to the world.

In his early studies of childhood autism, Kanner (1943) concluded that an innate disorder in the child is exacerbated by a cold and unresponsive mother, the first factor resulting in social withdrawal and the second tending to maintain the isolation syndrome. However, most investigators have failed to find the parents of autistic children to be "emotional refrigerators" (Schreibman & Koegel, 1975; Wolff & Morris, 1971). In a well-controlled study, McAdoo and De Myer (1978) found that the personality characteristics of parents of autistic children were not significantly different from those of parents of other types of disturbed children. He also discovered that the mothers of both autistic and disturbed children had significantly fewer psychological problems than did mothers who were themselves receiving treatment.

As Harlow (1969) has somewhat wryly pointed out, it is often extremely difficult to pinpoint cause and effect in studying relationships between mother and child:

"Possibly . . . some children are rendered autistic by maternal neglect and insufficiency, but it is even more likely that many more mothers are rendered autistic because of an inborn inability of their infants to respond affectionately to them in any semblance of an adequate manner." (p. 29)

On the basis of their intensive study of 53 autistic children, Clancy and McBride (1969) have suggested that the usual picture of the autistic child as lacking in language ability and being wholly withdrawn is probably oversimplified. They found that at least some autistic children *do* comprehend language, even though they may not use it to express themselves. These investigators also pointed to the occasional normal commencement of lan-

guage development, followed by its disappearance as the autistic process becomes manifest. Perhaps even more significantly, they found evidence that the autistic children they studied were very much aware of—and actively involved with—their environment:

"Autistic children actively seek to arrange the environment on their terms, and so as to exclude certain elements, e.g., intervention from other people and variety in any aspect of routine. They show a high degree of skill in manipulating people for their ends, and again this skill is usually obvious in the first year of life. In a socially inverted manner the children are as active and resourceful as normal children." (p. 243)

Tinbergen (1974) came to a somewhat similar conclusion, viewing autism as the result of an approach-avoidant conflict in which the child's natural tendency to explore and relate to the world has been overbalanced by aversive experiences and fear. According to this view, instead of venturing forth into the world, such children withdraw into a world they create for themselves. However, withdrawal is not as haphazard or disorderly as it may seem; rather it involves systematic avoidance of many stimuli and events in the real world, including people.

Clearly, much remains to be learned about the etiology of childhood autism. It would appear, however, that this disorder begins with an inborn defect or defects in brain functioning, regardless of what other causal factors may subsequently become involved.

Treatment and outcomes. A variety of procedures have been used with autistic children. Bettelheim (1967, 1969, 1974), at the Orthogenic School of the University of Chicago, has reported some success in treating autistic children with a program of warm, loving acceptance accompanied by reinforcement procedures (see HIGHLIGHT beginning on page 506). Similarly, Marchant and her associates (1974) in England have reported improvement using a method for introducing "graded change" into the environment of autistic children, thus tending to shift their behavior gradually from self-defeating to growth-oriented activities.

Another approach to treating autistic children is called *structural therapy*. Here the environment is structured to provide spontaneous

A young girl, diagnosed as autistic, receives a pretzel from her therapist as part of a reinforcement procedure in a therapy program.

physical and verbal stimulation to the children in a playful and game-like manner. The goal of this approach is to increase the amount and variety of stimuli for these children, gradually making them more aware of themselves and their environment and more related to it. The results of structural therapy have been encouraging, with 12 of 21 cases being considered improved enough to be able to return home after the three-year treatment program (Ward, 1978).

In an extensive study of autistic children who were mentally retarded, socially unresponsive, and behaviorally disturbed, Bartak and his colleagues at the Maudsley Hospital in England obtained significant results with educational procedures. Children who were assigned to a structured treatment unit focusing on formal schooling showed greater progress than those placed in units stressing play therapy, either free or structured (Bartak & Rutter, 1973; Russell, 1975). As a result of this work, Bartak (1978) suggests a "qualified optimism" for the educational progress of autistic children.

Behavior therapy in an institutional setting has been used successfully in the elimination of self-injurious behavior, the mastery of the fundamentals of social behavior, and the development of some language skills (Lovaas, 1977; Lovaas, Schaeffer, & Simmons, 1974).[4] One interesting finding of studies on the effectiveness of the use of behavior therapy with institutionalized children is that those children who were discharged to their parents continued to improve, whereas those who remained in the institution tended to lose much of what they had gained (Lovaas, 1977; Schreibman & Koegel, 1975).

Some of the most impressive results with autistic children have been obtained in projects that involve using the parent in the treatment program. Treatment "contracts" with the parents specify the desired behavior changes in the child and spell out the explicit techniques

---

[4]In a discussion of the disordered language of autistic children, Lord and Baker (in press) emphasize the importance of communicating clearly with them and offer some guidelines. For example, since only about half of these children have any meaningful speech, the clinician cannot assume that the words they utter are communicating anything consistently or that the words to which they respond at one time will be understood in a different context. Communications need to be kept as simple as possible; often gestures can help convey a message.

for bringing out these changes. Such contracting acknowledges the value of the parent as a potential change agent—in contrast with the previously held belief that the parents are somehow to blame for the child's disorder (Schopler, 1978).

Perhaps the most favorable results are those of Schreibman and Koegel (1975) who reported successful outcomes in the treatment of 10 of 16 autistic children. These investigators relied heavily on the use of parents as therapists in reinforcing normal behavior on the part of their children, and concluded that autism is potentially a "defeatable horror."

It is too early to evaluate the long-term effectiveness of these newer treatment methods or the degree of improvement actually brought about. Traditionally, the long-term results from the treatment of autism have been unfavorable. Even with intensive long-term care in a clinical facility, where gratifying improvements may be brought about in specific behaviors, the child is a long way from becoming "normal." Less than one-fourth of the autistic children who receive treatment appear to attain even marginal adjustment in later life.

Stuttering

Stuttering is a speech disorder that involves a blocking or repetition of, or sometimes a struggling with, speech sounds. The term *stuttering* is synonymous with the older term *stammering*, which has gradually fallen into disuse. The speaking behavior of the stutterer may vary from mild difficulty, with initial syllables of certain words, as in "D-d-d-don't do that," to violent contortions and momentary inability to utter any sound at all.

Every era has had its quota of these speech sufferers. Some of the more illustrious names on the roster are those of Moses, Aristotle, Vergil, Demosthenes, Charles Lamb, and Clara Barton. In our contemporary world, stuttering has been observed in diverse cultures—among the Bantu of South Africa and the Polynesians of the South Pacific, as well as among members of Oriental and Western societies (Lemert, 1962, 1970).

The actual incidence of stuttering is not known, but it has been estimated that in the Western world some 40 to 50 million children

Joey: a "mechanical boy"

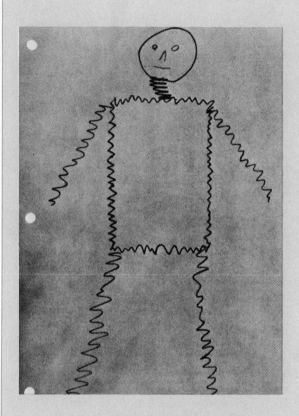

These four pictures were drawn by Joey, an autistic boy who entered the Sonia Shankman Orthogenic School of the University of Chicago at the age of 9. His unusual case history has been reported by Bettelheim (1959).

Joey presumably denied his own emotions because they were unbearably painful. Apparently not daring to be human in a world which he felt had rejected him, Joey withdrew into a world of fantasy and perceived himself as a machine that "functioned as if by remote control." This idea is brought out in the drawing above—a self-portrait in which Joey depicts himself as an electrical robot. Bettelheim interpreted this portrait as symbolizing Joey's rejection of human feelings.

So elaborately constructed and acted out was Joey's mechanical character that "entering the dining room, for example, he would string an imaginary wire from his 'energy source'—an imaginary electric

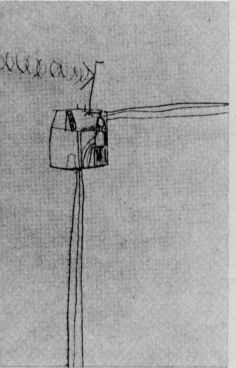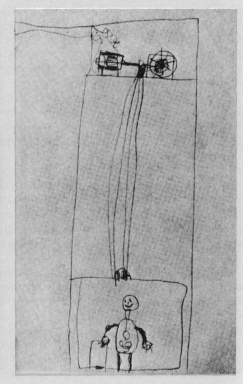

outlet—to the table. There he 'insulated' himself with paper napkins and finally plugged himself in. Only then could Joey eat, for he firmly believed that the 'current' ran his ingestive apparatus" (p. 117).

Joey's performance was convincing—so much so that others found themselves responding to him as a mechanical boy rather than as a human being: ". . . one had to look twice to be sure there was neither wire nor outlet nor plug. Children and members of our staff . . . avoided stepping on the 'wires' for fear of interrupting what seemed the source of his very life." When his machinery was idle, Joey "would sit so quietly that he would disappear from the focus of the most conscientious observation. Yet in the next moment he might be 'working' and the center of our captivated attention" (p. 117).

In his report on Joey, Bettelheim alluded to the painfully slow process by which Joey was eventually able to establish true relations with other human beings.

Three of the drawings (left to right above) depict part of the process. In the earliest of the three, Joey portrays himself "as an electrical 'papoose,' completely enclosed, suspended in empty space and operated by wireless signals." In the next one, he apparently demonstrates increasing self-esteem, for although he is still operated by wireless signals, he is much larger in stature. In the final drawing, Joey depicts "the machine which controls him," but in this one, unlike the previous drawings, "he has acquired hands with which he can manipulate his immediate environment" (p. 119).

When Joey was 12—three years after he had entered the school—". . . he made a float for our Memorial Day parade. It carried the slogan: 'Feelings are more important than anything under the sun.' Feelings, Joey had learned, are what make for humanity; their absence, for a mechanical existence. With this knowledge Joey entered the human condition" (p. 127).

stutter badly; in the United States the figure has been estimated to be between 2 and 3 million (Sheehan, 1970; Steinberg, 1975). Most stuttering begins early in life, the onset occurring before the age of 6 in 90 percent or more of the cases, with the highest incidence occurring between the ages of 2 and 4. More boys than girls stutter, in a ratio of about 4 or 5 to 1.

Clinical picture in stuttering.

The entire performance of the stutterer represents an "internal struggle" to speak. After the momentary disturbance, however, speech becomes smooth and fluent until the next stumbling block. Typically, stuttering increases both in severity and frequency in situations where the stutterer feels inferior, self-conscious, or anxious. On the other hand, most stutterers can articulate normally or with minimal difficulty when singing, whispering, or adopting some accent or drawl, or when they cannot hear the sound of their own voices. Usually, also, they have little or no difficulty in speaking aloud when they are alone, when addressing animals, or when reading aloud to the tempo of a metronome.

On the basis of his own early experiences as a stutterer, and also of his later studies in this field, Sheehan (1970) has pointed out that "for the child or adult who stutters, the production of a spoken word can be fraught with dread and difficulty" (p. vii). Certainly one can empathize with the young stutterer in the classroom who is eager to answer a question but fears the humiliation and ridicule that his or her stuttering may elicit. In a world organized around efficient verbal communication, stuttering can be highly stressful and self-devaluating. As Steinberg (1975) has expressed it, "this simple act of social interaction has been transformed into a frightening nightmare" (p. 30).

Causal factors in stuttering.

Stuttering has proved to be a most baffling disorder; attempts to explain it have focused largely on the following factors:

1. *Genetic and neurological factors.* In comparing a large group of children who stuttered with a matched group of nonstutterers, Johnson (1961) found that 9 times as many of the stutterers had siblings or parents—most fathers—who also stuttered. In a more recent review of research findings, Sheehan and Costley (1975) concluded that genetic factors

play a significant role in the etiology of stuttering. But these investigators did not rule out the key role of learning in the "familial transmission" of stuttering.

A neurological view that has received much emphasis relates stuttering to aberrations in auditory feedback. Since the experimental delay or withholding of auditory feedback greatly reduces or even eliminates severe stuttering, it seems possible that "in certain cases stuttering may be the result of minute physical imperfections in the feedback loop of the hearing mechanism" (Dinnan, McGuiness, & Perrin, 1970, p. 30). However, more recent research in this area has failed to delineate specific aberrations in auditory feedback.

Nor as a group do stutterers evidence brain damage or abnormal brain functioning. Brain damage may cause a different type of speech or language disorder called *aphasia,* defined as a loss or impairment of ability to use language because of brain lesions (see Chapter 13). For example, one common difficulty among aphasics is in finding the right word; the stutterer has the word in mind but has trouble getting it out.

2. *Learning and stress.* Currently, most investigators place strong emphasis on the roles of learning and stress as primary causal factors in stuttering.

The potential importance of learning in the development of stuttering was demonstrated some two decades ago by Flanagan, Goldiamond, and Azrin (1959), using operant conditioning procedures. A normally fluent subject received continual electric shock, but blockage of fluent speech turned off the shock for 10 seconds; each additional disfluency in speech that occurred during this 10-second interval further delayed the electroshock. Eventually the subject avoided the aversive stimulation almost entirely by continuous disfluent speech.[5] As Bandura (1969) has pointed out, however, "it is exceedingly improbable that parents of stutterers continuously punish their children's fluent verbal patterns, but respond nonpunitively whenever their children block and stutter" (p. 393).

While it appears that stuttering develops

---

[5]It may be noted here that MacDonald and Martin (1973) found distinctive differences between stuttering and disfluencies and consider them discrete types of language difficulties.

from the disfluencies that characterize normal speech, particularly during early stages of speech development, the actual learning processes involved still remain a puzzle though stress probably plays a role. Most of us have probably experienced blocking of thought and speech in stage fright or in situations where we have had to make unexpected introductions. In these situations it is probably safe to say that we were self-conscious and tense. Defective responses under these conditions are very common. Any stressful situation that leads to severe feelings of inadequacy, self-consciousness, anxiety, fear, and tension may also tend to impair psychomotor coordination and performance—including speech functions.

Why stressful situations affect such speech functions far more in some persons than others is not known—although this may be related to the constitutional vulnerability of specific organ systems, including those involved in speech. For example, the child who has been subjected to disruptive factors while learning the difficult motor coordinations needed for speech may be especially vulnerable to later speech difficulties. Then, once the pattern starts, the child expects to have trouble and becomes self-conscious and tense in situations calling for speech.

3. *Role behavior.* Sheehan (1970) and Sheehan and Lyon (1974) have pointed to the potential importance of role behavior—as well as learning and stress—in the development of stuttering. This role behavior may take either of two different forms, but the eventual result is the same.

In the first form the stutterers play a "false role" in that they attempt to conceal their stuttering, perhaps assuming a foreign accent or a regional dialect. Even when this enables them to deceive others at least temporarily, they are likely to experience guilt and doubt. These feelings, in turn, lead them to work even harder at denying their role as a stutterer and concentrating on their false role as a normal speaker. Ironically, however, as we have seen, stutterers usually have the greatest difficulty when they are thinking about their stuttering and trying to avoid it. Thus, their false role sooner or later fails in its protective function, confronting them in turn with the view of themselves as a stutterer.

In the second form, individuals simply see themselves as stutterers and resign themselves to that role. "I am a stutterer" becomes a permanent part of the self-concept—a view that is reinforced each time stuttering occurs. And presumably the expectations and reactions of those around them also tend to perpetuate the stuttering role and behavior.

Sheehan makes it clear that accepting the fact that one is a stutterer may have either positive or negative effects. For those who view stuttering as self-devaluating and a chronic affliction about which they can do nothing, the result is negative. On the other hand, in accepting the fact that they are stutterers, they have defined their problem and can begin to deal with it. In recognizing the problem, however, it is important that they not feel devaluated or obligated to play this role forever. Modern therapy places strong emphasis on self-acceptance, but not on self-resignation.

Treatment and outcomes. The following plea for help, written by a high-school youth, reveals the upset that may be caused by stuttering, and the need for effective therapy.

"I have stuttered since childhood, and it is spoiling my whole life. Is there any hope that I can overcome this affliction? Isn't there anything that can be done for boys like me?" (Greene, 1946, p. 120)

Fortunately, since this letter was written marked advances have been achieved. Treatment for stuttering has taken such varied forms as aversive conditioning, desensitization, rhythm exercises, assertiveness training, hypnosis, social reinforcement of fluency, and delay of auditory feedback.

These methods fall into two general categories: those involving direct elimination of the stuttering, and those involving acceptance first and then elimination. For example, methods such as Demosthenes' speaking with pebbles in his mouth, aversive conditioning, and the delay of auditory feedback fall into the first category. Here, the attempt is to achieve fluency by means of some special technique, with the hope that this fluency will generalize to the individual's life situation.

The second approach is based on the view that stuttering is an approach-avoidance conflict generated by certain situations viewed as stressful by the stutterer; as we have noted, this conflict tends to produce a vicious circle in which fear increases the likelihood of stuttering and the negative feedback in turn reinforces the fear response. The first step here is for the stutterer to accept himself or herself realistically as a person who now stutters but who can be helped. The second step then focuses on achieving speech fluency in stressful situations in which the individual formerly stuttered. Here desensitization, self-assertion, reinforcement, and other therapy approaches may be brought into use. Once fluency is achieved, the vicious circle is broken and positive feedback and reinforcement tend to maintain speech fluency.

Fortunately, about 4 out of 5 cases of stuttering clear up spontaneously (Sheehan & Martyn, 1970). Such recovery ordinarily occurs by the middle or late teens. Even in long-established cases, most stutterers can be completely relieved of their symptoms or be greatly helped by appropriate treatment. The term *appropriate* is important here, because a method that is effective with one stutterer may be ineffective with another.

Other symptom disorders

As in the case of stuttering, the behavior disorders we shall deal with here—enuresis, encopresis, sleepwalking, nail-biting, and tics—typically involve a single outstanding symptom, rather than a more pervasive maladaptive pattern.

Enuresis. The term *enuresis* refers to the habitual involuntary discharge of urine after the age of 3. It may occur during the day, but is most common at night (bed-wetting). Among older children enuresis often occurs in conjunction with dreams in which they imagine that they are urinating in a toilet, only to awaken and discover that they have wet the bed. Enuresis may vary in frequency, from nightly to occasional instances when the individual is under considerable stress or is unduly tired. Commonly, enuresis occurs from 2 to 5 times a week. The actual incidence of enuresis is unknown, but it has been estimated that some 4 to 5 million children and adolescents in the United States suffer from the inconvenience and embarrassment of this disorder (Turner & Taylor, 1974).

Although enuresis may result from a variety of organic conditions, most investigators have pointed to (a) faulty learning, resulting in the failure to acquire a needed adaptive response—that is, inhibition of reflex bladder emptying; (b) personal immaturity, associated with or stemming from emotional problems; and (c) disturbed family interactions, particularly those that lead to sustained anxiety and/or hostility. In some instances a child may regress to bed-wetting when a new baby enters the family and becomes the center of attention. Children also may resort to bed-wetting when they feel hostile toward their parents and want to get even, realizing that such behavior is annoying and upsetting to adults. In adolescence and adulthood, enuresis is often associated with other psychological problems.

Conditioning procedures have proven effective in the treatment of enuresis (Doleys, 1979). For example, a child may sleep on an electrified mattress that rings an alarm at the first few drops of urine, thus awakening the child and eliciting a reflex inhibition of urination. Fortunately, with or without treatment the incidence of enuresis tends to decrease significantly with age. Among 7-year-olds, an estimated 21.9 percent of boys and 15.5 percent of girls are enuretic, compared with only 3 percent of boys and 1.7 percent of girls at age 14 (Rutter, Yule, & Graham, 1973), and only 1 percent or less in young adulthood (Murphy et al., 1971). Nevertheless, many experts believe that enuresis should be treated in childhood, since there is currently no way of identifying which children will remain enuretic into adulthood.

Encopresis. Children who regularly have bowel movements in their clothing after age 3 are referred to as *encopretic*. This condition is less common than enuresis. However, about 2.3 percent of 8-year-old boys and 0.7 percent of 8-year-old girls are encopretic (Bellman, 1966). The list of following characteristics of encopretics was provided by Levine (1976) from a study of 102 cases of encopretic children:

a) The average age was 7, with a range from ages 4 to 13.
b) About one-third of encopretic children were also enuretic.
c) A large sex difference was found, with about six times more boys than girls in the sample.

d) Many of the children soiled their clothing when they were under stress. A common time was in the late afternoon after school. Very few children actually had this problem at school.

e) Most of the children reported that they did not know when they needed to have a bowel movement.

Many encopretic children suffer from constipation; thus an important element in the diagnosis of the disorder involves a physical examination to determine whether there are physiological factors contributing to the disorder. Treatment of encopresis usually involves both medical and psychological aspects. Levine and Bakow (1975) found that of the encopretic children they studied who were treated by medical and behavioral procedures, more than half were cured—that is, no additional incidents occurred within six months following treatment—and an additional 25 percent were improved.

Sleepwalking (somnambulism).   Statistics are meager but it would appear that some 5 percent of children experience regular or periodic sleepwalking episodes. Children subject to this problem usually go to sleep in a normal manner but arise during the second or third hour thereafter and walk in their sleep. They may walk to another room of the house or even outside, and may engage in rather complex activities. Finally they return to bed, and in the morning remember nothing that has taken place.

During the sleepwalking, their eyes are partially or fully open, and they avoid obstacles, hear when spoken to, and ordinarily respond to commands, such as to return to bed. Shaking sleepwalkers will usually awaken them, and they will be surprised and perplexed at finding themselves in an unexpected place. Such sleepwalking episodes usually last from 15 minutes to a half hour.

The risk of injury during sleepwalking episodes is illustrated by the following case study.

". . . 14-year-old Donald Elliot got up from his bunk in his sleep, looked in the refrigerator, then, still asleep, walked out the back door. It would have been just another sleepwalking episode except that Donald was in a camper-pickup truck traveling 50 miles an hour on the San Diego Freeway. Miraculously, he escaped with cuts and bruises. But his experience,

and that of many other sleepwalkers, disproves one of the myths about somnambulism: that people who walk in their sleep don't hurt themselves." (Taves, 1969, p. 41).

The causes of sleepwalking are not fully understood. Kales et al. (1966) have shown that sleepwalking takes place during NREM (non-rapid eye movement) sleep, but its relationship to dreaming remains unclear. In general, it would appear that sleepwalking is related to some anxiety-arousing situation that has just occurred or is expected to occur in the near future.

Very little attention has been given to the treatment of sleepwalking. However, Clement (1970) has reported on the treatment of a 7-year-old boy utilizing behavior therapy, as described in the HIGHLIGHT on page 512. And Nagaraja (1974) has reported the successful treatment of an 8-year-old boy and a 9-year-old girl utilizing a combination of tranquilizers and psychotherapy. But a good deal of additional research is needed before we can determine the most effective treatment procedures for sleepwalking.

Nail-biting.   Probably about a fifth of all children bite their fingernails at one time or another. The incidence appears to be highest among stutterers, children reared in institutions, and children confronted with stressful demands. Although about as many girls as boys bite their nails at early ages, males outnumber females in later age groups.

Nail-biting typically occurs in situations associated with anxiety and/or hostility, and appears to be a method of tension reduction that provides the individual with "something to do" (thumb-sucking is probably similarly motivated). It represents a learned maladaptive habit that is reinforced and maintained by its tension-reducing properties.

Little attention has been devoted to the treatment of nail-biting. While mild tranquilizers may prove helpful, it is generally agreed that restraint and bitter-tasting applications have yielded poor results. Behavior therapy appears to be more effective. Of course, initial development of this habit in a child may be checked if the child is helped to feel more adequate and secure, especially if he or she is going through some particularly difficult stress period.

Treatment of sleepwalking utilizing conditioning procedures

Bobby, a 7-year-old boy, walked in his sleep on an average of four times a week. His mother kept a record, indicating that Bobby's sleepwalking episodes were associated with nightmares, perspiring, and talking in his sleep. During the actual sleepwalking Bobby usually was glassy-eyed and unsteady on his feet. On one occasion he started out the front door. The sleepwalking had commenced about 6 weeks before the boy was brought for therapy, and usually an episode would begin about 45 to 90 minutes after he had gone to bed.

During treatment the therapist learned that just before each sleepwalking episode Bobby usually had a nightmare about being chased by "a big black bug." In his dream Bobby thought "the bug would eat off his legs if it caught him" (Clement, 1970, p. 23). Bobby's sleepwalking episodes usually showed the following sequence: after his nightmare began, he perspired freely, moaned and talked in his sleep, tossed and turned, and finally got up and walked through the house. He was amnesic for the sleepwalking episode when he awoke the next morning.

Assessment data revealed no neurological or other medical problems and indicated that Bobby was of normal intelligence. However, he was found to be "a very anxious, guilt-ridden little boy who avoided performing assertive and aggressive behaviors appropriate to his age and sex" (p. 23). Assertiveness training and related measures were used but were not effective. The therapist then focused treatment on having Bobby's mother awaken the boy each time he showed signs of an impending episode. Washing Bobby's face with cold water and making sure he was fully awake, the mother would return him to bed, where he was "to hit and tear up a picture of the big black bug." At the start of the treatment program, Bobby had made up several of these drawings.

Eventually, the nightmare was associated with awakening, and Bobby learned to wake up on most occasions when he was having a bad dream. Clement considered the basic behavior therapy model in this case to follow that used in the conditioning treatment for enuresis, where a waking response is elicited by an intense stimulus just as urination is beginning and becomes associated with and eventually prevents nocturnal bed-wetting.

Tics.   A tic is a persistent, intermittent muscle twitch or spasm, usually limited to a localized muscle group. The term *tic* is used rather broadly to include blinking the eye, twitching the mouth, licking the lips, shrugging the shoulders, twisting the neck, clearing the throat, blowing through the nostrils, and grimacing, among other actions. In some instances, as in clearing the throat, the individual may be aware of the tic when it occurs, but usually he or she performs the act habitually and does not notice it. In fact, many individuals do not even realize that they have a tic unless someone brings it to their attention. Tics occur most frequently between the ages of 6 and 14.

The psychological impact tics can have on an adolescent is exemplified in the following case:

An adolescent who had wanted very much to be a teacher told the school counselor that he was thinking of giving up his plans. When asked the reason, he explained that several friends told him he had a persistent twitching of the mouth muscles when he answered questions in class. He had been unaware of this muscle twitch, and even after being told about it, could not tell when it took place. However, he became acutely self-conscious, and was reluctant to answer questions or enter into class discussions. As a result, his general level of tension increased, and so did the frequency of the tic—which now became apparent even when he was talking to his friends. Thus, a vicious circle had been established. Fortunately, it proved amenable to treatment by conditioning and assertiveness training.

Although tics may have an organic basis, the great majority are psychological in origin— usually stemming from self-consciousness or tension in social situations. As in the case just described, the individual's awareness of the tic often increases the tension—and the tic. Tics have been successfully treated by means of drugs, psychotherapy, and conditioning techniques.

Delinquent behavior

One of the most troublesome and extensive problems in childhood and adolescence is delinquent behavior, such as destruction of property, violence against other people, and other behavior contrary to the needs and rights of others and in violation of the society's rules. Delinquent behavior thus ranges from truancy and "incorrigibility" to serious criminal offenses. Legally, the term is reserved for acts committed by individuals under the age of 16, 17, or 18 (depending on state law). Delinquency is generally regarded as calling for some punishment or corrective action.[6]

The actual incidence of juvenile delinquency is difficult to determine, since many delinquent acts are not reported. In addition, the states differ somewhat in their definitions of delinquent behavior—particularly regarding minor offenses—so that what is considered delinquent behavior in Texas may not be so considered in California or New York. Of the two million young people who go through the juvenile courts each year in the United States, about half are there for actions that would not be considered crimes at all in the case of an adult, such as running away (see HIGHLIGHT on page 514).

Incidence

Between 1968 and 1978, arrests of persons under 18 years of age for seven serious crimes increased more than 100 percent—some four times faster than the increase in population for this age group.[7] In 1977, juveniles accounted for over 1 out of every 3 arrests for robbery, 2 out of 3 arrests for crimes against property, 1 out of 5 arrests for rape, and 1 out of 10 arrests for murder. Although most of the "juvenile crime" was committed by males, the rate has risen sharply for females. In 1977, about 1 teenager out of every 15 in the nation was arrested.

Although delinquency rates are alarmingly high, there appears to be a moderating trend for violent youth crime in recent indicators. A seventeen-year survey of police records of violent youth crimes shows that arrests of young people between the ages of 13 and 20 for homicide, robbery, and aggravated assault increased greatly in the 1960s (as much as 84 percent in the case of homicide), then increased much more slowly from 1970 to 1975, and actually declined slightly from 1975 to 1977. Rape arrests increased 17 percent during the 1960s, only 1 percent between 1970 and 1975, and then stayed the same during the next two years (Zimring, 1979).

Well over half of the juveniles who are arrested each year have prior police records. Female delinquents are commonly apprehended for drug usage, sexual offenses, running away from home, and "incorrigibility," but crimes against property, such as stealing, have markedly increased among them. Male delinquents are commonly arrested for drug usage and crimes against property; to a lesser extent, they are arrested for armed robbery, aggravated assault, and other crimes against the person. However, crimes by juveniles are increasing in our large metropolitan centers to such an extent that the streets are considered unsafe after dark.

In general, it has been assumed that both the incidence and the severity of delinquent behavior are disproportionately high for slum and lower-class youth. This view has been supported by findings of the President's Commission on Law Enforcement and Administration of Justice (1967) as well as by later reports (Zimring, 1979). Other investigators, however, have found no evidence that delinquency is predominately a lower-class phenomenon. In a study of 433 teenagers who had committed almost 2500 delinquent acts, Haney and Gold (1973) found "no strong relationship between social status and delinquent behavior" (p. 52). It may also be noted that the delinquency rate for socially disadvantaged youth appears about equal for whites and nonwhites.

Causal factors in delinquency

Various conditions, singly and in combination, may be involved in the development of delin-

---

[6]It may be noted here that children under 8 who commit such acts are not considered delinquents, because it is assumed that they are too immature to understand the significance and consequences of their actions.

[7]Statistics in this section are based mainly on Uniform Crime Reports (1978).

Problems that lead children to run away

Of serious concern in the United States is the problem of youngsters who run away from home—an estimated million or more each year. While the average age is about 15, an increasing number are in the 11- to 14-year-old age bracket. Many of these runaways are from the suburbs, and at least half are girls. The following case illustrates this problem.

Joan, an attractive girl who looked older than her 12 years, came to the attention of juvenile authorities when her parents reported her as a "runaway." Twice before she had run away from home, but no report had been filed. In the first instance she had gone to the home of a girlfriend and returned two days later; in the second she had hitchhiked to another city with an older boy and returned home about a week later.

Investigation revealed that the girl was having difficulty in school and was living in a family situation torn by bickering and dissension. In explaining why she ran away from home, she stated simply that she "just couldn't take it anymore—all that quarreling and criticism, and no one really cared anyway."

Why do children and adolescents run away? English (1973) concluded that reasons for running away from home tend to fall into three categories: (a) getting out of a destructive family situation, as in the case of the girl who runs away to avoid sexual advances by her father or stepfather; (b) running away in an effort to better the family situation; and (c) having a secret, unsharable problem, such as, for girls, being pregnant.

In a study of runaway girls, Homer (1974) distinguished between "run from's," who had usually fought with their parents and run away because they were unable to resolve the situation or their anger, and "run to's," who were seeking something outside the home. The "run to's" were typically seekers of pleasure—sex, drugs, liquor, escape from school, and a peer group with similar interests. Usually they stayed with friends or at other "peer-established" facilities. The "run from's" usually ran away from home only once, while the "run to's" were more likely to be repetitive runaways.

An increasing number of children are "run froms" who are trying to get away from an intolerable home situation. In many instances, for economic or other reasons, they are actually encouraged to leave—and their parents do not want them back. These children have been referred to as the "throwaways" (*U.S. News & World Report*, May 12, 1975, pp. 49–50). Most do not feel that they can return to their parents but very much want a foster home where they will be treated well and respected.

The majority of runaways are not reported. Of those who are, about 90 percent or more are located by law enforcement officers and, where feasible, returned home. Beginning in late 1974, a toll-free "hot line" was established that informs runaways where the nearest temporary shelter is located and enables them to send messages to their parents if they wish.*

Treatment of the child runaway is similar to that for individuals who manifest other emotional problems in this life period. Often family therapy is an essential part of the treatment program. In some instances—as in those involving parental abuse, unconcern, or lack of cooperation—juvenile authorities may place the child in a foster home. However, parents are by no means always the primary reason for their child's running away; and a "what-have-we-done-wrong" attitude may lead to unnecessary feelings of guilt.

*Two of the nationwide toll-free numbers are 1-800-621-4000 and 1-800-231-6946. These hotlines do not operate from either Alaska or Hawaii.

quent behavior. In general, however, there appear to be several key variables: (a) personal pathology, (b) pathogenic family patterns, (c) undesirable peer relationships, (d) general sociocultural factors, and (e) special stress.

Personal pathology.   A number of investigators have attempted to "type" delinquents in terms of pervasive patterns of personal pathology.

1. *Brain damage and mental retardation.* In a distinct minority of cases of delinquency —an estimated 1 percent or less—brain pathology results in lowered inhibitory controls and a tendency toward episodes of violent behavior (Caputo & Mandell, 1970; Kiester, 1974). These youths are often hyperactive, impulsive, emotionally unstable, and unable to inhibit themselves when strongly stimulated. Fortunately their inner controls appear to improve during later adolescence and young adulthood.

In some 5 percent of delinquents, low intelligence appears to be of causal significance. These individuals may be unable to foresee the probable consequences of their actions or understand the significance of what they are doing. This is particularly true of mentally retarded, sexually delinquent girls, but it also applies to retarded delinquent males who typically commit impulsive offenses, such as petty thievery and minor acts of aggression. Frequently retarded delinquents fall prey to brighter psychopaths or delinquent gangs who dominate and exploit them.

2. *Neuroses and psychoses.* A small percentage of delinquent acts appear to be directly associated with neurotic or psychotic disorders. In delinquency associated with neurosis, acting-out behavior sometimes represents a masking of depression. In other cases, the delinquent acts take the form of a behavior like "peeping" or stealing things that are not needed. This behavior often seems related to deviant sexual gratification in overinhibited adolescents who have been indoctrinated in the belief that masturbation and other overt forms of sexual release are terribly evil and sinful. Often such individuals fight their inner impulses before committing the delinquent act, and then feel guilty afterward. Disturbances of this sort have shown a marked decline in recent years, possibly because parents are no longer so prone to induce sexual overinhibition in their children.

In delinquent acts associated with psychotic behavior (also a very small percentage), there is often a pattern of prolonged emotional hurt and turmoil, culminating after long frustration in an outburst of violent behavior (Bandura, 1973). In the case of both neurotic and psychotic delinquents, the delinquent act is a byproduct of severe personality maladjustment rather than a reflection of consistent antisocial attitudes.

3. *Psychopathic traits.* A sizable number of habitual delinquents appear to share the traits typical of the psychopathic personality —they are impulsive, defiant, resentful, devoid of feelings of remorse or guilt, incapable of establishing and maintaining close interpersonal ties, and seemingly unable to profit from experience. Because they lack needed reality and ethical controls, they often engage in seemingly "senseless" acts that are not planned but occur on the "spur of the moment." They may steal a small sum of money they do not need, or they may steal a car, drive it a few blocks, and abandon it. In some instances they engage in impulsive acts of violence that are not committed for personal gain but rather reflect underlying resentment and hostility toward their world. In essence, these individuals are "unsocialized."

Kendall, Deardorff, and Finch (1977) found that nonoffenders, first offenders, and repeat offenders differed on a measure of socialization, with the repeaters being the most poorly socialized. Ganzer and Sarason (1973) found that both male and female delinquents with multiple arrests were more frequently regarded as sociopathic than were nonrecidivists (those arrested only once).

The following case provides an extreme example of a juvenile with psychopathic traits.

At the age of 12, Benny hurled a brick from the roof of an apartment building, striking another boy on the head and killing him. Benny first told the police that "it was all an accident," the brick having slipped out of his hand. He later stated that a friend had hurled the brick and that he had tried to stop him. He absolutely refused to discuss the episode again.

Benny was a cherubic-looking boy who was superficially cheerful and seemed to relate easily to other people. Yet he had thrown puppies and kittens from the roof of the apartment building where he lived; had engaged in stealing, truancy, and glue-sniffing, and had frequently gotten into terrific fights with other boys, alternately experiencing savage beatings and bloody triumphs. He kept a flock of pigeons on the roof, and his concern for the birds appeared to be touching. However, when a pigeon was injured "in a bad fight," he would dispose of it by throwing it down the incinerator alive.

Over a period of time Benny had been sent to various juvenile correctional facilities. At each institution, the same behavior pattern was noted. Benny would be warm and charming for a time, but just when it appeared that he was responding to the treatment program, he would engage in defiant behavior culminating in escape. He escaped from various institutions more than twenty times and boasted that "the place hasn't been built that can hold me." His eventual course was a tragic one, ending in death when he escaped from a maximum security installation and slammed a stolen bicycle into a parked car, suffering a fatal cerebral injury. (Adapted from Greenberg & Blank, 1970)

Although research has focused primarily on

male delinquents, several investigators have also emphasized the high incidence of psychopathic personalities among females in state correctional institutions (Cloninger & Guze, 1970; Fine & Fishman, 1968; Konopka, 1964, 1967). In a study of 115 girls in a state correctional institution in Kentucky, Fine and Fishman (1968) emphasized a personality picture characterized by rebelliousness, impulsiveness, inadequacy, instability, and immaturity—characteristics commonly found in the psychopathic personality. In their study of male and female delinquents, Ganzer and Sarason noted that "Females more frequently came from personally and socially disorganized families than did males" (1973, p. 1).

4. *Drug abuse.* A sizable number of delinquent acts—particularly theft, prostitution, and assault—are directly associated with drug problems. Most adolescents who are addicted to hard drugs, such as heroin, are forced to steal in an attempt to maintain their habit, which can be very expensive. In the case of female addicts, theft may be combined with or replaced by prostitution as a means of obtaining money.

Pathogenic family patterns.   Of the various pathogenic family patterns that have been emphasized in the research on juvenile delinquency, the following appear to be the most important.

1. *Broken homes.* A number of investigators have pointed to the high incidence of broken homes and multiple or missing parental figures in the background of delinquent youths (Lefkowitz, Eron, Walder, & Huesmann, 1977). In general, delinquency appears to be much more common among youths coming from homes broken by parental separation or divorce than from homes broken by the death of a parent.

As we have seen, however, the effects of broken homes vary greatly. Even when the disruption is due to parental separation or divorce, the effects on the children may be more favorable than when they are raised in a home torn by parental conflict and dissension.

2. *Parental rejection and faulty discipline.* In many cases, one or both parents reject the child. When the father is the rejecting parent, it is difficult for a boy to identify with him and use him as a model for his own development. In an early study of 26 aggressively delinquent boys, Bandura and Walters (1963) delineated a pattern in which rejection by the father was combined with inconsistent handling of the boy by both parents. To complicate the pathogenic picture, the father typically used physically punitive methods of discipline, thus modeling aggressive behavior as well as augmenting the hostility the boy already felt toward him. The end result of such a pattern was a hostile, defiant, inadequately socialized youth who lacked normal inner controls and tended to act out his aggressive impulses in antisocial behavior.

The detrimental effects of parental rejection and inconsistent discipline are by no means attributable only to the father. Researchers have found that such behavior by either parent is associated with aggression, lying, stealing, running away from home, and a wide range of other difficulties (Langner et al., 1974; Lefkowitz et al., 1977; Pemberton & Benady, 1973). Often, too, inconsistent discipline may involve more complex family interactions, as when a mother imposes severe restrictions on a youth's behavior and then leaves "policing" to a timid or uncaring father who fails to follow through. In a study of middle-class families with a delinquent offspring, for example, Singer (1974) found that the result of such a family pattern was a buildup of resentment and tension on the part of the adolescent toward the mother followed by acting out in antisocial behavior.

3. *Psychopathic parental models.* Several investigators have found a high incidence of psychopathic traits in the parents of delinquents—particularly but not exclusively in the father (Bandura, 1973; Glueck & Glueck, 1969; Ulmar, 1971). These included alcoholism, brutality, antisocial attitudes, failure to provide, frequent unnecessary absences from home, and other characteristics that made the father an inadequate and unacceptable model. Elkind (1967), for example, cited the case of a "father who encouraged his 17-year-old son to drink, frequent prostitutes, and generally 'raise hell.' This particular father was awakened late one night by the police who had caught his son in a raid on a so-called 'massage' parlor. The father's reaction was, 'Why aren't you guys out catching crooks?' This same father would boast to his co-workers that his son was 'all boy' and a 'chip off the old block' " (p. 313).

Psychopathic fathers—and mothers—may contribute in various ways to delinquent behavior of girls as well. Covert encouragement of sexual promiscuity is fairly common, and in some instances there is actual incest with the daughter. In a study of 30 delinquent girls, Scharfman and Clark (1967) found evidence of serious psychopathology in one or both parents of 22 of the girls, including 3 cases of incest and many other types of early sexual experience. These investigators also reported a high incidence of broken homes (only 11 of the 30 girls lived with both parents) and harsh, irrational, and inconsistent discipline:

"Any form of consistent discipline or rational setting of limits was unknown to the girls in their homes. Rather, there was an almost regular pattern of indifference to the activities or whereabouts of these girls, often with the mother overtly or indirectly suggesting delinquent behavior by her own actions. This would alternate with unpredictable, irrational, and violent punishment." (p. 443)

Scharfman and Clark concluded that the key factors in the girls' delinquent behavior were (a) broken homes, combined with emotional deprivation; (b) irrational, harsh, and inconsistent parental discipline; and (c) patterns of early sexual and aggressive behavior modeled by psychopathic parents. Here we can readily see the interaction of pathogenic family conditions in the etiology of delinquent behavior.

In evaluating the role of pathogenic family patterns in delinquency, it may be emphasized that a given pattern is only one of many interacting factors. For example, the term "broken home" is a catchall term to describe the absence of one or both parents because of a variety of conditions, including desertion, separation, death, or imprisonment. A home may be "broken" at different times and under varying circumstances, and broken homes may have differing influences, depending on the individual involved and the total life situation. Consequently the effects of a given family pattern can be assessed adequately only in relation to the total situation.

Undesirable peer relationships. Delinquency tends to be a shared experience. In their study of delinquents in the Flint, Michi-

gan, area, Haney and Gold (1973) found that about two-thirds of delinquent acts were committed in association with one or two other persons, and most of the remainder involved three or four other persons. Usually the offender and the companion or companions were of the same sex. Interestingly enough, girls were more likely than boys to have a constant friend or companion in delinquency. The role of gang membership in delinquency is discussed in the next section.

General sociocultural factors. Here, we are concerned with broad social conditions that tend to produce or support delinquency. (See HIGHLIGHT on page 518 for a discussion of the possible influence of television on violent behavior.) Interrelated factors that appear to be of key importance include alienation and rebellion, social rejection, and the psychological support afforded by membership in a delinquent gang.

1. *Alienation and rebellion.* Feelings of alienation and rebellion are common to many teenagers from all socioeconomic levels. For example, we find middle-class youth who are uncommitted to the values of their parents or the "establishment" but at the same time are confused about their own values and sense of identity. Often they view the adult world as a hostile and phony place, inhabited by people who work at useless jobs that they pompously assume are meaningful and who try to "sell" the younger generation on a fraudulent and inevitably unfulfilling way of life. Alienated teenagers may outwardly submit passively to their elders' demands, or they may openly disobey parental and other adult authority and create no end of problems for themselves and their families. In either event, alienation from family and from the broader society exposes them to becoming "captives of their peers"—to whom they may turn for guidance and approval. Thus they are vulnerable to pressures to identify with and join peer groups that engage in the use of illegal drugs or other behavior considered delinquent.

In some instances these alienated youths may rebel, leave home, and drift into groups in which delinquent behavior is the way of life, as in the case of runaway teenage girls who become affiliated with organized prostitution. The alienated and rebellious behavior of eco-

Television and violence

Just how much the violence on television serves as a model for violent and criminal behavior has been widely argued. In 1977 the controversy entered the courtroom when a 15-year-old confessed killer was defended by an attorney who claimed that the youth had been brainwashed by TV. The attorney argued that the boy was living in a fantasy world which had been created by television programs that had given him a distorted sense of appropriate behavior. The defense alleged that the youth was intoxicated by television and "pulling the trigger became as common to him as killing a fly" (*Time*, October 10, 1977). The court did not accept the insanity plea but found the youth guilty of murder. In another case, in California, a lawyer argued (unsuccessfully) that the rape of his client, a young girl, had been a reenaction by a group of children of a scene from the TV movie *Born Innocent*, shown shortly before. And in Boston, after the showing of the TV movie *Fuzz*, a woman was set on fire in apparent imitation of a scene from that film.

A direct causal link between media violence and increased aggressiveness on the part of the viewer is difficult to prove. But the evidence of a relationship between TV violence and later aggressiveness is quite strong. As we saw in Chapter 5, early laboratory studies in the modeling of aggression showed that children who observed a display of aggression on film later demonstrated similar kicking and punching behavior themselves. Subsequent studies by the same investigator showed that when children viewed filmed aggression, they showed more aggressive behavior later (Bandura, 1973).

Other research has focused on the effects of TV on long-term attitudes and perceptions that might predispose a child toward later violent behavior. One such study found that violence on TV desensitized children so that they subsequently had less emotional arousal to violent scenes (Cline et al., 1973). Thus continued exposure to violence on TV might result in less fear of—or revulsion to—actual violence.

Well-controlled studies by Lefkowitz et al. (1977) demonstrated that children's preference for violent television at age 8 was highly associated with—and thus predictive of—aggressiveness in their behavior toward others: those who preferred violence on TV were more aggressive in their own behavior. Moreover, this relationship was still found to be significant in a ten-year follow-up when the children were young adults.

Even here, however, the direction of causation is not proven: it may have been the more aggressive children who preferred the violent TV in the beginning. But when, as has often happened, crimes occur that follow in detail a particular sequence that the individual has watched on TV or in a movie, it is hard to believe that the portrayed scene had no causal part in the tragedy. The researchers' conclusions in the Lefkowitz et al. study were that in most cases the TV violence was probably only a precipitating cause of aggressive behavior in the case of children already predisposed toward it.

nomically disadvantaged youth may lead to the same pattern, although its onset is much more likely to be directly associated with poverty, deprivation, and discrimination.

2. *The "social rejects."* Our society has become increasingly aware of young people who lack the motivation or ability to do well in school and "drop out" as soon as they can. With increasing automation and the demand for occupational skills—whether in the trades or in managerial or professional fields—there are few jobs for which they can qualify. Augmenting this group of youngsters are students who graduate from high school but whose training does not qualify them for available occupational opportunities.

Whether they come from upper-, middle-, or lower-class homes, and whether they drop out or continue through high school, they have one crucial problem in common—they discover they are not needed in our society. They are victims of "social progress"—"social rejects." While some are able to obtain training in specific job areas, others appear unable to find or hold jobs, and still others drift aimlessly from one unsatisfactory job to another.

In a study of 177 institutionalized teenage male delinquents, McCandless, Parsons, and Roberts (1972) found an average of 5 years' academic retardation, with reading at less than the fourth-grade level. With that academic handicap, such teenagers are at a

Children who grow up in poverty—as well as those who grow up in affluence—may become alienated and rebellious, confused about their own values and lacking a sense of personal identity.

serious disadvantage in the job market; many may engage in delinquent behavior partly as a result of underlying feelings of frustration, confusion, and hopelessness. Not surprisingly, Odell (1974) found a program that combined educational development and job placement —facilitating entry into the "opportunity structure"—more effective than traditional case-work methods in preventing juvenile recidivism.

3. *Delinquent gang cultures.* Here we are dealing not so much with personal psychopathology per se as with organized group pathology, involving rebellion against the norms of society. As Jenkins (1969) has expressed it,

"The socialized delinquent represents not a failure of socialization but a limitation of loyalty to a more or less predatory peer group. The basic capacity for social relations has been achieved. What is lacking is an effective integration with the larger society as a contributing member." (p. 73)

While the problem of delinquent gangs is most prevalent in lower socioeconomic areas, it is by no means restricted to them. Nor does the problem of juvenile delinquent gangs occur only in particular racial, ethnic, or social groups. It is pervasive, most particularly in inner city areas. While there are many reasons for joining delinquent gangs—including fear of personal injury by gang members if one does not join—most members of delinquent gangs appear to feel inadequate in and rejected by the larger society.

Gang membership gives them a sense of belonging and a means of gaining some measure of status and approval. It may also represent a means of committing robberies and other illegal acts for financial gain—acts that the individual could not successfully perform alone (Feldman & Weisfeld, 1973).

Juvenile and other law enforcement authorities in major U.S. cities have expressed concern about the increasing number and vio-

*There are many reasons why young people join
delinquent gangs, but most of them appear to feel
inadequate in and rejected by the larger society.
Gang membership gives them a sense of belonging
and a means of gaining some measure of status
and approval.*

lence of delinquent juvenile gangs. In Los
Angeles, for example, there are an estimated
200 such gangs, of which some 40 or more are
considered well organized and dangerous
(Hazlett, 1974). Police estimate that there are
over 800 hard-core leaders, each with a record
of 10 or more arrests. The typical gang activist
is between 14 and 22 years of age, but a sizable
and increasing number are as young as 10
years of age. The better organized and more
violent gangs have turned from knives and zip
guns to more lethal weapons, including
sawed-off shotguns and automatic rifles; their
activities range from "warfare" with rival
gangs to purse snatching, robbery, assault, and
homicide. As one Los Angeles police captain
expressed it to Hazlett (1974),

"We're caught up in an epidemic of violence, murder
has no meaning, killing has become a game, a way of
life. . . .
   "The whole attitude has changed. The kids aren't
afraid anymore—the public is!" (p. 1)

Nor is membership in delinquent gangs
confined to males. Female gangs that have developed in recent years provide much the same
function for confused, resentful, and defiant
girls as male gangs do for boys. In these gangs
the girls create their "own world" for purposes
of belonging, protection, and defiance. In the
gang they find acceptance, rules, loyalty, authority, discipline, and many of the other components that they cannot find or accept in the
adult world. Many of these female gangs are

affiliated with male gangs, while maintaining their own separate organizations.

It should be emphasized that the majority of delinquents do not belong to delinquent gangs, nor do the majority of juvenile gangs fall in the delinquent category. Many are organized for recreational and other constructive purposes. And not all delinquent gangs have been highly organized, cohesive groups. Observing several hundred black and Mexican-American gangs, both male and female, Klein (1968) found low cohesiveness, shifting roles, and little relation to adult criminal groups. More recently, however, there appears to be an increase in both the organization and cohesiveness of delinquent gangs as well as in the violent nature of their activities.

Unusual stress and other factors. We have noted that many delinquent acts reflect momentary impulses or are part of the regular activities of a delinquent gang. Delinquent behavior may also be precipitated by some relatively minor event, as when a riot is triggered by a fight between two youths. And, of course, it may sometimes be inadvertent, resulting from innocent pranks that backfire.

In some instances, traumatic experiences in the life of a boy or girl appear to act as precipitating events (Coleman, 1973). In an early study of 500 delinquent boys, Clarke (1961) found that in about a third of the cases it was possible to isolate especially stressful events that had preceded the delinquency, such as death of parents, disruption of family life, or discovery that they had been adopted. These events had proved highly disorganizing and often had led to poor school performance, truancy, brooding, and—eventually—delinquent behavior.

Burks and Harrison (1962) also emphasized the importance of stress as a precipitating factor in some cases of aggressive antisocial behavior, pointing out that the stress functioned to undermine the youths' feelings of adequacy and worth. In an analysis of 4 case histories —involving arson, murder, and breaking and entering—Finkelstein (1968) found an "accumulation of emotional tensions [leading] at times to temporary disintegration, or at least to a state in which the person in full awareness of what he is doing loses his ego control" (p.

310). Bandura (1973), Patterson (1974), and other investigators have concluded that with rare exceptions involving unusual brain damage, children are not born violent but learn to be that way.

Dealing with delinquency

If they have adequate facilities and personnel, juvenile institutions and training schools can be of great help to youths who need to be removed from aversive environments and given a chance to learn about themselves and their world, to further their education and develop needed skills, and to find purpose and meaning in their lives. In such settings the youths may have the opportunity to receive psychological counseling, group therapy, and guided group interaction. Here it is of key importance that peer-group pressures be channeled in the direction of resocialization, rather than toward repetitive delinquent behavior. Behavior therapy techniques—based on the assumption that delinquent behavior is learned, maintained, and changed according to the same principles as other learned behavior—have shown marked promise in the rehabilitation of juvenile offenders who require institutionalization.[8] Counseling with parents and related environmental changes are generally of vital importance in the total rehabilitation program.

Probation is widely used with juvenile offenders and may be granted either in lieu of or after a period of institutionalization. In keeping with the trend toward helping troubled persons in their own environments, the California Youth Authority conducted the Community Treatment Project, a 5-year experiment in which delinquents—other than those involved in such crimes as murder, rape, or arson— were granted immediate probation and supervised and assisted in their own communities. The 270 youths treated in this project showed a rehabilitation success rate of 72 percent during a 15-month follow-up period. In contrast, a comparable group of 357 delinquents who underwent institutional treatment and then were

---

[8]A review of studies dealing with the application of behavior therapy to juvenile delinquency may be found in Davidson and Seidman (1974).

released on probation showed a rehabilitation success rate of only 48 percent (Blake, 1967). Since 90 percent of the girls and 73 percent of the boys committed to the California Youth Authority by juvenile courts were found eligible for community treatment, it would appear that many delinquents can be guided into constructive behavior without being removed from their family or community. It may be noted, however, that a key factor in the success of this pioneering research project was a marked reduction in the case load of supervising probation officers.

The recidivism rate for delinquents—the most commonly used measure for assessing rehabilitation programs—depends heavily on the type of offenders being dealt with as well as on the particular facility or procedures used (Roberts, Erikson, Riddle, & Bacon, 1974). The overall recidivism rate for delinquents sent to training schools has been estimated to be as high as 80 percent (*Time*, June 30, 1975). And since many crimes are committed by juveniles who have been recently released from custody or were not incarcerated after being arrested, a number of state legal officials have become advocates of stiffer penalties for some types of juvenile crime. Individuals who commit crimes of senseless violence or armed assault or who have a long history of arrests are more often being given harsher penalties than they were a few years ago (*Time*, July 11, 1977).

Institutionalization seems particularly questionable in the case of "juvenile status offenders," youths whose offenses have involved acts that would not be considered criminal if committed by an adult, such as running away from home or engaging in sexual relations. In such instances, institutionalization may aggravate behavioral problems rather than correct them. Mixing status offenders with delinquents or adults who have committed violent and antisocial offenses may simply provide them with unfortunate learning experiences in how to become more seriously delinquent.

On the other hand, failure to institutionalize delinquents who have committed serious offenses such as robbery, assault, and murder may be a disservice to both the delinquents and the public. In essence, it seems essential to correct the "bizarre lumping" of major felonies, minor misdemeanors, and trivial violations of social norms under the general label of "juvenile delinquency." This would enable many delinquencies to be dealt with by educational and social-work agencies rather than by the justice system. It would also make it possible for treatment programs to meet the needs of individual young people, and society's need for protection would be better met in the long run.

One key task in dealing with troubled youth is that of opening lines of communication with them. The behavior of even some of the most "hard-core" delinquent gangs has shown marked improvement when social workers or police officers have managed to win their confidence and respect. Often such personnel can help channel the youths' activities into automobile or motorcycle rallies and other programs that provide both recreational and learning opportunities. Too often, however, as in the case of institutional and probation programs, lack of trained personnel and other resources prevent such programs.

Fortunately, there is growing concern about the inadequacies of our correctional system for juveniles, and the federal government has established the Office of Juvenile Justice and Delinquency Prevention to foster these and related goals. The big need, of course, is not only for more effective rehabilitation programs, but also for long-range programs aimed at the prevention of delinquency. This would mean alleviating slum conditions, providing adequate educational and recreational opportunities for disadvantaged youth, educating parents, and delineating a more meaningful societal role for adolescents—tasks for the whole society.

Planning better programs to help children and youth

In our discussion of several problems of childhood and adolescence, we have noted the wide range of treatment procedures that may be used as well as marked differences in outcomes. In concluding our chapter, let us note

(a) certain special factors associated with the treatment of children, and (b) the new emphasis on the "rights of children," which involves a social commitment to provide conditions conducive to their optimal development.

Special factors associated with treatment for children

Among the special factors to be considered here are these:

1. *The child's inability to seek assistance.* The great majority of emotionally disturbed children who need assistance are not in a position to ask for it themselves, or to transport themselves to and from child guidance clinics. Thus, unlike the adult or the adolescent, who usually can seek help during crisis periods, the child is dependent, primarily on his or her parents. Adults must realize when a child needs professional help and must take the initiative in obtaining it for the child.[9] Many children, of course, come to the attention of treatment agencies as a consequence of school referrals, delinquent acts, or parental abuse of the child.

2. *"Double deprivation" for children from pathogenic homes.* Many families provide an undesirable environment for their growing children. In fact, studies have shown that up to a fourth of our children may be living in inadequate homes (Joint Commission on the Mental Health of Children, 1968; Rutter, 1977). Yet the care of the child is traditionally the responsibility of the parents, and local and state agencies intervene only in extreme cases—usually those involving physical abuse. This means that children growing up in pathogenic homes are at a double disadvantage. Not only are they deprived from the standpoint of environmental influence on their personality development, but they also lack parents who will perceive their need for help and actively seek and participate in treatment programs.

3. *The need for treatment of the parents as well as the child.* Since most of the behavior disorders specific to childhood appear to grow out of pathogenic family interactions, it is usually essential for the parents, as well as the child, to receive treatment. In some instances, in fact, the treatment program may focus on the parents entirely. (See HIGHLIGHT beginning on page 524.)

Increasingly, then, the treatment of children has come to mean family therapy, in which one or both parents as well as the child and siblings may participate in all phases of the program. For working parents, however, and for parents who basically reject the child, such treatment may be difficult to arrange, especially in the case of poorer families, who lack transportation as well as money. Thus, both parental and economic factors help determine which emotionally disturbed children will receive assistance.

4. *The possibility of using parents as "change agents."* A recent trend, as we have seen, has been to teach the parents to be change agents. In essence, the parents are trained in techniques that enable them to help their child. Typically such training focuses on helping the parents understand the child's behavior disorder and learn to reinforce adaptive behavior while withholding reinforcement for undesirable behavior. Encouraging results have been obtained with parents who care about their children and want to help (Arnold, 1978; Johnson & Katz, 1973; Lexow & Aronson, 1975; Mash et al., 1976; O'Dell, 1974; Atkeson & Forehand, in press).

5. *The problem of placing the child outside the family.* Most communities have juvenile facilities which, day or night, will provide protective care and custody for child victims of unfit homes, abandonment, abuse, neglect, and related conditions. Depending on the home situation and the special needs of the child, he or she will later either be returned to the parents or placed elsewhere. In the latter instance, four types of facilities are commonly relied on: (a) a foster home; (b) a private institution for the care of children; (c) a county or state institution; or (d) the home of relatives. At any one time, about half a million children are living in foster-care facilities.

The quality of the child's new home, of course, is a crucial consideration in determining whether the child's problems will be alleviated or made worse. Although efforts are

---

[9]In an effort to lessen this dependence on initiative by adults, the Minnesota State Legislature in 1971 enacted a law giving minors the right to seek medical, dental, and mental health treatment without the consent of a parent or legal guardian.

made to screen the placement facilities and maintain contact with the situation through follow-up visits, there have been too many reported cases of mistreatment of children placed in foster homes and institutions. Perhaps the most dramatic example of unintended harm from placement of children in foster homes was the large number of children who perished in the Jonestown murder-suicide in Guyana in 1978. These youngsters had been placed in the care of Reverend James Jones, who had received large amounts of money for their care.

In cases of child abuse or child abandonment or serious behavior problems of children that the parents cannot control, it has often been assumed that the only feasible action was to take the child out of the home and find a temporary substitute. With the children's own homes so obviously inadequate, the hope has been that a more stable outside placement would be better. But when children are taken from their own homes and placed in an impersonal institution that promptly tries to change them or in a series of foster homes where they obviously do not really belong, they are likely to feel rejected by their own parents, unwanted by their new caretakers or anyone else, rootless, constantly insecure—and lonely and bitter.

Accordingly, the trend today is toward *permanent planning*. First, every effort is made to hold the family together and give the parents the support and guidance they need to be adequate for childrearing. If this is impossible, then efforts are made to free the child legally for adoption and to find an adoptive home as soon as possible. This, of course, means that the public agencies need specially trained staffs with reasonable caseloads and access to the resources that the families they work with may need.

Following a demonstration in Oregon (see HIGHLIGHT on page 526) that when these conditions are met, 90 percent of a group of children in foster care could be either returned to their homes or placed for adoption, the Children's Bureau of HEW is doing all it can to encourage the agencies in the various states to move in this direction. Currently it is funding projects in several states to provide intensive support services to "families at risk" in order to prevent the need for outside placement by improving

HIGHLIGHT

The problem of child abuse in contemporary society

There is a growing concern about child abuse in the United States. Over 200,000 cases are reported each year, and undoubtedly many more cases go unreported (Kempe & Kempe, 1979; President's Commission on Mental Health, 1978).

Of the reported cases, 20 to 40 percent of the children have been seriously injured. Although children and adolescents of all ages are physically abused, the most frequent cases involve children under 3 years of age. There is some evidence that boys are more often abused than girls. It is usually clear that children brought to the attention of legal agencies for abuse have been abused before.

The seriousness of the problem of child abuse in our society was not realized until the 1960s, when researchers began to report case after case like the following two:

The mother of a 29-month-old boy claimed he was a behavior problem, beat him with a stick and screwdriver handle, dropped him on the floor, beat his head on the wall or threw him against it, choked him to force his mouth open to eat, and burned him on the face and hands. After she had severely beaten him, the mother found the child dead.

Because her 2¹/₂-year-old daughter did not respond readily enough to toilet training, the mother became indignant and in a fit of temper over the child's inability to control a bowel movement gave her an enema with near scalding water. To save the child's life a doctor was forced to perform a colostomy (Earl, 1965).

Since the 1960s there has been a great deal of research aimed at finding out which parents abuse their children and why, in the hope ultimately of stopping or better yet preventing parents from abus-

the quality of children's lives in their homes. It is hoped that these projects will both provide training for the staffs in the various state agencies in the special skills needed for this kind of help and increase acceptance of the principle of permanent planning.

6. *The importance of intervening early before problems become acute.* Over the last

ing their children. We now know that parents who physically abuse their children tend to be young, with the majority under thirty. In the majority of the reported cases, they come from the lower socio-economic levels, though this may only reflect the fact that these parents are more likely to be reported to legal authorities than middle-class parents.

An important common factor among families with abusing parents is a higher-than-average degree of frustration, with many stressors in their lives, including marital discord, high unemployment, and alcohol abuse (Egeland, Cicchetti, & Taraldson, 1976). Although no clear and consistent personality pattern emerges as typical of child-abusing parents, they seem to show a higher-than-average rate of psychological disturbance. There is some evidence from personality testing to show that they tend to be aggressive, nonconforming, selfish, and lacking in appropriate impulse control (Lund, 1975).

Knowledge about causal factors in child abuse is limited and incomplete since most studies have involved retrospective analysis of cases identified through legal agencies. However, in a study currently in progress, 275 families in a population generally at risk for child abuse were identified before the birth of the child. From this group, the investigators then identified the 25 mothers at highest risk for child abuse and the 25 mothers most likely *not* to be child abusers.

These two groups have now been followed over several years. Eight of the highest-risk group have actually abused their children; none of the other group has done so, and there are many striking differences between the two groups. The mothers in the group identified as at lowest risk tend to be older, to show more understanding of the psychological complexity of their child, to have better caretaking skills, and to show more positive feeling for their child. The other mothers, in general, live a more chaotic life. Over twice as many are single (74 percent as compared with 32 percent). They are also more involved in disrupted relationships, physical fights, and heavy drinking in the immediate family. Continuing analysis of how the quality of care, the nature of the mother-child interaction, and personality characteristics of family members relate to child abuse in this group is planned (Egeland & Brunnquell, 1979).

Several kinds of efforts are being made to reduce the incidence of child abuse:

1. Community education to increase public awareness of the problem. Television advertisements have been especially effective here.

2. Organization of child protection teams by many state and county welfare departments to investigate and intervene in reported cases of child abuse.

3. Teams of mental health specialists in many community mental health centers to evaluate and provide psychological treatment for both abused children and their parents.

4. Parent support groups, often made up of former child abusers, who can offer abusing parents or those at risk for child abuse alternative ways of behaving toward their children.

5. A legal requirement, in many communities, for physicians and other professionals to report cases of child abuse that come to their attention.

Through such efforts on many levels it is hoped that children will be spared abuse and that abusing or potentially abusing parents will be helped to be more adequate and nurturant.

twenty years, a primary concern of many researchers and clinicians has been to identify and provide early help for children who are at special risk. Rather than wait until these children develop acute psychological problems that may require therapy or major changes in living arrangements, psychologists are attempting to identify conditions in such children's lives that seem likely to bring about or maintain behavior problems and, where such conditions exist, to intervene before the child's development has been seriously distorted.

The Milwaukee Project (Heber et al., 1972) reported in Chapter 13 (p. 487), in which a group of children at risk for mental retardation were given special training throughout their first five years, was an example of this approach. Another is provided in the work of Wallerstein and Kelly (1979):

These researchers identified children who were at risk for psychological disturbance as a result of the fact that their parents were going through a divorce. Each of the 66 participating families was seen by a clinician, and the children were seen separately for several sessions. The goals of the counseling sessions were to provide the children with a means of expressing their worries and frustrations and to strengthen their resources for dealing with them.

In addition to the counseling sessions, there were several follow-up sessions after the divorce to examine the psychological changes in the children and the changes in the family structure over time. The interventions were judged to be successful in lowering the tension levels in the family situations and in enhancing the children's adjustment to their new living arrangements.

Such early intervention has the double goal of reducing the stressors in the child's life and strengthening the child's coping mechanisms. If successful, it can effectively reduce the number and intensity of later problems, thus avoiding much grief for both the individuals concerned and the broader society.

It is apparent that children's needs can be met only if there are adequate preventive and treatment facilities for children and if it can be ensured that the children who need assistance will receive it. In our final section, we will look at the leadership that government agencies have been providing in spotlighting the special needs of children and youth and discuss the responsibility of the society to meet them.

Child advocacy programs

Today there are nearly 60 million children and young people under 18 in the United States. This would indicate that a massive social commitment is needed not only to provide adequate treatment facilities for children with problems but also to provide the physical and social conditions that will foster the optimal development of all children.

Unfortunately, however, both treatment and preventive programs in our society have been—and remain—inadequate. In 1970 the National Institute of Mental Health (1970)

HIGHLIGHT

Freeing children for permanent placement

Placement in a foster home, intended as a temporary expedient, too often is the beginning of a period of drifting from one foster home to another, denying the continuity in human relationships that the child acutely needs. In Oregon, staff members at the Regional Research Institute for Human Services carried out a pilot project to see whether it would be possible to reduce the numbers of children in foster care and give them permanent homes—either with their own parents or through adoption.

The project involved 509 children who at the start were in foster placement and were considered unlikely to return home. These cases were turned over to specially trained caseworkers, who made intensive efforts to locate the parent or parents and encourage their taking the child back, offering help to enable them to do so. Each case required a great deal of effort on the part of the caseworker—including counseling, legal aid, and so on. Every means of encouragement was exhausted before the caseworker gave up and recommended that the child be placed for adoption.

Many of these parents developed new motivation for taking responsibility for their children as a result of the help and support offered by the caseworkers, and three years after the project started, 131 of the children had been returned to their parents. An additional 184 had been adopted, with another 15 in the homes of relatives and 37 in contractual foster care. And 92 other children were moving toward one of these options, leaving only a probable 50 of the original 509 children for whom no permanent home seemed likely. This means a success rate of 90 percent.

Besides the immeasurable benefit to the children of at last being in permanent homes, the financial saving to the welfare system was also considerable. It was estimated that 4000 hours of foster care—at a cost of more than $1 million—had been saved. This suggests that some of the money now committed for foster care could be better spent in enabling staff members to work toward permanent planning for these children.

Interestingly, the new approach was also reflected in the fact that, in the state as a whole, fewer children were being placed in foster homes. Although foster care placement will remain an important option in some cases, it is encouraging to know that with concentrated effort by skilled staff, many children can be saved from "foster home drifting."

Based on Regional Research Institute for Human Services (1978).

pointed out that fewer than 1 percent of the disturbed children in our society were receiving any kind of treatment, and less than half of these were getting adequate help. In the same year, in its final report, *Crisis in Child Mental Health: Challenge for the 1970s,* the Joint Commission on the Mental Health of Children (1970) referred to our lack of commitment to our children and youth as a "national tragedy." The Commission's report concluded,

"Either we permit a fifth of the nation's children to go down the drain—with all that this implies for public disorder and intolerable inhumanity—or we decide, once and for all, that the needs of children have first priority on the nation's resources" (p. 408).

Unfortunately, eight years later, the President's Commission on Mental Health (NIMH, 1978) was still calling attention to the fact that children and adolescents were not receiving mental health services commensurate with their need. The Commission's report recommended again that greater efforts and financial resources be expended to serve the mental health needs of children and youth. It appears, however, that the needed financial support and redirected program foci have not materialized. (See HIGHLIGHT beginning on page 528.)

There are stirrings, however. A new approach to meeting mental health needs, known as *advocacy,* has been developing in recent years. Advocacy attempts to help children or others receive services that they need but often are unable to obtain for themselves. For example, advocacy might involve representing a retarded or mentally ill individual at a commitment hearing. In some cases, advocacy seeks to better conditions for underserved populations by changing the system (Biklen, 1976).

Twice in recent years the federal government has established a National Center for Child Advocacy to coordinate the many kinds of work for children's welfare that were going on in different government agencies. Both times the new agency proved ineffective and was given up after a year or so. Currently the physical welfare of children is the responsibility of the Children's Bureau of the Labor Department, and the mental health needs of children are the responsibility of the Alcoholism, Drug Abuse, and Mental Health Administration of the Public Health Service. Delinquents are dealt with by the Justice Department. This fragmentation

in services for children means that different agencies serve different needs of children, and there is no government agency charged with considering the whole child and planning comprehensively for children who need help.

Outside the federal government, until recently, advocacy efforts for children have been supported largely by legal and special-interest citizens' groups, such as the Children's Defense Fund, a public interest child advocacy organization based in Washington, D.C. Mental health professionals have typically not been involved. Today, however, there is greater interdisciplinary involvement in attempts to provide effective programs of advocacy for children.

In the state of New Jersey, for example, a Division of Mental Health Advocacy has been formed especially to provide advocacy services for disturbed and mentally handicapped children in the state. The staff consists of 15 lawyers and 16 mental health professionals. The aim of the agency is to provide two kinds of advocacy service: *individual case advocacy*— help for individual clients in obtaining specific services or treatment—and *class advocacy,* in which the focus is on problems that are common to many children. An example of class advocacy would be establishing the right to treatment for a retarded child who is a ward of the state, in order to obtain better treatment programs for retarded children generally (Siggers, 1979). The improvement in the delivery of mental health services for children in New Jersey since this program was established argues persuasively for the involvement of mental health professionals in such advocacy efforts.

Unfortunately, although such programs have made important local gains toward bettering conditions for mentally disabled children, there is still a great deal of confusion, inconsistency, and uncertainty in the advocacy movement as a whole (Biklen, 1976). And the present mood at both federal and state levels seems to be to cut back on funds for social services.

Clearly, the challenge issued by the Joint Commission on the Mental Health of Children in 1970 has not been adequately answered over the subsequent decade, but some important beginning steps have been taken in the work toward child advocacy, the new efforts to identify and help high-risk children, and the pres-

The rights of children

At the international level, as within nations and local communities, goals for children are far ahead of realities. As early as 1924 the League of Nations adopted a declaration formulated the year before by the International Union for Child Welfare affirming the right of every child to a home and family. In 1959 —35 years later—the United Nations General Assembly adopted the comprehensive statement of children's rights reprinted here. But like the UN's *Declaration of Human Rights*, it remains a statement of principles—a recognition of needs that the international community has not yet figured out how to meet.

A third of the world's burgeoning population are under 15; in some countries the proportion is over 40 percent. This poses an impossible problem for a poor country going through massive social and economic changes and eager for twentieth-century benefits that does not have adequate health services, education, and income-producing industries. There is no way that the rest of the population of such a nation can take adequate care of such a large dependent group—much less make progress toward "development."

Yet with no retirement benefits and with a high infant mortality rate, parents keep having many children in the hope that some will survive to care for them in their old age. Not until living conditions improve and infant mortality goes down can we expect the birth rates in such nations to slow appreciably. Meanwhile, throughout the world, it is the children who suffer most from poverty in warped physical and mental growth and lack of opportunity to meet their potential.

Designation of the year 1979 as the International Year of the Child, marking the 20th anniversary of *Declaration of the Rights of a Child*, was an attempt to heighten awareness of the special problems of children and the short-sightedness of the terrible waste of human potential that is being permitted throughout the world. But there was no International Conference or other focus for mobilization of effort or public education. So the International Year of the Child may be seen as the international community's recognition of the great unmet problems of the world's children—but also of the general unreadiness to do more at this time than acknowledge the need and the ideal. (The graphic symbol for the International Year of the Child, a child reaching up to be embraced, is shown opposite.)

Declaration of the Rights of a Child

. . . *The General Assembly proclaims this Declaration of the Rights of the Child to the end that he may* *have a happy childhood and enjoy for his own good and for the good of society the rights and freedoms herein set forth, and calls upon parents, upon men and women as individuals and upon voluntary organizations, local authorities and national governments to recognize and strive for the observance of these rights by legislative and other measures progressively taken in accordance with the following principles:*

Principle 1. The child shall enjoy all the rights set forth in this declaration. All children, without any exception whatsoever, shall be entitled to these rights, without distinction or discrimination on account of race, color, sex, language, religion, political or other opinion, national or social origin, property, birth or other status, whether of himself or of his family.

Principle 2. The child shall enjoy special protection, and shall be given opportunities and facilities, by law and by other means, to enable him to develop physically, mentally, morally, spiritually and socially in a healthy and normal manner and in conditions of freedom and dignity. In the enactment of laws for this purpose the best interests of the child shall be the paramount consideration.

Principle 3. The child shall be entitled from his birth to a name and a nationality.

Principle 4. The child shall enjoy the benefits of social security. He shall be entitled to grow up and develop in health; to this end special care and protection shall be provided both to him and to his mother, including adequate prenatal and post-natal care. The child shall have the right to adequate nutrition, housing, recreation and medical services.

Principle 5. The child who is physically, mentally or socially handicapped shall be given the special treatment, education and care required by his particular condition.

Principle 6. The child, for the full and harmonious development of his personality, needs love and understanding. He shall, wherever possible, grow up in the care and under the responsibility of his parents, and in any case in an atmosphere of affection and of moral and material security; a child of tender years shall not, save in exceptional circumstances, be separated from his mother. Society and the public authorities shall have the duty to extend particular care to children without a family and those without adequate means of support. Payment of state and other assistance toward the maintenance of children of large families is desirable.

Principle 7. *The child is entitled to receive education, which shall be free and compulsory at least in the elementary stages. He shall be given an education which will promote his general culture, and enable him on a basis of equal opportunity to develop his abilities, his individual judgment and his sense of moral and social responsibility, and to become a useful member of society.*

The best interests of the child shall be the guiding principle of those responsible for his education and upbringing; that responsibility lies in the first place with his parents.

The child shall have full opportunity for play and recreation, which should be directed to the same purposes as education; society and the public authorities shall endeavor to promote the enjoyment of this right.

Principle 8. *The child shall in all circumstances be among the first to receive protection and relief.*

Principle 9. *The child shall be protected against all forms of neglect, cruelty and exploitation. He shall not be the subject of traffic, in any form.*

The child shall not be admitted to employment before an appropriate minimum age; he shall in no case be caused or permitted to engage in any occupation or employment which would prejudice his health or education or interfere with his physical, mental or moral development.

Principle 10. *The child shall be protected from practices which may foster racial, religious and any other form of discrimination. He shall be brought up in a spirit of understanding, tolerance, friendship among peoples, peace and universal brotherhood and in full consciousness that his energy and talents should be devoted to the service of his fellow men.*

*Adopted by the General Assembly of the United Nations.

ent push toward permanent planning for children formerly sent to institutions or foster homes—the attempt to prevent outside placement if possible and, if not, to work toward adoption for the child. If the direction and momentum of these efforts can be maintained and if sufficient financial support for them can be procured, the next ten years could show substantially more gain in improving the psychological environment for children.

In this chapter we first looked at some of the differences in maladaptive behavior in different life periods, focusing on the special characteristics of childhood disorders. We then examined the clinical picture, causal factors, and treatment and likely outcomes in hyperactive (hyperkinetic) syndrome, unsocialized disturbance of conduct, anxiety and withdrawal disturbances, autism, stuttering, several other symptom disorders, and finally, in somewhat greater detail, the problem of delinquency.

We concluded the chapter by noting some of the special problems associated with the treatment of childhood behavior disorders, by commenting on the seeming lack of needed commitment to the welfare of children and youth in our society, and by briefly noting the encouraging trend toward child advocacy programs.

15

Sexual dysfunctions and variants

Sexual dysfunctions
Victimless sexual variants
Sexual variants involving nonconsent or assault
Treatment and outcomes

At lower levels on the phylogenetic scale of animal life, reproductive processes are not sexual and seem to be essentially preprogrammed and more or less "automatic." The individuals of a species show very little individuality or variation in their reproductive functioning.

As we move up the scale, reproduction becomes sexual in nature, thus becoming more complicated in requiring the cooperation and mutual participation of two or more organisms having differentiated roles in the procreative process. By the time we reach the level of the higher animals, we see the reproductive process richly infused with elements of behavioral distinctiveness: individuals differ considerably in their sexual behavior and show selectivity in choosing mates. Sexual functioning also incorporates other behavioral characteristics, such as aggressiveness in the case of males.

This expansion of the repertoire of reproductive behavior continues up to the human level, but the gap between humankind and even the highest of the other animals is a huge one. It is paralleled only in the advantage humans enjoy in intellectual power by virtue of their possession of conceptual language.

Several dimensions of variation underlie this phylogenetic progression in reproductive behavior. The most important of these, for our concerns, is the increasing freedom from rigidly programmed, instinctual, stereotyped forms of sexual behavior as we move up the scale. The freedom of the human female from recurrent, biologically based cycles of "heat" and nonreceptivity is but one example of this enhanced flexibility and independence from controlling neurobiological mechanisms. Of perhaps even greater importance is the enormously increased adaptability in human sexual needs themselves, as a result of their partial disengagement from their primary biological base. With a loosened connection between sex and procreation at the human level, sexual behavior is no longer simply the expression of instinct but has become at least as much a matter of *learned* patterns of attraction, activity, and consummation. To put it another way, human sexuality has to a large extent come under the control of "higher" neural processes.

These gains in flexibility and adaptability of the sexual functions have come at some cost. Nature is almost necessarily wise, at least in the long run; human cultures may or may not be. The varieties of human sexuality do indeed encompass an enormous range when compared with what is found for any species at a lower level, and much of the variation adds zest and richness to our lives, enhances our happiness, and intensifies our loves. But sexuality at the human level is also much more likely to go awry, causing profound misery for the individuals involved and for those close to them. This chapter is concerned with such "abnormalities" of human sexuality. They fall naturally into two distinct classes, the sexual *dysfunctions* and the sexual *variants*. Some of the sexual variants are basically "victimless," while others involve nonconsent or force.

Human societies have generally exhibited a kind of "double vision" regarding sexual behavior: on the one hand, there is typically a rather elaborate code limiting sexual behavior and directing that sexual acts shall encompass only certain narrowly defined "proprieties," while on the other there is an informal expectation, mostly followed in practice, that these limits will be regularly and routinely exceeded by at least the more venturesome of the society's members. It is only in recent times, thanks in large part to the pioneering work of Kinsey and his associates (1948, 1953), that we have come to understand how widespread and extreme are the personal problems with sexuality and the deviations from formal propriety within our own culture.

Sexual dysfunctions

The term *sexual dysfunction* refers to impairment either in the desire for sexual gratification or in the ability to achieve it. With but few exceptions, such impairments occur in the absence of anatomical or physiological pathology and are based on faulty psychosexual adjustment and learning. They vary markedly in degree and, regardless of which partner is alleged to be dysfunctional, the enjoyment of sex by both parties in the relationship is typically adversely affected.

Like sexuality in general, sexual dysfunctions of one sort or another were until recently either ignored entirely by polite society or—if discussed at all—were the subject of turgid medical treatises written by authors who were usually as ill informed and prejudiced as their readers. Then, with the popularization of Freud, there came an era in which all such difficulties in sexual functioning (and some that were not even "difficulties" in the normally accepted sense) were ascribed to unconscious conflicts of childhood origin—requiring years of psychoanalytic treatment for their resolution. We now know, thanks again to courageous work—chiefly by Masters and Johnson (1966, 1970, 1975)—that the common sexual dysfunctions are both more numerous and considerably less complex and mysterious than had once been believed. We shall first describe several of the most common ones and then discuss issues of causation and treatment.

Dysfunctions affecting the male

Here we shall briefly discuss several dysfunctions that may affect the male: erectile insufficiency, premature ejaculation, retarded ejaculation, and ejaculatory incompetence.

Erectile insufficiency. Inability to achieve or maintain an erection sufficient for successful sexual intercourse—formerly known as *impotence*—is known clinically as *erectile insufficiency*. In *primary insufficiency*, the male has *never* been able to sustain an erection long enough to accomplish a satisfactory duration of penetration—usually defined as including intravaginal ejaculation. In *secondary insufficiency*, the male has had a history of at least one successful attempt at coitus but is presently unable to produce or maintain the required level of penile rigidity. Primary insufficiency is a relatively rare disorder, but it has been estimated that half or more of the male population has experienced the secondary variety on at least a temporary basis, especially in the early years of sexual exploration.

Prolonged or permanent erectile insufficiency before the age of 60 is rare and almost always due to psychological factors. In fact, according to the findings of Kinsey and his associates, only about one-fourth of males become impotent by the age of 70 and even here

many cases are due to psychological factors. More recent studies have indicated that men and women in their 80s and 90s are quite capable of enjoying sex (Burros, 1974; Kaplan, 1975; Masters & Johnson, 1975).

Premature ejaculation. Often psychologically related to erectile insufficiency, premature ejaculation refers to an unsatisfactorily brief period between the commencement of sexual stimulation and the occurrence of ejaculation, the most serious result being the failure of the female partner to achieve satisfaction. Exact definition of prematurity is not possible, however, because of pronounced variations in both the likelihood and the latency of female orgasm in sexual intercourse. LoPiccolo (1978) suggests that an inability to tolerate as much as four minutes of stimulation without ejaculation is a reasonable indicator that the male may be in need of sex therapy. This suggested guideline is subject to numerous qualifications, however, including the age of the client—the alleged "quick trigger" of the younger male being more than a mere myth.

Retarded ejaculation or ejaculatory incompetence. It is of some interest that, while problems of female orgasmic dysfunction have received wide attention in the popular press, one rarely hears public mention of the corollary problem in males. It is as though there were a conspiracy of silence concerning the matter. As a result many males suffering from late ejaculation or inability to ejaculate during intercourse are condemned to worry needlessly about their supposedly unique defect, a type of worry likely to worsen the problem. In fact, relatively few cases of ejaculatory retardation or incompetence are seen by sex therapists, but our own clinical experience suggests that the problem is much more widespread than this observation would seem to indicate. It appears that many men are too embarrassed by the problem even to contemplate therapy for it.

Dysfunctions affecting the female

Somewhat paralleling the male sexual dysfunctions are arousal insufficiency, orgasmic dysfunction, vaginismus, and dyspareunia in women.

Arousal insufficiency.

This dysfunction, formerly and somewhat pejoratively referred to as *frigidity*, is in many ways the female counterpart of erectile insufficiency. Not uncommonly, it is accompanied by complaints of an absence of sexual feelings and of being unresponsive to most or all forms of erotic stimulation. Its chief physical manifestation is a failure to produce the characteristic lubrication of the vulva and vaginal tissues during sexual stimulation, a condition that may make intercourse quite uncomfortable.

Orgasmic dysfunction.

Many women who are readily sexually excitable and who otherwise enjoy sexual activity nevertheless experience greater or lesser difficulty in achieving orgasm. Of these women, many do not routinely experience orgasm during sexual intercourse without direct stimulation of the clitoris; indeed this pattern is so common that it can hardly be considered dysfunctional. A small proportion of women are able to achieve orgasm *only* through direct mechanical stimulation of the clitoris. Even fewer are unable to have the experience under any known conditions of stimulation; the latter condition is called *primary orgasmic dysfunction*, analogous to primary erectile insufficiency in the male. The diagnosis of orgasmic dysfunction is complicated by the fact that the subjective quality of orgasm varies widely among females and within the same female from time to time, making precise evaluations of occurrence and quality difficult (Singer & Singer, 1978).

Vaginismus.

An involuntary spasm of the muscles at the entrance to the vagina that prevents penetration and sexual intercourse is called *vaginismus*. In some cases, women who suffer from vaginismus also have arousal insufficiency, possibly as a result of conditioned fears associated with a traumatic rape experience; in other cases, however, they are sexually responsive, but are still afflicted with this disorder. This form of sexual dysfunction is relatively rare.

Dyspareunia.

"Dyspareunia" means *painful coitus*; it can occur in the male but is far more common in the female. This is the form of sexual dysfunction most likely to have an organic basis—for example, in association with infections or structural pathology of the sex organs. However, it often has a psychological basis, as in the case of women who have an aversion to sexual intercourse. This form of sexual dysfunction is also rare.

Causal factors in sexual dysfunction

Both sexual desire and genital functioning may be affected by a wide range of organic conditions including injuries to the genitals, disease, fatigue, excessive alcohol consumption, and abuse of certain drugs, including tranquilizers. Most cases of sexual dysfunction, however, seem traceable to psychosocial rather than physical causes. Although specific causal factors vary considerably from one type of sexual dysfunction to another, the following psychosocial factors are commonly found.

Faulty learning.

In some nonindustrialized societies, older members of the group instruct younger members in sexual techniques before marriage. But in our society, though we recognize that sexual behavior is an important aspect of marriage, the learning of sexual techniques and attitudes is too often left to chance. The result is that many young people start out with faulty expectations and a lack of needed information or harmful misinformation that can impair their sexual adequacy. In fact, Kaplan (1974) has concluded that couples with sexual problems are typically practicing insensitive, incompetent, and ineffective sexual techniques; this conclusion would be readily endorsed by most investigators in the field (LoPiccolo & LoPiccolo, 1978).

In our society many people, but perhaps especially females, have been subjected to early training that depicted sexual relations as lustful, dirty, and evil. The attitudes and inhibitions thus established can lead to a great deal of anxiety, conflict, and guilt about sexual relations, whether in or out of marriage. Faulty early conditioning may also have taken the form of indoctrination in the idea that the woman has a primary responsibility to satisfy the man sexually—and therefore to suppress her own needs and feelings. Masters and Johnson (1970) consider such faulty learning to be the primary cause of orgasmic dysfunction in females. In vaginismus a somewhat different conditioning patterning has occurred, leading the female to associate vaginal penetration with pain—either physical, psychological, or both. This defensive reflex comes into operation when penetration is attempted by the sexual partner (Kaplan, 1975).

Although males may also be subjected to early training emphasizing the evils of sex, such training apparently is a far less important factor for them. However, another type of faulty early conditioning was found by Masters and Johnson (1970) to be a key factor in premature ejaculation in males: a first sex experience with a prostitute or in a lovers' lane parking place or some other situation in which hurried ejaculation was necessary. Apparently, once this pattern was established, the individual had been unable to break the conditioned response. In other instances, initial difficulties in sexual functioning have led to conditioned anxieties which in turn have impaired subsequent performance. We shall elaborate on this point in the section that follows.

Feelings of fear, anxiety, and inadequacy.

In a study of 49 adult males with an erectile disorder, Cooper (1969) found anxiety to be a contributing factor in 94 percent of the cases and the primary problem for those whose erectile problems had started early. Similarly, Kaplan (1974) has concluded from her studies that "a man who suffers from impotence is often almost unbearably anxious, frustrated, and humiliated by his inability to produce or maintain an erection" (p. 80). Males who suffer from premature ejaculation may also experience acute feelings of inadequacy—and often feelings of guilt as well—stemming from their lack of control and inability to satisfy their sexual partner via intercourse.

Females may also feel fearful and inadequate in sexual relations. A woman may be uncertain whether her partner finds her sexually attractive, and this may lead to anxiety and tension that interfere with her sexual enjoyment. Or she may feel inadequate because she is unable to have an orgasm or does so infrequently. Sometimes a woman who is not climaxing will pretend to have orgasms in order to make her sexual partner feel that his

performance is fully adequate. The longer a woman maintains such a pretense, however, the more likely she is to become confused and frustrated; in addition, she is likely to feel resentful toward her partner for being so insensitive to her real feelings and needs. This, in turn, only adds to her sexual problems.

From a more general viewpoint, Masters and Johnson (1975) have concluded that most sexual dysfunctions are due to crippling fears, attitudes, and inhibitions concerning sexual behavior, often based on faulty early learning and then exacerbated by later aversive experiences. All this may lead to the adoption of a "spectator role" in sexual relations, rendering wholehearted participation impossible.

Interpersonal problems.

Interpersonal problems may cause a number of sexual dysfunctions. Lack of emotional closeness can lead to erectile or orgasmic problems. The individual may be in love with someone else, may find his or her sexual partner physically or psychologically repulsive, or may have hostile and antagonistic feelings as a result of prior misunderstandings, quarrels, and conflicts. A one-sided interpersonal relationship—in which one partner does most of the giving and the other most of the receiving—can lead to feelings of insecurity and resentment with resulting impairment in sexual performance (Friedman, 1974; Lobitz & Lobitz, 1978; Simon, 1975).

For the female, lack of emotional closeness often appears to result from intercourse with a partner who is a "sexual moron"—rough, unduly hasty, and concerned only with his own gratification. As Kaplan (1974) has pointed out,

"Some persons have as much difficulty giving pleasure as others do in receiving it. These individuals don't provide their partners with enough sexual stimulation because they lack either the knowledge and sensitivity to know what to do, or they are anxious about doing it." (p. 78)

In other instances the individual may be hostile toward and not want to please his or her sexual partner. This seems to occur rather frequently in unhappy and failing marital or other intimate relationships in which channels of communication have largely broken down and sexual relations continue as a sort of habit or duty or simply to gratify one's own sexual needs.

Many investigators feel that an individual should be able to experience pleasure and orgasm with any personally acceptable partner, providing, of course, that the individual has no emotional commitment to some other person. However, Switzer (1974) has aptly pointed to a generally agreed-on conclusion: "Orgasm has especially delightful overtones when you're with a person whom you love and when you can abandon yourself" (p. 36).

Changing male-female roles and relationships.

There was an increase in erectile problems during the 1970s which a number of investigators have related to two phenomena during that period: (a) the increasing changes being achieved by the women's movement in our society, and (b) the growing awareness of female sexuality (Burros, 1974). These trends have led women to want and expect more from their lives, including their sexual relationships. Women are no longer accepting the older concept of being the passive partner in sex, and many are taking a more aggressive and active role in sexual relations.

This new role appears to threaten the image many men have of themselves as the supposedly "dominant" partner who takes the initiative in sexual relations (Steinmann & Fox, 1974). In fact, some men appear to regard sexually assertive women who play an active role in sex as "castrating females" (Kaplan, 1974). In addition, the greater assertiveness and expectancy of women makes many men feel that they are under pressure to perform. As Ginsberg, Frosch, and Shapiro (1972) have expressed it,

"This challenge to manhood is most apparent in a sexually liberated society where women are not merely available but are perceived as demanding satisfaction from masculine performance." (p. 219)

The result may be not only impaired male performance but even erectile failure.

Changing male-female roles in sexual relationships also place greater demands on the female. The expectation of taking an active rather than a passive role may cause the female to make unrealistic demands on her own sexual responsiveness—such as expecting to have a highly pleasurable orgasm each time she engages in sexual relations. Such demands are likely to lead to some degree of un-

fulfilled aspirations, confusion, and self-devaluation, which in turn impair her actual sexual performance. This seems especially true when the female assumes a "spectator's role" and almost literally monitors her own sexual performance—thus depriving it of spontaneity and naturalness.

Homosexuality and other factors.

In some cases, sexual development takes a homosexual direction, and erotic desires come to be focused on members of one's own sex, with corresponding absence of erotic interest in members of the opposite sex. Although most male and female homosexuals seem able to achieve sexual gratification with members of either sex, some homosexuals seem able to achieve gratification only in homosexual relations, particularly during periods in their lives when their homosexual commitment is quite strong. Such individuals also may show an impairment in sexual adequacy in homosexual relationships if their commitment to this sexual pattern wanes.

Another condition that may lead to sexual inadequacy is a low sex drive; sometimes it is difficult to distinguish between persons with low sex drive and those who are actually dysfunctional. Cooper (1969) found that where erectile problems developed during later adulthood they came after a progressive decline in sexual interest and performance over months or years. In these cases, anxiety developed only after the disorder had become established, and thus appeared to be the result, rather than the cause, of the disorder.

Another possible causal factor in sexual dysfunction is a rejecting and disturbed family background that makes it difficult for the individual to give and receive affection in intimate interpersonal relationships. And as we noted in earlier chapters, sexual dysfunction is also common in cases of depression, schizophrenia, and other maladaptive behavior.

Treatment and outcomes

The treatment of sexual dysfunctions has undergone nothing less than a revolution during only the past few years. Once regarded as very difficult and intractable therapeutic challenges, most instances of sexual dysfunction now yield quite readily to programs of treatment involving new techniques that are still being developed and improved (LoPiccolo & LoPiccolo, 1978). As a result, success rates approaching 90 percent or more for many dysfunctions have become quite routine.

The turning point is uniformly considered to be the publication in 1970 of Masters and Johnson's *Human Sexual Inadequacy,* the product of an eleven-year search to develop truly effective treatment procedures for the common dysfunctions, both male and female. The carefully documented success rates claimed by this team of dedicated clinical researchers astonished the professional community and rapidly led to the widespread adoption of their general approach, which combines elements of traditional and behavioral therapy in a framework emphasizing direct intervention aimed at the dysfunction itself (see HIGH-LIGHT on page 537). Despite differences in emphasis and methods in different treatment programs, there seems to be general agreement on the importance of removing crippling misconceptions, inhibitions, and fears, and fostering attitudes toward and participation in sexual behavior as a pleasurable, natural, and meaningful experience.

Because of the manner in which sexual dysfunctions are presented and described by those suffering from them, it is easy to lose sight of a crucial issue emphasized by Masters and Johnson and by virtually all those who have followed in their footsteps. That is, sexual dysfunctions are *not* normally disorders of individuals, but rather of relationships between individuals. Thus, the new treatments for sexual dysfunction typically involve *both* parties to the relationship in which the disorder manifests itself, confirming in part the old adage that there are no "frigid" women apart from inept or clumsy men. J. LoPiccolo (1978) puts it this way:

"It must be stressed that all sexual dysfunctions are *shared disorders;* that is, the husband of an inorgasmic woman is partially responsible for creating or maintaining her dysfunction, and he is also a patient in need of help. Regardless of the cause of the dysfunction, both partners are responsible for future change and the solution of their problems." (p. 3)

With competent treatment, success rates vary between 60 and 100 percent, depending in part on the individual or couple and on the nature of the problem. For example, Masters and Johnson (1970) and Kaplan (1975) have reported success rates approaching 100 percent in the treatment of premature ejaculation and vaginismus, but considerably lower rates in the treatment of male erectile and female orgasmic dysfunctions. However, the term "competent" should be stressed here, since there are several thousand sex clinics in the United States, and the quality of treatment may range from sophisticated psychotherapy to sheer charlatanism. Indications are strong, in fact, that unqualified practitioners have entered this field in abundance in recent years, often charging astronomical fees for their inexpert services.

Victimless sexual variants

Our view of ourselves as male or female, the social demands made upon us for playing our expected sexual role, our concept of what sexual behavior is appropriate, and our anticipation of what will be exciting and pleasurable—all these are learned, and they help determine the sexual practices we develop as adults. And through conditioning, almost any object or situation can become sexually stimulating—particularly among preadolescents and adolescents—including erotic literature, sex scenes in plays and films, pictures of nude or partially nude individuals, and underclothing or other objects intimately associated with members of the opposite sex. Sexual arousal may also accompany strong emotional reactions—such as fear and excitement—especially if associated with the performance of some forbidden act.

Given the many channels that human sexual interests may take, especially when for some reason the usual patterning has become blocked, it is hardly surprising that many persons find their principal sexual satisfactions in

Treatment of sexual dysfunction

Masters and Johnson, widely known for their studies of sexual response and their therapeutic approach to problems of sexual inadequacy, are pictured counseling a couple at their clinic in St. Louis—the Reproductive Biology Research Foundation. These investigators have concluded from their research efforts (1970) that some 50 percent of American marriages suffer from sexual inadequacy, a factor they consider largely responsible for our high divorce rate. In their view, sexual inadequacy is a form of faulty communication which probably extends to other areas of a couple's relationship as well; consequently, their treatment program is oriented toward improving communication in a marriage and preventing it from being wrecked by ignorance and faulty attitudes about sex.

Stressing the concept that sex is an experience that both partners must enter into without reservation or shame, Masters and Johnson insist that fears or anxieties that either partner may have concerning intercourse—pressures that can turn it into a dreaded "command performance"—must be eliminated. In addition, they treat the married couple as a unit rather than as separate individuals.

Generally, the following steps appear to be basic to the treatment program of Masters and Johnson as well as to that of other prominent sex clinics: (a) a thorough medical examination to rule out the possibility of organic causes of the sexual dysfunction; (b) *sensate focus*—learning to experience pleasure in caressing each other's bodies and genitals while temporarily abstaining from intercourse; and (c) prescribed sexual experiences and therapy sessions. Beyond these basic principles, the formats employed by various major sex clinics vary considerably.

For the majority of couples participating in Masters and Johnson's treatment program, it appears that a change is effected in attitudes, feelings, and communication, and that sexual relations become an intimate, normal, and desirable experience. Five-year follow-up studies of 510 married couples and 57 unmarried men and women revealed that the program's rate of failure varied markedly with the type of sexual inadequacy—from zero for cases of vaginismus and 2.2 percent for cases of premature ejaculation to 40.6 percent for cases of primary ejaculatory insufficiency. Overall, the failure rate in treatment was only 20 percent.

Early experiences may shape our ideas and expectations about sex, perhaps determining the pattern of later sexual behavior.

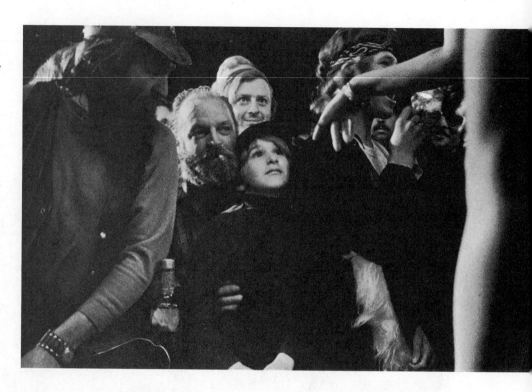

practices outside the range of what is considered acceptable in the given culture. The sexual drive is normally sufficiently powerful to override all but the most severe social sanctions; thus we see variant sexual needs frequently erupting into variant sexual behavior.

Variant sexual behavior is behavior in which satisfaction is dependent primarily on something other than a mutually desired sexual engagement with a sexually mature member of the opposite gender. So defined, the domain encompasses a vast array of preference patterns in which the psychosexual development of the affected individual has for some reason deviated from the standard, to-be-expected adult heterosexual course.

The specter of sexually variant behavior seems peculiarly threatening to many people in our society, and expressions of tolerance for such behavior as homosexuality, for example, can arouse intense emotion. It is certainly true that some forms of sexual variation, such as rape and child molestation, are contrary to the welfare of society and its members. Other forms, however, are generally victimless and thus constitute no obvious, rationally based threat to the public order. For this reason, we

will discuss separately the victimless variants and the patterns that involve varying degrees of nonconsent and assault—physical or psychological or both.

A key point—one particularly emphasized by Barlow (1974)—deserves mention at the outset. In considering these behaviors, we tend to focus our attention on the variant arousal patterns themselves to the exclusion of other, perhaps equally important factors that may help cause or maintain the variant behavior. Other factors that must often be given equal weight in most forms of variant sexuality are (a) the absence of a normal level of arousal to adults of the opposite sex; (b) significant deficits in the social skills normally needed for successful adult heterosexual relationships; and (c) failure to establish a firm psychological gender identity.

A good illustration of the importance of this broadened view for both understanding and therapy is provided in findings of several studies on therapy for homosexual individuals who wanted to change their arousal pattern. Adams and Sturgis (1977), reviewing the evidence, concluded that multiple-target treatment procedures aimed at the three factors mentioned above plus the variant arousal pattern greatly enhanced the likelihood of success of sexual reorientation therapy, as compared with approaches focused only on suppression of the variant sexual arousal pattern.

Male and female homosexuality

Homosexual behavior is sexual behavior directed toward a member of one's own sex; it is generally referred to as "lesbianism" for female relationships. Homosexuality has existed throughout recorded history and among some peoples has been tacitly accepted. The ancient Greek, Roman, Persian, and Moslem civilizations all condoned a measure of homosexuality, and the practice increased as these civilizations declined. In later Greece and Rome, for example, homosexual prostitution existed openly. In fact, it was quite popular for Roman matrons to engage in lesbian activities with their slaves. There is no evidence, however, that homosexuality was an important contributing factor in the decline of these civilizations, as some critics have charged (NAMH, 1971).

In Elizabethan England, an attitude of permissiveness was taken toward homosexuality without apparent harmful effects; in contemporary England, legislation has been passed making it legal for two consenting adults to engage privately in homosexual acts. Most cultures, however, have condemned homosexuality as socially undesirable. In the Netherlands and Denmark, for example, there are no laws against homosexuality, but it is strongly disapproved of (Weinberg & Williams, 1974).

In our own society, homosexual persons— particularly males—are still sometimes arrested and imprisoned under "crimes against nature" statutes as well as being subject to various forms of social disapproval and discrimination. Nevertheless, homosexuals may be otherwise well adjusted, well educated, and highly successful in their occupations. Many have made outstanding contributions in music, drama, and other fields. Not a few of the notable figures of history—including Alexander the Great, Sappho, Michelangelo, Oscar Wilde, Peter Tchaikovsky, Gertrude Stein, and Virginia Woolf—are thought to have been homosexuals.

Continuum of sexual behavior. Contrary to popular opinion, it is not possible to divide people into two clear-cut groups—homosexual and heterosexual. Rather, these two labels signify extreme poles on a continuum; in between, we find many individuals whose experiences and desires combine both heterosexual and homosexual components. Kinsey et al. (1948), in one of the first extensive studies of male homosexuality, found that of their white male subjects,

13 percent had reacted erotically to other males without having overt homosexual experiences after the onset of adolescence.

37 percent had had homosexual experience to the point of orgasm after the onset of adolescence.

50 percent of those who remained unmarried to the age of 35 had had overt homosexual experience to the point of orgasm since the onset of adolescence.

18 percent revealed as much of the homosexual as the heterosexual in their histories.

8 percent engaged exclusively in homosexual activities for at least three years between the ages of 16 and 55.

4 percent were exclusively homosexual from adolescence on.

Since the men in this study had volunteered to be interviewed, these figures may have been somewhat higher than for the general population. Homosexual relationships were found to be far less common among women and, of those reporting homosexual responses, only about a third had proceeded to the point of orgasm (Kinsey et al., 1953).

Recent investigators have concluded, however, that lesbianism is more common than previous data would indicate, and that homosexuality is on the increase among both males and females. However, the apparent increase may simply reflect our national climate of greater openness toward sex. As Hoover (1973) has pointed out, "No one is sure whether more women are becoming lesbians now or whether they are just more visible" (p. 9).

If we can assume that the number of homosexuals has not changed drastically since Kinsey's studies were made, something in excess of 2.6 million men and 1.4 million women in the United States are exclusively homosexual. If we add those who are exclusively homosexual during a period of several years in their lives or who consistently engage in homosexual acts even though they are not exclusively homosexual, the overall figure for men and women would probably exceed some 20 million persons. The most detailed information that we have about the physical aspects of homosexuality have been provided by Masters and Johnson (1979); their conclusions are summarized in the HIGHLIGHT on page 541.

Are homosexuals "sick"?

In our society, heterosexuality has been regarded as the "appropriate" mode of sexual behavior, while homosexuality has traditionally been seen as a mental disorder. Homosexuals have been regarded as "sick" persons in need of treatment.

However, research findings indicate that homosexuals usually manifest no more evidence of personality maladjustment than would be expected in any matched sample of heterosexuals (Bell, 1974; Freedman, 1975; Hooker, 1957; Thompson, McCandless, & Strickland, 1971; Weinberg & Williams, 1974). Somewhat curiously, nevertheless, data from a large sample of homosexuals, gathered several years ago but only recently made public, indicate a high rate of *self-diagnosed* maladjustment (Bell & Weinberg, 1978). Possibly this self-view reflected acceptance of the stereotype of the larger culture. In any case, it is by no means certain that researchers would find the same attitudes among current homosexuals of the "gay liberation" era.

The view of homosexuality as a mental disorder has been challenged by an increasing number of psychologists and psychiatrists. The trustees of the American Psychiatric Association voted to drop homosexuality from the official list of mental disorders in the DSM-II; on December 14, 1973, homosexuals were considered mentally disordered sexual deviants, but on December 15, 1973, they were no longer so considered. In effect, the millions of "gay" people in our society underwent an "instant cure" as a result of a vote by the trustees of the American Psychiatric Association!

To add to this somewhat bizarre tale, efforts were instituted almost immediately by a group of conservative psychiatrists to get homosexuality put back on the books as a mental disorder. The results of their lobbying efforts appear in DSM-III, where homosexuality is considered a mental disorder if the person is distressed about his or her homosexuality and would pre-fer to be more heterosexual—a condition called *ego-dystonic homosexuality*. The controversy over treating ego-dystonic homosexuality is discussed in the HIGHLIGHT on page 542.

Types of homosexuals.

Perspectives shared by members of the "straight" community concerning homosexuals are often unduly influenced by stereotypes arising from acquaintance with a limited range of homosexual life-styles—especially the more salient and "obvious" ones. As far as can be determined, the vast majority of homosexually oriented persons lead lives that are entirely unremarkable except for their preference of sexual partners. For example, the sexual orientation of large numbers of homosexual college students remain unknown to their campus friends and even their roommates, although in recent years there has been a trend on many campuses to encourage public "coming out." We summarize in the following sections the various kinds of homosexual adjustments that have been described in the pertinent literature and then discuss in some detail the most common variety—the "adjusted homosexual."

1. *"Blatant" homosexuals.* Here we are dealing with individuals who fit the popular stereotype of the homosexual—the lisping, limp-wristed, swishing caricature of femininity, in the case of the male. His lesbian counterpart, called a "dyke," "stud," or "butch," flaunts her masculinity, even to the point of trying to look like a man. Also included in this category are the "leather boys," who advertise their sadomasochistic homosexuality by wearing leather jackets, chains, and boots. Some transvestites, or "TVs"—individuals who enjoy wearing the clothes and often assuming the behavior of the opposite sex—fit in this category, too. However, as we shall see, many transvestites are not homosexuals, and in fact most homosexuals are not transvestites.

2. *"Desperate" homosexuals.* The so-called desperate homosexuals are males who tend to haunt public toilets ("tearooms") or steam baths, apparently driven to homosexual behavior but unable to face the strains of establishing and sustaining serious personal relationships in which to practice homosexuality. In his study of the "tearoom trade," Humphreys (1970) referred to such behavior as "impersonal sex in public places" and pointed

The Masters and Johnson perspective on homosexuality

In a recently published book, Masters and Johnson (1979) have provided new information on homosexuality and have offered new hope to individuals who wish to alter their sexual orientation. The publication of this book was awaited impatiently not only because Masters and Johnson are the acknowledged contemporary leaders in research into sexuality and its problems, but also because it promised to bring to the study of homosexuality the same objectivity based on precise physiological and behavioral measurement that characterized their earlier studies of heterosexual individuals.

Most of the data for this book were collected prior to 1968 from a sample of 176 "committed homosexuals"—94 men and 82 women—ranging in age from 21 to 54. The sexual performances of these individuals were compared with those of 681 heterosexual partners. Masters and Johnson acknowledge that their findings may be unrepresentative in two ways: (1) their volunteer samples may not be a true cross-section of people in general; and (2) in ways that are not discernible, sex in the laboratory may differ from sex in more accustomed surroundings. Nevertheless, their data are probably the best that can currently be obtained. Their study focused on the bodily processes in homosexual relations and they have little to say about causal factors except to emphasize the importance of learning in the development of this preference. Their major findings may be summarized as follows:

1. Among persons selected for "sexual efficiency," homosexuals and heterosexuals have about the same low rate of failure to achieve orgasm: 3 per 100 opportunities.

2. Heterosexual sex fantasies are common among homosexual lovemakers, and many heterosexual persons occasionally indulge in homosexual fantasies.

3. Homosexual lovers generally communicate better than their heterosexual counterparts concerning sexual needs and sources of satisfaction; they are less preoccupied with achieving orgasm and more aware of the partner's level of arousal. In lesbian lovemaking particularly, a large amount of time is devoted to foreplay, and breast stimulation does not enter into the lovemaking sequence until much later than is common in heterosexual lovemaking.

4. While the data on sexual fantasies are limited to only 132 cases and may thus be especially lacking in generalizability, certain interesting trends emerge. The theme of forced sex was a more popular fantasy for the homosexuals than for the heterosexuals and tended to be fantasied about in more violent terms. When heterosexual women fantasied about forced sex, which has been found by many researchers to be quite common, they tended to imagine being treated gently and admiringly—although without choice—by their attackers. Among lesbians, on the other hand, fantasies tended to involve revenge upon some other woman, in which attackers humiliated the woman while the fantasier looked on in enjoyment.

5. In a separate (and later) series of 54 homosexual men and 13 lesbians who wished to undergo reorientation therapy, the known failure rate for the treatment devised by Masters and Johnson stood at 35 percent; and it is not expected to exceed 45 percent when the five-year follow-ups have been completed. This finding is of considerable theoretical importance and, of course, offers hope to those who desire reorientation therapy.

out that barring unusual developments, "an occasionally whispered 'thanks' at the conclusion of the act constitutes the bulk of even whispered communication" (p. 13).

Of the subjects in Humphreys' study, 54 percent were married. Apparently the "tearoom" is used by many such individuals in an effort, through the anonymity of these contacts, to conceal their homosexuality from their wives—and perhaps even from themselves. Humphreys cited the case of a successful businessman who visited "tearooms" almost daily:

"I guess you might say I'm pretty highly sexed (he chuckled a little), but I really don't think that's why I go to tearooms. That's really not sex. Sex is something I have with my wife in bed. It's not as if I were committing adultery by getting my rocks off—or going down on some guy—in a tearoom. I get a kick out of it. Some of my friends go out for handball. I'd rather cruise the park. Does that sound perverse to you?" (p. 19)

3. *Secret homosexuals.* Although members of this group range across all class and racial lines, they tend to come from the middle class and to hold positions that they try to protect by concealing their homosexuality. Often they are married, wear wedding rings, and have spouses and employers who never know about their double lives. They are extremely skilled at camouflage and at "passing" as straight. They generally prefer subdued clothes and maintain a suitably conservative appearance.

Since they do not frequent "tearooms" or "gay bars," they may continue their homosexual behavior unsuspected throughout their adult lives. Only a few close friends, their lovers, and occasionally their psychotherapists know about their homosexuality. However, living in continuing fear of detection and possible social sanctions often adds to their adjustive problems. It appears that an important aim of the gay liberation movement, emphasizing as it does the desirability of allowing gays to "come out of the closet" with impunity, is to eradicate these anxiety-producing sanctions.

4. *Situational homosexuals.* There are a variety of situations in which individuals engage in homosexual behavior without any deep homosexual commitment. Both males and females may engage in homosexuality in prisons and other institutions, for example, but they usually resume heterosexual behavior on their release. Some prisoners act as homosexual prostitutes. Such individuals may not have homosexual inclinations themselves but may merely engage in homosexual practices for economic advantage.

Davis (1968) has also cited instances of homosexual rape among male prisoners in sheriff's vans, detention centers, and prisons. Typically, such assault involved anal intercourse, and apparently it is perpetrated by individuals or gangs who do not consider themselves homosexuals but are attempting to assert dominance and masculinity—motivation typical of the heterosexual rapist as well. Except in penal institutions, however, force appears rare in homosexual activity.

5. *Bisexuals.* Individuals who engage in both homosexual and heterosexual practices during a sustained period of their lives are considered "bisexual." Many "desperate homosexuals" would fit into this category, particularly those who are married.

The occurrence of bisexuality is not surprising, since homosexuality is not necessarily an all-or-nothing pattern and, as we have seen,

HIGHLIGHT

Should homosexuality be "treated"?

The question of whether homosexual persons should receive therapy to change their sexual orientation has been one of the key issues in the intense controversy over whether homosexuality is a personality disorder or only a normal sexual variant. In recent years a number of therapy programs have developed in which the explicit purpose is that of "reorienting" the sexual needs of homosexual individuals; many of these programs employ aversive conditioning techniques to suppress or eradicate the homosexual arousal pattern. Since the existence of treatment strongly implies that the condition being treated is undesirable, if not pathological, many supporters of the gay liberation movement object to treatment programs for homosexuality.

This issue has been forcefully brought to the attention of psychologists and other mental health professionals by Davison (1976, 1978), a leading researcher in the development of the new therapies for sexual difficulties. Davison argues that the very existence of sexual reorientation treatment programs strengthens prejudices against homosexual individuals and increases their self-hatred and embarrassment. Therefore, he concludes, the only ethical course is to stop offering this type of treatment—even to those individuals who voluntarily seek it.

Sturgis and Adams (1978) have taken the opposing position, arguing that the question of whether homosexuality is abnormal is entirely irrelevant to the question of whether an individual seeking treatment should have access to it. Sturgis and Adams charge that Davison's position will cause therapists to impose their own values—in this case, the belief that homosexuals should not receive treatment—on clients who may not share these values. For Sturgis and Adams, then, the primary issue is that of the "right to treatment" of those homosexual individuals who desire reorientation therapy. Davison (1978) acknowledges that his position is value-based, but he contends that values are the central consideration in the controversy. He also states that therapists have no absolute responsibility to provide what clients may request.

It seems likely that sexual reorientation programs will continue to be offered to those who request such treatment. In the meantime, the spirited exchange between researchers has sharpened the issues and has provoked a wide-ranging reexamination of attitudes within the professional community.

differing arousal patterns may be at least partially independent of one another. Weinberg and Williams (1974) found that about 1 gay male in 5 described himself as being significantly heterosexual as well. A given individual may have any combination of high or low arousability to homosexual and heterosexual erotic stimuli.

As contrasted with men who were exclusively homosexual, bisexual males were found by Weinberg and Williams (1974) to be more concerned about passing as heterosexual, to have less identification with the gay community, and to feel more guilty and anxious about their homosexual behavior. However, these investigators did not find bisexuals to be "marginal men"—to be suffering from psychological problems as a consequence of confusion about their sexual identity or lack of integration into the heterosexual or homosexual worlds. Rather, they seemed quite capable of adapting to their bisexual life-style.

In understanding these various patterns of homosexuality, it is useful to note the conclusion of Weinberg and Williams (1974) that " 'homosexual' can refer to a number of things—inclination, activity, status, role, or self-concept—and that a person need not be equally 'homosexual' in all respects. Thus, we find a variety of combinations of being homosexual which include some of these factors and exclude others, for example, hustlers who engage in homosexual activity but deny the self-concept, the married man who has the inclination but does not act on it, and so forth." (p. 208)

6. *Adjusted homosexuals.* The majority of homosexuals accept their homosexuality, fulfill responsible social roles, and closely associate with the gay community. We have previously pointed to research findings suggesting that, as a group, homosexuals evidence no more personality maladjustment than do heterosexuals. In their extensive study of male homosexuals, Weinberg and Williams (1974), too, failed to find any major differences in psychological well-being between homosexuals and the male population in general. And although there is little available research evidence, this finding would appear to apply to lesbians as well, when compared to the general female population (Ohlson, 1975).

Many homosexuals establish an intimate and stable relationship with one other person.

More and more homosexuals are openly proclaiming their sexual preferences and demanding an end to discrimination and harassment.

While this is more common among lesbians than among male homosexuals, the pattern is by no means exclusive to lesbians. For example, the findings of the Institute for Sex Research at Indiana University indicated that slightly over half of the male homosexual subjects were currently involved in an "affair," and half of these, in turn, were definitely "coupled" (Bell & Weinberg, 1978). A minority of such couples enter into a "homosexual marriage," often performed in a church ceremony by a homosexual minister, but generally without a marriage license.

Similarly, Jensen (1974) found that in the "real" world, as contrasted with controlled environments such as prisons and related institutional facilities,

"female homosexuals often form relatively long-lasting relationships with other female homosexuals with whom they share the same interests. When this relationship includes a common residence and economical cooperation as well as sexual relations, the marital union is established. . . . Other single homosexuals watch these unions closely, talk about them, sanction their conduct, and envy them, while at the same time hoping their own desire of finding a permanent, satisfying partner will materialize. By the way of illustration, when one of the unions was dissolved, all of the subjects in that town were concerned and disappointed. They visited the partner who was mistreated and tried to console her for her loss." (p. 366)

As in the case of male homosexuals, female homosexuals may exchange rings and marital vows in formal ceremonies. However, some homosexuals apparently consider such marriages a phony attempt to emulate the straight world.

In general, it would appear that lesbians place greater emphasis on the quality of their interpersonal relationship and less on its sexual aspects, while male homosexuals tend to place greater emphasis on the sexual aspects of their relationships—in this sense paralleling the male role in the traditional straight society. Interestingly enough, the findings of the Institute for Sex Research indicate that promiscuous gays and promiscuous straights are more like each other than they are like other members of their own groups (Bonnell, 1974).

In our discussion of the adjusted homosexual, it is relevant to note that special stresses are associated with the gay life-style. Thus, association with the supportive and protective institutions of the gay community appears to be an important aspect of coping with the stresses of a homosexual life-style.

The "gay community."   Broadly speaking, the gay community may be described as a

geographical area in which the homosexual subculture and its institutions are located. Thus the apartment buildings on certain streets may be rented exclusively to homosexuals; most of the homes in certain areas may be owned by homosexuals; clothing stores, bookstores, theaters, and other business establishments may cater primarily to homosexual clientele; and a variety of recreational facilities and groups, including ski and travel clubs, may be exclusively homosexual in their membership. In addition, there are churches, welfare organizations, service centers, and so on, for homosexuals. In essence, the homosexual community constitutes a subculture with unique customs, value systems, communication techniques, and supportive and protective institutions.

The cornerstone of the gay community, however, is the "gay bar"; it is also the most visible section of the homosexual community in the sense that any person may enter. In major cities, such as Los Angeles, New York, and San Francisco, there are relatively large numbers of such bars; for example, the Los Angeles area has more than 200 gay bars, the majority of which are for male homosexuals. In these bars friends are met, news and gossip exchanged, invitations to parties issued, and warnings about current police activities circulated. However, the crucial function of the bars, as is often the case with those that cater to heterosexual clientele, is to facilitate making sexual contacts. Typically, these contacts are between strangers, who agree to meet at a certain time and place for sexual purposes. Their relationship is usually transitory, and subsequently each is likely to find a new partner. A central feature of such relationships is the assumption that sexual gratification can be had without obligation or a long-term commitment. When asked what it means to be "gay," one man answered,

"To be gay is to go to the bar, to make the scene, to look, and look, and look, to have a one night stand, to never really love or be loved, and to really know this, and to do this night after night, and year after year." (Hooker, 1962, p. 9)

As we have noted, however, this viewpoint is not characteristic of the majority of homosexuals, but rather of those who find sexual variety of primary importance in their homosexual life-style.

As might be expected, there are many kinds of gay bars to serve both general and specific homosexual populations.

In a more general sense, the homosexual community is characterized by overlapping social networks of varying degrees of cohesiveness. There are, for example, loosely knit friendship groups and tightly knit cliques formed of homosexually married couples or of individuals who often are heterosexually married. In addition, there are organizations concerned with establishing and protecting the rights of homosexuals; of these, the best known are probably the Mattachine societies for male homosexuals, the first having been founded in Los Angeles in 1950 and named after sixteenth-century Spanish court jesters who wore masks. On the female side are the equally well-known Daughters of Bilitis, whose name is taken from *The Songs of Bilitis*, nineteenth-century lyrics that glorify lesbian love. There are also a number of other organizations and facilities, such as the Gay Community Service Centers, oriented primarily toward helping homosexuals deal with the practical problems associated with the gay life-style.

In general, homosexuals who are affiliated with the gay subculture—as well as most who are not—view homosexuality as an alternative sexual pattern or life-style and feel entitled to the same rights and protections as any minority group in society.

The question of causal factors. Proportionately there is far more research effort being devoted to trying to explain the development of homosexual than heterosexual life-styles, the latter usually being taken for granted as normal and natural. Thus, it is hardly surprising that many homosexuals feel subjected to discriminative and devaluating scrutiny. Nevertheless, since psychology is concerned with understanding human behavior—including alternative life-styles—it seems appropriate to comment briefly on possible conditions that may contribute to the development of the homosexual life-style.

While some investigators view biological factors as playing the key role in the development of homosexual behavior, a much larger number stress the importance of psychosocial and more general sociocultural factors. In this context, Money and Ehrhardt (1972) have described sexual differentiation as somewhat like a relay race—except instead of trying to beat other teams, the race is designed to complete a program.

Initially the XX or XY chromosomes pass the baton to the undifferentiated gonad to determine its destiny as ovary or testis. The gonad then differentiates and passes the baton to the hormonal secretion of its cells, and the process of fetal differentiation into the anatomy of a male or female continues. By birth, the first part of the program is completed. After birth, the baton is passed to environmental variables that play a determining role in shaping the individual's gender identity—usually, but not always, in accordance with his genetic sex.

Thus the initial part of the program is filled in by prenatal events, and the final part of the program by postnatal environmental ones, focusing primarily on learning. However, it is quite possible for the prenatal part of the program to markedly influence postnatal sexual differentiation. In any event, translated into actual sexual behavior, the total program may lead to heterosexual, bisexual, or homosexual patterns or life-styles (Adapted from Money & Ehrhardt, 1972).

1. *Genetic and hormonal factors.* Although Kallmann (1952) reported a 100 percent concordance rate for homosexuality in identical twins as contrasted with only 15 percent for fraternal twins, more recent investigators have not been able to corroborate the view that homosexual tendencies are inherited (Rosenthal, 1970).

Early research also led many investigators to conclude that homosexuality resulted from an abnormal androgen-estrogen ratio. Later studies, however, have failed to support these early findings (Tourney, Petrilli, & Hatfield, 1975). Furthermore, even in the occasional instances where hormonal imbalances do occur, they may have no causal significance: nonhomosexuals often show similar imbalances; individuals may shift from a homosexual to a heterosexual pattern or vice versa without a change in hormone balance; and treatment with sex hormones to change endocrine balance does not modify the direction of sexual behavior.

Nevertheless, the extensive research of Money and his associates (1969, 1972, 1974) provides a convincing demonstration of the effects of too little or too much male hormone during critical stages of fetal development on later sexual differentiation. For example, they cite examples of genetic females exposed to excessive androgen during fetal development. Although raised as girls, their behavior was "masculinized" in various ways as contrasted to the behavior of a control group of girls not exposed to excessive androgens. Presumably if the significant adults in the early postnatal environment of these androgenized girls provided unclear models or communicated unclear messages with respect to male and female sex identity, these girls *might* be more likely than girls in general to become homosexual. Similarly, genetic males exposed to insufficient prenatal androgen and subjected to an ambivalent postnatal environment concerning sexual identity *might* be more likely than males in general to become homosexual.

One of the basic hypotheses underlying the work of Money and his associates (1969, 1972, 1974) is that prenatal or early postnatal hormonal influences may actually affect the formation of brain pathways, leading to propensities toward a relatively masculine or feminine behavioral orientation. Evidence of such influences would not necessarily show up in hormonal imbalances at a later time. Their data are sufficiently strong that one would be ill-advised to dismiss this somewhat exotic conception out of hand. Should it prove to hold up under further scrutiny, it may provide a key to understanding some aspects of the development not only of homosexuality but also of other gender-role variants as well, such as transsexualism.

A great deal of research has also been done on supposed differences in the levels of plasma testosterone in homosexual and nonhomosexual males (Brodie et al., 1974; Kolodny et al., 1971). However, studies have produced widely varying results as to these alleged differences, and no agreement has been reached on the possible reasons for these discrepant findings.

2. *Homosexual experiences and their positive reinforcement.* The development of homosexuality is frequently associated with pleasant homosexual experiences during adolescence or early adulthood. In an early study of 79 male homosexuals, East (1946) found

early homosexual experiences to be the most common environmental factor. More recent studies have tended to support this finding. In a study of 65 lesbians, for example, Hedblom (1973) found that two-thirds engaged in their first homosexual contact before the age of 20 and had been willing and cooperative partners. Forty percent of the total group achieved orgasm at the time of their first homosexual experience.

In spite of these findings, it seems doubtful that early homosexual experiences lead to later homosexual life-styles except where they are reinforced by pleasurable repetition and/or meet the individual's emotional needs. This kind of emotional support is described in the following excerpt from the case of an adolescent girl who first entered into homosexual behavior in a correctional institution for delinquent girls.

"I have a girl, a simply wonderful girl. . . . I need her. . . . I feel better toward all people. I feel satisfied. Now I have somebody to care for. Now I have somebody I want to make happy and somebody I will work hard for. . . ." (Konopka, 1964, p. 23)

3. *Negative conditioning of heterosexual behavior.* A variety of circumstances may lead to conditioning in which heterosexual behavior becomes an aversive stimulus. For example, where a boy or girl is ridiculed, rebuffed, and humiliated in an early effort to approach members of the opposite sex, homosexuality may seem a safer source of affection and sexual outlet. If parents catch their son "playing with" a little girl and punish him for being "bad," they may be subtly telling him that heterosexual behavior is evil. Early sexual relations under unfortunate conditions may have a comparable effect. Konopka (1964) concluded: "Girls who have been raped by their fathers (and they are not rare among delinquent girls) find relationships with men either threatening or disgusting and often turn to other girls for the fulfillment of their emotional need for love" (p. 23).

Similarly, findings in the large-scale study of homosexuals by the Institute for Sex Research showed that some lesbians had shifted from heterosexual to homosexual behavior after disillusionment with their heterosexual partners; conversely, some lesbians shifted to heterosexuality after disillusionment with the gay life (Bell & Weinberg, 1978). It was also noted that more than a third of the gay females and 20 percent of the gay males had been married. In fact, the great majority of the subjects in this study had had heterosexual relationships prior to adopting a gay life-style.

4. *Family patterns.* A great deal of research attention has been given to the role of family relationships in the development of homosexuality. In a study of 106 male homosexuals who were undergoing psychoanalysis, Bieber et al. (1962) found a common family pattern involving a dominant, seductive mother and a weak or absent father. Typically the mother, frustrated by an unhappy marital relationship, established a relationship with the son that became seductive and romantic but stopped just short of physical contact. The son, overstimulated sexually, felt anxious and guilty over his incestuous feelings, and the mother, aware of his feelings and fearful of exposing her own incestuous impulses, discouraged overt signs of masculinity. The father, resenting the son as a rival, also made it clear that the son's developing masculinity was offensive. Often the father showed preference for a daughter, and the son, in envy, wished he were a girl. Bieber et al. described the end result as follows:

"By the time the H-son has reached the preadolescent period, he has suffered a diffuse personality disorder. Maternal overanxiety about health and injury, restriction of activities normative for the son's age and potential, interference with assertive behavior, demasculinizing attitudes and interference with sexuality—interpenetrating with paternal rejection, hostility, and lack of support—produce an excessively fearful child, pathologically dependent upon his mother and beset by feelings of inadequacy, impotence, and self-contempt. He is reluctant to participate in boyhood activities thought to be potentially physically injurious—usually grossly overestimated. His peer group responds with humiliating name-calling and often with physical attack which timidity tends to invite among children. His fear and shame of self, made worse by the derisive reactions of other boys, only drive him further away. . . .

"Failure in the peer group, and anxieties about a masculine, heterosexual presentation of self, pave the way for the prehomosexual's initiation into the less threatening atmosphere of homosexual society, its values, and way of life." (pp. 316–17)

Considerable doubt has been cast on the findings of Bieber et al. since the subjects studied were patients in psychoanalysis, the retrospective nature of many of the questions required the subjects to think back over several years for answers, and a high degree of inference was used in interpreting the data. On the other hand, the findings of several later investigators have generally supported the findings of Bieber and his associates (Evans, 1969; Snortum et al., 1969; Stephan, 1973; Thompson, Schwartz, McCandless, & Edwards, 1973). Typically the mothers were close-binding, controlling, and affectionate; the fathers were detached, rejecting, and often hostile. Neither parent fostered a masculine self-image or identity. As children, the male homosexuals in these studies tended to describe themselves as shy, fearful of physical injury, and loners who seldom entered into "rough" competitive sports such as baseball, basketball, or football.

In contrast, Siegelman (1974) examined the family constellation described by the preceding investigators among gay and nongay males and found that it did not distinguish among them; rather it was indicative of neuroticism or other psychopathology in both groups. Similarly, the well-designed Institute for Sex Research study has failed to turn up any consistent differences in the family backgrounds of homosexuals as compared with heterosexuals (Bell, 1974; Bell & Weinberg, 1978).

Although family patterns may create a wide range of adjustment problems and even severe maladjustment, there are insufficient research data to justify the conclusion that the family background of homosexuals as a group is significantly different from that of heterosexuals.

5. *General sociocultural factors.* It would appear that a variety of sociocultural factors, including the specificity of expected role behavior and the severity of social sanctions for deviations, may markedly influence the incidence of homosexual and other unconventional sexual life-styles. For example, Davenport (1965) has described the sexual mores of the Melanesians in the Southwest Pacific. Premarital intercourse is forbidden among them, and both males and females are encouraged to masturbate. In addition, all unmarried males engage in homosexual relations with the full knowledge of the community, but after marriage they are expected to assume a heterosexual pattern—a transition they appear to have little difficulty in making.

It would also appear that among certain

nonindustrialized groups living in areas with limited resources, homosexuality has actually been encouraged at one time or another to help control the population of the group; in other instances it has been encouraged among soldiers—as at one time in Greece and in the French Foreign Legion—because it was thought they would fight more fiercely to protect their lovers (Churchill, 1967). In any event, it seems clear that social inhibitions and reinforcements can markedly influence the incidence of homosexuality.

Homosexuality and society.   Since the general adjustment problems of homosexuals result in part from the self-devaluation fostered by society, the discrimination directed toward them, and the severe sanctions society often imposes on them, many investigators have urged the legalization of homosexual acts between consenting adults in private. For example, a task force of the National Institute of Mental Health concluded their report as follows:

"We believe that most professionals working in this area—on the basis of their collective research and clinical experience and the present overall knowledge of the subject—are strongly convinced that the extreme opprobrium our society has attached to homosexual behavior, by way of criminal statutes and restricted employment practices, has done more social harm than good and goes beyond what is necessary for the maintenance of public order and human decency." (Livingood, 1972, pp. 5–6)

As noted earlier, the centuries-old laws against homosexuality in England were repealed by Parliament in 1967, making homosexual acts between consenting adults in private none of the law's business. In the United States, Illinois in 1961 was the first state to repeal existing statutes against homosexual acts between consenting adults in private, followed by Connecticut, Oregon, Colorado, Hawaii, Delaware, Ohio, and California in the 1970s. Recently, a number of municipalities in this country have been the scene of often bitter struggles over the civil rights of homosexually oriented persons—including, for example, the issue of being allowed to teach in public schools. Unfortunately, these debates have often descended to patently absurd levels, as with the charge that male homosexuals are

cannibals because they swallow sperm, alleged to be the "most concentrated form" of human flesh. Such a charge is perhaps a measure of the amount of excess and extraneous emotion generated in many people by the increased assertiveness of organized homosexual groups.

While the long-range effects of such changes on society remain to be ascertained, there is no evidence to date that they have led to a significant increase in homosexuality or have proven detrimental to the general welfare. And, in general, heterosexual interests seem to remain alive and well through it all, so we need have little fear that our species will be decimated by rampant homoeroticism.

Transvestism and transsexualism

Both transvestism and transsexualism are in a general sense related to but essentially different from male homosexuality and lesbianism, and, proportionately, their incidence is relatively rare. However, it is instructive to examine these patterns briefly as part of our total picture of alternative sexual life-styles.

Transvestism.   Transvestism involves the achievement of sexual excitation by dressing as a member of the opposite sex. It is an uncommon condition in which the individual, usually a male, enjoys excursions into the social role of the other sex. Although a male transvestite, for example, regards himself as a man when dressed as a man, he may have feelings of being a woman when dressed in women's clothing. A medical researcher and transvestite himself for 35 years expressed it this way: "The transvestite finds that he is both a 'he' and a 'she' together—at the same time or alternating from one to the other when opportunity permits or desire compels" (*Los Angeles Times*, September 30, 1973).

Very little is known about transvestism. Most reports are based on studies of single cases, and most of those studied have been in therapy, which may make them an unrepresentative group. However, Buckner (1970) has formulated a description of the "ordinary" male transvestite from a survey of 262 transvestites conducted by the magazine *Transvestia*.

For many transvestites the switching of sex roles is a private matter; for others it is part of a more flamboyant life-style.

"He is probably married (about two thirds are); if he is married he probably has children (about two thirds do). Almost all of these transvestites said they were exclusively heterosexual—in fact, the rate of 'homosexuality' was less than the average for the entire population. The transvestic behavior generally consists of privately dressing in the clothes of a woman, at home, in secret. . . . The transvestite generally does not run into trouble with the law. His cross-dressing causes difficulties for very few people besides himself and his wife." (p. 381)

The most extensive studies to date of the personalities of male transvestites are those of Bentler and Prince (1969, 1970) and Bentler, Shearman, and Prince (1970). These investigators obtained replies to a standardized psychological inventory from a large sample of transvestites through the cooperation of a national transvestite organization. The transvestites, in comparison with matched control groups, showed no gross differences on neurotic or psychotic scales. However, they did present themselves as being more controlled in impulse expression, less involved with other individuals, more inhibited in interpersonal relationships, and more dependent.

It would appear that much transvestism can be explained in terms of a simple conditioning model. A male child may receive attention from females in the family who think it is cute for him to dress in feminine attire and hence reinforce this behavior with attention and praise. Such a conditioning process is well portrayed in the case of an adult transvestite studied by Stoller (1974):

"I have pictures of myself dressed as a little girl when I was a small child. My mother thought it was cute. She was right. I was a pretty little girl.

"The highlights of my life as a girl came when I was between the ages of 10 and 17. I had an aunt who was childless and wanted to take me through the steps from childhood to young womanhood. She knew of my desires to be a girl. I would spend every summer at her ranch. The first thing she would do was to give me a pixie haircut, which always turned out pretty good since I would avoid getting a haircut for two months before I went to her ranch. She then would take me into the bedroom and show me all my pretty new things she had bought me. The next day, dressed as a girl, I would accompany her to town and we would shop for a new dress for me. To everyone she met, she would introduce me as her 'niece.'

"This went on every year until I was 13 years old. Then she decided I should start my womanhood. I will never forget that summer. When I arrived I got the same pixie haircut as usual but when we went into the bedroom there laid out on the bed was a girdle, a garter belt and bra, size 32AA, and my first pair of nylons. She then took me over to the new dressing table she had bought me and slid back the top to reveal my very own makeup kit. I was thrilled to death. She said she wanted her 'niece' to start off right and it was about time I started to develop a bust.

"The next morning I was up early to ready myself for the usual shopping trip to town, only this time it was for a pair of high heels and a new dress. I remember I stuffed my bra with cotton, put on my garter belt, and slipped on my nylons with no effort. After all, I became an expert from practice the night before. My aunt applied my lipstick because I was so excited I couldn't get it on straight. Then off to town we went, aunt and 'niece.' What a wonderful day. I shall never forget it." (pp. 209–210)

The adult transvestite who marries faces problems that are well brought out in another case reported by Stoller (1974):

" 'We fell in love and as soon as I felt we could we were married. We have been as happy as two people can be and the best part of it is that she knows all about me and not only accepts me as I am but assists in my transformation and then admires me. . . .'

"This is the way the relationship looks at first, when the wife is pleased to see her husband's femininity. She does not know yet that as he becomes a more successful transvestite her enthusiasm will wane. Then he will be hurt that she is no longer interested in his dressing up, his sexual needs, his work. The fighting will start, neither will understand what has happened, and they will divorce." (p. 212)

Transsexualism. The transsexual is a person who feels trapped in a body of the opposite sex. Case histories of transsexuals indicate that their cross-gender identity began in childhood and continued into adulthood (Green, 1974; Money & Ehrhardt, 1972; Sabalis et al., 1974). The male-to-female transsexual, the most common variety, normally goes through stages of homosexuality and transvestism before arriving at the decision to seek sex-change surgery (Driscoll, 1977). As we have noted, several investigators have pointed out that gender identity does not automatically correspond to one's physical sex, but in most cases appears to be established early by experience —probably during the first 18 months of life— and is highly resistant to change thereafter.

In rare cases, when external genitalia are ambiguous or inconsistent with the genetic sex of the child, errors in sex assignment are made at birth. When such errors are discovered after approximately 18 to 36 months of age, the wisest course is often that of rearing the child in a manner consistent with the erroneous sex assignment. Reassignment after this age becomes increasingly difficult and is fraught with dangers to the psychological equilibrium of the child. Fortunately, surgical and endocrinological techniques exist for bringing external body structure into line with assigned sex, although male-to-female conversions are in these instances much more satisfactorily accomplished than those in the opposite direction; a functional vagina may be surgically fabricated, but there is no known means of creating artificially a fully serviceable penis.

Efforts to alter gender identity by means of behavior therapy and other psychotherapeutic procedures have generally proven unsuccessful. As a consequence, transsexuals who feel a complete inability to accept their sex identity have requested surgical sex change in increasing numbers during recent years.

The first transsexual operation is said to have been performed by F. Z. Abraham in the 1930s. While occasional reports of similar operations were forthcoming for the next two decades, it was not until 1953, when Hamburger reported the case of Christine Jorgensen, that surgical sex change became well known. Johns Hopkins Hospital and the University of Minnesota Hospital were among the first in this country to give official support to sex-change surgery; each has since received thousands of requests from individuals for evaluation and management of their cases.

In males, modern surgical procedures accomplish sex conversion through removal of male organs and their replacement with an artfully designed vagina that apparently works satisfactorily in many cases, even enabling the individual, now a woman, to achieve coital orgasm. Weekly injections of sex hormones stimulate breast development, give more feminine texture to the skin, and also lessen beard growth, though electrolysis is usually needed to remove excess hair. Surgery for female transsexuals generally has been less successful, for although surgeons can remove the breasts, ovaries, vagina, and uterus, and can insert a penis constructed from rib cartil-

Transsexual James Morris, an English writer and mountain climber, resolved the conflict between biological and perceived sex through a sex-change operation. Now Jan Morris, she has written a book entitled Conundrum *describing the transformation.*

age or plastic, the penis, as we have seen, does not function normally. Transplants of reproductive organs are not yet possible in either males or females, and the individual will be sterile after surgery.

Various evaluative studies of the outcome of such operations have been reported. One of the best known early studies is that of Benjamin (1966). This investigator questioned 50 transsexuals who had crossed the sex line from male to female. Their ages at the time of surgery ranged from 19 to 58, with an average age of 32. Of these subjects, 44 reported contentment sexually and socially with their new roles as women; 5 complained either about their ability to perform sexually or about their appearance; and 1 was totally dissatisfied with the results. In another study, Pauly (1968) reviewed the postoperative course of 121 male transsexuals who had received sex-reassignment surgery, and found that satisfactory outcomes outnumbered unsatisfactory ones at a ratio of 10 to 1. He also reported previous unsuccessful attempts by psychotherapy to help these patients achieve male-gender identity. Comparable re-

sults have been reported in later studies (Green, 1974).

There has been considerable controversy about sex-conversion surgery, however, and many physicians, as well as other professional persons, remain opposed to the operation. Newman and Stoller (1974) have pointed out that occasionally schizophrenics and other mentally disturbed individuals seek sexual reassignment, but that their desire is only transitory. For this and related reasons, it is recommended that those considering sex-reassignment surgery undergo a trial period first during which they receive hormone therapy and live in the new role to get a clearer understanding of the many psychological and social adjustments that will be required.

Prostitution

Prostitution is defined as the provision of sexual relations in return for money. Technically, there are four types of prostitution, the most common involving heterosexual relations for which the female is paid. There is also heterosexual prostitution for which the male is paid by the female, male homosexual prostitution for which a male provides sexual relations for another male (see HIGHLIGHT on page 553), and female homosexual prostitution for which a female provides sexual relations for another female. The last three types appear to be relatively rare. Hence our focus is on the first type—prostitution involving heterosexual relations for which the female is paid.

Prostitution has flourished throughout history, often being referred to as "the world's oldest profession." In some societies prostitutes are accorded high social status; where prostitution is governmentally regulated, they are accepted much as persons associated with any other social institution. In most segments of our own society, however, prostitution has traditionally been considered evil, and prostitutes have been subjected to legal sanctions and relegated to low social status. However, status does seem to vary somewhat among the different types of female prostitutes. It is highest for the "call girl" and lowest for the streetwalker, with the "house girl" falling in the middle. The "bar girl's" status seems largely determined by the status of the bars she frequents; but it is always lower than that of the call girl, whose working environment may be limited to her own, often lavish, apartment. There are an estimated 500,000 or more "career" prostitutes in the United States, as well as an equivalent number of persons who serve as part-time prostitutes.

For an indication of the proportion of men in this country who frequent prostitutes, we have only the findings of Kinsey et al. (1948), which, in turn, bear only on the white male population. According to these figures, 69 percent of white males had some experience with prostitutes; however, for many men there was only one such experience. The investigators estimated that contact with prostitutes provided less than 5 percent of the total sexual outlet of the population sampled—far lower than in countries where prostitution was governmentally controlled. Twenty years later, Packard (1968) reported a decrease in the number of young college males who frequented prostitutes as a consequence of changing sexual mores and the more ready availability of sexual relations with girlfriends.

Since there has been relatively little systematic research on prostitution in the United States, there are many questions for which we lack clear-cut answers. For example, one might ask: (a) Why do men frequent prostitutes? (b) Why and how do women become prostitutes? (c) What sort of relationship do prostitutes have with their clients? (d) What kind of social structure do most prostitutes enter when they become part of "the life"? and (e) What is the outcome for women who make a career of prostitution? Available evidence leads more to conjecture than to hard, fact, but it is evident that the answers will vary for different individuals. Most of what we know comes from studies of the "high-class" call girl, which may lead to a biased picture.

Why men frequent prostitutes. Among the reasons commonly reported for men's frequenting of prostitutes are (a) insufficient opportunity for other types of heterosexual experience, as is often the case with military personnel; (b) desire to discover what such an experience has to offer, and, in the case of some older men, to have sexual relations with a much younger woman; (c) desire to avoid the responsibilities generally associated with sexual relations; (d) difficulty in securing sexual relations with other women—possibly because of timidity or a physical defect; and (e) desire to find a partner willing to engage in otherwise unavailable variant or "kinky" sexual practices.

Proportionately it would appear that the largest numbers of males who go to prostitutes either are not married, or are separated or divorced—or are married to wives whom they do not find sexually attractive.

Why and how women become prostitutes. In a very basic sense, questioning why women become prostitutes inevitably involves questions about the special characteristics of their male clients. The one could not exist without the other. Beyond the obvious factors listed above, however, little is known about the men who frequent prostitutes and purchase their services. The personalities of prostitutes and their relationships with their clients have received greater attention.

Although there appears to be a higher-than-average incidence of psychopathology—including suicide—among prostitutes, Jackman,

HIGHLIGHT

Organized male homosexual prostitution

Organized prostitution is generally thought of as involving female prostitutes who report to a "madam" and provide sexual services for male clients. Most people do know that there are male prostitutes—for example, the "gigolo," who provides sexual favors for a woman in return for monetary support, and the men who work for "escort service" business establishments. But it is not well known that male prostitution can be as organized as the typical "house of prostitution." In this case, however, the clients are not women but are instead male homosexuals.

Pittman (1977) has provided a composite picture of one such house, which is operated by a "madam" named Jay. Jay is himself homosexual, but he does not mix business with pleasure. His employees, who are referred to as "models," are young, attractive males. They are required to be homosexually oriented, or at least bisexual, and are most likely to be employed by Jay if they are "versatile," which means having a range of the sexual skills and interests popular among male homosexuals. The models are paid approximately 70 percent of their fees; the other 30 percent goes to Jay. The models get to keep tips.

The clientele of Jay's establishment are socially heterogeneous; many clients are financially prosperous, lead conventional lives, and are married. Typically, they are in their 40s or early 50s. Their desires run the entire gamut of male homosexual practices, and models are expected to cater to every desire upon accepting a "call."

Jay feels that emotional attachments cause trouble and are bad for business, so he has taken precautions to avoid their development. He has a rule, apparently violated with some regularity, that models shall not have sexual relations with one another. "Dating" between models and clients is also forbidden, but this rule, too, is sometimes violated.

The models tend to be transient, and their popularity among regular clients wanes quickly as new models enter the establishment. Since the work is physically demanding, a model must save his energy for his job in order to retain his ability to satisfy clients. Sometimes models do not do so and are thus fired. As is the case with female prostitutes, many models are preoccupied with fantasies that a lover will rescue them from the "life" and thereafter provide love and security.

One former model recalled his feelings about the job as follows:

"The job was making me depressed. I was young and wanted to go out and have some fun. If I did, it would take me away from the job, and I would lose money. I could not start a romance—who would want a call boy as a lover. I wanted someone to love me for myself, not just my body" (p. 164).

O'Toole, and Geis (1963) have concluded that most prostitutes have normal intelligence and come from an average educational background. Especially as we go up the social scale to the "high-class" call girls, we appear to be dealing in the main with physically attractive, well-educated, and sophisticated young women who believe that prostitution is a perfectly acceptable business venture and is preferable to working at some other job. In some instances, of course, they actually do hold other jobs and work as prostitutes in their off-hours; in other cases, their jobs involve entertaining out-of-town businessmen, a responsibility that may or may not include sexual relations.

Research studies have ascribed widely different motives and characteristics to females who become prostitutes (Gagnon & Simon, 1973). In general, however, it would appear that the main consideration is money—the entry into what appears to be a quick, easy, and unpressured way to make a living. Additionally, assuming a modicum of physical attractiveness, it may appear virtually impossible to be a "failure" in this line of work in terms of performance and client satisfaction. There does not appear to be any systematic process of recruitment of call girls in the United Sates, but rather a process of "enlistment."

Females who enlist come from all social classes, although the majority appear to come from lower-class or lower-middle-class homes. However, some come from upper-middle and upper-class families and have had every "advantage" in terms of education and material resources. At the other extreme are females from the black ghettos and other poverty-stricken areas who have not been so fortunate and turn to streetwalking as the most accessible option for making money and maintaining at least a marginal way of life. In fact, Haggerty (1973) has concluded that "prostitution seems to be a natural 'dumping ground' for uneducated and unemployed women in a male-dominated society" (p. 7). Often prostitutes come from unstable families and have histories of frequent sexual episodes during adolescence. Somewhere along the line they may receive money as well as other presents for their sexual favors, and become interested in the possibility of a career in prostitution.

The inclination to become a prostitute must be implemented by some actual means of entering the profession. In a minority of cases, this may be achieved by entering a house of prostitution or brothel where training is provided. However, an increasing number of women gain entry to "the life" by establishing a dependent relationship with an experienced prostitute or with a man who operates as a pimp. All but 1 of the 33 call girls Bryan (1965) studied in the Los Angeles area had had a contact with someone engaged in call-girl activities. In some instances they had been friends; sometimes the contact had started with a homosexual relationship between the two. The initial contact usually determined the type or social level of prostitution at which the woman began, from streetwalking to serving a "select clientele" as a call girl.

Once the contact is acquired and the decision made to become a prostitute, the novice typically enters a period of apprenticeship, which may last for several months in the case of call girls. After acquiring the necessary skills and a clientele, she has completed her training period and can go into business for herself.

The prostitute-client relationship.

It has been assumed that the prostitute views her behavior strictly as a matter of business and does not experience orgasm or emotional arousal during a professional contact. However, the relationship appears to vary. For streetwalkers in large cities, who may expect never to see their clients again, the encounter is brief and business-like; for prostitutes who

have repeated contacts with the same client, there may be some emotional involvement. Bryan (1966) found a wide variety of relationships between prostitutes and their clients, ranging from coldness and hostility on the woman's part to friendship and sexual gratification. In general, however, the former picture is much more common than the latter, thus leading many prostitutes to develop consummate acting skills in an attempt to increase the likelihood of a customer's returning.

The world of prostitution.

The world of the prostitute is essentially a subculture with its own values, inhabitants, and required social skills. In general, great value is placed on achieving maximum gains from minimum effort and on cooperating with other working women—although prostitutes often do not like each other. The "johns" (customers) are pictured as basically exploitative, and therefore open to exploitation.

As Gagnon and Simon (1973) have pointed out, "The world of the prostitute is composed primarily of other prostitutes, clients, steerers, and procurers, and in some cases pimps; it may include lesbian lovers or madams; and—finally—the police and other agents of law enforcement" (p. 229). Steerers and procurers consist primarily of bellboys, desk clerks, taxi drivers, and other persons who act as "go-betweens" and, of course, receive some monetary or other reward for their services in steering clients to the prostitute.

The social skills required to adapt to the world of prostitution depend on the level of involvement. For example, streetwalkers, bar girls, and call girls need to acquire a much wider range of skills than prostitutes in bordellos where men come to them under some degree of supervision. Many streetwalkers and some bar girls rely heavily on pimps. Often a prostitute becomes emotionally attached to her pimp, usually because he is the only person she feels she can really trust and with whom she can share her experiences and problems. Possibly in an attempt to maintain his loyalty—or out of a vague sense that the money she earns is somehow "tainted"—she may turn over more of her earnings to him than she is required to.

In the decreasing number of cases where a madam is involved, she essentially serves as

Streetwalking is one form of prostitution that flourishes in present-day society despite legal sanctions.

the prostitute's employer and supervisor. Hirschi (1962) has described her role as follows:

"The madam . . . hires and fires, makes rules, punishes those who break them, and generally supervises the activities of girls on the job. She often keeps lists of customers and girls who may be available if extra help is needed. She may find it necessary to employ accessory personnel such as maids, cooks, bouncers, and spotters. Her contacts with madams in other cities enable her to assist girls in finding new positions. Her problems include those involved in meeting the sometimes rapidly changing tastes of her customers and of working out some sort of stable arrangement with city officials and the police." (p. 39)

In many instances, the world of prostitution is part of the larger world of organized crime. However, the picture appears to vary markedly from one city or region of the country to another.

The outcome of a career in prostitution. The great majority of prostitutes do not

spend their entire adult lives in "the life." However, some prostitutes, particularly the older and less attractive ones who have no other source of income, find it very difficult to get out of the profession until they are forced out by age. As Young (1967) has put it, "The older whores will say quite simply: 'There is no way out.' The younger ones will keep their chins up and pretend to themselves they're not like the rest. Nobody ever went on the game for keeps" (p. 123).

Gagnon and Simon (1973) have pointed out that conditions in the United States make leaving the life of prostitution more difficult than it is in many other countries. For example, in Denmark

"there is no statute against the act of taking pay for a sexual act as long as the female has another occupation. Danish authorities hope that through such a mechanism sufficient ties will be maintained to the conventional community so that the woman may have a past other than one of prostitution when she chooses to leave this career." (p. 233)

In the United States, the prostitute usually

lacks necessary skills for obtaining needed employment in other areas; in addition, she may find it hard to adapt to a new self-concept and to a new value orientation toward sex. Often, too, possible police records may have led to decreasing ties with the regular world and to a close identification and involvement with the world of prostitution. Nevertheless, many prostitutes do eventually marry and attempt to establish a more satisfying life pattern. Obviously serious problems may arise in the process of such a readjustment. However, in a study of 22 former prostitutes, Bess and Janus (1974) reported that an adequate readjustment can be achieved—both on interpersonal and occupational levels.

In any event, despite all the romanticizing of prostitution in movies and other mass media, the world of the prostitute is generally considered a difficult and ultimately unrewarding one (Gagnon & Simon, 1973). As Polly Adler (1953) summed it up in her book about her own experience, "Believe me, whoring is just a slow form of self-destruction."

Fetishism

We classify fetishism as a "victimless" sexual variant because, although it sometimes involves crimes such as thievery, its basic nature does not normally interfere with the rights of others except in an "incidental" way. In fetishism there is typically a centering of sexual interest on some body part or on an inanimate object, such as an article of clothing. Males are most commonly involved in cases of fetishism—reported cases of female fetishists are extremely rare. The range of fetishistic objects includes hair, ears, hands, underclothing, shoes, perfume, and similar objects associated with the opposite sex. The mode of using these objects for the achievement of sexual excitation and gratification varies considerably, but it commonly involves kissing, fondling, tasting, or smelling the object.

In order to obtain the required object, the fetishist may commit burglary, theft, or even assault. Probably the articles most commonly stolen by fetishists are women's underthings. One young boy was found to have accumulated over a hundred pairs of panties from a lingerie shop when he was apprehended. In such cases, the excitement and suspense of the criminal act itself typically reinforce the sexual stimulation, and in some cases actually constitute the fetish—the article stolen being of little importance. For example, one youth admitted entering a large number of homes in which the entering itself usually sufficed to induce an orgasm. When it did not, he was able to achieve sexual satisfaction by taking some "token," such as money or jewelry.

Not infrequently, fetishistic behavior consists of masturbation in association with the fetishistic object. Here, of course, it is difficult to draw a line between fetishistic activity and the effort to increase the sexual excitation and satisfaction of masturbation through the use of pictures and other articles associated with the desired sexual object. Utilization of such articles in masturbation is a common practice and not usually considered pathological. However, where antisocial behavior such as breaking and entering is involved, the practice is commonly referred to as fetishistic. For example, Marshall (1974) reported a rather unusual case of a young university student who had a "trouser fetish"; he would steal the trousers of teenagers and then use them in physical contact during masturbation.

A somewhat different, but not atypical pattern of fetishism is illustrated by the case of a man whose fetish was women's shoes and legs.

The fetishist in this case was arrested several times for loitering in public places, such as railroad stations and libraries, watching women's legs. Finally he chanced on a novel solution to his problem. Posing as an agent for a hosiery firm, he hired a large room, advertised for models, and took motion pictures of a number of girls walking and seated with their legs displayed to best advantage. He then used these pictures to achieve sexual satisfaction and found that they continued adequate for the purpose (Adapted from Grant, 1953).

Another type of fetishism involves setting fires. While people who set fires are a mixed group, a sizable number of fires—including some involving loss of life—are set by fetishists who have come to experience relief of sexual tension from setting and watching a fire burn. Such fires include brush and forest fires, as well as fires in buildings.

In approaching the causal factors in fetishism, we may again note that many stimuli can come to be associated with sexual excitation and gratification. Probably most people are stimulated to some degree by intimate articles of clothing and by perfumes and odors associated with the opposite sex. Thus the first prerequisite in fetishism seems to be a conditioning experience. In some instances this original conditioning may be quite accidental, as when sexual arousal and orgasm—which are reflexive responses—are elicited by a strong emotional experience involving some particular object or part of the body. More commonly, probably, the conditioning occurs during masturbatory fantasies.

The endowment of a formerly neutral stimulus with sexual arousal properties has been demonstrated in an interesting experiment by Rachman (1966), who created a mild fetish under laboratory conditions. A photograph of women's boots was repeatedly shown with slides of sexually stimulating nude females. In time, the subjects came to exhibit sexual arousal—as measured by changes in penile volume—to the boots alone; this response then generalized to other types of women's shoes.

In some instances, however, the associations involved in fetishism are not easy to explain. Bergler (1947) cited an unusual case in which a man's sex life was almost completely absorbed by a fetishistic fascination for exhaust pipes of automobiles. Nor would just any exhaust pipe do; it had to be in perfect shape, that is to say, undented and undamaged, and it had to emit softly blowing gases. This became far more attractive to him than sexual behavior with women.

Fetishistic patterns of sexual gratification usually become the preferred patterns only when they are part of a larger picture of maladjustment; such a picture typically involves doubts about one's masculinity and potency and fear of rejection and humiliation by members of the opposite sex. By his fetishistic practices and mastery over the inanimate object—which comes to symbolize for him the desired sexual object—the individual apparently safeguards himself and also compensates somewhat for his feelings of inadequacy.

Sexual variants involving nonconsent or assault

We come now to sexual variants in which there is a definite element of injury or significant risk of injury—physical or psychological—to one or more of the parties involved in a sexual encounter. Typically—and rightly so—these practices have strong legal sanctions against them. Furthermore, these sanctions tend to be enforced, which is not always the case in the milder variants. We shall consider only the most common forms of these variants, which include voyeurism, exhibitionism, sadism, masochism, incest, pedophilia, and rape.

Voyeurism

Voyeurism, scotophilia, and *inspectionalism* are synonymous terms referring to the achievement of sexual pleasure through clandestine peeping. Although children often engage in such behavior, it occurs as a sexual offense primarily among young males. These "peeping Toms," as they are commonly called, usually concentrate on females who are undressing, or on couples engaging in sexual relations. Frequently they masturbate during their peeping activity.

How do people develop this pattern? In the first place, viewing the body of an attractive female seems to be quite stimulating sexually for many males. The saying "He feasted his eyes upon her" attests to the appetitive quality of merely "looking" under certain conditions. In addition, the privacy and mystery that have traditionally surrounded sexual activities have tended to increase curiosity about them.

If a youth with such curiosity feels shy and inadequate in his relations with the other sex, it is not too surprising for him to accept the substitute of peeping. In this way he satisfies his curiosity and to some extent meets his sexual needs without the trauma of actually approaching a female, and thus without the failure and lowered self-status that such an approach might bring. As a matter of fact, peeping activities often provide important compensatory feelings of power and superiority over the one being looked at, which may contribute materially to the maintenance of this pattern. Also, of course, the suspense and danger associated with conditions of peeping may lead to emotional excitement and a reinforcement of the sexual stimulation.

If a peeper is married, he is rarely well adjusted sexually in his marriage.

A young married college student had an attic apartment which was extremely hot during the summer months. To enable him to attend school, his wife worked; she came home at night tired and irritable and not in the mood for sexual relations. In addition, "the damned springs in the bed squeaked." In order "to obtain some sexual gratification" the youth would peer through his binoculars at the room next door and occasionally saw the young couple there engaged in erotic scenes. This stimulated him greatly, and he thereupon decided to extend his activities to a sorority house. However, during his second venture he was reported and apprehended by the police. This offender was quite immature for his age, rather puritanical in his attitude toward masturbation, and prone to indulge in rich but immature sexual fantasies.

While more permissive laws concerning "adult" movies and magazines have probably removed much of the secrecy from sexual behavior and also provided an alternative source of gratification for would-be peepers, their actual effect on the incidence of voyeurism is a matter of speculation. For many voyeurs these movies and magazines probably do not provide an adequate substitute for secretly watching the "real life" sexual behavior of an unsuspecting couple. (See HIGHLIGHT on page 559 for a discussion of the controversy over the effects of pornography on sexual deviance.)

Although a voyeur may become somewhat reckless in his observation of courting couples and thus may be detected and assaulted by his subjects, peeping does not ordinarily have any serious criminal or antisocial aspects. In fact, many people probably have rather strong inclinations in the same direction, which are well checked by practical considerations such as the possibility of being caught and moral attitudes concerning the right to privacy.

Exhibitionism

Exhibitionism ("indecent exposure") is the most common sexual offense reported to the police in the United States, Canada, and Europe, accounting for about one-third of all sexual offenses (Rooth, 1974). Curiously enough, it is rare in most other countries. For example, in Argentina only 24 persons were convicted of exhibitionism during a five-year period; in Japan, only about 60 men are convicted of this offense each year. In still other countries, such as Burma and India, it is practically unheard of.

Exhibitionism involves the intentional exposure of the genitals to members of the opposite sex under inappropriate conditions. The exposure may take place in some secluded location, such as a park, or in a more public place, such as a department store, church, theater, or bus. In cities, the exhibitionist often drives by schools or bus stops, exhibits himself while in the car, and then drives rapidly away. In many instances, the exposure is repeated under fairly constant conditions, such as only in churches or buses, or in the same general vicinity and at the same time of day. In one case a youth exhibited himself only at the top of an escalator in a large department store. The kind of sex object too is usually fairly consistent for the individual exhibitionist. For the male offender this ordinarily involves a young or middle-aged female who is not known by the offender.

In some instances exposure of the genitals is accompanied by suggestive gestures or masturbatory activity, but more commonly there is only exposure. Although it is considered relatively rare, a hostile exposer may accompany exhibitionism with aggressive acts and may knock down or otherwise attack his victim. Despite the rarity of assaultive behavior in these cases, and the fact that most exhibitionists are anything but the aggressive and dangerous criminals they are often made out to be in newspaper stories, the exhibitionistic act nevertheless takes place without the viewer's consent and also may upset the viewer; thus, society considers exhibitionism to be a criminal offense.

Exhibitionism is most common during the warm spring and summer months, and most offenders are young adult males. Practically all occupational groups are represented. Among women, the exhibition of the genitals is rela-

HIGHLIGHT

Pornography and sexual deviance

Pornography is generally defined as sexually explicit materials—writings, pictures, or movies—whose primary aim is to arouse the viewer sexually. While this definition seems simple enough, it is subject to interpretation; for example, one person may view the painting of a nude woman as pornography while another views it as art. Even judges who officiate in obscenity trials may differ in their opinions concerning the pornographic nature of specific erotic materials.

In recent years a good deal of controversy and concern have focused on the permissive cultural climate in our society, a climate which permits "hard-core" X-rated films, erotic paperbacks, and a wide range of other "pornographic" materials to be marketed openly. Four questions are commonly raised here:

1. Does exposure to pornography lead to undesirable alterations in sexual orientation and to sex crimes?

2. Does exposure to pornography trigger antisocial sexual acts, such as pedophilia or rape?

3. Does exposure to pornography tend to divest sex of meaningful love relationships, so that it becomes an end in itself?

4. Does exposure to pornography threaten the family and the moral fabric of our society?

In terms of available evidence, the answer to each of the preceding questions would appear to be "no." For example, rapists and child molesters have reported less exposure to pornography during their formative years than normally curious young males; nor is there any evidence that exposure to pornographic materials alters an individual's orientation in the direction of maladaptive sexual patterns, or that it triggers transient antisocial acts such as pedophilia or rape. In fact, after Denmark legalized pornography, there was a significant reduction in sexual crimes, particularly in offenses against children.

After a thorough assessment of the scientific evidence, the U.S. Commission on Obscenity and Pornography concluded that "If a case is to be made against pornography, it will have to be made on grounds other than demonstrated effects of a damaging personal or social nature" (1970, p. 139). The commission recommended against the censorship of pornographic material for adults who seek it out; the commission did, however, support the view that there should be restricted access to such materials

for minors. The latter recommendation was made as a safeguard, even though there was no reliable evidence that such exposure was harmful.

While the recommendations of the commission were applauded by civil-liberty groups, they were condemned by church groups and other organizations who failed to see any merit in pornography and feared the possibility of long-range harm to American morals as well. So the controversy over pornography continued, and, in 1974, the Supreme Court ruled to permit local governments to censor pornography to conform to local views and sensibilities. Today the controversy over pornography continues at the community level.

Based on Goldstein (1974), Goldstein and Kant (with Hartman, 1973), Kutchinsky (1972), Nathan and Harris (1975), and U.S. Commission on Obscenity and Pornography (1970).

tively rare, and when it occurs it is less likely to be reported to the police.[1]

Usually exhibitionism by males in public or semipublic places is reported. Occasionally, however, such individuals are encouraged in their activity.

A rather handsome 17-year-old boy had been seating himself beside girls and women in darkened theaters and then exhibiting himself and masturbating. He had been repeatedly successful in obtaining approving collaboration from the "victims" before he finally made the mistake of exposing himself to a police woman. Out of an estimated 25 to 30 exposures, he was reported on only 3 occasions.

In general, cases of exhibitionism appear to fall into one of three categories:

1. *Exhibitionism associated with personal immaturity.* Witzig (1968) found that about 60 percent of the cases of exhibitionism referred by courts for treatment fall into this category. Here the exhibitionism seems to be based on inadequate information, feelings of shyness and inferiority in approaching the opposite sex, and puritanical attitudes toward masturbation. Commonly, there are strong bonds to an overly possessive mother. Often the exhibitionist states that he struggled against the impulse to expose himself in much the same way that the adolescent may struggle against the impulse to masturbate, but that, as sexual or other tensions increased, he felt compelled to carry out his exhibitionistic activities. Often he feels guilty and remorseful afterward, particularly if he has achieved ejaculation.

Although over half of all exhibitionists are married, they usually fail to achieve satisfactory sexual and personal relationships with their wives. Witzig (1968) has pointed out that

"These men almost never like to discuss sexual matters with their wives and frequently avoid undressing before them. The idea of living in a nudist colony is a repulsive thought to most exhibitionists, although they are periodically willing to show off their genitals in quite public places." (p. 78)

Many of these offenders state that they married

only because of family pressure, and many married at a late age. Thus we are dealing here with an individual who is essentially immature in his sex-role development, even though he may be well educated and competent in other life areas.

Closely related to the exhibitionist's personal immaturity appears to be a second factor: doubts and fears about his masculinity, combined with a strong need to demonstrate masculinity and potency. Apfelberg, Sugar, and Pfeffer (1944), for example, cited the case of an exhibitionist who achieved sexual satisfaction only when he accompanied the exposure of his genitals with a question to his victim as to whether she had ever seen such a large penis. On one occasion the woman, instead of evidencing shock and embarrassment, scornfully assured him that she had. On this occasion, the defendant stated, he received no sexual gratification.

It is worth noting that exhibitionism rarely takes place in a setting conducive to having sexual relations. The exhibitionist attempts to elicit a reaction that confirms his masculinity without entailing the risk of having to perform adequately in sexual intercourse.

In reviewing the role of personal immaturity and sexual ignorance in exhibitionism, it is interesting to note the conclusion of Rooth (1974) that the "sexual revolution" during the last decade in the Western world may have made matters worse for the exhibitionist: the growing assertiveness of women may make him even more insecure while at the same time he is being bombarded by sexually suggestive material from the "emancipated" mass media, thus increasing his frustration.

2. *Interpersonal stress and acting out.* Another causal factor is suggested by the high incidence of precipitating stress. Often the married exhibitionist appears to be reacting to some conflict or stress situation in his marriage, and his behavior is in the nature of a regression to adolescent masturbatory activity. In such instances, an exhibitionist may state that exhibiting himself during masturbation is more exciting and tension-reducing than utilizing pictures of nude women.

An interesting example of stress-induced exhibitionism was published several years ago in the autobiog-

---

[1]In certain instances, of course, as in some bars and discos, women—and less frequently, men—are paid wages to exhibit their sexual parts.

raphy of a prominent player in the National Football League. Intellectually and physically talented, attractive, wealthy, famous, and married to one of the most beautiful women in the entertainment field, this individual was nevertheless arrested on two occasions for exhibiting himself to preadolescent girls. By his own account, these incidents occurred only during periods of intense pressure, when he felt he was failing in those aspects of his life he most valued—his athletic career and his marriage (Rentzel, 1972).

Exhibitionism without genital arousal may take place following a period of intense conflict over some problem—often involving authority figures—with which the individual feels inadequate to cope.

"For example, a Marine who wanted to make a career of the service was having an experience with a superior that made it impossible for him to reenlist. He could not admit to himself that he could be hostile to either the corps or the superior. For the first time in his life, he exposed himself to a girl on the beach. Arrested, he was merely reprimanded and returned to the scene of conflict. A short time later he displayed his genitals to a girl in a parking lot. This time he was placed on probation with the stipulation that he seek treatment, and his enlistment was allowed to terminate in natural sequence. He never repeated the act. He was happily married and seemed to be acting out in this instance a vulgar expression of contempt." (Witzig, 1968, p. 77)

3. *Association with other psychopathology.* Exhibitionism may occur in association with a variety of more pervasive forms of psychopathology. Severely mentally retarded youths—both male and female—may exhibit themselves, being apparently unaware or only partially aware of the socially disapproved nature of their behavior. Some exhibitionists come from the ranks of older men with senile brain deterioration who evidence a lowering of inner reality and ethical controls.

In other cases exhibitionism is associated with psychopathic personality disorders. Here individuals usually have a history of poor school adjustment and erratic work records; often they have had difficulties with authorities as a consequence of other antisocial acts. Their exhibitionism appears to be just one more form of antisocial behavior, in connection with which they may or may not achieve sexual excitation and gratification. In some instances, exhibitionism is associated with manic or schizophrenic reactions. For example, the only women in a group of offenders studied by Witzig (1968) typically exposed herself prior to the onset of a full-blown psychotic episode.

Sadism

The term *sadism* is derived from the name of the Marquis de Sade (1740–1814), who for sexual purposes inflicted such cruelty on his victims that he was eventually committed as insane. Although the term's meaning has broadened to denote cruelty in general, we shall use it in its restricted sense, to denote achievement of sexual stimulation and gratification through the infliction of physical or psychic pain on a sexual partner. The pain may be inflicted by such means as whipping, biting, or pinching; the act may vary in intensity, from fantasy to severe mutilation and in extreme cases even murder. Mild degrees of sadism (and masochism) are involved in the sexual foreplay customs of many cultures, and some couples in our own society regularly engage in such practices. Males are ordinarily the aggressors, although Krafft-Ebing (1950) has reported a number of cases in which sadists were women. In one unusual case, the wife required her husband to cut himself on the arm before approaching her sexually. She would then suck the wound and become extremely aroused.

In some cases sadistic activities lead up to or terminate in actual sexual relations; in others, full sexual gratification is obtained from the sadistic practice alone. A sadist may slash a woman with a razor or stick her with a needle, experiencing an orgasm in the process. Showing the peculiar and extreme associations that may occur is the case of a young man who entered a strange woman's apartment, held a chloroformed rag to her face until she lost consciousness, and then branded her on the thigh with a hot iron. She was not molested in any other way.

Sometimes sadistic activities are associated with animals or with fetishistic objects instead of other human beings. East (1946) cited the case of a man who stole women's shoes, which he then slashed savagely with a knife. When he was in prison, he was found mutilating photographs that other prisoners kept in their cells by cutting the throats of the women in them. He admitted that he derived full sexual gratification from this procedure.

In other instances, gratification is achieved only if mutilation is performed directly on the victim's person. Chesser (1971) refers to such offenders as *pathological sadists* and notes that they are often extremely dangerous. The following is such a case:

The offender, Peter Kursten, was 47 years old at the time of his apprehension in Düsseldorf, Germany, for a series of lust murders. He was a skilled laborer, well groomed, modest, and had done nothing that annoyed his fellow workers.

Peter came from a disturbed family background, his father having been an alcoholic who had been sent to prison for having intercourse with Peter's older sister. Peter's own earliest sexual experiences were with animals. When he was about 13 years old, he attempted to have intercourse with a sheep, but the animal would not hold still and he took out a knife and stabbed her. At that moment he had an ejaculation.

After this experience, Peter found the sight of gushing blood sexually exciting, and he turned from animals to human females. Often he first choked his victim, but if he did not achieve an orgasm he then stabbed her. Initially he used scissors and a dagger, but later he took to using a hammer or an axe. After he achieved ejaculation, he lost interest in his victim, except for taking measures to cover up his crime.

The offender's sexual crimes extended over a period of some 30 years and involved over 40 victims. Finally apprehended . . . he expressed a sense of injustice at not being like other people who were raised in normal families (Adapted from Berg, 1954).

The news media have reported more recent cases in which the victims have been mutilated and killed in association with sadistic sexual practices. Included here would be the "horror story" of the sadistic homosexual murders of 27 teenage boys in Texas during the early 1970s. However, there is a lack of available case material on which to base definitive conclusions concerning the actual clinical picture or the causal factors involved in cases of sadism reported by the media.

The causal factors in sadism appear roughly comparable to those in fetishism.

1. *Experiences in which sexual excitation and possibly orgasm have been associated with the infliction of pain.* Such conditioned associations may occur under a variety of conditions. In their sexual fantasies many children visualize a violent attack by a man on a woman, and such ideas may be strengthened by newspaper articles of sadistic assaults on females. Perhaps more directly relevant are experiences in which an individual's infliction of pain on an animal or another person has given rise to strong emotions and, unintentionally, to sexual excitement. We have noted elsewhere the connection between strong emotional stimulation and sexual stimulation, especially during the adolescent period. Just as in fetishism—where simple conditioning seems to make it possible for almost any object or action to become sexually exciting— conditioning can also be an important factor in the development of sadistic tendencies.

2. *Negative attitudes toward sex and/or fears of impotence.* Sadistic activities may protect individuals with negative attitudes toward sex from the full sexual implications of their behavior, and at the same time may help them express their contempt and punishment of the other person for engaging in sexual relations. Several early investigators have described male sadists as timid, feminine, undersexed individuals, and sadistic behavior as apparently designed to arouse strong emotions in the sex object which, in turn, arouses the sadist and makes orgasm possible. The sadist apparently receives little or no satisfaction if the victim remains passive and unresponsive to the painful stimuli. In fact, the sadist usually wants the victim to find the pain exciting, and may even insist that the victim act pleasurably aroused when being stuck with pins, bitten, or otherwise hurt.

For many sexually inadequate and insecure individuals, the infliction of pain is apparently a "safe" means of achieving sexual stimulation. Strong feelings of power and superiority over the victim may for the time shut out underlying feelings of inadequacy and anxiety.

3. *Association with other psychopathology.* In schizophrenia and other severe forms of psychopathology, sadistic sexual behavior and sadistic rituals may result from the lowering of inner controls and the deviation of symbolic processes. Wertham (1949) cited an extreme case in which a schizophrenic individual with puritanical attitudes toward sex achieved full sexual gratification by castrating young boys and killing and mutilating young girls. He rationalized his actions as being the only way to save them from later immoral behavior.

Masochism

The term *masochism* is derived from the name of the Austrian novelist Leopold V. Sacher-Masoch (1836–1895), whose fictional characters dwelt lovingly on the sexual pleasure of pain. As in the case of the term *sadism,* the meaning of *masochism* has been broadened beyond sexual connotations, so that it includes the deriving of pleasure from self-denial, from expiatory physical suffering such as that of the religious flagellants, and from hardship and suffering in general. We shall restrict our present discussion to the sexual aspects of masochistic behavior.

The clinical picture in masochism is similar to that in sadistic practices, except that now pain is inflicted on the self instead of on others (Sack & Miller, 1975). For example, East (1946) cited the case of a young woman who frequently cut herself on the arms, legs, and breasts, and inserted pins and needles under her skin. She experienced sexual pleasure from the pain and from seeing the blood from the incisions.

Patterns of masochistic behavior usually come about through conditioned learning: as a result of early experiences, an individual comes to associate pain with sexual pleasure. For example, Gebhard (1965) cited the case of an adolescent boy who was having the fractured bones in his arm hurriedly set without an anesthetic. To comfort the boy, the physician's attractive nurse caressed him and held his head against her breast. As a consequence, he experienced a "powerful and curious combination of pain and sexual arousal," which led to masochistic—as well as sadistic—tendencies in his later heterosexual relations.

Such sayings as "being crushed in his arms" or "smothered with kisses" reveal the association commonly made between erotic arousal and pain or discomfort. Thus it is not surprising that many individuals resort to mild sadomasochistic acts such as biting in an attempt

The paraphernalia in this shop window is sold to some sadists and masochists for their sexual needs.

to increase the emotional excitement of the sexual act. For most people, however, such behavior does not result in serious physical injury, nor does it serve as a substitute for sexual relations. In actual masochism, by contrast, the individual experiences sexual stimulation and gratification from the experience of pain under certain conditions.

In the case of both sadism and masochism, it should be noted that gratification in many instances requires a shared, complementary interpersonal relationship—one sadist and one masochist or, in milder forms, one superior "disciplinarian" and one obedient "slave." Nor are such arrangements limited to heterosexual couples. On the contrary, they seem to be very popular in homosexual encounters (Tripp, 1975). One of the authors has treated a promiscuous male homosexual whose singular desire was to be penetrated anally in order to relive an exquisitely painful experience in which, as a boy, his father had administered an enema to him.

Incest

Culturally prohibited sexual relations, up to and including coitus, between family members, such as a brother and sister or a parent and child, are called *incestuous*. Although a few societies have approved incestuous relationships—at one time it was the established practice for Egyptian pharaohs to marry their sisters to prevent the royal blood from being "contaminated"—the incest taboo is virtually universal among human societies.[2]

An indication of the very real risks involved in such inbreeding has been provided by Adams and Neel (1967), who compared the offspring of 18 nuclear incest marriages—12 brother-sister and 6 father-daughter—with those of a control group matched for age, intelligence, socioeconomic status, and other relevant characteristics. At the end of 6 months, 5 of the infants of the incestuous marriages had died, 2 were severely mentally retarded and had been institutionalized, 3 showed evidence of borderline intelligence, and 1 had a cleft palate. Only 7 of the 18 infants were considered normal. In contrast, only 2 of the control-group infants were not considered normal—one showing indications of borderline intelligence and the other manifesting a physical defect. Lindzey (1967) concluded that

". . . the consequences of inbreeding are sufficiently strong and deleterious to make it unlikely that a

human society would survive over long periods of time if it permitted, or encouraged, a high incidence of incest. In this sense, then, one may say that the incest taboo (whatever other purposes it may serve) is biologically guaranteed." (p. 1055)

A number of investigators have also maintained that the incest taboo also serves to produce greater variability among offspring, and hence to increase the flexibility and long-term adaptability of the population (Schwartzman, 1974).

In our own society incestuous behavior does occur, but its actual incidence is unknown since it takes place in a family setting and comes to light only when reported to law enforcement or other agencies. It may well be more common than is generally believed, partly because many of the victims do not consider themselves victimized (Maisch, 1972). Kinsey et al. (1948, 1953) reported an incidence of 5 cases per 1000 persons in a sample of 12,000 subjects, and Gebhard et al. (1965) found 30 cases per 1000 subjects in a group of 3500 imprisoned sex offenders. In both these studies brother-sister incest was reported as being 5 times more common than the next most common pattern—father-daughter incest.[3] Mother-son incest is thought to be relatively rare. In a study of 78 cases of incest, which excluded brother-sister incest, Maisch (1972) found that the father-daughter and stepfather-stepdaughter varieties accounted for fully 85 percent of the sample; mother-son incest accounted for only 4 percent. Summit and Kryso (1978) estimate that some 36,000 cases of father-daughter incest occur each year in the United States. In occasional cases, there may be multiple patterns of incest within the same family.

For an understanding of incestuous behavior, it may be noted that incestuous fantasies and desires are common during the adolescent period, and it is not uncommon for fathers to have such feelings toward their daughters. However, social mores and prohibitions are usually so deeply ingrained that the desires are not often acted out. Bagley (1969) has suggested that several different causal patterns may be involved where incestuous be-

---

[2]Extensive reviews of the literature on incest which document its near-universality and cite the various reasons given for its taboo may be found in Devroye (1973) and Schwartzman (1974). Interestingly, the degree of relationship for which the taboo is invoked varies widely, in many instances extending beyond "blood relatives."

[3]Authorities are more likely to deal with cases of father-daughter incest than with cases of brother-sister incest, since the latter are less likely to be reported.

havior occurs. The following list represents a slight modification of his schema.

1. *Accidental incest.* When brothers and sisters share the same bedroom during the preadolescent or adolescent period (which is not uncommon among poorer families), they may tend to engage in sexual exploration and experimentation. In some cases older brothers seduce their younger sisters without any apparent understanding of the social prohibitions or possible consequences.

2. *Incest associated with severe psychopathology.* In the case of psychopathic fathers, the incest may simply be part of an indiscriminate pattern of sexual promiscuity; in other individuals, such as alcoholics and psychotics, the incestuous relations may be associated with the lowering of inner controls.

3. *Incest associated with pedophilia.* Here a father has an intense sexual craving for young children, including his own. It is evident, however, that pedophilic motivation is not a primary cause of incest, in that most victims are beyond puberty. (A discussion of disturbing exceptions appears in the HIGHLIGHT on this page.)

4. *Incest associated with a faulty paternal model.* Here a father sets an undesirable example for his son by engaging in incestuous relations with his daughter or daughters and may encourage his son to do so as well—either at the time with his sisters, or later in life with his own daughters.

5. *Incest associated with family pathology and disturbed marital relations.* Here a family has low morals or is disorganized. In some instances a rejecting, hostile wife may actually foster father-daughter incest. Most (but not all) cases of father-daughter incest, in fact, occur in a setting of marked family disorganization.

In general, incestuous fathers who come to the attention of authorities do not have a history of sexual offenses or other criminal behavior, nor do they show a disproportionate incidence of prior hospitalization for mental disorders (Cavillin, 1966). In fact, such fathers tend to restrict their sexual activity to family members, not seeking or engaging in extramarital sexual relations. For example, in his intensive study of 12 fathers convicted of incestuous relations with their daughters, Cavillin (1966) reported that only 2 of the 12 had resorted to extramarital relations, despite feeling

HIGHLIGHT

Sexual molestation of young children

While most incestuous contacts between parents and their children occur after the child has attained puberty, very young children—even infants—have been subjected to sexual molestation and abuse by parents or other adults. According to Sgroi (1977), these cases, like those involving adolescents, are markedly underreported. Even in the face of overwhelming evidence, this researcher claims, physicians are extremely reluctant to conclude that a child has been sexually attacked. Apparently it is considered "in bad taste" professionally to draw such a conclusion.

The cases Sgroi uses to illustrate the magnitude of the problem are truly disconcerting. She writes of one city's youngest known rape victim, a child 2 months old; of a 2½-year-old boy and his 4-year-old sister, both of whom acquired acute gonorrhea from their father; of a 17-month-old girl with a torn anus, dead of asphyxiation, with semen in her mouth and throat. In the face of such horror, one can only applaud Sgroi's attempt to break through the secrecy and "discretion" too often associated with this "last frontier" of child abuse.

Because many cases remain unreported, the actual incidence of child abuse of all types—and especially of sexual abuse—is unknown. In Connecticut, during fiscal years 1973 and 1974, approximately 10 percent of all cases of reported abuse were suspected to involve sexual assault or impropriety—a total of 248 separate incidents. The suspected perpetrator was most often the father or a male relative or boyfriend. This corroborates the earlier findings of De Francis (1969). Assuming Connecticut to be representative of the United States as a whole, many thousands of young children are sexually assaulted or abused each year, often by their own parents.

they were unloved and rejected by their wives.

Cavillin further reported that the youngest father in the group was 20 and the oldest 56, with an average age of 39. The average age of the daughters was 13, the youngest being 3 and the oldest 18. Five of the 12 fathers had had a relationship with more than 1 daughter, usually beginning with the oldest; in 11 of the cases the relationships had gone on for some time—from 3 months to 3 years—before being reported by the daughters. In all cases, too, the father felt rejected and threatened by his wife. Cavillin's findings are generally confirmed by Maisch (1972), who studied 78 cases of incest coming to the attention of officials in the Federal Republic of Germany.

The psychological effect of the incestuous relationship on the daughter appears to depend on her age at the time of the relationship and on how much anxiety and guilt she experiences. Most girls studied who were still adolescent expressed feelings of guilt and depression over this incestuous behavior. Some girls in this situation turn to promiscuity; others run away from home to escape the stressful situation. In some instances, no apparent long-range ill effects can be detected. Interestingly, in a case treated by one of the authors in which there had been long-standing sexual molestation by the young woman's father during her childhood and adolescence, she resolutely refused all further sexual contact with him after he provoked her first orgasm. Up to that time, as is often the case, she had assumed a passive, "blameless" position.

Pedophilia

In pedophilia the sex object is a child; the intimacy usually involves manipulation of the child's genitals, or, in the case of a female victim, partial or complete penetration of the vagina. Occasionally the child is induced to manipulate the sex organ of the pedophiliac or to engage in mouth-genital contacts.

Offenders are diverse in terms of the act committed, the intentionality of and general circumstances surrounding the act, and age, education, and developmental history. Most pedophiliacs are men, but women occasionally engage in such practices. The average age of

these offenders is about 40 years. Many offenders are or have been married, and many have children of their own. Indeed, as we saw in the Highlight on page 565, some choose their own children as victims. In an early study of 836 pedophiliac offenders in New Jersey, Revitch and Weiss (1962) found that the older offenders tended to seek out immature children, while younger offenders preferred adolescent girls between 12 and 15. Girls outnumbered boys as victims in the ratio of more than 2 to 1.

In most cases of pedophilia the victim is known to the offender, and the sexual behavior may continue over a sustained period of time; usually there is no physical coercion. Although in some cases the offenders may be encouraged or even seduced by their victims, Swanson (1968) found provocation or active participation by the victim in only 3 of the 25 cases he studied.

Whether or not there is an element of provocation by the victim, the onus is always on the offender. Since pedophiliacs may subject children to highly traumatic emotional experiences as well as physical injury, society's norms relating to pedophilia are explicit and uncompromising. An alleged offender is sometimes considered guilty until proven innocent, in fact, and a number of men have served time in penal institutions because children or their parents interpreted simple affection as attempted intimacy or rape. On the other hand, many cases of sexual assault on children undoubtedly go unreported to spare the child a further ordeal (Sgroi, 1977).

The following causal categories are based on (a) an intensive study of 38 pedophiliac offenders living in a segregated treatment center (Cohen, Seghorn, & Calmas, 1969), and (b) in-depth interviews with many pedophiliacs, some of whom had managed to avoid arrest and some of whom had been arrested and had served time (Rossman, 1973).

1. *The personally immature offender*, who has never been able to establish or maintain satisfactory interpersonal realtionships with male or female peers during his adolescent, young adult, or adult life. This was by far the most common type. He is sexually comfortable only with children, and in most cases knows the victim. Usually the act is not impulsive but begins with a type of disarming courtship which eventually leads to sexual play. Either male or female children may be the victims.

2. *The regressed offender,* who during adolescence has shown apparently normal development, with good peer relationships and some dating behavior and heterosexual experiences.

"However, throughout this period there exist increasing feelings of masculine inadequacy in sexual and nonsexual activities. And, as he enters adulthood, his social, occupational, and marital adjustment is quite tenuous and marginal. There is frequently a history of an inability to deal with the normal stresses of adult life and alcoholic episodes become increasingly more frequent and result in the breakdown of a relatively stable marital, social, and work adjustment. In almost all instances the pedophilic acts are precipitated by some direct confrontation of his sexual adequacy by an adult female or some threat to his masculine image by a male peer." (Cohen, Seghorn, & Calmas, 1969, p. 251)

The most frequent precipitating event is the offender's discovery that his wife or girlfriend is having an affair with another man. In most of these cases the victim selected is a female child, suggesting elements of both retaliation and affirmation of "manhood."

In contrast to the personally immature offender, the regressed offender is not acquainted with his victim, and the act is characteristically impulsive. For example, the offender may be driving a car, see a child, and become overwhelmed by sexual excitation.

3. *The "conditioned" offender.* Included here are individuals who have had their definitive sexual experiences with young boys, often in reformatories; this conditioned behavior continues into adulthood in terms of sexual preference. These individuals are usually callous and exploitative in their sexual behavior, and tend to cruise cheap motion picture theaters and other areas in search of vulnerable children. In many instances, they pick up young hustlers who are available in most large cities. Some of these men are careful about avoiding detection, while others are not and have a history of one or more arrests for such offenses.

4. *The psychopathic offender.* The individuals included here are psychopathic personalities who prey on children in search of new sexual thrills. In some instances, such individuals patronize child prostitutes who are usually available in large cities as well as in some foreign countries.

This category also includes aggressive psychopaths whose behavior is motivated by both aggressive and sexual components:

"The primary aim is aggression, and is expressed in cruel and vicious assaults on the genitalia or by introducing the penis or elongated objects into the victim orally or anally. The sexual excitement increases as an apparent function of the aggression, but the orgasm itself either does not occur or must be reached through masturbation." (Cohen, Seghorn, & Calmas, 1969, p. 251)

In a case known to one of the authors, for example, the offender's gratification centered on the screams of his young male victim as the penis was roughly thrust into the boy's anus.

Such offenders usually have a history of antisocial behavior and, in general, could be described as hostile, aggressive psychopaths. Ordinarily they select a boy as the object of their aggression. Psychopathic individuals—particularly those who use coercion—are prone to deny their offenses or place the blame on their victims.

A number of investigators have also pointed to other severe psychopathology in pedophiliac offenders. Some are alcoholic or schizophrenic. Many are older individuals in whom brain deterioration has led to a weakening of normal inhibitory controls. In fact, pedophilia and exhibitionism are the most common sexual offenses committed by individuals suffering senile and arteriosclerotic brain damage and displaying organic personality syndromes (Chapter 13).

Rape

In rape, sexual behavior is usually directed toward a culturally acceptable sex object but under antisocial conditions.[4] Almost exclusively in reported cases, the male is the offend-

---

[4]Here we are referring to heterosexual rape. Statistics on homosexual rapes, particularly among males, are not available, although scattered reports indicate that such incidents do occur, particularly in prisons.

er. Depending on the victim's age, such offenses are defined legally as (a) *statutory rape,* which involves the seduction of a minor; and (b) *forcible rape,* in which the unwilling partner is over 18. It is with the latter type that we are concerned in this section. Some of the facts about rape and rapists were summarized in the Highlight on page 298.

Rape has increased more rapidly in the last decade than any other type of violent crime, although part of the apparent rise may simply reflect better reporting. In any case, the FBI reported over 63,000 cases of forcible rape in 1977, up from 55,000 in 1974. The actual incidence is considered to be as much as four times higher, because many women wish to avoid the unfortunate consequences that in the past have often followed a complaint of having been raped. These include social stigmatization and, regrettably, crude and insensitive treatment by police. There is hope that the gap between actual and reported incidents of rape has been narrowed in recent years as women have banded together to call attention to these injustices.

Based on information gathered about arrested and convicted rapists, rape, relatively speaking, is a young man's crime. Fifty-six percent of all arrests are of persons under 25 years of age, and a third of these are under 20; the greatest concentration is in the 16 to 24 age group. Of the rapists who get into police records, about half are married and living with their wives at the time of the crime. As a group, they come from the low end of the socioeconomic ladder. Typically they are unskilled workers with low intelligence, low education, and low income. How representative they are of rapists as a whole we do not know.

Rape tends to be a repetitive activity rather than an isolated act, and most rapes are planned events. About 80 percent of rapists commit the act in the neighborhood in which they reside; most rapes take place in an urban setting at night. However, the specific scene of the rape varies greatly. The act may occur on a lonely street after dark, in an automobile in the parking lot of a large shopping center, in the elevator or hallway of a building, and in other situations where the victim has little chance of assistance. Rapists have also entered apartments or homes by pretending to be deliverymen or repairmen. In fact, as we have

seen, rapes most often occur in the woman's home.

About a third or more of all rapes involve more than one offender, and often they are accompanied by beatings. The remainder are single-offender rapes in which the victim and the offender may know each other; the closer the relationship, the more brutally the victim may be beaten. When the victim struggles against her attacker, she is also likely to receive more severe injuries or in occasional cases to be killed. On the other hand, one study found that when the victim was able to cry out and run away, she was more likely to be successful in avoiding the rape (Selkin, 1974).

In addition to the physical trauma inflicted on the victim, the psychological trauma may be severe (see HIGHLIGHT on page 570). One especially unfortunate factor in rape is the possibility of pregnancy; another is a sexually transmitted disease. Such an incident may also affect the victim's marriage or other intimate relationships. The situation is likely to be particularly upsetting to the husband or boyfriend if he has been forced to watch the rape, as is occasionally the case when a victim is raped by the members of a juvenile gang.

The concept of "victim-precipitated" rape, a favorite of defense attorneys and of some police and court jurisdictions, turns out on close examination to be a myth. According to this view, the victim, though often bruised both psychologically and physically—if not worse—is regarded as the *cause* of the crime, often on such flimsy grounds as the alleged provocativeness of her attire or her past sexual behavior. The attacker, on the other hand, is treated as a decerebrate organism, unable to quell his lust in the face of such "outrageous" provocation—and therefore incapable of any criminal act!

A number of typologies of rape incidents and of rapists have been proposed, most of them based on inadequate data of questionable representativeness. The system proposed by Groth, Burgess, and Holmstrom (1977) is the most adequately documented one to appear thus far, and it has the additional virtue of appearing to subsume the types identified in earlier work. It is based on the accounts of 133 convicted rapists and 92 victims of rapes occurring during a limited time period in Massachusetts.

Groth et al. noted that rape attacks combine psychological elements of power and anger as well as sexuality, and their strategy was to rank these elements in terms of their apparent salience for each of the 225 separate accounts of rape available to them. In doing so, they discovered *no case* in which sexual satisfaction appeared to be the dominant motive of the rapist; that is, all the rapes were characterized as involving either power motives or anger expression more than sexuality on the part of the rapists. The authors also noted that predominantly power- or anger-inspired rapes could each in turn be divided into two subtypes. These subdivisions form the basis of their classification scheme, as described below.

1. *Power-assertive type.* The essence of a rape in which power motives predominate is that of establishing control over the victim through intimidation; the mode of intimidation employed may involve use of a weapon, physical force not involving severe injury, or simply threats of harm. The achievement of penetration is regarded as a "conquest." The rape is frequently preceded by fantasies that the victim, once overpowered, will willingly participate with wild abandon. Because reality never matches the fantasy, the rapist is frustrated and is likely to repeat the act compulsively on another occasion. The power-assertive rapist tends to have a history of "hypermasculinity," striving always to assert power and domination over those with whom he comes in contact. We may surmise, of course, that such persons in fact have very serious questions about their manhood. In Groth el al.'s sample, 44 percent of the rapes were of the power-assertive variety.

2. *Power-reassurance type.* Like his power-assertive counterpart, the power-reassurance rapist seeks to intimidate and conquer his victim. In this case, however, the underlying sense of weakness, inadequacy, and indistinct gender identity is much more obvious. As in some cases of exhibitionism, the act not uncommonly takes place following some blow to the rapist's fragile ego; the rape is an attempt to "repair the damage." Rapes of the power-reassurance type accounted for 21 percent of Groth et al.'s sample.

3. *Anger-retaliation type.* In comparison with power-oriented rapists, who rarely inflict severe physical damage on their victims, predominantly anger-driven rapists are exceedingly dangerous—sometimes to the point of murdering the women they attack. Here, rage, contempt, and hatred dominate the assault, which is usually brutal and violent. Sexual satisfaction, if it occurs at all, is minimal. In fact, many anger-dominated rapists view normal sex with revulsion and disgust. Here the rape is an expression of hate and rage toward women in general, and the predominant motive is one of revenge for real or imagined slights suffered at the hands of females. Derogation and humiliation are prominent features of this type of attack. Of the rapes studied by Groth et al., 30 percent were of the anger-retaliation type.

4. *Anger-excitation type.* More than any other, this type of rapist fits the category of *pathological sadist.* His attack is one of eroticized aggression; he derives sexual pleasure, thrills, and excitement not from the sexual elements of his assault but from the suffering of his victim. The anger-excitation type accounted for only 5 percent of Groth et al.'s sample.

It might seem from the above descriptions of actual rape occurrences that rapists as a group are a very disturbed segment of the population, and that potential rapists should therefore be easy to recognize. This would be an erroneous and possibly dangerous conclusion, however. While it is true that a certain proportion of rapists are obviously abnormal on a chronic basis—some even being blatantly psychotic— the literature in this area abounds with instances of rape in which, prior to the attack, the rapist had given no hint whatever of being a dangerous person (Gager & Schurr, 1976; Medea & Thompson, 1974). Whatever the prevention of rape involves, it is not a matter of informal psychodiagnostic predictions.

As we have seen, conviction rates for rape are low, and most men who have raped are free in the community. Yet one study of rapists who were in the community found that the men had raped anywhere from 5 to 100 times (Abel, Blanchard, Becker, & Djenderedjian, 1978). Rape is an ugly, intrusive violation of another person's integrity and selfhood that deserves to be viewed with more gravity—and its victims with more sensitivity—than is customarily the case (Gager & Schurr, 1976; Medea & Thompson, 1974).

In recent years new rape laws have been adopted by 37 states, about a third of them based on the "Michigan model," which describes four degrees of criminal sexual conduct, with different levels of punishment for different degrees of seriousness. In calling the offense *criminal sexual conduct* rather than *rape*, the Michigan law also appropriately places the emphasis on the offender rather than the victim.

Treatment and outcomes

Research concerning effective treatment of variant sexual behavior has not progressed as far or as rapidly as in the case of the dysfunctions, but there are encouraging signs of progress. As was noted at the outset of this discussion, we now know that most sexually variant acts cannot adequately be conceptualized simply as aberrations of sexual arousal. In most instances we also need to look at the individual's level of response to adult heterosexual stimuli, overall degree of social skill with members of the other sex, and gender identity development. Only by taking all these factors into account is it possible to assess a given client's difficulties adequately and fashion treatment procedures for intervening on a broad enough front. On page 538 we noted the apparent effectiveness of such an approach to therapy in cases involving unwanted homosexual desires (Adams & Sturgis, 1977).

To date, unfortunately, such a broad-front intervention has been the exception rather than the rule in therapeutic attempts to change variant sexuality, and most treatment efforts still focus on the sexual arousal aspects. We are beginning to learn how to suppress a variant arousal pattern, as with aversive conditioning procedures. Similarly, we know something of how to develop or strengthen arousability to appropriate heterosexual stimuli (Barlow & Abel, 1976). Surely, we will be able to find ways to teach heterosocial skills where they are lacking. In fact, encouraging preliminary reports have emanated from a number of research cen-

HIGHLIGHT

Aftereffects of rape

Reactions to rape vary greatly among victims, depending on the relationship of the victim to the offender and the life circumstances of the victim, among other factors. Here we shall examine some of these factors and then look at typical coping behavior of rape victims, rape counseling, and possible long-term effects of rape.

Factors affecting reaction to rape

A woman's response to rape may vary depending on her relationship to the offender. In a "stranger" rape—one in which the victim does not know the offender—the victim is very likely to experience strong fear of physical harm and death. In an "acquaintance" rape situation, the reaction is apt to be slightly different (Ellison, 1977). In such a situation, the victim not only may feel fear but also may feel that she has been betrayed by someone she had trusted. She may feel more responsible for what happened and experience greater guilt. She may also be more hesitant to seek help or report the rape to the police out of fear that she will be held partially responsible for it.

The age and life circumstances of the victim may also influence her reaction to rape (Notman & Nadelson, 1976). For a young child who knows nothing about sexual behavior, rape can lead to sexual fears and confusion, particularly if the child is encouraged to forget about the experience without thoroughly talking it over first. For women between the ages of 17 and 24, rape can increase the conflicts over independence and separation that are normal in this age group. In an effort to be helpful, parents of young adult rape victims often encourage various forms of regression, such as moving back to the family home, which may in the long run prevent mastery of this developmental phase. Married rape victims with young children face the task of explaining their experience to their children. Sometimes the feelings of vulnerability that result from rape leave a woman feeling temporarily unable to care for her children.

Husbands and boyfriends can also influence rape victims' reactions by their attitudes and behavior. Rejection, blaming, uncontrolled anger at the offender, or insistence on early resumption of sexual activity can increase the woman's negative feelings.

Coping behavior of rape victims

Several researchers have interviewed rape victims in hospital emergency rooms and rape crisis centers soon after the rape (Burgess & Holmstrom, 1974, 1976; Holmstrom & Burgess, 1975; McCombie, 1976;

Sutherland & Scherl, 1970). Although based on small samples and nonstandardized interview formats, their findings are the best data currently available on the typical phases victims go through in coping with rape. The following represents an integration of these data.

1. Anticipatory phase. This is the period before the actual rape when the offender "sets up" the victim and the victim begins to perceive that a dangerous situation exists. In the early minutes of the anticipatory phase, victims often use defense mechanisms such as denial to preserve an illusion of invulnerability. Common thoughts are "Rape could never happen to me," and "He doesn't really mean that."

2. Impact phase. This phase begins with the victim's recognition that she is actually going to be raped and ends when the rape is over. The victim's first reaction is usually intense fear for her life, a fear much stronger than her fear of the sexual behavior itself. Symonds (1976) has described the paralytic effect of intense fear on victims of crime, showing that it usually leads to varying degrees of disintegration in the victim's functioning and possibly to complete inability to act. When the victim later recalls her behavior during this phase, she may feel guilty about not reacting more efficiently, and she needs to be reassured that her reaction is a common one. Major physiological reactions such as vomiting sometimes occur during this phase, but a woman who tries to simulate such reactions in order to escape generally discovers that she cannot produce them voluntarily.

3. Post-traumatic recoil phase. This phase begins immediately after the crime. Burgess and Holmstrom (1974, 1976) observed two emotional styles among the rape victims they interviewed in hospital emergency rooms. Some victims exhibited an *expressed style* where feelings of fear and anxiety were shown through crying, sobbing, and restlessness. Others demonstrated a *controlled style* in which feelings appeared to be masked by a calm, controlled, subdued façade. Regardless of style, most of the victims felt guilty about the way they had reacted to the offender and wished that they had reacted faster or fought harder. Feelings of dependency were increased, and victims often had to be encouraged and helped to call friends or parents and make other arrangements. Physical problems such as general tension, nausea, sleeplessness, and trauma directly related to the rape were common.

4. Re-constitution phase. This phase begins as the victim starts to make plans for leaving the emer-

gency room or crisis center and ends, often many months later, when the stress of the rape has been assimilated, the experience shared with significant others, and the victim's self-concept restored. Certain behaviors and symptoms are typical during this phase.

a) Motor activity, such as changing one's telephone number and moving to a new residence, is common. The victim's fear is often well justified at this point since, even if the offender has been arrested and charged with rape, he is often out on bail.

b) Frightening nightmares in which the rape is relived are common. As the victim moves closer toward assimilating the experience, the content of the dreams gradually shifts until the victim successfully fights off the assailant.

c) Phobias—including fear of the indoors or outdoors (depending on where the rape took place), fear of being alone, fear of crowds, fear of having people behind one, and sexual fears—have been observed to develop immediately following rape.

Counseling rape victims

The women's movement has played a crucial role in the establishment of specialized rape counseling services such as rape crisis centers and hotlines. Rape crisis centers are often staffed by trained paraprofessionals who provide general support for the victim, both individually and in groups. Crisis centers also have victim advocacy services, in which a trained volunteer accompanies the victim to the hospital or police station, helps her understand the procedures, and assists her with "red tape." The victim advocate may also accompany the victim to meetings with the district attorney and to the trial—experiences that tend to temporarily reactivate the trauma of the rape.

Long-term effects

Whether a rape victim will experience serious psychological decompensation depends to a large extent on her past coping skills and level of psychological functioning. The previously well-adjusted woman will regain her prior equilibrium, but rape can precipitate severe pathology in a woman with prior psychological difficulties. Comparisons of women who have been raped with those who have not indicate that, though victims feel that the rape has had and continues to have an impact on them, there are generally no significant differences in overall psychological adjustment between victims and nonvictims (Oros & Koss, 1978).

ters concerned with the problem (Hersen & Eisler, 1976). There is the remaining obstacle of learning how to strengthen an adult client's gender identity, not necessarily in an exclusively "masculine" or "feminine" direction but rather more in terms of overcoming amorphousness and immaturity in the individual's sense of being a man or a woman—an adult person. This promises to be a difficult challenge for clinical research. Having delineated the problem, however, we are in a much better position now than we were even a few short years ago.

A good example of the successful application of broadly based intervention is provided in the treatment by Barlow and his associates of a 17-year-old transsexual male (Barlow & Abel, 1976; Barlow, Reynolds, & Agras, 1973).

This young man had wished to be female for as long as he could recall. He had spontaneously begun cross-dressing before the age of 5; and when he appeared for therapy, his general behavior was markedly effeminate. At this time he was depressed and withdrawn, partly because people ridiculed his appearance and manner. Though he wanted to change his sex, he agreed to try therapy aimed at changing his gender identity.

The first part of the treatment involved the attempt to modify the young man's feminine gender role by teaching him masculine styles of sitting, walking, and standing. "Correct" behavior was modeled by a male therapist; errors in the client's attempts to reproduce this behavior were noted, and he was given abundant praise for his successes. For example, he was taught to cross his legs when sitting so that one ankle rested on the other knee instead of placing one knee atop the other. As his performance improved, the staring and ridicule of others diminished substantially, and the young man began to enjoy his new "masculine" image.

Attempts to improve the client's social skills, which were notably lacking even in his interactions with other males, also utilized behavioral rehearsal techniques and immediate feedback. Since he had affected a high-pitched, effeminate voice, he was also given voice retraining, which proved quite effective. By the end of this phase of the treatment program, the client was reporting much increased confidence and success in his relations with his peers, both male and female.

These gains were consolidated by a fantasy-retraining phase, in which the young man was taught to adopt a masculine role in his sexual and other fantasies. Continuing assessment of his re-

sponse to erotic stimuli, however, showed that he was still not aroused by heterosexually oriented materials and was still strongly attracted to males. In other words, at this point he was psychologically a male homosexual.

The next step, then, involved increasing the client's responsiveness to heterosexual stimuli and decreasing the variant arousal pattern. Enhancement of arousal to heterosexual stimuli was accomplished by a classical conditioning procedure that systematically paired arousal and orgasm with heterosexual stimuli. This procedure was successful in establishing heterosexual arousal; and at this stage in the treatment, the client was bisexual in terms of his erotic responsiveness. There remained only the therapeutic task of suppressing the homosexual arousal component, which was accomplished by a combination of electric shock and covert sensitization (having the client imagine repugnant scenes). At a follow-up two years later, the young man was attending college and was regularly dating young women.

The successful outcome of this case should not be taken as a routine occurrence. As we have mentioned before, many sexual variants —transsexualism in particular—are normally not amenable to therapeutic reversal. It should also be noted that Barlow and his associates encountered some procedural difficulties in this case, recommending refinements in techniques as a result (Barlow & Abel, 1976; Barlow & Agras, 1973). Furthermore, the techniques used to suppress variant arousal patterns—electric shock and covert sensitization—are highly controversial. However, such use of aversive stimuli is often the most successful method of eradicating unwanted desires.

In addition to the need to improve treatment for the various sexual problems, there is also a need for better treatment of the victims of sexually variant persons. Except in the case of rape, little attention has been given to this serious matter, and even in the case of rape much remains to be done.

In this chapter we have dealt with the highly complex and often controversial problems of sexual dysfunctions and variants, subdividing the latter into victimless variants and variants involving nonconsent or assault. We began by noting that the sexual needs and forms of expression of human beings are much more malleable and subject to learning and various environmental influences than are those of lower animals—an advantage that incurs the cost of much higher levels of dysfunction and aberrant development for human beings than for members of other species. At the human level, feelings, goal objects, and behaviors all vary greatly and are heavily dependent on the individual's experience.

The major types of male and female dysfunction were then surveyed in the light of current knowledge concerning incidence and causal patterns. Treatment of dysfunctions has undergone revolutionary changes, typically producing high levels of success today. Therapy usually involves both partners.

Both professional and popular attitudes toward "normality" and "abnormality" in sexual activity have changed in recent years, and the term *sexual deviation* is no longer in favor. Although some variant forms of sexual behavior, such as pedophilia and rape, are universally regarded as abnormal and undesirable, variant patterns which do not victimize other people— such as homosexuality and transsexualism— have gained greater acceptance as optional patterns if preferred by the individuals themselves.

Our discussion of victimless sexual variants included male and female homosexuality, transvestism, transsexualism, prostitution, and fetishism. Our discussion of sexual variants involving nonconsent or assault included voyeurism, exhibitionism, sadism, masochism, incest, pedophilia, and rape.

The treatment of both groups of sexual variants has lagged behind that of the dysfunctions. It appears that adequate treatment requires help in arousability to heterosexual stimuli, in development of greater social skill with members of the other sex, and in gaining a clearer sense of gender identity in addition to procedures aimed at curtailing the variant sexual desire.

16

Suicide

Clinical picture and causal pattern
Suicidal ambivalence
Suicide prevention

References to suicide—taking one's own life—are found throughout written history (Farberow, 1975). Dido, the founder and queen of Carthage, stabbed herself on a funeral pyre in grief and rage when Aeneas deserted her and led the Trojans onward toward their destiny; Zeno, founder of stoic philosophy, reportedly hanged himself at the age of 98 owing to disgust at stubbing his toe. More recently, we have had the examples of Ernest Hemingway, Sylvia Plath, Jimi Hendrix, and Freddie Prinze—all superbly talented people enjoying lives of success and public acclaim. And, among the less successful, we have witnessed the horror of large-scale self-massacre by members of the People's Temple in Jonestown, Guyana. How shall we account for such dramatic reversals of the fundamental will to live? The main purpose of the present chapter is to provide a partial answer to this disturbing and age-old question.

Attitudes toward suicide have varied greatly from one society to another. For example, the early Greeks considered suicide an appropriate solution to many stressful situations, such as dishonor, disappointment in love, and painful conditions in old age. The Romans also considered suicide an acceptable solution to such conditions, but it was forbidden when property rights or interests of the state were involved—as when a slave or soldier deprived the state of his services by killing himself. On the other hand, suicide was condemned by Judaism and even more severely by Islam.

With the advent of Christianity, suicide was denounced as a grievous sin in most of the Western world. Legal attitudes tended to follow those of the church; in early English law suicide was considered a crime, and it was directed that the body of a person who had committed suicide have a stake driven through the heart and be buried at a crossroads. The belief that suicide was morally and legally wrong prevailed throughout the Middle Ages in Western society.

During the Renaissance, however, some philosophers dared to challenge the prevailing views. Merian (1763) concluded that suicide was neither a sin nor a crime but a sign of disease—thus paving the way for a view of suicide as evidence of emotional disturbance. However, it remained for the French physician Jean Pierre Falret (1794–1870) to deal extensively with the subject of suicide as an indication of mental disorder (Fuller, 1973). In his review of suicide among outstanding historical personalities, Falret (1822) performed what has been called "the first psychological autopsy" when he examined the possibility that Jean Jacques Rousseau had taken his own life.

"In some people the idea of suicide tortures them for months, for a year or even for many years; this affliction seems to have taken a long time to sap the existence of the Geneva philosopher. Of a happy temperament but gifted by a high sensitivity, Rousseau becomes afflicted by the miserable state he finds himself in and the somberest of melancholy fills his heart. Apprehensive, faint-hearted, timid, suspicious, he avoids men because he believes they are all perverse, all his enemies. He seeks solitude and soon wishes for death. Let's look at some of his immortal writings to justify our assertion: 'Here am I all alone on earth, without parents, friends or society. Thus the most loving of men has been banished by unanimous agreement. I have been in this painful situation for more than twenty years, it still seems like a dream to me. I have headaches and continual indigestion, the least thing scares me, upsets me and saddens me. . . . Since my body is only an embarrassment, an obstacle to my rest, I shall seek a way to divest myself of it as soon as it will be possible.' " (Cited in Fuller, 1973, p. 60)

Falret then went on to describe the circumstances of Rousseau's death, concluding that "this great writer accomplished his fatal project."

At the present time, suicide ranks among the first ten causes of death in most Western countries. In the United States, estimates show that over 200,000 persons attempt suicide each year, and that over 5 million living Americans have made suicide attempts at some time in their lives. Official figures show that some 26,000 successful suicides occur each year, meaning that about every 20 minutes someone in the United States commits suicide. Indeed, the problem may be much more serious than these figures suggest, since many self-inflicted deaths are certified in official records as being attributable to other "more respectable" causes than suicide. Most experts agree that the number of actual suicides is at least twice—and possibly several times—as high as the number officially reported.

Nor can statistics, however accurate, begin to convey the tragedy of suicide in human terms. As we shall see, probably the great majority of persons who commit suicide are actually quite ambivalent about taking their own lives. The irreversible choice is made when they are alone and in a state of severe psychological stress, unable to see their problems objectively or to evaluate alternative courses of action. Thus a basic humanitarian problem in suicide is the seemingly senseless loss of life by an individual who may be ambivalent about living, or who does not really want to die. A second tragic concern arises from the long-lasting distress among those left behind that may result from such action. As Shneidman (1969) has put it, "The person who commits suicide puts his psychological skeleton in the survivor's emotional closet. . ." (p. 22).

In our present discussion, we shall focus in turn on some additional aspects of the incidence and clinical picture in suicide, on factors that appear to be of causal significance, on degrees of intent and ways of communicating it, and on issues of treatment and prevention.

Clinical picture and causal pattern

Since the clinical picture and etiology of suicide are so closely interrelated, it is useful to consider these topics under one general heading. This will lead us to a consideration of the following questions: Who commits suicide? What are the motives for taking one's own life? What general sociocultural variables appear to be relevant to an understanding of suicide?

Who commits suicide?

In the United States, the peak age for suicide attempts is between 24 and 44 (see HIGHLIGHT beginning on page 578). Three times as many men as women *commit* suicide, but more women make suicide *attempts*. Most attempts occur in the context of interpersonal discord or other severe life stress. For females, the most commonly used method is drug ingestion, usually barbiturates; males tend to use methods

more likely to be lethal, particularly firearms, which is probably the reason that successful suicides are higher among men. However, there is evidence that this long-established pattern may be changing; data from various Western countries, including the United States, indicate that the incidence of completed suicide has been increasing at a faster rate for women than for men in recent years. Also, more widows than widowers complete the act (Suter, 1976), although this seems due mainly to the disproportionate incidence of widowhood. The reasons for these trends are unknown but are almost certainly related to the changes that are occurring in differential sex roles. Another perplexing trend is that rates of completed suicide among teenagers and even children seem to be increasing at what many feel is an alarming pace (Klagsbrun, 1976; *Time*, September 25, 1978).

Thus, while the overall national rate has increased slightly but consistently in recent years, disproportionate increases have occurred among females and among younger members of the population. With respect to the age factor, the greatest increase has been among 15- to 24-year-olds; the rate for this age group has almost doubled in a decade and a half. An estimated 80,000 young people will attempt suicide in the next 12 months, and some 4,000 will succeed. In fact, suicide now ranks as the second most common cause of death for 15- to 24-year-olds (the first is auto accidents). Most of us feel that there is something especially tragic when a young person—physically healthy and having seemingly unlimited horizons—undertakes an irreversible self-destructive action.

Interestingly, there often seems to be an "epidemic" quality to suicide, as though the act of one person stimulates others to do the same thing. One of the first recorded instances of epidemic suicide peripherally involved no less a personage than Sigmund Freud. An outbreak of suicides among Viennese high-school students in 1910 was considered sufficiently serious to warrant the attention of the Vienna Psychoanalytical Society, of which Freud was founder and leader. The great man on that occasion, however, summed up the meeting by saying that, for him, the questions remained perplexing and unanswered (reported in Klagsbrun, 1976). And so they have largely remained since that time.

Many well-known creative people in the literary and entertainment world—apparently enjoying every external vestige of success—are known or strongly suspected of having committed suicide, including Ernest Hemingway, Marilyn Monroe, Freddie Prinze, and Jimi Hendrix.

Facts about suicide

Incidence

General

Suicide ranks among the first 10 causes of death in most Western countries, including the United States. Over 200,000 persons attempt suicide each year in the United States, and an estimated 5 million or more Americans have made suicide attempts at some time in their lives. Official figures show that about 26,000 successful suicides occur each year—a rate of about 12 persons per 100,000 within the population—although the actual incidence is considered to be at least twice as high as official figures indicate. The incidence of suicide is highest in the spring and summer, over weekends, and during special holidays.

Age and sex

Three times as many men as women commit suicide, but women make more suicide attempts, generally using less lethal means. The peak age for suicide attempts is between 24 and 44, but the peak age for completed suicides is 55 to 64. For males the incidence of suicide generally increases with age. For females the rate increases up to age 40 to 60, and then decreases. Over the past several years, however, the incidence of suicide has shown a marked increase among adolescents and young adults, and the proportion among women has similarly risen.

Marital and occupational status

Suicide rates are higher among divorced persons, followed by the widowed and the single, than among married persons except for married teenagers, who have quite high rates. Among certain professional and occupational groups, also, the rate is higher than average; e.g., it is high for physicians (particularly psychiatrists), lawyers, dentists, and psychologists. It is also high for unskilled laborers and persons with low employment security; and it is disproportionately high among black youth.

General sociocultural factors

The incidence of suicide varies significantly from one society to another as well as among subgroups within a society. In West Germany, Finland, and Hungary, for example, the annual suicide rate is over 20 persons per 100,000, whereas New Guinea and the Philippines have a rate of about 1 per 100,000. Religious beliefs are apparently one significant variable, as suggested by the fact that suicide rates are relatively low in both Catholic and Muslim countries—as they are among religious people generally. The incidence of suicide also varies over time with general sociocultural conditions. Contrary to popular belief, the incidence of suicide tends to decrease during wars, earthquakes, and certain other crises; however, it generally increases during economic depressions and periods of normlessness or social unrest. In the United States, as in other industrialized societies, the suicide rate is significantly greater in urban than in rural areas.

Method

Range of methods used

Every possible method of killing oneself is tried, including the use of barbiturates and other pills, inhalation of carbon monoxide and other poisonous gases, use of firearms and explosives, hanging, strangulation, suffocation, drowning, cutting and stabbing, jumping from high places, and automobile crashes. Firearms are used in more than 10,000 known suicides each year in the United States, 40 percent of the total.

Differences in methods used by men and women	Among men, the methods used in suicide attempts occur approximately in this order: gunshot, hanging, inhalation of carbon monoxide, drowning, use of barbiturates, jumping, use of other drugs, and cutting and stabbing. Among women, the most common methods are the use of barbiturates, hanging, and gunshot, followed by inhalation of carbon monoxide, use of other drugs, jumping, and cutting and stabbing.

Intent

Degree of intent	Most persons who attempt suicide either do not really want to kill themselves (approximately two-thirds of all who make such attempts) or are ambivalent about the consequences of their act (approximately one-third). Only a very small minority—estimated at from 3 to 5 percent—are intent on dying. Investigators have noted that the more violent the method used (such as jumping from high places or the use of firearms or explosives) the more serious the intent. The use of such methods also indicates that if one attempt fails, another is likely to follow.
Communication of intent	The great majority of persons who eventually attempt suicide make their distress and intentions known beforehand—either by threats or by such other cues as sudden increase in the consumption of alcohol or barbiturates, discussion of the methods of suicide, or a developing depression. Some write suicide notes which, if found in time, may prevent the suicide attempt from succeeding. Contrary to the popular belief that few persons who threaten suicide actually attempt to take their lives, the risk of suicide is very high among such individuals. In fact, the majority of suicide attempts are preceded by direct or indirect threats, predominantly the former.
Intervention	More than 200 Suicide Prevention Centers have been established throughout the United States for the purpose of helping people through suicidal crises. Emotionally disturbed individuals can call such centers around the clock and get help in dealing with their problems, depressions, and self-injurious impulses (see Highlight on page 591).

The preceding information relates to actual suicidal behavior. However, it would appear that many individuals, while not clearly suicidal in the ordinary sense, also engage in life-threatening behavior. Here, for example, may be those who "drink themselves to death," who are extremely accident-prone as a result of indifference or carelessness, or who engage in other behavior so injurious to mental and physical well-being that it may lead to their death.

Based on Berman (1975), Brown (1975), Browning (1974), Dizmang et al. (1974), Farberow (1974), Kidson and Jones (1968), Peck and Seiden (1975), Ross (1974), Shneidman (1973), Suter (1976), and Weissman (1974).

An "epidemic" quality is suggested by the multiple suicides among teenagers that have recently occurred in Ridgewood, New Jersey (*Time*, December 25, 1978) and in a suburb of Columbus, Ohio (Potts, 1978). Both communities would be classed as well-to-do by any reasonable standard, their youth populations being on the average distinctly "privileged" in respect to access to societal resources. And yet a number of youngsters in these communities have proceeded systematically and "cold-bloodedly" to kill themselves. It would seem that despair and hopelessness are not the exclusive province either of the downtrodden or of those whose possibilities have narrowed with advancing age.

In keeping with this paradoxical situation, many college students seem peculiarly vulnerable to the development of suicidal motivations, perhaps especially those attending the larger, more prestigious colleges. The rate seems to be higher in large universities than in community colleges and small liberal arts colleges (Peck & Schrut, 1971). The combined stressors of academic demands, problems of social interaction, and career choice—in interaction perhaps with challenges to their basic values—evidently make it impossible for such students to continue making the adjustive compromises their life situations demand (see HIGHLIGHT on page 581). Some 10,000 college students in the United States attempt suicide each year, and over 1000 of them succeed.

The greatest incidence of suicidal behavior among college students occurs at the beginning and the end of the school quarter or semester. Approximately three times more female than male students attempt suicide, but more males than females succeed. More than half of those who attempt suicide take pills, about one third cut themselves, and the remainder—mostly males—use other methods, such as hanging or gunshot (Klagsbrun, 1976; Ryle, 1969).

Other high-risk groups include depressed persons, the elderly (white), alcoholics, the separated or divorced, individuals living alone, migrants, people from socially disorganized areas, members of some Native American tribes, and certain professionals, such as physicians, dentists, lawyers, and psychologists. Both female physicians and female psychologists commit suicide at a rate about three times that of women in the general population; male physicians have a suicide rate about twice that of men in the general population (Ross, 1974; Schaar, 1974). The Highlight on page 594 provides more information on people at high risk for suicidal behavior. Summing up, Seiden (1974) has called suicide "the number one cause of unnecessary, premature, and stigmatizing death" in the United States.

Stress and suicide

The stressful situations associated with suicide are not particularly different from those found in the affective disorders. Thus crises commonly associated with suicide run the gamut from interpersonal disruptions through failure and self-devaluation to loss of meaning and hope. Paykel, Prusoff, and Myers (1975) found that suicide attempters reported 4 times as many recent aversive events as subjects from the general population, and there was a substantial peaking of such events in the month before the suicide attempt.

Depression and anger.   It would appear that the majority—about three fourths—of all persons who commit suicide are depressed at the time of the suicidal act (Leonard, 1974; Zung & Green, 1974). Often, there has been a retreat into self in an attempt to "comprehend" what is happening and to think through a course of action. Unfortunately, as we have seen, during periods of intense stress the individual's ability to think rationally is often impaired. As Farberow and Litman (1970) have expressed it,

"When clinical depression becomes acute, mental myopia is common. That is to say, a depressed person is emotionally incapable of perceiving realistic alternative solutions to a difficult problem. His thinking process is often limited to the point where he can see no other way out of a bad situation other than that of suicide." (p. 85)

One depressed and suicidal young woman described her feelings as "being like a dark fog drifting in and enveloping me, so that I can no longer see or think about anything but darkness and gloom."

In some instances the individual's thinking seems to involve depression coupled with in-

Warning signs for student suicide

A change in a student's mood and behavior is a significant warning of possible suicide. Characteristically, the student becomes depressed and withdrawn, undergoes a marked decline in self-esteem, and shows deterioration in habits of personal hygiene. This is accompanied by a profound loss of interest in studies. Often he or she stops attending classes and stays at home most of the day. Usually the student's distress is communicated to at least one other person, often in the form of a veiled suicide warning. A significant number of students who attempt suicide leave suicide notes.

When college students attempt suicide, one of the first explanations to occur to those around them is that they may have been doing poorly in school. As a group, however, they are superior students, and while they tend to expect a great deal of themselves in terms of academic achievement and to exhibit scholastic anxieties, grades, academic competition, and pressure over examinations are not regarded as significant precipitating stresses. Also, while many lose interest in their studies prior to the onset of suicidal behavior and their grades get lower, the loss of interest appears to be associated with depression and withdrawal caused by other problems. Moreover, when academic failure does appear to trigger suicidal behavior—in a minority of cases—the actual cause of the behavior is generally considered to be loss of self-esteem and failure to live up to parental expectations, rather than the academic failure itself.

For most suicidal students, both male and female, the major precipitating stressor appears to be either the failure to establish, or the loss of, a close interpersonal relationship. Often the breakup of a romance is the key precipitating factor. It has also been noted that there are significantly more suicide attempts and suicides by students from families where there has been separation, divorce, or the death of a parent. A particularly important precipitating factor among college males appears to be the existence of a close emotional involvement with a parent that is threatened when the student becomes involved with another person in college and tries to break this "parental knot."

Although most colleges and universities have mental health facilities to assist distressed students, few suicidal students seek professional help. Thus, it is of vital importance for those around a suicidal student to notice the warning signs and try to obtain assistance.

Sources drawn on for this description include Hendin (1975), Miller (1975), Murray (1973), Nelson (1971), Pausnau and Russell (1975), Peck and Schrut (1971), Shneidman, Parker, and Funkhouser (1970), and Stanley and Barter (1970).

tense anger and hostility and a desire to seek revenge on other persons. As Weissman, Fox, and Klerman (1973) have described it, "The suicide attempter is usually depressed, hostile, and immersed in a network of interpersonal relations that are frustrating and maladaptive" (p. 454). In still other instances, however, these individuals' thought processes are chaotic, and they are out of contact with reality when they attempt suicide. This may occur in certain forms of drug intoxication, schizophrenia, psychotic depressions, and states of extreme anxiety and panic.

Interpersonal crises. Interpersonal conflicts and disruptions—such as those associated with marital conflict, separation, divorce, or the loss of loved ones through death—may result in severe stress and suicidal behavior. The following was written by a 19-year-old college student:

Dear Jim:
I've just emptied 40 capsules and put the powder in a glass of water. I'm about to take it. I'm scared and I want to talk to someone but I just don't have anybody to talk to. I feel like I'm completely alone and nobody cares. I know our breakup was my fault but it hurts so bad. Nothing I do seems to turn out right, but nothing. My whole life has fallen apart. Maybe if, but I know.

I've thought about all of the trite phrases about how it will get brighter tomorrow and how suicide is copping out and really isn't a solution and maybe it isn't but I hurt so bad. I just want it to stop. I feel like my back is up against the wall and there is no other way out.

It's getting harder to think and my life is about to end. Tears are rolling down my face and I feel so scared and alone. Oh Jim . . . if you could put your arms around me and hold me close . . . just one last time. . . . . J. . .m.

Often such interpersonal difficulties include a combination of stressful factors—such as frustration and hostility over feeling rejected, a wish for revenge, and a desire to withdraw from the turmoil of a relationship that is highly conflictful and hurtful but on which the individual feels dependent. In other instances, suicidal behavior may follow the death of a loved one on whom the person felt dependent for emotional support and meaning in life.

Failure and self-devaluation.
Many suicides are associated with feelings of having failed in some important enterprise—often involving occupational aspirations and accomplishments—with resulting feelings of self-devaluation.

James Forrestal had been the Secretary of the Navy and the nation's first Secretary of Defense. In 1949 he took his life by jumping from his sixteenth-floor room at Bethesda Naval Hospital.

Forrestal was described as extremely conscientious, compulsively hard-working, and inclined to make excessive demands on himself; he was highly self-critical and suffered from feelings of inadequacy. Prior to taking his life, he apparently felt increasing pessimism concerning the world situation, and also felt that he had failed to achieve what he had hoped to accomplish in public office. During an episode of self-recrimination and depression, he committed suicide. (Adapted from Rogow, 1969)

A tragic aspect of this case is that James Forrestal was a highly respected man who was admired for his accomplishments in office. In fact, some of his friends thought that his political future might even include the White House.

Inner conflict.
Here the stressful situation is characterized by inner conflict and debate in the person's own mind, rather than by interpersonal difficulties or devaluating failures. He or she may be anxious and confused, struggle with the meaning of life and death, and decide that it is not worth it to continue the struggle any longer.

In this context, it is interesting to note the following comment made by Ernest Hemingway to a close friend:

"Hotch, if I can't exist on my own terms, then existence is impossible. Do you understand? That is how I've lived, and that is how I *must* live—or not live." (Hotchner, 1966, p. 297)

This letter was written shortly before Hemingway took his own life after receiving a diagnosis of a terminal illness. It is worth noting that Hemingway was in deep despair because he believed that a series of electroconvulsive shocks administered during depression had robbed him of his memory—an essential tool for a writer.

Loss of meaning and hope.
Several investigators have pointed out that of all the feelings associated with suicide, hopelessness is the most predominant (Boss, 1976; Kovacs, Beck, & Weissman, 1975; Melges & Bowlby, 1969; Minkoff et al., 1973; Wolman, 1976). As long as they see a chance that things will improve, and as long as they see meaning in their lives, most people continue to work toward valued goals. With the loss of hope and meaning, however, an individual may feel that life is futile and pointless. As a result, such a person may give up trying and use suicide as a way out.

The feeling that life has lost its meaning and that there really is no hope often occurs in chronic or terminal illnesses. In a study of surgical patients with malignant neoplasms, Farberow, Shneidman, and Leonard (1963) found that suicide may occur even when the patient has only a few hours or, at most, days to live. Similarly, Abram, Moore, and Westervelt (1971) found the suicide rate among chronic dialysis patients to be 400 times that of the general population. Here one is reminded of the haunting lines of Camus' *The Myth of Sisyphus:* "Is one to die voluntarily or to hope in spite of everything?"

Although the preceding categories include most of the key stresses associated with suicidal behavior, the specific factors in each category may take many forms. For example, one middle-aged man developed profound feelings of guilt after being promoted to the presidency of the bank for which he worked; shortly after his promotion, he fatally slit his throat. Similarly, suicide may be associated with severe financial reverses, loss of social status, imprisonment, or other difficult situations.

General sociocultural factors

Suicide rates vary considerably from one society to another. Hungary, with an annual incidence of 38.4 per 100,000, has the world's highest rate.[1] Other Western countries with high rates—20 per 100,000 or higher—include Czechoslovakia, Finland, Austria, and Sweden. The United States has a rate of 12.7 per 100,000, which is roughly comparable to that of Canada. In Mexico, New Guinea, and the Philippine Islands the rate drops to 1.1 per 100,000; and among certain groups, such as the aborigines of the Australian western desert, the suicide rate drops to zero—possibly as a result of a strong fear of death (Kidson & Jones, 1968).

Religious taboos concerning suicide as well as the attitudes of a society toward death are apparently important determinants of suicide rates. Both Catholicism and Mohammedanism strongly condemn suicide, and suicide rates in Catholic and Arab countries are correspondingly low. In fact, most societies have developed strong sanctions against suicide, and many still regard it as a crime as well as a sin.

Japan is one of the very few major societies in which suicide has been socially approved under certain circumstances—for example, in response to conditions that bring disgrace to the individual or the group. During World War II, large numbers of Japanese villagers were reported to have committed mass suicide when faced with imminent capture by Allied forces. There were also reported instances of group suicide by Japanese military personnel under threat of defeat. In the case of the *Kamikaze*, Japanese pilots who deliberately crashed their planes into American warships during the final stages of hostilities, self-destruction was a way of demonstrating complete personal commitment to the national purpose. It is estimated that approximately a thousand young Japanese males destroyed themselves in this exercise of patriotic zeal.

Societal norms cannot wholly explain differences in suicide rates, however, for the incidence of suicide often varies significantly among societies with similar cultures and also among different subgroups *within* given societies. For example, it is difficult to account for marked differences in suicide rates between Sweden and the United States, and we have noted differences in our own society with respect to sex, occupation, and age. In fact, the Scandinavian countries in general, sharing as they do a relatively common ethnic background and cultural pattern and overall high rates of suicide, pose a puzzling problem because the rate in Norway has remained stable and relatively low by world standards for the past century (Retterstøl, 1975)—thus exploding the myth that the high level of social welfare programs in Scandinavia is responsible for encouraging suicide by removing the challenge, and hope, of "making one's own way."

In a pioneering study of sociocultural factors in suicide, the French sociologist Émile Durkheim (1897) attempted to relate differences in suicide rates to differences in group cohesiveness. Analyzing records of suicides in different countries and for different historical periods, Durkheim concluded that the greatest barrier against committing suicide in times of personal stress is a sense of involvement and identity with other people. The likelihood of suicide increases, he maintained, among individuals who lack strong group ties (e.g., among single and divorced people as opposed to married ones, among the nonreligious as opposed to those who identify themselves with an organized faith), and it also increases under conditions of normlessness or *anomie*, when traditional group standards and expectations no longer seem to apply (e.g., during periods of economic depression, and after defeat in war). Durkheim termed these two patterns of suicide *egoistic* and *anomic* suicide, respectively. He identified a third pattern as *altruistic* suicide, in which the individual—far from lacking a sense of group involvement—feels closely identified with a group and willingly commits suicide for "the greater good." In modern times this pattern was illustrated not only by the *Kamikaze* pilots but also by Buddhist monks and nuns who burned themselves to death as a form of public protest in Vietnam.

Durkheim's theory takes little account of psychosocial factors other than group cohesion, but it does seem to help explain some of

---

[1]Incidence rate is calculated in terms of the number of completed suicides per 100,000 of the population per year. The figures given are approximations of those reported to the World Health Organization and cited in the UN's *Demographic Yearbook*, 1976.

As a form of public protest in Vietnam, a Buddhist monk turns himself into a burning torch as spectators solemnly watch.

the variations in suicide rates that have been observed. Thus, in our own society, as in those Durkheim studied, suicide rates have tended to increase during economic depressions, to remain constant during periods of domestic stability and prosperity, and to decrease during crises such as war, when people become united in a common purpose.

Durkheim's views also appear relevant to understanding the higher incidence of suicide among subgroups in our society who are subjected to conditions of uncertainty and social disorganization in the absence of strong group ties. In a study sponsored by the National Institute of Mental Health, Hall et al. (1970) found that low-income persons from large urban areas have an especially high rate of suicidal gestures and attempts. Similarly, suicide rates have been found to be higher than average among people who are "downwardly mobile" (or who fear they may become so) and among groups who are undergoing severe social pressures. For example, in 1932 at the height of

"the great depression" in the United States the suicide rate increased from less than 10 to 17.4 per 100,000; and during the early years of severe recession of the mid-1970s, the suicide rate increased to above 12 per 100,000 (NIMH, 1975). Following the same trend of thought, we could point to the environmental pressures that appear to contribute to the high rate of suicide among black youth in our society; and Parkin (1974) has noted the marked increase in suicide among Eskimo teenagers in Alaska, who appear to find themselves trapped in a sort of "no-man's-land" between their past culture and assimilation into the "white world."

A number of investigators, including Havighurst (1969) and Binstock (1974), have suggested that there is an inverse relationship between homicide and suicide in most cultures and ethnic groups. Where homicides are high, the suicide rate tends to be lower, and vice versa. Presumably, where homicide rates are high, frustration and hostility are turned outward against others rather than inward against the self. Further evidence is needed before any definite conclusions can be drawn, but in our society, where violence, homicide, and suicide rates are all high, the proposed inverse relationship is not apparent.

In any event, social forces as well as personal characteristics and life stress appear to be implicated as causal factors in suicidal behavior.

Suicidal ambivalence

From the standpoint of intent or motivation, suicide appears to be one method of obtaining relief from an aversive life situation. However, since most people undergoing severe stress do not commit suicide—for example, only a small number of patients who develop terminal cancer take their own lives—the question arises as to why an individual uses this method of coping rather than another. This is not an easy question to answer; it involves consideration not only of stress but also of other aspects of the individual's psychological state at the time of the suicide attempt.

Degree of intent

The ambivalence that typically accompanies thoughts of suicide finds classic expression in Hamlet's famous soliloquy:

To be, or not to be: that is the question:
Whether 'tis nobler in the mind to suffer
The slings and arrows of outrageous fortune,
Or to take arms against a sea of troubles,
And by opposing end them? To die: to sleep;
No more; and by a sleep to say we end
The heart-ache and the thousand natural shocks
That flesh is heir to, 'tis a consummation
Devoutly to be wish'd. To die, to sleep;
To sleep: perchance to dream: ay, there's the rub;
For in that sleep of death what dreams may come
When we have shuffled off this mortal coil,
Must give us pause. . . .

(*Hamlet*, Act III, scene i)

Recognizing that the vast majority of people who contemplate suicide do not in fact kill themselves, some investigators have focused on analyzing the degree of intent associated with suicidal behavior. Thus Farberow and Litman (1970)—echoing Hamlet—have classified suicidal behavior into three categories: "To be," "Not to be," and "To be or not to be."

The "To be" group involves individuals who do not really wish to die, but rather wish to communicate a dramatic message to others concerning their distress and contemplation of suicide. Their suicide attempts involve minimal drug ingestion, minor wrist slashing, and similar nonlethal methods. They usually arrange matters so that intervention by others is almost inevitable, although sometimes things do go awry. This group is estimated to make up about two thirds of the total suicidal population. As we have seen, a large—although decreasing—proportion of those who make unsuccessful attempts are women. It seems probable that traditional sex-role socialization of females predisposes many women to feel helpless and to fantasize being rescued—and thus to communicate in this mode (Suter, 1976).

In contrast, the "Not to be" group involves persons who seemingly are intent on dying. They give little or no warning of their intent to kill themselves, and they usually arrange the suicidal situation so that intervention is not possible. Although these persons use a variety of different methods for killing themselves, they generally rely on the more violent and certain means, such as shooting themselves or jumping from high places. It has been estimated that this group makes up only about 3 to 5 percent of the suicidal population. Successful preventive intervention with this group is at best a doubtful goal, even when the person is protectively incarcerated. In an interesting experiment, a pseudosuicidal "patient" (actually one of the investigators) gained admission to a mental hospital ward on "suicidal status." Though he was supposedly being carefully watched, he discovered multiple opportunities to do himself in (Reynolds & Farberow, 1976).

The "To be or not to be" group constitutes about 30 percent of the suicidal population. It is comprised of persons who are ambivalent about dying and tend to leave the question of death to chance, or, as they commonly view it, to fate. Although loss of a love object, strained interpersonal relationships, financial problems, or feelings of meaninglessness may be present, the individual still entertains some hope of working things out. The methods used for the suicide attempt are often dangerous but moderately slow acting, such as fairly high drug ingestion, or cutting oneself severely in nonvital parts of the body, thus allowing for the possibility of intervention. The feeling is apparently that, "If I die the conflict is settled, but if I am rescued that is what is meant to be." Often the persons in this group lead stormy, stress-filled lives and make repeated suicide attempts. After an unsuccessful attempt, there is usually a marked reduction in emotional turmoil. This reduction is not stable, however, and in a subsequent trial by fate, the verdict may well be death. In a follow-up study of 886 persons who had made suicidal attempts, Rosen (1970) classified them as serious (21 percent) or nonserious (79 percent). During the year following the attempts, the rate of successful suicide was twice as high among the group whose earlier attempts had been classified as serious.

Farberow and Litman's classification is largely descriptive and has little practical value in terms of predicting suicidal behavior. As we indicated, however, it does seem possible to infer the degree of intent from the lethality of the method used—a conclusion strongly supported by the more recent findings of Beck, Beck, and Kovacs (1975). The concept of intent is also a very useful reminder that most people who contemplate suicide retain at least some urge to live. Their hold on life, however tenuous, provides the key to successful suicide prevention programs.

Communication of suicidal intent

Research has clearly demonstrated the tragic fallacy of the belief that those who threaten to take their lives seldom do so. In fact, such people represent a very high-risk group in comparison with the general population. In a cross-cultural study, Rudestam (1971) conducted extensive interviews with close friends or relatives of 50 consecutive suicides in Stockholm and Los Angeles and found that at least 60 percent of the victims in both cities had made "direct" verbal threats of their intent. An additional 20 percent had made "indirect" threats.

In a similar study involving suicide deaths in Vienna and Los Angeles, Farberow and Simon (1975) found substantial differences between the two cities. In Los Angeles, 72 percent had made direct references to intent, versus only 27 percent in Vienna; the corresponding figures for indirect references were 25 percent and 2 percent. It would thus appear that cultural factors determine to some extent the likelihood that suicidal intent will be "signaled" to others.

Indirect threats typically include such behaviors as making statements about being better off dead, references to methods of committing suicide and to burial, making a point of saying "If I see you again . . . ," and making dire predictions about something happening to them.

Whether direct or indirect, communication of suicidal intent usually represents "a cry for help." The person is trying to express distress and ambivalence about suicide; the statements are both warnings and calls for help. Unfortunately, the message is often not received or is received with skepticism and denial. The latter pattern is particularly apt to occur when the suicidal person has given repeated warnings but has not made an actual suicide attempt. As a consequence, the recipients of the message may state that they did not think it would happen; or that they thought it might happen but only if the person became much more depressed. In this area, "crying wolf" needs to be taken seriously.

As several investigators have pointed out, many people who are contemplating suicide feel that living may be preferable if they can obtain the understanding and support of significant others. Failing to receive it, they go on to actual suicide.

Suicide notes

A number of investigators have analyzed the content of suicide notes in an effort to better understand the motives and feelings of persons who take their own lives. In a pioneering study of 742 suicides, Tuckman, Kleiner, and Lavell (1959) found that 24 percent left notes, usually addressed to relatives or friends. The notes were either mailed or found on the person of the deceased or near the suicide scene. With few exceptions, the notes were coherent and legible. In terms of emotional content, the suicide notes were categorized into those showing positive, negative, and neutral affect. And, of course, some notes showed combinations of these affective components.

1. *Positive emotional content.* Interestingly enough, 51 percent of the notes in the study by Tuckman et al. (1959) showed positive affect, expressing affection, gratitude, and concern for others. The following is a brief but somewhat typical example.

"Please forgive me and please forget me. I'll always love you. All I have was yours. No one ever did more for me than you, oh please pray for me please." (p. 60)

The following excerpts from a suicide note left by a 30-year-old psychiatrist also show positive affect and concern for others, but discouragement and hopelessness are apparent:

"I'm sorry, but somewhere I lost the road, and in my struggle to find it again, I just got further and further away.
    "There should be little sadness, and no searching for who is at fault; for the act and the result are not sad, and no one is at fault." (Shneidman, 1973, p. 379)

Here one is reminded of Darbonne's (1969) description of a suicide note as the "communication of the vanquished" (p. 49).

2. *Negative (hostile) emotional content.* Surprisingly, only 6 percent of the suicide notes were classified as involving pure hostility or negative affect. In most cases the hostility was directed toward others, as in the case of the following note:

"I hate you and all of your family and I hope you never have a piece of mind. I hope I haunt this house as long as you live here and I wish you all the bad luck in the world." (Tuckman et al., 1959, p. 60)

In other cases hostility was directed inward and accompanied by severe self-devaluation, as expressed in the following note.

"I know at last what I have to do. I pray to God to forgive me for all the many sins I have committed and for all the many people I have wronged, I no longer have the strength to go on, what I am about to do

The vast majority of people who contemplate suicide do not end up killing themselves. This young man, shown clinging to a cable of the Brooklyn Bridge, considered whether or not to jump for more than an hour before he was finally talked into climbing down to safety by his guardian and a member of the clergy.

might seem wrong to a lot of people, but I don't think so, I have given it plenty of sober consideration." (Tuckman, et al., 1959, p. 60)

3. *Neutral emotional content.* Suicide notes expressing neutral feeling commonly begin with "To whom it may concern," "To the police," or they may not be addressed to anyone. The following is an example.

"To Whom It May Concern,
    "I, Mary Smith, being of sound mind, do this day, make my last will as follows—I bequeath my rings, Diamond and Black Opal to my daughter-in-law, Doris Jones and any other of my personal belongings she might wish. What money I have in my savings account and my checking account goes to my dear father, as he won't have me to help him. To my husband, Ed Smith, I leave my furniture and car.

"I would like to be buried as close to the grave of John Jones as possible." (Darbonne, 1969, p. 50)

People who leave suicide notes of this type are often older persons who have lost a sense of having a meaningful role in life and wish to "check out" in an orderly way. In the study of Tuckman et al., 25 percent of the suicide notes were classified as emotionally neutral.

   4. *Mixed emotional content.* The note that follows contains a combination of positive and negative affect.

Dear Daddy:
   Please don't grieve for me or feel that you did something wrong, you didn't. I'll leave this life loving you and remembering the world's greatest father.
   I'm sorry to cause you more heartache but the reason I can't live anymore is because I'm afraid. Afraid of facing my life alone without love. No one ever knew how alone I am. No one ever stood by me when I needed help. No one brushed away the tears I cried for "help" and no one heard.

I love you Daddy,
Jeannie

Eighteen percent of the suicide notes in the study by Tuckman et al. involved a mixture of positive and negative affect.

   Shneidman and Farberow (1957), in another pioneering study, approached the question of the content of suicide notes by comparing 33 notes written by actual suicides with 33 composed by matched subjects who were asked to simulate a pre-suicidal state. The principal difference between the actual and the fictitious notes was that the actual ones had a greater number of thought units of a "neutral" quality. Evidently only the genuine writer tends to deal concretely with the idea of actually being gone; therefore he or she incorporates much more material of an instructional and admonishing sort to survivors. The genuine writers, however, also expressed more intense feelings of self-blame, hatred, demand, and vengeance.

   In a more recent study, Cohen and Fiedler (1974) compared 220 cases of completed suicides who left notes with 813 cases of non-note writers. In contrast to the findings of Tuckman et al.—who reported no differences with respect to such variables as sex, race, and marital status—these investigators found that 26 percent of female suicides left notes as con-

trasted with 19 percent of males. They also found that 40 percent of the separated or divorced females in their sample left notes as contrasted with approximately 31 percent of single females, 25 percent of married females, and 16 percent of widows. White suicide committers left notes almost three times as often as nonwhite committers. In terms of content, the use of emotional categories corresponded to those reported by Tuckman and his associates—with positive, neutral, mixed, and negative being used in that order of frequency. In the study by Farberow and Simon (1975) noted earlier, 46 percent of the residents of Los Angeles who committed suicide had left notes, but only 18 percent of the Viennese had done so. It would appear that the wish to communicate with survivors "after the fact" varies considerably with a host of demographic and cultural variables.

   An understanding of the reasons for or motives underlying note-writing (or its absence) could possibly help make the bases of the variations clearer. On this point, Cohen and Fiedler (1974) concluded,

"Many note writers seem to be motivated to influence the responses of survivors. The desire to be remembered positively by a survivor may account for the large number of statements expressing positive affect. By statements of love and concern, a note writer may try to reassure both the survivor and himself of the worth of their relationship and his own worth as a person." (pp. 93–94)

However, these investigators, as well as Shneidman (1973), expressed disappointment that suicide notes—written by persons on the brink of life's greatest mystery—failed to contain any "great insights" or "special messages" for the rest of us. As Cohen and Fiedler (1974) express it,

"the large quantity of references to the concrete, mundane features of everyday life is not congruent with the romantic conception of suicide as a grand, dramatic gesture preceded and accompanied by a corresponding state of the psyche into which the suicide note should serve as a kind of window. Perhaps all the drama takes place before the action is decided or it is anticipated in the act itself. Whatever role the dramatic elements may play, the large number of references to the commonplace squares

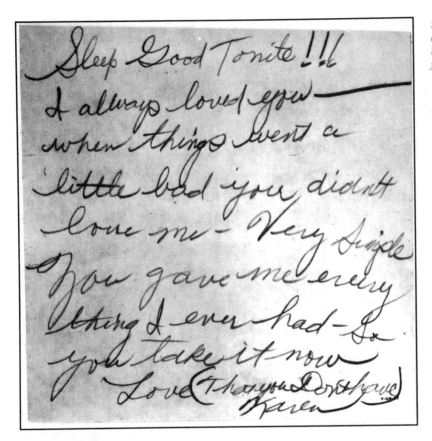

Suicide notes may have mixed emotional content, including both positive and negative feelings.

best with the conception of suicide notes as communications tailored to the needs of both the suicide and his survivors as these are perceived by the suicide under the existing circumstances." (pp. 94–95)

Suicide prevention

The prevention of suicide is an extremely difficult problem. One complicating factor is that most persons who are depressed and contemplating suicide do not realize that their thinking is restricted and irrational and that they are in need of assistance. Less than one third voluntarily seek psychological help; others are brought to the attention of mental health personnel by family members or friends who are concerned because the person appears depressed and/or has made suicide threats. The majority, however, do not receive the assistance they so desperately need. Yet, as we have seen, most persons who attempt suicide do not really want to die and give prior warning of their intentions; if the individual's "cry for help" can be heard in time, it is often possible to intervene successfully.

Currently the main thrust of preventive efforts is on crisis intervention. Efforts are gradually being extended, however, to the broader tasks of alleviating longer-term stressful conditions known to be associated with suicidal behavior and trying to better understand and cope with the suicide problem in "high-risk" groups.

Crisis intervention

The primary objective of crisis intervention is to help the individual cope with an immediate life crisis. If a serious suicide attempt has been made, the first step involves emergency medical treatment. Typically such treatment is given through the usual channels for handling medical emergencies—the emergency rooms of general hospitals or clinics. It would appear, however, that only about 10 percent of suicide attempts are considered of sufficient severity to warrant intensive medical care; the great majority of attempters, after initial treatment, are referred to inpatient or outpatient mental health facilities (Kirstein et al., 1975; Paykel et al., 1974).

When persons contemplating suicide are willing to discuss their problems with someone at a suicide prevention center, it is often possible to avert an actual suicide attempt. Here the primary objective is to help these individuals regain their ability to cope with their immediate problems—and to do so as quickly as possible. Emphasis is usually placed on (a) maintaining contact with the person over a short period of time—usually 1 to 6 contacts; (b) helping the person realize that acute distress is impairing his or her ability to assess the situation accurately and to choose among possible alternatives; (c) helping the person see that there are other ways of dealing with the problem that are preferable to suicide; (d) taking a highly directive as well as supportive role—for example, fostering a dependent relationship and giving specific suggestions to the person about what to do and what not to do; and (e) helping the person see that the present distress and emotional turmoil will not be endless (see HIGHLIGHT on page 591). When indicated and feasible, the understanding and emotional support of family members or friends may be elicited; and, of course, frequent use is made of relevant community agencies. Admittedly, however, these are "stopgap" measures rather than complete therapy.

In terms of long-range outcomes, people who have made previous suicide attempts are more likely to kill themselves than those who have not, although only about 10 percent of unsuccessful suicide attempters kill themselves at a later time (Seiden, 1974; WHO, 1974). As Seiden has expressed it, the suicidal crisis "is not a lifetime characteristic of most suicide attempters. It is rather an acute situation, often a matter of only minutes or hours at the most" (p. 2). Since the suicide rate for previous attempters is so much higher than that for the population in general, however, it is apparent that suicide attempters remain a relatively high-risk group.

Farberow (1974) has pointed out that it is important to distinguish between (a) individuals who have demonstrated relatively stable adjustment but have been overwhelmed by some acute stress—about 35 to 40 percent of persons coming to the attention of hospitals and suicide prevention centers; and (b) individuals who have been tenuously adjusted for some time and in whom the current suicidal crisis represents an intensification of ongoing problems—about 60 to 65 percent of suicidal cases. For individuals in the first group, crisis intervention is usually sufficient to help them cope with the immediate stress and regain their equilibrium. For individuals in the second group, crisis intervention may also be sufficient to help them deal with the present problem situation, but with their life-style of "staggering from one crisis to another," they are likely to require more comprehensive therapy.

During recent years the availability of competent assistance at times of suicidal crisis has been expanded through the establishment of suicide prevention centers. At present, there are over 200 such centers in the United States. These centers are geared primarily toward crisis intervention—usually via 24-hour-a-day availability of telephone contact. Some centers, however, offer longer-term therapy programs, and they can arrange for the referral of suicidal persons to other community agencies and organizations for special types of assistance. Such suicide prevention centers are staffed by a variety of personnel: psychologists, psychiatrists, social workers, clergy, and trained volunteers. Although there was initially some doubt about the wisdom of using nonprofessionals in the important first-contact role, experience has shown that the empathetic concern and peer-type relationships provided by volunteer workers can be highly effective in helping an individual through a suicidal crisis. For a guide to suicide prevention center personnel in gauging the seriousness of suicide threats, see the HIGHLIGHT on page 594.

It is difficult to evaluate the long-range impact of emergency aid provided by suicide prevention centers, but such facilities seem to have the potential, at least, for significantly reducing suicide rates. The Suicide Prevention

How a suicide prevention center answers calls for help

The first of the currently more than 200 professionally organized and operated suicide prevention centers in the United States was established in Los Angeles in 1958. Its founders, Norman L. Farberow and
Edwin S. Shneidman, realized the great need for the
services such a center could provide while collecting
data for a study on suicide on the wards of their local
county hospital. Patients who attempted suicide received adequate treatment for their physical injuries,
but little attention was given to their psychological
distress. On discharge they often returned to the same
environmental stresses which had produced their self-
destructive conflicts.

Initially the Suicide Prevention Center searched the
medical wards for persons who had attempted suicide and then, on the basis of interview and other assessment data, it helped them find a mental health
resource in the community for the kind of treatment
they needed. As the SPC became better known, people telephoned for help, and it soon became apparent
that the SPC could best serve as a crisis facility. To
do so, it has to be accessible and the staff has to be
trained in certain basic meanings of suicidal behavior
as well as in therapy procedures.

Taking calls for help centers on five steps, which may
or may not occur concomitantly. Farberow has enun-
ciated them as follows:

**1. Establish a relationship, maintain contact, and
obtain information.** The worker has to be able to listen nonjudgmentally and to assure the caller of interest, concern, and availability of help.

2. Identify and clarify the focal problem. Often the
caller is so disorganized and confused that he or she
is overwhelmed with all problems, both major and
minor, having seemingly lost the ability to determine
which is most important.

3. Evaluate the suicide potential. The staff person
must determine quickly how close the caller is to acting on self-destructive impulses, if he or she has not
already done so. The staff person does this by evaluating the information obtained from the caller against
a schedule of crucial items, such as age and sex, suicide plan, and so on, as shown in the Highlight on
page 594.

4. Assess the individual's strengths and resources.
A crisis often presents an opportunity for constructive change. The staff worker attempts to determine
the caller's strengths, capabilities, and other resources as he or she works out a therapeutic plan.

**5. Formulate a constructive plan and mobilize the
individual's own and other resources.** The staff person, together with the caller or significant others, determines the most appropriate course of action for the
caller. This may range from involvement of family
and friends to referral to a clinic or a social agency
or to recommendation of immediate hospitalization.

The emphasis is on crisis intervention and referral,
not on long-term therapy, although in recent years
therapy groups and other long-range treatment measures have been introduced.

In its organization and operation, the Los Angeles
Suicide Prevention Center has provided a prototype
for the other suicide prevention centers that have
been established throughout the United States.

Based on information supplied by the Los Angeles Suicide
Prevention Center.

Center of Los Angeles (Farberow & Litman, 1970) has reported that in comparison with an estimated suicide rate of 6 percent among persons judged to be high risks for suicide, the rate has been slightly less than 2 percent among approximately 8000 high-risk persons who used their services.

One difficult problem with which suicide prevention centers have to deal is that the majority of persons who are seen do not follow up their initial contact by seeking additional help from the center or other treatment agency. In a follow-up of 53 persons who committed suicide after contact with the Cleveland Suicide Prevention Center, Sawyer, Sudak, and Hall (1972) reported that none had recontacted the center just prior to death. They also found that "the interval between the time of last contact with the Center and the time of death ranged from 30 minutes to 32 months with a median interval of 4 months" (p. 232). Since this report was issued, systematic attempts have been made to expand the services of suicide prevention centers to help them better meet the needs of clients. Thus many centers have introduced long-range aftercare or maintenance therapy programs.

Focus on high-risk groups and other measures

Many investigators have emphasized the need for broadly based preventive programs aimed at alleviating the life problems of people who, on the basis of statistics, fall into high-risk groups with respect to suicide. Few such programs have actually been initiated, but one approach has been to involve older males—a very high-risk group—in social and interpersonal roles that contribute to others as a means of lessening their frequent feelings of isolation and meaninglessness. Among this group, such feelings often stem from forced retirement, financial problems, the death of loved ones, impaired physical health, and being unneeded and unwanted.

Another innovative approach to dealing with persons who are contemplating suicide—and in this sense represent a very high-risk group—was originated by a group of volunteers called the Samaritans, begun in England in 1953 by Reverend Chad Varah. The service

Jo Roman, 62, a painter and sculptor, took her own life in a planned suicide after suffering for more than a year with breast cancer. At the time of her death, her condition was not yet critical, but she had decided, "I would not subject myself nor those around me to the emotional strains and physical ravages of terminal cancer. Instead, I would make the best possible calculation of a time frame within which I might count reasonably on being able to function to my satisfaction."

Despite attempts to dissuade her by her husband, a professor of psychiatry, and her daughter, a geriatric social worker, Roman stuck to her decision and spent 15 months methodically planning her death. She wrote a book about suicide, explaining her views on the individual's right to choose death; videotaped 19 hours of conversation on the subject with her family and friends for use in medical training; prepared a coffin-like box with personal mementos—a "life sculpture," she called it. She also wrote a final explanatory letter to her friends and prepared her own obituary. Then, after bidding personal farewells to her husband, daughter, and a close friend, she swallowed 35 sleeping pills and a glass of champagne, quietly went to bed, and died.

extended by the Samaritans is simply that of "befriending." Befrienders offer support to the suicidal person with no strings attached. They are available to listen and help in whatever way needed, expecting nothing in return—not even gratitude. Since their founding, the Samaritans have spread throughout the British Commonwealth and to many other parts of the world as well, and preliminary findings concerning their effectiveness in suicide prevention seem most promising (Farberow, 1974; 1975).

Other measures to broaden the scope of suicide prevention programs include (a) the use of "psychological autopsies" as described in the HIGHLIGHT on this page; (b) assessment of the environments of high-risk groups, often including their work environments; and (c) training of clergy, nurses, police, teachers, and other professional personnel who come in contact with large numbers of people in the community. An important aspect of such training is to be alert for suicidal communications. For example, a parishioner might clasp the hand of a minister after church services and intensely say, "Pray for me." Since such a request is quite normal, the minister who is not alert to suicidal "cries for help" might reply with a simple "Yes, I will" and turn to the next person in line—only to receive the news a few days later that the parishioner has committed suicide.

Ethical issues in suicide prevention

Most of us respect the preservation and fulfillment of human life as a worthwhile value. Thus suicide is generally considered not only tragic but "wrong." However, efforts to prevent suicide also involve problems of ethics. If individuals wish to take their own lives, what obligation—or right—do others have to interfere? This question has been taken seriously by Thomas Szasz (1976), whose view of the problem is captured in the following:

"In regarding the desire to live as a legitimate human aspiration, but not the desire to die, the suicidologist stands Patrick Henry's famous exclamation . . . on its head. In effect, he says, 'Give *him* commitment, give *him* electroshock, give *him* lobotomy, give *him* life-long slavery, but *do not let*

The psychological autopsy

In cases where there is serious doubt about whether or not death was self-inflicted, a "psychological autopsy" may be performed. The psychological autopsy focuses on learning as much as possible about the personality makeup, life situation, and state of mind of the deceased, which may indicate the extent to which the person contributed to his or her own death. To obtain these data, interviews are usually arranged with members of the immediate family, relatives, employer, friends, physician, clergy, and other available persons who may be able to supply relevant information. Often, too, personal letters, paintings, literary works, and other sources may be utilized.

In a detailed and incisive psychological autopsy of Lenny Bruce, a well-known entertainer whose death had been officially listed as accidental, Deikel (1974) concluded:

"*. . . There can be no question that the death of Lenny Bruce was a self-administered act.*" *(p. 190)*

As one becomes familiar with the personality makeup and life-style of Lenny Bruce and is led through the poignant details of the stressful last years and months of his life, there seems little doubt that the above conclusion is warranted.

In this general context, Deikel cited a comment made by Bruce during a public interview several years before his death—a comment which was considered indicative of the ambivalent perspective in which he viewed himself, and in a sense prophetic of the future:

"*Sometimes I look at life in the fun mirror at the carnival. I see myself as a profound, incisive wit, concerned with man's inhumanity to man. Then I stroll to the next mirror and I see a pompous subjective ass whose humor is hardly spiritual. . . . I see traces of Mephistopheles. All my humor is based upon destruction and despair.*" *(Newsweek,* Jan. 2, 1961, p. 62)

him choose death!' By so radically illegitimizing another person's (not his own!) wish to die, the suicide-preventor redefines the aspiration of the other as not an aspiration at all." (p. 177)

Needless to say, Szasz's position is quite controversial.

Certainly a persuasive case can be made for the right of persons afflicted with a terminal illness, who suffer chronic and debilitating

"Lethality scale" for assessment of suicide potentiality

In assessing "suicide potentiality," or the probability that a person might carry out a threat of suicide, the Los Angeles Suicide Prevention Center uses a "lethality scale" consisting of ten categories:

1. Age and sex. The potentiality is greater if the individual is male rather than female, and is over 50 years of age. (The probability of suicide is also increasing for young adults aged 15 to 24.)

2. Symptoms. The potentiality is greater if the individual manifests such symptoms as sleep disturbances, depression, feelings of hopelessness, or alcoholism.

3. Stress. The potentiality is greater if the individual is under stress from the loss of a loved one through death or divorce, the loss of employment, increased responsibilities, or serious illness.

4. Acute vs. chronic aspects. The immediate potentiality is greater when there is a sudden onset of specific symptoms, such as those mentioned above. The long-term potentiality is greater when there is a recurrent outbreak of similar symptoms, or a recent increase in long-standing maladaptive traits.

5. Suicidal plan. The potentiality is greater in proportion to the lethality of the proposed method and the organizational clarity and detail of the plan.

6. Resources. The potentiality is greater if the person has no family or friends, or if they are unwilling to help.

7. Prior suicidal behavior. The potentiality is greater if the individual has made one or more prior attempts or has a history of repeated threats and depression.

8. Medical status. The potentiality is greater when there is chronic, debilitating illness or the individual has had many unsuccessful experiences with physicians.

9. Communication aspects. The potentiality is greater if communication between the individual and his or her relatives has been broken off and they reject efforts by the individual or others to reestablish communication.

10. Reaction of significant others. Potentiality is greater if a significant other, such as the husband or wife, evidences a defensive, rejecting, punishing attitude and denies that the individual needs help.

The final suicide potentiality rating is a composite score based on a weighting of each of the ten individual items.

Another interesting approach to the assessment of suicide potentiality involves the use of computers and actuarial methods to predict the risk not only of suicide but also of assaultive and other dangerous behaviors (Greist et al., 1974). Clinicians find this information helpful in making decisions regarding the amount of control needed or the amount of freedom that can safely be allowed. In a recent test of the system comparing computer accuracy with that of unaided judgments of clinicians, the computer predicted 90 percent of actual suicide attempts, versus only 30 percent for clinicians (*Time*, July 24, 1978).

Material concerning the lethality scale based on information supplied by the Los Angeles Suicide Prevention Center.

pain, to shorten their agony (see HIGHLIGHT on page 595). But what about the rights of persons who are not terminally ill and who have dependent children, parents, a spouse, or other loved ones who care about them and will be hurt by their death? Here the person's "right to suicide" becomes considerably less apparent, particularly in the case of those who are ambivalent about taking their lives, where intervention may help them regain their perspective and see alternative ways of dealing with their distress.

Here we may reemphasize that the great majority of persons who attempt suicide either do not really want to die or are ambivalent about taking their lives; and even for the minority who do wish to die, the desire is often a transient one. With improvement in the person's life situation, regaining of hope, and lifting of depression, the suicidal crisis is likely to pass and not recur. As Murphy (1973) has expressed it, "The 'right' to suicide is a 'right' desired only temporarily" (p. 472). Certainly in such cases intervention seems justified.

The dilemma becomes more intense, however, when prevention requires that the indi-

HIGHLIGHT

A "right" to suicide?

Every year millions of persons find out that they are suffering from a fatal disease, that they have no reasonable hope of living much longer, and that the near future will bring either agonizing pain or drug-induced clouding of consciousness, or both. What is a rational response to this awareness, and on what philosophical and moral grounds does one make it? What are the responsibilities of loved ones and professional caretakers in confronting the dilemma of the doomed person? Should nature simply be allowed to take its course? Should one submit passively to this apparent indication of "God's will"? Or should the individual take his or her own life before the pain becomes too agonizing and/or the medication too incapacitating?

There are, of course, no final, universal answers to such questions. But many people believe that, in such circumstances, suicide is an inviolable right and is in fact the most reasonable choice available. Some even take the position that healthy individuals have a moral obligation to help the stricken person take his or her life.

In our society, sanctions against helping a person commit suicide have been stronger than those against taking one's own life. Indeed, in most jurisdictions in the United States, aiding and abetting another person's suicide is a felony carrying rather severe penalties. Nevertheless, such assistance is rendered from time to time, and occasionally accounts of the circumstances are made public. Such was the case in the planned suicide of Carmen, whose sister, novelist Jessamyn West (1976), wrote poignantly of her active participation in Carmen's suicide.

Carmen was diagnosed as suffering from terminal cancer, and indications were strong that it would be a painful and prolonged death. She decided to commit suicide. At first she planned on doing it alone, but she subsequently decided that she wanted Jessamyn to be with her through it all. Jessamyn traveled to Carmen's home, and the sisters initiated a conspiracy to ensure that nothing would interfere with their plans. They knew that if they were discovered, others would try to intercede and prevent what each had decided was the only acceptable outcome. Though their extensive preparations were not accomplished joyously, neither were they characterized by inordinate gloom. Carmen and Jessamyn wanted, above all, to be certain that the method chosen would in fact be fatal. Finally, at the appointed time, Carmen died peacefully in the arms of her sister.

Was this a wrongful death?

vidual be hospitalized involuntarily; when personal items, such as belts and sharp objects, are taken away; and when calming medication is forcibly administered. Sometimes considerable restriction is needed to calm the individual. And even then the efforts may be fruitless. For example, in a study of hospitalized persons who were persistently suicidal, Watkins, Gilbert, and Bass (1969) reported that "almost one third used methods from which we cannot isolate them—seven head ramming, two asphyxia by aspiration of paper, one asphyxia by food, and three by exsanguination by tearing their blood vessels with their fingers" (p. 1593). Here again, however, as in the case of terminal illness and suffering, we are talking about a distinct minority of suicide cases.

Admittedly the preceding considerations do not resolve the issue of a person's "basic right to suicide." As in the case of most complex ethical issues, there does not seem to be any simple answer. But unless and until there is sufficient evidence to confirm this alleged right—and agreement on the conditions under which it may be appropriately exercised—it seems the wiser course to encourage existing suicide prevention programs and to foster research into suicidal behavior with the hope of reducing the toll in human life and misery taken each year by suicide in our society.

In this chapter we have dealt with the problem of suicidal behavior. We noted that the great majority of persons who attempt suicide do not want to die or are ambivalent about taking their lives. Often they give advance warning to others of their suicidal concern or intent. Feelings of depression and anger, interpersonal crises, failure, inner conflicts, a sense of hopelessness, and even sociocultural conditions may be causal factors in suicidal behavior. Finally, we examined the problems and methods of suicide prevention and the ethical issues involved in the concept of a person's "basic right to suicide."

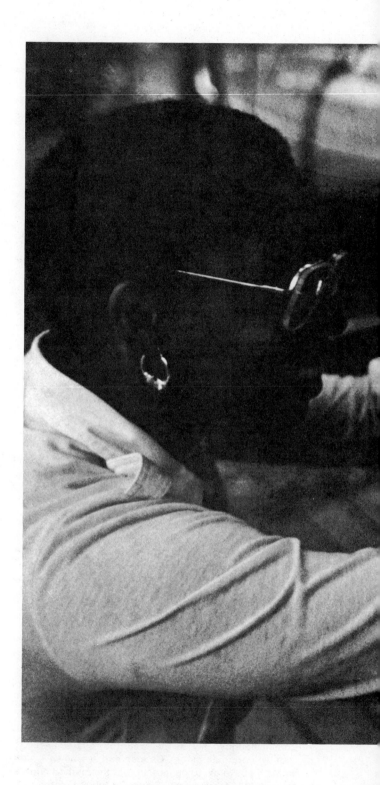

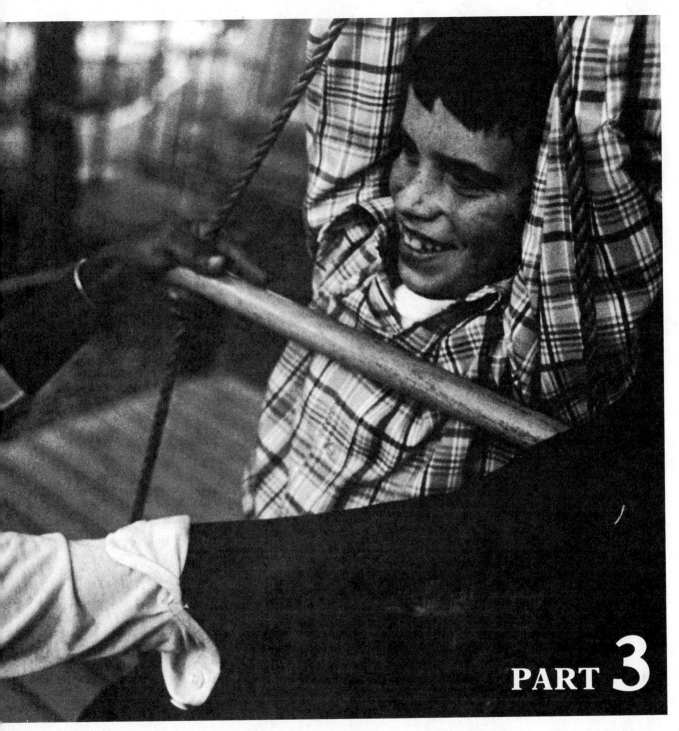

PART 3

Modern methods of assessment,
treatment, and prevention

17

Clinical assessment

The information sought in assessment
Interdisciplinary sources of assessment data
The use of computers in assessment

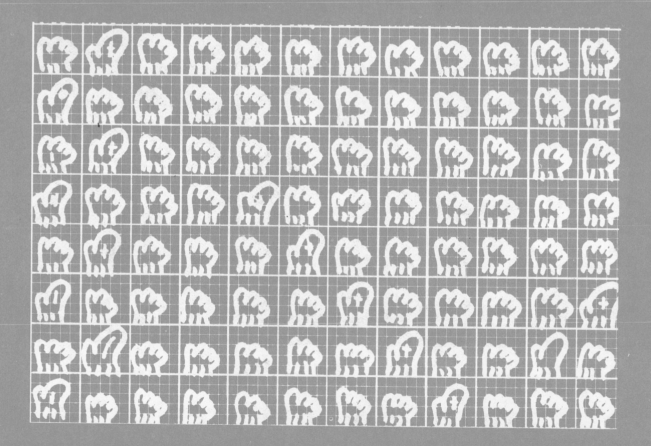

Clinical assessment is concerned with identifying the individual's current level of overall functioning; this includes determining the nature and severity of any maladaptive behavior and understanding the conditions that may have caused and/or may be maintaining it. Often assessment is a complex task, yet it is one of the most important activities in clinical work. The thoroughness and accuracy of assessment determines to a large extent how well the individual's problems are understood and his or her needs are met.

Usually within a brief period of time and often with limited information, the clinician must gather, weigh, and synthesize as much information as possible about the client. The individual may manifest a perplexing array of psychological problems, and his or her medical and social history may be unknown. In addition, there may be seemingly unsolvable problems in the individual's life situation. Equally important to evaluate are the individual's strengths and resources, including such personal factors as motivation for treatment, capacity for change, ability to participate in the treatment program, and available support from family and others. With all this information in hand, the clinician must then arrive at a working formulation concerning what can be done to promote the individual's well-being. It is an awesome but necessary task.

Depending on the setting, the severity of the problem, and practical considerations, the assessment process may be relatively comprehensive or selective and more problem-oriented, limited to identification of the key problems and the specific conditions that are maintaining or exacerbating them. In either event, it then provides a basis for making decisions concerning the best treatment program, be it hospitalization, the use of medication and/or psychotherapy, the modification of family patterns, or some other approach.

The initial clinical assessment also provides a "baseline" for comparison later with other measures obtained *during* and *following* treatment. This is an important but sometimes forgotten aspect of assessment. It makes it possible to check on the effectiveness of an ongoing treatment program to see if modifications may be needed; it also enables a comparison of the relative effectiveness of different therapeu-

tic and preventive approaches. In short, assessment is not a one-time venture: it is an ongoing process.

In this chapter we shall review some of the more commonly used assessment procedures —medical, psychological, and behavioral—and show how the data obtained may be integrated into a coherent clinical picture for use in making decisions about treatment. Then we shall examine some trends in clinical assessment, including the use of computers. But first we shall look at what, exactly, the clinician seeks to find in assessment.

The information sought in assessment

What does the clinician need to know? First, of course, the problem must be identified. Is it a particular self-defeating behavior or is it a more pervasive disorder? Does it fit into one of the categories of psychiatric disorder?

As we have seen, there has been a trend against overdependence on labeling because of the damage labels can do in setting up self-fulfilling prophecies for the individual and in blinding members of the therapeutic staff to other relevant behavior on the part of the individual. On the other hand, it is important to have an accurate classification for both clinical and administrative reasons. Clinically, knowledge of an individual's type of disorder can help in planning and managing the most appropriate treatment procedures. Administratively, it is essential to know the range of diagnostic problems that are represented among the patient or client population and for which treatment facilities need to be available. If the majority of patients at a facility have been diagnosed as schizophrenic, for example, then the staffing, physical environment, and treatment facilities should be arranged accordingly. Thus as clear a diagnosis as possible is needed, including a categorization if appropriate.

Adequate assessment includes other information as well. For example, it should include an objective description of the individual's behavior. How does the individual characteristically respond to other people? Are there *excesses* in behavior, such as eating or drinking too much? Are there notable *deficits,* as, for example, in social skills? How *appropriate* is the individual's behavior? Is the individual manifesting behavior that would be acceptable in some contexts but is considered abnormal in the contexts where it is displayed? Excesses, deficits, and appropriateness are key dimensions to be noted if the clinician is to understand the particular disorder that has brought the individual to the clinic or hospital.

In addition, assessment needs to include a description of any long-term personality characteristics that are relevant. Has the individual typically responded in certain deviant ways? Do there seem to be personality traits or action tendencies that predispose the individual to behave in maladaptive ways?

It is also important to analyze the social context in which the individual operates. What kinds of environmental demands are typically placed on the individual, and what supports or special stressors exist in the individual's life situation? As we have seen, the current DSM-III classification includes guidelines for rating both the severity of the stressors in the individual's current environment and the level of the individual's overall adjustment during the preceding year (see pages 18–19).

The diverse and often conflicting bits of information about the individual's behavior, action tendencies, environmental demands, and so on must then be integrated into a consistent and meaningful picture. Some clinicians refer to this picture as a *dynamic formulation* because it not only describes the current situation but includes information about why the person is behaving in maladaptive ways. For example, at this point in the assessment the clinician should have a plausible explanation for why a normally passive and mild-mannered man suddenly flew into a rage and started breaking up furniture.

The formulation should allow the clinician to develop hypotheses about the patient's future behavior as well. What is the likelihood of improvement or deterioration if the individual's problems are left untreated? Which behaviors

Important questions for clinical assessment

What are the presenting problems? Has the individual had these problems before? Are they of recent onset?

Were there important precipitating events—a recent trauma such as a death in the family or a severe economic loss?

Are there unusually difficult environmental circumstances such as chronic unemployment, traumatic family disturbance?

Does the individual or any family member have a history of psychological problems?

Is there a significant medical history—a precipitating physical disease, medication, or chemical abuse?

What is the patient's present mental and emotional status? Is he or she anxious, depressed? Are the thought processes disturbed? Is the person's affect appropriate? Is there a long-standing personality problem?

What are the individual's strengths? How has he or she successfully handled problems in the past?

Is the individual motivated for treatment? Can he or she be relied upon to take an active part in treatment—for example, to try alternative behaviors? Are there personality problems that may subvert treatment?

Are environmental resources available? Are there supportive friends or family members who might aid in the person's treatment or otherwise influence it positively?

should be the focus of change and what treatment methods are most likely to be successful? How much change might reasonably be expected from a particular type of treatment?

Where feasible, decisions about treatment are made with the consent and cooperation of the individual. In cases of severe disorder, however, they may have to be made without the patient's participation. As already indicated, important here is a knowledge of the strengths and resources of the patient; in short, what qualitites does the patient bring to the treatment program that can enhance the prognosis? (See HIGHLIGHT on this page.)

Interdisciplinary sources of assessment data

Since a wide range of factors may play important roles in causing and maintaining maladaptive behavior, assessment may involve the coordinated use of physical, psychological, and environmental assessment procedures. As we have indicated, however, the nature and comprehensiveness of clinical assessments vary depending on the problem and the facilities of the treatment agency. Assessment by phone in a suicide prevention center, for example, is quite different from assessment aimed at determining whether a particular hospitalized patient is intelligent and verbal enough to profit from individual psychotherapy. Our attempt here will be to provide a perspective about the way data are collected, with emphasis on psychosocial assessment procedures (see HIGHLIGHT on this page).

Physical evaluation

In some situations or with certain psychological problems, a medical examination is necessary to rule out physical abnormalities or to determine the extent to which physical problems are involved. The medical evaluation may include both general physical and special neurological examinations.

General physical examination. The physical examination consists of the kinds of procedures most of us have experienced in getting a "medical checkup." Typically, a medical history is obtained and the major systems of the body are checked.

Neurological examination. Since brain pathology is involved in some mental disorders, a specialized neurological examination is frequently given in addition to the general medi-

Terms commonly used in clinical assessment

Actuarial interpretation   Application of interpretations developed from a reference group with test scores similar to those of the subject to evaluate the subject's test performance.

Behavior observation   Direct observation of a subject's behavior in a clinical or real-life situation, often aided by the use of rating scales.

Behavior sample   Assessment data that presumably provide an accurate reflection of the subject's typical behavior.

Halo effect   Tendency when rating a specific trait to be influenced by another trait, such as appearance, or by one's overall impression of the subject.

Intelligence test   Test used for establishing a subject's level of intellectual capacity.

Neuropsychological assessment   The use of psychological tests that measure a subject's cognitive, perceptual, and motor performance to determine extent and locus of brain damage.

Performance test   Test in which perceptual-motor rather than verbal responses are emphasized.

Personality profile   A graphic summary of data from several tests or from subtests of the same test battery or scales that shows the personality configuration of an individual or a group of individuals.

Projective test   Technique using neutral or ambiguous stimuli that subject is encouraged to interpret, and from which the subject's personality characteristics can be analyzed.

Rating scale   Device for recording the rater's judgment of himself or herself or others on defined traits.

Self-monitoring   Self-observation and recording of behavior that is, typically, targeted for change.

Self-report inventory   Procedure in which subject is asked to sort statements in terms of their applicability to him or her.

Test reliability   Consistency with which a test measures a given trait on repeated administrations of the test to given subjects.

Test validity   Degree to which a test actually measures what it was designed to measure.

Verbal test   Test in which the subject's ability to understand and use words and concepts is important in making the required responses.

cal examination. This may involve getting an electroencephalograph (an EEG) to check on brain-wave patterns. Where EEG's reveal *dysrhythmias*—abnormal brain-wave patterns—or where other data indicate the possibility of brain pathology, a variety of specialized techniques may be used in an attempt to arrive at a precise diagnosis of the nature and extent of the problem.

In many instances, a neuropsychological test battery will be administered to a patient if organic brain damage is known or suspected to be present. Such a battery consists of a number of standard cognitive and perceptual-motor tasks known to be affected by brain pathology (see HIGHLIGHT on page 604). From the results of these tests, the clinician can often make inferences about the nature and extent of brain damage and even where it is probably located (Boll, 1978).

Medicine and allied sciences are contributing many new procedures of value in assessing conditions that can affect brain functioning. Radioactive isotopes can help locate brain lesions and other types of nervous system disturbances; techniques have been developed for the detection of rare metabolic disorders; and new methods have made it a simple matter to detect the use of heroin and other drugs of dependence. And as we have seen, it has become increasingly easy to identify genetic and chromosomal abnormalities. These techniques not only make it possible to diagnose conditions such as Down's syndrome in mental retardation, but also permit *preventive assessment*. For example, as we have seen, potential parents may be examined to see if they carry particular genetic aberrations that may adversely affect their offspring.

Psychosocial assessment

Psychosocial assessment attempts to provide a realistic picture of the individual in interaction with the environment. This picture includes relevant information concerning the individual's personality makeup and present level of functioning, as well as information about the stressors and resources in his or her life situation. The following are some of the psychosocial procedures that may be used.

Assessment interviews. The assessment interview usually involves a face-to-face conversation conducted in such a way that the clinician obtains information about various aspects of the patient's situation, behavior, and personality makeup. The interview may vary from a simple set of questions to a more formal format.

In order to minimize sources of error, an assessment interview is often carefully structured in terms of goals, content to be explored, and the type of relationship the interviewer attempts to establish with the subject. Here, the use of rating scales may help focus and score the interview data. For example, the subject may be rated on a three-point scale with respect to self-esteem, anxiety, and various other characteristics. Such a structured interview is particularly effective in giving an overall impression of the subject and his or her life situation and in revealing specific problems or crises—such as marital difficulties, drug dependence, or suicidal fantasies—that may require immediate therapeutic intervention (Matarazzo, 1978).

Clinical interviews have been criticized as an unreliable source of information on which to base important psychiatric decisions. Evidence of this unreliability lies in the fact that on the basis of interview data for a particular patient, different clinicians have often arrived at different diagnoses. For this reason, several investigators have attempted to improve the reliability of assessment interviews by specifying observable criteria for diagnosis and providing very specific guidelines for making judgments (Feighner et al., 1972). In one method, the questions are specified and take about an hour. They cover a wide range of topics in a fixed sequence, although the interviewer may phrase the questions in his or her own words. High agreement has been found for most diagnostic judgments among interviewers using this standard interview format (Helzer et al., 1977).

One of the rating scales most widely used for recording observations in clinical practice and in psychiatric research is the Brief Psychiatric Rating Scale (BPRS). The BPRS provides an objective and quantifiable format for rating clinical symptoms such as somatic concern, anxiety, emotional withdrawal, guilt feelings,

Interviews can provide a variety of useful data for psychological assessment. In general, the more carefully structured the interview format, the more reliable the results will be.

hostility, suspiciousness, and unusual thought patterns. It contains 18 scales which are scored from ratings made by the clinician following an interview with the patient. The distinct patterns of behavior reflected in the BPRS ratings enable clinicians to make a standardized comparison of their patients' symptoms with the behavior of other psychiatric patients (Overall & Klett, 1972). The BPRS has been found to be an extremely valuable instrument in clinical research, especially for the purpose of assigning patients to treatment groups on the basis of similarity in symptoms.

Psychological tests. Psychological tests are specialized instruments for ascertaining such characteristics as intellectual capacity, motive patterns, self-concept, perception of the environment, role behaviors, values, level of anxiety or depression, coping patterns, and general personality integration. Though more precise and often more dependable than interviews, psychological tests are far from perfect tools, and their value often depends heavily on

the competence of the clinician who interprets them. In general, however, they are useful diagnostic tools for psychologists in much the same way that blood tests or X rays are useful to physicians. In both cases, pathology may be revealed in persons who appear on the surface to be quite normal, or a general impression of "something wrong" can be checked against more precise information.

1. *Intelligence tests.* There is a wide range of intelligence tests from which the clinician can choose. The Wechsler Intelligence Scale for Children–Revised (WISC–R) and the Stanford-Binet Intelligence Scale are widely used in clinical settings for measuring the intellectual capacity of children. Probably the most commonly used test for measuring adult intelligence is the Wechsler Adult Intelligence Scale (WAIS). It includes both verbal and performance material and consists of ten subtests with one alternative subtest. A brief description of two of the subtests—one verbal and one performance—will serve to illustrate the type of functions the WAIS measures:

Neuropsychological examination: determining brain-behavior relationships

The effects of brain damage on behavior can be evaluated with a battery of psychological tests that measure cognitive, perceptual, and psychomotor performance. Inferences from the subject's test performance can aid the clinician in localizing the brain damage and in understanding the extent of the person's organic impairment.

The most widely used neuropsychological test is the Halstead-Reitan neuropsychology battery, which is composed of several tests and variables from which an index of impairment is computed (Boll, 1978; Filskov & Goldstein, 1974). In addition to the overall index of impairment, it provides specific information about the subject's functioning in several skill areas. The Halstead-Reitan neuropsychology battery for adults is made up of the following tests:

The *Halstead Category Test* measures the subject's ability to learn and remember material, and can provide clues as to his or her judgment and impulsivity. The subject is presented with a stimulus (on a screen) which suggests a number between one and four. The subject presses a button indicating which number is "correct." A correct choice is followed by the sound of a pleasant doorbell and an incorrect choice by a loud buzzer. The person is required to determine from the pattern of buzzers and bells what the underlying principle of the correct choice is.

The *Tactual Performance Test* measures the subject's motor speed, response to the unfamiliar, and learning and use of tactile and kinesthetic cues. The test consists of a board that has spaces for 10 blocks of varied shapes. The subject is blindfolded (and never actually sees the board) and asked to place the blocks into the correct grooves in the board. Later, the subject is asked to draw the blocks and the board from tactile memory.

The *Rhythm Test* is an auditory perception task used to measure attention and sustained concentration. It is a subtest of Seashore's Test of musical talent and includes 30 pairs of rhythmic beats that are presented on a tape recorder. The subject is required to determine if the pairs are the same or different.

The *Speech Sounds Perception Test* is a test to determine if the individual can identify spoken words. Nonsense words are presented on a tape recorder, and the subject is asked to identify the presented word from a list of four printed words. This task measures the subject's concentration, attention, and comprehension.

The *Finger Oscillation Task* measures the speed at which the individual can, with the index finger, depress a lever. Several trials are given with each hand.

In addition to the Halstead-Reitan Battery, other tests, referred to as *allied procedures,* may be used in a neuropsychology laboratory. For example, Boll (1980) recommends the use of the modified Halstead-Wepman Aphasia Screening Test for obtaining information about a subject's language abilities, and abilities to identify numbers and body parts, to follow directions, to spell, and to pantomime simple actions.

The neuropsychological examination typically takes 4 to 6 hours to complete. In spite of the substantial time necessary for administration, the neuropsychological examination is growing in usage in evaluating neurological status because it yields a great deal of useful information about the individual's cognitive and motor processes (Boll, 1980). Moreover, the neuropsychological examination provides valid information without the risk of injury or death that can accompany more direct neurological examinations (Filskov & Goldstein, 1974).

General information. This subtest consists of questions designed to tap the individual's range of information on material that is ordinarily encountered. For example, the individual is asked to do such things as tell how many weeks there are in a year, name the colors in the American flag, and tell who wrote *Hamlet.*

Picture completion. This subtest consists of 21 cards showing pictures, each with a part missing. The task for the subject is to indicate what is missing. This test is designed to measure the individual's ability to discriminate between essential and nonessential elements in a situation (Wechsler, 1955, pp. 33–35).

Analysis of scores on the various subtests reveals the individual's present level of intellectual functioning. In addition, the subject's behavior in the test situation may reveal much relevant information. For example, he or she may be very apprehensive about not doing well, may vacillate in responses, may seek continual reassurance from the clinician, or may be so disturbed that concentration on the tasks presented is difficult. These behaviors may tell the clinician as much as the actual test scores.

2. *Personality tests.* There are a great many tests designed to measure characteristics other than intellectual capacity. It is convenient to group these personality tests into *projective* and *structured* tests.

a) Projective tests are unstructured in that they rely on various ambiguous stimuli, such as inkblots or pictures rather than questions and answers. Through their interpretations of these ambiguous materials, individuals reveal a good deal about their personal conflicts, motives, coping techniques, and other personality characteristics.

An assumption underlying the use of projective techniques is that in trying to make sense out of vague, unstructured stimuli, individuals "project" their own problems, motives, and wishes into the situation. Thus projective tests are aimed at discovering the ways in which an individual's past learning and self-structure may lead him or her to organize and perceive ambiguous information. Prominent among the many projective tests in common usage are the Rorschach Test, the Thematic Apperception Test (TAT), and sentence completion tests.

The Rorschach Test is named after the Swiss psychiatrist Hermann Rorschach, who in-

itiated experimental use of inkblots in personality assessment in 1911. The test utilizes ten inkblot pictures to which the subject responds in succession after being instructed somewhat as follows (Klopfer & Davidson, 1962):

People may see many different things in these inkblot pictures; now tell me what you see, what it makes you think of, what it means to you.

The following excerpts are taken from the responses of a subject to the sample inkblot shown here.

"This looks like two men with genital organs exposed. They have had a terrible fight and blood has splashed up against the wall. They have knives or sharp instruments in their hands and have just cut up a body. They have already taken out the lungs and other organs. The body is dismembered . . . nothing remains but a shell . . . the pelvic region. They were fighting as to who will complete the final dismemberment . . . like two vultures swooping down. . . ."

From this response and other test results, this subject was diagnosed as an antisocial personality with strong hostility.

For several reasons, there has been a decreased use of the Rorschach Test over the past twenty years. The Rorschach takes several hours to administer and interpret, limiting its use to settings with high staff-patient ratio. Furthermore, the results of the Rorschach are often unreliable because of the subjective nature of the test interpretations. In addition, the types of clinical treatments used in mental health facilities generally require more specific behavioral descriptions rather than descriptions of general, often obscure, personality dynamics such as those that typically result from Rorschach Test interpretation.

The Rorschach has been criticized as an instrument with low or negligible validity, but in the hands of a skilled interpreter it has been shown to be quite useful in uncovering certain psychodynamic problems. Furthermore, there have been recent attempts to objectify Rorschach interpretation and demonstrate the clinical validity of the technique (Exner, 1974).

The Thematic Apperception Test (TAT) was introduced in 1935 by its coauthors, Morgan and Murray of the Harvard Psychological Clinic. It utilizes a series of simple pictures about which the subject is instructed to make up stories. The material is ambiguous and unstructured so that subjects tend to project their own conflicts and worries into it (Bellak, 1975).

Several scoring and interpretation systems have been developed to focus on different aspects of the subject's stories, such as expression(s) of needs (Atkinson, 1958; Winter, 1973), the individual's perception of reality (Arnold, 1962), and analysis of the individual's fantasies (Klinger, 1979). Most often, the clinician simply makes a qualitative and subjective determination of how the story content reflects the individual's underlying traits, motives, and preoccupations.

An example of the way an individual's problems may be reflected in TAT stories is shown in the following story based on Card 1 (a picture of a boy staring at a violin on a table in front of him). The client, David, was a 15-year-old male who had been referred to the clinic by his parents because of their concern about his withdrawal behavior and his poor work at school.

David was generally cooperative during the testing although he remained rather unemotional and unenthusiastic throughout. When he was given Card 1 of the TAT, he paused for over a minute, carefully scrutinizing the card.

"I think this is a . . . uh . . . machine gun . . . yeah, it's a machine gun. The guy is staring at it. Maybe he got it for his birthday or stole it or something." (Pause. The examiner reminded him that he was to make up a story about the picture.)

"OK. This boy, I'll call him Karl, found this machine gun . . . a Browning automatic rifle . . . in his garage. He kept it in his room for protection. One

In the Thematic Apperception Test (TAT), patients make up stories based on a series of drawings such as this one. The TAT is a method of revealing to the trained interpreter some of the dominant personality characteristics of the individual.

day he decided to take it to school to quiet down the jocks that lord it over everyone. When he walked into the locker hall, he cut loose on the top jock, Amos, and wasted him. Nobody bothered him after that because they knew he kept the BAR in his locker."

It was evident from this story that David was experiencing a high level of frustration and anger in his life. The extent of this anger was reflected in his perception of the violin in the picture as a machine gun—a potential instrument of violence. The clinician inferred that David was feeling threatened not only by people at school but even in his own home where he needed "protection."

This example shows how stories based on TAT cards may provide the clinician with information about the individual's own conflicts and worries, as well as clues to how the individual is handling these problems.

Another projective procedure that has proven useful in personality assessment is the sentence completion test. There are a number of such tests designed for children, adolescents, and adults. The material consists of the beginnings of sentences that the subject is asked to complete, as in these examples:

1. I wish _____ .
2. My mother _____ .
3. Sex _____ .
4. I hate _____ .
5. People _____ .

Sentence completion tests are somewhat more structured than the Rorschach and most other projective tests. They help examiners pinpoint topics that should be explored for an understanding of an individual's personality makeup and problems.

These projective tests provide situations to which an individual responds, however, and they do not sample the individual's own ongoing thoughts. In an attempt to get a sampling of naturally occurring thoughts, psychologists are experimenting with having individuals carry small electronic "beepers" that produce a signal, such as a soft tone, at unexpected intervals. At each signal, the individual is to write down whatever thoughts the signal interrupted. These thought reports can then be analyzed in various ways. It is possible that this method can eventually be used for some kinds of personality assessment and diagnosis as well as for monitoring progress in psychological therapy (Klinger, 1977).

b) Structured personality tests typically use questionnaires, self-inventories, or rating scales in which questions are carefully structured and possible responses are specified. One of the major structured inventories is the Minnesota Multiphasic Personality Inventory (MMPI). This inventory was developed in 1943 by Hathaway and McKinley and is the most widely used personality test today for both clinical assessment and research in psychopathology (Dahlstrom, Welsh, & Dahlstrom, 1975; Graham, 1978).

The inventory consists of 550 items covering topics from physical condition and psychological states to moral and social attitudes. Subjects are encouraged to answer all items either true or false. Some sample items follow:

I sometimes keep on at a thing until others lose their patience with me.   T F
Bad words, often terrible words, come into my mind and I cannot get rid of them.   T F
I often feel as if things were not real.   T F
Someone has it in for me.   T F

(Hathaway & McKinley, 1951, p. 28)

This inventory of items was originally administered to a large group of normal individuals and several groups of psychiatric patients, and item analyses were performed to see which items differentiated the various groups. On the basis of the results, several scales were constructed, each consisting of the items that were answered in a particular way by one of the groups. Thus the schizophrenia scale, for example, is made up of the items that the schizophrenic patients consistently answered in a particular direction. People who score high on this scale are often withdrawn and shy and have peculiar thoughts. They may have poor contact with reality and in severe cases may have delusions and hallucinations. In general, the higher the score on the schizophrenia scale, the more likely the individual is to be schizophrenic. Of the many such scales that have been prepared, the ten most often used in clinical practice are indicated along the top of the profile in the Highlight on page 615.

The MMPI also uses several *validity* scales to detect whether the patient has answered the questions in a straightforward, accurate way. When a patient is being assessed, his or her answers are scored on these validity scales as well as on the ten clinical scales, and the results are plotted against the scores for a normal population (as shown on page 615). By drawing a line connecting the scores for the different scales, the clinician can construct a profile that shows how far from normal the patient's performance is on the several dimensions.

Another kind of personality inventory utilizes the statistical technique of *factor analysis*. These tests are constructed to measure important and relatively independent personality traits. The goal is to measure one trait at a time with maximum precision and objectivity; a personality profile can then be drawn showing the degree to which several specific traits are characteristic of the individual, as well as their overall pattern. A well-known battery of tests of this type is Cattell's Sixteen Personality Factor Questionnaire. A profile obtained from a person's scores on this inventory is shown in the HIGHLIGHT on page 609.

A different kind of structured approach, widely used in clinical research, is called the *Q-sort*. Here a large number of statements are prepared concerning various traits, behavior patterns, or situations. For example, there might be statements like: "Is highly tense and anxious most of the time," and "Views sex as evil and strives to inhibit his/her sexual impulses." The subject or rater, such as a relative or therapist, is asked to sort these statements into piles according to whether or not they apply to the person being described; the piles range from "highly typical" to "highly untypical." A variety of statistical techniques can then be used to evaluate the results of the sorting.

Many psychological tests are available for clinical use to assess the individual's abilities, aptitudes, interests, temperament, anxiety level, self-concept, values, and other characteristics. Some in common use are the Strong-Campbell Vocational Interest Blank, an interest test used in occupational counseling; the Beck Depression Scale, used to determine the extent of an individual's depressed mood; and the Psychiatric Epidemiology Research Interview (PERI), a survey of stressful life events (Dohrenwend et al., 1978).

Clinical observation of behavior. Direct observation of the individual's characteristic behavior has long been considered important for adequate psychosocial assessment. The main purpose of direct observation is to find out more about the person's psychological makeup and level of functioning; though such observations would ideally occur within the individual's natural environment, they are typically confined to clinic or hospital settings. For example, a brief description is usually made of the subject's behavior on hospital admission, and more detailed observations are made periodically on the ward. These descriptions include concise notations of relevant information about the subject's personal hygiene, emotional behavior, delusions or hallucinations, anxiety, sexual behavior, aggressive or suicidal tendencies, and so on. To facilitate these observations, rating scales commonly used are

those that enable the observer to indicate not only the presence or absence of a trait or behavior but also its prominence. The following is an example of such a rating-scale item; the observer checks the most appropriate alternative.

Sexual behavior:
_____ 1. Sexually assaultive: aggressively approaches males or females with sexual intent.
_____ 2. Sexually soliciting: exposes genitals with sexual intent, makes overt sexual advances to other patients or staff, masturbates openly.
_____ 3. No overt sexual behavior: not preoccupied with discussion of sexual matters.
_____ 4. Avoids sex topics: made uneasy by discussion of sex, becomes disturbed if approached sexually by others.
_____ 5. Excessive prudishness about sex: considers sex filthy, condemns sexual behavior in others, becomes panic-stricken if approached sexually.

Like other assessment techniques, observation of the subject's behavior may be made not only to fill in the original picture but also to check on the course or outcome of treatment procedures.

Recently, a good deal of attention has focused on observing the subject's behavior in his or her natural surroundings. For example, children who have been showing behavior problems may be observed at school, in their peer groups, and in their homes. Here the purpose is to obtain a sampling of their behavior in ordinary situations in order to understand the problems they are facing, the coping patterns they are using, and the environmental conditions that may be reinforcing their maladaptive behavior.

In situations where it is not feasible to observe the subject's behavior in everyday settings—as when he or she is institutionalized—an entire family may be asked to meet together in the clinic or hospital where their interactions and difficulties can be observed and studied. In other cases a social worker may obtain relevant data by visiting the subject's home, talking with family members and others who are important to the subject, and observing the stressors and resources in the subject's life situation. Even in cases where considerable information about the subject's life situation has been collected in structured inter-

HIGHLIGHT

A profile based on factor analysis

By combining the test results of many people who show a particular type of maladaptive behavior, it is possible to discover whether they have a characteristic pattern of personality traits that distinguishes them from the general population. For example, this is a composite profile based on the scores of 937 drug addicts serving prison terms. The measures were obtained on the Sixteen Personality Factor Questionnaire. This profile is interpreted as indicating lower-than-average emotional stability (Factor C) and higher-than-average unrealistic thinking (Factor M) and apprehensiveness (Factor O).

Since the testing was done entirely on prison inmates, we do not know whether this profile is representative of all drug addicts. Also, it must be borne in mind that such profiles are only descriptive: they indicate a *probability* of finding certain traits associated with certain behavior but do not tell us whether one *caused* the other.

PERSONALITY PROFILE OF DRUG ADDICTS

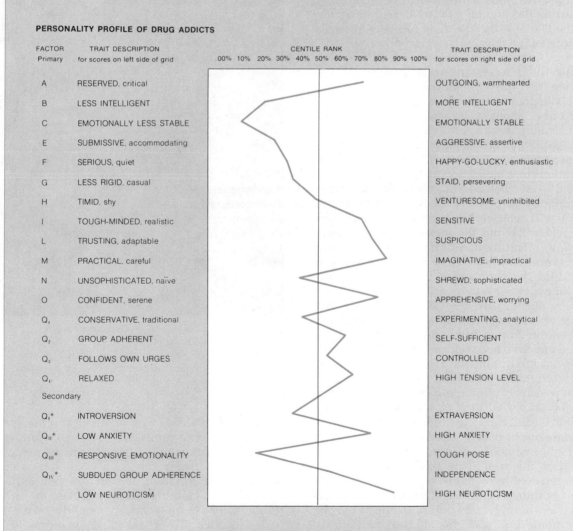

FACTOR Primary	TRAIT DESCRIPTION for scores on left side of grid	CENTILE RANK	TRAIT DESCRIPTION for scores on right side of grid
A	RESERVED, critical		OUTGOING, warmhearted
B	LESS INTELLIGENT		MORE INTELLIGENT
C	EMOTIONALLY LESS STABLE		EMOTIONALLY STABLE
E	SUBMISSIVE, accommodating		AGGRESSIVE, assertive
F	SERIOUS, quiet		HAPPY-GO-LUCKY, enthusiastic
G	LESS RIGID, casual		STAID, persevering
H	TIMID, shy		VENTURESOME, uninhibited
I	TOUGH-MINDED, realistic		SENSITIVE
L	TRUSTING, adaptable		SUSPICIOUS
M	PRACTICAL, careful		IMAGINATIVE, impractical
N	UNSOPHISTICATED, naïve		SHREWD, sophisticated
O	CONFIDENT, serene		APPREHENSIVE, worrying
Q_1	CONSERVATIVE, traditional		EXPERIMENTING, analytical
Q_2	GROUP ADHERENT		SELF-SUFFICIENT
Q_3	FOLLOWS OWN URGES		CONTROLLED
Q_4	RELAXED		HIGH TENSION LEVEL

Centile Rank scale: 00% 10% 20% 30% 40% 50% 60% 70% 80% 90% 100%

Secondary

Q_I*	INTROVERSION		EXTRAVERSION
Q_{II}*	LOW ANXIETY		HIGH ANXIETY
Q_{III}*	RESPONSIVE EMOTIONALITY		TOUGH POISE
Q_{IV}*	SUBDUED GROUP ADHERENCE		INDEPENDENCE
	LOW NEUROTICISM		HIGH NEUROTICISM

*Roman subscripts denote "second-order" traits, which are derived from weighted combinations of the first-order trait scores and are broader and more extensive in their effects. (IPAT Personality Profile Series, Copyright 1971, IPAT, Champaign, Illinois. Reproduced by permission.)

views or in psychological tests, the collection of supplemental observational data is regarded as desirable.

Extending the use of such data a bit further, the social worker may analyze situations with which the subject is likely to be confronted in the future. For example, a patient with little education and a history of chronic unemployment might improve sufficiently to leave the institution but be little better off than before unless treatment has included training in job skills. Thus knowledge of troubled individuals' life situations not only helps in understanding their present maladaptive behavior but is often essential for planning a treatment program that will enable them to meet future challenges in more adaptive ways.

Behavioral assessment techniques.

Behavior therapists deemphasize the use of psychological tests because they want to avoid inferences about underlying personality traits that might predispose the person to the maladaptive response pattern. Their interest is in the response pattern itself and the particular situations in which it occurs. Thus they depend heavily on behavioral assessment, using techniques that enable them to determine the functional relationship between the maladaptive behavior and the environmental stimuli that are affecting it. Skinner has called this a *functional analysis of behavior* because it identifies the function of the individual's behavior in getting reinforcement.

More specifically, the behaviorally oriented clinician attempts to collect information that will enable him or her to determine (a) which of the patient's behaviors require modification; (b) what environmental factors are serving to maintain those maladaptive behaviors; (c) what positively reinforcing or punishing events can be employed to alter the individual's behavior; (d) what techniques of behavior therapy might best be used to bring about the desired behavior change; and, later, (e) whether the treatment techniques have, in fact, resulted in a change in behavior. Assessment is thus a central and integral part of all behavior therapies, not only at the beginning of treatment, but also during the intervening phases, in order to keep checking on the effectiveness of the procedure being used.

A number of clinical procedures have been

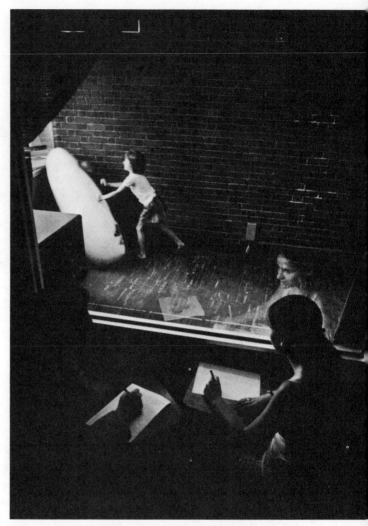

The very presence of an observer may well influence the behavior being assessed. Special facilities with one-way mirrors or similar devices are frequently used to minimize the impact of the observers' presence.

adapted or developed to provide information for such behavioral analysis. The behaviorally oriented clinician relies heavily on the structured *clinical interview* as a main source of behavioral information. In order to elicit quite specific behavioral descriptions, he or she would likely ask many questions of the "what" variety, such as "What did you do when you became irritated?"

The behaviorist also employs objective *observation techniques* wherever possible. Observations made in natural settings by trained observers provide useful behavioral data but are time consuming and beyond the means of most clinical staffs. It is also helpful to obtain observations of the individual's behavior from significant others in the person's family. In addition to providing important assessment data, this procedure incorporates the "observers" into the treatment program, thereby enhancing the therapy.

Patterson and his colleagues (Jones, Reid, & Patterson, 1975) have developed a method for coding and quantifying the observations of a child's behavior at school and at home. Concrete instances of behavior and interaction are observed, recorded, and coded, either by trained observers or by the parents themselves. This provides the clinician with information about the stimuli that are controlling the child's interactions, which in turn makes it possible for the clinician to evaluate the quantity and quality of the child's interactions and identify the situations that result in behavior problems.

When observation in the natural setting is not possible, the clinician may construct or contrive an observational situation that can provide information about the individual's response to a particular situation. For example, an individual who has a phobia for snakes might be placed in a situation where snakelike objects and pictures are presented.

An often-used procedure that enables the clinician to observe the client's behavior directly is *role playing*. The client is instructed to play a part—for example, someone standing up for his or her rights. Role playing a situation like this not only can provide assessment information for the clinician but also can serve as a vehicle for new learning for the client.

Another approach to behavioral assessment employs *self-report*. This approach recognizes that individuals are an excellent source of information about themselves. Assuming that the right questions are asked and that people are willing to disclose information about themselves, the results can be quite valuable. One of the most efficient instruments for obtaining specific information about an individual's problem area is the *self-report schedule* or *problem checklist*. Such checklists may include items that measure fears, problems, moods, and conditions that are operating as reinforcements in the person's life. Thus they can provide useful information for structuring a behavioral treatment plan.

Another type of self-report—which serves as a therapeutic strategy as well as an assessment procedure—is *self-monitoring*. With this technique clients are asked to observe and record their own behavior. Using journals, they record particular behaviors that they are trying to decrease or increase. For example, they might be asked to record the number of times during the week that they were appropriately assertive.

Some self-monitoring techniques involve the use of a "golf counter," which may be worn on the wrist or carried in the pocket and enables the individual to record easily instances of certain behavior. Monitoring one's behavior in this way also has a direct effect on the behavior itself. For example, individuals who record negative behaviors, such as overeating, usually reduce the amount of their food intake over the period of self-observation. Thus the assessment technique of self-monitoring has become a major strategy in the treatment of problem behavior.

Integration of assessment data

As assessment data are collected, their significance must be interpreted so that they can be integrated into a coherent "working model" for use in planning or changing treatment.

In a clinic or hospital setting, assessment data are usually evaluated in a staff conference attended by members of the interdisciplinary team (perhaps a psychiatrist, a clinical psychologist, a social worker, and other mental health personnel) who are concerned with the decisions to be made regarding treatment. By putting together all the information they have gathered, they can see whether the findings complement each other and form a definitive clinical picture or whether there are gaps or discrepancies that necessitate further investigation.

At the time of the original assessment, integration of all the data may lead to agreement on a tentative diagnostic classification for the individual—such as *paranoid schizophrenia*. In any case, the findings of each member of the interdisciplinary team, as well as the recommendations for treatment, are entered in the case record, so that it will always be possible to check back and see why a certain course of therapy was undertaken, how accurate the clinical assessment was, and how valid the treatment decision turned out to be.

New assessment data collected during the course of therapy provide feedback on its effectiveness, as well as a basis for making needed modifications in an ongoing treatment program. As we have noted, clinical assessment data are also commonly used in evaluating the final outcome of therapy as well as in comparing the effectiveness of different therapeutic and preventive approaches. Summers (1979), among others, has pointed out the importance of assessing a patient's level of functioning prior to hospital discharge. Too often, individuals who cannot function well outside the mental hospital are released to the community with little or no provision for continuing mental health care.

The decisions made on the basis of assessment data may have far-reaching implications for the persons under study. The staff decision may determine whether a depressed person will be hospitalized or remain with his or her family; whether divorce will be accepted as a solution to an unhappy marriage or a further attempt will be made to salvage the marriage; or whether an accused person will be declared competent to stand trial. Thus a valid decision, based on accurate assessment data, is of far more than theoretical importance. Because of the impact that assessment can have, it is important that those involved keep in mind factors that may limit the accuracy of assessment. Some of these factors are suggested in the HIGH-LIGHT on page 613.

The use of computers in assessment

Perhaps the most dramatic innovation in clinical assessment during the last decade has been the increasing sophistication and use of computers in individual assessment. Computers are used in assessment both to gather information directly from the individual and to put together and evaluate all the information that has been gathered previously through interviews, tests, and other assessment procedures. By comparing the incoming information with data previously stored in its memory banks, the computer can perform a wide range of assessment tasks. It can supply a diagnosis, indicate the likelihood of certain kinds of behavior, suggest the most appropriate form of treatment, predict the outcome, and print out a summary report concerning the subject.

In many of these functions, the computer is actually superior to the individual clinician because it is more efficient at recall of stored material. And over time, the computer builds an increasingly large data base covering many cases, which makes possible a continual refinement of its probability statements.

In producing test evaluations or making predictions about individuals, the computer can sometimes employ an *actuarial* procedure. Here, descriptions of typical behavior of a large number of individuals with particular patterns of test scores have been stored in the computer. Then, whenever an individual turns up with one of these test score patterns, the appropriate description is printed out in the computer's evaluation. Such descriptions have been written and stored for a number of different test score patterns, most of them based on MMPI scores. Examples of these prepared descriptions appear in the computer evaluation reprinted in the HIGHLIGHT on page 614. Sometimes the different paragraphs picked up in this way by the computer will have elements that seem inconsistent, as occurred in this case where one paragraph described the individual's "rigidity" after another had mentioned an "original or inventive orientation." This is due to the fact that different parts of the individual's test pattern call up different paragraphs from the computer. The computer simply prints out blindly what has been found to be typical for individuals making similar scores on the various clinical scales. The computer cannot *integrate* the descriptions it picks up and is dealing only with averages, which may not be accurate for the given individual.

There are several centers in the country to

Limitations of psychosocial assessment

Despite the need for assessment to understand an individual's problems and to plan appropriate treatment, the assessment process has several limitations and possible risks.

1. *Cultural bias of the instrument or the clinician.* Psychological tests may not elicit valid information from a patient of an ethnic minority, or a clinician from one sociocultural background may have trouble assessing objectively the behavior of an individual from another background (Dahlstrom, 1978; Gynther, 1979).

2. *Theoretical orientation of the clinician.* Assessment is inevitably influenced by the assumptions, perceptions, and theoretical orientation of the clinician. For example, a psychoanalyst and a behaviorist might assess the same behaviors quite differently.

3. *Overemphasis on internal traits.* Many clinicians overemphasize personality traits as the cause of patients' problems without due attention to the possible role of stressors in their life situations.

4. *Insufficient validation.* Many psychological assessment procedures have not been sufficiently validated. For example, unlike many of the personality scales, widely used procedures for behavioral observation and behavioral self-report have not been subjected to strict psychometric validation. The tendency on the part of clinicians to accept the results of these procedures at face value has recently been giving way to a broader recognition of the need for more explicit validation.

5. *Inaccurate data or premature evaluation.* There is always the possibility that some assessment data—and any label or treatment based on them—may be inaccurate. For example, some risk is always involved in making predictions for an individual on the basis of group data or averages. Inaccurate data or premature conclusions not only may lead to a misunderstanding of the patient's problem but may close off attempts to get further information, with possibly grave harm for the patient.

which clinicians and other professionals can send MMPI score sheets for such actuarial interpretations. Some give interpretations with a special focus—for example, to evaluate and make predictions about individuals in a prison setting, or to detect psychological problems in a medical setting, or to make a general psychiatric evaluation.

So far, actuarial systems have been developed with adequate validation for only about twenty discrete personality types. This is only about a third of the personality types that might appear in a given clinical setting. To interpret scores that fall outside the computer's "experience tables," the computer is programmed with interpretive statements written by a clinician on the basis of his or her experience with individuals who have had particular test scores. Here the computer constructs a clinical report by printing out the statements that are appropriate for the individual's scores.

The essential difference between the actuarial program and the "automated clinician" program is that the first has been more directly and thoroughly validated for personality types; the clinical interpretations of the automated program are based instead on the clinical experience of the program developer. In practice, most computerized personality systems rely heavily on this latter type of information.

In this chapter we have attempted to gain an overall perspective on clinical assessment. The value of assessment—including identifying the important factors in a case, planning appropriate treatment, and conducting research —was cited, and the need to evaluate both personal characteristics and the stressors and reinforcements in the individual's environment was emphasized.

Evaluating the effects of psychotherapy with automated MMPI interpretation

In the case reported here, the computerized interpretation of the individual's MMPI scores revealed a problem that the patient was not recognizing—depression. This test interpretation was quite helpful in guiding the clinician to an appropriate treatment program centered around alleviation of the conditions producing the depression rather than treatment for a "speech phobia."

Mr. D., a 38-year-old businessman, was referred for psychotherapy because he had recently developed what he referred to as a "speech phobia." As a result of his recent promotion to manager, he was required to speak in front of small groups of employees. He found that he choked up and could not think of anything to say.

In the first assessment interview, Mr. D. spoke at length about his new responsibilities and his desire to perform well in his new position, but he said very little about his own personal life. Not until later sessions did Mr. D. talk about his extensive personal distress. Just prior to his referral to the clinic, he and his wife had separated at her request. To add insult to injury, another man had moved into their new home with her. She was also awarded custody of their two-year-old son, a judgment which Mr. D. resented and fought in court. Having been raised in an orphanage after losing his parents, Mr. D. placed a great deal of value on being in a family. His present situation—losing another family—had resulted in his feeling deserted.

Besides his "unrecognized" depression, there were other psychological symptoms, including feelings of inadequacy, and also some physical problems. He had begun to spend considerable time drinking alone in bars and on one recent occasion had picked up a woman in a bar and been unable to have successful intercourse with her. Since this episode, he had become even more introverted and isolated, with the belief (a false one in his case) that he was sexually impotent.

Mr. D.'s MMPI profile and the computer evaluation of it made before therapy (and prepared by the Roche Psychiatric Service Institute) are reprinted here. On most of the scales his scores are above the mean, which is a T-score of 50. On Scale 2 (Depression) and Scale 5 (Masculinity-Femininity) his scores were 70. About 2 percent of the normal population score higher than 70.

Mr. D. was seen in six sessions of brief cognitive-behavioral therapy (see Chapter 19). The sense of guilt he felt in losing his family was found to be the central theme in his depression. The sessions were devoted in large part to exploring his self-defeating beliefs and giving him a different perspective on his problem. One important focus of therapy was on activity scheduling to get him involved in pleasurable activities again. For example, he was given homework assignments, such as calling three people or having a certain number of other social contacts before the next therapy session.

Within two sessions, he was beginning to get involved in several activities—for example, jogging and attending some social gatherings—and was feeling more confident in his work. At the end of treatment his mood had changed significantly, and he had resolved most of the problems centering around his dissolved marriage.

It is interesting to note that his fear of public speaking, which had brought him into therapy, was not a central theme of the treatment. However, by the end of the therapy, he had been successful at several difficult public presentations. He was no longer worried about this aspect of his new job.

The MMPI was readministered to Mr. D. again at the end of treatment. His new profile has been plotted on the same grid for comparison, and the change is impressive. On most of the scales, he has dropped below the mean. Most clearly, there is a significant reduction in depressed affect. This is shown by the sharp drop on Scale 2 (Depression) and also by the

---

Interdisciplinary sources of assessment data include physical and neurological examinations, often including neuropsychological tests, and a range of psychosocial techniques, including interviews, intelligence tests, personality tests (both projective and structured), observation of the individual's behavior, and assessment of the conditions in the individual's environment that are inducing or maintaining maladaptive behavior. Data gathered by these

rise on Scale 9 (Hypomania), which is often elevated at this point in very active, energetic, normal individuals. His score on Scale 5 (Masculinity-Feminity) remains high. As the original computer report pointed out, a high score on this scale is consistent with that of a well-educated person who has a wide range of interests.

MMPI computer report (before therapy)

Case No: 865696   RPSI. No: 10000
Age 38   Male   _____, 1978

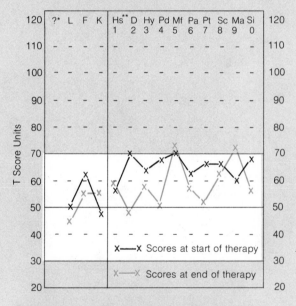

*The question mark, L, F, and K are validity scores: high scores indicate, respectively: evasiveness, lying to oneself to put oneself in a favorable light, faking illness, and subtle defensiveness.

**The ten scales to the right of the vertical line indicate, respectively: Hypochondriasis, Depression, Hysteria, Psychopathic Deviate, Masculinity-Femininity, Paranoia, Psychasthenia, Schizophrenia, Hypomania, and Social Introversion-Extroversion.

The test results of this patient appear to be valid. He seems to have made an effort to answer the items truthfully and to follow the instructions accurately. To some extent, this may be regarded as a favorable diagnostic sign, since it indicates that he is capable of following instructions and able to respond relevantly and truthfully to personal inquiry.

This patient appears to be somewhat depressed and restless. He may be a person who has difficulty maintaining control over his impulses. When his behavior does deviate from established norms, he feels guilt, but this does not seem to prevent recurrence. His expressed intentions to improve seem genuine, but the pattern is a persistent one. Frequently, his behavior shows a self-defeating and self-punitive tendency.

There are some unusual qualities in this patient's thinking which may represent an original or inventive orientation or perhaps some schizoid tendencies. Further information would be required to make this determination.

He is a rigid person who may express his anxiety in fears, compulsive behavior, and rumination. He may be chronically worried and tense, with marked resistance to treatment despite obvious distress.

He appears to be an idealistic, inner-directed person who may be seen as quite socially perceptive and sensitive to interpersonal interactions. His interest patterns are quite different from those of the average male. In a person with a broad educational and cultural background this is to be expected and may reflect such characteristics as self-awareness, concern with social issues, and an ability to communicate ideas clearly and effectively. In some men, however, the same interest pattern may reflect a rejection of masculinity accompanied by a relatively passive, effeminate noncompetitive personality.

This person may be hesitant to become involved in social relationships. He is sensitive, reserved, and somewhat uncomfortable, especially in new and unfamiliar situations.

Some aspects of this patient's test pattern are similar to those of psychiatric patients. Appropriate professional evaluation is recommended.

Note: Although not a substitute for the clinician's professional judgment and skill, the MMPI can be a useful adjunct in the evaluation and management of emotional disorders. The report is for professional use only and should not be shown or released to the patient.

various means are integrated by the clinical team and form the basis for treatment decisions. Further assessment data may be collected during the course of treatment.

Computers are used both to gather information from the patient and to integrate and evaluate information obtained from other sources. Computers have been programmed to provide evaluations based on both actuarial data and clinically derived rules.

18

Biologically based therapies

Early attempts at biological intervention
Emergence of pharmacological methods
Other biological therapies

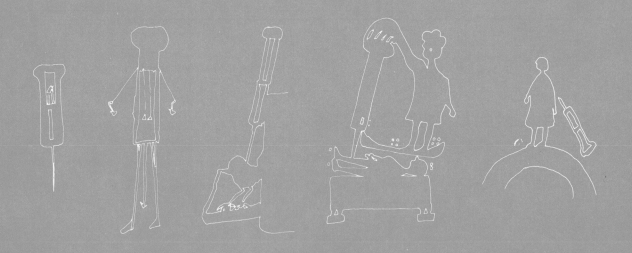

Therapy is directed toward modifying maladaptive behavior and fostering adaptive behavior. There are, of course, a great many other approaches to behavior change, such as formal education, political propaganda, and brainwashing. In therapy, however, the primary goal is to help an individual overcome maladaptive patterns and achieve more effective coping behavior.

The concept of therapy is not new. Throughout recorded history, human beings have tried to help each other with problems of living— including mental disorders—in both informal and formal ways. In Chapter 2 we noted the wide range of procedures that have, throughout history, been advocated for helping the mentally disturbed—from trephining and exorcism to incarceration and torture, from understanding and kindliness to the most extreme cruelty.

Today both biological and psychological procedures are used in attempts to help individuals overcome psychopathology. In this chapter we shall focus on biological methods that have evolved for the treatment of mental disorders such as the schizophrenias, affective psychoses, and disorders in which severe anxiety is central. Then, in the next chapter we shall focus on psychological approaches.

Early attempts at biological intervention

The idea that a disordered mind might be set straight by treatment directed at the body goes back, as we have seen, to ancient times. Beginning with those early "medicine men" who trephined skulls, through Hippocrates and Kraepelin, and on into the present era, there have always been those who believed that, ultimately, the route to the cure of mental aberration would have to be through alteration of the biological state of the organism. The dictum "no twisted thought without a twisted molecule," while philosophically and scientifically naive in certain respects, has been

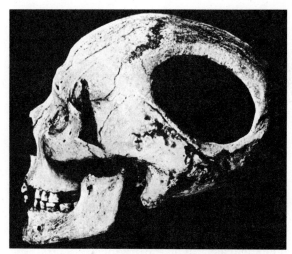

Above, a trephined skull from neolithic times. Trephination—perforating the skull with a sharp instrument—has long been a means of treating mental disorder. By boring a hole in the patient's skull, people hoped the "evil spirits" causing the mental disturbance would be driven out.

deeply internalized by many workers in the field. For those who do hold this belief, it is but a small step to conclude that the search for treatment methods should concentrate on finding effective means of rearranging or reconstituting aberrant "molecules"—of changing the presumed physical substrate of abnormal mentality.

However sincere the intent behind the earliest formal methods of treatment for mental disorders, they often involved harrowing physical abuse, as we have seen in Chapter 2. The fundamental purpose seems to have been not so much to frighten the person out of his or her madness, but rather either to punish the demon in residence in the patient's body or to alter the patient's physical or biological state, which was presumed to be the underlying cause of the disorder. The latter rationale still forms the basis of biological treatments of the present day, though methods have become more sophisticated and more guided by scientific advances.

These early methods of treatment—in essence, of "assaulting" the affected body—may also have reflected the conviction that stubbornly persistent abnormal behavior would obviously require very potent forms of intervention. It seems likely that this same reasoning was behind the centuries-old practice of blood-letting as a therapeutic technique for varied physical ailments—a process that doubtless hastened the demise of many patients.

During the nineteenth century, the paradoxical idea of fighting disease by "assaulting" the diseased organism gained additional credence. This was due in large part to the work of Louis Pasteur, who discovered that it was possible to immunize an organism against a severe form of disease by inoculating it with a benign strain of the microorganisms that produce the disease. Furthermore, in the psychiatric field, Wagner-Jauregg's development in 1917 of malarial fever treatment for general paresis provided enormous impetus to the practice of biological assault on the organism. In brief, the fever produced by the malaria organisms in the bloodstream markedly diminished the destructive activity of the syphilitic spirochetes. Thus, by the early years of the twentieth century, conditions were ripe for the introduction of more sophisticated forms of assaultive therapeutic intervention. Here we shall look at two of these, shock therapies and psychosurgery.

Shock therapies

Insulin shock therapy, little used today, was introduced by Sakel in 1932 as a physiological treatment for schizophrenia. The technique involves administration of increasing amounts of insulin (a hormone that regulates sugar metabolism in the body) on a daily basis until a point is reached at which the patient goes into "shock"—actually hypoglycemic coma, caused by an acute deficiency of glucose (sugar) in the blood. Coma-inducing doses of insulin are administered daily thereafter until the patient has experienced approximately 50 comas, each an hour or more in duration. Comas are terminated by the administration of glucose. This treatment involves profound physiological stress, especially to the cardiovascular and nervous systems. The patient being treated must be closely monitored both during and after the comatose state because of a variety of medical complications that may ensue, including some that are fatal.

Results of insulin shock therapy have been generally disappointing. Where the patient has shown improvement, it has been difficult to de-termine whether it was due to the coma or to some other feature associated with the treatment, such as the markedly increased attention of the medical staff. Moreover, patients who do show some improvement tend to be those who would improve readily under other treatment regimens as well; the severe, chronic schizophrenic patient remains for the most part unimproved. Finally, the relapse rate for those who have improved has been very high. With such a record—and in the face of the marked medical risks—it is hardly surprising that the use of insulin shock as a therapeutic method has largely disappeared in recent years (Kalinowski & Hippius, 1969).

Electroconvulsive therapy (ECT) has been more widely used—many would say regrettably. It developed after an early observation—erroneous, as it turned out—that schizophrenia rarely occurred in individuals with epilepsy. This observation led to the inference that schizophrenia and epilepsy were somehow incompatible, and that therefore one might be able to cure schizophrenia by inducing convulsions. Various methods of convulsion-induction were tried until 1938 when two Italian psychiatrists, Cerletti and Bini, tried the simplest method of all—that of passing an electric current through the patient's head.

Despite modest variations in the placing of electrodes and the introduction of safeguards, the standard form of the technique remains basically as Cerletti and Bini had determined it: an electric current of approximately 160 volts is passed from one side of the patient's head to the other for up to about one and one-half seconds. The patient immediately loses consciousness and undergoes a marked tonic (extensor) seizure of the muscles, followed by a lengthy series of clonic (contractile) ones of lesser amplitude. In the days before muscle-relaxant premedication, the initial seizure was sometimes so violent as to fracture vertebrae, one of several potential complications of this method of therapy.

After awakening several minutes later, the patient has amnesia for the period immediately preceding the shock, and is usually somewhat confused for the next hour or so. With repeated treatments, usually administered three times weekly, the patient gradually becomes generally disoriented, a state that clears after termination of treatments. Memory impairment, however, is likely to remain for months (Squire, Slater, & Chase, 1975), or apparently, in some instances, even years.

Normally, a treatment series consists of less than a dozen shocks, although in times past there was widespread overuse of the technique as a means of controlling excited or violent behavior. Even today, there are chronic patients on the "back wards" of mental hospitals whose treatment history includes the administration of literally hundreds of shocks. As was suggested in Chapter 11, it is not unlikely that so much electroconvulsive shock has led to significant brain damage in some cases (Allen, 1951; Alpers & Hughes, 1942; Brengelmann, 1959; Corsellis & Meyer, 1954; Fink, 1977, 1979; Heilbrun & Liebert, 1941).

Despite the violence of the method and the not uncommon complications that arise, a dispassionate appraisal of treatment results forces one to the conclusion that the procedure is sometimes almost miraculously effective in resolving psychotic states—particularly the affective psychoses but also, occasionally and unpredictably, the schizophrenias. In some cases, however, the benefits are short lived. As has been true with some other techniques, the mechanism by which therapeutic effects are brought about has never been adequately explained. Indeed, one early observer (Gordon, 1948) was able to count fifty separate theories about how ECT can produce a therapeutic effect. More recently, there seems to be some consensus that the therapeutic effect is mediated by induced changes in the biochemistry of brain synapses (Fink, 1979; Fink, Kety, McGaugh, & Williams, 1974).

A dramatic example of the unprecedented early success of ECT that sometimes occurred following its introduction is provided in the autobiographical account of Lenore McCall (1947), who suffered a severe depressive disorder in her middle years.

Ms. McCall, a well-educated woman of affluent circumstances and the mother of three children, noticed a feeling of persistent fatigue as the first sign of her impending descent into depression. Too fearful to seek help, she at first attempted to fight off her increasingly profound apathy by engaging in excessive activity, a defensive strategy that accomplished little but the depletion of her remaining strength and emotional reserves.

In due course, she noticed that her mental process-es seemed to be deteriorating—her memory appeared impaired and she could concentrate only with great difficulty. Emotionally, she felt an enormous loneliness, bleakness of experience, and increasingly intense fear about what was happening to her mind. She came to view her past small errors of commission and omission as the most heinous of crimes and increasingly withdrew from contact with her husband and children. Eventually, at her husband's and her physician's insistence, she was hospitalized despite her own vigorous resistance. She felt betrayed, and shortly thereafter attempted suicide by shattering a drinking glass and ingesting its fragments; to her great disappointment, she survived.

Ms. McCall thereafter spent nearly four years continuously in two separate mental hospitals, during which she deteriorated further. She was silent and withdrawn, behaved in a mechanical fashion, lost an alarming amount of weight, and underwent a seemingly premature aging process. She felt she emitted an offensive odor. At this time, ECT was introduced into the therapeutic procedures in use at her hospital.

A series of ECT treatments was given to Ms. McCall over a period of about three months. Then, one day, she woke up in the morning with a totally changed outlook: "I sat up suddenly, my heart pounding. I looked around the room and a sweep of wonder surged over me. God in heaven, I'm well. I'm myself . . . . " After a brief period of convalescence, she went home to her husband and children to try to pick up the threads of their lives that had been so painfully severed. She did so, and then wrote the engrossing and informative book from which this history is taken.

Some years ago, a modification in the standard method of administering ECT was introduced. Instead of placing the electrodes on each side of the head in the temple region, thereby causing a transverse flow of current through both cerebral hemispheres, the new procedure involves limiting current flow through only one side of the brain, typically the nondominant (right, for most people) side. This is called *unilateral ECT,* and there is good evidence that it lessens distressing side effects (such as memory impairment) without decreasing therapeutic effectiveness (Squire, 1977; Squire & Slater, 1978). Unfortunately, it is estimated that some 75 percent of psychiatrists who employ ECT still use the original, bilateral method exclusively (American Psychiatric Association, 1978).

ECT is used much less frequently today than heretofore, having yielded to advances in pharmacological approaches. However, it is still employed when other methods prove ineffective, or sometimes as a stopgap measure when slow-acting medication has not yet produced the desired result.

Psychosurgery

In 1935 in Portugal, Moniz introduced the surgical procedure known as *prefrontal lobotomy*. This operation, in which the nerve fibers connecting the frontal lobes and deeper centers of the brain are severed, stands as a dubious tribute to the levels to which professionals have sometimes been driven in their search for effective treatments of the psychoses. In retrospect, it seems somewhat surprising that this procedure—which results in permanent brain damage to the patient—won for its originator the Nobel Prize in Medicine for the year 1949.

In the two decades between 1935 and 1955 (when the new antipsychotic drugs became widely available) tens of thousands of mental patients in this country and abroad were subjected to prefrontal lobotomy and related neurosurgical procedures. In fact, in some settings, as many as 50 patients were treated at a facility in a single day (Freeman, 1959)! As is often the case with newly developed techniques of therapy, initial reports of results tended to be enthusiastic, downplaying complications (including a 1 to 4 percent death rate) and undesirable side effects. It was eventually recognized, however, that the "side effects" of psychosurgery could be very undesirable indeed. In some instances they included a permanent inability to inhibit impulses; in others, an unnatural "tranquility," with undesirable shallowness or absence of feeling. By 1951 the Soviet Union had banned all such operations; they are still permitted in the United States and in many other countries (see HIGH-LIGHT on this page).

The advent of the major antipsychotic drugs caused an almost immediate halt in the widespread use of psychosurgical procedures. Such operations are extremely rare today and are used only as a last resort for the intractable psychoses, severely and chronically debilitating obsessional neuroses, and occasionally for the control of severe pain in cases of terminal illness. In addition, contemporary psycho-

HIGHLIGHT

Transorbital lobotomy made simple

As a concrete example of the surgical techniques involved in psychosurgery in the early 1950s, we reproduce here the recommendations offered in a widely used text of that time concerning a supposed improvement of Moniz' procedure—that of transorbital lobotomy. It is heralded as a technique psychiatrists can employ by themselves, without the help of neurosurgeons.

It is first recommended that the patient be administered two to four electroconvulsive shock treatments prior to surgery, primarily for anaesthetic purposes. When a suitable level of "anaesthesia" is thereby achieved, the recommended procedure is as follows:

"The upper eye lid is lifted away from the eye ball, and the point of a leucotome introduced into the conjunctival sac until it rests in the vault of the orbit. This is usually 3 cm. from the midline. The shaft of the instrument is aimed parallel to the bony ridge of the nose and the base of the instrument driven with a hammer through the orbital plate. At a depth of 5 cm. from the margin of the upper lid, i.e., 3 cm. within the frontal lobe, the handle is moved as far laterally as the orbit will permit. This movement severs the basal portion of the thalamofrontal fibers. Returned to the midline, the instrument is then driven until a 7 cm. mark is reached and the handle is moved 20 degrees medially and 30 degrees laterally in order to sever the superior portion of the thalamofrontal radiation. . . .

"The deep frontal cut is performed when the handle of the instrument is in the lateral position at the 7 cm. mark. At this moment the handle is strongly elevated until the shaft lies as nearly parallel as possible to the orbital plate. From this position the handle is then returned to the parasagital plane and withdrawn. The operation is always performed on both sides.

"Sometimes it is difficult to withdraw the ['ice pick-like'] instrument when the bone is very thick. Therefore the instrument has been replaced with a 'transorbitoma' whose shaft is elliptical in cross section and has a gentle increase in caliber from the point to the hilt, thus preventing the instrument from running through the orbital plate too fast when struck with a mallet, and also allowing easy removal" (Kalinowski & Hoch, 1952, p. 228).

surgery, when it is employed, is a much more circumspect procedure than was true in the heyday of lobotomies. The technique involves the selective destruction of very minute areas; for example, in the "cingulotomy" procedure—which seems to relieve the subjective experience of pain, including "psychic" pain—a very small bundle of nerve fibers connecting the frontal lobes with a deeper structure known as the limbic system is interrupted with virtually pinpoint precision.

Despite these advances, continuing concern has been voiced about such operations, and in the mid-1970s the Congress of the United States called for a special national commission to evaluate their effects. The report of that commission indicated some surprisingly beneficial effects that had been achieved with modern psychosurgery—for example, the alleviation of chronic depression—but it also warned that such benefits were often achieved at the expense of the loss of certain cognitive capacities (Culliton, 1976). We may be reasonably assured that such careful surveillance will continue.

It would appear that at long last the use of severe assaults on the body to treat major behavioral disorders is coming to an end. One can only hope that it will never be revived. At the same time, it should be noted that, for the most part, the individuals who practiced these methods were using the best knowledge and theory that were available to tackle difficult problems that no one understood. Their intent was to help their patients. It is in retrospect that we are just now beginning to understand the harm their methods sometimes caused.

Emergence of pharmacological methods

A long-term goal of medicine has been to discover drugs that can effectively combat the ravages of mental disorder. This goal, one of the pursuits of *pharmacology*, the science of drugs, has until fairly recently remained very

elusive. Early efforts in this direction were limited largely to a search for chemical compounds that would have soothing, calming, or sleep-inducing effects. Such drugs, if they could be found, would make it easier to manage distraught, excited, and sometimes violent patients. Little thought was given to the possibility that the status and course of the disorder itself might actually be brought under control by appropriate medication; the focus was on rendering the patient's overt behavior more manageable and thereby making restraint devices such as straitjackets unnecessary.

As the field of psychopharmacology developed, many such compounds were introduced and tried in the mental hospital setting. Almost without exception, however, those that produced the desired calming effects proved to have very serious shortcomings. At effective dosage levels they often produced severe drowsiness if not outright sleep, and many of them were dangerously addicting. On the whole, little real progress was made in this field until the mid-1950s, at which point, as we shall see, a genuine revolution in treatment of the more severe disorders occurred. This breakthrough was followed shortly by the discovery of compounds helpful in the treatment of the less severe, anxiety-based disorders, and eventually by recognition of the therapeutic benefits of lithium salts for manic states.

Types of drugs used in therapy

In this section we will trace the discovery of the four types of chemical agents now commonly used in therapy for mental disorders—antipsychotic compounds, antidepressant compounds, antianxiety compounds (minor tranquilizers), and lithium, which is used principally to combat manic disorders.

Antipsychotic compounds. The antipsychotic compounds as a group are sometimes called "major tranquilizers," but this term is somewhat misleading. They are used with the major disorders, such as the schizophrenias, but they do more than tranquilize. While they do indeed produce a calming effect on many patients, their unique quality is that of somehow alleviating or reducing the intensity of schizophrenic symptoms, including delusions and hallucinations. The antianxiety compounds, to be described shortly, are by contrast effective in reducing tension without in any way affecting psychotic symptoms.

Although the benefits of the antipsychotic compounds have often been exaggerated, it is difficult to convey the truly enormous influence they have had in altering the environment of the mental hospital. One of the authors, as part of his training, worked several months in the maximum security ward of one such hospital immediately prior to the introduction of this type of medication in 1955. The ward patients fulfilled the oft-heard stereotypes of individuals "gone mad." Bizarreness, nudity, wild screaming, and an ever present threat of violence pervaded the atmosphere. Fearfulness and a near-total preoccupation with the maintenance of control characterized the attitudes of staff. Such staff attitudes were not unrealistic in terms of the frequency of occurrence of serious physical assaults by patients, but they were hardly conducive to the development or maintenance of an effective therapeutic program.

Then, quite suddenly—within a period of perhaps a month—all of this dramatically changed. The patients were receiving antipsychotic medication. The ward became a place in which one could seriously get to know one's patients on a personal level and perhaps even initiate programs of "milieu therapy"[1] and the like, promising reports of which had begun to appear in the professional literature. A new era in hospital treatment had arrived, aided enormously and in many instances actually made possible by the development of these extraordinary drugs.

The beginnings of this development were quite commonplace. For centuries the root of the plant *rauwolfia* (snakeroot) had been used in India for the treatment of mental disorders. In 1943, the *Indian Medical Gazette* reported improvement in manic reactions, schizophrenia, and other types of psychopathology following the use of *reserpine*, a drug derived

from rauwolfia. Reserpine was first used in the United States in the early 1950s, after it was found to have a "calming" effect on mental patients (Kline, 1954). Early enthusiasm for the drug was tempered, however, by the finding that it also might produce low blood pressure, nasal congestion, and, perhaps most seriously, severe depression. More recently, reanalysis of this latter finding suggests that the danger of serious depression is mainly for patients with a prior history of depression (Mendels & Frazer, 1974). However, widespread use of reserpine in this field continues to be unlikely, especially in view of recent findings that it may produce cancer.

Meanwhile, the first of the phenothiazine family of drugs, chlorpromazine (Thorazine), was being synthesized in the early 1950s by one of the major pharmaceutical houses. It was first marketed at about the same time that reserpine was introduced, and it quickly proved to have virtually the same benefits but fewer undesirable side effects. It soon became the treatment of choice for schizophrenia.

The remarkable early successes reported with chlorpromazine led quickly to a bandwagon effect among other pharmaceutical companies, who began to manufacture and market their own variants of the basic phenothiazine compound. Some of the best known variants are trifluoperazine (Stelazine), prochlorperazine (Compazine), thioridazine (Mellaril), perphenazine (Trilafon), and fluphenazine (Prolixin). Recently, too, several nonphenothiazine antipsychotic agents have become available, of which the best known is haloperidol (Haldol).

With persistent use or at high dosage, however, all of these preparations have various troublesome side effects, such as dryness of mouth and throat, muscular stiffness, jaundice, and a Parkinson-like syndrome involving tremors of the extremities and immobility of the facial muscles. Which side effects develop appears to depend on the particular compound used in relation to the particular vulnerabilities of the treated patient. Many of these side effects are temporary and may be relieved by substitution of another drug of the same class, by a different class of drug, or by reduction in dosage.

Until very recently, a particularly serious and worrisome potential side effect of taking

---

[1]In *milieu therapy* the entire facility is regarded as a therapeutic community, and the emphasis is on developing a meaningful and constructive environment in which the patients participate in the regulation of their own activities. Self-reliance and the formation of socially acceptable interpersonal relationships are encouraged.

antipsychotic drugs has been that of *tardive dyskinesia,* a disfiguring disturbance of motor control formerly believed to be irreversible. However, new techniques involving replacement of brain acetylcholene (which is believed to be depleted by these drugs or by drugs commonly used to control their side effects) show considerable promise in overcoming this difficulty (Kolata, 1979).

Compared to anything we have known before, the effects of these substances in the treatment of schizophrenic disorders are clearly remarkable. At the same time, we must acknowledge that they are not a panacea. Indeed, while the more striking symptoms of schizophrenic psychoses frequently abate under active treatment with these drugs, the behavioral residual is usually less than impressive; the patient still does not become the alert, competent person one might hope. Though no longer overtly psychotic, the individual's symptoms are only being suppressed: withdrawal of the drug not uncommonly results in a reappearance of schizophrenic symptomatology. In short, the pharmacologic approach has yet to produce a "cure" for schizophrenia (Berger, 1978).

The range of effects achieved by the antipsychotic drugs may be illustrated by two brief case histories of patients who served as subjects in a clinical research project designed to evaluate differing treatment approaches to the schizophrenias (Grinspoon, Ewalt, & Shader, 1972).

Ms. W. was a 19-year-old, white, married woman who was admitted to the treatment unit as a result of gradually increasing agitation and hallucinations over a three-month period. Her symptoms had markedly intensified during the four days prior to admission, partly as a result of a homosexual seduction she had undergone while under the influence of marijuana. She had had a deprived childhood, but had managed to function reasonably well up to the point of her breakdown.

At the outset of her hospitalization, Ms. W. continued to have auditory and visual hallucinations and appeared frightened, angry, and confused. She believed she had some special, unique relationship with God or the devil. Her thought content displayed loosening of associations, and her affect was inappropriate to this content. Her condition continued to deteriorate for more than two weeks, at which point medication was begun.

Ms. W. was assigned to a treatment group in which the patients were receiving thioridazine (Mellaril). She responded quite dramatically during the first week of treatment. Her behavior became, for the most part, quiet and appropriate, and she made some attempts at socialization. She continued to improve, but by the fourth week of treatment began to show signs of mild depression. Her medication was increased, and she resumed her favorable course. By the sixth week she was dealing with various reality issues in her life in a reasonably effective manner, and by the ninth week she was spending considerable time at home, returning to the hospital in a pleasant and cheerful mood. She was discharged exactly 100 days after her admission, being then completely free of symptoms.

Mr. S., the eldest of three sons in a fairly religious Jewish family, was admitted to the hospital after developing marked paranoid ideation and hallucinations during his first weeks of college. He had looked forward to going to college, an elite New England school, but his insecurity once on campus caused him to become unduly boastful about his prowess with drinking and women. He stayed up late at night to engage in "bull sessions," and he neglected his studies and other responsibilities. Within ten days he had panicked about his ability to keep up and tried frantically to rearrange his course schedule and his life, to no avail.

His sense of incompetence was transformed over time into the idea that others—including all the students in his dormitory—were against him, and that fellow male students were perhaps flirting homosexually with him. By the time of his referral to the college infirmary, he was convinced the college was a fraud he would have to expose, that the CIA was plotting against him, and that someone was going to kill him. He heard voices and smelled strange odors. He also showed a marked loosening of associations and flat, inappropriate affect. At the time of his transfer to the hospital, he was diagnosed as an acute paranoid schizophrenic.

Mr. S. was assigned to a treatment group receiving haloperidol (Haldol). His initial response to treatment was rapid and favorable, but observers noted that his behavior remained quite immature. Then quite suddenly during the fifth week of treatment, he became very tense, negativistic, and hostile. Thereafter, he gradually became less defiant and angry, and he responded well to a day-care program prescribed by his therapist, although he was nervous and apprehensive about being outside the hospital. He was discharged as improved ten weeks after initiation of his drug therapy.

Three months later Mr. S. was readmitted to the hospital. While he had done well at first, he then had begun to deteriorate, concurrently with his planned withdrawal from haloperidol. His behavior showed increasing signs of lack of effective control, including setting fires, and was described by the investigators as "sociopathic." Two days after his readmission, he signed himself out of the hospital "against medical advice." His parents immediately arranged for his confinement in another hospital, and the investigators subsequently lost contact with him.

Antidepressant compounds.

The antidepressant drugs made their appearance some two years after the introduction of reserpine and chlorpromazine. There are two basic classes of these compounds: the monoamine oxidase (MAO) inhibitors and the tricyclics. While they differ considerably in their chemical makeup, it is currently believed that they accomplish a common biochemical result—namely, that of increasing the concentrations of the biogenic amines serotonin and norepinephrine at pertinent synaptic sites in the brain (Berger, 1978). The abundant availability of these neurotransmitter substances, in turn, is thought somehow to mitigate, abort, or terminate the fundamental biological conditions that accompany the depressive state. The evidence for this view remains highly circumstantial and indirect, however; as in the case of the antipsychotic drugs, a clear understanding of how these drugs work must await further research.

Of the two main classes of antidepressants, the tricyclics are by far the more often used. This is largely because the MAO inhibitors are more toxic and require troublesome dietary restrictions; in addition, they are widely believed to have less potent therapeutic effects. Nevertheless, some patients who do not respond favorably to tricyclics will subsequently do well on an MAO inhibitor. A minority of severely depressed patients respond to neither type of antidepressant compound, in which case alternative modes of intervention, such as ECT, may be used. Commonly used tricyclics are imipramine (Tofranil), amitriptyline (Elavil), and nortriptyline (Aventyl). MAO inhibitors include isocarboxazid (Marplan), phenelzine (Nardil), and tranylcypromine (Parnate).

Pharmacological treatment of depression often produces a dramatic and fully satisfactory result. This is in sharp contrast to the effect of the antipsychotic drugs in merely suppressing schizophrenic symptoms. However, this statement must be tempered with the observation that individuals suffering from severe depressive disorders often respond to any treatment—or even no treatment at all. That is distinctly less true in the case of the schizophrenias.

Antianxiety compounds (the minor tranquilizers).

If it is true, as we have observed, that ours is the age of anxiety, it is certainly no less true that ours is also the age of the search for anxiety-reducers. At the present time, literally millions of physician-prescribed pills alleged to contain anxiety- and tension-relieving substances are consumed daily by the American public, to say nothing of the manifold alternative methods people employ to reduce their anxiety—ranging from biofeedback to the practice of ancient Eastern religious rituals—that promise to relieve "uptight" feelings. The nonprescription drug market, which includes traffic in alcoholic beverages, marijuana, and decidedly more problematic substances, has had an unprecedented growth rate in recent years—much of it presumably due to the same widespread wish to be somehow relieved of "hassle."

Besides the long-used barbiturates (see Chapter 10), which have high addictive potential and a low margin of dosage safety, two additional classes of prescription antianxiety compounds have gained widespread acceptance in recent years. One of these, the meprobamates, seems to operate mainly through the reduction of muscular tension, which in turn is experienced by the patient as calming and emotionally soothing. Meprobamate drugs are marketed under the trade names Miltown and Equanil.

The other class of antianxiety compounds, with a level of use in this country and elsewhere that almost exceeds belief, is the benzodiazepine derivatives (see HIGHLIGHT on page 625). Under this rubric are included chlordiazepoxide (Librium), diazepam (Valium), oxazepam (Serax), clorazepate (Tranxene), and flurazepam (Dalmane). In experimental studies on animals, the most striking effect of these compounds has been the recurrence of behavior previously inhibited by conditioned fears but without serious impairment in overall behavioral efficiency. Benzodiazepine derivatives, in other words, have the important property of somehow selectively diminishing generalized fear (or anxiety) and leaving adaptive behaviors largely intact. They are thus far superior to many other types of anxiety-reducing chemicals, which tend to produce widespread negative effects on adaptive functioning.

Nevertheless, all of the antianxiety drugs have a basically sedative effect on the organism, and many patients treated with them complain of drowsiness and lethargy. This has been a particular problem among schoolchildren treated with these compounds. Also to be noted is that all of these drugs have the potential of inducing dependence when used unwisely or in excess (Bassuk & Schoonover, 1977).

The range of application of the antianxiety compounds is quite broad. They are used in all manner of conditions in which tension and anxiety may be significant components, including neurotic and psychosomatic disorders. They are also used as supplementary treatment in certain neurological disorders in order to control such symptoms as convulsive seizures, but they have little place in the treatment of the psychoses. They are now the most widely prescribed of all of the drugs available to physicians, a fact that has caused concern among some leaders in the medical and psychiatric fields.

Lithium for the affective psychoses.
Lithium is a simple mineral salt that was discovered—as early as 1949 by J. Cade in Australia—to be effective in treating manic disorders. Some twenty years passed before this treatment was introduced in the United States. This may have been, in part, for two reasons. First, if not used at the proper dosage, lithium can be very toxic to the individual, causing numerous troublesome side effects, such as delirium and convulsions. And yet lithium must be used at a critical-level dosage—which is very close to the toxic level—if it is to have any therapeutic benefit whatever. To add to these difficulties, different individuals require different amounts of lithium to be at the critical-level dosage. Thus at the onset of lithium treatment each patient's blood level must be carefully monitored to determine the exact dosage of lithium appropriate for him or her.

A second possible reason for the delay in widespread usage of lithium in the United

---

HIGHLIGHT

Chemically induced sleep: is it worth the risks?

Prescriptions for the benzodiazepine class of antianxiety compounds currently exceed 70 million per year in the United States. Of these, a huge proportion are written for the ostensible purpose of enabling persons to sleep better at night. The most common benzodiazepine prescribed specifically for this purpose is flurazepam (Dalmane). Some 8 million individuals use this general class of drug sometime during any one year, and up to 2 million persons take these pills nightly for more than two months at a time.

Recently, the Institute of Medicine (IOM) of the National Academy of Sciences issued a report outlining the hazards of this remedy for sleeping difficulties—difficulties that in any case they found to be severely overestimated on a routine basis by the persons allegedly suffering from them. Noting that the barbiturates justly deserve their reputation as dangerous drugs, the IOM report indicated that the benzodiazepines may be just as risky, and in some cases more so. For example, flurazepam, while not quite as addicting as the barbiturates, remains in the body in the form of metabolites far longer than do the barbiturates, resulting in a build-up of toxic substances in the body that may reach a critical level within a week of regular ingestion of the drug at bedtime. While flurazepam overdose is usually not in itself lethal, it may interact with other drugs, such as alcohol, to produce lethal effects. Because of these readily misunderstood characteristics, the IOM concludes that, overall, flurazepam does not diminish the number of deaths attributable to sleeping pill medication, relative to earlier types of "hypnotic" drugs such as the barbiturates.

A particularly worrisome aspect of this problem is the fact that a certain amount of benign "insomnia" naturally accompanies advancing age. And yet elderly persons currently receive some 39 percent of all sleeping pill prescriptions. For these individuals there is a real danger that the side effects of these drugs, such as daytime lethargy and clouding of consciousness, may be considered indicators of senile deterioration by family members and even by professional caretakers.

Considering the risks involved in taking these drugs, it seems appropriate to keep in mind an observation of one of the IOM members: losing some sleep now and then is *not* a life-threatening problem (Smith, 1979).

States may have been the simple fact that researchers were skeptical that it was the lithium itself that was producing the beneficial results: the lithium compounds used in treatment are simple inorganic salts that have no known physiological function (Berger, 1978). Lithium, then, is a somewhat peculiar drug.

Its curious qualities notwithstanding, there can be no doubt at this point concerning lithium's remarkable effectiveness in promptly resolving about 70 percent of all manic states. In addition, as we saw in Chapter 11, lithium is sometimes successful in relieving depressions, although possibly only in those patients who are subject to both manic and depressive episodes—that is, who are bipolar in type (Bassuk & Schoonover, 1977; Berger, 1978; Segal, Yager, & Sullivan, 1976). The drug has been a boon, especially to those persons who heretofore have experienced repeated bouts with mania and/or depression throughout their adult lives. For many, these cycles can now be modulated or even prevented by regular maintenance doses of lithium. Psychiatry may thus have achieved its first essentially preventive treatment method.

One of Cade's (1949) own cases will serve well as an illustration of the effects of lithium treatment:

Mr. W. B. was a 51-year-old man who had been in a state of chronic manic excitement for five years. So obnoxious and destructive was his behavior that he had long been regarded as the most difficult patient on his ward in the hospital.

He was started on treatment with a lithium compound, and within three weeks his behavior had improved to the point that transfer to the convalescent ward was deemed appropriate. He remained in the hospital for another two months, during which his behavior continued to be essentially normal. Prior to discharge, he was switched to another form of lithium salts, because the one he had been taking had caused stomach upset.

He was soon back at his job and living a happy and productive life. In fact, he felt so well off that, contrary to instructions, he stopped taking his lithium. Thereafter he steadily became more irritable and erratic; some six months following his discharge, he had to cease work. In another five weeks he was back in the hospital in an acute manic state.

Lithium therapy was immediately reestablished, with prompt positive results. In another month Mr. W. B. was pronounced ready to return to home and work, provided he continued taking a prescribed dosage of lithium.

The biochemical basis of the therapeutic effect of lithium is unknown. One well-received hypothesis is that it achieves its effects by limiting the availability of norepinephrine, which functions as a neural transmitter or modulator at certain synapses in the brain. This effect is opposite that of antidepressant compounds and presumably reduces the individual's ability to process the amount of input typical during a manic state. Of course, this still leaves unexplained the fact that lithium can also alleviate some depressions. Clearly, the riddle will be solved only by more and better research.

Drug therapy for children

Our discussion of the use of drugs in treating maladaptive behavior would be incomplete without some reiteration of their role in the management of childhood disturbances and disorders. We have already addressed this matter to some extent in Chapter 14. While our society has often been too quick to label as deviant, and to proceed to "treat," various annoying or inconvenient behaviors in which children sometimes indulge, it is nevertheless true that *some* children do evidence more or less serious behavior disorders. It is also true that some of them may be helped by judicious use of medication.

Antianxiety, antipsychotic, and antidepressant medications have all been used effectively with children who are, respectively, excessively anxious or "nervous," psychotic, or depressed. Considerable caution must be exercised in the use of these powerful compounds with children, however, in order to be certain that dosage levels are within tolerable limits for a small and as yet biologically immature organism. Not only are excessive blood levels of these drugs physically dangerous, but in some instances they may produce paradoxical reversal effects—that is, the child's problem may become *more* severe (Bassuk & Schoonover, 1977).

We have already mentioned the apparently widespread problem of excessively tranquilized elementary-school pupils. While the diagnostic terms "hyperactivity," "hyperkinesis," "minimal brain dysfunction," and "specific learning disability" have been used somewhat haphazardly in recent years, there appears to be a subset of highly distractable youngsters of normal but unevenly developed cognitive ability who benefit rather dramatically, and paradoxically, from drugs that stimulate the central nervous system. As we saw in Chapter 14, the most widely used of these stimulants are the amphetamines; a closely related compound known as methylphenidate (Ritalin) is also used. In certain instances, these drugs produce a prompt termination of hyperactivity, which typically results in an increase in attention span and in ability to do schoolwork (Sprague, Barnes, & Werry, 1970). Normally, the child thus helped is kept on the drug until adolescence, when hyperactivity tends to diminish by an as yet unknown natural process (Bassuk & Schoonover, 1977).

The danger, of course, is that restless, overactive children will be summarily diagnosed as "hyperkinetic" or "minimally brain damaged" and treated with drugs whether or not the problem is essentially a physical one. If such is the case, the option to use less extreme but potentially effective psychological approaches in treating these children may be forgotten (see Chapter 14).

A perspective on pharmacological therapy

Modern psychopharmacology has brought a reduction in the severity and chronicity of many types of psychopathology, particularly the psychoses. It has helped many individuals who would otherwise require hospitalization to function in their family and community setting; it has led to the earlier discharge of those who do require hospitalization and to the greater effectiveness of aftercare programs; and it has made restraints and locked wards largely methods of the past. All in all, pharmacological therapy not only has outmoded more drastic forms of treatment but has led to a much more favorable hospital climate for patients and staff alike (see HIGHLIGHT beginning on page 628).

However, there are a number of complications and limitations in the use of psychoactive drugs. Aside from possible undesirable side effects, the problem of matching drug and dosage to the needs of a given individual is often a difficult one, and it is sometimes necessary to change medication in the course of treatment. In addition, as many investigators have pointed out, these drugs tend to alleviate symptoms rather than bring the individual to grips with personal or situational factors that may be reinforcing maladaptive behaviors. Although the reduction in anxiety, disturbed thinking, and other symptoms may tempt therapists to regard a patient as "recovered," it would seem wise to include psychotherapy in the total program if such gains are to be maintained or improved upon.

The judicious combining of chemical and psychological forms of treatment, however, is a somewhat more complicated challenge than it might at first appear. For example, there may be complex interactions—not all of them necessarily positive in effect—between the two types of influence, such that the potential positive effects of either could be mitigated or compromised by the influence of the other treatment. Research into the problems of combined treatments is still in its infancy, and is characterized by much confusion and contradiction (Hollon & Beck, 1978).

Other biological therapies

Our still incomplete understanding of the biological bases of mental disorders, particularly the major psychoses, renders the field a fertile one for speculative thought and for continuation of the search for new innovations in biological intervention. By and large, despite the gains described above, the history of these innovations has been a disappointing one; when subjected to rigorous evaluation, most new treatment techniques for which hopeful claims have been made have proven ineffective except by virtue of the power of suggestion—the so-called placebo effect. Nevertheless, it would be folly to condemn out of hand all new proposed therapies: witness, for instance, the unnecessary and unfortunately long delay in the introduction of lithium therapy in the United States. In this section we shall briefly review some of the more widely used of these less established biological treatments.

Frequently used drugs in the treatment of mental and behavioral disorders

Class	Generic name	Trade name	Used to treat	Effects
Antipsychotic a) phenothiazines	chlorpromazine thioridazine promazine trifluoperazine prochlorperazine perphenazine fluphenazine	Thorazine Mellaril Sparine Stelazine Compazine Trilafon Prolixin	Psychotic (especially schizophrenic) symptoms such as extreme agitation, delusions, and hallucinations; aggressive or violent behavior.	Somewhat variable in achieving intended purpose of suppression of psychotic symptoms. Side effects, such as dry mouth, are often uncomfortable. In long-term use may produce motor disturbances such as Parkinsonism and tardive dyskinesia.
b) butyrophenones	haloperidol	Haldol		
c) thioxanthenes	thiothixine chlorprothixene	Navane Taractan		
Antidepressant a) tricyclics	imipramine amitriptyline nortriptyline protriptyline doxepin	Tofranil Elavil Aventyl Vivactil Sinequan	Relatively severe depressive symptoms, especially of psychotic severity and unipolar in type.	Somewhat variable in alleviating depressive symptoms, and noticeable effects may be delayed up to three weeks. Multiple side effects—some of them dangerous. Use of MAO inhibitors requires dietary restrictions.
b) monoamine oxidase (MAO) inhibitors	isocarboxazid phenelzine tranylcypromine	Marplan Nardil Parnate		

1. *Megavitamin therapy.* In megavitamin therapy, treatment includes large dosages of vitamins, particularly niacin (vitamin B_3, nicotinic acid), which have been alleged to have curative properties for schizophrenic patients by correcting certain imbalances in brain biochemistry. In addition, the treatment regimen usually involves large-scale ingestion of other vitamins besides the B group (especially ascorbic acid, vitamin C), as well as various special diets in what is known as the "orthomolecular" approach.

There is no reliable evidence that the orthomolecular approach by itself (that is, without accompanying standard antipsychotic medication) produces any benefit to patients. In fact, an American Psychiatric Association Task Force, charged with conducting an evaluation of this approach, issued the following unusually harsh judgment after a lengthy review of the available evidence:

"In the end the credibility of the megavitamin proponents and the orthomolecular psychiatrists becomes

Class	Generic name	Trade name	Used to treat	Effects
Antimanic (bipolar)	lithium carbonate	Eskalith Lithane Lithonate Lithotabs Phi-Lithium	Manic episodes and some severe depressions, particularly recurrent ones or those alternating with mania.	Usually effective in resolving manic episodes, but highly variable in effects on depression, probably because the latter is a less homogeneous grouping. Multiple side effects unless carefully monitored; high toxicity potential.
Antianxiety (minor tranquilizers)	diazepam chlordiazepoxide flurazepam oxazepam clorazepate	Valium Librium Dalmane Serax Tranxene	Nonpsychotic personality problems in which anxiety and tension are prominent features; also used as anticonvulsants and as sleep-inducers (especially flurazepam).	Somewhat variable in achieving intended purpose of tension reduction. Side effects include drowsiness and lethargy. Dependence and toxicity are dangers.
Stimulant	dextroamphetamine amphetamine methylphenidate	Dexedrine Benzedrine Ritalin	Hyperactivity, distractability, specific learning disabilities, and, occasionally, extreme hypoactivity.	Rather unpredictable. When maximally effective, can enable otherwise uneducable children to attend regular schools. Side effects often troublesome, including recently discovered retardation of growth.

the crucial issue because it is never possible to fully prove or disprove a therapeutic procedure. Rather the theory and practice gain or lose credibility as their premises, methods, and results are examined, and attempts are made at clinical replication by independent investigators. This review and critique has carefully examined the literature produced by megavitamin proponents and by those who have attempted to replicate their basic and clinical work. It concludes that in this regard the credibility of the megavitamin proponents is low.

"Their credibility is further diminished by a consistent refusal over the past decade to perform controlled experiments and to report their new results in a scientifically acceptable fashion.

"Under these circumstances, this Task Force considers the massive publicity which they promulgate via radio, the lay press, and popular books, using catch phrases which are really misnomers like 'megavitamin therapy' and 'orthomolecular treatment' to be deplorable" (Lipton et al., 1973, p. 48)

2. *Electrosleep therapy.* Although it has received little attention in the United States,

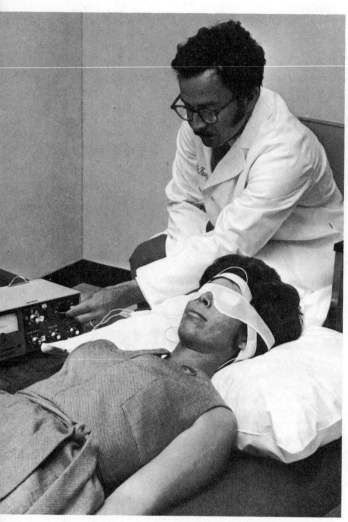

In electrosleep therapy, a mild electric current is passed through the individual's brain. The procedure has been the subject of extensive research in the Soviet Union but has received little attention in the United States. In the studies that have been done, the effectiveness of the therapy has been mixed.

electrosleep, or *cerebral electrotherapy*, has been the subject of extensive research in the U.S.S.R. In this procedure, a soft mask containing electrodes is placed over the upper part of the individual's face. A mild electric current—just enough to cause a slight tingling sensation—is administered. The individual does not lose consciousness or experience convulsions and may or may not actually fall asleep during the treatment. Usually, half-hour treatments are administered daily for one or two weeks.

In one of the first studies of electrosleep in the United States, Rosenthal and Wulfsohn (1970) reported favorable preliminary results with a group of more than 40 outpatients suffering from chronic anxiety, depressive states, and associated insomnia.

Unfortunately, later studies have shown less promising results, and the types of disorders for which electrosleep may be appropriate, as well as its long-range effectiveness, remain to be ascertained (Astrup, 1974; Brown, 1975; Hearst et al., 1974). However, international efforts to evaluate this form of therapy are being made, and it may well prove to be a useful treatment in and of itself or as an adjunct to a broader treatment program.

3. *Continuous sleep therapy.* Introduced in 1922 by Kläsi, this technique involves the administration of sleep-inducing medication on a schedule that will cause the patient to remain asleep for approximately 20 hours daily over a period of about 10 days. The treatment is somewhat dangerous, with a mortality rate approaching 1 percent. Research on this treatment method has yet to be validated, but it appears to have no benefit in the schizophrenias; it may be of some use in treating chronic anxiety states (Freedman, Kaplan, & Sadock, 1976).

4. *Carbon dioxide therapy.* This method involves inhalation of a mixture of 30 percent carbon dioxide and 70 percent oxygen for 20 to 100 breathing cycles. The patient becomes unconscious and undergoes generalized muscular rigidity. Twenty to 150 such treatments are usually administered at intervals of one to several days. There have been scattered reports of positive results with the treatment, particularly in anxiety and personality disorders. However, controlled studies with neurotic patients have failed to substantiate these claims of benefit (Freedman et al., 1976).

5. *Hemodialysis therapy.* One of the new biological treatments in psychiatry, as of this writing, is that of hemodialysis—blood purification by means of the artificial kidney machine. In November of 1977, Ervin and Palmour announced that they had isolated a certain peptide molecule from the blood of schizophrenic patients and suggested that this allegedly psychotoxic substance could be removed by dialysis (*Time*, November 21, 1977). Actually, dialysis treatment of schizophrenia had already been begun some five years earlier by R. Cade at the University of Florida. Greenberg (1978) reported that Cade and his former colleague Wagemaker claimed recovery or significant improvement for two-thirds of treated patients. Greenberg also noted that The National Institute of Mental Health has taken an interested but cautious approach to these claims, pending the results of further research now underway to determine the effectiveness of this method. In view of the long history of premature announcements about discoveries of a blood toxin responsible for schizophrenia, the reader is advised against undue optimism regarding this approach.

In this chapter we have taken a historical approach to the biologically based treatment of mental disorder. We noted that earlier tendencies to employ harsh, assaultive methods on the body seem largely to have run their course—fortunately for contemporary victims of mental disorders. The current revolution in pharmacological therapy was described in some detail. Finally, we noted some of the still experimental forms of biological intervention, including the recently developed use of hemodialysis for schizophrenia.

19

Psychological therapies

Psychoanalytic therapy

Behavior therapy

Cognitive-behavioral therapy

Humanistic-experiential therapies

Therapy for interpersonal relationships

Evaluation of "success" in psychotherapy

When mental disorders and emotional disturbances were seen as possession by demons or punishment for sin, they were regarded as generally beyond human power to change. Then, as brain damage and other physical pathology were found to be causally involved in certain types of mental disorder, attitudes changed. Mental disorders were assumed to be physically caused diseases, with the implication that where cure was possible, it too would be through physical means. As the role of both psychological and sociocultural factors became apparent, however, psychopathology was increasingly recognized as a natural phenomenon in which biological, psychological, and sociocultural factors could each play a role in causation and therapeutic intervention.

Psychotherapy is therapy directed primarily at the psychological factors in this trio. Its use is based on the assumption that even in cases where physical pathology is present, the individual's perceptions, evaluations, expectations, and coping strategies have also played a role in the development of the disorder and will probably need to be changed if recovery is to take place. The belief that individuals with psychological problems *can* change—can learn more adaptive ways of perceiving, evaluating, and behaving—is the central belief underlying all psychotherapy.

Most of us have experienced a time or situation when we were dramatically helped by a bit of advice from a relative or friend. Or perhaps we made a drastic change in our life-style after a particular experience that had led to a new insight. As Alexander (1946) has pointed out, psychotherapy is not far removed from the experience of most of us:

". . . Everyone who tries to console a despondent friend [or] calm down a panicky child in a sense practices psychotherapy. He tries by psychological means to restore the disturbed emotional equilibrium of another person. Even these commonsense, everyday methods are based on the understanding of the nature of the disturbance, although on an intuitive and not a scientific understanding. . . . Methodological psychotherapy to a large degree is nothing but a systematic, conscious application of methods by which we influence our fellow men in our daily life."

In general, psychotherapy aims toward (a) changing maladaptive behavior patterns, (b) minimizing or eliminating environmental conditions that may be causing and/or maintaining such behavior, (c) improving interpersonal and other competencies, (d) resolving handicapping or disabling inner conflicts and alleviating personal distress, (e) modifying individuals' inaccurate assumptions about themselves and their world, and (f) fostering a clear-cut sense of self-identity. All these are ways of opening pathways to a more meaningful and fulfilling existence.

These goals are by no means easy to achieve. Often an individual's distorted view of the world and unhealthy self-concept are the end products of faulty parent-child relationships reinforced by many years of life experiences. In other instances, inadequate occupational, marital, or social adjustment requires major changes in the person's life situation in addition to psychotherapy. It would be too much to expect that a psychotherapist could in a short time undo the individual's entire past history and prepare him or her to cope with a difficult life situation in a fully adequate manner.

The psychotherapist does have certain assets to start with, however—the major one being the apparent inner drive of the human organism toward physical and mental health. Just as physical medicine, properly used, essentially frees and cooperates with the body's own healing mechanisms, the most important ally of the psychotherapist is the individual's own drive toward wholeness and toward the development of unrealized potentialities. Although this inner drive is often obscured in severely disturbed patients, the majority of anxious and confused people are sufficiently discouraged with their situation to be eager to cooperate in any program that holds hope for improvement. Some degree of cooperation on the part of the individual receiving help is considered essential if psychotherapy is to have much chance of success.

Psychological treatment methods are effective in helping troubled individuals for several other reasons, too. Despite their differing theoretical orientations and particular methods, they all help individuals to see themselves and their situations more objectively—that is, to gain a different perspective. Yet insight and new perspective are only a start and not usually enough alone to bring about the necessary changes in behavior. So besides helping the individual toward a new perspective, most therapy situations also provide a protected setting in which he or she is helped to practice new ways of feeling and acting, gradually developing both the courage and the ability to take responsibility for acting in more effective and satisfying ways in the world.

And finally, an important ingredient in psychotherapeutic change is the patient's *expectation* of receiving help. This expectancy is often sufficient in itself to bring about some improvement (Frank, 1961). Just as a placebo can lessen pain for the individual who believes it will do so, the individual who expects to be helped by psychotherapy is likely to be helped, almost regardless of the particular methods used by the therapist. Those in the "helping professions" are the first to admit how inexact the state of their art is and how dependent it is on what the "patient" brings to the experience of psychotherapy.

Psychotherapy with severely disturbed individuals usually takes place in a hospital setting. Most of those who receive psychotherapy for neuroses, alcohol abuse problems, or personality disorders, however, do so on an outpatient basis, either in an outpatient clinic or with psychiatrists or clinical psychologists in private practice. Thus the various therapeutic procedures we shall be discussing might take place in any of these settings.

Even in the treatment of physical disorders, we sometimes find that "doctors disagree." In psychopathology, this is even more the case. The differing perspectives on human motivation and behavior outlined in Chapter 3 lead, as might be expected, to quite different diagnoses of what "the problem" is and how the individual should be helped to overcome it. In this chapter we shall review several of the chief approaches among the many psychological therapies that are being used today in an effort to help individuals overcome psychological problems and lead more satisfying lives. The HIGHLIGHT on page 635 provides an overview of some of the key dimensions in this somewhat complex area of study.[1]

---

[1]Comprehensive but concise descriptions of the major types of psychotherapy may be found in Morse and Watson (1977) and Sahakian (1976).

Psychoanalytic therapy

Psychoanalytic therapy is better known as *psychoanalysis,* and the therapists who practice it are often called *psychoanalysts* or just *analysts*. As developed by Freud, psychoanalytic therapy is an intensive, long-term procedure for uncovering repressed memories, thoughts, fears, and conflicts—presumably stemming from problems in early psychosexual development—and helping the individual come to terms with them in the light of adult reality. It is felt that gaining insight into such repressed material will free individuals from the need to keep squandering their energies on repression and other defense mechanisms. Instead, they can bring their personality resources to bear on consciously resolving the anxieties that prompted the repression in the first place. Freed from this load of threatening material and from the effort of keeping it out of consciousness, they can turn their energies to better personality integration and more effective living.

Freudian psychoanalysis

Psychoanalysis is a system of therapy that evolved over a period of years during Sigmund Freud's long career. It is not an easy system of therapy to describe, and the problem is complicated by the fact that most people have some more-or-less inaccurate conceptions of it based on cartoons and movies. The best way to begin our discussion is to describe the four basic techniques of this form of therapy: free association, dream interpretation, analysis of resistance, and analysis of transference. Then we shall note some of the changes that have taken place in psychoanalytic therapy since Freud's time.

1. *Free association.* As we saw in Chapter 3, Freud used hypnosis in his early work to free repressed thoughts from his patients' unconscious (see HIGHLIGHT on page 636). Later, he

HIGHLIGHT

Key dimensions of psychotherapy

The forms of psychotherapy discussed in this chapter can be classified in a number of ways. Listed below are a few "key dimensions" that will be useful to bear in mind as we examine various approaches to psychotherapy.

1. Individual/group. In individual, or one-to-one, therapy, the therapist treats one person at a time. The effectiveness of such therapies depends to a great extent on the patient-therapist relationship. In group therapy, several persons are treated at the same time in a group setting. Here the interactions and relationships of the group members to one another are important aspects of therapy.

2. Cognitive change/behavior change. Some approaches to psychotherapy focus on changes in the patient's values and other assumptions, on the premise that such cognitive change will lead to more effective behavior. Other approaches focus directly on changing particular behaviors and include chances to develop new skills, on the premise that behavior change will in turn result in cognitive change. Increasingly, today, therapists are working toward both goals.

3. Directive/nondirective. Therapists differ widely with respect to the amount of responsibility they place upon the individual being treated as contrasted with the degree to which they themselves direct the course of therapy. In directive therapy, the therapist takes an "active" role, asking questions and offering interpretations; in nondirective therapy, the major responsibility is placed on the client, and the therapist may simply try to help clients clarify and understand their feelings and values.

4. Inner control of behavior/outer control of behavior. In some instances, psychotherapy is aimed at establishing environmental control of the individual's behavior through planned reinforcement. In other instances, the primary goal of psychotherapy is to change the individual's value assumptions in such a way as to foster the inner cognitive control of behavior. Of course, external controls may be used as an emergency measure with the expectation that inner controls will eventually be developed and take over.

5. Brief/long term. Most psychotherapy today is brief, lasting only between 6 and 10 sessions (Butcher & Kolotkin, 1979). Brief approaches to therapy begin with the assumption that the problem is a specific one that will not require a major restructuring of the personality. Relief from particular worries or symptoms is a major goal of the therapy. Long-term therapy, on the other hand, aims at personality reconstruction.

6. Historical focus/here-and-now emphasis. Some approaches to psychological intervention explore patients' early life experiences and attempt to get patients to integrate their childhood feelings, attitudes, and conflicts into their present outlook and perspective. Other treatment approaches focus more on the "here and now" and minimize early experiences. This latter focus often emphasizes present interpersonal relationships and current problem-solving efforts.

---

stopped using hypnosis in favor of a more direct method of gaining access to the individual's hidden thoughts and fears—*free association.*

The basic rule of free association is that the individual must say whatever comes into his or her mind, regardless of how personal, painful, or seemingly irrelevant it may be. Usually the patient sits comfortably in a chair or lies in a relaxed position on a couch and gives a running account of all the thoughts, feelings, and desires that come to mind as one idea leads to another. The therapist usually takes a position behind the patient so as not to distract or disrupt the free flow of associations.

Although such a running account of whatever comes into one's head may seem random, Freud did not view it as such; rather, he believed that associations are determined like other events. And, as we have seen, he also thought that the conscious represents a relatively small part of the mind, while the unconscious, like the submerged part of an iceberg, is much the larger portion. The purpose of the free association is to bring to light these long-submerged motives and conflicts. The therapist then interprets this material to the individual, guiding him or her toward increased awareness and understanding of these long-repressed feelings.

2. *Dream interpretation.* Another important procedure for uncovering unconscious material is dream analysis. When a person is asleep, repressive defenses are lowered and forbidden desires and feelings may find an out-

The use of hypnosis in therapy

Hypnosis was known among the ancient Egyptians and other early peoples, but its modern use in psychotherapy dates only from the time of Mesmer, as we saw in Chapter 3. Since that time, there have been periodic fluctuations in the popularity of hypnosis in psychotherapy, and differing viewpoints have arisen concerning the exact nature of hypnotic phenomena. In general, hypnosis may be defined as an altered state of consciousness involving extreme suggestibility. Hypnotic induction procedures are designed to bring about a heightened state of selective attention in which the subject "tunes out" irrelevant stimuli and concentrates solely on the hypnotist's suggestions. The induction of hypnosis and some of its therapeutic uses are briefly outlined below.

1. Induction of hypnosis. Hypnosis may be induced by a variety of techniques, most of which involve the following factors: (a) enlisting the cooperation of the subject and allaying any fears of hypnosis; (b) having the subject assume a comfortable position and relax completely; (c) narrowing and focusing the subject's attention, perhaps by having him or her gaze on some bright object; and (d) directing the subject's activities by means of suggestions. The latter often involves establishing the assumption that normal bodily reactions have in fact come about at the direction of the hypnotist. For example, the subject may be directed to gaze upward toward an object and then be told, "your eyelids are starting to feel heavy." This is a normal reaction to the strain of looking upward, but the subject interprets it as being caused by the hypnotist; thus the way is paved for the acceptance of additional suggestions.

2. Recall of buried memories. Traumatic experiences that have been repressed from consciousness may be recovered under hypnosis. This technique was used in treating combat-exhaustion cases during World War II, as we saw in Chapter 6. Under hypnosis, the amnesic soldier could relive his battle experience, thus discharging the emotional tensions associated with it and permitting the experience to be assimilated into his self-structure. Civilian shock reactions involving amnesia may be similarly handled.

3. Age regression. Closely related to memory recall is hypnotic age regression. A hypnotized woman may be told that she is now a six-year-old child again and will subsequently act, talk, and think very much as she did at the age of six years. Regression to the age just preceding the onset of phobias often brings to light the traumatic experiences that precipitated them. Here again reliving the traumatic experience may desensitize the subject to it.

4. Dream induction. Dreams can be induced through hypnosis, although some investigators consider hypnotic dreams to more nearly resemble fantasies than nocturnal dreams. In any event, hypnotic dreams may be used to explore intrapsychic conflicts along the lines of dream analysis worked out by Freud. Perhaps the particular value of such dreams is that the therapist can suggest the theme about which the hypnotic dream should center, using it much like a projective technique in exploring the individual's inner conflicts.

5. Posthypnotic suggestion. One of the hypnotic phenomena most widely used in psychotherapy is posthypnotic suggestion. Here suggestions are made by the therapist during the hypnotic state for behavior to be carried out later in the waking state, with the subject remaining unaware of the source of the behavior. For example, a subject may be told that he or she will no longer have a desire to smoke upon coming out of the hypnotic state. While such suggestions do carry over into the waking state, their duration is usually short. That is, the individual may again experience a desire to smoke in a few hours or a few days. This time factor can be partially compensated for, however, by regular reinforcement of the posthypnotic suggestion in booster sessions.

Some investigators attribute the altered state of consciousness in hypnosis to the subject's strong motivation to meet the demand characteristics of the situation. Barber (1969) has shown that many of the behaviors induced under hypnosis can be replicated in nonhypnotized subjects simply by giving instructions which they are strongly motivated to follow. However, the preponderance of research evidence indicates that behavior induced in hypnotized subjects does differ significantly from that evidenced during simulated hypnosis or role enactment (Diamond, 1974; Fromm & Shor, 1972; Hilgard, 1973, 1974; Miller & Springer, 1974; Nace, Orne, & Hammer, 1974). For example, a number of investigators have offered dramatic evidence that the pain response can be brought almost completely under hypnotic control in many subjects, permitting a degree of pain reduction well beyond that produced in nonhypnotized subjects.

Such drugs as sodium pentothal can be used to produce phenomena similar to those manifested in the hypnotic trance. This form of biological therapy is referred to as *narcoanalysis* or *narcosynthesis*. In Chapter 6 we noted the use of sodium pentothal in the treatment of severe cases of combat exhaustion involving amnesia.

Psychoanalysis relies heavily on the analyst's interpretation of the patient's account of thoughts, feelings and desires that come to mind in the relaxed setting of the consulting room.

let in dreams. For this reason dreams have been referred to as the "royal road to the unconscious." But some motives are so unacceptable to the individual that even in dreams they are not revealed openly but are expressed in disguised or symbolic form. Thus a dream has two kinds of content: *manifest* content, which is the dream as it appears to the dreamer, and *latent* content, composed of the actual motives that are seeking expression but are so painful or unacceptable that they are disguised.

It is the task of the therapist to uncover these disguised meanings by studying the symbols that appear in the manifest content of the dream. For example, a patient's dream of being engulfed in a tidal wave may be interpreted by the therapist as indicating that the patient feels in danger of being overwhelmed by inadequately repressed fears and hostilities.

3. *Analysis of resistance.* During the process of free association or of associating to dreams, an individual may evidence *resistance*—an unwillingness or inability to talk about certain thoughts, motives, or experiences. For example, a patient may be talking about an important childhood experience and then suddenly switch topics, perhaps stating

that "It really isn't that important," or that "It is too absurd to discuss." Resistance may also be evidenced by the patient's giving a too-glib interpretation of some association, or coming late to an appointment, or even "forgetting" an appointment altogether. Since resistance prevents painful and threatening material from entering awareness, its sources must be sought if the individual is to face the problem and learn to deal with it in a realistic manner.

4. *Analysis of transference.* As patient and therapist interact, the relationship between them may become complex and emotionally involved. Often people carry over and apply to the therapist attitudes and feelings that they had in their relations with a parent or other person close to them in the past. Thus they may react to the analyst as they did to that earlier person and feel the same hostility and rejection that they felt long ago in relation to the other person.

By recognizing the transference relationship, the therapist may provide the individual with the experience of having a "good" father or mother. This may make it possible for the individual to work through the conflict in feelings about the real parent or perhaps to overcome feelings of hostility and self-devaluation that stemmed from the earlier parental rejection. In essence, the pathogenic effects of an undesirable early relationship are counteracted by working through a similar emotional conflict in a therapeutic setting. Since the person's reliving of a pathogenic past relationship in a sense recreates the neurosis in real life, this experience is often referred to as a *transference neurosis*.

It is not possible here to consider at length the complexities of transference relationships, but it may be stressed that the patient's attitudes toward the therapist do not always follow simple patterns. Often the patient is ambivalent—distrusting the therapist and feeling hostile toward him or her as a symbol of authority, but at the same time seeking acceptance and love. In addition, the problems of transference are by no means confined to the patient, for the therapist may also have a mixture of feelings toward the patient. This is known as *countertransference* and must be recognized and handled properly by the therapist. For this reason, it is considered important that therapists have an understanding of their own motives, conflicts, and "weak spots"; in fact, all psychoanalysts themselves undergo psychoanalysis before they begin practice.

Particularly during the early stages, psychoanalytic therapy is directed toward uncovering unconscious desires and conflicts and helping patients integrate them into the conscious dimension of their personality. However, the new insights patients have achieved about their past problems do not automatically generalize to their present day-to-day relationships. Thus as the therapy progresses toward its terminal phase, it is increasingly directed toward furthering patients' emotional reeducation and helping ensure the generalization of new insights and behaviors into current real-life situations.

Psychoanalytic therapy since Freud

Although some psychoanalysts still adhere to standard long-term psychoanalysis—which may take years—most analysts have worked out modifications in procedure designed to shorten the time and expense required. Other differences have appeared also. For example,

analytic therapists tend to place more emphasis on current ego functioning and see the ego as a developing and controlling agent in the individual's life (Hartmann, 1958). Thus the individual is seen as capable of being more in control and less dominated by early repressed sexuality. Although childhood events are still viewed as important formative experiences, most modern analysts also place more emphasis on patients' current interpersonal relationships and life situations and less on their childhood experiences.

Evaluation of psychoanalysis

Despite such modifications, psychoanalytic therapy is still commonly criticized for being relatively time-consuming and expensive, for being based on a questionable theory of human nature, for neglecting the patient's immediate problems in the search for unconscious conflicts in the remote past, and for inadequate proof of effectiveness. Because it expects the individual to achieve insight and major personality change, it is also limited in its applicability. For example, it is best suited for persons who are average or above in intelligence and economically well off and who do not suffer from severe psychopathology. Nevertheless, many individuals do feel that they have profited from psychoanalytic therapy—particularly in terms of greater self-understanding, relief from inner conflict and anxiety, and improved interpersonal relationships.

Behavior therapy

It has been over 50 years since Mary Cover Jones first used conditioning to overcome a little boy's conditioned fear of a rabbit (described in Chapter 3), but it was not until the 1960s that behavior therapy really came into its own. The major reason for the long delay was the dominant position of psychoanalysis in the field of psychological therapy. In recent years, however, the therapeutic potentialities of behavior-therapy techniques have been strikingly demonstrated in dealing with a wide variety of maladaptive behaviors, and there have been literally thousands of research publications dealing with the systematic application of conditioning principles to the modification of maladaptive behavior.

In the behavioristic perspective, as we saw in Chapter 3, the maladjusted person (unless suffering from brain pathology) is seen as differing from other people only in (a) having failed to acquire competencies needed for coping with the problems of living and/or (b) having learned faulty coping patterns that are being maintained by some kind of reinforcement. Thus the behavior therapist specifies in advance the precise maladaptive behaviors to be modified and the adaptive behaviors to be achieved, as well as the specific learning principles or procedures to be utilized.

Instead of exploring past traumatic events or inner conflicts in order to bring about cognitive change, behavior therapists attempt to modify behavior directly by manipulating environmental contingencies—that is, by the use of reward and punishment. Behavior-therapy techniques seem especially effective in altering maladaptive behavior when the reinforcement is administered immediately following the desired response, and when the person knows what is expected and why the reinforcement is given. The ultimate goal, of course, is not only to achieve the desired responses but to bring them under the control and self-monitoring of the individual.

We have cited many examples of the application of behavior therapy in earlier chapters. In this section, we shall elaborate briefly on the key techniques of behavior therapy.

Simple extinction

Since learned behavior patterns tend to weaken and disappear over time if they are not reinforced, often the simplest way to eliminate a maladaptive pattern is to remove the reinforcement for it. This is especially true in situations where maladaptive behavior has been reinforced unknowingly by others.

Billy, a 6-year-old first grader, was brought to a psychological clinic by his parents because he "hated school," and his teacher had told them that his showing-off behavior was disrupting the class and making him unpopular. It became apparent in observing Billy and his parents during the initial interview that both his mother and father were noncritical and approving of everything he did. After further assessment, a three-phase program of therapy was undertaken: (a) the parents were helped to discriminate between showing-off behavior and appropriate behavior on Billy's part; (b) the parents were instructed to show a loss of interest and attention when Billy engaged in showing-off behavior while continuing to evidence their approval of appropriate behavior; and (c) Billy's teacher was instructed to ignore Billy, insofar as it was feasible, when he engaged in showing-off behavior and to devote her attention at those times to children who were behaving more appropriately.

Although Billy's showing-off behavior in class increased during the first few days of this therapy program, it diminished markedly thereafter when it was no longer reinforced by his parents and teacher. As his maladaptive behavior diminished, he was better accepted by his classmates, which in turn, helped reinforce more appropriate behavior patterns and change his negative attitude toward school.

Systematic desensitization

In the preceding section we dealt with the extinction of behavior that was being *positively reinforced*. Behavior that is being *negatively reinforced*—reinforced by the successful *avoidance* of a painful situation—is harder to deal with. In this case, since the individual becomes anxious and withdraws at the first sign of the painful situation, he or she never gets a chance to find out whether the expected aversive consequences would in fact come about. In addition, the avoidance is anxiety reducing and hence is itself reinforced.

One commonly used technique for extinguishing negatively reinforced behavior involves eliciting an antagonistic or competing response. Since it is difficult to feel both pleasant and anxious at the same time, the method of desensitization is aimed at teaching the individual to relax or behave in some other way that is inconsistent with anxiety while in the presence (real or imagined) of the anxiety-producing stimulus.

The prototype of this approach is the classic experiment of Jones (1924) already mentioned, in which she successfully eliminated a small boy's conditioned fears of a white rabbit and other furry animals. First she brought the rabbit just inside the door at the far end of the

Desensitization techniques begin by teaching clients to relax through a series of graduated exercises.

room while the boy, Peter, was eating. On successive days the rabbit was gradually brought closer until Peter could pat it with one hand while eating with the other.

The term *systematic desensitization* has been applied to a specific approach developed by Wolpe[2] (1961, 1963, 1969). On the assumption that most neurotic patterns are, fundamentally, conditioned anxiety responses, Wolpe worked out a way to train the client to remain calm and relaxed in situations that formerly produced anxiety. Wolpe's approach is elegant in its simplicity, and the carrying out of his method is equally straightforward.

1. Training in relaxation. The first step in therapy is training the individual to relax. This is usually done in the first six sessions and con-

sists of having the individual contract and then gradually relax different muscles until a state of complete relaxation can be achieved at will. The basic technique follows the principles of "progressive relaxation" outlined by Jacobson (1938) and is described in detail by Wolpe (1969). Other techniques that are sometimes used to facilitate complete relaxation include meditation, hypnosis, and drugs.

2. The construction of hierarchies. During the early sessions of therapy, time is also spent constructing a hierarchy of the individual's anxieties. This anxiety hierarchy is a list of related stimuli ranked in descending order according to the amount of anxiety they evoke in the client. For example, if a client is overly possessive or jealous of her husband, she describes the situations in which she feels this jealousy. The highest anxiety-producing situation might be observing him at a cocktail party talking intimately with an attractive woman. Further down the list might be hearing him comment favorably about a waitress; the lowest anxiety-evoking stimulus might be noticing him look casually at a young female hitchhiker. In some instances the anxiety is easier to quantify, as in the case of acrophobia (fear of high places) or of a student's examination anxiety;

[2]In an attempt to clarify the confusion in terminology relating to desensitization, Van Egeren (1971) has noted that *reciprocal inhibition* has been applied in classical neurophysiology to momentary, reversible inhibition of one nerve process by another, as in the inhibition of antagonistic skeletal muscles. *Counterconditioning* implies the permanent inhibition of a reaction by means of an incompatible or antagonistic response—as, for example, in the inhibition of anxiety in a fear-arousing situation by the repetitive presentation of food. Wolpe, although referring to his method of desensitization as involving reciprocal inhibition, achieves long-lasting changes in response by means of planned repetition, and thus, in effect, produces counterconditioning.

and, of course, anxiety may focus around more than one theme, as when the client shows a variety of phobias.

3. *Desensitization procedure.* When the client has mastered the relaxation techniques and the therapist has established an appropriate anxiety hierarchy, the actual process of desensitization begins. While the client relaxes completely in a comfortable chair with closed eyes, the therapist describes a series of scenes, starting with a neutral one, then moving to one at the bottom of the client's anxiety hierarchy and progressing gradually up it. The client, while remaining relaxed, is directed to imagine each situation as it is described. As soon as the client reports experiencing anxiety, the session is terminated. Treatment continues until the client is able to remain in a relaxed state while vividly imagining the scenes that formerly evoked the greatest anxiety.

The usual duration of a desensitization session is 15 to 30 minutes, and the sessions are ordinarily given 2 to 3 times per week. The overall therapy program may, of course, take a number of weeks or even months. Kennedy and Kimura (1974) have shown, however, that even patients who have progressed only 25 to 50 percent of the way through their anxiety hierarchy show significant therapeutic gains, as evidenced by a marked reduction in specific avoidance behaviors when compared with their pretreatment levels.

Several variants of systematic desensitization have been devised. One variation involves the use of a tape recorder to enable a client to carry out the desensitization process at home. Another utilizes group desensitization procedures—as in "marathon" desensitization groups, in which the entire program is compressed into a few days of intensive treatment. Perhaps the most important variation is *in vivo* desensitization, in which the client is asked to enter real-life situations similar to the ones he or she has just successfully imagined during the desensitization sessions.

Wolpe (1969) has noted three types of client-related problems that would suggest that desensitization techniques would be an ineffective therapeutic choice: the client demonstrates (a) difficulties in relaxation, (b) misleading or irrelevant hierarchies, and (c) inadequacies of imagery. Desensitization procedures have, however, been used successfully in dealing with a wide range of maladaptive behaviors, including examination anxieties, phobias, anxiety neuroses, and certain cases of impotence and frigidity.

Implosive therapy

Another method of behavior therapy used increasingly in recent years is implosive therapy. Like systematic desensitization, this approach regards neurotic behavior as involving the conditioned avoidance of anxiety-arousing stimuli, and clients are asked to imagine and relive aversive scenes associated with their anxiety.

In this case, however, instead of trying to banish anxiety from the treatment sessions, the therapist deliberately attempts to elicit a massive flood or "implosion" of anxiety. With repeated exposure in a "safe" setting, the stimulus loses its power to elicit anxiety and the neurotic avoidance behavior is extinguished.

Stampfl and Levis (1967, 1973), who were the early developers of this approach, usually devote the first two or three therapy sessions to ascertaining the nature of the anxiety-arousing stimuli. They describe the procedure as follows:

"Once the implosive procedure is begun, every effort is made to encourage the patient to 'lose himself' in the part that he is playing and 'live' the scenes with genuine emotion. . . . The scenes which contain the hypothesized cues are described at first by the therapist. The more involved and dramatic the therapist becomes in describing the scenes, the more realistic the presentation, and the easier it is for the patient to participate. At each stage of the process an attempt is made by the therapist to attain a maximal level of anxiety evocation from the patient. When a high level anxiety is achieved, the patient is held on this level until some sign of spontaneous reduction in the anxiety-inducing value of the cues appears (extinction). The process is repeated, and again, at the first sign of spontaneous reduction of fear, new variations are introduced to elicit an intense anxiety response. This procedure is continued until a significant diminution in anxiety has resulted. . . . Between sessions the patient is instructed to reenact in his imagination the scenes which were presented during the treatment session." (1967, p. 500)

In a report of an actual case, Stampfl (1975) described a young woman who could not swim and was terrified of water—particularly of sinking under the water. Although she knew it was irrational, she was so terrified of water "that she wore a life preserver when she took a bath" (p. 66). She was instructed by the therapist to imagine in minute detail taking a bath without a life preserver in a "bottomless" tub, and slipping under the water. Initially, the patient showed intense anxiety, and the scene was repeated over and over. In addition, she was given a "homework" assignment in which she was asked to imagine herself drowning. Eventually, after imagining the worst and finding that nothing happened, her anxiety diminished; after the fourteenth therapy session, she was able to take baths without feelings of anxiety or apprehension.

As in the case of systematic desensitization, hypnosis or drugs may be used to enhance suggestibility under implosive therapy, and here, too, *in vivo* procedures may be used with individuals who do not imagine scenes realistically. For example, a client with a phobia of airplanes may be instructed to take a short flight in an airplane. This is another means of exposing the client to the anxiety-eliciting stimulus and demonstrating that the feared consequences do not occur. In a study of patients with agoraphobia (fear of open spaces), Emmelkamp and Wessels (1975) concluded that "prolonged exposure *in vivo* plainly proved to be superior to flooding in the imagination" (p. 7).

Reports on the effectiveness of implosive therapy have generally been quite favorable. In fact, a number of therapists consider implosive therapy superior to systematic desensitization in the treatment of neurotic phobias, since it results in more rapid improvement. However, some investigators have reported unfavorable as well as favorable results with implosive therapy (Emmelkamp & Wessels, 1975; Mealiea, 1967; Wolpe, 1969). This appears to be particularly true of flooding *in vivo*. For example, Emmelkamp and Wessels (1975) found that flooding *in vivo* was terrifying for some clients. In one case, the agoraphobic client "hid in a cellar out of fear of being sent into the street for 90 minutes by the therapist" (p. 14).

In general, it would appear that while most patients respond favorably to implosive therapy, some do not respond, and a few suffer an exacerbation of their phobias. This finding

suggests a need for caution in the use of this method, particularly since it involves procedures that may be highly traumatic.

Aversion therapy

This approach involves the modification of undesirable behavior by the old-fashioned method of punishment. Punishment may involve either the removal of positive reinforcers or the use of aversive stimuli, but the basic idea is to reduce the "temptation value" of stimuli that elicit undesirable behavior. The most commonly used aversive stimulus is electric shock, although drugs may also be used. As we shall see, however, punishment is rarely employed as the sole method of treatment.

Apparently the first formal use of aversion therapy was made by Kantorovich (1930), who administered electric shocks to alcoholics in association with the sight, smell, and taste of alcohol. Since that time aversion therapy has been used in the treatment of a wide range of maladaptive behaviors, including smoking, drinking, overeating, drug dependence, gambling, sexual variants, and bizarre psychotic behavior. Since we have described the use of aversion therapy in the course of our discussion of abnormal behavior patterns, we shall restrict ourselves here to a review of a few brief examples and principles.

A leading exponent of punishment to inhibit maladaptive behavior is Lovaas (1977), who has worked mostly with severely disturbed autistic children. He has found punishment by electric shock to be effective even in extreme cases of self-destructive behavior among such children. In one case a 7-year-old autistic boy, diagnosed as severely retarded, had had to be kept in restraints 24 hours a day because he would continually beat his head with his fists or bang it against the walls of his crib, inflicting serious injuries. Though it is difficult to understand why punishment should reduce the frequency of self-destructive behavior, electric shock following such behavior was nevertheless quite effective, bringing about complete inhibition of this maladaptive behavior pattern in a relatively short time (Bucher & Lovaas, 1967). In earlier chapters we have noted that irrational and maladaptive thoughts—obsessions, delusions, and hallucinations—may also be minimized or extinguished by means of electric shock or other aversive control measures.

Electric shock as an aversive stimulus has generally diminished in use in recent years (Harris & Ersner-Hershfield, 1978) because of the ethical problems involved in its use and because the new behaviors induced by it do not automatically generalize to other settings. Also, less dangerous and more effective procedures have been found. The method of choice today is probably differential reinforcement of other responses (DOR), in which behaviors alternative to the undesired behavior and incompatible with it are reinforced. For example, for a child who indulges in antisocial, destructive behavior, positive reinforcement might be used for every sign of constructive play. At the same time, any reinforcement that has been maintaining maladaptive behavior is removed.

Aversion therapy is primarily a way of stopping maladaptive responses for a period of time during which there is an opportunity for changing a life-style by encouraging more adaptive alternative patterns that will prove reinforcing in themselves. This point is particularly important, since otherwise the client may simply refrain from maladaptive responses in "unsafe" therapy situations, where such behavior leads to immediate aversive results, but keep making them in "safe" real-life situations, where there is no fear of immediate discomfort.

The systematic use of positive reinforcement

Systematic programs for the application of positive reinforcement are achieving notable success, particularly in institutional settings. Response shaping, modeling, and token economies are among the most widely used of such techniques.

1. *Response shaping.* Positive reinforcement is often used in response shaping; that is, in establishing a response that is not initially in the individual's behavior repertoire. This technique has been used extensively in working with the behavior problems of children. The following case reported by Wolf, Risley, and Mees (1964) is illustrative:

A 3-year-old autistic boy lacked normal verbal and social behavior. He did not eat properly, engaged in

These two autistic boys were enrolled in an intensive behavior-therapy program at the UCLA Neuropsychiatric Institute. Here the boy pulling the wagon is shown receiving immediate positive reinforcement in the form of food for his participation in the activity. Other reinforcement techniques used included punishment and modeling.

self-destructive behavior such as banging his head and scratching his face, and manifested ungovernable tantrums. He had recently had a cataract operation, and required glasses for the development of normal vision. He refused to wear his glasses, however, and broke pair after pair.

The technique of shaping was decided upon to counteract the problem of glasses. Initially, the boy was trained to expect a bit of candy or fruit at the sound of a toy noisemaker. Then training was begun with empty eyeglass frames. First the boy was reinforced with the candy or fruit for picking them up, then for holding them, then for carrying them around, then for bringing the frames closer to his eyes, and then for putting the empty frames on his head at any angle. Through successive approximations, the boy finally learned to wear his glasses up to twelve hours a day.

2. *Modeling.* Response shaping can be tedious and time consuming, especially when complex responses are to be learned. And yet, as Bandura (1977) pointed out,

"Learning would be exceedingly laborious, not to mention hazardous, if people had to rely solely on the effects of their own actions to inform them what to do. Fortunately, most human behavior is learned observationally through modeling: from observing others one forms an idea of how new behaviors are performed, and on later occasions this coded information serves as a guide for action. Because people can learn from example what to do, at least in approximate form, before performing any behavior, they are spared needless error." (p. 22)

Although reinforcement of modeled behavior can influence whether the observer-learner attends to the model's actions and strengthens the response imitated, observational learning does not seem to require extrinsic reinforcement. Rather, according to Bandura, reinforcement functions as a facilitative condition to learning. Anticipation of a reinforcement may also make the individual more likely to perform the behavior.

As we have noted, modeling and imitation are used in various forms of behavior therapy. Bandura (1964) has found that live modeling combined with instruction and guided participation is the most effective desensitization treatment, resulting in the elimination of snake phobias in over 90 percent of the cases.

3. *Token economies.* Approval and other intangible reinforcers often prove ineffective in behavior-therapy programs, especially those dealing with severely maladaptive behavior. In such instances, appropriate behaviors may be rewarded with tangible reinforcers in the form of tokens that can later be exchanged for desired objects or privileges. In working with hospitalized schizophrenic patients, for example, Ayllon and Azrin (1968) found that using the commissary, listening to records, and going to movies were considered highly desirable activities by most patients. Consequently, these activities were chosen as reinforcers for socially appropriate behavior. To participate in any of them, the patient had to earn a number of tokens by demonstrating appropriate ward behavior. In Chapter 20 we will describe another successful token economy program with chronic hospitalized patients who had been considered resistant to treatment (Paul & Lentz, 1977).

Token economies have been used to establish adaptive behaviors ranging from elementary responses such as eating and making one's bed to the daily performance of responsible hospital jobs. In the latter instance, the token economy resembles the outside world where the individual is paid for his or her work in tokens (money) that can later be exchanged for desired objects and activities.

The use of tokens as reinforcers for appropriate behavior has a number of distinct advantages: (a) the number of tokens earned depends directly on the amount of desirable behavior shown; (b) tokens are not readily subject to satiation and hence tend to maintain their incentive value; (c) tokens can reduce the delay that often occurs between appropriate performance and reinforcement; (d) the number of tokens earned and the way in which they are "spent" are largely up to the patient, and (e) tokens tend to bridge the gap between the institutional environment and the demands and system of payment that will be encountered in the outside world.

The ultimate goal in token economies, as in other programs of extrinsic reinforcement, is not only to achieve desired responses but to bring such responses to a level where their adaptive consequences will be reinforcing in their own right—thus enabling natural rather than artificial reward contingencies to maintain the desired behavior. For example, extrinsic reinforcers may be used initially to help children overcome reading difficulties, but once the child becomes proficient in reading skills, these skills will presumably provide intrinsic reinforcement as the child comes to enjoy reading for its own sake.

Behavioral contracting

Behavioral contracting is a technique used in some types of psychotherapy and behavior therapy to identify and agree on the behaviors that are to be changed, and to maximize the probability that the behavioral changes will occur and be maintained (Nelson & Mowry, 1976). By definition, a contract is an agreement between two or more parties—such as a therapist and a client, or a parent and a teenager—that governs the nature of the treatment program. The agreement, often in writing, specifies the client's obligations to change, as well as the responsibilities of the other person to provide something the client wants in return, such as tangible rewards, privileges, or therapeutic attention. Behavior therapists frequently make behavioral contracting an explicit focus of treatment, thus helping establish the treatment as a joint enterprise for which both parties have responsibility.

Behavioral contracting can facilitate therapy in several ways: (a) the structuring of the treatment relationship can be explicitly stated, giving the client a clear idea of each person's role in the treatment; (b) the actual responsibilities of the client are outlined along with a system of rewards built in for changed behavior; (c) the limitations of the treatment in terms of the length and focus of the sessions are specified; (d) by agreement, some behaviors may be eliminated from the treatment focus, thereby establishing the "appropriate content" of the treatment sessions; (e) clear treatment goals can be defined; and (f) criteria for determining success or failure in achieving these goals can be built into the program. A classic case of behavioral contracting is described in the HIGHLIGHT on this page.

Sometimes a contract is negotiated between a disruptive child and the teacher, according to which the child will maintain or receive certain privileges as long as he or she behaves in accordance with the responsibilities set forth in the contract. Usually the school principal is also a party to such a contract to ensure the enforcement of certain conditions which the teacher may not be in a position to enforce, such as removing the child from the classroom for engaging in certain types of misbehavior.

Behavioral contracting

Candy was a 16-year-old girl who had been admitted to a psychiatric hospital following alleged exhibitionism, drug abuse, truancy from home, and promiscuity (Stuart, 1971). Candy's parents also complained that she was chronically antagonistic in her verbal exchanges with them and was near failing in her schoolwork. Because of the cost of private psychiatric care, they requested that she be made a ward of the juvenile court. They were advised that their allegations would probably not stand up in court and agreed to let her remain at home under the terms of a behavioral contract.

An initial contract, based on unrealistic parental demands, failed when Candy consistently violated its terms by sneaking out at night. A new, more realistic contract between Candy and her parents was then negotiated, and a monitoring form containing a checklist of chores, curfew conditions, and bonus time for each day of the month was provided. Some of the provisions of this contract were as follows:

"In exchange for the privilege of going out at 7:00 p.m. on one weekend evening without having to account for her whereabouts Candy must maintain a weekly average of "B" in the academic ratings of all of her classes and must return home by 11:30 p.m.

"In exchange for the privilege of having Candy complete household chores and maintain her curfew Mr. and Mrs. Bremer agree to pay Candy $1.50 on the morning following days on which the money is earned.

"If Candy is 31–60 minutes late she loses the privilege of going out the following day and does forfeit her money for the day." (Stuart, 1971, p. 9)

Behavioral contracting proved to be a constructive means of structuring the interaction between Candy and her parents, and Candy's behavior improved steadily. By removing the issues of privileges and responsibilities from the realm of contention, many intrafamilial arguments were avoided, and those that did occur tended to be tempered by the specified options. Through the contract, privileges such as money and free time were established as effective environmental contingencies in fostering desired behavior (p. 11).

Assertiveness training

Assertiveness training has been used as a method of desensitization as well as a means of developing more effective coping techniques. It appears particularly useful in helping individuals who have difficulties in interpersonal interactions because of conditioned anxiety responses that may prevent them from "speaking up" or even from showing appropriate affection. Such inhibition may lead to continual inner turmoil, particularly if the individual feels strongly about the situation. Assertiveness training may also be indicated in cases where individuals consistently allow other people to take advantage of them or maneuver them into situations which they find uncomfortable.

The expression of assertive behavior—first by role-playing in the therapy setting and then by practice in real-life situations—is guided by the therapist. Often attention is focused on developing more effective interpersonal skills; in some instances, the client is taught to use techniques of "gamesmanship" in situations where he or she seems at a disadvantage. For example, a client may learn to ask the other person such questions as "Is anything wrong? You don't seem to be your usual self today." Such questions put the focus on the other person without indicating an aggressive or hostile intent on the part of the speaker. Each act of intentional assertion inhibits the anxiety associated with the situation and therefore weakens the maladaptive anxiety response pattern. At the same time, it tends to foster more adaptive interpersonal behaviors.

Although assertiveness training is a highly useful therapeutic procedure in certain types of situations, it does have limitations. For example, Wolpe (1969) has pointed out that it is largely irrelevant for phobias involving nonpersonal stimuli. It may also be of little use in some types of interpersonal situations; for instance, if the individual has in fact been rejected by someone, assertive behavior may tend to aggravate rather than resolve the problem. However, in interpersonal situations where maladaptive anxiety can be traced to lack of self-assertiveness, this type of therapy appears particularly effective.

Biofeedback training

Until relatively recently it was generally believed that voluntary control over physiological processes such as heart rate, galvanic skin response, and blood pressure was not possible. However, in the early 1960s this view began to change. A number of investigators, aided by the development of sensitive electronic instruments that could accurately measure physiological responses, demonstrated that many of the processes formerly thought to be "involuntary" were modifiable by learning procedures—operant learning as well as classical conditioning. Schearn (1962) showed that

Assertiveness training begins with role-playing situations in which the client practices particular behaviors—perhaps complaining to a "sales clerk" about a defective "purchase."

This young woman is linked to both a thermal biofeedback device and one that monitors muscle activity.

heart rate could be conditioned by operant techniques; Miller (1969) demonstrated that internal visceral and glandular processes could be conditioned;[3] and Kimmel (1974) demonstrated that the galvanic skin response could be conditioned by operant learning techniques.

The importance of the autonomic nervous system in the development of abnormal behavior had long been recognized. For example, autonomic arousal is an important factor in anxiety states. Thus many researchers were quick to apply techniques developed in the autonomic conditioning studies in an attempt to modify the "internal environment" of troubled individuals in order to bring about more adaptive behavior—for instance, to reduce the frequency and severity of migraine headaches, to lower blood pressure, and to manage anxiety or "fear" responses by reducing heart rate.

This treatment approach—in which the person is taught to influence his or her own physiological processes—is referred to as *biofeedback*. Several steps are typical in the process of biofeedback treatment: (a) monitor-

ing the physiological response that is to be modified (perhaps blood pressure or skin temperature); (b) converting the information to a visual or auditory signal; and (c) providing a means of prompt feedback—indicating to the subject as rapidly as possible when the desired change is taking place (Blanchard & Epstein, 1978).

For example, in attempts to change skin temperature—by producing a constriction of the blood vessels—small thermometers called *thermistors*, which are sensitive to temperature changes of about a tenth of a degree, are taped to the subject's skin. Their signal is then amplified and converted to an easily interpreted medium, such as a digital readout display. One investigator (Hunter, 1974) used an electric train display to feed back information to children she was training to control hand temperature: when the children made the desired changes in temperature, the toy train ran around the track with lights flashing and whistle blowing.

Biofeedback has been used in a wide range of situations from programs to modify heart rate in patients with irregular heartbeat (Weiss & Engel, 1971) to the treatment of stuttering by

---

[3]These early findings were, however, not replicated in later studies (Miller & Dworkin, 1974).

feeding back information on electric potential of muscles in the speech apparatus (Lanyon, Barrington, & Newman, 1976).

The psychologically based problems with which biofeedback is most frequently used are migraine headache, hypertension, and the control of anxiety. The following illustrates such a case.

"The patient [was] a 30-year-old married female with a history of 'spells' since age 14, at which age she was raped by her sister's boyfriend. Repulsed by this event and feeling guilty, she concealed it from her family. The 'spells' began shortly thereafter and, although having some variability, they generally were associated with a feeling of nausea and vomiting, a choking sensation with the onset of tachycardia (rapid heartbeat), and a numbness of the extremities. The patient reported a vague sense of altered state of consciousness, had lost control of her bladder on one occasion, but had never lost control of bowels during a 'spell.' She reported no loss of consciousness, that is, she was able to hear what was occurring around her, but she was simply unresponsive for a minute or two. A number of months following the rape, the patient became aware that she was pregnant and concealed this from her parents until her seventh month of gestation. Great turmoil developed within the home, eventually leading to the patient's leaving town during the latter stages of pregnancy, delivering the child, and giving it up for adoption. On returning to her home town, the patient perceived that others began thinking of her as the town slut. Her thoughts of guilt about the rape continued unabated, as did the spells.

"Her history from the age of 20 to her initial psychiatric contact with the experimenters was an endless repetition of numerous organic evaluations. She [had been] followed for approximately 15 years as having a possible convulsive disorder. . . . Cardiovascular evaluations were likewise extensive with numerous possible diagnoses being entertained, but physical evaluations plus electrocardiograms . . . failed to confirm any specific cardiac disorder.

"The subject's extensive medical evaluations (running $3–4,000 per year) eventually led to her psychiatric referral. During the sessions which followed, she was able to identify the antecedents of her symptoms as thoughts and ruminations about having been raped, and more importantly, how individuals in her natural environment (especially her home town) might perceive her. Thoughts of returning home frequently preceded episodes of tachycardia. In the last 10 years, her fears were aggravated when she was propositioned by men in her home town, events she interpreted as directly resulting from her having been raped at age 14.

"The patient's therapy initially involved group therapy to increase her verbalization regarding chronic marital problems and her marked passivity regarding her symptomatology. In the course of therapy, the specific stimuli that elicited her spells became more apparent. Since they were rather easily circumscribed to the sexual area, and since the patient focused so strongly on her somatic problems, particularly the tachycardia episodes, a biofeedback treatment designed specifically to help the patient in this area was instituted. Throughout this treatment, the patient continued in group therapy and was stabilized on Dilantin, 100 mg. twice per day." (Blanchard & Abel, 1976, p. 114)

The biofeedback equipment used was a polygraph and electronic counters to time and measure heart rate. The patient was given visual feedback about her heart rate and was seen in 40-minute sessions which alternated between training her to control the rate of her heart beat and listening to audiotapes describing her rape ordeal and the negative aftereffects of the situation. In the training sessions, the first 15 minutes were devoted to adaptation to the setting, the next 5 minutes to obtaining a baseline of her heart rate, and the remaining 20 minutes to the biofeedback training itself.

During the treatment the patient gradually experienced a reduction in anxiety over the tapes, and her tachycardia episodes disappeared. Several weeks after treatment ended, she returned to her home town and actually met some of the men who had propositioned her years before without experiencing anxiety or "spells." The fact that she was able to control the tachycardia while she was not receiving biofeedback information suggests that the biofeedback training may have generalized to the natural environment. However, the investigators did not rule out the possibility that her improvement may have been attributable to some other process, such as relaxation or becoming desensitized to the rape-related stimuli.

Biofeedback training is one of the most rapidly spreading treatment approaches, with many clinics and hospitals spending large sums of money to purchase complicated equipment, with the formation of new professional organizations to advance biofeedback research and practice, with the growth of small companies to market biofeedback systems, and with efforts to train a semiprofessional cadre of biofeedback technicians to perform the treatment.

Unfortunately, however, although there is general agreement that many physiological processes can be regulated to some extent by learning, the application of biofeedback procedures to alter abnormal behavior has produced equivocal results. Demonstrations of incidents of clinical biofeedback applications abound, but carefully controlled research has not sufficiently supported earlier clinical impressions of improvement. Blanchard and Young (1973, 1974) pointed out that the effects of biofeedback procedures are generally small and often do not generalize to situations outside the laboratory, where the biofeedback devices are not present. And two recent, well-controlled studies have failed to show a treatment effect for biofeedback with migraine patients (Kewman & Roberts, 1979) and Raynaud's disease patients (Gugliemi, 1979).

In addition, biofeedback has not been shown to be any more effective than relaxation training, leading to the suggestion that biofeedback may simply be only a more elaborate means of teaching subjects relaxation (Blanchard & Epstein, 1978; Blanchard & Young, 1974; Tarler-Benlolo, 1978).

In a recent review of the findings on visceral learning and biofeedback, Miller (1978) concluded:

"The studies . . . give enough evidence of an effect of some kind to justify the more rigorous studies that are needed to prove that the effect is indeed produced specifically by the biofeedback and is of more therapeutic value, at least in certain cases, than currently available treatments. They do not justify any widespread, unevaluated applications." (p. 396)

Thus with the relatively small effects that biofeedback training produces in many treatment situations, and the finding that other, less expensive behavioral treatments—such as relaxation training—may be just as effective, biofeedback appears not to be the panacea that many had hoped.

Evaluation of behavior therapy

As compared with psychoanalytic and other interview psychotherapies, behavior therapy appears to have three distinct advantages. First is the precision of the treatment approach. The target behaviors to be modified are specified, the methods to be used are clearly delineated,

and the results can be readily evaluated. Second is the use of explicit, well-understood principles of learning. Third is the economy of time, cost, and personnel. Behavior therapy usually achieves results in a short period of time, leading to faster relief of personal distress for the individual, as well as lower financial cost. In addition, more people can be treated by a given therapist.

Different kinds of behavior therapy vary in their effectiveness for particular problems: desensitization seems most useful in treating conditioned avoidance responses; aversive techniques in establishing impulse control; and modeling combined with positive reinforcement in the acquisition of complex responses. In addition, behavior therapy techniques are the backbone of modern approaches to the treatment of sexual dysfunctions, discussed in Chapter 15. Like other forms of psychological intervention, behavior therapy has proven somewhat unsuccessful in the treatment of such patterns as childhood autism, schizophrenia, and severe depression, although dramatic results have been shown in some cases by Lovaas (1977) and Paul and Lentz (1977).

But although behavior therapy is not a "cure-all," it has proven effective in the treatment of a wide range of maladaptive behaviors, and typical reports indicate a success rate of well over 50 percent and sometimes as high as 90 percent, depending largely on the type of maladaptive pattern being treated.

Cognitive-behavioral therapy

Early behavior therapists focused on observable behavior. They regarded the inner thoughts of their clients as not really part of the causal chain, and in their zeal to be objective they focused on the relationship between observable behaviors and observable reinforcing conditions. Thus they were often viewed as mechanistic technicians who simply manipulated their subjects without considering them as people. More recently, however, a number of behavior therapists have reappraised the importance of "private events"—thoughts, perceptions, evaluations, and self-statements—seeing them as processes that mediate the effects of objective stimulus conditions and thus help determine behavior (Mahoney & Arnkoff, 1978).

Homme (1965), a student of Skinner, began this exodus from strict behaviorism in a paper arguing that these private events were behaviors that could be objectively analyzed. He proposed that thoughts be regarded as emitted internal events comparable to emitted external behaviors, and that a technology be developed for modifying thoughts by use of the same principles of learning that were proving so effective in changing outer behavior. These internal, private events he called *coverants,* considering them to be operants of the mind. Following Homme's "coverant behaviorism," many investigators began to apply conditioning principles to covert events, such as thoughts and assumptions.

Cognitive-behavioral therapy, as the term suggests, stems from both cognitive psychology, with its emphasis on the effects of thoughts on behavior, and behaviorism, with its rigorous methodology and performance-oriented focus. At the present time there is no single method of operation in cognitive-behavioral therapy: numerous methods are being developed with varying foci. Two main themes seem to characterize them all, however: (a) the conviction that cognitive processes influence both motivation and behavior, and (b) the use of behavior-change techniques in a pragmatic (hypothesis-testing) manner. That is, the therapy sessions are analogous to experiments in which the therapist and client apply learning principles to alter the client's cognitions, continuously evaluating the effects that the changes in cognitions have on both thoughts and outer behavior. In our discussion we shall focus on three approaches to cognitive-behavioral therapy: the rational-emotive therapy of Ellis, the cognitive therapy of Beck, and stress inoculation training, as illustrated by the work of Meichenbaum.[4]

---

[4]For an extended discussion of cognitive-behavioral treatment, the following references would be informative: Beck (1976); Foreyt and Rathjen (1978); Goldfried and Davidson (1976); Kendall and Hollon (1979); Lazarus (1971); Mahoney and Arnkoff (1978); Meichenbaum (1977).

Rational-emotive therapy (RET)

One of the earliest behaviorally oriented cognitive therapies was the rational-emotive therapy (RET) of Ellis (1958, 1973, 1975). RET attempts to change the client's basic maladaptive thought processes. In its infancy, RET was viewed skeptically by many professionals who doubted its effectiveness, but it has now become one of the most widely used therapeutic approaches (Garfield & Kurtz, 1976).

Ellis considers the well-functioning individual as one who is behaving rationally and in tune with empirical reality. Unfortunately, many of us have learned unrealistic beliefs and perfectionistic values that cause us to expect too much of ourselves, leading us to behave irrationally and then to feel unnecessarily that we are worthless failures. For example, a person may continually think, "I should be able to win everyone's love and approval" or "I should be thoroughly adequate and competent in everything I do." Such unrealistic assumptions and self-demands inevitably lead to ineffective and self-defeating behavior and then to the emotional response of self-devaluation. The emotional response of self-devaluation is thus the consequence not of real-life events but of an individual's faulty expectations, interpretations, and self-demands.

As a more specific example, consider the case in which a man has a very intense emotional reaction of despair with deep feelings of worthlessness, unlovability, and self-devaluation when he is jilted by his fiancée. With a stronger self-concept and a more realistic picture of both himself and his fiancée, as well as of their actual relationship, his emotional reaction might have been one of relief. It is his interpretation of the situation and of himself rather than the objective situation that has led to his intense emotional reaction. For an idea of how Ellis might diagram such a situation schematically, see the HIGHLIGHT on page 651.

Ellis (1970) believes that one or more of the core irrational beliefs below are at the root of most psychological maladjustment.

a) One should be loved by everyone for everything one does.

b)   Certain acts are awful or wicked, and people who perform them should be severely punished.

c)   It is horrible when things are not the way we would like them to be.

d)   Human misery is produced by external causes, or outside persons, or events rather than by the view that one takes of these conditions.

e)   If something may be dangerous or fearsome, one should be terribly upset about it.

f)   It is better to avoid life problems if possible than to face them.

g)   One needs something stronger or more powerful than oneself to rely on.

h)   One should be thoroughly competent, intelligent, and achieving in all respects.

i)   Because something once affected one's life, it will indefinitely affect it.

j)   One must have certain and perfect self-control.

k)   Happiness can be achieved by inertia and inaction.

l)   We have virtually no control over our emotions and cannot help having certain feelings.

The task of rational-emotive therapy is to restructure the individual's belief system and self-evaluation, especially with respect to the irrational "shoulds," "oughts," and "musts" that are preventing a more positive sense of self-worth and a creative, emotionally satisfying, and fulfilling life. Several methods are used.

One way is to *dispute* the person's false beliefs through rational confrontation. For example, the therapist dealing with the case above might ask the young man, "Why should your fiancée's changing her mind mean that *you* are worthless?" Here the therapist would teach the client to identify and dispute the beliefs that were producing the negative emotional consequences.

The rational-emotive therapist also uses behaviorally oriented techniques to bring about changed thoughts and behaviors. Sometimes, for example, homework assignments are given in order to encourage clients to have new experiences and break negative chains of behavior. For example, clients might be instructed to reward themselves by an external reinforcer such as a food treat after working 15 minutes at disputing their beliefs. Another method of self-reinforcement might be through covert statements such as "You are doing a really good job."

In some ways rational-emotive therapy can

Ellis' ABC theory of disturbance

A person has an emotional reaction at C following an event (jilting by a loved one) at Point A. The emotional consequences at C, however, are not produced by the events at point A but by the person's *beliefs* at Point B.

Legend:
⟶ = Observed sequence
⟶ = Ellis' postulated relationship

be viewed as a *humanistic* therapy (to be discussed in the next section) because it takes a clear stand on personal worth and human values. Rational-emotive therapy aims at increasing the individual's feelings of self-worth and clearing the way for self-actualization by removing the false beliefs that have been stumbling blocks to personal growth.

Cognitive restructuring therapy

Beck's cognitive restructuring therapy was developed for the treatment of depression (Beck et al., 1979; Hollon & Beck, 1978). One basic assumption underlying this approach is that problems like depression result from patients' negative beliefs about themselves, the world they live in, and the future. These false beliefs are maintained even in the face of contradictory evidence because the individuals typically engage in self-defeating and self-fulfilling behaviors in which they (a) *selectively perceive* the world as harmful while ignoring evidence to the contrary; (b) *over-generalize* on the basis of limited examples—for example, seeing themselves as totally worthless because they were laid off at work; (c) *magnify* the significance of undesirable events—for example, seeing the job loss as the end of the world for them; and (d) engage in *absolutistic,* "all-or-none" thinking—for example, exaggerating the importance of someone's casual comment and perceiving it as final proof of their worthlessness.

In Beck's cognitive restructuring therapy, however, clients are not persuaded to change their beliefs by debate as in rational-emotive therapy; rather, they are encouraged to gather information about themselves through unbiased experiments that allow them to disconfirm their false beliefs. Together, the therapist and the individual identify the individual's assumptions, beliefs, and expectations and formulate them as hypotheses to be tested. They then design ways in which the individual can check out these hypotheses in the world. These behavioral-disconfirmation experiments are planned to give the individual successful experiences. They are arranged according to difficulty, so that the least difficult tasks will be accomplished successfully before the more difficult ones are attempted (see HIGHLIGHT on page 653).

Sometimes the client and the therapist schedule the patient's daily activities on an hour-by-hour basis. Such activity scheduling is an important part of therapy with depressed individuals because by reducing the patient's inactivity, it interrupts the tendency of depressed individuals to ruminate about themselves. An important part of the arrangement is the scheduling of pleasurable events because many depressed patients have lost the capacity for gaining pleasure from their own activities. Both the scheduled pleasurable activities and the rewarding experiences from carrying out the behavioral experiments tend to increase the individual's satisfaction and positive mood.

Besides planning the behavioral assignments, evaluating the results in subsequent sessions, and planning further disconfirmation experiments, there are several other cognitive foci in the therapy sessions. The individual is encouraged to discover underlying assumptions and "automatic thoughts" that may be leading to self-defeating tendencies. With this background, the individual is taught to self-monitor his or her thought content and keep challenging its validity.

Stress-inoculation training

A third cognitive-behavioral approach to treatment is stress-inoculation training—a type of self-instructional training focused on altering self-statements that the individual is routinely making in order to restructure his or her characteristic approach to stress-producing situations (Meichenbaum, 1974). Like other cognitive-behavioral therapies, stress-inoculation training assumes that the individual's problems result from maladaptive beliefs which are leading to negative emotional states and maladaptive behavior (see HIGHLIGHT on page 654).

Stress-inoculation training usually involves three stages. In the initial phase, *cognitive preparation,* client and therapist together explore the client's beliefs and attitudes about the problem situation and the self-statements to which they are leading. The focus is on how the individual's self-talk can influence later performance and behavior. Together, the therapist and the client agree on new self-statements that would be more adaptive. Then the second phase of the stress inoculation, *skill acquisition and rehearsal,* is begun. In this phase, more adaptive self-statements are learned and practiced. For example, an individual undergoing stress-inoculation training for coping with the "feeling of being overwhelmed" would rehearse self-statements such as,

"When fear comes, just pause.
Keep the focus on the present; what is it you have to do?
Label your fear from 0 to 10 and watch it change.
You should expect your fear to rise.
Don't try to eliminate fear totally; just keep it manageable.
You can convince yourself to do it. You can reason fear away.
It will be over shortly.
It's not the worst thing that can happen.
Just think about something else.
Do something that will prevent you from thinking about fear.
Describe what is around you. That way you won't think about worrying." (Meichenbaum, 1974, p. 16)

Cognitive-behavioral therapy for depression

Rush, Khatami, and Beck (1975) have reported several cases of successful treatment using cognitive clarification and behavioral assignments for patients with recurring chronic depression. The following case illustrates their approach:

"A 53-year-old white male engineer's initial depressive episode 15 years ago necessitated several month's absence from work. Following medication and psychotherapy, he was asymptomatic up to four years ago. At that time, sadness, pessimism, loss of appetite and weight, and heavy use of alcohol returned.

"Two years later, he was hospitalized for six weeks and treated with lithium and imipramine. He had three subsequent hospitalizations with adequate trials of several different tricyclics. During his last hospitalization, two weeks prior to initiating cognitive-behavioral therapy, he was treated with 10 sessions of ECT. His symptoms were only partially relieved with these various treatments.

"When the patient started cognitive-behavioral therapy, he showed moderate psychomotor retardation. He was anxious, sad, tearful, and pessimistic. He was self-depreciating and self-reproachful without any interest in life. He reported decreased appetite, early morning awakening, lack of sexual interest, and worries about his physical health. Initially he was treated with weekly sessions for 3 months, then biweekly for 2 months. Treatment, terminated after 5 months, consisted of 20 sessions. He was evaluated 12 months after the conclusion of therapy.

"Therapist and patient set an initial goal of his becoming physically active (i.e., doing more things no matter how small or trivial). The patient and his wife kept a separate list of his activities. The list included raking leaves, having dinner, and assisting his wife in apartment sales, etc. His cognitive distortions were identified by comparing his assessment of each activity with that of his wife. Alternative ways of interpreting his experiences were then considered.

"In comparing his wife's resumé of his past experiences, he became aware that he had (1) undervalued his past by failing to mention many previous accomplishments, (2) regarded himself as far more responsible for his "failures" than she did, and (3) concluded that he was worthless since he had not succeeded in attaining certain goals in the past. When the two accounts were contrasted he could discern many of his cognitive distortions. In subsequent sessions, his wife continued to serve as an 'objectifier.'

"In midtherapy, the patient compiled a list of new attitudes that he had acquired since initiating therapy. These included:

1) I am starting at a lower level of functioning at my job, but it will improve if I persist.

2) I know that once I get going in the morning, everything will run all right for the rest of the day.

3) I can't achieve everything at once.

4) I have my periods of ups and down, but in the long run I feel better.

5) My expectations from my job and life should be scaled down to a realistic level.

6) Giving in to avoidance never helps and only leads to further avoidance.

"He was instructed to re-read this list daily for several weeks even though he already knew the content. The log was continued, and subsequent assumptions reflected in the log were compared to the assumptions listed above.

"As the patient became gradually less depressed, he returned to his job for the first time in 2 years. He undertook new activities (e.g., camping, going out of town) as he continued his log." (pp. 400–401)

The focus of the therapy was on encouraging the patient to restructure his thought content—to reduce the negative self-judgments and to evaluate his actual achievements more realistically. Making and reviewing the list of new attitudes gave the patient more perspective on his life situation, which resulted in an improved mood, less self-blame, and more willingness to risk alternative behavior.

Stress inoculation in the control of severe anger

Many clinicians believe that intense anger typically underlies depression. Novaco (1977) recently employed a stress-inoculation procedure in the treatment of a severely depressed man by focusing on this hypothesized relationship between severe anger and depression.

"The client was a 38-year-old male who had been admitted to the psychiatric ward of a community hospital with the diagnosis of depressive neurosis. Upon admission he was judged to be grossly depressed, having suicidal ruminations and progressive beliefs of worthlessness and inadequacy. He was a credit manager for a national business firm and had been under considerable job pressure. Quite routinely, he developed headaches by midafternoon at work. He had recurrent left anterior chest pain that was diagnosed by a treadmill stress test procedure as due to muscle tension.

"The client had been hospitalized for 3 weeks when the attending psychiatrist referred him to me for the treatment of anger problems. At that time I had initiated a staff training program for the treatment of anger. The principal behavior settings in which problems with anger control emerged were at work, at home, and at church. The client was married and had six children, one of which was hyperactive.

"Circumstances at work had progressively generated anger and hostility for this man's superiors, colleagues, and supervisees. His anger at work was typically overcontrolled. He would actively suppress his anger and would then periodically explode with a verbal barrage of epithets, curses, and castigations when a conflict arose. At home, he was more impulsively aggressive. The accumulated tensions and frustrations at work resulted in his being highly prone to provocation at home, particularly in response to the disruptive behavior of the children. Noise, disorders, and the frequent fights among the children were high anger elicitors. Unlike his behavior at work, he would quickly express his anger in verbal and physical outbursts. Although not an abusive parent, he would readily resort to physical means and threats of force (e.g., 'I'll knock your goddamn head off') as a way to control the behavior of his children. The children's unruly behavior often became a problem during church services. The client's former training in a seminary disposed him to value family attendance at church, but serious conflict was often the result. In an incident just prior to hospitalization, the client abruptly removed two of his boys from church for creating a disturbance and threatened them to the extent that one ran away. At this point he had begun to realize that he was reacting 'out of proportion,' but he felt helpless about instituting the desired changes in behavior.

"During hospitalization, treatment sessions were conducted three times per week for 3½ weeks. Following discharge, follow-up sessions were conducted biweekly for a 2-month period. During these sessions, anger diary incidents were discussed, and there was continued modeling, rehearsal, and practice of coping procedures." (pp. 602–3)

The stress-inoculation program consisted of three phases: (a) In the cognitive preparation period, the client was educated about how anger operates—that is, how it is triggered, how to recognize one's anger, how anger affects one's physical state, and what coping strategies can be learned to control anger. He was taught to see anger as an emotional state that was induced by external events but could be altered by his own problem-solving behavior. (b) In the skill acquisition and rehearsal period, the therapist modeled effective coping techniques which the client then practiced. For example, he was taught to see possible alternatives to anger in particular situations, thus changing his view about the importance of certain events that had been making him angry. Self-instructions were used to modify his appraisals of anger-producing events and to guide his coping behavior when he felt himself becoming angry. He also was given relaxation training. (c) Finally, in the application and practice phase, a task-oriented response set was taught in which the client learned to regulate his anger by managing provocative situations in practice sessions. He was given "manageable doses of anger stimuli" in a series of role-play situations, working through a hierarchy of anger-producing situations until the coping skills had been sufficiently learned and rehearsed.

The client's proneness to provocation was evaluated prior to treatment, during treatment, and following treatment by a questionnaire dealing with anger-inducing situations. His behavior was also observed during nine observation periods by a trained clinician. In addition, the client self-monitored his own anger by keeping a diary of anger experiences.

The results were truly dramatic. The client improved on all measures over the course of treatment: antagonism and anger (both overt or restrained) decreased over the period while more positive, constructive behaviors and more relaxed appearance increased. His self-reported anger was also considerably reduced over the three-month period.

The third phase of stress-inoculation training, *application and practice,* involves applying the new coping strategies in actual situations. This practice is graduated in such a way that the individual is placed in easier situations first and is only gradually introduced to more stressful life situations as he or she feels confident of mastering them.

Stress-inoculation training has been successfully employed with a number of clinical problems, especially anxiety (Meichenbaum, 1975); pain (Turk, 1974); and impulsive behavior in children (Kendall & Finch, 1976). This approach is particularly suited to increasing the adaptive capabilities of individuals who have shown a vulnerability to developing problems in certain stressful situations. In addition to its value as a therapeutic technique for identified problems, stress-inoculation training may be a viable method for preventing behavior disorders. Although the preventive value of this and other cognitive-behavioral therapy procedures has not been demonstrated by empirical study, many believe that the incidence of maladjustment might be reduced if more individuals' general coping skills were improved (Mahoney & Arnkoff, 1978).

Evaluation of cognitive-behavioral therapy

An evaluation of cognitive-behavioral treatments at this time must necessarily be tentative, since the treatment approach is still being systematized and is too new to have been thoroughly evaluated empirically. There is even a question as to whether these approaches should be considered "behavioral," since the focus is primarily upon cognitive rather than behavioral changes (Ledwidge, 1978). This criticism may be premature, however, since many behavioral theorists are clearly integrating behavioral techniques into cognitive-behavioral treatment programs (Kendall & Hollon, 1979).

The more serious criticism that cognitive-behavioral therapy is no more effective than either cognitively oriented or behaviorally oriented therapy separately (Ledwidge, 1978) has been answered in part by recent empirical studies which have found it more effective

(Fuchs & Rehm, 1977; Shaw, 1977; Taylor & Marshall; 1977). However, it is much too early to arrive at firm conclusions about the relative effectiveness of cognitive-behavioral therapy until a wider range of clinical studies has been completed (Hobbs, Mogluin, Tyroller, & Lahey, in press).

It is quite possible that some techniques associated with cognitive-behavioral therapy will prove to be more effective than others in bringing about behavior change. Mahoney and Arnkoff (1978), reviewing cognitive-behavioral therapy research, reported that self-reinforcement procedures have demonstrated consistent effects over a wide range of populations and behaviors, whereas the effects of self-monitoring are more variable. He also cautions that "in the realm of covert conditioning we found a high ratio of theory to evidence, with a variety of extrapolation problems and theoretical dilemmas" (p. 710).

The combining of cognitive and behavioral therapy approaches is nevertheless growing rapidly. It is expected that the next few years will see a greater endeavor to demonstrate the relative merits of cognitive-behavioral therapy as a medium of therapeutic change, as well as a greater effort at explaining the processes through which cognitive restructuring results in changed behavior.

Humanistic-experiential therapies

The humanistic perspective and humanistic-experiential therapies have emerged as a "third force" in psychology during the last two decades. To a large extent, they developed in reaction to the psychoanalytic and behavioristic perspectives, which many feel do not accurately take into account either the existential problems or the full potentialities of human beings. In a society dominated by computerized technology and mass bureaucracy, proponents of the humanistic-experiential therapies see psychopathology as stemming in many cases from problems of alienation, depersonalization, loneliness, and a failure to find meaning and fulfillment in life—problems that are not solved either by delving into forgotten memories or by correcting specific responses.

The humanistic-experiential therapies follow some variant of the general humanistic and existential viewpoints spelled out in Chapter 3. They are based on the assumption that we have the freedom to control our own behavior— that we can reflect upon our problems, make choices, and take positive action. Whereas some behavior therapists see themselves as "behavioral engineers," responsible for changing specific behaviors by appropriate modifications in the individual's environment, humanistic-experiential therapists feel that the client must take most of the responsibility for the success of therapy, with the therapist serving as counselor, guide, and facilitator. These therapies may be carried out with individual clients or with groups of clients (see HIGHLIGHT on page 657).

Carl Rogers' nondirective techniques gave the client rather than the therapist the primary role in the therapeutic relationship. Many of today's humanistic therapies are based on this approach.

Client-centered therapy

The client-centered therapy of Carl Rogers (1951, 1961, 1966) actually antedated both the current emphasis on behavior therapy and the "humanistic revolution" of the 1960s. It was developed in the 1940s as a truly innovative alternative to psychoanalysis, the only major psychotherapy of the time.

Rogers rejected both Freud's view of the primacy of irrational instinct and the therapist's role of prober, interpreter, and director of the therapeutic process. Instead, believing in the natural power of the organism to heal itself, he saw psychotherapy as a process of removing the constraints and hobbling restrictions that often prevent this process from operating. These constraints, he believed, grow out of unrealistic demands that people tend to place on themselves when they believe they should not have certain kinds of feelings, such as hostility. By denying that they do in fact have such feelings, they become unaware of their actual "gut" reactions. As they lose touch with their own genuine experience, the result is lowered integration, impaired personal relationships, and various forms of maladjustment.

The primary objective of Rogerian therapy is to resolve this incongruence—to help clients become able to accept and be *themselves*. To this end, the therapist establishes a psychological climate in which clients can feel unconditionally accepted, understood, and valued as persons. In this climate they can begin to feel free for the first time to explore their real feelings and thoughts and to accept hates and angers and "ugly feelings" as parts of themselves. As their self-concept becomes more congruent with their actual experiencing, they become more self-accepting and more open to new experience and new perspectives; in short, they become better integrated people.

In client-centered therapy, also called *nondirective* therapy, it is not the therapist's task to direct the course of therapy. Thus the therapist does not give answers or interpret what the client says or probe for unconscious conflicts or even steer the client onto certain topics. Rather he or she simply listens attentively and acceptingly to what the client wants to talk about, interrupting only to restate in other words what the client is saying. Such restatements, without any judgment or interpretation by the therapist, help the client clarify

Group therapy

Treatment of patients in groups first received impetus in the military during World War II, when psychotherapists were in short supply. Group therapy was found to be effective in dealing with a variety of problems, and it rapidly became an important therapeutic approach in civilian life. In fact, all the major systematic approaches to psychotherapy that we have discussed—psychoanalysis, behavior therapy, and so on—have been applied in group as well as individual settings.

Group therapy has traditionally involved a relatively small group of patients in a clinic or hospital setting, using a variety of procedures depending upon the age, needs, and potentialities of the patients and the orientation of the therapists. The degree of structure and of patient participation in the group process varies in different types of groups.

Most often, groups are informal, and many follow the format of encounter groups. Occasionally, however, more or less formal lectures and visual materials will be presented to patients as a group. For example, a group of alcoholic patients may be shown a film depicting the detrimental effects of excessive drinking on the human body, with a group discussion afterwards. While this approach by itself has not proven effective in combating alcoholism, it is often a useful adjunct to other forms of group therapy.

An interesting form of group therapy is *psychodrama,* based on role-playing techniques. The patient, assisted by staff members or other patients, is encouraged to act out problem situations in a theater-like setting. This technique frees the individual to express anxieties and hostilities or relive traumatic experiences in a situation that simulates real life but is more sheltered. The goal is to help the patient achieve emotional catharsis, increased understanding, and improved interpersonal competencies. This form of therapy, developed initially by Moreno (1959), has proved beneficial for the patients who make up the audience as well as for those who participate on the stage (Sundberg & Tyler, 1962; Yablonsky, 1975).

It may be noted that group therapy may also be nearly completely unstructured, as in activity groups where children with emotional problems are allowed to act out their aggressions in the safety and control of the therapeutic group setting.

further the feelings and ideas that he or she is exploring—really to look at them and acknowledge them.

The following excerpt from a counselor's second interview with a young woman will serve to illustrate these techniques of reflection and clarification.

> "**Alice:** I was thinking about this business of standards. I somehow developed a sort of a knack, I guess, of—well—habit—of trying to make people feel at ease around me, or to make things go along smoothly. . . .
>
> **Counselor:** In other words, what you did was always in the direction of trying to keep things smooth and to make other people feel better and to smooth the situation.
>
> **Alice:** Yes. I think that's what it was. Now the reason why I did it probably was—I mean, not that I was a good little Samaritan going around making other people happy, but that was probably the role that felt easiest for me to play. I'd been doing it around home so much. I just didn't stand up for my own convictions, until I don't know whether I have any convictions to stand up for.
>
> **Counselor:** You feel that for a long time you've been playing the role of kind of smoothing out the frictions or differences or what not. . . .
>
> **Alice:** M-hm.
>
> **Counselor:** Rather than having any opinion or reaction of your own in the situation. Is that it?
>
> **Alice:** That's it. Or that I haven't been really honestly being myself, or actually knowing what my real self is, and that I've been just playing a sort of false role. Whatever role no one else was playing, and that needed to be played at the time, I'd try to fill it in." (Rogers, 1951, pp. 152–53)

Rogers was also a pioneer in attempting to carry out empirical research on psychotherapy. Using recordings of therapy sessions, he was able to make objective analyses later of what was said, of the client-counselor relationship, and of many aspects of the ongoing processes in these therapy sessions. He was also able to compare a client's behavior and attitudes at different stages of therapy. These comparisons revealed a typical sequence that clients tended to go through. Early sessions were dominated by negative feelings and discouragement. Then, after a time, tentative statements of hope and greater self-acceptance began to appear. Eventually, positive feelings, a reaching out toward others, greater self-confidence, and interest in future plans appeared. This characteristic sequence gave support to Rogers'

hypothesis that once freed to do so, individuals have the capacity to lead themselves to psychological health.

Pure nondirective psychotherapy, as originally practiced, is rarely used today, but it opened the way for a variety of humanistically oriented therapies in which the focus is the client's present conscious problems and in which it is assumed that the client is the primary actor in the curative process, with the therapist essentially just the facilitator. The newer humanistic therapies thus accept Rogers' concept of an active self, capable of sound value choices; they also emphasize the importance of a high degree of empathy, genuine warmth, and unconditional positive regard on the part of the therapist. They differ from original client-centered therapy in having found various short-cuts by which the therapist, going beyond simple reflection and clarification, can hasten and help focus the client's search for wholeness. But it is still the client's search and the client's insights that are seen as central in therapy.

Existential therapy

Several important concepts underlie existential psychotherapy. As we noted in Chapter 3, the existentialists emphasize the importance of the human situation as experienced by the individual: they are deeply concerned about the predicament of humankind, the breakdown of traditional faith, the alienation and depersonalization of the individual in contemporary society, and the lack of meaning in the lives of many people. But they see individuals as having a high degree of freedom and thus as both capable of doing something about their predicament and responsible for doing the best they can. The unique ability of human beings to be aware of, reflect on, and question their existence confronts them with the responsibility for *being*—for deciding what kind of person to become, for establishing their own values, and for actualizing their potentialities.

Existential therapists do not follow any rigidly prescribed procedures, but emphasize the uniqueness of each individual and his or her "way-of-being-in-the-world." They stress the importance of *confrontation*—challenging the individual directly with questions concerning the meaning and purpose of existence—

and the *encounter*—the complex relationship established between two interacting human beings in the therapeutic situation as they both try to be open and "authentic." In contrast to behavior therapy, existential therapy calls for therapists to share themselves—their feelings, their values, and their own existence.

Besides being authentic themselves, it is the task of existential therapists to keep the client responding authentically to the present reality (Havens, 1974; May, 1969). For example, if the client says, "I hate you just like I hated my father," the therapist might respond by saying, "I am not your father, I am me, and you have to deal with me as Dr. S., not as your father." The focus is on the here and now—on what the individual is choosing to do, and therefore be, at this moment. This sense of immediacy, of the urgency of experience, is the touchstone of existential therapy and sets the stage for the individual to clarify and choose between alternative ways of being.

The existential approach is illustrated by the treatment of Hilda, a 29-year-old woman whose case was diagnosed as "chronic undifferentiated schizophrenia." This was the third time she had been hospitalized for mental illness.

"Prior to this current hospitalization she had been unemployed; had 'floated around and almost starved.' Her relationships with females were negative and hostile; with men, always rather 'shady, mistress types of things.' She expressed feelings of failure, inadequacy, anger and dread. She was loud, boisterous, brutally frank and blistering to anyone who 'crossed' her. . . .

"The questions that interested me most were: What was her world? What was she to herself? . . . I knew that I would have to encounter her where she was before she would be able to accept me as a helping person, who was—in essence—criticizing her way of being. My 'treatment goal' was, therefore, to encounter her in her own world, which seemed to be constructed upon a series of negative reflections which made unauthentic being in the world the only existence possible for her. . . .

"We then began to explore, in earnest, 'the world of Hilda,' as she termed it, and I followed where she led. She proved to be unsure of where she had been or where she was. As she grew more and more related to me, I began to ask her: 'Where are you?' It was not very long before she stopped saying 'in the nuttery . . .'; and started telling me things which made me wonder if she were not trying to give me something; trying to tell me about Hilda. She began to disorganize but could write:

" 'I'm glad I'm young in heart. You're at this time my strongest contact with reality. You are it. This "epistle" represents my "search for reality." Ha, ha. Let's call it that: one fool's search. . . .'

"Finally, she evaluated my relationship to her:

" '. . . I wanted to give you my illness . . . but you don't want it. You want me to just lose it and work it out of my system . . . Keep watching the light up there above San Francisco like a beacon! Guide me, please guide me out of this . . . I'm mesmerized today. . . . Now I'm going ashore, the bridge will be my vehicle. . . .'

"Shortly after this 'prophecy,' she became so disorganized that I could not read her writings, nor follow her arguments. However, I tried, spending time with her almost every day. She was put on an increased dosage of Thorazine but still managed to get to group meetings and to our interviews. Even in her disorganization, she clung to her relationship with me, and managed to write:

" '. . . I must listen when you talk, I'm not always there. . . .'

"She had encountered me, perhaps long before I became fully aware of it. The idea of love—love without purpose—was emerging from deep within her. On 800 milligrams of tranquilizer, she gradually became less disorganized. With a burst of unbelievable energy, she began to plan for a 'future'; took hospital jobs, as she said, 'fighting to stay awake.'

"When the patients on her ward elected her president of the government group, she got up and ran out of the room, crying violently. I felt that I had lost; she had recoiled from letting herself be liked. But she returned to the room, accepting the role of president.

"She was in the midst of turning from her futureless, pseudo-world of distortions to the world of possibility, in which one could find hope and meaning; in which one could establish an authentic relationship!

"One of the last things she wrote, before she gave up writing, was a poem which began:

Glorious night all is right
No time for flight too tired to fight . . .

and ended:

I'm awake I'm awake
A happy wake for a former fake. . . .

"Hilda remained on leave for one year, received her discharge and managed extremely well for approximately another year. She experienced a slight relapse and was rehospitalized elsewhere for about three months. After this, she once again returned to the community." (Curry, 1962, pp. 129–35)

Like psychoanalysis, existential psychotherapy is a therapy for the few. It is a therapy that is directed primarily toward the intelligent and verbal individual who appears to be having an existential crisis. The existential treatment approach works best with individuals who have problems at the level of neurosis or personality disorder, although success with more seriously disturbed individuals has been reported, as in the case of Hilda.

Gestalt therapy

The term *gestalt* means "whole," and gestalt therapy emphasizes the unity of mind and body—placing strong emphasis on the need for integration of thought, feeling, and action. Gestalt therapy was developed by Frederick (Fritz) Perls (1967, 1969) as a means of teaching clients to recognize the bodily processes and emotional modalities they had been blocking off from awareness. The main goal of gestalt therapy is to increase the individual's self-awareness and self-acceptance.

Although gestalt therapy is commonly used in a group setting, the emphasis is on one individual at a time with whom the therapist works intensively, attempting to help identify aspects of the individual's self or world that are not being acknowledged in awareness. The individual may be asked to act out fantasies concerning feelings and conflicts, or to "be" one part of a conflict while sitting in one chair and then switch chairs to take the part of the "adversary." Often the therapist or other group members will ask questions like, "What are you aware of in your body now?" or "What does it feel like in your gut when you think of that?"

In Perls' approach to therapy, a good deal of emphasis is also placed on dreams:

". . . all the different parts of the dream are fragments of our personalities. Since our aim is to make every one of us a wholesome person, which means a unified person, without conflicts, what we have to do is put the different fragments of the dream together. We have to *re-own* these projected, fragmented parts of our personality, and *re-own* the hidden potential that appears in the dream." (1967, p. 67)

In the following dialogue, taken from the transcript of a "dreamwork seminar," Perls (Fritz) helps a young woman (Linda) discover the meaning of her dream:

"**Linda:** I dreamed that I watch . . . a lake . . . drying up, and there is a small island in the middle of the lake, and a circle of . . . porpoises—they're like porpoises except that they can stand up, so they're like porpoises that are like people, and they're in a circle, sort of like a religious ceremony, and it's very sad—I feel very sad because they can breathe, they are sort of dancing around the circle, but the water, their element, is drying up. So it's like a dying—like watching a race of people, or a race of creatures, dying. And they are mostly females, but a few of them have a small male organ, so there are a few males there, but they won't live long enough to reproduce, and their element is drying up. And there is one that is sitting over here near me and I'm talking to this porpoise and he has prickles on his tummy, sort of like a porcupine, and they don't seem to be a part of him. And I think that there's one good point about the water drying up, I think—well, at least at the bottom, when all the water dries up, there will probably be some sort of treasure there, because at the bottom of the lake there should be things that have fallen in, like coins or something, but I look carefully and all that I can find is an old license plate . . . That's the dream.

Fritz: Will you please play the license plate.

L: I am an old license plate, thrown in the bottom of a lake. I have no use because I'm no value—although I'm not rusted—I'm outdated, so I can't be used as a license plate . . . and I'm just thrown on the rubbish heap. That's what I did with a license plate, I threw it on a rubbish heap.

F: Well, how do you feel about this?

L: (quietly) I don't like it. I don't like being a license plate—useless.

F: Could you talk about this. That was such a long dream until you come to find the license plate, I'm sure this must be of great importance.

L: (sighs) Useless. Outdated . . . The use of a license plate is to allow—give a car permission to go . . . and I can't give anyone permission to do anything because I'm outdated . . . In California, they just paste a little—you buy a sticker—and stick it on the car on the old license plate. (faint attempt at humor) So maybe someone could put me on their car and stick this sticker on me, I don't know . . .

F: Okeh, now play the lake.

L: I'm a lake . . . I'm drying up, and disappearing, soaking into the earth . . . (with a touch of surprise) *dying* . . . But when I soak into the earth, I become a part of the earth—so maybe I water the surrounding area, so . . . even in the lake, even in my bed, flowers can grow (sighs) . . . New life can grow . . . from me (cries) . . .

F: You get the existential message?

L: Yes. (sadly, but with conviction) I can paint—I can create—I can create beauty. I can no longer reproduce, I'm like the porpoise . . . but I . . . I'm . . . I . . . keep wanting to say I'm *food* . . . I . . . as water becomes . . . I water the earth, and give life—growing things, the water—they need both the earth and water, and the . . . and the air and the sun, but as the water from the lake, I can play a part in something, and producing—feeding.

F: You see the contrast: On the surface, you find something, some artifact—the license plate, the artificial you—but then when you go deeper, you find the apparent death of the lake is actually fertility . . .

L: And I don't need a license plate, or a permission, a license in order to . . .

F: (gently) Nature doesn't need a license plate to grow. You don't have to be useless, if you are organismically creative, which means if you are involved.

L: And I don't need permission to be creative . . . Thank you." (Perls, 1969, 81–82)

In gestalt therapy sessions, the focus is on the more obvious elements of the person's behavior. Such sessions are often called "gestalt awareness training," since the therapeutic results of the experience stem from the process of becoming more aware of one's total self and environment. The technique of working through unresolved conflicts is called "taking care of unfinished business." We all go through life, according to Perls, with unfinished or unresolved traumas and conflicts. We carry the excess baggage of these unfinished situations into new relationships and tend to reenact them in our relations with other people. If we are able to complete our past unfinished business, we then have less psychological tension to cope with and can be more realistically aware of ourselves and our world.

Expressing themselves in front of the group, perhaps taking the part of first one and then another fragment of a scene, and denied the use of their usual techniques for avoiding self-awareness, individuals are brought to an "impasse," at which point they must confront their feelings and conflicts. According to Perls, "In the safe emergency of the therapeutic situation, the neurotic discovers that the world does not fall to pieces if he or she gets angry, sexy, joyous, mournful" (1967, p. 331). Thus, individuals find that they can, after all, get beyond impasses on their own.

Gestalt therapy has become a widely used form of therapy, perhaps because it blends many of the strong points of psychoanalysis (working through intrapsychic conflicts), behaviorism (the focus on overt behavior), and the humanistic-existential orientation (the importance of self-awareness and personal growth).[5]

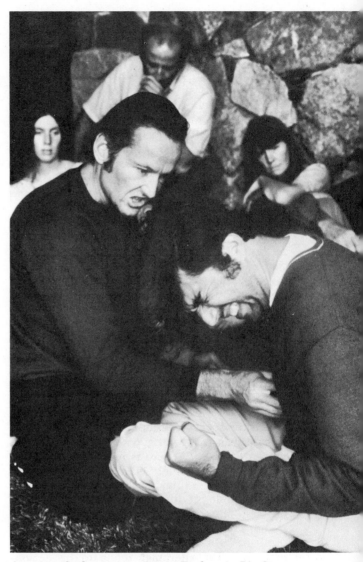

At a gestalt therapy session at Esalen, in Big Sur, California, the leader (left) encourages a member to express his pent-up feelings of anger.

Reality therapy

As formulated by Glasser (1965, 1976), reality therapy assumes that in early life the individual develops a basic sense of right and

---

[5]An extensive discussion of the principles and procedures of gestalt therapy may be found in Perls (1969) and Stephenson (1975).

wrong that provides the basis for later value choices. Difficulties arise when the individual's actual behavior is in conflict with this basic sense of right or wrong.

Reality therapy focuses on helping clients clarify their basic values and evaluate their current behavior and future plans in relation to these values. One of the first tasks of therapy is to get the client to clarify his or her goals in life—both short-term goals and longer-term directions. Once these are identified, the therapy examines ways in which the person is blocking his or her own progress toward these goals.

The therapist in this form of therapy thus functions as a moral agent and model but encourages the client to identify his or her own true values and then live responsibly—fulfilling personal needs without hurting others. The therapist helps the individual perceive both the aversive consequences of living irresponsibly and the sense of personal fulfillment that results from living in accordance with one's basic values and life goals.

In reality therapy, the therapist establishes a warm, caring, supportive relationship and encourages the client to evaluate his or her own behavior on the basis of whether it is the best choice that could be made among the possible alternatives in keeping with the individual's chosen life goals. There is more concern with what the individual is *doing* than with thoughts or feelings or repressed material. For example, if the client says, "I feel depressed—just miserable!" the therapist asks, "What are you doing to make yourself depressed?" Rather than spend time discussing problems, the therapist tends to be action-oriented and supportive, and the focus for the client is on planning responsible actions.

Favorable results with a wide range of clients have been reported for reality therapy. Of particular interest is Glasser's (1967) report of successful results with reality therapy in dealing with delinquents, and the report of its successful application on a group basis in helping the wives of military personnel through the crisis of widowhood (Glasser & Zunin, 1973).

Encounter groups

In the '60s and '70s, the entire field of group therapy was changed by the advent of en-

counter groups. Some encounter groups follow the pattern of the sensitivity training or "T-groups" started over thirty years ago at the National Training Laboratories (NTL) in Bethel, Maine, for training in more effective leadership and group interaction. Others stem from patterns developed at the Esalen Institute in California and similar "growth centers." Their overall focus varies depending on their origin, with the NTL groups focusing more on verbal expression and cognitive modes of interacting and with the Esalen-model groups focusing more on emotional-experiential expression.

Some encounter groups are directed toward helping normal individuals learn more about how their feelings and behavior affect themselves and others, while others are directed primarily toward treating personal problems and hence tend to be an extension of traditional group therapy. It is these therapeutically oriented encounter groups with which we are presently concerned, although many of the aspects of group process described here are characteristic of all encounter groups.

1. *Format and goals.* There has always been a great deal of flexibility and experimentation in encounter groups, and a variety of formats have emerged. Usually encounter groups consist of some 6 to 12 participants with one or two group leaders; the physical setting is relatively bare, permitting maximum freedom of movement and activity. Specific goals in encounter-group therapy vary considerably, depending on the nature and orientation of the group. However, the focus is on providing an intensive group experience that helps members work through emotional problems and achieve more effective coping techniques. The group situation, with its intensive give-and-take, is much closer to social reality than is traditional individual therapy; in fact, it typically goes beyond conventional social reality in the honesty and frankness it demands in interpersonal interactions.

The encounter-group leader—more appropriately described as a leader-participant since his or her function is not highly directive—is usually responsible for screening group members and for scheduling meetings. Other responsibilities of the group leader include establishing a climate of "psychological safety" in which members feel safe to drop their façades, to express their real feelings, and to try out new ways of interacting with others. Also, group

Warming-up exercises that involve some form of physical rather than verbal interaction are frequently used to open up lines of communication within an encounter group.

leaders serve as models by expressing their own feelings openly and honestly, and accepting expressions of hostility or other negative feelings directed toward them without becoming defensive. They encourage group members to give *descriptive* feedback ("It made me uncomfortable when you said that") rather than *evaluative* feedback ("You are being obnoxious"). It is also the responsibility of a group leader to see that confrontations among group members are resolved in a constructive way, and in general to serve as a resource person when the group needs guidance or comes to an impasse.

2. *Group process.* The emphasis in encounter groups is on the removal of masks, the free and honest expression of feelings, and the resolution of confrontations and other interactions that emerge within the group. This in turn requires prompt and honest feedback, both negative and positive, from other group members. Usually a good deal of mutual support and affection develop within the group, especially for members who are experiencing periods of crisis.

Nonverbal techniques may be used as "warming-up" exercises to facilitate aware-ness and group interaction. Such techniques include *eyeball-to-eyeball*, in which two participants gaze into each other's eyes for 60 to 90 seconds; the *blind mill*, in which all of the group members walk around with their eyes closed, learning how to communicate by touch; and *trusting exercises*, in which participants take turns being lifted and passed around the circle formed by other group members. Partial or total disrobing has also been used: it is reported to enhance feelings of spontaneity and confidence rather than eliciting sexual excitement.

Verbal techniques may also be used to facilitate group interaction, to provide feedback, and to focus on personal problems. One method—echoing a technique developed by Perls—is to have a member occupy the "hot seat" while the others provide feedback about their reactions to his or her behavior. A variation of this technique is called *positive and negative bombardment,* in which the members are instructed to say only positive or only negative things about the person on the "hot seat," with the proviso that they must be sincere. This may help members gain remarkably different impressions of themselves than before. Here we are reminded of the words of the poet Robert Burns:

O wad some Pow'r the giftie gie us
To see oursels as ithers see us!

Most encounter-group leaders consider such warming-up exercises as useful in getting people to "open up" and to develop feelings of trust and mutual support. Others consider any type of structured technique to be "gimmicky" and counterproductive and prefer to allow group interaction to take its natural course. So far, there is no conclusive evidence as to which approach works better.

Encounter group experiences may be intensified by the use of the *marathon* format, in which the group meets for a live-in weekend with only a brief break for sleep. The "opening-up" process appears to be hastened by the continuous contact as well as the lowering of inhibitions that accompanies fatigue. Presumably the participants become too tired to "play games," and there is more immediacy, openness, and honesty of expression. This intensive, unbroken format also helps members focus on the immediate group experience—on the here and now rather than the past or future. Thus the marathon encounter group has been called a "pressure cooker" because of the emotional tension it builds up and the reduced amount of time apparently required to achieve therapeutic goals.

3. *Termination and reentry.* The term *reentry* refers to the return of group members from the new climate of the encounter group to their everyday world. It is often difficult for them to return to the mundane patterns of everyday life, where their new understandings and ways of behaving may not be readily accepted. For example, there is considerable risk in being completely open with others and giving honest feedback in family, work, or social groups.

As yet, there is no simple strategy for overcoming the reentry problem. Some group leaders utilize a final session of the group for "reflections," during which participants share their feelings about the group experience and how it may carry over into their lives. In some cases, follow-up sessions are scheduled. Of course, for many encounter groups there is no set termination date. For example, an encounter group for alcoholics or drug addicts may be more or less continuous, with the membership changing over time as new members enter the group and old ones leave it.

In sum, the potency of encounter groups is indicated by the fact that a group of strangers can learn, in a relatively short period of time, to function with a high degree of honesty, trust, and supportiveness. Participants frequently attest that the intensive group experience has had a profound influence on their lives. A typical reaction upon termination of the group is "I feel I know each of you better and feel closer to you than to most people I have known or worked with for years."

The complexity of the encounter-group process defies rigorous scientific scrutiny. Much of the published research on outcomes of such groups is not well controlled, and there are few objective conclusions (Bednar & Kaul, 1978). Demonstration of the efficacy of encounter groups as a means of bringing about important positive and lasting life changes awaits future research. However, there appears to be near universal agreement that encounter groups, like other therapies, can result in casualties (Bednar & Kaul, 1978). There are many potential problems, including discouragement after reentry into the world of reality, aggravation of personal problems that are brought out but not adequately resolved in the group, and development of sexual involvements among group members that may jeopardize their marriages. Similarly, one hears references to "encounter freaks" who wander like lost souls from one encounter group to another, always seeking an intimacy and belonging that they never really capture.

A particularly relevant research study involving "encounter-group casualties" is summarized in the HIGHLIGHT on page 665. Since these casualties were "ordinary" college students, one wonders what might be expected in a setting where all the members are there because they have been judged to be "emotionally disturbed."

From their review of the available research, Bednar and Kaul (1978) concluded that to minimize the potential for such casualties, the leaders of encounter groups should (a) screen potential group members to eliminate individuals who are unlikely to get along with each other, and (b) spend time early in the sessions shaping the expectations of the members. Adequate qualification for group leaders should also be ensured by adherence to the guidelines established by the American Psychological Association (APA, 1973).

Evaluation of the humanistic-experiential therapies

The humanistic-experiential therapies have been criticized for their lack of a highly systematized model of human behavior, their lack of agreed-upon therapeutic procedures, and their vagueness about what is supposed to happen between client and therapist. It is these very features, however, that are seen by many proponents of this general approach as contributing to its strength and vitality. Systematized theories can reduce individuals to abstractions, which can result in diminishing their perceived worth and denying their uniqueness as individuals. Because people are so different, we should expect that different techniques would be appropriate for different cases.

In any event, many of the humanistic-experiential concepts—the uniqueness of each individual, the satisfaction that comes from developing and using one's potentials, the importance of the search for meaning and fulfillment, and the human power for choice and self-direction—have had a major impact on our contemporary views of both human nature and psychotherapy.

Therapy for interpersonal relationships

In Chapter 3 we noted the emphasis of the interpersonal perspective on the role of faulty communications, interactions, and relationships in maladaptive behavior. This viewpoint has had an important impact on approaches to therapy—particularly on the behavioristic and

Encounter-group "casualties"

Encounter groups encourage, support, and frequently pressure members toward increased awareness of feelings, interpersonal interactions, and potential for change. The result is often a more positive self-concept, increased competency, and the opening of pathways toward personal growth. Unfortunately, failure in the face of group pressure can be a crushing experience, confirming and intensifying an individual's negative self-evaluation.

In a study of 16 "encounter-group casualties," Yalom and Lieberman (1971) found that 3 of the subjects had psychotic experiences during or shortly after the termination of the group experience. Apparently these individuals were unable to handle the intensive emotional stimulation, feedback about unrecognized aspects of self, and pressure to "open up"—at a time when their need was for support of their tenuous inner control. The other subjects were referred to as casualties because they became more depressed or evidenced more maladaptive effects persisting through the time of a follow-up interview 8 months later.

The major tragedy uncovered by this study was the suicide of a student shortly after the second meeting of his group. This suicide was not considered an encounter-group casualty, because the person had had a long history of emotional difficulties and his suicide could not necessarily be attributed to his group experience. Nevertheless, his suicide note vividly illustrates the extreme difficulty that a vulnerable person can have in an encounter group:

"I felt great pain that I could not stop any other way. It would have been helpful if there had been anyone to understand and care about my pain, but there wasn't. People did not believe me when I told them about my problems or pain or else that it was just self pity; or if there had been someone to share my feelings with, but all they said was that I was hiding myself, not showing my true feelings, talking to myself. They kept saying this no matter how hard I tried to reach them. This is what I mean when I say they do not understand or care about my pain; they just discredited it or ignored it and I was left alone with it. I ask that anyone who asks about me see this; it is my only last request." (p. 19)

Couple counseling can help husbands and wives learn to listen—perhaps for the first time—to the feelings their partner has been trying to express.

humanistic-experiential therapies. For example, in behavior therapy we have seen the emphasis on modifying social reinforcements that may be maintaining maladaptive responses; in humanistic-experiential therapies we have seen the concern with such problems as lack of acceptance, relatedness, and love in the individual's life.

In many cases, however, disordered interpersonal relationships are at the very center of an individual's problems. Such cases require therapeutic techniques that focus on relationships rather than on individuals. In this section we shall explore the growing fields of couple and family therapy and then examine in some detail the popular interpersonal technique of transactional analysis.

Couple counseling (marital therapy)

The large numbers of couples seeking assistance with problems centering around their relationship have made this a growing field of therapy. Typically the partners are seen together, and therapy focuses on clarifying and improving the interactions and relationships between them. Therapy for only one of the partners has proved very ineffective for resolving such problems (Gurman & Kniskern, 1978).

Couple counseling includes a wide range of concepts and procedures. Most therapists emphasize mutual need gratification, social role expectations, communication patterns, and similar interpersonal factors. Not surprisingly, happily married couples tend to differ from unhappily married couples in that they talk more to each other, keep channels of communication open, make more use of nonverbal techniques of communication, and show more sensitivity to each other's feelings and needs.

Faulty role expectations often play havoc with marital adjustment. For example, Paul (1971) cited the case of a couple who came for marital therapy when the 39-year-old husband was about to divorce his wife to marry a much younger woman. During therapy he broke into sobs of grief as he recalled the death of his Aunt Anna, who had always accepted him as he was and created an atmosphere of peace and contentment. In reviewing this incident, the husband realized that his girlfriend represented his life-long search for another Aunt Anna. This led to a reconciliation with his wife, who was now more understanding of his needs, feelings, and role expectations.

One of the difficulties in couple therapy is the intense emotional involvement of the marital partners, which makes it difficult for them to perceive and accept the realities of their relationship. Often wives can see clearly what is "wrong" with their husbands but not what attitudes and behavior of their own are contributing to the relationship, while husbands tend to have remarkable "insight" into their wives' flaws but not their own. To help correct this problem, videotape recordings have been used increasingly to recapture crucial moments of intense interaction between the partners. By watching these tapes the partners can gain a fuller awareness of the nature of their interactions. Thus a husband may realize for the first time that he tries to dominate rather than listen to his wife and consider her needs and expectations; or a wife may realize that she is continually undermining her husband's feelings of worth and esteem. The following statement was made by a young wife after viewing a videotape playback of the couple's first therapy session:

"See! There it is—loud and clear! As usual you didn't let me express *my* feelings or opinions, you just interrupted me with your own. You're always *telling* me what I think without *asking* me what I think. And I can see what I have been doing in response—withdrawing into silence. I feel like, what's the use of talking."

This insight was shared with the husband, and the couple were able to work out a much more satisfactory marital relationship within a few months.

Other relatively new and innovative approaches to couple therapy include training the partners to use Rogerian nondirective techniques in listening to each other and helping each other clarify and verbalize their feelings and reactions. A mutual readiness to really listen and try to understand what the other one is experiencing—and acceptance of whatever comes out in this process—can be both therapeutic for the individuals and productive of a more open and honest relationship in the future.

Eisler et al. (1974) have used an interesting combination of videotape playbacks and assertiveness training.

In one case, a 45-year-old high-school teacher was responding passively and ineffectively to his highly critical wife at the beginning of therapy. By watching videotapes of their interactions, they both received feedback on their roles in the interactions. The husband received training in assertiveness and practiced being more assertive, continuing to watch videotapes of the gradually changing interactions between him and his wife.

In contrast to the videotapes made at the beginning of therapy, those made at the end showed such positive results as improved communication, an increased frequency of expressions of affection and approval, and a marked increase in the amount of smiling in their interactions. Both spouses stated that their posttreatment marital adjustment seemed more satisfying.

Behavior therapy has also been used to bring about desired changes in marital relationships. Here the spouses are taught to reinforce instances of desired behavior while withdrawing reinforcement for undesired behavior (see HIGHLIGHT on page 668).

Family therapy

Therapy for the family group overlaps with marital therapy but has somewhat different roots. Whereas marital therapy developed in response to the large number of clients who came for assistance with marital problems, family therapy had its roots in the finding that many people who had shown marked improvement in individual therapy—often in institutional settings—had a relapse upon their return home. It soon became apparent that many of these people came from disturbed family settings that required modification if they were to maintain their gains.

A pioneer in the field of family therapy has described the problem as follows:

"Psychopathology in the individual is a product of the way he deals with his intimate relations, the way they deal with him, and the way other family members involve him in their relations with each other. Further, the appearance of symptomatic behavior in an individual is necessary for the continued function of a particular family system. Therefore changes in the individual can occur only if the family system changes. . . ." (Haley, 1962, p. 70)

This viewpoint led to an important concept in the field of psychotherapy, namely, that the problem or disorder shown by the "identified patient" is often only a symptom of a larger family problem. A careful study of the family of a disturbed child may reveal that the child is merely reflecting the pathology of the family unit. As a result, most family therapists share the view that the family—not simply the designated person—should be directly involved

Structured behavior therapy for couples

Weiss (1975) has developed a brief, highly structured form of couple therapy organized around six topics or modules. The sequence takes about ten weeks.

1. Pinpointing contingencies   In an intensive period, the problem behaviors and the conditions maintaining them are identified.

2. Training in communication skills   Several techniques to improve communication, such as paraphrasing and reflecting the partner's feelings, are taught through modeling by the therapist, behavioral rehearsal, and video-feedback.

3. Training in conflict resolution   Partners view videotapes of other couples illustrating good and bad ways to deal with conflicts. Sometimes a poor method such as sidetracking or name-calling is followed by a constructive approach.

4. Formation of utility matrices   Here the partners identify rewards and penalties that they can use in contracts with each other about what they will and will not do.

5. Negotiating and "contingency contracting"   This is one of the most important phases. Practicing their new communication skills, the couple negotiate agreements on behavioral contracts that will provide a more rewarding and less punishing relationship for both of them.

6. Termination and maintenance   Once the agreements go into effect, the therapist helps promptly with any problems that arise to ensure that the learned skills are being practiced and the improved relationship maintained. In fact, throughout the course of the therapy sequence, evening phone contacts supplement the laboratory sessions for obtaining information on the partners' interactions, problems, and use of new skills. Treatment is terminated gradually as the spouses assume their new roles.

Follow-up is an important part of this therapy. The therapist may make weekly telephone contacts for the first weeks following termination. Booster sessions may be scheduled after termination if they are needed.

This form of behavioral marital therapy has been shown to be one of the most effective approaches to improving marriage relationships (Gurman & Kniskern, 1978; Jacobson & Martin, 1976). Moreover, its relatively well-structured modules can be precisely applied and taught readily to beginning therapists. The relatively specific interventions also lend themselves to empirical verification more easily than other, nonbehavioral methods; thus research into marital therapy, a previously neglected area, may now be encouraged. A more recent general exposition of this approach is presented in Weiss and Birchler (1978).

---

in therapy if lasting improvement is to be achieved.

Perhaps the most widely used approach to family therapy is the "conjoint family therapy" of Satir (1967). Her emphasis is on improving faulty communications, interactions, and relationships among family members and fostering a family system that better meets the needs of all the family members. The following example shows Satir's emphasis on the problem of faulty communication.

"**Husband:** She never comes up to me and kisses me. I am always the one to make the overtures.
Therapist: Is this the way you see yourself behaving with your husband?
Wife: Yes, I would say he is the demonstrative one. I didn't know he wanted me to make the overtures.

T: Have you told your wife that you would like this from her—more open demonstration of affection?
H: Well, no you'd think she'd know.
W: No, how would I know? You always said you didn't like aggressive women.
H: I don't, I don't like *dominating* women.
W: Well, I thought you meant women who make the overtures. How am I to know what you want?
Th: You'd have a better idea if he had been able to *tell* you." (Satir, 1967, pp. 72–73)

Another encouraging approach to resolving family disturbance is called *structured family therapy* (Minuchin, 1974). This approach, based on "systems theory," assumes that the family system itself is more influential than individual personality or intrapsychic conflicts in producing abnormal behavior. It assumes that the family system has contributed to the characteristic behaviors that individual family members have developed; if the family context changes, then the individual members will have a changed experience in the family and will behave differently in accordance with the changed requirements of the new family context. Thus an important goal of structured family therapy is to change the organization of the family in such a way that the family members will behave more positively and supportively toward each other.

Structured family therapy is focused on present interactions and requires an active but not directive approach on the part of the therapist. Initially, the therapist gathers information about the family—a "structural map" of the typical family interaction patterns—by acting like one of the family, and participating in the family interactions as an insider. In this way the therapist discovers whether the family system has rigid or flexible boundaries, who dominates the power structure, who gets blamed when things go wrong, and so on.

Armed with this understanding, the therapist then uses himself or herself as a "change medium" for altering the interaction among the family members. For example, Aponte and Hoffman (1973) report the successful use of structured family therapy in treating an anorexic 14-year-old girl.

Analyzing the communications in the family, the therapists saw a competitive struggle for the father's attention and observed that the girl, Laura, was able to succeed in this competition and get "cuddly" attention from her father by not eating. To bring the hidden dynamics out into the open, they worked at getting the family members to express their desires more directly—in words instead of through hidden behavioral messages. In time, Laura became much more able to verbalize her wishes for affection and gave up the unacceptable and dangerous method of not eating.

Similarly, Minuchin et al. (1975) reported a study in which structured family therapy was used successfully with families in which children had developed psychosomatic illnesses. And Stanton and Todd (1976) reported dramatic improvement rates with its use in several families in which one member was an identified heroin addict. Finally, after reviewing family therapy approaches, Gurman and Kniskern (1978) concluded that structured family therapy had had more impressive results than most other experientially and analytically oriented approaches they had reviewed.

As with couple problems, maladaptive family relationships have also been successfully overcome by behavioristically oriented therapies.[6] Here Huff (1969) has suggested that the task of the therapist is to reduce the aversive value of the family for the identified client as well as that of the client for other family members. "The therapist does this by actively manipulating the *relationship* between members so that the relationship changes to a more positively reinforcing and reciprocal one" (p. 26).

Hurwitz (1974) has elaborated on the role of the family therapist as an intermediary whose functions include "interpreter, clarifier, emissary, go-between, messenger, catalyst, mediator, arbitrator, negotiator, and referee" (p. 145). These role demands are most exacting, and are commonly shared by cotherapists, one male and one female.

Transactional analysis

Eric Berne (1964, 1972) developed an innovative technique of interpersonal therapy based on the notion that our personalities are composed of three "ego states"—Child, Adult, and Parent—which correspond roughly to Freud's id, ego, and superego. Our Parent is that part of our personality which we have incorporated from our own parents or from other parental models whom we have inadvertently learned to emulate. Statements such as "You shouldn't eat so much" or "Put on a sweater if you're going outside in the cold" are examples of our Parent talking. Such statements may be appropriate when spoken to a child, but if they are used with a spouse, it may well be that the speaker is playing too active a Parent role.

Our Child is that part of us which is a carry-over from our childhood feelings. "I'll eat as much as I want, and don't always yell at me!" is an example of the Child responding to the first Parent statement above. A Child response to the second command might be simply to break down and cry—behavior possibly appropriate for a real child, but not for a mature adult.

---

[6]A more extended discussion of behaviorally oriented approaches to family therapy can be found in Patterson, Weiss, & Hops (1976) and Weiss (1975).

These boys are using transactional analysis to become aware of the roles they take in one-to-one interactions. The two boys in chairs —the communicators— sit in one of the three chairs, depending on whether they feel they are acting as a Child, a Parent, or an Adult. The observers sitting on the tables watch and listen and, when they think a communicator is wrong, signal him to move to the appropriate chair.

Finally, the Adult in each of us is that part of us which processes information rationally and appropriately for the present unique set of circumstances. An Adult response to the Parent's sweater command might be, "I really don't think it is cold enough for a sweater."

In transactional analysis, the therapist analyzes the interactions among group members (often married couples) and helps the partipants understand the ego states in which they are communicating with each other. As long as each participant reacts to the other by accepting the role assigned and responding accordingly—as a Child, for example, if addressed as a child—the transactions may continue indefinitely. Many couples find out that they have been having "complementary" transactions for years, but that they have always been communicating as mother to son or father to daughter. However, when one party decides to discontinue playing Child to the spouse's Parent, the game ceases, and conflicts develop that must be worked out. Since analysis is done in a group setting, other members are encouraged to participate; the method of their participation often invites analysis of how they, in turn, communicate with other people.

Berne characterized many of our social interactions as "games"—not because they are played "for fun," but because they are played according to a set of unspoken rules. In *Games People Play* (1964), he described a number of these, most of which are deadly serious and highly destructive in their effects.

1. *Why Don't You—Yes But (WDYB).* This is considered the prototype game in transactional analysis and involves what is commonly referred to as "gamesmanship" or "one-up-manship." The game is perpetrated by A who adopts a docile stance toward B (the victim) and presents some personal problem in such a way that B is induced to offer advice—for example, to adopt a counterstance of Therapist. Once the advice has been offered, A responds by saying "Yes, but . . . ," and proceeds to add additional information about the problem that renders B's advice erroneous or irrelevant. At this point B may come back with an alternative solution, still believing that A is sincere in offering him or her the Therapist role. A again follows the same procedure and "shoots" B down again. This game may go on for several rounds until B finally realizes he or she has been defeated; at this point, B may assume a self-effacing stance, perhaps acknowledging that A "sure has a tough problem." In this game, A has perpetrated a transactional role reversal in which he or she has achieved competitive satisfaction at B's expense. A has, so to speak, "put B down."

2. *Wooden Leg.* This game involves the adoption of a "sick" role—much like that in conversion disorders. In essence, the individual asks "What do you expect from a person with a 'wooden leg'?" (a personality deficiency, physical deformity, slum background, or whatever). As we have seen, our society relaxes its demands on persons who are "sick"—who are temporarily or permanently incapable of meeting usual social standards of performance by virtue of some serious misfortune or handicap. It is a "helpless" game played by the Child who wants sympathy but does not really want to get better. The payoff is, "Oh yes, I understand: don't worry, we'll take care of you and give you whatever comfort you need." Of course, this kind of game is maladaptive in that the individual—whether or not he or she actually has the handicap claimed—avoids acquiring the competencies and sense of responsibility needed for independence and self-direction.

3. *Now I've Got You, You Son of a Bitch (NIGYSOB).* This game involves an aggressive payoff in which the perpetrator adopts a self-effacing stance that invites competitive exploitation from the victim. Since there is presumably "a little larceny in all of us," the victim unwisely accepts the proffered role and initiates a program of exploitation. The perpetrator plays along for a while, but at a certain point suddenly reverses his or her stance and reveals the exploitation; with an appropriate show of anger and indignation, the perpetrator assumes his or her justly deserved aggressive position of NIGYSOB. The victim, in turn, is forced into the apologetic and devaluating role of guilty self-effacement.

By analyzing the "games" we play, transactional analysis makes us aware of our habitual coping patterns and their consequences on our interpersonal relationships and life adjustment. In holding up a mirror so that we can see our behavior for what it really is, transactional analysis reveals how we often unthinkingly manipulate and harm other people as well as ourselves. And as a strategy of therapy, it holds out the possibility of eliminating these subterfuges and deceits and achieving more authentic, meaningful, and satisfying interpersonal relationships.

Evaluation of "success" in psychotherapy

Some years ago, Eysenck (1952) cited evidence that people who were simply placed on a waiting list for psychotherapy improved about as much as those who actually received therapy. Reevaluation of the research reviewed by Eysenck, however, along with more recent research on outcomes of therapy, has painted a very different and more positive picture of the effectiveness of psychotherapy (Bergin & Lambert, 1978; Smith & Glass, 1977).

Problems of evaluation

Evaluating the effectiveness of treatment is a difficult enterprise for several reasons. At best, it is an inexact process, dependent on inexact and inevitably somewhat subjective data. For example, attempts at evaluation generally depend on one or more of the following sources of information: (a) the therapist's impression of changes that have occurred, (b) the patient's reports of change, (c) reports from the patient's family or friends, (d) comparison of pretreatment and posttreatment personality test scores, and (e) measures of change in selected overt behaviors.

Unfortunately, each of these sources has serious limitations. The therapist may not be the best judge of the patient's progress, since any therapist is likely to be biased in favor of seeing himself or herself as competent and successful. Furthermore, therapists can inflate improvement averages by consciously or unconsciously encouraging difficult patients to discontinue therapy. It has also been somewhat facetiously remarked that the therapist often thinks the patient is getting better because he or she is getting used to the patient's symptoms.

The patient, too, is an unreliable source concerning the outcomes of therapy. Patients may not only want to think that they are getting better but may report that they are being helped in an attempt to please the therapist. Family and relatives may also be inclined to "see" the improvement they had hoped for, although they often seem to be more realistic than either the therapist or the patient in their long-term evaluations.

Outside clinical ratings by an independent observer are sometimes used in psychotherapy outcome research to evaluate the progress of a patient; these may be more objective than ratings by those directly involved in the therapy. Another widely used objective measure of patient change is performance on psychological tests. The patient takes a battery of tests before and after therapy and the differences in scores are assumed to reflect progress or deterioration. But although such tests may indeed show changes, they are likely to focus on the particular measures in which the therapist is interested. They are not necessarily valid predictors of how the client will behave in real-life situations, nor can they give any indication of whether the changes that have occurred are likely to be enduring.

Changes in selected behaviors appear to be the safest measures of outcome, but even this criterion is subject to limitations, for changes in behavior in the therapy situation may not generalize to other situations. In addition, the changes selected reflect the goals of the individual therapist. For example, one therapist may consider therapy "successful" if a patient becomes more manageable on the ward; another, if an individual becomes a more growth-oriented and self-directing person. To complicate matters further, such terms as "recovery," "marked improvement," and "fair improvement" are open to considerable differences in interpretation, and there is always the possibility that spontaneous improvement will be attributed to the particular form of treatment used.

In spite of these difficulties, however, it is possible to study the effectiveness of various treatment approaches separately—determining what procedures work best with various types of individuals. In the course of our discussion of abnormal behavior patterns we have mentioned a number of such studies, most of which have demonstrated positive outcomes from psychotherapy.

In this context, it is relevant to ask what happens to people who do not obtain formal treatment. In view of the many ways that people can help each other, it is not surprising that there is often considerable improvement without therapeutic intervention. Some forms of psychopathology, such as manic and depressive psychoses and some types of schizophrenia, appear to run a fairly predictable course with or without treatment, and there are many other instances in which disturbed persons improve over time for reasons that are not apparent.

But even if many emotionally disturbed individuals tend to improve over time without psychotherapy, it seems clear that psychotherapy can often accelerate improvement or ensure desired behavior change that might not otherwise occur (Bergin & Lambert, 1978). Most researchers today would agree that psychotherapy is more effective than no treatment. The rate of improvement given in most studies of therapy outcome, regardless of approach, is usually about 70 to 80 percent. No one approach or orientation has been shown to be clearly superior to other types (Sloane et al., 1975). Nonetheless, the issue of treatment evaluation remains a vital one—both ethically and practically—if psychologists and other mental health personnel are to be justified in intervening in other persons' lives.

The issue of values

Many persons—both inside and outside the mental health professions—have come to see psychotherapy primarily as an attempt to get people adjusted to a "sick" society, rather than encouraging them to work toward its improvement. As a consequence, psychotherapy has often been considered the guardian of the status quo. Such charges, of course, bring us back to the question we raised in Chapter 1: What do we mean by "abnormal"? Our answer to that question can only be made in the light of our values.

In a broader perspective, of course, we are concerned with the complex and controversial issue of the role of values in science. For psychotherapy is not a system of ethics but a set of tools to be used at the discretion of the therapist. Thus mental health professionals are confronted with the same kind of question that confronts scientists in general. Should the physical scientist who helps develop thermonuclear weapons be morally concerned about how they are used? Similarly, should the psychologist or behavioral scientist who develops powerful techniques of behavior control be concerned about how they are used?

Many psychologists and other scientists try to sidestep this issue by insisting that science is value free—that it is concerned only with gathering "facts," not with how they are applied. But each time therapists decide that one behavior should be eliminated or substituted for another, they are making a value choice. And the increasing social awareness of today's mental health professionals has brought into sharp focus ethical questions concerning their roles as therapists and value models as well as their roles as agents for maintaining the status quo or fostering social change. For therapy takes place in a context that involves the values of the therapist, the client, and the society in which they live. There are strong pressures on the therapist—from parents, schools, courts, and other social institutions—to help people adjust to "the world as it is." At the same time there are many counterpressures, particularly from young people who are seeking support in their attempts to become authentic persons rather than blind conformists.

The dilemma in which contemporary therapists often find themselves is well illustrated by the following case example.

A 15-year-old high-school sophomore is sent to a therapist because her parents have discovered that she has been having sexual intercourse with her boyfriend. The girl tells the therapist that she thoroughly enjoys such relations and feels no guilt or remorse over her behavior, even though her parents strongly disapprove. In addition, she reports that she is acutely aware of the danger of becoming pregnant and is very careful to take contraceptive measures.

What is the role of the therapist? Should the girl be encouraged to conform to her parents' mores and postpone the gratification of her sexual needs until she is older and more mature? Or should the parents be helped to adjust to the pattern of sexual behavior she has chosen? What should be the therapist's goal?

It becomes apparent that there are diametrically opposed ways of dealing with the same problems in therapy. Society must enforce conformity to certain norms if it is to maintain its organization and survive. But how does one distinguish between those norms that are relevant and valid and those that are irrelevant and outmoded? It is often up to individual therapists to decide what path to take, and this requires value decisions on their part concerning what is best for the individual and for the larger society. Thus mental health professionals find themselves confronted with the problem of "controlling the controller"; that is, of developing ethical standards and societal safeguards to prevent misuse of the techniques they have developed for modifying individual and group behavior.

In this chapter, we have described a wide range of approaches to psychological therapy for maladaptive behavior. Our survey of individual therapies discussed *psychoanalysis* as developed by Freud and modified by later analytic therapists; several techniques of *behavior therapy* for changing specific behaviors through the use of reinforcement, including extinction, desensitization, implosive therapy, aversion therapy, systematic use of positive reinforcement, behavior contracting, assertiveness training, and biofeedback; *cognitive-behavioral therapies*, which use behavioral methods to change cognitions and self-statements; and several *humanistic-experiential therapies*, which are aimed at fostering self-understanding, self-acceptance, and a more satisfying life.

Many therapies today focus on interpersonal relationships rather than individuals and try to change patterns that are uncomfortable and pathological for those involved. Several types of couple and family therapy were reviewed.

Finally, we looked at the problem of evaluating "success" in psychotherapy and glanced briefly at the value problems that arise when a therapist intervenes to change another human being's attitudes and behavior.

In our final chapter, which now follows, we shall take up the problems of preventing mental disorders, fostering comprehensive health, and building a good future for humankind. These are problems that pose a challenge for all of us who share the dream of a better society in a better world.

Action for mental health and a better world

Perspectives on prevention
Organized efforts for mental health
Challenges for the future

As the President's Commission on Mental Health (1978) has pointed out, efforts toward mental health have in the past been largely *restorative,* geared toward helping people only after they have already developed serious problems. Until recently, mental health professionals have not become involved until an individual has suffered a breakdown, and then have often sent such individuals for treatment far away from their home communities, compounding their distress and the disruption of their lives.

Increasingly today, however, professionals are trying to catch problems before they become acute or better still to establish conditions in which breakdowns will not occur. Where preventive efforts fail and a serious problem develops, they emphasize the importance of prompt treatment, if possible in the individual's own community in order to utilize whatever family and other familiar supports may be available and to cause as little disruption as possible in the individual's life pattern. If hospitalization becomes necessary, every effort is made to prevent the disorder from becoming chronic and to return the individual to the community as soon as possible, with whatever aftercare and continued supportive help may be needed.

Thus just as medical science has developed vaccines and antitoxins and other procedures for preventing infection and disease, the contemporary behavioral sciences are attempting to formulate and apply principles that can help prevent maladaptive behavior and foster more supportive and health-inducing conditions for all people. Already our knowledge of the causal factors in mental disorders gives us many clues as to how to prevent disorder and foster positive mental health. But greater effort needs to be expended toward training professionals in preventive roles and in developing more effective research strategies if mental disorder is to be reduced (Murphy & Frank, 1979).

In this, our final chapter, we shall examine the kinds of measures that are being taken to prevent maladaptive behavior or limit its seriousness. Our discussion will include a brief survey of the scope of organized efforts for mental health both in the United States and throughout the world and, finally, a consideration of what the average person can do to prevent mental disorder and help build a good future for all of us.

Perspectives on prevention

In our present discussion we shall utilize the concepts of primary, secondary, and tertiary prevention, which are widely used in public health medicine to describe general strategies of disease prevention. *Primary* prevention is aimed at reducing the possibility of disease and fostering positive health. *Secondary* prevention involves efforts to reduce the impact, duration, or spread of a problem that has already developed—if possible, catching it before it has become serious. *Tertiary* prevention seeks to reduce the long-term consequences to individuals of having had a disorder or serious problem.

Primary prevention

In primary prevention we are concerned with two key tasks: seeking out and eradicating conditions that can cause or contribute to mental disorders, and establishing conditions that foster positive mental health. Thus it includes biological, psychosocial, and sociocultural measures. As Kessler and Albee (1975) have noted, "everything aimed at improving the human condition, at making life more fulfilling and meaningful, may be considered to be part of primary prevention of mental or emotional disturbance" (p. 557).

Physical measures. Here primary prevention begins with help in family planning and includes both prenatal and postnatal care. A good deal of current emphasis is being placed on guidance in family planning—how many children to have, when to have them in relation to marital and other family conditions, and even whether to have children at all. Such guidance may include genetic counseling, in which tests for diagnosing genetic defects may be administered to potential parents to assess their risk of having defective children.

Breakthroughs in genetic research have also made it possible to detect and often alleviate genetic defects before the baby is born; when

Young women here wait for help in family planning and prenatal and postnatal care at a community health center. Primary prevention of mental health problems involves not only eradicating conditions that cause or contribute to mental disorders but also establishing conditions that foster positive mental health.

in utero treatment is not feasible, such information provides the parents with the choice of having an abortion rather than a seriously defective baby. Continued progress in genetic research may make it possible to identify genetic disorders early (Lyle & Gottesman, 1977) or even to correct faulty genes, thus providing humankind with fantastic new power to prevent hereditary pathology.

Psychosocial measures. In regarding normality as "optimal development and functioning" rather than as mere absence of pathology, we imply that the individual will require opportunities for learning needed competencies—physical, intellectual, emotional, and social. As we have seen, failure to develop the skills required for effective problem solving, for handling emotions constructively, and for establishing satisfying interpersonal relationships places the individual at a serious disadvantage in coping with life problems.

A second crucial requirement for psychosocial health is that the individual acquire an accurate frame of reference—in terms of reality, possibility, and value assumptions. We have seen repeatedly that when people's assumptions about themselves or their world are inaccurate, their behavior is likely to be maladap-

tive. Likewise, inability to find satisfying values that foster a meaningful and fulfilling life constitutes a fertile source of maladjustment and mental disorders.

Psychosocial health measures also require preparation for the types of problems an individual is likely to encounter during given life stages. For example, pregnancy and childbirth usually have a great deal of emotional significance for both parents and may disturb family equilibrium or exacerbate an already disturbed marital situation. Young people who want to marry and have children should have had preparation for the tasks of building a mutually satisfying relationship and helping children develop their potentialities. Similarly, the individual needs to be prepared adequately for other developmental tasks characteristic of given life periods, including old age.

General sociocultural measures. The relationship between the individual and the community is a reciprocal one, a fact we sometimes forget in our prizing of individualism. We need autonomy and "space of free movement" to be ourselves, but we also need to belong and contribute to a community. Without a nourishing community, the development of individuals is blighted. At the same time, without responsible, psychologically healthy individuals, the community withers and cannot be a nourishing one. Sociocultural efforts toward primary prevention are focused on making the community as nourishing as possible for the individuals within it.

With our growing realization of the importance of pathological social conditions in producing maladaptive behavior, increased attention is being devoted to creating social conditions that will foster healthy development and functioning in individuals. Efforts to create these conditions are seen in a wide spectrum of social measures ranging from public education and social security to economic planning and social legislation directed toward ensuring adequate health care for all citizens. Such measures, of course, must take into account the stressors and health problems we are likely to encounter in the future in our rapidly changing society.

Primary prevention through social change in the community is difficult. Although the whole psychological climate can ultimately be changed by a social movement such as the civil rights movement of the 1960s, the "payoff" of such efforts is generally far in the future and may be difficult or impossible to measure. Thus some feel that, to be meaningful, the term *primary prevention* should be reserved for policies in which the initiator clearly specifies (a) how today's program is intended to improve conditions for future health, and (b) how the impact is to be assessed (Kelly, Snowden, & Muñoz, 1977). Of this redefined and delimited concept of primary prevention in the mental health field Kelly and associates have written:

"There are glimmers in the literature that the elusive goal of primary prevention can be realized if long-term impact is an intrinsic element in the work, if systematic factors for personal and social development are the focus, and if people's integration with their community is fostered. In the final analysis, primary prevention requires a radically different kind of psychology, that is, one which commits itself to long term intervention in people's natural habitat." (1977, p. 333)

Primary preventive measures also include working with individuals who are at special risk, in order to make their environment more supportive and to improve their coping skills.

Examples of efforts to prevent such individuals from developing mental disorders were described in Chapter 14 and another is presented in the HIGHLIGHT on page 678.

Secondary prevention

Secondary prevention emphasizes the early detection and prompt treatment of maladaptive behavior in the individual's family and community setting. Thus it requires a knowledge of the incidence and scope of maladaptive behavior in specific populations, facilities for the early detection of such behavior, and available treatment facilities in the community.

Epidemiological studies. Science has found that most contagious physical diseases can be brought under control once their distribution and modes of communication are discovered by way of epidemiological studies. Epidemiological studies are also helping investigators obtain information concerning the incidence and distribution of various maladaptive behaviors in our society. For example, such studies have shown that recently divorced people (Bloom et al., 1978), the physically disabled (Freeman, Malkin, & Hastings, 1975), and elderly persons living alone (Neugarten, 1977) are high-risk groups for various disorders. Epidemiological studies tell us what to look for and where to look.

Sometimes no formal study to detect psychological problems is required since problems seem "epidemic." For example, our society has witnessed several difficult periods in which widespread social problems—such as extensive unemployment during the great depression of the 1930s and the "antiestablishment" movement during the 1960s—resulted in widespread individual psychological problems. In both of these periods, however, adequate psychological resources were unavailable to most of the people in need. There were few agencies and not enough qualified professionals to deal with the problems that emerged.

Comprehensive community mental health centers. Since the 1960s we have witnessed a marked increase in the variety and

Primary prevention following a crisis

In 1977, 154 people were held hostage at three locations in Washington, D.C., by members of the Hanafi Muslim sect. The largest group of hostages, about 100 people, were subjected to a great deal of humiliation and harassment over the 39-hour period of their confinement, including physical violence, verbal abuse, hunger, physical restraint, and threats of death.

Even before their release, the Health Maintenance Organization to which many of them belonged was making plans for short-term, crisis-oriented, broad-spectrum group therapy, which it offered to all the hostages on release, in most cases in their workplace, which had been the scene of their confinement. Sessions began a few days later and continued twice a week for four weeks, with four groups of about 12 members each. The goal was to prevent existing symptoms from becoming serious, and, where no symptoms had appeared, to forestall or minimize trouble later.

Some of those who accepted the invitation were indeed suffering from symptoms following their ordeal, and therapy was planned to deal directly with each type of symptom. For example,

"in vivo and systematic desensitization were employed for avoidance behaviors; deep muscle relaxation was taught for sleep disturbances, anxiety attacks, multiple somatic complaints, and as a substitute for minor tranquilizers and hypnotic agents; assertion imagery and rational-emotive therapy were used for disturbing images and recurrent irrational thoughts; and assertiveness training and outside referrals were used for disruptive familial relations." (Sank, 1979, p. 336)

One of the women who was experiencing symptoms at the start of therapy sessions was Shirley, a 47-year-old woman who had been at her desk when several Hanafis burst into the room. She was herded up the stairs with others to the room that was to serve as their prison. On the way she heard screams and saw the bloodied machete that had been used on another employee. The men were separated from the women and roughly bound; several were humiliated. There were times of overwhelming fear when the Hanafi leader came and made grisly threats to individuals and then to the entire group.

After release, Shirley had great trouble returning to the building to work. She also had trouble sleeping and dreamed of the takeover and the bloodied faces and clothes. She cried frequently and suffered from persistent depression and anxiety.

"In the group sessions, Shirley was able to review, along with her co-hostages, the events of the takeover and siege. All were encouraged to speak freely about what had occurred, something they had not been able to do while hostages. Shirley was able to give and get feedback about how she and others had really appeared—how brave, how foolish, how cowardly, and so forth. What were others thinking and feeling then and now? How unique were her postsiege symptoms?

"Shirley's aftereffects were not uncommon among the hostages. She reported that the content and availability of the group sessions were extremely helpful to her. She did not feel alone. There was a forum for the expression of her difficulties and a format for dealing with them. It was especially comforting to find the commonality of what she had feared were unique and embarrassing symptoms." (Sank, 1979, p. 337)

The response of the other hostages, too, was highly positive. They appreciated having been sought out and followed professionally whether they seemed to need it or not.

Three months later there was an additional series of sessions for these who still felt the need of help, and approximately a year after the frightening experience an additional session was conducted.

Those in charge of the program felt that offering help through the Health Maintenance Organization and at the scene of the harrowing experience made the help more accessible, less stigmatizing, and more informal than is often the case with psychiatric help. They also felt that their approach had capitalized on a powerful tool in using and strengthening the natural mutual support system of the employees who had suffered the ordeal together and would be continuing to work together in the same building.

availability of comprehensive community mental health centers. These are of particular significance because they mark a distinct trend away from the traditional state mental hospital approach.

In 1963 President Kennedy sent a message to Congress calling for "a bold new approach" to mental disorders. From this message came the Community Mental Health Centers Act providing federal assistance to communities for constructing such centers. Since that time, over 700 mental health centers have been built, providing services for millions of Americans in their home communities.

These centers offer at least five types of services: (a) *inpatient care* for persons requiring short-term hospitalization; (b) *partial hospitalization,* with day hospitalization for patients able to return home evenings, or night hospitalization for patients able to work but in need of futher care; (c) *outpatient therapy* permitting patients to live at home and go about their daily activities; (d) *emergency care,* with psychiatric services around the clock; and (e) *consultation and education* for professionals who have contact with members of the community. These services are provided without discrimination for all those who are in need of them—young or old, well-to-do or unable to pay.

Community mental health centers are highly flexible and have a number of advantages over the facilities previously available. For example, the emotionally disturbed individual need no longer face the choice between being admitted to a distant hospital or receiving no treatment at all. If a disturbance is severe, the individual may be able to enter a center's inpatient facility for short-term hospitalization; if he or she can remain on the job or at home with supportive care, partial hospitalization may be the answer; and if outpatient therapy is sufficient, it is available at the center.

Such community centers usually utilize an interdisciplinary approach to therapy, involving psychologists, psychiatrists, social workers, nurses, and other mental health personnel. They usually have many resources at their disposal, thus enabling the individual to obtain most or all of the needed services at one agency instead of having to travel around the city to several agencies to obtain different kinds of help.

In addition to the federally funded centers, there are now community mental health centers funded by states, by cities, and by private groups. Thus emergency psychological services in the community are now much more widely available than in the past. A survey in 1976 by the National Institute of Mental Health (NIMH, 1976) showed that emergency psychological care was available in 50 percent of general hospitals, 46 percent of local outpatient psychiatric clinics, 29 percent of state and community mental hospitals, and 98 percent of federally funded community mental health clinics.

Free clinics. During the "counterculture" movement in the 1960s, many young people developed serious psychological and physical problems, often associated with the heavy use of psychedelic and other drugs. Yet because of their rejection of the "establishment," they were reluctant to utilize the usual private and public mental health facilities—and usually unable to afford them.

In response to the need for free, anonymous treatment facilities, the Haight-Ashbury and Berkeley Free Clinics were organized and staffed by volunteer physicians, psychiatrists, psychologists, and other health personnel. No charge was made for treatment; no information was given out to parents or relatives; and no questions were asked about drug usage, sexual behavior, or truancy. This freedom from being "hassled" appeared to have a constructive effect on these young people, whose problems were often associated with feeling oppressed by an "uptight" society. Following the establishment of the free clinics in the San Francisco area, many similar clinics, offering a wide range of services, opened throughout the country. While focusing on the needs of young people, these clinics offered assistance to clients of all ages (Smith, 1976).

The growth of the free clinics peaked in the late 1970s, and with the waning of the counterculture movement, fewer alternative agencies have been opened. Many of the free clinics that opened in the 1960s have ceased to operate, while others have become more like traditional mental health facilities, often charging fees for their services and receiving grant support from federal and local government agencies. Some have also developed into agencies

A counselor leads a discussion session for young people with problems in a special mobile van, part of an innovative community service project that makes professional help available in whatever area of the community it is needed. Such health care—aimed at the early detection and prompt treatment of maladaptive behavior in a community setting—is called secondary prevention.

serving special populations, such as the gay community.

During the last decade, a number of community service agencies have developed in which imaginative and concerned members of the community attempt to cope with the interrelated problems of unemployment, delinquency, crime, family disorganization, and mental health. For example, community youth centers have been established for hard-to-reach teenagers in poverty areas. These youth centers have provided such services as job counseling, remedial education, drug programs staffed by former addicts, discussion sessions for dealing with personal problems, leadership training, and home counseling for the young people and their families. Another development has been community coordinating councils concerned with delineating the problems in their areas, improving the quality of family and neighborhood life, fostering community involvement, and developing needed facilities.

Crisis intervention. Crisis intervention emerged as a response to a widespread need for immediate help for individuals and families confronted with especially stressful situations (Golan, 1978; Rosenbaum & Beebe, 1975). Often such people are in a state of acute turmoil and feel overwhelmed and incapable of dealing with the stress by themselves. They do

not have time to wait for the customary initial therapy appointment, nor are they usually in a position to continue therapy over a sustained period. They need immediate assistance.

To meet this need, two modes of therapeutic intervention have been developed: (a) short-term crisis therapy involving face-to-face discussion, and (b) the telephone "hot line." These forms of crisis intervention are usually handled either by professional mental health personnel or by paraprofessionals—lay persons who have been trained for this work (see HIGHLIGHT on page 681).

1. *Short-term crisis therapy.* The sole concern of short-term crisis therapy is the current problem with which the individual or family is having difficulty. Although medical problems may also require emergency treatment, we are concerned here with personal or family problems of an emotional nature. In such crisis situations the therapist is usually very active, helping clarify the problem, suggesting plans of action, providing reassurance, and otherwise giving needed information and support. In essence, the therapist tries to provide as much help as the individual or family will accept.

If the problem involves psychological disturbance in one of the family members, emphasis is usually placed on mobilizing the support of other family members. Often this enables the person to avoid hospitalization and disruption of family life. Crisis intervention may

HIGHLIGHT

The use of paraprofessionals

While many professionals in the field of mental health believe that only thoroughly trained and experienced personnel are qualified to undertake the complex task of therapeutic work with disturbed individuals, it has become increasingly clear that there are simply not enough professional personnel to do the job. As a consequence, there has been increased interest in the possibility of training nonprofessionals in therapy procedures. In addition, programs have been instituted to train and make more effective use of nurses, clergy, police officers, and members of other occupational groups. And, of course, student volunteers provide another reservoir of human resources for community service as paraprofessionals.

Currently there would appear to be three primary nontraditional sources of mental health workers.

1. Community college trainees. Many community colleges offer two-year programs leading to an Associate of Arts (AA) degree with specialized training in some mental health area; some also provide opportunities for upgrading and extending skills of hospital attendants, nurses, police officers, and other personnel already working in this area or related fields. Other colleges and universities have established four-year programs along similar lines: Such programs are roughly analogous to the training of paramedical personnel.

2. Lay volunteers. The use of lay volunteers in working with mental patients goes back many years, but until recently this approach has not been subjected to systematic study and evaluation. The contribution such lay volunteers can make is well illustrated in a study by Katkin and his colleagues (1971). They utilized female volunteers who functioned primarily in supportive roles in providing posthospital therapy for former patients. In comparison with a control group of released patients who had a recidivism rate of 34 percent within a one-year period, the recidivism rate in the experimental group was only 11 percent. Yet the program did not involve extensive training, relying primarily on supervision that the volunteers received while working with the patients. After reporting positive results in a similar training program, Nicoletti and Flater (1975) concluded that the utilization of volunteers is not a panacea but that it is a vital contributor to meeting the increasing demands in the mental health area.

3. Former patients. Perhaps the most creative and exciting work being done in recruiting nonprofessional mental health workers is the use of former mental patients, prison inmates, delinquents, drug addicts, or other previously disturbed individuals to treat those with similar problems. We have also commented on the use of actual patients who are progressing favorably in helping those who are more seriously disturbed and the "pyramid approach" in which less severely mentally retarded individuals assist in the training of more severely retarded ones. These "therapists" often get as much benefit from the process of giving therapy as their trainees do from receiving it.

In essence, we appear to be creating a new breed of therapist who will ordinarily be a resident of the community in which he or she serves, who will have lived much the same kind of life as the clients being served, and who thus will understand and be able to communicate with them through "speaking their language."

also involve bringing other mental health or medical personnel into the treatment picture.

Most individuals and families who come for short-term crisis therapy do not continue in treatment for more than one to six sessions. Often, in fact, they come to the therapist or clinic for an "emotional Band-Aid," and after receiving guidance and support in the initial session do not return.

2. *The "hot line."* As we noted in Chapter 16, the Suicide Prevention Center in Los Angeles opened up a whole new approach to dealing with people undergoing crisis. All major cities in the United States and most smaller ones have developed some form of telephone hot line to help individuals undergoing periods of deep stress. While the threat of suicide is the most dramatic example, the range of problems that people call about is virtually unlimited— from breaking up with someone to being on a bad drug "trip." In addition, there are specific hot lines in various communities for rape victims and for runaways who need assistance.

As with other crisis intervention, the person handling hot-line calls is confronted with the problem of rapidly assessing "what's wrong" and "how bad it is." But even if an accurate assessment is possible and the hot-line therapist does everything within his or her power to help the individual—within the confines imposed by the telephone—a distraught caller may hang up without leaving any name, telephone number, or address. This can be a deeply disturbing experience for the therapist—particularly if, for example, the caller has announced that he or she has just swallowed a lethal dose of sleeping pills. Even in less severe cases, of course, the hot-line therapist may never learn whether the caller's problem has been solved. In other instances, however, the caller may be induced to come in for counseling, making more personal contact possible.

Crisis intervention is probably the most discouraging for the therapist of any treatment approach that we have discussed. Free clinics have reported that their counselors—most of whom are volunteers—tend to "burn out" on counseling after a rather short period of time. Despite the high frustration level of this work, however, crisis intervention therapists fill a crucial need in the mental health field—particularly for the young people who make up the majority of their clients. For thousands of individuals in desperate trouble an invaluable social support is provided by the fact that there is somewhere they can go for immediate help or someone they can call who will listen to their problems and try to help them. Thus the proliferation of crisis intervention services and telephone hot lines is not surprising.

Consultation and education of intermediaries. Often community mental health professionals, such as psychologists and psychiatrists, are able to reach a larger group of individuals in need of psychological attention by working through primary care professionals, such as teachers, social workers, and police personnel.[1] Here the mental health professionals identify a population at risk for the development of psychological disorder and then work with personnel in community institutions who have frequent contact with members of this population. For example, the mental health professional might train police officers in effective ways of intervening in domestic quarrels.

It was originally intended that consultation and education (C & E) would be included among the services offered by all community mental health centers so that part of their impact on problems would be indirect—helping individuals at high risk by increasing the skill and sensitivity of those who come into contact with them in the community and are in a position to make their lives either more stressful or less so. Currently, however, most community mental health centers provide little such service: only about 4 percent of their total effort is devoted to consultation with and education of primary care professionals. Typically, half or more of this involves working with the schools or with other juvenile services; less than a tenth of such consultation time is spent with police and correctional personnel (NIMH, 1978b).

Tertiary prevention

Although crisis intervention services and other secondary prevention measures have been effective in making hospitalization unnecessary in many cases where individuals would formerly have been hospitalized, they have not eliminated the need for hospitalization for some individuals. Tertiary prevention involves prompt and intensive inpatient treatment for patients whose disorders require it.[2] Its double aim is to prevent the disorder from becoming chronic and to enable the individual to return home as soon as possible. It includes assessment, therapy, and provisions for aftercare following release.

In many cases, intensive inpatient treatment can be given in the local community mental health center or in a nearby general hospital. But even where the individual requires treatment in a state mental hospital—which is usually a considerable distance from home—the emphasis is on brief hospitalization and long-range follow-up care.

---

[1]Issues and methods in such consultation and education are discussed in Iscoe, Bloom, and Spielberger (1977); Mann (1978); and Mannino, McLennan, and Shore (1975).

[2]The preponderance of resident patients in mental hospitals today are either schizophrenic (49 percent) or patients with organic brain disorders (about 17 percent). This means only about 34 percent for all other disorders (NIMH, 1978a).

Tertiary prevention involves prompt and intense inpatient therapy for patients whose disorders require it. Such therapy may take the form of recreational therapy (top right) or group therapy (center right) as well as a variety of other forms of treatment that prevent a disorder from becoming chronic and enable an individual to return home as soon as possible. Tertiary prevention also involves provisions for aftercare, such as this halfway house (below right), to help smooth the transition from institutional to community life.

The mental hospital as a therapeutic community. Most of the traditional forms of therapy that we discussed in Chapters 18 and 19 may, of course, be used in the hospital setting. In addition, in more and more mental hospitals these techniques are being supplemented by an effort to make the hospital environment itself a *therapeutic community* (Gunn et al., 1978; Jones, 1953; Paul & Lentz, 1977). That is, all the ongoing activities of the hospital are brought into the total treatment program, and the environment, or *milieu,* is a crucial aspect of the therapy.

Three general therapeutic principles guide the milieu approach to treatment:

a) Staff expectations are clearly communicated to the patient. Both positive and negative feedback are used to encourage appropriate verbalizations and actions on the part of patients.

b) Patients are encouraged to become involved in all decisions made and all actions taken concerning them. A "do-it-yourself attitude" prevails.

c) All patients belong to social groups on the ward. The experience of group cohesiveness gives each patient group support and encouragement, and the related process of group pressure helps exert control over the patient's behavior.

In the therapeutic community, as few restraints as possible are placed on the freedom of the patient, and the orientation is toward encouraging patients to take responsibility for their behavior as well as to participate actively in their treatment programs. Open wards permit patients the use of grounds and premises. Self-government programs give them responsibility for managing their own affairs and those of the ward. All hospital personnel are expected to treat the patients as human beings who merit consideration and courtesy. A number of studies have shown the beneficial effects of such staff attitudes on everyone concerned, staff and patients alike. Some of the psychotherapeutic aids that may be used are described in the HIGHLIGHT on page 685.

The interaction among patients—whether in encounter groups, social events, or other activities—is planned in such a way as to be of therapeutic benefit. In fact, it is becoming apparent that often the most beneficial aspect of the therapeutic community is the interaction among the patients themselves. Differences in social roles and backgrounds may make empathy between staff and patients difficult, but fellow patients have "been there"—they have had similar problems and breakdowns and have experienced the anxiety and humiliation of being labeled "mentally ill" and hospitalized. Thus constructive and helping relationships frequently develop among patients in a warm, encouraging milieu.

Another highly successful method for helping patients take increased responsibility for their own behavior is the use of *social learning programs.* These programs use learning principles and techniques such as token economies to shape more socially acceptable behavior.

A persistent danger with hospitalization is that the mental hospital may become a permanent refuge from the world, either because it offers total escape from the demands of everyday living or because it encourages patients to settle into a chronic "sick role" with a permanent excuse for letting other people take care of them (see HIGHLIGHT on page 686).

To keep the focus on returning the patient to the community and on preventing the disorder from becoming chronic, hospital staffs try to establish close ties with the family and community and to maintain a "recovery-expectant" attitude. Between 70 and 90 percent of patients labeled as psychotic and admitted to mental hospitals can now be discharged within a few weeks, or at most months.

Even where disorders have become chronic, effective treatment methods are being developed.

In one of the most extensive and well-controlled studies of chronic hospitalized patients, Paul and Lentz (1977) compared the relative effectiveness of three treatment approaches:

a) *Milieu therapy,* focused upon structuring the patient's environment to provide clear communications of expectations, and to get the patient involved in the treatment and participating in the therapeutic community through the group process.

b) *A social learning treatment program,* organized around learning principles—using a token economy system, with ward staff as reinforcing agents. Undesirable behavior was not reinforced.

c) *Traditional mental hospital treatments,* in-

Psychotherapeutic aids

There are a number of procedures which have proved of therapeutic value, particularly in hospital settings, but which are usually considered aids or adjuncts to the total therapy program rather than systematic approaches to psychotherapy.

1. Bibliotherapy. Books, pamphlets, and other reading material are often of value in helping the patient realize that others have had similar problems and in increasing his or her self-understanding and motivation to improve. Specific reading materials are usually selected in terms of the needs and intellectual abilities of the patient. Related to this type of therapy is the practice of providing patients or prison inmates with the opportunity to take extension or correspondence courses for credit, and in some instances to attend educational institutions.

2. Audio-visual aids. Videotape playbacks of excerpts from marital, encounter group, and other forms of therapy are often extremely helpful in reviewing and integrating critical events and processes in therapy sessions. In addition, there are many fine films dealing with alcoholism, drug abuse, and other maladaptive patterns that can be utilized in overall treatment programs.

3. Occupational therapy. This may involve constructive work which contributes to the operation of the hospital or clinic, formal training in actual job skills, or the supervision of the patient in a therapeutic role in helping other patients—often with the expectation that the patient may later become a paraprofessional.

4. Social events. Many mental hospitals and clinics have a regular schedule of social events including dances, teas, and "cocktail hours." In some instances patients may operate a closed-circuit television program featuring items of interest to patients. In addition, theatrical productions may be put on by patients. Such social events help the patients feel less isolated and more involved in their environment.

5. Athletics. Regularly scheduled athletic events for patient participation may include softball, basketball, and other team sports. Where facilities are available, a physical conditioning program may be worked out to meet individual needs.

6. Music therapy. Patients are commonly given opportunities to listen to music and to play an instrument—often as part of a musical group. Traditional music and folk singing have been found especially effective in fostering patient interest and group cohesiveness.

7. Art therapy. Painting, clay sculpturing, and other art media may facilitate the communication of feelings and assist in the resolution of inner conflicts, as may creative writing of prose or poetry. In addition, patients commonly experience a sense of pride and accomplishment in their creative productions. In some instances, art exhibitions are held and prizes are awarded, and there may be competition between different hospital or clinic facilities in such exhibitions.

---

cluding chemotherapy, occupational therapy, recreational therapy, activity therapy, and individual or group therapy. No systematic application of milieu therapy or social learning therapy was given to this group.

The treatment project covered a period of six years, with an initial phase of staff training, patient assessment, and base-line recording, a treatment phase, an aftercare phase, and a long (year and a half) follow-up. The changes targeted included resocialization, the learning of new roles, and the reduction or elimination of bizarre behavior. There were 28 chronic schizophrenic patients in each treatment group, matched for age, sex, socioeconomic level, symptoms, and duration of hospitalization.

The results of the study were quite impressive. Both milieu therapy and social learning therapy produced significant improvement in overall function-ing and resulted in more successful hospital releases than the traditional hospital care. However, the behaviorally based social learning program was clearly superior to the more diffuse program of milieu therapy, as evidenced by the fact that over 90 percent of the released patients from the social learning program remained continuously in the community as compared with 70 percent of the released patients who had had milieu therapy. The figure for the traditional treatment program was less than 50 percent.

Provisions for aftercare.   Even where hospitalization has successfully modified maladaptive behavior and the patient has learned needed occupational and interpersonal skills, readjustment in the community following release may still be very difficult. Many studies have shown that in the past up to 45 percent of schizophrenic patients have been readmitted within the first year after their discharge. (One exception to this general rule—the successful adaptation of Israeli mental patients suddenly released during the 1973 Arab-Israeli war, as described in the HIGHLIGHT on page 687—may have been due in part to feelings of unity among Israeli citizens during that national crisis.)

Today, aftercare programs are helping smooth the transition from institutional to community life and are markedly reducing the number of relapses. A recent study showed that only 16 percent of patients who received adequate aftercare were readmitted within the first six months as compared with 37 percent for patients not receiving aftercare. By the end of 5 years, more of both groups had been readmitted, but 47 percent of the aftercare group were still in the community, as compared with only 30 percent of the group who had not received aftercare (Glasscote, 1978).

Aftercare is the responsibility of community mental health facilities and personnel as well as of the community as a whole and, of course, the person's family. Its goal is to ensure that released patients will be helped to make an adequate readjustment and return to full participation in their home and community with a minimum of delay and difficulty.

Sometimes aftercare includes a "halfway" period in which the released patient has a gradual return to the outside world. Thus the last decade has seen a trend toward the establishment of *day hospitals* and *halfway houses* for released patients. Since the founding of the first day hospital in Moscow in 1932, there has been a marked growth in this type of facility in Europe and more recently in the United States (Silverman & Val, 1975).

As we have seen, day hospital facilities in community mental health centers may also be used as alternatives to full hospitalization in the beginning. For example, Penk, Charles, and Van Hoose (1978) showed that partial hospitalization in a day treatment setting resulted in as much improvement as full inpatient psychiatric treatment at a lower cost in a group of patients they studied.

Halfway houses are live-in facilities which serve as a home base for former patients as they make the transition back to adequate

HIGHLIGHT

The hospitalization syndrome

Although individuals differ markedly in their response to hospitalization, some who reside in large mental hospitals over long periods of time tend to adopt a passive role, losing the self-confidence and motivation required for reentering the outside world. In fact, a sizable number of chronic patients become adept at manipulating their symptoms and making themselves appear "sicker" than they are in order to avoid the possibility of discharge from the sheltered hospital environment. This pattern is not ordinarily considered to be the result of hospitalization alone, but rather is attributed to an interaction between the patient and the hospital milieu. The following are some of the steps which have been delineated in the development of this hospitalization syndrome or, as it is also called, *social breakdown syndrome*.

1. Deficiency in self-concept. A precondition for the development of the social breakdown syndrome is the presence of severe self-devaluation and inner confusion concerning social roles and responsibilities.

2. Social labeling. During an acute crisis period in the person's life he or she has probably been labeled *psychotic* and perhaps even *dangerous* and has been sent involuntarily to a mental hospital, legally certified as incompetent and lacking in self-control.

3. Induction into the "sick" role. Admission procedures, diagnostic labeling, and treatment by staff members and other patients all too often initiate the individual into the role of a "sick" person—helpless, passive, and requiring care and external control.

4. Atrophy of work and social skills. In institutions that serve primarily as "storage bins" for the emotionally disturbed, basic work and social skills may atrophy through disuse. And during prolonged hospitalization, technological changes in the outside world may contribute to the obsolescence of the individual's work skills.

5. Development of the chronic sick role. Eventually the confused and devaluated patient becomes a full member of the sick community in which passive dependence and "crazy" behavior are not only common but expected.

The staffs of large mental hospitals today are more aware of the pitfalls of chronicity than in the past and are introducing various corrective procedures for remotivation and resocialization, as well as stressing a recovery-expectant attitude.

functioning in the community. Typically halfway houses are run not by professional mental health personnel, but by the residents themselves.

In a pilot program with a group of newly released mental patients, Fairweather and his colleagues (1969) demonstrated that these patients could function in the community in a patient-run halfway house. Initially, a member of the research staff coordinated the daily operations of the lodge, but he was shortly replaced by a lay person. The patients were given full responsibility for operating the lodge, for regulating each other's behavior, for earning money, and for purchasing and preparing food.

Forty months after their discharge, a comparison was made of these ex-patients and a comparable group of 75 patients who had been discharged at the same time but had not had the halfway house experience. Whereas most members of the halfway house were able to hold income-producing jobs, to manage their daily lives, and to adjust in the outside world, the majority of those who had not had the halfway house experience were unable to adjust to life on the outside and required rehospitalization.

Similar halfway houses have been established for alcoholics and drug addicts and other persons attempting to make an adjustment in the community after institutionalization. Such houses may be said to be specialized in the sense that all residents share similar backgrounds and problems, and this seems to contribute to their effectiveness.

One of the chief problems of halfway houses is that of gaining the acceptance and support of community residents. As Denner (1974) has pointed out, this requires educational and other social measures directed toward increasing community understanding, acceptance, and tolerance of troubled people who may differ somewhat from community norms. That such an approach is not necessarily unrealistic, however, is demonstrated in the example of Gheel—"the town that cares"—which we discussed in Chapter 2 (Aring, 1975).

The trend toward deinstitutionalization.

The introduction of the major antipsychotic and antidepressant drugs, as we have seen, has made it possible for many patients to be released from mental hospitals even though they are still psychotic. These patients can often get along outside the hospital indefinitely as long as they continue their medication. Having daily decisions to make and being responsi-

HIGHLIGHT

Adjustment of hospitalized patients following sudden discharge

What would happen to chronic hospitalized psychiatric patients if with little notice they were suddenly released into the community?

In the early hours of the Yom Kippur war in Israel in 1973, all psychiatric patients were released from hospitals in order to make room for war casualties being received from the front, only a few miles away. Thirty of these patients (about 90 percent), half of whom were schizophrenic, were later followed up by Merbaum and Hefez (1975).

Contrary to what one might expect, these investigators found that the patients had adjusted extremely well to the community. Some had even gotten actively involved in the war effort, transporting materials or doing clerical tasks. Psychiatric interviews ten months after their release showed that most of them were not experiencing psychological deterioration, and that only 4 had been rehospitalized. Of the others, only 8 were taking tranquilizers or antidepressant medication, and very few were receiving psychological therapy.

ble for their day-to-day routines can prevent such individuals from developing the passivity and dependence that the hospital environment encourages, and recovery may be speeded.

Unfortunately, however, many of these individuals have no families or meaningful roles to return to. Thus the custom has developed of releasing many patients to "board-and-care" facilities—hotels or boarding houses where they can have their own rooms and lead independent lives. The community mental health centers are responsible for keeping in touch with them to monitor their condition, see that they continue their medication, and offer them group therapy or other psychological support as needed. Thus the greater availability of community mental health centers, as well as the new drugs, is given credit for the trend toward deinstitutionalization in recent years (Klerman, 1979).

Has this large-scale return of patients to the community resulted in better treatment for them than that formerly provided in institutions? After interviewing 101 patients in a board-and-care facility, Lamb (1979) concluded that they were not receiving better treatment but had

"come to what one might call adaptation by decompression. They have found a place of asylum from life's pressures but at the same time a place where there is support, structure, and some treatment, especially in the form of psychotropic medications. For a large proportion of long-term psychiatric patients, the board-and-care home has not only replaced but taken over the functions of the state hospital." (p. 132)

Recent controversy, however, suggests that many new problems have been created and that many chronic patients may be no better off in their new surroundings. There is some evidence that former patients living in the community are generally not receiving sufficient care and that many require readmission to the hospital (Ozarin, 1976). Summers (1979), in a study of ex-patients in an urban aftercare facility, found a "group of chronically unemployed, socially isolated patients who had been hospitalized numerous times, and whose problems derived more from empty lives and inability to function than from psychopathological symptoms" (p. 199). He concluded that aftercare clinics are generally unprepared to meet the needs of such patients and questioned programs that continue to discharge patients who will shortly require rehospitalization.

Organized efforts for mental health

With increasing public awareness of the magnitude and severity of our contemporary mental health problem, a large number of governmental, professional, and lay organizations have joined in a concerted attack on mental disorders—a broad-based attack directed toward better understanding, more effective treatment, and long-range prevention. This trend is apparent not only in our society but also in many other countries. And international as well as national and local organizations and measures are involved.

Governmental, professional, and lay organizations in the United States

Traditionally, dealing with mental disorders has been primarily the responsibility of state and local agencies. During World War II, however, the extent of mental disorders in the United States was brought to public attention when a large number of young men—2 out of every 7 recruits—were rejected for military service for psychiatric reasons. This discovery led to a variety of organized measures for coping with the mental health problem.

The government and mental health. Aware of the need for more research, training, and services in the field of mental health, Congress in 1946 passed its first comprehensive mental health bill, the National Mental Health Act, which laid the basis for the federal government's present mental health program.

The 1946 bill provided for the establishment of a National Institute of Mental Health (NIMH) in or near Washington, D.C., to serve as a central research and training center and headquarters for the administration of a grant-in-aid program. The grant-in-aid feature was designed to foster research and training elsewhere in the nation and to help state and local communities expand and improve their own mental health services. New powers were conferred on NIMH in 1956, when Congress, under Title V of the Health Amendments Act, authorized the Institute to provide "mental health project grants" for experimental studies, pilot projects, surveys, and general research having to do with the understanding, assessment, treatment, and aftercare of mental disorders.

As a result of organizational changes since then, NIMH is now one of three Institutes under the Alcoholism, Drug Abuse, and Mental Health Administration, a division of the Public Health Service. NIMH (a) conducts and supports research on the biological, psychosocial, and sociocultural aspects of mental disorders; (b) supports the training of professional and paraprofessional personnel in the mental health field; (c) assists communities in planning, establishing, and maintaining more effective mental health programs; and (d) provides information on mental health to the public and to the scientific community. Its two companion institutes—the National Institute on Alcohol Abuse and Alcoholism and the National Institute on Drug Abuse (NIDA)—perform comparable functions in their respective fields. They are centralized in their administration, whereas much of the work of NIMH is carried out in ten regional offices. As we have seen, a central concept in the federal government's mental health program is that of comprehensive care in the community.

Although the federal government provides leadership and financial aid, the states and localities actually plan and run most NIMH programs. In addition, the states establish, maintain, and supervise their own mental hospitals and clinics. A number of states have also pioneered, through their own legislation, in the development of community mental health centers, rehabilitation services in the community for ex-patients, and facilities for dealing with alcoholism, drug abuse, and other special mental health problems. Thus through the combination of federal grants and state funds, a wide range of vital mental health facilities and activities has been made possible, including financing of badly needed basic research in the field of mental disorders.

Professional organizations and mental health.

There are a number of professional organizations in the mental health field. Some of the most influential of these are listed in the HIGHLIGHT on pages 690–691.

One of the most important functions of these organizations is to set and maintain high professional and ethical standards within their special areas. This function may include: (a) establishing and reviewing training qualifications for professional and paraprofessional personnel; (b) setting standards and procedures for accreditation of undergraduate and graduate training programs; (c) setting standards for accreditation of clinic, hospital, or other service operations and carrying out inspections to

see that the standards are followed; and (d) investigating reported cases of unethical or unprofessional conduct, and taking disciplinary action where necessary.

A second key function of these professional organizations involves communication and information exchange within their fields via meetings, symposia, workshops, refresher courses, the publication of professional and scientific journals, and related activities. In addition, all such organizations sponsor programs of public education as a means of advancing the interests of their professions, drawing attention to mental health needs, and attracting students to careers in their professional fields.

A third key function of professional organizations, which is receiving increasing attention, is that of applying their insights and methods to contemporary social problems. In the 1970s we saw the growing involvement of professional mental health organizations in social problems and even international issues. In 1974, for example, the Board of Trustees of the American Psychiatric Association endorsed the United Nations program for a decade of action to combat racism and racial discrimination and directed that efforts be made to implement this program as it applies to conditions in the United States. In addition, it has tried to call world attention to the use of psychiatric treatment for political dissidents in the Soviet Union. The major professional organizations have also taken strong stands on equal opportunities for women and on the provision of adequate health services for all people.

Composed as they are of qualified personnel, professional mental health organizations are in a unique position to serve as consultants on mental health problems and programs not only on the national level but also on state and local levels. Increasingly, they are establishing a closer liaison with one another as well as with both governmental and voluntary agencies concerned with mental health.

Role of voluntary mental health organizations and agencies.

While professional mental health personnel and organizations can give expert technical advice in regard to mental health needs and programs, real progress in helping plan and implement these programs must come from an informed and concerned

Professional organizations concerned with mental health

American Psychological Association (APA)

An association of professionally trained psychologists. Its purpose is to advance psychology as a science, as a profession, and as a means of promoting human welfare. It has over 30 divisions concerned with various special areas within psychology, and it establishes and monitors standards for the training and practice of psychologists in mental health work.

American Psychiatric Association (APA)

An association of physicians with training in psychiatry. Its purpose is to further the study of the nature, treatment, and prevention of mental disorders; to help set, improve, and maintain standards of practice and service in mental hospitals, clinics, general hospital psychiatric units, and institutions for the mentally retarded; to further psychiatric research and education; and to foster enlightened views with regard to the social and legal aspects of psychopathology and the role of psychiatry in fostering human welfare.

American Medical Association (AMA)

An association of physicians who are members of constituent state medical associations. In addition to its myriad other functions, it is concerned with mental disorder as a general health problem and with fostering research, education, and legislation to advance comprehensive health efforts in the United States.

American Psychoanalytic Association (APA)

An association of analytically trained psychiatrists. It sets standards for the training of psychoanalysts.

American Sociological Association (ASA)

An association of sociologists, social scientists, and other professional persons interested in research, teaching, and applications of sociology. Its sections on Social Psychology, Medical Sociology, and Criminology have special pertinence to mental health.

National Association of Social Workers (NASW)

An association of professionally trained social workers, organized to promote the quality and effectiveness of social work and to foster mental health. It establishes and monitors standards for training and practice, encourages research, and interprets the role of social work in the community.

American Nurses Association (ANA) and National League for Nursing (NLN)

An association of registered nurses concerned with high standards of professional practice (ANA). Two of its clinical committee groups (one on Psychiatric Nursing Practice and one on Maternal and Child Health Nursing) have special mental health concerns. A Coordinating Council unites its program with that of the National League for Nursing, a voluntary organization of professional, semi-professional, and lay persons and of institutions and organizations; the National League is the principal standard-setting group in the nursing field.

American Occupational Therapy Association (AOTA)

A society of registered occupational therapists administering medically supervised activities to physically or mentally ill persons. It maintains standards of education and training, makes surveys and recommendations on request, and works with its state associations in the preparation and certification of occupational therapy volunteer assistants.

National Rehabilitation Association (NRA)	An association of physicians, counselors, therapists, and others (including organizations) concerned with rehabilitation of the physically and mentally handicapped. Reviews existing services and makes recommendations for improved rehabilitation programs.
American Orthopsychiatric Association (AOA)	An organization of psychiatrists, psychologists, social workers, sociologists, and members of other disciplines working in a collaborative approach to the study and treatment of human behavior, primarily in clinical settings. Its focus is on the problems of children. The AOA encourages research and is directly concerned with fostering human welfare.
National Council for Family Relations (NCFR)	Composed primarily of and directed toward practitioners serving couples and families through counseling, therapy, education, and community service. The NCFR fosters research and the application of its findings to practice.
American Association on Mental Deficiency (AAMD)	An interdisciplinary association of physicians, educators, administrators, social workers, psychologists, psychiatrists, and others interested in assisting the mentally retarded. It works with the American Psychiatric Association in setting standards for hospitals and schools for the mentally retarded.
Council for Exceptional Children (CEC)	Made up largely of professional workers in fields dealing with mentally retarded, physically handicapped, and emotionally disturbed children. It fosters research and its applications, education, and social legislation relating to exceptional children.
Group for the Advancement of Psychiatry (GAP)	An invitational association of limited membership (approximately 185 psychiatrists at any one time). Members are organized into small committees for the purpose of studying and reporting on various aspects of psychiatry and on the applications of current knowledge. Its influential, action-directed reports are often developed through consultation and collaboration with experts from many other disciplines.
American Association for the Advancement of Science (AAAS)	Composed of scientists from many disciplines. Its objectives include furthering the work and mutual cooperation of scientists, improving the effectiveness of science and its contribution to human welfare, and increasing understanding and appreciation of the importance and promise of scientific methods in human progress.
Society for Research in Child Development (SRCD)	An association of psychologists whose aim is to study normal processes of child development. Members are concerned with issues related to improving the welfare of children as well as with encouraging scientific research on developmental processes.

Most of these organizations sponsor national conventions, workshops, symposia, and public educational programs and publish journals in their respective areas. They are also concerned with broad social problems as well as with the special problems in their professional areas.

citizenry. In fact, it has been repeatedly stated that it has been nonprofessionals who have blazed the trail in the mental health field.

Prominent among the many voluntary mental health agencies is the National Association for Mental Health (NAMH). This organization was founded in 1950 by the merger of the National Committee for Mental Hygiene, the National Mental Health Foundation, and the Psychiatric Foundation; and it was further expanded in 1962 by amalgamation with the National Organization for Mentally Ill Children. Through its national governing body and some 1000 local affiliates, the NAMH works for the improvement of services in community clinics and mental hospitals; it helps recruit, train, and place volunteers for service in treatment and aftercare programs; and it works for enlightened mental health legislation and provision of needed facilities and personnel. It also carries on special educational programs aimed at fostering positive mental health and helping people understand mental disorders.

In addition, the National Association for Mental Health has been actively involved in many court decisions affecting patient rights (NAMH, 1979). In several cases the NAMH has sponsored litigation or served as amicus curiae (friend of the court) in efforts to establish the rights of mental patients to treatment, freedom from custodial confinement, freedom to live in the community, and protection of their confidentiality (see HIGHLIGHT on page 693).

With a program and organization similar to that of the NAMH, the National Association for Retarded Children (NARC) works to reduce the incidence of mental retardation, to seek community and residential treatment centers and services for the retarded, and to carry on a program of education aimed at better public understanding of retarded individuals and greater support for legislation on their behalf. The NARC also fosters scientific research into mental retardation, the recruitment and training of volunteer workers, and programs of community action. On the local level, it is especially interested in forming groups of parents of retarded children in order to help such parents better understand, accept, and deal with their children's limited capabilities.

These and other voluntary health organizations, such as Alcoholics Anonymous, are particularly American in their development of extensive programs of research, service, and training of volunteers financed by donations from interested individuals and foundations. To succeed in their objectives, of course, they need the backing of a wide constituency of knowledgeable and involved citizens.

International efforts for mental health

Mental health is a major problem not only in the United States but in the rest of the world as well. Indeed, many of the unfavorable conditions in this country with regard to the causes and treatment of mental disorders are greatly magnified in poorer countries and countries with repressive governments. According to the World Health Organization (WHO, 1978a), 40 million people in the world suffer from severe mental illness, over 80 million from alcohol and drug addiction, mental retardation, and organic brain disorders, and another 80 million suffer from other mental disorders, such as the neuroses. The severity of the world mental health problem is shown in the estimates that mental disorders affect more than 200 million people worldwide.

It was the knowledge of this great problem that served to bring about the formation of several international organizations at the end of World War II. We shall briefly review here the World Health Organization and the United Nations Educational, Scientific, and Cultural Organization (both UN agencies), as well as the World Federation for Mental Health.

The World Health Organization (WHO). The World Health Organization defines health as not simply absence of disease but a positive state of physical, mental, and social well-being. From the first, it has been keenly aware of the close interrelationships between physical, psychosocial, and sociocultural factors—such as the influence of rapid change and social disruption on both physical and mental health; the impossibility of major progress toward mental health in societies where a large proportion of the population suffer from malnutrition, parasites, and disease; and the frequent psychological and cultural barriers to successful programs in family planning and public health.

Formed after World War II as part of the UN system, WHO's earliest focus was on physical

Patient advocacy: important court decisions in establishing patient rights

Several important court decisions in recent years have helped establish certain basic rights for individuals suffering from mental disorders.

Right to treatment
In 1972 a U.S. District Court in Alabama made a landmark decision in the case of *Wyatt* v. *Stickney*. The ruling held that a mentally ill or mentally retarded individual had a right to receive treatment. Since the decision, the State of Alabama has increased its budget for treatment of mental health and mental retardation by 300 percent.

Freedom from custodial confinement
In 1975 the U.S. Supreme Court upheld the principle that patients have a right to freedom from custodial confinement if they are not dangerous to themselves or others and if they can safely survive outside of custody. In the *Donaldson* v. *O'Connor* decision, the defendants were required to pay Donaldson $10,000 for having kept him in custody without providing treatment.

Right to compensation for work
In 1973 a U.S. District Court ruled in the case of *Souder* v. *Brennan* (Secretary of Labor) that a patient in a nonfederal mental institution who performed work must be paid according to the Fair Labor Standards Act. Although a 1976 Supreme Court ruling nullified the part of the lower court's decision dealing with state hospitals, the ruling still

applies to mentally ill and mentally retarded patients in private facilities.

Right to legal counsel at commitment hearings
The State Supreme Court in Wisconsin decided in 1976 in the case of *Memmel* v. *Mundy* that an individual had the right to legal counsel during the commitment process.

Right to live in a community
In 1974, the U.S. District Court decided, in the case of *Stoner* v. *Miller*, that released state mental hospital patients had a right to live in "adult homes" in the community.

Right to refuse treatment
Several court decisions have provided rulings and some states have enacted legislation permitting patients to refuse certain treatments, such as electroconvulsive therapy and psychosurgery.

Right to less restrictive treatment
In 1975 a U.S. District Court issued a landmark decision in the case of *Dixon* v. *Weinberger*. The ruling establishes the right of individuals to receive treatment in less restrictive facilities than mental institutions.

Based on Bernard (1979), National Association for Mental Health (1979), and Mental Health Law Project (1976).

---

diseases, and through its efforts dramatic progress has been made toward the conquest of ancient scourges like smallpox and malaria. Over the years, however, mental health has become an increasing concern of the member countries, and they not only have requested help in prevention and control of mental disorders and the psychosocial problems related to them but also have sought help in ensuring the healthy psychosocial development of their children, in preserving the protective aspects of traditional cultural values and family relationships in the face of rapid industrialization, and in fostering attitudes and forms of community participation that will enable public health programs to succeed. WHO's present mental health program thus integrates

mental health concerns with the broad problems of overall health and socioeconomic development member countries currently face. (WHO, 1978a).

WHO has headquarters in Geneva and regional offices for Africa, the Americas, Southeast Asia, Europe, the Eastern Mediterranean, and the Western Pacific. Hence its activities extend into areas with diverse physical environments, types of social organization, and mental health facilities. It enters a country only on invitation, helping identify the basic health needs of each country and working with the local authorities to plan and carry out the most useful and appropriate programs. Where possible, it strives to make its services available over a period of several years to ensure continuity and success for the programs that are undertaken.

Another important contribution of WHO has been its International Classification of Diseases, which enables clinicians and researchers in different countries to use a uniform set of diagnostic categories (WHO, 1978b). The American Psychiatric Association's latest classification, DSM-III, has been coordinated with the current revision of the WHO classification (ICD-9).

The United Nations Educational, Scientific, and Cultural Organization (UNESCO).
The constitution of UNESCO (1945) contains a statement that seems to strike many people with the force of a spiritual conversion: "Since wars begin in the minds of men, it is in the minds of men that the defenses of peace must be constructed." By promoting collaboration among nations through educational, cultural, and scientific channels, UNESCO attempts to foster peace and respect for human rights, with fundamental freedoms for all.

Over 135 UN member countries belong to UNESCO. In general, UNESCO programs are divided into three main areas: (a) *international intellectual cooperation* aimed at the communication of information and the exchange of ideas among member countries; (b) *operational assistance* through the provision of specialists to advise governments in the planning of educational and other projects and to provide day-by-day assistance in their implementation; and (c) *promotion of peace* through increased knowledge of international problems, emphasis on human rights, and mutual understanding among peoples. On many problems UNESCO works cooperatively with other agencies—sometimes as instigator or catalyst, sometimes as consultant, sometimes as one of several cooperating groups. For example, the use of satellites for educational and mental health purposes was initially arranged by UNESCO.

UNESCO is also working to provide better opportunities for young people to participate actively in the social, economic, and cultural life of their own countries and of the world. It helps in the training of scientists and technicians, as well as in the development of scientific research in developing countries. Thus on many fronts UNESCO is working for the progress of education, culture, and research and for the intellectual and moral unity of humankind in a peaceful world.

The World Federation for Mental Health.
The World Federation for Mental Health was established in 1948 at an international congress of nongovernmental organizations and individuals concerned with mental health. Its purpose is to further cooperation at the international level between governmental and nongovernmental mental health agencies, and its membership now extends to more than 50 countries. The Federation has been granted consultative status by both WHO and UNESCO, and it assists the UN agencies by collecting information on mental health conditions all over the world.

We have now seen something of the maze of local, national, and international measures that are being undertaken in the mental health field. It is the first time in history that mental health problems have been viewed as having discoverable causes and as being amenable to treatment and prevention by scientific means, and it is also the first time that a systematic attack has been waged against these problems on a worldwide level. Many people now believe the statement Julian Huxley (1959) made two decades ago, that through the advances of modern science and technology "human life could gradually be transformed from a competitive struggle against blind fate into a great collective enterprise, consciously undertaken . . . for greater fulfillment through the better realization of human potentialities" (p. 409).

Challenges for the future

Our society has a long way to go before the dreams of a better world are realized. Many question whether the United States or any other technologically advanced nation can achieve mental health for the majority of its citizens in our time. Racism, poverty, and other social problems that contribute to mental disorder sometimes seem unsurmountable.

What happens in the rest of the world affects us also, both directly and indirectly. Worldwide economic instability and shortages and the possibilities of nuclear war and even of destruction of the life-support system of our planet breed widespread anxiety about the future, and our military defenses against perceived threats from other parts of the world absorb vast funds and energy that otherwise might be turned to meeting human and social needs here and elsewhere in the world.

The need for planning

It seems imperative that more effective planning be done at community, national, and international levels before it is too late. Many challenges must be met if we are to create a better world for ourselves and future generations. Without slackening our efforts to meet needs at home, we shall probably find it increasingly essential to participate in international measures toward reducing group tensions and promoting mental health and a better world for people everywhere. At the same time, we can expect that measures undertaken to reduce international conflict and improve the general condition of humankind will make their contribution to our own nation's social progress and mental health. But both kinds of measures will require understanding and moral commitment from concerned citizens.

Unfortunately, some people, including many individuals in positions of power, consider the cost of such social programs too high and their outcomes too remote. Elected officials need to show results before the next election and often feel they cannot afford to work for long-term goals. The 1970s closed on a pessimistic note—a widespread concern about inflation, economic instability, and energy shortages and a generally conservative mood. A sign of this new conservatism was the great taxpayers' revolt in which voters supported extreme tax cuts in state and local funds in spite of appeals that such measures might close off important ongoing social programs. Concerned individuals and organizations may have to increase their efforts if the great gain in the mental health movement made during the last thirty years is to keep its momentum.

To some people in our society, social planning seems contrary to the American way of life and the ideal of individual freedom. Yet as the NIMH (1969) has emphasized:

"Social planning does not imply authoritarian control; a planned society does not mean a closed society. Techniques are now emerging to guarantee that planning will enhance, not diminish, the power and influence of individuals in controlling their destinies and achieving their personal goals. 'Advocacy planning' and 'participatory democracy' provide for the inclusion of all interested groups and individuals in the planning and decision-making process." (p. 117)

In fact, to be planless in our complex, interdependent, and rapidly changing world is to invite—and perhaps ensure—disaster.

The enduring problem of values

We are all concerned not only with *whether* the human race will survive but also with *how*—with the quality of life that will be possible. It will not be enough to preserve human life for a future world of "unsanity" or lockstep regimentation or bare subsistence. For many years we have been creating an increasing part of our own future but often without realizing it and foreseeing only some of the results of our actions. As we increasingly take the future consciously into our own hands, it is critical that we consider the entire range of options open to us and make wise value judgments in choosing among the alternatives.

Why these goals rather than other goals? Why these means rather than other means? The answers to these questions involve value judgments. Although science can specify the conditions that will foster passivity, creativity, or other personality traits, it is our values that determine the kind of children we want to rear, the kind of lives we want to live, and the type of world we want to live in.

Where we lack values for making choices, are confused about our values, or put our faith in false values, the results are likely to be destructive and maladaptive. Although it would be both arrogant and premature to attempt a formulation of universal values, it would appear that we are likely to have to come to grips with the following tentative value assumptions as minimal essentials:

1. A belief in the worth of the individual and of human survival
2. A belief that personal growth and social progress are possible and worthwhile
3. A belief in equal justice and in the desirability of opportunities for all persons to fulfill their potentialities
4. A belief in the value of the "truth" that we try to approach by means of scientific inquiry
5. A belief in the maxim "love one another" and other basic ethical tenets of the world's religious philosophies
6. A belief in the right and responsibility of all people to have a voice in decisions that will affect their lives
7. A belief in humankind as a functional part of the universe with potentialities for evolution that can be fulfilled
8. A belief in the responsibility of all individuals for carrying forward the progress made by preceding generations and for contributing to the creation of a good future for all

These value assumptions are not universally accepted, and, being assumptions, they are not subject to proof. They are suggested simply as guidelines that may merit consideration by those who are seeking a new ethic that can match the impact of science on society. If we have no faith in the worth or growth potential of the individual, in the possibility or value of greater social justice, or in the potentiality of a meaningful role in the universe for humankind, then these value assumptions will be useless. However, people do not easily adopt the doctrine of despair so vividly portrayed by Shakespeare, that life is

"a tale
Told by an idiot, full of sound and fury,
Signifying nothing." (*Macbeth*, Act V, Scene v)

As we embark upon the great adventure of shaping the future, let us hope that we will learn to change what needs to be changed while preserving what is valid of our heritage from the past. For it has taken many thousands of years to achieve the imperfect level of freedom and opportunity that we have reached in our society. As Haskins (1968) has pointed

out, we must be continually aware of the danger that "in embracing new and experimental courses on myriad fronts of movement with the ardor that we must, we do not at the same time discard long-tested values and long-tried adaptive courses, which, if they are lost, will only have, one day, to be rewon—and probably at enormous cost."

This book can go no further toward a value orientation. Beyond this point, we will each be confronted with the challenge of exploring the world of values and making our own value judgments and choices.

The individual's contribution

> "Each man can make a difference, and each man should try."
> John F. Kennedy

When students become aware of the tremendous scope of the mental health problem both nationally and internationally and the woefully inadequate facilities for coping with it, they often ask, "What can I do?" This is not an idle question, for much of the progress that has been achieved in the treatment of mental disorders has resulted from the work of concerned citizens. Thus it seems appropriate to suggest a few of the lines of action interested students can profitably take.

Many opportunities in mental health work are open to trained personnel, both professional and paraprofessional. Social work, clinical psychology, psychiatry, and other mental health occupations are rewarding in terms of personal fulfillment. And as we have seen, there is a shortage of trained personnel in the mental health field. In addition, there are many occupations, ranging from law enforcement to teaching and the ministry, that can and do play key roles in the mental health and well-being of many people. Training in all these fields usually offers individuals opportunities to work in community clinics and related facilities, to gain experience in understanding the needs and problems of people in distress, and to become familiar with community resources.

Citizens can find many ways to be of direct service if they are familiar with national and international resources and programs and invest the effort necessary to learn about their

Volunteer workers like this young college student can do a great deal to augment the programs of mental hospitals and other institutions. One important function is simply to provide companionship and social interaction for patients who might otherwise have only minimal contact with overworked staff members.

community's special needs and problems. Whatever their roles in life—student, teacher, police officer, lawyer, homemaker, business executive, or trade unionist—their interests are directly at stake. For although the mental health of a nation may be manifested in many ways—in its purposes, courage, moral responsibility, scientific and cultural achievements, and quality of daily life—its health and resources derive ultimately from the individuals within it. In a participatory democracy, it is they who plan and implement its goals.

Besides accepting some measure of responsibility for the mental health of others through the quality of one's own interpersonal relationships, there are several other constructive courses of action open to each citizen, including: (a) serving as a volunteer in a mental hospital, community mental health center, or service organization; (b) supporting realistic measures for ensuring comprehensive health services for all age groups; and (c) working toward improved public education, responsible government, the alleviation of group prejudice, and the establishment of a more sane and harmonious world.

All of us are concerned with mental health for personal as well as altruistic reasons, for we want to overcome the harassing problems of contemporary living and find our share of happiness in a meaningful and fulfilling life. To do so, we may sometimes need the courage to admit that our problems are too much for us. When existence seems futile or the going becomes too difficult, it may help to remind ourselves of the following basic facts, which have been emphasized in the course of the present text.

1. From time to time each of us has serious difficulties in coping with the problems of living.

2. During such crisis periods, we may need psychological and related assistance.

3. Such difficulties are not a disgrace; they can happen to anyone if the stress is sufficiently severe.

4. The early detection and correction of maladaptive behavior is of great importance in preventing the development of more severe or chronic conditions.

5. Preventive measures—primary, secondary, and tertiary—are the most effective long-range approach to the solution of both individual and group mental health problems.

To recognize these facts is essential because statistics show that almost all of us will at some time in our lives have to deal with severely maladaptive behavior or mental disorder in ourselves or those close to us. The interdependence among us and the loss to us all, individually and collectively, when any one of us fails to achieve his or her potential are eloquently expressed in the famous lines of John Donne (1624):

"No man is an island, entire of itself; every man is a piece of the continent, a part of the main. If a clod be washed away by the sea, Europe is less, as well as if a promontory were, as well as if a manor of thy friends or of thine own were: any man's death diminishes me, because I am involved in mankind, and therefore never send to know for whom the bell tolls; it tolls for thee."

Appendix:
Systems used in
the classification of
mental disorders

DSM/II classification

DSM/III classification

Classification of mental disorders (Rutter, Shaffer, & Sturge, n.d.)

DSM/II CLASSIFICATION

The DSM-II, in use since 1968, is now superseded by DSM-III. It is printed here for purposes of comparison.

From the *Diagnostic and statistical manual of mental disorders, Second Edition (DSM-II).* Washington, D.C.: American Psychiatric Association, 1968. Reprinted by permission of the American Psychiatric Association.

MENTAL RETARDATION
Borderline
Mild
Moderate
Severe
Profound
Unspecified
  With each: Following or associated with
Infection or intoxication
Trauma or physical agent
Disorders of metabolism, growth or nutrition
Gross brain disease (postnatal)
Unknown prenatal influence
Chromosomal abnormality
Prematurity
Major psychiatric disorder
Psycho-social (environmental) deprivation
Other condition

ORGANIC BRAIN SYNDROMES (OBS)
A PSYCHOSES
Senile and pre-senile dementia
Senile dementia
Pre-senile dementia

Alcoholic psychosis
Delirium tremens
Korsakov's psychosis
Other alcoholic hallucinosis
Alcohol paranoid state
Acute alcohol intoxication
Alcoholic deterioration
Pathological intoxication
Other alcoholic psychosis

Psychosis associated with intracranial infection
General paralysis
Syphilis of central nervous system
Epidemic encephalitis
Other and unspecified encephalitis
Other intracranial infection

Psychosis associated with other cerebral condition
Cerebral arteriosclerosis
Other cerebrovascular disturbance
Epilepsy
Intracranial neoplasm
Degenerative disease of the CNS
Brain trauma
Other cerebral condition

Psychosis associated with other physical condition
Endocrine disorder
Metabolic or nutritional disorder
Systemic infection
Drug or poison intoxication (other than alcohol)
Childbirth
Other and unspecified physical condition

B NONPSYCHOTIC OBS
Intracranial infection
Alcohol (simple drunkenness)
Other drug, poison, or systemic intoxication
Brain trauma
Circulatory disturbance
Epilepsy
Disturbance of metabolism, growth or nutrition
Senile or pre-senile brain disease
Intracranial neoplasm
Degenerative disease of the CNS
Other physical condition

PSYCHOSES NOT ATTRIBUTED TO PHYSICAL CONDITIONS LISTED PREVIOUSLY
Schizophrenia
Simple
Hebephrenic
Catatonic
Catatonic type, excited
Catatonic type, withdrawn
Paranoid
Acute schizophrenic episode
Latent
Residual
Schizo-affective
Schizo-affective, excited
Schizo-affective, depressed
Childhood
Chronic undifferentiated
Other schizophrenic

Major affective disorders
Involutional melancholia
Manic-depressive illness, manic
Manic-depressive illness, depressed
Manic-depressive illness, circular
Manic-depressive, circular, manic
Manic-depressive, circular, depressed
Other major affective disorder

Paranoid states
Paranoia
Involutional paranoid state
Other paranoid state

Other psychoses
Psychotic depressive reaction

NEUROSES
Anxiety
Hysterical
Hysterical, conversion type
Hysterical, dissociative type
Phobic
Obsessive compulsive
Depressive
Neurasthenic
Depersonalization
Hypochondriacal
Other neurosis

PERSONALITY DISORDERS AND CERTAIN OTHER NONPSYCHOTIC MENTAL DISORDERS
Personality disorders
Paranoid
Cyclothymic
Schizoid
Explosive
Obsessive compulsive
Hysterical
Asthenic
Antisocial
Passive-aggressive
Inadequate
Other specified types

Sexual deviation
Homosexuality
Fetishism
Pedophilia
Transvestism
Exhibitionism
Voyeurism
Sadism
Masochism
Other sexual deviation

Alcoholism
Episodic excessive drinking
Habitual excessive drinking
Alcohol addiction
Other alcoholism

Drug dependence
Opium, opium alkaloids and their derivatives
Synthetic analgesics with morphinelike effects
Barbiturates
Other hypnotics and sedatives or "tranquilizers"
Cocaine
Cannabis sativa (hashish, marihuana)
Other psycho-stimulants
Hallucinogens
Other drug dependence

PSYCHOPHYSIOLOGIC DISORDERS
Skin
Musculoskeletal
Respiratory
Cardiovascular
Hemic and lymphatic
Gastro-intestinal
Genito-urinary
Endocrine
Organ of special sense
Other type

SPECIAL SYMPTOMS
Speech disturbance
Specific learning disturbance
Tic
Other psychomotor disorder
Disorders of sleep
Feeding disturbance
Enuresis
Encopresis
Cephalalgia
Other special symptom

TRANSIENT SITUATIONAL DISTURBANCES
Adjustment reaction of infancy
Adjustment reaction of childhood
Adjustment reaction of adolescence
Adjustment reaction of adult life
Adjustment reaction of late life

BEHAVIOR DISORDERS OF CHILDHOOD AND ADOLESCENCE
Hyperkinetic reaction
Withdrawing reaction
Overanxious reaction
Runaway reaction
Unsocialized aggressive reaction
Group delinquent reaction
Other reaction

CONDITIONS WITHOUT MANIFEST PSYCHIATRIC DISORDER AND NONSPECIFIC CONDITIONS
Social maladjustment without manifest psychiatric disorder
Marital maladjustment
Social maladjustment
Occupational maladjustment
Dyssocial behavior
Other social maladjustment

Non-specific conditions
Non-specific conditions

No mental disorder
No mental disorder

NONDIAGNOSTIC TERMS FOR ADMINISTRATIVE USE
Diagnosis deferred
Boarder
Experiment only
Other

DSM/III CLASSIFICATION

Reproduced here are Axes I and II of the DSM-III classification. The Axis II categories are in the two colored boxes; all other categories are on Axis I.

DISORDERS USUALLY FIRST EVIDENT IN INFANCY, CHILDHOOD, OR ADOLESCENCE
Mental retardation
Mild mental retardation
Moderate mental retardation
Severe mental retardation
Profound mental retardation
Unspecified mental retardation

Attention deficit disorder
with hyperactivity
without hyperactivity
residual type

Conduct disorder
undersocialized, aggressive
undersocialized, nonaggressive
socialized, aggressive
socialized, nonaggressive
atypical

Anxiety disorders of childhood or adolescence
Separation anxiety disorder
Avoidant disorder of childhood or adolescence
Overanxious disorder

Other disorders of infancy, childhood, or adolescence
Reactive attachment disorder of infancy
Schizoid disorder of childhood or adolescence
Elective mutism
Oppositional disorder
Identity disorder

Eating disorders
Anorexia nervosa
Bulimia
Pica
Rumination disorder of infancy
Atypical eating disorder

Stereotyped movement disorders
Transient tic disorder
Chronic motor tic disorder
Tourette's disorder
Atypical tic disorder
Atypical stereotyped movement disorder

From the *Diagnostic and statistical manual of mental disorders, Third Edition.* Washington, D.C.: American Psychiatric Association, 1980. Reprinted by permission.

Other disorders with physical manifestations
Stuttering
Functional enuresis
Functional encopresis
Sleepwalking disorder
Sleep terror disorder

Pervasive developmental disorders
Infantile autism
Childhood onset pervasive developmental disorder
Atypical

AXIS II
Specific developmental disorders
Developmental reading disorder
Developmental arithmetic disorder
Developmental language disorder
Developmental articulation disorder
Mixed specific developmental disorder
Atypical specific developmental disorder

ORGANIC MENTAL DISORDERS
Section 1. Organic mental disorders in whose etiology or pathophysiological process is listed below.

Senile and presenile dementias arising in the senium and presenium
Primary degenerative dementia, senile onset
with delirium
with delusions
with depression
uncomplicated

Primary degenerative dementia, presenile onset
Multi-infarct dementia

Substance-induced
Alcohol
intoxication
idiosyncratic intoxication
withdrawal
withdrawal delirium
hallucinosis
amnestic disorder
Dementia associated with alcoholism

Barbiturate or similarly acting sedative or hypnotic
intoxication
withdrawal
withdrawal delirium
amnestic disorder

Opioid
intoxication
withdrawal

Cocaine
intoxication

Amphetamine or similarly acting sympathomimetic
intoxication
delirium
delusional disorder
withdrawal

Phencyclidine (PCP) or similarly acting arylcyclohexylamine
intoxication
delirium
mixed organic mental disorder

Hallucinogen
hallucinosis
delusional disorder
affective disorder

Cannabis
intoxication
delusional disorder

Tobacco
withdrawal

Caffeine
intoxication

Other or unspecified substance
intoxication
withdrawal
delirium
dementia
amnestic disorder
delusional disorder
hallucinosis
affective disorder
personality disorder
atypical or mixed organic mental disorder

Section 2. Organic brain syndromes whose etiology or pathophysiological process is either noted as an additional diagnosis or is unknown.
Delirium
Dementia
Amnestic syndrome
Organic delusional syndrome
Organic hallucinosis
Organic affective syndrome
Organic personality syndrome
Atypical or mixed organic brain syndrome

SUBSTANCE USE DISORDERS
Alcohol abuse
Alcohol dependence (Alcoholism)
Barbiturate or similarly acting sedative or hypnotic abuse
Barbiturate or similarly acting sedative or hypnotic dependence
Opioid abuse
Opioid dependence
Cocaine abuse
Amphetamine or similarly acting sympathomimetic abuse
Amphetamine or similarly acting sympathomimetic dependence
Phencyclidine (PCP) or similarly acting arylcyclohexylamine abuse
Hallucinogen abuse
Cannabis abuse
Cannabis dependence
Tobacco dependence
Other, mixed or unspecified substance abuse
Other specified substance dependence
Unspecified substance dependence

Dependence on combination of opioid and other non-alcohol substance
Dependence on combination of substances, excluding opioids and alcohol

SCHIZOPHRENIC DISORDERS
Disorganized
Catatonic
Paranoid
Undifferentiated
Residual

PARANOID DISORDERS
Paranoia
Shared paranoid disorder
Acute paranoid disorder
Atypical paranoid disorder

PSYCHOTIC DISORDERS NOT ELSEWHERE CLASSIFIED
Schizophreniform disorder
Brief reactive psychosis
Schizoaffective disorder
Atypical psychosis

NEUROTIC DISORDERS
These are included in Affective, Anxiety, Somatoform, Dissociative, and Psychosexual Disorders. In order to facilitate the identification of the categories that in DSM-II were grouped together in the class of Neuroses, the DSM-II terms are included separately in parentheses after the corresponding DSM-III categories.

AFFECTIVE DISORDERS
Major affective disorders
Bipolar disorder
  mixed
  manic
  depressed
Major depression
  single episode
  recurrent

Other specific affective disorders
Cyclothymic disorder
Dysthymic disorder *(Depressive neurosis)*

Atypical Affective Disorders
Atypical bipolar disorder
Atypical depression

ANXIETY DISORDERS
Phobic disorders *(Phobic neuroses)*
Agoraphobia with panic attacks
Agoraphobia without panic attacks
Social phobia
Simple phobia

Anxiety states *(Anxiety neuroses)*
Panic disorder
Generalized anxiety disorder
Obsessive-compulsive disorder
  (Obsessive-compulsive neurosis)

Post-traumatic stress disorder
  acute
  chronic or delayed
Atypical anxiety disorder

SOMATOFORM DISORDERS
Somatization disorder
Conversion disorder *(Hysterical neurosis, conversion type)*
Psychogenic pain disorder
Hypochondriasis *(Hypochondriacal neurosis)*
Atypical somatoform disorder

DISSOCIATIVE DISORDERS *(Hysterical neuroses, dissociative type)*
Psychogenic amnesia
Psychogenic fugue
Multiple personality
Depersonalization disorder
  (Depersonalization neurosis)
Atypical dissociative disorder

PSYCHOSEXUAL DISORDERS
Gender identity disorders
Transsexualism
Gender identity disorder of childhood
Atypical gender identity disorder

Paraphilias
Fetishism
Transvestism
Zoophilia
Pedophilia
Exhibitionism
Voyeurism
Sexual masochism
Sexual sadism
Atypical paraphilia

Psychosexual dysfunctions
Inhibited sexual desire
Inhibited sexual excitement
Inhibited female orgasm
Inhibited male orgasm
Premature ejaculation
Functional dyspareunia
Functional vaginismus
Atypical psychosexual dysfunction

Other psychosexual disorders
Ego-dystonic homosexuality
Psychosexual disorder not elsewhere classified

FACTITIOUS DISORDERS
Factitious disorder with psychological symptoms
Chronic factitious disorder with physical symptoms
Atypical factitious disorder with physical symptoms

DISORDERS OF IMPULSE CONTROL NOT ELSEWHERE CLASSIFIED
Pathological gambling
Kleptomania
Pyromania
Intermittent explosive disorder
Isolated explosive disorder
Atypical impulse control disorder

ADJUSTMENT DISORDER
  with depressed mood
  with anxious mood
  with mixed emotional features
  with disturbance of conduct
  with mixed disturbance of emotions and conduct
  with work (or academic) inhibition
  with withdrawal
  with atypical features

PSYCHOLOGICAL FACTORS AFFECTING PHYSICAL CONDITION
Specify physical condition on Axis III.

Psychological factors affecting physical condition

AXIS II
Personality Disorders
Paranoid
Schizoid
Schizotypal

Histrionic
Narcissistic
Antisocial
Borderline

Avoidant
Dependent
Compulsive
Passive-Aggressive

Atypical, mixed, or other personality disorder

CONDITIONS NOT ATTRIBUTABLE TO A MENTAL DISORDER THAT ARE A FOCUS OF ATTENTION OR TREATMENT
Malingering
Borderline intellectual functioning
Adult antisocial behavior
Childhood or adolescent antisocial behavior
Academic problem
Occupational problem
Uncomplicated bereavement
Noncompliance with medical treatment
Phase of life problem or other life circumstance problem
Marital problem
Parent-child problem
Other specified family circumstances
Other interpersonal problem

ADDITIONAL CLASSIFICATIONS
Unspecified mental disorder (nonpsychotic)
No diagnosis or condition on Axis I
Diagnosis or condition deferred on Axis I

Classification of Mental Disorders
(Rutter, Shaffer, & Sturge, n.d.)

AXIS I[1]
CLINICAL PSYCHIATRIC SYNDROMES

Psychoses

Senile and presenile organic psychotic
   conditions (includes arteriosclerotic
   dementia)
Alcoholic psychoses
Drug-induced psychoses
Transient organic psychotic conditions
Other organic psychotic conditions
   (chronic)
Schizophrenic psychoses
   Simple/hebephrenic/catatonic/
   paranoid/acute episode/latent/residual/
   schizoaffective, other/unspecified
Affective psychoses
   Manic/depressed/circular
Paranoid states
Other non-organic psychoses
Psychoses with origin specific to
   childhood
   Infantile autism/disintegrative
   psychosis/other (stereotyped repetitive
   movements, hyperkinesis, echolalia,
   retarded speech or social
   development)/unspecified

**Neurotic disorders, personality disorders,
and other nonpsychotic mental disorders**

Neurotic disorders
   Anxiety states/hysteria/phobic state/
   obsessive-compulsive disorder/
   neurotic depression/neurasthenia/
   depersonalization syndrome/
   hypochondriasis/other/unspecified
Personality (or character) disorders
Sexual deviations and disorders
Alcohol dependence
Drug dependence
Nondependent abuse of drugs
Physical conditions arising from mental
   factors (not involving tissue damage)
Special symptoms or syndromes not
   elsewhere classified
   Stammering and stuttering, anorexia
   nervosa/tics/stereotyped repetitive
   movements/specific disorders of
   sleep/other disorders of eating/
   enuresis/encopresis/psychalgia/other
   and unspecified

Acute reaction to stress
   Catastrophic/combat fatigue/
   exhaustion delirium
Adjustment reaction
Specific nonpsychotic mental disorders
   following organic brain damage
Depressive disorder, not elsewhere classified
Disturbance of conduct not elsewhere
   classified (aggressive, destructive, any
   age)
   Unsocialized/socialized (to
   subgroup)/compulsive (kleptomania)/
   mixed/other/unspecified

Disturbance of emotions specific to
   childhood and adolescence
   With anxiety and fearfulness/with misery and unhappiness/with sensitivity,
   shyness, and social withdrawal/
   relationship problems/other or
   mixed/unspecified

Hyperkinetic syndrome of childhood
   Simple disturbance of activity and
   attention/hyperkinesis with developmental delay/hyperkinetic conduct
   disorder/other/unspecified

Psychic factors associated with diseases
   classified elsewhere (psychosomatic)

AXIS II
SPECIFIC DELAYS IN DEVELOPMENT

No specific delay
Specific reading retardation
Specific arithmetical retardation
Other specific learning difficulties
Developmental speech/language
   disorder
Specific motor retardation
Mixed developmental disorder

AXIS III
INTELLECTUAL LEVEL

Normal variation
Mild mental retardation
Moderate mental retardation
Severe mental retardation
Profound mental retardation
Unspecified mental retardation
Intellectual level unknown

AXIS IV
MEDICAL CONDITIONS

AXIS V
**ABNORMAL PSYCHOSOCIAL
SITUATIONS**

No significant distortion or inadequacy
   of psychosocial environment
Mental disturbance in other family
   members
Discordant intra-familial relationships
Lack of warmth in intra-familial
   relationships
Familial over-involvement
Inadequate or inconsistent parental
   control
Inadequate social, linguistic, or
   perceptual stimulation
Inadequate living conditions
Inadequate or distorted intra-familial
   communications
Anomalous family situations
Stresses or disturbances in school or
   work environment
Migration or social transplantation
Natural disaster
Other intra-familial psychosocial stress
Other extra-familial psychosocial stress
Persecution or adverse discrimination
Other psychosocial disturbance in
   society in general
Other (specified)
Not known

Adapted from Rutter, M. L., Shaffer, D., &
Sturge, C. A guide to a multi-axial
classification scheme for psychiatric disorders
in childhood and adolescence. Department of
Child and Adolescent Psychiatry, Institute of
Psychiatry, De Crespigny Park, London SE5
8AF, England, n.d. Reprinted by permission of
Professor Michael Rutter.

[1]Axis I consists of Chapter V categories of the
ICD-9 (The International Classification of
Diseases, Ninth Revision, a World Health
Organization 1978 publication) except for the
categories of Specific Delays in Development
and Mental Retardation, which have been
placed in Axes II and III, respectively.

Glossary

Abnormal. Maladaptive behavior detrimental to the individual and/or the group.

Abreaction. Expression of pent-up emotions.

Accommodation. The cognitive process whereby new information causes a reorganization of previously existing cognitive maps or structures.

Acting-out. Reaction in which individual reduces anxiety, hostility, or other unpleasant emotions by permitting their expression in overt behavior.

Activation (arousal). Energy mobilization required for organism to pursue its goals and meet its needs.

Actualization strivings. Strivings toward growth and fulfillment.

Actuarial approach. Application of probability statistics to human behavior, as in insurance.

Acute. Term used to describe a disorder of sudden onset and relatively short duration, usually with intense symptoms.

Acute alcoholic hallucinosis. State of alcoholic intoxication characterized by hallucinations.

Adaptability. Flexibility in meeting changed circumstances or demands.

Adipose cells. Fat cells in the body.

Adjustive behavior. Behavior by which the individual attempts to deal with stress and meet his or her needs, including efforts to maintain harmonious relationships with the environment.

Adjustment. Outcome of the individual's efforts to deal with stress and meet his or her needs.

Adrenal cortex. Outer layer of the adrenal glands; secretes the adrenal steroids and other hormones.

Adrenal glands. Endocrine glands located at the upper end of the kidneys; consist of inner adrenal medulla and outer adrenal cortex.

Adrenaline. Hormone secreted by the adrenal medulla during strong emotion; causes such bodily changes as an increase in blood sugar and a rise in blood pressure. Also called *epinephrine*.

Advocacy programs. Programs aimed at helping people in underserved populations to obtain aid with which to improve their situations.

Affect. Experience of emotion or feeling.

Affective disorder. Psychosis and related thought disturbances characterized by severe disturbances of feeling or mood.

Aftercare. Follow-up therapy after release from a hospital.

Aggression. Behavior aimed at hurting or destroying someone or something.

Agitated depression. Type of psychotic depressive reaction characterized by both severely depressed mood and hyperactivity.

Agitation. Marked restlessness and psychomotor excitement.

Agoraphobia. Morbid fear of large, open places.

Alarm reaction. First stage of the general-adaptation-syndrome, characterized by the mobilization of defenses to cope with a stressful situation.

Alcoholic deterioration. Personality deterioration, including impaired judgment, associated with alcoholism.

Alcoholic intoxication. State reached when alcohol content of blood is 0.1 percent or above.

Alcoholism. Dependence on alcohol to the extent that it seriously interferes with life adjustment.

Algophobia. Irrational fear of pain.

Alienation. Lack or loss of relationships to others.

Alpha waves. Brain waves having a frequency of 8 to 12 cycles per second and accompanied by a state of wakeful relaxation.

Alzheimer's disease. A presenile dementia.

Ambivalence. Simultaneous existence of contradictory emotional attitudes toward the same person, e.g., love and hate.

Amnesia. Total or partial loss of memory.

Amniocentesis. A technique that involves drawing fluid from the amniotic sac of a pregnant woman so that the sloughed-off fetal cells can be examined for chromosomal irregularities, including that of Down's syndrome.

Amphetamine. One type of drug that produces a psychologically stimulating and energizing effect.

Analgesia. Insensitivity to pain without loss of consciousness.

Anal stage. In psychoanalytic theory, stage of psychosexual development in which behavior is presumably focused on anal pleasure and activities.

Analytic psychology. The school or system of psychology developed by Carl Jung.

Androgen. Hormones associated with the development and maintenance of male characteristics.

Anesthesia. Loss or impairment of sensitivity (usually to touch but often applied to sensitivity to pain and other senses as well).

Anhedonia. Inability to experience pleasure or joy; believed by some to be a basic characteristic of schizophrenic individuals.

Anomie. State of disregulation of social norms and values.

Anorexia nervosa. Loss or severe diminishment

of appetite, apparently of psychogenic origin.

Anoxia.   Lack of sufficient oxygen.

Antabuse.   Drug used in the treatment of alcoholism.

Anterograde amnesia.   Loss of memory for events *following* trauma or shock.

Antianxiety drugs.   Drugs which are used primarily for alleviating anxiety.

Antidepressant drugs.   Drugs which are used primarily to elevate mood and relieve depression.

Antisocial (psychopathic) personality.   Personality disorder involving a marked lack of ethical or moral development.

Anxiety.   Generalized feelings of fear and apprehension.

Anxiety attack.   Acute episode of intense anxiety.

Anxiety disorder.   Type of neurosis characterized by chronic anxiety and apprehension.

Anxiety disturbance.   A childhood disorder marked by oversensitivity, self-consciousness, unrealistic fears, and a high level of anxiety.

Anxiety hierarchy.   Ranking of anxiety-eliciting situations utilized in systematic desensitization therapy.

Aphasia.   Loss or impairment of ability to communicate and understand language symbols—involving loss of power of expression by speech, writing, or signs, or loss of ability to comprehend written or spoken language—resulting from brain injury or disease.

Approach-avoidance conflict.   Type of stress situation involving both positive and negative features.

Apraxia.   Loss of ability to perform purposeful movements.

Arousal.   See **Activation.**

Arteriosclerosis.   Degenerative thickening and hardening of the walls of the arteries, occurring usually in old age.

Assertiveness training.   Behavior therapy technique for helping individuals become more self-assertive in interpersonal relationships.

Assimilation.   The cognitive process whereby new information is fitted into previously existing cognitive maps or structures.

Astasia-abasia.   Inability to stand or walk without the legs wobbling about and collapsing, although the person has normal control of legs while sitting or lying down; no associated organic pathology.

Asthma.   A respiratory disorder.

Ataxia.   Muscular incoordination, particularly of the arms and legs. See **Locomotor ataxia.**

Atrophy.   Wasting away or shrinking of a bodily organ, particulary muscle tissue.

Attention deficit disorder.   A term suggested as a replacement for "hyperactive syndrome" or "hyperkinetic syndrome."

Attitude.   A consistent, learned, emotionalized predisposition to respond in a particular way to a given object, person, or situation.

Attribution theory.   Theory by which causes in the behavior of others are interpreted, based on unseen or unrecognized qualities in ourselves.

Aura.   Subjective sensations, such as a peculiar odor, preceding an epileptic seizure.

Autism.   Disorder beginning in infancy characterized by inability of child to relate to others or form normal self-concept.

Automated assessment.   Psychological test interpretation by electronic computer or some other mechanical means.

Autonomic nervous system.   The section of the nervous system that regulates the internal organs; consists primarily of ganglia connected with the brain stem and spinal cord and may be subdivided into the sympathetic and parasympathetic systems.

Autonomic reactivity.   Individual's characteristic degree of emotional reactivity to stress.

Autonomy.   Self-reliance; the sense of being an individual in one's own right.

Autosome.   Any chromosome other than those determining sex.

Aversion therapy.   Form of behavior therapy in which punishment or aversive stimulation is used to eliminate undesired responses.

Aversive conditioning.   Use of noxious stimuli to suppress unwanted behavior.

Aversive stimulus.   A stimulus that elicits psychic or physical pain.

Avoidance conditioning.   Form of conditioning in which the subject learns to behave in a certain way in order to avoid an unpleasant stimulus.

Avoidant personality.   A personality disorder characterized by hypersensitivity to rejection, limited social relationships, and low self-esteem.

"Bad trip."   An unpleasant or traumatic experience while under the influence of a hallucinogenic drug, such as LSD.

Barbiturate.   Type of commonly used synthetic sedative drug.

Baseline.   In behavior therapy, the initial level of responses emitted by the individual.

Bedlam.   Popular contraction of the name of the early London asylum of St. Mary of Bethlehem.

Behavioral assessment.   A technique to determine the functional relationships between an individual's behavior and environmental stimuli.

Behavioral contract.   A contract, often between family members, stipulating privileges and responsibilities.

Behavioral medicine.   A rapidly developing discipline concerned with relations between physical health and the psychological aspects of individuals who have, or are at risk for, physical disease.

Behavioral sciences.   The various interrelated disciplines, including psychology, sociology, and anthropology, that focus on human behavior.

Behavior control.   Shaping and manipulation of behavior by drugs, persuasion, and other techniques.

Behavior disorder.   Synonym for psychological problem.

Behaviorism.   School of psychology that formerly restricted itself primarily to study of overt behavior.

Behavior modification.   See **Behavior therapy.**

Behavior therapy.   Therapeutic procedures based primarily on application of principles of respondent and operant conditioning.

Benign.   Of a mild, self-limiting nature; not malignant.

Bereavement. Grief and sorrow following the death of a loved one.

Bestiality. Sexual relations with animals.

Beta waves. Brain waves having a frequency of 18 to 30 cycles per second and associated with problem solving and feelings of tension.

Biochemical disorders. Disorders involving disturbances in internal chemical regulation.

Biofeedback. Treatment technique by which individuals are taught to change and control internal bodily processes formerly thought to be involuntary (e.g., blood pressure and skin temperature); involves giving the individual immediate feedback about the bodily changes as they occur.

Biogenic amines. Chemicals that serve as neurotransmitters or modulators.

Biological clocks. The 24-hour rhythmic fluctuations in metabolic processes of plants and animals. Also called *circadian cycles*.

Biological viewpoint. An approach to mental disorders emphasizing biological causation.

Bipolar disorder. A manic or depressive episode believed to be a manifestation of an underlying condition predisposing the individual to severe mood swings; has largely replaced the term "manic-depressive psychosis."

Bisexual. A person sexually attracted to both females and males.

Blocking. Involuntary inhibition of recall, ideation, or communication (including sudden stoppage of speech).

Body image. A person's image of his or her body in terms of attractiveness and other characteristics.

Borderline personality. A personality disorder characterized by instability and drastic mood shifts; such individuals are impulsive and at times may appear psychotic.

Brain pathology. Diseased or disordered condition of the brain.

Brainwashing. Extreme form of thought modification and control.

Brain waves. Minute oscillations of electrical potential given off by neurons in the cerebral cortex and measured by the electroencephalograph.

Brief Psychiatric Rating Scale (BPRS). Objective method of rating clinical symptoms that provides scores on eighteen variables (e.g., somatic concern, anxiety, withdrawal, hostility, and bizarre thinking).

Brief psychotherapy. Short-term therapy, usually 8 to 10 sessions, focused upon restoring the individual's functioning and offering emotional support.

Butch. Slang term for *lesbian,* particularly one who assumes a masculine appearance.

Cardiovascular. Pertaining to the heart and blood vessels.

Case study. Assessment information on a specific individual.

Castrating. Refers to any source of injury to or deprivation of the genitals, or more broadly, to a threat to the masculinity or feminity of the individual.

Catalepsy. A condition in which the muscles are waxy and semirigid, tending to maintain the limbs in any position in which they are placed.

Catatonic schizophrenia. Type of schizophrenia characterized by periods of extreme excitement and extreme withdrawal.

Catecholamine. Class of amines sharing a similar chemical structure and involved chiefly in neural transmission.

Catharsis. Discharge of emotional tension associated with repressed traumatic material, e.g., by "talking it out."

Central nervous system (CNS). The brain and spinal cord.

Cerebral arteriosclerosis. Hardening of the arteries in the brain.

Cerebral concussion. Mild head injury that disrupts brain functions.

Cerebral contusion. Brain damage resulting from head injury severe enough to shift brain and compress it against skull.

Cerebral cortex. The surface layers of the cerebrum.

Cerebral hemorrhage. Bleeding into brain tissue from a ruptured blood vessel.

Cerebral laceration. Tearing of brain tissue associated with severe head injury.

Cerebral syphillis. Syphilitic infection of the brain.

Cerebral thrombosis. The formation of a clot or thrombus in the vascular system of the brain.

Cerebrovascular accident (CVA). Blockage or rupture of large blood vessel in brain leading to both focal and generalized impairment of brain function. Also called *stroke.*

Cerebrum. Main part of brain; divided into left and right hemispheres.

Character disorder. See **Personality disorder.**

Chemotherapy. Use of drugs in treatment of mental disorders.

Child abuse. The infliction of physical damage upon a child by parents or other adults.

Child advocacy. Movement concerned with protecting rights and ensuring well-being of children.

Childhood depression. An affective disorder occurring in children often in a masked form, e.g., as acting-out behavior.

Chlorpromazine. One of the major antipsychotic drugs.

Chorea. A pathological condition characterized by jerky, irregular, involuntary movements. See also **Huntington's chorea.**

Chromosomes. Chainlike structures within cell nucleus that contain genes.

Chronic. Referring to relatively permanent maladaptive pattern or condition.

Circadian rhythms. Regular biological cycle of sleep and activity characteristic of each species.

Civil commitment. Procedure whereby an individual certified as mentally disordered can be hospitalized, either voluntarily or against his will.

Classical (respondent) conditioning. Basic form of learning in which a previously neutral stimulus comes to elicit a given response.

Claustrophobia. Irrational fear of small enclosed places.

Client-centered psychotherapy. A nondirective approach to psychotherapy developed chiefly by Carl Rogers and based on his personality theory.

Climacteric. The life period associated with the menopause in women and various related glandular and bodily changes in men.

Clinical picture. Diagnostic picture formed by observation of patient's behavior or by all available assessment data.

Clinical psychology. Field of psychology concerned with the understanding, assessment, treatment, and prevention of maladaptive behavior.

Cocaine. A stimulating and pain-reducing psychoactive drug.

Cognition. The act, process, or product of knowing or perceiving.

Cognitive-behavior therapy. A treatment approach in which behavioral methods or learning principles are applied to thought processes (cognitions).

Cognitive derailment ("slippage"). The tendency for thoughts and associations not to follow one another in logical order; believed to be a basic characteristic of schizophrenic disorders.

Cognitive dissonance. Condition existing when new information is contradictory to one's assumptions.

Cognitive map. See **Frame of reference.**

Cognitive mediation. Thought processes in the individual that occur between the stimulus and the response.

Cognitive process (cognition). Mental processes, including perception, memory, and reasoning, by which one acquires knowledge, solves problems, and makes plans.

Cognitive restructuring therapy. A cognitive behavior therapy that aims to alter the individual's false or maladaptive frame of reference.

Cohabitation. A male and female living together without being married.

Coitus. Sexual intercourse.

Collective unconscious. Term used by Carl Jung to refer to that portion of the unconscious which he considered common to all humanity.

Coma. Profound stupor with unconsciousness.

Community mental health. Application of psychosocial and sociocultural principles to the improvement of given environments.

Community psychology. Use of community resources in dealing with maladaptive behavior; tends to be more concerned with community intervention rather than with personal or individual change.

Compensation. Type of ego-defense mechanism in which an undesirable trait is covered up by exaggerating a desirable trait.

Complex. Group of emotionally toned attitudes, desires, or memories which are partially or totally repressed.

Compulsion. An irrational and repetitive impulse to perform some act.

Compulsive personality. A personality disorder characterized by excessive concern with rules, order, efficiency, and work.

Computer assessment. Use of computers to obtain or interpret assessment data.

Computer model. Use of computer to simulate psychological functioning.

Conceived values. The individual's conception of the ideal values.

Concept. General idea based on similarities among different objects, events, etc.

Concordance. Similarity in diagnosis or other traits in a twin pair.

Concussion. See **Cerebral concussion.**

Conditioned reinforcer. A reinforcer that derives its value from basic unconditioned reinforcers.

Conditioning. See **Classical conditioning** and **Operant conditioning.**

Confabulation. The filling in of memory gaps with false and often irrelevant details.

Confidentiality. Commitment on part of professional person to keep information he or she obtains from a client confidential.

Conflict. Simultaneous arousal of opposing impulses, desires, or motives.

Congenital. Existing at birth or before birth but not necessarily hereditary.

Conscience. The functioning of an individual's system of moral values in the approval or disapproval of his or her own thoughts and actions. Roughly equivalent to Freudian concept of superego.

Consciousness. Awareness of inner and/or outer environment.

Constitution. The relatively constant biological makeup of the individual, resulting from the interaction of heredity and environment.

Consultation. A community intervention approach that aims at helping individuals at risk for disorder by working indirectly through caretaker institutions (e.g., police and teachers).

Contingency. Relationship, usually causal, between two events in which one is usually followed by the other.

Continuous reinforcement. Reward or reinforcement given regularly after each correct response.

Control group. A group of subjects compared with experimental group in assessing effects of independent variables.

Controlled drinking therapy. Behavioral treatment approach aimed at reducing the individual's drinking by self-control methods.

Convulsion. Pathological, involuntary, muscular contractions.

Corpus callosum. Nerve fibers that connect the two hemispheres of the brain.

Correlational studies. Studies dealing with the extent to which two or more variables co-vary.

Corticovisceral control mechanisms. Brain mechanisms that regulate autonomic and other bodily functions.

Counseling psychology. Field of psychology that focuses on helping persons with problems pertaining to education, marriage, or occupation.

Counterconditioning. Relearning by using a particular stimulus to establish a new (and generally more adaptive) response.

Counterculture. Subculture in conflict with established culture in a given society.

Countertransference. Arousal by the client of inappropriate feelings of transference on the part of the analyst during the course of psychoanalytic therapy.

Couple counseling. Treatment for disordered

interpersonal relationships involving sessions with both members of the relationship present.

Covert. Concealed, disguised, not directly observable.

Covert sensitization. A behavioral treatment method for extinguishing undesirable behavior by associating noxious mental images with that behavior.

Crazy. Mentally disordered (term not used in scientific circles).

Cretinism. Condition arising from thyroid deficiency in early life and marked by mental retardation and distinctive physical characteristics.

Criminal responsibility. Legal question of whether an individual should be permitted to use insanity as a defense after having committed some criminal act.

Crisis. Stress situation which approaches or exceeds adaptive capacities of individual or group.

Crisis intervention. Various methods for rendering therapeutic assistance to an individual or group during a period of crisis.

Critical period. Period of development during which organism most needs certain inputs or is most ready for acquisition of a given response.

Cultural-familial mental retardation. Mental retardation resulting from inherited limitation or lack of needed environmental stimulation, with no evidence of brain pathology.

Cultural lag. The tendency for formal conceptions of reality and "appropriate" behavior within a given culture to change more slowly than the actual thinking and actions of a society's members.

Cushing's syndrome. An endocrine disorder resulting from oversecretion of *cortisone* and marked by mood swings, irritability, and other mental symptoms.

Cyclothymic (affective) personality. Personality type characterized by extreme mood swings, i.e., alternating periods of depression and elation.

Day hospital. A community-based mental hospital where the patients are treated during the day, returning to their homes at night.

Decompensation. Ego or personality disorganization under excessive stress.

Defense mechanism. See **Ego-defense mechanism.**

Defense-oriented reaction. Reaction involving one's feelings of adequacy and worth rather than objective handling of the stress situation.

Deficiency motivation. Motivation directed primarily toward maintaining or restoring physiological or psychological equilibrium rather than toward personal growth.

Delinquency. Antisocial or illegal behavior by a minor.

Delirium. State of mental confusion characterized by clouding of consciousness, disorientation, restlessness, excitement, and often hallucinations.

Delirium tremens. Acute delirium associated with prolonged alcoholism; characterized by intense anxiety, tremors, and hallucinations.

Delusion. Firm belief opposed to reality but maintained in spite of strong evidence to the contrary.

Delusion of persecution. False belief that one is being mistreated or interfered with by one's enemies. Often found in schizophrenia.

Delusion system. An internally coherent, systematized pattern of delusions.

Dementia. Severe mental disorder involving impairment of mental ability; not congenital.

Dementia praecox. Older term for schizophrenia.

Demonology. Viewpoint emphasizing supernatural causation of mental disorder, especially "possession" by evil spirits or forces.

Denial of reality. Ego-defense mechanism by means of which the individual protects himself or herself from unpleasant aspects of reality by refusing to acknowledge them.

Dependency. The tendency to rely overly upon others.

Dependent personality. A personality disorder marked by lack of self-confidence and feelings of acute panic or discomfort at having to be alone.

Dependent variable. In an experiment, the factor which the hypothesis predicts will change with changes in the independent variable.

Depersonalization. Loss of sense of personal identity, often with a feeling of being something or someone else.

Depersonalization disorder. A dissociative neurotic disorder, usually occurring in adolescence, in which individuals lose their sense of self and feel unreal or displaced to a different location.

Depression. Emotional state characterized by extreme dejection, gloomy ruminations, feelings of worthlessness, loss of hope, and often apprehension.

Depressive disorder. Neurotic reaction characterized by persistent dejection and discouragement.

Depressive stupor. Extreme degree of depression characterized by marked psychomotor underactivity.

Desensitization. Therapeutic process by means of which reactions to traumatic experiences are reduced in intensity by repeatedly exposing the individual to them in mild form, either in reality or in fantasy.

Deterrence. The premise that punishment for criminal offenses will deter that criminal and others from future criminal acts.

Detox. A center or facility for receiving and detoxifying alcohol- or drug-intoxicated individuals.

Detoxification. Treatment directed toward ridding the body of alcohol or other drugs.

Developmental task. A competency that is considered essential to master during a particular life period, e.g., learning to talk during infancy.

Deviant behavior. Behavior which deviates markedly from the average or norm.

Dexedrine. An amphetamine drug; a stimulant used to curb appetite or elevate mood.

Diagnosis. Determination of the nature and extent of a specific disorder.

Didactic group therapy. Group therapy consisting of more or less formal group lectures and discussions.

Differential reinforcement of other behavior (DOR). Behavior modification technique for extinguishing undesirable behavior by reinforcing incompatible behaviors.

Dilantin. An anti-convulsant medication often used in controlling epileptic seizures.

Directive therapy. Type of therapeutic approach in which the therapist supplies direct answers to problems and takes much of the responsibility for the progression of therapy.

Discrimination learning.   Learning to interpret and respond differently to two or more similar stimuli.

Diseases of adaptation.   Stomach ulcers and other disease conditions resulting from the stresses of life.

Disintegration.   Loss of organization or integration in any organized system.

Disorganization.   Severely impaired integration.

Disorientation.   Mental confusion with respect to time, place, or person.

Displacement.   Ego-defense mechanism in which an emotional attitude or symbolic meaning is transferred from one object or concept to another.

Dissociation.   Separation or "isolation" of mental processes in such a way that they become split off from the main personality or lose their normal thought-affect relationships.

Dissociative disorder.   Psychoneurotic disorder characterized by amnesia, fugue, somnambulism, or multiple personality.

Dizygotic (fraternal) twins.   Twins that develop from two separate eggs.

DNA.   Deoxyribonucleic acid, principal component of genes.

Dominant gene.   A gene whose hereditary characteristics prevail in the offspring.

Dopamine.   A catecholamine neural transmitter substance.

Double-approach conflict.   Type of conflict in which individual is confronted with choosing between two or more desirable alternatives.

Double-avoidant conflict.   Type of conflict in which individual is confronted with choosing between two or more aversive alternatives.

Double-bind.   Situation in which an individual will be disapproved for performing a given act and equally disapproved if he or she does not perform it.

Down's syndrome (mongolism).   Form of mental retardation associated with chromosomal anomalies.

Dramatization.   A defense against anxiety in which the individual engages in attention-getting behavior and self-dramatization.

Dream analysis.   Psychotherapeutic technique involving the interpretation of the patient's dreams.

Drive.   Internal conditions directing organism toward a specific goal, usually involving biological rather than psychological motives.

Drug abuse.   Use of a drug to extent that it interferes with health and/or occupational or social adjustment.

Drug addiction (dependence).   Physiological and/or psychological dependence on a drug.

Drug therapy.   See **Chemotherapy, Pharmacotherapy.**

DSM-III.   Current diagnostic manual of the American Psychiatric Association.

Dual personality.   See **Multiple personality.**

Dwarfism.   A condition of arrested growth and very short stature.

Dyad.   A two-person group.

Dynamic formulation.   An integrated evaluation of a patient's traits, attitudes, conflicts, and symptoms that attempts to explain the individual's problem.

Dysfunction.   Impairment or disturbance in the functioning of an organ.

Dyslexia.   Impairment of the ability to read.

Dyspareunia.   Painful coitus in male or female.

Dyssocial personality.   Behavior pattern characterized by criminal values but good ego strength.

Echolalia.   Meaningless repetition of words by an individual, usually of whatever has been said to that person.

Echopraxia.   Repetition of another person's actions or gestures.

Ecology.   Relation or interaction between organisms and their physical environment.

Economy, principle of.   Theory that the individual meets stress in the simplest way possible.

EEG.   See **Electroencephalogram.**

Ego.   In psychoanalytic theory, the rational subsystem of the personality which mediates between id and superego demands and reality. More generally, the individual's self-concept.

Ego-defense mechanism (reaction).   Type of reaction designed to maintain the individual's feelings of adequacy and worth rather than to cope directly with the stress situation; usually unconscious and reality distorting.

Ego-ideal (self-ideal).   The person or "self" the individual thinks he or she could and should be.

Ego involvement.   Perception of a situation in terms of its importance to the individual.

Egocentric.   Preoccupied with one's own concerns and relatively insensitive to the concerns of others.

Ejaculatory incompetence.   A male's inability to ejaculate.

Electra complex.   In psychoanalytic theory, an excessive emotional attachment (love) of a daughter for her father.

Electroconvulsive therapy (ECT).   Use of electricity to produce convulsions and unconsciousness; also called *electroshock therapy.*

Electroencephalogram (EEG).   A recording of the brain waves by an electroencephalograph.

Electrotherapy.   Methods of therapy which involve the influence of electric current on the central nervous system.

Embolism.   Lodgment of a blood clot in a blood vessel too small to permit its passage.

Emotion.   A strong feeling accompanied by physiological changes.

Emotional disturbance.   Psychological disorder.

Emotional inoculation.   Therapeutic procedures designed to prepare persons who face stress situations, such as surgery, by providing such persons with adaptive techniques.

Emotional insulation.   Ego-defense mechanism in which the individual reduces the tensions of need and anxiety by withdrawing into a shell of passivity.

Empathy.   Ability to understand and to some extent share the state of mind of another person.

Encephalitis.   Inflammation of the brain.

Encopresis.   Disorder defined by having bowel movements in one's clothing after the age of 3.

Encounter.   Term applied to the interaction between client and therapist (in existential therapy) or between patients (in encounter-group therapy).

Encounter group.   Small group designed to provide an

intensive interpersonal experience focusing on feelings and group interactions; used in therapy or to promote personal growth.

Endocrine glands. Ductless glands which secrete hormones directly into the lymph or bloodstream.

Endogenous factors. Factors originating within the organism that affect behavior.

Endorphins. Opium-like substances produced in the brain and pituitary gland in response to stimulation; thought to be neurotransmitters.

Energizer. Drug which has a stimulating effect.

Engram. Hypothesized physiological change in nervous system thought to be responsible for memory.

Entrophy. Deterioration and eventual disintegration or death of a living system.

Enuresis. Bed-wetting; involuntary discharge of urine.

Environmental psychology. Field of psychology focusing on the effects of environmental setting on an individual's feelings and behavior.

Enzyme. Catalyst regulating metabolic activities.

Epidemiology. Study of the distribution of physical or mental disorders in a population.

Epilepsy. Group of disorders varying from momentary lapses of consciousness to generalized convulsions.

Epinephrine. Hormone secreted by the adrenal medulla; also called **adrenaline.**

Equilibrium. Steady state; balance.

Erotic. Pertaining to sexual stimulation and gratification.

Escape learning. Conditioned response in which the subject learns to terminate or escape an aversive stimulus.

Essence. Existential term referring to the fact that one's existence is given but what is made of it is up to the individual and becomes that person's essence.

Essential hypertension. High blood pressure, presumably of a psychological or emotional origin.

Estrogens. Female hormones produced by the ovaries.

Ethnic group. Group of people who are treated as distinctive in terms of culture and group patterns.

Ethnocentrism. Belief that one's own country and race are superior to other countries and races.

Etiology. Causation; the systematic study of the causes of disorders.

Eugenics. The application of methods of selective breeding of human beings with the intent of improving the species.

Euphoria. Exaggerated feeling of well-being and contentment.

Exacerbate. Intensify.

Excitation. Process whereby activity is elicited in a nerve.

Exhibitionism. Public display or exposure of genitals for conscious or unconscious purpose of sexual excitement and pleasure.

Existential anxiety. Anxiety concerning one's ability to find a satisfying and fulfilling way of life.

Existential neurosis. Disorder characterized by feelings of alienation, meaninglessness, and apathy.

Existential therapy. Therapy based on existential concepts, emphasizing the development of a sense of self-direction and meaning in one's existence.

Existentialism. A view of human beings that emphasizes the individual's responsibility for becoming the kind of person he or she should be.

Exogenous. Originating from or due to external causes.

Exorcism. A religiously inspired treatment procedure designed to drive out evil spirits or forces from a "possessed" person.

Expanded consciousness. Sensation caused by psychedelic drugs or meditation in which individual feels the mind is opened to new types of experience.

Experimental method. Rigorous scientific procedure by which hypotheses are tested.

Experimental neurosis. Neurotic behavior produced in animals by inescapable conflicts and other types of stress.

Extinction. Gradual disappearance of conditioned response when it is no longer reinforced.

Extrapunitive. Characterized by a tendency to evaluate the source of frustrations as external and to direct hostility outward.

Extraversion. Personality type oriented toward the outer world of people and things rather than concepts and intellectual concerns.

Fabrication. Relating imaginary events as if they were true without intent to deceive; confabulation.

Factor analysis. Statistical technique used in identifying and measuring the relative importance of the underlying variables, or factors, which contribute to a complex ability, trait, or form of behavior.

Fading. A technique whereby a stimulus causing some reaction is gradually replaced by a previously neutral stimulus, such that the latter acquires the property of producing the reaction in question.

Familial. Pertaining to characteristics which tend to run in families and have a higher incidence in certain families than in the general population.

Family therapy. Form of interpersonal therapy focusing on relationships within the family.

Fantasy. Daydream; also, an ego-defense mechanism by means of which the individual escapes from the world of reality and gratifies his desires in fantasy achievements.

Feedback. Explicit information pertaining to internal physiological processes or to the social consequences of one's overt behavior.

Fetal alcohol syndrome. Observed pattern in infants of alcoholic mothers in which there is a characteristic facial or limb irregularity, low body weight, and behavioral abnormality.

Fetishism. Maladaptive sexual deviation in which an individual achieves sexual gratification by means of some inanimate object or nonsexual part of the body.

Fetus. Embryo after the sixth week following conception.

Field properties. Characteristics of the environment surrounding a living system.

Fixation. Unreasonable or exaggerated attachment to some person or arresting of emotional development on a childhood or adolescent level.

Fixed-interval schedule. Schedule of reinforcement based on fixed period of time after previous reinforced response.

Fixed-ratio schedule. Schedule of reinforcement based on reinforcement after fixed number of nonreinforced responses.

Flashback. The recurrence of a drug experience, usually in a negative manner, without further ingestion of the drug.

Flight of ideas. Rapid succession of ideas without logical association or continuity.

Flooding. Anxiety-eliciting technique used in implosive therapy.

Folie à deux. A psychotic interpersonal relationship involving two people; e.g., husband and wife both become psychotic with similar or complementary symptomatology.

Follow-up study. Research procedure in which individuals are studied over a period of time or are recontacted at a later time after initial study.

Forensic psychiatry. Branch of psychiatry dealing with legal problems relating to mental disorders.

Frame of reference. The reality, ethical, and possibility assumptions which form the individual's "cognitive map" for interpreting and coping with his world.

Fraternal twins. Dizygotic twins; fertilized by separate germ cells, thus not having same genetic inheritance. May be of the same or opposite sex.

Fraudulent interpersonal contract. Violation of rules or norms governing healthy interpersonal relationships.

Free association. Psychoanalytic procedure for probing the unconscious in which individual gives a running account of his every thought and feeling.

Free-floating anxiety. Anxiety not referable to any specific situation or cause.

Frigidity. Inability to experience sexual pleasure or orgasm on the part of the female. Now called *arousal insufficiency* or *orgasmic dysfunction.*

Frontal lobe. Portion of the brain active in reasoning and other higher thought processes.

Frustration. Thwarting of a need or desire.

Fugue. Neurotic dissociative disorder; entails loss of memory accompanied by actual physical flight from one's present life situation to a new environment or less threatening former one.

Functional psychoses. Severe mental disorders attributed primarily to psychological stress.

Furor. Transitory outbursts of excitement or anger during which the individual may be quite dangerous.

Future shock. Condition brought about when social change proceeds so rapidly that the individual cannot cope with it adequately.

Gay. Synonym for "homosexual."

Gender identity. Individual's identification as being male or female.

General-adaptation-syndrome. Reaction of the individual to excessive stress; consists of the alarm reaction, the stage of resistance, and the stage of exhaustion.

General paresis. Mental disorder associated with syphilis of the brain.

General systems theory. A comprehensive theoretical model embracing all living systems.

Generalization. Tendency of a response that has been conditioned to one stimulus to become associated with other similar stimuli.

Generalized reinforcer. Reinforcer such as money which may influence a wide range of stimuli and behaviors.

Genes. Ultramicroscopic areas of DNA which are responsible for transmission of hereditary traits.

Genetic code. Means by which DNA controls the sequence and structure of proteins manufactured within each cell and also makes exact duplicates of itself.

Genetic counseling. Counseling prospective parents concerning the probability of their having defective offspring as a result of genetic defects.

Genetics. Science of heredity.

Genital stage. In psychoanalytic theory, the final stage of psychosexual development involving shift from autoeroticism to heterosexual interest.

Genitalia. Organs of reproduction, especially the external organs.

Genotype. Genetic characteristics inherited by an individual.

Geriatrics. Science of the diseases and treatment of the aged.

Germ cells. Reproductive cells (female ovum and male sperm) which unite to produce a new individual.

Gerontology. Science dealing with the study of old age.

Gestalt psychology. School of psychology which emphasizes patterns rather than elements or connections, taking the view that the whole is more than the sum of its parts.

Gestalt therapy. Type of psychotherapy emphasizing wholeness of the person and integration of thought, feeling, and action.

Gigantism. Abnormally tall stature resulting from hyperfunctioning of the pituitary.

Glucocorticoids. Adrenocortical hormones involved in sugar metabolism but also having widespread effects on injury-repair mechanisms and resistance to disease; they include hydrocortisone, corticosterone, and cortisone.

Gonads. The sex glands.

Grand mal epilepsy. Type of epilepsy characterized by generalized convulsive seizures.

Grief work. Necessary period of mourning for an individual to assimilate personal loss into the self-structure and view it as an event of the past.

Group therapy. Psychotherapy with two or more individuals at the same time.

Guilt. Feelings of culpability arising from behavior or desires contrary to one's ethical principles. Involves both self-devaluation and apprehension growing out of fears of punishment.

Habit. Any product of learning, whether it is a customary or transitory mode of response.

Habituation. Process whereby an individual's response to the same stimulus lessens with repeated presentations.

Halfway house. Facility which provides aftercare following institutionalization, seeking to ease the individual's adjustment to the community.

Hallucination. Sense perception for which there is no appropriate external stimulus.

Hallucinogens. Drugs or chemicals capable of producing hallucinations.

Hashish. The strongest drug derived from the hemp plant; a relative of marijuana.

Hebephrenic schizophrenia. Type of schizophrenia characterized by severe personality decompensation or disintegration.

Hemiplegia. Paralysis of one lateral half of the body.

Hemophobia. Pathological fear of blood. Also called *hematophobia*.

Heredity. Genetic transmission of characteristics from parents to their children.

Hermaphroditism. Anatomical sexual abnormality in which an individual has sex organs of both sexes.

Heterosexuality. Sexual interest in a member of the opposite sex.

Hierarchy of needs. The concept that needs arrange themselves in a hierarchy in terms of importance or "prepotence," from the most basic biological needs to those psychological needs concerned with self-actualization.

High-risk group. Group showing great vulnerability to physical or mental disorders.

Histrionic personality. Personality pattern characterized by excitability, emotional instability, and self-dramatization.

Holistic. A systematic approach to science involving the study of the whole or total configuration; the view of human beings as unified psychobiological organisms inextricably immersed in a physical and sociocultural environment.

Homeostasis. Tendency of organisms to maintain conditions making possible a constant level of physiological functioning.

Homosexuality. Sexual preference for member of one's own sex.

Hormones. Chemicals released by the endocrine glands that regulate development of and activity in various bodily organs.

Hostility. Emotional reaction or drive toward the destruction or damage of an object interpreted as a source of frustration or threat.

Humanistic-existential therapy. Type of psychotherapy emphasizing personal growth and self-direction.

Human potential movement. Movement concerned with enrichment of experience, increased sensory awareness, and fulfillment of human potentials.

Huntington's chorea. Incurable disease, presumably of hereditary origin, which is manifested in jerking, twitching movements and mental deterioration.

Hydrocephalus. Organic condition associated with brain damage and mental retardation.

Hydrotherapy. Use of hot or cold baths, ice packs, etc., in treatment.

Hyper-. Prefix meaning *increased* or *excessive*.

Hyperkinetic (hyperactive) reaction. Disorder of childhood characterized by overactivity, restlessness, and distractibility.

Hyperobesity. Extreme overweight; more than 100 pounds over ideal body weight.

Hypertension. High blood pressure.

Hyperventilation. Rapid breathing associated with intense anxiety.

Hypesthesia. Partial loss of sensitivity.

Hypnosis. Trancelike mental state induced in a cooperative subject by suggestion.

Hypnotherapy. Use of hypnosis in psychotherapy.

Hypnotic regression. Process by which a subject is brought to relive, under hypnosis, early forgotten or repressed experiences.

Hypo-. Prefix meaning *decreased* or *insufficient*.

Hypochondriacal delusions. Delusions concerning various horrible disease conditions, such as the belief that one's brain is turning to dust.

Hypochondriacal disorder. Condition dominated by preoccupation with bodily processes and fear of presumed diseases.

Hypomania. Mild form of manic reaction, characterized by moderate psychomotor activity.

Hypothalamus. Key structure at the base of the brain; important in emotion and motivation.

Hypothesis. Statement or proposition, usually based on observation, which is tested in an experiment; may be denied or supported by experimental results but never conclusively proved.

Hysteria. Older term used to include conversion disorders; involves the appearance of symptoms of organic illness in the absence of any related organic pathology.

Hysterical disorder. Disorder characterized by involuntary psychogenic dysfunction of motor, sensory, or visceral processes.

ICD-9. See **International Classification of Diseases.**

Id. In psychoanalytic terminology, the reservoir of instinctual drives; the most inaccessible and primitive stratum of the mind.

Identical twins. Monozygotic twins; developed from a single fertilized egg.

Identification. Ego-defense mechanism in which the individual identifies himself or herself with some person or institution, usually of an illustrious nature.

Ideology. System of beliefs.

Idiot. Older term referring to severe and profound degrees of mental retardation (IQ below 25).

Idiot savant. A mental retardate who can perform unusual mental feats, usually involving music or manipulation of numbers.

Illusion. Misinterpretation of sensory data; false perception.

Imipramine. Antidepressant medication.

Implosive therapy. Type of behavior therapy in which desensitization is achieved by eliciting a massive "flood" or implosion of anxiety.

Impotence. Inability of male to achieve erection.

Impulse. Tendency to action.

Incentive. External inducement to behave in a certain way.

Incest. Sexual relations between close relatives such as father and daughter or brother and sister.

Independent variable. Factor whose effects are being examined in an experiment; it is manipulated in some way while the other variables are held constant.

Index case. In a genetic study, the individual who evidences the trait in which the investigator is interested. Same as *proband*.

Infantile autism. See **Autism.**

Inferiority complex. Strong feelings of inadequacy and insecurity which color an individual's entire adjustive efforts.

Inhibition. Conscious restraint of impulse or desire.

Innate. Inborn.

Inner controls. Reality, value, and possibility assumptions which serve to inhibit dangerous or undesirable behavior; could also apply to conditioned avoidance reactions.

Inpatient. Hospitalized patient.

Insanity. Legal term for mental disorder, implying lack of responsibility for one's acts and inability to manage one's affairs.

Insight. Clinically, the individual's understanding of his or her illness or of the motivations underlying a behavior pattern; in general psychology, the sudden grasp or understanding of meaningful relationships in a situation.

Insight therapy. Type of psychotherapy focusing on helping the patient achieve greater self-understanding with respect to his or her motives, values, coping patterns, and so on.

Insomnia. Difficulty in sleeping.

Instinct. Inborn tendency to particular behavior patterns under certain conditions in absence of learning; characteristic of species.

Instrumental act. Act directed toward achieving specific goals and meeting needs.

Instrumental (operant) conditioning. Type of conditioning in which the subject is reinforced for making a predetermined response, such as pressing a lever.

Integration. Organization of parts (psychological, biological functions) to make a functional whole.

Integrative properties. Tendency of living systems to maintain their organization and functional integrity.

Integrity. Quality of being unified and honest with self and others.

Intellectualization. Ego-defense mechanism by which the individual achieves some measure of insulation from emotional hurt by cutting off or distorting the emotional charge which normally accompanies hurtful situations.

Intelligence. Pertaining to ability to learn, reason, and adapt.

Intelligence quotient (IQ). Measurement of "intelligence" expressed as a number or position on a scale. Comparable to term *intellectual level*.

Interdisciplinary (multidisciplinary) approach. Integration of various scientific disciplines in understanding, assessing, treating, and preventing mental disorders.

Intermittent reinforcement. Reinforcement given intermittently rather than after every response.

International Classification of Diseases (ICD-9). System of classification of disorders published by the World Health Organization.

Interpersonal accommodation. A reciprocal process of give and take meant to promote satisfactory interpersonal relationships.

Intrapsychic conflict. Psychoanalytic concept referring to conflict between id, ego, and superego.

Introjection. Incorporation of qualities or values of another person or group into one's own ego structure with a tendency to identify with them and to be affected by what happens to them.

Intromission. Insertion of the penis into the vagina or anus.

Intropunitive. Responding to frustration by tending to blame oneself.

Introspection. Observing (and often reporting on) one's inner experiencing.

Introversion. Direction of interest toward one's inner world of experience and toward concepts rather than external events and objects.

In vivo. Taking place in a real-life situation as opposed to the therapeutic or laboratory setting.

Involutional melancholia (involutional psychotic reaction). Depressive psychotic reaction characterized by depression, agitation, and apprehension.

Ionizing radiation. Form of radiation; major cause of gene mutations.

Isolation. Ego-defense mechanism by means of which contradictory attitudes or feelings which normally accompany particular attitudes are kept apart, thus preventing conflict or hurt.

Jejunal bypass operation. A surgical treatment for extreme obesity which involves disconnecting and bypassing a large portion of the small intestine.

Juvenile delinquency. Legally prohibited behavior committed by minors.

Juvenile paresis. General paresis in children, usually of congenital origin.

Klinefelter's syndrome. Type of mental retardation associated with sex chromosome anomaly.

Korsakoff's psychosis. Psychosis usually associated with chronic alcoholism and characterized by disorientation, gross memory defects, and confabulation.

Labeling. Assigning an individual to a particular diagnostic category, such as schizophrenia.

Lability. Instability, particularly with regard to affect.

Latent. Inactive or dormant.

Latent content. In psychoanalytic theory, repressed wishes indirectly expressed in the manifest content of dreams.

Latent learning. Learning that becomes evident only after an incentive is introduced.

Law of effect. Principle that responses that have rewarding consequences are strengthened and those that have aversive consequences are weakened or eliminated.

Learning. Modification of behavior as a consequence of experience.

Lesbian. Female homosexual.

Lesion. Anatomically localized area of tissue pathology in an organ.

Lethality scale. Criteria used to assess the likelihood of an individual's committing suicide. .

Level of aspiration. Standard by which the individual

judges success or failure of his or her behavior.

Libido. In general psychoanalytic terminology, the instinctual drives of the id. In a narrow sense, the drive for sexual gratification.

Life crisis. Stress situation that approaches or exceeds the individual's adjustive capacity.

Life history method. Technique of psychological observation in which the development of particular forms of behavior is traced by means of records of the subject's past or present behavior.

Life-style. The general pattern of assumptions, motives, cognitive styles, and coping techniques that characterize the behavior of a given individual and give it consistency.

Lobotomy. Drastic form of psychosurgery rarely used at present. It involves cutting the nerve fibers that connect the frontal lobes to limbic system.

Locomotor ataxia. Muscular incoordination usually resulting from syphilitic damage to the spinal-cord pathways.

Logic-tight compartments. Form of intellectualization in which contradictory desires or attitudes are "sealed off" in separate areas of consciousness.

Lunacy. Old term roughly synonymous with insanity.

Lycanthropy. The delusion of being a wolf.

Lysergic acid diethylamide-25 (LSD). A potent hallucinogen.

Macrocephalic. Having an abnormally large cranium.

Madness. Nontechnical synonym for severe mental disorder.

Mainstreaming. Placement of mentally retarded children in regular school classrooms to avoid certain negative effects of "special education."

Maintaining cause. Environmental reinforcers or contingencies that tend to maintain maladaptive behavior.

Maintenance strivings. Strivings directed toward maintenance of physiological and psychological equilibrium and integration.

Major depressive disorder. See **Unipolar disorder.**

Major tranquilizers. Antipsychotic drugs, such as the phenothiazines.

Maladaptive (abnormal) behavior. Behavior which is detrimental to well-being of the individual and/or group.

Maladjustment. A more or less enduring failure of adjustment; lack of harmony with self or environment.

Malinger. To fake illness or disability symptoms consciously.

Malleus Malleficarum. Infamous handbook prepared by two monks dealing with the "diagnosis" and "treatment" of witches and witchcraft.

-mania. Suffix denoting a compulsive or morbid preoccupation with some impulse or activity; e.g., compulsive stealing is called klepto*mania*.

Manic-depressive psychoses. Older term denoting a group of psychotic disorders characterized by prolonged periods of excitement and overactivity (mania) or by periods of depression and underactivity (depression) or by alternation of the two.

Manifest content. In psychoanalytic theory, the apparent meaning of a dream; masks the latent content.

Mannerism. Recurring stereotyped gesture, posture, or movement.

Marathon encounter group. Intensive group experience lasting for 2 or more days with only brief breaks for sleep.

Marijuana. Drug derived from the plant *cannabis indica;* often used in cigarettes called "reefers" or "joints."

Marital schism. Marriage characterized by severe chronic discord which threatens continuation of marital relationship.

Marital skew. Marriage maintained at expense of distorted relationship.

Marital therapy. Therapy directed toward improving communication and interaction between marital partners.

Masked deprivation. Rejection of child by mother; does not involve separation.

Masked disorder. "Masking" of underlying depression or other emotional disturbance by delinquent behavior or other patterns seemingly unrelated to the basic disturbance.

Masochism. Sexual variant in which an individual obtains sexual gratification through infliction of pain.

Mass hysteria. Group outbreak of hysterical reactions.

Masturbation. Self-stimulation of genitals for sexual gratification.

Maternal deprivation. Lack of adequate care and stimulation by the mother or mother surrogate.

Maturation. Process of development and body change resulting from heredity rather than learning.

Medical model. The view of disordered behavior as a symptom of a more basic process, rather than a pattern representing faulty learning. Also associated with approaches to disorder that involve medical ideology, procedures, and rituals—such as the "white coat."

Megalomania. Delusions of grandeur.

Melancholia. Mental disorder characterized by severe depression. Term now rarely used.

Meninges. Membranes which envelop the brain and spinal cord.

Mental age (MA). A scale unit indicating level of intelligence in relation to chronological age.

Mental deficiency. Synonym for mental retardation; the latter term is now preferred.

Mental disorder. Entire range of abnormal behavior patterns.

Mental illness. Once used synonymously with mental disorder but now ordinarily restricted to psychoses.

Mental retardation. Below-normal intelligence, usually meaning an IQ below 68.

Mescaline. One of the hallucinogenic drugs.

Mesmerism. Theories of "animal magnetism" (hypnosis) formulated by Anton Mesmer.

Methadone. An orally administered narcotic which replaces the craving for heroin and weans the individual from heroin addiction.

Microcephaly. Form of mental retardation characterized by abnormally small cranium and retarded development of brain.

Micturate, micturition. Pertaining to urination.

Migraine headache. Type of psychosomatic disorder characterized by recurrent headaches, usually on one side of head only, and associated with emotional tension.

Milieu.   The immediate environment, physical or social or both; sometimes used to include the internal state of an organism.

Minimal brain dysfunction (MBD).   Controversial term referring to various "soft" neurological signs presumably indicative of malfunctioning of brain.

Minnesota Multiphasic Personality Inventory (MMPI).   A widely used and empirically validated personality scale.

Minor tranquilizers.   Antianxiety drugs such as the meprobramates and benzodiazepines.

Model.   An analogy that helps a scientist order findings and see important relationships among them.

Modeling.   Form of learning in which individual learns by watching someone else (the model) perform the desired response.

Model psychoses.   Psychoticlike states produced by various hallucinogenic drugs such as LSD.

Modus operandi.   Manner or mode of behavior; a criminal's typical pattern of performing crimes.

Mongolism.   See **Down's syndrome.**

Monozygotic twins.   Identical twins, developed from one fertilized egg.

Moral nihilism.   Doctrine which denies any objective or real ground for moral beliefs, and holds that the individual is not bound by obligation to others or society.

Moral therapy.   Therapy based on provision of kindness, understanding, and favorable environment; prevalent during early part of 19th century.

Morbid.   Unhealthy, pathological.

Morita therapy.   Treatment of neuroses involving deprivation of external stimulation and other procedures.

Moron.   Term formerly used to refer to mild degrees of mental retardation.

Morphine.   Addictive opiate drug.

Motivation.   Often used as synonym for drive or activation; implies that the organism's actions are partly determined in direction and strength by its own inner nature.

Motivational selectivity.   Influence of motives on perception and other cognitive processes.

Motive.   Internal condition which directs action toward some goal; term usually used to include both the drive and the goal to which it is directed.

Multiple personality.   Type of dissociative disorder characterized by the development of two or more relatively independent personality systems in the same individual.

Mutant gene.   Gene that has undergone some change in structure.

Mutation.   Change in the composition of a gene, usually causing harmful or abnormal characteristics to appear in the offspring.

Mutism.   Refusal or inability to speak.

Myxedema.   Disorder due to thyroid deficiency in adult life, characterized by mental dullness.

Narcissism.   Self-love.

Narcissistic personality.   A personality disorder characterized by grandiosity and an exaggerated sense of self-importance; arrogance and exploitation of others which covers up a frail self-concept.

Narcolepsy.   Disorder characterized by transient, compulsive states of sleepiness.

Narcotherapy (narcoanalysis, narcosynthesis).   Psychotherapy carried on while the patient is in a sleeplike state of relaxation induced by a drug such as sodium pentothal.

Narcotic drugs.   Drugs such as morphine which lead to physiological dependence and increased tolerance.

Need.   Biological or psychological condition whose gratification is necessary for the maintenance of homeostasis or for self-actualization.

Negativism.   Form of aggressive withdrawal which involves refusing to cooperate or obey commands, or doing the exact opposite of what has been requested.

Neologism.   A new word; commonly coined by persons labeled as schizophrenic.

Neonate.   Newborn infant.

Neoplasm.   Tumor.

Nervous breakdown.   Refers broadly to lowered integration and inability to deal adequately with one's life situation.

Neurasthenic neurosis.   Neurotic disorder characterized by complaints of chronic weakness, easy fatigability, and lack of enthusiasm.

Neurodermatitis.   A skin eruption frequently accompanied by intense itching and often considered to be psychosomatically caused.

Neurological examination.   Examination to determine presence and extent of organic damage to the nervous system.

Neurology.   Field concerned with study of brain and nervous system and disorders thereof.

Neuron.   Individual nerve cell.

Neurophysiology.   The branch of biology concerned with the functioning of nervous tissue and the nervous system.

Neuropsychological assessment.   Use of psychological tests to determine extent of organic brain damage.

Neurosis.   Nonpsychotic emotional disturbance characterized by exaggerated use of avoidance behavior and defense mechanisms against anxiety.

Neurosyphilis.   Syphilis affecting the central nervous system.

Neurotic nucleus.   Basic personality characteristics underlying neurotic disorders.

Neurotic paradox.   Failure of neurotic patterns to extinguish despite their self-defeating nature.

Neurotransmitters.   Chemical substances which transmit nerve impulses from one neuron to another.

Night hospital.   Mental hospital in which an individual may receive treatment during all or part of the night while carrying on his usual occupation in the daytime.

Nihilistic delusion.   Fixed belief that everything is unreal.

Nomadism.   Withdrawal reaction in which the individual continually attempts to escape frustration by moving from place to place or job to job.

Nondirective therapy.   An approach to psychotherapy in which the therapist refrains from advice or direction of the therapy. See also **Client-centered psychotherapy.**

Norepinephrine. A catecholamine neurotransmitter substance.

Norm. Standard based on measurement of a large group of persons; used for comparing the scores of an individual with those of others in a defined group.

Normal. Conforming to the usual or norm; healthy.

Normal distribution. Tendency for most members of a population to cluster around a central point or average with respect to a given trait, with the rest spreading out to the two extremes.

NREM sleep. Stages of sleep not characterized by the rapid eye movements that accompany dreaming.

Obsession. Persistent idea or thought which the individual recognizes as irrational but cannot get rid of.

Obsessive-compulsive neurosis. Disorder characterized by persistent intrusion of unwanted desires, thoughts, or actions.

Obsessive-compulsive personality. Personality disorder characterized by excessive concern with conformity and adherence to ethical values.

Occipital lobe. Portion of cerebrum concerned chiefly with visual function.

Occupational therapy. Use of occupational training or activity in psychotherapy.

Oedipus complex. Desire for sexual relations with parent of opposite sex, specifically that of a boy for his mother.

Olfactory hallucinations. Hallucinations involving the sense of smell, as of poison gas.

Operant conditioning. Form of learning in which a particular response is reinforced and becomes more likely to occur.

Operational definition. Defining a concept on the basis of a set of operations that can be observed and measured.

Opium. Narcotic drug which leads to physiological dependence and the building up of tolerance; derivatives are morphine, heroin, paregoric, and codeine.

Oral stage. First stage of psychosexual development in Freudian theory, in which mouth or oral activities are primary source of pleasure.

Organic brain syndromes. Mental disorders associated with organic brain pathology.

Organic viewpoint. Concept that all mental disorders have an organic basis. See **Biological viewpoint.**

Orgasm. Peak sexual tension followed by relaxation.

Outcome research. Studies of effectiveness of treatment.

Outpatient. An ambulatory patient who visits a hospital or clinic for examination and treatment, as distinct from a hospitalized patient.

Ovaries. Female gonads.

Overanxious. Disorder of childhood characterized by chronic anxiety, unrealistic fears, sleep disturbances, and exaggerated autonomic responses.

Overloading. Subjecting organism to excessive stress, e.g., forcing the organism to handle or "process" an excessive amount of information.

Overprotection. Shielding a child to the extent that he or she becomes too dependent on the parent.

Overt behavior. Activities which can be observed by an outsider.

Ovum. Female gamete or germ cell.

Pain cocktail. A concoction of all the medication a pain patient is taking in a single liquid that can be systematically controlled and reduced in strength.

Panic. Severe personality disorganization involving intense anxiety and usually either paralyzed immobility or blind flight.

Paradigm. A model or pattern; in research, a basic design specifying concepts considered legitimate and procedures to be used in the collection and interpretation of data.

Paranoia. Psychosis characterized by a systematized delusional system.

Paranoid personality. Individual showing behavior characterized by projection (as a defense mechanism), suspiciousness, envy, extreme jealousy, and stubbornness.

Paranoid schizophrenia. Type of schizophrenia in which delusions are usually prominent.

Paranoid state. Transient psychotic disorder in which the main element is a delusion, usually persecutory or grandiose in nature.

Paraphasia. Garbled speech.

Paraprofessional. Individual who has been trained in mental health services, but not at the professional level.

Parasympathetic nervous system. Division of the autonomic nervous system that controls most of the basic metabolic functions essential for life.

Paresis. See **General paresis.**

Paresthesia. Exceptional sensations, such as tingling.

Parkinson's disease (Paralysis agitans). Progressive disease characterized by a masklike, expressionless face and various neurological symptoms such as tremors.

Partial reinforcement. Intermittent reinforcement of a response.

Passive-aggressive personality. Personality pattern characterized by passively expressed aggressiveness.

Pathogenic. Pertaining to conditions which lead to pathology.

Pathological gambling. A pattern of addictive behavior in which the individual habitually gambles.

Pathological intoxication. Severe cerebral and behavioral disturbance in an individual whose tolerance to alcohol is extremely low.

Pathology. Abnormal physical or mental condition.

PCP. Phencyclidine; developed as a tranquilizer but not marketed because of its unpredictability. Known on the streets as "angel dust," this drug produces stuporous conditions and, at times, prolonged comas or psychoses.

Pederasty. Sexual intercourse between males via the anus.

Pedophilia. Sexual variant in which an adult engages in or desires sexual relations with a child.

Peer group. Social group of equivalent age and status.

Perception. Interpretation of sensory input.

Perceptual defense. A process in which threatening

stimuli are filtered out and not perceived by the organism.

Perceptual filtering. Processes involved in selective attention to aspects of the great mass of incoming stimuli which continually impinge on organism.

Peripheral nervous system. Nerve fibers passing between the central nervous system and the sense organs, muscles, and glands.

Permanent planning. Placing children who are drifting through foster homes back into their original families.

Perseveration. Persistent continuation of a line of thought or activity once it is under way. Clinically, inappropriate repetition.

Personality. The unique pattern of traits which characterizes the individual.

Personality disorder. A group of maladaptive behavioral syndromes originating in the developmental years and not characterized by neurotic or psychotic symptoms.

Perversion. Deviation from normal.

Petit mal. Relatively mild form of epilepsy involving a temporary partial lapse of consciousness.

Phallic stage. In psychoanalytic theory, the stage of psychosexual development during which genital exploration and manipulation occur.

Phallic symbol. Any object which resembles the erect male sex organ.

Pharmacotherapy. Treatment by means of drugs.

Phenomenological. Referring to the immediate perceiving and experiencing of the individual.

Phenylketonuria (PKU). Type of mental retardation resulting from a metabolic deficiency.

Phobia. Irrational fear; the individual may realize its irrationality but nevertheless be unable to dispel it.

Phobic neurosis. Disorder characterized by intense fear of an object or situation which the individual consciously realizes poses no real danger.

Physiological dependence. Type of drug dependence involving withdrawal symptoms when drug is discontinued.

Pick's disease. Form of presenile dementia.

Pineal gland. Small gland at the base of the brain which helps regulate body's biological clock and may also pace sexual development.

Pituitary gland. Endocrine gland associated with many regulatory functions.

Placebo. An inactive treatment administered in such a way that individual thinks he or she is receiving an active treatment.

Play therapy. Use of play activities in psychotherapy with children.

Pleasure principle. In psychoanalysis, the demand that an instinctual need be immediately gratified regardless of reality.

Positive reinforcer. A reinforcer that increases the probability of recurrence of a given response.

Posthypnotic amnesia. Subject's lack of memory for the period during which he or she was hypnotized.

Posthypnotic suggestion. Suggestion given during hypnosis to be carried out by the subject after he or she is brought out of hypnosis.

Postpartum disturbances. Emotional disturbances associated with childbirth.

Posttraumatic disorders. Residual symptoms following traumatic experience.

Precipitating cause. The particular stress which triggers a disorder.

Predisposing cause. Factor which lowers the individual's stress tolerance and paves the way for the appearance of a disorder.

Predisposition. Likelihood that an individual will develop certain symptoms under given stress conditions.

Prejudice. Emotionally toned conception favorable or unfavorable to some person, group, or idea—typically in the absence of sound evidence.

Premature ejaculation. Inability of male to inhibit ejaculation long enough to satisfy his partner.

Prematurity. Birth of an infant before the end of normal period of pregnancy.

Premorbid. Existing prior to onset of mental disorder.

Prenatal. Before birth.

Presenile dementia. Brain deterioration occurring at an early age and accompanied by mental disorder.

Pressure. Demand made on an organism.

Primary cause. Cause without which a disorder would not have occurred.

Primary erectile dysfunction. Form of dysfunction in which male has never been able to sustain an erection long enough to have successful intercourse.

Primary orgasmic dysfunction. Inability on the part of a woman to have an orgasm.

Primary prevention. Establishing conditions designed to prevent occurrence of mental disorders.

Primary process. The gratification of an instinctual id demand by means of imagery or fantasy; a psychoanalytic concept.

Primary reaction tendencies. Constitutional tendencies apparent in infancy, such as sensitivity and activity level.

Privileged communication. Freedom from the obligation to report to the authorities information concerning legal guilt revealed by a client or patient.

Proband. In a genetic study, the original individual who evidences the trait in which the investigator is interested. Same as *index case*.

Problem checklist. Inventory used in behavioral assessment to determine an individual's fears, moods, and other problems.

Problem drinker. Behavioral term referring to one who has serious problems associated with drinking. Term is currently preferable to *alcoholic*.

Process-reactive. Dimensions of schizophrenia referring to gradual or acute onset of symptoms.

Prognosis. Prediction as to the probable course and outcome of a disorder.

Programmed learning. Method of instruction or learning in which the student is guided through the subject matter step by step.

Projection. Ego-defense mechanism in which individual attributes unacceptable desires and impulses to others.

Projective technique. Any psychological technique for the diagnosis of personality organization utilizing relatively unstructured stimuli which reveal the individual's basic attitudes, conflicts, and so on.

Prostitution. Sexual service for financial gain.

Pseudo-community. Delusional social environment developed by a paranoiac.

Pseudo-mutuality. Relationship among family members that appears to be mutual, understanding, and open, but in fact is not.

Psilocybin. Hallucinogenic drug derived from a mushroom.

Psychedelic drugs. "Mind expanding" drugs, such as LSD, which often result in hallucinations.

Psychedelic therapy. Use of LSD as an adjunct in treatment of severe obsessive or alcoholic individuals.

Psychiatric nursing. Field of nursing primarily concerned with mental disorders.

Psychiatrist. Medical doctor who specializes in the diagnosis and treatment of mental disorders.

Psychiatry. Field of medicine concerned with understanding, assessing, treating, and preventing mental disorders.

Psychic pain. Synonym for *anxiety*.

Psychic trauma. Stressful psychological experience of a severely traumatic nature.

Psychoactive drug. Any drug that primarily affects mental functioning.

Psychoanalysis. Theoretical model and therapeutic approach developed by Freud.

Psychodrama. Psychotherapeutic technique in which the acting of various roles is a cardinal part.

Psychodynamic. A term in psychoanalytic theory referring to the psychic forces and processes developed through the individual's childhood experiences and which influence adult thinking and behavior.

Psychogenic. Of psychological origin: originating in the psychological functioning of the individual.

Psychogenic pain disorder. A neurotic disorder in which pain is the predominant complaint.

Psychological autopsy. An analytical procedure used to determine whether or not death was self-inflicted.

Psychological need. Need emerging out of environmental interactions, e.g., the need for social approval.

Psychological test. Standardized procedure designed to measure the subject's performance on a specified task.

Psychomotor. Involving both psychological and physical activity.

Psychomotor epilepsy. State of disturbed consciousness in which the individual may perform various actions, sometimes of a homicidal nature, for which he or she is later amnesic.

Psychomotor retardation. Slowing down of psychological and motor functions.

Psychopathic (antisocial) personality. Sociopathic disorder characterized by lack of moral development and inability to show loyalty to other persons or groups.

Psychopathology. Mental disorder.

Psychopharmacological drugs. Drugs used in treatment of mental disorders.

Psychophysiologic disorders. See **Psychosomatic disorders.**

Psychosexual development. Freudian view of development as involving a succession of stages, each characterized by a dominant mode of achieving libidinal pleasure.

Psychosis. Severe psychological disorder involving loss of contact with reality and gross personality distortion. Hospitalization is ordinarily required.

Psychosocial. Pertaining to interpersonal interactions and relations which influence the individual's development and/or behavior.

Psychosocial deprivation. Lack of needed stimulation and interaction during early life.

Psychosomatic (psychophysiologic) disorders. Physical symptoms, which may involve actual tissue damage, resulting from continued emotional mobilization under stress.

Psychosurgery. Brain surgery used in treatment of functional mental disorders or occasionally to relieve pain.

Psychotherapy. Treatment of mental disorders by psychological methods.

Puberty. Stage of physical development when reproduction first becomes possible.

Punishment. Application of aversive stimulation in response to behavior considered undesirable.

Q-sort. A personality inventory in which subject, or clinician, sorts a number of statements into piles according to their applicability to the subject.

Racism. Prejudice and discrimination directed toward individuals or groups because of their racial background.

Random sample. Sample drawn in such a way that each member of population has equal chance of being selected; hopefully representative of population from which drawn.

Rape. An act of violence in which sexual relations are forced upon another person.

Rapport. Interpersonal relationship characterized by a spirit of cooperation, confidence, and harmony.

Rating scale. Device for evaluating oneself or someone else in regard to specific traits.

Rational-emotive therapy. Form of psychotherapy focusing on cognitive and emotional restructuring to foster adaptive behavior.

Rationalization. Ego-defense mechanism in which the individual thinks up "good" reasons to justify his or her actions.

Reaction formation. Ego-defense mechanism in which individual's conscious attitudes and overt behavior are opposite to repressed unconscious wishes.

Reality assumptions. Assumptions which relate to the gratification of needs in the light of environmental possibilities, limitations, and dangers.

Reality principle. Awareness of the demands of the environment and adjustment of behavior to meet these demands.

Reality testing. Behavior aimed at testing or exploring the nature of the individual's social and physical environment; often used more specifically to refer to the testing of the limits of permissiveness of his social environment.

Reality therapy. Form of therapy based on assumption that emotional difficulties arise when an individual violates his or her basic sense of right and wrong.

Recessive gene. Gene which is effective only when paired with an identical gene.

Recidivism. A shift back to one's original behavior (often delinquent or criminal) after a period of treatment or rehabilitation.

Reciprocal inhibition.   Technique of desensitization used in behavior therapy in which responses antagonistic to anxiety are paired with anxiety-eliciting stimuli.

Recompensation.   Increase in integration or inner organization. Opposite of *decompensation*.

Reentry.   Return from the openness of an encounter group to the real world, which is presumably less open and honest.

Referral.   Sending or recommending an individual and/or family for psychological assessment and/or treatment.

Regression.   Ego-defense mechanism in which the individual retreats to the use of less mature responses in attempting to cope with stress and maintain ego integrity.

Rehabilitation.   Use of reeducation rather than punishment to overcome behavioral deficits.

Reinforcement.   In classical conditioning, the process of following the conditioned stimulus with the unconditioned stimulus; in operant conditioning, the rewarding of desired responses.

Reinforcing cause.   A circumstance tending to maintain behavior that is ultimately maladaptive, as in **secondary gain.**

Rejection.   Lack of acceptance of another person, usually referring to such treatment of a child by the parents.

Reliability.   Degree to which a test or measuring device produces the same result each time it is used to measure the same thing.

REM sleep.   Stage of sleep involving rapid eye movements (REM), associated with dreaming.

Remission.   Marked improvement or recovery appearing in the course of a mental illness; may or may not be permanent.

Representative sample.   Small group selected in such a way as to be representative of the larger group from which it is drawn.

Repression.   Ego-defense mechanism by means of which dangerous desires and intolerable memories are kept out of consciousness.

Reserpine.   One of the early antipsychotic drugs, now largely supplanted by newer drugs.

Resistance.   Tendency to maintain symptoms and resist treatment or uncovering of repressed material.

Resistance to extinction.   Tendency of a conditioned response to persist despite lack of reinforcement.

Respondent conditioning.   See **Classical conditioning.**

Reticular activating system (RAS).   Fibers going from the reticular formation to higher brain centers and presumably functioning as a general arousal system.

Reticular formation.   Neural nuclei and fibers in the brain stem which apparently play an important role in arousing and alerting the organism and in controlling attention.

Retrograde amnesia.   Loss of memory for events during a circumscribed period prior to brain injury or damage.

Retrospective study.   Research approach which attempts to retrace earlier events in the life of the subject.

Reverse tolerance.   Situation in which a decreased amount of some psychoactive drug brings about the effects formerly achieved by a larger dose.

Reynaud's disease.   A potentially serious constriction of the small blood vessels of the extremities, cutting off adequate blood flow to them; sometimes considered psychosomatic.

Rigid control.   Coping patterns involving reliance upon inner restraints, such as inhibition, suppression, repression, and reaction formation.

Rigidity.   Tendency to follow established coping patterns, with failure to see alternatives or extreme difficulty in changing one's established patterns.

Ritalin.   A central nervous system stimulant often used to treat hyperactivity in children.

Role.   See **Social role.**

Role distortion.   Violation of expected role behavior in an undesirable way.

Role obsolescence.   Condition occurring when the ascribed social role of a given individual is no longer of importance to the social group.

Role playing.   Form of psychotherapy in which the individual acts out a social role other than his or her own or tries out a new role.

Rorschach test.   A series of inkblots to which the subject responds with associations that come to mind. Analysis of these productions enables the clinician to infer personality characteristics.

Sadism.   Sexual variant in which sexual gratification is obtained by the infliction of pain upon others.

St. Vitus' dance.   Hysterical chorea of common occurrence during the Middle Ages.

Sample.   Group upon which measurements are taken; should normally be representative of the population about which an inference is to be made.

Scapegoating.   Displacement of aggression onto some object, person, or group other than the source of frustration.

Schedule of reinforcement.   Program of rewards for requisite behavior.

Schizo-affective psychosis.   Disorder characterized by schizophrenic symptoms in conjunction with pronounced depression or elation.

Schizoid personality.   Personality pattern characterized by shyness, oversensitivity, seclusiveness, and eccentricity.

Schizophrenia.   Psychosis characterized by the breakdown of integrated personality functioning, withdrawal from reality, emotional blunting and distortion, and disturbances in thought and behavior.

Schizotypal personality.   Personality disorder in which egocentricity, avoidance of others, and eccentricity of thought and perception are distinguishing traits.

School phobia.   Term used to denote refusal to go to school, a condition which results from the child's overdependency and fearfulness.

Secondary cause.   Factor which contributes to a mental illness but which in and of itself would not have produced it, as distinct from the *primary cause*.

Secondary erectile dysfunction.   Condition in which male has been capable of successful intercourse but is currently dysfunctional.

Secondary gain.   Indirect benefit from neurotic or other symptoms.

Secondary prevention.   Preventive techniques

focusing on early detection and correction of maladaptive patterns within context of individual's present life situation.

Secondary process. Reality-oriented rational processes of the ego.

Secondary reinforcer. Reinforcement provided by a stimulus that has gained reward value by being associated with a primary reinforcing stimulus.

Security. Maintenance of conditions necessary to need gratification.

Sedative. Drug used to reduce tension and induce relaxation and sleep.

Selective attention. A tuning of attentional and perceptual processes towards stimuli relevant or central to goal-directed behavior, with decreased sensitivity to stimuli irrelevant or peripheral to this purpose.

Self (ego). The integrating core of the personality which mediates between needs and reality.

Self-acceptance. Being satisfied with one's attributes and qualities while remaining aware of one's limitations.

Self-actualization. Fulfillment of one's potentialities as a human being.

Self-concept. The individual's sense of his or her own identity, worth, capabilities, and limitations.

Self-devaluation. Lowered feelings of worth and self-esteem.

Self-differentiation. Degree to which the individual achieves a sense of unique identity apart from the group.

Self-direction. Basing one's behavior on inner assumptions rather than external contingencies.

Self-esteem. Feeling of personal worth.

Self-evaluation. Way in which the individual views the self, in terms of worth, adequacy, etc.

Self-fulfillment. Living a meaningful, actualizing, and fulfilling life.

Self-ideal. See **Ego-ideal.**

Self-identity. Individual's delineation and awareness of his or her continuing identity as a person.

Self-instructional training. A cognitive behavioral method aimed at teaching the individual to alter his or her covert behavior.

Self-monitor. To observe and record one's own behavior.

Self-recrimination. Self-condemnation and blame.

Self-reinforcement. Reward of self for desired or appropriate behavior.

Self-statements. Implicit "verbalizations" of what a person is experiencing.

Self-theory. Personality theory which utilizes the self-concept as the integrating core of personality organization and functioning.

Self-worth. The individual's evaluation of himself or herself.

Senile. Pertaining to old age.

Senile dementia. A form of psychosis caused in part by deteriorative brain changes due to aging.

Sensate focus training. Training to derive pleasure from touching one's partner and being touched by him or her; used in sexual therapy to enhance sexual feelings and help overcome sexual dysfunction.

Sensitivity training group (T-group). One type of small group designed to provide intensive group experience and foster self-understanding and personal growth.

Sensory awareness. Openness to new ways of experiencing and feeling.

Sensory deprivation. Restriction of sensory stimulation below the level required for normal functioning of the central nervous system.

Sentence-completion test. Form of projective technique utilizing incomplete sentences that the subject is to complete, analysis of which enables the clinician to infer personality dynamics.

Separation anxiety. Intense fear experienced when individual is separated from someone on whom he or she feels dependent.

Sequelae. Symptoms remaining as the aftermath of a disorder.

Sexual deviate. Individual who manifests nonconforming sexual behavior, often of a pathological nature.

Sexual dysfunction. Inability or impaired ability to experience or give sexual gratification.

Shaping. Form of instrumental conditioning; at first, all responses resembling the desired one are reinforced, then only the closest approximations, until finally the desired response is attained.

Sheltered workshops. Workshops where mentally retarded or otherwise handicapped individuals can engage in constructive work in the community.

"Shock" reaction. Transient personality decompensation in the face of sudden acute stress.

Shock therapy. Use of electroshock or related methods in treating mental disorders.

Siblings. Offspring of the same parents.

Sick role. Protected role provided by society via medical model for individual suffering from severe physical or mental disorder.

Situational orgasmic dysfunction. Inability of a woman to have an orgasm with a particular person or in a particular situation.

Situational stress reaction (acute). Superficial maladjustment to newly experienced life situations which are especially difficult or trying.

Situational test. Test which measures performance in a simulated life situation.

Social exchange. Model of interpersonal relationships based on the premise that such relationships are formed for mutual need gratification.

Social introversion. A trait characterized by shy, withdrawn, and inhibited behavior.

Socialization. The process by which a child acquires the values and impulse controls deemed appropriate by his or her culture.

Social learning programs. Behavioral treatment techniques using learning principles, especially token economies, to help chronic patients assume more responsibility for their own behavior.

Social norms. Group standards concerning behaviors viewed as acceptable or unacceptable.

Social pathology. Abnormal patterns of social organization, attitudes, or behavior; undesirable social conditions which tend to produce individual pathology.

Social role. Behavior expected of individual occupying given position in group.

Social sanction. Punishment by group for violation of social norms.

"Social" self.   The facade the individual displays to others as contrasted with the private self.

Social worker.   Person in mental health field with a master's degree in social work (MSW) plus supervised training in clinical or social service agencies.

Sociocultural.   Pertaining to broad social conditions which influence the development and/or behavior of individuals and groups.

Socioeconomic status.   Position on social and economic scale in community; determined largely by income and occupational level.

Sociogenic.   Having its roots in sociocultural conditions or causes.

Sociopathic disorder.   Lack of social responsibility and inability to conform to prevailing social norms even when such norms are adaptive.

Sociotherapy.   Treatment of interpersonal aspects of the individual's life situation.

Sodium pentothal.   Barbiturate drug sometimes used in psychotherapy to produce a state of relaxation and suggestibility.

Sodomy.   Sexual intercourse via the anus.

Somatic.   Pertaining to the body.

Somatic weakness.   Special vulnerability of given organ systems to stress.

Somatotype.   Physique or build of a person, as assessed by various theories relating temperament to physical characteristics.

Somnambulism.   Sleepwalking.

Spasm.   Intense, involuntary, usually painful contraction of muscle or group of muscles.

Spasticity.   Marked hypertonicity or continual over-contraction of muscles, causing stiffness, awkwardness, and motor incoordination.

Special vulnerability.   Low tolerance for specific types of stress.

Sperm.   Male gamete or germ cell.

Split-brain research.   Research associated with split-brain surgery, which cuts off transmission of information from one cerebral hemisphere to the other.

Spontaneous recovery (remission).   Recovery of a mental patient without treatment or with minimal treatment.

S-R psychologists.   Psychologists who emphasize the role of stimulus-response (S-R) connections in learning. Also called *associationists*.

Stage of exhaustion.   Third and final stage in the general-adaptation-syndrome, in which the organism is no longer able to resist continuing stress; may result in death.

Stage of resistance.   Second stage of the general-adaptation-syndrome.

Standardization.   Procedure for establishing the expected performance range on a test.

Stanford-Binet.   A standardized intelligence test for children.

Startle reaction.   Sudden involuntary motor reaction to intense unexpected stimuli; may result from mild stimuli if person is hypersensitive.

Status comparison.   A process by which an individual estimates his or her own worth by measuring it against the achievements of others.

Statutory rape.   Sexual intercourse with a minor.

Stereotype.   A generalized notion of how people of a given race, religion, or other group will appear, think, feel, or act.

Stereotypy.   Persistent and inappropriate repetition of phrases, gestures, or acts.

Stimulants.   Drugs that tend to increase feelings of alertness, reduce feelings of fatigue, and enable individual to stay awake over sustained periods of time.

Stimulus generalization.   The spread of a conditioned response to some stimulus similar to, but not identical with, the conditioned stimulus.

Stress.   The internal responses caused by application of a stressor.

Stress-decompensation model.   View of abnormal behavior which emphasizes progressive disorganization of behavior under excessive stress.

Stress-inoculation training.   A cognitive-behavioral treatment that prepares people to handle stressful situations by altering their attitudes toward themselves and the stressor.

Stress interview.   Interview of a subject in which stressors are introduced.

Stressor.   Any adjustive demand that requires coping behavior on the part of individual or group.

Stress tolerance (frustration tolerance).   Nature, degree, and duration of stress which an individual can tolerate without undergoing serious personality decompensation.

Stroke.   See **Cerebrovascular accident.**

Structural therapy.   A treatment for autistic children in which the environment is structured to provide spontaneous physical and verbal stimulation to autistic children.

Structured family therapy.   Treatment of the entire family by analysis of communication between family members.

Student's disease.   Common belief among students of abnormal psychology that they have the symptoms of the disorders they are studying.

Stupor.   Condition of lethargy and unresponsiveness, with partial or complete unconsciousness.

Stuttering.   Speech disorder characterized by a blocking or repetition of initial sounds of words.

Sublimation.   Ego-defense mechanism by means of which frustrated sexual energy is partially channeled into substitutive activities.

Substance use disorder.   Patterns of maladaptive behavior centered around drug consumption.

Substitution.   Acceptance of substitute goals or satisfactions in place of those originally sought after or desired.

Successive approximation.   See **Shaping.**

Suicide.   Taking one's own life.

Suicidology.   The study of the causes and prevention of suicide.

Superego.   Conscience; ethical or moral dimensions (attitudes) of personality.

Suppression.   Conscious forcing of desires or thoughts out of consciousness; conscious inhibition of desires or impulses.

Surrogate.   Substitute parent, child, or mate.

Survey methods.   Procedures for obtaining opinions or other data concerning a given population.

Swinging. Mate swapping and other group sex practices.

Symbol. Image, word, object, or activity that is used to represent something else.

Symbolism. Representation of one idea or object by another.

Sympathetic division. Division of the autonomic nervous system which is active in emergency conditions of extreme cold, violent effort, and emotions.

Symptom. An observable manifestation of a physical or mental disorder.

Syncope. Temporary loss of consciousness resulting from cerebral anoxia.

Syndrome. Group or pattern of symptoms which occur together in a disorder and represent the typical picture of the disorder.

Syphilophobia. Morbid fear of syphilis.

System. An assemblage of interdependent parts, living or nonliving.

Systematic desensitization. A behavior therapy technique for eliminating maladaptive anxiety responses.

Tachycardia. Rapid heartbeat.

Tactual hallucinations. Hallucinations involving the sense of touch, such as feeling cockroaches crawling over one's body.

Tarantism. Type of hysterical dancing occurring in epidemic form during the Middle Ages.

Task-oriented reaction. Realistic rather than ego-defensive approach to stressors.

Tay-Sachs disease. Genetic disorder of lipoid metabolism usually resulting in death by age 3.

Telepathy. Communication from one person to another without use of any known sense organs.

Temporal lobe. Portion of cerebrum located in front of occipital lobe and separated from frontal and parietal lobes by the fissure of Sylvius.

Tension. Condition arising out of the mobilization of psychobiological resources to meet a threat; physically, involves an increase in muscle tonus and other emergency changes; psychologically, is characterized by feelings of strain, uneasiness, and anxiety.

Tertiary prevention. Preventive techniques focusing on short-term hospitalization and intensive aftercare when an emotional breakdown has occurred, with aim of returning individual to his or her family and community setting as soon as possible.

Testes. Male reproductive glands or gonads.

Testosterone. Male sex hormone.

Thematic Apperception Test (TAT). A psychological test composed of a series of pictures based on which the subject makes up a story. Analysis of the story gives the clinician clues about the individual's conflicts, traits, personality dynamics, and so on.

Therapeutic. Pertaining to treatment or healing.

Therapeutic community. The hospital environment used for therapeutic purposes.

Therapy. Treatment; application of various treatment techniques.

Theta wave. Brain wave having a frequency of only 5 to 7 cycles per second.

Threat. Real or imagined danger to individual or group.

Thyroids. Endocrine glands located in neck which influence body metabolism, rate of physical growth, and development of intelligence.

Thyroxin. Hormone secreted by the thyroid glands.

Tic. Intermittent twitching or jerking, usually of facial muscles.

Token economy. Reinforcement technique often used in hospital or institutional settings in which individuals are rewarded for socially constructive behavior with tokens that can then be exchanged for desired objects or activities.

Tolerance. Physiological condition in which increased dosage of an addictive drug is needed to obtain effects previously produced by smaller dose.

Tonic. Pertaining to muscle tension or contraction; muscle tone.

Toxic. Poisonous.

Toxic deliria (psychoses). Severe disturbances in cerebral functions resulting from toxins.

Trait. Characteristic of individual which can be observed or measured.

Trance. Sleeplike state in which the range of consciousness is limited and voluntary activities are suspended; a deep hypnotic state.

Tranquilizers. Drugs used for antipsychotic purposes and/or reduction of anxiety and tension. See also **Major tranquilizers, Minor tranquilizers.**

Transactional analysis. Form of interpersonal therapy based on interaction of "Child," "Adult," and "Parent" ego states.

Transference. Process whereby client projects attitudes and emotions applicable to another significant person onto the therapist; emphasized in psychoanalytic therapy.

Transient situational disorder. Temporary mental disorder developing under conditions of overwhelming stress, as in military combat or civilian catastrophes.

Transsexualism. Identification of oneself with members of opposite sex, as opposed to acceptance of one's anatomical sexual identity.

Transvestism. Persistent desire to dress in clothing of the opposite sex, often accompanied by sexual excitement.

Trauma. Severe psychological or physiological stressor.

Traumatic. Pertaining to a wound or injury, or to psychic shock.

Traumatic neurosis. See **"Shock" reaction.**

Treatment contract. Explicit arrangement between therapist and client designed to bring about specific behavioral changes.

Tremor. Repeated fine spastic movement.

Turner's syndrome. Form of mental retardation associated with sex chromosome anomaly.

Ulcer. Open sore in mucosa lining of the stomach.

Unconscious. As used by Freud, psychological material that has been repressed. Also, loss of consciousness; lack of awareness.

Unconscious motivation. Motivation for an individual's behavior of which he or she is unaware.

Underarousal. Inadequate physiological response to a given stimulus.

Undoing. Ego-defense mechanism by means of which the individual performs activities designed to atone for his or her misdeeds, thereby, in a sense, "undoing" them.

Unipolar disorder. A severe affective disorder in which only depressive episodes occur, as opposed to *bipolar* disorder in which both manic and depressive processes are assumed to occur.

Unsocialized disturbance of conduct. Childhood disorder in which the child is disobedient, hostile, and highly aggressive.

Vaginismus. An involuntary muscle spasm at the entrance to the vagina that prevents penetration and sexual intercourse.

Validity. Extent to which a measuring instrument actually measures what it purports to measure.

Values. Assumptions concerning good and bad, right and wrong.

Variable. A characteristic or property that may assume any one of a set of different qualities or quantities.

Vasomotor. Pertaining to the walls of the blood vessels.

Vegetative. Withdrawn or deteriorated to the point where the individual leads a passive, vegetablelike existence.

Verbigeration. Prolonged and monotonous repetition of meaningless words and phrases.

Vertigo. Dizziness.

Vicarious living. Attempt to evade efforts toward self-fulfillment by repressing one's own individuality and identifying with some hero or ideal.

Vicious circle. Chain reaction in which individual resorts to an unhealthy defensive reaction in trying to solve his or her problems, which only serves to complicate them and make them harder to solve.

Virilism. Accentuation of masculine secondary sex characteristics, especially in a woman or young boy, caused by hormonal imbalance.

Viscera. Internal organs.

Visual hallucinations. Hallucinations involving sense of sight.

Voyeurism. Achievement of sexual pleasure through clandestine "peeping," usually watching other persons disrobe and/or engage in sexual activities.

Waxy flexibility. Condition in which a patient will maintain the position in which his or her limbs are placed for an unusually long period of time.

Wechsler Intelligence Scale for Children (WISC). A standardized intelligence scale for children.

Withdrawal. Intellectual, emotional, or physical retreat.

Withdrawal disturbance. Disorder of childhood in which the child becomes aloof and detached from a world he or she sees as dangerous.

Withdrawal symptoms. Wide range of symptoms evidenced by addicts when the drug on which they are physiologically dependent is not available.

Word salad. Jumbled or incoherent use of words by psychotic or disoriented individuals.

Working through. Confronting and dealing with a problem situation until satisfactory adjustments are achieved and established.

Worry. Persistent concern about past behavior or about anticipated dangers in the present or future.

X chromosome. Sex-determining chromosome: all female gametes contain X chromosomes, and if fertilized ovum has also received an X chromosome from its father it will be female.

XYY syndrome. A chromosomal anomaly in males (presence of an extra Y chromosome) possibly related to impulsive behavior.

Y chromosome. Sex-determining chromosome found in half of the total number of male gametes; uniting with X chromosome always provided by female produces a male offspring.

Zygote. Fertilized egg cell formed by union of male and female gametes.

Acknowledgments and references

The reference list includes not only the sources from which the authors have drawn material, but also acknowledgments of the permission granted by authors and publishers to quote directly from their works.

Journal Abbreviations

ACTA PSYCHIATR. SCANDIN.— *Acta Psychiatrica Scandinavica*
AIR UNIVER. QUART. REV.— *Air University Quarterly Review*
AMER. J. MED. SCI.— *American Journal of Medical Science*
AMER. J. MENT. DEF.— *American Journal of Mental Deficiency*
AMER. J. NURS.— *American Journal of Nursing*
AMER. J. OCCUPA. THER.— *American Journal of Occupational Therapy*
AMER. J. ORTHOPSYCHIAT.— *American Journal of Orthopsychiatry*
AMER. J. PSYCHIAT.— *American Journal of Psychiatry*
AMER. J. PSYCHOTHER.— *American Journal of Psychotherapy*
AMER. PSYCHOLOGIST— *American Psychologist*
AMER. SCIEN.— *American Scientist*
ANN. AMER. ACAD. POLIT. SOC. SCI.— *Annals of the American Academy of Political and Social Science*
ANN. N. Y. ACAD. SCI.— *Annals of the New York Academy of Science*
ANNU. REV. PSYCHOL.— *Annual Review of Psychology*
ARCH. GEN. PSYCHIAT.— *Archives of General Psychiatry*
ARCH. INT. MED.— *Archives of Internal Medicine*
ARCH. NEUROL. PSYCHIAT.— *Archives of Neurology and Psychiatry*
BEHAV. RES. THER.— *Behavior Research and Therapy*
BEHAV. SCI.— *Behavioral Science*
BEHAV. TODAY.— *Behavior Today*
BRIT. J. EDUC. PSYCHOL.— *British Journal of Educational Psychology*
BRIT. J. MED. PSYCHOL.— *British Journal of Medical Psychology*
BRIT. J. OPHTHALMOL.— *British Journal of Ophthalmology*
BRIT. J. PSYCHIAT.— *British Journal of Psychiatry*
BRIT. MED. J.— *British Medical Journal*
BULL. MENNINGER CLIN.— *Bulletin of the Menninger Clinic*
CHARACT. & PERS.— *Character and Personality*
CHILD DEVELOP.— *Child Development*
COMM. MENT. HLTH. J.— *Community Mental Health Journal*
DEVELOP. MED. CHILD NEUROL.— *Developmental Medicine & Child Neurology*
DEVELOP. PSYCHOL.— *Developmental Psychology*
DIS. NERV. SYS.— *Diseases of the Nervous System*
GEN. PSYCHIAT.— *General Psychiatry*
GROUP PSYCHOTHER.— *Group Psychotherapy*
HARVARD ED. REV.— *Harvard Educational Review*
HUMAN DEVELOP.— *Human Development*
INTER. J. GROUP PSYCHOTHER.— *International Journal of Group Psychotherapy*
INTER. J. PSYCHIAT.— *International Journal of Psychiatry*
INTER. J. PSYCHOANAL.— *International Journal of Psychoanalysis*
J. ABNORM. PSYCHOL.— *Journal of Abnormal Psychology*
J. ABNORM. SOC. PSYCHOL.— *Journal of Abnormal and Social Psychology*
JAMA— *Journal of the American Medical Association*

J. AMER. ACAD. CHILD PSYCHIAT.— *Journal of the American Academy of Child Psychiatry*
J. APPL. BEH. ANAL.— *Journal of Applied Behavior Analysis*
J. BEHAV. RES. EXP. PSYCHIAT.— *Journal of Behavior Research and Experimental Psychiatry*
J. BEHAV. THER. EXP. PSYCHIAT.— *Journal of Behavior Therapy and Experimental Psychiatry*
J. CHILD PSYCHOL. PSYCHIAT.— *Journal of Child Psychology and Psychiatry*
J. CLIN. PSYCHOL.— *Journal of Clinical Psychology*
J. CLIN. PSYCHOPATH.— *Journal of Clinical Psychopathology*
J. COMPAR. PHYSIOL. PSYCHOL.— *Journal of Comparative and Physiological Psychology*
J. CONS. CLIN. PSYCHOL.— *Journal of Consulting and Clinical Psychology*
J. COUNS. PSYCHOL.— *Journal of Counseling Psychology*
J. CRIM. LAW CRIMINOL. POLICE SCI.— *Journal of Criminal Law, Criminology, and Police Science*
J. CRIM. PSYCHOPATH. PSYCHOTHER.— *Journal of Criminal Psychopathology and Psychotherapy*
J. EXPER. ANAL. BEHAV.— *Journal of Experimental Analysis of Behavior*
J. EXPER. CHILD PSYCHOL.— *Journal of Experimental Child Psychology*
J. EXPER. PSYCHOL.— *Journal of Experimental Psychology*
J. EXPER. RES. PERSON.— *Journal of Experimental Research in Personality*
J. GEN. PSYCHOL.— *Journal of General Psychology*
J. GENET. PSYCHOL.— *Journal of Genetic Psychology*
J. GERIAT. PSYCHOL.— *Journal of Geriatric Psychology*
J. HLTH. SOC. BEHAV.— *Journal of Health and Social Behavior*
J. LEARN. DIS.— *Journal of Learning Disabilities*
J. MARR. FAM.— *Journal of Marriage and the Family*
J. MENT. SCI.— *Journal of Mental Science*
J. NERV. MENT. DIS.— *Journal of Nervous and Mental Disease*
J. PERSONAL.— *Journal of Personality*
J. PERS. SOC. PSYCHOL.— *Journal of Personality and Social Psychology*
J. PSYCHIAT.— *Journal of Psychiatry*
J. PSYCHIAT. RES.— *Journal of Psychiatric Research*
J. PSYCHOL.— *Journal of Psychology*
J. PSYCHOSOM. MED.— *Journal of Psychosomatic Medicine*
J. PSYCHOSOM. RES.— *Journal of Psychosomatic Research*
J. SOC. PSYCHOL.— *Journal of Social Psychology*
J. SPEC. ED.— *Journal of Special Education*
J. SPEECH HEAR. DIS.— *Journal of Speech and Hearing Disorders*
J. SPEECH HEAR. RES.— *Journal of Speech and Hearing Research*
MENT. HLTH. DIG.— *Mental Health Digest*
MENT. HLTH. PROG. REP.— *Mental Health Program Reports*
MENT. HYG.— *Mental Hygiene*
MONOGR. SOC. RES. CHILD DEVELOP.— *Monographs of the Society for Research in Child Development*
N.C. MED. J.— *North Carolina Medical Journal*
NEW ENGL. J. MED.— *New England Journal of Medicine*
N.Y. ST. J. MED.— *New York State Journal of Medicine*

PSYCHIAT. DIG.— *Psychiatry Digest*
PSYCHIAT. QUART.— *Psychiatric Quarterly*
PSYCHIAT. SOC. SCI. REV.— *Psychiatry and Social Science Review*
PSYCHOANAL. QUART.— *Psychoanalytic Quarterly*
PSYCHOANAL. REV.— *Psychoanalytic Review*
PSYCHOL. BULL.— *Psychological Bulletin*
PSYCHOL. REC.— *Psychological Record*
PSYCH. REP.— *Psychological Reports*
PSYCH. REV.— *Psychological Review*
PSYCHOSOM. MED.— *Psychosomatic Medicine*
PSYCH. TODAY — *Psychology Today*
PUBL. MASS. MED. SOC.— *Publication of the Massachusetts Medical Society*
QUART. J. STUD. ALCOHOL.— *Quarterly Journal of Studies in Alcoholism*
SAT. REV.— *Saturday Review*
SCI. J.— *Science Journal*
SCI. NEWS— *Science News*
SCI. NEWSLETTER— *Science Newsletter*
SCI. TECH.— *Science and Technology*
SCIENTIF. AMER.— *Scientific American*
SOC. PSYCHIAT.— *Social Psychiatry*
SOCIOL. QUART.— *Sociological Quarterly*
WORLD MENT. HLTH.— *World Mental Health*

1. Abnormal Behavior in Our Times

American Psychiatric Association. *Diagnostic and statistical manual of mental disorders.* Third Edition *(DSM-III Draft).* Washington, D.C.: American Psychiatric Association, 1979. Reprinted by permission of the American Psychiatric Association.

American Psychological Association. *Ethical standards of psychologists.* Washington, D.C.: APA, 1972.

Bluemel, C. S. *War, politics, and insanity.* Denver: World Press, 1948.

Born, W. Great artists who suffered from mental disorders. *Ciba Symposia,* 1946, **7,** 225–33.

Edwards, J. Sinners in the hands of an angry God. *The works of President Edwards in eight volumes* (Vol. 7). Worcester: Isiah Thomas, 1809.

Hirsch, S. et al. (Eds.). *Madness network news reader.* San Francisco: New Glide Publications, 1974. Poem entitled "Self-knowledge" from VISIONS OF A MADMAN by P. G. Harrison. Reprinted by permission of the author.

Kaplan, A. A philosophical discussion of normality. *Arch. Gen Psychiat.,* 1967, **17,** 325–30.

Kesey, K. *One flew over the cuckoo's nest.* New York: Viking Press, 1973.

Langer, E. J., & Abelson, R. P. A patient by any other name . . . ; Clinician group difference in labeling bias. *J. Cons. Clin. Psychol.* Feb. 1974, **42**(1), 4–9.

Lombroso, C. *Man of genius.* New York: Scribner's, 1891.

Marks, J. *Genius and disaster.* New York: Greenberg, 1925.

Martindale, C. Father's absence, psychopathology, & poetic eminence. *Psych. Rep.,* Dec. 1972, **31**(3), 843–47.

President's Commission on Mental Health. *Report.* Washington: U.S. Government Printing Office, 1978.

Rabkin, J. G. Opinions about mental illness: A review of the literature. *Psychol. Bull.,* Mar. 1972, **77**(3), 153–71.

Rabkin, J. G. Criminal behavior of discharged mental patients: A critical appraisal of the research. *Psychol. Bull.,* 1979, **86**(1), 1–27.

Rogers, C. R. *Client-centered therapy.* Boston: Houghton-Mifflin, 1951.

Rosenhan, D. L. On being sane in insane places. *Science,* 1973, **179**(4070), 365–69.

Sewell, W. S. (Ed.). *Famous personalities.* Philadelphia: Blakiston, 1943.

Ullmann, L. P., & Krasner, L. *Psychological approach to abnormal behavior* (2nd ed.). Englewood Cliffs, N.J.: Prentice-Hall, 1975.

United States Department of Health, Education and Welfare. National health survey. *Roche Report,* 1971,**1**(9), 2.

Vonnegut, K. *Breakfast of champions.* New York: Delacorte, 1974.

Whitwell, J. R. *Historical notes on psychiatry.* London: H. K. Lewis, 1936.

Zilboorg, G., & Henry, G. W. *A history of medical psychology.* New York: Norton, 1941.

Zitrin, A., Hardesty, A. S., Burdock, E. I., & Drossman, A. K. Crime and violence among mental patients. *Amer. J. Psychiat.,* 1976, **133**(2), 142–49.

2. From Demonology to the Biological Viewpoint

Alexander, F. G., & Selesnick, S. T. *History of psychiatry.* New York: Harper & Row, 1966.

Aring, C. D. The Gheel experience: Eternal spirit of the chainless mind! *JAMA,* 1974, **230**(7), 998–1001.

Aring, C. D. Science and the citizen. *Scientif. Amer.,* Jan. 1975, **232**(1), 48–49; 52–53.

Belgian Consulate. Los Angeles, California. Personal communication, Jan. 2, 1975.

Bennett, A. E. Mad doctors. *J. Nerv. Ment. Dis.,* 1947, **106,** 11–18.

Bockhoven, J. S. *Moral treatment in community mental health.* New York: Springer, 1972.

Bromberg, W. *The mind of man.* New York: Harper, 1937.

Browne, E. G. *Arabian medicine.* New York: Macmillan, 1921.

Campbell, D. *Arabian medicine and its influence on the Middle Ages.* New York: Dutton, 1926.

Castiglioni, A. *Adventures of the mind.* New York: Knopf, 1946.

Cockayne, T. O. *Leechdoms, wort cunning, and star craft of early England.* London: Longman, Green, Longman, Roberts & Green, 1864–1886.

Deutsch, A. *The mentally ill in America.* New York: Columbia University Press, 1946.

Gloyne, H. F. Tarantism. *American Imago,* 1950, **7,** 29–42.

Guthrie, D. J. *A history of medicine.* Philadelphia: Lippincott, 1946.

Karnosh, L. J. (with collaboration of Zucker, E. M.). *Handbook of psychiatry.* St. Louis: C. V. Mosby, 1945. Reprinted by permission.

Lewis, N. D. C. *A short history of psychiatric achievement.* New York: Norton, 1941.

Mora, G. Paracelsus' psychiatry. *Amer. J. Psychiat.,* 1967, **124,** 803–14.

Plato. *The laws* (Vol. 5). G. Burges (Tr.). London: George Bell & Sons, n.d.

Polvan, N. Historical aspects of mental ills in Middle East discussed. *Roche Reports,* 1969, **6**(12), 3.

Rees, T. P. Back to moral treatment and community care. *J. Ment. Scien.,* 1957, **103,** 303–13. In H. B. Adams, "Mental illness" or interpersonal behavior? *Amer. Psychologist,* 1964, **19,** 191–97.

Rosen, G. Emotion and sensibility in ages of anxiety. *Amer. J. Psychiat.,* 1967, **124,** 771–84.

Russell, W. L. A psychopathic department of an American general hospital in 1808. *Amer. J. Psychiat.,* 1941, **98,** 229–37.

Sarbin, T. R., & Juhasz, J. B. The historical background of the concept of hallucination. *Journal of the History of the Behavioral Sciences,* 1967, **3,** 339–58.

Selling, L. S. *Men against madness.* New York: Garden City Books, 1943.

Sigerist, H. E. *Civilization and disease.* Ithaca, N.Y.: Cornell University Press, 1943.

Stone, S. Psychiatry through the ages. *J. Abnorm. Soc. Psychol.,* 1937, **32,** 131–60.

Tseng, W. S. The development of psychiatric concepts in

traditional Chinese medicine. *Arch. Gen. Psychiat.,* Oct. 1973, **29**(4), 569–75.

White, A. D. *A history of the warfare of science with theology in Christendom.* New York: Appleton, 1896.

Whitwell, J. R. *Historical notes on psychiatry.* London: H. K. Lewis, 1936.

Zilboorg, G., & Henry, G. W. *A history of medical psychology.* New York: Norton, 1941.

3. Psychosocial and Sociocultural Viewpoints

Bandura, A. Behavior theory and the models of man. *Amer. Psychologist,* Dec. 1974, **29**(12), 859–69.

Bem, D. J. Self-perception theory. In L. Berkowitz (Ed.), *Advances in experimental social psychology* (Vol. 6). New York: Academic Press, 1972.

Benedict, R. Anthropology and the abnormal. *J. Gen. Psychol.,* 1934, **10**, 59–82.

Berne, E. *Games people play: The psychology of human relationships.* New York: Grove Press, 1964.

Berne, E. *What do you say after you say hello?* New York: Grove Press, 1972.

Brehm, S. S. *The application of social psychology to clinical practice.* New York: Halsted Press, 1976.

Brown, J. F., & Menninger, K. A. *Psychodynamics of abnormal behavior.* New York: McGraw-Hill, 1940.

Butcher, J. N., & Pancheri, P. *Handbook of international MMPI research.* Minneapolis: University of Minnesota Press, 1976.

Cautela, J. R. Covert processes and behavior modification. *J. Nerv. Ment. Dis.,* 1973, **157**(1), 27–36.

Cooper, J. R. M., Kendall, R. E., Gurland, B. J., Sharp, L., Copeland, J. R. M., & Simon, R. *Psychiatric diagnosis in New York and London.* London: Oxford University Press, 1972.

Dohrenwend, B. P., & Dohrenwend, B. P. Social and cultural influences on psychopathology. *Annu. Rev. Psychol.,* 1974, **25**, 417–52.

Draguns, J. G. Culture and personality. In A. J. Marsella, R. Tharp, & T. Cibowrowski (Eds.), *Perspectives in cross-cultural psychology.* New York: Academic Press. 1979.

Faris, R. E. L., & Dunham, H. W. *Mental disorders in urban areas.* Chicago: University of Chicago Press, 1939. (Reprinted, 1965.)

Goldfried, M. R., & Davison, G. C. *Clinical behavior therapy.* New York: Holt, Rinehart & Winston, 1976.

Goldfried, M. R., Lineham, M. M., & Smith, J. L. Reduction of test anxiety through cognitive restructuring. *J. Cons. Clin. Psychol.,* 1978, **46**(1), 32–39.

Heider, F. *The psychology of interpersonal relations.* New York: Wiley, 1958.

Homans, G. C. *Social behavior: Its elementary forms.* New York: Harcourt Brace Jovanovich, 1961.

Jaco, E. G. *The social epidemiology of mental disorders.* New York: Russell Sage Foundation, 1960.

James, W. *The principles of psychology* (Vols. 1 & 2). New York: Holt, 1890.

Jones, E. E., & Davis, K. E. From acts to dispositions: The attribution process in person perception. In L. Berkowitz (Ed.), *Advances in experimental social psychology* (Vol. 2). New York: Academic Press, 1965.

Jones, M. C. A laboratory study of fear: The case of Peter. *Pedagogical Seminary,* 1924, **31**, 308–15.

Kiev, A. *Transcultural psychiatry.* New York: Free Press, 1972.

Lazarus, A. A. *Behavior therapy and beyond.* New York: McGraw-Hill, 1971.

Lebra, W. (Ed.). Culture-bound syndromes, ethnopsychiatry and alternate therapies. In *Mental health research in Asia and the Pacific* (Vol. 4). Honolulu: University Press of Hawaii, 1976.

Lehmann, H. E. Psychiatric disorders not in standard nomenclature. In A. M. Freedman, H. I. Kaplan, & H. S. Kaplan (Eds.), *Comprehensive textbook of psychiatry.* Baltimore, Md.: Williams & Wilkins, 1967.

Lennard, H. L., & Bernstein, A. *Patterns in human interaction.* San Francisco: Jossey-Bass, 1969.

Levy, L., & Rowitz, L. Mapping out schizophrenia. *Human Behavior,* May 1974, **3**(5), 39–40.

Lovaas, O. I., Frietag, G., Gold, V. J., & Kassorla, I. C. Experimental studies in childhood schizophrenia. *J. Exper. Child. Psychol.,* 1965, **2**, 67–84.

Malinowski, B. *Sex and repression in savage society.* New York: Humanities, 1927.

Marsella, A. J. Cross-cultural studies of mental disorders. In A. J. Marsella, R. Tharp, & T. Cibowrowski (Eds.), *Perspectives in cross-cultural psychology.* New York: Academic Press, 1979.

Maslow, A. H. *Toward a psychology of being.* New York: Van Nostrand, 1962.

Maslow, A. H. Toward a humanistic biology. *Amer. Psychologist,* 1969, **24**(8), 734–35.

Mead, G. H. *Mind, self, and society: From the standpoint of a social behaviorist.* Chicago: University of Chicago Press, 1934.

Meichenbaum, D. H. *Cognitive-behavior modification.* New York: Plenum, 1977.

Morris, M. G. Psychological miscarriage: An end to mother love. *Trans-action,* 1966, **3**(2), 8–13.

Murphy, H. B. M., & Hall, B. Chronicity, community and culture. Paper presented at the Colloque sur traitments au long cours des états psychotiques, Paris, France, 1972.

Murphy, J. M. Psychiatric labeling in cross-cultural perspective. *Science,* 1976, **191**(4231), 1019–28.

Opler, M. K., & Singer, J. L. Ethnic differences in behavior and psychopathology. *International Journal of Social Psychiatry,* 1959, **2**, 11–23.

Pavlov, I. P. [*Lectures on conditioned reflexes*] (W. H. Gantt, trans.). New York: International Publishers, 1928.

Rekers, G. A., Lovaas, O. I., & Low, B. The behavioral treatment of a "transsexual" preadolescent boy. *J. Abnorm. Psychol.,* 1975, **2**(1), 99–116.

Selling, L. S. *Men against madness.* New York: Garden City Books, 1943.

Skinner, B. F. *Walden two.* New York: Macmillan, 1948.

Skinner, B. F. *Science and human behavior.* New York: Macmillan, 1953.

Skinner, B. F. *Beyond freedom and dignity.* New York: Knopf, 1971.

Skinner, B. F. *About behaviorism.* New York: Knopf, 1974.

Smith, M. B. The revolution in mental health care—A "bold new approach"? *Trans-action,* 1968, **5**(5), 19–23.

Strauss, T. S. Social and cultural influences on psychopathology. *Annu. Rev. Psychol.,* 1979, **30**(4). 397–415.

Sullivan, H. S. *The interpersonal theory of psychiatry.* H. S. Perry & M. L. Gawel (Eds.). New York: Norton, 1953.

Szasz, T. S. *The myth of mental illness.* New York: Harper & Row, 1961.

Szasz, T. S. *The manufacture of madness.* New York: Harper & Row, 1970.

Thibaut, J. W., & Kelley, H. H. *The social psychology of groups.* New York: Wiley, 1959.

Thorndike, E. L. *The psychology of learning.* New York: Teachers College, 1913.

Wahler, R. G. Behavior therapy for oppositional children: Love is not enough. Paper presented at Eastern Psychological Assn. meeting, Washington, D.C., April 1968.

Watson, J. B., & Rayner, R. Conditioned emotional reactions. *J. Exper. Psychol.,* 1920, **3**, 1–14.

Wilson, G. T., & Evans, I. M. The therapist-client relationship in behavior therapy. In A. S. Gurmon & A. M. Razin (Eds.), *Effective psychotherapy.* New York: Pergamon Press, 1977.

Wolpe, J. Conditioned inhibition of craving in drug addiction. *Behav. Res. Ther.,* 1965, **2**, 285–88.

World Health Organization. *Report of the international pilot study of schizophrenia.* Geneva: World Health Organization, 1973.

Yap, P. M. Mental diseases peculiar to certain cultures: A survey of comparative psychiatry. *J. Ment. Sci.*, 1951, **97**(3), 313.

Zola, I. K. Culture and symptoms—An analysis of patients' presenting complaints. *American Sociological Review*, 1966, **31,** 615–30.

4. Personality Development and Adjustment: An Overview

Aronson, E. The rationalizing animal. *Psych. Today*, May 1973, **6**(12), 46–50, 52.

Averill, J. R. Personal control over aversive stimuli and its relationship to stress. *Psychol. Bull.*, Oct. 1973, **80**(4), 286–303.

Bandura, A. Self-efficacy: Toward a unifying theory of behavioral change. *Psychol. Rev.*, 1977, **84**(2), 191–215.

Bandura, A. The self-system in reciprocal determinism. *Amer. Psychologist*, 1978, **33**(4), 344–58.

Bard, M. The price of survival for cancer victims. *Transaction*, 1966, **3**(3), 10–14.

Berger, R. J. Morpheus descending. *Psych. Today*, 1970, **4**(1), 33–36.

Berkowitz, L. Some determinants of impulsive aggression. *Psych. Rev.*, Mar. 1974, **81**(2), 165–76.

Berlyne, D. E. *Conflict, arousal, and curiosity.* New York: McGraw-Hill, 1960.

Bettelheim, B. Individual and mass behavior in extreme situations. *J. Abnorm. Soc. Psychol.*, 1943, **38**, 417–52.

Bluestone, H., & McGahee, C. L. Reaction to extreme stress. *Amer. J. Psychiat.*, 1962, **119**, 393–96.

Bombard, A. *The voyage of the Hérétique.* New York: Simon and Schuster, 1954.

Butcher, J. N., & Koss, M. P. Research on brief and crisis-oriented psychotherapies. In S. L. Garfield & A. E. Bergin (Eds.), *Handbook of psychotherapy and behavior change* (2nd ed.). New York: Wiley, 1978. Pp. 725–67.

Cantril, H. A fresh look at the human design. In J. F. T. Bugental (Ed.), *Challenges of humanistic psychology.* New York: McGraw-Hill, 1967.

Cochrane, R., & Robertson, A. The life events inventory: A measure of the relative severity of psycho-social stressors. *J. Psychosom. Res.*, Mar. 1973, **17**(2), 135–40.

Coleman, J. C. Life stress and maladaptive behavior. *Amer. J. Occupa. Ther.*, May–June 1973, **27**(4), 169–80.

Dor-Shav, N. K. On the long-range effects of concentration camp internment on Nazi victims: 25 years later. *J. Cons. Clin. Psychol.*, 1978, **46**, 1–11.

Engel, G. L. *Psychological development in health and disease.* New York: Saunders, 1962.

Epstein, S., & Fenz, W. D. Theory and experiment on the measurement of approach-avoidance conflict. *J. Abnorm. Soc. Psychol.*, 1962, **64**(1), 97–112.

Epstein, S., & Fenz, W. D. Steepness of approach and avoidance gradients in humans as a function of experience: Theory and experiment. *J. Exper. Psychol.*, 1965, **70**(1), 1–12.

Erdelyi, M. H. A new look at the new look: Perceptual defense and vigilance. *Psych. Rev.*, Jan. 1974, **81**(1), 1–25.

Erickson, M. H. Experimental demonstrations of the psychopathology of everyday life. *The Psychoanalytic Quarterly*, 1939, **8**, 342–45. Reprinted by permission.

Freud, A. *Ego and the mechanisms of defense* (Rev. ed.). New York: International Universities Press, 1967.

Friedman, P. Some aspects of concentration camp psychology. *Amer. J. Psychiat.*, 1949, **105**, 601–5.

Fromm, E. *The sane society.* New York: Holt, Rinehart, & Winston, 1955.

Gesell, A. Human infancy and the embryology of behavior. In A. Weider (Ed.), *Contributions toward medical psychology.* New York: Ronald, 1953.

Gleser, G., & Sacks, M. Ego defenses and reaction to stress: A validation study of the Defense Mechanisms Inventory. *J. of Cons. Clin. Psychol.*, Apr. 1973, **40**(2), 181–87.

Gottschalk, L. A., Haer, J. L., & Bates, D. E. Effect of sensory

overload on psychological state: Changes in social alienation—personal disorganization and cognitive-intellectual impairment. *Arch. Gen. Psychiat.*, 1972, **27**(4), 451–56.

Harlow, H. F., & Harlow, M. K. Learning to love. *Amer. Scien.*, 1966, **54**, 244–72.

Haythorn, W. W., & Altman, I. Together in isolation. *Transaction*, 1967, **4**(3), 18–22.

Hebb, D. O. The American revolution. *Amer. Psychologist*, 1960, **15**, 735–45.

Holmes, D. S. Investigations of repression: Differential recall of material experimentally or naturally associated with ego threat. *Psychol. Bull.*, Oct. 1974, **81**(10), 632–53.

Holmes, T. S., & Holmes, T. H. Short-term intrusions into the life style routine. *J. Psychosom. Res.*, June 1970, **14**(2), 121–32.

Holmes, T. H., & Rahe, R. H. The social readjustment rating scale. *J. Psychosom. Res.*, Apr. 1967, **11**(2), 213–18.

Hunt, J. McV. *Intelligence and experience.* New York: Ronald Press, 1961.

Huxley, A. Human potentialities. In R. E. Farson (Ed.), *Science and human affairs.* Palo Alto, Calif.: Science and Behavior Books, 1965.

Huxley, J. *Evolution in action.* New York: Harper & Row. 1953.

Janis, I. L., & Leventhal, H. Psychological aspects of physical illness and hospital care. In B. B. Wolman (Ed.), *Handbook of clinical psychology.* New York: McGraw-Hill, 1965. Pp. 1360–77.

Katz, J. L., Weiner, H., Gallagher, T., & Hellman, L. Stress, distress, and ego defenses. *Arch. Gen. Psychiat.*, 1970, **23**, 131–42.

Keys, A., Brožek, J., Henschel, A., Mickelson, O., & Taylor, H. L. *The biology of human starvation.* Minneapolis: University of Minnesota Press, 1950.

Kobasa, S. C. Stressful life events, personality, and health: An inquiry into hardiness. *J. Pers. Soc. Psychol.*, 1979, **37**(1), 1–11.

Kübler-Ross, E. *Death: The final stage of growth.* Englewood Cliffs, New Jersey: Prentice-Hall, 1975.

Langsley, D. G. Crisis intervention. *Amer. J. Psychiat.*, Dec. 1972, **129**(6), 110–12.

Lazarus, R. S. *Psychological stress and the coping process.* New York: McGraw-Hill, 1966.

Lefkowitz, M. M., Evon, L. D., Walder, L. O., & Huesmann, L. R. *Growing up to be violent: A longitudinal study of the development of aggression.* New York: Pergamon Press, 1977.

Maslow, A. H. (Ed.). *Motivation and personality.* New York: Harper & Row, 1954, 1970.

Maslow, A. H. *Farther reaches of human nature.* Escalen Institute Book Publishing Program, New York: Viking Press, 1971.

Masserman, J. H. *Principles of dynamic psychiatry* (2nd ed.). Philadelphia: W. B. Saunders Company, 1961.

Mead, M. *Male and female.* New York: Morrow, 1949.

Mechanic, D. *Students under stress.* New York: Free Press, 1962.

Miller, J. G. Living systems: Basic concepts. *Behav. Sci.*, 1965, **10**, 193–237.

Mischel, W. Toward a cognitive social learning reconceptualization of personality. *Psychol. Rev.*, 1973, **80**(4), 252–83.

Nardini, J. E. Survival factors in American prisoners of war of the Japanese. *Amer. J. Psychiat.*, 1952, **109**, 241–48.

Nardini, J. E. Psychiatric concepts of prisoners of war confinement. The William C. Porter Lecture—1961. *Military Medicine*, 1962, **127**, 299–307.

Piaget, J. *Genetic epistemology.* New York: Columbia University Press, 1970.

Popkin, M. K., Stillner, V., Osborn, L. W., Pierce, C. M., & Shurley, J. T. Novel behaviors in an extreme environment. *Amer. J. Psychiat.*, June 1974, **131**(6), 651–54.

Rahe, R. H., & Arthur, R. J. Life change and illness studies: Past history and future directions. *Journal of Human Stress*, 1978, **4**, 3–15.

Rohrer, J. H. Interpersonal relations in isolated small groups. In B. E. Flaherty (Ed.), *Psychophysiological aspects of space flight.* New York: Columbia University Press, 1961.

Sargent, D. A. Loss of identity in prison. *Sci. News,* June 16, 1973, **103**(24), 390.

Sears, R. R., Maccoby, E. E., & Levin, H. *Patterns of child rearing.* New York: Harper & Row, 1957.

Selye, H. *The stress of life* (2nd ed.). New York: McGraw-Hill, 1976.

Skeels, H. M. Adult status of children with contrasting early life experiences. *Monogr. Soc. Res. Child Develop.,* 1966, **31**(3).

Sommerschield H., & Reyher, J. Posthypnotic conflict, repression and psychopathology. *J. Abnorm. Psychol.,* Oct. 1973, **82**(2), 278–90.

Sullivan, H. S. *The interpersonal theory of psychiatry.* H. S. Perry & M. L. Gawel (Eds.). New York: Norton, 1953.

Uhlenhuth, E. H., & Paykel, E. S. Symptom intensity and life events. *Arch. Gen. Psychiat.,* Apr. 1973, **28**(4), 473–77.

U.S. News & World Report. How the POW's fought back. May 14, 1973, **74**(20), 46–52; 110–15.

Weiss, P. A., & Taylor, A. C. Shuffled cells can reconstruct same organs, *Sci. Newsletter,* 1960, **78**, 263.

White, R. W. Motivation reconsidered: The concept of competence. *Psychol. Rev.,* 1959, **66**(3), 297–334.

White, W. A. Medical philosophy from the viewpoint of a psychiatrist. *Psychiatry,* 1947, **10**(1–2), 77–98; 191–210.

Wilson, E. B. *The cell in development and heredity* (3rd ed.). New York: Macmillan, 1925.

5. Causes of Abnormal Behavior

Alexander, J. F. Defensive and supportive communications in normal and deviant families. *J. Couns. Clin. Psychol.,* Apr. 1973, **40**(2), 223–31.

Anthony, J. E. A clinical evaluation of children with psychotic parents. *Amer. J. Psychiat.,* 1969, **126**(2), 177–84.

Bandura, A., Ross, D., & Ross, S. A. Imitation of film-mediated aggressive models. *J. Abnorm. Soc. Psychol.,* 1963, **66**, 3–11.

Bardwick, K. (Ed.). *Psychology of women: A study of bio-cultural conflicts.* New York: Harper & Row, 1971.

Bateson, G. Minimal requirements for a theory of schizophrenia. *Arch. Gen. Psychiat.,* 1960, **2**, 477–91.

Baumrind, D. Current patterns of parental authority. *Developmental Psychology,* 1971, **4**(1), 1–103.

Beach, F. A., & Jaynes, J. Effects of early experience upon the behavior of animals. *Psychol. Bull.,* 1954, **51**, 239–63.

Becker, W. C. Consequences of different kinds of parental discipline. In M. L. Hoffman & L. W. Hoffman (Eds.), *Review of child development research* (Vol. 1). New York: Russell Sage Foundation, 1964.

Beres, D., & Obers, S. J. The effects of extreme deprivation in infancy on psychic structure in adolescence. In R. S. Eissler et al. (Eds.), *The psychoanalytic study of the child.* Vol. 5. New York: International University Press, 1950.

Bergsma, D. (Ed.). *Medical genetics today* (National Foundation Series). Baltimore: Johns Hopkins University Press, 1974.

Blau, A., Slaff, B., Easton, K., Welkowitz, J., Springarn, J., & Cohen, J. The psychogenic etiology of premature births. *Psychosom. Med.,* 1963, **25**, 201–11.

Bleuler, M. Offspring of schizophrenics. *Schizophrenia Bulletin,* 1974, Issue #8, 93–107.

Bloom, B. L., Asher, S. J., & White, S. W. Marital disruption as a stressor: A review and analysis. *Psychol. Bull.,* 1978, **85**(4), 867–94.

Bowlby, J. Separation anxiety. *Inter. J. Psychoanal.,* 1960, **41**, 89–93.

Bowlby, J. Separation: Anxiety and anger. *Psychology of attachment and loss series* (Vol. 3). New York: Basic Books, 1973.

Brenner, M. H. *Mental illness and the economy.* Cambridge, Mass.: Harvard University Press, 1973.

Bronfenbrenner, U. The origins of alienation. *Scientif. Amer.,* Aug. 1974, **231**(2), 53, 57, 60–61.

Brown, L. *The twenty-ninth day.* New York: Norton, 1978.

Brown, L. R. Global food insecurity. *The Futurist,* Apr. 1974. **8**(2), 56–64.

Buck, V. E. *Working under pressure.* New York: Crane, Russak, 1972.

Bullard, D. M., Glaser, H. H., Heagarty, M. C., & Pivcheck, E. C. Failure to thrive in the neglected child. *Amer. J. Orthopsychiat.,* 1967, **37**, 680–90.

Buss, A., & Plomin, R. *A temperament theory of personality development.* New York: Wiley, 1975.

Caine, L. Widow. New York: Morrow, 1974.

Calhoun, J. B. Population density and social pathology. *Scientif. Amer.,* Feb. 1962, **206**(2), 139–46; 148.

Calhoun, J. B., & Marsden, H. Not with a bang but with a whimper. *Sci. News,* Feb. 3, 1973, **103**(5), 73.

Chess, S., Thomas, A., & Birch, H. G. *Your child is a person.* New York: Viking, 1965.

Coopersmith, S. *The antecedents of self-esteem.* San Francisco: Freeman, 1967.

Cravioto, J., & de Licardie, E. R. Environmental and nutritional deprivation in children with learning disabilities. In W. M. Cruickshank & D. P. Hallahan (Eds.), *Perceptual and learning disabilities in children* (Vol. 2): *Research and Theory.* Syracuse, New York: Syracuse University Press, 1975.

Creasy, M. R., & Crolla, J. A. Prenatal mortality of trisomy 21 (Down's syndrome). *Lancet,* Mar. 23, 1974, **1**(7856), 473–74.

Davenport, R. K., Rogers, C. M., & Rumbaugh, D. M. Long-term cognitive deficits in chimpanzees associated with early impoverished rearing. *Develop. Psychol.,* Nov. 1973, **9**(3), 343–47.

Denenberg, V., Rosenberg, K., Haltmeyer, G., & Whimbey, A. Programming life histories: Effects of stress in ontogeny upon emotional reactivity. *Merrill-Palmer Quarterly,* 1970, **15**, 109–16.

Dennis, W. Spaulding's experiment on the flight of birds repeated with another species. *J. Compar. Physiol. Psychol.,* 1941, **31**, 337–48.

Deur, J. I., & Parke, R. D. Effects of inconsistent punishment on aggression in children. *Develop. Psychol.,* 1970, **2**, 403–11.

Dobbing, J. Growth of the brain. *Sci. J.,* 1967, **3**(5), 81–86.

Eisenberg, L. Student unrest: Sources and consequences. *Science,* Mar. 27, 1970, **167**(3926), 1688–92.

Erikson, E. H. Identity and identity diffusion. In C. Gordon & K. J. Gergen (Eds.), *The self in social interaction* (Vol. I). New York: Wiley, 1968. Pp. 197–205.

Eron, L. D., Huesmann, L. R., Lefkowitz, M. M., & Walder, L. O. How learning conditions in early childhood—including mass media—relate to aggression in late adolescence. *Amer. J. Orthopsychiat.,* Apr. 1974, **44**(3), 412–23.

Fish, B. Biologic antecedents of psychosis in children. In D. X. Freedman (Ed.), *Biology of the major psychoses.* New York: Raven, 1975.

Freedman, A. M., Kaplan, H. I., & Sadock, B. J. *Modern synopsis of comprehensive textbook of psychiatry* (2nd ed.). Baltimore: Williams & Wilkins, 1976.

Gartner, A., & Riessman, F. Is there a new work ethic? *Amer. J. Orthopsychiat.,* July 1974, **44**(4), 563–67.

Gelven, M. Guilt and human meaning. *Humanitas,* Feb. 1973, **9**(1), 69–81.

Glueck, S., & Glueck, E. *Non-delinquents in perspective.* Cambridge: Harvard University Press, 1968.

Green, A. H., Gaines, R. W., & Sandgrund, A. Child abuse: Pathological syndrome of family interaction. *Amer. J. Psychiat.,* Aug. 1974, **131**(8), 882–86.

Haley, J. The family of the schizophrenic: A model system. *Journal of Nervous and Mental Disease,* 1959, **129**, 357–74. Copyright © 1959 by The Williams & Wilkins Co., Baltimore. Reprinted by permission.

Hanerton, J. L., Canning, N., Ray, M., & Smith, S. A cytogenetic survey of 14,069 newborn infants: Incidence of chromosome abnormalities. *Clinical Genetics,* 1975, **8,** 223–43.

Hanson, D. R., Gottesman, I. I., & Meehl, P. E. Genetic theories and the validation of psychiatric diagnoses: Implications for the study of children of schizophrenics. *J. Abnorm. Psychol.,* 1977, **86**(6), 575–88.

Harlow, H. F. Sexual behavior in the rhesus monkey. In F. Beach (Ed.), *Sex and behavior.* New York: Wiley, 1965.

Harlow, H. F. *Learning to love.* San Francisco: Albion, 1973.

Harlow, H. F., & Harlow, M. Learning to love. *Amer. Scien.,* 1966, **54,** 244–72.

Harlow, H. F., & Suomi, S. J. Nature of love—simplified. *Amer. Psychologist,* 1970, **25**(1), 161–68.

Harmeling, P. C. Therapeutic theater of Alaska Eskimos. *Group Psychother.,* 1950, **3,** 74–76.

Harvey, C. D., & Bahr, H. M. Widowhood, morale, and affiliation. *J. Marr. Fam.,* Feb. 1974, **36**(1), 97–106.

Hersher, L., Moore, U., Richmond, J. B., & Blauvelt, H. The effects of maternal deprivation during the nursing period on the behavior of young goats. *Amer. Psychologist,* 1962, **17,** 307.

Hetherington, E. M. Girls without fathers. *Psych. Today,* Feb. 1973, **6**(9), 47; 49–52.

Hetherington, E. M., Cox, M., & Cox, R. *Family interaction and the social, emotional and cognitive development of children following divorce.* Symposium on The family: Setting priorities, Institute for Pediatric Service, Johnson & Johnson Baby Food Company. Washington, D.C., May 17–20, 1978.

Holmes, T. S., & Holmes, T. H. Short-term intrusions into the life-style routine. *J. Psychosom. Res.,* June 1970, **14**(2), 121–32.

Horner, M. S. Sex differences in achievement motivation and performance in competitive and non-competitive situations. Unpublished doctoral dissertation, University of Michigan, 1968.

Horner, M. S. Femininity and successful achievement: A basic inconsistency. In J. M. Bardwick, E. Douvan, M. S. Horner, & D. Gutman (Eds.), *Feminine personality and conflict.* Belmont, Calif.: Brooks/Cole, 1970.

Hurley, J. R. Parental acceptance-rejection and children's intelligence. *Merrill-Palmer Quart.,* 1965, **11**(1), 19–32.

Inself, P. M., & Moos, R. H. Psychological environments: Expanding the scope of human ecology. *Amer. Psychologist,* Mar. 1974, **29**(3), 179–88.

Jenkins, R. L. Psychiatric syndromes in children and their relation to family background. *Amer. J. Orthopsychiat.,* 1966, **36,** 450–57.

Jenkins, R. L. The varieties of children's behavioral problems and family dynamics. *Amer. J. Psychiat.,* 1968, **124,** 1440–45.

Kadushin, A. Reversibility of trauma: A follow-up study of children adopted when older. *Social Work,* 1967, **12**(4), 22–23.

Kagan, J. In B. Pratt (Ed.), Kagan counters Freud, Piaget theories on early childhood deprivation effects. *APA Monitor,* 1973, **4**(2), 1;7.

Kagan, J., Kearsley, R. B., & Zelazo, P. R. *The effects of infant day-care on psychological development.* Symposium on The effect of early experience on child development, American Association for the Advancement of Science. Boston, February, 1976.

Kaiser Foundation Health Plan, Inc. *Planning for health.* Summer 1970, 1–2.

Kaplan, B. J. Malnutrition and mental deficiency. *Psychol. Bull.,* Nov. 1972, **78**(5), 321–34.

Kaplun, D., & Reich, R. The murdered child and his killers. *Amer. J. Psychiat.,* 1976, **133**(7), 809–13.

Klerman, G. L., & Izen, J. E. The effects of bereavement and grief on physical health and general well-being. In S. Kasl & F. Reichsman (Eds.), *Advances in psychosomatic medicine* (Vol. 9). Basel, Switzerland: S. Karger, 1977. Pp. 63–104.

Langner, T. S., Gersten, J. C., Greene, E. L., Eisenberg, J. G., Herson, J. H., & McCarthy, E. D. Treatment of psychological disorders among urban children. *J. Cons. Clin. Psychol.,* Apr. 1974, **42**(2), 170–79.

Langner, T. S., & Michael. S. T. *Life stress and mental health* (Vol. 20). New York: Free Press, 1963.

Lefkowitz, M. M., Huesmann, L. R., Walder, L. O., Eron, L. D. Developing and predicting aggression. *Sci. News,* Jan. 1973, **103**(3), 40.

Lefkowitz, M. M., Evon, L. D., Walder, L. O., & Huesmann, L. R. *Growing up to be violent: A longitudinal study of the development of aggression.* New York: Pergamon Press, 1977.

Leiderman, P. H., & Leiderman, G. F. Affective and cognitive consequences of polymatric infant care in the East African highlands. In A. Pick (Ed.), *Minnesota symposium on child development* (Vol. 8). Minneapolis: University of Minnesota Press, 1974.

Lessac, M., & Solomon, R. L. Effects of early isolation on the later adaptive behavior of beagles. *Develop. Psychol.,* 1969, **1**(1), 14–25.

Levy, D. M. Maternal overprotection, In N. D. C. Lewis & B. L. Pacella (Eds.), *Modern trends in child psychiatry.* New York: International University Press, 1945.

Lidz, T., Fleck, S., & Cornelison, A. R. *Schizophrenia and the family.* New York: International University Press, 1965.

Loyd, G. F. Finally, facts on malnutrition in the United States. *Today's Health,* 1969, **47**(9), 32–33.

Lynch, H. T., Harlan, W. L., & Dyhrberg, J. S. Subjective perspective of a family with Huntington's chorea. *Arch. Gen. Psychiat.,* July 1972, **27**(1), 67–72.

Matsunaga, E., Tonomura, A., Hidetsune, O., & Yasumoto, K. Reexamination of paternal age effect in Down's syndrome. *Human Genetics,* 1978, **40,** 259–68.

Minde, K. K., Hackett, J. D., Killou, D., & Silver, S. How they grow up: 41 physically handicapped children and their families. *Amer. J. Psychiat.,* June 1972, **128**(12), 104–10.

Moody, S., & Graham, V. Why? *Sunday Sun Times,* November 26, 1978, pp. 8–10.

National Institute of Mental Health. *The mental health of urban America.* Washington, D.C.: Public Hlth. Serv. Publ. No. 1906, 1969.

Nelson, H. How to be successfully fired. *Behav. Today,* Apr. 29, 1974, **5**(17), 118–19.[a]

Nicholson, S. International future studies program involves kids. *Brain/Mind Bulletin,* Jan. 15, 1979, **4**(5), 1–2.

Pemberton, D. A., & Benady, D. R. Consciously rejected children. *Brit. J. Psychiat.,* Nov. 1973, **123**(576), 575–78.

Peterson, G. C. Organic brain syndromes: Differential diagnostic and investigative procedures in adults. *Psychiatric Clinics of North America,* 1978, **1,** 21–36.

Pollack, J. H. Five frequent mistakes of parents. *Today's Health,* 1968, **46**(5), 14–15; 26–29.

Poznanski, E. O. Children with excessive fears. *Amer. J. Orthopsychiat.,* Apr. 1973, **43**(3), 428–38.

President's Commission on Mental Health. *Report.* Washington: U.S. Government Printing Office, 1978.

Pringle, M. L. K. *Deprivation and education.* New York: Humanities Press, 1965.

Provence, S., & Lipton, R. C. *Infants in institutions.* New York: International University Press, 1962.

Reice, S. Editorial. *Family Health,* Apr. 1974, **6**(4), 4.

Reisen, A. H. The development of visual perception in men and chimpanzee. *Science,* 1947, **106,** 107–8.

Ribble, M. A. Infantile experience in relation to personality development. In J. McV. Hunt (Ed.), *Personality and the behavior disorders* (Vol. 2). New York: Ronald, 1944. Pp. 621–51.

Ribble, M. A. Anxiety in infants and its disorganizing effects. In N. D. C. Lewis & B. L. Pacella (Eds.), *Modern trends in child psychiatry.* New York: International University Press, 1945.

Rice, R. D. Neurophysiological development in premature infants following stimulation. *Develop. Psychol.,* 1977, **13,** 69–76.

Robinson, N. M., & Robinson, H. B. *The mentally retarded child* (2nd ed.). New York: McGraw-Hill, 1976.

Robinson, S., & Winnik, H. Z. Severe psychotic disturbances following crash diet weight loss. *Arch. Gen. Psychiat.,* Oct. 1973, **29**(4), 559–62.

Romer, N. The motive to avoid success and its effects on performance in school-age males and females. *Develop. Psychol.,* 1975, **11**, 689–99.

Rutter, M. Maternal deprivation reconsidered. *J. Psychosom. Res.,* Aug. 1972, **16**(4), 241–50.

Sanderson, F. H. The great food fumble. *Science,* May 9, 1975, **188**(4188), 503–9.

Schopler, E. Changing parental involvement in behavioral treatment. In M. Rutter & E. Schopler (Eds.), *Autism: A reappraisal of concepts and treatment.* New York: Plenum Press, 1978.

Seaman, M. Antidote for alienation. *Trans-action,* 1966, **3**(4), 35–39.

Sears, R. R. Relation of early socialization experiences to aggression in middle childhood. *J. Abnorm. Soc. Psychol.,* 1961, **63**, 466–92.

Sears, R. R., Maccoby, E. E., & Levin, H. *Patterns of child rearing.* New York: Harper & Row, 1957.

Seligman, M. E. P. *Helplessness: On depression, development, and death.* San Francisco: W. H. Freeman, 1975.

Selye, H. *The stress of life* (2nd ed.). New York: McGraw-Hill, 1976.

Sergovich, F., Valentine, G. H., Chen, A. T., Kinch, R., & Smout, M. Chromosomal aberrations in 2159 consecutive newborn babies. *New Engl. J. Med.,* 1969, **280**(16), 851–54.

Sheldon, W. H. (with the collaboration of C. W. Dupertuis & E. McDermott). *Atlas of men.* New York: Harper & Row, 1954.

Snyder, M., Tanke, E. D., & Berscheid, E. Social perception and interpersonal behavior: On the self-fulfilling nature of social stereotypes. *J. Pers. Soc. Psychol.,* 1977, **35**(9), 656–66.

Solomon, J. Sea of drugs. *The Sciences,* May 1973, **13**(4), 23–28.

Sontag, L. W., Steele, W. G., & Lewis, M. The fetal and maternal cardiac response to environmental stress. *Human Develop.,* 1969, **12**, 1–9.

Spencer, S. M. The disease we've overlooked. *Family Health,* Jan. 1973, **5**(1), 38; 40; 42–43.

Steinmetz, S. K., & Straus, M. A. The family as cradle of violence. *Society,* Sept./Oct. 1973, **10**(6), 50–56.

Stierlin, H. A family perspective on adolescent runaways. *Ment. Hlth. Dig.,* Oct. 1973, **5**(10), 1–4.

Tart, C. T. (Ed.) *Transpersonal psychologies.* Harper & Row, 1975.

Terr, L. A family study of child abuse. *Amer. J. Psychiat.,* 1970, **127**, 665–71.

Thomas, A., & Chess, S. *Temperament and development.* New York: Brunner/Mazel, 1977.

Thomas, A., Chess, S., & Birch, H. *Temperament and behavior disorders in children.* New York: New York University Press, 1968.

Time. On being an American parent. Dec. 15, 1967, **90**(24), 30–31.

Time. From "Cannibalism on the Cordillera" from *Time,* January 8, 1973, p. 27. Reprinted by permission from *Time,* The Weekly Newsmagazine; Copyright © Time Inc., 1973.

Tizard, B., & Rees, J. The effect of early institutional rearing on the behavior problems and affectional relationships of four-year-old children. *J. Child Psychol. Psychiat.,* Jan. 1975, **16**(1), 61–73.

Toffler, A. *Future shock.* New York: Random House, 1970.

Traub, E. Quote from "What can happen if you're an overprotective parent" by E. Traub. Reprinted with permission, *Today's Health* Magazine, April 1974 ©. All rights reserved.

Winick, C. The beige epoch: Depolarization of sex roles in America. *Ann. Amer. Acad. Polit. Soc. Sci.,* 1978, **376**, 18–24.

Winick, M., & Rosso, P. Effects of malnutrition on brain development. *Biology of Brain Dysfunction,* 1973, **1**, 301–17.

Wolkind, S. N. The components of "affectionless psychotherapy"

in institutionalized children. *J. Child Psychol. Psychiat.,* July 1974, **15**(3), 215–20.

Wolkind, S. N., & Rutter, M. Children who have been "in care": An epidemiological study. *J. Child Psychol. Psychiat.,* June 1973, **14**(2), 97–105.

Zimbardo, P. G., Haney, C., Banks, W. C., & Jaffe, D. The psychology of imprisonment: Privation, power, and pathology. In D. Rosenhan & P. London (Eds.), *Theory and research in abnormal psychology* (2nd ed.). New York: Holt, Rinehart & Winston, 1975. Pp. 270–87.

6. Transient Reactions to Severe Stress

Adler, A. Neuropsychiatric complications in victims of Boston's Cocoanut Grove disaster. *JAMA,* 1943, **123**, 1098–1101.

Allerton, W. S. Psychiatric casualties in Vietnam. *Roche Medical Image and Commentary,* 1970, **12**(8), 27.

Archibald, H. C., & Tuddenham, R. D. Persistent stress reaction after combat. *Arch. Gen. Psychiat.,* 1965, **12**(5), 475–81.

Bartemeier, L. H., Kubie, L. S., Menninger, K. A., Romano, J., & Whitehorn, J. C. Combat exhaustion. *Journal of Nervous and Mental Disease,* 1946, **104**, 385–89; 489–525. Published by The Williams & Wilkins Co. Copyright 1946 and reprinted by permission of The Smith Ely Jelliffe Trust.

Bell, E., Jr. The basis of effective military psychiatry. *Dis. Nerv. System,* 1958, **19**, 283–88.

Bettelheim, B. Individual and mass behavior in extreme situations. *J. Abnorm. Soc. Psychol.,* 1943, **38**, 417–52.

Bettelheim, B. *The informed heart.* New York: Free Press, 1960.

Bloch, H. S. Army clinical psychiatry in the combat zone— 1967–1968. Reprinted from *The American Journal of Psychiatry,* volume *126,* pages 289–98, 1969. Copyright, 1969, the American Psychiatric Association.

Borus, J. F. Incidence of maladjustment in Vietnam returnees. *Arch. Gen. Psychiat.,* Apr. 1974, **30**(4), 554–57.

Bourne, P. G. Military psychiatry and the Vietnam experience. *Amer. J. Psychiat.,* 1970, **127**(4), 481–88.

Chambers, R. E. Discussion of "Survival factors. . . ." *Amer. J. Psychiat.,* 1952, **109**. 247–48.

Chodoff, P. The German concentration camp as a psychological stress. *Arch. Gen. Psychiat.,* 1970, **22**(1), 78–87.

Davidson, A. D. Coping with stress reactions in rescue workers: A program that worked. *Police Stress,* Spring 1979.[a]

Davidson, A. D. Personal communication, 1979. [b]

Defazio, V. J., Rustin, S., & Diamond, A. Symptom development in Vietnam era veterans. *Amer. J. Orthopsychiat.,* Jan. 1975, **45**(1), 158–63.

Egbert, L., Battit, G., Welch, C., & Bartlett, M. Reduction of postoperative pain by encouragement and instruction of patients. *New Engl. J. Med.,* 1964, **270**, 825–27.

Eitinger, L. Pathology of the concentration camp syndrome. *Arch. Gen. Psychiat.,* 1961, **5**, 371–79.

Eitinger, L. Concentration camp survivors in the postwar world. *Amer. J. Orthopsychiat.,* 1962, **32**, 367–75.

Eitinger, L. *Concentration camp survivors in Norway and Israel.* New York: Humanities Press, 1964.

Eitinger, L. Psychosomatic problems in concentration camp survivors. *J. Psychosom. Res.,* 1969, **13**, 183–90.

Eitinger, L. A follow-up study of the Norwegian concentration camp survivors: Mortality and morbidity. *Israel Annals of Psychiatry and Related Disciplines,* Sept. 1973, **11**, 199–210.

Farber, I. E., Harlow, H. F., & West, L. J. Brainwashing, conditioning, and DDD (debility, dependency and dread). *Sociometry,* 1956, **19**, 271–85.

Frankl, V. E. *Man's search for meaning* (Rev. ed.). Boston: Beacon Press, 1963.

Friedman, P. The effects of imprisonment. *Acta Medica Orientalia,* Jerusalem, 1948, 163–67.

Friedman, P., & Linn, L. Some psychiatric notes on the Andrea Doria disaster. *Amer. J. Psychiat.,* 1957, **114**, 426–32.

Goldsmith, W., & Cretekes, C. Unhappy odysseys: Psychiatric hospitalization among Vietnam returnees. *Amer. J. Psychiat.*, 1969, **20**, 78–83.

Grinker, R. R. An essay on schizophrenia and science. *Arch. Gen. Psychiat.*, 1969, **20**, 1–24.

Grinker, R. R., & Spiegel, J. P. *War neuroses.* Philadelphia: Blakiston, 1945.

Hafner, H. Psychological disturbances following prolonged persecution. *Soc. Psychiat.*, 1968, **3**(3), 80–88.

Haley, S. A. Treatment implications of post-combat stress response syndromes for mental health professionals. In C. R. Figley (Ed.), *Stress disorders among Vietnam veterans.* New York: Brunner/Mazel, 1978.

Hausman, W., & Rioch, D. M. Military psychiatry. *Arch. Gen. Psychiat.*, 1967, **16**, 727–39.

Haythorn, W. W., & Altman, I. Together in isolation. *Transaction*, 1967, **4**(3), 18–22.

Hinkle, L. E., Jr., & Wolff, H. G. Communist interrogation and indoctrination of "enemies of the states." *Arch. Neurol. Psychiat.*, 1956, **76**, 115–74.

Horowitz, M. J. Psychic trauma. *Arch. Gen. Psychiat.*, 1969, **20**, 552–59.

Horowitz, M. J., & Solomon, G. F. Delayed stress response in Vietnam veterans. In C. R. Figley (Ed.), *Stress disorders among Vietnam veterans.* New York: Brunner/Mazel, 1978.

Hunter, E. *Brain-washing in Red China.* New York: Vanguard, 1954.

Hunter, E. J. The prisoner of war: Coping with the stress of isolation. In R. H. Moos (Ed.), *Human adaptation: Coping with life crises.* Lexington, Mass.: D. C. Heath & Company, 1976.

Hunter, E. J. The Vietnam POW veteran: Immediate and long-term effects. In C. R. Figley (Ed.), *Stress disorders among Vietnam veterans.* New York: Brunner/Mazel, 1978.

Janis, I. L. *Psychological stress: Psychoanalytic and behavioral studies of surgical patients.* New York: Wiley, 1958.

Janis, I. L., Mahl, G. F., Kagan, J., & Holt, R. R. From *Personality: Dynamics, development, and assessment.* Published by Harcourt Brace Jovanovich, Inc., 1969. Reprinted by permission.

Keiser, L. *The traumatic neurosis.* Philadelphia: Lippincott, 1968.

Kinkead, E. *In every war but one.* New York: Norton, 1959.

Kormos, H. R. The nature of combat stress. In C. R. Figley (Ed.), *Stress disorders among Vietnam veterans.* New York: Brunner/Mazel, 1978.

Kushner, F. H. All of us bear the scars. *U.S. News & World Report*, Apr. 16, 1973, **74**(16), 41.

Leopold, R. L., & Dillon, H. Psychoanatomy of a disaster: A long term study of post-traumatic neuroses in survivors of a marine explosion. *Amer. J. Psychiat.*, 1963, **119**, 913–21.

Lifton, R. J. Home by ship: Reaction patterns of American prisoners of war repatriated from North Korea. *Amer. J. Psychiat.*, 1954, **110**, 732–39.

Lifton, R. J. *Thought reform and the psychology of totalism: A study of "brainwashing" in China.* New York: Norton, 1961.

Lifton, R. J. The "Gook syndrome" and "numbed warfare." *Sat. Rev.*, Dec. 1972, **55**(47), 66–72.

Ludwig, A. O., & Ranson, S. W. A statistical follow-up of treatment of combat-induced psychiatric casualties. I and II. *Military Surgeon*, 1947, **100**, 51–62; 169–75.

McDavid, J. W., & Harari, H. *Social psychology: Individuals, groups, societies.* New York: Harper & Row, 1968.

Meichenbaum, D., & Cameron, R. Stress inoculation: A skills training approach to anxiety management. Unpublished manuscript, University of Waterloo, 1973.

Meichenbaum, D., Turk, D., & Burstein, S. The nature of coping with stress. In I. Sarason & C. Spielberger (Eds.), *Stress and anxiety* (Vol. 2). New York: Wiley, 1975.

Menninger, W. C. *Psychiatry in a troubled world.* New York: Macmillan, 1948.

Merbaum, M. Some personality characteristics of soldiers exposed to extreme war stress: A follow-up study of post-hospital adjustment. *J. Clin. Psychol.*, 1977, **33**, 558–62.

Merbaum, M., & Hefez, A. Some personality characteristics of soldiers exposed to extreme war stress. *J. Cons. Clin. Psychol.*, 1976, **44**(1), 1–6.

Modlin, H. C. The postaccident anxiety syndrome: Psychosocial aspects. *Amer. J. Psychiat.*, 1967, **123**, 1008–21.

Nardini, J. E. Survival factors in American prisoners of war of the Japanese. Reprinted from *The American Journal of Psychiatry*, volume **109**, pages 241–48, 1952. Copyright 1952, the American Psychiatric Association.

Nardini, J. E. Psychiatric concepts of prisoners of war confinement. The William C. Porter Lecture—1961. *Military Medicine*, 1962, **127**, 299–307.

O'Brien, D. Mental anguish: An occupational hazard. *Emergency*, March 1979, pp. 61–64.

O'Connell, P. Trends in psychological adjustment: Observations made during successive psychiatric follow-up interviews of returned Navy-Marine Corps POWs (R. Spaulding, Ed.). *Proceedings of the 3rd Annual Joint Meeting Concerning POW/MIA matters*, San Diego, Calif., November 1975, 1976, 16–22.

Okura, K. P. Mobilizing in response to a major disaster. *Comm. Ment. Hlth. J.*, Summer 1975, **2**(2), 136–44.

Orwell, G. *1984.* New York: Harcourt, 1949.

O'Toole, P. Casualties in the classroom. *New York Times Magazine*, December 10, 1978, pp. 59, 78–90.

Perlberg, M. Adapted from Trauma at Tenerife: The psychic aftershocks of a jet disaster. From *Human Behavior*, April 1979, pp. 49–50. Reprinted by permission of *Human Behavior* magazine.

Polner, M. Vietnam War stories. *Transaction*, 1968, **6**(1), 8–20. Quote published by permission of Transaction, Inc., from *Transaction*, Vol. 6, #1. Copyright © 1968, by Transaction, Inc.

Rachman, S. J. *Fear and courage.* San Francisco, Calif.: Freeman, 1978.

Rios, P. Quote from The Vietnam casualties are prisoners of war—for life, by Pete Rios from *The Chicago Daily News* (June 3, 1973). Reprinted by permission.

Saul, L. J. Psychological factors in combat fatigue. *Psychosom. Med.*, 1945, **7**, 257–72.

Schanche, D. A. The emotional aftermath of "the largest tornado ever." *Today's Health*, Aug. 1974, **52**(8), 16–19; 61; 63–64.

Schein, E. H., Schneier, I., & Barker, C. H. *Coercive persuasion.* New York: Norton, 1961.

Segal, H. A. Initial psychiatric findings of recently repatriated prisoners of war. *Amer. J. Psychiat.*, 1954, **111**, 358–63.

Selkin, J., & Loya, F. Issues in the psychological autopsy of controversial public figures. *Professional Psychology*, **10**(1), 87–93.

Shatan, C. F. Stress disorders among Vietnam veterans: The emotional content of combat continues. From *Stress disorders among Vietnam veterans: Theory, research and treatment*, edited by Charles R. Figley, Ph.D. Copyright © 1978 by Charles R. Figley. Reprinted by permission of Brunner/Mazel, Publishers.

Sobel, Maj. R. Anxiety-depressive reactions after prolonged combat experience—The old sergeant syndrome. *Bull. U.S. Army Med. Dept., Combat Psychiat. Suppl.*, Nov. 1949, 137–46.

Stern, R. L. Diary of a war neurosis. *Journal of Nervous and Mental Disease*, 1947, **106**, 583–86. Published by the Williams & Wilkins Co. Copyright 1947 and reprinted by permission of The Smith Ely Jelliffe Trust.

Strange, R. E., & Brown, D. E., Jr. Home from the wars. *Amer. J. Psychiat.*, 1970, **127**(4), 488–92.

Strassman, H. D., Thaler, M. B., & Schein, E. H. A prisoner of war syndrome: Apathy as a reaction to severe stress. *Amer. J. Psychiat.*, 1956, **112**, 998–1003.

Terkel, S. *Hard times: An oral history of the Great Depression.* Copyright © 1970 by Studs Terkel. Reprinted by permission of Pantheon Books, a Division of Random House, Inc. and Penquin Books Ltd.

Tuohy, W. Drugs fight shell shock in Vietnam. *Los Angeles*

Times, July 30, 1967, F, 12–13.

Tuohy, W. Combat fatigue: U.S. lessens its toll in Vietnam. *Los Angeles Times*, Dec. 1, 1968, A, 1.

Uhlenhuth, E. Free therapy said to be helpful to Chicago train wreck victims. *Psychiatric News*, Feb. 7, 1973, **8**(3), 1; 27.

Warnes, H. The traumatic syndrome. *Ment. Hlth. Dig.*, Mar. 1973, **5**(3), 33–34.

Watzlawick, P., Beavin, J., & Jackson, D. D. *Pragmatics of human communication*. New York: Norton, 1967.

West, L. J. Psychiatric aspects of training for honorable survival as a prisoner of war. *Amer. J. Psychiat.*, 1958, **115**, 329–36.

Wilbur, R. S. In S. Auerbach (Ed.), POWs found to be much sicker than they looked upon release. *Los Angeles Times*, June 2, 1973, Part I, p. 4.

Williams, A. H. A psychiatric study of Indian soldiers in the Arakan. *Brit. J. Med. Psychol.*, 1950, **23**, 130–81.

Worthington, E. R. Demographic and pre-service variables as predictors of post-military adjustment. In C. R. Figley (Ed.), *Stress disorders among Vietnam veterans*. New York: Brunner/Mazel, 1978.

7. The Neuroses: Anxiety, Somatoform, and Dissociative Disorders

Abse, D. W. Hysteria. In S. Arieti (Ed.), *American handbook of psychiatry* (Vol. 1). New York: Basic Books, 1959. Pp. 272–92.

Agras, S., Sylvester, D., & Oliveau, D. The epidemiology of common fears and phobias. Unpublished manuscript, 1969.

Alarcon, R. D. Hysteria and hysterical personality: How come one without the other? *Psychiat. Quart.*, 1973, **47**(2), 258–75.

American Psychiatric Association (APA). *Diagnostic and statistical manual of mental disorders (DSM-III)*. Washington, D.C.: APA, 1979.

Bandura, A. *Principles of behavior modification*. New York: Holt, Rinehart & Winston, 1969.

Bandura, A. *Aggression: A social learning analysis*. Englewood Cliffs, N.J.: Prentice-Hall, 1973.

Bandura, A. *Social learning theory*. Englewood Cliffs, N.J.: Prentice-Hall, 1977.

Bandura, A., Blanchard, E. B., & Ritter, B. Relative efficacy of desensitization and modeling approaches for inducing behavioral, affective, and attitudinal changes. *J. Pers. Soc. Psychol.*, 1969, **13**, 173–79.

Beck, A. T., Laude, R., & Bohnert, M. Ideational components of anxiety neurosis. *Arch. Gen. Psychiat.*, Sept. 1974, **31**(3), 319–25.

Bergin, A. E., & Lambert, M. J. The evaluation of outcomes in psychotherapy. In S. L. Garfield & A. E. Bergin (Eds.), *Handbook of psychotherapy and behavior change: An empirical analysis*. New York: Wiley, 1978.

Berman, E. Tested and documented split personality: Veronica and Nelly. Reprinted from *Psychology Today*, August 1975, pp. 78–81. Copyright © 1975 by Ziff Davis Publishing Company.

Blanchard, E. B., & Epstein, L. H. *A biofeedback primer*. Reading, Mass.: Addison-Wesley, 1978.

Blanchard, E. B., & Young, L. D. Clinical applications of biofeedback training: A review. *Arch. Gen. Psychiat.*, May 1974, **30**(5), 573–89.

Button, J. H., & Reivich, R. S. Obsession of infanticide. A review of 42 cases. Reprinted from *Archives of General Psychiatry*, Aug. 1972, **27**(2), 235–40. Copyright 1972, American Medical Association.

Carr, A. T. Compulsive neurosis: Two psychophysiological studies. *Bulletin of the British Psychological Society*, 1971, **24**, 256–57.

Chodoff, P. The diagnosis of hysteria: An overview. *Amer. J. Psychiat.*, Oct. 1974, **131**(10), 1073–78.

Cohen, D. B. On the etiology of neurosis. *J. Abnorm. Psychol.*, Oct. 1974, **83**(5), 473–79.

Cohen, S. The use of psychedelics as adjuncts to psychotherapy. In U. Binder, A. Binder, & B. Rimland (Eds.),

Modern therapies. New York: Prentice-Hall, 1976.

Covi, L., Lipman, R. S., Derogatis, L. R., Smith, J. E., III, & Pattison, J. H. Drugs and group psychotherapy in neurotic depression. *Amer. J. Psychiat.*, Feb. 1974, **131**(2), 191–97.

Cox, G. B., Chapman, C. R., & Black, R. G. The MMPI and chronic pain: The diagnosis of psychogenic pain. *Journal of Behavioral Medicine*, 1978, 4, 437–43.

Downing, R. W., & Rickels, K. Mixed anxiety-depression: Fact or myth? *Arch. Gen. Psychiat.*, Mar. 1974, **30**(3), 312–17.

Engelhardt, D. M. Pharmacologic basis for use of psychotropic drugs: An overview. *N.Y. St. J. Med.*, Feb. 1974, **74**(2), 360–66.

Eysenck, H. J. The learning theory model of neurosis: A new approach. *Behav. Res. Ther.*, 1976, **14**, 251–67.

Fordyce, W. E. Use of the MMPI in the assessment of clinical pain. Nutley, N. J.: *Roche Laboratories Monograph*, 1979.

Fox, R. E. Family therapy. In I. Weiner (Ed.), *Clinical methods in psychology*. New York: Wiley, 1976.

Frankel, A. S. Treatment of a multisymptomatic phobic by a self-directed, self-reinforced imagery technique: A case study. Reprinted from the *Journal of Abnormal Psychology*, 1970, Vol. **76**, pp. 496–99, "Treatment of a Multisymptomatic Phobic by a Self-Directed, Self-Reinforced Imagery Technique" by A. S. Frankel, by permission of the American Psychological Association.

Gibson, H. B. Morita therapy and behavior therapy. *Behav. Res. Ther.*, Nov. 1974, **12**(4), 347–55.

Gurman, A. S., & Kniskern, D. P. Research on marital and family therapy: Progress, perspective and prospect. In S. L. Garfield & A. E. Bergin (Eds.), *Handbook of psychotherapy and behavior change*. New York: Wiley, 1978.

Halleck, S. L. Hysterical personality traits. Reprinted from *Archives of General Psychiatry*, 1967, **16**, 750–57. Copyright 1967, American Medical Association.

Halpern, H. J. Hysterical amblyopia. *Bull. U.S. Army Med. Dept.*, 1944, No. 72, 84–87.

Hammer, H. Astasia-abasia: A report of two cases at West Point. *Amer. J. Psychiat.*, 1967, **124**(5), 671–74.

Hearst, E. D., Cloninger, C. R., Crews, E. L., & Cadoret, R. J. Electrosleep therapy. *Arch. Gen. Psychiat.*, Apr. 1974, **30**(4), 463–66.

Hodgson, R. J., & Rachman, S. The effects of contamination and washing in obsessional patients. *Behav. Res. Ther.*, May 1972, **10**(2), 111–17.

Ironside, R., & Batchelor, I. R. C. The ocular manifestations of hysteria in relation to flying. *Brit. J. Ophthalmol.*, 1945, **29**, 88–98.

Jeans, R. F. An independently validated case of multiple personality. From the *Journal of Abnormal Psychology*, 1976, **85**(3), 249–55. Reprinted by permission.

Jenkins, R. L. Psychiatric syndromes in children and their relation to family background. *Amer. J. Orthopsychiat.*, 1966, **36**, 450–57.

Jenkins, R. L. The varieties of children's behavioral problems and family dynamics. *Amer. J. Psychiat.*, 1968, **124**(10), 1440–45.

Jenkins, R. L. Classification of behavior problems of children. *Amer. J. Psychiat.*, 1969, **125**(8), 1032–39.

Jones, M. C. A laboratory study of fear: The case of Peter. *Pedagogical Seminary*, 1924, **31**, 308–15.

Kaufmann, W. *Without guilt and justice: From decidophobia to autonomy*. New York: Peter H. Wyden, 1973.

Kerckhoff, A. C., & Back, K. W. The bug. *Psych. Today*, 1969, **3**(1), 46–49.

Kidson, M. A., & Jones, I. H. Psychiatric disorders among aborigines of the Australian Western Desert. *Arch. Gen. Psychiat.*, 1952, the American Psychiatric Association.

Kiersch, T. A. Amnesia: A clinical study of ninety-eight cases. *Amer. J. Psychiat.*, 1962, **119**, 57–60.

Kline, N. S. Drug treatment of phobic disorders. *Amer. J. Psychiat.*, 1967, **123**(11), 1447–50.

Kora, T., & Ohara, K. Morita therapy. *Psych. Today*, Mar. 1973, **6**(10), 63–68.

Kraines, S. H. *The therapy of the neuroses and psychoses* (3rd ed.). Philadelphia: Lea & Febiger, 1948. Reprinted by permission.

Lader, M., & Mathews, A. Physiological changes during spontaneous panic attacks. *J. Psychosom. Res.,* 1970, **14**(4), 377–82.

Lewis, W. C. Hysteria: The consultant's dilemma. *Arch. Gen. Psychiat.,* Feb. 1974, **30**(2), 145–51.

Liebson, I. Conversion reaction: A learning theory approach. *Behav. Res. Ther.,* 1969, **7**, 217–18.

Lipton, S. Dissociated personality: A case report. *Psychiatric Quarterly,* 1943, **17**, 35–36. Reprinted by permission of Human Science Press, 72 Fifth Avenue, New York, N.Y. 10011.

Maddi, S. R. The existential neurosis. *J. Abnorm. Psychol.,* 1967, **72**, 311–25.

Mahoney, M. J. *Cognition and behavior modification.* Cambridge, Mass.: Ballinger, 1974.

Malmo, R. B. Emotions and muscle tension: The story of Anne. *Psych. Today,* Mar. 1970, **3**(10), 64–67; 83.

Marks, I. Phobias and obsessions: Clinical phenomena in search of a laboratory model. In J. D. Maser & M. E. P. Seligman (Eds.), *Psychopathology: Experimental models.* San Francisco: W. H. Freeman & Company, 1977.

Marks, I. Behavorial psychotherapy of adult neurotics. In S. L. Garfield & A. E. Bergin (Eds.), *Handbook of psychotherapy and behavior change: An empirical analysis.* New York: Wiley, 1978.

Masserman, J. H. *Principles of dynamic psychiatry* (2nd ed.). Philadelphia: W. B. Saunders Company, 1961. Reproduced by permission of the author and publisher.

Mather, M. D. The treatment of an obsessive-compulsive patient by discrimination learning and reinforcement of decision-making. *Behav. Res. Ther.,* 1970, **8**(3), 315–18.

Meichenbaum, D. A self-instructional approach to stress management: A proposal for stress-inoculation training. In C. Spielberger & I. Sarason (Eds.), *Stress and anxiety* (Vol. 2). New York: Wiley, 1977.

Melville, K. Changing the family game. *The Sciences,* Apr. 1973, **13**(3), 17–19.

Menninger, K. A. *The human mind* (3rd ed.). New York: Knopf, 1945. From pages 139–140 in *The Human Mind,* by Karl Menninger. Copyright 1930, 1937, 1945 and renewed 1958, 1965 by Karl Menninger. Reprinted by permission of Alfred A. Knopf, Inc.

Mucha, T. F., & Reinhardt, R. F. Conversion reactions in student aviators. *Amer. J. Psychiat.,* **127**, 1970, 493–97.

Natale, M., Kowitt, M., Dahlberg, C. C., & Jaffe, J. Effects of psychotomimetics (LSD and dextroamphetamine) on the use of figurative language during psychoanalysis. *J. Cons. Clin. Psychol.,* 1978, **46**(6), 1579–80.

Nemiah, J. C. Obsessive-compulsive reaction. In A. M. Freedman & H. I. Kaplan (Eds.), *Comprehensive textbook of psychiatry.* Baltimore: Williams & Wilkins, 1967.

O'Neill, M., & Kempler, B. Approach and avoidance responses of the hysterical personality to sexual stimuli. *J. Abnorm. Psychol.,* 1969, **74**, 300–305.

Osgood, C. E., & Luria, Z. A blind analysis of a case of multiple personality using the semantic differential. *J. Abnorm. Soc. Psychol.,* 1954, **49**, 579–91.

Osgood, C. E., Luria, Z., Jeans, R. F., & Smith, S. W. The three faces of Evelyn: A case report. *Journal of Abnormal Psychology,* 1976, Vol. 85, pp. 249–70. Copyright © 1976 by the American Psychological Association. Reprinted by permission.

Pollak, J. M. Obsessive-compulsive personality: A review. *Psychol. Bull.,* 1979, **86**(2), 225–41.

Pollin, W., Allen, M. G., Hoffer, A., Stabenau, J. R., & Hrubec, Z. Psychopathology in 15,909 pairs of veteran twins. *Amer. J. Psychiat.,* 1969, **126**, 597–609.

Portnoy, I. The anxiety states. In S. Arieti (Ed.), *American handbook of psychiatry* (Vol. 1). New York: Basic Books, 1959. Pp. 307–23.

Prusoff, B., & Klerman, G. L. Differentiating depressed from anxious neurotic outpatients. *Arch. Gen. Psychiat.,* Mar. 1974, **30**(3), 302–9.

Rosenthal, S. H., & Wulfsohn, N. L. Electrosleep—A clinical trial. *Amer. J. Psychiat.,* 1970, **127**(4), 533–34.

Salzman, L. Obsessions and phobias. *Inter. J. Psychiat.,* 1968, **6**, 451–68.

Schreiber, F. R. *Sybil.* Warner Books, 1974.

Schwartz, G. E. Psychobiological foundations of psychotherapy and behavior change. In S. L. Garfield & A. E. Bergin (Eds.), *Handbook of psychotherapy and behavior change: An empirical analysis.* New York: Wiley, 1978.

Slavney, P. R., & McHugh, P. R. The hysterical personality. *Arch. Gen. Psychiat.,* Mar. 1974, **30**(3), 325–29.

Sloane, R. B., Staples, F. R., & Cristol, A. H. *Psychotherapy versus behavior therapy.* Cambridge: Harvard University Press, 1975.

Solomon, P., Leiderman, P. H., Mendelson, J., & Wexler, D. Sensory deprivation. *Amer. J. Psychiat.,* 1957, **114**, 357–63.

Stern, R. S., Lipsedge, M. S., & Marks, I. M. Obsessive ruminations: A controlled trial of thought-stopping technique. *Behav. Res. Ther.,* Nov. 1973, **11**(4), 659–62.

Templer, D. I., & Lester, D. Conversion disorders: A review of research findings. *Comprehensive Psychiatry,* July/Aug. 1974, **15**(4), 285–94.

Teoh, J. I., Soewondo, S., & Sidharta, M. Epidemic hysteria in Malaysian schools: An illustrative episode. *Psychiatry,* August 1975, **38**, 258–68. Reprinted by permission of the William Alanson White Psychiatric Foundation.

Theodor, L. H., & Mandelcorn, M. S. Hysterical blindness: A case report and study using a modern psychophysical technique. *J. Abnorm. Psychol.,* Dec. 1973, **82**(3), 552–53.

Thigpen, C. H., & Cleckley, H. M. *Three Faces of Eve.* New York: McGraw-Hill, 1957.

Verbeek, E. Hysteria. *Psychiatria clinica,* 1973, **6**(2), 104–20.

Weiss, E., & English, O. S. *Psychosomatic medicine.* Philadelphia: W. B. Saunders, 1943.

Woodruff, R. A. Jr., Guze, S. B., & Clayton, P. J. Anxiety neurosis among psychotic patients. *Comprehensive Psychiatry,* 1972, **13**, 165–70.

8. Psychological Factors and Physical Illness

Ainslie, G. Specious reward: A behavioral theory of impulsiveness and impulse control. *Psychol. Bull.,* 1975, **82**, 463–96.

Alexander, A. B. Chronic asthma. In R. B. Williams, Jr. & W. D. Gentry (Eds.), *Behavioral approaches to medical treatment.* Cambridge, Mass.: Ballinger, 1977. Pp. 7–24.

Alexander, F. *Psychosomatic medicine.* New York: Norton, 1950.

Astor, G. From sitting on top of the world to sitting in a wheelchair. *Today's Health,* Mar. 1973, **51**(3), 20–26.

Bachrach, A. J., Erwin, W. J., & Mohr, J. P. The control of eating behavior in an anorexic by operant conditioning techniques. In L. P. Ullmann & L. Krasner (Eds.), *Case studies in behavior modification,* New York: Holt, Rinehart & Winston, 1965. Pp. 153–63.

Basedow, H. *The Australian aboriginal.* London: Adelaide, 1927.

Bemis, K. M. Current approaches to the etiology and treatment of anorexia nervosa. *Psychol. Bull.,* 1978, **85**, 593–617.

Berk, S. N., Moore, M. E., & Resnick, J. H. Psychosocial factors as mediators of acupuncture therapy. *J. Cons. Clin. Psychol.,* 1977, **45**, 612–19.

Blanchard, E. B., & Young, L. D. Clinical applications of biofeedback training: A review of evidence. *Arch. Gen. Psychiat.,* May 1974, **30**(5), 573–89.

Bleeker, E. Many asthma attacks psychological. *Sci. News,* 1968, **93**(17), 406.

Bliss, E. L., & Branch, C. H. H. *Anorexia nervosa: Its history, psychology, and biology.* Copyright © 1960, by Paul B. Hoeber, Inc. Medical Division of Harper & Row, Publishers, Inc. Reprinted by permission.

Bloom, B. L., Asher, S. J., & White, S. W. Marital disruption as a stressor: A review and analysis. *Psychol. Bull.*, 1978, **85,** 867–94.

Brady, J. V. Personal communication to F. L. Ruch & P. G. Zimbardo, 1970. In F. L. Ruch & P. G. Zimbardo, *Psychology and life* (8th ed.). Glenview, III.: Scott, Foresman, 1971. P. 48.

Brady, J. V., Porter, R. W., Conrad, D. G., & Mason, J. W. Avoidance behavior and the development of gastroduodenal ulcers. *J. Exper. Anal. Behav.*, 1958, **1,** 69–73.

Bresler, D. Personal correspondence with author re ongoing acupuncture research project at UCLA, funded by NIMH, 1975.

Brown, B. B. *New mind, new body bio-feedback: New directions for the mind.* New York: Harper & Row, 1974.

Brown, D. G. Stress as a precipitant factor of eczema. *J. Psychosom. Res.*, Aug. 1972, **16**(5), 321–27.

Brown, G. W. Life-events and psychiatric illness: Some thoughts on methodology and causality. *J. Psychosom. Res.*, Aug. 1972, **16**(5), 311–20.

Bruch, H. *The golden cage: The enigma of anorexia nervosa.* Cambridge, Mass.: Harvard University Press, 1978.

Budzynski, T. In M. Schneider, Some cheering news about a very painful subject. *The Sciences*, May 1974, **14**(4), 6–12.

Bulatov, P. K. The higher nervous activity in persons suffering from bronchial asthma. In Problems of interrelationship between psyche and soma in psychoneurology and general medicine. *Institute Bechtereva*, 1963, 317–28. *Inter. J. Psychiat.*, Sept. 1967, p. 245.

Byassee, J. E. Essential hypertension. In R. B. Williams, Jr. & W. D. Gentry (Eds.), *Behavioral approaches to medical treatment.* Cambridge, Mass.: Ballinger, 1977. Pp. 113–37.

Cailliet, R. *Low back pain syndrome* (2nd ed.). Philadelphia: F. A. Davis Co., 1968.

Cannon, W. B. "Voodoo" death. *American Anthropologist*, 1942, **44**(2), 169–81.

Chaves, J. F., & Barber, T. X. Needles and knives: Behind the mystery of acupuncture and Chinese meridians. *Human Behavior*, 1973, **2**(1), 18–24.

Cox, D. J., Freundlich, A., & Meyer, R. G. Differential effectiveness of electromyographic feedback, verbal relaxation instructions, and medication placebo with tension headaches. *J. Cons. Clin. Psychol.*, 1975, **43,** 892–98.

Crisp, A. H. Premorbid factors in adult disorders of weight, with particular reference to primary anorexia nervosa (weight phobia). *J. Psychosom. Med.*, 1970, **14**(1), 1–22.

Crisp, A. H. The prevalence of anorexia nervosa and some of its associations in the general population. In S. Kasl & F. Reichsman (Eds.), *Advances in psychosomatic medicine* (Vol. 9): *Epidemiologic studies in psychosomatic medicine*, Basel, Switzerland: S. Karger, 1977. Pp. 38–47.

Crown, S., & Crown, J. M. Personality in early rheumatoid disease. *J. Psychosom. Res.*, July 1973, **17**(3), 189–96.

Davis, M. H., Saunders, D. R., Creer, T. L., & Chai, H. Relaxation training facilitated by biofeedback apparatus as a supplemental treatment in bronchial asthma. *J. Psychosom. Res.*, Mar. 1973, **17**(2), 121–28.

Day, G. The psychosomatic approach to pulmonary tuberculosis. *Lancet*, May 12, 1951, p. 6663.

Dunbar, F. *Psychosomatic diagnosis.* New York: Harper & Row, 1943.

Dunbar, F. *Emotions and bodily changes* (4th ed.). New York: Columbia University Press, 1954.

Edwards, C. C. What you can do to combat high blood pressure. *Family Health*, Nov. 1973, **5**(11), 24–26.

Ellis, E. F. Asthma—The demon that thrives on myths. *Today's Health*, 1970, **48**(6), 63–64.

Engel, G. Is grief a disease? *Psychosom. Med.*, 1961, **23,** 18–23.

Erwin, W. J. A 16-year follow-up of a case of severe anorexia nervosa. *J. Behav. Ther. Exp. Psychiat.*, 1977, **8,** 157–60.

Faris, R. E. L., & Dunham, H. W. *Mental disorders in urban areas.* Chicago: University of Chicago Press, 1939.

Feighner, J. P., Robins, E., Guze, S. B., Woodruff, R. A., Jr., Winokur, G., & Muñoz, R. Diagnostic criteria for use in psychiatric research. Reprinted from *Archives of General Psychiatry*, 1972, **26,** 61. Copyright 1972, American Medical Association.

Fischer, H. K., & Dlin, B. M. Psychogenic determination of time of illness or death by anniversary reactions and emotional deadlines. *Psychosomatics*, May/June 1972, **13**(3), 170–73.

Friar, L. R., & Beatty, J. Migraine: Management by trained control of vasoconstriction. *J. Cons. Clin. Psychol.*, 1976, **44,** 46–53.

Friedman, M., & Rosenman, R. Association of specific overt behavior pattern with blood and cardiovascular findings. *JAMA*, 1959, **169,** 1286.

Friedman, R., & Iwai, J. Genetic predisposition and stress-induced hypertension. *Science*, 1976, **193,** 161–92.

Fuller, G. D. Current status of biofeedback in clinical practice. *Amer. Psychologist*, 1978, **33**(1), 39–78.

Gaw, A. C., Chang, L. W., & Shaw, L. Efficacy of acupuncture on osteoarthritic pain: A controlled, double-blind study. *New Engl. J. Med.*, 1975, **293,** 375–78.

Goldfried, M. R., & Merbaum, M. (Eds.), *Behavior change through self control.* New York: Holt, Rinehart and Winston, 1973.

Goldstein, M. J., & Palmer, J. O. The case of George P. Adapted from *The experience of anxiety: A casebook*, Second Edition. Copyright © 1963, 1975 by Michael J. Goldstein and James O. Palmer. Reprinted by permission of Oxford University Press, Inc.

Gottlieb, A. A., Gleser, G. C., & Gottschalk, L. A. Verbal and physiological responses to hypnotic suggestion of attitudes. *Psychosom. Med.*, 1967, **29,** 172–83.

Graham, D. T. Some research on psychophysiologic specificity and its relation to psychosomatic disease. In R. Roessler & N. S. Greenfield (Eds.), *Physiological correlates of psychological disorder.* Madison: University of Wisconsin Press, 1962. Pp. 221–38.

Graham, D. T., Kabler, J. D., & Graham, F. Physiological responses to the suggestion of attitudes specific for hives and hypertension. *Psychosom. Med.*, 1962, **24,** 159–69.

Gregory, I., & Rosen, E. *Abnormal psychology.* Philadelphia: W. B. Saunders, 1965.

Halberstam, M. Can you make yourself sick? A doctor's report on psychosomatic illness. *Today's Health*, Dec. 1972, **50**(12), 24–29.

Harburgh, E., Erfurt, J. C., Hauenstein, L. S., Chape, C., Schull, W. J., & Schork, M. A. Socioecological stress, suppressed hostility, skin color, and black-white male blood pressure: Detroit, *Psychosom. Med.*, 1973, **35,** 276–96.

Hearst, E. D., Cloninger, C. R., Crews, E. L., & Cadoret, R. J. Electrosleep therapy: A double-blind trial. *Arch. Gen. Psychiat.*, Apr. 1974, **30**(4), 463–66.

Hokanson, J. E., & Burgess, M. The effects of three types of aggression on vascular process. *J. Abnorm. Soc. Psychol.*, 1962, **64,** 446–49.

Holmes, T. H., & Masuda, M. Life change and illness susceptibility. In B. P. Dohrenwend & B. S. Dohrenwend (Eds.), *Stressful life events: Their nature and effects.* New York: Wiley, 1974. Pp. 45–72.

Ikemi, Y., Ago, Y., Nakagawa, S., Mori, S., Takahashi, N., Suematsu, H., Sugita, M., & Matsubara, H. Psychosomatic mechanism under social changes in Japan. *J. Psychosom. Res.*, Feb. 1974, **18**(1), 15–24.

Jones, R. A. *Self-fulfilling prophecies: Social, psychological, and physiological effects of expectancies.* Hillsdale, N.J.: Erlbaum Associates, 1977.

Jenkins, C. D. Behavior that triggers heart attacks. *Sci. News*, June 22, 1974, **105**(25), 402.

Kahn, R. L. Stress: from 9 to 5. *Psych. Today*, 1969, **3**(4), 34–38.

Katkin, E. S., & Obrist, P. A. An inaccurate picture. *Amer. Psychologist*, 1978, **33,** 963.

Kidson, M. A. Personality and hypertension. *J. Psychosom. Res.*, Jan. 1973, **17**(1), 35–41.

Klerman, G. L., & Izen, J. E. The effects of bereavement and grief on physical health and general well-being. In S. Kasl & F. Reichsman (Eds.), *Advances in psychosomatic medicine* (Vol.

9): *Epidemiologic studies in psychosomatic medicine.* Basel, Switzerland: S. Karger, 1977. Pp. 63–104.

Kushner, M. The operant control of intractable sneezing. In C. D. Spielberger (Ed.), *Contributions to general psychology: Selected readings for introductory psychology.* New York: Ronald Press, 1968.

Lang, P. Autonomic control. *Psych. Today,* 1970, **4**(5), 37–41.

Lang, P. J., Stroufe, L. A., & Hastings, J. E. Effects of feedback and instructional set on the control of cardiac-rate variability. *J. Exp. Psychol.,* 1967, **75,** 425–31.

Lebedev, B. A. Corticovisceral psychosomatics. *Inter. J. Psychiat.,* 1967, **4**(3), 241–46.

Leonard, A. G. *The lower Niger and its tribes.* London: Barnes & Noble, 1906.

Le Shan, L. L., & Worthington, R. E. Some psychologic correlates of neoplastic disease: Preliminary report. *Journal of Clinical and Experimental Psychopathology,* 1955, **16,** 281–88.

Liebman, R., Minuchin, S., & Baker, L. An integrated treatment program for anorexia nervosa. *Amer. J. Psychiat.,* Apr. 1974, **131**(4), 432–36.

Liljefors, I., & Rahe, R. H. An identical twin study of psychosocial factors in coronary heart disease in Sweden. *Psychosom. Med.,* Sept./Oct. 1970, **32**(5), 523–42.

Lipton, E. L., Steinschneider, A., & Richmond, J. B. Psychophysiologic disorders in children. In L. W. Hoffman & M. L. Hoffman (Eds.), *Review of child development research.* Russell Sage Foundation, 1966. Pp. 169–220.

Mays, J. A. High blood pressure, soul food. *Los Angeles Times,* Jan. 16, 1974, II, 7.

McLelland, D. C. Inhibited power motivation and high blood pressure in men. *J. Abnorm. Psychol.,* 1979, **88**(2), 182–90.

Miller, J. P. Relax! The brain machines are here. *Human Behavior,* Aug. 1974, **3**(8), 16–23.

Murase, T., & Johnson, F. Naikan, Morita, and western psychotherapy. *Arch. Gen. Psychiat.,* July 1974, **31**(1), 121–28.

Murata, S. New help for the headache that won't go away. *Family Health,* Feb. 1973, **5**(2), 29–31; 55–56.

Nelson, H. High blood pressure found in third of adults in survey. *Los Angeles Times,* March 27, 1973, II, 1; 3.

Nemiah, J. C. The case of Mary S. from *Foundations of psychopathology.* Copyright © 1961 by Oxford University Press, Inc. Reprinted by permission.

Olds, S. Say it with a stomach ache. *Today's Health,* 1970, **48**(11), 41–43; 88.

Ostfeld, A. M., & D'Atri, D. A. Rapid sociocultural change and high blood pressure. In S. Kasl & F. Reichsman (Eds.), *Advances in psychosomatic medicine* (Vol. 9): *Epidemiologic studies in psychosomatic medicine.* Basel, Switzerland: S. Karger, 1977. Pp. 20–37.

Palazzoli, M. S. *Self-starvation: From individual to family therapy in the treatment of anorexia nervosa.* New York: Jason Aronson, 1978.

Parkes, C. M., Benjamin, B., & Fitzgerald, R. G. Broken heart: A statistical study of increased mortality among widowers. *Brit. Med. J.,* Mar. 22, 1969, **1,** 740–43.

Pasamanick, B. Prevalence and distribution of psychosomatic conditions in an urban population according to social class. *Psychosom. Med.,* 1962, **24,** 352–56.

Payne, R. L. Recent life changes and the reporting of psychological states. *J. Psychosom. Res.,* Feb. 1975, **19**(1), 99–103.

Peters, J. E., & Stern, R. M. Specificity of attitude hypothesis in psychosomatic medicine. *J. Psychosom. Res.,* 1971, **15,** 129–35.

Philipp, R. L., Wilde, G. J. S., & Day, J. H. Suggestion and relaxation in asthmatics. *J. Psychosom. Res.,* June 1972, **16**(3), 193–204.

Rahe, R. H. Life change and subsequent illness reports. In K. E. Gunderson & R. H. Rahe (Eds.), *Life stress and illness.* Springfield, Ill.: Thomas, 1974.

Rahe, R. H., & Arthur, R. J. Life change and illness studies. *Journal of Human Stress,* 1978, **4,** 3–15.

Rahe, R. H., & Lind, E. Psychosocial factors and sudden cardiac death. *J. Psychosom. Res.,* 1971, **15**(1), 19–24.

Rawitch, R. Oscar winner dies on day he predicted. *Los Angeles Times,* July 5, 1973, II, 2.

Rennie, T. A. C., & Srole, L. Social class prevalence and distribution of psychosomatic conditions in an urban population. *Psychosom. Med.,* 1956, **18,** 449–56.

Rimm, D. C., & Masters, J. C. *Behavior therapy: Techniques and empirical findings.* New York: Academic Press, 1974.

Robinson, H., Kirk, R. F., Jr., Frye, R. F., & Robertson, J. T. A psychological study of patients with rheumatoid arthritis and other painful diseases. *J. Psychosom. Res.,* Feb. 1972, **16**(1), 53–56.

Romo, M., Siltanen, P., Theorell, T., & Rahe, R. H. Work behavior, time urgency, and life dissatisfactions in subjects with myocardial infarction: A cross-cultural study. *J. Psychosom. Res.,* Feb. 1974, **18**(1), 1–8.

Rosenthal, S. H. Electrosleep: A double-bind clinical study. *Biological Psychiatry,* Apr. 1972, **4**(2), 179–85.

Schmale, A. H. Hopelessness as a predictor of cervical cancer. *Social Science and Medicine,* 1971, **5,** 95–100.

Schwartz, G. E. Psychobiological foundations of psychotherapy and behavior change. In S. L. Garfield & A. E. Bergin (Eds.), *Handbook of psychotherapy and behavior change* (2nd Ed.). New York: Wiley, 1978. Pp. 63–99.

Senay, E. C., & Redlich, F. C. Cultural and social factors in neuroses and psychosomatic illnesses. *Social Psychiatry,* 1968, **3**(3), 89–97.

Seligman, M. E. P. *Helplessness: On depression, development, and death.* San Francisco: Freeman, 1975.

Selye, H. *The stress of life* (2nd ed.). New York: McGraw-Hill, 1976.

Shapiro, A. K., & Morris, L. A. The placebo effect in medical and psychological therapies. In S. L. Garfield & A. E. Bergin (Eds.) *Handbook of psychotherapy and behavior change* (2nd Ed.). New York: Wiley, 1978. Pp. 369–410.

Simonton, O. C., Matthews-Simonton, S., & Creighton, J. *Getting well again.* Los Angeles: J. P. Tarper (Distributed by St. Martin's Press, New York), 1978.

Stein, J. *Neurosis in contemporary society: Process and treatment.* Belmont, Calif.: Brooks/Cole, 1970.

Suinn, R. M. Type A behavior pattern. In R. B. Williams, Jr., & W. D. Gentry (Eds.), *Behavioral approaches to medical treatment.* Cambridge, Mass.: Ballinger, 1977. Pp. 55–56.

Surwit, R. S., Shapiro, D., & Good, M. I. Comparison of cardiovascular biofeedback, neuromuscular biofeedback, and meditation in the treatment of borderline essential hypertension. *J. Cons. Clin. Psychol.,* 1978, **46,** 252–63.

Tasto, D. L., & Hinkle, J. E. Muscle relaxation treatment for tension headaches. *Beh. Res. Ther.,* 1973, **11,** 347–50.

Thiel, H., Parker, D., & Bruce, T. A. Stress factors and the risk of myocardial infarction. *J. Psychosom. Res.,* Jan. 1973, **17**(1), 43–57.

Time. From Shocks to stop sneezes. *Time,* (June 17, 1966) p. 72. Reprinted by permission from *Time,* The Weekly Newsmagazine; Copyright Time Inc.

Watson, A. A. Death by cursing—A problem for forensic psychiatry. *Medicine, Science and the Law,* July 1973, **13**(3), 192–94.

Weiner, H. F., Thaler, M., Reiser, M. F., & Mirsky, I. A. Etiology of duodenal ulcer: I. Relation of specific psychological characteristics to rate of gastric secretion (Serum pepsenogen). *Psychosom. Med.,* 1957, **19,** 1–10.

Weisenberg, M. Pain and pain control. *Psychol. Bull.,* 1977, **84,** 1008–44.

Weisman, A. Psychosocial death. *Psych. Today,* Nov. 1972, **6**(6), 77–78; 83–84; 86.

Weitzman, E. D., & Luce, G. Biological rhythms: Indices of pain, adrenal hormones, sleep, and sleep reversal. In NIMH, *Behavioral sciences and mental health.* Washington, D.C.: Govt. Printing Office, 1970.

Williams, R. B., Jr. Headache. In R. B. Williams, Jr. & W. D.

Gentry (Eds.), *Behavioral approaches to medical treatment.* Cambridge, Mass.: Ballinger, 1977. Pp. 41–53.

Williams, R. B., Jr., & Gentry, W. D. (Eds.). *Behavioral approaches to medical treatment.* Cambridge, Mass.: Ballinger, 1977.

Wolff, H. G. *Headache and other head pain.* Cambridge: Oxford University Press, 1948.

Wolff, H. G. Life stress and cardiovascular disorders. *Circulation,* 1950, **1**, 187–203.

Wolpe, J. For phobia: A hair of the hound. *Psych. Today,* 1969, **3**(1), 34–37.

9. Personality Disorders and Crime

Abel, G. G., Blanchard, E. B., Becker, J. V., & Djenderedjian, A. Differentiating sexual aggressives with penile measures. *Criminal Justice and Behavior,* 1978, **5**, 315–32.

Alexander, S. Under the rock. *Newsweek,* July 8, 1974, **84**(2), 35.

American Psychiatric Association (APA). *Diagnostic and statistical manual of mental disorders (DSM-III).* Washington, D.C.: APA, 1979.

Arief, A. J., & Bowie, C. G. Some psychiatric aspects of shoplifting. *J. Clin. Psychopath.,* 1947, **7**, 565–76.

Bandura, A. *Principles of behavior modification.* New York: Holt, Rinehart & Winston, 1969.

Bluemel, C. S. *War, politics, and insanity.* Denver: World Press, 1948. Reprinted by permission of Mrs. Andrew Bluemel.

Bolen, D. W., & Boyd, W. H. Gambling and the gambler. *Arch. Gen. Psychiat.,* 1968, **18**(5), 617–30.

Borkovec, T. D. Autonomic reactivity to sensory stimulation in psychopathic, neurotic, and normal juvenile delinquents. *J. Cons. Clin. Psychol.,* 1970, **35**, 217–22.

Buss, A. H. *Psychopathology.* New York: Wiley, 1966.

Chesno, F. A., & Kilmann, P. R. Effects of stimulation on sociopathic avoidance learning. *J. Abnorm. Psychol.,* Apr. 1975, **84**(2), 144–50.

Climent, C. E., Rollins, A., Ervin, F. R., & Plutchik, R. Epidemiological studies of women prisoners, I: medical and psychiatric variables related to violent behavior. *Amer. J. Psychiat.,* Sept. 1973, **130**(9), 985–90.

Cohen, J., & Hansel, M. *Risk and gambling: A study of subjective probability.* New York: Philosophical Library, 1956.

Cressey, D. R. *Theft of the nation: The structure and operations of organized crime in America.* New York: Harper & Row, 1969.

Crichton, R. *The great imposter.* New York: Random House, 1959. Summarized from *The Great Imposter,* by Robert Crichton © Copyright 1959 by Robert Crichton. Used by permission of Random House, Inc.

Devereaux, G. Psychodynamics of Mohave gambling. *American Imago,* 1950, **7**, 55–56.

Doleschal, E., & Klapmuts, N. New criminology. *Behav. Today,* Jan. 21, 1974, **5**(3), 18–19.

Ellis, A. The treatment of a psychopath with rational therapy. In S. J. Morse & R. I. Watson (Eds.), *Psychotherapies: A comparative casebook.* New York: Holt, Rinehart & Winston, 1977.

Eysenck, H. J. *Behaviour therapy and the neuroses.* London: Pergamon Press, 1960.

Feild, H. S. Attitudes toward rape: A comparative analysis of police, rapists, crisis counselors, and citizens. *J. Pers. Soc. Psychol.,* 1978, **36**, 156–79.

Fenz, W. D. Heart rate responses to a stressor: A comparison between primary and secondary psychopaths and normal controls. *J. Exper. Res. Person.,* 1971, **5**(1), 7–13.

Franklin, B. The autobiography of Benjamin Franklin. In C. W. Eliot (Ed.), *The Harvard classics* (Vol. 1). New York: P. F. Collier & Sons, 1909 [1771].

Ginsburg, B. E Cited in E. Kiester, Jr., Violence in America: The latest theories and research. *Today's Health,* Jan. 1974, **52**(1), 52–53.

Gluckstern, N. Personal communication, June 11, 1979.

Goldfarb, R. L. American prisons: Self-defeating concrete.

Psych. Today, Jan. 1974, **7**(8), 20; 22; 24; 85; 88–89.

Greenacre, P. Conscience in the psychopath. *Amer. J. Orthopsychiat.,* 1945, **15**, 495–509.

Greer, S. Study of parental loss in neurotics and sociopaths. *Arch. Gen. Psychiat.,* Aug. 1964, **11**(2), 177–80.

Group for the Advancement of Psychiatry (GAP). *Misuses of psychiatry in the criminal courts: Competency to stand trial.* New York: GAP Publications Office, 1974.

Gunn, J., Robertson, G., Dell, S., & Way, C. *Psychiatric aspects of imprisonment.* New York: Academic Press, 1978.

Gurman, A. S., & Kniskern, D. P. Research on marital and family therapy: Progress, perspectives, and prospects. In S. L. Garfield & A. E. Bergin (Eds.), *Handbook of psychotherapy and behavior change: An empirical analysis.* New York: Wiley, 1978.

Guthrie, P. D. California copes with change. *Los Angeles Times,* May 25, 1975, IV, 5.

Guze, S. B., Goodwin, D. W., & Crane, J. B. Criminality and psychiatric disorders. *Arch. Gen. Psychiat.,* 1969, **20**, 592–97.

Hare, R. D. Psychopathy, autonomic functioning and the orienting response. *J. Abnorm. Psychol.,* 1968, **73**(Monogr. Suppl. 3, part 2), 1–24.

Hare, R. D. From *Psychopathy: Theory and research* by Robert D. Hare. New York: Wiley, 1970. Copyright © 1970, by John Wiley & Sons, Inc. Reprinted by permission of John Wiley & Sons, Inc.

Heaver, W. L. A study of forty male psychopathic personalities before, during and after hospitalization. *Amer. J. Psychiat.,* 1943, **100**, 342–46.

Henley, A. Muggers of the mind. *Today's Health,* 1971, **49**(2), 39–41; 71.

Holden, C. Prisons: faith in "rehabilitation" is suffering a collapse. *Science,* May 23, 1975, **188**(4190), 815–17.

Horton, P. C., Louy, J. W., & Coppolillo, H. P. Personality disorder and transitional relatedness. *Arch. Gen. Psychiat.,* May 1974, **30**(5), 618–22.

Hotchkiss, S. The realities of rape. *Human Behavior,* 1978, **7**, 18–23.

Jacobs, P. A., Brunton, M., & Melville, M. M. Aggressive behavior, mental sub-normality, and the XYY male. *Nature,* 1965, **208**, 1351–52.

Jarvik, L. F., Klodin, V., & Matsuyama, S. S. Human aggression and the extra Y chromosome: fact or fantasy? *Amer. Psychologist,* Aug. 1973, **28**(8), 674–82.

Kiester, E., Jr. Explosive youngsters: What to do about them. *Today's Health,* Jan. 1974, **52**(1), 49–53; 64–65.

Kirkpatrick, C., & Kanin, E. J. Male sexual aggression on a university campus. *American Sociological Review,* 1957, **22**, 52–58.

Kretschmer, E. [*Physique and character*] (W. J. H. Spratt, trans.). New York: Harcourt Brace Jovanovich, 1925. (Originally published, 1921.)

Leeman, C. P., & Mulvey, C. H. Brief psychotherapy of the dependent personality: Specific techniques. *Psychonometrics,* 1973, **25**, 36–42.

Life. The kid with the bad eye. 1951, **30**(5), 17–21.

Livingston, J. Compulsive gamblers: A culture of losers. *Psych. Today,* Mar. 1974, 51–55.

Lubin, B. Group therapy. In I. Weiner (Ed.), *Clinical methods in psychology.* New York: Wiley, 1976.

Lombroso-Ferrero, G. *Criminal man.* New York: Putnam's, 1911.

Lykken, D. T. A study of anxiety in the sociopathic personality. *J. Abnorm. Soc. Psychol.,* July 1957, **55**(1), 6–10.

MacDonald, J. M. A psychiatric study of check offenders. *Amer. J. Psychiat.,* 1959, **116**, 438–42.

McCord, W., & McCord, J. *The psychopath: An essay on the criminal mind.* New York: Van Nostrand Reinhold, 1964.

McNeil, E. B. *The quiet furies.* Englewood Cliffs, N.J.: Prentice-Hall, 1967.

Megargee, E. An MMPI-based classification system for prisoners. In J. N. Butcher (Ed.), *New directions in the use of the MMPI.* Minneapolis: University of Minnesota Press, 1979.

Melges, F. T., & Bowlby, J. Types of hopelessness in psychopathological process. *Arch. Gen. Psychiat.*, 1969, **20**, 690–99.

Melville, K. Capital punishment. *The Sciences*, May 1973, **13**(4), 20–22.

Menninger, K. *The crime of punishment.* New York: Viking Press, 1968.

Mischel, W. *Personality and assessment.* New York: Wiley, 1968.

Monohan, J. (Ed.). *Community mental health and the criminal justice system.* Elmsford, N.Y.: Pergamon, 1976.

Murphy, P. V. Crime and its causes—A need for social change. *Los Angeles Times*, Dec. 13, 1970, H, 1–2.

Murray, H. A. *Explorations in personality.* New York: Oxford University Press, 1938.

Pollak, J. M. Obsessive-compulsive personality: A review. *Psychol. Bull.*, 1979, **86**(2), 225–41.

Quay, H. C. Psychopathic personality as pathological stimulation seeking. *Amer. J. Psychiat.*, 1965, **122**(2), 180–83.

Rosten, R. A. Some personality characteristics of compulsive gamblers. Unpublished dissertation, UCLA, 1961.

Saxbe, W. Cited in Ostrow, R. J. Soaring crime rate is severe. setback: Saxbe warns U.S. *Los Angeles Times*, Aug. 28, 1974, I, 1; 12.

Schmauk, F. J. Punishment, arousal, and avoidance learning in sociopaths. *J. Abnorm. Psychol.*, Dec. 1970, **76**(3), 325–35.

Schwartz, B. The effect in Philadelphia of Pennsylvania's increased penalties for rape and attempted rape. *J. Crim. Law, Criminol. Police Sci.*, 1968, **59**(4), 509–15.

Schwartz, H. Danger ahead in get-tough policy. *Los Angeles Times*, May 25, 1975, IV, 5.

Sheldon, W. H. (with the collaboration of C. W. Dupertuis & E. McDermott). *Atlas of men.* New York; Harper & Row, 1954.

Sherrod, B. *Dallas Times Herald*, n.d. Quoted in D. Bolen & W. H. Boyd, Gambling and the gambler. *Arch. Gen. Psychiat.*, 1968, **18**(5), 617–30.

Silber, D. E. Controversy concerning the criminal justice system and its implications for the role of mental health workers. *Amer. Psychologist*, Apr. 1974, **29**(4), 239–44.

Silverman, H. Determinism, choice, responsibility, and the psychologist's role as an expert witness. *Amer. Psychologist*, 1969, **24**(1), 5–9.

Small, I. F., & Small, J. G. Sex and the passive-aggressive personality. *Medical Aspects of Human Sexuality*, 1971, **5**(12), 78–89.

Small, J. G. The organic dimensions of crime. *Arch. Gen. Psychiat.*, 1966, **55**(1), 82–89.

Smith, R. J. *The psychopath in society.* New York: Academic Press, 1978.

Smith, R. L. Strange tales of medical imposters. *Today's Health*, 1968, **46**(10), 44–47; 69–70.

Solomon, J. Why gamble? A psychological profile of pathology. *The Sciences*, July/Aug. 1972, **12**(6), 20–21.

Stojanovich, K. Antisocial and dyssocial. *Arch. Gen. Psychiat.*, 1969, **21**(5), 561–67.

Strine, G. Compulsive gamblers pursue elusive dollar forever. *Los Angeles Times*, Mar. 30, 1971, III, 1; 6.

Sutherland, E. H., & Cressey, D. R. *Principles of criminology* (7th ed.). Philadelphia: Lippincott, 1966.

Sutker, P. B., Archer, R. P., & Kilpatrick, D. G. Sociopathy and antisocial behavior: Theory and treatment. In S. M. Turner, K. S. Calhoun, & H. E. Adams (Eds.), *Handbook of clinical behavior therapy.* New York: Wiley, 1979.

Sutker, P. B., & Moan, C. E. A psychosocial description of penitentiary inmates. *Arch. Gen. Psychiat.*, Nov. 1973, **29**(5), 663–67.

Time. Young man with a gun. Jan. 22, 1951, 19–20.

Time. Billy's last words. Dec. 22, 1952.

Uniform Crime Reports. *Federal Bureau of Investigation, U.S. Dept. of Justice.* Washington, D.C.: U.S. Government Printing Office, 1978.

Vaillant, G. E. Sociopathy as a human process: A viewpoint.

Arch. Gen. Psychiat., 1975, **32**(2), 178–83.

Widom, C. S. A methodology for studying noninstitutionalized psychopaths. *J. Cons. Clin. Psychol.*, 1977, **45**, 674–83.

Witkin, H. A. et al. Criminality in XYY and XXY men. *Science*, 1976, **193**(4253), 547–55.

Wolkind, S. N. The components of "affectionless psychopathy" in institutionalized children. *J. Child Psychol. Psychiat.*, July 1974, **15**(3), 215–20.

Yablonsky, L. *The violent gang.* New York: Macmillan, 1962.

Zimbardo, P. G. A field experiment in autoshaping. In C. Ward (Ed.), *Vandalism.* London: Architectural Press, 1973.

10. Addictive Disorders: Substance Abuse, Obesity, and Pathological Gambling

Akil, H., Watson, S., Sullivan, S., & Barchas, J. D. Enkephalin-like material in normal human cerebrospinal fluid: Measurement and levels. *Life Sciences*, 1978, **23**, 121–26.

Alander, R., & Campbell, T. An evaluation of an alcohol and drug recovery program: A case study of the Oldsmobile Experience. *Human Resource Management*, 1975 (Spring), 14–18.

Al-Anon. *Al-Anon—Family treatment tool in alcoholism.* New York: Al-Anon Family Group Headquarters, Inc., 1971.

American Medical Association, Committee on Alcoholism and Drug Dependency. *The illness called alcoholism.* Chicago: AMA, 1969.

American Medical Association, Department of Mental Health. The crutch that cripples: Drug dependence, Part I. *Today's Health*, 1968, **46**(9), 11–12; 70–72.[a]

American Medical Association, Department of Mental Health. The crutch that cripples: Drug dependence, Part II. *Today's Health*, 1968, **46**(10), 12–15; 73–75.[b]

Bales, R. F. Cultural differences in rates of alcoholism. *Quart. J. Stud. Alcohol.*, 1946, **6**, 480–99.

Bandura, A. *Principles of behavior modification.* New York: Holt, Rinehart & Winston, 1969.

Bandura, A. *Aggression: A social learning analysis.* Englewood Cliffs, N.J.: Prentice-Hall, 1973.

Bannister, G., Jr. Cognitive and behavior therapy in a case of compulsive gambling. *Cognitive therapy and research*, 1975, **1**, 223–27.

Bayh, B. Cited in Barbiturate abuse held U.S. epidemic. *Los Angeles Times*, Dec. 5, 1972, I, 1; 9.

Bazell, R. J. Drug abuse: Methadone becomes the solution and the problem. *Science*, Feb. 23, 1973, **179**(4975), 772–75.

Beckman, L. J. Self-esteem of women alcoholics. *Journal of Studies on Alcohol*, 1978, **3**, 491–98.

Behavior Today. . . . And a drug that makes marijuana look "benign." November 1977, p. 3.

Bengelsdorf, I. S. Alcohol, morphine addictions believed chemically similar. *Los Angeles Times*, Mar. 5, 1970, II, 7.

Berzins, J. I., Ross, W. F., English, G. E., & Haley, J. V. Subgroups among opiate addicts: A typological investigation. *J. Abnorm. Psychol.*, Feb. 1974, **83**(1), 65–73.

Blacker, K. H., Jones, R. T., Stone, G. C., & Pfefferbaum, D. Chronic users of LSD: The "acidheads." *Amer. J. Psychiat.*, 1968, **125**(3), 97–107.

Blum, R. *Society and drugs* (Vol. 1). San Francisco: Jossey-Bass, 1969.

Boehm, G. At last—a nonaddicting substitute for morphine? *Today's Health*, 1968, **46**(4), 69–72.

Bolen, D. W., & Boyd, W. H. Gambling and the gambler. *Arch. Gen. Psychiat.*, 1968, **18**(5), 617–30.

Bolen, D. W., Caldwell, A. B., & Boyd, W. H. *Personality traits of pathological gamblers.* Paper presented at the Second Annual Conference on Gambling, Lake Tahoe, Nevada, June 1975.

Boyd, W. H., & Bolen, D. W. The compulsive gambler and spouse in group psychotherapy. *Inter. J. Group Psychother.*, 1970, **20**, 77–90.

Braden, W., Stillman, R. C., & Wyatt, R. J. Effects of marijuana on contingent negative variation and reaction times. *Arch. Gen. Psychiat.*, Oct. 1974, **31**(4), 537–41.

Bruch, H. *Eating disorders: Obesity, anorexia nervosa and the person within.* New York: Basic Books, 1973.

Bumbalo, J. H., & Young, D. E. The self-help phenomenon. *Amer. J. Nurs.*, 1973, **73**, 1588–91.

Bychowski, G. On neurotic obesity. *Psychoanal. Rev.*, 1950, **37**, 301–19.

Caldwell, A. B., Bolen, D. W., & Boyd, W. H. Pathologic gamblers not necessarily obsessive. *Roche Report: Frontiers of Psychiatry*, Oct. 15, 1972, **2**(17), 3.

Cappell, H. D., & Pliner, P. L. Volitional control of marijuana intoxication: A study of the ability to "come down" on command. *J. Abnorm. Psychol.*, Dec. 1973, **82**(3), 428–34.

Carlin, A. S., & Stauss, F. F. Descriptive and functional classification of drug abusers. *J. Cons. Clin. Psychol.*, 1977, **45**, 222–77.

Cautela, J. R. Covert sensitization. *Psych. Rep.*, 1967, **20**, 459–68.

Celentano, D. D., & McQueen, D. V. Comparison of alcoholism prevalence rates obtained by survey and indirect estimators. *Journal of Studies on Alcohol*, 1978, **39**, 420–34.

Chinlund, S. The female addict. *Sci. News*, 1969, **95**(14), 578.

Claeson, L. E., & Malm, U. Electro-aversion therapy of chronic alcoholism. *Behav. Res. Ther.*, 1973, **11**(4), 663–65.

Cohen, J., & Hansel, M. *Risk and gambling: A study of subjective probability.* New York: Philosophical Library, 1956.

Cohen, S. The use of psychedelics as adjuncts to psychotherapy. In V. Binder, A. Binder, & B. Rimland (Eds.), *Modern therapies.* Englewood Cliffs, N.J.: Prentice-Hall, 1976.

Commission of Inquiry into the Non-Medical Use of Drugs. *Interim report.* Ottawa, Canada: Crown, 1970.

Cotler, S. B. The use of different behavioral techniques in treating a case of compulsive gambling. *Behavior Therapy*, 1971, **2**, 579–81.

Crisp, A. H., Douglas, J. W. B., Ross, J. M., & Stonehill, E. Some developmental aspects of disorders of weight. *J. Psychosom. Res.*, 1970, **14**, 313–20.

Culliton, B. J. Pot facing stringent scientific examination. *Sci. News*, Jan. 24, 1970, **97**(4), 102–5.

Curlee, J. Alcoholism and the "empty nest." *Bull. Menninger Clin.*, 1969, **33**(3), 165–71.

Custer, R. L. *Personality and social aspects of compulsive gambling.* Paper presented at the American Psychological Association, Washington, D.C., 1976.

Davidson, W. S. Studies of aversive conditioning for alcoholics: A critical review of theory and research methodology. *Psychol. Bull.*, Sept. 1974, **81**(9), 571–81.

DeLint, J., & Schmidt, U. Alcoholism and mortality. In B. Kissin and H. Begleiter (Eds.), *The biology of alcoholism* (Vol. 4): *Social Aspects of Alcoholism.* New York: Plenum, 1976.

Devereaux, G. Psychodynamics of Mohave gambling. *American Imago*, 1950, **7**, 55–56.

Dole, V. P., & Nyswander, M. The miracle of methadone in the narcotics jungle. *Roche Report*, 1967, **4**(11), 1–2; 8; 11.

Dole, V. P., Nyswander, M., & Warner, A. Successful treatment of 750 criminal addicts. *JAMA*, 1968, **206**, 2709–11.

Dole, V. P., & Robinson, J. W. Methadone treatment of randomly selected criminal addicts. *New Engl. J. Med.*, 1969, **280**(25), 1372–75.

Drug Enforcement Administration, Department of Justice. *Controlled Substance Inventory List.* Washington, D.C., 1979.

Efron, V., Keller, M., & Gurioli, C. *Statistics on consumption of alcohol and on alcoholism.* New Brunswick, N.J.: Rutgers Center of Alcohol Studies, 1974.

Ellinwood, E. H. Assault and homicide associated with amphetamine abuse. *Amer. J. Psychiat.*, 1971, **127**(9), 90–95.

Feeney, D. M. The marijuana window: A theory of cannabis use. *Behavioral Biology*, 1976, **18**, 455–71.

Fenna, D. et al. Ethanol metabolism in various racial groups. *Canadian Medical Association Journal*, 1971, **105**, 472–75.

Fontana, A. F., & Dowds, B. N. Assessing treatment outcomes. *J. Nerv. Ment. Dis.*, 1975, **161**, 221–30.

Foulks, E. F., & Katz, S. The mental health of Alaskan natives. *ACTA Psychiatrica Scandinavica*, 1973, **49**, 91–96.

Furlong, W. B. How "speed" kills athletic careers. *Today's Health*, Feb. 1971, **49**(2), 30–33; 62; 64; 66.

Garb, J. R., & Stunkard, A. J. Effectiveness of a self-help group in obesity control: A further assessment. *Arch. Int. Med.*, 1974, **134**, 716–20.

Gearing, F. R. Methadone project called success after five years. *Psychiatric News*, 1970, **5**(12), 18.

Gershon, E. S., Dunner, D. L., & Goodwin, F. K. Toward a biology of affective disorders. *Arch. Gen. Psychiat.*, 1971, **25**, 1–15.

Gilbert, J. G., & Lombardi, D. N. Personality characteristics of young male narcotic addicts. *J. Couns. Psychol.*, 1967, **31**, 536–38.

Goldstein, A., et al. Researchers isolate opiate receptor. *Behav. Today*, Mar. 4, 1974, **5**(9), 1.

Goodwin, D. W. *Is alcoholism hereditary?* New York: Oxford University Press, 1976.

Goodwin, D. W. Alcoholism and heredity. *Arch. Gen. Psychiat.*, 1979, **36**, 57–61.

Goodwin, D. W., Schulsinger, F., Hermansen, L., Guze, S. B., & Winokur, G. Alcohol problems in adoptees raised apart from alcoholic biological parents. *Arch. Gen. Psychiat.*, Feb. 1973, **28**(2), 238–43.

Goodwin, D. W., Schulsinger, F., Moller, N., Hermansen, L., Winokur, G., & Guze, S. B. Drinking problems in adopted and nonadopted sons of alcoholics. *Arch. Gen. Psychiat.*, Aug. 1974, **31**(2), 164–69.

Graham, D. L., & Cross, W. C. Values and attitudes of high school drug users. *Journal of Drug Education*, 1975, **5**, 97–107.

Graham, J. R. *MMPI characteristics of alcoholics, drug abusers and pathological gamblers.* Paper presented at the 13th Annual Symposium on Recent Developments in the Use of the MMPI. Puebla, Mexico, March 1978.

Greene, M. H., Brown, B. S., & Dupont, R. L. Controlling the abuse of illicit methadone in Washington, D.C. *Arch. Gen. Psychiat.*, Feb. 1975, **32**(2), 221–26.

Greene, M. H., & Dupont, R. L. Heroin addiction trends. *Amer. J. Psychiat.*, May 1974, **131**(5), 545–50.

Grossman, J. C., Goldstein, R., & Eisenman, R. Undergraduate marijuana and drug use as related to openness of experience. *Psychiat. Quart.*, 1974, **48**(1), 86–92.

Guerra, F. *The pre-columbian mind.* New York: Seminar Press, 1971.

Hamburg, S. Behavior therapy in alcoholism: A critical review of brood-spectrum approaches. *Journal of Studies on Alcohol*, 1975, **36**, 69–87.

Hazlett, B. Two who played with death—and lost the game. *Los Angeles Times*, Mar. 2, 1971, II, 1; 5.

Hekimian, L. J., & Gershon, S. Characteristics of drug abusers admitted to a psychiatric hospital. *JAMA*. 1968, **205**(3), 125–30.

HEW. Physical damage of pot yet unproven, says HEW. *Psychiatric News*, 1971, **6**(7), 3.

HEW. *The alcoholism report: The authoritative newsletter for professionals.* Washington, D.C.: U.S. Government Printing Office, 1978, **7**(3), 2.

Hirsch, J. Can we modify the number of adipose cells? *Postgraduate Medicine*, 1972, **51**, 83–86.

Hoffer, A., & Osmond, H. *The hallucinogens.* New York: Academic Press, 1967.

Hoffman, A. LSD discoverer disputes "chance" factor in finding. *Psychiatric News*, 1971, **6**(8), 23–26.

Hogan, R., Mankin, D., Conway, J., & Fox, S. Personality correlates of undergraduate marijuana use. *J. Cons. Clin. Psychol.*, 1970, **35**(1), 58–73.

Hollt, V., Dum, J., Blasig, J., Schubert, J. P., & Herz, A. Comparison of in vivo and in vitro parameters of opiate receptor binding in naive and tolerant dependent rodents. *Life Sciences,* 1975, **16,** 1823–28.

Horowitz, M. J. Flashbacks: Recurrent intrusive images after the use of LSD. *Amer. J. Psychiat.,* 1969, **126**(4), 147–51.

Horton, D. The functions of alcohol in primitive societies: a cross-cultural study. *Quart. J. Stud. Alcohol.,* 1943, **4,** 199–320.

Jarvik, M. E. The psychopharmacological revolution. *Psych. Today,* 1967, **1**(1), 51–58.

Jeffrey, D. B., & Katz, R. C. *Take it off and keep it off: A behavioral program for weight loss and healthy living.* Englewood Cliffs, N.J.: Prentice-Hall, 1977.

Jeffery, R. W., Wing, R. R., & Stunkard, A. J. Behavioral treatment of obesity: The state of the art, 1978. *Behavior Therapy,* **9,** 189–99.

Jellinek, E. M. Phases of alcohol addiction. *Quart. J. Stud. Alcohol.,* 1952, **13,** 673–78.

Jellinek, E. M. Phases of alcohol addiction, In G. D. Shean (Ed.), *Studies in abnormal behavior.* Chicago: Rand McNally, 1971. Pp. 86–98.

Johnson, C. Does maternal alcoholism affect offspring? *Clinical Pediatrics,* 1974, **13,** 633–34.

Jones, K. L., & Smith, B. W. The fetal alcohol syndrome. *Teratology,* 1975, **12,** 1–10.

Jones, K. L., Smith, B. W., & Hanson, J. W. Fetal alcohol syndrome: A clinical delineation. *Ann. N.Y. Acad. Sci.,* 1976, **273,** 130–37.

Jones, M. C. Personality correlates and antecedents of drinking patterns in adult males. *J. Cons. Clin. Psychol.,* 1968, **32**(1), 2–12.

Jones, M. C. Personality antecedents and correlates of drinking patterns in women. *J. Cons. Clin. Psychol.,* 1971, **36**(1), 61–69.

Jordan, H. A., & Levitz, L. S. Behavior modification in a self-help group. *Journal of the American Dietetic Association,* 1975, **62,** 27–29.

Kamien, M. Aborigines and alcohol: Intake, effects, and social implications in a rural community in western New South Wales. *Medical Journal of Australia,* 1975, **1,** 291–98.

Katz, M. M., Waskow, E. E., & Olsson, J. Characteristics of the psychological state produced by LSD. *J. Abnorm. Psychol.,* 1968, **73**(1), 1–14.

Kay, E. J., Lyons, A., Newman, W., Mankin, D., & Loeb, R. C. A longitudinal study of personality correlates of marijuana use. *J. Cons. Clin. Psychol.,* 1978, **46,** 470–1.

King, L. J., Murphy, G., Robins, L,, & Darvish, H. Alcohol abuse: A crucial factor in the social problems of Negro men. *Amer. J. Psychiat.,* 1969, **125**(12), 96–104.

Kingsley, R. G., & Wilson, G. T. Behavior therapy for obesity: A comparative investigation of long-term efficacy. *J. Cons. Clin. Psychol.,* 1977, **45,** 288–98.

Kunnes, R. Double dealing in dope. *Human Behavior,* Oct. 1973, **2**(10), 22–27.

Kurland, H. D. Extreme obesity: A psychophysiological disorder. *Psychosomatics,* 1967, **8,** 108–11.

Leon, G. Current directions in the treatment of obesity. *Psychol. Bull.,* 1976, **83,** 557–78.

Leon, G. R., & Chamberlain, K. Emotional arousal, eating patterns, and body image as differential factors associated with varying success in maintaining a weight loss. *J. Cons. Clin. Psychol.,* 1973, **40,** 474–80.

Leon, G. R., Eckert, E. D., Teed, D., & Buckwald, H. Changes in body image and other psychological factors after intestinal bypass surgery for massive obesity, 1978.

Leon, G. R. & Roth, L. Obesity. Psychological causes, correlations and speculations. *Psychol. Bull.,* 1977, **84,** 117–39.

Levitt, L. P. *Illinois State Plan for the Prevention, Treatment, and Control of Alcohol Abuse and Alcoholism* (Vol. 1). Objectives—Plan of Action—Basic Data. Department of Mental Health and Developmental Disabilities, State of Illinois.

Apr. 1, 1974, 1–364.

Levitz, L. S., & Stunkard, A. J. A therapeutic coalition for obesity: Behavior modification and patient self-help. *Amer. J. Psychiat.,* 1974, **131,** 423–27.

Livingston, J. Compulsive gamblers: A culture of losers. *Psych. Today,* Mar. 1974, 51–55.

Lloyd, R. W., Jr., & Salzberg, H. C. Controlled social drinking: An alternative to abstinence as a treatment goal for some alcohol abusers. *Psychol. Bull.,* 1975, **82,** 815–42.

Loper, R. G., Kammeier, M. L., & Hoffman, H. MMPI characteristics of college freshmen males who later became alcoholics. *J. Abnorm. Psychol.,* 1973, **82,** 159–62.

Los Angeles Police Department. *Youth and narcotics.* Reprinted by Los Angeles City School District, 1952, 3–4.

Lovibond, S. H., & Caddy, G. R. Discriminated aversive control in the moderation of alcoholics' drinking behavior. *Behavior Therapy,* 1970, **1,** 437–44.

Marijuana Research Findings. National Institute on Drug Abuse Research Monograph, 1976, No. 14.

Maugh, T. H., II. Marijuana: The grass may no longer be greener. *Science,* Aug. 23, 1974, **185**(4152), 683–85.

McClelland, D. C., Davis, W. N., Kalin, R., & Wanner, E. *The drinking man.* New York: The Free Press, 1972.

McWilliams, S. A., & Tuttle, R. J. Long-term psychological effects of LSD. *Psychol. Bull.,* June 1973, **79**(6), 341–51.

Miller, W. R. *Behavioral self-management: Strategies, techniques and outcome.* New York: Brunner/Mazel, 1977.

Miller, W. R. Behavioral treatment of problem drinkers: A comparative outcome study of three controlled drinking therapies. *J. Cons. Clin. Psychol.,* 1978, **46,** 74–86.

Miller, W. R. Problem drinking and substance abuse: Behavioral perspectives. In N. Krasnegar (Ed.), *Behavioral approaches to analysis and treatment of substance abuse,* in press.

Miller, W. R., & Caddy, G. R. Abstinence and controlled drinking in the treatment of problem drinking. *Journal of Studies on Alcohol,* 1977, **38,** 986–1003.

Miller, W. R., & Muñoz, R. F. *How to control your drinking.* Englewood Cliffs, N.J.: Prentice-Hall, 1976.

Moran, E. Gambling as a form of dependency. *British Journal of Addiction,* 1970, **64,** 419–28.

Munro, J. F., & Duncan, L. J. P. Fasting in the treatment of obesity. *The Practitioner,* 1972, **208,** 493–98.

Nathan, P. E. An overview of behavioral treatment approaches. In G. A. Marlatt & P. E. Nathan (Eds.), *Behavioral approaches to alcoholism.* New Brunswick, N.J.: Rutgers Center of Alcohol Studies, 1977.

National Institute on Alcohol Abuse and Alcoholism. *Report.* Washington, D.C.: U.S. Government Printing Office, 1978.

National Institute of Drug Abuse. *Marijuana and health, 3rd annual report to Congress from the Secretary of Health, Education, and Welfare.* Washington, D.C.: U.S. Government Printing Office, 1976.

Nelson, H. Study compares drug dangers. *Los Angeles Times,* Oct. 6, 1969, I, 3; 25.

Newman, M. G., & Cates, M. S. *Methadone treatment in narcotic addiction.* New York: Academic Press, 1977.

NIDA. Research Monograph No. 14: Marijuana Research Findings, 1976.

NIDA. *Drug abuse statistics in 1977,* March 17, 1978.

NIMH. *Third report on alcohol and health,* October 1978.

Payne, J. H., Dewind, L. T., & Commons, R. R. Metabolic observations in patients with jejunocolic shunts. *American Journal of Surgery,* 1963, **106,** 273–89.

Pert, C. B., & Snyder, S. H. Opiate receptor: Demonstration in nervous tissue. *Science,* Mar. 9, 1973, **179**(4077), 1011–14.

Pliner, P. L., & Cappell, H. D. Modification of affective consequences of alcohol: A comparison of social and solitary drinking. *J. Abnorm. Psychol.,* Aug. 1974, **83**(4), 418–25.

Post, R. M. Cocaine psychoses: A continuum model. *Amer. J. Psychiat.,* Mar. 1975, **132**(3), 225–31.

Pratt, B. Studies reveal alcoholism differs in males and females.

APA Monitor, July 1972, **3**(7), 1.

President's Commission on Mental Health. *Report to the President.* Washington, D.C.: U.S. Government Printing Office, 1978.

Project Dawn Drug Enforcement Agency. *Drug Abuse Warning Network: Project DAWN V.,* May 1976–April 1977.

Rinkel, M. Psychedelic drugs. *Amer. J. Psychiat.,* June 1966, **122**(6), 1415–16.

Rodin, J. *Obesity and external responsiveness.* Paper presented at the meeting of the Eastern Psychological Association, Philadelphia, April 1974.

Roe, A., Burks, B. S., & Mittelmann, B. Adult adjustment of foster children of alcoholic and psychotic parentage and the influence of the foster home. *Memorial Section on Alcohol Studies,* No. 3., New Haven: Yale University Press, 1945.

Roeder, F., et al. Cited in Brain surgery for addiction. *Sci. News,* Feb. 16, 1974, **105**(7), 106.

Rorvik, D. M. Do drugs lead to violence? *Look,* Apr. 7, 1970, 58–61.

Rose, A., & Burks, B. Roundup of current research: Is the child really the father of the man? *Trans-action,* 1968, **5**(6), 6.

Rosten, R. A. Some personality characteristics of compulsive gamblers. Unpublished dissertation, UCLA, 1961.

Runcie, J., & Thompson, T. J. Prolonged starvation—A dangerous procedure? *Brit. Med. J.,* 1970, **3**, 432–35.

Schachter, S. Some extraordinary facts about obese humans and rats. *Amer. Psychologist,* 1971, **26**, 129–44.

Schachter, S. & Rodin, J. *Obese humans and rats.* Potomac, Md.: Erlbaum, 1974.

Schaefer, H. H. Accepted theories disproven. *Sci. News,* 1971, **99**(11), 182.

Schaefer, J. M. Drunkenness and culture stress: A holocultural test. Abstract published in *Transcultural Psychiatric Research Review,* 1972, **9**(1), 62–64.

Schaefer, J. M. Drunkenness and culture stress: A holocultural test. *Transcultural Psychiatric Research Review,* 1974, **11**, 127–29.

Schaefer, J. M. Firewater myths revisited: Towards a second generation of ethanol metabolism studies. Paper presented at Cross-cultural Approaches to Alcoholism. Physiological variation: Invited Symposium. NATO Conference Os, Bergen, Norway, August 30, 1977.

Schaefer, J. M. Alcohol metabolism reactions among the Reddis of South India. *Alcoholism: Clinical and experimental research,* 1978, **2**(1), 61–69.

Schmidt, W. Cirrhosis and alcohol consumption: An epidemiological perspective. In G. Edwards & M. Grant (Eds.), *Alcoholism: New knowledge and new responses.* London: Croom Itall, 1977.

Seixas, F. A., & Cadoret, R. What is the alcoholic man? *New York Academy of Sciences,* Apr. 15, 1974, **223**, 13–14.

Sherrod, B. *Dallas Times Herald,* n.d. Quoted in D. Bolen & W. H. Boyd, Gambling and the gambler. *Arch. Gen. Psychiat.,* 1968, **18**(5), 617–30.

Siegler, M., Osmond, H., & Newell, S. Models of alcoholism. *Quart. J. Stud. Alcohol.,* 1968, **29**(3-A), 571–91.

Silverston, J. T., & Lascelles, B. D. Dieting and depression. *Brit. J. Psychiat.,* 1966, **112**, 513–19.

Skelton, G. Oregonians stand behind new law on marijuana. *Los Angeles Times,* Feb. 10, 1975, I, 16–17.

Smith, D. W., Jones, K. L. & Hanson, J. W. Perspectives on the cause and frequency of the fetal alcohol syndrome. *Ann. N.Y. Acad. Sci.,* 1976, **273**, 138–39.

Sobell, M. B., & Sobell, L. C. Alcoholics treated by individualized behavior therapy: One year treatment outcome. *Behav. Res. Ther.,* Nov. 1973, **11**(4), 599–618.

Sobell, M. B., & Sobell, L. C. *Behavioral treatment of alcohol problems.* New York: Plenum, 1978.

Solomon, J. Why gamble? A psychological profile of pathology. *The Sciences,* July/Aug. 1972, **12**(6), 20–21.

Steiner, C. *Games alcoholics play.* New York: Ballantine, 1977.

Stephens, R., & Cottrell, E. A follow-up study of 200 narcotic addicts committed for treatment under the narcotic addict rehabilitation act. *British Journal of Addiction,* 1972, **67**, 45–53.

Streissguth, A. P. Maternal alcoholism and the outcome of pregnancy: A review of the fetal alcohol syndrome. In M. Greenblatt & M. A. Schuckit (Eds.), *Alcoholism: Problems in Women and Children.* New York: Grune & Stratton, 1976.

Strine, G. Compulsive gamblers pursue elusive dollar forever. *Los Angeles Times,* Mar. 30, 1971, III, 1; 6.

Stuart, R. B. Behavioral control of overeating. *Beh. Res. Ther.,* 1967, **5**, 357–65.

Stuart, R. B. A three-dimensional program for the treatment of obesity. *Beh. Res. Ther.,* 1971, **9**, 177–86.

Stunkard, A., D'Aquili, E., Fox, S., & Filion, R. D. L. Influence of social class on obesity and thinness in children. *JAMA,* 1972, **221**, 579–84.

Su, C. V., Lin, S., Wang, Y. T., Li, C. H., Hung, L. H., Lin, C. S., & Lin, B. C. Effects of B-endorphin on narcotic abstinence syndrome in man. *Taiwan I Hoven Hui Tsa Chih,* 1978, **77**, 133–41.

Sutker, P. B., & Archer, R. P. MMPI characteristics of opiate addicts, alcoholics and other drug abusers. In C. S. Newmark (Ed.), *MMPI: Current clinical and research trends.* Praeger Publishers, 1979.

Swanson, D. W., & Dinello, F. A. Severe obesity as a habituation syndrome. *Arch. Gen. Psychiat.,* 1970, **22**, 120–27.

Tavel, M. E. A new look at an old syndrome: Delirium tremens. *Arch. Int. Med.,* 1962, **109**, 129–34.

Thornton, W. E., & Thornton, B. P. Narcotic poisoning: A review of the literature. *Amer. J. Psychiat.,* Aug. 1974, **131**(8), 867–69.

Time. Alcoholism: New victims, new treatment. Apr. 22, 1974, **103**(16), 75–81.

Ulleland, C. N. The offspring of alcoholic mothers. *Ann. N.Y. Acad. Sci.,* 1972, **197**, 167–69.

U.S. Department of Health, Education, and Welfare (HEW). *Alcohol and health.* Morris E. Chafetz, Chairman of the Task Force. Washington, D.C.: U.S. Government Printing Office, 1974.

U.S. News & World Report. School-age drunks—A fresh worry. Apr. 14, 1975, **78**(15), 40.

Watson, S., & Akil, H. Endorphins: Clinical issues. In R. Pickens & L. Heston (Eds.), *Psychiatric factors in drug abuse.* New York: Grune and Stratton, 1979.

Weissman, M. M., Pottenger, M., Kleber, H., Ruben, H. L., Williams, D., & Thompson, D. Symptom pattern in primary and secondary depression. *Arch. Gen. Psychiat.,* 1977, **34**, 854–62.

Westermeyer, J. Use of alcohol and opium by the Meo of Laos. *Amer. J. Psychiat.,* Feb. 1971, **127**(8), 1019–23.

Westermeyer, J. Opium dens: A social resource for addicts in Laos. *Arch. Gen. Psychiat.,* Aug. 1974, **31**(2), 237–40.

Wetli, C. V., & Wright, R. K. Death caused by recreational cocaine use. *JAMA,* 1979, **241**(23), 2519–22.

Wikler, A. Dynamics of drug dependence: Implications of a conditioning theory for research and treatment. *Arch. Gen. Psychiat.,* May 1973, **28**(5), 611–16.

Wilsnack, S. C. Feminity by the bottle, *Psych. Today,* Apr. 1973, **6**(11), 39–43; 96.[a]

Wilsnack, S. C. Sex role identity in female alcoholism, *J. Abnorm. Psychol.,* Oct. 1973, **82**(2), 253–61.[b]

Winokur, G., Reich, T., Rimmer, J., & Pitts, F. N., Jr. Alcoholism. III: diagnosis and familial psychiatric illness in 259 alcoholic probands. *Arch. Gen. Psychiat.,* 1970, **23**(2), 104–11.

Wolff, P. H. Ethnic differences in alcohol sensitivity. *Science,* 1972, **175**, 449–50.

Woodruff, R. A., Guze, S. B., Clayton, P. J., & Carr, D. Alcoholism and depression. *Arch. Gen. Psychiat.,* Jan. 1973, **28**(1), 97–100.

Yolles, S. Cited in Pop drugs: The high as a way of life. *Time,* Sept. 26, 1969, **94**(13), 74.

11. Affective Disorders

Abrams, R., & Taylor, M. A. Unipolar mania: A preliminary report. *Arch. Gen. Psychiat.*, Apr. 1974, **30**(4), 441–43.

Akiskal, H. S., & McKinney, W. T., Jr., Overview of recent research in depression: Integration of ten conceptual models into a comprehensive clinical frame. *Arch. Gen. Psychiat.*, Mar. 1975, **32**(3), 285–305.

Allen, M. G., Cohen, S., Pollin, W., & Greenspan, S. I. Affective illness in veteran twins: A diagnostic review. *Amer. J. Psychiat.*, Nov. 1974, **131**(11), 1234–39.

American Psychiatric Association (APA). *Diagnostic and statistical manual of mental disorders. (DSM-III).* Washington, D.C.: APA, 1979.

Bagley, C. Occupational class and symptoms of depression. *Social Science and Medicine*, May 1973, **7**(5), 327–40.

Barchas, J. D., Akil, H., Elliott, G. R., Holman, R. B., & Watson, S. J. Behavioral neurochemistry: Neuroregulators and behavioral states. *Science.* Vol. 200, pp. 964–973, 26 May 1978. Copyright 1978 by the American Association for the Advancement of Science. Reprinted by permission.

Beard, G. M. *A practical treatise on nervous exhaustion (neurasthenia), its symptoms, nature, sequences, treatment* (5th ed.). New York: E. B. Treat, 1905.

Beck, A. T. *Depression: Causes and treatment.* Philadelphia: University of Pennsylvania Press, 1967.

Beck, A. T. Cognition, affect, and psychopathology. *Arch. Gen. Psychiat.*, June 1971, **24**(6), 495–500.

Becker, J. *Affective disorders.* Morristown, N. J.: General Learning Press, 1977.

Becker, J., & Altrocchi, J. Peer conformity and achievement in female manic-depressives. *J. Abnorm. Psychol.*, 1968, **73**(6), 585–89.

Berger, P. A. Medical treatment of mental illness. *Science,* 1978, **200**, 974–81.

Bibring, E. The mechanism of depression. In P. Greenacre (Ed.), *Affective disorders.* New York: International University Press, 1953.

Blaney, P. H. Contemporary theories of depression: Critique and comparison. *J. Abnorm. Psychol.*, 1977, **86**(2), 203–23.

Blatt, S. J., D'Afflitti, J. P., & Quinlan, D. M. Experiences of depression in normal young adults. *J. Abnorm. Psychol.*, 1976, **85**, 383–89.

Bloom, B. L., Asher, S. J., & White, S. W. Marital disruption as a stressor: A review and analysis. *Psychol. Bull.*, 1978, **85,** 867–94.

Briscoe, C. W., Smith, J. B., Robins, E., Marten, S., & Gaskin, F. Divorce and psychiatric illness. *Arch. Gen. Psychiat.*, July 1973, **29**(1), 119–25.

Brown, B. Depression roundup. *Behav. Today,* Apr. 29, 1974, **5**(17), 117.

Brown, G. W. Life-events and psychiatric illness: Some thoughts on methodology and causality. *J. Psychosom. Res.*, Aug. 1972, **16**(5), 311–20.

Bunney, W. E., Jr., Murphy, D. L., Goodwin, F. K., & Borge, G. F. The "switch process" in manic-depressive illness: A systematic study of sequential behavioral changes. *Arch. Gen. Psychiat.*, Sept. 1972, **27**(3), 295–302.

Bunney, W. E., Jr., Paul, M. I., & Cramer, H. Biological trigger of "switch" from depression to mania may be CAMP. *Roche Reports,* 1971, **1**(6), 1–2, 8. Reprinted by permission of Dr. W. E. Bunney, Jr., and Dr. M. I. Paul.

Carlson, G., & Goodwin, F. K. The stages of mania: A longitudinal analysis of the manic episode. *Arch. Gen. Psychiat.*, Feb. 1973, **28**(2), 221–28.

Carothers, J. C. A study of mental derangement in Africans, and an attempt to explain its peculiarities, more especially in relation to the African attitude of life. *J. Ment. Sci.*, 1947, **93**, 548–97.

Carothers, J. C. Frontal lobe function and the African. *J. Ment. Sci.*, 1951, **97**, 12–48.

Carothers, J. C. The African mind in health and disease. In *A study in ethnopsychiatry.* Geneva: World Health Organization, 1953, No. 17.

Carothers, J. C. Culture, psychiatry, and the written word. *Psychiatry*, 1959, **22**, 307–20.

Chodoff, P. The depressive personality: A critical review. *Arch. Gen. Psychiat.*, Nov. 1972, **27**(2), 666–73.

Cole, J. O. Depression. *Amer. J. Psychiat.*, Feb. 1974, **131**(2), 204–5.

Coyne, J. C. Depression and the response of others. *J. Abnorm. Psychol.*, 1976, **55**(2), 186–93.

Davis, J. M. Overview; Maintenance therapies in psychiatry: Affective disorder (Vol. 2). *Amer. J. Psychiat.*, 1976, **133**(1), 1–13.

Depue, R. A., & Monroe, S. M. The unipolar-bipolar distinction in the depressive disorders. *Psychol. Bull.*, 1978, **85**, 1001–29.

Downing, R. W., & Rickels, K. Mixed anxiety-depression: Fact or myth? *Arch. Gen. Psychiat.*, Mar. 1974, **30**(3), 312–17.

Eastman, C. Behavioral formulations of depression. *Psychol. Rev.*, 1976, **83**, 277–91.

Engel, G. L. *Psychological development in health and disease.* New York: Saunders, 1962.

Ferster, C. B. A functional analysis of depression. *Amer. Psychologist,* Oct. 1973, **28**(10), 857–70.

Fink, M. *Convulsive therapy: Theory and practice.* New York: Raven Press, 1979.

Hammen, C. L., & Peters, S. D. Differential responses to male and female depressive reactions. *J. Cons. Clin. Psychol.*, 1977, **45**, 994–1001.

Hammen, C. L., & Peters, S. D. Interpersonal consequences of depression: Responses to men and women enacting a depressed role. *J. Abnorm. Psychol.*, 1978, **87**(3), 322–32.

Hartmann, E. Longitudinal studies of sleep and dream patterns in manic-depressive patients. *Arch. Gen. Psychiat.*, 1968, **19**, 312–29.

Hauri, P. Depression. *Behav. Today,* Apr. 29, 1974. **5**(17), 123.

Hauri, P., Chernik, D., Hawkins, D., & Mendels, J. Sleep of depressed patients in remission. *Arch. Gen. Psychiat.*, Sept. 1974, **31**(3). 386–91.

Helzer, J. E., & Winokur, G. A family interview study of male manic depressives. *Arch. Gen. Psychiat.*, July 1974, **31**(1), 73–77.

Hill, D. Depression: Disease, reactions, or posture? *Amer. J. Psychiat.*, 1968, **125**(4), 445–57.

Hiroto, D. S., & Seligman, M. E. P. Generality of learned helplessness in man. *J. Pers. Soc. Psychol.*, Feb. 1975, **31**(2), 311–27.

Hollon, S. *Status and efficacy of behavior therapies for depression: Comparisons and combinations with alternative approaches.* Paper presented at conference on Research Recommendations for the Behavioral Treatment of Depression, University of Pittsburgh, April 1979.

Hollon, S., & Beck, A. T. Psychotherapy and drug therapy: Comparisons and combinations. In S. L. Garfield & A. E. Bergin (Eds.), *Handbook of psychotherapy and behavior change.* New York: Wiley, 1978.

Hurwitz, T. D. Electroconvulsive therapy: A review. *Comprehensive Psychiatry,* July/Aug. 1974, **15**(4), 303–14.

Jaco, E. G. *The social epidemiology of mental disorders.* New York: Russell Sage Foundation, 1960.

Janowsky, D. S., El-Yousef, M. K., & Davis, J. M. Interpersonal maneuvers of manic patients. *Amer. J. Psychiat.*, Mar. 1974, **131**(3), 250–55.

Janowsky, D. S., Leff, M., & Epstein, R. Playing the manic game. *Arch. Gen. Psychiat.*, 1970, **22**, 252–61.

Jenner, F. A., Gjessing, L. R., Cox, J. R., Davies-Jones, A., & Hullin, R. P. A manic-depressive psychotic with a 48 hour cycle. *Brit. J. Psychiat.*, 1967, **113**(501), 859–910.

Johnson, W. B. Euphoric and depressed moods in normal subjects. I. *Charact. & Pers.*, 1937, **6**, 212–16.

Kallmann, F. J. The use of genetics in psychiatry. *J. Ment. Sci.*, 1958, **104**, 542–49.

Karnosh, L. J. (with collaboration of Zucker, E. M.). *Handbook* *of psychiatry.* St. Louis: Mosby, 1945. Reprinted by permission of the C. V. Mosby Co.

Kidson, M., & Jones, I. Psychiatric disorders among aborigines of the Australian Western Desert. *Arch. Gen. Psychiat.,* 1968, **19,** 413–22.

Kraepelin, E. *Clinical psychiatry* (6th ed.). New York: Macmillan, 1937. Originally published 1899.

Lazarus, A. P. Learning theory in the treatment of depression. *Behav. Res. Ther.,* 1968, **8,** 83–89.

Leff, M. J., Roatch, J. F., & Bunney, W. E., Jr. Environmental factors preceding the onset of severe depressions. *Psychiatry,* 1970, **33**(3), 298–311.

Lehmann, H. E. Clinical perspectives on anti-depressant therapy. *Amer. J. Psychiat.,* May 1968, **124**(11, Suppl.), 12–21.

Leonard, C. V. Depression and suicidality. *J. Cons. Clin. Psychol.,* Feb. 1974, **42**(1), 98–104.

Levi, L. D., Fales, C. H., Stein, M., & Sharp, V. H. Separation and attempted suicide. *Arch. Gen. Psychiat.,* 1966, **15**(2), 158–65.

Lewinsohn, P. M. A behavioral approach to depression. In R. J. Friedman & M. M. Katz (Eds.), *The psychology of depression: Contemporary theory and research.* New York: Halstead Press, 1974.

Lewinsohn, P. M., & Graf, M. Pleasant activities and depression. *J. Cons. Clin. Psychol.,* Oct. 1973, **41**(2), 261–68.

Liberman, R. P., & Raskin, D. E. Depression: A behavioral formulation. Reprinted from *Archives of General Psychiatry,* June 1971, **24**(6), 515–23. Copyright 1971, American Medical Association.

Libet, J. M., & Lewinsohn, P. M. Concept of social skill with special reference to the behavior of depressed persons. *J. Cons. Clin. Psychol.,* Apr. 1973, **40**(2), 304–12.

Lorr, M., Klett, C. J. Cross-cultural comparison of psychotic syndromes. *J. Abnorm. Psychol.,* 1968, **74**(4), 531–43.

Marsella, A. J. Depressive experience and disorder across cultures. In H. Triandis & J. Draguns (Eds.), *Handbook of cross-cultural psychology* (Vol. 5). Boston: Allyn & Bacon, 1979.

Masserman, J. H. *Principles of dynamic psychiatry.* Philadelphia: W. B. Saunders Company, 1961.

Paykel, E. S. Life events and acute depression. In J. P. Scott & E. C. Senay (Eds.), *Separation and depression.* Washington: American Association for the Advancement of Science, 1973. Pp. 215–36.

Peto, A. Body image and depression. *Inter. J. Psychoanal.,* 1972, **53**(2), 259–63.

Potts, T. L. *Activity valence as a function of mood change.* Unpublished thesis, University of Georgia, 1977.

Poznanski, E., & Zrull, J. P. Childhood depression. *Arch. Gen. Psychiat.,* 1970, **23**(1), 8–15.

Prange, A. J. The use of drugs in depression: Its practical and theoretical aspects. *Psychiatric Annals,* 1973, **3,** 56–75.

President's Commission on Mental Health. *Report to the President.* Washington, D.C.: U.S. Government Printing Office, 1978.

Prien, R. F., Klett, C. J., & Caffey, E. M. Lithium carbonate and imipramine in prevention of affective episodes. *Arch. Gen. Psychiat.,* Sept. 1973, **29**(3), 420–25.

Prusoff, B., & Klerman, G. L. Differentiating depressed from anxious neurotic outpatients. *Arch. Gen. Psychiat.,* Mar. 1974, **30**(3), 302–9.

Raskin, A. A guide for drug use in depressive disorders. *Amer. J. Psychiat.,* Feb. 1974, **131**(2), 181–85.

Reich, T., Clayton, P. J., & Winokur, G. Family history studies: The genetics of mania. *Amer. J. Psychiat.,* 1969, **125**(10), 1358–69.

Reich, L. H., Davies, R. K., & Himmelhoch, J. M. Excessive alcohol use in manic-depressive illness. *Amer. J. Psychiat.,* Jan. 1974, **131**(1), 83–86.

Rosenthal, S. H. The involutional depressive syndrome. *Amer. J. Psychiat.,* 1968, **124**(11, Suppl.), 21–34.

Rush, A. J., Beck, A. T., Kovacs, M., & Hollon, S. The comparative efficacy of cognitive therapy and imipramine in the treatment of depressed out-patients. *Cognitive Therapy and Research,* 1977, **1**(1), 17–37.

Segal, D. S., Yager, J., & Sullivan, J. L. *Foundations of biochemical psychiatry.* Boston: Butterworth, 1976.

Seligman, M. E. P. Fall into hopelessness. *Psych. Today,* June 1973, **7**(1), 43–47; 48.

Seligman, M. E. P. *Helplessness.* San Francisco: Freeman, 1975.

Slater. E. T. O. Genetics in psychiatry. *J. Ment. Sci.,* 1944, **90,** 17–35.

Stainbrook, E. J. Depression: The psychological context. In G. Usdin (Ed.), *Depression: Clinical, biological and psychological perspectives.* New York: Brunner/Mazel, 1977. Pp. 28–51.

Strickland, B. R., Hale, W. D., & Anderson, L. K. Effect of induced mood states on activity and self-reported affect. *J. Cons. Clin. Psychol.,* 1975, **43,** 587.

Sullivan, H. S. *Clinical studies in psychiatry.* New York: Norton, 1956.

Taylor, M., & Abrams, R. Manic states: A genetic study of early and late onset affective disorders. *Arch. Gen. Psychiat.,* May 1973, **28**(5), 656–58.

Thompson, K. C., & Hendrie, H. C. Environmental stress in primary depressive illness. *Arch. Gen. Psychiat.,* 1972, **26**(2), 130–2.

Travis, J. H. Precipitating factors in manic-depressive psychoses. *Psychiat. Quart.,* 1933, **7,** 411–18.

Weiss, J. M. Cited in Depressing situations. *Sci. News,* Apr. 6, 1974, **105**(14), 224.

White, R. B., Davis, H. K., & Cantrell, W. A. Psychodynamics of depression: Implications for treatment. In G. Usdin (Ed.), *Depression: Clinical, biological and psychological perspectives.* New York: Brunner/Mazel, 1977. Pp. 308–38.

Volkan, V. Regriefing therapy. *Behav. Today,* June 18, 1973, **4**(25), 2.

Winokur, G., & Pitts, F. N. Affective disorder: Is reactive depression an entity? *J. Nerv. Ment. Dis.,* 1964, **138,** 541–47.

Zung, W. W. K. A cross-cultural survey of symptoms in depression. *Amer. J. Psychiat.,* 1969, **126**(1), 116–21.

Zung, W. W. K. & Green, R. L., Jr. Seasonal variations of suicide and depression. *Gen. Psychiat.,* Jan. 1974, **30**(1), 89–91.

12. Schizophrenia and Paranoia

Anthony, E. J. Concluding comments on treatment implications. In L. C. Wynne, R. L. Cromwell & S. Matthysse (Eds.), *The nature of schizophrenia: New approaches to research and treatment.* New York: Wiley, 1978. Pp. 481–84.

Arieti, S. An overview of schizophrenia from a predominantly psychological approach. *Amer. J. Psychiat.,* Mar. 1974, **131**(3), 241–49.

Bannister, D. Schizophrenia: Carnival mirror of coherence. *Psych. Today,* 1971, **4**(8), 66–69; 84.

Bateson, G. Cultural problems posed by a study of schizophrenic process. In A. Auerback (Ed.), *Schizophrenia: an integrated approach.* New York: Ronald Press, 1959.

Bateson, G. Minimal requirements for a theory of schizophrenia, *Arch. Gen. Psychiat.,* 1960, **2,** 477–91.

Bender, L. The life course of children with schizophrenia. *Amer. J. Psychiat.,* July 1973, **130**(7), 783–86.

Berger, P. A. Medical treatment of mental illness. *Science,* 1978, **200,** 974–81.

Bettelheim, B. *Truants from life: The rehabilitation of emotionally disturbed children.* New York: Free Press, 1955.

Bleuler, E. *Dementia praecox or the group of schizophrenias.* New York: International Universities Press, 1950.

Bleuler, M. The offspring of schizophrenics. *Schizophrenia Bulletin,* NIMH, Spring 1974, **8,** 93–107.

Bleuler, M. The long-term course of schizophrenic psychoses. In

L. C. Wynne, R. L. Cromwell, & S. Matthysse (Eds.), *The nature of schizophrenia: New approaches to research and treatment*. New York: Wiley, 1978. Pp. 631–36.

Born, W. Artistic behavior of the mentally deranged; and Great Artists who suffered from mental disorders. *Ciba Symposia*, 1946, **8**, 207–16; 225–32.

Bowen, M. Family relationships in schizophrenia. In A. Auerback (Ed.), *Schizophrenia: An integrated approach*. New York: Ronald Press, 1959.

Bowen, M. A family concept of schizophrenia. In D. D. Jackson (Ed.), *The etiology of schizophrenia*, New York: Basic Books, 1960.

Bowers, M., Jr. The onset of psychosis—A diary account. *Psychiatry*, 1965, **28**, 346–58. Permission granted by author and The William Alanson White Psychiatric Foundation.

Braginsky, B. M., Braginsky, D. D., & Ring, K. *Methods of madness: The mental hospital as a last resort*. New York: Holt, Rinehart, and Winston, 1969.

Brodey, W. M. Some family operations and schizophrenia. *Arch. Gen. Psychiat.*, 1959, **1**, 379–402.

Brown, G. W. Life-events and psychiatric illness: Some thoughts on methodology and causality. *J. Psychosom. Res.*, Aug. 1972, **16**(5), 311–20.

Buber, M. Distance and relation. *Psychiatry*, 1957, **20**, 97–104.

Buchsbaum, M. S., Murphy, D. L., Coursey, R. D., Lake, C. R., & Zeigler, M. G. Platelet monoamine oxidase, plasma dopamine betahydroxylase and attention in a "biochemical high-risk" sample. In L. C. Wynne, R. L. Cromwell, & S. Matthysse (Eds.), *The nature of schizophrenia: New approaches to research and treatment*. New York: Wiley, 1978. Pp. 387–96.

Caffey, E. M., Galbrecht, C. R., & Klett, C. J. Brief hospitalization and aftercare in the treatment of schizophrenia. *Arch. Gen. Psychiat.*, 1971, **21**(1), 81–86.

Cameron, N. Paranoid conditions and paranoia. In S. Arieti (Ed.), *American handbook of psychiatry*. New York: Basic Books, 1959.

Cameron, N., & Margaret, A. Experimental studies in thinking. I. Scattered speech in the responses of normal subjects to incomplete sentences. *J. Exper. Psychol.*, 1949, **39**(5), 617–27.

Cameron, N., & Margaret, A. *Behavior pathology*. Boston: Houghton Mifflin, 1951.

Carothers, J. C. The African mind in health and disease. In *A study in ethnopsychiatry*. Geneva: World Health Organization, 1953, No. 17.

Carothers, J. C. Culture, psychiatry, and the written word. *Psychiatry*, 1959, **22**, 307–20.

Carson, R. C. Disordered interpersonal behavior. In W. A. Hunt (Ed.), *Human behavior and its control*. Cambridge, Mass.: Schenkman (Distributed by General Learning Press, Morristown, N. J.), 1971. Pp. 134–57.

Carson, T. P., & Adams, H. E. Affective disorders: Behavioral perspectives. In S. M. Turner, K. S. Calhoun, & H. E. Adams (Eds.), *Handbook of clinical behavior therapy*. New York: Wiley, 1980.

Cohen, S. M., Allen, M. G., Pollin, W., & Hrubec, Z. Relationship of schizo-affective psychosis to manic depressive psychosis and schizophrenia. *Arch. Gen. Psychiat.*, June 1972, **26**(6), 539–46.

Copeland, J. Aspects of mental illness in West African students. *Soc. Psychiat.*, 1968, **3**(1), 7–13.

Davis, J. M. Dopamine theory of schizophrenia: A two-factor theory. In L. C. Wynne, R. L. Cromwell, & S. Matthysse (Eds.), *The nature of schizophrenia; New approaches to research and treatment*. New York: Wiley, 1978. Pp. 105–15.

Diamond, B. L. Sirhan B. Sirhan: A conversation with T. George Harris. *Psych. Today*, 1969, **3**(4), 48–56.

Drake, R. E., & Wallach, M. A. Will mental patients stay in the community: A social psychological perspective. *J. Cons. Clin. Psychol.*, 1979, **47**(2), 285–94.

Enders, L. J., & Flinn, D. E. Clinical problems in aviation medicine: Schizophrenic reaction, paranoid type. *Aerospace Medicine*, 1962, **33**, 730–32. Reprinted by permission.

Erlenmeyer-Kimling, L., & Cornblatt, B. Attentional measures in a study of children at high risk for schizophrenia. In L. C. Wynne, R. L. Cromwell, & S. Matthysse (Eds.), *The nature of schizophrenia: New approaches to research and treatment*. New York: Wiley, 1978. Pp. 359–65.

Feinsilver, D. Communication in families of schizophrenic patients. *Arch. Gen. Psychiat.*, 1970, **22**(2), 143–48.

Fenz, W. D., & Velner, J. Physiological concomitants of behavior indexes in schizophrenia. *J. Abnorm. Psychol.*, 1970, **76**(1), 27–35.

Field, M. J. *Search for security: An ethnopsychiatric study of rural Ghana*. Evanston: Northwestern University Press, 1960.

Forgus, R. H., & DeWolfe, A. S. Coding of cognitive input in delusional patients. *J. Abnorm. Psychol.*, June 1974, **83**(3), 278–84.

Freedman, B., & Chapman, L. J. Early subjective experience in schizophrenic episodes. *J. Abnorm. Psychol.*, 1973, **82**(1), 46–54.

Freeman, T. On the psychopathology of schizophrenia. *J. Ment. Sci.*, 1960, **106**, 925–37.

Garmezy, N. Current status of other high-risk research programs. In L. C. Wynne, R. L. Cromwell, & S. Matthysse (Eds.), *The nature of schizophrenia: New approaches to research and treatment*. New York: Wiley, 1978.[a]

Garmezy, N. Observations on high-risk research and premorbid development in schizophrenia. In L. C. Wynne, R. L. Cromwell, & S. Matthysse (Eds.), *The nature of schizophrenia: New approaches to research and treatment*. New York: Wiley, 1978.[b]

Gottesman, I. I. Schizophrenia and genetics: Where are we? Are you sure? In L. C. Wynne, R. L. Cromwell, & S. Matthysse (Eds.), *The nature of schizophrenia: New approaches to research and treatment*. New York: Wiley, 1978. Pp. 59–69.

Gottesman, I. I., & Shields, J. *Schizophrenia and genetics*. New York: Academic Press, 1972.

Gralnick, A. Folie a deux—The psychosis of association: A review of 103 cases and the entire English literature, with case presentations. *Psychiat. Quart.*, 1942, **14**, 230–63.

Gross, G., & Huber, G. Zur prognose der schizophenier. *Psychiatria Clinica*, 1973, **6**(1), 1–16.

Grunebaum, H., & Perlman, M. S. Paranoia and naivete. *Arch. Gen. Psychiat.*, Jan. 1973, **28**(1), 30–32.

Gurland, B., & Kuriansky, J. Some observations on British and American concepts of schizophrenia. In L. C. Wynne, R. L. Cromwell, & S. Matthysse (Eds.), *The nature of schizophrenia: New approaches to research and treatment*. New York: Wiley, 1978. Pp. 686–89.

Hawk, A. B., Carpenter, W. T., & Strauss, J. S. Diagnostic criteria and five-year outcome in schizophrenia. *Arch. Gen. Psychiat.*, Mar. 1975, **32**(3), 343–47.

Heston, L. Psychiatric disorders in foster home reared children of schizophrenic mothers. *Brit. J. Psychiat.*, 1966, **112**, 819–25.

Hoffman, J. L. Psychotic visitors to government offices in the national capital. *Amer. J. Psychiat.*, 1943, **99**, 571–75.

Huxley, A. *The doors of perception*. New York: Harper & Row, 1954.

Jacob, T. Family interaction in disturbed and normal families: A methodological and substantive review. *Psychol. Bull.*, Jan. 1975, **82**(1), 33–65.

Katz, M. M., Sanborn, K. O., Lowery, H. A., & Ching, J. Ethnic studies in Hawaii: On psychopathology and social deviance. In L. C. Wynne, R. L. Cromwell, & S. Matthysse (Eds.), *The nature of schizophrenia: New approaches to research and treatment*. New York: Wiley, 1978. Pp. 572–85.

Kaufman, I., Frank, T., Heims, L., Herrick, J., Reiser, D., & Willer, L. Treatment implications of a new classification of parents of schizophrenic children. *Amer. J. Psychiat.*, 1960, **116**, 920–24.

Kety, S. S., Rosenthal, D., Wender, P. H., Schulsinger, F., & Jacobsen, B. The biologic and adaptive families of adopted individuals who become schizophrenic: Prevalence of mental illness and other characteristics. In L. C. Wynne, R. L. Cromwell, & S. Matthysse (Eds.), *The nature of schizophrenia: New approaches to research and treatment.* New York: Wiley, 1978. Pp. 25–37.

Kinney, D. K., & Jacobsen, B. Environmental factors in schizophrenia: New adoption study evidence. In L. C. Wynne, R. L. Cromwell, & S. Matthysse (Eds.), *The nature of schizophrenia: New approaches to research and treatment.* New York: Wiley, 1978. Pp. 38–51.

Kinzie, J. D., & Bolton, J. M. Psychiatry with the aborigines of West Malaysia. *Amer. J. Psychiat.,* July 1973, **130**(7), 769–73.

Kohn, M. L. Social class and schizophrenia: A critical review and a reformulation. *Schizophrenia Bulletin,* 1973, No. 7, 60–79.

Kringlen, E. *Heredity and environment in the functional psychosis: An epidemiological-clinical twin study.* Oslo: Universitsforlaget, 1967.

Kringlen, E. Adult offspring of two psychotic parents, with special reference to schizophrenia. In L. C. Wynne, R. L. Cromwell, & S. Matthysse (Eds.), *The nature of schizophrenia: New approaches to research and treatment.* New York: Wiley, 1978. Pp. 9–24.

Laing, R. D. Schizophrenic split. *Time,* Feb. 3, 1967, 56.

Laing, R. D. *The divided self.* New York: Pantheon, 1969.

Laing, R. D. Quoted in J. S. Gordon, Who is mad? Who is sane? R. D. Laing: In search of a new psychiatry. *Atlantic,* 1971, **227**(1), 50–66.

Laing, R. D., & Esterson, A. *Sanity, madness, and the family,* London: Tavistock, 1964.

Lemert, E. M. Paranoia and the dynamics of exclusion. *Sociometry,* 1962, **25**, 2–25.

Levy, L., & Rowitz, L. *The ecology of mental disorders.* New York: Behavioral Publications, 1972.

Levy, S. M. Schizophrenic symptomatology: Reaction or strategy? A study of contextual antececents. *J. Abnorm. Psychol.,* 1976, **85**, 435–45.

Lewinson, T. S. Dynamic disturbances in the handwriting of psychotics; with reference to schizophrenic, paranoid, and manic-depressive psychoses. Reprinted from *The American Journal of Psychiatry,* volume **97**, pages 102–35, 1940.

Lidz, T. The family, language, and the transmission of schizophrenia. In D. Rosenthal & S. S. Kety (Eds.), *The transmission of schizophrenia.* Elmsford, N.Y.: Pergamon Press, 1968. Pp. 175–84.

Lidz, T. *The origin and treatment of schizophrenoid disorders.* New York: Basic Books, 1973.

Lidz, T. Egocentric cognitive regression and the family setting of schizophrenic disorders. In L. C. Wynne, R. L. Cromwell, & S. Matthysse (Eds.), *The nature of schizophrenia: New approaches to research and treatment.* New York: Wiley, 1978. Pp. 526–33.

Lidz, T., Fleck, S., & Cornelison, A. R. *Schizophrenia and the family.* New York: International Universities Press, 1965.

Liem, J. H. Effects of verbal communications of parents and children: A comparison of normal and schizophrenic families. *J. Cons. Clin. Psychol.,* 1974, **42**, 438–50.

Matthysse, S. Missing links. In L. C. Wynne, R. L. Cromwell, & S. Matthysse (Eds.), *The nature of schizophrenia: New approaches to research and treatment.* New York: Wiley, 1978. Pp. 148–51.

McNeil, T. F., & Kaij, L. Obstetrical factors in the development of schizophrenia: Complications in the births of preschizophrenics and in reproduction by schizophrenic parents. In L. C. Wynne, R. L. Cromwell, & S. Matthysse (Eds.), *The nature of schizophrenia: New approaches to research and treatment.* New York: Wiley, 1978.

Mednick, S. A. Berkson's fallacy and high-risk research. In L. C. Wynne, R. L. Cromwell, & S. Matthysse (Eds.), *The nature of schizophrenia: New approaches to research and treatment.* New York: Wiley, 1978. Pp. 442–52.

Mednick, S. A., & Schulsinger, F. Some premorbid

characteristics related to breakdown in children with schizophrenic mothers. In D. Rosenthal & S. S. Kety (Eds.), *The transmission of schizophrenia.* Oxford: Pergamon, 1968. Pp. 267–91.

Meehl, P. E. Schizotaxia, schizotypy, schizophrenia. *Amer. Psychologist,* 1962, **17**, 827–38.

Meissner, W. W. *The paranoid process.* New York: Jason Aronson, 1978.

Menninger, K. Diagnosis and treatment of schizophrenia. Reprinted with permission from the *Bulletin of the Menninger Clinic,* vol. **12**, 101–04, copyright 1948 by The Menninger Foundation.

Milner, K. O. The environment as a factor in the aetiology of criminal paranoia, *J. Ment. Sci.,* 1949, **95**, 124–32.

Mishler, E. G., & Waxler, N. E. *Interaction in families: An experimental study of family processes and schizophrenia.* New York: Wiley, 1968.

Morrison, J. R. Catatonia: Retarded and excited types. *Arch. Gen. Psychiat.,* Jan. 1973, **28**(1), 39–41.

Morrison, J. R. Catatonia: Prediction of outcome. *Comprehensive Psychiatry,* July/Aug. 1974, **15**(4), 317–24.

Murphy, H. B. Cultural factors in the genesis of schizophrenia. In D. Rosenthal & S. S. Kety (Eds.), *The transmission of schizophrenia.* Elmsford, N.Y.: Pergamon Press, 1968. Pp. 137–52.

Murphy, H. B. Cultural influences on incidence, course, and treatment response. In L. C. Wynne, R. L. Cromwell, & S. Matthysse (Eds.), *The nature of schizophrenia: New approaches to research and treatment.* New York: Wiley, 1978. Pp. 586–94.

Paul, G. L., & Lentz, R. J. *Psychosocial treatment of chronic mental patients: Milieu vs. social-learning programs.* Cambridge, Mass.: Harvard University Press, 1977.

President's Commission on Mental Health. *Report to the President.* Washington, D.C.: U.S. Government Printing Office, 1978.

Rieder, R. O. The offspring of schizophrenic parents: A review. *J. Nerv. Ment. Dis.,* Sept. 1973, **157**(3), 179–90.

Ritchie, P. L. *The effect of the interviewer's presentation on some schizophrenic symptomatology.* Unpublished doctoral dissertation, Duke University, 1975.

Roff, J. D. Adolescent schizophrenia: Variables related to differences in long-term adult outcome. *J. Cons. Clin. Psychol.,* Apr. 1974, **42**(2), 180–83.

Rosen, H., & Kiene, H. E. Paranoia and paranoiac reaction types. *Diseases of the Nervous System,* 1946, **7**, 330–37. Reprinted by permission of the Physicians Postgraduate Press.

Rosenhan, D. L. On being sane in insane places. *Science,* 1973, **179**, 250–58.

Rosenthal, D. (Ed.). *The Genain quadruplets.* New York: Basic Books, 1963.

Rosenthal, D. *Genetic theory and abnormal behavior.* New York: McGraw-Hill, 1970.

Rosenthal, D., Wender, P. H., Kety, S. S., Welner, J., & Schulsinger, F. The adopted-away offspring of schizophrenics. *Amer. J. Psychiat.,* Sept. 1971, **128**(3), 307–11.

Sachar, E. J., Gruen, P. H., Altman, N., Langer, G., & Halpern, F. S. Neuroendocrine studies of brain dopamine blockade in humans. In L. C. Wynne, R. L. Cromwell, & S. Matthysse (Eds.), *The nature of schizophrenia: New approaches to research and treatment.* New York: Wiley, 1978. Pp. 95–104.

Sarvis, M. A. Paranoid reactions: Perceptual distortion as an etiological agent. *Arch. Gen. Psychiat.,* 1962, **6**, 157–62.

Schwartz, D. A. A re-view of the "paranoid" concept. *Gen. Psychiat.,* 1963, **8**, 349–61.

Shakow, D. On doing research in schizophrenia. *Arch. Gen. Psychiat.,* 1969, **20**(6), 618–42.

Shimkunas, A. M. Demand for intimate self-disclosure and pathological verbalizations in schizophrenia. *J. Abnorm. Psychol.,* 1972, **80**, 197–205.

Singer, M., & Wynne, L. C. Differentiating characteristics of the parents of childhood schizophrenics, childhood neurotics and young adult schizophrenics. *Amer. J. Psychiat.,* 1963, **120,** 234–43.

Singer, M., & Wynne, L. C. Thought disorder and family relations of schizophrenics. III. Methodology using projective techniques. *Arch. Gen. Psychiat.,* 1965, **12,** 182–200.[a]

Singer, M., & Wynne, L. C. Thought disorder and family relations of schizophrenics. IV. Results and implications. *Arch. Gen. Psychiat.,* 1965, **12,** 201–12.[b]

Singer, M. T., Wynne, L. C., & Toohey, M. I. Communication disorders and the families of schizophrenics. In L. C. Wynne, R. L. Cromwell, & S. Matthysse (Eds.), *The nature of schizophrenia: New approaches to research and treatment.* New York: Wiley, 1978. Pp. 499–511.

Snyder, S. H. Dopamine and schizophrenia. In L. C. Wynne, R. L. Cromwell, & S. Matthysse (Eds.), *The nature of schizophrenia: New approaches to research and treatment.* New York: Wiley, 1978. Pp. 87–94.

Soni, S. D., & Rockley, G. J. Socio-cultural substrates of folie à deux. *Brit. J. Psychiat.,* Sept. 1974, **125**(9), 230–35.

Spring, B. J., & Zubin, J. Attention and information-processing as indicators of vulnerability to schizophrenic episodes. In L. C. Wynne, R. L. Cromwell, & S. Matthysse (Eds.), *The nature of schizophrenia: New approaches to research and treatment.* New York: Wiley, 1978. Pp. 366–75.

Stabenau, J. R., Tupin, J., Werner, M., & Pollin, W. A comparative study of families of schizophrenics, delinquents, and normals. *Psychiatry,* 1965, **28,** 45–59.

Stephens, J. H., Astrup, C., & Mangrum, J. C. Prognostic factors in recovered and deteriorated schizophrenics. *Amer. J. Psychiat.,* 1966, **122**(10), 1116–21.

Swanson, D. W., Bohnert, P. J., & Smith, J. A. *The paranoid.* Boston: Little, Brown, 1970.

Tanna, V. L. Paranoid states: A selected review. *Comprehensive Psychiatry,* Nov./Dec. 1974, **15**(6), 453–70.

Tienari, P. Schizophrenia in monozygotic male twins. In D. Rosenthal & S. S. Kety (Eds.), *The transmission of schizophrenia.* Oxford: Pergamon, 1968. Pp. 27–36.

Torrey, E. F. Is schizophrenia universal? An open question. *Schizophrenia Bulletin,* Winter 1973, **7,** 53–59.

Tsuang, M. T., Fowler, R. C., Cadoret, R. J., & Monnelly, E. Schizophrenia among first-degree relatives of paranoid and nonparanoid schizophrenics. *Comprehensive Psychiatry,* July/Aug. 1974, **15**(4), 295–302.

Turner, R., Dopkeen, L., & Labreche, G. Marital status and schizophrenia: A study of incidence and outcome. *J. Abnorm. Psychol.,* 1970, **76**(1), 110–16.

Wender, P. H. In R. Cancro, Genetics of schizophrenia: Some misconceptions clarified. *Roche Report, Frontiers of Psychiatry,* Jan. 1, 1972, **2**(4), 1–2; 8.

Wender, P. H., Rosenthal, D., Kety, S. S., Schulsinger, F., & Welner, J. Cross-fostering: A research strategy for clarifying the role of genetic and experiential factors in the etiology of schizophrenia. *Arch. Gen. Psychiat.,* Jan. 1974, **30**(1), 121–28.

Wilson, J. R. *The mind.* New York: Time-Life, Inc., 1969.

Wynne, L. C., Cromwell, R. L., & Matthysse, S. (Eds.). *The nature of schizophrenia: New approaches to research and treatment.* New York: Wiley, 1978.

Wynne, L. C., Ryckoff, I. M., Day, J., & Hirsch, S. I. Pseudomutuality in the family relations of schizophrenics. *Psychiatry,* 1958, **21,** 205–20.

Yarden, P. E. Observations on suicide in chronic schizophrenics. *Comprehensive Psychiatry,* July/Aug. 1974, **15**(4), 325–33.

Yerbury, E. C., & Newell, N. Genetic and environmental factors in psychoses of children. *Amer. J. Psychiat.,* 1943, **100,** 599–605.

Yolles, S. F. Quote from "Unraveling the mystery of schizophrenia." Reprinted with permission from *Today's Health,* April 1967 ©. All rights reserved.

Zubin, J. Concluding comments. In L. C. Wynne, R. L. Cromwell, & S. Matthysse (Eds.), *The nature of schizophrenia.* Copyright © 1978 by John Wiley & Sons, Inc. Reprinted by permission.

Zubin, J., & Spring, B. J. Vulnerability: A new view of schizophrenia. *J. Abnorm. Psychol.,* 1977, **86,** 103–26.

13. Organic Mental Disorders and Mental Retardation

American Association on Mental Deficiency (AAMD). *Manual on terminology and classification in mental retardation* (Rev. ed.). H. J. Grossman (Ed.). Special Publication Series No. 2, 1973, 11+. Washington, D.C., 1973.

American Psychiatric Association. *Diagnostic and statistical manual of mental disorders* (2nd ed.). Washington, D.C.: APA, 1968.

American Psychiatric Association. Classification of mental retardation. Supplement to the *Amer. J. Psychiat.,* May 1972, **128**(11), 1–45.

American Psychological Association. Psychology and mental retardation. *Amer. Psychologist,* 1970, **25,** 267–68.

Annals of the American Academy of Political and Social Science. Political consequences of aging. Sept. 1974, **415.**

Anonymous. The animal school. *Adolescence: The prevention and treatment of emotional disturbances.* Morganton, N. C.: Broughton Hospital, 1977, p. 4.

Batchelor, I., & Campbell, R. *Henderson and Gillespie's textbook of psychiatry for students and practitioners* (10th ed.). New York: Oxford University Press, 1969.

Benenson, A. S. (Ed.). *Control of communicable diseases in man* (12th Ed.). Washington: American Public Health Association, 1975.

Benson, D. F. The hydrocephalic dementias. In D. F. Benson & D. Blumer (Eds.), *Psychiatric aspects of neurological disease.* New York: Grune & Stratton, 1975. Pp. 83–98.

Bijou, S. W. A functional analysis of retarded development. In N. R. Ellis (Ed.), *International review of research in mental retardation.* (Vol. 1). New York: Academic Press, 1966.

Birns, B., & Bridger, W. Cognitive development and social class. In J. Wortis (Ed.), *Mental retardation and developmental disabilities* (Vol. 9). New York: Brunner/Mazel, 1977. Pp. 203–33.

Blau, D. The course of psychiatric hospitalization in the aged. *J. Geriat. Psychol.,* 1970, **3**(2), 210–23.

Blumer, D., & Benson, D. F. Personality changes with frontal and temporal lobe lesions. In D. F. Benson & D. Blumer (Eds.), *Psychiatric aspects of neurological disease.* New York: Grune & Stratton, 1975. Pp. 151–70.

Braginsky, B. M., & Braginsky, D. D. The mentally retarded: Society's Hansels and Gretels. *Psych. Today,* Mar. 1974, **7**(10), 18; 20–21; 24; 26; 28–30.

Brebner, A., Hallworth, H. J., & Brown, R. I. Computer-assisted instruction programs and terminals for the mentally retarded. In P. Mittler (Ed.), *Research to practice in mental retardation* (Vol. 2). Baltimore: University Park Press, 1977. Pp. 421–26.

Brickner, R. M. *The intellectual functions of the frontal lobes.* New York: Macmillan, 1936.

Brooks, D. N. Recognition, memory, and head injury. *Journal of Neurology, Neurosurgery, & Psychiatry,* July 1974, **37**(7), 794–801.

Brown, R. I. An integrated program for the mentally handicapped. In P. Mittler (Ed.), *Research to practice in mental retardation* (Vol. 2). Baltimore: University Park Press, 1977. Pp. 387–93.

Budoff, M. The mentally retarded child in the mainstream of the public school: His relation to the school administration, his teachers, and his age-mates. In P. Mittler (Ed.), *Research to practice in mental retardation.* (Vol. 2). Baltimore: University Park Press, 1977. Pp. 307–13.

Burns, G. W. *The science of genetics.* New York: Macmillan, 1972.

Centerwall, W. R., & Centerwall, S. A. Phenylketonuria (Folling's disease): The story of its discovery. *Journal of the*

History of Medicine, 1961, **16**, 292–96.

Christodorescu, D., Collins, S., Zellingher, R., & Tautu, C. Psychiatric disturbances in Turner's syndrome: Report of three cases. *Psychiatrica Clinica*, 1970, **3**(2), 114–24.

Clark, G. R., Kivitz, M. S., & Rosen, N. Program for mentally retarded. *Sci. News*, 1969, **96**, 82.

De Beauvoir, S. The terrors of old age. *Newsweek*, Feb. 9, 1970, p. 54.

Dobrokhotova, T. A. On the pathology of the emotional sphere in tumorous lesion of the frontal lobes of the brain. *Zhurnal Nevropatologii i Psikhiartrii*, 1968, **68**(3), 418–22.

Donoghue, E. C., Abbas, K. A., & Gal, E. The medical assessment of mentally retarded children in hospital. *Brit. J. Psychiat.*, 1970, **117**(540), 531–32.

Dorfman, D. D. The Cyril Burt question: New findings. *Science*, 1978, **201**, 1177–86.

Earl, H. G. Head injury: The big killer. *Today's Health*, 1966, **44**(12), 19–21.

Ernst, P., Beran, B., Badash, D., Kosovsky, R., & Kleinhauz, M. Treatment of the aged mentally ill: Further unmasking of the effects of a diagnosis of chronic brain syndrome. *Journal of the American Geriatric Society*, 1977, **10**, 466–69.

Falls, H. F. Ocular changes in Down's syndrome help in diagnosis. *Roche Report*, 1970, **7**(16), 5.

Fetterman, J. L. *Practical lessons in psychiatry.* Courtesy of Charles C Thomas, Publisher, Springfield, Illinois.

Feuerstein, R. Mediated learning experience: A theoretical basis for cognitive modifiability during adolescence. In P. Mittler (Ed.), *Research to practice in mental retardation* (Vol. 2). Baltimore: University Park Press, 1977. Pp. 105 –16.

Flor-Henry, P. Temporal lobe epilepsy: Etiological factors. *Amer. J. Psychiat.*, 1969, **126**(3), 400–403.

Forssman, H., & Akesson, H. O. Mortality in patients with Down's syndrome. *Journal of Mental Deficiency Research*, 1965, **9**, 146–61.

Freedman, A. M., Kaplan, H. I., & Sadock, B. J. *Modern synopsis of comprehensive textbook of psychiatry* (Vol. 2). Baltimore: Williams & Wilkins, 1976.

Gal, P. Mental disorders of advanced years. *Geriatrics*, 1959, **14**, 224–28.

Geisz, D., & Steinhausen, H. On the "psychological development of children with hydrocephalus." (German) *Praxis der Kinderpsychologie und Kinderpsychiatrie*, May-June 1974, **23**(4), 113–18.

German, W. J. Initial symptomatology in brain tumors. *Connecticut Medicine*, 1959, **23**, 636–37.

Geschwind, N. The borderland of neurology and psychiatry: Some common misconceptions. In D. F. Benson & D. Blumer (Eds.), *Psychiatric aspects of neurological disease.* New York: Grune & Stratton, 1975. Pp. 1–9.

Golden, D. A., & Davis, J. G. Counseling parents after the birth of an infant with Down's syndrome. *Children Today*, Mar.–Apr. 1974, **3**(2), 7–11.

Goldfarb, A. *Aging and the organic brain syndrome.* Fort Washington, Pa.: McNeill Labs, 1974.

Greenfield, J. C., & Wolfson, J. M. Microcephalia vera. *Arch. Neurol. Psychiat.*, 1935, **33**, 1296–1316.

Guerney, B. G., Jr. (Ed.). *Psychotherapeutic agents: New roles for nonprofessionals, parents, and teachers.* New York: Holt, Rinehart & Winston, 1969.

Gunther, J. *Death be not proud.* New York: Harper, 1949.

Hagan, J. W., & Huntsman, N. J. Selective attention in mental retardation. *Develop. Psychol.*, 1971, **5**(1), 151–60.

Hallworth, H. J. Computer-assisted instruction for the mentally retarded. In P. Mittler (Ed.), *Research to practice in mental retardation* (Vol. 2). Baltimore: University Park Press, 1977. Pp. 419–20.

Harlow, J. M. Recovery from the passage of an iron bar through the head. *Publ. Mass. Med. Soc.*, 1868, **2**, 327.

Heber, R. *Epidemiology of mental retardation.* Springfield, Ill.: Charles C Thomas, 1970.

Heber, R., Garber, H., Harrington, S., & Hoffman, C. *Rehabilitation of families at risk for mental retardation.* Progress Report, Social Rehabilitation Service, U.S. Department of Health, Education, and Welfare, 1972.

Hecaen, H., & Albert, M. L. Disorders of mental functioning related to frontal lobe pathology. In D. F. Benson, & D. Blumer (Eds.), *Psychiatric aspects of neurological disease.* New York: Grune & Stratton, 1975. Pp. 137–49.

Hill, A. L. Investigation of calendar calculating by an idiot savant. *Amer. J. Psychiat.*, May 1975, **132**(5), 557–59.

Holmes, L. B., Moser, H. W., Halldorsson, S., Mack, C., Pant, S., & Matzilevich, B. *Mental retardation: An atlas of diseases with associated physical abnormalities.* New York: Macmillan, 1972.

Holvey, D. N., & Talbott, J. H. (Eds.). *The Merck manual of diagnosis and therapy* (12th ed.). Rahway, N.J.: Merck, Sharp, & Dohme Research Laboratories, 1972.

Hyatt, R., & Rolnick, N. (Eds.). *Teaching the mentally handicapped child.* New York: Behavioral Publications, 1974.

Isaacson, R. L. When brains are damaged. *Psych. Today*, 1970, **3**(4), 38–42.

Itard, J. *The wild boy of Aveyron.* Paris, 1799. G. Humphrey & M. Humphrey (Tr.). New York: Century, 1932.

Jasper, H. (Ed.). *Basic mechanisms of the epilepsies.* Boston: Little, Brown, 1969.

Jennet, B. et al. Predicting outcome in individual patients after severe head injury. *Lancet*, 1976, **1**, 1031.

Johnson, H. R., Myhre, S. A., Riwalcaba, R. H. A., Thuline, H. C., & Kelley, V. C. Effects of testosterone on body image and behavior in Klinefelter's syndrome: A pilot study. *Develop. Med. Child Neurol.*, 1970, **12**(4), 454–60.

Johnson, J. The EEG in the traumatic encephalography of boxers. *Psychiatrica Clinica*, 1969, **2**(4), 204–11.

Kahana, B., & Kahana, E. Changes in mental status of elderly patients in age-integrated and age-segregated hospital milieus. *J. Abnorm. Psychol.*, 1970, **75**, 177–81.

Kaiser Permanente Medical Care Program. *Planning for health.* Los Angeles: Kaiser Foundation Health Plan, Inc., 1973.

Kallman, F. J. Genetic factors in aging: Comparative and longitudinal observations on a senescent twin population. In P. H. Hoch & J. Zubin (Eds.), *Psychopathology of aging.* New York: Grune & Stratton, 1961. Pp. 227–47.

Karnes, M. B., Teska, J. A., & Hodgins, A. S. The effects of four programs of classroom intervention on the intellectual and language development of 4-year-old disadvantaged children. *Amer. J. Orthopsychiat.*, 1970, **40**, 58–76.

Keniston, K. Meeting the needs of children: I, The necessity of politics. *Christianity and Crisis*, Nov. 28, 1977, pages 247–8. Copyright © 1977 by Christianity and Crisis, Inc. Reprinted by permission.

Kennedy, J. F. Message from the President of the United States relative to mental illness and mental retardation. *Amer. Psychologist*, 1963, **18**, 280–89.

Koch, R. The multidisciplinary approach to mental retardation. In A. A. Baumeister (Ed.), *Mental retardation: Appraisal, education, and rehabilitation.* Chicago: Aldine, 1967.

Krugman, S., & Ward, R. *Infectious diseases of children and adults.* St. Louis: C. V. Mosby, 1973.

Levin, S. Brain tumors in mental hospital patients. *Amer. J. Psychiat.*, 1949, **105**, 897–900.

Los Angeles Times. Prostitute's diary aids in syphilis hunt. Apr. 1, 1970, III, 16.

Lyle, O. E., & Gottesman, I. I. Premorbid psychometric indicators of the gene for Huntington's disease. *J. Cons. Clin. Psychol.*, 1977, **45**, 1011–22.

MacDonald, A. D. Intelligence in children of very low birth weight. *British Journal of Preventive Social Medicine*, 1964, **18**, 59–74.

MacMillan, D. L., & Keogh, B. K. Normal and retarded children's expectancy for failure. *Develop. Psychol.*, 1971, **4**(3), 343–48.

Malamud, N. Organic brain disease mistaken for psychiatric disorder: A clinicopathologic study. In D. F. Benson & D. Blumer (Eds.), *Psychiatric aspects of neurological disease.* New York: Grune & Stratton, 1975. Pp. 287–307.

Matsunaga, E., Tonomura, A., Hidetsune, O., & Yasumoto, K. Reexamination of the paternal age effect in Down's syndrome. *Human Genetics,* 1978, **40,** 259–68.

Mayer-Gross, W. Arteriosclerotic, senile, and presenile psychoses. *J. Ment. Sci.,* 1944, **90,** 316–27.

Miller, R. Does Down's syndrome predispose children to leukemia? *Roche Report,* 1970, **7**(16), 5.

Mittler, P. (Ed.). *Research to practice in mental retardation* (3 Volumes). Baltimore: University Park Press, 1977.

Morishima, A. His spirit raises the ante for retardates. *Psych. Today,* June 1975, **9**(1), 72–73.

Neugarten, B. L. Age groups in American society and the rise of the young-old. *The Annals of the American Academy of Political and Social Science,* Sept. 1974, **415,** 187–98.

Nielsen, J., Bjarnason, S., Friedrich, U., Froland, A., Hansen, V. H., & Sorensen, A. Klinefelter's syndrome in children. *J. Child Psychol. Psychiat.,* 1970, **11**(2), 109–20.

Offir, C. Old people's revolt—"At 65, work becomes a four-letter word." *Psych. Today,* Mar. 1974, **7**(10), 40.

Penrose, L. S. *Biology of mental defect* (3rd ed.). New York: Grune & Stratton, 1963.

Perry, T. The enigma of PKU. *The Sciences,* 1970, **10**(8), 12–16.

Peterson, G. C. Organic brain syndrome: Differential diagnosis and investigative procedures. *Psychiatric Clinics of North America,* 1978, **1,** 21–36.

Plater, F. *Praxeos medical Tomi tres.* (Basil 1656), *Histories and Observations.* London: Culpeper and Cole, 1664.

Porter, J. F., & Kane, P. Sexually transmitted diseases. *Research in Reproduction,* 1975, **7.**

Post, F. Some problems arising from a study of mental patients over the age of sixty years. *J. Ment. Sci.,* 1944, **90,** 554–65.

President's Committee on Mental Retardation. *The decisive decade.* Washington, D.C.: U.S. Government Printing Office, 1970.

Pryse-Phillips, W. *Epilepsy.* London: Bristol-Wright, 1969.

Robinson, N. M., & Robinson, H. B. *The mentally retarded child* (2nd Ed.). New York: McGraw-Hill, 1976.

Rodin, E. A. Psychomotor epilepsy and aggressive behavior. *Arch. Gen. Psychiat.,* Feb. 1973, **28**(2), 210–13.

Rodin, E. A. Psychiatric disorder associated with epilepsy. *Psychiatric Clinics of North America,* 1978, **1,** 101–15.

Rodman, D. H., & Collins, M. J. A community residence program; an alternative to institutional living for the mentally retarded. *Training School Bulletin,* May 1974, **71**(1), 41–48.

Rothschild, B. F. Incubator isolation as a possible contributing factor to the high incidence of emotional disturbance among prematurely born persons. *J. Genet. Psychol.,* 1967, **110**(2), 287–304.

Sasaki, M., & Hara, Y. Paternal origin of the extra chromosome in Down's syndrome. *Lancet,* 1973, **2**(7840), 1257–58.

Schild, S. Parents of children with PKU. *Children Today,* July/Aug. 1972, **1**(4), 20–22.

Schwab, J. J. Comprehensive medicine and the concurrence of physical and mental illness. *Psychosomatics,* 1970, **11**(6), 591–95.

Seidl, F. W. Community oriented residential care: The state of the art. *Child Care Quarterly,* Fall 1974, **3**(3), 150–63.

Sherwin, I., & Geschwind, N. Neural substrates of behavior. In A. M. Nicholi (Ed.), *The Harvard guide to modern psychiatry.* Cambridge, Mass.: Harvard University Press, 1978. Pp. 59–80.

Silberstein, R. M., & Irwin, H. Jean-Marc-Gaspard Itard and the savage of Aveyron: An unsolved diagnostic problem in child psychiatry. *J. Amer. Acad. Child Psychiat.,* 1962, **1**(2), 314–22.

Skigen, J., & Solomon, J. R. Community resources and facilities for the elderly patient with organic mental disease. *Psychiatric Clinics of North America,* 1978, **1,** 169–77.

Smith, G. F., & Berg, J. M. *Down's anomaly.* New York: Churchill Livingstone (Distributed by Longman, Inc.), 1976.

Stearman, M. B. Cited in Controlling epilepsy by biofeedback. *Sci. News,* Sept. 1, 1973, **104**(9), 132–33.

Stene, J., Fischer, G., Stene, E., Mikkelsen, M., & Petersen, E. Paternal age effect in Down's syndrome. *Annals of Human Genetics,* 1977, **46,** 299–306.

Strage, M. VD: The clock is ticking. *Today's Health,* 1971, **49**(4), 16–18; 69–71.

Sullivan, J. P., & Batareh, G. J. Educational therapy with the severely retarded. *The Training School Bulletin,* May 1973, **70**(1), 5–9.

Sutherland, J. M., & Trait, H. *The epilepsies: Modern diagnosis and treatment.* Edinburgh: Livingstone, 1969.

Tarjan, G., & Eisenberg, L. Some thoughts on the classification of mental retardation in the United States of America. *Amer. J. Psychiat.,* May 1972 Supplement, **128**(11), 14–18.

Tarjan, G., Wright, S. W., Eyman, R. K., & Keeran, C. V. Natural history of mental retardation: some aspects of epidemiology. *Amer. J. Ment. Def.,* Oct. 1973, **77**(4), 369–79.

Tarver, S. G., & Hallahan, D. P. Attention deficits in children with learning disabilities: A review. *J. Learn. Dis.,* Nov. 1974, **7**(9), 560–69.

Terry, R., & Wisniewski, H. Sans teeth, sans eyes, sans taste, sans everything. *Behav. Today,* Mar. 25, 1974, **5**(12), 84. Summary of paper delivered at the American Association for the Advancement of Science, San Francisco, Mar. 1974.

Thacher, M. First steps for the retarded. *Human Behavior.* April 1978. Copyright © 1978 by *Human Behavior* Magazine. Reprinted by permission.

Uchida, I. A. Paternal origin of the extra chromosome in Down's syndrome. *Lancet,* 1973, **2**(7840), 1258.

Ullmann, M., & Gruen, A. Behavioral changes in patients with strokes. *Amer. J. Psychiat.,* 1961, **117,** 1004–9.

Viscott, D. S. A musical idiot savant. *Psychiatry,* 1970, **33**(4), 494–515.

Volpe, A., & Kastenbaum, R. TLC. *Amer. J. Nurs.* 1967, **67,** 100–103.

Warrington, E. K., & Weiskrantz, L. An analysis of short-term and long-term memory defects in man. In J. A. Deutsch (Ed.), *The psychological basis of memory.* New York: Academic Press, 1973.

Whalen, C. K., & Henker, B. A. Pyramid therapy in a hospital for the retarded. *Amer. J. Ment. Def.,* 1971, **75**(4), 414–34.

Wortis, J. Comments on the ICD classification of mental retardation. *Amer. J. Psychiat.,* May 1972 Supplement, **128**(11), 21–24.

Wortis, J. (Ed.). *Mental retardation and developmental disabilities: An annual review* (Vol. 5). New York: Brunner/Mazel, 1973.

Zucker, S. H., and Altman, R. An on-the-job training program for adolescent trainable retardates. *Training School Bulletin,* Aug. 1973, **70**(2), 106–10.

14. Behavior Disorders of Childhood and Adolescence

Arnold, L. E. Is this label necessary? *Journal of School Health,* Oct. 1973, **43**(8), 510–14.

Arnold, L. E. Helping parents help their children. New York: Brunner/Mazel, 1978.

Atkeson, B. M., & Forehand, R. Home-based reinforcement programs to modify classroom behavior: A review and methodological evaluation. *Psychol. Bull.,* in press.

Bandura, A., & Walters, R. H. Social learning and personality development. New York: Holt, Rinehart & Winston, 1963.

Bandura, A. Principles of behavior modification. New York: Holt, Rinehart & Winston, 1969.

Bandura, A. Aggression: A social learning analysis. Englewood Cliffs, N.J.: Prentice-Hall, 1973.

Bartak, L. Educational approaches. In M. Rutter & E. Schopler (Eds.), *Autism: A reappraisal of concepts and treatment.* New York: Plenum, 1978.

Bartak, L., & Rutter, M. Special education treatment of autistic children: A comparative study, I: Design of study and characteristics of unit. *J. Child Psychol. Psychiat.*, 1973, **14,** 161–79.

Beck, L., Langford, W. S., Mackay, M., & Sum, G. Childhood chemotherapy and later drug abuse and growth curve: A follow-up study of 30 adolescents. *Amer. J. Psychiat.*, Apr. 1975, **132**(4), 436–38.

Bellman, M. Studies on encopresis. *Acta Paediatrica Scandanovica Suppl.*, 1966, **170,** 121.

Bender, L. The life course of children with schizophrenia. *Amer. J. Psychiat.*, July 1973, **130**(7), 783–86.

Bettelheim, B. Joey: A "mechanical boy." *Scientif. American,* 1959, **200,** 116–27. From "Joey: A 'Mechanical Boy' " by Bruno Bettelheim. Copyright © March 1959 by Scientific American, Inc. All rights reserved.

Bettelheim, B. *The empty fortress.* New York: Free Press, 1967.

Bettelheim, B. Laurie. *Psych. Today,* 1969, **2**(12), 24–25; 60.

Bettelheim, B. *A home for the heart.* New York: Alfred A. Knopf, 1974.

Biklen, D. Advocacy comes of age. *Exceptional Children,* 1976, **42,** 308–13.

Blake, G. Community treatment plan aids delinquents. Five year experiment. *Los Angeles Times,* Jan. 26, 1967, I; 6.

Bolen, D. W., & Boyd, W. H. Gambling and the gambler. *Arch. Gen. Psychiat.*, 1968, **18**(5), 617–30.

Boyd, W. H., & Bolen, D. W. The compulsive gambler and spouse in group psychotherapy. *Inter. J. Group Psychother.*, 1970, **20,** 77–90.

Bryan, T. H. Learning disabilities: A new stereotype. *J. Learn. Dis.,* May 1974, **7**(5), 46–51.

Burks, H. L., & Harrison, S. I. Aggressive behavior as a means of avoiding depression. *Amer. J. Orthopsychiat.*, 1962, **32,** 416–22.

Caldwell, A. B., Bolen, D. W., & Boyd, W. H. Pathologic gamblers not necessarily obsessive. *Roche Report: Frontiers of Psychiatry,* Oct. 15, 1972, **2**(17), 3.

Caputo, D. V., & Mandell, W. Consequences of low birth weight. *Develop. Psychol.,* 1970, **3**(3), 363–83.

Chalfant, J. C., & Scheffelin, M. A. *Central processing dysfunctions in children: A review of research.* INNDS monogr. no. 9. Washington, D.C.: U.S. Government Printing Office, 1969.

Clancy, H., & McBride, G. The autistic process and its treatment. *J. Child Psychol. Psychiat.,* 1969, **10**(4), 233–44.

Clarke, J. The precipitation of juvenile delinquency. *J. Ment. Sci.,* 1961, 107, 1033–34.

Clement, P. Elimination of sleepwalking in a seven-year-old boy. *J. Cons. Clin. Psychol.,* 1970, **34**(1), 22–26.

Clements, S. D. *Minimal brain dysfunction in children — Terminology and identification.* Washington, D.C.: HEW, 1966.

Cline, V. B., Croft, R. G., & Courrier, S. Desensitization of children to television violence. *J. Pers. Soc. Psychol.,* 1973, **27,** 360–65.

Cloninger, C. R., & Guze, S. Psychiatric illness and female criminality: The role of sociopathy and hysteria in the antisocial woman. *Amer. J. Psychiat.,* 1970, **127**(3), 303–11.

Cole, S. O. Hyperkinetic children: The use of stimulant drugs evaluated. *Amer. J. Orthopsychiat.,* Jan. 1975, **45**(1), 28–37.

Coleman, J. C. Life stress and maladaptive behavior. *Amer. J. Occupa. Ther.,* May/June 1973, **27**(4), 169–80.

Cytryn, L., & McKnew, D. H., Jr. Factors influencing the changing clinical expression of the depressive process in children. *Amer. J. Psychiat.,* Aug. 1974, **131**(8), 879–81.

Davidson, W. S., & Seidman, E. Studies of behavior modification and juvenile delinquency: A review, methodological critique, and social perspective. *Psychol. Bull.,* Dec. 1974, **81**(12), 998–1011.

Dinnan, J. A., McGuiness, E., & Perrin, L. Auditory feedback— Stutterers versus nonstutterers. *J. Learn. Dis.,* 1970, **3**(4), 30–34.

Doleys, D. M. Assessment and treatment of childhood enuresis.

In R. J. Finch & P. C. Kendall (Eds.), *Clinical treatment and research in child psychopathology*. New York: Spectrum Publications, 1979.

Earl, H. G. 10,000 children battered and starved: Hundreds die. *Today's Health,* 1965, **43**(9), 24–31.

Edwards, R. P., Alley, G. R., & Snider, W. Academic achievement and minimal brain dysfunction. *J. Learn, Dis.,* 1971, **4**(3), 134–38.

Egeland, B., & Brunnquell, D. An at-risk approach to the study of child abuse: Some preliminary findings. *J. Amer. Acad. Child Psychiat.,* 1979, **18,** 219–35.

Egeland, B., Cicchetti, D., & Taraldson, B. Child abuse: A family affair. *Proceedings of the N. P. Masse Research Seminar on Child Abuse,* 1976, 28–52. Paper presented April 26, 1976, Paris, France.

Eisenberg, L. Principles of drug therapy in child psychiatry with special reference to stimulant drugs. *Amer. J. Orthopsychiat.,* 1971, **4**(3). 371–79.

Elkind, D. Middle-class delinquency. *Mental Hygiene,* 1967, **51,** 80–84.

Elkind, D., & Weiner, I. B. *Development of the child.* New York: Wiley, 1978.

Elmer, E. *Fragile families, troubled children.* Pittsburgh: University of Pittsburgh Press, 1977.

English, C. J. Leaving home: A typology of runaways. *Society,* July/Aug. 1973, **10**(5), 22–24.

Feighner, A. C., & Feighner, J. P. Multimodality treatment of the hyperkinetic child. *Amer. J. Psychiat.,* Apr. 1974, **131**(4), 459–63.

Feldman, R., & Weisfeld, G. An interdisciplinary study of crime. *Crime and Delinquency.* Apr. 1973, **19**(2), 150–62.

Fine, R. H., & Fishman, J. J. Institutionalized girl delinquents. *Dis. Nerv. Sys.,* 1968, **29**(1), 17–27.

Finkelstein, B. Offenses with no apparent motive. *Dis. Nerv. Sys.,* 1968, **29**(5), 310–14.

Flanagan, B., Goldiamond, I., & Azrin, N. H. Instatement of stuttering in normally fluent individuals through operant procedures. *Science,* 1959, 130, 979–81.

Gajzago, C., & Prior, M. Two cases of "recovery" in Kanner syndrome. *Arch. Gen. Psychiat.,* Aug. 1974, **31**(2), 264–68.

Ganzer, V. J., & Sarason, I. G. Variables associated with recidivism among juvenile delinquents. *J. Cons. Clin. Psychol.,* Feb. 1973, **40**(1), 1–5.

Garmezy, N. DSM III: Never mind the psychologists; Is it good for the children? *The Clinical Psychologist,* 1978, **31,** 1–6.

General Assembly of the United Nations. *Declaration of the rights of a child,* November 20, 1959. Reprinted by permission.

Glueck, S., & Glueck, E. T. Delinquency prediction method reported highly accurate. *Roche Reports,* 1969, **6**(15), 3.

Goodman, J. A case study of an "autistic-savant": Mental function in the psychotic child with markedly discrepant abilities. *J. Child Psychol. Psychiat.,* Oct. 1972, **13**(4), 267–78.

Greenberg, H., & Blank, H. R. Murder and self-destruction by a twelve-year-old boy. *Adolescence,* 1970, **5**(20), 391–6.

Greene, J. S. Hope for the stutterer. *Hygeia,* 1946, **24**(2), 120–21.

Grunewald-Züberbier, E., Grunewald, G., & Rasche, E. Hyperactive behavior and EEG arousal reactions in children's electroencephalograms. *Clinical Neurophysiology,* 1975, **38,** 149–59.

Haney, B., & Gold, M. The juvenile delinquent nobody knows. *Psychol. Today,* Sept. 1973, **7**(4), 48–52; 55.

Hanson, D. R., & Gottesman, I. I. The genetics, if any, of infantile autism and childhood schizophrenia. *Journal of Autism and Childhood Schizophrenia,* 1976, **6,** 209–34.

Harlow, H. A brief look at autistic children. *Psychiat. Soc. Sci. Rev.,* 1969, **3**(1), 27–29.

Hatzenbuehler, L. C., & Schroeder, H. E. Desensitization procedures in the treatment of childhood disorders. *Psychol. Bull.,* 1978, **85,** 831–44.

Hayes, T. A., Panitch, M. L., & Barker, E. Imipramine dosage in children: A comment on "Imipramine and electrocardiographic abnormalities in hyperactive children." *Amer. J. Psychiat.,* May 1975, **132**(5), 546–47.

Hazlett, B. Juvenile gangs: Violence and fatal assaults on increase. *Los Angeles Times,* Apr. 14, 1974, II, 1; 3.

Heber, F. R. Sociocultural mental retardation: A longitudinal study. In G. W. Albee & J. M. Joffe (Eds.), *Primary prevention of psychopathology: The issues* (Vol. 1). Hanover, N.H.: University Press of New England, 1978.

Heber, R. *Epidemiology of mental retardation.* Springfield, Ill.: Charles C Thomas, 1970.

Hewett, F. M., & Forness, S. R. *Education of exceptional learners.* Boston: Allyn & Bacon, 1974.

Homer, L. E. The anatomy of a runaway. *Human Behavior,* Apr. 1974, **3**(4), 37.

Jenkins, R. L. The varieties of children's behavioral problems and family dynamics. *Amer. J. Psychiat.,* 1968, **124**(10), 134–39.

Jenkins, R. L. Classification of behavior problems of children. *Amer. J. Psychiat.,* 1969, **125**(8), 68–75.

Jenkins, R. L. Diagnostic classification in child psychiatry. *Amer. J. Psychiat.,* 1970, **127**(5), 140–41.

Johnson, C. A., & Katz, R. C. Using parents as change agents for their children: A review. *J. Child Psychol. Psychiat.,* July 1973, **14**(3), 181–200.

Johnson, W. *Stuttering and what you can do about it.* Minneapolis: University of Minnesota Press, 1961.

Joint Commission on the Mental Health of Children. Position statement: Statement of the American Orthopsychiatric Association on the work of the Joint Commission on the Mental Health of Children. *Amer. J. Orthopsychiat.,* 1968, **38**(3), 402–9.

Joint Commission on the Mental Health of Children. Crisis in child mental health: Challenge for the 1970's. New York: Harper & Row, 1970.

Judd, L., & Mandell, A. Chromosome studies in early infantile autism. *Arch. Gen. Psychiat.,* 1968, **18**(4), 450–57.

Kales, A., Paulson, M. J., Jacobson, A., & Kales, J. Somnambulism: Psychophysiological correlates. *Arch. Gen. Psychiat.,* 1966, **14**(6), 595–604.

Kanner, L. Autistic disturbances of affective content. *Nervous Child,* 1943, **2**, 217–40.

Kempe, R., & Kempe, H. *Child Abuse.* London: Fontana/Open Books, 1979.

Kendall, P. C., Deardorff, P. A., & Finch, A. J. Empathy and socialization in first and repeat juvenile offenders and normals. *J. Abnorm. Psychol.,* 1977, **5**, 93–97.

Kendall, P. C., & Finch, A. J. A cognitive-behavioral treatment for impulse control: A case study. *J. Cons. Clin. Psychol.,* 1976, **44**, 852–57.

Kendall, P. C., & Finch, A. J. A cognitive-behavioral treatment for impulsivity: A group comparison study. *J. Cons. Clin. Psychol.,* 1978, **46**, 110–18.

Kendall, P. C., & Finch, A. J. Developing nonimpulsive behavior in children: Cognitive-behavioral strategies for self-control. In P. C. Kendall and S. D. Hollon (Eds.), *Cognitive-behavioral intervention: Theory, research, and procedures.* New York: Academic Press, 1979.

Keniston, K. Meeting the needs of children: I, The need for politics. *Christianity and Crisis,* Nov. 28, 1977, pages 274–8. Copyright © 1977 by Christianity and Crisis, Inc. Reprinted by permission.

Kiester, E., Jr. Explosive youngsters: What to do about them. *Today's Health,* Jan. 1974, **52**(1), 49–53; 64–65.

Klein, M. W. Impressions of juvenile gang members. *Adolescence,* 1968, **3**(9), 53–78.

Konopka, G. Adolescent delinquent girls. *Children,* 1964, **11**(1), 21–26.

Konopka, G. Rehabilitation of the delinquent girl. *Adolescence,* 1967, **2**(5), 69–82.

Kovacs, M., & Beck, A. T. An empirical clinical approach towards a definition of childhood depression. In J. G. Schulterbrand & A. Raskin (Eds.), *Depression in children: Diagnosis, treatment and conceptual models.* New York: Raven

Press, 1977.

Langner, T. S., Gersten, J. C., Greene, E. L., Eisenberg, J. G., Herson, J. H., & McCarthy, E. D. Treatment of psychological disorders among urban children. *J. Cons. Clin. Psychol.,* Apr. 1974, **42**(2), 70–79.

Lefkowitz, M. M., & Burton, N. Childhood depression: A critique of the concept. *Psychol. Bull.,* 1978, **85**, 716–26.

Lefkowitz, M. M., Eron, L. D., Walder, L. O., & Huesmann, L. R. *Growing up to be violent: A longitudinal study of the development of aggression.* New York: Pergamon Press, 1977.

Lemert, E. M. Stuttering and social structure in two Pacific societies, *J. Speech Hear. Dis.,* 1962, **27**, 3–10.

Lemert, E. M. Sociological perspective. In J. Sheehan (Ed.), *Stuttering: Research and therapy.* New York: Harper & Row, 1970.

Levine, M. D. Children with encopresis: A descriptive analysis. *Pediatrics,* 1976, **56**, 412.

Levine, M. D., & Bakow, H. Children with encopresis: A study of treatment outcomes. *Pediatrics,* 1975, **58**, 845.

Lexow, G. A., & Aronson, S. S. Health advocacy: A need, a concept, a model. *Children Today,* Jan./Feb. 1975, **4**(1), 2–6; 36.

Lievens, P. The organic psychosyndrome of early childhood and its effects on learning. *J. Learn. Dis.,* Dec. 1974, **7**(10), 626–31.

Life. The kid with the bad eye. 1951, **30**(5), 17–21.

Livingston, J. Compulsive gamblers: A culture of losers. *Psych. Today,* Mar. 1974, 51–55.

Loney, J. The intellectual functioning of hyperactive elementary school boys: A cross-sectional investigation. *Amer. J. Orthopsychiat.,* Oct. 1974, **44**(5), 754–62.

Lord, C., & Baker, A. F. Communicating with autistic children. *Journal of Pediatric Psychology,* in press.

Lovaas, O. I. *The autistic child: Language development through behavior modification.* New York: Irvington Publishers, 1977.

Lovaas, O. I., Schaeffer, B., & Simmons, J. Q. In O. I. Lovaas & B. D. Bucker (Eds.), *Perspectives in behavior modification with deviant children.* Englewood Cliffs, N.J.: Prentice-Hall, 1974.

Lund, S. N. *Personality and personal history factors of child abusing parents.* Unpublished doctoral dissertation, University of Minnesota, 1975.

MacDonald, J. D., & Martin, R. R. Stuttering and disfluency as two reliable and unambiguous response classes. *J. Speech Hear. Res.,* 1973, **16**(4), 691–99.

MacFarlane, J. W., Allen, L., & Honzik, M. P. *A developmental study of the behavior problems of normal children between 21 months and 14 years.* Berkeley: University of California Press, 1954.

Makita, K. The rarity of "depression" in childhood. *Acta Psychiatrica,* 1973, **40**, 37–44.

Marchant, R., Howlin, P., Yule, W., & Rutter, M. Graded change in the treatment of the behavior of autistic children. *J. Child Psychol. Psychiat.,* July 1974, **15**(3), 221–27.

Marsella, A. Depressive experience and disorder across cultures. In H. Triandis & J. Draguns (Eds.), *Handbook of cross-cultural psychology: Culture and psychopathology* (Vol. 5), 1979.

Martin, G. I., & Zaug, P. J. Electrocardiographic monitoring of enuretic children receiving therapeutic doses of imipramine. *Amer. J. Psychiat.,* May 1975, **132**(5), 540–42.

Mash, E. J., Handy, L. C., & Hamerlynck, L. A. *Behavior modification approaches to parenting.* New York: Brunner/Mazel, 1976.

Mayer, C. L., & Scheffelin, M. State-wide planning for special education in California. *J. Learn. Dis.,* Apr. 1975, **8**(4), 50–54.

McAdoo, W. G., & DeMyer, M. K. Personality characteristics of parents. In M. Rutter & E. Schopler (Eds.), *Autism: A reappraisal of concepts and treatment.* New York: Plenum, 1978.

McCandless, B. R., Parsons, W. S., & Roberts, A. Perceived opportunity, delinquency, race and body build among delinquent youth, *J. Cons. Clin. Psychol.,* 1972, **38**(2), 281–87.

McGlannan, F. K. Learning disabilities: The decade ahead. *J. Learn. Dis.,* Feb. 1975, **8**(2), 56–59.

Meichenbaum, D. *Cognitive-behavior modification: An integrative approach.* New York: Plenum, 1977.

Meichenbaum, D. H., and Goodman, J. Training impulsive children to talk to themselves: A means of developing self-control. *J. Abnorm. Psychol.,* 1971, **77,** 115–26.

Montenegro, H. Severe separation anxiety in two preschool children: Successfully treated by reciprocal inhibition. *J. Child Psychol. Psychiat.,* 1968, **9**(2), 93–103.

Murphy, S., Nichols, J., Eddy, R., & Umphress, A. Behavioral characteristics of adolescent enuretics, *Adolescence,* 1971, **6**(21), 1–18.

Nagaraja, J. Somnambulism in children: Clinical communication. *Child Psychiatry Quarterly,* Jan. 1974, **7**(1), 18–19.

NIMH. United States Department of Health, Education, and Welfare. Mental Health Publication No. 5027. Washington, D. C.: U.S. Government Printing Office, 1970.

NIMH. Amphetamines approved for children. *Sci. News,* 1971, **99**(4), 240.

O'Dell, S. Training parents in behavior modification: A review. *Psychol. Bull.,* July 1974, **81**(7), 418–33.

Ossofsky, H. J. Endogenous depression in infancy and childhood. *Comprehensive Psychiatry,* Jan./Feb. 1974, **15**(1), 19–25.

Paine, R. S. *Minimal brain dysfunction.* National Project on Learning Disabilities. Public Health Service Publication No. 2015. Washington, D.C.: U.S. Government Printing Office, 1969.

Patterson, G. Cited in Kiester, E., Jr., Explosive youngsters: What to do about them. *Today's Health,* Jan. 1974, **52**(1), 48–53; 64–65.

Patterson, G. R., & Reid, J. B. Intervention for families of aggressive boys: A replication study. *Beh. Res. Ther.,* 1973, **11,** 383–94.

Pelham, W. E., Jr. Hyperactive children. *Psychiatric Clinics of North America,* 1978, **1,** 227–45.

Pemberton, D. A., & Benady, D. R. Consciously rejected children. *Brit. J. Psychiat.,* Nov. 1973, **123**(576), 575–78.

Poznanski, E., & Zrull, J. Childhood depression. *Arch. Gen. Psychiat.,* 1970, **23**(1), 8–15.

President's Commission on Law Enforcement and Administration of Justice. Katzenbach, N.D. (Chairman), *The challenge of crime in a free society.* Washington, D.C.: U.S. Government Printing Office, 1967.

President's Commission on Mental Health. *Report to the President.* Washington, D.C.: U.S. Government Printing Office, 1978.

Rapoport, J. L., Buchsbaum, M. S., Zahn, T. P., Weingarten, H., Ludlow, C., & Mikkelsen, E. J. Dextroamphetamine: Cognitive and behavioral effects in normal prepubertal boys. *Science,* 1978, **199,** 560–63.

Regional Research Institute for Human Services. *Overcoming barriers to planning for children in foster care.* U.S. Department of Health, Education, and Welfare, 1978.

Ritvo, E., & Ornitz, E. A new look at childhood autism points to CNS disease. *Roche Report,* 1970, **7**(18), 6–8.

Roberts, A. H., Erikson, R. V., Riddle, M., & Bacon, J. G. Demographic variables, base rates, and personality characteristics associated with recidivism in male delinquents. *J. Cons. Clin. Psychol.,* Dec. 1974, **42**(6), 833–41.

Robins, L. N. The adult development of the antisocial child. *Seminars in Psychiatry,* Nov. 1970, **2**(4), 420–34.

Roff, J. D. Adolescent schizophrenia: Variables related to differences in long-term adult outcome. *J. Cons. Clin. Psychol.,* Apr. 1974, **42**(2), 180–83.

Rolf, J. E., & Hasazi, J. E. Identification of preschool children at risk and some guidelines for primary prevention. In E. W. Albee & J. M. Joffee (Eds.), *Primary prevention of psychopathology: The Issues* (Vol. 1). Hanover, N.H.: University Press of New England, 1977.

Rosenthal, R. H., & Allen, T. W. An examination of attention, arousal, and learning dysfunctions of hyperkinetic children. *Psychol. Bull.,* 1978, **85,** 689–715.

Rosten, R. A. Some personality characteristics of compulsive gamblers. Unpublished dissertation, UCLA, 1961.

Russell, S. The development and training of autistic children in separate training centres and in centres for retarded children. *Special Publication No. 6.* Victoria: Mental Health Authority, 1975.

Rutter, M. Parent-child separation: Psychological effects on the children. *J. Child Psychol. Psychiat.,* 1971, **12,** 233–60.

Rutter, M. Surveys to answer questions: Some methodological considerations. In P. J. Graham (Ed.), *Epidemiological approaches in child psychiatry.* New York: Academic Press, 1977.

Rutter, M. Diagnosis and definition. In M. Rutter & E. Schopler (Eds.), *Autism: A reappraisal of concepts and treatment.* New York: Plenum, 1978.

Rutter, M., & Schopler, E. (Eds.). *Autism: A reappraisal of concepts and behavior.* New York: Plenum, 1978.

Rutter, M., Shaffer, D., & Shepherd, M. A multi-axial classification of child psychiatric disorders. Geneva: *WHO,* 1975.

Rutter, M., Shaffer, D., & Sturge, C. A guide to the multi-axial classification scheme for psychiatric disorders in childhood and adolescence, n.d.

Rutter, M., Yule, W., & Graham, P. Enuresis and behavioral deviance: Some epidemiological considerations. In I. Kolvin, R. C. MacKeith, & S. R. Meadow (Eds.), *Bladder control and enuresis.* Philadelphia: J. B. Lippincott, 1973.

Safer, D. J., & Allen, R. P. Stimulant drugs said to suppress height, weight. *Psychiatric News,* May 2, 1973, **8**(9), 9.

Satterfield, J. H., Cantwell, D. P., Saul, R. E. & Yusin, A. Intelligence, academic achievement, and EEG abnormalities in hyperactive children. *Amer. J. Psychiat.,* Apr. 1974, **131**(4), 391–95.

Scharfman, M., & Clark, R. W. Delinquent adolescent girls: Residential treatment in a municipal hospital setting. *Arch. Gen. Psychiat.,* 1967, **17**(4), 441–47.

Schnackenberg, R. C. Caffeine as a substitute for Schedule II stimulants in hyperkinetic children. *Amer. J. Psychiat.,* July 1973, **130**(7), 796–98.

Schopler, E. Changing parental involvement in behavioral treatment. In M. Rutter & E. Schopler (Eds.), *Autism: A reappraisal of concepts and treatment.* New York: Plenum, 1978.

Schreibman, L., & Koegel, R. L. Autism: A defeatable horror. *Psych. Today,* Mar. 1975, **8**(10), 61–67.

Schulterbrandt, J. D., & Raskin, A. (Eds.). *Depression in children: Diagnosis, treatment and conceptual models.* New York: Raven Press, 1977.

Sheehan, J. G. (Ed.). *Stuttering: Research and therapy.* New York: Harper & Row, 1970.

Sheehan, J. G. & Costley, M. S. A reexamination of the role of heredity in stuttering. *J. Speech Hear. Dis.,* 1975, **40.**

Sheehan, J. G., & Lyon, M. A. Role perception in stuttering. *Journal of Communication Disorders,* 1974, **7**(2), 113–26.

Sheehan, J. G., & Martyn, M. Stuttering and its disappearance. *J. Speech Hear. Dis.,* 1970, **13**(2), 279–89.

Sherrod, B. *Dallas Times Herald,* n.d. Quoted in D. Bolen & W. H. Boyd, Gambling and the gambler. *Arch. Gen. Psychiat.,* 1968, **18**(5), 617–30.

Shoemaker, M. E., & Paulson, T. L. Group assertion training for mothers: A family intervention strategy. In E. J. Mash, L. C. Handy, & L. A. Hamerlynck (Eds.), *Behavior modification approaches to parenting.* New York: Brunner/Mazel, 1976.

Siggers, W. W. The role of the psychologist in advocacy for the handicapped. *Professional Psychology,* 1979, **10**(1), 80–86.

Singer, M. Delinquency and family disciplinary configurations: An elaboration of the superego Lacunae concept. *Arch. Gen. Psychiat.,* Dec. 1974, **31**(6), 795–98.

Solomon, J. Why gamble? A psychological profile of pathology.

The Sciences, July/Aug. 1972, **12**(6), 20–21.

Spitz, R. A. Anaclitic depression. In *Psychoanalytic study of the child* (Vol. 2). New York: International Universities Press, 1946.

Steinberg, H. Helping the stutterer. *Family Health,* May 1975, **7**(5), 30–33; 64.

Strine, G. Compulsive gamblers pursue elusive dollar forever. *Los Angeles Times,* March 30, 1971, III, 1; 6.

Taves, I. Is there a sleepwalker in the house? *Today's Health,* 1969, **47**(5), 41; 76.

Time. Young man with a gun. Jan. 22, 1951, 19–20.

Time. Billy's last words. Dec. 22, 1952.

Tinbergen, N. Ethology and stress disease. *Science,* July 5, 1974, **185**(4145), 20–27.

Treffert, D. A. Epidemiology of infantile autism. *Arch. Gen. Psychiat.,* 1970, **22**, 431–38.

Trotter, S. Labeling: It hurts more than it helps. *APA Monitor,* Jan. 1975, **6**(1), 5.

Turner, R. K., & Taylor, P. D. Conditioning treatment of nocturnal enuresis in adults: Preliminary findings. *Behav. Res. Ther.,* Feb. 1974, **12**(1), 41–52.

Tymchuk, A. J., Knights, R. M., & Hinton, G. G. The behavioral significance of differing EEG abnormalities in children with learning and/or behavior problems. *J. Learn. Dis.,* 1970, **3**(11), 547–52.

Ulmar, G. Adolescent girls who steal. *Psychiat. Diag.,* 1971, **32**(3), 27–28.

Uniform Crime Reports. Federal Bureau of Investigation. U.S. Dept. of Justice. Washington, D.C.: U.S. Government Printing Office, 1978.

United Nations. *Declaration of the rights of a child.* Adopted by the General Assembly of the United Nations, November 20, 1959.

U.S. News & World Report. More kids on the road—Now it's the "throwaways." May 12, 1975, **78**(19), 49–50.

Wallerstein, J. S., & Kelly, J. B. *Children of divorce: Preventions in parent-child relationships,* 1979.

Ward, A. J. Early childhood autism and structural therapy: Outcome after 3 years. *J. Cons. Clin. Psychol.,* 1978, **46**, 586–87.

Weiss, G., Kruger, E., & Danielson, U. Effect of long-term treatment of hyperactive children with methylphenidate. *Canadian Medical Association Journal,* 1975, **112**, 159.

Werry, J. S., & Quay, H. C. The prevalence of behavior symptoms in younger elementary school children. *Amer. J. Orthopsychiat.,* 1971, **41**, 136–43.

Whalen, C. K., & Henker, B. Pyramid theory in a hospital for the retarded. *Amer. J. Ment. Def.,* 1971, **75**(4), 414–34.

Whalen, C. K., & Henker, B. Psychostimulants and children: A review and analysis. *Psychol. Bull.,* 1976, **83**, 1113–30.

Wing, L. K. Diagnosis, clinical description and prognosis. In L. Wing (Ed.), *Early childhood autism.* London: Pergamon Press, 1976.

Winsberg, B. G., Goldstein, S., Yepes, L. E., & Perel, J. M. Imipramine and electrocardiographic abnormalities in hyperactive children. *Amer. J. Psychiat.,* May 1975, **132**(5), 542–45.

Wolff, W. M., & Morris, L. A. Intellectual personality characteristics of parents of autistic children. *J. Abnorm. Psychol.,* 1971, **77**(2), 155–61.

Wolkind, S. N. The components of "affectionless psychopathy" in institutionalized children. *J. Child Psychol. Psychiat.,* July 1974, **15**(3), 215–20.

Zimring, F. *American Youth Violence.* Chicago: University of Chicago Press, 1979.

15. Sexual Dysfunctions and Variants

Abel, G. G., Blanchard, E. B., Becker, J. V., & Djendéredjian, A. Differentiating sexual aggressives with penile measures. *Criminal Justice and Behavior,* 1978, **5**, 315–32.

Adams, M. S. & Neel, J. V. Children of incest, *Pediatrics,* 1967, **40**, 55–62.

Adams, H. E., & Sturgis, E. T. Status of behavioral reorientation techniques in the modification of homosexuality: A review. *Psychol. Bull.,* 1977, **84**, 1171–88.

Adler, P. *A house is not a home.* New York: Holt, Rinehart & Winston, 1953.

Apfelberg, B., Sugar, C., & Pfefer, A. Z. A psychiatric study of 250 sex offenders. *Amer. J. Psychiat.,* 1944, **100**, 762–70.

Bagley, C. Incest behavior and incest taboo. *Social Problems,* 1969, **16**(4), 505–19.

Barlow, D. H. The treatment of sexual deviation: Toward a comprehensive behavioral approach. In K. S. Calhoun, H. E. Adams, & K. M. Mitchell (Eds.), *Innovative treatment methods in psychopathology.* New York: Wiley Interscience Series, 1974.

Barlow, D. H., & Abel, G. G. Sexual deviation. In W. E. Craighead, A. E. Kazdin, & M. J. Mahoney (Eds.), *Behavior modification: Principles, issues, and applications.* Boston: Houghton Mifflin, 1976.

Barlow, D. H., & Agras, W. S. Fading to increase heterosexual responsiveness in homosexuals. *J. Appl. Beh. Anal.,* 1973, **6**, 355–66.

Barlow, D. H., Reynolds, E. J., & Agras, W. S. Gender identity change in a transsexual. *Arch. Gen. Psychiat.,* Apr. 1973, **28**(4), 569–76.

Bell, A. O. Homosexualities: Their range and character. In J. K. Cole and R. Dienstbier (Eds.), *Nebraska symposium on motivation, 1973.* Lincoln, Neb.: University of Nebraska Press, 1974. Pp. 1–26.

Bell, A. O., & Weinberg, M. S. *Homosexualities: A study of diversity among men and women.* New York: Simon & Schuster, 1978.

Benjamin, H. *The transsexual phenomenon.* New York: Julian Press, 1966.

Bentler, P. M., & Prince, C. Personality characteristics of male transvestites. III. *J. Abnorm. Psychol.,* 1969, **74**(2), 140–43.

Bentler, P. M., & Prince, C. Psychiatric symptomology in transvestites. *J. Clin. Psychol.,* 1970, **26**(4), 434-35.

Bentler, P. M., Shearman, R. W., & Prince, C. Personality characteristics of male transvestites. *J. Clin. Psychol.,* 1970, **126**(3), 287–91.

Berg, A. *The sadist.* O. Illner & G. Godwin (trans.). New York: Medical Press of New York, 1954.

Bergler, E. Analysis of an unusual case of fetishism. *Bull. Menninger Clin.,* 1947, **2**, 67–75.

Bess, B. E., & Janus, S. S. Factors in successful renunciation of prostitution. Paper delivered at 1974 Annual Convention of American Psychiatric Association, Preliminary Program, Detroit, Mich., May 6–10, 1974.

Bieber, I., Dain, H., Dince, P., Drellech, M., Grand, H., Grundlach, R., Kremer, M., Ritkin, A., Wilbur, C., & Bieber, T. Quote from *Homosexuality: A psychoanalytic study,* by Irving Bieber et al., © 1962 by the Society of Medical Psychoanalysts, Basic Books, Inc., Publishers, New York.

Bonnell, C. Preliminary results reported. New Kinsey study may scrap more myths. *The Advocate,* Dec. 18, 1974, 4.

Brodie, H. K. H., Gartrell, N., Doering, C., & Rhue, T. Plasma testosterone levels in heterosexual and homosexual men. *Amer. J. Psychiat.,* Jan. 1974, **131**(1), 82–83.

Bryan, J. H. Apprenticeships in prostitution. *Social Problems,* 1965, **12**, 287–97.

Bryan, J. H. Occupational ideologies and individual attitudes of call girls. *Social Problems,* 1966, **13**, 441–50.

Buckner, H. T. The transvestic career path. *Psychiatry,* 1970, **33**(3), 381–89.

Burgess, A. W., & Holmstrom, L. Rape trauma syndrome. *Amer. J. Psychiat.,* 1974, **131**, 981–86.

Burgess, A. W., & Holmstrom, L. Coping behavior of the rape victim. *Amer. J. Psychiat.,* 1976, **133**, 413–18.

Burros, W. M. The growing burden of impotence. *Family Health,* May 1974, **6**(5), 18–21.

Cavallin, H. Incestuous fathers: A clinical report. *Amer. J. Psychiat.,* 1966, **122**(10), 1132–38.

Chesser, E. *Strange loves: The human aspects of sexual deviation.* New York: William Morrow, 1971.

Churchill, W. *Homosexual behavior among males: A cross-cultural and cross-species investigation.* New York: Hawthorne, 1967.

Cohen, M., Seghorn, T., & Calmas, W. Sociometric study of the sex offender. *Journal of Abnormal Psychology,* 1969, **74**(2), 249–55. Copyright 1969 by the American Psychological Association and reproduced by permission.

Cooper, A. J. A clinical study of "coital anxiety" in male potency disorders. *J. Psychosom. Res.,* 1969, **13**(2), 143–47.

Davenport, W. Sexual patterns and their regulation in a society of the Southwest Pacific. In F. Beach (Ed.), *Sex and behavior.* New York: Wiley, 1965.

Davis, A. J. Sexual assault in the Philadelphia prisons and sheriff's vans. *Trans-action,* 1968, **6**(2), 28–35.

Davison, G. C. Homosexuality: The ethical challenge. *J. Cons. Clin. Psychol.,* 1976, **44**(2), 157–62.

Davison, G. C. Not can but ought: The treatment of homosexuality. *J. Cons. Clin. Psychol.,* 1978, **46**(1), 170–2.

DeFrancis, V. *Protecting the child victim of sex crimes committed by adults.* Denver: Children Division, American Humane Association, 1969.

Devroye, A. Incest: Bibliographical review (French). *Acta Psychiatrica Belgica,* Nov. 1973, **73**(6), 661–712.

Driscoll, J. P. Transsexuals. In J. M. Henslin (Ed.), *Deviant life-styles.* New Brunswick, N.J.: Transaction Books, 1977.

East, W. N. Sexual offenders. *J. Nerv. Ment. Dis.,* 1946, **103**, 626–66.

Ellison, K. Personal communication, 1977.

Evans, R. B. Childhood parental relationships of homosexual men. *J. Cons. Clin. Psychol.,* 1969, **33**(2), 129–35.

Freedman, M. Homosexuals may be healthier than straights. *Psych. Today,* March 1975, **8**(10), 28–32.

Friedman, J. H. Woman's role in male impotence. *Medical Aspects of Human Sexuality,* June 1974, **8**(6), 8–23.

Gager, N., & Schurr, C. *Sexual assault: Confronting rape in America.* New York: Grosset & Dunlap, 1976.

Gagnon, J. H., & Simon, W. *Sexual conduct: The social sources of human sexuality.* Chicago: Aldine, 1973.

Gebhard, P. H. Situational factors affecting human sexual behavior. In F. Beach (Ed.), *Sex and behavior.* New York: Wiley, 1965.

Gebhard, P. H., Gagnon, J. H., Pomeroy, W. B. & Christenson, C. V. *Sex offenders: An analysis of types.* New York: Harper & Row, 1965.

Ginsberg, G. L., Frosch, W. A., & Shapiro, T. The new impotence. *Arch. Gen. Psychiat.,* Mar. 1972, **26**(3), 218–20.

Goldstein, M. J. Pornography, sex deviancy: An exaggerated link. *The Los Angeles Times,* Oct. 23, 1974, II, 7.

Goldstein, M. J., & Kant, H. S. (with collaboration of Hartman, J. J.). *Pornography and sexual deviance.* Berkeley, Calif.: University of California Press, 1973.

Grant, V. W. A case study of fetishism. *J. Abnorm. Soc. Psychol.,* 1953, **48**, 142–49.

Green, R. *Sexual identity conflict in children and adults.* New York: Basic Books, 1974.

Groth, A. N., Burgess, A. W., & Holmstrom, L. L. Rape: Power, anger, and sexuality. *Amer. J. Psychiat.,* 1977, **134**, 1239–43.

Haggerty, S. The oldest profession. *Los Angeles Times,* June 19, 1973, II, 7.

Hedblom, J. H. Dimensions of lesbian experience. *Archives of Sexual Behavior,* Dec. 1973, **2**(4), 329–41.

Hersen, M., & Eisler, R. M. Social skills training. In W. E. Craighead, A. E. Kazdin, & M. J. Mahoney (Eds.), *Behavior modification: Principles, issues, and applications.* Boston: Houghton Mifflin, 1976.

Hirschi, T. The professional prostitute. *Berkeley Journal of Sociology,* 1962, **7**, 37–41; 47–48.

Holmstrom, L., & Burgess, A. W. Assessing trauma in the rape victim. *Amer. J. Nurs.,* 1975, **75**, 1288.

Hooker, E. The adjustment of the male overt homosexual.

Journal of Projective Techniques, 1957, **21**, 18–31.

Hooker, E. The homosexual community. In *Proceedings of the XIV International Congress of Applied Psychology* (Vol. II).. *Personality research.* Copenhagen: Munksgaard, 1962.

Hoover, E. L. Lesbianism: Reflections of a "straight" woman. *Human Behavior,* Oct. 1973, **2**(10), 9.

Humphreys, L. Tearoom trade: Impersonal sex in public places. *Trans-action,* 1970, **7**(3), 10–25.

Jackman, N. R., O'Toole, R., & Geis, G. The self-image of the prostitute. *Sociol. Quart.,* 1963, **4**(2), 150–61.

Jensen, M. S. Role differentiation in female homosexual quasi-marital unions. *J. Marr. Fam.,* May 1974, **36**(2), 360–67.

Kallmann, F. J. Twin and sibship study of overt male homosexuality. *American Journal of Human Genetics,* June 1952, **4**(2), 136–46.

Kaplan, H. S. No-nonsense therapy for six sexual malfunctions. *Psych. Today,* Oct. 1974, **8**(5), 76–80; 83–84; 86.

Kaplan, H. S. *The illustrated manual of sex therapy.* New York: Quadrangle/The New York Times Book Company, 1975.

Kinsey, A. C., Pomeroy, W. B., & Martin, C. E. *Sexual behavior in the human male.* Philadelphia: W. B. Saunders, 1948.

Kinsey, A. C., Pomeroy, W. B., & Martin, C. E. *Sexual behavior in the human female.* Philadelphia: W. B. Saunders, 1953.

Kolodny, R. C., Masters, W. H., Hendrys, J., & Toro, G. Plasma testosterone and semen analysis in male homosexuals. *New Engl. J. Med.,* Nov. 18, 1971, **285**(21), 1170–74.

Konopka, G. Adolescent delinquent girls. *Children,* 1964, **11**(1), 21–26.

Krafft-Ebing, R. V. *Psychopathica sexualis.* New York: Pioneer Publications, 1950.

Kutchinsky, B. The effect of easy availability of pornography on the incidence of sex crimes: The Danish experience. Institute of Criminal Science. University of Copenhagen, 1972.

Lindzey, G. Some remarks concerning incest, the incest taboo, and psychoanalytic theory. *Amer. Psychologist,* 1967, **22**(12), 1051–59.

Livingood, J. M. (Ed.). *National Institute of Mental Health Task Force on Homosexuality: Final report and background papers.* Rockville, Md.: National Institute of Mental Health, 1972.

Lobitz, W. C., & Lobitz, G. K. Clinical assessment in the treatment of sexual dysfunctions. In J. Lo Piccolo & L. LoPiccolo (Eds.), *Handbook of sex therapy.* New York: Plenum Press, 1978. Pp. 85–102.

LoPiccolo, J. Direct treatment of sexual dysfunction. In J. LoPiccolo & L. LoPiccolo (Eds.), *Handbook of sex therapy.* New York: Plenum Press, 1978. Pp. 1–17.

LoPiccolo, J., & LoPiccolo, L. (Eds.). *Handbook of sex therapy.* New York: Plenum Press, 1978.

Los Angeles Times. A transvestite's plea for understanding and tolerance. Sept. 30, 1973, IV, 7.

Maisch, H. *Incest.* New York: Stein & Day, 1972.

Marshall, W. L. A combined treatment approach to the reduction of multiple fetish-related behaviors. *J. Cons. Clin. Psychol.,* Aug. 1974, **42**(4), 613–16.

Masters, W. H., & Johnson, V. E. *Human sexual response.* Boston: Little, Brown, 1966.

Masters, W. H., & Johnson, V. E. *Human sexual inadequacy.* Boston: Little, Brown, 1970.

Masters, W. H., & Johnson, V. E. *The pleasure bond: A new look at sexuality and commitment.* Boston: Little, Brown, 1975.

Masters, W. H., & Johnson, V. E. *Homosexuality in perspective.* Boston: Little, Brown, 1979.

McCombie, S. L. Characteristics of rape victims seen in crisis intervention. *Smith College Studies in Social Work,* 1976, **46**, 137–58.

Medea, A., & Thompson, K. *Against rape.* New York: Farrar, Straus, and Giroux, 1974.

Money, J. Prenatal hormones and postnatal socialization in gender identity differentiation. In J. K. Cole & R. Dienstbier (Eds.), *Nebraska symposium on motivation, 1973.* Lincoln, Neb.: University of Nebraska Press, 1974. Pp. 221–95.

Money, J. & Alexander, D. Psychosexual development and

absence of homosexuality in males with precocious puberty. *J. Nerv. Ment. Dis.*, 1969, **148**(2), 111–23.

Money, J., & Ehrhardt, A. A. *Man & woman, boy & girl: Differentiation and dimorphism of gender identity*. Baltimore: Johns Hopkins University Press, 1972.

NAMH. NAMH supports repeal of homosexual status. *Psychiatric News*, 1971, **6**(3), 1.

Nathan, P. E., & Harris, S. L. *Psychopathology and society.* McGraw-Hill, 1975.

Newman, L. E. & Stoller, R. J. Nontranssexual men who seek sex reassignment. *Amer. J. Psychiat.*, Apr. 1974, **131**(4), 437–41.

Notman, N. T. & Nadelson, C. C. The rape victim: Psychodynamic considerations. *Amer. J. Psychiat.*, 1976, **133**(4), 408–13.

Ohlson, E. L. In R. Cole & S. G. Lewis, Studies challenge myths on gay men, women. *The Advocate*, Jan. 1, 1975, 3; 10.

Oros, C. J., & Koss, M. P. *Women as rape victims.* Paper presented at the American Psychological Association Annual Meeting, Toronto, August 1978.

Packard, V. *The sexual wilderness.* New York: David McKay, 1968.

Pauly, I. B. The current status of the change of sex operation. *J. Nerv. Ment. Dis.*, 1968, **147**(5), 460–71.

Pittman, D. J. The male house of prostitution. In J. M. Henslin (Ed.), *Deviant life styles.* New Brunswick, N.J.: Transaction Books, 1977.

Rachman, S. Sexual fetishism: An experimental analogue. *Psychol. Rec.*, 1966, **16**, 293–96.

Rentzel, L. *When all the laughter died in sorrow.* New York: Saturday Review Press, 1972.

Revitch, E., & Weiss, R. G. The pedophiliac offender. *Dis. Nerv. Sys.*, 1962, **23**, 73–78.

Rooth, G. Exhibitionists around the world. *Human Behavior,* May 1974, **3**(5), 61.

Rosenthal, D. *Genetic theory and abnormal behavior.* New York: McGraw-Hill, 1970.

Rossman, P. The pederasts. *Society,* Mar./Apr. 1973, **10**(3), 28–32; 34–35.

Sabalis, R. F., Frances, A., Appenzeller, S. N., & Moseley, W. B. The three sisters: Transsexual male siblings. *Amer. J. Psychiat.*, Aug. 1974, **131**(8), 907–9.

Sack, R. L. & Miller, W. Masochism: A clinical and theoretical overview. *Psychiatry,* Aug. 1975, **38**(3), 244–57.

Schwartzman, J. The individual, incest, and exogamy. *Psychiatry,* May 1974, **37**, 171–80.

Selkin, J. Rape. *Psychology Today,* 1975, **8**(8), 70–72.

Sgroi, S. M. Sexual molestation of children. *Children Today,* May-June 1975, **4**(3), 18–21; 44.

Sgroi, S. M. Sexual molestation of children: The last frontier in child abuse. In S. Chess & A. Thomas (Eds.), *Annual progress in child psychiatry and child development: 1976.* New York: Brunner/Mazel, 1977.

Siegelman, M. Parental background of male homosexuals and heterosexuals. *Archives of Sexual Behavior,* Jan. 1974, **3**, 3–18.

Simon, W. Male sexuality: The secret of satisfaction. *Today's Health,* Apr. 1975, **53**(4). 32–34; 50–52.

Singer, J., & Singer, I. Types of female orgasm. In J. LoPiccolo & L. LoPiccolo (Eds.), *Handbook of sex therapy.* New York: Plenum Press, 1978. Pp. 175–86.

Snortum, J. R., Marshall, J. E., Gillespie, J. E., McLaughlin, J. P., & Mosberg, L. Family dynamics and homosexuality. *Psych. Rep.*, 1969, **24**(3), 763–70.

Steinmann, A., & Fox, D. J. *The male dilemma: How to survive the sexual revolution.* New York: Jason Aronson, 1974.

Stephan, W. G. Parental relationships and early social experiences of activist male homosexuals and male heterosexuals. *J. Abnorm. Psychol.*, 1973, **82**(3), 506–13.

Stoller, R. J. *Sex and gender* (Vol. 1): *The development of masculinity and femininity.* Published by Jason Aronson, New York. Copyright © 1968, 1974, by Robert J. Stoller. Reprinted by permission of the author.

Sturgis, E. T., & Adams, H. E. The right to treatment: Issues in the treatment of homosexuality. *J. Cons. Clin. Psychol.*, 1978, **46**(1), 165–69.

Summit, R., & Kryso, J. Sexual abuse of children: A clinical spectrum. *Amer. J. Orthopsychiat.*, 1978, **48**, 237–51.

Sutherland, S., & Scherl, D. J. Patterns of response among victims of rape. *Amer. J. Orthopsychiat.*, 1970, **40**, 503–11.

Swanson, D. W. Adult sexual abuse of children: The man and circumstances. *Dis. Nerv. Sys.*, 1968, **29**(10), 677–83.

Switzer, E. Female sexuality. *Family Health,* Mar. 1974, **6**(3), 34–36; 38.

Symonds, M. The rape victim: Psychological patterns of response. *American Journal of Psychoanalysis,* 1976, **36**(1), 27–34.

Thompson, N. L., Jr., & McCandless, B. R. & Strickland, B. R. Personal adjustment of male and female homosexuals and heterosexuals. *J. Abnorm. Psychol.*, 1971, **78**(2), 237–40.

Thompson, N. L., Jr., Schwartz, D. M., McCandless, B. R., & Edwards, D. A. Parent-child relationships and sexual identity in male and female homosexuals and heterosexuals. *J. Cons. Clin. Psychol.,* Aug. 1973, **41**(1), 120–27.

Tourney, G., Petrilli, A. J., & Hatfield, L. N. Hormonal relationships in homosexual men. *Amer. J. Psychiat.,* Mar. 1975, **132**(3), 288–90.

Tripp, C. A. *The homosexual matrix.* New York: McGraw-Hill, 1975.

U.S. Commission on Obscenity and Pornography. *The Report of the Commission on Obscenity and Pornography.* Washington, D.C.: Government Printing Office, 1970.

Young, W. Prostitution. In J. H. Gagnon & W. Simon (Eds.), *Sexual deviance.* New York: Harper & Row, 1967.

Weinberg, M., & Williams, C. J. *Male homosexuals: Their problems and adaptations in three societies.* New York: Oxford University Press, 1974.

Wertham, F. *The show of violence.* New York: Doubleday, 1949.

Witzig, J. S. The group treatment of male exhibitionists. *Amer. J. Psychiat.*, 1968, **125**, 75–81.

16. Suicide

Abram, H. S., Moore, G. L., & Westervelt, F. B., Jr. Suicidal behavior in chronic dialysis patients. *Amer. J. Psychiat.,* Mar. 1971, **127**(9), 119–21.

Beck, A. T., Beck, R., & Kovacs, M. Classification of suicidal behaviors: I. Qualifying intent and medical lethality. *Amer. J. Psychiat.,* Mar. 1975, **132**(3), 285–87.

Berman, A. L. The epidemiology of life-threatening events. *Suicide,* Summer 1975, **5**(2), 67–77.

Binstock, J. Choosing to die: The decline of aggression and the rise of suicide. *The Futurist,* Apr. 1974, **8**(2), 68–71.

Boss, M. Flight from death—mere survival; and flight into death—suicide. In B. B. Wolman & H. H. Krauss (Eds.), *Between survival and suicide.* New York: Gardner, 1976. Pp. 1–23.

Brown, J. H. Reporting of suicide: Canadian statistics. *Suicide,* Spring 1975, **5**(1), 21–28.

Browning, C. H. Epidemiology of suicide: Firearms. *Comprehensive Psychiatry,* Nov./Dec. 1974, **15**(6), 549–53.

Cohen, S. L., & Fiedler, J. E. Quote from "Content analysis of multiple messages in suicide notes" by Stuart L. Cohen and J. E. Fiedler from *Life-Threatening Behavior,* Summer 1974, **4**(2), 75–95. © Human Sciences Press, 72 Fifth Avenue, New York, N.Y. 10011, 1974.

Darbonne, A. R. Suicide and age: A suicide note analysis. *J. Cons. Clin. Psychol.,* 1969, **33**, 46–50.

Deikel, S. M. The life and death of Lenny Bruce: A psychological autopsy. *Life-Threatening Behavior,* Fall 1974, **4**(3), 176–92.

Dizmang, L. H., Watson, J., May, P. A., & Bopp, J. Adolescent suicide at an Indian reservation. *Amer. J. Orthopsychiat.*, Jan. 1974, **44**(1), 43–49.

Durkheim, E. *Suicide: A study in sociology*. Trans. J. A. Spaulding & G. Simpson. Ed. G. Simpson. New York: Free Press, 1951. Originally published 1897.

Falret, J. P. *De l'hypocondrie et du suicide*. Paris: Caroullebois. Libraire de la Société de Médecine, 1822.

Farberow, N. L. *Suicide*. Morristown, N.J.: General Learning Press, 1974.

Farberow, N. L. Cultural history of suicide. In N. L. Farberow (Ed.), *Suicide in different cultures*. Baltimore: University Park Press, 1975. Pp. 1–15.

Farberow, N. L., & Litman, R. E. A comprehensive suicide prevention program. Suicide Prevention Center of Los Angeles, 1958–1969. Unpublished final report DHEW NIMH Grants No. MH 14946 & MH 00128. Los Angeles, 1970.

Farberow, N. L., Shneidman, E. S., & Leonard, C. Suicide among general medical and surgical hospital patients with malignant neoplasms. Veterans Administration, Dept. of Medicine and Surgery, *Medical Bulletin* MB–9, Feb. 25, 1963, 1–11.

Farberow, N. L., & Simon, M. D. Suicide in Los Angeles and Vienna. In N. L. Farberow (Ed.), *Suicide in different cultures*. Baltimore: University Park Press, 1975. Pp. 185–204.

Fuller, M. From Suicide past and present: A note on Jean Pierre Falret, by Marielle Fuller. *Life-Threatening Behavior*, Spring 1973, **3**(1), 58–65. © Human Sciences Press, 72 Fifth Avenue, New York, N.Y. 10011, 1973.

Griest, J. H., Gustafson, D. H., Stauss, F. F., Rowse, G. L., Laughren, T. P., & Chiles, J. A. Suicide risk prediction: A new approach. *Life-Threatening Behavior*, Winter 1974, **4**(4), 212–23.

Hall, J. C., Bliss, M., Smith, K., & Bradley, A. Suicide gestures, attempts found high among poor. *Psychiatric News*, July 1, 1970, 20.

Havighurst, R. J. Suicide and education. In E. S. Shneidman (Ed.), *On the nature of suicide*. San Francisco: Jossey-Bass, 1969.

Hendin, H. Student suicide: Death as a life-style. *J. Nerv. Ment. Dis.*, Mar. 1975, **160**(3), 204–19.

Hotchner, A. E. *Papa Hemingway*. New York: Random House, 1966.

Kidson, M., & Jones, I. Psychiatric disorders among aborigines of the Australian Western Desert. *Arch. Gen. Psychiat.*, 1968, **19**, 413–22.

Kirstein, L., Prusoff, B., Weissman, M., & Dressler, D. M. Utilization review of treatment for suicide attempters. *Amer. J. Psychiat.*, Jan. 1975, **132**(1), 22–27.

Klagsbrun, F. *Too young to die: Youth and suicide*. Boston: Houghton-Mifflin, 1976.

Kovacs, M., Beck, A. T., & Weissman, A. Hopelessness: An indicator of suicidal risk. *Suicide*, Summer 1975, **5**(2), 95–103.

Leonard, C. V. Depression and suicidality. *J. Cons. Clin. Psychol.*, Feb. 1974, **42**(1), 98–104.

Melges, F. T., & Bowlby, J. Types of hopelessness in psychopathological process. *Arch. Gen. Psychiat.*, June 1969, **20**(6), 690–99.

Merian. Sur la creinte de la mort, sur le mepris de la mort, sur le suicide: Memoire. *Histoire de l'Academie Royale des Sciences et Belles-Lettres de Berlin*, 1763, XIX: 385, 392, 403.

Miller, J. P. Suicide and adolescence. *Adolescence*, Spring 1975, **10**(37), 11–24.

Minkoff, K., Bergman, E., Beck, A. T., & Beck, R. Hopelessness, depression and attempted suicide. *Amer. J. Psychiat.*, Apr. 1973, **130**(4), 455–59.

Murphy, G. E. Suicide and the right to die. *Amer. J. Psychiat.*, Apr. 1973, **130**(4), 472–73.

Murray, D. C. Suicidal and depressive feelings among college students. *Psych. Rep.*, Aug. 1973, **33**(1), 175–81.

National Institute of Mental Health (NIMH). Rising suicide rate linked to economy. *Los Angeles Times*, Apr. 20, 1976, VIII, 2; 5.

Nelson, H. County suicide rate up sharply among young. *Los Angeles Times*, Jan. 26, 1971, II, 1.

Parkin, M. Suicide and culture in Fairbanks: A comparison of three cultural groups in a small city of interior Alaska. *Psychiatry*, Feb. 1974, **37**(1), 60–67.

Pausnau, R. O., & Russell, A. T. Psychiatric resident suicide: An analysis of five cases. *Amer. J. Psychiat.*, Apr. 1975, **132**(4), 402–6.

Paykel, E. S., Hallowell, C., Dressler, D. M., Shapiro, D. L., & Weissman, M. M. Treatment of suicide attempters. *Arch. Gen. Psychiat.*, Oct. 1974, **31**(4), 487–91.

Paykel, E. S., Prusoff, B. A., & Myers, J. K. Suicide attempts and recent life events. *Arch. Gen. Psychiat.*, Mar. 1975, **32**(3), 327–33.

Peck, M. A., & Schrut, A. Suicidal behavior among college students. *HSMHA Health Reports*, Feb. 1971, **86**(2), 149–56.

Peck, M., & Seiden, R. Youth suicide. *ExChange*. Sacramento, Calif.: California State Department of Health, May 1975. Pp. 17–20.

Potts, P. Personal communication, January 1978.

Retterstøl, N. Suicide in Norway. In N. L. Farberow (Ed.). *Suicide in different cultures*. Baltimore: University Park Press, 1975, Pp. 77–94.

Reynolds, D. K., & Farberow, N. L. *Suicide: Inside and out*. Berkeley: University of California Press, 1976.

Rogow, A. A. Private illness and public policy: The cases of James Forrestal and John Winant. *Amer. J. Psychiat.*, 1969, **125**(8), 1093–97.

Rosen, D. H. The serious suicide attempt: Epidemiological and follow-up study of 886 patients. *Amer. J. Psychiat.*, 1970, **127**(6), 64–70.

Ross, M. This doctor will self-destruct . . . *Human Behavior*, Feb. 1974, **3**(2), 54.

Rudestam, K. E. Stockholm and Los Angeles: A cross-cultural study of the communication of suicidal intent. *J. Cons. Clin. Psychol.*, 1971, **36**(1), 82–90.

Ryle, A. *Student Casualties*. London: Penguin, 1969.

Sawyer, J. B., Sudak, H. S., & Hall, S. R. A follow-up study of 53 suicides known to a suicide prevention center. *Life-Threatening Behavior*, Winter 1972, **2**(4), 227–38.

Schaar, K. Suicide rate high among women psychologists. *APA Monitor*, July 1974, **5**(7), 1; 10.

Seiden, R. H. Suicide: preventable death. *Public Affairs Report*, Aug. 1974, **15**(4), 1–5.

Shneidman, E. S. Fifty-eight years. In E. S. Shneidman (Ed.), *On the nature of suicide*. San Francisco: Jossey-Bass, 1969. Pp. 1–30.

Shneidman, E. S. Suicide notes reconsidered. *Psychiatry*, Nov. 1973, **36**(4), 379–94. Copyright 1973, The William Alanson White Psychiatric Foundation, Inc. Reprinted by permission of the author and The William Alanson White Psychiatric Foundation, Inc.

Shneidman, E. S., & Farberow, N. L. (Eds.), *Clues to suicide*. New York: McGraw-Hill, 1957.

Shneidman, E. S., Parker, E., & Funkhouser, G. R. You and death. *Psych. Today*, 1970, **4**(3), 67–72.

Stanley, E. J., & Barter, J. T. Adolescent suicidal behavior. *Amer. J. Orthopsychiat.*, 1970, **40**(1), 87–96.

Suter, B. Suicide and women. In B. B. Wolman & H. H. Krauss (Eds.), *Between survival and suicide*. New York: Gardner, 1976. Pp. 129–61.

Szasz, T. S. The ethics of suicide. In B. B. Wolman & H. H. Krauss (Eds.), *Between survival and suicide*. New York: Gardner, 1976. Pp. 163–85.

Tuckman, J., Kleiner, R., & Lavell, M. Emotional content of suicide notes. Reprinted from *The American Journal of Psychiatry*, volume **116**, pages 59–63, 1959. Copyright 1959, the American Psychiatric Association.

Watkins, C., Gilbert, J. E., & Bass, W. The persistent suicidal patient. *Amer. J. Psychiat.*, 1969, **125,** 1590–93.

Weissman, M. M. The epidemiology of suicide attempts, 1960–1971. *Arch. Gen. Psychiat.*, June 1974, **30**(6), 737–46.

Weissman, M. M., Fox, K., & Klerman, G. L. Hostility and depression associated with suicide attempts. *Amer. J. Psychiat.*, Apr. 1973, **130**(4), 450–55.

West, J. *The woman said yes: Encounters with life and death.* New York: Harcourt Brace Jovanovich, 1976.

Wolman, B. B. The anticulture of suicide. In B. B. Wolman & H. H. Krauss (Eds.), *Between survival and suicide.* New York: Gardner, 1976. Pp. 77–94.

World Health Organization (WHO). In W. Tuohy, World health agency zeroes in on suicide. *Los Angeles Times,* Oct. 25, 1974, VI, 1–3.

Zung, W. W. K., & Green, R. L., Jr. Seasonal variations of suicide and depression. *Gen. Psychiat.,* Jan. 1974, **30**(1), 89–91.

17. The Role of Assessment in Clinical Decisions

Arnold, M. B. *Story sequence analysis: A new method of measuring motivation and predicting achievement.* New York: Columbia University Press, 1962.

Atkinson, J. W. (Ed.). *Motives in fantasy, action, and society.* Princeton, N.J.: Van Nostrand, 1958.

Bellak, L. *The Thematic Apperception Test, the Children's Apperception Test, and the Senior Apperception Technique in clinical use* (3rd ed.). New York: Grune & Stratton, 1975.

Boll, T. J. The Halstead-Reitan neurophysiology battery. In S. B. Filskov & T. J. Boll (Eds.), *Handbook of neurophysiology.* New York: Wiley Interscience Series, 1980.

Boll, T. J. Diagnosing brain impairment. In B. B. Wolman, (Ed.), *Clinical diagnosis of mental disorders: A handbook.* New York: Plenum, 1978.

Dahlstrom, W. G., Welsh, G. S., & Dahlstrom, L. E. *An MMPI handbook: Research applications* (Vol. 2). Minneapolis: University of Minnesota Press, 1975.

Dahlstrom, W. G. *Minority status and MMPI scores: MMPI score patterns and background characteristics of black adults.* Paper presented at the meeting of the American Psychological Association, Toronto, August 1978.

Dohrenwend, B. S., Krasnoff, L., Askenasy, A., & Dohrenwend, B. P. Exemplification of a method for scaling life events: The PERI life events scale, *J. Hlth. Soc. Beh.,* 1978, **19,** 205–29.

Exner, J. E. *The Rorschach: A comprehensive system.* New York: Wiley, 1974.

Feighner, J. P., Robins, E., Guze, S. B., Woodruff, R. A., Winokur, G., & Muñoz, R. Diagnostic criteria for use in psychiatric research. *Arch. Gen. Psychiat.,* 1972, **26,** 57–63.

Filskov, S. B., & Goldstein, S. G. Diagnostic validity of the Halstead-Reitan Neuropsychology battery. *J. Cons. Clin. Psychol.,* 1974, **42,** 383–88.

Graham, J. R. *The Minnesota Multiphasic Personality Inventory.* In B. B. Wolman (Ed.), *Clinical diagnosis of mental disorders: A handbook.* New York: Plenum, 1978.

Gynther, M. D. Ethnicity and personality. In J. N. Butcher (Ed.), *New directions in MMPI research.* Minneapolis: University of Minnesota Press, 1979.

Hathaway, S. R., & McKinley, J. C. *The Minnesota multiphasic personality inventory* (Rev. ed.). New York: Psychological Corporation, 1951.

Helzer, J. E., Robins, L. N., Taibleson, M., Woodruff, R. A., Jr., Reich, T., & Wish, E. D. Reliability of psychiatric diagnosis: A methodological review. *Arch. Gen. Psychiat.,* 1977, **34,** 129–33.

Jones, R. R., Reid, J. B., & Patterson, G. R. Naturalistic observation in clinical assessment. In P. M. Reynolds (Ed.), *Advances in psychological assessment* (Vol. 3). San Francisco: Jossey-Bass, 1975.

Klinger, E. *Structure and functions of fantasy.* New York: Wiley, 1971.

Klinger, E. *Meaning and void: Inner experience and the incentives in peoples' lives.* Minneapolis: University of Minnesota Press, 1978.

Klinger, E. Modes of normal conscious flow. In K. S. Pope & J. L. Singer (Eds.), *The stream of consciousness: Scientific investigations into the flow of human experience.* New York: Plenum, 1979.

Klopfer, B., & Davidson, H. *The Rorschach technique: An introductory manual.* New York: Harcourt Brace Jovanovich, Inc., 1962.

Matarazzo, J. D. The interview: Its reliability and validity in psychiatric diagnosis. In B. Wolman (Ed.), *Clinical diagnosis of mental disorders: A handbook.* New York: Plenum Press, 1978.

Overall, J. E., & Klett, C. J. *Applied multivariate analysis.* New York: McGraw-Hill, 1972.

Summers, F. Characteristics of new patient admissions to aftercare. *Hospital and Community Psychiatry,* 1979, **30**(3), 199–202.

Wechsler, D. *Manual for the Wechsler Adult Intelligence Scale.* New York: Psychological Corporation, 1955.

Winter, D. G. *The power motive.* New York: Free Press, 1973.

18. Biologically Based Therapies

Allen, I. M. Cerebral injury with shock treatment. *New Zealand Medical Journal,* 1951, **50,** 356–64.

Alpers, B. J., & Hughes, J. Changes in the brain after electrically induced convulsions in cats. *Arch. Neurol. Psychiat.,* 1942, **47,** 385–98.

American Psychiatric Association, Task Force on Electroconvulsive Therapy. *Report: Electroconvulsive therapy.* Washington: American Psychiatric Association, 1978.

Astrup, C. A follow-up study of electrosleep. *Biological Psychiatry,* Feb. 1974, **8**(1), 115–17.

Bassuk, E. L., & Schoonover, S. C. *The practitioner's guide to psychoactive drugs.* New York: Plenum Medical, 1977.

Berger, P. A. Medical treatment of mental illness. *Science,* 1978, **200,** 974–81.

Brengelmann, J. C. *The effect of repeated electroshock on learning in depressives.* Munich: Springer, 1959.

Brown, C. C. Electroanesthesia and electrosleep. *Amer. Psychologist,* Mar. 1975, **30**(3), 402–10.

Cade, J. F. J. Lithium salts in the treatment of psychotic excitement. *Medical Journal of Australia,* **36** (part II): 349–352, 1949. Reprinted by permission.

Corsellis, J. A. N., & Meyer, A. Histological changes in the brain after uncomplicated electro-convulsant treatment. *Journal of Mental Science,* 1954, **100,** 375–83.

Culliton, B. J. Psychosurgery: National Commission issues surprisingly favorable report. *Science,* 1976, **194,** 299–301.

Fink, M. CNS sequellae of EST: Risks of therapy and their prophylaxis. In C. Shagass & A. Friedhoff (Eds.), *Psychopathology and brain dysfunction.* New York: Raven Press, 1977. Pp. 223–39.

Fink, M. *Convulsive therapy: Theory and practice.* New York: Raven Press, 1979.

Fink, M., Kety, S., McGaugh, I., & Williams, T. A. (Eds.), *Psychobiology of convulsive therapy.* New York: Wiley, 1974.

Freedman, A. M., Kaplan, H. I., & Sadock, B. J. *Modern synopsis of comprehensive textbook of psychiatry/ II* (2nd Ed.). Baltimore: Williams & Wilkins, 1976.

Freeman, W. Psychosurgery. In S. Arieti (Ed.), *American handbook of psychiatry* (Vol. 2). New York: Basic Books, 1959. Pp. 1521–40.

Gordon, H. L. Fifty shock therapy theories. *Military Surgeon,* 1948, **103,** 397–408.

Greenberg, J. Dialysis: Aid for schizophrenia? *APA Monitor,* 1978, **9,** 8.

Grinspoon, L., Ewalt, J. R., & Shader, R. I. *Schizophrenia: Pharmacotherapy and psychotherapy.* Copyright © 1972, The Williams & Wilkins Co., Baltimore. Reprinted by permission.

Hearst, E. D., Cloninger, C. R., Crews, E. L., & Cadoret, R. J. Electrosleep therapy: A double-blind trial. *Arch. Gen. Psychiat.,* Apr. 1974, **30**(4), 463–66.

Heilbrun, G., & Liebert, E. Biopsy studies of the brain following artificially produced convulsions. *Arch. Neurol. Psychiat.,* 1941, **46,** 548–50.

Hollon, S., & Beck, A. T. Psychotherapy and drug therapy: Comparisons and combinations. In S. L. Garfield & A. E. Bergin (Eds.), *Handbook of psychotherapy and behavior change.* New York: Wiley, 1978. Pp. 437–90.

Kalinowski, L. B., & Hippius, H. *Pharmacological, convulsive and other somatic treatments in psychiatry.* New York: Grune & Stratton, 1969.

Kalinowski, L. B., & Hoch, P. H. From *Shock treatments, psychosurgery, and other somatic treatments in psychiatry,* Second Revised and Enlarged Edition. Published by Grune & Stratton, New York, 1952.

Kline, N. S. Use of *Rauwolfia serpentina* in neuropsychiatric conditions. *Ann. N.Y. Acad. Sci.,* 1954, **54,** 107–32.

Kolata, G. B. Mental disorders: A new approach to treatment? *Science,* 1979, **203,** 36–38.

Lipton, M. A., Ban, T. A., Kane, F. J., Levine, J., Loren, R., & Wittenborn, R. *Megavitamin and orthomolecular therapy in psychiatry.* A report of the APA Task Force on Vitamin Therapy in Psychiatry. Copyright 1973 by the American Psychiatric Association. Reprinted by permission.

McCall, L. *Between us and the dark* (originally published in 1947). Summary in W. C. Alvarez, *Minds that came back,* 1961. Reprinted by permission of Gladys A. Muirhead, Executor.

Mendels, J., & Frazer, A. Brain biogenic amine depletion and mood. *Arch. Gen. Psychiat.,* 1974, **30,** 447–51.

Rosenthal, S. H., & Wulfsohn, N. L. Electrosleep—A clinical trial. *Amer. J. Psychiat.,* 1970, **127**(4), 175–76.

Segal, D. S., Yager, J., & Sullivan, J. L. *Foundations of biochemical psychiatry.* Boston: Butterworths, 1976.

Smith, R. J. Study finds sleeping pills overprescribed. *Science,* 1979, **204,** 287–88.

Sprague, R. L., Barnes, K. R., & Werry, J. S. Methylphenidate and thioridazine: Learning, reaction time, activity, and classroom behavior in disturbed children. *Amer. J. Orthopsychiat.,* 1970, **40,** 615–28.

Squire, L. R. ECT and memory loss. *Amer. J. Psychiat.,* 1977, **134,** 997–1001.

Squire, L. R., & Slater, P. C. Bilateral and unilateral ECT: Effects on verbal and nonverbal memory. *Amer. J. Psychiat.,* 1978, **135,** 1316–20.

Squire, L. R., Slater, P. C., & Chase, P. M. Retrograde amnesia: Temporal gradient in very long-term memory following electroconvulsive therapy. *Science,* 1975, **187,** 77–79.

19. Psychological Therapies

Alexander, F. Individual psychotherapy. *Psychosom. Med.,* 1946, **8,** 110–15.

American Psychological Association. Guidelines for psychologists conducting growth groups. *Amer. Psychologist,* Oct. 1973, **28**(10), 933.

Aponte, H., & Hoffman, L. The open door: A structural approach to a family with an anorectic child. *Family Process,* 1973, **12,** 1–44.

Ayllon, T., & Azrin, N. H. *The token economy: A motivational system for therapy and rehabilitation.* New York: Appleton-Century-Crofts, 1968.

Bandura, A. *Principles of behavior modification.* New York: Holt, Rinehart & Winston, 1964.

Bandura, A. *Social learning theory.* Published by Prentice-Hall, Inc., 1977.

Barber, T. X. *Hypnosis: A scientific approach.* New York: Van Nostrand Reinhold, 1969.

Beck, A. *Cognitive therapy and emotional disorders.* New York: International Universities Press, 1976.

Beck, A. T., Rush, A. J., Shaw, B., & Emery, G. *Cognitive therapy of depression: A treatment manual.* New York: Gilford Press, 1979.

Bednar, R. L., & Kaul, T. J. Experiential group research: Current perspectives. In S. L. Garfield & A. E. Bergin (Eds.), *Handbook of psychotherapy and behavior change: An empirical analysis.* New York: Wiley, 1978.

Bergin, A. E., & Lambert, M. J. The evaluation of therapeutic outcomes. In S. L. Garfield & A. E. Bergin (Eds.), *Handbook of psychotherapy and behavior change: An empirical analysis.* New York: Wiley, 1978.

Bergin, A. E., & Suinn, R. M. Individual psychotherapy and behavior therapy. *Ann. Rev. Psychol.,* 1975, **26,** 509–56.

Berne, E. *Games people play.* New York: Grove Press, 1964.

Berne, E. *What do you say after you say hello?* New York: Grove Press, 1972.

Blanchard, E. B., & Abel, G. G. An experimental case study of the biofeedback treatment of a rape-induced psychophysiological cardiovascular disorder. *Behavior Therapy,* 1976, **7,** 113–19. Copyright © 1976 by the Association for the Advancement of Behavior Therapy. Reprinted by permission of the authors and Academic Press, Inc.

Blanchard, E. B., & Epstein, L. H. *A biofeedback primer.* Reading, Mass.: Addison-Wesley, 1978.

Blanchard, E. B., & Young, L. D. Self-control of cardiac functioning: A promise as yet unfulfilled. *Psychol. Bull.,* 1973, **79,** 145–63.

Blanchard, E. B., & Young, L. Clinical applications of biofeedback training: A review of evidence. *Arch. Gen. Psychiat.,* 1974, **30,** 573–89.

Bucher, B., & Lovaas, O. I. Use of aversive stimulation in behavior modification. In M. R. Jones (Ed.), *Miami symposium on the prediction of behavior 1967: Aversive stimulation.* Coral Gables: University of Miami Press, 1967. Pp. 77–145.

Butcher, J. N., & Kolotkin, R. Evaluation of outcome in grief psychotherapy. *Psychiatric Clinics of North America,* 1979, **3**(1), 157–69.

Curry, A. E. The world of a schizophrenic woman. *The Psychoanalytic Review,* Vol. 49, No. 1, 1962. Reprinted by permission of Human Science Press, 72 Fifth Avenue, New York, N.Y. 10011.

Diamond, M. J. Modification of hypnotizability: A review. *Psychol. Bull.,* Mar. 1974, **81**(3), 180–98.

Eisler, R. M., Miller, P. M., Hersen, M., & Alford, H. Effects of assertive training on marital interaction. *Arch. Gen. Psychiat.,* May 1974, **30**(5), 643–49.

Ellis, A. Rational psychotherapy. *J. Gen. Psychol.,* 1958, **59,** 35–49.

Ellis, A. *Reason and emotion in psychotherapy.* New York: Lyle Stuart, 1970.

Ellis, A. Rational-emotive therapy. In R. J. Corsini (Ed.), *Current psychotherapies.* Itasca, Ill.: Peacock Publishers, 1973.

Ellis, A. Creative job and happiness: The humanistic way. *The Humanist,* Jan.-Feb. 1975, **35**(1), 11–13.

Emmelkamp, P. M. G., & Wessels, H. Flooding in imagination vs. flooding *in vivo:* A comparison with agoraphobics. *Behav. Res. Ther.,* Feb. 1975, **13**(1), 7–15.

Eysenck, H. J. The effects of psychotherapy: An evaluation. *Journal of Consulting Psychology,* 1952, **16,** 319–24.

Foreyt, J., & Rathjen, D. (Eds.), *Cognitive behavior therapy: Research and application.* New York: Plenum Press, 1978.

Frank, J. D. *Persuasion and healing.* Baltimore: Johns Hopkins University Press, 1961.

Fromm, E., & Shor, R. E. *Hypnosis: Research developments and perspectives.* Chicago: Aldine, 1972.

Fuchs, C. Z., & Rehm, L. P. A self-control behavior therapy program for depression. *J. Cons. Clin. Psychol.,* 1977, **45,** 206–15.

Garfield, S. L., & Kurtz, R. Clinical psychologists in the 1970s. *Amer. Psychologist,* 1976, **31,** 1–9.

Glasser, W. *Reality therapy.* New York: Harper & Row, 1965.

Glasser, W. Reality therapy—A new approach. In O. H. Mowrer (Ed.), *Morality and mental health.* Skokie, Ill.: Rand McNally, 1967. Pp. 126–34.

Glasser, W. Reality therapy. In V. Binder, A. Binder, & R. Rimland (Eds.), *Modern therapies.* Englewood Cliffs, N.J.: Prentice-Hall, 1976.

Glasser, W., & Zunin, L. N. Reality therapy. In R. Corsini (Ed.), *Current psychotherapies.* Itasca, Ill.: Peacock Publishers, 1973.

Goldfried, M., & Davidson, G. *Clinical behavior therapy.* New York: Holt, Rinehart & Winston, 1976.

Gugliemi, R. S. *A double-blind study of the effectiveness of skin temperature biofeedback as a treatment for Raynaud's disease.* Unpublished doctoral dissertation, University of Minnesota, 1979.

Gurman, A. S., & Kniskern, D. P. Research on marital and family therapy: Progress, perspective and prospect. In S. L. Garfield & A. E. Bergin (Eds.), *Handbook of psychotherapy and behavior change: An empirical analysis* (2nd ed.). New York: Wiley, 1978.

Haley, J. Whither family therapy. *Family Process,* 1962, **1,** 69–100.

Harris, S. L., & Ersner-Hershfield, R. Behavioral suppression of seriously disruptive behavior in psychotic and retarded patients: A review of punishment and its alternatives. *Psychol. Bull.,* 1978, **85,** 1352–75.

Hartmann, H. *Ego psychology and the problem of adaptation.* New York: International Universities Press, 1958.

Havens, L. L. The existential use of the self. *Amer. J. Psychiat.,* Jan. 1974, **131**(1), 1–10.

Hilgard, E. R. The domain of hypnosis: With some comments on alternative paradigms. *Amer. Psychologist,* Nov. 1973, **28**(11), 972–82.

Hilgard, E. R. Weapon against pain: Hypnosis is no mirage. *Psych. Today,* Nov. 1974, **8**(6), 120–22; 126; 128.

Hobbs, S. A., Mogluin, L. E., Tyroller, M., & Lahey, D. Cognitive behavior therapy with children: Has clinical utility been demonstrated? *Psychol. Bull.,* in press.

Hollon, S., & Beck, A. T. Psychotherapy and drug therapy: Comparisons and combinations. In S. L. Garfield & A. E. Bergin (Eds.), *Handbook of psychotherapy and behavior change.* New York: Wiley, 1978. Pp. 437–90.

Homme, L. E. Perspectives in psychology: Control of coverants, the operants of the mind (Vol. 24). *Psychol. Rec.,* 1965, **15,** 501–11.

Huff, F. W. A learning theory approach to family therapy. *The Family Coordinator,* 1969, **18**(1), 22–26.

Hunter, S. *Self-regulation of fingertip temperature increases in normal and learning-disabled children.* Unpublished doctoral dissertation, University of Minnesota, 1974.

Hurwitz, N. The family therapist as intermediary. *The Family Coordinator,* Apr. 1974, **23**(2), 145–58.

Jacobson, E. *Progressive relaxation.* Chicago: University of Chicago Press, 1938.

Jacobson, N. S., & Martin, B. Behavioral marriage therapy: Current status. *Psychol. Bull.,* 1976, **83,** 540–56.

Jones, M. C. A laboratory study of fear: The case of Peter. *Pedagogical Seminary,* 1924, **31,** 308–15.

Kantorovich, F. An attempt at associative reflex therapy in alcoholism. *Psychological Abstracts,* 1930, **4282.**

Kendall, P. C., & Finch, A. J. A cognitive-behavioral treatment for impulse control: A case study. *J. Cons. Clin. Psychol.,* 1976, **44,** 852–57.

Kendall, P. C., & Hollon, S. D. (Eds.), *Cognitive behavioral intervention: Theory, research and procedures.* New York: Academic Press, 1979.

Kennedy, T. D., & Kimura, H. K. Transfer, behavioral improvement, and anxiety reduction in systematic desensitization. *J. Cons. Clin. Psychol.,* Oct. 1974, **42**(5), 720–28.

Kewman, D., & Roberts, A. H. Skin temperature biofeedback

and migraine headaches. Paper presented at the Annual Conference of the Biofeedback Society of America, San Diego, 1979.

Kimble, G. A. *Hilgard and Marquis' conditioning and learning.* New York: Appleton-Century-Crofts, 1961.

Kimmel, H. D. Instrumental conditioning of autonomically mediated responses. *Amer. Psychologist,* 1974, **29,** 325–35.

Lanyon, R. I., Barrington, C. C., & Newman, A. C. Modification of stuttering through EMG biofeedback: A preliminary study. *Behavior therapy,* 1976, **7,** 96–103.

Lazarus, A. *Behavior therapy and beyond.* New York: McGraw-Hill, 1971.

Ledwidge, B. Cognitive behavior modification: A step in the wrong direction? *Psychol. Bull.,* 1978, **85,** 353–75.

Lovaas, O. I. *The autistic child.* New York: Halstead Press, 1977.

Mahoney, M., & Arnkoff, D. Cognitive and self-control therapies. In S. Garfield & A. Bergin (Eds.), *Handbook of psychotherapy and behavior change: An empirical analysis.* New York: Wiley, 1978.

May, R. *Love and will.* New York: Norton, 1969.

Mealiea, W. L., Jr. *The comparative effectiveness of systematic desensitization and implosive therapy in the elimination of snake phobia.* Unpublished doctoral dissertation, University of Missouri, 1967.

Meichenbaum, D. *Cognitive behavior modification,* p. 16. © 1974 by General Learning Corporation. Reprinted by permission.

Meichenbaum, D. A self-instructional approach to stress management: A proposal for stress-inoculation training. In C. Spielberger & I. Sarason (Eds.), *Stress and anxiety* (Vol. 2). New York: Wiley, 1975.

Meichenbaum, D. *Cognitive-behavior modification: An integrative approach.* New York: Plenum Press, 1977.

Miller, N. E. Learning of visceral and glandular responses. *Science,* 1969, **163,** 434–45.

Miller, N. E., & Dworkin, B. R. Visceral learning: Recent difficulties with curarized rats and significant problems for human research. In D. A. Obrist et al. (Eds.), *Cardiovascular psychophysiology.* Chicago: Aldine, 1974.

Miller, N. E. Biofeedback and visceral learning, In M. R. Rosenzweig & L. W. Porter (Eds.), *Annual Review of Psychology.* Palo Alto, Calif.: Annual Reviews, 1978.

Miller, R. R., & Springer, A. D. Implications of recovery from experimental amnesia. *Psych. Rev.,* Sept. 1974, **81**(5), 470–73.

Minuchin, S. *Families and family therapy.* Cambridge, Mass.: Harvard University Press, 1974.

Minuchin, S., Baker, L., Rosman, B., Liebman, R., Milman, L., & Todd, T. A conceptual model of psychosomatic illness in children. *Arch. Gen. Psychiat.,* 1975, **32,** 1031–38.

Moreno, J. L. Psychodrama. In S. Arieti et al. (Eds.), *American handbook of psychiatry* (Vol. 2). New York: Basic Books, 1959.

Morse, S. J., & Watson, R. I., Jr. *Psychotherapies: A comparative casebook.* New York: Holt, Rinehart & Winston, 1977.

Nace, E. P., Orne, M. T., & Hammer, A. G. Posthypnotic amnesia as an active psychic process. *Arch. Gen. Psychiat.,* Aug. 1974, **31**(2), 257–60.

Nelson, Z. P., & Mowry, D. D. Contracting in crisis intervention. *Community Mental Health Journal,* 1976, **12,** 37–43.

Novaco, R. W. Stress inoculation: A cognitive therapy for anger and its application to a case of depression. *Journal of Counseling and Clinical Psychology,* 1977, Vol. 45, pp. 600–8. Copyright © 1977 by the American Psychological Association. Reprinted by permission.

Patterson, G. R., Weiss, R. L., & Hops, H. Training of marital skills. In H. Leitenberg (Ed.), *Handbook of behavior modification and behavior therapy.* New York: Prentice-Hall, 1976.

Paul, G. L., & Lentz, R. J. *Psychosocial treatment of chronic* *mental patients.* Cambridge, Mass.: Harvard University Press, 1977.

Paul, N. The family as patient. *Time,* May 31, 1971, 60.

Perls, F. S. Group vs. individual therapy. *ETC: A review of general semantics,* 1967, **34,** 306–12.

Perls, F. S. *Gestalt therapy verbatim.* Lafayette, California: Real People Press, 1969. Reprinted by permission.

Rogers, C. R. *Client-centered therapy.* Boston: Houghton Mifflin, 1951. Reprinted by permission of Houghton Mifflin Company and Constable & Company Limited.

Rogers, C. R. The necessary and sufficient conditions of therapeutic personality change. *Journal of Consulting Psychology,* 1957, **21,** 95–103.

Rogers, C. R. *On becoming a person: A client's view of psychotherapy.* Boston: Houghton Mifflin, 1961.

Rogers, C. R. Client-centered therapy. In S. Arieti et al. (Eds.), *American handbook of psychiatry* (Vol. 3). New York: Basic Books, 1966.

Rush, A. J., Khatami, M., & Beck, A. T. Cognitive and behavior therapy in chronic depression. *Behavior Therapy,* 1975, **6,** 398–404. Copyright © 1975 by Academic Press, Inc. Reprinted by permission.

Sahakian, W. S. *Psychotherapy and counseling* (2nd Ed.). Chicago: Rand McNally, 1976.

Satir, V. *Conjoint family therapy* (Rev. ed.). Palo Alto: Science and Behavior Books, 1967.

Schearn, D. W. Operant conditioning of heart rate. *Science,* 1962, **137,** 530–31.

Shaw, B. F. Comparison of cognitive therapy and behavior therapy in the treatment of depression. *J. Cons. Clin. Psychol.,* 1977, **45,** 543–51.

Sloane, R. B., Staples, F. R., Cristol, A. H., Yorkston, N. J., & Whipple, K. *Psychotherapy versus behavior therapy.* Cambridge, Mass.: Harvard University Press, 1975.

Smith, M. L., & Glass, G. V. Meta-analysis of psychotherapy outcome studies. *Amer. Psychologist,* 1977, **32,** 752–60.

Stampfl, T. G. Implosive therapy: Staring down your nightmares. *Psych. Today,* Feb. 1975, **8**(9), 66–68; 72–73.

Stampfl, T. G., & Levis, D. J. Essentials of implosive therapy: A learning-theory-based psychodynamic behavioral therapy. *J. Abnorm. Psychol.,* 1967, **72,** 496–503.

Stampfl, T. G., & Levis, D. J. *Implosive therapy: Theory and technique.* Morristown, N.J.: General Learning Press, 1973.

Stanton, M. D., & Todd, T. C. *Structural family therapy with heroin addicts: Some outcome data.* Paper presented at the Society for Psychotherapy Research, San Diego, June 1976.

Stephenson, F. D. (Ed.), *Gestalt therapy primer.* Springfield, Ill.: Charles C Thomas, 1975.

Stuart, R. B. Behavioral contracting within the families of delinquents. *Journal of Behavior Therapy and Experimental Psychiatry,* 1971, **2,** 1–11. Copyright 1971, Pergamon Press.

Sullivan, H. S. *The interpersonal theory of psychiatry.* New York: Norton, 1953

Sundberg, N. D., & Tyler, L. E. *Clinical psychology.* New York: Appleton-Century-Crofts, 1962.

Tarler-Benlolo, L. The role of relaxation in biofeedback training: A critical review of the literature. *Psychol. Bull.,* 1978, **85**(4), 727–55.

Taylor, F. G., & Marshall, W. L. Experimental analysis of a cognitive-behavioral therapy for depression. *Cognitive Therapy and Research,* 1977, **1,** 59–72.

Turk, D. *Cognitive control of pain: A skills training approach.* Unpublished manuscript, University of Waterloo, Ontario, Canada, 1974.

Van Egeren, L. F. Psychophysiologic aspects of systematic desensitization. *Behav. Res. Ther.,* 1971, **9**(1), 65–77.

Weiss, R. L. Contracts, cognition, and change: A behavioral approach to marriage. *The Counseling Psychologist,* 1975, **5**(3), 15–26. Margolin, G., Christensen, A., & Weiss, R. L. Contracts, cognition, and change: A behavioral approach to marriage therapy. *The Counseling Psychologist,* 1975, **5,**

15–26. Reprinted by permission.

Weiss, R. L., & Birchler, G. R. Adults with marital dysfunction. In M. Hersen & A. Bellack (Eds.), *Behavior therapy in the psychiatric setting.* Baltimore: Williams & Williams, 1978.

Weiss, T., & Engel, B. T. Operant conditioning of heart rate in patients with premature ventricular contractions. *Psychosomatic Medicine,* 1971, **33,** 301–21.

Wolf, M., Risley, T., & Mees, H. Application of operant conditioning procedures to the behavior problems of an autistic child. *Behavior Research and Therapy,* 1964, **1,** 305–12. Permission granted by Maxwell International Microforms Corporation.

Wolpe, J. The systematic desensitization treatment of neuroses. *J. Nerv. Ment. Dis.,* 1961, **132,** 189–203.

Wolpe, J. Quantitative relationships in the systematic desensitization of phobias. *Amer. J. Psychiat.,* 1963, **119,** 1062.

Wolpe, J. *The practice of behavior therapy.* New York: Pergamon, 1969.

Yablonsky, L. Psychodrama lives. *Human Behavior,* Feb. 1975, **4**(2), 24–29.

Yalom, I. D., & Lieberman, M. A. A study of encounter group casualties. *Arch. Gen. Psychiat.,* 1971, **25,** 16–30.

20. Action for Mental Health and a Better World

Aring, C. D. Gheel: The town that cares. *Family Health,* Apr. 1975, **7**(4), 54–55; 58; 60.

Bernard, J. L. Reply to Siegal. *Amer. Psychologist,* 1979, **34**(3), 280–82.

Bloom, B. L., Asher, S. J., & White, S. W. Marital disruption as a stressor: A review and analysis. *Psychol. Bull.,* 1978, **85,** 867–94.

Caplan, G. *Principles of preventive psychiatry.* New York: Basic Books, 1964.

Denner, B. Returning madness to an accepting community. *Comm. Ment. Hlth. J.,* 1974, **10**(2), 163–72.

Donne, J. Meditation XVII. *Devotions upon emergent occasions.* London, 1624.

Fairweather, G. W., Sanders, D. H., Maynard, H., & Cressler, D. L. *Community life for the mentally ill: An alternative to institutional care.* Chicago: Aldine, 1969.

Freeman, R. D., Malkin, S. F., & Hastings, J. O. Psychosocial problems of deaf children and their families: A comparative study. *American Annals of the Deaf,* 1975, **120,** 391–405.

Glasscote, R. What programs work and what programs do not work for chronic mental patients? In J. A. Talbott (Ed.), *The chronic mental patient: Problems, solutions and recommendations for a public policy.* Washington, D.C.: American Psychiatric Association, 1978.

Golan, N. *Treatment in crisis situations.* New York: The Free Press, 1978.

Guglielmi, R. S. *A double-blind study of the effectiveness of skin temperature biofeedback as a treatment for Raynaud's disease.* Unpublished doctoral dissertation, University of Minnesota, 1979.

Gunn, J., Robertson, G., Dell, S., & Way, C. *Psychiatric aspects of imprisonment.* London: Academic Press, 1978.

Haskins, C. P. *Report to the president, 1966–1967.* Washington, D.C.: Carnegie Institute, 1968.

Huxley, J. The future of man. *Bulletin of the Atomic Scientists,* 1959, **15,** 402–9.

Iscoe, I., Bloom, B. L., & Spielberger, C. D. (Eds.), *Community psychology in transition.* Washington, D.C.: Hemisphere, 1977.

Jones, M. *The therapeutic community.* New York: Basic Books, 1953.

Katkin, S., Ginsburg, M., Rifkin, M., & Scott, J. Effectiveness of female volunteers in the treatment of outpatients. *J. Couns. Psychol.,* 1971, **18**(2), 97–100.

Kelly, J. G., Snowden, L. R., & Muñoz, R. F. Social and community interventions. *Ann. Rev. Psychol.,* 1977, **28,** 323–61.

Kessler, M., & Albee, G. W. Primary prevention. *Ann. Rev. Psychol.,* 1975, **26,** 557–91.

Kewman, D., & Roberts, A. H. *Skin temperature biofeedback and migraine headaches.* Paper presented at the Annual Conference of the Biofeedback Society of America, San Diego, 1979.

Klerman, G. L. National trends in hospitalization. *Hospital and Community Psychiatry,* 1979, **30**(2), 110–13.

Lamb, H. R. The new asylums in the community. *Arch. Gen. Psychiat.,* 1979, **36,** 129–34.

Lyle, O. E., & Gottesman, I. I. Premorbid psychometric indicators of the gene for Huntington's disease. *J. Cons. Clin. Psychol.,* 1977, **45**(6), 1011–22.

Mann, P. A. *Community psychology: Concepts and applications.* New York: The Free Press, 1978.

Mannino, F. V., McLennan, B. W., & Shore, M. F. *The practice of mental health consultation.* New York: Gardner, 1975.

Mental Health Law Project. *Summary of Activities,* June 1976, Vol. II, No. 2.

Merbaum, M., & Hefez, A. Emotional adjustment of psychiatric patients following their unexpected discharge due to war: Short- and long-term effects. *J. Abnorm. Psychol.,* 1975, **84,** 709–14.

Murphy, L. B., & Frank, C. Prevention: The clinical psychologist. *Ann. Rev. Psychol.,* 1979, **30,** 173–207.

NAMH. Bulletin #103, March 23, 1979.

Neugarten, B. L. Personality and aging. In J. E. Birren & K. W. Schaie (Eds.), *Handbook of the psychology of aging.* New York: Van Nostrand, 1977.

Nicoletti, J., & Flater, L. A community-oriented program for training and using volunteers. *Comm. Ment. Hlth. J.,* Apr. 1975, **11** (1), 58–63.

NIMH. *The mental health of urban America.* Washington, D.C.: U.S. Government Printing Office, 1969.

NIMH. *Emergency services in psychiatric facilities.* Washington, D.C.: U.S. Government Printing Office, 1976.

NIMH. *Changes in the age, sex, and diagnostic composition of the resident population of state and county mental hospitals* (Statistical note #146). Washington, D.C.: U.S. Government Printing Office, March 1978. [a]

NIMH. *Indirect services* (Statistical Note #147). Washington, D.C.: U.S. Government Printing Office, 1978. [b]

Ozarin, L. D. Community alternatives to institutional care. *Amer. J. Psychiat.,* 1976, **133**(1), 69–72.

Paul, G. L., & Lentz, R. J. *Psychosocial treatment of chronic mental patients: Milieu versus social-learning programs.* Cambridge, Mass.: Harvard University Press, 1977.

Penk, W. E., Charles, H. L., & Van Hoose, T. A. Comparative effectiveness of day hospital and inpatient psychiatric treatment. *J. Cons. Clin. Psychol.,* 1978, **46,** 94–101.

President's Commission on Mental Health. *Report to the President.* Washington, D.C.: U.S. Government Printing Office, 1978.

Rosenbaum, C. P., & Beebe, J. E. *Psychiatric treatment: Crisis, clinic and consultation.* New York: McGraw-Hill, 1975.

Sank, L. I. Community disasters: Primary prevention and treatment in a Health Maintenance Organization. *Amer. Psychologist,* April 1979, **34**(4), 334–38.

Silverman, W. H., & Val, E. Day hospital in the context of a community mental health program. *Comm. Ment. Hlth. J.,* Spring 1975, **11**(1), 82–90.

Smith, D. E. The free clinic in the United States: A ten year perspective. *Journal of Drug Issues,* Fall, 1976.

Summers, F. Characteristics of new patient admissions to aftercare. *Hospital and Community Psychiatry,* 1979, **30**(3), 199–202.

UNESCO. *Constitution.* Paris: UNESCO, 1945.

World Health Organization (WHO). *Report of the director-general,* April, 1978. [a]

World Health Organization (WHO). *Mental disorders: Glossary and guide to their classification in accordance with the ninth revision of the International Classification of Diseases.* Geneva: World Health Organization, 1978. [b]

Picture Credits

Cover (detail) and front endsheet (entire painting): "Ravine in the Peyroulets," oil on canvas by Vincent van Gogh, 1889. The Rijksmuseum Kröller-Müller, Otterlo, The Netherlands

xii–1 Ron Mesaros: "Muscle Beach," 1968
2 "Mon cochon s'appelle Rafi" by Anton M. Heinrich. Courtesy the Collection de la Compagnie de l'Art Brut
5 Historical Pictures Service, Inc.
7 (left) The Bettmann Archive
7 (right) Culver Pictures
8 The Bettmann Archive
9 The Bettmann Archive
11 James H. Karales/Peter Arnold, Inc.
15 David Herman/DPI
20 Tom Damman NYT PICTURES
24 "Château avec deux personnages" by Paul End. Courtesy the Collection de la Compagnie de l'Art Brut
26 The Bettmann Archive
30 The Bettmann Archive
31 Historical Pictures Service, Inc.
35 (right) The Bettmann Archive
35 (bottom left) Historical Pictures Service, Inc.
35 (bottom right) Historical Pictures Service, Inc.
37 The Bettmann Archive
38 From Reginald Scot's Discovery of Witchcraft, reproduced from A History of Medical Psychology, by Gregory Zilboorg and W. Henry, W. W. Norton, 1941. Copyright 1941 by W. W. Norton & Company, Inc. Copyright renewed 1968 by Margaret Stone Zilboorg and George W. Henry
40 (top) Historical Pictures Service, Inc.
40 (bottom left) Historical Pictures Service, Inc.
40 (bottom right) National Library of Medicine, Bethesda, Maryland
42 Culver Pictures
43 (top) Historical Pictures Service, Inc.
43 (bottom) James H. Karales/Peter Arnold, Inc.
44 (top) National Library of Medicine, Bethesda, Maryland
44 (bottom) National Library of Medicine, Bethesda, Maryland
45 Historical Pictures Service, Inc.
46 (left) Historical Pictures Service, Inc.
46 (right) Historical Pictures Service, Inc.

47 (left) The Bettmann Archive
47 (center) Historical Pictures Service, Inc.
47 (right) Historical Pictures Service, Inc.
50 "Dreams and Lies of Franco," etching by Pablo Picasso. Courtesy of The Art Institute of Chicago
52 Historical Pictures Service, Inc.
53 Historical Pictures Service, Inc.
56 (left) Historical Pictures Service, Inc.
56 (center left) The Bettmann Archive
56 (center right) Historical Pictures Service, Inc.
56 (right) Association for the Advancement of Psychoanalysis of the Karen Horney Psychoanalytic Institute and Center
57 (left) Dr. Karl Menninger, courtesy the Menninger Clinic Foundation
57 (center) UPI
57 (right) Photo by Jon Erikson
58 The Bettmann Archive
61 Charles Biasiny-Rivera
62 (top left) Historical Pictures Service, Inc.
62 (top right) Historical Pictures Service, Inc.
62 (center left) Ken Heyman
62 (center right) Courtesy of Dr. Albert Bandura
62 (bottom left) Courtesy of Dr. Donald Meichenbaum
68 (top left) The Bettmann Archive
68 (top right) The Bettmann Archive
68 (center left) The Bettmann Archive
68 (center right) Courtesy of Dr. Thomas S. Szasz
68 (bottom left) Hugh L. Wilkerson
71 (left) UPI
71 (center) Courtesy of Dr. Rollo May, photo by Bernard Gotfryd
71 (right) Courtesy of The William Alanson White Psychiatric Foundation, Inc.
73 Ken Heyman
78 Courtesy of the Institute of Interculteral Studies, Inc., photo by Theodore Schwartz
82 "William Tell" by Jules Dou. Reproduced from Though this be Madness (Insania Pingens) by A. Bader, H. Steck, G. Schmidt, J. Cocteau. Thames and Hudson, London 1961
84 Historical Pictures Service, Inc.
86 Suzanne Szasz/Photo Researchers, Inc.
89 J. R. Holland/Stock, Boston, Inc.

91 Shirley Zeiberg/Taurus Photos
92 Paul Sequeira
94 Fred Conrad/Leo de Wys, Inc.
97 (left) Richard Kalvar/Magnum Photos
97 (right) Leonard Freed/Magnum Photos
99 (top) Erika Stone/Peter Arnold, Inc.
99 (bottom) Joel Gordon
100 Jay Hoops/Leo de Wys, Inc.
103 Lily Solmssen/Photo Researchers, Inc.
105 Bob Combs/Photo Researchers, Inc.
109 Lynn Karlin/Leo de Wys, Inc.
111 Charles Gatewood
113 Richard Kalvar/Magnum Photos
120 Courtesy of Dr. John Romano, Dr. Jules Masserman, and the W. B. Saunders Company
126 "Façade de chateau avec petite fille" by Paul End. Courtesy the Collection de la Compagnie de l'Art Brut
131 © The Washington Post 1978, Frank Johnston/Woodfin Camp and Associates
132 Courtesy of Dr. James L. German III
134 Museum of the City of New York
136 Stern/Black Star
137 (left) Ellis Herwig/Stock, Boston, Inc.
137 (right) Jay Hoops/Leo de Wys, Inc.
141 Wide World Photos
145 Courtesy of Dr. H. F. Harlow, University of Wisconsin Primate Laboratory
152 Courtesy of Dr. Albert Bandura and The American Psychological Association
153 UPI
155 UPI
158 Cary Wolinsky/Stock, Boston, Inc.
159 Pat Vine/Leo de Wys, Inc.
162 Martha Cooper
164 Courtesy of Dr. Philip G. Zimbardo
165 Courtesy of Dr. Philip G. Zimbardo
168–169 Daniel S. Brody/Stock, Boston, Inc.
170 "Three Figures" by Johann Knüpfer. Prinzhorn collection, Psychiatric Clinic, Heidelberg
174 Wide World Photos
177 Arthur Greenspon/Nancy Palmer Photo Agency, Inc.
182 Philip Jones Griffiths/Magnum Photos
185 Alex Webb/Magnum Photos
188 UPI
189 (left) UPI
189 (right) UPI

Charts and graphs credits

Name index

Subject index

Feedback, please!

We need your reactions and ideas if *Abnormal Psychology and Modern Life* is to serve you and others better. What did you like best and least? What would you like to have more or less of? How could it have been handled better? Please jot down your suggestions, cut out this page, fold and tape or staple it, and mail it to us. No postage is needed.

Many thanks!
The authors

For every chapter that you read, please make a check mark on each line to indicate your evaluation of it. It is ideal if you can do this as soon as you finish reading each chapter.

	Informational Value			Interest		
Chapter	high	average	low	high	average	low
1 Abnormal Behavior in Our Times						
2 Demonology to Biological Viewpoint						
3 Psychosocial/Sociocultural Viewpoints						
4 Personality Development/Adjustment						
5 Causes of Abnormal Behavior						
6 Transient Reactions to Severe Stress						
7 The Neuroses						
8 Psychological Factors and Illness						
9 Personality Disorders and Crime						
10 Addictive Disorders						
11 Affective Disorders						
12 The Schizophrenias and Paranoia						
13 Organic Mental Disorders/Retardation						
14 Disorders of Childhood/Adolescence						
15 Sexual Dysfunctions and Variants						
16 Suicide						
17 Clinical Assessment						
18 Biologically Based Therapies						
19 Psychological Therapies						
20 Action for Mental Health						
Appendix Classification Systems						

What did you like best about *Abnormal Psychology and Modern Life*?

How could *Abnormal Psychology and Modern Life* be improved?

Your name and address (if you wish)

_____

_____

Size of your psychology class _____

Male _____ Female _____ Age _____   Were you in a discussion section? _____

Your course grade _____   Besides the text, did you use:

Will you take more psychology? _____   *Student's Guide to accompany Abnormal*

Your probable major _____   *Psychology and Modern Life* 6th _____

School _____   Other supplementary material _____

---

fold here

Overall evaluation of *Abnormal Psychology and Modern Life* 6th

All things considered, how does *Abnormal Psychology and Modern Life* compare to texts you have used in other courses?

| much better | better | about average | worse | much worse |

Would you recommend its continued use at your school?

_____ Definitely yes
_____ Yes
_____ Uncertain
_____ No
_____ Definitely no

fold here

BUSINESS REPLY MAIL

FIRST CLASS   PERMIT NO. 31   GLENVIEW, IL

POSTAGE WILL BE PAID BY ADDRESSEE

NO POSTAGE
NECESSARY
IF MAILED
IN THE
UNITED STATES

Scott, Foresman and Company
    College Division, Dept. Abn Psy-1
1900 East Lake Avenue
Glenview, Illinois 60025

cut page out

Maladaptive Behaviors Discussed in

ABNORMAL PSYCHOLOGY AND MODERN LIFE, Sixth Edition

Transient Reactions to Severe Stress

Traumatic reactions to combat

Reactions to civilian catastrophes

Reactions to sustained or difficult stressors

Neurotic Patterns

Anxiety disorders

> Generalized anxiety disorder
> Obsessive-compulsive disorder
> Phobic disorder

Somatoform disorders

> Hypochondriasis
> Psychogenic pain disorder
> Conversion disorder

Dissociative disorders

> Psychogenic amnesia and fugue
> Multiple personality
> Depersonalization disorder

Psychosomatic Disorders

Peptic ulcers

Anorexia nervosa

Migraine and tension headaches

Hypertension

Heart attacks

Other specific reaction patterns

Personality Disorders

Types of personality disorder

> Paranoid
> Schizoid
> Schizotypal
> Histrionic
> Narcissistic
> Antisocial
> Borderline
> Avoidant
> Dependent
> Compulsive
> Passive-aggressive

Criminal behavior

Addictive Disorders

Alcohol abuse and dependence

Drug abuse and dependence

> Opium and its derivatives
> Barbiturates
> Amphetamines and cocaine
> LSD
> Mescaline
> Psilocybin
> Marijuana

Extreme obesity

Pathological gambling

Affective Disorders

Normal depression

Neurotic depression

Affective psychoses

> Major depressive disorder
> Bipolar affective disorder

Suicide